The Sporting News

PRO FOOTBALL REGISTER

1998 EDITION

Editors/Pro Football Register
MARK BONAVITA
BRENDAN ROBERTS

The Sporting News

Efrem Zimbalist III, President and Chief Executive Officer, Times Mirror Magazines; **James H. Nuckols,** President, The Sporting News; **Francis X. Farrell,** Senior Vice President, Publisher; **John D. Rawlings,** Senior Vice President, Editorial Director; **John Kastberg,** Vice President, General Manager; **Kathy Kinkeade,** Vice President, Operations; **Steve Meyerhoff,** Executive Editor; **Mike Huguenin,** Assistant Managing Editor; **Marilyn Kasal,** Production Director; **Michael Bruner,** Prepress Director; **Terry Shea,** Database Analyst; **Michael Behrens,** Art Director, Special Projects; **Christen Webster,** Macintosh Production Artist; **Ryan Basen, Amanda Kuehner, Brandiss Schacher, Steve Sigel,** and **David Walton,** Editorial Interns.

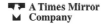
A Times Mirror
Company

S0-DVD-636

CONTENTS

EXPLANATION OF ABBREVIATIONS AND TERMS

LEAGUES: AFL: American Football League. **Ar.FL., Arena Football:** Arena Football League. **CFL:** Canadian Football League. **CoFL:** Continental Football League. **NFL:** National Football League. **USFL:** United States Football League. **WFL:** World Football League. **W.L.:** World League. **WLAF:** World League of American Football.

TEAMS: Birm.: Birmingham. **Jack.:** Jacksonville. **L.A. Raiders:** Los Angeles Raiders. **L.A. Rams:** Los Angeles Rams. **New Eng.:** New England. **N.Y. Giants:** New York Giants. **N.Y. Jets:** New York Jets. **N.Y./N.J.:** New York/New Jersey. **San Ant.:** San Antonio. **San Fran.:** San Francisco. **Sask.:** Saskatchewan. **StL.:** St. Louis.

STATISTICS: Att.: Attempts. **Avg.:** Average. **Blk.:** Blocked punts. **Cmp.:** Completions. **FGA:** Field goals attempted. **FGM:** Field goals made. **50+:** Field goals of 50 yards or longer. **F., Fum.:** Fumbles. **G:** Games. **In. 20:** Punts inside 20-yard line. **Int.:** Interceptions. **Lg.:** Longest made field goal. **L:** Lost. **Net avg.:** Net punting average. **No.:** Number. **Rat.:** Passer rating. **Pct.:** Percentage. **Pts.:** Points scored. **T:** Tied. **TD:** Touchdowns. **2-pt.:** Two-point conversions. **W:** Won. **XPA:** Extra points attempted. **XPM:** Extra points made. **Yds.:** Yards.

POSITIONS: C: Center. **CB:** Corner back. **DB:** Defensive back. **DE:** Defensive end. **DT:** Defensive tackle. **FB:** Full back. **G:** Guard. **K:** Kicker. **LB:** Linebacker. **OL:** Offensive lineman. **OT:** Offensive tackle. **P:** Punter. **QB:** Quarterback. **RB:** Running back. **S:** Safety. **TE:** Tight end. **WR:** Wide receiver.

SINGLE GAME HIGHS (regular season): If a player reached a single game high on numerous occasions—had one rushing touchdown in a game, for example—the most recent occurrence is listed.

EXPLANATION OF AWARDS

AWARDS: Butkus Award: Nation's top college linebacker. **Davey O'Brien Award:** Nation's top college quarterback. **Doak Walker Award:** Nation's top college junior or senior running back. **Fred Biletnikoff Award:** Nation's top college wide receiver. **Harlon Hill Trophy:** Nation's top college Division II player. **Heisman Trophy:** Nation's top college player. **Jim Thorpe Award:** Nation's top college defensive back. **Lombardi Award:** Nation's top college lineman. **Lou Groza Award:** Nation's top college kicker. **Maxwell Award:** Nation's top college player. **Outland Trophy:** Nation's top college interior lineman. **Walter Payton Award:** Nation's top college Division I-AA player.

ON THE COVER: John Elway. (Photo by Ed Nessen/THE SPORTING NEWS.)

Spine photo of Brett Favre by Albert Dickson/THE SPORTING NEWS.

ISBN: 0-89204-597-3   10 9 8 7 6 5 4 3 2 1

VETERAN PLAYERS

Please note for statistical comparisons: In 1982, only nine of 16 games were played due to the cancellation of games because of a player's strike. In 1987, only 15 of 16 games were played due to the cancellation of games in the third week because of a player's strike. Most NFL players also missed games scheduled in the fourth, fifth and sixth weeks.

Sacks became an official NFL statistic in 1982.

Two-point conversions became an official NFL statistic in 1994.

* Indicates league leader.	† Indicates tied for league lead.	... Statistics unavailable, unofficial, or mathematically
‡ Indicates NFC leader.	§ Indicates AFC leader.	impossible to calculate.
∞ Indicates tied for NFC lead.	▲ Indicates tied for AFC lead.	

ABDUL-JABBAR, KARIM   RB   DOLPHINS

PERSONAL: Born June 28, 1974, in Los Angeles. ... 5-10/200. ... Formerly known as Sharmon Shah.
HIGH SCHOOL: Dorsey (Los Angeles).
COLLEGE: UCLA.
TRANSACTIONS/CAREER NOTES: Selected after junior season by Miami Dolphins in third round (80th pick overall) of 1996 NFL draft. ... Signed by Dolphins (July 18, 1996).
HONORS: Named running back on THE SPORTING NEWS college All-America second team (1995).
SINGLE GAME HIGHS (regular season): Attempts—30 (December 22, 1996, vs. New York Jets); yards—152 (December 22, 1996, vs. New York Jets); and rushing touchdowns—3 (November 23, 1997, vs. New England).
STATISTICAL PLATEAUS: 100-yard rushing games: 1996 (4), 1997 (2). Total: 6.

			RUSHING				RECEIVING				TOTALS			
Year Team	G	GS	Att.	Yds.	Avg.	TD	No.	Yds.	Avg.	TD	TD	2pt.	Pts.	Fum.
1996—Miami NFL	16	14	307	1116	3.6	11	23	139	6.0	0	11	0	66	4
1997—Miami NFL	16	14	283	892	3.2	†15	29	261	9.0	1	*16	0	†96	3
Pro totals (2 years)	32	28	590	2008	3.4	26	52	400	7.7	1	27	0	162	7

ABRAHAM, CLIFTON   CB

PERSONAL: Born December 9, 1971, in Dallas. ... 5-9/185. ... Full name: Clifton Eugene Abraham.
HIGH SCHOOL: David W. Carter (Dallas).
COLLEGE: Florida State.
TRANSACTIONS/CAREER NOTES: Selected by Tampa Bay Buccaneers in fifth round (143rd pick overall) of 1995 NFL draft. ... Signed by Buccaneers (May 3, 1995). ... Released by Buccaneers (August 25, 1996). ... Signed by Chicago Bears (October 31, 1996). ... On injured reserve with hamstring injury (December 4, 1996-remainder of season). ... Claimed on waivers by Carolina Panthers (February 14, 1997). ... Released by Panthers (April 15, 1998).
PLAYING EXPERIENCE: Tampa Bay NFL, 1995; Chicago NFL, 1996; Carolina NFL, 1997. ... Games/Games started: 1995 (6/0), 1996 (2/0), 1997 (1/0). Total: 9/0.
HONORS: Named defensive back on THE SPORTING NEWS college All-America first team (1994).

ABRAHAM, DONNIE   CB   BUCCANEERS

PERSONAL: Born October 8, 1973, in Orangeburg, S.C. ... 5-10/190. ... Full name: Nathaniel Donnell Abraham.
HIGH SCHOOL: Wilkinson (Orangeburg, S.C.).
COLLEGE: East Tennessee State
TRANSACTIONS/CAREER NOTES: Selected by Tampa Bay Buccaneers in third round (71st pick overall) of 1996 NFL draft. ... Signed by Buccaneers (July 13, 1996).
PRO STATISTICS: 1996—Recovered two fumbles for three yards. 1997—Recovered one fumble for two yards.

			INTERCEPTIONS			
Year Team	G	GS	No.	Yds.	Avg.	TD
1996—Tampa Bay NFL	16	12	5	27	5.4	0
1997—Tampa Bay NFL	16	16	5	16	3.2	0
Pro totals (2 years)	32	28	10	43	4.3	0

ABRAMS, KEVIN   CB   LIONS

PERSONAL: Born February 28, 1974, in Tampa. ... 5-8/175. ... Full name: Kevin R. Abrams.
HIGH SCHOOL: Hillsborough (Tampa).
COLLEGE: Syracuse.
TRANSACTIONS/CAREER NOTES: Selected by Detroit Lions in second round (54th pick overall) of 1997 NFL draft. ... Signed by Lions (July 14, 1997).
HONORS: Named defensive back on THE SPORTING NEWS college All-America first team (1995).
PRO STATISTICS: 1997—Credited with two sacks.

			INTERCEPTIONS			
Year Team	G	GS	No.	Yds.	Avg.	TD
1997—Detroit NFL	15	4	1	29	29.0	0

ACKERMAN, TOM   C   SAINTS

PERSONAL: Born September 6, 1972, in Bellingham, Wash. ... 6-3/290. ... Full name: Thomas Michael Ackerman.
HIGH SCHOOL: Nooksack (Wash.).
COLLEGE: Eastern Washington.
TRANSACTIONS/CAREER NOTES: Selected by New Orleans Saints in fifth round (145th pick overall) of 1996 NFL draft. ... Signed by Saints (July 14, 1996).
PLAYING EXPERIENCE: New Orleans NFL, 1996 and 1997. ... Games/Games started: 1996 (2/0), 1997 (14/0). Total: 16/0.

ADAMS, MIKE   WR   STEELERS

PERSONAL: Born March 25, 1974, in Dallas. ... 5-11/184. ... Full name: Michael Adams.
HIGH SCHOOL: Sam Houston (Arlington, Texas).
COLLEGE: Texas.
TRANSACTIONS/CAREER NOTES: Selected by Pittsburgh Steelers in seventh round (223rd pick overall) of 1997 NFL draft. ... Signed by Steelers (July 14, 1997). ... On injured reserve with knee injury (October 22, 1997-remainder of season).
SINGLE GAME HIGHS (regular season): Receptions—1 (September 20, 1997, vs. Tennessee); yards—39 (September 28, 1997, vs. Tennessee); and touchdown receptions—0.

			RECEIVING				KICKOFF RETURNS				TOTALS		
Year Team	G	GS	No.	Yds.	Avg.	TD	No.	Yds.	Avg.	TD	TD	2pt.	Pts.	Fum.
1997—Pittsburgh NFL	6	0	1	39	39.0	0	10	215	21.5	0	0	0	0	1

ADAMS, SAM   DT   SEAHAWKS

PERSONAL: Born June 13, 1973, in Houston. ... 6-3/300. ... Full name: Sam Aaron Adams. ... Son of Sam Adams Sr., guard with New England Patriots (1972-80) and New Orleans Saints (1981).
HIGH SCHOOL: Cypress Creek (Houston).
COLLEGE: Texas A&M.
TRANSACTIONS/CAREER NOTES: Selected after junior season by Seattle Seahawks in first round (eighth pick overall) of 1994 NFL draft. ... Signed by Seahawks (July 30, 1994).
HONORS: Named defensive lineman on THE SPORTING NEWS college All-America first team (1993).
PRO STATISTICS: 1996—Recovered one fumble for two yards.

Year Team	G	GS	SACKS
1994—Seattle NFL	12	7	4.0
1995—Seattle NFL	16	5	3.5
1996—Seattle NFL	16	15	5.5
1997—Seattle NFL	16	16	7.0
Pro totals (4 years)	60	43	20.0

ADAMS, SCOTT   OT   FALCONS

PERSONAL: Born September 28, 1966, in Lake City, Fla. ... 6-5/315. ... Full name: Scott Alexander Adams.
HIGH SCHOOL: Columbia (Lake City, Fla.).
COLLEGE: Georgia (degree in marketing).
TRANSACTIONS/CAREER NOTES: Signed as non-drafted free agent by Dallas Cowboys (April 25, 1989). ... Released by Cowboys (September 5, 1989). ... Signed by Atlanta Falcons (1990). ... Released by Falcons (February 1990). ... Signed by WLAF (January 2, 1991). ... Selected by Barcelona Dragons in third round (16th offensive lineman) of 1991 WLAF positional draft. ... Signed by Minnesota Vikings (June 22, 1991). ... Released by Vikings (August 26, 1991). ... Re-signed by Vikings to practice squad (August 27, 1991). ... Activated (December 20, 1991). ... On inactive list for one game (1991). ... Released by Vikings (August 31, 1992). ... Re-signed by Vikings to practice squad (September 1, 1992). ... Activated (September 8, 1992). ... Granted free agency (February 17, 1994). ... Re-signed by Vikings (July 12, 1994). ... Released by Vikings (August 22, 1994). ... Signed by New Orleans Saints (September 28, 1994). ... Granted free agency (February 17, 1995). ... Signed by Chicago Bears (March 21, 1995). ... Granted unconditional free agency (February 16, 1996). ... Signed by Tampa Bay Buccaneers (March 23, 1996). ... Released by Buccaneers (October 22, 1996). ... Signed by Denver Broncos (January 23, 1997). ... Released by Broncos (February 14, 1997). ... Re-signed by Broncos (March 21, 1997). ... Released by Broncos (September 9, 1997). ... Signed by Falcons (September 18, 1997). ... Granted unconditional free agency (February 13, 1998). ... Re-signed by Falcons (February 19, 1998).
PLAYING EXPERIENCE: Barcelona W.L., 1991; Minnesota NFL, 1992 and 1993; New Orleans NFL, 1994; Chicago NFL, 1995; Tampa Bay NFL, 1996; Atlanta NFL, 1997. ... Games/Games started: 1991 (10/10), 1992 (15/0), 1993 (15/10), 1994 (11/0), 1995 (4/0), 1996 (7/2), 1997 (6/0). Total W.L.: 10/10. Total NFL: 58/12. Total Pro: 68/22.
PRO STATISTICS: NFL: 1992—Returned one kickoff for no yards and fumbled once. 1994—Recovered one fumble.

ADAMS, VASHONE   S   CHIEFS

PERSONAL: Born September 12, 1973, in Aurora, Colo. ... 5-10/196. ... Full name: Vashone LaRey Adams. ... Name pronounced vash-ON.
HIGH SCHOOL: Overland (Kan.) Christian.
JUNIOR COLLEGE: Butte College (Calif.).
COLLEGE: Fort Hays State (Kan.), then Eastern Michigan.
TRANSACTIONS/CAREER NOTES: Signed as non-drafted free agent by Cleveland Browns (May 2, 1995). ... Released by Browns (August 21, 1995). ... Re-signed by Browns to practice squad (August 30, 1995). ... Activated (November 4, 1995). ... Browns franchise moved to Baltimore and renamed Ravens for 1996 season (March 11, 1996). ... Granted unconditional free agency (February 14, 1997). ... Signed by New Orleans Saints (April 7, 1997). ... Released by Saints (September 29, 1997). ... Signed by Kansas City Chiefs (April 7, 1998).
PLAYING EXPERIENCE: Cleveland NFL, 1995; Baltimore NFL, 1996; New Orleans NFL, 1997. ... Games/Games started: 1995 (8/6), 1996 (16/2), 1997 (5/4). Total: 29/12.
PRO STATISTICS: 1996—Intercepted one pass for 16 yards.

AGNEW, RAY — DT — RAMS

PERSONAL: Born December 9, 1967, in Winston-Salem, N.C. ... 6-3/285. ... Full name: Raymond Mitchell Agnew.
HIGH SCHOOL: Carver (Winston-Salem, N.C.).
COLLEGE: North Carolina State.
TRANSACTIONS/CAREER NOTES: Selected by New England Patriots in first round (10th pick overall) of 1990 NFL draft. ... Signed by Patriots (July 19, 1990). ... On injured reserve with knee injury (December 29, 1990-remainder of season). ... Granted unconditional free agency (February 17, 1995). ... Signed by New York Giants (March 10, 1995). ... Released by Giants (June 4, 1997). ... Signed by Carolina Panthers (June 12, 1997). ... Released by Panthers (August 19, 1997). ... Signed by Giants (August 21, 1997). ... Granted unconditional free agency (February 13, 1998). ... Signed by St. Louis Rams (February 26, 1998).
PRO STATISTICS: 1990—Recovered one fumble. 1992—Recovered one fumble. 1995—Recovered one fumble. 1996—Intercepted one pass for 34 yards and a touchdown. 1997—Recovered one fumble.

Year Team	G	GS	SACKS
1990—New England NFL	12	9	2.5
1991—New England NFL	13	10	2.0
1992—New England NFL	14	14	1.0
1993—New England NFL	16	1	1.5
1994—New England NFL	11	3	0.5
1995—New York Giants NFL	16	15	1.0
1996—New York Giants NFL	13	2	0.5
1997—New York Giants NFL	15	0	2.0
Pro totals (8 years)	110	54	11.0

AGUIAR, LOUIE — P — CHIEFS

PERSONAL: Born June 30, 1966, in Livermore, Calif. ... 6-2/218. ... Full name: Louis Raymond Aguiar. ... Name pronounced AG-ee-ar.
HIGH SCHOOL: Granada (Livermore, Calif.).
COLLEGE: Utah State.
TRANSACTIONS/CAREER NOTES: Signed as non-drafted free agent by Buffalo Bills (May 8, 1989). ... Released by Bills (August 14, 1989). ... Re-signed by Bills (March 27, 1990). ... Released by Bills (August 7, 1990). ... Signed by WLAF (January 8, 1991). ... Selected by Barcelona Dragons in first round (first punter) of 1991 WLAF positional draft. ... Signed by New York Jets (June 14, 1991). ... Granted free agency (February 17, 1994). ... Signed by Kansas City Chiefs (April 1994). ... Granted unconditional free agency (February 14, 1997). ... Re-signed by Chiefs (April 18, 1997).
PRO STATISTICS: NFL: 1991—Made one of two field goal attempts (23 yards), rushed once for 18 yards and recovered one fumble. 1993—Rushed three times for minus 27 yards, attempted two passes without a completion and an interception, fumbled twice and recovered one fumble for minus 10 yards. 1997— Rushed twice for 11 yards and attempted one pass with one completion for 35 yards.

Year Team	G	GS	PUNTING No.	Yds.	Avg.	Net avg.	In. 20	Blk.
1991—Barcelona W.L.	10	0	49	2029	41.4	33.7	15	1
—New York Jets NFL	16	0	64	2521	39.4	34.6	14	0
1992—New York Jets NFL	16	0	73	2993	41.0	37.6	21	0
1993—New York Jets NFL	16	0	73	2806	38.4	34.3	21	0
1994—Kansas City NFL	16	0	85	3582	42.1	34.5	15	0
1995—Kansas City NFL	16	0	91	3990	43.8	36.5	†29	0
1996—Kansas City NFL	16	0	88	3667	41.7	33.7	25	0
1997—Kansas City NFL	16	0	82	3465	42.3	38.2	▲28	0
W.L. totals (1 year)	10	0	49	2029	41.4	33.7	15	1
NFL totals (7 years)	112	0	556	23024	41.4	35.6	153	0
Pro totals (8 years)	122	0	605	25053	41.4	35.5	168	1

AHANOTU, CHIDI — DE — BUCCANEERS

PERSONAL: Born October 11, 1970, in Modesto, Calif. ... 6-2/283. ... Full name: Chidi Obioma Ahanotu. ... Name pronounced chee-DEE a-HA-nah-TWO.
HIGH SCHOOL: Berkeley (Calif.).
COLLEGE: California (degree in physical education).
TRANSACTIONS/CAREER NOTES: Selected by Tampa Bay Buccaneers in sixth round (145th pick overall) of 1993 NFL draft. ... Signed by Buccaneers (July 9, 1993). ... Granted free agency (February 16, 1996). ... Re-signed by Buccaneers (February 20, 1996).
PRO STATISTICS: 1996—Recovered one fumble. 1997—Recovered two fumbles.

Year Team	G	GS	SACKS
1993—Tampa Bay NFL	16	10	1.5
1994—Tampa Bay NFL	16	16	1.0
1995—Tampa Bay NFL	16	15	3.0
1996—Tampa Bay NFL	13	13	5.5
1997—Tampa Bay NFL	16	15	10.0
Pro totals (5 years)	77	69	21.0

AIKMAN, TROY — QB — COWBOYS

PERSONAL: Born November 21, 1966, in West Covina, Calif. ... 6-4/219. ... Full name: Troy Kenneth Aikman.
HIGH SCHOOL: Henryetta (Okla.).
COLLEGE: Oklahoma, then UCLA.
TRANSACTIONS/CAREER NOTES: Selected by Dallas Cowboys in first round (first pick overall) of 1989 NFL draft. ... Signed by Cowboys (April 20, 1989). ... On injured reserve with shoulder injury (December 28, 1990-remainder of season).
CHAMPIONSHIP GAME EXPERIENCE: Played in NFC championship game (1992-1995 seasons). ... Member of Super Bowl championship team (1992, 1993 and 1995 seasons).

HONORS: Named quarterback on THE SPORTING NEWS college All-America second team (1987). ... Davey O'Brien Award winner (1988). ... Named quarterback on THE SPORTING NEWS college All-America first team (1988). ... Played in Pro Bowl (1991, 1992 and 1994 seasons). ... Named Most Valuable Player of Super Bowl XXVII (1992 season). ... Named quarterback on THE SPORTING NEWS NFL All-Pro team (1993). ... Named to play in Pro Bowl (1993 season); replaced by Bobby Hebert due to injury. ... Named to play in Pro Bowl (1995 season); replaced by Warren Moon due to injury. ... Named to play in Pro Bowl (1996 season); replaced by Gus Frerotte due to injury.

POST SEASON RECORDS: Holds Super Bowl career record for highest percentage of passes completed (minimum 40 attempts)—70.0. ... Holds NFL postseason career records for highest percentage of passes completed (minimum 150 attempts)—66.5; and longest pass completion (to Alvin Harper)—94 yards (January 8, 1995, vs. Green Bay).

PRO STATISTICS: 1989—Caught one pass for minus 13 yards, fumbled six times and recovered three fumbles. 1990—Fumbled five times and recovered one fumble. 1991—Caught one pass for minus six yards and fumbled four times. 1992—Fumbled four times and recovered one fumble. 1993—Fumbled seven times and recovered three fumbles for minus three yards. 1994—Fumbled twice and recovered two fumbles. 1995—Fumbled five times and recovered two fumbles for minus 15 yards. 1996—Fumbled six times and recovered two fumbles for minus eight yards. 1997—Fumbled six times for minus five yards.

SINGLE GAME HIGHS (regular season): Attempts—53 (December 14, 1997, vs. Cincinnati); completions—34 (October 5, 1997, vs. New York Giants); yards—379 (November 12, 1989, vs. Phoenix); and touchdown passes—4 (August 31, 1997, vs. Pittsburgh).

STATISTICAL PLATEAUS: 300-yard passing games: 1989 (1), 1990 (1), 1991 (1), 1993 (1), 1994 (1), 1995 (2), 1996 (1), 1997 (2). Total: 10.

MISCELLANEOUS: Regular-season record as starting NFL quarterback: 76-53 (.589). ... Postseason record as starting NFL quarterback: 11-2 (.846). ... Holds Dallas Cowboys all-time record for most yards passing (26,016).

Year Team	G	GS	PASSING								RUSHING				TOTALS		
			Att.	Cmp.	Pct.	Yds.	TD	Int.	Avg.	Rat.	Att.	Yds.	Avg.	TD	TD	2pt.	Pts.
1989—Dallas NFL	11	11	293	155	52.9	1749	9	18	5.97	55.7	38	302	7.9	0	0	0	0
1990—Dallas NFL	15	15	399	226	56.6	2579	11	∞18	6.46	66.6	40	172	4.3	1	1	0	6
1991—Dallas NFL	12	12	363	237	‡65.3	2754	11	10	7.59	86.7	16	5	0.3	1	1	0	6
1992—Dallas NFL	16	16	473	∞302	63.8	3445	23	14	7.28	89.5	37	105	2.8	1	1	0	6
1993—Dallas NFL	14	14	392	271	*69.1	3100	15	6	7.91	99.0	32	125	3.9	0	0	0	0
1994—Dallas NFL	14	14	361	233	64.5	2676	13	12	7.41	84.9	30	62	2.1	1	1	0	6
1995—Dallas NFL	16	16	432	280	64.8	3304	16	7	7.65	93.6	21	32	1.5	1	1	0	6
1996—Dallas NFL	15	15	465	296	63.7	3126	12	13	6.72	80.1	35	42	1.2	1	1	0	6
1997—Dallas NFL	16	16	‡518	292	56.4	3283	19	12	6.34	78.0	25	79	3.2	0	0	0	0
Pro totals (9 years)	129	129	3696	2292	62.0	26016	129	110	7.04	82.3	274	924	3.4	6	6	0	36

ALBRIGHT, ETHAN   OL   BILLS

PERSONAL: Born May 1, 1971, in Greensboro, N.C. ... 6-5/283. ... Full name: Lawrence Ethan Albright.
HIGH SCHOOL: Grimsley (Greensboro, N.C.).
COLLEGE: North Carolina.
TRANSACTIONS/CAREER NOTES: Signed as non-drafted free agent by Miami Dolphins (April 28, 1994). ... Released by Dolphins (August 22, 1994). ... Re-signed by Dolphins to practice squad (August 29, 1994). ... Released by Dolphins (September 14, 1994). ... Re-signed by Dolphins to practice squad (September 28, 1994). ... Released by Dolphins (November 2, 1994). ... Re-signed by Dolphins (February 16, 1995). ... On injured reserve with knee injury (November 15, 1995-remainder of season). ... Released by Dolphins (August 20, 1996). ... Signed by Buffalo Bills (August 26, 1996). ... Granted free agency (February 13, 1998). ... Re-signed by Bills (April 15, 1998).
PLAYING EXPERIENCE: Miami NFL, 1995; Buffalo NFL, 1996 and 1997. ... Games/Games started: 1995 (10/0), 1996 (16/0), 1997 (16/0). Total: 42/0.

ALDRIDGE, ALLEN   LB   LIONS

PERSONAL: Born May 30, 1972, in Houston. ... 6-1/255. ... Full name: Allen Ray Aldridge. ... Son of Allen Aldridge, defensive end, Houston Oilers and Cleveland Browns (1971, 1972 and 1974).
HIGH SCHOOL: Willowridge (Sugar Land, Texas).
COLLEGE: Houston.
TRANSACTIONS/CAREER NOTES: Selected by Denver Broncos in second round (51st pick overall) of 1994 NFL draft. ... Signed by Broncos (July 12, 1994). ... Granted free agency (February 14, 1997). ... Re-signed by Broncos (April 15, 1997). ... Granted unconditional free agency (February 13, 1998). ... Signed by Detroit Lions (February 17, 1998).
PLAYING EXPERIENCE: Denver NFL, 1994-1997. ... Games/Games started: 1994 (16/2), 1995 (16/12), 1996 (16/16), 1997 (16/15). Total: 64/45.
CHAMPIONSHIP GAME EXPERIENCE: Played in AFC championship game (1997 season). ... Member of Super Bowl championship team (1997 season).
PRO STATISTICS: 1995—Credited with 1 1/2 sacks and recovered one fumble.

ALEAGA, INK   LB   SAINTS

PERSONAL: Born April 27, 1973, in Honolulu. ... 6-1/225.
HIGH SCHOOL: Marynoll (Honolulu).
COLLEGE: Washington.
TRANSACTIONS/CAREER NOTES: Signed as non-drafted free agent by New Orleans Saints (April 25, 1997). ... Released by Saints (August 24, 1997). ... Re-signed by Saints to practice squad (August 25, 1997). ... Activated (October 17, 1997).
PLAYING EXPERIENCE: New Orleans NFL, 1997. ... Games/Games started: 3/1.

ALEXANDER, BRENT   S   PANTHERS

PERSONAL: Born July 10, 1970, in Gallatin, Tenn. ... 5-11/186.
HIGH SCHOOL: Gallatin (Tenn.).
COLLEGE: Tennessee State.
TRANSACTIONS/CAREER NOTES: Signed as non-drafted free agent by Arizona Cardinals (April 28, 1994). ... Granted unconditional free agency (February 13, 1998). ... Signed by Carolina Panthers (March 19, 1998).
PRO STATISTICS: 1995—Credited with 1/2 sack and recovered one fumble.

Year Team	G	GS	No.	Yds.	Avg.	TD
			INTERCEPTIONS			
1994—Arizona NFL	16	7	0	0	...	0
1995—Arizona NFL	16	13	2	14	7.0	0
1996—Arizona NFL	16	15	2	3	1.5	0
1997—Arizona NFL	16	15	0	0	...	0
Pro totals (4 years)	64	50	4	17	4.3	0

ALEXANDER, DERRICK — DE — VIKINGS

PERSONAL: Born November 3, 1973, in Jacksonville. ... 6-4/286.
HIGH SCHOOL: Raines (Jacksonville).
COLLEGE: Florida State.
TRANSACTIONS/CAREER NOTES: Selected after junior season by Minnesota Vikings in first round (11th pick overall) of 1995 NFL draft. ... Signed by Vikings (August 16, 1995).
HONORS: Named defensive lineman on THE SPORTING NEWS college All-America second team (1994).
PRO STATISTICS: 1995—Recovered one fumble. 1996—Recovered one fumble for three yards. 1997—Recovered one fumble.

Year Team	G	GS	SACKS
1995—Minnesota NFL	15	12	2.0
1996—Minnesota NFL	12	9	3.5
1997—Minnesota NFL	14	14	4.5
Pro totals (3 years)	41	35	10.0

ALEXANDER, DERRICK — WR — CHIEFS

PERSONAL: Born November 6, 1971, in Detroit. ... 6-2/195. ... Full name: Derrick Scott Alexander.
HIGH SCHOOL: Benedictine (Detroit).
COLLEGE: Michigan.
TRANSACTIONS/CAREER NOTES: Selected by Cleveland Browns in first round (29th pick overall) of 1994 NFL draft. ... Signed by Browns (August 3, 1994). ... Browns franchise moved to Baltimore and renamed Ravens for 1996 season (March 11, 1996). ... Granted unconditional free agency (February 13, 1998). ... Signed by Kansas City Chiefs (March 2, 1998).
PRO STATISTICS: 1995—Fumbled three times and recovered one fumble. 1997—Fumbled once.
SINGLE GAME HIGHS (regular season): Receptions—8 (September 7, 1997, vs. Cincinnati); yards—198 (December 1, 1996, vs. Pittsburgh); and touchdown receptions—2 (September 21, 1997, vs. Cincinnati).
STATISTICAL PLATEAUS: 100-yard receiving games: 1994 (3), 1996 (3), 1997 (3). Total: 9.
MISCELLANEOUS: Shares Baltimore Ravens all-time records for most touchdown receptions (18) and touchdowns (18).

Year Team	G	GS	RUSHING				RECEIVING				PUNT RETURNS				KICKOFF RETURNS				TOTALS		
			Att.	Yds.	Avg.	TD	No.	Yds.	Avg.	TD	No.	Yds.	Avg.	TD	No.	Yds.	Avg.	TD	TD	2pt.	Pts.
1994—Cleveland NFL	14	12	4	38	9.5	0	48	828	17.3	2	0	0	...	0	0	0	...	0	2	1	14
1995—Cleveland NFL	14	2	1	29	29.0	0	15	216	14.4	0	9	122	13.6	†1	21	419	20.0	0	1	0	6
1996—Baltimore NFL	15	14	3	0	0.0	0	62	1099	17.7	9	1	15	15.0	0	1	13	13.0	0	9	1	56
1997—Baltimore NFL	15	13	1	0	0.0	0	65	1009	15.5	9	1	34	34.0	0	0	0	...	0	9	0	54
Pro totals (4 years)	58	41	9	67	7.4	0	190	3152	16.6	20	11	171	15.5	1	22	432	19.6	0	21	2	130

ALEXANDER, ELIJAH — LB — COLTS

PERSONAL: Born August 8, 1970, in Fort Worth, Texas. ... 6-2/237. ... Full name: Elijah Alfred Alexander III.
HIGH SCHOOL: Dunbar Senior (Fort Worth, Texas).
COLLEGE: Kansas State.
TRANSACTIONS/CAREER NOTES: Selected by Tampa Bay Buccaneers in 10th round (254th pick overall) of 1992 NFL draft. ... Signed by Buccaneers (June 3, 1992). ... Released by Buccaneers (August 31, 1992). ... Re-signed by Buccaneers (September 1, 1992). ... Released by Buccaneers (October 16, 1992). ... Re-signed by Buccaneers to practice squad (October 22, 1992). ... Activated (November 10, 1992). ... Claimed on waivers by Denver Broncos (August 31, 1993). ... On injured reserve with shoulder injury (November 22, 1995-remainder of season). ... Granted unconditional free agency (February 16, 1996). ... Signed by Indianapolis Colts (August 6, 1996).
PRO STATISTICS: 1994—Recovered one fumble for nine yards.

Year Team	G	GS	No.	Yds.	Avg.	TD	No.
			INTERCEPTIONS				SACKS
1992—Tampa Bay NFL	12	0	0	0	...	0	0.0
1993—Denver NFL	16	0	0	0	...	0	0.0
1994—Denver NFL	16	16	1	2	2.0	0	1.0
1995—Denver NFL	9	8	2	5	2.5	0	0.5
1996—Indianapolis NFL	14	3	0	0	...	0	1.0
1997—Indianapolis NFL	13	11	1	43	43.0	1	1.0
Pro totals (6 years)	80	38	4	50	12.5	1	3.5

ALEXANDER, KEVIN — WR — DOLPHINS

PERSONAL: Born January 23, 1975, in Denver. ... 5-9/185.
HIGH SCHOOL: Goldwater (Phoenix).
JUNIOR COLLEGE: Glendale (Ariz.) Community College.
COLLEGE: Utah State.
TRANSACTIONS/CAREER NOTES: Signed as non-drafted free agent by New York Giants (April 27, 1996). ... Released by Giants (August 19, 1996). ... Re-signed by Giants to practice squad (August 28, 1996). ... Activated (October 25, 1996). ... Granted free agency (February 13, 1998). ... Signed by Miami Dolphins (March 2, 1998).

SINGLE GAME HIGHS (regular season): Receptions—5 (October 26, 1997, vs. Cincinnati); yards—100 (October 26, 1997, vs. Cincinnati); and touchdown receptions—1 (September 28, 1997, vs. New Orleans).
STATISTICAL PLATEAUS: 100-yard receiving games: 1997 (1).

				RECEIVING				KICKOFF RETURNS				TOTALS		
Year Team	G	GS	No.	Yds.	Avg.	TD	No.	Yds.	Avg.	TD	TD	2pt.	Pts.	Fum.
1996—New York Giants NFL	4	0	4	88	22.0	0	2	27	13.5	0	0	0	0	0
1997—New York Giants NFL	14	8	18	276	15.3	1	3	30	10.0	0	1	0	6	0
Pro totals (2 years)	18	8	22	364	16.5	1	5	57	11.4	0	1	0	6	0

ALEXANDER, PATRISE — LB — REDSKINS

PERSONAL: Born October 23, 1972, in Galveston, Texas. ... 6-1/244.
HIGH SCHOOL: Ball (Galveston, Texas).
COLLEGE: Southwestern Louisiana.
TRANSACTIONS/CAREER NOTES: Signed as non-drafted free agent by Washington Redskins (April 26, 1995). ... Released by Redskins (August 22, 1995). ... Re-signed by Redskins to practice squad (November 21, 1995).
PLAYING EXPERIENCE: Washington NFL, 1996 and 1997. ... Games/Games started: 1996 (16/1), 1997 (16/0). Total: 32/1.

ALLEN, ERIC — CB — RAIDERS

PERSONAL: Born November 22, 1965, in San Diego. ... 5-10/180. ... Full name: Eric Andre Allen.
HIGH SCHOOL: Point Loma (San Diego).
COLLEGE: Arizona State (degree in broadcasting, 1988).
TRANSACTIONS/CAREER NOTES: Selected by Philadelphia Eagles in second round (30th pick overall) of 1988 NFL draft. ... Signed by Eagles (July 19, 1988). ... Granted free agency (February 1, 1992). ... Re-signed by Eagles (September 2, 1992). ... Granted roster exemption (September 2-4, 1992). ... Designated by Eagles as transition player (February 25, 1993). ... Tendered offer sheet by New Orleans Saints (March 20, 1995). ... Eagles declined to match offer (March 27, 1995). ... Traded by Saints to Oakland Raiders for fourth-round pick (DB Fred Weary) in 1998 draft (March 5, 1998).
HONORS: Played in Pro Bowl (1989 and 1991-1995 seasons).
RECORDS: Shares NFL single-season record for most touchdowns by interception—4 (1993). ... Shares NFL single-game record for most touchdowns by interception—2 (December 26, 1993, vs. New Orleans).
PRO STATISTICS: 1989—Fumbled once for seven yards. 1990—Returned one kickoff for two yards and recovered one fumble. 1991—Recovered one fumble. 1992—Recovered two fumbles. 1993—Credited with two sacks. 1994—Recovered one fumble for 30 yards.
MISCELLANEOUS: Shares Philadelphia Eagles all-time record for most interceptions (34).

			INTERCEPTIONS			
Year Team	G	GS	No.	Yds.	Avg.	TD
1988—Philadelphia NFL	16	16	5	76	15.2	0
1989—Philadelphia NFL	15	15	‡8	38	4.8	0
1990—Philadelphia NFL	16	15	3	37	12.3	1
1991—Philadelphia NFL	16	16	5	20	4.0	0
1992—Philadelphia NFL	16	16	4	49	12.3	0
1993—Philadelphia NFL	16	16	6	*201	33.5	*4
1994—Philadelphia NFL	16	16	3	61	20.3	0
1995—New Orleans NFL	16	16	2	28	14.0	0
1996—New Orleans NFL	16	16	1	33	33.0	0
1997—New Orleans NFL	16	16	2	27	13.5	0
Pro totals (10 years)	159	158	39	570	14.6	5

ALLEN, JAMES — RB — BEARS

PERSONAL: Born March 28, 1975, in Wynnewood, Okla. ... 5-10/215.
HIGH SCHOOL: Wynnewood (Okla.).
COLLEGE: Oklahoma.
TRANSACTIONS/CAREER NOTES: Signed as non-drafted free agent by Tennessee Oilers (May 14, 1997). ... Released by Oilers (August 20, 1997). ... Signed by Philadelphia Eagles to practice squad (August 27, 1997). ... Released by Eagles (September 2, 1997). ... Re-signed by Eagles to practice squad (September 10, 1997). ... Signed by Chicago Bears off Eagles practice squad (December 9, 1997). ... Inactive for two games (1997).

ALLEN, LARRY — OT/G — COWBOYS

PERSONAL: Born November 27, 1971, in Los Angeles. ... 6-3/326. ... Full name: Larry Christopher Allen.
HIGH SCHOOL: Vintage (Napa, Calif.).
JUNIOR COLLEGE: Butte College (Calif.).
COLLEGE: Sonoma State (Calif.).
TRANSACTIONS/CAREER NOTES: Selected by Dallas Cowboys in second round (46th pick overall) of 1994 NFL draft. ... Signed by Cowboys (July 16, 1994).
PLAYING EXPERIENCE: Dallas NFL, 1994-1997. ... Games/Games started: 1994 (16/10), 1995 (16/16), 1996 (16/16), 1997 (16/16). Total: 64/58.
CHAMPIONSHIP GAME EXPERIENCE: Played in NFC championship game (1994 and 1995 seasons). ... Member of Super Bowl championship team (1995 season).
HONORS: Named guard on THE SPORTING NEWS NFL All-Pro team (1995-97). ... Played in Pro Bowl (1995-1997 seasons).
PRO STATISTICS: 1995—Recovered one fumble.

ALLEN, MARCUS   RB   A

PERSONAL: Born March 26, 1960, in San Diego. ... 6-2/210. ... Brother of Damon Allen, quarterback, B.C. Lions of CFL.
HIGH SCHOOL: Lincoln (San Diego).
COLLEGE: Southern California.
TRANSACTIONS/CAREER NOTES: Selected by Los Angeles Raiders in first round (10th pick overall) of 1982 NFL draft. ... On reserve/did not report list (July 26-August 30, 1989). ... On injured reserve with knee injury (October 13-November 29, 1989). ... Moved to developmental squad (November 30, 1989). ... Activated (December 2, 1989). ... Granted free agency (February 1, 1990). ... Re-signed by Raiders (July 27, 1990). ... Granted free agency (February 1, 1991). ... Re-signed by Raiders (July 13, 1991). ... On injured reserve with knee injury (September 4-October 30, 1991). ... Granted free agency (February 1, 1992). ... Re-signed by Raiders (August 12, 1992). ... Granted unconditional free agency (March 1, 1993). ... Signed by Kansas City Chiefs (June 9, 1993). ... Granted unconditional free agency (February 16, 1996). ... Re-signed by Chiefs (April 24, 1996). ... Announced retirement (April 9, 1998).
CHAMPIONSHIP GAME EXPERIENCE: Played in AFC championship game (1983, 1990 and 1993 seasons). ... Member of Super Bowl championship team (1983 season).
HONORS: Heisman Trophy winner (1981). ... Maxwell Award winner (1981). ... Named College Football Player of the Year by THE SPORTING NEWS (1981). ... Named running back on THE SPORTING NEWS college All-America first team (1981). ... Named NFL Rookie of the Year by THE SPORTING NEWS (1982). ... Played in Pro Bowl (1982, 1984, 1985, 1987 and 1993 seasons). ... Named Most Valuable Player of Super Bowl XVIII (1983 season). ... Named NFL Player of the Year by THE SPORTING NEWS (1985). ... Named running back on THE SPORTING NEWS NFL All-Pro team (1985). ... Named to play in Pro Bowl (1986 season); replaced by Sammy Winder due to injury.
RECORDS: Holds NFL career records for most rushing touchdowns—123; and most receptions by a running back—587.
POST SEASON RECORDS: Holds Super Bowl career records for highest average gain (minimum 20 attempts)—9.5; longest touchdown run—74 yards; and longest run from scrimmage—74 yards (January 22, 1984, vs. Washington).
PRO STATISTICS: 1982—Attempted four passes with one completion for 47 yards and recovered two fumbles. 1983—Attempted seven passes with four completions for 111 yards and three touchdowns and recovered two fumbles (including one in end zone for a touchdown). 1984—Attempted four passes with one completion for 38 yards and recovered three fumbles. 1985—Attempted two passes with one completion for 16 yards and recovered two fumbles. 1986—Recovered one fumble. 1987—Attempted two passes with one completion for 23 yards. 1988—Attempted two passes with one completion for 21 yards. 1990—Attempted one pass without a completion and recovered one fumble. 1991—Attempted two passes with one completion for 11 yards and a touchdown. 1993—Recovered one fumble. 1995—Recovered one fumble. 1996—Attempted one pass without a completion. 1997—Attempted two passes with two completions for 15 yards and two touchdowns and recovered two fumbles.
SINGLE GAME HIGHS (regular season): Attempts—33 (December 24, 1994, vs. Los Angeles Raiders); yards—173 (November 24, 1985, vs. Denver); and rushing touchdowns—3 (December 5, 1993, vs. Seattle).
STATISTICAL PLATEAUS: 100-yard rushing games: 1982 (2), 1983 (1), 1984 (3), 1985 (11), 1986 (2), 1987 (1), 1988 (1), 1994 (1), 1995 (2). Total: 24. ... 100-yard receiving games: 1983 (1), 1984 (1), 1986 (1). Total: 3.
MISCELLANEOUS: Holds Raiders franchise all-time records for most yards rushing (8,545) and most touchdowns (98). ... Holds Kansas City Chiefs all-time record for most rushing touchdowns (44).

			RUSHING				RECEIVING				TOTALS			
Year Team	G	GS	Att.	Yds.	Avg.	TD	No.	Yds.	Avg.	TD	TD	2pt.	Pts.	Fum.
1982—Los Angeles Raiders NFL	9	9	160	697	4.4	*11	38	401	10.6	3	*14	...	*84	5
1983—Los Angeles Raiders NFL	15	14	266	1014	3.8	9	68	590	8.7	2	12	...	72	*14
1984—Los Angeles Raiders NFL	16	16	275	1168	4.2	§13	64	758	11.8	5	†18	...	108	8
1985—Los Angeles Raiders NFL	16	16	§380	*1759	4.6	▲11	67	555	8.3	3	14	...	84	3
1986—Los Angeles Raiders NFL	13	10	208	759	3.6	5	46	453	9.8	2	7	...	42	7
1987—Los Angeles Raiders NFL	12	12	200	754	3.8	5	51	410	8.0	0	5	...	30	3
1988—Los Angeles Raiders NFL	15	15	223	831	3.7	7	34	303	8.9	1	8	...	48	5
1989—Los Angeles Raiders NFL	8	5	69	293	4.2	2	20	191	9.6	0	2	...	12	2
1990—Los Angeles Raiders NFL	16	15	179	682	3.8	12	15	189	12.6	1	13	...	78	1
1991—Los Angeles Raiders NFL	8	2	63	287	4.6	2	15	131	8.7	0	2	...	12	1
1992—Los Angeles Raiders NFL	16	0	67	301	4.5	2	28	277	9.9	1	3	...	18	1
1993—Kansas City NFL	16	10	206	764	3.7	*12	34	238	7.0	3	§15	...	90	4
1994—Kansas City NFL	13	13	189	709	3.8	7	42	349	8.3	0	7	1	44	3
1995—Kansas City NFL	16	15	207	890	4.3	5	27	210	7.8	0	5	0	30	2
1996—Kansas City NFL	16	15	206	830	4.0	9	27	270	10.0	0	9	0	54	2
1997—Kansas City NFL	16	0	124	505	4.1	11	11	86	7.8	0	11	0	66	4
Pro totals (16 years)	221	167	3022	12243	4.1	123	587	5411	9.2	21	145	1	872	65

ALLEN, TAJE   DB   RAMS

PERSONAL: Born November 6, 1973, in Lubbock, Texas. ... 5-10/185. ... Full name: Taje LaQuane Allen. ... Name pronounced TAH-jee.
HIGH SCHOOL: Estacado (Lubbock, Texas).
COLLEGE: Texas.
TRANSACTIONS/CAREER NOTES: Selected by St. Louis Rams in fifth round (158th pick overall) of 1997 NFL draft. ... Signed by Rams (July 3, 1997).
PLAYING EXPERIENCE: St. Louis NFL, 1997. ... Games/Games started: 14/1.

ALLEN, TERRY   RB   REDSKINS

PERSONAL: Born February 21, 1968, in Commerce, Ga. ... 5-10/208. ... Full name: Terry Thomas Allen Jr.
HIGH SCHOOL: Banks County (Homer, Ga.).
COLLEGE: Clemson.
TRANSACTIONS/CAREER NOTES: Selected after junior season by Minnesota Vikings in ninth round (241st pick overall) of 1990 NFL draft. ... Signed by Vikings (July 2, 1990). ... On injured reserve with knee injury (August 28, 1990-entire season). ... On injured reserve with knee injury (August 23, 1993-entire season). ... Released by Vikings (May 8, 1995). ... Signed by Washington Redskins (June 15, 1995). ... Granted free agency (February 16, 1996). ... Re-signed by Redskins (July 17, 1996). ... Granted unconditional free agency (February 14, 1997). ... Re-signed by Redskins (February 26, 1997).
HONORS: Played in Pro Bowl (1996 season).

PRO STATISTICS: 1991—Returned one kickoff for 14 yards and recovered one fumble. 1992—Recovered two fumbles. 1994—Recovered two fumbles for four yards. 1995—Recovered one fumble. 1997—Recovered one fumble.

SINGLE GAME HIGHS (regular season): Attempts—36 (September 28, 1997, vs. Jacksonville); yards—172 (December 20, 1992, vs. Pittsburgh); and rushing touchdowns—3 (December 22, 1996, vs. Dallas).

STATISTICAL PLATEAUS: 100-yard rushing games: 1991 (1), 1992 (3), 1994 (3), 1995 (4), 1996 (5), 1997 (3). Total: 19. ... 100-yard receiving games: 1992 (1).

Year Team	G	GS	RUSHING				RECEIVING				TOTALS			
			Att.	Yds.	Avg.	TD	No.	Yds.	Avg.	TD	TD	2pt.	Pts.	Fum.
1990—Minnesota NFL							Did not play.							
1991—Minnesota NFL	15	6	120	563	‡4.7	2	6	49	8.2	1	3	...	18	4
1992—Minnesota NFL	16	16	266	1201	4.5	13	49	478	9.8	2	15	...	90	9
1993—Minnesota NFL							Did not play.							
1994—Minnesota NFL	16	16	255	1031	4.0	8	17	148	8.7	0	8	1	50	3
1995—Washington NFL	16	16	338	1309	3.9	10	31	232	7.5	1	11	0	66	6
1996—Washington NFL	16	16	347	1353	3.9	*21	32	194	6.1	0	*21	0	126	4
1997—Washington NFL	10	10	210	724	3.4	4	20	172	8.6	1	5	0	30	2
Pro totals (6 years)	89	80	1536	6181	4.0	58	155	1273	8.2	5	63	1	380	28

ALLEN, TREMAYNE — TE — BEARS

PERSONAL: Born August 9, 1974, in Knoxville, Tenn. ... 6-2/244. ... Full name: Tremayne Aubrey Allen. ... Cousin of Bryant Stith, guard, Denver Nuggets.

HIGH SCHOOL: Brentwood (Tenn.) Academy.

COLLEGE: Florida.

TRANSACTIONS/CAREER NOTES: Signed as non-drafted free agent by Chicago Bears (April 25, 1997). ... Released by Bears (August 24, 1997). ... Re-signed by Bears (August 27, 1997). ... Released by Bears (September 9, 1997). ... Re-signed by Bears to practice squad (September 11, 1997). ... Activated (October 7, 1997).

PLAYING EXPERIENCE: Chicago NFL, 1997. ... Games/Games started: 2/0.

PRO STATISTICS: 1997—Caught one pass for nine yards.

SINGLE GAME HIGHS (regular season): Receptions—1 (December 21, 1997, vs. Tampa Bay); yards—2 (December 21, 1997, vs. Tampa Bay); and touchdown receptions—0.

ALLRED, JOHN — TE — BEARS

PERSONAL: Born September 9, 1974, in Del Mar, Calif. ... 6-4/249.

HIGH SCHOOL: Torrey Pines (Encinitas, Calif.).

COLLEGE: Southern California.

TRANSACTIONS/CAREER NOTES: Selected by Chicago Bears in second round (38th pick overall) of 1997 NFL draft. ... Signed by Bears (July 14, 1997).

PRO STATISTICS: 1997—Returned two kickoffs for 21 yards.

SINGLE GAME HIGHS (regular season): Receptions—2 (September 14, 1997, vs. Detroit); yards—26 (September 14, 1997, vs. Detroit); and touchdown receptions—0.

Year Team	G	GS	RECEIVING				TOTALS			
			No.	Yds.	Avg.	TD	TD	2pt.	Pts.	Fum.
1997—Chicago NFL	15	4	8	70	8.8	0	0	0	0	0

ALSTOTT, MIKE — FB — BUCCANEERS

PERSONAL: Born December 21, 1973, in Joliet, Ill. ... 6-1/248. ... Full name: Michael Joseph Alstott.

HIGH SCHOOL: Catholic (Joliet, Ill.).

COLLEGE: Purdue.

TRANSACTIONS/CAREER NOTES: Selected by Tampa Bay Buccaneers in second round (35th pick overall) of 1996 NFL draft. ... Signed by Buccaneers (July 21, 1996).

HONORS: Played in Pro Bowl (1997 season).

PRO STATISTICS: 1996—Returned one kickoff for 14 yards. 1997—Returned one kickoff for no yards.

SINGLE GAME HIGHS (regular season): Attempts—18 (September 21, 1997, vs. Miami); yards—95 (September 21, 1997, vs. Miami); and rushing touchdowns—1 (November 30, 1997, vs. New York Giants).

Year Team	G	GS	RUSHING				RECEIVING				TOTALS			
			Att.	Yds.	Avg.	TD	No.	Yds.	Avg.	TD	TD	2pt.	Pts.	Fum.
1996—Tampa Bay NFL	16	16	96	377	3.9	3	65	557	8.6	3	6	0	36	4
1997—Tampa Bay NFL	15	15	176	665	3.8	7	23	178	7.7	3	10	0	60	5
Pro totals (2 years)	31	31	272	1042	3.8	10	88	735	8.4	6	16	0	96	9

AMBROSE, ASHLEY — CB — BENGALS

PERSONAL: Born September 17, 1970, in New Orleans. ... 5-10/185. ... Full name: Ashley Avery Ambrose.

HIGH SCHOOL: Fortier (New Orleans).

COLLEGE: Mississippi Valley State.

TRANSACTIONS/CAREER NOTES: Selected by Indianapolis Colts in second round (29th pick overall) of 1992 NFL draft. ... Signed by Colts (August 11, 1992). ... On injured reserve with leg injury (September 14-October 29, 1992); on practice squad (October 21-29, 1992). ... Granted free agency (February 17, 1995). ... Re-signed by Colts (April 29, 1995). ... Granted unconditional free agency (February 16, 1996). ... Signed by Cincinnati Bengals (February 25, 1996).

CHAMPIONSHIP GAME EXPERIENCE: Played in AFC championship game (1995 season).

HONORS: Played in Pro Bowl (1996 season).

PRO STATISTICS: 1992—Returned eight kickoffs for 126 yards. 1994—Recovered one fumble. 1997—Credited with one sack and recovered two fumbles.

Year Team	G	GS	No.	Yds.	Avg.	TD
				INTERCEPTIONS		
1992—Indianapolis NFL	10	2	0	0	...	0
1993—Indianapolis NFL	14	6	0	0	...	0
1994—Indianapolis NFL	16	4	2	50	25.0	0
1995—Indianapolis NFL	16	0	3	12	4.0	0
1996—Cincinnati NFL	16	16	8	63	7.9	1
1997—Cincinnati NFL	16	16	3	56	18.7	0
Pro totals (6 years)	88	44	16	181	11.3	1

A

ANDERS, KIMBLE — FB — CHIEFS

PERSONAL: Born September 10, 1966, in Galveston, Texas. ... 5-11/230. ... Full name: Kimble Lynard Anders.
HIGH SCHOOL: Ball (Galveston, Texas).
COLLEGE: Houston.
TRANSACTIONS/CAREER NOTES: Signed as non-drafted free agent by Pittsburgh Steelers (April 25, 1990). ... Released by Steelers (September 3, 1990). ... Signed by Kansas City Chiefs (March 13, 1991). ... On injured reserve with hand injury (September 15, 1991-remainder of season). ... On injured reserve with knee injury (September 12-October 17, 1992); on practice squad (October 7-17, 1992). ... Granted unconditional free agency (February 16, 1996). ... Re-signed by Chiefs (April 1, 1996).
CHAMPIONSHIP GAME EXPERIENCE: Played in AFC championship game (1993 season).
HONORS: Played in Pro Bowl (1995-1997 seasons).
PRO STATISTICS: 1994—Recovered two fumbles. 1997—Recovered one fumble.
SINGLE GAME HIGHS (regular season): Attempts—13 (November 13, 1994, vs. San Diego); yards—75 (November 5, 1995, vs. Washington); and rushing touchdowns—1 (November 17, 1996, vs. Chicago).

Year Team	G	GS	RUSHING Att.	Yds.	Avg.	TD	RECEIVING No.	Yds.	Avg.	TD	KICKOFF RETURNS No.	Yds.	Avg.	TD	TOTALS TD	2pt.	Pts.	Fum.
1991—Kansas City NFL	2	0	0	0	...	0	2	30	15.0	0	0	0	...	0	0	...	0	0
1992—Kansas City NFL	11	2	1	1	1.0	0	5	65	13.0	0	1	20	20.0	0	0	...	0	1
1993—Kansas City NFL	16	13	75	291	3.9	0	40	326	8.2	1	1	47	47.0	0	1	...	6	1
1994—Kansas City NFL	16	13	62	231	3.7	2	67	525	7.8	1	2	36	18.0	0	3	0	18	1
1995—Kansas City NFL	16	13	58	398	6.9	2	55	349	6.3	1	0	0	...	0	3	0	18	1
1996—Kansas City NFL	16	15	54	201	3.7	2	60	529	8.8	2	2	37	18.5	0	4	0	24	0
1997—Kansas City NFL	15	14	79	397	5.0	0	59	453	7.7	2	1	0	0.0	0	2	0	12	3
Pro totals (7 years)	92	70	329	1519	4.6	6	288	2277	7.9	7	7	140	20.0	0	13	0	78	7

ANDERSEN, MORTEN — K — FALCONS

PERSONAL: Born August 19, 1960, in Struer, Denmark. ... 6-2/225.
HIGH SCHOOL: Ben Davis (Indianapolis).
COLLEGE: Michigan State.
TRANSACTIONS/CAREER NOTES: Selected by New Orleans Saints in fourth round (86th pick overall) of 1982 NFL draft. ... On injured reserve with sprained ankle (September 15-November 20, 1982). ... Designated by Saints as transition player (February 25, 1993). ... Released by Saints (July 19, 1995). ... Signed by Atlanta Falcons (July 21, 1995).
HONORS: Named kicker on The Sporting News college All-America first team (1981). ... Named kicker on The Sporting News NFL All-Pro team (1985-1987 and 1995). ... Played in Pro Bowl (1985-1988, 1990, 1992 and 1995 seasons).
RECORDS: Holds NFL career record for most made field goals of 50 or more yards—33. ... Holds NFL record for most consecutive games scoring—190 (December 11, 1983-December 24, 1995). ... Holds NFL single-season record for most made field goals of 50 or more yards—8 (1995). ... Holds NFL single-game record for most made field goals of 50 or more yards—3 (December 11, 1983, at Philadelphia). ... Shares NFL record for most seasons with 100 or more points—11 (1985-1989, 1991-1995 and 1997).

Year Team	G	GS	KICKING XPM	XPA	FGM	FGA	Lg.	50+	Pts.
1982—New Orleans NFL	8	0	6	6	2	5	45	0-1	12
1983—New Orleans NFL	16	0	37	38	18	24	52	3-4	91
1984—New Orleans NFL	16	0	34	34	20	27	53	2-3	94
1985—New Orleans NFL	16	0	27	29	31	35	55	3-4	120
1986—New Orleans NFL	16	0	30	30	26	30	53	2-5	108
1987—New Orleans NFL	12	0	37	37	*28	*36	52	2-6	121
1988—New Orleans NFL	16	0	32	33	26	36	51	1-4	110
1989—New Orleans NFL	16	0	44	45	20	29	49	0-4	104
1990—New Orleans NFL	16	0	29	29	21	27	52	3-4	92
1991—New Orleans NFL	16	0	38	38	25	32	60	2-4	113
1992—New Orleans NFL	16	0	33	34	29	34	52	3-3	∞120
1993—New Orleans NFL	16	0	33	33	28	35	56	1-5	117
1994—New Orleans NFL	16	0	32	32	28	†39	48	0-6	116
1995—Atlanta NFL	16	0	29	30	‡31	37	59	8-9	122
1996—Atlanta NFL	16	0	31	31	22	29	54	1-5	97
1997—Atlanta NFL	16	0	35	35	23	27	55	2-3	104
Pro totals (16 years)	244	0	507	514	378	482	60	33-70	1641

ANDERSON, ANTONIO — DT — COWBOYS

PERSONAL: Born June 4, 1973, in Brooklyn, N.Y. ... 6-6/318. ... Full name: Antonio Kenneth Anderson. ... Cousin of Keith Jennings, tight end with Montreal Machine of World League (1991) and Chicago Bears (1991-97); cousin of Stanford Jennings, running back with Cincinnati Bengals (1984-1990), New Orleans Saints (1991) and Tampa Bay Buccaneers (1992); and cousin of John Salley, forward with four NBA teams (1980-1995).
HIGH SCHOOL: Midwood (Brooklyn, N.Y.), then Milford (Conn.) Academy.
COLLEGE: Syracuse.

TRANSACTIONS/CAREER NOTES: Selected by Dallas Cowboys in fourth round (101st pick overall) of 1997 NFL draft. ... Signed by Cowboys (July 14, 1997).

Year Team	G	GS	SACKS
1997—Dallas NFL	16	5	2.0

ANDERSON, CURTIS · CB · JAGUARS

PERSONAL: Born September 29, 1973, in Lynchburg, Va. ... 6-0/203. ... Full name: Jerome Curtis Anderson.
HIGH SCHOOL: E.C Glass (Lynchburg, Va.).
COLLEGE: Pittsburgh (degree in legal studies, 1997).
TRANSACTIONS/CAREER NOTES: Signed as non-drafted free agent by Jacksonville Jaguars (April 21, 1997). ... Released by Jaguars (August 20, 1997). ... Re-signed by Jaguars to practice squad (August 25, 1997). ... Activated (October 24, 1997).
PLAYING EXPERIENCE: Jacksonville NFL, 1997. ... Games/Games started: 9/0.

ANDERSON, DARREN · CB

PERSONAL: Born January 11, 1969, in Cincinnati. ... 5-10/189. ... Full name: Darren Hunter Anderson.
HIGH SCHOOL: Walnut Hills (Cincinnati).
COLLEGE: Toledo.
TRANSACTIONS/CAREER NOTES: Selected by New England Patriots in fourth round (93rd pick overall) of 1992 NFL draft. ... Signed by Patriots (July 21, 1992). ... Released by Patriots (September 3, 1992). ... Re-signed by Patriots to practice squad (September 9, 1992). ... Activated (September 26, 1992). ... Released by Patriots (October 2, 1992). ... Re-signed by Patriots to practice squad (October 6, 1992). ... Released by Patriots (October 28, 1992). ... Signed by Tampa Bay Buccaneers to practice squad (October 31, 1992). ... Activated (December 26, 1992). ... Traded by Buccaneers to Kansas City Chiefs for seventh-round pick (DE Jeffrey Rodgers) in 1995 draft (August 23, 1994). ... Granted free agency (February 16, 1996). ... Re-signed by Chiefs (April 9, 1996). ... Released by Chiefs (April 24, 1998).
PLAYING EXPERIENCE: New England (1)-Tampa Bay (1) NFL, 1992; Tampa Bay NFL, 1993; Kansas City NFL 1994-1997. ... Games/Games started: 1992 (N.E.-1/0; T.B.-1/0; Total: 2/0), 1993 (14/1), 1994 (15/1), 1995 (16/0), 1996 (11/3), 1997 (11/0). Total: 69/5.
PRO STATISTICS: 1993—Intercepted one pass for six yards. 1994—Recovered one fumble. 1996—Recovered one fumble. 1997—Intercepted one pass for 55 yards and a touchdown and credited with two sacks.

ANDERSON, DUNSTAN · DE · DOLPHINS

PERSONAL: Born December 31, 1970, in Fort Worth, Texas. ... 6-4/254. ... Full name: Dunstan Evrette Anderson.
HIGH SCHOOL: O.D. Wyatt (Fort Worth, Texas).
COLLEGE: Tulsa (degree in recreational management).
TRANSACTIONS/CAREER NOTES: Signed as non-drafted free agent by Kansas City Chiefs (May 2, 1994). ... Released by Chiefs (August 28, 1994). ... Re-signed by Chiefs to practice squad (September 1, 1994). ... Released by Chiefs (November 16, 1994). ... Signed by Atlanta Falcons to practice squad (November 22, 1994). ... Released by Falcons (December 9, 1994). ... Re-signed by Falcons (December 21, 1994). ... Released by Falcons (August 27, 1995). ... Signed by New Orleans Saints to practice squad (September 21, 1995). ... Granted free agency after 1995 season. ... Signed by Dallas Cowboys to practice squad (January 9, 1996). ... Selected by Rhein Fire in 1996 World League draft (February 22, 1996). ... Signed by Houston Oilers (July 20, 1996). ... Released by Oilers (August 14, 1996). ... Signed by Miami Dolphins (July 8, 1997). ... Released by Dolphins (November 10, 1997). ... Re-signed by Dolphins for 1998 season.

Year Team	G	GS	SACKS
1994—Atlanta NFL	1	0	0.0
1995—New Orleans NFL	Did not play.		
1996—Rhein W.L.	...	...	7.5
1997—Rhein W.L.	...	...	4.0
—Miami NFL	9	1	0.0
W.L. totals (2 years)	...	...	11.5
NFL totals (2 years)	10	1	0.0
Pro totals (4 years)	...	...	11.5

ANDERSON, EDDIE · S

PERSONAL: Born July 22, 1963, in Warner Robins, Ga. ... 6-1/210. ... Full name: Eddie Lee Anderson Jr.
HIGH SCHOOL: Warner Robins (Ga.).
COLLEGE: Fort Valley (Ga.) State.
TRANSACTIONS/CAREER NOTES: Selected by Seattle Seahawks in sixth round (153rd pick overall) of 1986 NFL draft. ... Signed by Seahawks (July 16, 1986). ... On injured reserve with back injury (September 11-November 21, 1986). ... Released by Seahawks (September 1, 1987). ... Signed as replacement player by Los Angeles Raiders (September 24, 1987). ... Granted free agency (February 1, 1991). ... Re-signed by Raiders (July 12, 1991). ... Raiders franchise moved to Oakland (July 21, 1995). ... Released by Raiders (February 19, 1998).
CHAMPIONSHIP GAME EXPERIENCE: Played in AFC championship game (1990 season).
PRO STATISTICS: 1987—Recovered one fumble. 1990—Recovered one fumble. 1991—Recovered one fumble. 1993—Recovered one fumble. 1994—Recovered one fumble. 1995—Recovered two fumbles.

Year Team	G	GS	INTERCEPTIONS No.	Yds.	Avg.	TD	SACKS No.
1986—Seattle NFL	5	0	0	0	...	0	0.0
1987—Los Angeles Raiders NFL	13	3	1	58	58.0	0	0.0
1988—Los Angeles Raiders NFL	16	5	2	-6	-3.0	0	0.0
1989—Los Angeles Raiders NFL	15	10	5	*233	46.6	*2	0.0
1990—Los Angeles Raiders NFL	16	16	3	49	16.3	0	0.0
1991—Los Angeles Raiders NFL	16	16	2	14	7.0	0	0.0
1992—Los Angeles Raiders NFL	16	16	3	131	43.7	0	1.0
1993—Los Angeles Raiders NFL	16	16	2	52	26.0	0	1.0
1994—Los Angeles Raiders NFL	14	14	0	0	...	0	2.0

Year Team	G	GS	INTERCEPTIONS No.	Yds.	Avg.	TD	SACKS No.
1995—Oakland NFL	14	14	1	0	0.0	0	0.0
1996—Oakland NFL	7	5	0	0	...	0	0.0
1997—Oakland NFL	11	1	0	0	...	0	0.0
Pro totals (12 years)	159	116	19	531	27.9	3	4.0

ANDERSON, FLIPPER — WR

PERSONAL: Born March 7, 1965, in Philadelphia. ... 6-0/176. ... Full name: Willie Lee Anderson Jr.
HIGH SCHOOL: Paulsboro (N.J.).
COLLEGE: UCLA.
TRANSACTIONS/CAREER NOTES: Selected by Los Angeles Rams in second round (46th pick overall) of 1988 NFL draft. ... Signed by Rams (July 17, 1988). ... Granted unconditional free agency (February 17, 1995). ... Signed by Indianapolis Colts (March 7, 1995). ... On injured reserve with knee injury (September 14, 1995-remainder of season). ... Released by Colts (July 7, 1996). ... Signed by Washington Redskins (October 7, 1996). ... Granted unconditional free agency (February 14, 1997). ... Signed by Denver Broncos (June 5, 1997). ... Released by Broncos (October 6, 1997). ... Re-signed by Broncos (October 7, 1997). ... Released by Broncos (November 18, 1997).
CHAMPIONSHIP GAME EXPERIENCE: Played in NFC championship game (1989 season).
RECORDS: Holds NFL single-game record for most yards receiving—336 (November 26, 1989, OT, at New Orleans).
PRO STATISTICS: 1989—Rushed once for minus one yard. 1990—Rushed once for 13 yards and recovered one fumble. 1991—Recovered one fumble. 1992—Returned one kickoff for nine yards. 1993—Recovered one fumble. 1994—Rushed once for 11 yards and recovered one fumble for seven yards.
SINGLE GAME HIGHS (regular season): Receptions—15 (November 26, 1989, vs. New Orleans); yards—336 (November 26, 1989, vs. New Orleans); and touchdown receptions—2 (September 3, 1995, vs. Cincinnati).
STATISTICAL PLATEAUS: 100-yard receiving games: 1989 (2), 1990 (4), 1991 (1), 1994 (2). Total: 9.

Year Team	G	GS	RECEIVING No.	Yds.	Avg.	TD	TOTALS TD	2pt.	Pts.	Fum.
1988—Los Angeles Rams NFL	16	1	11	319	29.0	0	0	...	0	0
1989—Los Angeles Rams NFL	16	13	44	1146	*26.0	5	5	...	30	0
1990—Los Angeles Rams NFL	16	10	51	1097	*21.5	4	4	...	24	0
1991—Los Angeles Rams NFL	12	9	32	530	16.6	1	1	...	6	2
1992—Los Angeles Rams NFL	15	9	38	657	17.3	7	7	...	42	1
1993—Los Angeles Rams NFL	15	15	37	552	14.9	4	4	...	24	0
1994—Los Angeles Rams NFL	16	16	46	945	20.5	5	5	0	30	0
1995—Indianapolis NFL	2	2	8	111	13.9	2	2	0	12	0
1996—Washington NFL	2	0	0	0	...	0	0	0	0	0
1997—Denver NFL	4	0	0	0	...	0	0	0	0	0
Pro totals (10 years)	114	75	267	5357	20.1	28	28	0	168	3

ANDERSON, GARY — K — VIKINGS

PERSONAL: Born July 16, 1959, in Parys, Orange Free State, South Africa. ... 5-11/178. ... Full name: Gary Allan Anderson. ... Son of Rev. Douglas Anderson, former professional soccer player in England.
HIGH SCHOOL: Brettonwood (Durban, South Africa).
COLLEGE: Syracuse (degree in management and accounting, 1982).
TRANSACTIONS/CAREER NOTES: Selected by Buffalo Bills in seventh round (171st pick overall) of 1982 NFL draft. ... Claimed on waivers by Pittsburgh Steelers (September 7, 1982). ... Designated by Steelers as transition player (February 15, 1994). ... On reserve/did not report list (August 23-25, 1994). ... Free agency status changed by Steelers from transition to unconditional (February 17, 1995). ... Signed by Philadelphia Eagles (July 23, 1995). ... Released by Eagles (April 22, 1997). ... Signed by San Francisco 49ers (June 11, 1997). ... Granted unconditional free agency (February 13, 1998). ... Signed by Minnesota Vikings (February 19, 1998).
CHAMPIONSHIP GAME EXPERIENCE: Played in AFC championship game (1984 and 1994 seasons). ... Played in NFC championship game (1997 season).
HONORS: Played in Pro Bowl (1983, 1985 and 1993 seasons).
RECORDS: Holds NFL career record for most field goals—385.
PRO STATISTICS: 1994—Rushed once for three yards.

Year Team	G	GS	KICKING XPM	XPA	FGM	FGA	Lg.	50+	Pts.
1982—Pittsburgh NFL	9	0	22	22	10	12	48	0-1	52
1983—Pittsburgh NFL	16	0	38	39	27	31	49	0-0	§119
1984—Pittsburgh NFL	16	0	45	45	24	32	55	2-3	117
1985—Pittsburgh NFL	16	0	40	40	*33	*42	52	1-4	§139
1986—Pittsburgh NFL	16	0	32	32	21	32	45	0-3	95
1987—Pittsburgh NFL	12	0	21	21	22	27	52	2-2	87
1988—Pittsburgh NFL	16	0	34	35	28	36	52	1-2	118
1989—Pittsburgh NFL	16	0	28	28	21	30	49	0-0	91
1990—Pittsburgh NFL	16	0	32	32	20	25	48	0-2	92
1991—Pittsburgh NFL	16	0	31	31	23	33	54	1-6	100
1992—Pittsburgh NFL	16	0	29	31	28	36	49	0-2	113
1993—Pittsburgh NFL	16	0	32	32	28	30	46	0-0	116
1994—Pittsburgh NFL	16	0	32	32	24	29	50	1-2	104
1995—Philadelphia NFL	16	0	32	33	22	30	43	0-3	98
1996—Philadelphia NFL	16	0	40	40	25	29	46	0-0	115
1997—San Francisco NFL	16	0	38	38	29	36	51	1-3	125
Pro totals (16 years)	245	0	526	531	385	490	55	9-33	1681

A

ANDERSON, JAMAL RB FALCONS

PERSONAL: Born September 30, 1972, in Woodland Hills, Calif. ... 5-11/234. ... Full name: Jamal Sharif Anderson.
HIGH SCHOOL: El Camino Real (Monterey Park, Calif.).
COLLEGE: Utah.
TRANSACTIONS/CAREER NOTES: Selected by Atlanta Falcons in seventh round (201st pick overall) of 1994 NFL draft. ... Signed by Falcons (June 21, 1994).
PRO STATISTICS: 1996—Recovered one fumble. 1997—Attempted four passes with one completion and one interception for 27 yards and one touchdown and recovered one fumble.
SINGLE GAME HIGHS (regular season): Attempts—33 (December 21, 1997, vs. Arizona); yards—162 (November 2, 1997, vs. St. Louis); and rushing touchdowns—3 (October 6, 1996, vs. Detroit).
STATISTICAL PLATEAUS: 100-yard rushing games: 1996 (3), 1997 (2). Total: 5.

Year Team	G	GS	RUSHING				RECEIVING				KICKOFF RETURNS				TOTALS			
			Att.	Yds.	Avg.	TD	No.	Yds.	Avg.	TD	No.	Yds.	Avg.	TD	TD	2pt.	Pts.	Fum.
1994—Atlanta NFL	3	0	2	-1	-0.5	0	0	0	...	0	1	11	11.0	0	0	0	0	0
1995—Atlanta NFL	16	0	39	161	4.1	1	4	42	10.5	0	24	541	22.5	0	1	0	6	0
1996—Atlanta NFL	16	12	232	1055	4.5	5	49	473	9.7	1	4	80	20.0	0	6	0	36	4
1997—Atlanta NFL	16	15	290	1002	3.5	7	29	284	9.8	3	0	0		0	10	0	60	4
Pro totals (4 years)	51	27	563	2217	3.9	13	82	799	9.7	4	29	632	21.8	0	17	0	102	8

ANDERSON, RICHIE RB/FB JETS

PERSONAL: Born September 13, 1971, in Sandy Spring, Md. ... 6-2/225. ... Full name: Richard Darnoll Anderson.
HIGH SCHOOL: Sherwood (Sandy Spring, Md.).
COLLEGE: Penn State.
TRANSACTIONS/CAREER NOTES: Selected after junior season by New York Jets in sixth round (144th pick overall) of 1993 NFL draft. ... Signed by Jets (June 10, 1993). ... On injured reserve with ankle injury (December 31, 1993-remainder of season). ... On injured reserve with ankle injury (November 30, 1995-remainder of season).
PRO STATISTICS: 1993—Recovered one fumble. 1994—Recovered one fumble. 1995—Attempted one pass without a completion. 1996—Recovered one fumble. 1997—Recovered one fumble.
SINGLE GAME HIGHS (regular season): Attempts—9 (November 13, 1994, vs. Green Bay); yards—74 (November 13, 1994, vs. Green Bay); and rushing touchdowns—1 (October 27, 1996, vs. Arizona).

Year Team	G	GS	RUSHING				RECEIVING				KICKOFF RETURNS				TOTALS			
			Att.	Yds.	Avg.	TD	No.	Yds.	Avg.	TD	No.	Yds.	Avg.	TD	TD	2pt.	Pts.	Fum.
1993—New York Jets NFL	7	0	0	0	...	0	0	0	...	0	4	66	16.5	0	0	...	0	1
1994—New York Jets NFL	13	5	43	207	4.8	1	25	212	8.5	1	3	43	14.3	0	2	0	12	1
1995—New York Jets NFL	10	0	5	17	3.4	0	5	26	5.2	0	0	0	...	0	0	0	0	2
1996—New York Jets NFL	16	13	47	150	3.2	1	44	385	8.8	0	0	0	...	0	1	0	6	0
1997—New York Jets NFL	16	3	21	70	3.3	0	26	150	5.8	1	0	0	...	0	1	0	6	2
Pro totals (5 years)	62	21	116	444	3.8	2	100	773	7.7	2	7	109	15.6	0	4	0	24	6

ANDERSON, WILLIE OT BENGALS

PERSONAL: Born July 11, 1975, in Mobile, Ala. ... 6-5/335. ... Full name: Willie Aaron Anderson.
HIGH SCHOOL: Vigor (Mobile, Ala.).
COLLEGE: Auburn.
TRANSACTIONS/CAREER NOTES: Selected after junior season by Cincinnati Bengals in first round (10th pick overall) of 1996 NFL draft. ... Signed by Bengals (August 5, 1996).
PLAYING EXPERIENCE: Cincinnati NFL, 1996 and 1997. ... Games/Games started: 1996 (16/10), 1997 (16/16). Total: 32/26.

ANTHONY, REIDEL WR BUCCANEERS

PERSONAL: Born October 20, 1976, in South Bay, Fla. ... 5-11/178. ... Full name: Reidel Clarence Anthony. ... Name pronounced REE-dell.
HIGH SCHOOL: Glades Central (Fla.).
COLLEGE: Florida.
TRANSACTIONS/CAREER NOTES: Selected after junior season by Tampa Bay Buccaneers in first round (16th pick overall) of 1997 NFL draft. ... Signed by Buccaneers (July 20, 1997).
HONORS: Named wide receiver on THE SPORTING NEWS college All-America first team (1996).
PRO STATISTICS: 1997—Rushed five times for 84 yards.
SINGLE GAME HIGHS (regular season): Receptions—5 (October 26, 1997, vs. Minnesota); yards—92 (October 26, 1997, vs. Minnesota); and touchdown receptions—1 (November 23, 1997, vs. Chicago).

Year Team	G	GS	RECEIVING				KICKOFF RETURNS				TOTALS			
			No.	Yds.	Avg.	TD	No.	Yds.	Avg.	TD	TD	2pt.	Pts.	Fum.
1997—Tampa Bay NFL	16	12	35	448	12.8	4	25	592	23.7	0	4	0	24	0

ARAGUZ, LEO P RAIDERS

PERSONAL: Born January 18, 1970, in Pharr, Texas. ... 6-0/185. ... Full name: Leobardo Jaime Araguz.
HIGH SCHOOL: Harlingen (Texas).
COLLEGE: Stephen F. Austin.
TRANSACTIONS/CAREER NOTES: Signed as non-drafted free agent by Miami Dolphins (March 28, 1994). ... Released by Dolphins prior to 1994 season. ... Signed by San Diego Chargers (1995). ... Released by Chargers prior to 1995 season. ... Signed by Rhein Fire of World League for 1996 season. ... Signed by Oakland Raiders (December 4, 1996).
PRO STATISTICS: 1996—Rushed once for no yards and recovered one fumble. 1997—Rushed once for no yards, fumbled once and recovered one fumble for minus 21 yards.

Year Team	G	GS	No.	Yds.	PUNTING Avg.	Net avg.	In. 20	Blk.
1996—Rhein W.L.	...	...	41	1735	42.3	37.8	17	0
—Oakland NFL	3	0	13	534	41.1	34.5	4	0
1997—Oakland NFL	16	0	§93	§4189	45.0	§39.1	▲28	0
W.L. totals (1 year)	...	...	41	1735	42.3	37.8	17	0
NFL totals (2 years)	19	0	106	4723	44.6	38.5	32	0
Pro totals (3 years)	...	...	147	6458	43.9	38.3	49	0

ARCHAMBEAU, LESTER   DE   FALCONS

PERSONAL: Born June 27, 1967, in Montville, N.J. ... 6-5/275. ... Full name: Lester Milward Archambeau.
HIGH SCHOOL: Montville (N.J.).
COLLEGE: Stanford (degree in industrial engineering).
TRANSACTIONS/CAREER NOTES: Selected by Green Bay Packers in seventh round (186th pick overall) of 1990 NFL draft. ... Signed by Packers (July 22, 1990). ... On injured reserve with back injury (October 6, 1990-remainder of season). ... Granted free agency (February 1, 1992). ... Re-signed by Packers (August 12, 1992). ... Traded by Packers to Atlanta Falcons for WR James Milling (June 3, 1993). ... Granted unconditional free agency (February 17, 1994). ... Re-signed by Falcons (March 7, 1994). ... Granted unconditional free agency (February 14, 1997). ... Re-signed by Falcons (March 3, 1997).
PRO STATISTICS: 1995—Recovered one fumble. 1997—Intercepted one pass for no yards and recovered three fumbles.

Year Team	G	GS	SACKS
1990—Green Bay NFL	4	0	0.0
1991—Green Bay NFL	16	0	4.5
1992—Green Bay NFL	16	0	1.0
1993—Atlanta NFL	15	11	0.0
1994—Atlanta NFL	16	12	2.0
1995—Atlanta NFL	16	7	3.0
1996—Atlanta NFL	15	15	2.0
1997—Atlanta NFL	16	16	8.5
Pro totals (8 years)	114	61	21.0

ARCHIE, MIKE   RB   OILERS

PERSONAL: Born October 14, 1972, in Sharon, Pa. ... 5-8/211. ... Full name: Michael Lamont Archie.
HIGH SCHOOL: Sharon (Pa.).
COLLEGE: Penn State.
TRANSACTIONS/CAREER NOTES: Selected by Houston Oilers in seventh round (218th pick overall) of 1996 NFL draft. ... Signed by Oilers (July 12, 1996). ... Oilers franchise moved to Tennessee for 1997 season.
PRO STATISTICS: 1997—Returned one punt for five yards and recovered one fumble.
SINGLE GAME HIGHS (regular season): Attempts—0; yards—0; and rushing touchdowns—0.

Year Team	G	GS	KICKOFF RETURNS No.	Yds.	Avg.	TD	TOTALS TD	2pt.	Pts.	Fum.
1996—Houston NFL	2	0	2	24	12.0	0	0	0	0	0
1997—Tennessee NFL	5	0	2	24	12.0	0	0	0	0	0
Pro totals (2 years)	7	0	4	48	12.0	0	0	0	0	0

ARMOUR, JUSTIN   WR   BRONCOS

PERSONAL: Born January 1, 1973, in Colorado Springs, Colo. ... 6-4/209. ... Full name: Justin Hugh Armour.
HIGH SCHOOL: Manitou Springs (Colo.).
COLLEGE: Stanford.
TRANSACTIONS/CAREER NOTES: Selected by Buffalo Bills in fourth round (113th pick overall) of 1995 NFL draft. ... Signed by Bills (June 27, 1995). ... Inactive for 11 games (1996). ... On injured reserve with foot injury (November 22, 1996-remainder of season). ... Released by Bills (August 24, 1997). ... Signed by Philadelphia Eagles (September 23, 1997). ... Released by Eagles (September 27, 1997). ... Re-signed by Eagles (September 29, 1997). ... Released by Eagles (November 4, 1997). ... Signed by Denver Broncos (February 24, 1998).
CHAMPIONSHIP GAME EXPERIENCE: Member of 49ers for NFC championship game (1997 season); inactive.
PRO STATISTICS: 1995—Rushed four times for minus five yards, attempted one pass without a completion, and recovered two fumbles.
SINGLE GAME HIGHS (regular season): Receptions—6 (November 26, 1995, vs. New England); yards—66 (November 26, 1995, vs. New England); and touchdown receptions—1 (December 24, 1995, vs. Houston).

Year Team	G	GS	RECEIVING No.	Yds.	Avg.	TD	TOTALS TD	2pt.	Pts.	Fum.
1995—Buffalo NFL	15	9	26	300	11.5	3	3	0	18	1
1996—Buffalo NFL					Did not play.					
1997—Philadelphia NFL	1	0	0	0	...	0	0	0	0	0
Pro totals (2 years)	16	9	26	300	11.5	3	3	0	18	1

ARMSTEAD, JESSIE   LB   GIANTS

PERSONAL: Born October 26, 1970, in Dallas. ... 6-1/232. ... Full name: Jessie W. Armstead.
HIGH SCHOOL: David W. Carter (Dallas).
COLLEGE: Miami, Fla. (degree in criminal justice, 1992).
TRANSACTIONS/CAREER NOTES: Selected by New York Giants in eighth round (207th pick overall) of 1993 NFL draft. ... Signed by Giants (July 19, 1993).
HONORS: Named outside linebacker on THE SPORTING NEWS NFL All-Pro team (1997). ... Played in Pro Bowl (1997 season).
PRO STATISTICS: 1995—Recovered one fumble. 1996—Fumbled once and recovered two fumbles. 1997—Recovered one fumble.

Year Team	G	GS	INTERCEPTIONS No.	Yds.	Avg.	TD	SACKS No.
1993—New York Giants NFL	16	0	1	0	0.0	0	0.0
1994—New York Giants NFL	16	0	1	0	0.0	0	3.0
1995—New York Giants NFL	16	2	1	58	58.0	1	0.5
1996—New York Giants NFL	16	16	2	23	11.5	0	3.0
1997—New York Giants NFL	16	16	2	57	28.5	1	3.5
Pro totals (5 years)	80	34	7	138	19.7	2	10.0

ARMSTRONG, BRUCE   OT   PATRIOTS

PERSONAL: Born September 7, 1965, in Miami. ... 6-4/295. ... Full name: Bruce Charles Armstrong.
HIGH SCHOOL: Central (Miami).
COLLEGE: Louisville.
TRANSACTIONS/CAREER NOTES: Selected by New England Patriots in first round (23rd pick overall) of 1987 NFL draft. ... Signed by Patriots (July 23, 1987). ... On injured reserve with knee injury (November 2, 1992-remainder of season). ... On active/physically unable to perform list (July 16-July 27, 1993). ... Granted unconditional free agency (February 13, 1998). ... Re-signed by Patriots (February 23, 1008).
PLAYING EXPERIENCE: New England NFL, 1987-1997. ... Games: 1987 (12/12), 1988 (16/16), 1989 (16/16), 1990 (16/16), 1991 (16/16), 1992 (8/8), 1993 (16/16), 1994 (16/16), 1995 (16/16), 1996 (16/16), 1997 (16/16). Total: 164/164.
CHAMPIONSHIP GAME EXPERIENCE: Played in AFC championship game (1996 season). ... Played in Super Bowl XXXI (1996 season).
HONORS: Named offensive tackle on THE SPORTING NEWS NFL All-Pro team (1988). ... Played in Pro Bowl (1990, 1991 and 1994-1997 seasons).
PRO STATISTICS: 1990—Recovered two fumbles for four yards. 1992—Recovered one fumble. 1993—Recovered one fumble for one yard. 1995—Recovered one fumble.

ARMSTRONG, TRACE   DE   DOLPHINS

PERSONAL: Born October 5, 1965, in Bethesda, Md. ... 6-4/267. ... Full name: Raymond Lester Armstrong.
HIGH SCHOOL: John Carroll (Birmingham, Ala.).
COLLEGE: Arizona State, then Florida (degree in psychology, 1989).
TRANSACTIONS/CAREER NOTES: Selected by Chicago Bears in first round (12th pick overall) of 1989 NFL draft. ... Signed by Bears (August 18, 1989). ... On injured reserve with knee injury (September 24-November 3, 1991). ... Granted free agency (March 1, 1993). ... Re-signed by Bears (March 14, 1993). ... Traded by Bears to Miami Dolphins for second- (P Todd Sauerbrun) and third-round (G Evan Pilgrim) picks in 1995 draft (April 4, 1995).
HONORS: Named defensive lineman on THE SPORTING NEWS college All-America first team (1988).
PRO STATISTICS: 1989—Recovered one fumble. 1990—Recovered two fumbles. 1992—Recovered one fumble. 1993—Recovered three fumbles for three yards. 1995—Recovered one fumble. 1996—Recovered two fumbles. 1997—Recovered three fumbles.

Year Team	G	GS	SACKS
1989—Chicago NFL	15	14	5.0
1990—Chicago NFL	16	16	10.0
1991—Chicago NFL	12	12	1.5
1992—Chicago NFL	14	14	6.5
1993—Chicago NFL	16	16	11.5
1994—Chicago NFL	15	15	7.5
1995—Miami NFL	15	0	4.5
1996—Miami NFL	16	9	12.0
1997—Miami NFL	16	16	5.5
Pro totals (9 years)	135	112	64.0

ARMSTRONG, TYJI   TE   RAMS

PERSONAL: Born October 3, 1970, in Inkster, Mich. ... 6-4/250. ... Full name: Tyji Donrapheal Armstrong. ... Name pronounced TY-JAY.
HIGH SCHOOL: Robichaud (Dearborn, Mich.).
JUNIOR COLLEGE: Iowa Central Community College.
COLLEGE: Mississippi.
TRANSACTIONS/CAREER NOTES: Selected by Tampa Bay Buccaneers in third round (79th pick overall) of 1992 NFL draft. ... Signed by Buccaneers (July 27, 1992). ... Granted free agency (February 17, 1995). ... Re-signed by Buccaneers (May 19, 1995). ... Released by Buccaneers (August 25, 1996). ... Signed by Dallas Cowboys (August 27, 1996). ... Granted unconditional free agency (February 14, 1997). ... Signed by St. Louis Rams (January 21, 1998). ... Assigned by Rams to Amsterdam Admirals in 1998 NFL Europe enhancement allocation program (February 18, 1998).
PRO STATISTICS: 1993—Rushed twice for five yards. 1994—Rushed once for minus one yard, returned one kickoff for six yards and recovered one fumble. 1995—Returned one kickoff for six yards and recovered one fumble.
SINGLE GAME HIGHS (regular season): Receptions—4 (December 24, 1994, vs. Green Bay); yards—81 (December 6, 1992, vs. Los Angeles Rams); and touchdown receptions—1 (December 24, 1994, vs. Green Bay).

Year Team	G	GS	RECEIVING No.	Yds.	Avg.	TD	TOTALS TD	2pt.	Pts.	Fum.
1992—Tampa Bay NFL	15	7	7	138	19.7	1	1	...	6	0
1993—Tampa Bay NFL	12	7	9	86	9.6	1	1	...	6	0
1994—Tampa Bay NFL	16	9	22	265	12.0	1	1	0	6	2
1995—Tampa Bay NFL	16	3	7	68	9.7	0	0	0	0	1
1996—Dallas NFL	16	7	2	10	5.0	0	0	0	0	0
1997—					Did not play.					
Pro totals (5 years)	75	33	47	567	12.1	3	3	0	18	3

ARNOLD, JAHINE   WR   STEELERS

PERSONAL: Born June 19, 1973, in Rockville, Conn. ... 6-0/187.
HIGH SCHOOL: Homestead (Cupertino, Calif.).
JUNIOR COLLEGE: DeAnza (Cupertino, Calif.).
COLLEGE: Fresno State.
TRANSACTIONS/CAREER NOTES: Selected by Pittsburgh Steelers in fourth round (132nd pick overall) of 1996 NFL draft. ... Signed by Steelers (July 16, 1996). ... On injured reserve with knee injury (August 19, 1997-entire season).
PRO STATISTICS: 1996—Rushed once for minus three yards and returned two punts for six yards.
SINGLE GAME HIGHS (regular season): Receptions—2 (December 22, 1996, vs. Carolina); yards—26 (October 7, 1996, vs. Kansas City); and touchdown receptions—0.

| | | | RECEIVING | | | | KICKOFF RETURNS | | | | TOTALS | | |
Year Team	G	GS	No.	Yds.	Avg.	TD	No.	Yds.	Avg.	TD	TD	2pt.	Pts.	Fum.
1996—Pittsburgh NFL	9	0	6	76	12.7	0	19	425	22.4	0	0	0	0	1
1997—Pittsburgh NFL							Did not play.							

ASHER, JAMIE   TE   REDSKINS

PERSONAL: Born October 31, 1972, in Indianapolis. ... 6-3/245.
HIGH SCHOOL: Warren Central (Indianapolis).
COLLEGE: Louisville.
TRANSACTIONS/CAREER NOTES: Selected by Washington Redskins in fifth round (137th pick overall) of 1995 NFL draft. ... Signed by Redskins (June 1, 1995). ... Granted free agency (February 13, 1998). ... Re-signed by Redskins (April 23, 1998).
PRO STATISTICS: 1995—Returned one kickoff for 13 yards. 1996—Returned one kickoff for 13 yards and recovered two fumbles. 1997—Returned one kickoff for 17 yards and recovered two fumbles.
SINGLE GAME HIGHS (regular season): Receptions—6 (September 7, 1997, vs. Pittsburgh); yards—55 (November 28, 1996, vs. Dallas); and touchdown receptions—2 (November 17, 1996, vs. Philadelphia).

| | | | RECEIVING | | | | TOTALS | | | |
Year Team	G	GS	No.	Yds.	Avg.	TD	TD	2pt.	Pts.	Fum.
1995—Washington NFL	7	1	14	172	12.3	0	0	0	0	0
1996—Washington NFL	16	12	42	481	11.5	4	4	0	24	0
1997—Washington NFL	16	13	49	474	9.7	1	1	0	6	0
Pro totals (3 years)	39	26	105	1127	10.7	5	5	0	30	0

ASHMORE, DARRYL   OT   RAIDERS

PERSONAL: Born November 1, 1969, in Peoria, Ill. ... 6-7/310. ... Full name: Darryl Allan Ashmore.
HIGH SCHOOL: Peoria (Ill.) Central.
COLLEGE: Northwestern (degree in business).
TRANSACTIONS/CAREER NOTES: Selected by Los Angeles Rams in seventh round (171st pick overall) of 1992 NFL draft. ... Signed by Rams (July 13, 1992). ... On injured reserve with knee injury (September 3-October 7, 1992). ... On practice squad (October 7, 1992-remainder of season). ... Granted free agency (February 17, 1995). ... Rams franchise moved to St. Louis (April 12, 1995). ... Re-signed by Rams (July 20, 1995). ... Released by Rams (October 14, 1996). ... Signed by Washington Redskins (October 26, 1996). ... Granted unconditional free agency (February 14, 1997). ... Re-signed by Redskins (May 9, 1997). ... Granted unconditional free agency (February 13, 1998). ... Signed by Oakland Raiders (April 23, 1998).
PLAYING EXPERIENCE: Los Angeles Rams NFL, 1993 and 1994; St. Louis NFL, 1995; St. Louis (6)-Washington (5) NFL, 1996; Washington NFL, 1997. ... Games/Games started: 1993 (9/7), 1994 (11/3), 1995 (16/15), 1996 (St.L-6/0; Wash.-5/0; Total: 11/0), 1997 (11/2). Total: 58/27.

ASKA, JOE   RB   RAIDERS

PERSONAL: Born July 14, 1972, in St. Croix, Virgin Islands ... 5-11/230.
HIGH SCHOOL: Putnam City (Okla.).
JUNIOR COLLEGE: Cisco (Texas) Junior College, then Coffeyville (Kan.) Community College.
COLLEGE: Central Oklahoma.
TRANSACTIONS/CAREER NOTES: Selected by Los Angeles Raiders in third round (86th pick overall) of 1995 NFL draft. ... Signed by Raiders (June 1, 1995). ... Raiders franchise moved to Oakland (July 21, 1995).
PRO STATISTICS: 1996—Caught eight passes for 63 yards and returned one kickoff for 17 yards. 1997—Returned two kickoffs for 46 yards.
SINGLE GAME HIGHS (regular season): Attempts—21 (October 6, 1996, vs. New York Jets); yards—136 (October 6, 1996, vs. New York Jets); and rushing touchdowns—1 (October 6, 1996, vs. New York Jets).
STATISTICAL PLATEAUS: 100-yard rushing games: 1996 (1).

| | | | RUSHING | | | | TOTALS | | | |
Year Team	G	GS	Att.	Yds.	Avg.	TD	TD	2pt.	Pts.	Fum.
1995—Oakland NFL	1	0	0	0	...	0	0	0	0	0
1996—Oakland NFL	15	2	62	326	5.3	1	1	0	6	1
1997—Oakland NFL	7	0	12	10	0.8	0	0	0	0	0
Pro totals (3 years)	23	2	74	336	4.5	1	1	0	6	1

ATKINS, JAMES   G   RAVENS

PERSONAL: Born January 28, 1970, in Amite, La. ... 6-6/306.
HIGH SCHOOL: Woodland (Amite, La.).
COLLEGE: Southwestern Louisiana.

TRANSACTIONS/CAREER NOTES: Signed as non-drafted free agent by Houston Oilers (May 26, 1993). ... Released by Oilers (August 31, 1993). ... Signed by Seattle Seahawks to practice squad (October 11, 1993). ... Released by Seahawks (February 27, 1998). ... Signed by Baltimore Ravens (March 25, 1998).
PLAYING EXPERIENCE: Seattle NFL, 1994-1997. ... Games/Games started: 1994 (4/2), 1995 (16/16), 1996 (16/16), 1997 (13/3). Total: 49/37.
PRO STATISTICS: 1995—Recovered one fumble. 1996—Recovered two fumbles. 1997—Recovered one fumble.

ATWATER, STEVE   S   BRONCOS

PERSONAL: Born October 28, 1966, in Chicago. ... 6-3/216. ... Full name: Stephen Dennis Atwater. ... Cousin of Mark Ingram, wide receiver with four NFL teams (1987-1996).
HIGH SCHOOL: Lutheran North (St. Louis).
COLLEGE: Arkansas (degree in business administration, 1989).
TRANSACTIONS/CAREER NOTES: Selected by Denver Broncos in first round (20th pick overall) of 1989 NFL draft. ... Signed by Broncos (August 1, 1989). ... Designated by Broncos as transition player (February 25, 1993). ... Designated by Broncos as franchise player (February 15, 1995).
CHAMPIONSHIP GAME EXPERIENCE: Played in AFC championship game (1989, 1991and 1997 seasons). ... Played in Super Bowl XXIV (1989 season). ... Member of Super Bowl championship team (1997 season).
HONORS: Named defensive back on THE SPORTING NEWS college All-America second team (1988). ... Played in Pro Bowl (1990-1995 seasons). ... Named free safety on THE SPORTING NEWS NFL All-Pro team (1992). ... Named to play in Pro Bowl (1996 season); replaced by Eric Turner due to injury.
PRO STATISTICS: 1989—Recovered one fumble for 29 yards. 1990—Returned one kickoff for no yards. 1991—Recovered one fumble. 1992—Recovered two fumbles for one yard. 1994—Recovered two fumbles for 17 yards. 1996—Fumbled once. 1997—Recovered two fumbles.

			INTERCEPTIONS				SACKS
Year Team	G	GS	No.	Yds.	Avg.	TD	No.
1989—Denver NFL	16	16	3	34	11.3	0	0.0
1990—Denver NFL	15	15	2	32	16.0	0	1.0
1991—Denver NFL	16	16	5	104	20.8	0	1.0
1992—Denver NFL	15	15	2	22	11.0	0	1.0
1993—Denver NFL	16	16	2	81	40.5	0	1.0
1994—Denver NFL	14	14	1	24	24.0	0	0.0
1995—Denver NFL	16	16	3	54	18.0	0	0.0
1996—Denver NFL	16	16	3	11	3.7	0	0.0
1997—Denver NFL	15	15	2	42	21.0	1	1.0
Pro totals (9 years)	139	139	23	404	17.6	1	5.0

AUSTIN, RAYMOND   DB   JETS

PERSONAL: Born December 21, 1974, in Lawton, Okla. ... 5-11/190. ... Full name: Raymond Demont Austin.
HIGH SCHOOL: Eisenhower (Lawton, Okla.).
COLLEGE: Tennessee.
TRANSACTIONS/CAREER NOTES: Selected by New York Jets in fifth round (145th pick overall) of 1997 NFL draft. ... Signed by Jets (June 15, 1997).
PLAYING EXPERIENCE: New York Jets NFL, 1997. ... Games/Games started: 16/0.

AUTRY, DARNELL   RB   BEARS

PERSONAL: Born June 19, 1976, in Weisbaden, West Germany ... 5-10/210. ... Full name: Harrington Darnell Autry.
HIGH SCHOOL: Tempe (Ariz.).
COLLEGE: Northwestern.
TRANSACTIONS/CAREER NOTES: Selected after junior season by Chicago Bears in fourth round (105th pick overall) of 1997 NFL draft. ... Signed by Bears (July 14, 1997).
HONORS: Named running back on THE SPORTING NEWS college All-America second team (1995 and 1996).
SINGLE GAME HIGHS (regular season): Attempts—26 (December 14, 1997, vs. St. Louis); yards—62 (December 14, 1997, vs. St. Louis); and rushing touchdowns—1 (December 21, 1997, vs. Tampa Bay).

			RUSHING				RECEIVING				TOTALS			
Year Team	G	GS	Att.	Yds.	Avg.	TD	No.	Yds.	Avg.	TD	TD	2pt.	Pts.	Fum.
1997—Chicago NFL	13	3	112	319	2.8	1	9	59	6.6	0	1	1	8	2

BADGER, BRAD   G   REDSKINS

PERSONAL: Born January 11, 1975, in Corvallis, Ore. ... 6-4/298.
HIGH SCHOOL: Corvallis (Ore.).
COLLEGE: Stanford.
TRANSACTIONS/CAREER NOTES: Selected by Washington Redskins in fifth round (162nd pick overall) of 1997 NFL draft. ... Signed by Redskins (May 5, 1997).
PLAYING EXPERIENCE: Washington NFL, 1997. ... Games/Games started: 12/2.

BAILEY, AARON   WR   COLTS

PERSONAL: Born October 24, 1971, in Ann Arbor, Mich. ... 5-10/185. ... Full name: Aaron Duane Bailey.
HIGH SCHOOL: Pioneer (Ann Arbor, Mich.).
COLLEGE: College of DuPage (Ill.), then Louisville.
TRANSACTIONS/CAREER NOTES: Signed as non-drafted free agent by Indianapolis Colts (May 5, 1994).
CHAMPIONSHIP GAME EXPERIENCE: Played in AFC championship game (1995 season).

PRO STATISTICS: 1995—Rushed once for 34 yards and recovered one fumble. 1996—Recovered one fumble. 1997—Rushed three times for 20 yards, returned one punt for 19 yards and recovered one fumble.

SINGLE GAME HIGHS (regular season): Receptions—7 (September 21, 1997, vs. Buffalo); yards—96 (September 21, 1997, vs. Buffalo); and touchdown receptions—1 (November 30, 1997, vs. New England).

Year Team	G	GS	RECEIVING No.	Yds.	Avg.	TD	KICKOFF RETURNS No.	Yds.	Avg.	TD	TOTALS TD	2pt.	Pts.	Fum.
1994—Indianapolis NFL	13	0	2	30	15.0	0	0	0	...	0	0	0	0	0
1995—Indianapolis NFL	15	3	21	379	18.0	3	21	495	23.6	1	4	0	24	0
1996—Indianapolis NFL	14	2	18	302	16.8	0	43	1041	24.2	▲1	1	0	6	3
1997—Indianapolis NFL	13	4	26	329	12.7	3	55	1206	21.9	0	3	0	18	2
Pro totals (4 years)	55	9	67	1040	15.5	6	119	2742	23.0	2	8	0	48	5

BAILEY, CARLTON — LB — B

PERSONAL: Born December 15, 1964, in Baltimore. ... 6-3/242. ... Full name: Carlton Wilson Bailey.

HIGH SCHOOL: Woodlawn (Baltimore).

COLLEGE: North Carolina (degree in sociology, 1988).

TRANSACTIONS/CAREER NOTES: Selected by Buffalo Bills in ninth round (235th pick overall) of 1988 NFL draft. ... Signed by Bills (July 15, 1988). ... On injured reserve with knee injury (August 30-November 14, 1988). ... Granted unconditional free agency (March 1, 1993). ... Signed by New York Giants (March 22, 1993). ... Released by Giants (April 5, 1995). ... Signed by Carolina Panthers (May 2, 1995). ... Granted unconditional free agency (February 14, 1997). ... Re-signed by Panthers (September 1, 1997). ... Granted unconditional free agency (February 13, 1998).

CHAMPIONSHIP GAME EXPERIENCE: Played in AFC championship game (1988 and 1990-1992 seasons). ... Played in Super Bowl XXV (1990 season), Super Bowl XXVI (1991 season) and Super Bowl XXVII (1992 season). ... Played in NFC championship game (1996 season).

PRO STATISTICS: 1989—Intercepted one pass for 16 yards. 1990—Recovered one fumble. 1991—Recovered one fumble. 1993—Fumbled once and recovered one fumble. 1994—Recovered one fumble for two yards.

Year Team	G	GS	SACKS
1988—Buffalo NFL	6	0	0.0
1989—Buffalo NFL	16	0	0.0
1990—Buffalo NFL	16	6	2.0
1991—Buffalo NFL	16	16	0.0
1992—Buffalo NFL	16	10	1.0
1993—New York Giants NFL	16	16	1.5
1994—New York Giants NFL	16	11	0.0
1995—Carolina NFL	16	14	3.0
1996—Carolina NFL	16	14	2.5
1997—Carolina NFL	8	0	0.0
Pro totals (10 years)	142	87	10.0

BAILEY, HENRY — WR/KR — STEELERS

PERSONAL: Born February 28, 1973, in Chicago. ... 5-8/176. ... Full name: Henry C. Bailey.

HIGH SCHOOL: John F. Kennedy (Chicago), then George W. Collins (Chicago).

COLLEGE: UNLV.

TRANSACTIONS/CAREER NOTES: Selected by Pittsburgh Steelers in seventh round (235th pick overall) of 1995 NFL draft. ... Signed by Steelers (June 8, 1995). ... Released by Steelers (August 27, 1995). ... Re-signed by Steelers to practice squad (August 29, 1995). ... Granted free agency after 1995 season. ... Signed by Buffalo Bills (February 20, 1996). ... Released by Bills (August 25, 1996). ... Signed by New York Jets to practice squad (August 27, 1996). ... Activated (September 24, 1996). ... Granted unconditional free agency (February 14, 1997). ... Signed by Steelers (April 8, 1997). ... On injured reserve with knee injury (August 25, 1997-entire season).

PRO STATISTICS: 1996—Rushed once for minus four yards and caught five passes for 65 yards.

SINGLE GAME HIGHS (regular season): Receptions—3 (October 6, 1996, vs. Oakland); yards—42 (October 6, 1996, vs. Oakland); and touchdown receptions—0.

Year Team	G	GS	INTERCEPTIONS No.	Yds.	Avg.	TD	TOTALS TD	2pt.	Pts.	Fum.
1996—New York Jets NFL	8	0	0	0	...	0	0	0	0	0
1997—Pittsburgh NFL						Did not play.				

BAILEY, ROBERT — CB — LIONS

PERSONAL: Born September 3, 1968, in Miami. ... 5-9/174. ... Full name: Robert Martin Bailey.

HIGH SCHOOL: Miami Southridge Senior.

COLLEGE: Miami (Fla.).

TRANSACTIONS/CAREER NOTES: Selected by Los Angeles Rams in fourth round (107th pick overall) of 1991 NFL draft. ... Signed by Rams (July 17, 1991). ... On injured reserve with broken hand (August 27-October 11, 1991). ... On injured reserve with finger injury (November 19, 1991-remainder of season). ... On injured reserve with knee injury (December 11, 1993-remainder of season). ... Granted free agency (February 17, 1994). ... Re-signed by Rams (June 10, 1994). ... Released by Rams (August 22, 1995). ... Signed by Washington Redskins (September 11, 1995). ... Released by Redskins (October 17, 1995). ... Signed by Dallas Cowboys (October 19, 1995). ... Granted unconditional free agency (February 16, 1996). ... Signed by Miami Dolphins (March 7, 1996). ... Released by Dolphins (March 20, 1997). ... Signed by Lions (April 24, 1997). ... Released by Lions (June 20, 1997). ... Re-signed by Lions (July 22, 1997). ... Granted unconditional free agency (February 13, 1998). ... Re-signed by Lions (March 4, 1998).

CHAMPIONSHIP GAME EXPERIENCE: Played in NFC championship game (1995 season). ... Member of Super Bowl championship team (1995 season).

RECORDS: Holds NFL record for longest punt return—103 yards, touchdown (October 23, 1994, at New Orleans).

PRO STATISTICS: 1994—Returned one punt for 103 yards and a touchdown and recovered one fumble. 1996—Credited with one sack. 1997—Credited with two sacks.

Year Team	G	GS	INTERCEPTIONS			
			No.	Yds.	Avg.	TD
1991—Los Angeles Rams NFL	6	0	0	0	...	0
1992—Los Angeles Rams NFL	16	6	3	61	20.3	1
1993—Los Angeles Rams NFL	9	3	2	41	20.5	0
1994—Los Angeles Rams NFL	16	2	0	0	...	0
1995—Washington NFL	4	0	0	0	...	0
—Dallas NFL	9	0	0	0	...	0
1996—Miami NFL	14	0	0	0	...	0
1997—Detroit NFL	15	0	1	0	0.0	0
Pro totals (7 years)	89	11	6	102	17.0	1

BAKER, DONNELL — WR — RAMS

PERSONAL: Born December 21, 1973, in Baton Rouge, La. ... 6-0/200.
HIGH SCHOOL: Baker (Baton Rouge, La.).
COLLEGE: Southern (La.).
TRANSACTIONS/CAREER NOTES: Selected by Carolina Panthers in seventh round (217th pick overall) of 1996 NFL draft. ... Signed by Panthers (July 17, 1996). ... Released by Panthers (August 25, 1996). ... Re-signed by Panthers to practice squad (August 27, 1996). ... Signed by St. Louis Rams (December 18, 1996). ... Released by Rams (August 19, 1997). ... Signed by Jacksonville Jaguars to practice squad (September 24, 1997). ... Released by Jaguars (October 22, 1997). ... Signed by St. Louis Rams to practice squad (November 11, 1997).

BAKER, MYRON — LB — COLTS

PERSONAL: Born January 6, 1971, in Haughton, La. ... 6-1/232. ... Full name: Myron Tobias Baker.
HIGH SCHOOL: Haughton (La.).
COLLEGE: Louisiana Tech.
TRANSACTIONS/CAREER NOTES: Selected by Chicago Bears in fourth round (100th pick overall) of 1993 NFL draft. ... Signed by Bears (July 15, 1993). ... Granted free agency (February 16, 1996). ... Re-signed by Bears (April 18, 1996). ... Claimed on waivers by Carolina Panthers (August 21, 1996). ... Granted unconditional free agency (February 14, 1997). ... Signed by Bears (July 21, 1997). ... Released by Bears (August 18, 1997). ... Signed by Panthers (December 10, 1997). ... Granted unconditional free agency (February 13, 1998). ... Signed by Indianapolis Colts (March 12, 1998).
PLAYING EXPERIENCE: Chicago NFL, 1993-1995; Carolina NFL, 1996 and 1997. ... Games/Games started: 1993 (16/0), 1994 (16/3), 1995 (16/0), 1996 (16/0), 1997 (2/0). Total: 66/3.
CHAMPIONSHIP GAME EXPERIENCE: Played in NFC championship game (1996 season).
PRO STATISTICS: 1993—Returned blocked punt for five yards and a touchdown and recovered two fumbles for eight yards and a touchdown. 1996—Returned one kickoff for 11 yards and recovered one fumble.

BALL, JERRY — DT — VIKINGS

PERSONAL: Born December 15, 1964, in Beaumont, Texas. ... 6-1/320. ... Full name: Jerry Lee Ball. ... Related to Mel Farr Sr., running back, Detroit Lions (1967-1973); cousin of Mel Farr Jr., running back, Los Angeles Rams (1989) and Sacramento Surge of World League (1991); and cousin of Mike Farr, wide receiver, Detroit Lions (1990-1992).
HIGH SCHOOL: Westbrook (Texas).
COLLEGE: Southern Methodist.
TRANSACTIONS/CAREER NOTES: Selected by Detroit Lions in third round (63rd pick overall) of 1987 NFL draft. ... Signed by Lions (July 6, 1987). ... On injured reserve with knee injury (December 12, 1991-remainder of season). ... On injured reserve with ankle injury (December 13, 1992-remainder of season). ... Traded by Lions to Cleveland Browns for third-round pick (LB Antonio London) in 1993 draft (April 23, 1993). ... Granted unconditional free agency (February 17, 1994). ... Signed by Los Angeles Raiders (June 21, 1994). ... Raiders franchise moved to Oakland (July 21, 1995). ... Released by Raiders (February 14, 1997). ... Signed by Minnesota Vikings (September 24, 1997).
HONORS: Played in Pro Bowl (1989 and 1990 seasons). ... Named to play in Pro Bowl (1991 season); replaced by Henry Thomas due to injury.
PRO STATISTICS: 1987—Returned two kickoffs for 23 yards. 1989—Recovered three fumbles. 1991—Credited with a safety. 1992—Recovered three fumbles for 21 yards and a touchdown. 1994—Recovered one fumble. 1995—Recovered one fumble. 1996—Intercepted one pass for 66 yards and a touchdown and recovered one fumble. 1997—Recovered two fumbles.

Year Team	G	GS	SACKS
1987—Detroit NFL	12	12	1.0
1988—Detroit NFL	16	16	2.0
1989—Detroit NFL	16	16	9.0
1990—Detroit NFL	15	16	2.0
1991—Detroit NFL	13	13	2.0
1992—Detroit NFL	12	12	2.5
1993—Cleveland NFL	16	7	3.0
1994—Los Angeles Raiders NFL	16	14	3.0
1995—Oakland NFL	15	15	3.0
1996—Oakland NFL	16	0	3.0
1997—Minnesota NFL	12	6	0.0
Pro totals (11 years)	159	127	30.5

BALLARD, HOWARD — OT — SEAHAWKS

PERSONAL: Born November 3, 1963, in Ashland, Ala. ... 6-6/325. ... Full name: Howard Louis Ballard. ... Nickname: The House.
HIGH SCHOOL: Clay County (Ashland, Ala.).
COLLEGE: Alabama A&M.
TRANSACTIONS/CAREER NOTES: Selected by Buffalo Bills in 11th round (283rd pick overall) of 1987 NFL draft (elected to return to college for final year of eligibility). ... Signed by Bills (March 30, 1988). ... Granted unconditional free agency (February 17, 1994). ... Signed by Seattle Seahawks (February 28, 1994).

PLAYING EXPERIENCE: Buffalo NFL, 1988-1993; Seattle NFL, 1994-1997. ... Games: 1988 (16/0), 1989 (16/16), 1990 (16/16), 1991 (16/16), 1992 (16/16), 1993 (16/16), 1994 (16/16), 1995 (16/16), 1996 (16/16), 1997 (10/10). Total: 154/138.
CHAMPIONSHIP GAME EXPERIENCE: Played in AFC championship game (1988 and 1990-1993 seasons). ... Played in Super Bowl XXV (1990 season), Super Bowl XXVI (1991 season), Super Bowl XXVII (1992 season) and Super Bowl XXVIII (1993 season).
HONORS: Played in Pro Bowl (1992 and 1993 seasons).
PRO STATISTICS: 1996—Recovered one fumble.

BALLARD, JIM — QB — BILLS

PERSONAL: Born April 16, 1972, in Cuyahoga, Ohio. ... 6-3/223. ... Full name: James R. Ballard.
HIGH SCHOOL: Cuyahoga (Ohio).
COLLEGE: Wilmington (Ohio), then Mount Union (Ohio).
TRANSACTIONS/CAREER NOTES: Signed as non-drafted free agent by Miami Dolphins (April 28, 1993). ... Released by Dolphins prior to 1994 season. ... Signed by Cincinnati Bengals to practice squad (October 19, 1994). ... Released by Bengals following 1994 season. ... Played with London Monarchs (1995) and Scottish Claymores (1995 and 1996) of World League. ... Signed by Atlanta Falcons prior to 1996 season. ... Released by Falcons (August 18, 1996). ... Signed by Buffalo Bills (February 5, 1997). ... Released by Bills (August 19, 1997). ... Re-signed by Bills (October 15, 1997). ... Inactive for nine games (1997). ... Assigned by Bills to Scottish Claymores in 1998 NFL Europe enhancement allocation program (February 18, 1998).

			PASSING							RUSHING				TOTALS		
Year	Team	G	GS	Att.	Comp.	Pct.	Yds.	TD	Int.	Avg.	Rat.	Att.	Yds.	Avg.	TD	TD	2pt.	Pts.
1995—London W.L.	...	...	14	10	71.4	102	0	1	7.29	62.2	0	0	...	0	0	0	0
—Scotland W.L.	...	...	8	4	50.0	39	1	0	4.87	103.7	0	0	...	0	0	0	0
1996—Scotland W.L.	...	...	67	50	74.6	787	8	2	11.75	143.5	13	49	3.8	0	0	0	0
1997—Buffalo NFL								Did not play.									
W.L. totals (2 years)	...	...	89	64	71.9	928	9	3	10.43	125.1	13	49	3.8	0	0	0	0

BANKS, ANTONIO — DB — VIKINGS

PERSONAL: Born March 12, 1973, in Ivor, Va. ... 5-10/199. ... Full name: Antonio Dontral Banks.
HIGH SCHOOL: Warwick (Newport News, Va.).
COLLEGE: Virginia Tech.
TRANSACTIONS/CAREER NOTES: Selected by Minnesota Vikings in fourth round (113th pick overall) of 1997 NFL draft. ... Signed by Vikings (June 9, 1997). ... On injured reserve with foot injury (August 18, 1997-entire season). ... Assigned by Vikings to Amsterdam Admirals in 1998 NFL Europe enhancement allocation program (February 18, 1998).

BANKS, TONY — QB — RAMS

PERSONAL: Born April 5, 1973, in San Diego. ... 6-4/215. ... Full name: Anthony Lamar Banks. ... Cousin of Chip Banks, linebacker with Cleveland Browns (1982-1986), San Diego Chargers (1987) and Indianapolis Colts (1989-1992).
HIGH SCHOOL: Hoover (San Diego).
JUNIOR COLLEGE: San Diego Mesa College.
COLLEGE: Michigan State.
TRANSACTIONS/CAREER NOTES: Selected by St. Louis Rams in second round (42nd pick overall) of 1996 NFL draft. ... Signed by Rams (July 15, 1996).
RECORDS: Holds NFL single-season record for most fumbles—21 (1996).
PRO STATISTICS: 1996—Led league with 21 fumbles and recovered four fumbles for minus 17 yards. 1997—Tied for NFC lead with 15 fumbles and recovered three fumbles for minus 27 yards.
SINGLE GAME HIGHS (regular season): Attempts—49 (September 28, 1997, vs. Oakland); completions—26 (October 27, 1996, vs. Baltimore); yards—401 (November 2, 1997, vs. Atlanta); and touchdown passes—3 (December 7, 1997, vs. New Orleans).
STATISTICAL PLATEAUS: 300-yard passing games: 1996 (2), 1997 (1). Total: 3.
MISCELLANEOUS: Regular-season record as starting NFL quarterback: 10-19 (.345).

			PASSING							RUSHING				TOTALS		
Year	Team	G	GS	Att.	Cmp.	Pct.	Yds.	TD	Int.	Avg.	Rat.	Att.	Yds.	Avg.	TD	TD	2pt.	Pts.
1996—St. Louis NFL	14	13	368	192	52.2	2544	15	15	6.91	71.0	61	212	3.5	0	0	1	2
1997—St. Louis NFL	16	16	487	252	51.7	3254	14	13	6.68	71.5	47	186	4.0	1	1	0	6
Pro totals (2 years)	30	29	855	444	51.9	5798	29	28	6.78	71.3	108	398	3.7	1	1	1	8

RECORD AS BASEBALL PLAYER

TRANSACTIONS/CAREER NOTES: Threw right, batted right. ... Selected by Minnesota Twins organization in 10th round of free-agent draft (June 3, 1991).

			BATTING											FIELDING		
Year	Team (League)	Pos.	G	AB	R	H	2B	3B	HR	RBI	Avg.	BB	SO	SB	PO	A	E	Avg.
1991—GC Twins (GCL)	DH	17	57	7	13	3	0	0	1	.228	4	16	2	...	...	...	...

BANKSTON, MICHAEL — DE — BENGALS

PERSONAL: Born March 12, 1970, in East Bernard, Texas. ... 6-3/280.
HIGH SCHOOL: East Bernard (Texas).
COLLEGE: Sam Houston State.
TRANSACTIONS/CAREER NOTES: Selected by Phoenix Cardinals in fourth round (100th pick overall) of 1992 NFL draft. ... Signed by Cardinals (July 20, 1992). ... Cardinals franchise renamed Arizona Cardinals for 1994 season. ... Granted unconditional free agency (February 14, 1997). ... Re-signed by Cardinals (April 2, 1997). ... Granted unconditional free agency (February 13, 1998). ... Tendered offer sheet by Cincinnati Bengals (February 13, 1998). ... Cardinals declined to match offer (February 14, 1998).
PRO STATISTICS: 1993—Recovered five fumbles for 16 yards. 1994—Recovered one fumble for two yards. 1995—Intercepted one pass for 28 yards and fumbled once. 1996—Recovered one fumble.

Year Team	G	GS	SACKS
1992—Phoenix NFL	16	6	2.0
1993—Phoenix NFL	16	12	3.0
1994—Arizona NFL	16	16	7.0
1995—Arizona NFL	16	16	2.0
1996—Arizona NFL	16	16	0.5
1997—Arizona NFL	16	16	2.0
Pro totals (6 years)	96	82	16.5

BANTA, BRAD — TE — COLTS

PERSONAL: Born December 14, 1970, in Baton Rouge, La. ... 6-6/260. ... Full name: Dennis Bradford Banta.
HIGH SCHOOL: University (Baton Rouge, La.).
COLLEGE: Southern California.
TRANSACTIONS/CAREER NOTES: Selected by Indianapolis Colts in fourth round (106th pick overall) of 1994 NFL draft. ... Signed by Colts (July 22, 1994). ... Granted free agency (February 14, 1997). ... Re-signed by Colts (May 14, 1997).
PLAYING EXPERIENCE: Indianapolis NFL, 1994-1997. ... Games/Games started: 1994 (16/0), 1995 (16/2), 1996 (13/0), 1997 (15/0). Total: 60/2.
CHAMPIONSHIP GAME EXPERIENCE: Played in AFC championship game (1995 season).
PRO STATISTICS: 1995—Caught one pass for six yards.
SINGLE GAME HIGHS (regular season): Receptions—1 (December 17, 1995, vs. San Diego); yards—6 (December 17, 1995, vs. San Diego); and touchdown receptions—0.

BARBER, MICHAEL — LB — SEAHAWKS

PERSONAL: Born November 9, 1971, in Edgemore, S.C. ... 6-1/246.
HIGH SCHOOL: Lewisville (Richburg, S.C.).
COLLEGE: Auburn.
TRANSACTIONS/CAREER NOTES: Signed as non-drafted free agent by Seattle Seahawks (April 26, 1995). ... Granted free agency (February 13, 1998). ... Re-signed by Seahawks (May 13, 1998).
PLAYING EXPERIENCE: Seattle NFL, 1995-1997. ... Games/Games started: 1995 (2/0), 1996 (13/7), 1997 (8/2). Total: 23/9.
PRO STATISTICS: 1996—Returned one kickoff for 12 yards and recovered one fumble. 1997—Recovered one fumble.

BARBER, RONDE — CB — BUCCANEERS

PERSONAL: Born April 7, 1975, in Montgomery County, Va. ... 5-10/186. ... Full name: Ronde Oronde Barber. ... Twin brother of Tiki Barber, running back, New York Giants. ... Name pronounced RON-day.
HIGH SCHOOL: Cave Spring (Roanoke, Va.).
COLLEGE: Virginia.
TRANSACTIONS/CAREER NOTES: Selected after junior season by Tampa Bay Buccaneers in third round (66th pick overall) of 1997 NFL draft. ... Signed by Buccaneers (July 18, 1997).
PLAYING EXPERIENCE: Tampa Bay NFL, 1997. ... Games/Games started: 1/0.

BARBER, TIKI — RB — GIANTS

PERSONAL: Born April 7, 1975, in Montgomery County, Va. ... 5-10/205. ... Full name: Atiim Kiambu Barber. ... Twin Brother of Ronde Barber, cornerback, Tampa Bay Buccaneers. ... Name pronounced TEE-kee.
HIGH SCHOOL: Cave Spring (Roanake, Va.).
COLLEGE: Virginia.
TRANSACTIONS/CAREER NOTES: Selected by New York Giants in second round (36th pick overall) of 1997 NFL draft.
SINGLE GAME HIGHS (regular season): Attempts—21 (December 7, 1997, vs. Philadelphia); yards—114 (December 7, 1997, vs. Philadelphia); and rushing touchdowns—1 (September 14, 1997, vs. Baltimore).
STATISTICAL PLATEAUS: 100-yard rushing games: 1997 (1).

Year Team	G	GS	RUSHING				RECEIVING				TOTALS			
			Att.	Yds.	Avg.	TD	No.	Yds.	Avg.	TD	TD	2pt.	Pts.	Fum.
1997—NY Giants NFL	12	6	136	511	3.8	3	34	299	8.8	1	4	1	26	3

BARKER, BRYAN — P — JAGUARS

PERSONAL: Born June 28, 1964, in Jacksonville Beach, Fla. ... 6-2/200. ... Full name: Bryan Christopher Barker.
HIGH SCHOOL: Miramonte (Orinda, Calif.).
COLLEGE: Santa Clara (degree in economics).
TRANSACTIONS/CAREER NOTES: Signed as non-drafted free agent by Denver Broncos (May 1988). ... Released by Broncos (July 19, 1988). ... Signed by Seattle Seahawks (1989). ... Released by Seahawks (August 30, 1989). ... Signed by Kansas City Chiefs (May 1, 1990). ... Released by Chiefs (August 28, 1990). ... Re-signed by Chiefs (September 26, 1990). ... Granted unconditional free agency (February 1-April 1, 1991). ... Re-signed by Chiefs for 1991 season. ... Granted unconditional free agency (February 1-April 1, 1992). ... Re-signed by Chiefs for 1992 season. ... Released by Chiefs (1994). ... Signed by Minnesota Vikings (May 18, 1994). ... Released by Vikings (August 30, 1994). ... Signed by Philadelphia Eagles (October 11, 1994). ... Granted unconditional free agency (February 17, 1995). ... Signed by Jacksonville Jaguars (March 7, 1995).
CHAMPIONSHIP GAME EXPERIENCE: Played in AFC championship game (1993 and 1996 seasons).
HONORS: Played in Pro Bowl (1997 season).
PRO STATISTICS: 1997—Rushed once for no yards, attempted one pass with one completion for 22 yards and fumbled once for minus 19 yards.

				PUNTING					
Year Team	G	GS	No.	Yds.	Avg.	Net avg.	In. 20	Blk.	
1990—Kansas City NFL	13	0	64	2479	38.7	33.3	16	0	
1991—Kansas City NFL	16	0	57	2303	40.4	35.0	14	1	
1992—Kansas City NFL	15	0	75	3245	43.3	35.2	16	1	
1993—Kansas City NFL	16	0	76	3240	42.6	35.3	19	1	
1994—Philadelphia NFL	11	0	66	2696	40.8	‡36.2	20	0	
1995—Jacksonville NFL	16	0	82	3591	43.8	*38.6	19	0	
1996—Jacksonville NFL	16	0	69	3016	43.7	35.6	16	0	
1997—Jacksonville NFL	16	0	66	2964	44.9	38.8	27	0	
Pro totals (8 years)	119	0	555	23534	42.4	36.1	147	2	

BARKER, ROY   DE   49ERS

B

PERSONAL: Born February 14, 1969, in New York. ... 6-5/290.
HIGH SCHOOL: Central Islip (N.Y.).
COLLEGE: North Carolina (degree in speech communications).
TRANSACTIONS/CAREER NOTES: Selected by Minnesota Vikings in fourth round (98th pick overall) of 1992 NFL draft. ... Signed by Vikings (July 16, 1992). ... On injured reserve with knee injury (September 1-30, 1992). ... Granted unconditional free agency (February 16, 1996). ... Signed by San Francisco 49ers (February 28, 1996).
CHAMPIONSHIP GAME EXPERIENCE: Played in NFC championship game (1997 season).
PRO STATISTICS: 1993—Recovered one fumble. 1994—Recovered one fumble. 1995—Intercepted one pass for minus two yards.

Year Team	G	GS	SACKS
1992—Minnesota NFL	8	0	0.0
1993—Minnesota NFL	16	16	6.0
1994—Minnesota NFL	16	15	3.5
1995—Minnesota NFL	16	16	3.0
1996—San Francisco NFL	16	16	12.5
1997—San Francisco NFL	13	12	5.5
Pro totals (6 years)	85	75	30.5

BARLOW, REGGIE   WR/KR   JAGUARS

PERSONAL: Born January 22, 1973, in Montgomery, Ala. ... 5-11/191. ... Full name: Reggie Devon Barlow.
HIGH SCHOOL: Lanier (Montgomery, Ala.).
COLLEGE: Alabama State.
TRANSACTIONS/CAREER NOTES: Selected by Jacksonville Jaguars in fourth round (110th pick overall) of 1996 NFL draft. ... Signed by Jaguars (May 28, 1996).
CHAMPIONSHIP GAME EXPERIENCE: Played in AFC championship game (1996 season).
PRO STATISTICS: 1997—Recovered one fumble.
SINGLE GAME HIGHS (regular season): Receptions—2 (September 22, 1997, vs. Pittsburgh); yards—29 (October 26, 1997, vs. Pittsburgh); and touchdown receptions—0.

			RECEIVING				PUNT RETURNS				KICKOFF RETURNS				TOTALS			
Year Team	G	GS	No.	Yds.	Avg.	TD	No.	Yds.	Avg.	TD	No.	Yds.	Avg.	TD	TD	2pt.	Pts.	Fum.
1996—Jacksonville NFL	7	0	0	0	...	0	0	0	...	0	0	0	...	0	0	0	0	0
1997—Jacksonville NFL	16	0	5	74	14.8	0	36	412	11.4	0	10	267	26.7	▲1	2	0	12	2
Pro totals (2 years)	23	0	5	74	14.8	0	36	412	11.4	0	10	267	26.7	1	2	0	12	2

BARNDT, TOM   DT   CHIEFS

PERSONAL: Born March 14, 1972, in Mentor, Ohio. ... 6-3/301. ... Full name: Thomas Allen Barndt.
HIGH SCHOOL: Mentor (Ohio).
COLLEGE: Pittsburgh.
TRANSACTIONS/CAREER NOTES: Selected by Kansas City Chiefs in sixth round (207th pick overall) of 1995 NFL draft. ... Signed by Chiefs for 1995 season. ... Released by Chiefs (August 27, 1995). ... Re-signed by Chiefs to practice squad (August 29, 1995). ... Assigned by Chiefs to Scottish Claymores in 1996 World League enhancement allocation program (February 19, 1996).
PLAYING EXPERIENCE: Kansas City NFL, 1996 and 1997. ... Games/Games started: 1996 (13/0), 1997 (16/1). Total: 29/1.
PRO STATISTICS: 1997—Credited with two sacks.

BARNES, DERRICK   LB

PERSONAL: Born September 11, 1974, in Hattiesburg, Miss. ... 6-1/267. ... Full name: Derrick Cornelious Barnes.
HIGH SCHOOL: Prospect (Saratoga, Calif.).
COLLEGE: Oregon.
TRANSACTIONS/CAREER NOTES: Signed as non-drafted free agent by Tennessee Oilers (April 23, 1997). ... Released by Oilers (August 11, 1997). ... Signed by New Orleans Saints to practice squad (December 10, 1997). ... Activated (December 20, 1997). ... Assigned by Saints to England Monarchs in 1998 NFL Europe enhancement allocation program (February 18, 1998). ... Released by Saints (April 14, 1998).
PLAYING EXPERIENCE: New Orleans NFL, 1997. ... Games/Games started: 1/0.

BARNES, PAT   QB   CHIEFS

PERSONAL: Born February 23, 1975, in Arlington Heights, Ill. ... 6-3/215. ... Full name: Patrick Barnes.
HIGH SCHOOL: Trabuco Hills (Calif.).
COLLEGE: California.
TRANSACTIONS/CAREER NOTES: Selected by Kansas City Chiefs in fourth round (110th pick overall) of 1997 NFL draft. ... Signed by Chiefs (May 8, 1997). ... Active for one game (1997); did not play.

BARNES, TOMUR — CB

PERSONAL: Born September 8, 1970, in McNair, Texas. ... 5-10/188.
HIGH SCHOOL: Ross Sterling (Baytown, Texas).
COLLEGE: North Texas.
TRANSACTIONS/CAREER NOTES: Signed as non-drafted free agent by San Francisco 49ers (May 7, 1993). ... Released by 49ers (July 16, 1993). ... Re-signed by 49ers (August 12, 1993). ... Released by 49ers (August 24, 1993). ... Re-signed by 49ers to practice squad (September 22, 1993). ... Released by 49ers (November 8, 1993). ... Re-signed by 49ers to practice squad (December 1, 1993). ... Released by 49ers (December 15, 1993). ... Re-signed by 49ers (May 4, 1994). ... Released by 49ers (August 23, 1994). ... Signed by Houston Oilers to practice squad (August 30, 1994). ... Activated (December 23, 1994). ... Released by Oilers (October 7, 1996). ... Signed by Minnesota Vikings (October 14, 1996). ... Released by Vikings (November 5, 1996). ... Signed by Washington Redskins (November 6, 1996). ... Released by Redskins (August 18, 1997). ... Signed by Tennessee Oilers (August 26, 1997). ... Released by Oilers (September 29, 1997). ... Signed by Denver Broncos (January 30, 1998). ... Released by Broncos (June 9, 1998).
PRO STATISTICS: 1995—Returned one kickoff for minus four yards and recovered one fumble.

			INTERCEPTIONS		
Year Team	G	GS	No.	Yds.	Avg.	TD
1993—San Francisco NFL			Did not play.			
1994—Houston NFL	1	0	0	0	...	0
1995—Houston NFL	15	0	2	6	3.0	0
1996—Houston NFL	5	0	0	0	...	0
—Minnesota NFL	2	0	0	0	...	0
—Washington NFL	3	0	0	0	...	0
1997—Tennessee NFL	3	0	0	0	...	0
Pro totals (4 years)	29	0	2	6	3.0	0

BARNETT, FRED — WR

PERSONAL: Born June 17, 1966, in Shelby, Miss. ... 6-0/199. ... Full name: Fred Lee Barnett Jr. ... Nephew of John Barnett, running back with Los Angeles Express of USFL (1983); and cousin of Tim Barnett, wide receiver with Kansas City Chiefs (1991-1993) and Scottish Claymores of World League (1995).
HIGH SCHOOL: Rosedale (Miss.).
COLLEGE: Arkansas State.
TRANSACTIONS/CAREER NOTES: Selected by Philadelphia Eagles in third round (77th pick overall) of 1990 NFL draft. ... Signed by Eagles (August 13, 1990). ... Granted free agency (March 1, 1993). ... Re-signed by Eagles (August 21, 1993). ... On injured reserve with knee injury (October 4, 1993-remainder of season). ... Granted unconditional free agency (February 16, 1996). ... Signed by Miami Dolphins (March 11, 1996). ... Released by Dolphins (October 13, 1997).
HONORS: Played in Pro Bowl (1992 season).
PRO STATISTICS: 1990—Rushed twice for 13 yards and returned four kickoffs for 65 yards. 1991—Rushed once for no yards and recovered one fumble. 1992—Rushed once for minus 15 yards. 1995—Recovered one fumble.
SINGLE GAME HIGHS (regular season): Receptions—11 (November 6, 1994, vs. Arizona); yards—193 (September 13, 1992, vs. Arizona); and touchdown receptions—2 (November 10, 1996, vs. Indianapolis).
STATISTICAL PLATEAUS: 100-yard receiving games: 1990 (3), 1991 (3), 1992 (3), 1994 (3), 1995 (1), 1996 (1). Total: 14.

			RECEIVING				TOTALS			
Year Team	G	GS	No.	Yds.	Avg.	TD	TD	2pt.	Pts.	Fum.
1990—Philadelphia NFL	16	11	36	721	20.0	8	8	...	48	0
1991—Philadelphia NFL	15	15	62	948	15.3	4	4	...	24	2
1992—Philadelphia NFL	16	16	67	1083	16.2	6	6	...	36	1
1993—Philadelphia NFL	4	4	17	170	10.0	0	0	...	0	1
1994—Philadelphia NFL	16	16	78	1127	14.4	5	5	0	30	1
1995—Philadelphia NFL	14	14	48	585	12.2	5	5	1	32	0
1996—Miami NFL	9	7	36	562	15.6	3	3	0	18	1
1997—Miami NFL	6	5	17	166	9.8	1	1	0	6	1
Pro totals (8 years)	96	88	361	5362	14.9	32	32	1	194	7

BARNHARDT, TOMMY — P — BUCCANEERS

PERSONAL: Born June 11, 1963, in Salisbury, N.C. ... 6-2/228. ... Full name: Tommy Ray Barnhardt.
HIGH SCHOOL: South Rowan (China Grove, N.C.).
COLLEGE: East Carolina, then North Carolina (degree in industrial relations, 1986).
TRANSACTIONS/CAREER NOTES: Selected by Baltimore Stars in 1986 USFL territorial draft. ... Selected by Tampa Bay Buccaneers in ninth round (223rd pick overall) of 1986 NFL draft. ... Released by Buccaneers (July 16, 1986). ... Released by Buccaneers (August 25, 1986). ... Re-signed by Buccaneers (February 6, 1987). ... Released by Buccaneers (August 5, 1987). ... Signed as replacement player by New Orleans Saints (September 23, 1987). ... Released by Saints (November 3, 1987). ... Signed by Chicago Bears (December 16, 1987). ... Released by Bears (August 24, 1988). ... Signed by Washington Redskins (September 9, 1988). ... On injured reserve with pulled quadricep (October 11, 1988-remainder of season). ... Granted unconditional free agency (February 1-April 1, 1989). ... Re-signed by Redskins (May 11, 1989). ... Released by Redskins (June 27, 1989). ... Signed by Detroit Lions (July 20, 1989). ... Released by Lions (August 30, 1989). ... Signed by Saints (October 11, 1989). ... Granted unconditional free agency (February 1-April 1, 1992). ... Re-signed by Saints for 1992 season. ... Granted unconditional free agency (March 1, 1993). ... Re-signed by Saints (July 15, 1993). ... Granted unconditional free agency (February 17, 1995). ... Signed by Carolina Panthers (March 2, 1995). ... Released by Panthers (May 7, 1996). ... Signed by Buccaneers (May 13, 1996). ... On injured reserve with broken collarbone (October 9, 1997-remainder of season).
PRO STATISTICS: 1987—Had 35.2-net-punting average and rushed once for minus 13 yards. 1991—Rushed once for no yards. 1992—Rushed four times for minus two yards and fumbled twice for minus 16 yards. 1993—Rushed once for 18 yards and attempted one pass with one completion for seven yards. 1994—Rushed once for 21 yards and attempted one pass without a completion. 1996—Rushed twice for 27 yards. 1997—Attempted one pass with one completion for 25 yards.

Year Team	G	GS	No.	Yds.	Avg.	Net avg.	In. 20	Blk.
					PUNTING			
1987—New Orleans NFL	3	0	11	483	43.9	...	4	0
—Chicago NFL	2	0	6	236	39.3	35.2	2	0
1988—Washington NFL	4	0	15	628	41.9	34.2	1	0
1989—New Orleans NFL	11	0	55	2179	39.6	35.0	17	0
1990—New Orleans NFL	16	0	70	2990	42.7	36.2	20	1
1991—New Orleans NFL	16	0	86	*3743	43.5	35.2	20	1
1992—New Orleans NFL	16	0	67	2947	44.0	37.7	19	0
1993—New Orleans NFL	16	0	77	3356	43.6	37.5	26	0
1994—New Orleans NFL	16	0	67	2920	43.6	33.5	14	0
1995—Carolina NFL	16	0	‡95	‡3906	41.1	35.2	27	0
1996—Tampa Bay NFL	16	0	70	3015	43.1	37.7	24	1
1997—Tampa Bay NFL	6	0	29	1304	45.0	39.1	12	0
Pro totals (11 years)	138	0	648	27707	42.8	35.5	186	3

B

BARROW, MICHEAL · LB · PANTHERS

PERSONAL: Born April 19, 1970, in Homestead, Fla. ... 6-2/236. ... Full name: Micheal Calvin Barrow.
HIGH SCHOOL: Homestead (Fla.) Senior.
COLLEGE: Miami, Fla (degree in accounting, 1992).
TRANSACTIONS/CAREER NOTES: Selected by Houston Oilers in second round (47th pick overall) of 1993 NFL draft. ... Signed by Oilers (July 30, 1993). ... Granted free agency (February 16, 1996). ... Re-signed by Oilers (August 9, 1996). ... Granted unconditional free agency (February 14, 1997). ... Signed by Carolina Panthers (February 20, 1997).
HONORS: Named linebacker on THE SPORTING NEWS college All-America first team (1992).
PRO STATISTICS: 1995—Recovered one fumble. 1996—Recovered one fumble. 1997—Recovered two fumbles.

Year Team	G	GS	SACKS
1993—Houston NFL	16	0	1.0
1994—Houston NFL	16	16	2.5
1995—Houston NFL	13	12	3.0
1996—Houston NFL	16	16	6.0
1997—Carolina NFL	16	16	8.5
Pro totals (5 years)	77	60	21.0

BARTON, HARRIS · OT · 49ERS

PERSONAL: Born April 19, 1964, in Atlanta. ... 6-4/292. ... Full name: Harris Scott Barton.
HIGH SCHOOL: Dunwoody (Ga.).
COLLEGE: North Carolina (bachelor of science degree, 1987).
TRANSACTIONS/CAREER NOTES: Selected by San Francisco 49ers in first round (22nd pick overall) of 1987 NFL draft. ... Signed by 49ers (July 22, 1987). ... Granted free agency (February 1, 1990). ... Re-signed by 49ers (July 30, 1990). ... On injured reserve with knee injury (October 31, 1997-remainder of season). ... Inactive for eight games (1997).
PLAYING EXPERIENCE: San Francisco NFL, 1987-1996. ... Games/Games started: 1987 (12/9), 1988 (16/15), 1989 (16/16), 1990 (16/16), 1991 (16/16), 1992 (13/13), 1993 (15/15), 1994 (9/9), 1995 (12/12), 1996 (13/13). Total: 138/134.
CHAMPIONSHIP GAME EXPERIENCE: Played in NFC championship game (1988-1990 and 1992-1994 seasons). ... Member of Super Bowl championship team (1988, 1989 and 1994 seasons). ... Member of 49ers for NFC championship game (1997 season); inactive.
HONORS: Named offensive tackle on THE SPORTING NEWS college All-America second team (1986). ... Named offensive tackle on THE SPORTING NEWS NFL All-Pro team (1993). ... Played in Pro Bowl (1993 season).
PRO STATISTICS: 1987—Recovered one fumble. 1991—Recovered one fumble.

BARTRUM, MIKE · TE · PATRIOTS

PERSONAL: Born June 23, 1970, in Gallipolis, Ohio. ... 6-5/245. ... Full name: Michael Weldon Bartrum.
HIGH SCHOOL: Meigs (Pomeroy, Ohio).
COLLEGE: Marshall (degree in education).
TRANSACTIONS/CAREER NOTES: Signed as non-drafted free agent by Kansas City Chiefs (May 5, 1993). ... Released by Chiefs (August 30, 1993). ... Re-signed by Chiefs to practice squad (August 31, 1993). ... Activated (October 27, 1993). ... Released by Chiefs (August 23, 1994). ... Signed by Green Bay Packers (January 20, 1995). ... On injured reserve with broken arm (October 11, 1995-remainder of season). ... Traded by Packers with DE Walter Scott to New England Patriots for past considerations (August 25, 1996). ... On injured reserve with forearm injury (November 12, 1997-remainder of season). ... Granted unconditional free agency (February 13, 1998). ... Re-signed by Patriots (April 7, 1998).
PLAYING EXPERIENCE: Kansas City NFL, 1993; Green Bay NFL, 1995; New England NFL, 1996 and 1997. ... Games/Games started: 1993 (3/0), 1995 (4/0), 1996 (16/0), 1997 (9/0). Total: 32/0.
CHAMPIONSHIP GAME EXPERIENCE: Member of Chiefs for AFC championship game (1993 season); inactive. ... Played in AFC championship game (1996 season). ... Played in Super Bowl XXXI (1996 season).
PRO STATISTICS: 1996—Caught one pass for one yard and a touchdown.
SINGLE GAME HIGHS (regular season): Receptions—1 (October 6, 1996, vs. Baltimore); yards—1 (October 6, 1996, vs. Baltimore); and touchdown receptions—1 (October 6, 1996, vs. Baltimore).

BATES, BILL · S

PERSONAL: Born June 6, 1961, in Knoxville, Tenn. ... 6 1/213. ... Full name: William Frederick Bates.
HIGH SCHOOL: Farragut (Knoxville, Tenn.).
COLLEGE: Tennessee.

TRANSACTIONS/CAREER NOTES: Selected by New Jersey Generals in 1983 USFL territorial draft. ... Signed as non-drafted free agent by Dallas Cowboys (April 28, 1983). ... On injured reserve with hip injury (September 3-28, 1984). ... Granted unconditional free agency (February 1-April 1, 1991). ... Re-signed by Cowboys for 1991 season. ... Granted unconditional free agency (February 1-April 1, 1992). ... Re-signed by Cowboys for 1992 season. ... On injured reserve with knee injury (October 14, 1992-remainder of season). ... Granted unconditional free agency (March 1, 1993). ... Released by Cowboys (June 15, 1993). ... Re-signed by Cowboys (August 30, 1993). ... Re-signed by Cowboys (August 31, 1993). ... Granted unconditional free agency (February 17, 1994). ... Re-signed by Cowboys (July 14, 1994). ... Granted unconditional free agency (February 16, 1996). ... Re-signed by Cowboys (March 29, 1996). ... Granted unconditional free agency (February 14, 1997). ... Re-signed by Cowboys (June 2, 1997). ... Granted unconditional free agency (February 13, 1998).

CHAMPIONSHIP GAME EXPERIENCE: Played in NFC championship game (1993-1995 seasons). ... Member of Super Bowl championship team (1992, 1993 and 1995 seasons).

HONORS: Played in Pro Bowl (1984 season).

PRO STATISTICS: 1983—Fumbled once and recovered two fumbles. 1984—Recovered one fumble. 1985—Returned 22 punts for 152 yards. 1988—Recovered one fumble. 1989—Rushed once for no yards. 1990—Rushed once for four yards. 1991—Recovered two fumbles. 1993—Recovered one fumble. 1997—Credited with one sack.

			INTERCEPTIONS			
Year Team	G	GS	No.	Yds.	Avg.	TD
1983—Dallas NFL	16	1	1	29	29.0	0
1984—Dallas NFL	12	2	1	3	3.0	0
1985—Dallas NFL	16	0	4	15	3.8	0
1986—Dallas NFL	15	15	0	0	...	0
1987—Dallas NFL	12	11	3	28	9.3	0
1988—Dallas NFL	16	16	1	0	0.0	0
1989—Dallas NFL	16	0	1	18	18.0	0
1990—Dallas NFL	16	0	1	4	4.0	0
1991—Dallas NFL	16	0	0	0	...	0
1992—Dallas NFL	5	0	0	0	...	0
1993—Dallas NFL	16	0	2	25	12.5	0
1994—Dallas NFL	15	0	0	0	...	0
1995—Dallas NFL	16	0	0	0	...	0
1996—Dallas NFL	14	0	0	0	...	0
1997—Dallas NFL	16	0	0	0	...	0
Pro totals (15 years)	217	45	14	122	8.7	0

BATES, MARIO — RB — CARDINALS

PERSONAL: Born January 16, 1973, in Tucson, Ariz. ... 6-1/217. ... Full name: Mario Doniel Bates. ... Brother of Michael Bates, kick returner/wide receiver, Carolina Panthers.

HIGH SCHOOL: Amphitheater (Tucson, Ariz.).

COLLEGE: Arizona State.

TRANSACTIONS/CAREER NOTES: Selected after junior season by New Orleans Saints in second round (44th pick overall) of 1994 NFL draft. ... Signed by Saints (July 6, 1994). ... Granted free agency (February 14, 1997). ... Re-signed by Saints (June 12, 1997). ... Granted unconditional free agency (February 13, 1998). ... Signed by Arizona Cardinals (March 6, 1998).

PRO STATISTICS: 1994—Returned one kickoff for 20 yards and recovered one fumble. 1995—Recovered one fumble. 1997—Attempted one pass with one completion for 21 yards and a touchdown.

SINGLE GAME HIGHS (regular season): Attempts—32 (December 15, 1996, vs. New York Giants); yards—162 (September 21, 1997, vs. Detroit); and rushing touchdowns—3 (December 4, 1994, vs. Los Angeles Rams).

STATISTICAL PLATEAUS: 100-yard rushing games: 1994 (1), 1995 (3), 1996 (1), 1997 (1). Total: 6.

			RUSHING				RECEIVING				TOTALS			
Year Team	G	GS	Att.	Yds.	Avg.	TD	No.	Yds.	Avg.	TD	TD	2pt.	Pts.	Fum.
1994—New Orleans NFL	11	7	151	579	3.8	6	8	62	7.8	0	6	0	36	3
1995—New Orleans NFL	16	16	244	951	3.9	7	18	114	6.3	0	7	0	42	2
1996—New Orleans NFL	14	10	164	584	3.6	4	13	44	3.4	0	4	0	24	4
1997—New Orleans NFL	12	7	119	440	3.7	4	5	42	8.4	0	4	0	24	2
Pro totals (4 years)	53	40	678	2554	3.8	21	44	262	6.0	0	21	0	126	11

BATES, MICHAEL — KR/WR — PANTHERS

PERSONAL: Born December 19, 1969, in Tucson, Ariz. ... 5-10/189. ... Full name: Michael D. Bates. ... Brother of Mario Bates, running back, Arizona Cardinals.

HIGH SCHOOL: Amphitheater (Tucson, Ariz.).

COLLEGE: Arizona.

TRANSACTIONS/CAREER NOTES: Selected after sophomore season by Seattle Seahawks in sixth round (151st pick overall) of 1992 NFL draft. ... Missed 1992 season due to contract dispute. ... Signed by Seahawks (March 7, 1993). ... Claimed on waivers by Carolina Panthers (August 28, 1995). ... Traded by Panthers to Cleveland Browns for LB Travis Hill (August 29, 1995). ... Granted unconditional free agency (February 16, 1996). ... Signed by Panthers (March 12, 1996). ... Granted unconditional free agency (February 13, 1998). ... Re-signed by Panthers (February 22, 1998).

CHAMPIONSHIP GAME EXPERIENCE: Played in NFC championship game (1996 season).

HONORS: Named kick returner on THE SPORTING NEWS NFL All-Pro team (1996 and 1997). ... Played in Pro Bowl (1996 and 1997 seasons).

PRO STATISTICS: 1993—Rushed twice for 12 yards and recovered two fumbles for three yards. 1994—Rushed twice for minus four yards. 1997—Returned one punt for eight yards and recovered two fumbles.

SINGLE GAME HIGHS (regular season): Receptions—1 (December 24, 1994, vs. Cleveland); yards—40 (September 11, 1994, vs. Los Angeles Raiders); and touchdown receptions—1 (September 11, 1994, vs. Los Angeles Raiders).

MISCELLANEOUS: Won bronze medal in 200-meter dash in 1992 Summer Olympics.

			RECEIVING				KICKOFF RETURNS				TOTALS			
Year Team	G	GS	No.	Yds.	Avg.	TD	No.	Yds.	Avg.	TD	TD	2pt.	Pts.	Fum.
1992—Seattle NFL							Did not play.							
1993—Seattle NFL	16	1	1	6	6.0	0	30	603	20.1	0	0	...	0	1
1994—Seattle NFL	15	0	5	112	22.4	1	26	508	19.5	0	1	0	6	3

				RECEIVING			KICKOFF RETURNS			TOTALS			
Year Team	G	GS	No.	Yds.	Avg.	TD	No.	Yds.	Avg.	TD	TD	2pt.	Pts.	Fum.
1995—Cleveland NFL	13	0	0	0	...	0	9	176	19.6	0	0	0	0	0
1996—Carolina NFL	14	0	0	0	...	0	33	998	*30.2	1	1	0	6	2
1997—Carolina NFL	16	0	0	0	...	0	47	1281	*27.3	0	0	0	0	4
Pro totals (5 years)	74	1	6	118	19.7	1	145	3566	24.6	1	2	0	12	10

BATES, PATRICK　　　　　S　　　　　RAIDERS

PERSONAL: Born November 27, 1970, in Galveston, Texas. ... 6-3/220. ... Full name: Patrick James Bates.
HIGH SCHOOL: Ball (Galveston, Texas).
COLLEGE: Texas A&M.
TRANSACTIONS/CAREER NOTES: Selected after junior season by Los Angeles Raiders in first round (12th pick overall) of 1993 NFL draft. ... Signed by Raiders for 1993 season. ... Raiders franchise moved to Oakland (July 21, 1995). ... Inactive for 16 games (1995). ... Traded by Raiders to Atlanta Falcons for second-round pick (traded to Houston) in 1996 draft (April 18, 1996). ... Released by Falcons (Aprill 22, 1997). ... Signed by Raiders (May 1998).
PLAYING EXPERIENCE: Los Angeles Raiders NFL, 1993 and 1994; Atlanta NFL, 1996. ... Games/Games started: 1993 (13/0), 1994 (16/9), 1996 (15/9). Total: 44/18.
HONORS: Named defensive back on THE SPORTING NEWS college All-America first team (1992).
PRO STATISTICS: 1993—Intercepted one pass for no yards. 1994—Recovered two fumbles. 1996—Recovered one fumble.

BATISTE, MICHAEL　　　　　G　　　　　REDSKINS

PERSONAL: Born December 24, 1970, in Beaumont, Texas. ... 6-3/325.
HIGH SCHOOL: Westbrook (Texas).
COLLEGE: Tulane.
TRANSACTIONS/CAREER NOTES: Signed as non-drafted free agent by Dallas Cowboys (April 28, 1994). ... Released by Cowboys (August 23, 1994). ... Re-signed by Cowboys (April 10, 1995). ... Released by Cowboys (August 25, 1996). ... Signed by Washington Redskins (February 27, 1997). ... Released by Redskins (August 24, 1997). ... Re-signed by Redskins (February 11, 1998).
PLAYING EXPERIENCE: Dallas NFL, 1995. ... Games/Games started: 2/0.
CHAMPIONSHIP GAME EXPERIENCE: Member of Cowboys for NFC championship game (1995 season); inactive.

BATTAGLIA, MARCO　　　　　TE　　　　　BENGALS

PERSONAL: Born January 25, 1973, in Howard Beach, N.Y. ... 6-3/250.
HIGH SCHOOL: St. Francis (Queens, N.Y.).
COLLEGE: Rutgers.
TRANSACTIONS/CAREER NOTES: Selected by Cincinnati Bengals in second round (39th pick overall) of 1996 NFL draft. ... Signed by Bengals (July 15, 1996).
HONORS: Named tight end on THE SPORTING NEWS college All-America first team (1995).
PRO STATISTICS: 1996—Returned one kickoff for eight yards and recovered one fumble. 1997—Recovered two fumbles.
SINGLE GAME HIGHS (regular season): Receptions—3 (November 9, 1997, vs. Indianapolis); yards—42 (December 21, 1997, vs. Baltimore); and touchdown receptions—1 (December 21, 1997, vs. Baltimore).

			RECEIVING				TOTALS			
Year Team	G	GS	No.	Yds.	Avg.	TD	TD	2pt.	Pts.	Fum.
1996—Cincinnati NFL	16	0	8	79	9.9	0	0	0	0	0
1997—Cincinnati NFL	16	0	12	149	12.4	1	1	0	6	2
Pro totals (2 years)	32	0	20	228	11.4	1	1	0	6	2

BATTLE, TERRY　　　　　RB　　　　　LIONS

PERSONAL: Born February 7, 1976, in Dallas. ... 5-11/197. ... Full name: Terrence Leshaun Battle.
HIGH SCHOOL: Sweetwater Union (San Diego).
COLLEGE: Arizona State.
TRANSACTIONS/CAREER NOTES: Selected after junior season by Detroit Lions in seventh round (206th pick overall) of 1997 NFL draft. ... Signed by Lions (June 13, 1997). ... Inactive for 16 games (1997).
HONORS: Named kick returner on THE SPORTING NEWS college All-America first team (1996).

BAXTER, FRED　　　　　TE　　　　　JETS

PERSONAL: Born June 14, 1971, in Brundidge, Ala. ... 6-3/265. ... Full name: Frederick Denard Baxter.
HIGH SCHOOL: Pike County (Brundidge, Ala.).
COLLEGE: Auburn.
TRANSACTIONS/CAREER NOTES: Selected by New York Jets in fifth round (115th pick overall) of 1993 NFL draft. ... Signed by Jets (July 13, 1993).
PRO STATISTICS: 1994—Returned one kickoff for 20 yards and recovered one fumble. 1995—Returned six kickoffs for 36 yards and recovered two fumbles for eight yards. 1997—Returned one kickoff for no yards.
SINGLE GAME HIGHS (regular season): Receptions—6 (September 17, 1995, vs. Jacksonville); yards—99 (September 17, 1995, vs. Jacksonville); and touchdown receptions—1 (November 23, 1997, vs. Minnesota).

B

Year Team	G	GS	No.	Yds.	Avg.	TD	TD	2pt.	Pts.	Fum.
				RECEIVING					TOTALS		
1993—New York Jets NFL	7	0	3	48	16.0	1	1	...	6	0
1994—New York Jets NFL	11	1	3	11	3.7	1	1	0	6	0
1995—New York Jets NFL	15	3	18	222	12.3	1	1	0	6	1
1996—New York Jets NFL	16	4	7	114	16.3	0	0	0	0	1
1997—New York Jets NFL	16	9	27	276	10.2	3	3	0	18	1
Pro totals (5 years)	65	17	58	671	11.6	6	6	0	36	3

BAYNE, CHRIS　　　　DB　　　　FALCONS

PERSONAL: Born March 22, 1975, in Riverside, Calif. ... 6-1/205. ... Full name: Christopher Oliver Bayne.
HIGH SCHOOL: North (Bakersfield, Calif.).
JUNIOR COLLEGE: San Bernardino Valley (Calif.).
COLLEGE: Fresno State.
TRANSACTIONS/CAREER NOTES: Selected by Atlanta Falcons in seventh round (222nd pick overall) of 1997 NFL draft. ... Signed by Falcons (June 11, 1997).
PLAYING EXPERIENCE: Atlanta NFL, 1997. ... Games/Games started: 13/0.

BEASLEY, AARON　　　　DB　　　　JAGUARS

PERSONAL: Born July 7, 1973, in Pottstown, Pa. ... 6-0/196. ... Full name: Aaron Bruce Beasley.
HIGH SCHOOL: Pottstown (Pa.), then Valley Forge Military Academy (Wayne, Pa.).
COLLEGE: West Virginia.
TRANSACTIONS/CAREER NOTES: Selected by Jacksonville Jaguars in third round (63rd pick overall) of 1996 NFL draft. ... Signed by Jaguars (May 24, 1996).
CHAMPIONSHIP GAME EXPERIENCE: Played in AFC championship game (1996 season).

Year Team	G	GS	No.	Yds.	Avg.	TD	No.
				INTERCEPTIONS			SACKS
1996—Jacksonville NFL	9	7	1	0	0.0	0	1.0
1997—Jacksonville NFL	9	7	1	5	5.0	0	0.0
Pro totals (2 years)	18	14	2	5	2.5	0	1.0

BECH, BRETT　　　　WR　　　　SAINTS

PERSONAL: Born August 20, 1971, in Slidell, La. ... 6-1/184. ... Full name: Brett Lamar Bech.
HIGH SCHOOL: Slidell (La.).
COLLEGE: Louisiana State.
TRANSACTIONS/CAREER NOTES: Signed as non-drafted free agent by Jacksonville Jaguars (April 24, 1995). ... Released by Jaguars (June 7, 1995). ... Signed by San Antonio Texans of CFL (July 1995). ... Signed by New Orleans Saints to practice squad (November 13, 1996). ... Activated (December 19, 1996). ... Released by Saints (August 24, 1997). ... Re-signed by Saints to practice squad (August 25, 1997). ... Activated (September 27, 1997). ... On injured reserve with hand and shoulder injury (December 12, 1997-remainder of season).
PRO STATISTICS: 1997—Recovered one fumble.
SINGLE GAME HIGHS (regular season): Receptions—1 (November 23, 1997, vs. Atlanta); yards—22 (November 23, 1997, vs. Atlanta); and touchdown receptions—0.

Year Team	G	GS	No.	Yds.	Avg.	TD	No.	Yds.	Avg.	TD	TD	2pt.	Pts.	Fum.
				RECEIVING				KICKOFF RETURNS					TOTALS		
1995—San Antonio CFL	5	...	0	0	...	0	0	0	...	0	0	0	0	0
1996—New Orleans NFL							Did not play.							
1997—New Orleans NFL	10	0	3	50	16.7	0	3	47	15.7	0	0	0	0	0
CFL totals (1 year)	5	...	0	0		0	0	0	...	0	0	0	0	0
NFL totals (1 year)	10	0	3	50	16.7	0	3	47	15.7	0	0	0	0	0
Pro totals (2 years)	15	...	3	50	16.7	0	3	47	15.7	0	0	0	0	0

BECKLES, IAN　　　　G　　　　EAGLES

PERSONAL: Born July 20, 1967, in Montreal. ... 6-1/304. ... Full name: Ian Harold Beckles.
HIGH SCHOOL: Lindsay Place (Montreal).
JUNIOR COLLEGE: Waldorf Junior College (Iowa).
COLLEGE: Indiana (degree in general studies).
TRANSACTIONS/CAREER NOTES: Selected by Tampa Bay Buccaneers in fifth round (114th pick overall) of 1990 NFL draft. ... Signed by Buccaneers (July 19, 1990). ... Granted free agency (February 1, 1992). ... Re-signed by Buccaneers (July 17, 1992). ... On injured reserve with knee injury (September 1-October 16, 1992). ... On injured reserve with knee injury (December 22, 1993-remainder of season). ... Granted unconditional free agency (February 17, 1994). ... Re-signed by Buccaneers (March 29, 1994). ... Granted unconditional free agency (February 14, 1997). ... Signed by Philadelphia Eagles (June 4, 1997).
PLAYING EXPERIENCE: Tampa Bay NFL, 1990-1997. ... Games/Games started: 1990 (16/16), 1991 (16/16), 1992 (11/7), 1993 (14/14), 1994 (16/16), 1995 (15/15), 1996 (13/13), 1997 (9/8). Total: 110/105.
PRO STATISTICS: 1993—Recovered one fumble. 1994—Recovered two fumbles. 1995—Recovered two fumbles. 1997—Recovered two fumbles.

BEEBE, DON　　　　WR

PERSONAL: Born December 18, 1964, in Aurora, Ill. ... 5-11/183. ... Full name: Don Lee Beebe. ... Name pronounced BEE-BEE.
HIGH SCHOOL: Kaneland (Maple Park, Ill.).
COLLEGE: Western Illinois, then Aurora, Ill. (did not play football), then Chadron (Neb.) State College.

B

TRANSACTIONS/CAREER NOTES: Selected by Buffalo Bills in third round (82nd pick overall) of 1989 NFL draft. ... Signed by Bills (May 8, 1989). ... On injured reserve with broken leg (December 29, 1990-remainder of season). ... On injured reserve with broken collarbone (November 23, 1991-January 5, 1992). ... Granted free agency (February 1, 1992). ... Re-signed by Bills (1992). ... On injured reserve with pulled hamstring (September 19-October 26, 1992). ... Granted unconditional free agency (February 17, 1995). ... Signed by Carolina Panthers (April 25, 1995). ... Released by Panthers (February 14, 1996). ... Signed by Green Bay Packers (April 1, 1996). ... Granted unconditional free agency (February 14, 1997). ... Re-signed by Packers (March 20, 1997). ... On injured reserve with hamstring injury (January 23, 1998-remainder of 1997 playoffs). ... Released by Packers (February 11, 1998).

CHAMPIONSHIP GAME EXPERIENCE: Played in AFC championship game (1991-1993 seasons). ... Played in Super Bowl XXVI (1991 season), Super Bowl XXVII (1992 season) and Super Bowl XXVIII (1993 season). ... Played in NFC championship game (1996 season). ... Member of Super Bowl championship team (1996 season). ... Member of Packers for NFC championship game (1997 season); inactive.

PRO STATISTICS: 1990—Rushed once for 23 yards. 1992—Rushed once for minus six yards. 1993—Recovered one fumble. 1994—Rushed twice for 11 yards. 1996—Recovered one fumble in end zone for a touchdown.

SINGLE GAME HIGHS (regular season): Receptions—11 (October 14, 1996, vs. San Francisco); yards—220 (October 14, 1996, vs. San Francisco); and touchdown receptions—4 (September 8, 1991, vs. Pittsburgh).

STATISTICAL PLATEAUS: 100-yard receiving games: 1991 (1), 1992 (4), 1993 (1), 1994 (1), 1996 (2). Total: 9.

			RECEIVING				KICKOFF RETURNS				TOTALS		
Year Team	G	GS	No.	Yds.	Avg.	TD	No.	Yds.	Avg.	TD	TD	2pt.	Pts.	Fum.
1989—Buffalo NFL	14	0	17	317	18.6	2	16	353	22.1	0	2	...	12	1
1990—Buffalo NFL	12	4	11	221	20.1	1	6	119	19.8	0	1	...	6	0
1991—Buffalo NFL	11	7	32	414	12.9	6	7	121	17.3	0	6	...	36	3
1992—Buffalo NFL	12	8	33	554	16.8	2	0	0	...	0	2	...	12	1
1993—Buffalo NFL	14	14	31	504	16.3	3	10	160	16.0	0	3	...	18	1
1994—Buffalo NFL	13	11	40	527	13.2	4	12	230	19.2	0	4	0	24	3
1995—Carolina NFL	14	1	14	152	10.9	1	9	215	23.9	0	1	0	6	0
1996—Green Bay NFL	16	6	39	699	17.9	4	15	403	26.9	1	6	0	36	1
1997—Green Bay NFL	10	0	2	28	14.0	0	6	134	22.3	0	0	0	0	0
Pro totals (9 years)	116	51	219	3416	15.6	23	81	1735	21.4	1	25	0	150	10

BEEDE, FRANK   G   SEAHAWKS

PERSONAL: Born May 1, 1973, in Antioch, Calif. ... 6-4/296.
HIGH SCHOOL: Antioch (Calif.).
COLLEGE: Panhandle State (Okla.).
TRANSACTIONS/CAREER NOTES: Signed as non-drafted free agent by Seatle Seahawks (April 22, 1996).
PLAYING EXPERIENCE: Seattle NFL, 1996 and 1997. ... Games/Games started: 1996 (14/2), 1997 (16/6). Total: 30/8.
PRO STATISTICS: 1997—Returned one kick for no yards and fumbled once.

BELL, MYRON   S

PERSONAL: Born September 15, 1971, in Toledo, Ohio. ... 5-11/203. ... Full name: Myron C. Bell.
HIGH SCHOOL: Macomber-Whitney (Toledo, Ohio).
COLLEGE: Michigan State.
TRANSACTIONS/CAREER NOTES: Selected by Pittsburgh Steelers in fifth round (140th pick overall) of 1994 NFL draft. ... Signed by Steelers (July 18, 1994). ... Granted free agency (February 14, 1997). ... Re-signed by Steelers (April 15, 1997). ... Granted unconditional free agency (February 13, 1998).
CHAMPIONSHIP GAME EXPERIENCE: Played in AFC championship game (1994, 1995 and 1997 seasons). ... Played in Super Bowl XXX (1995 season).
PRO STATISTICS: 1995—Recovered one fumble. 1996—Credited with two sacks and recovered two fumbles. 1997—Credited with $1\frac{1}{2}$ sacks and recovered one fumble.

			INTERCEPTIONS			
Year Team	G	GS	No.	Yds.	Avg.	TD
1994—Pittsburgh NFL	15	0	0	0	...	0
1995—Pittsburgh NFL	16	9	2	4	2.0	0
1996—Pittsburgh NFL	16	4	0	0	...	0
1997—Pittsburgh NFL	16	8	1	10	10.0	0
Pro totals (4 years)	63	21	3	14	4.7	0

BELL, RICKY   CB   BEARS

PERSONAL: Born October 2, 1974, in Columbia, S.C. ... 5-10/194.
HIGH SCHOOL: Eau Claire (Columbia, S.C.).
COLLEGE: North Carolina State.
TRANSACTIONS/CAREER NOTES: Signed as non-drafted free agent by Pittsburgh Steelers (April 29, 1996). ... Released by Steelers (August 24, 1996). ... Re-signed by Steelers to practice squad (August 27, 1996). ... Activated (September 10, 1996); did not play. ... Claimed on waivers by Jacksonville Jaguars (September 25, 1996). ... Released by Jaguars (August 19, 1997). ... Signed by Chicago Bears (September 9, 1997). ... On non-football injury list (October 25, 1997-remainder of season).
PLAYING EXPERIENCE: Jacksonville NFL, 1996; Chicago NFL, 1997. ... Games/Games started: 1996 (12/0), 1997 (5/0). Total: 17/0.
CHAMPIONSHIP GAME EXPERIENCE: Played in AFC championship game (1996 season).
PRO STATISTICS: 1996—Returned six kickoffs for 119 yards and fumbled once.

BELLAMY, JAY   S   SEAHAWKS

PERSONAL: Born July 8, 1972, in Perth Amboy, N.J. ... 5-11/199. ... Full name: John Lee Bellamy.
HIGH SCHOOL: Matawan (N.J.).
COLLEGE: Rutgers.

TRANSACTIONS/CAREER NOTES: Signed as non-drafted free agent by Seattle Seahawks (April 27, 1994). ... On injured reserve with shoulder injury (November 11, 1994-remainder of season).
PRO STATISTICS: 1997—Credited with two sacks.

| | | | INTERCEPTIONS | | | |
Year Team	G	GS	No.	Yds.	Avg.	TD
1994—Seattle NFL	3	0	0	0	...	0
1995—Seattle NFL	14	0	0	0	...	0
1996—Seattle NFL	16	0	3	18	6.0	0
1997—Seattle NFL	16	7	1	13	13.0	0
Pro totals (4 years)	49	7	4	31	7.8	0

BELLISARI, GREG — LB — BUCCANEERS

PERSONAL: Born June 21, 1975, in Boca Raton, Fla. ... 6-0/236.
HIGH SCHOOL: Boca Raton (Fla.).
COLLEGE: Ohio State.
TRANSACTIONS/CAREER NOTES: Signed as non-drafted free agent by Tampa Bay Buccaneers (April 21, 1997).
PLAYING EXPERIENCE: Tampa Bay NFL, 1997. ... Games/Games started: 14/0.

BELSER, JASON — DB — COLTS

PERSONAL: Born May 28, 1970, in Kansas City, Mo. ... 5-9/196. ... Full name: Jason Daks Belser. ... Son of Caeser Belser, defensive back with Kansas City Chiefs (1968-1971) and linebacker with San Francisco 49ers (1974).
HIGH SCHOOL: Raytown (Mo.) South.
COLLEGE: Oklahoma.
TRANSACTIONS/CAREER NOTES: Selected by Indianapolis Colts in eighth round (197th pick overall) of 1992 NFL draft. ... Signed by Colts (July 22, 1992). ... Granted free agency (February 17, 1995). ... Tendered offer sheet by Carolina Panthers (April 17, 1995). ... Offer matched by Colts (April 19, 1995).
CHAMPIONSHIP GAME EXPERIENCE: Played in AFC championship game (1995 season).
PRO STATISTICS: 1992—Fumbled once and recovered two fumbles. 1993—Recovered three fumbles. 1995—Returned one kickoff for 15 yards and recovered two fumbles. 1996—Credited with one sack and recovered one fumble. 1997—Credited with one sack.

| | | | INTERCEPTIONS | | | |
Year Team	G	GS	No.	Yds.	Avg.	TD
1992—Indianapolis NFL	16	2	3	27	9.0	0
1993—Indianapolis NFL	16	16	1	14	14.0	0
1994—Indianapolis NFL	13	12	1	31	31.0	0
1995—Indianapolis NFL	16	16	1	0	0.0	0
1996—Indianapolis NFL	16	16	4	81	20.3	†2
1997—Indianapolis NFL	16	16	2	121	60.5	1
Pro totals (6 years)	93	78	12	274	22.8	3

BENDER, WES — FB — SAINTS

PERSONAL: Born August 2, 1970, in Van Nuys, Calif. ... 5-10/249.
HIGH SCHOOL: Burbank (Calif.), then John Burroughs (Burbank, Calif.).
JUNIOR COLLEGE: Glendale (Calif.) Community College.
COLLEGE: Southern California.
TRANSACTIONS/CAREER NOTES: Signed as non-drafted free agent by Kansas City Chiefs (May 5, 1993). ... On injured reserve with foot injury (August 24-September 7, 1993). ... Released by Chiefs (September 7, 1993). ... Signed by Los Angeles Raiders (May 6, 1994). ... Released by Raiders (August 23, 1994). ... Re-signed by Raiders to practice squad (August 29, 1994). ... Activated (October 26, 1994). ... Released by Raiders (August 27, 1995). ... Selected by Frankfurt Galaxy in 1996 World League draft (February 22, 1996). ... Re-signed by Raiders (June 27, 1996). ... Released by Raiders (August 20, 1996). ... Signed by New Orleans Saints (March 5, 1997).
SINGLE GAME HIGHS (regular season): Attempts—3 (September 14, 1997, vs. San Francisco); yards—8 (September 14, 1997, vs. San Francisco); and rushing touchdowns—0.

| | | | RUSHING | | | | RECEIVING | | | | TOTALS | | | |
Year Team	G	GS	Att.	Yds.	Avg.	TD	No.	Yds.	Avg.	TD	TD	2pt.	Pts.	Fum.
1993—Kansas City NFL								Did not play.						
1994—Los Angeles Raiders NFL	9	0	0	0	...	0	2	14	7.0	0	0	0	0	0
1995—								Did not play.						
1996—Frankfurt W.L.	...	...	16	41	2.6	1	19	119	6.3	0	1	0	6	...
1997—New Orleans NFL	11	0	5	9	1.8	0	0	0	...	0	0	0	0	1
W.L. totals (1 year)	...	...	16	41	2.6	1	19	119	6.3	0	1	0	6	...
NFL totals (2 years)	20	0	5	9	1.8	0	2	14	7.0	0	0	0	0	1
Pro totals (3 years)	...	...	21	50	2.4	1	21	133	6.3	0	1	0	6	...

BENNETT, CORNELIUS — LB — FALCONS

PERSONAL: Born August 25, 1965, in Birmingham, Ala. ... 6-2/238. ... Full name: Cornelius O'landa Bennett.
HIGH SCHOOL: Ensley (Birmingham, Ala.).
COLLEGE: Alabama.
TRANSACTIONS/CAREER NOTES: Selected by Indianapolis Colts in first round (second pick overall) of 1987 NFL draft. ... Placed on reserve/unsigned list (August 31-October 30, 1987). ... Rights traded by Colts to Buffalo Bills in exchange for Bills trading first-round pick (RB Gaston Green) in 1988 draft, first-(RB Cleveland Gary) and second-round (CB Darryl Henley) picks in 1989 draft and RB Greg Bell to Los Angeles Rams (October 31, 1987); Rams also traded RB Eric Dickerson to Colts for first-(WR Aaron Cox) and second-round (LB Fred Strickland) picks in 1988 draft, second-round pick (LB Frank Stams) in 1989 draft and RB Owen Gill. ... Signed by Bills (October 31, 1987).

... Granted roster exemption (October 31-November 7, 1987). ... Granted free agency (February 1, 1992). ... Re-signed by Bills (August 31, 1992). ... Designated by Bills as franchise player (February 15, 1995). ... Granted unconditional free agency (February 16, 1996). ... Signed by Atlanta Falcons (March 1, 1996).

CHAMPIONSHIP GAME EXPERIENCE: Played in AFC championship game (1988 and 1990-1993 seasons). ... Played in Super Bowl XXV (1990 season), Super Bowl XXVI (1991 season), Super Bowl XXVII (1992 season) and Super Bowl XXVIII (1993 season).

HONORS: Named linebacker on THE SPORTING NEWS college All-America first team (1984-1986). ... Lombardi Award winner (1986). ... Named outside linebacker on THE SPORTING NEWS NFL All-Pro team (1988). ... Played in Pro Bowl (1988 and 1990-1993 seasons).

PRO STATISTICS: 1988—Recovered three fumbles. 1989—Recovered two fumbles for five yards. 1990—Returned blocked field-goal attempt 80 yards for a touchdown and recovered two fumbles. 1991—Recovered two fumbles for nine yards and a touchdown. 1992—Recovered three fumbles. 1993—Recovered two fumbles for 40 yards and fumbled once. 1994—Recovered three fumbles for 14 yards. 1995—Recovered two fumbles. 1996—Recovered two fumbles. 1997—Recovered one fumble.

Year Team	G	GS	No.	Yds.	Avg.	TD	No.
			INTERCEPTIONS				SACKS
1987—Buffalo NFL	8	7	0	0	...	0	8.5
1988—Buffalo NFL	16	16	2	30	15.0	0	9.5
1989—Buffalo NFL	12	12	2	5	2.5	0	5.5
1990—Buffalo NFL	16	16	0	0	...	0	4.0
1991—Buffalo NFL	16	16	0	0	...	0	9.0
1992—Buffalo NFL	15	15	0	0	...	0	4.0
1993—Buffalo NFL	16	16	1	5	5.0	0	5.0
1994—Buffalo NFL	16	16	0	0	...	0	5.0
1995—Buffalo NFL	14	14	1	69	69.0	▲1	2.0
1996—Atlanta NFL	13	13	1	3	3.0	0	3.0
1997—Atlanta NFL	16	16	0	0	...	0	7.0
Pro totals (11 years)	158	157	7	112	16.0	1	62.5

BENNETT, DARREN　　　　P　　　　CHARGERS

PERSONAL: Born January 9, 1965, in Sydney, Australia. ... 6-5/235. ... Full name: Darren Leslie Bennett.

HIGH SCHOOL: Applecross (Western Australia).

COLLEGE: None.

TRANSACTIONS/CAREER NOTES: Played Australian Rules Football (1987-1993). ... Signed as non-drafted free agent by San Diego Chargers (April 14, 1994). ... Released by Chargers (August 28, 1994). ... Re-signed by Chargers to practice squad (August 29, 1994). ... Granted free agency after 1994 season. ... Re-signed by Chargers (February 18, 1995). ... Assigned by Chargers to Amersterdam Admirals in 1995 World League enhancement allocation program (February 20, 1995).

HONORS: Named punter on THE SPORTING NEWS NFL All-Pro team (1995). ... Played in Pro Bowl (1995 season).

Year Team	G	GS	No.	Yds.	Avg.	Net avg.	In. 20	Blk.
					PUNTING			
1995—Amsterdam W.L.	...	...	60	2296	38.3	35.1	24	1
—San Diego NFL	16	0	72	3221	44.7	36.6	28	0
1996—San Diego NFL	16	0	87	3967	45.6	37.2	23	0
1997—San Diego NFL	16	0	89	3972	44.6	37.7	26	1
W.L. totals (1 year)	...	...	60	2296	38.3	35.1	24	1
NFL totals (3 years)	48	0	248	11160	45.0	37.2	77	1
Pro totals (4 years)	...	...	308	13456	43.7	36.8	101	2

BENNETT, DONNELL　　　　FB　　　　CHIEFS

PERSONAL: Born September 14, 1972, in Fort Lauderdale. ... 6-0/232.

HIGH SCHOOL: Cardinal Gibbons (Fort Lauderdale).

COLLEGE: Miami (Fla.).

TRANSACTIONS/CAREER NOTES: Selected after junior season by Kansas City Chiefs in second round (58th pick overall) of 1994 NFL draft. ... Signed by Chiefs (May 6, 1994). ... On injured reserve with knee injury (December 20, 1994-remainder of season). ... On physically unable to perform list with knee injury (August 22-October 31, 1995). ... Granted free agency (February 14, 1997). ... Re-signed by Chiefs (April 22, 1997).

PRO STATISTICS: 1994—Returned one kickoff for 12 yards and recovered one fumble.

SINGLE GAME HIGHS (regular season): Attempts—24 (December 7, 1997, vs. Oakland); yards—85 (December 7, 1997, vs, Oakland); and rushing touchdowns—1 (December 7, 1997, vs. Oakland).

Year Team	G	GS	Att.	Yds.	Avg.	TD	No.	Yds.	Avg.	TD	TD	2pt.	Pts.	Fum.
			RUSHING				RECEIVING				TOTALS			
1994—Kansas City NFL	15	0	46	178	3.9	2	7	53	7.6	0	2	0	12	2
1995—Kansas City NFL	3	1	7	11	1.6	0	1	12	12.0	0	0	0	0	0
1996—Kansas City NFL	16	0	36	166	4.6	0	8	21	2.6	0	0	0	0	0
1997—Kansas City NFL	14	1	94	369	3.9	1	7	5	0.7	0	1	0	6	0
Pro totals (4 years)	48	2	183	724	4.0	3	23	91	4.0	0	3	0	18	2

BENNETT, EDGAR　　　　FB　　　　BEARS

PERSONAL: Born February 15, 1969, in Jacksonville. ... 6-0/218. ... Full name: Edgar Bennett III.

HIGH SCHOOL: Robert E. Lee Senior (Jacksonville).

COLLEGE: Florida State.

TRANSACTIONS/CAREER NOTES: Selected by Green Bay Packers in fourth round (103rd pick overall) of 1992 NFL draft. ... Signed by Packers (July 22, 1992). ... Granted free agency (February 17, 1995). ... Re-signed by Packers (May 5, 1995). ... On injured reserve with knee injury (August 18, 1997/-entire season). ... Granted unconditional free agency (February 13, 1998). ... Signed by Chicago Bears (February 20, 1998).

CHAMPIONSHIP GAME EXPERIENCE: Played in NFC championship game (1995 and 1996 seasons). ... Member of Super Bowl championship team (1996 season).

PRO STATISTICS: 1992—Returned five kickoffs for 104 yards. 1993—Recovered one fumble. 1994—Recovered one fumble. 1995—Recovered one fumble. 1996—Recovered one fumble.
SINGLE GAME HIGHS (regular season): Attempts—30 (September 11, 1995, vs. Chicago); yards—121 (October 29, 1995, vs. Detroit); and rushing touchdowns—2 (October 31, 1994, vs. Chicago).
STATISTICAL PLATEAUS: 100-yard rushing games: 1992 (1), 1994 (3), 1995 (1), 1996 (1). Total: 6. ... 100-yard receiving games: 1994 (1).

Year Team	G	GS	RUSHING				RECEIVING				TOTALS			
			Att.	Yds.	Avg.	TD	No.	Yds.	Avg.	TD	TD	2pt.	Pts.	Fum.
1992—Green Bay NFL	16	2	61	214	3.5	0	13	93	7.2	0	0	...	0	2
1993—Green Bay NFL	16	14	159	550	3.5	9	59	457	7.7	1	10	...	60	0
1994—Green Bay NFL	16	15	178	623	3.5	5	78	546	7.0	4	9	0	54	1
1995—Green Bay NFL	16	16	316	1067	3.4	3	61	648	10.6	4	7	0	42	2
1996—Green Bay NFL	16	15	222	899	4.0	2	31	176	5.7	1	3	2	22	2
1997—Green Bay NFL						Did not play.								
Pro totals (5 years)	80	62	936	3353	3.6	19	242	1920	7.9	10	29	2	178	7

BENNETT, TOMMY   S   CARDINALS

PERSONAL: Born February 19, 1973, in Las Vegas. ... 6-2/219.
HIGH SCHOOL: Morse (San Diego).
COLLEGE: UCLA.
TRANSACTIONS/CAREER NOTES: Signed as a non-drafted free agent by Arizona Cardinals (April 23, 1996).
PRO STATISTICS: 1997—Recovered blocked punt in end zone for a touchdown.

Year Team	G	GS	INTERCEPTIONS				TOTALS			
			No.	Yds.	Avg.	TD	TD	2pt.	Pts.	Fum.
1996—Arizona NFL	16	1	0	0	...	0	0	0	0	0
1997—Arizona NFL	13	7	1	0	0.0	0	1	0	6	0
Pro totals (2 years)	29	8	1	0	0.0	0	1	0	6	0

BENNETT, TONY   LB   COLTS

PERSONAL: Born July 1, 1967, in Alligator, Miss. ... 6-2/250. ... Full name: Tony Lydell Bennett.
HIGH SCHOOL: Coahoma County (Clarksdale, Miss.).
COLLEGE: Mississippi (degree in physical education and recreation).
TRANSACTIONS/CAREER NOTES: Selected by Green Bay Packers in first round (18th pick overall) of 1990 NFL draft. ... Signed by Packers (July 22, 1990). ... Granted free agency (March 1, 1993). ... Re-signed by Packers to practice squad (October 27, 1993). ... Activated (October 30, 1993). ... Granted unconditional free agency (February 17, 1994). ... Signed by Indianapolis Colts (March 26, 1994). ... On injured reserve with knee injury (October 29, 1997-remainder of season). ... Designated by Colts as transition player (February 13, 1998).
CHAMPIONSHIP GAME EXPERIENCE: Played in AFC championship game (1995 season).
HONORS: Named defensive end on THE SPORTING NEWS college All-America second team (1989).
PRO STATISTICS: 1990—Recovered one fumble. 1992—Recovered three fumbles for 18 yards and a touchdown. 1994—Recovered one fumble for 75 yards and a touchdown. 1995—Credited with a safety and recovered one fumble for 32 yards and a touchdown.

Year Team	G	GS	SACKS
1990—Green Bay NFL	14	0	3.0
1991—Green Bay NFL	16	16	13.0
1992—Green Bay NFL	16	16	13.5
1993—Green Bay NFL	10	7	6.5
1994—Indianapolis NFL	16	15	9.0
1995—Indianapolis NFL	16	16	10.5
1996—Indianapolis NFL	14	13	6.0
1997—Indianapolis NFL	6	6	3.0
Pro totals (8 years)	108	89	64.5

BENSON, DARREN   DT   COWBOYS

PERSONAL: Born August 25, 1974, in Memphis ... 6-7/308.
HIGH SCHOOL: Craigmont (Memphis).
JUNIOR COLLEGE: Trinity Valley Community College (Texas).
COLLEGE: Arkansas State (did not play football).
TRANSACTIONS/CAREER NOTES: Selected by Dallas Cowboys in third round of 1995 NFL supplemental draft. ... Signed by Cowboys (July 21, 1995). ... On injured reserve with knee injury (August 20, 1996-entire season).
PLAYING EXPERIENCE: Dallas NFL, 1995 and 1997. ... Games/Games started: 1995 (6/0), 1997 (6/0).
CHAMPIONSHIP GAME EXPERIENCE: Played in NFC championship game (1995 season). ... Member of Super Bowl championship team (1995 season).

BENTLEY, SCOTT   K   FALCONS

PERSONAL: Born April 10, 1974, in Dallas. ... 6-0/203.
HIGH SCHOOL: Aurora (Colo.).
COLLEGE: Florida State.
TRANSACTIONS/CAREER NOTES: Signed as non-drafted free agent by Arizona Cardinals (April 21, 1997). ... Released by Cardinals (August 19, 1997). ... Signed by Denver Broncos to practice squad (October 1, 1997). ... Activated (October 6, 1997). ... Released by Broncos (October 7, 1997). ... Signed by Atlanta Falcons to practice squad (December 2, 1997). ... Activated (December 14, 1997). ... Granted free agency (February 13, 1998).

Year Team	G	GS	KICKING						
			XPM	XPA	FGM	FGA	Lg.	50+	Pts.
1997—Denver NFL	1	0	4	4	2	3	33	0-0	10
—Atlanta NFL	2	0	0	0	0	0		0-0	0
Pro totals (1 years)	3	0	4	4	2	3	33	0-0	10

BERCICH, PETE LB VIKINGS

PERSONAL: Born December 23, 1971, in Joliet, Ill. ... 6-1/239. ... Full name: Peter James Bercich. ... Son of Bob Bercich, safety with Dallas Cowboys (1960 and 1961). ... Name pronounced BURR-sitch.
HIGH SCHOOL: Providence Catholic (New Lenox, Ill.).
COLLEGE: Notre Dame.
TRANSACTIONS/CAREER NOTES: Selected by Minnesota Vikings in seventh round (211th pick overall) of 1994 NFL draft. ... Signed by Vikings (July 11, 1994). ... Released by Vikings (August 28, 1994). ... Re-signed by Vikings to practice squad (August 29, 1994). ... Granted free agency after 1994 season. ... Re-signed by Vikings (March 27, 1995). ... Granted free agency (February 13, 1998). ... Re-signed by Vikings (April 28, 1998).
PLAYING EXPERIENCE: Minnesota NFL, 1995-1997. ... Games/Games started: 1995 (9/0), 1996 (15/1), 1997 (16/0). Total: 40/1.
PRO STATISTICS: 1996—Recovered one fumble.

BERGER, MITCH P VIKINGS

B

PERSONAL: Born June 24, 1972, in Kamloops, British Columbia. ... 6-2/218.
HIGH SCHOOL: North Delta (Vancouver).
JUNIOR COLLEGE: Tyler (Texas) Junior College.
COLLEGE: Colorado.
TRANSACTIONS/CAREER NOTES: Selected by Philadelphia Eagles in sixth round (193rd pick overall) of 1994 NFL draft. ... Signed by Eagles (July 11, 1994). ... Released by Eagles (October 10, 1994). ... Signed by Cincinnati Bengals to practice squad (October 13, 1994). ... Released by Bengals (November 30, 1994). ... Signed by Chicago Bears (March 7, 1995). ... Released by Bears (May 4, 1995). ... Signed by Indianapolis Colts (May 16, 1995). ... Claimed on waivers by Green Bay Packers (August 24, 1995). ... Released by Packers (August 27, 1995). ... Signed by Bears (November 7, 1995). ... Released by Bears (November 13, 1995). ... Signed by Minnesota Vikings (April 19, 1996).
PRO STATISTICS: 1997—Rushed once for no yards and fumbled once for minus nine yards.

					PUNTING			
Year Team	G	GS	No.	Yds.	Avg.	Net avg.	In. 20	Blk.
1994—Philadelphia NFL	5	0	25	951	38.0	31.3	8	0
1995—				Did not play.				
1996—Minnesota NFL	16	0	88	3616	41.1	32.3	26	2
1997—Minnesota NFL	14	0	73	3133	42.9	34.1	22	0
Pro totals (3 years)	35	0	186	7700	41.4	32.9	56	2

BERNSTEIN, ALEX G RAVENS

PERSONAL: Born August 11, 1975, in Aspen, Colo. ... 6-3/325. ... Full name: Alexander Douglas Bernstein.
HIGH SCHOOL: The Blake School (Minneapolis).
COLLEGE: Colby College (Maine), then Amherst (Mass.).
TRANSACTIONS/CAREER NOTES: Signed as non-drafted free agent by Baltimore Ravens (April 25, 1997). ... Released by Ravens (August 24, 1997). ... Re-signed by Ravens to practice squad (August 26, 1997) ... Activated (December 21, 1997). ... Inactive for two games (1997).

BERRY, BERT LB COLTS

PERSONAL: Born August 15, 1975, in Houston. ... 6-2/248. ... Full name: Bertrand D. Berry.
HIGH SCHOOL: Humble (Texas).
COLLEGE: Notre Dame.
TRANSACTIONS/CAREER NOTES: Selected by Indianapolis Colts in third round (86th pick overall) of 1997 NFL draft. ... Signed by Colts (July 9, 1997).

Year Team	G	GS	SACKS
1997—Indianapolis NFL	10	1	0.0

BERTI, TONY OT/OG CHARGERS

PERSONAL: Born June 21, 1972, in Rock Springs, Wyo. ... 6-6/300. ... Full name: Charles Anton Berti Jr.
HIGH SCHOOL: Skyview (Thornton, Colo.).
COLLEGE: Colorado.
TRANSACTIONS/CAREER NOTES: Selected by San Diego Chargers in sixth round (200th pick overall) of 1995 NFL draft. ... Signed by Chargers (July 12, 1995).
PLAYING EXPERIENCE: San Diego NFL, 1995-1997. ... Games/Games started: 1995 (1/0), 1996 (16/14), 1997 (16/16). Total: 33/30.
PRO STATISTICS: 1997—Recovered one fumble.

BETTIS, JEROME RB STEELERS

PERSONAL: Born February 16, 1972, in Detroit. ... 5-11/243. ... Full name: Jerome Abram Bettis. ... Nickname: The Bus.
HIGH SCHOOL: Mackenzie (Detroit).
COLLEGE: Notre Dame.
TRANSACTIONS/CAREER NOTES: Selected after junior season by Los Angeles Rams in first round (10th pick overall) of 1993 NFL draft. ... Signed by Rams (July 22, 1993). ... Rams franchise moved to St. Louis (April 12, 1995). ... Traded by Rams with third-round pick (LB Steven Conley) in 1996 draft to Pittsburgh Steelers for second-round pick (TE Ernie Conwell) in 1996 draft and fourth-round pick (traded to Miami) in 1997 draft (April 20, 1996). ... Granted unconditional free agency (February 14, 1997). ... Re-signed by Steelers (February 17, 1997).
CHAMPIONSHIP GAME EXPERIENCE: Played in AFC championship game (1997 season).

HONORS: Named NFL Rookie of the Year by THE SPORTING NEWS (1993). ... Played in Pro Bowl (1993, 1994, 1996 and 1997 seasons).
PRO STATISTICS: 1994—Recovered three fumbles. 1995—Recovered two fumbles. 1996—Recovered two fumbles. 1997—Recovered one fumble.
SINGLE GAME HIGHS (regular season): Attempts—39 (January 2, 1994, vs. Chicago); yards—212 (December 12, 1993, vs. New Orleans); and rushing touchdowns—3 (November 30, 1997, vs. Arizona).
STATISTICAL PLATEAUS: 100-yard rushing games: 1993 (7), 1994 (4), 1996 (10), 1997 (10). Total: 31.

				RUSHING				RECEIVING				TOTALS		
Year Team	G	GS	Att.	Yds.	Avg.	TD	No.	Yds.	Avg.	TD	TD	2pt.	Pts.	Fum.
1993—Los Angeles Rams NFL	16	12	‡294	1429	4.9	7	26	244	9.4	0	7	...	42	4
1994—Los Angeles Rams NFL	16	16	319	1025	3.2	3	31	293	9.5	1	4	2	28	5
1995—St. Louis NFL	15	13	183	637	3.5	3	18	106	5.9	0	3	0	18	4
1996—Pittsburgh NFL	16	12	320	1431	4.5	11	22	122	5.5	0	11	0	66	7
1997—Pittsburgh NFL	15	15	*375	1665	4.4	7	15	110	7.3	2	9	0	54	6
Pro totals (5 years)	78	68	1491	6187	4.1	31	112	875	7.8	3	34	2	208	26

BEUERLEIN, STEVE   QB   PANTHERS

PERSONAL: Born March 7, 1965, in Hollywood, Calif. ... 6-3/220. ... Full name: Stephen Taylor Beuerlein. ... Name pronounced BURR line.
HIGH SCHOOL: Servite (Anaheim, Calif.).
COLLEGE: Notre Dame (degree in American studies, 1987).
TRANSACTIONS/CAREER NOTES: Selected by Los Angeles Raiders in fourth round (110th pick overall) of 1987 NFL draft. ... Signed by Raiders (July 24, 1987). ... On injured reserve with elbow and shoulder injuries (September 7, 1987-entire season). ... Granted free agency (February 1, 1990). ... Re-signed by Raiders (September 3, 1990). ... Granted roster exemption (September 3-16, 1990). ... On inactive list for all 16 games (1990). ... Granted free agency (February 1, 1991). ... Re-signed by Raiders (July 8, 1991). ... Traded by Raiders to Dallas Cowboys for fourth-round pick (traded to Indianapolis) in 1992 draft (August 25, 1991). ... Granted unconditional free agency (March 1, 1993). ... Signed by Phoenix Cardinals (April 21, 1993). ... Cardinals franchise renamed Arizona Cardinals for 1994 season. ... Selected by Jacksonville Jaguars from Cardinals in NFL expansion draft (February 15, 1995). ... Granted free agency (February 16, 1996). ... Signed by Carolina Panthers (April 10, 1996).
CHAMPIONSHIP GAME EXPERIENCE: Member of Raiders for AFC championship game (1990 season); inactive. ... Played in NFC championship game (1992 season). ... Member of Super Bowl championship team (1992 season). ... Member of Panthers for NFC championship game (1996 season); did not play.
PRO STATISTICS: 1988—Caught one pass for 21 yards, fumbled six times and recovered two fumbles for minus one yard. 1989—Fumbled six times and recovered three fumbles for minus eight yards. 1993—Fumbled eight times and recovered two fumbles. 1994—Fumbled eight times and recovered three fumbles for minus 13 yards. 1995—Fumbled three times. 1996—Fumbled nine times and recovered two fumbles for minus seven yards. 1997—Fumbled once.
SINGLE GAME HIGHS (regular season): Attempts—53 (December 19, 1993, vs. Seattle); completions—34 (December 19, 1993, vs. Seattle); yards—431 (December 19, 1993, vs. Seattle); and touchdown passes—3 (November 24, 1996, vs. Houston).
STATISTICAL PLATEAUS: 300-yard passing games: 1988 (1), 1993 (2). Total: 3.
MISCELLANEOUS: Regular-season record as starting NFL quarterback: 26-27 (.491). Postseason record as starting NFL quarterback: 1-1 (.500).

					PASSING							RUSHING				TOTALS	
Year Team	G	GS	Att.	Cmp.	Pct.	Yds.	TD	Int.	Avg.	Rat.	Att.	Yds.	Avg.	TD	TD	2pt.	Pts.
1987—L.A. Raiders NFL						Did not play.											
1988—L.A. Raiders NFL	10	8	238	105	44.1	1643	8	7	6.90	66.6	30	35	1.2	0	0	...	0
1989—L.A. Raiders NFL	10	7	217	108	49.8	1677	13	9	7.73	78.4	16	39	2.4	0	0	...	0
1990—L.A. Raiders NFL						Did not play.											
1991—Dallas NFL	8	4	137	68	49.6	909	5	2	6.64	77.2	7	-14	-2.0	0	0	...	0
1992—Dallas NFL	16	0	18	12	66.7	152	0	1	8.44	69.7	4	-7	-1.8	0	0	...	0
1993—Phoenix NFL	16	14	418	258	61.7	3164	18	17	7.57	82.5	22	45	2.0	0	0	...	0
1994—Arizona NFL	9	7	255	130	51.0	1545	5	9	6.06	61.6	22	39	1.8	1	1	0	6
1995—Jacksonville NFL	7	6	142	71	50.0	952	4	7	6.70	60.5	5	32	6.4	0	0	0	0
1996—Carolina NFL	8	4	123	69	56.1	879	8	2	7.15	93.5	12	17	1.4	0	0	0	0
1997—Carolina NFL	7	3	153	89	58.2	1032	6	3	6.75	83.6	4	32	8.0	0	0	0	0
Pro totals (9 years)	91	53	1701	910	53.5	11953	67	57	7.03	75.1	122	218	1.8	1	1	0	6

BIAKABUTUKA, TSHIMANGA   RB   PANTHERS

PERSONAL: Born January 24, 1974, in Zaire. ... 6-0/210. ... Name pronounced Tee-MONG-uh Bee-ock-uh-bah-TWO-kah. ... Nickname: Tim.
HIGH SCHOOL: Vanier (Longueuil, Que.) College.
COLLEGE: Michigan.
TRANSACTIONS/CAREER NOTES: Selected after junior season by Carolina Panthers in first round (eighth pick overall) of 1996 NFL draft. ... Signed by Panthers (August 16, 1996). ... On injured reserve with knee injury (October 1, 1996-remainder of season).
SINGLE GAME HIGHS (regular season): Attempts—26 (September 1, 1996, vs. Atlanta); yards—104 (October 26 1997, vs. Atlanta); and rushing touchdowns—2 (October 26, 1997, vs. Atlanta).
STATISTICAL PLATEAUS: 100-yard rushing games: 1997 (1).

			RUSHING				TOTALS			
Year Team	G	GS	Att.	Yds.	Avg.	TD	TD	2pt.	Pts.	Fum.
1996—Carolina NFL	4	4	71	229	3.2	0	0	0	0	0
1997—Carolina NFL	8	2	75	299	4.0	2	2	0	12	1
Pro totals (2 years)	12	6	146	528	3.6	2	2	0	12	1

BIEKERT, GREG   LB   RAIDERS

PERSONAL: Born March 14, 1969, in Iowa City, Iowa. ... 6-2/240. ... Name pronounced BEEK-ert.
HIGH SCHOOL: Longmont (Colo.).
COLLEGE: Colorado (degree in marketing, 1992).

TRANSACTIONS/CAREER NOTES: Selected by Los Angeles Raiders in seventh round (181st pick overall) of 1993 NFL draft. ... Signed by Raiders (July 13, 1993). ... Raiders franchise moved to Oakland (July 21, 1995).

PRO STATISTICS: 1996—Recovered one fumble. 1997—Returned one kickoff for 16 yards.

Year Team	G	GS	INTERCEPTIONS				SACKS
			No.	Yds.	Avg.	TD	No.
1993—Los Angeles Raiders NFL	16	0	0	0	...	0	0.0
1994—Los Angeles Raiders NFL	16	14	1	11	11.0	0	1.5
1995—Oakland NFL	16	14	0	0	...	0	1.0
1996—Oakland NFL	16	15	0	0	...	0	0.0
1997—Oakland NFL	16	16	0	0	...	0	2.5
Pro totals (5 years)	80	59	1	11	11.0	0	5.0

BIENIEMY, ERIC — RB — BENGALS

B

PERSONAL: Born August 15, 1969, in New Orleans. ... 5-7/205. ... Full name: Eric Bieniemy Jr.

HIGH SCHOOL: Bishop Amat (La Puente, Calif.).

COLLEGE: Colorado.

TRANSACTIONS/CAREER NOTES: Selected by San Diego Chargers in second round (39th pick overall) of 1991 NFL draft. ... Signed by Chargers (July 19, 1991). ... Granted free agency (February 17, 1994). ... Re-signed by Chargers (June 6, 1994). ... Granted unconditional free agency (February 17, 1995). ... Signed by Cincinnati Bengals (March 27, 1995).

CHAMPIONSHIP GAME EXPERIENCE: Played in AFC championship game (1994 season). ... Played in Super Bowl XXIX (1994 season).

HONORS: Named running back on THE SPORTING NEWS college All-America first team (1990).

PRO STATISTICS: 1992—Fumbled four times and recovered one fumble. 1993—Fumbled once. 1994—Fumbled once and recovered one fumble. 1995—Attempted two passes without a completion, fumbled once and recovered one fumble. 1996—Fumbled once. 1997—Fumbled twice.

SINGLE GAME HIGHS (regular season): Attempts—19 (November 12, 1995, vs. Houston); yards—65 (September 10, 1995, vs. Jacksonville); and rushing touchdowns—1 (December 14, 1997, vs. Dallas).

YearTeam	G	GS	RUSHING				RECEIVING				PUNT RETURNS				KICKOFF RETURNS				TOTALS		
			Att.	Yds.	Avg.	TD	No.	Yds.	Avg.	TD	No.	Yds.	Avg.	TD	No.	Yds.	Avg.	TD	TD	2pt.	Pts.
1991—San Diego NFL	15	0	3	17	5.7	0	0	0	...	0	0	0	...	0	0	0	...	0	0	...	0
1992—San Diego NFL	15	0	74	264	3.6	3	5	49	9.8	0	30	229	7.6	0	15	257	17.1	0	3	...	18
1993—San Diego NFL	16	0	33	135	4.1	1	1	0	0.0	0	0	0	...	0	7	110	15.7	0	1	...	6
1994—San Diego NFL	16	0	73	295	4.0	0	5	48	9.6	0	0	0	...	0	0	0	...	0	0	0	0
1995—Cincinnati NFL	16	1	98	381	3.9	3	43	424	9.9	0	7	47	6.7	0	8	168	21.0	0	3	0	18
1996—Cincinnati NFL	16	0	56	269	4.8	2	32	272	8.5	0	0	0	...	0	0	0	...	0	2	0	12
1997—Cincinnati NFL	16	0	21	97	4.6	1	31	249	8.0	0	0	0	...	0	34	789	23.2 ▲1		2	0	12
Pro totals (7 years)	110	1	358	1458	4.1	10	117	1042	8.9	0	37	276	7.5	0	64	1324	20.7	1	11	0	66

BINN, DAVE — C — CHARGERS

PERSONAL: Born February 6, 1972, in San Mateo, Calif. ... 6-3/240. ... Full name: David Aaron Binn.

HIGH SCHOOL: San Mateo (Calif.).

COLLEGE: California.

TRANSACTIONS/CAREER NOTES: Signed as non-drafted free agent by San Diego Chargers (April 28, 1994). ... Granted unconditional free agency (February 13, 1998). ... Re-signed by Chargers (February 25, 1998).

PLAYING EXPERIENCE: San Diego NFL, 1994-1997. ... Games/Games started: 1994 (16/0), 1995 (16/0), 1996 (16/0), 1997 (16/0). Total: 64/0.

CHAMPIONSHIP GAME EXPERIENCE: Played in AFC championship game (1994 season). ... Played in Super Bowl XXIX (1994 season).

BISHOP, BLAINE — S — OILERS

PERSONAL: Born July 24, 1970, in Indianapolis. ... 5-9/197. ... Full name: Blaine Elwood Bishop.

HIGH SCHOOL: Cathedral (Indianapolis).

COLLEGE: Saint Joseph's (Ind.) College, then Ball State (degree in insurance, 1993).

TRANSACTIONS/CAREER NOTES: Selected by Houston Oilers in eighth round (214th pick overall) of 1993 NFL draft. ... Signed by Oilers (July 16, 1993). ... Granted free agency (February 16, 1996). ... Re-signed by Oilers (June 17, 1996). ... Designated by Oilers as franchise player (February 14, 1997). ... Oilers franchise moved to Tennessee for 1997 season. ... Re-signed by Oilers (August 27, 1997).

HONORS: Played in Pro Bowl (1995 and 1997 seasons). ... Named to play in Pro Bowl (1996 season); replaced by Tyrone Braxton due to injury.

PRO STATISTICS: 1993—Fumbled once and recovered one fumble. 1994—Returned two kickoffs for 18 yards and recovered one fumble. 1995—Recovered four fumbles for six yards. 1997—Recovered two fumbles.

Year Team	G	GS	INTERCEPTIONS				SACKS
			No.	Yds.	Avg.	TD	No.
1993—Houston NFL	16	2	1	1	1.0	0	1.0
1994—Houston NFL	16	13	1	21	21.0	0	1.5
1995—Houston NFL	16	16	1	62	62.0	▲1	1.5
1996—Houston NFL	15	15	1	6	6.0	0	0.0
1997—Tennessee NFL	14	14	0	0	...	0	1.5
Pro totals (5 years)	77	60	4	90	22.5	1	5.5

BISHOP, GREG — G — GIANTS

PERSONAL: Born May 2, 1971, in Stockton, Calif. ... 6-5/315. ... Full name: Gregory Lawrence Bishop

HIGH SCHOOL: Lodi (Calif.).

COLLEGE: Pacific.

TRANSACTIONS/CAREER NOTES: Selected by New York Giants in fourth round (93rd pick overall) of 1993 NFL draft. ... Signed by Giants (July 19, 1993).
PLAYING EXPERIENCE: New York Giants NFL, 1993-1997. ... Games/Games started: 1993 (8/0), 1994 (16/1), 1995 (16/16), 1996 (16/16), 1997 (16/16). Total: 72/49.
PRO STATISTICS: 1994—Recovered two fumbles. 1995—Recovered one fumble. 1996—Recovered one fumble. 1997—Recovered one fumble.

BJORNSON, ERIC   TE   COWBOYS

PERSONAL: Born December 15, 1971, in San Francisco. ... 6-4/236. ... Name pronounced buh-YORN-sun.
HIGH SCHOOL: Bishop O'Dowd (Oakland).
COLLEGE: Washington.
TRANSACTIONS/CAREER NOTES: Selected by Dallas Cowboys in fourth round (110th pick overall) of 1995 NFL draft. ... Signed by Cowboys (July 18, 1995). ... Granted free agency (February 13, 1998).
CHAMPIONSHIP GAME EXPERIENCE: Played in NFC championship game (1995 season). ... Member of Super Bowl championship team (1995 season).
SINGLE GAME HIGHS (regular season): Receptions—8 (November 10, 1996, vs. San Francisco); yards—72 (October 5, 1997, vs. New York Giants); and touchdown receptions—1 (November 10, 1996, vs. San Francisco).

| | | | RECEIVING | | | | TOTALS | | |
Year Team	G	GS	No.	Yds.	Avg.	TD	TD	2pt.	Pts.	Fum.
1995—Dallas NFL	14	1	7	53	7.6	0	0	0	0	0
1996—Dallas NFL	14	10	48	388	8.1	3	3	1	20	1
1997—Dallas NFL	14	14	47	442	9.4	0	0	1	2	2
Pro totals (3 years)	42	25	102	883	8.7	3	3	2	22	3

BLACKMAN, KEN   G   BENGALS

PERSONAL: Born November 8, 1972, in Abilene, Texas. ... 6-6/315.
HIGH SCHOOL: Wylie (Abilene, Texas).
COLLEGE: Illinois.
TRANSACTIONS/CAREER NOTES: Selected by Cincinnati Bengals in third round (69th pick overall) of 1996 NFL draft. ... Signed by Bengals (July 16, 1996).
PLAYING EXPERIENCE: Cincinnati NFL, 1996 and 1997. ... Games/Games started: 1996 (14/10), 1997 (13/13). Total: 27/23.

BLACKMON, ROBERT   S   COLTS

PERSONAL: Born May 12, 1967, in Bay City, Texas. ... 6-0/208. ... Full name: Robert James Blackmon.
HIGH SCHOOL: Van Vleck (Texas).
COLLEGE: Baylor (degree in therapy recreation).
TRANSACTIONS/CAREER NOTES: Selected by Seattle Seahawks in second round (34th pick overall) of 1990 NFL draft. ... Signed by Seahawks (July 29, 1990). ... Granted free agency (March 1, 1993). ... Tendered offer sheet by Philadelphia Eagles (April 21, 1993). ... Offer matched by Seahawks (April 23, 1993). ... Designated by Seahawks as franchise player (February 16, 1996). ... Granted unconditional free agency (February 14, 1997). ... Signed by Indianapolis Colts (June 3, 1997).
PRO STATISTICS: 1990—Recovered one fumble. 1991—Recovered one fumble. 1992—Recovered one fumble for nine yards. 1993—Recovered one fumble for five yards and a touchdown. 1993—Recovered one fumble for five yards. 1994—Recovered three fumbles for 18 yards. 1996—Returned blocked field-goal attempt 61 yards for a touchdown and recovered one fumble for five yards. 1997—Recovered one fumble for 18 yards and a touchdown.

| | | | INTERCEPTIONS | | | | SACKS |
Year Team	G	GS	No.	Yds.	Avg.	TD	No.
1990—Seattle NFL	15	5	0	0	...	0	0.0
1991—Seattle NFL	16	16	3	59	19.7	0	1.0
1992—Seattle NFL	15	15	1	69	69.0	0	3.5
1993—Seattle NFL	16	16	2	0	0.0	0	0.0
1994—Seattle NFL	15	15	1	24	24.0	0	0.0
1995—Seattle NFL	13	13	5	46	9.2	0	1.0
1996—Seattle NFL	16	16	3	48	16.0	0	1.0
1997—Indianapolis NFL	14	14	1	2	2.0	0	3.0
Pro totals (8 years)	120	110	16	248	15.5	0	9.5

BLACKSHEAR, JEFF   G   RAVENS

PERSONAL: Born March 29, 1969, in Fort Pierce, Fla. ... 6-6/323.
HIGH SCHOOL: Fort Pierce (Fla.) Westwood.
JUNIOR COLLEGE: Northeast Mississippi Junior College.
COLLEGE: Northeast Louisiana.
TRANSACTIONS/CAREER NOTES: Selected by Seattle Seahawks in eighth round (197th pick overall) of 1993 NFL draft. ... Signed by Seahawks (July 15, 1993). ... Traded by Seahawks to Cleveland Browns for fourth-round pick (traded to Atlanta) in 1997 draft (March 12, 1996). ... Browns franchise moved to Baltimore and renamed Ravens for 1996 season (March 11, 1996). ... Granted unconditional free agency (February 14, 1997). ... Re-signed by Ravens (March 13, 1997).
PLAYING EXPERIENCE: Seattle NFL, 1993 and 1994; Cleveland NFL, 1995; Baltimore NFL, 1996 and 1997. ... Games/Games started: 1993 (15/2), 1994 (16/16), 1995 (16/3), 1996 (16/12), 1997 (16/16). Total: 79/49.

BLACKWELL, WILL — WR — STEELERS

PERSONAL: Born July 9, 1975, in Texarkana, Texas. ... 6-0/184. ... Full name: William H. Blackwell Jr.
HIGH SCHOOL: Skyline (Oakland).
COLLEGE: San Diego State.
TRANSACTIONS/CAREER NOTES: Selected after junior season by Pittsburgh Steelers in second round (53rd pick overall) of 1997 NFL draft. ... Signed by Steelers (July 15, 1997).
CHAMPIONSHIP GAME EXPERIENCE: Played in AFC championship game (1997 season).
PRO STATISTICS: 1997—Recovered two fumbles.
SINGLE GAME HIGHS (regular season): Receptions—4 (November 23, 1997, vs. Philadelphia); yards—68 (September 28, 1997, vs. Tennessee); and touchdown receptions—1 (November 23, 1997, vs. Philadelphia)..

			RECEIVING				PUNT RETURNS				KICKOFF RETURNS				TOTALS			
Year Team	G	GS	No.	Yds.	Avg.	TD	No.	Yds.	Avg.	TD	No.	Yds.	Avg.	TD	TD	2pt.	Pts.	Fum.
1997—Pittsburgh NFL	14	0	12	168	14.0	1	23	149	6.5	0	32	791	24.7	▲1	2	0	12	3

B

BLADES, BENNIE — S

PERSONAL: Born September 3, 1966, in Fort Lauderdale. ... 6-1/221. ... Full name: Horatio Benedict Blades. ... Brother of Brian Blades, wide receiver, Seattle Seahawks; and cousin of Daryl Porter, cornerback, Detroit Lions.
HIGH SCHOOL: Piper (Sunrise, Fla.).
COLLEGE: Miami (Fla.).
TRANSACTIONS/CAREER NOTES: Selected by Detroit Lions in first round (third pick overall) of 1988 NFL draft. ... Signed by Lions (July 14, 1988). ... Granted free agency (February 1, 1992). ... Re-signed by Lions (August 26, 1992). ... Granted roster exemption (August 26-September 4, 1992). ... Designated by Lions as transition player (February 25, 1993). ... On injured reserve (January 7, 1994-remainder of 1993 playoffs). ... Granted unconditional free agency (February 14, 1997). ... Signed by Seattle Seahawks (March 5, 1997). ... On injured reserve with back injury (December 2, 1997-remainder of season). ... Released by Seahawks (June 11, 1998).
CHAMPIONSHIP GAME EXPERIENCE: Played in NFC championship game (1991 season).
HONORS: Named defensive back on THE SPORTING NEWS college All-America first team (1986 and 1987). ... Jim Thorpe Award co-winner (1987). ... Played in Pro Bowl (1991 season).
PRO STATISTICS: 1988—Recovered four fumbles for 22 yards. 1989—Recovered one fumble. 1990—Recovered one fumble. 1991—Recovered three fumbles for 21 yards. 1992—Returned blocked punt seven yards for a touchdown. 1994—Recovered two fumbles. 1995—Credited with a safety.

			INTERCEPTIONS				SACKS
Year Team	G	GS	No.	Yds.	Avg.	TD	No.
1988—Detroit NFL	15	14	2	12	6.0	0	1.0
1989—Detroit NFL	16	16	0	0	...	0	0.0
1990—Detroit NFL	12	12	2	25	12.5	0	1.0
1991—Detroit NFL	16	16	1	14	14.0	0	0.0
1992—Detroit NFL	16	16	3	56	18.7	0	0.0
1993—Detroit NFL	4	4	0	0	...	0	0.0
1994—Detroit NFL	16	16	1	0	0.0	0	1.0
1995—Detroit NFL	16	16	1	0	0.0	0	1.0
1996—Detroit NFL	15	15	2	112	56.0	1	0.0
1997—Seattle NFL	10	9	2	11	5.5	0	1.0
Pro totals (10 years)	136	134	14	230	16.4	1	5.0

BLADES, BRIAN — WR — SEAHAWKS

PERSONAL: Born July 24, 1965, in Fort Lauderdale. ... 5-11/190. ... Full name: Brian Keith Blades. ... Brother of Bennie Blades, cornerback with Detroit Lions (1988-96) and Seattle Seahawks (1997); and cousin of Daryl Porter, cornerback, Detroit Lions.
HIGH SCHOOL: Piper (Sunrise, Fla.)
COLLEGE: Miami (Fla.).
TRANSACTIONS/CAREER NOTES: Selected by Seattle Seahawks in second round (49th pick overall) of 1988 NFL draft. ... Signed by Seahawks (May 19, 1988). ... Granted free agency (February 1, 1992). ... Re-signed by Seahawks (September 2, 1992). ... Granted roster exemption (September 2-5, 1992). ... On injured reserve with broken clavicle (September 8-November 25, 1992); on practice squad (November 18-25, 1992). ... Designated by Seahawks as transition player (February 25, 1993). ... Free agency status changed from transitional to unconditional (February 17, 1994). ... Re-signed by Seahawks (May 17, 1994). ... Granted unconditional free agency (February 16, 1996). ... Re-signed by Seahawks (April 10, 1996). ... On injured reserve with hand injury (November 19, 1997-remainder of season).
HONORS: Played in Pro Bowl (1989 season).
PRO STATISTICS: 1988—Recovered one fumble. 1989—Recovered one fumble. 1994—Recovered two fumbles.
SINGLE GAME HIGHS (regular season): Receptions—12 (September 1, 1991, vs. New Orleans); yards—160 (September 1, 1991 vs. New Orleans); and touchdown receptions—2 (November 5, 1995, vs. New York Giants).
STATISTICAL PLATEAUS: 100-yard receiving games: 1988 (2), 1989 (5), 1991 (3), 1992 (1), 1993 (2), 1994 (1), 1995 (3). Total: 17.

			RUSHING				RECEIVING				TOTALS			
Year Team	G	GS	Att.	Yds.	Avg.	TD	No.	Yds.	Avg.	TD	TD	2pt.	Pts.	Fum.
1988—Seattle NFL	16	7	5	24	4.8	0	40	682	17.1	8	8	...	48	1
1989—Seattle NFL	16	14	1	3	3.0	0	77	1063	13.8	5	5	...	30	3
1990—Seattle NFL	16	16	3	19	6.3	0	49	525	10.7	3	3	...	18	0
1991—Seattle NFL	16	16	2	17	8.5	0	70	1003	14.3	2	2	...	12	1
1992—Seattle NFL	6	5	1	5	5.0	0	19	256	13.5	1	1	...	6	1
1993—Seattle NFL	16	14	5	52	10.4	0	80	945	11.8	3	3	...	18	1
1994—Seattle NFL	16	16	2	32	16.0	0	81	1086	13.4	4	4	1	26	1
1995—Seattle NFL	16	16	2	4	2.0	0	77	1001	13.0	4	4	0	24	0
1996—Seattle NFL	11	9	0	0	...	0	43	556	12.9	2	2	0	12	1
1997—Seattle NFL	11	3	0	0	...	0	30	319	10.6	2	2	0	12	1
Pro totals (10 years)	140	116	21	156	7.4	0	566	7436	13.1	34	34	1	206	10

BLAKE, JEFF   QB   BENGALS

PERSONAL: Born December 4, 1970, in Daytona Beach, Fla. ... 6-0/205. ... Son of Emory Blake, running back, Toronto Argonauts of CFL (1974).
HIGH SCHOOL: Seminole (Sanford, Fla.).
COLLEGE: East Carolina.
TRANSACTIONS/CAREER NOTES: Selected by New York Jets in sixth round (166th pick overall) of 1992 NFL draft. ... Signed by Jets (July 14, 1992). ... Claimed on waivers by Cincinnati Bengals (August 29, 1994). ... Granted free agency (February 17, 1995). ... Re-signed by Bengals (May 8, 1995).
HONORS: Played in Pro Bowl (1995 season).
PRO STATISTICS: 1992—Fumbled once. 1994—Fumbled six times. 1995—Fumbled 10 times for minus seven yards. 1996—Fumbled seven times and recovered one fumble for minus five yards. 1997—Fumbled seven times.
SINGLE GAME HIGHS (regular season): Attempts—46 (December 17, 1995, vs. Cleveland); completions—31 (November 6, 1994, vs. Seattle); yards—387 (November 6, 1994, vs. Seattle); and touchdown passes—4 (November 24, 1996, vs. Atlanta).
STATISTICAL PLATEAUS: 300-yard passing games: 1994 (2), 1995 (1), 1996 (2), 1997 (1). Total: 6.
MISCELLANEOUS: Regular-season record as starting NFL quarterback: 21-31 (.404).

				PASSING							RUSHING			TOTALS		
Year Team	G	GS	Att.	Cmp.	Pct.	Yds.	TD	Int.	Avg.	Rat.	Att.	Yds.	Avg.	TD	TD	2pt.	Pts.
1992—New York Jets NFL	3	0	9	4	44.4	40	0	1	4.44	18.1	2	-2	-1.0	0	0	...	0
1993—New York Jets NFL							Did not play.										
1994—Cincinnati NFL	10	9	306	156	51.0	2154	14	9	7.04	76.9	37	204	5.5	1	1	1	8
1995—Cincinnati NFL	16	16	567	§326	57.5	3822	§28	17	6.74	82.1	53	309	5.8	2	2	1	14
1996—Cincinnati NFL	16	16	549	308	56.1	3624	24	14	6.60	80.3	72	317	4.4	2	2	0	12
1997—Cincinnati NFL	11	11	317	184	58.0	2125	8	7	6.70	77.6	45	234	5.2	3	3	0	18
Pro totals (5 years)	56	52	1748	978	55.9	11765	74	48	6.73	79.4	209	1062	5.1	8	8	2	52

BLANCHARD, CARY   K   COLTS

PERSONAL: Born November 5, 1968, in Fort Worth, Texas. ... 6-1/227. ... Full name: Robert C. Blanchard.
HIGH SCHOOL: L.D. Bell (Hurst, Texas).
COLLEGE: Oklahoma State.
TRANSACTIONS/CAREER NOTES: Signed as non-drafted free agent by Dallas Cowboys (April 25, 1991). ... Released by Cowboys (August 4, 1991). ... Signed by Sacramento Surge of World League (1992). ... Signed by New Orleans Saints (July 7, 1992). ... Released by Saints (August 31, 1992). ... Re-signed by Saints to practice squad (September 7, 1992). ... Activated (September 14, 1992). ... Active for one game with Saints (1992); did not play. ... Claimed on waivers by New York Jets (September 29, 1992). ... Released by Jets (June 24, 1994). ... Signed by Minnesota Vikings (July 12, 1994). ... Released by Vikings (August 28, 1994). ... Signed by New Orleans Saints (April 18, 1995). ... Released by Saints (August 27, 1995). ... Signed by Indianapolis Colts (October 3, 1995).
CHAMPIONSHIP GAME EXPERIENCE: Played in AFC championship game (1995 season).
HONORS: Named kicker on THE SPORTING NEWS NFL All-Pro team (1996). ... Played in Pro Bowl (1996 season).

			KICKING						
Year Team	G	GS	XPM	XPA	FGM	FGA	Lg.	50+	Pts.
1991—					Did not play.				
1992—Sacramento W.L.	4	0	17	17	5	8	42	0-0	32
—New York Jets NFL	11	0	17	17	16	22	47	0-1	65
1993—New York Jets NFL	16	0	31	31	17	26	45	0-2	82
1994—					Did not play.				
1995—Indianapolis NFL	12	0	25	25	19	24	50	1-1	82
1996—Indianapolis NFL	16	0	27	27	§36	§40	52	5-5	§135
1997—Indianapolis NFL	16	0	21	21	§32	†41	50	1-3	117
W.L. totals (1 year)	4	0	17	17	5	8	42	0-0	32
NFL totals (4 years)	71	0	121	121	120	153	52	7-12	481
Pro totals (5 years)	75	0	138	138	125	161	52	7-0	513

BLAND, TONY   WR   VIKINGS

PERSONAL: Born December 12, 1972, in St. Petersburg, Fla. ... 6-3/213.
HIGH SCHOOL: Pinellas Park (St. Petersburg, Fla.).
COLLEGE: Florida A&M.
TRANSACTIONS/CAREER NOTES: Signed as non-drafted free agent by Minnesota Vikings (April 26, 1996). ... Released by Vikings (August 20, 1996). ... Re-signed by Vikings to practice squad (August 26, 1996). ... Activated (December 20, 1996); did not play. ... Released by Vikings (August 24, 1997). ... Re-signed by Vikings to practice squad (August 25, 1997). ... Activated (November 29, 1997).
PLAYING EXPERIENCE: Minnesota NFL, 1997. ... Games/Games started: 2/0.
SINGLE GAME HIGHS (regular season): Receptions—0; yards—0; and touchdown receptions—0.

BLANTON, SCOTT   K   REDSKINS

PERSONAL: Born July 1, 1973, in Norman, Okla. ... 6-2/221.
HIGH SCHOOL: Norman (Okla.).
COLLEGE: Oklahoma.
TRANSACTIONS/CAREER NOTES: Signed as non-drafted free agent by Washington Redskins (April 26, 1995). ... On injured reserve with groin injury (August 27, 1995-entire season). ... Granted free agency (February 13, 1998). ... Re-signed by Redskins (May 7, 1998).
PRO STATISTICS: 1997—Recovered one fumble.

			KICKING						
Year Team	G	GS	XPM	XPA	FGM	FGA	Lg.	50+	Pts.
1995—Washington NFL					Did not play.				
1996—Washington NFL	16	0	40	40	26	32	53	2-3	118
1997—Washington NFL	15	0	34	34	16	24	50	1-4	82
Pro totals (2 years)	31	0	74	74	42	56	53	3-7	200

BLEDSOE, DREW — QB — PATRIOTS

PERSONAL: Born February 14, 1972, in Ellensburg, Wash. ... 6-5/233.
HIGH SCHOOL: Walla Walla (Wash.).
COLLEGE: Washington State.
TRANSACTIONS/CAREER NOTES: Selected after junior season by New England Patriots in first round (first pick overall) of 1993 NFL draft. ... Signed by Patriots (July 6, 1993).
CHAMPIONSHIP GAME EXPERIENCE: Played in AFC championship game (1996 season). ... Played in Super Bowl XXXI (1996 season).
HONORS: Played in Pro Bowl (1994, 1996 and 1997 seasons).
RECORDS: Holds NFL single-season record for most passes attempted—691 (1994). ... Holds NFL single-game records for most passes completed—45; most passes attempted—70; and most passes attempted without an interception—70 (November 13, 1994, vs. Minnesota).
POST SEASON RECORDS: Shares Super Bowl single-game record for most passes intercepted—4 (January 26, 1997, vs. New England).
PRO STATISTICS: 1993—Fumbled eight times and recovered five fumbles for minus 23 yards. 1994—Fumbled nine times and recovered three fumbles for minus five yards. 1995—Caught one pass for minus one yard, fumbled 11 times and recovered one fumble for minus eight yards. 1996—Fumbled nine times and recovered one fumble for minus two yards. 1997—Fumbled four times and recovered three fumbles for minus four yards.
SINGLE GAME HIGHS (regular season): Attempts—70 (November 13, 1994, vs. Minnesota); completions—45 (November 13, 1994, vs. Minnesota); yards—426 (November 13, 1994, vs. Minnesota; and touchdown passes—4 (September 7, 1997, vs. Indianapolis).
STATISTICAL PLATEAUS: 300-yard passing games: 1993 (1), 1994 (6), 1995 (2), 1996 (4), 1997 (3). Total: 16.
MISCELLANEOUS: Regular-season record as starting NFL quarterback: 42-33 (.560). Postseason record as starting NFL quarterback: 3-3 (.500).

Year Team	G	GS	Att.	Cmp.	Pct.	Yds.	TD	Int.	Avg.	Rat.	Att.	Yds.	Avg.	TD	TD	2pt.	Pts.
1993—New England NFL........	13	12	429	214	49.9	2494	15	15	5.81	65.0	32	82	2.6	0	0	—	0
1994—New England NFL........	16	16	*691	*400	57.9	*4555	25	*27	6.59	73.6	44	40	0.9	0	0	0	0
1995—New England NFL........	15	15	*636	323	50.8	3507	13	16	5.51	63.7	20	28	1.4	0	0	0	0
1996—New England NFL........	16	16	*623	*373	59.9	4086	27	15	6.56	83.7	24	27	1.1	0	0	0	0
1997—New England NFL........	16	16	522	314	60.2	3706	28	15	7.10	87.7	28	55	2.0	0	0	0	0
Pro totals (5 years)............	76	75	2901	1624	56.0	18348	108	88	6.32	74.9	148	232	1.6	0	0	0	0

BLOEDORN, GREG — G — SEAHAWKS

PERSONAL: Born November 15, 1972, in Elmhurst, Ill. ... 6-6/278.
HIGH SCHOOL: Glenbard South (Glen Ellyn, Ill.).
COLLEGE: Cornell (degree in economics).
TRANSACTIONS/CAREER NOTES: Signed as non-drafted free agent by Seattle Seahawks (April 25, 1996). ... Released by Seahawks (August 13, 1996). ... Re-signed by Seahawks to practice squad (September 11, 1996). ... Released by Seahawks (August 26, 1997). ... Re-signed by Seahawks to practice squad (August 27, 1997). ... Activated (October 31, 1997). ... Returned to practice squad (November 5, 1997). ... Activated (November 21, 1997). ... Returned to practice squad (November 25, 1997). ... Activated (November 28, 1997). ... Assigned by Seahawks to England Monarchs in 1998 NFL Europe enhancement allocation program (February 18, 1998).
PLAYING EXPERIENCE: Seattle NFL, 1997. ... Games/Games started: 3/0.

BLUNDIN, MATT — QB

PERSONAL: Born March 7, 1969, in Darby, Pa. ... 6-6/233. ... Full name: Matthew Brent Blundin. ... Nephew of Barry Blundin, minor league pitcher (1987-88).
HIGH SCHOOL: Ridley Senior (Folsom, Pa.).
COLLEGE: Virginia (degree in mathematics).
TRANSACTIONS/CAREER NOTES: Selected by Kansas City Chiefs in second round (40th pick overall) of 1992 NFL draft. ... Signed by Chiefs (July 22, 1992). ... On inactive list for all 16 games (1992). ... Assigned by Chiefs to Scottish Claymores in 1995 World League enhancement allocation program (February 20, 1995). ... Granted unconditional free agency (February 16, 1996). ... Signed by Chicago Bears (July 22, 1996). ... Released by Bears (August 13, 1996). ... Signed by Detroit Lions (March 27, 1997). ... Granted unconditional free agency (February 13, 1998).
CHAMPIONSHIP GAME EXPERIENCE: Member of Chiefs for AFC championship game (1993 season); inactive.

Year Team	G	GS	Att.	Cmp.	Pct.	Yds.	TD	Int.	Avg.	Rat.	Att.	Yds.	Avg.	TD	TD	2pt.	Pts.
1992—Kansas City NFL.........							Did not play.										
1993—Kansas City NFL.........	1	0	3	1	33.3	2	0	0	0.67	42.4	0	0	...	0	0	...	0
1994—Kansas City NFL.........	1	0	5	1	20.0	13	0	1	2.60	0.0	0	0	...	0	0	0	0
1995—Scottish W.L.	...	...	221	107	48.4	1228	6	11	5.56	53.9	6	33	5.5	0	0	0	0
1996—							Did not play.										
1997—Detroit NFL...............	1	0	1	0	0.0	0	0	1	...	0.0	0	0	...	0	0	0	0
W.L. totals (1 year)..............	...	...	221	107	48.4	1228	6	11	5.56	53.9	6	33	5.5	0	0	0	0
NFL totals (3 years).............	3	0	9	2	22.2	15	0	2	1.67	0.0	0	0	...	0	0	0	0
Pro totals (4 years).............	...	...	230	109	47.4	1243	6	13	5.40	49.2	6	33	5.5	0	0	0	0

BOBO, ORLANDO — G — VIKINGS

PERSONAL: Born February 9, 1974, in Westpoint, Miss. ... 6-3/296.
HIGH SCHOOL: Westpoint (Miss.).
JUNIOR COLLEGE: East Mississippi Community College.
COLLEGE: Northeast Louisiana.
TRANSACTIONS/CAREER NOTES: Signed as non-drafted free agent by Minnesota Vikings (April 26, 1996). ... Released by Vikings (August 20, 1996). ... Re-signed by Vikings to practice squad (August 26, 1996). ... Released by Vikings (August 27, 1997). ... Re-signed by Vikings to practice squad (August 29, 1997). ... Activated (September 12, 1997).
PLAYING EXPERIENCE: Minnesota NFL, 1997. ... Games/Games started: 5/0.

BOCK, JOHN   C   DOLPHINS

PERSONAL: Born February 11, 1971, in Crystal Lake, Ill. ... 6-3/295. ... Full name: John Matthew Bock. ... Nephew of Wayne Bock, tackle with Chicago Cardinals (1957).
HIGH SCHOOL: Crystal Lake (Ill.).
COLLEGE: Louisville, then Indiana State.
TRANSACTIONS/CAREER NOTES: Signed as non-drafted free agent by Buffalo Bills (May 7, 1994). ... Released by Bills (August 22, 1994). ... Selected by Amsterdam Admirals in 1995 World League draft. ... Signed by New York Jets (June 22, 1995). ... Released by Jets (August 29, 1996). ... Signed by Miami Dolphins (October 16, 1996).
PLAYING EXPERIENCE: Amsterdam W.L., 1995; New York Jets NFL, 1995; Miami NFL, 1996 and 1997. ... Games/Games started: W.L.: 1995 (10/10); NFL: 1995 (10/7), 1996 (2/0), 1997 (14/3). Total W.L.: 10/10. Total NFL: 26/10. Total Pro: 36/20.
PRO STATISTICS: 1995—Fumbled once for minus one yard.

BOLDEN, JURAN   CB   FALCONS

PERSONAL: Born June 27, 1974, in Tampa. ... 6-2/201.
HIGH SCHOOL: Hillsborough (Tampa).
JUNIOR COLLEGE: Mississippi Delta Community College.
TRANSACTIONS/CAREER NOTES: Selected by Atlanta Falcons in fourth round (127th pick overall) of 1996 NFL draft. ... Signed by Falcons (July 20, 1996). ... On injured reserve with knee injury (December 9, 1996-remainder of season).
PRO STATISTICS: CFL: 1995—Intercepted six passes for 28 yards.

Year Team	G	GS	KICKOFF RETURNS				TOTALS			
			No.	Yds.	Avg.	TD	TD	2pt.	Pts.	Fum.
1995—Winnipeg CFL	9	9	1	2	2.0	0	0	0	0	0
1996—Atlanta NFL	9	0	0	0	...	0	0	0	0	0
1997—Atlanta NFL	14	1	5	106	21.2	0	0	0	0	0
CFL totals (1 year)	9	9	1	2	2.0	0	0	0	0	0
NFL totals (2 years)	23	1	5	106	21.2	0	0	0	0	0
Pro totals (3 years)	32	10	6	108	18.0	0	0	0	0	0

BONHAM, SHANE   DL   49ERS

PERSONAL: Born October 18, 1970, in Fairbanks, Alaska. ... 6-2/286. ... Full name: Steven Shane Bonham.
HIGH SCHOOL: Lathrop (Fairbanks, Alaska).
COLLEGE: Air Force, then Tennessee.
TRANSACTIONS/CAREER NOTES: Selected by Detroit Lions in third round (93rd pick overall) of 1994 NFL draft. ... Signed by Lions (July 21, 1994). ... Granted free agency (February 14, 1997). ... Re-signed by Lions (May 22, 1997). ... Granted unconditional free agency (February 13, 1998). ... Signed by San Francisco 49ers (April 21, 1998).

Year Team	G	GS	SACKS
1994—Detroit NFL	15	1	0.0
1995—Detroit NFL	15	0	1.0
1996—Detroit NFL	15	2	2.0
1997—Detroit NFL	16	0	1.0
Pro totals (4 years)	61	3	4.0

BONIOL, CHRIS   K   EAGLES

PERSONAL: Born December 9, 1971, in Alexandria, La. ... 5-11/167.
HIGH SCHOOL: Alexandria (La.).
COLLEGE: Louisiana Tech.
TRANSACTIONS/CAREER NOTES: Signed as non-drafted free agent by Dallas Cowboys (April 28, 1994). ... Granted free agency (February 14, 1997). ... Tendered offer sheet by Philadelphia Eagles (March 7, 1997). ... Cowboys declined to match offer (March 14, 1997).
CHAMPIONSHIP GAME EXPERIENCE: Played in NFC championship game (1994 and 1995 season). ... Member of Super Bowl championship team (1995 season).
RECORDS: Holds NFL career record for highest field-goal percentage—83.06. ... Shares NFL single-game record for most field goals—7 (November 18, 1996, vs. Green Bay).
PRO STATISTICS: 1995—Punted twice for 77 yards.

Year Team	G	GS	KICKING						
			XPM	XPA	FGM	FGA	Lg.	50+	Pts.
1994—Dallas NFL	16	0	48	48	22	29	47	0-1	114
1995—Dallas NFL	16	0	†46	48	27	28	45	0-0	127
1996—Dallas NFL	16	0	24	25	32	36	52	1-2	120
1997—Philadelphia NFL	16	0	33	33	22	31	49	0-1	99
Pro totals (4 years)	64	0	151	154	103	124	52	1-4	460

BONO, STEVE   QB   RAMS

PERSONAL: Born May 11, 1962, in Norristown, Pa. ... 6-4/212. ... Full name: Steven Christopher Bono.
HIGH SCHOOL: Norristown (Pa.).
COLLEGE: UCLA.
TRANSACTIONS/CAREER NOTES: Selected by Memphis Showboats in 1985 USFL territorial draft. ... Selected by Minnesota Vikings in sixth round (142nd pick overall) of 1985 NFL draft. ... Signed by Vikings (July 10, 1985). ... Released by Vikings (October 4, 1986). ... Re-signed by Vikings (November 19, 1986). ... Released by Vikings (December 9, 1986). ... Signed by Pittsburgh Steelers (March 25, 1987). ... Released by Steelers (September 7, 1987). ... Re-signed as replacement player by Steelers (September 24, 1987). ... Released by Steelers (April 13,

1989). ... Signed by San Francisco 49ers (June 13, 1989). ... Active for seven games (1990); did not play. ... Granted free agency (February 1, 1991). ... Re-signed by 49ers (1991). ... Granted unconditional free agency (March 1, 1993). ... Re-signed by 49ers (April 7, 1993). ... Released by 49ers (April 29, 1994). ... Re-signed by 49ers and traded to Kansas City Chiefs for conditional draft pick (May 2, 1994). ... Released by Chiefs (June 12, 1997). ... Signed by Green Bay Packers (June 20, 1997). ... Traded by Packers to St. Louis Rams for conditional pick in 1999 draft (April 5, 1998).

CHAMPIONSHIP GAME EXPERIENCE: Member of 49ers for NFC championship game (1989 and 1990 seasons); inactive. ... Member of Super Bowl championship team (1989 season). ... Played in NFC championship game (1992 and 1993 seasons). ... Member of Packers for NFC championship game (1997 season); did not play. ... Member of Packers for Super Bowl XXXII (1997 season); did not play.

HONORS: Played in Pro Bowl (1995 season).

PRO STATISTICS: 1987—Caught one pass for two yards, fumbled five times and recovered three fumbles. 1991—Fumbled seven times for minus eight yards. 1992—Fumbled twice and recovered one fumble for minus three yards. 1995—Fumbled 10 times and recovered one fumble for minus five yards. 1996—Fumbled five times. 1997—Fumbled once.

SINGLE GAME HIGHS (regular season): Attempts—55 (December 12, 1994, vs. Miami); completions—33 (December 12, 1994, vs. Miami; yards—347 (December 1, 1991, vs. New Orleans); and touchdown passes—3 (September 15, 1996, vs. Seattle).

STATISTICAL PLATEAUS: 300-yard passing games: 1991 (2), 1994 (2). Total: 4.

MISCELLANEOUS: Regular-season record as starting NFL quarterback: 28-12 (.700). ... Postseason record as starting NFL quarterback: 0-1 (.000).

				PASSING						RUSHING				TOTALS		
Year Team	G	GS	Att.	Cmp.	Pct.	Yds.	TD	Int.	Avg.	Rat.	Att.	Yds.	Avg.	TD	TD	2pt.	Pts.
1985—Minnesota NFL...........	1	0	10	1	10.0	5	0	0	0.50	39.6	0	0	...	0	0	...	0
1986—Minnesota NFL...........	1	0	1	1	100.0	3	0	0	3.00	79.2	0	0	...	0	0	...	0
1987—Pittsburgh NFL...........	3	3	74	34	45.9	438	5	2	5.92	76.3	8	27	3.4	1	1	...	6
1988—Pittsburgh NFL...........	2	0	35	10	28.6	110	1	2	3.14	25.9	0	0	...	0	0	...	0
1989—San Francisco NFL......	1	0	5	4	80.0	62	1	0	12.40	157.9	0	0	...	0	0	...	0
1990—San Francisco NFL......							Did not play.										
1991—San Francisco NFL......	9	6	237	141	59.5	1617	11	4	6.82	88.5	17	46	2.7	0	0	...	0
1992—San Francisco NFL......	16	0	56	36	64.3	463	2	2	8.27	87.1	15	23	1.5	0	0	...	0
1993—San Francisco NFL......	8	0	61	39	63.9	416	0	1	6.82	76.9	12	14	1.2	1	1	...	6
1994—Kansas City NFL.........	7	2	117	66	56.4	796	4	4	6.80	74.6	4	-1	-0.3	0	0	0	0
1995—Kansas City NFL.........	16	16	520	293	56.3	3121	21	10	6.00	79.5	28	113	4.0	5	5	0	30
1996—Kansas City NFL.........	13	13	438	235	53.7	2572	12	13	5.87	68.0	26	27	1.0	0	0	0	0
1997—Green Bay NFL...........	2	0	10	5	50.0	29	0	0	2.90	56.3	3	-3	-1.0	0	0	0	0
Pro totals (12 years)...........	79	40	1564	865	55.3	9632	57	38	6.16	75.9	113	246	2.2	7	7	0	42

BOOKER, MICHAEL — DB — FALCONS

PERSONAL: Born April 27, 1975, in Oceanside, Calif. ... 6-2/203. ... Full name: Michael Allen Booker.
HIGH SCHOOL: El Camino (Calif.).
COLLEGE: Nebraska.
TRANSACTIONS/CAREER NOTES: Selected by Atlanta Falcons in first round (11th pick overall) of 1997 NFL draft. ... Signed by Falcons (July 16, 1997).

			INTERCEPTIONS			
Year Team	G	GS	No.	Yds.	Avg.	TD
1997—Atlanta NFL	15	2	3	16	5.3	0

BOOKER, VAUGHN — DE — PACKERS

PERSONAL: Born February 24, 1968, in Cincinnati. ... 6-5/295. ... Full name: Vaughn Jamel Booker.
HIGH SCHOOL: Taft (Cincinnati).
COLLEGE: Cincinnati.
TRANSACTIONS/CAREER NOTES: Signed as non-drafted free agent by Winnipeg Blue Bombers of CFL (June 1992). ... Granted free agency after 1994 season. ... Signed as free agent by Kansas City Chiefs (May 2, 1994). ... Traded by Chiefs to Green Bay Packers for DT Darius Holland (May 13, 1998).
PRO STATISTICS: CFL: 1992—Recovered four fumbles and returned one kickoff for three yards. NFL: 1994—Recovered two fumbles for six yards and returned two kickoffs for 10 yards. 1995—Recovered one fumble for 14 yards and a touchdown. 1996—Recovered one fumble. 1997—Recovered one fumble.
MISCELLANEOUS: Served in U.S. Army (1988-90).

Year Team	G	GS	SACKS
1992—Winnipeg CFL	15	...	2.0
1993—Winnipeg CFL	9	...	4.0
1994—Kansas City NFL	13	0	0.0
1995—Kansas City NFL	16	10	1.5
1996—Kansas City NFL	14	12	1.0
1997—Kansas City NFL	13	13	4.0
CFL totals (2 years)...	24	...	6.0
NFL totals (4 years)...	56	35	6.5
Pro totals (6 years)...	80	...	12.5

BORDELON, BEN — OT — CHARGERS

PERSONAL: Born April 9, 1974, in Mathews, La. ... 6-4/291. ... Full name: Benjamin Gerald Bordelon.
HIGH SCHOOL: Central Lafourche (Mathews, La.).
COLLEGE: Louisiana State.
TRANSACTIONS/CAREER NOTES: Signed as non-drafted free agent by San Diego Chargers (April 21, 1997).
PLAYING EXPERIENCE: San Diego NFL, 1997. ... Games/Games started: 16/2.
PRO STATISTICS: 1997—Returned two kickoffs for no yards.

BOSELLI, TONY   OT   JAGUARS

PERSONAL: Born April 17, 1972, in Boulder, Colo. ... 6-7/322. ... Full name: Don Anthony Boselli Jr.
HIGH SCHOOL: Fairview (Boulder, Colo.).
COLLEGE: Southern California.
TRANSACTIONS/CAREER NOTES: Selected by Jacksonville Jaguars in first round (second pick overall) of 1995 NFL draft. ... Signed by Jaguars (June 1, 1995).
PLAYING EXPERIENCE: Jacksonville NFL, 1995-1997. ... Games/Games started: 1995 (13/12), 1996 (16/16), 1997 (12/12). Total: 41/40.
CHAMPIONSHIP GAME EXPERIENCE: Played in AFC championship game (1996 season).
HONORS: Named offensive lineman on THE SPORTING NEWS college All-America first team (1994). ... Played in Pro Bowl (1996 and 1997 seasons). ... Named offensive tackle on THE SPORTING NEWS NFL All-Pro team (1997).
PRO STATISTICS: 1996—Recovered one fumble.

B

BOSTIC, JAMES   RB   CHIEFS

PERSONAL: Born March 13, 1972, in Fort Lauderdale. ... 5-11/225. ... Full name: James Edwards Bostic.
HIGH SCHOOL: Dillard (Fort Lauderdale).
COLLEGE: Auburn.
TRANSACTIONS/CAREER NOTES: Selected after junior season by Los Angeles Rams in third round (83rd pick overall) of 1994 NFL draft. ... Signed by Rams (July 6, 1994). ... Active for 10 games with Rams (1994); did not play. ... On injured reserve with right wrist injury (November 16, 1994-remainder of season). ... Rams franchise moved to St. Louis (April 12, 1995). ... Released by Rams (August 27, 1995). ... Signed by Green Bay Packers (January 10, 1996). ... On injured reserve with knee injury (August 20, 1996-entire season). ... Released by Packers (June 24, 1997). ... Signed by Kansas City Chiefs (April 7, 1998).

BOTKIN, KIRK   TE   STEELERS

PERSONAL: Born March 19, 1971, in Baytown, Texas. ... 6-3/245. ... Full name: Kirk Randal Botkin.
HIGH SCHOOL: Robert E. Lee (Baytown, Texas).
COLLEGE: Arkansas.
TRANSACTIONS/CAREER NOTES: Signed as non-drafted free agent by New England Patriots (April 25, 1994). ... Released by Patriots (August 24, 1994). ... Signed by New Orleans Saints to practice squad (September 28, 1994). ... Activated (December 9, 1994). ... Claimed on waivers by Pittsburgh Steelers (August 26, 1996). ... Granted free agency (February 13, 1998).
CHAMPIONSHIP GAME EXPERIENCE: Played in AFC championship game (1997 season).
SINGLE GAME HIGHS (regular season): Receptions—2 (December 15, 1996, vs. San Francisco); yards—26 (December 15, 1996, vs. San Francisco); and touchdown receptions—0.

				RECEIVING		
Year Team	G	GS	No.	Yds.	Avg.	TD
1994—New Orleans NFL	3	0	0	0	...	0
1995—New Orleans NFL	16	0	1	8	8.0	0
1996—Pittsburgh NFL	16	0	4	36	9.0	0
1997—Pittsburgh NFL	13	1	1	11	11.0	0
Pro totals (4 years)	48	1	6	55	9.2	0

BOUIE, KEVIN   RB

PERSONAL: Born August 18, 1971, in Pahokee, Fla. ... 6-1/230. ... Full name: Kevin Lamount Bouie.
HIGH SCHOOL: Pahokee (Fla.).
JUNIOR COLLEGE: Garden City (Kan.) Community College.
COLLEGE: Mississippi State.
TRANSACTIONS/CAREER NOTES: Selected by Philadelphia Eagles in seventh round (210th pick overall) of 1995 NFL draft. ... Signed by Eagles (July 10, 1995). ... On injured reserve with shoulder injury (August 22, 1995-entire season). ... Released by Eagles (November 22, 1996). ... Signed by San Diego Chargers (December 4, 1996). ... Released by Chargers (June 2, 1997). ... Signed by Arizona Cardinals (June 4, 1997). ... Released by Cardinals (November 17, 1997).
SINGLE GAME HIGHS (regular season): Attempts—5 (September 14, 1997, vs. Washington); yards—25 (September 14, 1997, vs. Washington);and rushing touchdowns—0.

			RUSHING				KICKOFF RETURNS				TOTALS			
Year Team	G	GS	Att.	Yds.	Avg.	TD	No.	Yds.	Avg.	TD	TD	2pt.	Pts.	Fum.
1995—Philadelphia NFL							Did not play.							
1996—San Diego NFL	1	0	0	0	...	0	0	0	...	0	0	0	0	0
1997—Arizona NFL	5	0	11	26	2.4	0	6	136	22.7	0	0	0	0	0
Pro totals (2 years)	6	0	11	26	2.4	0	6	136	22.7	0	0	0	0	0

BOUIE, TONY   S   BUCCANEERS

PERSONAL: Born August 7, 1972, in New Orleans. ... 5-10/193. ... Full name: Tony Vanderson Bouie.
HIGH SCHOOL: Holy Cross (New Orleans).
COLLEGE: Arizona.
TRANSACTIONS/CAREER NOTES: Signed as non-drafted free agent by Tampa Bay Buccaneers (April 26, 1995). ... Released by Buccaneers (August 21, 1995). ... Re-signed by Buccaneers to practice squad (October 4, 1995). ... Activated (October 17, 1995). ... Granted free agency (February 13, 1998). ... Re-signed by Buccaneers (June 16, 1998).
PLAYING EXPERIENCE: Tampa Bay NFL, 1995-1997. ... Games/Games started: 1995 (9/3), 1996 (16/0), 1997 (16/1). Total: 41/4.
HONORS: Named defensive back on THE SPORTING NEWS college All-America second team (1994).
PRO STATISTICS: 1995—Intercepted one pass for 19 yards. 1997—Caught one pass for 25 yards and recovered one fumble.

BOULWARE, PETER — LB — RAVENS

PERSONAL: Born December 18, 1974, in Columbia, S.C. ... 6-4/255. ... Name pronounced BOWL-ware.
HIGH SCHOOL: Spring Valley (Columbia, S.C.).
COLLEGE: Florida State (degree in management information systems, 1997).
TRANSACTIONS/CAREER NOTES: Selected after junior season by Baltimore Ravens in first round (fourth pick overall) of 1997 NFL draft. ... Signed by Ravens (August 16, 1997).
HONORS: Named defensive end on THE SPORTING NEWS college All-America first team (1996).
MISCELLANEOUS: Holds Baltimore Ravens all-time record for most sacks (11.5).

Year Team	G	GS	SACKS
1997—Baltimore NFL	16	16	11.5

BOUTTE, MARC — DT — REDSKINS

B

PERSONAL: Born July 26, 1969, in Lake Charles, La. ... 6-4/307. ... Full name: Marc Anthony Boutte. ... Name pronounced BOO-TAY.
HIGH SCHOOL: Lake Charles (La.)-Boston.
COLLEGE: Louisiana State.
TRANSACTIONS/CAREER NOTES: Selected by Los Angeles Rams in third round (57th pick overall) of 1992 NFL draft. ... Signed by Rams (July 13, 1992). ... Claimed on waivers by Washington Redskins (August 29, 1994). ... Granted free agency (February 17, 1995). ... Re-signed by Redskins (April 21, 1995). ... Granted unconditional free agency (February 16, 1996). ... Re-signed by Redskins (February 17, 1996). ... On injured reserve with knee injury (October 13, 1996-remainder of season).
PRO STATISTICS: 1993—Recovered one fumble. 1995—Recovered one fumble. 1996—Intercepted one pass for no yards. 1997—Intercepted one pass for 10 yards.

Year Team	G	GS	SACKS
1992—Los Angeles Rams NFL	16	15	1.0
1993—Los Angeles Rams NFL	16	16	1.0
1994—Washington NFL	9	3	0.0
1995—Washington NFL	16	16	2.0
1996—Washington NFL	10	10	0.0
1997—Washington NFL	16	13	2.0
Pro totals (6 years)	83	73	6.0

BOWDEN, JOE — LB — OILERS

PERSONAL: Born February 25, 1970, in Dallas. ... 5-11/224. ... Full name: Joseph Tarrod Bowden.
HIGH SCHOOL: North Mesquite (Mesquite, Texas).
COLLEGE: Oklahoma.
TRANSACTIONS/CAREER NOTES: Selected by Houston Oilers in fifth round (133rd pick overall) of 1992 NFL draft. ... Signed by Oilers (July 16, 1992). ... Granted free agency (February 17, 1995). ... Re-signed by Oilers (June 6, 1995). ... Granted unconditional free agency (February 16, 1996). ... Re-signed by Oilers (March 4, 1996). ... Oilers franchise moved to Tennessee for 1997 season.
PRO STATISTICS: 1993—Recovered one fumble. 1995—Returned one kickoff for six yards and recovered one fumble. 1997—Recovered one fumble.

Year Team	G	GS	SACKS
1992—Houston NFL	14	0	0.0
1993—Houston NFL	16	6	1.0
1994—Houston NFL	14	1	0.0
1995—Houston NFL	16	14	1.0
1996—Houston NFL	16	16	3.0
1997—Tennessee NFL	16	16	2.5
Pro totals (6 years)	92	53	7.5

BOWENS, TIM — DT — DOLPHINS

PERSONAL: Born February 7, 1973, in Okolona, Miss. ... 6-4/315. ... Full name: Timothy L. Bowens.
HIGH SCHOOL: Okolona (Miss.).
JUNIOR COLLEGE: Itawamba Junior College (Miss.).
COLLEGE: Mississippi.
TRANSACTIONS/CAREER NOTES: Selected after junior season by Miami Dolphins in first round (20th pick overall) of 1994 NFL draft. ... Signed by Dolphins (June 2, 1994). ... Designated by Dolphins as franchise player (February 13, 1998).
PRO STATISTICS: 1994—Recovered one fumble. 1995—Recovered two fumbles. 1996—Recovered one fumble. 1997—Recovered one fumble in end zone for touchdown.

Year Team	G	GS	SACKS
1994—Miami NFL	16	15	3.0
1995—Miami NFL	16	16	2.0
1996—Miami NFL	16	16	3.0
1997—Miami NFL	16	16	5.0
Pro totals (4 years)	64	63	13.0

BOWIE, LARRY — RB — REDSKINS

PERSONAL: Born March 21, 1973, in Anniston, Ala. ... 6-0/249.
HIGH SCHOOL: Anniston (Ala.).
COLLEGE: Georgia.

TRANSACTIONS/CAREER NOTES: Signed as non-drafted free agent by Washington Redskins (May 1, 1996).
PRO STATISTICS: 1997—Returned one kickoff for 15 yards and recovered one fumble.
SINGLE GAME HIGHS (regular season): Attempts—6 (December 7, 1997, vs. Arizona); yards—23 (December 21, 1997, vs. Philadelphia); and rushing touchdowns—1 (December 21, 1997, vs. Philadelphia).

Year Team	G	GS	RUSHING Att.	Yds.	Avg.	TD	RECEIVING No.	Yds.	Avg.	TD	TOTALS TD	2pt.	Pts.	Fum.
1996—Washington NFL	3	0	0	0	...	0	3	17	5.7	0	0	0	0	0
1997—Washington NFL	15	13	28	100	3.6	2	34	388	11.4	2	4	0	24	2
Pro totals (2 years)	18	13	28	100	3.6	2	37	405	10.9	2	4	0	24	2

BOWNES, FABIEN — WR — BEARS

PERSONAL: Born February 29, 1972, in Aurora, Ill. ... 5-11/190. ... Name pronounced BOW-ens.
HIGH SCHOOL: Waubonsie Valley (Aurora, Ill.).
COLLEGE: Western Illinois.
TRANSACTIONS/CAREER NOTES: Signed as non-drafted free agent by Chicago Bears (April 27, 1995). ... Released by Bears (August 27, 1995). ... Re-signed by Bears to practice squad (August 29, 1995). ... Activated (December 14, 1995). ... Released by Bears (August 19, 1996). ... Re-signed by Bears to practice squad (October 15, 1996).
PRO STATISTICS: 1997—Recovered one fumble.
SINGLE GAME HIGHS (regular season): Receptions—4 (November 2, 1997, vs. Washington); yards—54 (November 2, 1997, vs. Washington); and touchdown receptions—0.

Year Team	G	GS	RECEIVING No.	Yds.	Avg.	TD	KICKOFF RETURNS No.	Yds.	Avg.	TD	TOTALS TD	2pt.	Pts.	Fum.
1995—Chicago NFL	1	0	0	0	...	0	0	0	...	0	0	0	0	0
1996—Chicago NFL							Did not play.							
1997—Chicago NFL	16	0	12	146	12.2	0	19	396	20.8	0	0	0	0	0
Pro totals (2 years)	17	0	12	146	12.2	0	19	396	20.8	0	0	0	0	0

BOYD, STEPHEN — LB — LIONS

PERSONAL: Born August 22, 1972, in Valley Stream, N.Y. ... 6-0/247. ... Full name: Stephen Gerard Boyd.
HIGH SCHOOL: Valley Stream (N.Y.).
COLLEGE: Boston College.
TRANSACTIONS/CAREER NOTES: Selected by Detroit Lions in fifth round (141st pick overall) of 1995 NFL draft. ... Signed by Lions (July 19, 1995). ... Granted free agency (February 13, 1998). ... Re-signed by Lions (April 17, 1998).
PLAYING EXPERIENCE: Detroit NFL, 1995-1997. ... Games/Games started: 1995 (16/0), 1996 (8/5), 1997 (16/16). Total: 40/21.
HONORS: Named linebacker on THE SPORTING NEWS college All-America first team (1994).
PRO STATISTICS: 1997—Intercepted one pass for four yards and recovered one fumble for 42 yards and a touchdown.

BOYD, TOMMIE — WR — LIONS

PERSONAL: Born December 21, 1971 ... 6-0/195.
HIGH SCHOOL: Lansing (Mich.) Eastern.
COLLEGE: Toledo (degree in communications).
TRANSACTIONS/CAREER NOTES: Signed as non-drafted free agent by Detroit Lions (April 24, 1995). ... Released by Lions (August 18, 1995). ... Played with Rhein Fire of World League (1996). ... Re-signed by Lions (January 22, 1996). ... Released by Lions (August 21, 1996). ... Re-signed by Lions (February 19, 1997).
PRO STATISTICS: W.L.: 1996—Returned 17 punts for 164 yards.
SINGLE GAME HIGHS (regular season): Receptions—3 (December 21, 1997, vs. New York Jets); yards—32 (December 14, 1997, vs. Minnesota); and rushing touchdowns—0.

Year Team	G	GS	RECEIVING No.	Yds.	Avg.	TD
1996—Rhein W.L.	...	...	22	204	9.3	1
1997—Detroit NFL	16	1	10	142	14.2	0
Pro totals (2 years)	...	...	32	346	10.8	1

BOYER, BRANT — LB — JAGUARS

PERSONAL: Born June 27, 1971, in Ogden, Utah. ... 6-1/230. ... Full name: Brant T. Boyer.
HIGH SCHOOL: North Summit (Coalville, Utah).
JUNIOR COLLEGE: Snow College (Utah).
COLLEGE: Arizona.
TRANSACTIONS/CAREER NOTES: Selected by Miami Dolphins in sixth round (177th pick overall) of 1994 NFL draft. ... Signed by Dolphins (July 11, 1994). ... Released by Dolphins (September 21, 1994). ... Re-signed by Dolphins to practice squad (September 22, 1994). ... Activated (October 5, 1994). ... Selected by Jacksonville Jaguars from Dolphins in NFL expansion draft (February 15, 1995). ... Released by Jaguars (August 27, 1995). ... Re-signed by Jaguars (December 13, 1995). ... Released by Jaguars (August 25, 1996). ... Re-signed by Jaguars (September 24, 1996). ... Released by Jaguars (September 25, 1996). ... Re-signed by Jaguars (September 27, 1996). ... Granted free agency (February 13, 1998).
PLAYING EXPERIENCE: Miami NFL, 1994; Jacksonville NFL, 1995-1997. ... Games/Games started: 1994 (14/0), 1995 (2/0), 1996 (12/0), 1997 (16/2). Total: 44/2.
CHAMPIONSHIP GAME EXPERIENCE: Played in AFC championship game (1996 season).
PRO STATISTICS: 1997—Credited with 1 1/2 sacks.

BRACKENS, TONY — DE — JAGUARS

PERSONAL: Born December 26, 1974, in Fairfield, Texas. ... 6-4/258. ... Full name: Tony Lynn Brackens Jr.
HIGH SCHOOL: Fairfield (Texas).
COLLEGE: Texas.
TRANSACTIONS/CAREER NOTES: Selected after junior season by Jacksonville Jaguars in second round (33rd pick overall) of 1996 NFL draft. ... Signed by Jaguars (May 28, 1996).
CHAMPIONSHIP GAME EXPERIENCE: Played in AFC championship game (1996 season).
HONORS: Named defensive lineman on THE SPORTING NEWS college All-America first team (1995).
PRO STATISTICS: 1996—Recovered three fumbles. 1997—Recovered one fumble.

| | | | INTERCEPTIONS | | | | SACKS |
Year Team	G	GS	No.	Yds.	Avg.	TD	No.
1996—Jacksonville NFL	16	1	1	27	27.0	0	7.0
1997—Jacksonville NFL	15	3	0	0	...	0	7.0
Pro totals (2 years)	31	4	1	27	27.0	0	14.0

BRADFORD, PAUL — DB — CHARGERS

PERSONAL: Born April 20, 1974, in East Palo Alto, Calif. ... 5-9/185.
HIGH SCHOOL: Carlmont (East Palo Alto, Calif.).
JUNIOR COLLEGE: College of San Mateo (Calif.).
COLLEGE: Portland State.
TRANSACTIONS/CAREER NOTES: Selected by San Diego Chargers in fifth round (146th pick overall) of 1997 NFL draft. ... Signed by Chargers (June 2, 1997).
PRO STATISTICS: 1997—Recovered one fumble for 78 yards and a touchdown.

| | | | INTERCEPTIONS | | | |
Year Team	G	GS	No.	Yds.	Avg.	TD
1997—San Diego NFL	15	4	2	56	28.0	1

BRADFORD, RONNIE — CB — FALCONS

PERSONAL: Born October 1, 1970, in Minot, N.D. ... 5-10/188. ... Full name: Ronald L. Bradford.
HIGH SCHOOL: Adams City (Commerce City, Colo.).
COLLEGE: Colorado.
TRANSACTIONS/CAREER NOTES: Selected by Miami Dolphins in fourth round (105th pick overall) of 1993 NFL draft. ... Signed by Dolphins (July 14, 1993). ... Released by Dolphins (August 24, 1993). ... Signed by Denver Broncos to practice squad (September 1, 1993). ... Activated (October 12, 1993). ... On injured reserve with knee injury (September 28, 1995-remainder of season). ... Released by Broncos (August 25, 1996). ... Signed by Arizona Cardinals (August 27, 1996). ... Granted unconditional free agency (February 14, 1997). ... Signed by Atlanta Falcons (April 11, 1997).
PRO STATISTICS: 1993—Returned one punt for no yards and fumbled once. 1994—Credited with one sack and recovered two fumbles. 1996—Recovered one fumble.

| | | | INTERCEPTIONS | | | |
Year Team	G	GS	No.	Yds.	Avg.	TD
1993—Denver NFL	10	3	1	0	0.0	0
1994—Denver NFL	12	0	0	0	...	0
1995—Denver NFL	4	0	0	0	...	0
1996—Arizona NFL	15	11	1	0	0.0	0
1997—Atlanta NFL	16	15	4	9	2.3	0
Pro totals (5 years)	57	29	6	9	1.5	0

BRADY, DONNY — DB — RAVENS

PERSONAL: Born November 24, 1973, in North Bellmore, N.Y. ... 6-2/195.
HIGH SCHOOL: Mepham (Bellmore, N.Y.).
JUNIOR COLLEGE: Nassau Community College (N.Y.).
COLLEGE: Wisconsin.
TRANSACTIONS/CAREER NOTES: Signed as non-drafted free agent by Cleveland Browns (May 2, 1995). ... Released by Browns (August 21, 1995). ... Re-signed by Browns to practice squad (December 13, 1995). ... Activated (December 16, 1995). ... Browns franchise moved to Baltimore and renamed Ravens for 1996 season (March 11, 1996).
PLAYING EXPERIENCE: Cleveland NFL, 1995; Baltimore NFL, 1996 and 1997. ... Games/Games started: 1995 (2/0), 1996 (16/13), 1997 (16/5). Total: 34/18.
PRO STATISTICS: 1996—Recovered one fumble. 1997—Recovered one fumble.

BRADY, JEFF — LB

PERSONAL: Born November 9, 1968, in Cincinnati. ... 6-1/243. ... Full name: Jeffrey Thomas Brady.
HIGH SCHOOL: Newport (Ky.) Central Catholic.
COLLEGE: Kentucky (degree in telecommunications, 1990).
TRANSACTIONS/CAREER NOTES: Selected by Pittsburgh Steelers in 12th round (323rd pick overall) of 1991 NFL draft. ... Signed by Steelers (July 10, 1991). ... Granted unconditional free agency (February 1, 1992). ... Signed by Green Bay Packers (March 30, 1992). ... On injured reserve with knee injury (September 26-November 21, 1992). ... Claimed on waivers by Los Angeles Rams (August 31, 1993). ... Released by Rams (October 20, 1993). ... Signed by San Diego Chargers (October 25, 1993). ... Granted free agency (February 17, 1994). ... Signed

by Tampa Bay Buccaneers (May 4, 1994). ... Granted unconditional free agency (February 17, 1995). ... Signed by Minnesota Vikings (April 13, 1995). ... Granted unconditional free agency (February 16, 1996). ... Re-signed by Vikings (February 28, 1996). ... Granted unconditional free agency (February 14, 1997). ... Re-signed by Vikings (March 1, 1997). ... On injured reserve with hamstring injury (December 30, 1997-remainder of playoffs). ... Released by Vikings (February 13, 1998).

PRO STATISTICS: 1993—Recovered one fumble. 1995—Recovered two fumbles. 1996—Recovered three fumbles. 1997—Recovered three fumbles for 30 yards and one touchdown.

			INTERCEPTIONS				SACKS
Year Team	G	GS	No.	Yds.	Avg.	TD	No.
1991—Pittsburgh NFL	16	0	0	0	...	0	0.0
1992—Green Bay NFL	8	0	0	0	...	0	0.0
1993—Los Angeles Rams NFL	6	0	0	0	...	0	0.0
—San Diego NFL	3	0	0	0	...	0	0.0
1994—Tampa Bay NFL	16	0	0	0	...	0	0.0
1995—Minnesota NFL	16	7	2	7	3.5	0	3.0
1996—Minnesota NFL	16	16	3	20	6.7	0	1.5
1997—Minnesota NFL	15	14	0	0	...	0	0.0
Pro totals (7 years)	96	37	5	27	5.4	0	4.5

BRADY, KYLE — TE — JETS

PERSONAL: Born January 14, 1972, in New Cumberland, Pa. ... 6-6/268. ... Full name: Kyle James Brady.
HIGH SCHOOL: Cedar Cliff (Camp Hill, Pa.).
COLLEGE: Penn State.
TRANSACTIONS/CAREER NOTES: Selected by New York Jets in first round (ninth pick overall) of 1995 NFL draft. ... Signed by Jets (July 17, 1995).
HONORS: Named tight end on THE SPORTING NEWS college All-America second team (1994).
PRO STATISTICS: 1995—Returned two kickoffs for 25 yards. 1996—Returned two kickoffs for 26 yards.
SINGLE GAME HIGHS (regular season): Receptions—5 (September 17, 1995, vs. Jacksonville); yards—48 (September 17, 1995, vs. Jacksonville); and touchdown receptions—1 (November 9, 1997, vs. Dallas).

			RECEIVING				TOTALS			
Year Team	G	GS	No.	Yds.	Avg.	TD	TD	2pt.	Pts.	Fum.
1995—New York Jets NFL	15	11	26	252	9.7	2	2	0	12	0
1996—New York Jets NFL	16	16	15	144	9.6	1	1	1	8	1
1997—New York Jets NFL	16	14	22	238	10.8	2	2	0	12	1
Pro totals (3 years)	47	41	63	634	10.1	5	5	1	32	2

BRAHAM, RICH — C/G — BENGALS

PERSONAL: Born November 6, 1970, in Morgantown, W.Va. ... 6-4/302. ... Name pronounced bray-HAM.
HIGH SCHOOL: University (Morgantown, W.Va.).
COLLEGE: West Virginia.
TRANSACTIONS/CAREER NOTES: Selected by Arizona Cardinals in third round (76th pick overall) of 1994 NFL draft. ... Signed by Cardinals (July 30, 1994). ... Claimed on waivers by Cincinnati Bengals (November 18, 1994). ... On injured reserve with ankle injury (August 29, 1995-entire season). ... Granted free agency (February 14, 1997). ... Tendered offer sheet by New England Patriots (April 8, 1997). ... Offer matched by Bengals (April 15, 1997).
PLAYING EXPERIENCE: Cincinnati NFL, 1994, 1996 and 1997. ... Games/Games started: 1994 (3/0), 1996 (16/16), 1997 (16/16). Total: 35/32.
HONORS: Named offensive lineman on THE SPORTING NEWS college All-America second team (1993).

BRANCH, CALVIN — RB — RAIDERS

PERSONAL: Born May 8, 1974, in Versilles, Ky. ... 5-11/200. ... Full name: Calvin Stanley Branch.
HIGH SCHOOL: Klein (Spring, Texas).
COLLEGE: Iowa State, then Colorado State.
TRANSACTIONS/CAREER NOTES: Selected by Oakland Raiders in sixth round (172nd pick overall) of 1997 NFL draft. ... Signed by Raiders (July 21, 1997).
PLAYING EXPERIENCE: Oakland NFL, 1997. ... Games/Games started: 6/0.

BRANDENBURG, DAN — LB — BILLS

PERSONAL: Born February 16, 1973, in Rensselaer, Ind. ... 6-3/240.
HIGH SCHOOL: Rensselaer (Ind.) Central.
COLLEGE: Indiana State.
TRANSACTIONS/CAREER NOTES: Selected by Buffalo Bills in seventh round (237th pick overall) fo 1996 NFL draft. ... Signed by Bills (July 9, 1996). ... Released by Bills (August 20, 1996). ... Re-signed by Bills to practice squad (August 26, 1996). ... Activated (November 22, 1996). ... Inactive for five games (1996).
PRO STATISTICS: 1997—Recovered one fumble.

Year Team	G	GS	SACKS
1996—Buffalo NFL	Did not play.		
1997—Buffalo NFL	12	0	0.0

BRANDON, DAVID — LB — FALCONS

PERSONAL: Born February 9, 1965, in Memphis. ... 6-4/238. ... Full name: David Sherrod Brandon.
HIGH SCHOOL: Mitchell (Memphis).
COLLEGE: Memphis State.

TRANSACTIONS/CAREER NOTES: Selected by Buffalo Bills in third round (60th pick overall) of 1987 NFL draft. ... Signed by Bills (July 25, 1987). ... Traded by Bills with fourth-round pick (OL Stacy Searels) in 1988 draft to San Diego Chargers for WR Trumaine Johnson and seventh-round pick (NT Jeff Wright) in 1988 draft (August 31, 1987). ... On injured reserve with knee injury (July 23, 1990-entire season). ... Granted unconditional free agency (February 1, 1991). ... Signed by Cleveland Browns (April 1, 1991). ... Granted free agency (February 1, 1992). ... Re-signed by Browns (July 19, 1992). ... Granted unconditional free agency (March 1, 1993). ... Re-signed by Browns (April 20, 1993). ... Released by Browns (October 26, 1993). ... Signed by Seattle Seahawks (November 10, 1993). ... Granted unconditional free agency (February 17, 1994). ... Re-signed by Seahawks (April 6, 1994). ... Released by Seahawks (August 27, 1995). ... Signed by San Diego Chargers (August 28, 1995). ... Granted unconditional free agency (February 16, 1996). ... Signed by Atlanta Falcons (May 3, 1996). ... Granted unconditional free agency (February 14, 1997). ... Re-signed by Falcons (April 25, 1997). ... Granted unconditional free agency (February 13, 1998). ... Re-signed by Falcons (April 14, 1998).

PRO STATISTICS: 1987—Recovered blocked punt in end zone for a touchdown. 1992—Recovered three fumbles for 32 yards and a touchdown.

			INTERCEPTIONS				SACKS
Year Team	G	GS	No.	Yds.	Avg.	TD	No.
1987—San Diego NFL	8	1	0	0	...	0	0.0
1988—San Diego NFL	8	1	0	0	...	0	0.0
1989—San Diego NFL	13	0	0	0	...	0	0.0
1990—San Diego NFL				Did not play.			
1991—Cleveland NFL	16	8	2	70	35.0	1	3.0
1992—Cleveland NFL	16	13	2	123	61.5	1	1.0
1993—Cleveland NFL	6	3	0	0	...	0	0.0
—Seattle NFL	7	0	0	0	...	0	0.0
1994—Seattle NFL	13	0	0	0	...	0	0.0
1995—San Diego NFL	15	1	0	0	...	0	1.0
1996—Atlanta NFL	16	2	0	0	...	0	1.0
1997—Atlanta NFL	4	4	0	0	...	0	1.0
Pro totals (10 years)	122	33	4	193	48.3	2	7.0

BRATZKE, CHAD DE GIANTS

PERSONAL: Born September 15, 1971, in Brandon, Fla. ... 6-4/285. ... Full name: Chad Allen Bratzke.

HIGH SCHOOL: Bloomingdale (Valcro, Fla.).

COLLEGE: Eastern Kentucky.

TRANSACTIONS/CAREER NOTES: Selected by New York Giants in fifth round (155th pick overall) of 1994 NFL draft. ... Signed by Giants (July 17, 1994). ... On injured reserve with knee injury (November 12, 1997-remainder of season).

PRO STATISTICS: 1996—Recovered two fumbles. 1997—Recovered two fumbles.

Year Team	G	GS	SACKS
1994—New York Giants NFL	2	0	0.0
1995—New York Giants NFL	6	0	0.0
1996—New York Giants NFL	16	16	5.0
1997—New York Giants NFL	10	10	3.5
Pro totals (4 years)	34	26	8.5

BRAXTON, TYRONE CB BRONCOS

PERSONAL: Born December 17, 1964, in Madison, Wis. ... 5-11/185. ... Full name: Tyrone Scott Braxton. ... Related to Jim Braxton, fullback with Buffalo Bills (1971-1977) and Miami Dolphins (1978).

HIGH SCHOOL: James Madison Memorial (Madison, Wis.).

COLLEGE: North Dakota State.

TRANSACTIONS/CAREER NOTES: Selected by Denver Broncos in 12th round (334th pick overall) of 1987 NFL draft. ... Signed by Broncos (July 18, 1987). ... On injured reserve with shoulder injury (September 1-December 18, 1987). ... On injured reserve with knee injury (September 25, 1990-remainder of season). ... Granted unconditional free agency (February 17, 1994). ... Signed by Miami Dolphins (May 13, 1994). ... Released by Dolphins (April 20, 1995). ... Signed by Broncos (May 5, 1995). ... Granted unconditional free agency (February 16, 1996). ... Re-signed by Broncos (March 1, 1996).

CHAMPIONSHIP GAME EXPERIENCE: Played in AFC championship game (1987, 1989, 1991 and 1997 seasons). ... Played in Super Bowl XXII (1987 season) and Super Bowl XXIV (1989 season). ... Member of Super Bowl championship team (1997 season).

HONORS: Played in Pro Bowl (1996 season).

PRO STATISTICS: 1988—Recovered one fumble. 1989—Recovered two fumbles for 35 yards. 1991—Fumbled once and recovered one fumble. 1993—Recovered two fumbles for six yards. 1994—Returned one kickoff for 34 yards. 1996—Recovered one fumble for 20 yards. 1997—Recovered three fumbles for 45 yards.

			INTERCEPTIONS				SACKS
Year Team	G	GS	No.	Yds.	Avg.	TD	No.
1987—Denver NFL	2	0	0	0	...	0	0.0
1988—Denver NFL	16	0	2	6	3.0	0	1.0
1989—Denver NFL	16	16	6	103	17.2	1	0.0
1990—Denver NFL	3	2	1	10	10.0	0	0.0
1991—Denver NFL	16	15	4	55	13.8	1	1.0
1992—Denver NFL	16	14	2	54	27.0	0	0.0
1993—Denver NFL	16	16	3	37	12.3	0	0.0
1994—Miami NFL	16	0	2	3	1.5	0	0.0
1995—Denver NFL	16	16	2	36	18.0	0	0.0
1996—Denver NFL	16	16	†9	128	14.2	1	0.0
1997—Denver NFL	16	16	4	113	28.3	1	0.5
Pro totals (11 years)	149	111	35	545	15.6	4	2.5

BREW, DORIAN CB CHARGERS

PERSONAL: Born July 19, 1974, in St. Louis. ... 5-10/182. ... Full name: Dorian C. Brew.
HIGH SCHOOL: McCluer North (Florissant, Mo.).
COLLEGE: Kansas.

TRANSACTIONS/CAREER NOTES: Selected by Miami Dolphins in third round (79th pick overall) of 1996 NFL draft. ... Signed by Dolphins (July 16, 1996). ... Released by Dolphins (August 20, 1996). ... Signed by Kansas City Chiefs to practice squad (August 28, 1996). ... Signed by Baltimore Ravens off Chiefs practice squad (October 29, 1996). ... Released by Ravens (September 16, 1997). ... Signed by San Diego Chargers (October 29, 1997).
PLAYING EXPERIENCE: Baltimore NFL, 1996; Baltimore (3)-San Diego (7) NFL, 1997. ... Games/Games started: 1996 (7/0), 1997 (Balt.-3/0; S.D.-7/0; Total: 10/0). Total: 17/0.
PRO STATISTICS: 1997—Returned five kickoffs for 88 yards.

BRICE, ALUNDIS — CB — EAGLES

PERSONAL: Born May 1, 1970, in Brookhaven, Miss. ... 5-10/178.
HIGH SCHOOL: Brookhaven (Miss.).
COLLEGE: Mississippi.
TRANSACTIONS/CAREER NOTES: Selected by Dallas Cowboys in fourth round (129th pick overall) of 1995 NFL draft. ... Signed by Cowboys (July 19, 1995). ... On injured reserve with knee injury (December 12, 1996-remainder of season). ... Released by Cowboys (August 21, 1997). ... Signed by Philadelphia Eagles (April 24, 1998).
CHAMPIONSHIP GAME EXPERIENCE: Played in NFC championship game (1995 season). ... Member of Super Bowl championship team (1995 season).

Year Team	G	GS	INTERCEPTIONS No.	Yds.	Avg.	TD
1995—Dallas NFL	11	1	1	2	2.0	0
1996—Dallas NFL	14	1	0	0	...	0
1997—			Did not play.			
Pro totals (2 years)	25	2	1	2	2.0	0

BRICE, WILL — P — GIANTS

PERSONAL: Born October 24, 1974, in Lancaster, S.C. ... 6-4/225. ... Full name: William Jamison Brice.
HIGH SCHOOL: Lancaster (S.C.).
COLLEGE: Virginia.
TRANSACTIONS/CAREER NOTES: Signed as non-drafted free agent by St. Louis Rams (April 29, 1997). ... Released by Rams (October 12, 1997). ... Signed by New York Giants (February 19, 1998). ... Assigned by Giants to Amsterdam Admirals in 1998 NFL Europe enhancement allocation program (February 18, 1998).

Year Team	G	GS	PUNTING No.	Yds.	Avg.	Net avg.	In. 20	Blk.
1997—St. Louis NFL	6	0	41	1713	41.8	30.5	6	1

BRIEN, DOUG — K — SAINTS

PERSONAL: Born November 24, 1970, in Bloomfield, N.J. ... 6-0/180. ... Full name: Douglas Robert Zachariah Brien.
HIGH SCHOOL: De La Salle Catholic (Concord, Calif.).
COLLEGE: California.
TRANSACTIONS/CAREER NOTES: Selected by San Francisco 49ers in third round (85th pick overall) of 1994 NFL draft. ... Signed by 49ers (July 27, 1994). ... Released by 49ers (October 16, 1995). ... Signed by New Orleans Saints (October 31, 1995). ... Granted free agency (February 14, 1997). ... Re-signed by Saints (July 17, 1997).
CHAMPIONSHIP GAME EXPERIENCE: Played in NFC championship game (1994 season). ... Member of Super Bowl championship team (1994 season).
POST SEASON RECORDS: Shares Super Bowl single-game record for most extra points—7 (January 29, 1995, vs. San Diego).

Year Team	G	GS	KICKING XPM	XPA	FGM	FGA	Lg.	50+	Pts.
1994—San Francisco NFL	16	0	*60	*62	15	20	48	0-1	105
1995—San Francisco NFL	6	0	19	19	7	12	51	1-1	40
—New Orleans NFL	8	0	16	16	12	17	47	0-1	52
1996—New Orleans NFL	16	0	18	18	21	25	54	3-4	81
1997—New Orleans NFL	16	0	22	22	23	27	53	4-5	91
Pro totals (4 years)	62	0	135	137	78	101	54	8-12	369

BRIGANCE, O.J. — LB — DOLPHINS

PERSONAL: Born September 29, 1969, in Houston. ... 6-0/236. ... Full name: Orenthial James Brigance.
HIGH SCHOOL: Willowridge (Sugar Land, Texas).
COLLEGE: Rice (degree in managerial studies).
TRANSACTIONS/CAREER NOTES: Signed as free agent by B.C. Lions of CFL (May 1991). ... Granted free agency (February 1994). ... Signed by Baltimore Stallions of CFL (April 1994). ... Granted free agency (February 16, 1996). ... Signed by Miami Dolphins (May 17, 1996).
PRO STATISTICS: CFL: 1991—Intercepted one pass for seven yards. 1992—Returned five kickoffs for 40 yards and recovered three fumbles. 1993—Recovered one fumble for 27 yards. 1994—Recovered two fumbles. 1995—Intercepted one pass for 13 yards and recovered three fumbles for 10 yards. 1997—Recovered one fumble.

Year Team	G	GS	SACKS
1991—British Columbia CFL	18	...	2.0
1992—British Columbia CFL	18	...	0.0
1993—British Columbia CFL	18	...	20.0
1994—Baltimore CFL	18	...	6.0
1995—Baltimore CFL	18	...	7.0
1996—Miami NFL	12	0	0.0
1997—Miami NFL	16	0	0.0
CFL totals (5 years)	90	...	35.0
NFL totals (2 years)	28	0	0.0
Pro totals (7 years)	118	...	35.0

BRIGGS, GREG   S   VIKINGS

PERSONAL: Born October 1, 1968, in Meadville, Miss. ... 6-3/215.
HIGH SCHOOL: Franklin (Meadville, Miss.).
JUNIOR COLLEGE: Copiah-Lincoln Junior College (Miss.).
COLLEGE: Arkansas-Pine Bluff, then Texas Southern.
TRANSACTIONS/CAREER NOTES: Selected by Dallas Cowboys in fifth round (120th pick overall) of 1992 NFL draft. ... Signed by Cowboys (June 10, 1992). ... On physically unable to perform list with right hip injury (August 25, 1992-entire season). ... Released by Cowboys (August 23, 1993). ... Signed by Cleveland Browns to practice squad (December 15, 1993). ... Granted free agency after 1993 season. ... Re-signed by Browns (March 18, 1994). ... Released by Browns (July 21, 1994). ... Signed by Frankfurt Galaxy of World League (1995). ... Signed by Cowboys (August 14, 1995). ... Released by Cowboys (August 27, 1995). ... Re-signed by Cowboys (September 20, 1995). ... Granted unconditional free agency (February 16, 1996). ... Signed by Chicago Bears (June 7, 1996). ... Released by Bears (October 1, 1996). ... Re-signed by Bears (October 15, 1996). ... Granted unconditional free agency (February 14, 1997). ... Signed by Minnesota Vikings (April 11, 1997).
PLAYING EXPERIENCE: Frankfurt W.L., 1995; Dallas NFL, 1995; Chicago NFL, 1996; Minnesota NFL, 1997. ... Games/Games started: W.L.— 1995 (games played unavailable); NFL: 1995 (11/0), 1996 (14/0), 1997 (14/0). Total NFL: 39/0.
CHAMPIONSHIP GAME EXPERIENCE: Played in NFC championship game (1995 season). ... Member of Super Bowl championship team (1995 season).
PRO STATISTICS: 1997—Recovered one fumble.

B

BRILZ, DARRICK   C   BENGALS

PERSONAL: Born February 14, 1964, in Richmond, Calif. ... 6-3/295. ... Full name: Darrick Joseph Brilz.
HIGH SCHOOL: Pinole (Calif.) Valley.
COLLEGE: Oregon State.
TRANSACTIONS/CAREER NOTES: Signed as non-drafted free agent by Washington Redskins (May 1, 1987). ... Released by Redskins (August 31, 1987). ... Re-signed as replacement player by Redskins (September 23, 1987). ... On injured reserve with pinched nerve in neck (December 12, 1987-remainder of season). ... Claimed on waivers by San Diego Chargers (August 30, 1988). ... Released by Chargers (August 1, 1989). ... Signed by Seattle Seahawks (August 16, 1989). ... Released by Seahawks (September 5, 1989). ... Re-signed by Seahawks (September 21, 1989). ... Granted unconditional free agency (February 17, 1994). ... Signed by Cincinnati Bengals (March 28, 1994).
PLAYING EXPERIENCE: Washington NFL, 1987; San Diego NFL, 1988; Seattle NFL, 1989-1993; Cincinnati NFL, 1994-1997. ... Games/Games started: 1987 (7/4), 1988 (14/0), 1989 (14/0), 1990 (16/5), 1991 (16/7), 1992 (16/16), 1993 (16/16), 1994 (15/15), 1995 (16/16), 1996 (13/13), 1997 (16/16). Total: 159/108.
PRO STATISTICS: 1991—Recovered one fumble. 1994—Recovered one fumble. 1997—Recovered one fumble.

BRISBY, VINCENT   WR   PATRIOTS

PERSONAL: Born January 25, 1971, in Lake Charles, La. ... 6-3/193. ... Full name: Vincent Cole Brisby.
HIGH SCHOOL: Washington-Marion Magnet (Lake Charles, La.).
COLLEGE: Northeast Louisiana.
TRANSACTIONS/CAREER NOTES: Selected by New England Patriots in second round (56th pick overall) of 1993 NFL draft. ... Signed by Patriots (July 30, 1993). ... Granted free agency (February 16, 1996). ... Re-signed by Patriots (May 31, 1996).
CHAMPIONSHIP GAME EXPERIENCE: Played in AFC championship game (1996 season). ... Played in Super Bowl XXXI (1996 season).
PRO STATISTICS: 1993—Recovered one fumble.
SINGLE GAME HIGHS (regular season): Receptions—9 (October 1, 1995, vs. Atlanta); yards—161 (October 1, 1995, vs. Atlanta); and touchdown receptions—2 (December 18, 1994, vs. Buffalo).
STATISTICAL PLATEAUS: 100-yard receiving games: 1994 (2), 1995 (3). Total: 5.

| | | | RECEIVING | | | | TOTALS | | | |
Year Team	G	GS	No.	Yds.	Avg.	TD	TD	2pt.	Pts.	Fum.
1993—New England NFL	16	12	45	626	13.9	2	2	...	12	1
1994—New England NFL	14	11	58	904	15.6	5	5	0	30	1
1995—New England NFL	16	16	66	974	14.8	3	3	0	18	0
1996—New England NFL	3	0	0	0	...	0	0	0	0	0
1997—New England NFL	16	4	23	276	12.0	2	2	0	12	0
Pro totals (5 years)	65	43	192	2780	14.5	12	12	0	72	2

BRISTER, BUBBY   QB   BRONCOS

PERSONAL: Born August 15, 1962, in Alexandria, La. ... 6-3/205. ... Full name: Walter Andrew Brister III.
HIGH SCHOOL: Neville (Monroe, La.).
COLLEGE: Tulane, then Northeast Louisiana.
TRANSACTIONS/CAREER NOTES: Selected by Pittsburgh Steelers in third round (67th pick overall) of 1986 NFL draft. ... Selected by New Jersey Generals in 11th round (80th pick overall) of 1986 USFL draft; did not sign. ... Signed by Steelers (July 25, 1986). ... Granted free agency (February 1, 1992). ... Re-signed by Steelers (June 16, 1992). ... Signed by Philadelphia Eagles (July 19, 1993). ... Granted unconditional free agency (February 17, 1994). ... Re-signed by Eagles (April 6, 1994). ... Granted unconditional free agency (February 17, 1995). ... Signed by New York Jets (March 17, 1995). ... Released by Jets (February 29, 1996). ... Signed by Denver Broncos (April 7, 1997).
CHAMPIONSHIP GAME EXPERIENCE: Member of Broncos for AFC championship game (1997 season); did not play. ... Member of Super Bowl championship team (1997 season); did not play.
PRO STATISTICS: 1986—Fumbled once. 1988—Recovered two fumbles. 1989—Caught one pass for minus 10 yards, fumbled eight times and recovered one fumble. 1990—Fumbled nine times. 1991—Fumbled four times and recovered two fumbles. 1992—Fumbled twice and recovered two fumbles for minus two yards. 1993—Fumbled three times. 1995—Caught one pass for two yards, fumbled four times and recovered three fumbles for minus nine yards.

SINGLE GAME HIGHS (regular season): Attempts—48 (December 12, 1993, vs. Buffalo); completions—28 (December 12, 1993, vs. Buffalo); yards—353 (October 14, 1990, vs. Denver); and touchdown passes—4 (December 23, 1990, vs. Los Angeles Rams).
STATISTICAL PLATEAUS: 300-yard passing games: 1988 (2), 1993 (1), 1994 (1). Total: 4.
MISCELLANEOUS: Regular-season record as starting NFL quarterback: 33-38 (.465). ... Postseason record as starting NFL quarterback: 1-1 (.500).

Year Team	G	GS	PASSING Att.	Cmp.	Pct.	Yds.	TD	Int.	Avg.	Rat.	RUSHING Att.	Yds.	Avg.	TD	TOTALS TD	2pt.	Pts.
1986—Pittsburgh NFL	2	2	60	21	35.0	291	0	2	4.85	37.6	6	10	1.7	1	1	...	6
1987—Pittsburgh NFL	2	0	12	4	33.3	20	0	3	1.67	2.8	0	0	...	...	0	...	0
1988—Pittsburgh NFL	13	13	370	175	47.3	2634	11	14	7.12	65.3	45	209	4.6	6	6	...	36
1989—Pittsburgh NFL	14	14	342	187	54.7	2365	9	10	6.92	73.1	27	25	0.9	0	0	...	0
1990—Pittsburgh NFL	16	16	387	223	57.6	2725	20	14	7.04	81.6	25	64	2.6	0	0	...	0
1991—Pittsburgh NFL	8	8	190	103	54.2	1350	9	9	7.11	72.9	11	17	1.5	0	0	...	0
1992—Pittsburgh NFL	6	4	116	63	54.3	719	2	5	6.20	61.0	10	16	1.6	0	0	...	0
1993—Philadelphia NFL	10	8	309	181	58.6	1905	14	5	6.17	84.9	20	39	2.0	0	0	...	0
1994—Philadelphia NFL	7	2	76	51	67.1	507	2	1	6.67	89.1	1	7	7.0	0	0	0	0
1995—New York Jets NFL	9	4	170	93	54.7	726	4	8	4.27	53.7	16	18	1.1	0	0	0	0
1996—									Did not play.								
1997—Denver NFL	1	0	9	6	66.7	48	0	0	5.33	79.9	4	2	0.5	0	0	0	0
Pro totals (11 years)	88	71	2041	1107	54.2	13290	71	71	6.51	71.5	165	407	2.5	7	7	0	42

RECORD AS BASEBALL PLAYER

TRANSACTIONS/CAREER NOTES: Threw right, batted right. ... Selected by Detroit Tigers organization in fourth round of free-agent draft (June 8, 1981). ... On suspended list (June 22, 1982-entire season). ... Placed on restricted list (October 7, 1982).

Year Team (League)	Pos.	G	AB	R	H	BATTING 2B	3B	HR	RBI	Avg.	BB	SO	SB	FIELDING PO	A	E	Avg.
1981—Bristol (Appal.)	OF-SS	39	111	12	20	7	0	0	10	.180	16	27	5	46	11	9	.864
1982—								Did not play.									

BROCK, FRED   WR   CARDINALS

PERSONAL: Born November 15, 1974, in Montgomery, Ala. ... 5-11/181.
HIGH SCHOOL: Jefferson Davis (Montgomery, Ala.).
COLLEGE: Southern Mississippi.
TRANSACTIONS/CAREER NOTES: Signed as non-drafted free agent by Arizona Cardinals (April 23, 1996). ... Released by Cardinals (August 20, 1996). ... Re-signed by Cardinals to practice squad (August 27, 1996). ... Inactive for all 16 games during 1996 season.
PLAYING EXPERIENCE: Arizona NFL, 1997. ... Games/Games started: 2/0.
PRO STATISTICS: 1997—Caught one pass for 29 yards.
SINGLE GAME HIGHS (regular season): Receptions—1 (November 9, 1997, vs. Dallas); yards—29 (November 9, 1997, vs. Dallas); and touchdown receptions—0.

BROCKERMEYER, BLAKE   OT   PANTHERS

PERSONAL: Born April 11, 1973, in Fort Worth, Texas. ... 6-4/300. ... Full name: Blake Weeks Brockermeyer.
HIGH SCHOOL: Arlington Heights (Texas).
COLLEGE: Texas.
TRANSACTIONS/CAREER NOTES: Selected after junior season by Carolina Panthers in first round (29th pick overall) of 1995 NFL draft. ... Signed by Panthers (July 14, 1995).
PLAYING EXPERIENCE: Carolina NFL, 1995-1997. ... Games/Games started: 1995 (16/16), 1996 (12/12), 1997 (16/13). Total: 44/41.
CHAMPIONSHIP GAME EXPERIENCE: Played in NFC championship game (1996 season).
HONORS: Named offensive lineman on THE SPORTING NEWS college All-America first team (1994).

BROHM, JEFF   QB   BUCCANEERS

PERSONAL: Born April 24, 1971, in Louisville, Ky. ... 6-1/205.
HIGH SCHOOL: Trinity (Louisville).
COLLEGE: Louisville.
TRANSACTIONS/CAREER NOTES: Signed as non-drafted free agent by Washington Redskins (September 5, 1995). ... Released by Redskins (September 11, 1995). ... Signed by San Francisco 49ers (December 6, 1995). ... Signed by Tampa Bay Buccaneers (April 18, 1998).
CHAMPIONSHIP GAME EXPERIENCE: Member of 49ers for NFC championship game (1997 season); did not play.
PRO STATISTICS: 1996—Fumbled once and recovered one fumble. 1997—Fumbled three times.
SINGLE GAME HIGHS (regular season): Attempts—30 (October 27, 1996, vs. Houston); completions—19 (October 27, 1996, vs. Houston); yards—176 (October 27, 1996, vs. Houston); and touchdown passes—1 (October 27, 1996, vs. Houston).

Year Team	G	GS	PASSING Att.	Cmp.	Pct.	Yds.	TD	Int.	Avg.	Rat.	RUSHING Att.	Yds.	Avg.	TD	TOTALS TD	2pt.	Pts.
1996—San Francisco NFL	3	0	34	21	61.8	189	1	0	5.56	86.5	16	43	2.7	0	0	0	0
1997—San Francisco NFL	5	0	24	16	66.7	164	0	1	6.83	68.8	4	11	2.8	0	0	0	0
Pro totals (2 years)	8	0	58	37	63.8	353	1	1	6.09	79.2	20	54	2.7	0	0	0	0

BRONSON, ZACK   S   49ERS

PERSONAL: Born January 28, 1974 ... 6-1/191.
HIGH SCHOOL: Jasper (Texas).
COLLEGE: McNeese State.

TRANSACTIONS/CAREER NOTES: Signed as non-drafted free agent by San Francisco 49ers (May 2, 1997).
PLAYING EXPERIENCE: San Francisco NFL, 1997. ... Games/Games started: 16/0.
CHAMPIONSHIP GAME EXPERIENCE: Played in NFC championship game (1997 season).
PRO STATISTICS: 1997—Intercepted one pass for 22 yards and recovered one fumble for three yards.

BROOKS, BARRETT — OT — EAGLES

PERSONAL: Born May 5, 1972, in St. Louis. ... 6-4/309.
HIGH SCHOOL: McCluer North (Florissant, Mo.).
COLLEGE: Kansas State.
TRANSACTIONS/CAREER NOTES: Selected by Philadelphia Eagles in second round (58th pick overall) of 1995 NFL draft. ... Signed by Eagles (July 19, 1995). ... Granted free agency (February 13, 1998). ... Re-signed by Eagles (April 21, 1998).
PLAYING EXPERIENCE: Philadelphia NFL, 1995-1997. ... Games/Games started: 1995 (16/16), 1996 (16/15), 1997 (16/14). Total: 48/45.
PRO STATISTICS: 1996—Returned one kickoff for no yards and recovered one fumble. 1997—Recovered two fumbles.

B

BROOKS, BUCKY — CB — CHIEFS

PERSONAL: Born January 22, 1971, in Raleigh, N.C. ... 6-0/201. ... Full name: William Eldridge Brooks Jr.
HIGH SCHOOL: Millbrook (Raleigh, N.C.).
COLLEGE: North Carolina.
TRANSACTIONS/CAREER NOTES: Selected by Buffalo Bills in second round (48th pick overall) of 1994 NFL draft. ... Signed by Bills (July 15, 1994). ... On injured reserve (November 17, 1994-remainder of season). ... Released by Bills (August 22, 1995). ... Signed by Green Bay Packers (December 12, 1995). ... Claimed on waivers by Jacksonville Jaguars (October 29, 1996). ... Claimed on waivers by Packers (September 24, 1997). ... Released by Packers (November 25, 1997). ... Signed by Kansas City Chiefs (December 3, 1997).
CHAMPIONSHIP GAME EXPERIENCE: Member of Packers for NFC championship game (1995 season); inactive. ... Played in AFC championship game (1996 season).
PRO STATISTICS: 1994—Recovered one fumble.

| | | | KICKOFF RETURNS | | | | TOTALS | | | |
Year Team	G	GS	No.	Yds.	Avg.	TD	TD	2pt.	Pts.	Fum.
1994—Buffalo NFL	3	0	9	162	18.0	0	0	0	0	1
1995—Green Bay NFL						Did not play.				
1996—Green Bay NFL	2	0	0	0	...	0	0	0	0	0
—Jacksonville NFL	6	1	17	412	24.2	0	0	0	0	0
1997—Jacksonville NFL	3	0	0	0	...	0	0	0	0	0
—Green Bay NFL	3	0	0	0	...	0	0	0	0	0
—Kansas City NFL	3	0	0	0	...	0	0	0	0	0
Pro totals (3 years)	20	1	26	574	22.1	0	0	0	0	1

BROOKS, DERRICK — LB — BUCCANEERS

PERSONAL: Born April 18, 1973, in Pensacola, Fla. ... 6-0/235. ... Full name: Derrick Dewan Brooks.
HIGH SCHOOL: Washington (Pensacola, Fla.).
COLLEGE: Florida State (degree in communications, 1994).
TRANSACTIONS/CAREER NOTES: Selected by Tampa Bay Buccaneers in first round (28th pick overall) of 1995 NFL draft. ... Signed by Buccaneers (May 3, 1995).
HONORS: Named linebacker on THE SPORTING NEWS college All-America first team (1993 and 1994). ... Played in Pro Bowl (1997 season).
PRO STATISTICS: 1997—Fumbled once and recovered one fumble.

| | | | INTERCEPTIONS | | | | SACKS |
Year Team	G	GS	No.	Yds.	Avg.	TD	No.
1995—Tampa Bay NFL	16	13	0	0	...	0	1.0
1996—Tampa Bay NFL	16	16	1	6	6.0	0	0.0
1997—Tampa Bay NFL	16	16	2	13	6.5	0	1.5
Pro totals (3 years)	48	45	3	19	6.3	0	2.5

BROOKS, ETHAN — OT — RAMS

PERSONAL: Born April 27, 1972, in Simsbury, Conn. ... 6-6/299.
HIGH SCHOOL: Westminster (Simsbury, Conn.).
COLLEGE: Williams (Conn.).
TRANSACTIONS/CAREER NOTES: Selected by Atlanta Falcons in seventh round (229th pick overall) of 1996 NFL draft. ... Signed by Falcons (June 7, 1996). ... Assigned by Falcons to Frankfurt Galaxy in 1997 World League enhancement allocation program (February 19, 1997). ... Released by Falcons (August 27, 1997). ... Signed by St. Louis Rams (November 20, 1997). ... Inactive for five games (1997).
PLAYING EXPERIENCE: Atlanta NFL, 1996. ... Games/Games started: 1996 (2/0).

BROOKS, MACEY — WR — COWBOYS

PERSONAL: Born February 2, 1975, in Hampton, Va. ... 6-5/220. ... Full name: Barry Macey Brooks.
HIGH SCHOOL: Kecoughtan (Hampton, Va.).
COLLEGE: James Madison.
TRANSACTIONS/CAREER NOTES: Selected by Dallas Cowboys in fourth round (127th pick overall) of 1997 NFL draft. ... Signed by Cowboys (July 14, 1997). ... On injured reserve with arm injury (August 27, 1997-entire season).
MISCELLANEOUS: Selected by San Francisco Giants organization in second round of free-agent draft (June 2, 1993); did not sign. ... Selected by Kansas City Royals organization in 55th round of free-agent draft (June 4, 1996); did not sign.

BROOKS, ROBERT   WR   PACKERS

PERSONAL: Born June 23, 1970, in Greenwood, S.C. ... 6-0/180. ... Full name: Robert Darren Brooks.
HIGH SCHOOL: Greenwood (S.C.).
COLLEGE: South Carolina (bachelor of science degree in retailing).
TRANSACTIONS/CAREER NOTES: Selected by Green Bay Packers in third round (62nd pick overall) of 1992 NFL draft. ... Signed by Packers (July 22, 1992). ... Granted free agency (February 17, 1995). ... Re-signed by Packers (June 1, 1995). ... On injured reserve with knee injury (October 26, 1996-remainder of season). ... Granted unconditional free agency (February 13, 1998). ... Re-signed by Packers (February 13, 1998).
CHAMPIONSHIP GAME EXPERIENCE: Played in NFC championship game (1995 and 1997 seasons). ... Member of Super Bowl championship team (1996 season); inactive. ... Played in Super Bowl XXXII (1997 season).
RECORDS: Shares NFL record for longest pass reception (from Brett Favre)—99 yards, touchdown (September 11, 1995, at Chicago).
POST SEASON RECORDS: Holds NFL posteason career record for highest average punt return (minimum 10 returns)—15.3.
PRO STATISTICS: 1993—Fumbled once and recovered one fumble. 1994—Fumbled four times and recovered one fumble.
SINGLE GAME HIGHS (regular season): Receptions—11 (December 24, 1995, vs. Pittsburgh); yards—164 (September 28, 1997, vs. Detroit); and touchdown receptions—2 (September 9, 1996, vs. Philadelphia).
STATISTICAL PLATEAUS: 100-yard receiving games: 1994 (1), 1995 (9), 1996 (2), 1997 (1). Total: 13.

			RUSHING				RECEIVING				PUNT RETURNS				KICKOFF RETURNS				TOTALS		
Year/Team	G	GS	Att.	Yds.	Avg.	TD	No.	Yds.	Avg.	TD	No.	Yds.	Avg.	TD	No.	Yds.	Avg.	TD	TD	2pt.	Pts.
1992—Green Bay NFL....	16	1	2	14	7.0	0	12	126	10.5	1	11	102	9.3	0	18	338	18.8	0	1	...	6
1993—Green Bay NFL....	14	0	3	17	5.7	0	20	180	9.0	0	16	135	8.4	0	23	611	*26.6	†1	1	...	6
1994—Green Bay NFL....	16	16	1	0	0.0	0	58	648	11.2	4	40	352	8.8	1	9	260	28.9	1	6	0	36
1995—Green Bay NFL....	16	15	4	21	5.3	0	102	1497	14.7	13	0	0	...	0	1	28	28.0	0	13	0	78
1996—Green Bay NFL....	7	7	4	2	0.5	0	23	344	15.0	4	0	0	...	0	0	0	...	0	4	0	24
1997—Green Bay NFL....	15	15	2	19	9.5	0	60	1010	‡16.8	7	0	0	...	0	0	0	...	0	7	0	42
Pro totals (6 years)........	84	54	16	73	4.6	0	275	3805	13.8	29	67	589	8.8	1	51	1237	24.3	2	32	0	192

BROSTEK, BERN   C

PERSONAL: Born September 11, 1966, in Honolulu. ... 6-3/300. ... Name pronounced BRAH-stek.
HIGH SCHOOL: Iolani (Honolulu).
COLLEGE: Washington.
TRANSACTIONS/CAREER NOTES: Selected by Los Angeles Rams in first round (23rd pick overall) of 1990 NFL draft. ... Signed by Rams (July 29, 1990). ... Rams franchise moved to St. Louis (April 12, 1995). ... On injured reserve with back injury (October 9, 1997-December 17, 1997). ... Released by Rams (December 17, 1997).
PLAYING EXPERIENCE: Los Angeles Rams NFL, 1990-1994; St. Louis NFL, 1995-1997. ... Games/Games started: 1990 (16/2), 1991 (14/8), 1992 (16/16), 1993 (16/16), 1994 (10/10), 1995 (16/16), 1996 (16/16), 1997 (1/1). Total: 105/85.
HONORS: Named center on THE SPORTING NEWS college All-America first team (1989).
PRO STATISTICS: 1992—Recovered one fumble. 1993—Fumbled once.

BROUSSARD, STEVE   RB/KR   SEAHAWKS

PERSONAL: Born February 22, 1967, in Los Angeles. ... 5-7/201. ... Full name: Steve N. Broussard. ... Name pronounced BREW-sard.
HIGH SCHOOL: Manual Arts (Los Angeles).
COLLEGE: Washington State.
TRANSACTIONS/CAREER NOTES: Selected by Atlanta Falcons in first round (20th pick overall) of 1990 NFL draft. ... Signed by Falcons (July 12, 1990). ... Released by Falcons (February 17, 1994). ... Signed by Cincinnati Bengals (April 8, 1994). ... On injured reserve with concussion (December 21, 1994-remainder of season). ... Released by Bengals (May 3, 1995). ... Signed by Seattle Seahawks (June 13, 1995). ... Granted unconditional free agency (February 13, 1998). ... Re-signed by Seahawks (March 2, 1998).
HONORS: Named running back on THE SPORTING NEWS college All-America second team (1988).
PRO STATISTICS: 1992—Recovered one fumble for minus two yards. 1994—Attempted one pass without a completion and recovered one fumble. 1995—Recovered one fumble.
SINGLE GAME HIGHS (regular season): Attempts—26 (December 19, 1993, vs. Washington); yards—162 (December 19, 1993, vs. Washington); and rushing touchdowns—2 (October 5, 1997, vs. Tennessee).
STATISTICAL PLATEAUS: 100-yard rushing games: 1991 (2), 1993 (1), 1997 (1). Total: 4.

			RUSHING				RECEIVING				KICKOFF RETURNS				TOTALS			
Year Team	G	GS	Att.	Yds.	Avg.	TD	No.	Yds.	Avg.	TD	No.	Yds.	Avg.	TD	TD	2pt.	Pts.	Fum.
1990—Atlanta NFL	13	10	126	454	3.6	4	24	160	6.7	0	3	45	15.0	0	4	...	24	6
1991—Atlanta NFL	14	5	99	449	4.5	4	12	120	10.0	1	0	0	...	0	5	...	30	1
1992—Atlanta NFL	15	1	84	363	4.3	1	11	96	8.7	1	0	0	...	0	2	...	12	3
1993—Atlanta NFL	8	0	39	206	5.3	1	1	4	4.0	0	0	0	...	0	1	...	6	0
1994—Cincinnati NFL	13	3	94	403	4.3	2	34	218	6.4	0	7	115	16.4	0	2	1	14	5
1995—Seattle NFL	15	1	46	222	4.8	1	10	94	9.4	0	43	1064	24.7	0	1	0	6	4
1996—Seattle NFL	12	0	15	106	7.1	1	6	26	4.3	0	43	979	22.8	0	1	0	6	2
1997—Seattle NFL	16	1	70	418	6.0	5	24	143	6.0	1	50	1076	21.5	0	6	0	36	0
Pro totals (8 years)	106	21	573	2621	4.6	19	122	861	7.1	3	146	3279	22.5	0	22	1	134	21

BROWN, ANTHONY   OT/OG   BENGALS

PERSONAL: Born November 6, 1972, in Okinawa, Japan. ... 6-5/315.
HIGH SCHOOL: American (Wurzburg, West Germany).
COLLEGE: Utah.
TRANSACTIONS/CAREER NOTES: Signed as non-drafted free agent by Cincinnati Bengals (April 26, 1995). ... Granted free agency (February 13, 1998). ... Re-signed by Bengals (April 13, 1998).
PLAYING EXPERIENCE: Cincinnati NFL, 1995-1997. ... Games/Games started: 1995 (7/1), 1996 (7/0), 1997 (6/0). Total: 20/1.

BROWN, CHAD   LB   SEAHAWKS

PERSONAL: Born July 12, 1970, in Pasadena, Calif. ... 6-2/240. ... Full name: Chadwick Everett Brown.
HIGH SCHOOL: John Muir (Pasadena, Calif.).
COLLEGE: Colorado (degree in marketing, 1992).
TRANSACTIONS/CAREER NOTES: Selected by Pittsburgh Steelers in second round (44th pick overall) of 1993 NFL draft. ... Signed by Steelers (July 26, 1993). ... Granted unconditional free agency (February 14, 1997). ... Signed by Seattle Seahawks (February 15, 1997).
CHAMPIONSHIP GAME EXPERIENCE: Played in AFC championship game (1994 and 1995 seasons). ... Played in Super Bowl XXX (1995 season).
HONORS: Named linebacker on THE SPORTING NEWS NFL All-Pro team (1996). ... Played in Pro Bowl (1996 season).
PRO STATISTICS: 1996—Fumbled once and recovered two fumbles. 1997—Recovered four fumbles for 68 yards and two touchdowns.

			INTERCEPTIONS			SACKS
Year Team	G	GS	No.	Yds.	Avg.	TD	No.
1993—Pittsburgh NFL	16	9	0	0	...	0	3.0
1994—Pittsburgh NFL	16	16	1	9	9.0	0	8.5
1995—Pittsburgh NFL	10	10	0	0	...	0	5.5
1996—Pittsburgh NFL	14	14	2	20	10.0	0	13.0
1997—Seattle NFL	15	15	0	0	...	0	6.5
Pro totals (5 years)	71	64	3	29	9.7	0	36.5

B

BROWN, CORNELL   LB   RAVENS

PERSONAL: Born March 15, 1975, in Englewood, N.J. ... 6-0/240. ... Full name: Cornell Desmond Brown. ... Brother of Ruben Brown, offensive tackle, Buffalo Bills.
HIGH SCHOOL: E.C. Glass (Lynchburg, Va.).
COLLEGE: Virginia Tech.
TRANSACTIONS/CAREER NOTES: Selected by Baltimore Ravens in sixth round (194th pick overall) of 1997 NFL draft. ... Signed by Ravens (July 10, 1997).
HONORS: Named defensive lineman on THE SPORTING NEWS college All-America first team (1995).
PRO STATISTICS: 1997—Intercepted one pass for 21 yards.

Year Team	G	GS	SACKS
1997—Baltimore NFL	16	1	0.5

BROWN, CORWIN   S   JETS

PERSONAL: Born April 25, 1970, in Chicago. ... 6-1/200. ... Full name: Corwin Alan Brown.
HIGH SCHOOL: Percy L. Julian (Chicago).
COLLEGE: Michigan.
TRANSACTIONS/CAREER NOTES: Selected by New England Patriots in fourth round (110th pick overall) of 1993 NFL draft. ... Signed by Patriots (July 16, 1993). ... Granted free agency (February 16, 1996). ... Re-signed by Patriots (February 27, 1996). ... Released by Patriots (August 24, 1997). ... Signed by New York Jets (August 25, 1997).
PLAYING EXPERIENCE: New England NFL, 1993-1996; New York Jets NFL, 1997. ... Games/Games started: 1993 (15/12), 1994 (16/0), 1995 (16/2), 1996 (14/0), 1997 (16/0). Total: 77/14.
CHAMPIONSHIP GAME EXPERIENCE: Played in AFC championship game (1996 season). ... Played in Super Bowl XXXI (1996 season).
PRO STATISTICS: 1993—Recovered one fumble. 1995—Recovered one fumble. 1996—Recovered one fumble for 42 yards and a touchdown. 1997—Caught one pass for 26 yards.

BROWN, DAVE   QB   CARDINALS

PERSONAL: Born February 25, 1970, in Summit, N.J. ... 6-5/230. ... Full name: David Michael Brown.
HIGH SCHOOL: Westfield (N.J.).
COLLEGE: Duke.
TRANSACTIONS/CAREER NOTES: Selected by New York Giants in first round of 1992 NFL supplemental draft. ... Signed by Giants (August 12, 1992). ... On injured reserve with thumb injury (December 18, 1992-remainder of season). ... Granted unconditional free agency (February 16, 1996). ... Re-signed by Giants (May 3, 1996). ... Released by Giants (February 21, 1998). ... Signed by Arizona Cardinals (April 29, 1998).
PRO STATISTICS: 1994—Punted twice for 57 yards, fumbled 11 times and recovered four fumbles for minus 15 yards. 1995—Punted once for 15 yards, fumbled 10 times and recovered two fumbles for minus eight yards. 1996—Fumbled nine times and recovered one fumble for minus three yards. 1997—Fumbled once.
SINGLE GAME HIGHS (regular season): Attempts—50 (September 17, 1995, vs. Green Bay); completions—28 (September 14, 1997, vs. Baltimore); yards—299 (November 5, 1995, vs. Seattle); and touchdown passes—2 (September 28, 1997, vs. New Orleans).
MISCELLANEOUS: Regular-season record as starting NFL quarterback: 23-30 (.434).

			PASSING							RUSHING				TOTALS		
Year Team	G	GS	Att.	Cmp.	Pct.	Yds.	TD	Int.	Avg.	Rat.	Att.	Yds.	Avg.	TD	TD	2pt.	Pts.
1992—N.Y. Giants NFL	2	0	7	4	57.1	21	0	0	3.00	62.2	2	-1	-0.5	0	0	...	0
1993—N.Y. Giants NFL	1	0	0	0	...	0	0	0	...	...	3	-4	-1.3	0	0	...	0
1994—N.Y. Giants NFL	15	15	350	201	57.4	2536	12	16	7.25	72.5	60	196	3.3	2	2	0	12
1995—N.Y. Giants NFL	16	16	456	254	55.7	2814	11	10	6.17	73.1	45	228	5.1	4	4	0	24
1996—N.Y. Giants NFL	16	16	398	214	53.0	2412	12	20	6.06	61.3	50	170	3.4	0	0	0	0
1997—N.Y. Giants NFL	8	6	180	93	51.7	1023	5	3	5.68	71.1	17	29	1.7	1	1	0	6
Pro totals (6 years)	58	53	1391	766	55.1	8806	40	49	6.33	69.3	177	618	3.5	7	7	0	42

BROWN, DEAUNTAE   CB   STEELERS

PERSONAL: Born April 28, 1974, in Detroit. ... 5-10/195.
HIGH SCHOOL: Osborne (Detroit).
COLLEGE: Central State (Ohio).
TRANSACTIONS/CAREER NOTES: Selected by Philadelphia Eagles in seventh round (227th pick overall) of 1997 NFL draft. ... Signed by Eagles (June 4, 1997). ... Released by Eagles (September 2, 1997). ... Signed by Pittsburgh Steelers to practice squad (October 22, 1997).
PLAYING EXPERIENCE: Philadelphia NFL, 1997. ... Games/Games started: 1/0.

BROWN, DEREK   TE   RAIDERS

PERSONAL: Born March 31, 1970, in Fairfax, Va. ... 6-6/267. ... Full name: Derek Vernon Brown.
HIGH SCHOOL: Merritt Island (Fla.).
COLLEGE: Notre Dame.
TRANSACTIONS/CAREER NOTES: Selected by New York Giants in first round (14th pick overall) of 1992 NFL draft. ... Signed by Giants (July 29, 1992). ... Selected by Jacksonville Jaguars from Giants in NFL expansion draft (February 15, 1995). ... On injured reserve with rib injury (October 10, 1995-remainder of season). ... Granted unconditional free agency (February 14, 1997). ... Re-signed by Jaguars (February 26, 1997). ... Granted unconditional free agency (February 13, 1998). ... Signed by Oakland Raiders (May 13, 1998).
CHAMPIONSHIP GAME EXPERIENCE: Played in AFC championship game (1996 season).
PRO STATISTICS: 1994—Returned one kickoff for one yard and recovered one fumble.
SINGLE GAME HIGHS (regular season): Receptions—3 (December 22, 1996, vs. Atlanta); yards—33 (December 22, 1996, vs. Atlanta); and touchdown receptions—1 (October 19, 1997, vs. Dallas).

Year Team	G	GS	RECEIVING				TOTALS			
			No.	Yds.	Avg.	TD	TD	2pt.	Pts.	Fum.
1992—New York Giants NFL	16	7	4	31	7.8	0	0	...	0	0
1993—New York Giants NFL	16	0	7	56	8.0	0	0	...	0	0
1994—New York Giants NFL	13	0	0	0	...	0	0	0	0	0
1995—Jacksonville NFL						Did not play.				
1996—Jacksonville NFL	16	14	17	141	8.3	0	0	0	0	0
1997—Jacksonville NFL	13	7	8	84	10.5	1	1	0	6	0
Pro totals (5 years)	74	28	36	312	8.7	1	1	0	6	0

BROWN, GARY   RB   GIANTS

PERSONAL: Born July 1, 1969, in Williamsport, Pa. ... 5-11/230. ... Full name: Gary Leroy Brown.
HIGH SCHOOL: Williamsport (Pa.) Area.
COLLEGE: Penn State.
TRANSACTIONS/CAREER NOTES: Selected by Houston Oilers in eighth round (214th pick overall) of 1991 NFL draft. ... Signed by Oilers (July 15, 1991). ... Granted free agency (February 17, 1994). ... Re-signed by Oilers (July 15, 1994). ... Released by Oilers (April 19, 1996). ... Signed by San Diego Chargers (February 24, 1997). ... Granted unconditional free agency (February 13, 1998). ... Signed by New York Giants (April 21, 1998).
PRO STATISTICS: 1992—Recovered one fumble. 1993—Recovered two fumbles for four yards. 1995—Recovered one fumble.
SINGLE GAME HIGHS (regular season): Attempts—36 (October 5, 1997, vs. Oakland); yards—194 (November 21, 1993, vs. Cleveland); and rushing touchdowns—2 (September 11, 1994, vs. Dallas).
STATISTICAL PLATEAUS: 100-yard rushing games: 1993 (5), 1995 (1), 1997 (2). Total: 8.

Year Team	G	GS	RUSHING				RECEIVING				KICKOFF RETURNS				TOTALS			
			Att.	Yds.	Avg.	TD	No.	Yds.	Avg.	TD	No.	Yds.	Avg.	TD	TD	2pt.	Pts.	Fum.
1991—Houston NFL	11	0	8	85	10.6	1	2	1	0.5	0	3	30	10.0	0	1	...	6	0
1992—Houston NFL	16	0	19	87	4.6	1	1	5	5.0	0	1	15	15.0	0	1	...	6	0
1993—Houston NFL	16	8	195	1002	§5.1	6	21	240	11.4	2	2	29	14.5	0	8	...	48	4
1994—Houston NFL	12	8	169	648	3.8	4	18	194	10.8	1	0	0	...	0	5	0	30	6
1995—Houston NFL	9	4	86	293	3.4	0	6	16	2.7	0	0	0	...	0	0	0	0	2
1996—										Did not play.								
1997—San Diego NFL	15	14	253	945	3.7	4	21	137	6.5	0	0	0	...	0	4	0	24	2
Pro totals (6 years)	79	34	730	3060	4.2	16	69	593	8.6	3	6	74	12.3	0	19	0	114	14

BROWN, GILBERT   DT   PACKERS

PERSONAL: Born February 22, 1971, in Farmington, Mich. ... 6-2/345. ... Full name: Gilbert Jesse Brown.
HIGH SCHOOL: Mackenzie (Detroit).
COLLEGE: Kansas.
TRANSACTIONS/CAREER NOTES: Selected by Minnesota Vikings in third round (79th pick overall) of 1993 NFL draft. ... Signed by Vikings (July 16, 1993). ... Claimed on waivers by Green Bay Packers (August 31, 1993). ... On injured reserve with knee injury (December 6, 1994-remainder of season). ... Granted unconditional free agency (February 14, 1997). ... Re-signed by Packers (February 18, 1997).
CHAMPIONSHIP GAME EXPERIENCE: Played in NFC championship game (1995-97 seasons). ... Member of Super Bowl championship team (1996 season). ... Played in Super Bowl XXXII (1997 season).

Year Team	G	GS	SACKS
1993—Green Bay NFL	2	0	0.0
1994—Green Bay NFL	13	1	3.0
1995—Green Bay NFL	13	7	0.0
1996—Green Bay NFL	16	16	1.0
1997—Green Bay NFL	12	12	3.0
Pro totals (5 years)	56	36	7.0

B

BROWN, J.B.   CB   STEELERS

PERSONAL: Born January 5, 1967, in Washington, D.C. ... 6-0/191. ... Full name: James Harold Brown.

HIGH SCHOOL: DeMatha Catholic (Hyattsville, Md.).

COLLEGE: Maryland.

TRANSACTIONS/CAREER NOTES: Selected by Miami Dolphins in 12th round (315th pick overall) of 1989 NFL draft. ... Signed by Dolphins (July 16, 1989). ... Granted free agency (February 1, 1991). ... Re-signed by Dolphins to practice squad (August 29, 1991). ... Activated (September 7, 1991). ... Granted free agency (March 1, 1993). ... Re-signed by Dolphins (July 21, 1993). ... Released by Dolphins (February 3, 1997). ... Signed by Pittsburgh Steelers (February 7, 1997).

CHAMPIONSHIP GAME EXPERIENCE: Played in AFC championship game (1992 and 1997 seasons).

PRO STATISTICS: 1990—Credited with one sack. 1992—Recovered one fumble. 1993—Fumbled once. 1995—Fumbled once and recovered two fumbles.

				INTERCEPTIONS		
Year Team	G	GS	No.	Yds.	Avg.	TD
1989—Miami NFL	16	0	0	0	...	0
1990—Miami NFL	16	16	0	0	...	0
1991—Miami NFL	15	11	1	0	0.0	0
1992—Miami NFL	16	16	4	119	29.8	1
1993—Miami NFL	16	16	5	43	8.6	0
1994—Miami NFL	16	16	3	82	27.3	0
1995—Miami NFL	13	12	2	20	10.0	0
1996—Miami NFL	14	1	1	29	29.0	0
1997—Pittsburgh NFL	13	0	0	0	...	0
Pro totals (9 years)	**135**	**88**	**16**	**293**	**18.3**	**1**

BROWN, JAMES   OT   DOLPHINS

PERSONAL: Born January 3, 1970, in Philadelphia. ... 6-6/330. ... Full name: James Lamont Brown.

HIGH SCHOOL: Mastbaum Area Vo-Tech (Philadelphia).

COLLEGE: Virginia State.

TRANSACTIONS/CAREER NOTES: Selected by Dallas Cowboys in third round (82nd pick overall) of 1992 NFL draft. ... Signed by Cowboys (July 15, 1992). ... Released by Cowboys (August 17, 1992). ... Signed by Indianapolis Colts (August 19, 1992). ... Released by Colts (August 31, 1992). ... Signed by New York Jets to practice squad (September 2, 1992). ... Traded by Jets to Miami Dolphins for fifth-round pick (DB Raymond Austin) in 1997 draft (March 4, 1996). ... Granted unconditional free agency (February 13, 1998). ... Re-signed by Dolphins (March 3, 1998).

PLAYING EXPERIENCE: New York Jets NFL, 1993-1995; Miami NFL, 1996 and 1997. ... Games/Games started: 1993 (14/1), 1994 (16/6), 1995 (14/12), 1996 (16/16), 1997 (16/16). Total: 76/51.

PRO STATISTICS: 1994—Recovered one fumble.

BROWN, JAMIE   OT   49ERS

PERSONAL: Born April 24, 1972, in Miami. ... 6-8/318.

HIGH SCHOOL: Miami Killian.

COLLEGE: Florida A&M.

TRANSACTIONS/CAREER NOTES: Selected by Denver Broncos in fourth round (121st pick overall) of 1995 NFL draft. ... Signed by Broncos (May 25, 1995). ... On injured reserve with foot injury (November 29, 1995-remainder of season). ... Granted free agency (February 13, 1998). ... Re-signed by Broncos (April 15, 1998). ... Traded by Broncos to San Francisco 49ers for second-round pick in 1999 draft (April 15, 1998).

PLAYING EXPERIENCE: Denver NFL, 1995-1997. ... Games/Games started: 1995 (6/0), 1996 (12/2), 1997 (11/2). Total: 29/4.

CHAMPIONSHIP GAME EXPERIENCE: Member of Broncos for AFC championship game (1997 season); inactive. ... Member of Super Bowl championship team (1997 season); inactive.

BROWN, LANCE   CB   STEELERS

PERSONAL: Born February 2, 1972, in Jacksonville. ... 6-2/200.

HIGH SCHOOL: Terry Parker (Jacksonville).

COLLEGE: Indiana.

TRANSACTIONS/CAREER NOTES: Selected by Pittsburgh Steelers in fifth round (161st pick overall) of 1995 NFL draft. ... Signed by Steelers (July 18, 1995). ... Claimed on waivers by Arizona Cardinals (September 25, 1995). ... Released by Cardinals (September 10, 1996). ... Signed by New York Jets to practice squad (November 19, 1996). ... Released by Jets (August 7, 1997). ... Signed by Steelers (February 13, 1998).

PLAYING EXPERIENCE: Arizona NFL, 1995 and 1996. ... Games/Games started: 1995 (11/5), 1996 (1/0). Total: 12/5.

PRO STATISTICS: 1995—Recovered one fumble.

BROWN, LARRY   CB   VIKINGS

PERSONAL: Born November 30, 1969, in Miami. ... 5-11/186. ... Full name: Larry Brown Jr.

HIGH SCHOOL: Los Angeles.

JUNIOR COLLEGE: Southwestern College (Calif.).

COLLEGE: Texas Christian (degree in criminal justice).

TRANSACTIONS/CAREER NOTES: Selected by Dallas Cowboys in 12th round (320th pick overall) of 1991 NFL draft. ... Granted unconditional free agency (February 16, 1996). ... Signed by Oakland Raiders (February 20, 1996). ... Released by Raiders (June 3, 1998). ... Signed by Minnesota Vikings (June 16, 1998).

CHAMPIONSHIP GAME EXPERIENCE: Played in NFC championship game (1992-1995 seasons). ... Member of Super Bowl championship team (1992, 1993 and 1995 seasons).

HONORS: Named Most Valuable Player of Super Bowl XXX (1995 season).

POST SEASON RECORDS: Holds Super Bowl career and single-game records for most interception return yards—77. ... Shares Super Bowl career record for most interceptions—3.

PRO STATISTICS: 1991—Recovered one fumble. 1992—Recovered one fumble.

Year Team	G	GS	INTERCEPTIONS			
			No.	Yds.	Avg.	TD
1991—Dallas NFL	16	13	2	31	15.5	0
1992—Dallas NFL	16	15	1	30	30.0	0
1993—Dallas NFL	16	16	0	0	...	0
1994—Dallas NFL	15	15	4	21	5.3	0
1995—Dallas NFL	16	15	6	124	20.7	†2
1996—Oakland NFL	8	1	1	4	4.0	0
1997—Oakland NFL	4	0	0	0	...	0
Pro totals (7 years)	91	75	14	210	15.0	2

BROWN, LOMAS   OT   CARDINALS

PERSONAL: Born March 30, 1963, in Miami. ... 6-4/290. ... Full name: Lomas Brown Jr. ... Cousin of Joe Taylor, defensive back with Chicago Bears (1967-1974); cousin of Guy McIntyre, guard with San Francisco 49ers (1984-1993) and Green Bay Packers (1994) and Philadelphia Eagles (1995 and 1996); and cousin of Eric Curry, defensive end, Green Bay Packers.

HIGH SCHOOL: Miami Springs Senior.

COLLEGE: Florida.

TRANSACTIONS/CAREER NOTES: Selected by Orlando Renegades in second round (18th pick overall) of 1985 USFL draft. ... Selected by Detroit Lions in first round (sixth pick overall) of 1985 NFL draft. ... Signed by Lions (August 9, 1985). ... Designated by Lions as franchise player (February 25, 1993). ... Granted roster exemption (September 1-3, 1993). ... Designated by Lions as franchise player (February 15, 1995). ... Re-signed by Lions (September 7, 1995). ... Granted unconditional free agency (February 16, 1996). ... Signed by Arizona Cardinals (February 28, 1996).

PLAYING EXPERIENCE: Detroit NFL, 1985-1995; Arizona NFL, 1996 and 1997. ... Games/Games started: 1985 (16/16), 1986 (16/16), 1987 (11/11), 1988 (16/16), 1989 (16/16), 1990 (16/16), 1991 (15/15), 1992 (16/16), 1993 (11/11), 1994 (16/16), 1995 (15/14), 1996 (16/16), 1997 (14/14). Total: 194/193.

CHAMPIONSHIP GAME EXPERIENCE: Played in NFC championship game (1991 season).

HONORS: Named tackle on THE SPORTING NEWS college All-America first team (1984). ... Played in Pro Bowl (1990-1996 seasons). ... Named offensive tackle on THE SPORTING NEWS NFL All-Pro team (1992).

PRO STATISTICS: 1989—Rushed once for three yards and recovered one fumble. 1991—Recovered one fumble.

BROWN, ORLANDO   OT   RAVENS

PERSONAL: Born December 12, 1970, in Washington, D.C. ... 6-7/340. ... Full name: Orlando Claude Brown.

HIGH SCHOOL: Howard D. Woodson (Washington, D.C.).

COLLEGE: Central State (Ohio), then South Carolina State.

TRANSACTIONS/CAREER NOTES: Signed as non-drafted free agent by Cleveland Browns (May 13, 1993). ... On injured reserve with shoulder injury (August 30, 1993-entire season). ... Browns franchise moved to Baltimore and renamed Ravens for 1996 season (March 11, 1996).

PLAYING EXPERIENCE: Cleveland NFL, 1994 and 1995; Baltimore NFL, 1996 and 1997. ... Games/Games started: 1994 (14/8), 1995 (16/16), 1996 (16/16), 1997 (16/16). Total: 62/56.

PRO STATISTICS: 1995—Recovered one fumble.

BROWN, RAY   G   49ERS

PERSONAL: Born December 12, 1962, in West Memphis, Ark. ... 6-5/318. ... Full name: Leonard Ray Brown Jr.

HIGH SCHOOL: Marion (Ark.).

COLLEGE: Memphis State, then Arizona State, then Arkansas State.

TRANSACTIONS/CAREER NOTES: Selected by St. Louis Cardinals in eighth round (201st pick overall) of 1986 NFL draft. ... Signed by Cardinals (July 14, 1986). ... On injured reserve with knee injury (October 17-November 21, 1986). ... Released by Cardinals (September 7, 1987). ... Re-signed by Cardinals as replacement player (September 25, 1987). ... On injured reserve with finger injury (November 12-December 12, 1987). ... Cardinals franchise moved to Phoenix (March 15, 1988). ... Granted unconditional free agency (February 1, 1989). ... Signed by Washington Redskins (March 10, 1989). ... On injured reserve with knee injury (September 5-November 4, 1989). ... On injured reserve with knee injury (September 4, 1990-January 4, 1991). ... Granted unconditional free agency (February 1-April 1, 1991). ... Re-signed by Redskins for 1991 season. ... On injured reserve with elbow injury (August 27, 1991-entire season). ... Granted unconditional free agency (February 16, 1996). ... Signed by San Francisco 49ers (March 1, 1996).

PLAYING EXPERIENCE: St. Louis NFL, 1986 and 1987; Phoenix NFL, 1988; Washington NFL, 1989, 1992-1995; San Francisco NFL, 1996 and 1997. ... Games/Games started: 1986 (11/4), 1987 (7/3), 1988 (15/1), 1989 (7/0), 1992 (16/8), 1993 (16/14), 1994 (16/16), 1995 (16/16), 1996 (16/16), 1997 (15/15). Total: 135/93.

CHAMPIONSHIP GAME EXPERIENCE: Played in NFC championship game (1997 season).

BROWN, REGGIE   FB   SEAHAWKS

PERSONAL: Born June 26, 1973, in Detroit. ... 6-0/244. ... Full name: Regilyn Brown.

HIGH SCHOOL: Henry Ford (Detroit).

JUNIOR COLLEGE: College of the Desert (Calif.).

COLLEGE: Fresno State.

TRANSACTIONS/CAREER NOTES: Selected by Seattle Seahawks in third round (91st pick overall) of 1996 NFL draft. ... Signed by Seahawks (July 23, 1996). ... On injured reserve with knee injury (October 23, 1996-remainder of season). ... On injured reserve with knee injury (December 17, 1997-remainder of season).

PLAYING EXPERIENCE: Seattle NFL, 1996 and 1997. ... Games/Games started: 1996 (7/0), 1997 (11/0). Total: 18/0.

PRO STATISTICS: 1996—Returned four kickoffs for 51 yards. 1997—Returned one kickoff for 16 yards.

SINGLE GAME HIGHS (regular season): Attempts—0; yards—0; and rushing touchdowns—0.

BROWN, REGGIE — LB

PERSONAL: Born September 28, 1974, in Austin, Texas. ... 6-2/241. ... Full name: Reginald Dwayne Brown.
HIGH SCHOOL: Reagan (Austin, Texas).
COLLEGE: Texas A&M.
TRANSACTIONS/CAREER NOTES: Selected by Detroit Lions in first round (17th pick overall) of 1996 NFL draft. ... Signed by Lions for 1996 season. ... On injured reserve with neck injury (December 23, 1997-remainder of season). ... Suffered career-ending neck injury (December 21, 1997). ... Released by Lions (June 16, 1998).

			INTERCEPTIONS			SACKS
Year Team	G	GS	No.	Yds.	Avg.	TD	No.
1996—Detroit NFL	10	10	0	0	...	0	0.0
1997—Detroit NFL	16	16	2	83	41.5	∞2	2.5
Pro totals (2 years)	26	26	2	83	41.5	2	2.5

BROWN, ROD — FB — CARDINALS

PERSONAL: Born February 28, 1974, in Lithonia, Ga. ... 5-11/247. ... Full name: Roderick Jamar Brown.
HIGH SCHOOL: Lithonia (Ga.).
COLLEGE: North Carolina State.
TRANSACTIONS/CAREER NOTES: Selected by Arizona Cardinals in sixth round (175th pick overall) of 1997 NFL draft. ... Signed by Cardinals (June 4, 1997). ... Released by Cardinals (August 24, 1997). ... Re-signed by Cardinals to practice squad (August 26, 1997).

BROWN, RUBEN — G — BILLS

PERSONAL: Born February 13, 1972, in Lynchburg, Va. ... 6-3/304. ... Full name: Ruben Pernell Brown. ... Brother of Cornell Brown, linebacker, Baltimore Ravens.
HIGH SCHOOL: E.C. Glass (Lynchburg, Va.).
COLLEGE: Pittsburgh.
TRANSACTIONS/CAREER NOTES: Selected by Buffalo Bills in first round (14th pick overall) of 1995 NFL draft. ... Signed by Bills (June 20, 1995).
PLAYING EXPERIENCE: Buffalo NFL, 1995-1997. ... Games/Games started: 1995 (16/16), 1996 (14/14), 1997 (16/16). Total: 46/46.
HONORS: Named offensive lineman on THE SPORTING NEWS college All-America second team (1994). ... Played in Pro Bowl (1996 and 1997 seasons).
PRO STATISTICS: 1997—Recovered one fumble.

BROWN, TIM — WR — RAIDERS

PERSONAL: Born July 22, 1966, in Dallas. ... 6-0/195. ... Full name: Timothy Donell Brown.
HIGH SCHOOL: Woodrow Wilson (Dallas).
COLLEGE: Notre Dame (degree in sociology).
TRANSACTIONS/CAREER NOTES: Selected by Los Angeles Raiders in first round (sixth pick overall) of 1988 NFL draft. ... Signed by Raiders (July 14, 1988). ... On injured reserve with knee injury (September 12, 1989-remainder of season). ... Granted free agency (February 1, 1992). ... Re-signed by Raiders (August 13, 1992). ... Designated by Raiders as transition player (February 25, 1993). ... Tendered offer sheet by Denver Broncos (March 11, 1994). ... Offer matched by Raiders (March 16, 1994). ... Raiders franchise moved to Oakland (July 21, 1995).
CHAMPIONSHIP GAME EXPERIENCE: Played in AFC championship game (1990 season).
HONORS: Named wide receiver on THE SPORTING NEWS college All-America first team (1986 and 1987). ... Heisman Trophy winner (1987). ... Named College Football Player of the Year by THE SPORTING NEWS (1987). ... Named kick returner on THE SPORTING NEWS NFL All-Pro team (1988). ... Played in Pro Bowl (1988, 1991 and 1993-1997 seasons). ... Named wide receiver on THE SPORTING NEWS NFL All-Pro team (1997).
RECORDS: Holds NFL rookie-season record for most combined yards gained—2,317 (1988).
PRO STATISTICS: 1988—Fumbled five times and recovered one fumble for seven yards. 1989—Fumbled once. 1990—Fumbled three times. 1991—Fumbled once. 1992—Fumbled six times and recovered one fumble. 1993—Fumbled once. 1994—Fumbled three times. 1995—Recovered one fumble for three yards. 1996—Fumbled three times and recovered one fumble. 1997—Fumbled once.
SINGLE GAME HIGHS (regular season): Receptions—14 (December 21, 1997, vs. Jacksonville); yards—183 (December 5, 1993, vs. Buffalo); and touchdown receptions—3 (August 31, 1997, vs. Tennessee).
STATISTICAL PLATEAUS: 100-yard receiving games: 1988 (1), 1991 (1), 1992 (1), 1993 (4), 1994 (4), 1995 (6), 1996 (2), 1997 (7). Total: 26.
MISCELLANEOUS: Holds Raiders franchise all-time record for most receptions (599).

			RUSHING				RECEIVING				PUNT RETURNS				KICKOFF RETURNS				TOTALS		
YearTeam	G	GS	Att.	Yds.	Avg.	TD	No.	Yds.	Avg.	TD	No.	Yds.	Avg.	TD	No.	Yds.	Avg.	TD	TD	2pt.	Pts.
1988—LA Raiders NFL	16	9	14	50	3.6	1	43	725	16.9	5	§49	§444	9.1	0	*41	*1098	*26.8	†1	7	...	42
1989—LA Raiders NFL	1	1	0	0	...	0	1	8	8.0	0	4	43	10.8	0	3	63	21.0	0	0	...	0
1990—LA Raiders NFL	16	0	0	0	...	0	18	265	14.7	3	34	295	8.7	0	0	0	...	0	3	...	18
1991—LA Raiders NFL	16	1	5	16	3.2	0	36	554	15.4	5	29	§330	11.4	▲1	1	29	29.0	0	6	...	36
1992—LA Raiders NFL	15	12	3	-4	-1.3	0	49	693	14.1	7	37	383	10.4	0	2	14	7.0	0	7	...	42
1993—LA Raiders NFL	16	16	2	7	3.5	0	80	§1180	14.8	7	40	§465	11.6	1	0	0	...	0	8	...	48
1994—LA Raiders NFL	16	16	0	0	...	0	89	§1309	14.7	9	40	*487	12.2	0	0	0	...	0	9	0	54
1995—Oakland NFL	16	16	0	0	...	0	89	§1342	15.1	10	36	364	10.1	0	0	0	...	0	10	0	60
1996—Oakland NFL	16	16	6	35	5.8	0	90	1104	12.3	9	32	272	8.5	0	1	24	24.0	0	9	0	54
1997—Oakland NFL	16	16	5	19	3.8	0	†104	§1408	13.5	5	0	0	...	0	1	7	7.0	0	5	1	32
Pro totals (10 years)	144	103	35	123	3.5	1	599	8588	14.3	60	301	3083	10.2	2	49	1235	25.2	1	64	1	386

BROWN, TROY — WR — PATRIOTS

PERSONAL: Born July 2, 1971, in Blackville, S.C. ... 5-10/190. ... Full name: Troy Fitzgerald Brown.
HIGH SCHOOL: Blackville (S.C.)-Hilda.
COLLEGE: Lees-McRae College (N.C.), then Marshall.

TRANSACTIONS/CAREER NOTES: Selected by New England Patriots in eighth round (198th pick overall) of 1993 NFL draft. ... Signed by Patriots (July 16, 1993). ... On injured reserve with quadriceps injury (December 31, 1993-remainder of season). ... Released by Patriots (August 28, 1994). ... Re-signed by Patriots (October 19, 1994). ... Granted unconditional free agency (February 14, 1997). ... Re-signed by Patriots (March 10, 1997).

CHAMPIONSHIP GAME EXPERIENCE: Played in AFC championship game (1996 season). ... Member of Patriots for Super Bowl XXXI (1996 season); inactive.

PRO STATISTICS: 1993—Recovered one fumble. 1994—Recovered two fumbles. 1995—Recovered one fumble for 75 yards and a touchdown. 1997—Rushed once for minus 18 yards.

SINGLE GAME HIGHS (regular season): Receptions—7 (December 21, 1996, vs. New York Giants); yards—125 (October 19, 1997, vs. New York Jets); and touchdown receptions—1 (December 7, 1997, vs. Jacksonville).

STATISTICAL PLATEAUS: 100-yard receiving games: 1997 (2).

			RECEIVING				PUNT RETURNS				KICKOFF RETURNS				TOTALS			
Year Team	G	GS	No.	Yds.	Avg.	TD	No.	Yds.	Avg.	TD	No.	Yds.	Avg.	TD	TD	2pt.	Pts.	Fum.
1993—New England NFL	12	0	2	22	11.0	0	25	224	9.0	0	15	243	16.2	0	0	...	0	2
1994—New England NFL	9	0	0	0	...	0	24	202	8.4	0	1	14	14.0	0	0	0	0	2
1995—New England NFL	16	0	14	159	11.4	0	0	0	...	0	31	672	21.7	0	1	0	6	1
1996—New England NFL	16	0	21	222	10.6	0	0	0	...	0	29	634	21.9	0	0	0	0	0
1997—New England NFL	16	6	41	607	14.8	6	0	0	...	0	0	0	...	0	6	0	36	0
Pro totals (5 years)	69	6	78	1010	12.9	6	49	426	8.7	0	76	1563	20.0	0	7	0	42	5

BROWNING, JOHN   DT   CHIEFS

PERSONAL: Born September 30, 1973, in Miami. ... 6-4/290.
HIGH SCHOOL: North Miami.
COLLEGE: West Virginia.
TRANSACTIONS/CAREER NOTES: Selected by Kansas City Chiefs in third round (68th pick overall) of 1996 NFL draft. ... Signed by Chiefs (July 24, 1996).
PRO STATISTICS: 1997—Recovered one fumble.

Year Team	G	GS	SACKS
1996—Kansas City NFL	13	2	2.0
1997—Kansas City NFL	14	13	4.0
Pro totals (2 years)	27	15	6.0

BRUCE, AUNDRAY   DE   RAIDERS

PERSONAL: Born April 30, 1966, in Montgomery, Ala. ... 6-5/265. ... Uncle of Ricky Shaw, linebacker with New York Giants (1988 and 1989) and Philadelphia Eagles (1989 and 1990).
HIGH SCHOOL: George Washington Carver (Montgomery, Ala.).
COLLEGE: Auburn.
TRANSACTIONS/CAREER NOTES: Signed by Atlanta Falcons (April 6, 1988). ... Selected officially by Falcons in first round (first pick overall) of 1988 NFL draft. ... Granted unconditional free agency (February 1, 1992). ... Signed by Los Angeles Raiders (February 14, 1992). ... Granted unconditional free agency (February 17, 1995). ... Re-signed by Oakland Raiders (September 6, 1995). ... Raiders franchise moved to Oakland (July 21, 1995). ... Released by Raiders (August 24, 1997). ... Re-signed by Raiders (October 1, 1997).
HONORS: Named linebacker on THE SPORTING NEWS college All-America first team (1987).
PRO STATISTICS: 1989—Returned one kickoff for 15 yards. 1991—Caught one pass for 11 yards. 1993—Recovered one fumble. 1996—Recovered one fumble for three yards.

			INTERCEPTIONS				SACKS
Year Team	G	GS	No.	Yds.	Avg.	TD	No.
1988—Atlanta NFL	16	16	2	10	5.0	0	6.0
1989—Atlanta NFL	16	13	1	0	0.0	0	6.0
1990—Atlanta NFL	16	3	0	0	...	0	4.0
1991—Atlanta NFL	14	2	0	0	...	0	0.0
1992—Los Angeles Raiders NFL	16	4	0	0	...	0	3.5
1993—Los Angeles Raiders NFL	16	0	0	0	...	0	2.0
1994—Los Angeles Raiders NFL	16	0	0	0	...	0	0.0
1995—Oakland NFL	14	0	1	1	1.0	▲1	5.5
1996—Oakland NFL	16	0	0	0	...	0	4.0
1997—Oakland NFL	10	3	0	0	...	0	1.0
Pro totals (10 years)	150	41	4	11	2.8	1	32.0

BRUCE, ISAAC   WR   RAMS

PERSONAL: Born November 10, 1972, in Fort Lauderdale. ... 6-0/188. ... Full name: Isaac Isidore Bruce. ... Cousin of Derrick Moore, running back with Detroit Lions (1993 and 1994) and Carolina Panthers (1995).
HIGH SCHOOL: Dillard (Fort Lauderdale).
COLLEGE: Memphis State.
TRANSACTIONS/CAREER NOTES: Selected by Los Angeles Rams in second round (33rd pick overall) of 1994 NFL draft. ... Signed by Rams (July 13, 1994). ... On injured reserve with sprained right knee (December 9, 1994-remainder of season). ... Rams franchise moved to St. Louis (April 12, 1995).
HONORS: Played in Pro Bowl (1996 season).
PRO STATISTICS: 1995—Ran 52 yards with lateral from punt return and recovered one fumble. 1996—Attempted two passes with one completion for 15 yards and an interception.
SINGLE GAME HIGHS (regular season): Receptions—15 (December 24, 1995, vs. Miami); yards—233 (November 2, 1997, vs. Atlanta); and touchdown receptions—2 (December 7, 1997, vs. New Orleans).
STATISTICAL PLATEAUS: 100-yard receiving games: 1995 (9), 1996 (4), 1997 (2). Total: 15.

Year Team	G	GS	RUSHING				RECEIVING				TOTALS			
			Att.	Yds.	Avg.	TD	No.	Yds.	Avg.	TD	TD	2pt.	Pts.	Fum.
1994—Los Angeles Rams NFL	12	0	1	2	2.0	0	21	272	13.0	3	3	0	18	0
1995—St. Louis NFL	16	16	3	17	5.7	0	119	1781	15.0	13	13	1	80	2
1996—St. Louis NFL	16	16	1	4	4.0	0	84	*1338	15.9	7	7	0	42	1
1997—St. Louis NFL	12	12	0	0	...	0	56	815	14.6	5	5	0	30	1
Pro totals (4 years)	56	44	5	23	4.6	0	280	4206	15.0	28	28	1	170	4

BRUENER, MARK — TE — STEELERS

PERSONAL: Born September 16, 1972, in Olympia, Wash. ... 6-4/258. ... Name pronounced BREW-ner.
HIGH SCHOOL: Aberdeen (Wash.).
COLLEGE: Washington.
TRANSACTIONS/CAREER NOTES: Selected by Pittsburgh Steelers in first round (27th pick overall) of 1995 NFL draft. ... Signed by Steelers (July 25, 1995). ... On injured reserve with knee injury (November 29, 1996-remainder of season).
CHAMPIONSHIP GAME EXPERIENCE: Played in AFC championship game (1995 and 1997 seasons). ... Played in Super Bowl XXX (1995 season).
PRO STATISTICS: 1995—Returned two kickoffs for 19 yards.
SINGLE GAME HIGHS (regular season): Receptions—5 (December 13, 1997, vs. New England); yards—43 (December 13, 1997, vs. New England); and touchdown receptions—1 (December 13, 1997, vs. New England).

Year Team	G	GS	RECEIVING				TOTALS			
			No.	Yds.	Avg.	TD	TD	2pt.	Pts.	Fum.
1995—Pittsburgh NFL	16	13	26	238	9.2	3	3	0	18	0
1996—Pittsburgh NFL	12	12	12	141	11.8	0	0	1	2	0
1997—Pittsburgh NFL	16	16	18	117	6.5	6	6	0	36	1
Pro totals (3 years)	44	41	56	496	8.9	9	9	1	56	1

BRUMFIELD, SCOTT — G — BENGALS

PERSONAL: Born August 19, 1970, in Salt Lake City. ... 6-8/325.
HIGH SCHOOL: Spanish Fork (Utah).
JUNIOR COLLEGE: Dixie College (Utah).
COLLEGE: Brigham Young.
TRANSACTIONS/CAREER NOTES: Signed as non-drafted free agent by Cincinnati Bengals (April 28, 1993). ... Released by Bengals (August 29, 1994). ... Re-signed by Bengals (November 7, 1994). ... Granted free agency (February 16, 1996). ... Re-signed by Bengals (April 26, 1996). ... On injured list with spinal cord concussion (November 8, 1996-entire season). ... Granted unconditional free agency (February 14, 1997). ... Re-signed by Bengals (April 21, 1997).
PLAYING EXPERIENCE: Cincinnati NFL, 1993-1997. ... Games/Games started: 1993 (16/7), 1994 (2/0), 1995 (13/11), 1996 (9/8), 1997 (15/3). Total: 55/29.

BRUNELL, MARK — QB — JAGUARS

PERSONAL: Born September 17, 1970, in Los Angeles. ... 6-1/214. ... Full name: Mark Allen Brunell.
HIGH SCHOOL: St. Joseph (Santa Maria, Calif.).
COLLEGE: Washington (degree in history).
TRANSACTIONS/CAREER NOTES: Selected by Green Bay Packers in fifth round (118th pick overall) of 1993 NFL draft. ... Signed by Packers (July 1, 1993). ... Traded by Packers to Jacksonville Jaguars for third- (FB William Henderson) and fifth-round (RB Travis Jervey) picks in 1995 draft (April 21, 1995).
CHAMPIONSHIP GAME EXPERIENCE: Played in AFC championship game (1996 season).
HONORS: Played in Pro Bowl (1996 and 1997 seasons). ... Named Outstanding Player of Pro Bowl (1996 season).
PRO STATISTICS: 1994—Fumbled once. 1995—Fumbled five times and recovered three fumbles. 1996—Fumbled 14 times and recovered five fumbles for minus 14 yards. 1997—Fumbled four times for minus five yards.
SINGLE GAME HIGHS (regular season): Attempts—52 (October 20, 1996, vs. St. Louis); completions—37 (October 20, 1996, vs. St. Louis); yards—432 (September 22, 1996, vs. New England); and touchdown passes—3 (October 19, 1997, vs. Dallas).
STATISTICAL PLATEAUS: 300-yard passing games: 1995 (2), 1996 (6), 1997 (3). Total: 11.
MISCELLANEOUS: Regular-season record as NFL starting quarterback: 21-19 (.525). ... Postseason record as NFL starting quarterback: 2-2 (.500). ... Holds Jacksonville Jaguars all-time record for most yards passing (9,816) and most touchdown passes (52).

Year Team	G	GS	PASSING								RUSHING				TOTALS		
			Att.	Cmp.	Pct.	Yds.	TD	Int.	Avg.	Rat.	Att.	Yds.	Avg.	TD	TD	2pt.	Pts.
1993—Green Bay NFL							Did not play.										
1994—Green Bay NFL	2	0	27	12	44.4	95	0	0	3.52	53.8	6	7	1.2	1	1	0	6
1995—Jacksonville NFL	13	10	346	201	58.1	2168	15	7	6.27	82.6	67	480	7.2	4	4	0	24
1996—Jacksonville NFL	16	16	557	353	§63.4	*4367	19	§20	*7.84	84.0	80	396	5.0	3	3	2	22
1997—Jacksonville NFL	14	14	435	264	60.7	3281	18	7	§7.54	§91.2	48	257	5.4	2	2	0	12
Pro totals (4 years)	45	40	1365	830	60.8	9911	52	34	7.26	85.3	201	1140	5.7	10	10	2	64

BRUSCHI, TEDY — LB — PATRIOTS

PERSONAL: Born June 9, 1973, in San Francisco. ... 6-1/245. ... Full name: Tedy Lacap Bruschi. ... Stepson of Ronald Sandys, former professional tennis player. ... Name pronounced BREW-ski.
HIGH SCHOOL: Roseville (Calif.).
COLLEGE: Arizona.
TRANSACTIONS/CAREER NOTES: Selected by New England Patriots in third round (86th pick overall) of 1996 NFL draft. ... Signed by Patriots (July 17, 1996).

CHAMPIONSHIP GAME EXPERIENCE: Played in AFC championship game (1996 season). ... Played in Super Bowl XXXI (1996 season).
HONORS: Named defensive lineman on THE SPORTING NEWS college All-America first team (1994 and 1995).
PRO STATISTICS: 1996—Returned blocked punt four yards for a touchdown. 1997—Recovered two fumbles.

Year Team	G	GS	SACKS
1996—New England NFL	16	0	4.0
1997—New England NFL	16	1	4.0
Pro totals (2 years)	32	1	8.0

BRYANT, JUNIOR — DE — 49ERS

PERSONAL: Born January 16, 1971, in Omaha, Neb. ... 6-4/278. ... Full name: Edward E. Bryant.
HIGH SCHOOL: Creighton Prep (Omaha, Neb.).
COLLEGE: Notre Dame.
TRANSACTIONS/CAREER NOTES: Signed as non-drafted free agent by San Francisco 49ers (May 3, 1993). ... Released by 49ers (August 30, 1993). ... Re-signed by 49ers to practice squad (August 31, 1993). ... Released by 49ers (August 27, 1994). ... Re-signed by 49ers to practice squad (August 31, 1994).
PLAYING EXPERIENCE: San Francisco NFL, 1995-1997. ... Games/Games started: 1995 (16/4), 1996 (16/1), 1997 (16/3). Total: 48/8.
CHAMPIONSHIP GAME EXPERIENCE: Played in NFC championship game (1997 season).
PRO STATISTICS: 1995—Credited with one sack. 1996—Recovered one fumble. 1997—Credited with 2$^1/_2$ sacks.

BRYANT, KEIF — DT — PACKERS

PERSONAL: Born March 12, 1973, in Largo, Fla. ... 6-4/285.
HIGH SCHOOL: Largo (Fla.).
COLLEGE: Rutgers.
TRANSACTIONS/CAREER NOTES: Selected by Seattle Seahawks in seventh round (216th pick overall) of 1995 NFL draft. ... Signed by Seahawks (June 8, 1995). ... Released by Seahawks (August 21, 1995). ... Re-signed by Seahawks to practice squad (August 28, 1995). ... On injured reserve with heel injury (August 12, 1996-entire season). ... Released by Seahawks (August 18, 1997). ... Signed by Green Bay Packers (February 5, 1998).

BUCHANAN, RAY — DB — FALCONS

PERSONAL: Born September 29, 1971, in Chicago. ... 5-9/195. ... Full name: Raymond Louis Buchanan.
HIGH SCHOOL: East Proviso (Ill.).
COLLEGE: Louisville.
TRANSACTIONS/CAREER NOTES: Selected by Indianapolis Colts in third round (65th pick overall) of 1993 NFL draft. ... Signed by Colts (July 26, 1993). ... Designated by Colts as transition player (February 13, 1997). ... Tendered offer sheet by Atlanta Falcons (February 25, 1997). ... Colts declined to match offer (March 3, 1997).
CHAMPIONSHIP GAME EXPERIENCE: Played in AFC championship game (1995 season).
PRO STATISTICS: 1994—Credited with one sack and recovered one fumble. 1995—Returned one kickoff for 22 yards, credited with one sack and recovered two fumbles. 1996—Returned one kickoff for 20 yards.

			INTERCEPTIONS				PUNT RETURNS				TOTALS		
Year Team	G	GS	No.	Yds.	Avg.	TD	No.	Yds.	Avg.	TD	TD	2pt.	Pts.	Fum.
1993—Indianapolis NFL	16	5	4	45	11.3	0	0	0	...	0	0	...	0	0
1994—Indianapolis NFL	16	16	8	221	27.6	†3	0	0	...	0	3	0	18	0
1995—Indianapolis NFL	16	16	2	60	30.0	0	16	113	7.1	0	0	0	0	1
1996—Indianapolis NFL	13	13	2	32	16.0	0	12	201	16.8	0	0	0	0	0
1997—Atlanta NFL	16	16	5	49	9.8	0	0	37	...	0	0	0	0	0
Pro totals (5 years)	77	66	21	407	19.4	3	28	351	12.5	0	3	0	18	1

BUCKEY, JEFF — OT — DOLPHINS

PERSONAL: Born August 7, 1974, in Bakersfield, Calif. ... 6-5/305.
HIGH SCHOOL: Bakersfield (Calif.).
COLLEGE: Stanford (degree in economics).
TRANSACTIONS/CAREER NOTES: Selected by Miami Dolphins in seventh round (230th pick overall) of 1996 NFL draft. ... Signed by Dolphins for 1996 season.
PLAYING EXPERIENCE: Miami NFL, 1996 and 1997. ... Games/Games started: 1996 (15/1), 1997 (16/12). Totals: 31/13.

BUCKLEY, CURTIS — S — 49ERS

PERSONAL: Born September 25, 1970, in Oakdale, Calif. ... 6-0/182. ... Full name: Curtis Ladonn Buckley.
HIGH SCHOOL: Silsbee (Texas).
JUNIOR COLLEGE: Kilgore (Texas) College.
COLLEGE: East Texas State.
TRANSACTIONS/CAREER NOTES: Signed as non-drafted free agent by Tampa Bay Buccaneers (May 3, 1993). ... Released by Buccaneers (August 30, 1993). ... Re-signed by Buccaneers (August 31, 1993). ... Released by Buccaneers (September 7, 1993). ... Re-signed by Buccaneers to practice squad (September 9, 1993). ... Activated (November 5, 1993). ... Released by Buccaneers (August 30, 1994). ... Re-signed by Buccaneers (September 7, 1994). ... Released by Buccaneers (September 17, 1994). ... Re-signed by Buccaneers (September 30, 1994). ... Granted free agency (February 16, 1996). ... Tendered offer sheet by San Francisco 49ers (February 21, 1996). ... Buccaneers declined to match offer (February 28, 1996).
CHAMPIONSHIP GAME EXPERIENCE: Played in NFC championship game (1997 season).
PRO STATISTICS: 1994—Recovered two fumbles. 1996—Recovered two fumbles. 1997—Recovered one fumble.

Year Team	G	GS	INTERCEPTIONS				TOTALS			
			No.	Yds.	Avg.	TD	TD	2pt.	Pts.	Fum.
1993—Tampa Bay NFL	10	2	0	0	...	0	0	0	0	0
1994—Tampa Bay NFL	13	0	8	177	22.1	...	0	0	0	1
1995—Tampa Bay NFL	15	0	2	29	14.5	0	0	0	0	0
1996—San Francisco NFL	15	0	0	0	...	0	0	0	0	0
1997—San Francisco NFL	15	0	0	0	...	0	0	0	0	0
Pro totals (5 years)	68	2	10	206	20.6	0	0	0	0	1

BUCKLEY, MARCUS LB GIANTS

PERSONAL: Born February 3, 1971, in Fort Worth, Texas. ... 6-3/240. ... Full name: Marcus Wayne Buckley.
HIGH SCHOOL: Eastern Hills (Fort Worth, Texas).
COLLEGE: Texas A&M.
TRANSACTIONS/CAREER NOTES: Selected by New York Giants in third round (66th pick overall) of 1993 NFL draft. ... Signed by Giants (July 23, 1993). ... Granted free agency (February 16, 1996). ... Re-signed by Giants (April 15, 1996). ... Granted unconditional free agency (February 13, 1998). ... Re-signed by Giants (February 19, 1998).
PLAYING EXPERIENCE: New York Giants NFL, 1993-1997. ... Games/Games started: 1993 (16/2), 1994 (16/1), 1995 (16/5), 1996 (15/2), 1997 (12/3). Total: 75/13.
HONORS: Named linebacker on THE SPORTING NEWS college All-America first team (1992).
PRO STATISTICS: 1993—Recovered one fumble. 1995—Recovered one fumble. 1997—Recovered one fumble.

BUCKLEY, TERRELL CB DOLPHINS

PERSONAL: Born June 7, 1971, in Pascagoula, Miss. ... 5-9/180. ... Full name: Douglas Terrell Buckley.
HIGH SCHOOL: Pascagoula (Miss.).
COLLEGE: Florida State.
TRANSACTIONS/CAREER NOTES: Selected after junior season by Green Bay Packers in first round (fifth pick overall) of 1992 NFL draft. ... Signed by Packers (September 11, 1992). ... Granted roster exemption for one game (September 1992). ... Traded by Packers to Miami Dolphins for past considerations (April 3, 1995).
HONORS: Named defensive back on THE SPORTING NEWS college All-America second team (1990). ... Jim Thorpe Award winner (1991). ... Named defensive back on THE SPORTING NEWS college All-America first team (1991).
PRO STATISTICS: 1992—Recovered four fumbles. 1994—Recovered one fumble. 1995—Returned one kickoff for 16 yards. 1996—Returned one kickoff for 48 yards and recovered two fumbles. 1997—Recovered two fumbles for 23 yards and one touchdown.

Year Team	G	GS	INTERCEPTIONS				PUNT RETURNS				TOTALS			
			No.	Yds.	Avg.	TD	No.	Yds.	Avg.	TD	TD	2pt.	Pts.	Fum.
1992—Green Bay NFL	14	12	3	33	11.0	1	21	211	10.0	1	2	...	12	7
1993—Green Bay NFL	16	16	2	31	15.5	0	11	76	6.9	0	0	...	0	1
1994—Green Bay NFL	16	16	5	38	7.6	0	0	0	...	0	0	0	0	0
1995—Miami NFL	16	4	1	0	0.0	0	0	0	...	0	0	0	0	0
1996—Miami NFL	16	16	6	*164	27.3	1	3	24	8.0	0	1	0	6	1
1997—Miami NFL	16	16	4	26	6.5	0	4	58	14.5	0	1	0	6	0
Pro totals (6 years)	94	80	21	292	13.9	2	39	369	9.5	1	4	0	24	9

BUCKNER, BRENTSON DE 49ERS

PERSONAL: Born September 30, 1971, in Columbus, Ga. ... 6-2/315. ... Full name: Brentson Andre Buckner.
HIGH SCHOOL: Carver (Columbus, Ga.).
COLLEGE: Clemson.
TRANSACTIONS/CAREER NOTES: Selected by Pittsburgh Steelers in second round (50th pick overall) of 1994 NFL draft. ... Signed by Steelers (July 23, 1994). ... Traded by Steelers to Kansas City Chiefs for seventh-round pick (traded to San Diego) in 1997 draft (April 4, 1997). ... Claimed on waivers by Cincinnati Bengals (August 25, 1997). ... Granted unconditional free agency (February 13, 1998). ... Signed by San Francisco 49ers (May 26, 1998).
CHAMPIONSHIP GAME EXPERIENCE: Played in AFC championship game (1994 and 1995 seasons). ... Played in Super Bowl XXX (1995 season).
PRO STATISTICS: 1994—Recovered one fumble. 1995—Recovered one fumble for 46 yards and a touchdown. 1996—Fumbled once and recovered one fumble for 13 yards.

Year Team	G	GS	SACKS
1994—Pittsburgh NFL	13	5	2.0
1995—Pittsburgh NFL	16	16	3.0
1996—Pittsburgh NFL	15	14	3.0
1997—Cincinnati NFL	14	5	0.0
Pro totals (4 years)	58	40	8.0

BURGER, TODD G JETS

PERSONAL: Born March 20, 1970, in Clark, N.J. ... 6-3/303. ... Full name: Todd R. Burger.
HIGH SCHOOL: A.L. Johnson Regional (Clark, N.J.).
COLLEGE: Penn State.
TRANSACTIONS/CAREER NOTES: Signed as non-drafted free agent by Chicago Bears (April 29, 1993). ... Released by Bears (August 30, 1993). ... Re-signed by Bears to practice squad (August 31, 1993). ... Activated (December 12, 1993). ... Granted free agency (February 14, 1997). ... Re-signed by Bears (March 7, 1997). ... Granted unconditional free agency (February 13, 1998). ... Signed by New York Jets (February 25, 1998).
PLAYING EXPERIENCE: Chicago NFL, 1994-1997. ... Games/Games started: 1994 (4/0), 1995 (16/1), 1996 (11/8), 1997 (15/15). Total: 46/24.
PRO STATISTICS: 1996—Recovered one fumble. 1997—Recovered one fumble.

BURGESS, JAMES   LB   CHARGERS

PERSONAL: Born March 31, 1974, in Miami. ... 5-11/230. ... Full name: James Paul Burgess. ... Half-brother of Fernanza Burgess, wide receiver with New York Jets (1984) and Miami Dolphins (1984).
HIGH SCHOOL: Homestead (Fla.).
COLLEGE: Miami (Fla.).
TRANSACTIONS/CAREER NOTES: Signed as non-drafted free agent by Kansas City Chiefs (April 25, 1997). ... Released by Chiefs (August 19, 1997). ... Signed by Dallas Cowboys to practice squad (August 28, 1997). ... Signed by San Diego Chargers off Cowboys practice squad (September 2, 1997).
PLAYING EXPERIENCE: San Diego NFL, 1997. ... Games/Games started: 15/4.

BURKE, JOHN   TE   CHARGERS

PERSONAL: Born September 7, 1971, in Elizabeth, N.J. ... 6-3/248. ... Full name: John Richard Burke.
HIGH SCHOOL: Holmdel (N.J.).
COLLEGE: Virginia Tech.
TRANSACTIONS/CAREER NOTES: Selected by New England Patriots in fourth round (121st pick overall) of 1994 NFL draft. ... Signed by Patriots (May 25, 1994). ... Granted free agency (February 14, 1997). ... Re-signed by Patriots (June 20, 1997). ... Claimed on waivers by New York Jets (August 25, 1997). ... Granted unconditional free agency (February 13, 1998). ... Signed by San Diego Chargers (April 7, 1998).
CHAMPIONSHIP GAME EXPERIENCE: Played in AFC championship game (1996 season). ... Played in Super Bowl XXXI (1996 season).
PRO STATISTICS: 1995—Recovered one fumble.
SINGLE GAME HIGHS (regular season): Receptions—4 (October 8, 1995, vs. Denver); yards—41 (December 18, 1994, vs. Buffalo); and touchdown receptions—0.

			RECEIVING				KICKOFF RETURNS				TOTALS			
Year Team	G	GS	No.	Yds.	Avg.	TD	No.	Yds.	Avg.	TD	TD	2pt.	Pts.	Fum.
1994—New England NFL	16	6	9	86	9.6	0	3	11	3.7	0	0	0	0	0
1995—New England NFL	16	4	15	136	9.1	0	1	7	7.0	0	0	0	0	0
1996—New England NFL	11	2	1	19	19.0	0	0	0	...	0	0	0	0	0
1997—New York Jets NFL	7	1	0	0	...	0	0	0	...	0	0	0	0	0
Pro totals (4 years)	50	13	25	241	9.6	0	4	18	4.5	0	0	0	0	0

BURNETT, ROB   DE   RAVENS

PERSONAL: Born August 27, 1967, in Livingston, N.J. ... 6-4/280. ... Full name: Robert Barry Burnett.
HIGH SCHOOL: Newfield (Selden, N.Y.).
COLLEGE: Syracuse.
TRANSACTIONS/CAREER NOTES: Selected by Cleveland Browns in fifth round (129th pick overall) of 1990 NFL draft. ... Signed by Browns (July 22, 1990). ... Granted free agency (March 1, 1993). ... Re-signed by Browns (June 11, 1993). ... Browns franchise moved to Baltimore and renamed Ravens for 1996 season (March 11, 1996).
HONORS: Played in Pro Bowl (1994 season).
PRO STATISTICS: 1991—Recovered one fumble for nine yards. 1992—Recovered two fumbles. 1993—Recovered two fumbles. 1994—Recovered one fumble. 1995—Recovered one fumble. 1997—Recovered one fumble.

Year Team	G	GS	SACKS
1990—Cleveland NFL	16	6	2.0
1991—Cleveland NFL	13	8	3.0
1992—Cleveland NFL	16	16	9.0
1993—Cleveland NFL	16	16	9.0
1994—Cleveland NFL	16	16	10.0
1995—Cleveland NFL	16	16	7.5
1996—Baltimore NFL	6	6	3.0
1997—Baltimore NFL	15	15	4.0
Pro totals (8 years)	114	99	47.5

BURNS, KEITH   LB   BRONCOS

PERSONAL: Born May 16, 1972, in Greelyville, S.C. ... 6-2/236. ... Full name: Keith Bernard Burns.
HIGH SCHOOL: T. C. Williams (Alexandria, Va.).
JUNIOR COLLEGE: Navarro College (Texas).
COLLEGE: Oklahoma State.
TRANSACTIONS/CAREER NOTES: Selected by Denver Broncos in seventh round (210th pick overall) of 1994 NFL draft. ... Signed by Broncos (July 12, 1994). ... Granted free agency (February 14, 1997). ... Re-signed by Broncos (June 30, 1997).
PLAYING EXPERIENCE: Denver NFL, 1994-1997. ... Games/Games started: 1994 (11/1), 1995 (16/0), 1996 (16/0), 1997 (16/0). Total: 59/1.
CHAMPIONSHIP GAME EXPERIENCE: Played in AFC championship game (1997 season). ... Member of Super Bowl championship team (1997 season).
PRO STATISTICS: 1995—Credited with 1 1/2 sacks, returned one kickoff for five yards and recovered two fumbles. 1997—Returned four kickoffs for 45 yards.

BURNS, LAMONT   G   JETS

PERSONAL: Born March 16, 1974, in Greensboro, N.C. ... 6-4/300. ... Full name: Lamont Antonio Burns.
HIGH SCHOOL: Page (Greensboro, N.C.).
COLLEGE: East Carolina.
TRANSACTIONS/CAREER NOTES: Selected by New York Jets in fifth round (131st pick overall) of 1997 NFL draft. ... Signed by Jets (July 9, 1997).
PLAYING EXPERIENCE: New York Jets NFL, 1997. ... Games/Games started: 4/3.

BURRIS, JEFF   CB/PR   COLTS

PERSONAL: Born June 7, 1972, in York, S.C. ... 6-0/190. ... Full name: Jeffrey Lamar Burris.
HIGH SCHOOL: Northwestern (Rock Hill, S.C.).
COLLEGE: Notre Dame.
TRANSACTIONS/CAREER NOTES: Selected by Buffalo Bills in first round (27th pick overall) of 1994 NFL draft. ... Signed by Bills (July 18, 1994). ... On injured reserve (November 20, 1995-remainder of season). ... Granted unconditional free agency (February 13, 1998). ... Signed by Indianapolis Colts (February 18, 1998).
HONORS: Named defensive back on THE SPORTING NEWS college All-America second team (1993).
PRO STATISTICS: 1994—Recovered one fumble. 1996—Recovered one fumble. 1997—Returned one kickoff for 10 yards and recovered one fumble.

| | | | INTERCEPTIONS | | | | PUNT RETURNS | | | | TOTALS | | |
Year Team	G	GS	No.	Yds.	Avg.	TD	No.	Yds.	Avg.	TD	TD	2pt.	Pts.	Fum.
1994—Buffalo NFL	16	0	2	24	12.0	0	32	332	10.4	0	0	0	0	2
1995—Buffalo NFL	9	9	1	19	19.0	0	20	229	11.5	0	0	0	0	0
1996—Buffalo NFL	15	15	1	28	28.0	0	27	286	10.6	0	0	0	0	1
1997—Buffalo NFL	14	14	2	19	9.5	0	21	198	9.4	0	0	0	0	3
Pro totals (4 years)	54	38	6	90	15.0	0	100	1045	10.5	0	0	0	0	6

BURROUGH, JOHN   DL   FALCONS

PERSONAL: Born May 17, 1972, in Laramie, Wyo. ... 6-5/275.
HIGH SCHOOL: Pinedale (Wyo.).
COLLEGE: Wyoming.
TRANSACTIONS/CAREER NOTES: Selected by Atlanta Falcons in seventh round (245th pick overall) of 1995 NFL draft. ... Signed by Falcons (June 30, 1995). ... Granted free agency (February 13, 1998). ... Re-signed by Falcons (April 1, 1998).
PLAYING EXPERIENCE: Atlanta NFL, 1995-1997. ... Games/Games started: 1995 (16/0), 1996 (16/1), 1997 (16/1). Total: 48/2.
PRO STATISTICS: 1997—Returned one kickoff for six yards and credited with one sack.

BURROUGHS, SAMMIE   LB   COLTS

PERSONAL: Born June 21, 1973, in Pomona, Calif. ... 6-0/227.
HIGH SCHOOL: Pomona (Calif.).
JUNIOR COLLEGE: Mt. San Antonio (Calif.).
COLLEGE: Portland State.
TRANSACTIONS/CAREER NOTES: Signed as non-drafted free agent by Indianapolis Colts (April 26, 1996).
PLAYING EXPERIENCE: Indianapolis NFL, 1996 and 1997. ... Games/Games started: 1996 (16/1), 1997 (16/1). Total: 32/2.
PRO STATISTICS: 1997—Credited with one sack.

BURTON, JAMES   CB   SEAHAWKS

PERSONAL: Born April 27, 1971, in Torrance, Calif. ... 5-9/184.
HIGH SCHOOL: Polytechnic (Long Beach, Calif.).
COLLEGE: Fresno State.
TRANSACTIONS/CAREER NOTES: Selected by Kansas City Chiefs in fifth round (151st pick overall) of 1994 NFL draft. ... Signed by Chiefs (July 20, 1994). ... Released by Chiefs (August 29, 1994). ... Signed by Chicago Bears (August 31, 1994). ... On injured reserve with shoulder injury (November 22, 1995-remainder of season). ... On injured reserve (November 11-26, 1997). ... Released by Bears (November 26, 1997). ... Signed by Seattle Seahawks for 1998 season.
PLAYING EXPERIENCE: Chicago NFL, 1994-1997. ... Games/Games started: 1994 (13/1), 1995 (11/2), 1996 (16/3), 1997 (5/1). Total: 40/6.
PRO STATISTICS: 1996—Intercepted one pass for 11 yards.

BURTON, KENDRICK   DE   OILERS

PERSONAL: Born September 7, 1973, in Decatur, Ala. ... 6-5/288. ... Full name: Kendrick Duran Burton.
HIGH SCHOOL: Hartselle (Ala.).
COLLEGE: Alabama.
TRANSACTIONS/CAREER NOTES: Selected by Houston Oilers in fourth round (107th pick overall) of 1996 NFL draft. ... Signed by Oilers (July 16, 1996). ... Oilers franchise moved to Tennessee for 1997 season. ... On suspended list for violating league substance abuse policy (July 16, 1997-entire season).
PLAYING EXPERIENCE: Houston NFL, 1996. ... Games/Games started: 1996 (4/2).
PRO STATISTICS: 1996—Recovered one fumble for nine yards.

BURTON, SHANE   DT   DOLPHINS

PERSONAL: Born January 18, 1974, in Catawba, N.C. ... 6-6/310. ... Full name: Franklin Shane Burton.
HIGH SCHOOL: Bandys (Catawba, N.C.).
COLLEGE: Tennessee.
TRANSACTIONS/CAREER NOTES: Selected by Miami Dolphins in fifth round (150th pick overall) of 1996 NFL draft. ... Signed by Dolphins (June 18, 1996).
PRO STATISTICS: 1996—Recovered one fumble. 1997—Recovered one fumble.

Year Team	G	GS	SACKS
1996—Miami NFL	10	0	3.0
1997—Miami NFL	16	4	4.0
Pro totals (2 years)	32	12	7.0

BUSH, DEVIN   S   FALCONS

PERSONAL: Born July 3, 1973, in Miami. ... 5-11/210.
HIGH SCHOOL: Hialeah Miami Lakes.
COLLEGE: Florida State.
TRANSACTIONS/CAREER NOTES: Selected after junior season by Atlanta Falcons in first round (26th pick overall) of 1995 NFL draft. ... Signed by Falcons (August 8, 1995).
PRO STATISTICS: 1995—Recovered one fumble. 1996—Recovered one fumble. 1997—Recovered one fumble.

			INTERCEPTIONS			
Year Team	G	GS	No.	Yds.	Avg.	TD
1995—Atlanta NFL	11	5	1	0	0.0	0
1996—Atlanta NFL	16	15	1	2	2.0	0
1997—Atlanta NFL	16	16	1	4	4.0	0
Pro totals (3 years)	43	36	3	6	2.0	0

BUSH, LEW   LB   CHARGERS

PERSONAL: Born December 2, 1969, in Atlanta. ... 6-2/245. ... Full name: Lewis Fitzgerald Bush.
HIGH SCHOOL: Washington (Tacoma, Wash.).
COLLEGE: Washington State.
TRANSACTIONS/CAREER NOTES: Selected by San Diego Chargers in fourth round (99th pick overall) of 1993 NFL draft. ... Signed by Chargers (July 9, 1993). ... Granted free agency (February 16, 1996). ... Re-signed by Chargers (June 14, 1996). ... Granted unconditional free agency (February 14, 1997). ... Re-signed by Chargers (May 13, 1997).
PLAYING EXPERIENCE: San Diego NFL, 1993-1997. ... Games/Games started: 1993 (16/0), 1994 (16/0), 1995 (16/15), 1996 (16/16), 1997 (14/13). Total: 78/44.
CHAMPIONSHIP GAME EXPERIENCE: Played in AFC championship game (1994 season). ... Played in Super Bowl XXIX (1994 season).
PRO STATISTICS: 1994—Recovered one fumble. 1995—Intercepted one pass and recovered two fumbles. 1996—Credited with one sack and recovered two fumbles.

BUSH, STEVE   TE   BENGALS

PERSONAL: Born July 4, 1974, in Phoenix. ... 6-3/258. ... Full name: Steven Jack Bush.
HIGH SCHOOL: Paradise Valley (Phoenix).
COLLEGE: Arizona State.
TRANSACTIONS/CAREER NOTES: Signed as non-drafted free agent by Cincinnati Bengals (April 25, 1997).
PLAYING EXPERIENCE: Cincinnati NFL, 1997. ... Games/Games started: 16/0.
SINGLE GAME HIGHS (regular season): Receptions—0; yards—0; and touchdown receptions—0.

BUTLER, DUANE   S   VIKINGS

PERSONAL: Born November 29, 1973 ... 6-1/203.
HIGH SCHOOL: Madison (Trotwood, Ohio).
COLLEGE: Eastern Michigan, then Illinois State.
TRANSACTIONS/CAREER NOTES: Signed as a non-drafted free agent by New York Jets (April 25, 1997). ... Released by Jets (August 10, 1997). ... Signed by Minnesota Vikings (August 13, 1997). ... Released by Vikings (August 18, 1997). ... Re-signed by Vikings to practice squad (August 25, 1997). ... Activated (October 8, 1997). ... Released by Vikings (November 13, 1997). ... Re-signed by Vikings to practice squad (November 14, 1997). ... Activated (November 26, 1997). ... Assigned by Vikings to England Monarchs in 1998 NFL Europe enhancement allocation program (February 18, 1998).
PLAYING EXPERIENCE: Minnesota NFL, 1997. ... Games/Games started: 3/0.

BUTLER, KEVIN   K

PERSONAL: Born July 24, 1962, in Savannah, Ga. ... 6-1/200. ... Full name: Kevin Gregory Butler.
HIGH SCHOOL: Redan (Stone Mountain, Ga.).
COLLEGE: Georgia.
TRANSACTIONS/CAREER NOTES: Selected by Jacksonville Bulls in 1985 USFL territorial draft. ... Selected by Chicago Bears in fourth round (105th pick overall) of 1985 NFL draft. ... Signed by Bears (July 23, 1985). ... Granted free agency (February 1, 1991). ... Re-signed by Bears (August 6, 1991). ... Granted unconditional free agency (February 17, 1994). ... Re-signed by Bears (June 4, 1994). ... Released by Bears (August 20, 1996). ... Signed by Arizona Cardinals (November 5, 1996). ... Released by Cardinals (October 15, 1997).
CHAMPIONSHIP GAME EXPERIENCE: Played in NFC championship game (1985 and 1988 seasons). ... Member of Super Bowl championship team (1985 season).
HONORS: Named kicker on THE SPORTING NEWS college All-America second team (1984).
RECORDS: Holds NFL rookie-season record for most points—144 (1985).

			KICKING						
Year Team	G	GS	XPM	XPA	FGM	FGA	Lg.	50+	Pts.
1985—Chicago NFL	16	0	51	51	‡31	‡37	46	0-2	*144
1986—Chicago NFL	16	0	36	37	‡28	†41	52	1-6	‡120
1987—Chicago NFL	12	0	28	30	19	28	52	2-6	85
1988—Chicago NFL	16	0	37	38	15	19	45	0-0	82
1989—Chicago NFL	16	0	43	45	15	19	46	0-1	88
1990—Chicago NFL	16	0	36	37	26	37	52	4-7	114

B

Year Team	G	GS	XPM	XPA	FGM	FGA	Lg.	50+	Pts.
						KICKING			
1991—Chicago NFL	16	0	32	34	19	29	50	1-3	89
1992—Chicago NFL	16	0	34	34	19	26	50	1-3	91
1993—Chicago NFL	16	0	21	22	27	36	55	5-8	102
1994—Chicago NFL	15	0	24	24	21	29	52	2-4	87
1995—Chicago NFL	16	0	45	45	23	31	47	0-2	114
1996—Arizona NFL	7	0	17	19	14	17	41	0-0	59
1997—Arizona NFL	6	0	9	10	8	12	49	0-0	33
Pro totals (13 years)	184	0	413	426	265	361	55	16-42	1208

BUTLER, LeROY   S   PACKERS

B

PERSONAL: Born July 19, 1968, in Jacksonville. ... 6-0/200. ... Full name: LeRoy Butler III.

HIGH SCHOOL: Robert E. Lee Senior (Jacksonville).

COLLEGE: Florida State.

TRANSACTIONS/CAREER NOTES: Selected by Green Bay Packers in second round (48th pick overall) of 1990 NFL draft. ... Signed by Packers (July 25, 1990). ... On suspended list (December 9, 1992). ... Designated by Packers as transition player (February 15, 1994).

CHAMPIONSHIP GAME EXPERIENCE: Played in NFC championship game (1995-97 seasons). ... Member of Super Bowl championship team (1996 season). ... Played in Super Bowl XXXII (1997 season).

HONORS: Named strong safety on THE SPORTING NEWS NFL All-Pro team (1993, 1996 and 1997). ... Played in Pro Bowl (1993, 1996 and 1997 seasons).

PRO STATISTICS: 1991—Recovered one fumble. 1992—Recovered one fumble for 17 yards. 1993—Ran 25 yards with lateral from fumble recovery for a touchdown. 1996—Recovered two fumbles for two yards. 1997—Recovered one fumble.

Year Team	G	GS	INTERCEPTIONS No.	Yds.	Avg.	TD	SACKS No.
1990—Green Bay NFL	16	0	3	42	14.0	0	0.0
1991—Green Bay NFL	16	16	3	6	2.0	0	0.0
1992—Green Bay NFL	15	15	1	0	0.0	0	0.0
1993—Green Bay NFL	16	16	6	131	21.8	0	1.0
1994—Green Bay NFL	13	13	3	68	22.7	0	1.0
1995—Green Bay NFL	16	16	5	105	21.0	0	1.0
1996—Green Bay NFL	16	16	5	149	29.8	1	6.5
1997—Green Bay NFL	16	16	5	4	0.8	0	3.0
Pro totals (8 years)	124	108	31	505	16.3	1	12.5

BYARS, KEITH   FB   JETS

PERSONAL: Born October 14, 1963, in Dayton, Ohio. ... 6-1/255. ... Full name: Keith Alan Byars.

HIGH SCHOOL: Nettie Lee Roth (Dayton, Ohio).

COLLEGE: Ohio State.

TRANSACTIONS/CAREER NOTES: Selected by New Jersey Generals in 1986 USFL territorial draft. ... Selected by Philadelphia Eagles in first round (10th pick overall) of 1986 NFL draft. ... Signed by Eagles (July 25, 1986). ... Granted free agency (February 1, 1990). ... Re-signed by Eagles (August 10, 1990). ... Granted unconditional free agency (March 1, 1993). ... Signed by Miami Dolphins (July 15, 1993). ... On injured reserve with knee injury (November 9, 1994-remainder of season). ... Released by Dolphins (February 15, 1996). ... Re-signed by Dolphins (March 21, 1996). ... Released by Dolphins (October 1, 1996). ... Signed by New England Patriots (October 15, 1996). ... Granted unconditional free agency (February 13, 1998). ... Signed by New York Jets (February 25, 1998).

CHAMPIONSHIP GAME EXPERIENCE: Played in AFC championship game (1996 season). ... Played in Super Bowl XXXI (1996 season).

HONORS: Named running back on THE SPORTING NEWS college All-America first team (1984). ... Played in Pro Bowl (1993 season).

PRO STATISTICS: 1986—Attempted two passes with one completion for 55 yards and a touchdown, returned two kickoffs for 47 yards and recovered two fumbles. 1987—Recovered two fumbles. 1988—Attempted two passes without a completion, returned two kickoffs for 20 yards and recovered two fumbles for 14 yards. 1989—Recovered four fumbles for six yards and returned one kickoff for 27 yards. 1990—Attempted four passes with four completions for 53 yards and four touchdowns and recovered one fumble. 1991—Attempted two passes without a completion and with one interception. 1992—Attempted one pass without a completion and recovered one fumble. 1993—Attempted two passes with one completion for 11 yards and a touchdown.

SINGLE GAME HIGHS (regular season): Attempts—24 (December 7, 1986, vs. St. Louis); yards—127 (December 7, 1986, vs. St. Louis); and rushing touchdowns—2 (October 29, 1989, vs. Denver).

STATISTICAL PLATEAUS: 100-yard rushing games: 1986 (1), 1987 (1). Total: 2. ... 100-yard receiving games: 1989 (2), 1990 (2), 1991 (1). Total: 5.

Year Team	G	GS	RUSHING Att.	Yds.	Avg.	TD	RECEIVING No.	Yds.	Avg.	TD	TOTALS TD	2pt.	Pts.	Fum.
1986—Philadelphia NFL	16	8	177	577	3.3	1	11	44	4.0	0	1	...	6	3
1987—Philadelphia NFL	10	8	116	426	3.7	3	21	177	8.4	1	4	...	24	3
1988—Philadelphia NFL	16	16	152	517	3.4	6	72	705	9.8	4	10	...	60	5
1989—Philadelphia NFL	16	15	133	452	3.4	5	68	721	10.6	0	5	...	30	4
1990—Philadelphia NFL	16	15	37	141	3.8	0	81	819	10.1	3	3	...	18	4
1991—Philadelphia NFL	16	16	94	383	4.1	1	62	564	9.1	3	4	...	24	5
1992—Philadelphia NFL	15	15	41	176	4.3	1	56	502	9.0	2	3	...	18	1
1993—Miami NFL	16	16	64	269	4.2	3	61	613	10.0	3	6	...	36	3
1994—Miami NFL	9	9	19	64	3.4	2	49	418	8.5	5	7	0	42	0
1995—Miami NFL	16	16	15	44	2.9	1	51	362	7.1	2	3	0	18	0
1996—Miami NFL	4	4	0	0	...	0	5	40	8.0	0	0	0	0	0
—New England NFL	10	6	2	2	1.0	0	27	249	9.2	2	2	1	14	0
1997—New England NFL	16	8	11	24	2.2	0	20	180	0.5	3	3	0	18	1
Pro totals (12 years)	176	152	861	3075	3.6	23	584	5403	9.3	28	51	1	308	29

BYNER, EARNEST   RB

PERSONAL: Born September 15, 1962, in Milledgeville, Ga. ... 5-10/225. ... Full name: Earnest Alexander Byner.
HIGH SCHOOL: Baldwin (Milledgeville, Ga.).
COLLEGE: East Carolina.
TRANSACTIONS/CAREER NOTES: Selected by Cleveland Browns in 10th round (280th pick overall) of 1984 NFL draft. ... On injured reserve with ankle injury (October 21, 1986-January 10, 1987). ... Granted free agency (February 1, 1989). ... Re-signed by Browns and traded to Washington Redskins for RB Mike Oliphant (April 23, 1989). ... Granted unconditional free agency (February 17, 1994). ... Signed by Browns (May 5, 1994). ... Browns franchise moved to Baltimore and renamed Ravens for 1996 season (March 11, 1996). ... Granted unconditional free agency (February 16, 1996). ... Re-signed by Ravens (April 26, 1996). ... Released by Ravens (March 27, 1998). ... Announced retirement following 1997 season.
CHAMPIONSHIP GAME EXPERIENCE: Played in AFC championship game (1986 and 1987 seasons). ... Played in NFC championship game (1991 season). ... Member of Super Bowl championship team (1991 season).
HONORS: Played in Pro Bowl (1990 and 1991 seasons).
PRO STATISTICS: 1984—Recovered two fumbles for 55 yards and a touchdown. 1985—Recovered four fumbles. 1987—Recovered one fumble. 1988—Recovered two fumbles. 1990—Attempted one pass without a completion and recovered two fumbles. 1990—Attempted two passes with one completion for 31 yards and a touchdown and recovered one fumble. 1991—Attempted four passes with one completion for 18 yards and a touchdown and recovered one fumble. 1992—Attempted three passes with one completion for 41 yards and a touchdown. 1993—Recovered one fumble. 1995—Recovered three fumbles.
SINGLE GAME HIGHS (regular season): Attempts—39 (December 15, 1990, vs. New England); yards—188 (December 16, 1984, vs. Houston); and rushing touchdowns—3 (December 2, 1990, vs. Miami).
STATISTICAL PLATEAUS: 100-yard rushing games: 1984 (1), 1985 (2), 1989 (1), 1990 (5), 1991 (4), 1992 (2), 1995 (1), 1996 (1). Total: 17.

			RUSHING				RECEIVING				KICKOFF RETURNS				TOTALS			
Year Team	G	GS	Att.	Yds.	Avg.	TD	No.	Yds.	Avg.	TD	No.	Yds.	Avg.	TD	TD	2pt	Pts.	Fum.
1984—Cleveland NFL	16	3	72	426	5.9	2	11	118	10.7	0	22	415	18.9	0	3	...	18	3
1985—Cleveland NFL	16	13	244	1002	4.1	8	45	460	10.2	2	0	0	...	0	10	...	60	5
1986—Cleveland NFL	7	7	94	277	2.9	2	37	328	8.9	2	0	0	...	0	4	...	24	1
1987—Cleveland NFL	12	12	105	432	4.1	4	52	552	10.6	2	1	2	2.0	0	10	...	60	5
1988—Cleveland NFL	16	16	157	576	3.7	3	59	576	9.8	2	0	0	...	0	5	...	30	5
1989—Washington NFL	16	13	134	580	4.3	7	54	458	8.5	2	0	0	...	0	9	...	54	2
1990—Washington NFL	16	16	*297	1219	4.1	6	31	279	9.0	1	0	0	...	0	7	...	42	2
1991—Washington NFL	16	16	274	1048	3.8	5	34	308	9.1	0	0	0	...	0	5	...	30	3
1992—Washington NFL	16	16	262	998	3.8	6	39	338	8.7	1	0	0	...	0	7	...	42	1
1993—Washington NFL	16	3	23	105	4.6	1	27	194	7.2	0	0	0	...	0	1	...	6	0
1994—Cleveland NFL	16	1	75	219	2.9	2	11	102	9.3	0	0	0	...	0	2	0	12	0
1995—Cleveland NFL	16	2	115	432	3.8	2	61	494	8.1	2	5	98	19.6	0	4	0	24	1
1996—Baltimore NFL	16	8	159	634	4.0	4	30	270	9.0	1	4	61	15.3	0	5	0	30	1
1997—Baltimore NFL	16	6	84	313	3.7	0	21	128	6.1	0	1	0	0.0	0	0	1	2	2
Pro totals (14 years)	211	132	2095	8261	3.9	56	512	4605	9.0	15	33	576	17.5	0	72	1	434	31

BYNUM, KENNY   RB   CHARGERS

PERSONAL: Born May 29, 1974, in Gainesville, Fla. ... 5-11/191. ... Full name: Kenneth Bynum.
HIGH SCHOOL: Gainesville (Fla.).
COLLEGE: South Carolina State.
TRANSACTIONS/CAREER NOTES: Selected by San Diego Chargers in fifth round (138th pick overall) of 1997 NFL draft. ... Signed by Chargers (June 16, 1997).
SINGLE GAME HIGHS (regular season): Attempts—11 (November 23, 1997, San Francisco); yards—64 (November 23, 1997, vs. San Francisco); and rushing touchdowns—0.

			RUSHING				RECEIVING				KICKOFF RETURNS				TOTALS		
Year Team	G	GS	Att.	Yds.	Avg.	TD	No.	Yds.	Avg.	TD	No.	Yds.	Avg.	TD	TD	2pt	Pts.
1997—San Diego NFL	13	0	30	97	3.2	0	2	4	2.0	0	38	814	21.4	0	0	0	0

BYRD, ISAAC   WR   OILERS

PERSONAL: Born November 11, 1974, in St. Louis. ... 6-0/173. ... Full name: Isaac Byrd III. ... Brother of Israel Byrd, cornerback, New Orleans Saints (1994 and 1995).
HIGH SCHOOL: Parkway Central (Chesterfield, Mo.).
COLLEGE: Kansas.
TRANSACTIONS/CAREER NOTES: Selected by Kansas City Chiefs in sixth round (195th pick overall) of 1997 NFL draft. ... Signed by Chiefs (May 6, 1997). ... Released by Chiefs (August 23, 1997). ... Re-signed by Chiefs to practice squad (August 25, 1997). ... Signed by Tennessee Oilers off Chiefs practice squad (November 7, 1997).
PLAYING EXPERIENCE: Tennessee NFL, 1997. ... Games/Games started: 2/0.

RECORD AS BASEBALL PLAYER

TRANSACTIONS/CAREER NOTES: Selected by San Diego Padres organization in 24th round of free-agent draft (June 3, 1993); did not sign. ... Drafted by St. Louis Cardinals organization in 11th round of free agent draft (June 2, 1996).

							BATTING							FIELDING		
Year Team (League)	Pos.	G	AB	R	H	2B	3B	HR	RBI	Avg.	BB	SO	SB	PO	A	E	Avg.
1996—Johnson City (Appal.)	OF	24	94	16	26	6	1	2	15	.277	8	19	5	37	1	1	.974

CADREZ, GLENN   LB   BRONCOS

PERSONAL: Born January 2, 1970, in El Centro, Calif. ... 6-3/249. ... Full name: Glenn E. Cadrez. ... Name pronounced kuh-DREZ.
HIGH SCHOOL: El Centro (Calif.) Central Union.
JUNIOR COLLEGE: Chaffey College (Calif.).
COLLEGE: Houston.

TRANSACTIONS/CAREER NOTES: Selected by New York Jets in sixth round (154th pick overall) of 1992 NFL draft. ... Signed by Jets (July 13, 1992). ... Released by Jets (September 19, 1995). ... Signed by Denver Broncos (September 27, 1995).
PLAYING EXPERIENCE: New York Jets NFL, 1992-1994; New York Jets (1)-Denver (10) NFL, 1995; Denver NFL, 1996 and 1997. ... Games/Games started: 1992 (16/0), 1993 (16/0), 1994 (16/0), 1995 (NYJ: 1/0; Den.:10/7; Total: 11/7), 1996 (16/0), 1997 (16/0). Total: 91/7.
CHAMPIONSHIP GAME EXPERIENCE: Played in AFC championship game (1997 season). ... Member of Super Bowl championship team (1997 season).
PRO STATISTICS: 1992—Recovered one fumble. 1994—Returned one kickoff for 10 yards and recovered one fumble. 1995—Credited with two sacks and recovered one fumble. 1996—Recovered one fumble.

CAIN, JOE　　　　LB　　　　SEAHAWKS

PERSONAL: Born June 11, 1965, in Los Angeles. ... 6-1/242. ... Full name: Joseph Harrison Cain Jr.
HIGH SCHOOL: Compton (Calif.).
COLLEGE: Stanford, then Oregon Tech.
TRANSACTIONS/CAREER NOTES: Selected by Minnesota Vikings in eighth round (210th pick overall) of 1988 NFL draft. ... Signed by Vikings (July 24, 1988). ... Released by Vikings (August 30, 1988). ... Signed by Seattle Seahawks (March 31, 1989). ... Released by Seahawks (September 5, 1989). ... Re-signed by Seahawks to developmental squad (September 6, 1989). ... Activated (October 13, 1989). ... Granted unconditional free agency (February 1-April 1, 1992). ... Re-signed by Seahawks (July 23, 1992). ... Granted free agency (March 1, 1993). ... Tendered offer sheet by Chicago Bears (March 10, 1993). ... Seahawks declined to match offer (March 15, 1993); Seahawks received eighth-round pick (DE Antonio Edwards) in 1993 draft as compensation. ... Granted unconditional free agency (February 17, 1995). ... Re-signed by Bears (February 27, 1995). ... Granted unconditional free agency (February 14, 1997). ... Signed by Seahawks (May 15, 1997).
PRO STATISTICS: 1992—Recovered one fumble. 1994—Recovered one fumble. 1996—Credited with one sack. 1997—Recovered one fumble.

			INTERCEPTIONS		
Year　Team	G	GS	No.	Yds.	Avg.	TD
1989—Seattle NFL	9	0	0	0	...	0
1990—Seattle NFL	16	5	0	0	...	0
1991—Seattle NFL	16	0	1	5	5.0	0
1992—Seattle NFL	16	8	2	3	1.5	0
1993—Chicago NFL	15	15	0	0	...	0
1994—Chicago NFL	16	15	0	0	...	0
1995—Chicago NFL	16	16	0	0	...	0
1996—Chicago NFL	16	15	0	0	...	0
1997—Seattle NFL	12	0	0	0	...	0
Pro totals (9 years)	132	74	3	8	2.7	0

CALDWELL, MIKE　　　　LB　　　　EAGLES

PERSONAL: Born August 31, 1971, in Oak Ridge, Tenn. ... 6-2/237. ... Full name: Mike Isiah Caldwell.
HIGH SCHOOL: Oak Ridge (Tenn.).
COLLEGE: Middle Tennessee State.
TRANSACTIONS/CAREER NOTES: Selected by Cleveland Browns in third round (83rd pick overall) of 1993 NFL draft. ... Signed by Browns (July 14, 1993). ... Granted free agency (February 16, 1996). ... Browns franchise moved to Baltimore and renamed Ravens for 1996 season (March 11, 1996). ... Re-signed by Ravens for 1996 season. ... Granted unconditional free agency (February 14, 1997). ... Signed by Arizona Cardinals (July 16, 1997). ... Granted unconditional free agency (February 13, 1998). ... Signed by Philadelphia Eagles (April 9, 1998).
PRO STATISTICS: 1993—Recovered one fumble. 1994—Returned one punt for two yards.

			INTERCEPTIONS			SACKS
Year　Team	G	GS	No.	Yds.	Avg.	TD	No.
1993—Cleveland NFL	15	1	0	0	...	0	0.0
1994—Cleveland NFL	16	1	1	0	0.0	0	0.0
1995—Cleveland NFL	16	6	2	24	12.0	1	0.0
1996—Baltimore NFL	9	9	1	45	45.0	1	4.5
1997—Arizona NFL	16	0	1	5	5.0	0	2.0
Pro totals (5 years)	72	17	5	74	14.8	2	6.5

CALICCHIO, LONNY　　　　P

PERSONAL: Born October 24, 1972, in Plantation, Fla. ... 6-3/230.
HIGH SCHOOL: South Plantation (Plantation, Fla.).
JUNIOR COLLEGE: Northwest Mississippi Community College.
COLLEGE: Mississippi.
TRANSACTIONS/CAREER NOTES: Signed as non-drafted free agent by Washington Redskins (June 12, 1996). ... Released by Redskins (July 30, 1996). ... Signed by Dallas Cowboys (March 26, 1997). ... Released by Cowboys (August 17, 1997). ... Signed by Philadelphia Eagles to practice squad (September 23, 1997). ... Activated (September 27, 1997). ... Released by Eagles (September 29, 1997). ... Re-signed by Eagles to practice squad (October 2, 1997). ... Activated (October 29, 1997). ... Released by Eagles (November 4, 1997). ... Signed by Buffalo Bills to practice squad (December 1, 1997). ... Granted free agency after 1997 season.
PLAYING EXPERIENCE: Philadelphia NFL, 1997. ... Games/Games started: (2/0).

CALLOWAY, CHRIS　　　　WR　　　　GIANTS

PERSONAL: Born March 29, 1968, in Chicago. ... 5-10/191. ... Full name: Christopher Fitzpatrick Calloway.
HIGH SCHOOL: Mount Carmel (Chicago).
COLLEGE: Michigan (degree in communications and film, 1990).
TRANSACTIONS/CAREER NOTES: Selected by Pittsburgh Steelers in fourth round (97th pick overall) of 1990 NFL draft. ... Signed by Steelers (July 18, 1990). ... On injured reserve with knee injury (November 25, 1991-remainder of season). ... Granted unconditional free agency (February 1, 1992). ... Signed by New York Giants (April 1, 1992). ... Granted unconditional free agency (February 17, 1994). ... Re-signed by Giants (July 18, 1994). ... Granted unconditional free agency (February 16, 1996). ... Re-signed by Giants (April 2, 1996).

PRO STATISTICS: 1991—Recovered one fumble. 1992—Returned two kickoffs for 29 yards. 1993—Returned six kickoffs for 89 yards and recovered one fumble. 1996—Recovered one fumble for seven yards.
SINGLE GAME HIGHS (regular season): Receptions—9 (October 20, 1996, vs. Washington); yards—145 (October 19, 1997, vs. Detroit); and touchdown receptions—1 (November 10, 1996, vs. Carolina).
STATISTICAL PLATEAUS: 100-yard receiving games: 1995 (1), 1996 (1), 1997 (1). Total: 3.

Year Team	G	GS	RUSHING				RECEIVING				TOTALS			
			Att.	Yds.	Avg.	TD	No.	Yds.	Avg.	TD	TD	2pt.	Pts.	Fum.
1990—Pittsburgh NFL	16	2	0	0	...	0	10	124	12.4	1	1	...	6	0
1991—Pittsburgh NFL	12	0	0	0	...	0	15	254	16.9	1	1	...	6	0
1992—New York Giants NFL	16	1	0	0	...	0	27	335	12.4	1	1	...	6	0
1993—New York Giants NFL	16	9	0	0	...	0	35	513	14.7	3	3	...	18	0
1994—New York Giants NFL	16	14	8	77	9.6	0	43	666	15.5	2	2	0	12	1
1995—New York Giants NFL	16	15	2	-9	-4.5	0	56	796	14.2	3	3	0	18	0
1996—New York Giants NFL	16	15	1	2	2.0	0	53	739	13.9	4	4	0	24	1
1997—New York Giants NFL	16	16	1	-1	-1.0	0	58	849	14.6	8	8	0	48	0
Pro totals (8 years)	124	72	12	69	5.8	0	297	4276	14.4	23	23	0	138	2

CAMPBELL, JESSE   S   REDSKINS

PERSONAL: Born April 11, 1969, in Washington, N.C. ... 6-1/211.
HIGH SCHOOL: West Craven (Vanceboro, N.C.).
COLLEGE: North Carolina State.
TRANSACTIONS/CAREER NOTES: Selected after junior season by Philadelphia Eagles in second round (48th pick overall) of 1991 NFL draft. ... Signed by Eagles (July 17, 1991). ... On injured reserve with knee injury (August 27-October 23, 1991). ... On practice squad (October 23, 1991-remainder of season). ... Released by Eagles (September 4, 1992). ... Signed by New York Giants (September 7, 1992). ... Released by Giants (September 21, 1992). ... Signed by Giants to practice squad (September 23, 1992). ... Activated (October 21, 1992). ... Granted free agency (February 17, 1994). ... Re-signed by Giants (July 17, 1994). ... Granted unconditional free agency (February 17, 1995). ... Re-signed by Giants (February 24, 1995). ... Released by Giants (February 14, 1997). ... Signed by Washington Redskins (April 5, 1997).
HONORS: Named defensive back on The Sporting News college All-America first team (1990).
PRO STATISTICS: 1992—Recovered one fumble. 1994—Recovered two fumbles for three yards. 1996—Recovered one fumble. 1997—Recovered two fumbles for minus one yard.

Year Team	G	GS	INTERCEPTIONS			
			No.	Yds.	Avg.	TD
1991—Philadelphia NFL				Did not play.		
1992—New York Giants NFL	11	0	0	0	...	0
1993—New York Giants NFL	16	0	1	0	0.0	0
1994—New York Giants NFL	14	10	2	3	1.5	0
1995—New York Giants NFL	16	16	0	0	...	0
1996—New York Giants NFL	16	16	2	14	7.0	0
1997—Washington NFL	16	16	1	7	7.0	0
Pro totals (6 years)	89	58	6	24	4.0	0

CAMPBELL, MARK   DE   FALCONS

PERSONAL: Born September 12, 1972, in Jamaica. ... 6-1/293. ... Full name: Mark Anthony Campbell.
HIGH SCHOOL: Sunset (Miami).
COLLEGE: Florida.
TRANSACTIONS/CAREER NOTES: Selected by Denver Broncos in third round (78th pick overall) of 1996 NFL draft. ... Signed by Broncos (July 16, 1996). ... Released by Broncos (August 14, 1997). ... Signed by Arizona Cardinals for 1997 season. ... Released by Cardinals (February 12, 1998). ... Signed by Atlanta Falcons (April 22, 1998).

Year Team	G	GS	SACKS
1997—Arizona NFL	5	0	0.0

CAMPBELL, MATHEW   OT   PANTHERS

PERSONAL: Born July 14, 1972, in North Augusta, S.C. ... 6-4/270. ... Full name: Mathew Thomas Campbell.
HIGH SCHOOL: North Augusta (S.C.).
COLLEGE: South Carolina.
TRANSACTIONS/CAREER NOTES: Signed as non-drafted free agent by New Orleans Saints (April 28, 1994). ... Released by Saints (August 23, 1994). ... Re-signed by Saints to practice squad (August 30, 1994). ... Signed by Saints (September 20, 1994). ... Signed by Carolina Panthers (December 15, 1994). ... Granted free agency (February 13, 1998). ... Tendered offer sheet by Miami Dolphins (February 20, 1998). ... Offer matched by Panthers (February 27, 1998).
PLAYING EXPERIENCE: Carolina NFL, 1995-1997. ... Games/Games started: 1995 (10/1), 1996 (9/8), 1997 (16/14). Total: 35/23.
CHAMPIONSHIP GAME EXPERIENCE: Played in NFC championship game (1996 season).
PRO STATISTICS: 1995—Caught three passes for 32 yards and fumbled once.
MISCELLANEOUS: Played tight end during 1995 season.

CANTY, CHRIS   CB   PATRIOTS

PERSONAL: Born March 30, 1976, in Voorhees, N.J. ... 5-9/185. ... Full name: Christopher Shawn Patrick Canty.
HIGH SCHOOL: Eastern (Voorhees, N.J.).
COLLEGE: Kansas State.
TRANSACTIONS/CAREER NOTES: Selected after junior season by New England Patriots in first round (29th pick overall) of 1997 NFL draft. ... Signed by Patriots (July 17, 1997).
HONORS: Named defensive back on The Sporting News college All-America first team (1995). ... Named cornerback on The Sporting News college All-America first team (1996).
PLAYING EXPERIENCE: New England NFL, 1997. ... Games/Games started: 16/1.
PRO STATISTICS: 1997—Returned four kickoffs for 115 yards, credited with two sacks and recovered two fumbles for nine yards.

CARNEY, JOHN | K | CHARGERS

PERSONAL: Born April 20, 1964, in Hartford, Conn. ... 5-11/170. ... Full name: John Michael Carney.
HIGH SCHOOL: Cardinal Newman (West Palm Beach, Fla.).
COLLEGE: Notre Dame (degree in marketing, 1987).
TRANSACTIONS/CAREER NOTES: Signed as non-drafted free agent by Cincinnati Bengals (May 1, 1987). ... Released by Bengals (August 10, 1987). ... Signed as replacement player by Tampa Bay Buccaneers (September 24, 1987). ... Released by Buccaneers (October 14, 1987). ... Re-signed by Buccaneers (April 5, 1988). ... Released by Buccaneers (August 23, 1988). ... Re-signed by Buccaneers (November 22, 1988). ... Granted unconditional free agency (February 1-April 1, 1989). ... Re-signed by Buccaneers (April 13, 1989). ... Released by Buccaneers (September 5, 1989). ... Re-signed by Buccaneers (December 13, 1989). ... Granted unconditional free agency (February 1, 1990). ... Signed by San Diego Chargers (April 1, 1990). ... Released by Chargers (August 28, 1990). ... Signed by Los Angeles Rams (September 21, 1990). ... Released by Rams (September 26, 1990). ... Signed by Chargers (October 3, 1990). ... Granted free agency (February 1, 1992). ... Re-signed by Chargers (July 27, 1992). ... Granted free agency (March 1, 1993). ... Re-signed by Chargers (June 9, 1993). ... Granted unconditional free agency (February 17, 1994). ... Re-signed by Chargers (April 6, 1994). ... On injured reserve with knee injury (November 15, 1997-remainder of season).
CHAMPIONSHIP GAME EXPERIENCE: Played in AFC championship game (1994 season). ... Played in Super Bowl XXIX (1994 season).
HONORS: Named kicker on THE SPORTING NEWS NFL All-Pro team (1994). ... Played in Pro Bowl (1994 season).
PRO STATISTICS: 1993—Punted four times for 155 yards (38.8-yard average).

| | | | KICKING | | | | | | |
Year Team	G	GS	XPM	XPA	FGM	FGA	Lg.	50+	Pts.
1988—Tampa Bay NFL	4	0	6	6	2	5	29	0-0	12
1989—Tampa Bay NFL	1	0	0	0	0	0	...	0-0	0
1990—Los Angeles Rams NFL	1	0	0	0	0	0	...	0-0	0
—San Diego NFL	12	0	27	28	19	21	43	0-1	84
1991—San Diego NFL	16	0	31	31	19	29	54	2-4	88
1992—San Diego NFL	16	0	35	35	26	32	50	1-3	113
1993—San Diego NFL	16	0	31	33	31	40	51	2-3	124
1994—San Diego NFL	16	0	33	33	†34	§38	50	2-2	*135
1995—San Diego NFL	16	0	32	33	21	26	45	0-2	95
1996—San Diego NFL	16	0	31	31	29	36	53	3-3	118
1997—San Diego NFL	4	0	5	5	7	7	41	0-0	26
Pro totals (10 years)	118	0	231	235	188	234	54	10-18	795

CARPENTER, CHAD | WR | CARDINALS

PERSONAL: Born July 17, 1973, in Ontario, Ore. ... 5-11/198. ... Full name: Chad M. Carpenter.
HIGH SCHOOL: Weiser (Idaho).
COLLEGE: Washington State.
TRANSACTIONS/CAREER NOTES: Selected by Arizona Cardinals in fifth round (139th pick overall) of 1997 NFL draft. ... Signed by Cardinals (June 4, 1997). ... Released by Cardinals (August 24, 1997). ... Re-signed by Cardinals to practice squad (August 26, 1997).

CARRIER, MARK | WR | PANTHERS

PERSONAL: Born October 28, 1965, in Lafayette, La. ... 6-0/185. ... Full name: John Mark Carrier. ... Related to Mark Carrier, safety, Detroit Lions.
HIGH SCHOOL: Church Point (La.).
COLLEGE: Nicholls State (La.).
TRANSACTIONS/CAREER NOTES: Selected by Tampa Bay Buccaneers in third round (57th pick overall) of 1987 NFL draft. ... Signed by Buccaneers (July 18, 1987). ... Granted free agency (February 1, 1990). ... Re-signed by Buccaneers (August 13, 1990). ... Granted unconditional free agency (March 1, 1993). ... Signed by Cleveland Browns (April 7, 1993). ... Selected by Carolina Panthers from Browns in NFL expansion draft (February 15, 1995). ... Granted unconditional free agency (February 16, 1996). ... Re-signed by Panthers (April 2, 1996). ... Granted unconditional free agency (February 14, 1997). ... Re-signed by Panthers (September 17, 1997). ... On injured reserve with hand injury (December 5, 1997-remainder of season). ... Granted unconditional free agency (February 13, 1998). ... Re-signed by Panthers (February 19, 1998).
CHAMPIONSHIP GAME EXPERIENCE: Played in NFC championship game (1996 season).
HONORS: Played in Pro Bowl (1989 season).
PRO STATISTICS: 1987—Returned one kickoff for no yards. 1991—Recovered one fumble. 1993—Rushed four times for 26 yards and a touchdown. 1994—Rushed once for 14 yards and a touchdown and recovered one fumble. 1995—Rushed three times for minus four yards and recovered one fumble.
SINGLE GAME HIGHS (regular season): Receptions—10 (December 10, 1989, vs. Houston); yards—212 (December 6, 1987, vs. New Orleans); and touchdown receptions—2 (September 29, 1996, vs. Jacksonville).
STATISTICAL PLATEAUS: 100-yard receiving games: 1987 (1), 1988 (1), 1989 (8), 1990 (1), 1991 (1), 1992 (1), 1993 (2), 1995 (3), 1996 (1). Total: 19.
MISCELLANEOUS: Holds Carolina Panthers all-time records for most yards receiving (2,246) and most receptions (157).

| | | | RECEIVING | | | | PUNT RETURNS | | | | TOTALS | | |
Year Team	G	GS	No.	Yds.	Avg.	TD	No.	Yds.	Avg.	TD	TD	2pt.	Pts.	Fum.
1987—Tampa Bay NFL	10	5	26	423	16.3	3	0	0	...	0	3	...	18	0
1988—Tampa Bay NFL	16	16	57	970	17.0	5	0	0	...	0	5	...	30	2
1989—Tampa Bay NFL	16	15	86	1422	16.5	9	0	0	...	0	9	...	54	1
1990—Tampa Bay NFL	16	16	49	813	16.6	4	0	0	...	0	4	...	24	0
1991—Tampa Bay NFL	16	16	47	698	14.9	2	0	0	...	0	2	...	12	2
1992—Tampa Bay NFL	14	12	56	692	12.4	4	0	0	...	0	4	...	24	1
1993—Cleveland NFL	16	16	43	746	17.3	3	6	92	15.3	1	5	...	30	0
1994—Cleveland NFL	16	6	29	452	15.6	5	9	112	12.4	0	6	0	36	1
1995—Carolina NFL	16	15	66	1002	15.2	3	6	25	4.2	0	3	0	18	0
1996—Carolina NFL	16	15	58	808	13.9	6	0	0	...	0	6	0	36	0
1997—Carolina NFL	9	6	33	436	13.2	2	0	0	...	0	2	0	12	1
Pro totals (11 years)	161	138	550	8462	15.4	46	21	229	10.9	1	49	0	294	8

CARRIER, MARK   S   LIONS

PERSONAL: Born April 28, 1968, in Lake Charles, La. ... 6-1/192. ... Full name: Mark Anthony Carrier. ... Related to Mark Carrier, wide receiver, Carolina Panthers.
HIGH SCHOOL: Polytechnic (Long Beach, Calif.).
COLLEGE: Southern California (degree in communications).
TRANSACTIONS/CAREER NOTES: Selected after junior season by Chicago Bears in first round (sixth pick overall) of 1990 NFL draft. ... Signed by Bears (April 22, 1990). ... Designated by Bears as transition player (February 25, 1993). ... Released by Bears (June 1, 1997). ... Signed by Detroit Lions (June 20, 1997).
HONORS: Named defensive back on THE SPORTING NEWS college All-America second team (1988). ... Jim Thorpe Award winner (1989). ... Named defensive back on THE SPORTING NEWS college All-America first team (1989). ... Played in Pro Bowl (1990, 1991 and 1993 seasons). ... Named free safety on THE SPORTING NEWS NFL All-Pro team (1991).
PRO STATISTICS: 1990—Recovered two fumbles for 16 yards. 1991—Recovered one fumble for two yards. 1992—Recovered two fumbles. 1995—Recovered one fumble. 1996—Recovered one fumble. 1997—Returned one punt for no yards and fumbled once.
STATISTICAL PLATEAUS: 100-yard receiving games: 1995 (3).

			INTERCEPTIONS			
Year Team	G	GS	No.	Yds.	Avg.	TD
1990—Chicago NFL	16	16	*10	39	3.9	0
1991—Chicago NFL	16	16	2	54	27.0	0
1992—Chicago NFL	16	14	0	0	...	0
1993—Chicago NFL	16	16	4	94	23.5	1
1994—Chicago NFL	16	15	2	10	5.0	0
1995—Chicago NFL	16	15	0	0	...	0
1996—Chicago NFL	13	13	2	0	0.0	0
1997—Detroit NFL	16	16	5	94	18.8	0
Pro totals (8 years)	125	121	25	291	11.6	1

CARRUTH, RAE   WR   PANTHERS

PERSONAL: Born January 20, 1974, in Sacramento. ... 5-11/194. ... Full name: Rae Lamar Carruth.
HIGH SCHOOL: Valley (Sacramento).
COLLEGE: Colorado.
TRANSACTIONS/CAREER NOTES: Selected by Carolina Panthers in first round (27th pick overall) of 1997 NFL draft. ... Signed by Panthers (July 18, 1997).
HONORS: Named wide receiver on THE SPORTING NEWS college All-America first team (1996).
SINGLE GAME HIGHS (regular season): Receptions—8 (September 21, 1997, vs. Kansas City); yards—110 (September 21, 1997, vs. Kansas City); and touchdown receptions—1 (December 20, 1997, vs. St. Louis).
STATISTICAL PLATEAUS: 100-yard receiving games: 1997 (2).

			RUSHING				RECEIVING				TOTALS			
Year Team	G	GS	Att.	Yds.	Avg.	TD	No.	Yds.	Avg.	TD	TD	2pt.	Pts.	Fum.
1997—Carolina NFL	15	14	6	23	3.8	0	44	545	12.4	4	4	0	24	2

CARSWELL, DWAYNE   TE   BRONCOS

PERSONAL: Born January 18, 1972, in Jacksonville. ... 6-3/260.
HIGH SCHOOL: University Christian (Jacksonville).
COLLEGE: Liberty (Va.).
TRANSACTIONS/CAREER NOTES: Signed as non-drafted free agent by Denver Broncos (May 2, 1994). ... Released by Broncos (August 26, 1994). ... Re-signed by Broncos to practice squad (August 30, 1994). ... Activated (November 25, 1994).
CHAMPIONSHIP GAME EXPERIENCE: Played in AFC championship game (1997 season). ... Member of Super Bowl championship team (1997 season).
PRO STATISTICS: 1994—Returned one kickoff for no yards and recovered one fumble. 1997—Recovered one fumble.
SINGLE GAME HIGHS (regular season): Receptions—4 (September 14, 1997, vs. St. Louis); yards—47 (September 14, 1997, vs. St. Louis); and touchdown receptions—1 (September 14, 1997, vs. St. Louis).

			RECEIVING				TOTALS			
Year Team	G	GS	No.	Yds.	Avg.	TD	TD	2pt.	Pts.	Fum.
1994—Denver NFL	4	0	0	0	...	0	0	0	0	0
1995—Denver NFL	9	2	3	37	12.3	0	0	0	0	0
1996—Denver NFL	16	2	15	85	5.7	0	0	0	0	0
1997—Denver NFL	16	3	12	96	8.0	1	1	0	6	0
Pro totals (4 years)	45	7	30	218	7.3	1	1	0	6	0

CARTER, CHRIS   S   PATRIOTS

PERSONAL: Born September 27, 1974, in Tyler, Texas. ... 6-1/201. ... Full name: Christopher Cary Carter. ... Cousin of Joe Carter, first baseman/outfielder, Baltimore Orioles.
HIGH SCHOOL: John Tyler (Tyler, Texas).
COLLEGE: Texas.
TRANSACTIONS/CAREER NOTES: Selected by New England Patriots in third round (89th pick overall) of 1997 NFL draft. ... Signed by Patriots (July 15, 1997).
PLAYING EXPERIENCE: New England NFL, 1997. ... Games/Games started: 16/0.

CARTER, CRIS   WR   VIKINGS

PERSONAL: Born November 25, 1965, in Middletown, Ohio. ... 6-3/216. ... Full name: Christopher D. Carter. ... Brother of Butch Carter, guard/forward with four NBA teams (1980-81 through 1985-86).
HIGH SCHOOL: Middletown (Ohio).
COLLEGE: Ohio State.
TRANSACTIONS/CAREER NOTES: Selected by Philadelphia Eagles in fourth round of 1987 NFL supplemental draft (September 4, 1987). ... Signed by Eagles (September 17, 1987). ... Granted roster exemption (September 17-October 26, 1987). ... Claimed on waivers by Minnesota Vikings (September 4, 1990). ... Granted free agency (February 1, 1991). ... Re-signed by Vikings (July 9, 1991). ... Granted free agency (February 1, 1992). ... Re-signed by Vikings (July 26, 1992). ... On injured reserve with collarbone injury (December 4-30, 1992).
HONORS: Played in Pro Bowl (1993-1997 seasons). ... Named wide receiver on THE SPORTING NEWS NFL All-Pro team (1994).
PRO STATISTICS: 1987—Attempted one pass without a completion and returned 12 kickoffs for 241 yards. 1988—Recovered one fumble in end zone for a touchdown. 1989—Recovered one fumble. 1993—Recovered one fumble. 1996—Returned one kickoff for three yards and recovered one fumble.
SINGLE GAME HIGHS (regular season): Receptions—14 (October 2, 1994, vs. Arizona); yards—167 (October 2, 1994, vs. Arizona); and touchdown receptions—3 (December 21, 1997, vs. Indianapolis).
STATISTICAL PLATEAUS: 100-yard receiving games: 1988 (1), 1989 (1), 1990 (2), 1991 (4), 1992 (1), 1993 (3), 1994 (5), 1995 (5), 1996 (1), 1997 (4). Total: 27.
MISCELLANEOUS: Holds Minnesota Vikings all-time records for most yards receiving (7,986), most receptions (667) and most touchdown receptions (70).

| | | | RUSHING | | | | RECEIVING | | | | TOTALS | | | |
Year Team	G	GS	Att.	Yds.	Avg.	TD	No.	Yds.	Avg.	TD	TD	2pt.	Pts.	Fum.
1987—Philadelphia NFL	9	0	0	0	...	0	5	84	16.8	2	2	...	12	0
1988—Philadelphia NFL	16	16	1	1	1.0	0	39	761	19.5	6	7	...	42	0
1989—Philadelphia NFL	16	15	2	16	8.0	0	45	605	13.4	11	11	...	66	1
1990—Minnesota NFL	16	5	2	6	3.0	0	27	413	15.3	3	3	...	18	0
1991—Minnesota NFL	16	16	0	0	...	0	72	962	13.4	5	5	...	30	1
1992—Minnesota NFL	12	12	5	15	3.0	0	53	681	12.8	6	6	...	36	1
1993—Minnesota NFL	16	16	0	0	...	0	86	1071	12.5	9	9	...	54	0
1994—Minnesota NFL	16	16	0	0	...	0	*122	1256	10.3	7	7	2	46	4
1995—Minnesota NFL	16	16	1	0	0.0	0	122	1371	11.2	17	17	0	102	0
1996—Minnesota NFL	16	16	0	0	...	0	96	1163	12.1	10	10	0	60	1
1997—Minnesota NFL	16	16	0	0	...	0	89	1069	12.0	13	13	3	84	3
Pro totals (11 years)	165	144	11	38	3.5	0	756	9436	12.5	89	90	5	550	11

CARTER, DALE   CB   CHIEFS

PERSONAL: Born November 28, 1969, in Covington, Ga. ... 6-1/188. ... Full name: Dale Lavelle Carter. ... Brother of Jake Reed, wide receiver, Minnesota Vikings.
HIGH SCHOOL: Newton County (Covington, Ga.).
JUNIOR COLLEGE: Ellsworth (Iowa) Community College.
COLLEGE: Tennessee.
TRANSACTIONS/CAREER NOTES: Selected by Kansas City Chiefs in first round (20th pick overall) of 1992 NFL draft. ... Signed by Chiefs (June 2, 1992). ... Designated by Chiefs as transition player (February 25, 1993). ... On injured reserve with broken arm (January 7, 1994-remainder of 1993 playoffs). ... Tendered offer sheet by Minnesota Vikings (July 12, 1996). ... Offer matched by Chiefs (July 19, 1996).
HONORS: Named kick returner on THE SPORTING NEWS college All-America first team (1990). ... Named defensive back on THE SPORTING NEWS college All-America first team (1991). ... Played in Pro Bowl (1994, 1995 and 1997 seasons). ... Named cornerback on THE SPORTING NEWS NFL All-Pro team (1996). ... Named to play in Pro Bowl (1996 season); replaced by Terry McDaniel due to injury.
PRO STATISTICS: 1992—Recovered two fumbles. 1993—Rushed once for two yards and recovered two fumbles. 1994—Recovered one fumble. 1995—Recovered two fumbles. 1996—Rushed once for three yards, caught six passes for 89 yards and a touchdown, and recovered two fumbles for seven yards.

| | | | INTERCEPTIONS | | | | PUNT RETURNS | | | | KICKOFF RETURNS | | | | TOTALS | | | |
Year Team	G	GS	No.	Yds.	Avg.	TD	No.	Yds.	Avg.	TD	No.	Yds.	Avg.	TD	TD	2pt.	Pts.	Fum.
1992—Kansas City NFL	16	9	7	65	9.3	1	38	390	10.5	†2	11	190	17.3	0	3	...	18	7
1993—Kansas City NFL	15	11	1	0	0.0	0	27	247	9.1	0	0	0	...	0	0	...	0	4
1994—Kansas City NFL	16	16	2	24	12.0	0	16	124	7.8	0	0	0	...	0	0	0	0	1
1995—Kansas City NFL	16	14	4	45	11.3	0	0	0	...	0	0	0	...	0	0	0	0	0
1996—Kansas City NFL	14	14	3	17	5.7	0	2	18	9.0	0	0	0	...	0	1	0	6	1
1997—Kansas City NFL	16	15	2	9	4.5	0	0	0	...	0	0	0	...	0	0	0	0	0
Pro totals (6 years)	93	79	19	160	8.4	1	83	787	9.5	2	11	190	17.3	0	4	0	24	13

CARTER, DARYL   LB   BEARS

PERSONAL: Born February 24, 1975. ... 6-2/232.
HIGH SCHOOL: Washington (Milwaukee).
COLLEGE: Wisconsin.
TRANSACTIONS/CAREER NOTES: Signed as non-drafted free agent by Chicago Bears (April 21, 1997). ... Released by Bears (August 18, 1997). ... Re-signed by Bears to practice squad (August 26, 1997). ... Released by Bears (September 4, 1997). ... Re-signed by Bears to practice squad (September 30, 1997). ... Activated (December 17, 1997).
PLAYING EXPERIENCE: Chicago NFL, 1997. ... Games/Games started: 1/0.

CARTER, KEVIN   DE   RAMS

PERSONAL: Born September 21, 1973, in Tallahassee, Fla. ... 6-5/280. ... Full name: Kevin Louis Carter. ... Brother of Bernard Carter, linebacker with Jacksonville Jaguars (1995).
HIGH SCHOOL: Lincoln (Tallahassee, Fla.).
COLLEGE: Florida.

TRANSACTIONS/CAREER NOTES: Selected by St. Louis Rams in first round (sixth pick overall) of 1995 NFL draft. ... Signed by Rams (July 17, 1995).

HONORS: Named defensive lineman on THE SPORTING NEWS college All-America first team (1994).

PRO STATISTICS: 1995—Recovered one fumble. 1996—Recovered two fumbles. 1997—Recovered two fumbles for five yards.

Year Team	G	GS	SACKS
1995—St. Louis NFL	16	16	6.0
1996—St. Louis NFL	16	16	9.5
1997—St. Louis NFL	16	16	7.5
Pro totals (3 years)	48	48	23.0

CARTER, KI-JANA   RB   BENGALS

PERSONAL: Born September 12, 1973, in Westerville, Ohio. ... 5-10/222. ... Full name: Kenneth Leonard Carter. ... Name pronounced ki-JOHN-ah.

HIGH SCHOOL: Westerville (Ohio) South.

COLLEGE: Penn State.

TRANSACTIONS/CAREER NOTES: Selected after junior season by Cincinnati Bengals in first round (first pick overall) of 1995 NFL draft. ... Signed by Bengals (July 19, 1995). ... On injured reserve with knee injury (August 22, 1995-entire season).

HONORS: Named running back on THE SPORTING NEWS college All-America first team (1994).

PRO STATISTICS: 1996—Recovered two fumbles for minus eight yards. 1997—Attempted one pass without a completion, returned one kick-off for nine yards and recovered two fumbles.

SINGLE GAME HIGHS (regular season): Attempts—19 (August 13, 1997, vs. Arizona); yards—104 (September 21, 1997, vs. Denver); and rushing touchdowns—2 (August 31, 1997, vs. Arizona).

STATISTICAL PLATEAUS: 100-yard rushing games: 1997 (1).

Year Team	G	GS	RUSHING Att.	Yds.	Avg.	TD	RECEIVING No.	Yds.	Avg.	TD	TOTALS TD	2pt.	Pts.	Fum.
1995—Cincinnati NFL							Did not play.							
1996—Cincinnati NFL	16	4	91	264	2.9	8	22	169	7.7	1	9	0	54	2
1997—Cincinnati NFL	15	10	128	464	3.6	7	21	157	7.5	0	7	0	42	3
Pro totals (2 years)	31	14	219	728	3.3	15	43	326	7.6	1	16	0	96	5

CARTER, MARTY   S   BEARS

PERSONAL: Born December 17, 1969, in LaGrange, Ga. ... 6-1/214. ... Full name: Marty LaVincent Carter.

HIGH SCHOOL: LaGrange (Ga.).

COLLEGE: Middle Tennessee State.

TRANSACTIONS/CAREER NOTES: Selected by Tampa Bay Buccaneers in eighth round (207th pick overall) of 1991 NFL draft. ... Signed by Buccaneers (July 19, 1991). ... Granted unconditional free agency (February 17, 1995). ... Signed by Chicago Bears (March 3, 1995).

PRO STATISTICS: 1993—Recovered two fumbles. 1994—Caught one pass for 21 yards and returned one kickoff for no yards. 1995—Recovered one fumble.

Year Team	G	GS	INTERCEPTIONS No.	Yds.	Avg.	TD	SACKS No.
1991—Tampa Bay NFL	14	11	1	5	5.0	0	0.0
1992—Tampa Bay NFL	16	16	3	1	0.3	0	2.0
1993—Tampa Bay NFL	16	14	1	0	0.0	0	0.0
1994—Tampa Bay NFL	16	14	0	0	...	0	1.0
1995—Chicago NFL	16	16	2	20	10.0	0	...
1996—Chicago NFL	16	16	3	34	11.3	0	0.0
1997—Chicago NFL	15	15	1	14	14.0	0	1.0
Pro totals (7 years)	109	102	11	74	6.7	0	4.0

CARTER, PAT   TE

PERSONAL: Born August 1, 1966, in Sarasota, Fla. ... 6-4/265. ... Full name: Wendell Patrick Carter.

HIGH SCHOOL: Riverview (Sarasota, Fla.).

COLLEGE: Florida State.

TRANSACTIONS/CAREER NOTES: Selected by Detroit Lions in second round (32nd pick overall) of 1988 NFL draft. ... Signed by Lions (June 13, 1988). ... Traded by Lions to Los Angeles Rams for fourth-round pick (LB Rob Hinckley) in 1990 draft (August 18, 1989). ... Granted free agency (February 1, 1992). ... Re-signed by Rams (July 21, 1992). ... Granted unconditional free agency (February 17, 1994). ... Signed by Houston Oilers (March 30, 1994). ... Released by Oilers (August 27, 1995). ... Signed by St. Louis Rams (August 29, 1995). ... Granted unconditional free agency (February 16, 1996). ... Signed by Arizona Cardinals (April 22, 1996). ... Granted unconditional free agency (February 14, 1997). ... Re-signed by Cardinals (June 19, 1997). ... Granted unconditional free agency (February 13, 1998).

CHAMPIONSHIP GAME EXPERIENCE: Played in NFC championship game (1989 season).

HONORS: Named tight end on THE SPORTING NEWS college All-America first team (1987).

PRO STATISTICS: 1991—Returned one kickoff for 18 yards.

SINGLE GAME HIGHS (regular season): Receptions—4 (November 10, 1996, vs. Washington); yards—52 (December 1, 1996, vs. Minnesota); and touchdown receptions—1 (September 7, 1997, vs. Dallas).

Year Team	G	GS	RECEIVING No.	Yds.	Avg.	TD	TOTALS TD	2pt.	Pts.	Fum.
1988—Detroit NFL	15	14	13	145	11.2	0	0	...	0	0
1989—Los Angeles Rams NFL	16	0	0	0	...	0	0	...	0	0
1990—Los Angeles Rams NFL	16	4	8	58	7.3	0	0	...	0	0
1991—Los Angeles Rams NFL	16	5	8	69	8.6	2	2	...	12	1
1992—Los Angeles Rams NFL	16	16	20	232	11.6	3	3	...	18	0
1993—Los Angeles Rams NFL	11	10	14	166	11.9	1	1	...	6	0

Year Team	G	GS	RECEIVING				TOTALS			
			No.	Yds.	Avg.	TD	TD	2pt.	Pts.	Fum.
1994—Houston NFL	16	13	11	74	6.7	1	1	0	6	0
1995—St. Louis NFL	16	6	0	0	...	0	0	0	0	0
1996—Arizona NFL	16	16	26	329	12.7	1	1	0	6	0
1997—Arizona NFL	16	10	7	44	6.3	1	1	0	6	0
Pro totals (10 years)	154	94	107	1117	10.4	9	9	0	54	1

CARTER, PERRY   CB   RAIDERS

PERSONAL: Born August 15, 1971, in McComb, Miss. ... 5-11/206. ... Full name: Perry Lynn Carter.
HIGH SCHOOL: McComb (Miss.).
COLLEGE: Southern Mississippi.
TRANSACTIONS/CAREER NOTES: Selected by Arizona Cardinals in fourth round (107th pick overall) of 1994 NFL draft. ... Signed by Cardinals for 1994 season. ... Released by Cardinals (August 27, 1994). ... Re-signed by Cardinals to practice squad (August 30, 1994). ... Released by Cardinals (September 5, 1994). ... Signed by Washington Redskins to practice squad (September 13, 1994). ... Released by Redskins (September 20, 1994). ... Signed by Kansas City Chiefs to practice squad (December 15, 1994). ... Granted free agency after 1994 season. ... Re-signed by Chiefs (February 28, 1995). ... Released by Chiefs (August 22, 1995). ... Re-signed by Chiefs to practice squad (August 29, 1995). ... Activated (December 10, 1995). ... Released by Chiefs (August 25, 1996). ... Signed by Oakland Raiders (November 20, 1996).
PLAYING EXPERIENCE: Kansas City NFL, 1995; Oakland NFL, 1996 and 1997. ... Games/Games started: 1995 (2/0), 1996 (4/0), 1997 (16/7). Total: 22/7.

CARTER, TOM   CB   BEARS   C

PERSONAL: Born September 5, 1972, in St. Petersburg, Fla. ... 6-0/189. ... Full name: Thomas Carter III.
HIGH SCHOOL: Lakewood Senior (St. Petersburg, Fla.).
COLLEGE: Notre Dame.
TRANSACTIONS/CAREER NOTES: Selected after junior season by Washington Redskins in first round (17th pick overall) of 1993 NFL draft. ... Signed by Redskins for 1993 season. ... Designated by Redskins as transition player (February 15, 1994). ... Designated by Redskins as transition player (February 12, 1997). ... Tendered offer sheet by Chicago Bears (March 31, 1997). ... Redskins declined to match offer (April 7, 1997).

Year Team	G	GS	INTERCEPTIONS			
			No.	Yds.	Avg.	TD
1993—Washington NFL	14	11	6	54	9.0	0
1994—Washington NFL	16	16	3	58	19.3	0
1995—Washington NFL	16	16	4	116	29.0	1
1996—Washington NFL	16	16	5	24	4.8	0
1997—Chicago NFL	16	16	3	12	4.0	0
Pro totals (5 years)	78	75	21	264	12.6	1

CARTER, TONY   FB   PATRIOTS

PERSONAL: Born August 23, 1972, in Columbus, Ohio. ... 5-11/236. ... Full name: Antonio Carter.
HIGH SCHOOL: South (Columbus, Ohio).
COLLEGE: Minnesota.
TRANSACTIONS/CAREER NOTES: Signed as non-drafted free agent by Chicago Bears (April 28, 1994). ... Granted unconditional free agency (February 13, 1998). ... Signed by New England Patriots (February 25, 1998).
PRO STATISTICS: 1996—Recovered one fumble. 1997—Recovered one fumble.
SINGLE GAME HIGHS (regular season): Attempts—6 (October 13, 1996, vs. New Orleans); yards—37 (October 13, 1996, vs. New Orleans); and rushing touchdowns—0.

Year Team	G	GS	RUSHING				RECEIVING				KICKOFF RETURNS				TOTALS			
			Att.	Yds.	Avg.	TD	No.	Yds.	Avg.	TD	No.	Yds.	Avg.	TD	TD	2pt.	Pts.	Fum.
1994—Chicago NFL	14	0	0	0	...	0	1	24	24.0	0	6	99	16.5	0	0	0	0	0
1995—Chicago NFL	16	11	10	34	3.4	0	40	329	8.2	1	3	24	8.0	0	1	0	6	1
1996—Chicago NFL	16	11	11	43	3.9	0	41	233	5.7	0	0	0	...	0	0	0	0	1
1997—Chicago NFL	16	10	9	56	6.2	0	24	152	6.3	0	2	34	17.0	0	0	0	0	0
Pro totals (4 years)	62	32	30	133	4.4	0	106	738	7.0	1	11	157	14.3	0	1	0	6	2

CARVER, SHANTE   DE

PERSONAL: Born February 12, 1971, in Stockton, Calif. ... 6-5/253. ... Name pronounced shon-TAY.
HIGH SCHOOL: Lincoln (Stockton, Calif.).
COLLEGE: Arizona State.
TRANSACTIONS/CAREER NOTES: Selected by Dallas Cowboys in first round (23rd pick overall) of 1994 NFL draft. ... Signed by Cowboys (July 16, 1994). ... On suspended list for violating league substance abuse policy (August 26-October 14, 1996). ... Granted unconditional free agency (February 13, 1998).
CHAMPIONSHIP GAME EXPERIENCE: Member of Cowboys for NFC championship game (1994 season); inactive. ... Played in NFC championship game (1995 season). ... Member of Super Bowl championship team (1995 season).
HONORS: Named defensive lineman on THE SPORTING NEWS college All-America first team (1993).

Year Team	G	GS	SACKS
1994—Dallas NFL	10	0	0.0
1995—Dallas NFL	15	3	2.5
1996—Dallas NFL	10	7	3.0
1997—Dallas NFL	16	16	6.0
Pro totals (4 years)	51	26	11.5

CASCADDEN, CHAD — LB — JETS

PERSONAL: Born May 14, 1972, in Chippewa Falls, Wis. ... 6-1/240.
HIGH SCHOOL: Chippewa Falls (Wis.).
COLLEGE: Wisconsin.
TRANSACTIONS/CAREER NOTES: Signed as non-drafted free agent by New York Jets (April 28, 1995). ... Released by Jets (August 27, 1995). ... Re-signed by Jets to practice squad (August 29, 1995). ... Activated (September 19, 1995). ... Granted free agency (February 13, 1998). ... Tendered offer sheet by St. Louis Rams (April 7, 1998). ... Offer matched by Jets (April 13, 1998).
PRO STATISTICS: 1996—Recovered one fumble. 1997—Recovered one fumble.

Year Team	G	GS	SACKS
1995—New York Jets NFL	12	0	0.0
1996—New York Jets NFL	16	8	3.0
1997—New York Jets NFL	15	0	0.0
Pro totals (3 years)	43	8	3.0

CASE, STONEY — QB — CARDINALS

PERSONAL: Born July 7, 1972, in Odessa, Texas. ... 6-3/201. ... Full name: Stoney Jarrod Case.
HIGH SCHOOL: Permian (Odessa, Texas).
COLLEGE: New Mexico.
TRANSACTIONS/CAREER NOTES: Selected by Arizona Cardinals in third round (80th pick overall) of 1995 NFL draft. ... Signed by Cardinals for 1995 season. ... Inactive for 16 games (1996). ... Assigned by Cardinals to Barcelona Dragons in 1997 World League enhancement allocation program (February 19, 1997). ... Granted free agency (February 13, 1998). ... Re-signed by Cardinals (April 28, 1998).
PRO STATISTICS: 1997—Fumbled three times.
SINGLE GAME HIGHS (regular season): Attempts—33 (October 12, 1997, vs. New York Giants); completions—18 (October 12, 1997, vs. New York Giants); yards—222 (October 12, 1997, vs. New York Giants); and touchdown passes—0.
MISCELLANEOUS: Regular-season record as starting NFL quarterback: 0-1.

Year Team	G	GS	PASSING Att.	Cmp.	Pct.	Yds.	TD	Int.	Avg.	Rat.	RUSHING Att.	Yds.	Avg.	TD	TOTALS TD	2pt.	Pts.
1995—Arizona NFL	2	0	2	1	50.0	19	0	1	9.50	43.8	1	4	4.0	0	0	0	0
1996—Arizona NFL								Did not play.									
1997—Arizona NFL	3	1	55	29	52.7	316	0	2	5.75	54.8	7	8	1.1	1	1	0	6
Pro totals (2 years)	5	1	57	30	52.6	335	0	3	5.88	48.5	8	12	1.5	1	1	0	6

CASILLAS, TONY — DT

PERSONAL: Born October 26, 1963, in Tulsa, Okla. ... 6-3/278. ... Full name: Tony Steven Casillas.
HIGH SCHOOL: East Central (Tulsa, Okla.).
COLLEGE: Oklahoma (degree in communications, 1986).
TRANSACTIONS/CAREER NOTES: Selected by Atlanta Falcons in first round (second pick overall) of 1986 NFL draft. ... Selected by Arizona Outlaws in first round (second pick overall) of 1986 USFL draft. ... Signed by Falcons (July 20, 1986). ... Granted roster exemption (September 13-24, 1990). ... On reserve//suspended list (October 23-November 5, 1990). ... On injured reserve with fractured elbow (December 27, 1990-remainder of season). ... Traded by Falcons to Dallas Cowboys for second- (DE Chuck Smith) and eighth-round (TE Reggie Dwight) picks in 1992 draft (July 22, 1991). ... Granted unconditional free agency (February 17, 1994). ... Signed by Kansas City Chiefs (April 5, 1994). ... Released by Chiefs (August 4, 1994). ... Signed by New York Jets (September 19, 1994). ... Granted unconditional free agency (February 17, 1995). ... Re-signed by Jets (March 7, 1995). ... Released by Jets (March 1, 1996). ... Signed by Cowboys (July 15, 1996). ... Announced retirement (February 24, 1998).
CHAMPIONSHIP GAME EXPERIENCE: Played in NFC championship game (1992 and 1993 seasons). ... Member of Super Bowl championship team (1992 and 1993 seasons).
HONORS: Named defensive lineman on THE SPORTING NEWS college All-America first team (1984 and 1985). ... Lombardi Award winner (1985).
PRO STATISTICS: 1986—Recovered one fumble. 1987—Recovered one fumble. 1988—Recovered one fumble. 1989—Recovered three fumbles. 1991—Recovered one fumble. 1992—Recovered one fumble for three yards. 1993—Recovered one fumble.

Year Team	G	GS	SACKS
1986—Atlanta NFL	16	16	1.0
1987—Atlanta NFL	9	9	2.0
1988—Atlanta NFL	16	16	2.0
1989—Atlanta NFL	16	16	2.0
1990—Atlanta NFL	9	0	1.0
1991—Dallas NFL	16	16	2.5
1992—Dallas NFL	15	15	3.0
1993—Dallas NFL	15	14	2.0
1994—New York Jets NFL	12	11	1.5
1995—New York Jets NFL	11	5	3.0
1996—Dallas NFL	16	3	0.0
1997—Dallas NFL	15	14	3.0
Pro totals (12 years)	166	135	23.0

CAVIL, BEN — G — RAVENS

PERSONAL: Born January 31, 1972, in Galveston, Texas. ... 6-2/310. ... Name pronounced Gavel. ... Nickname: Big Ben.
HIGH SCHOOL: LaMarque (Texas).
COLLEGE: Oklahoma.
TRANSACTIONS/CAREER NOTES: Signed as non-drafted free agent by San Diego Chargers (April 27, 1995). ... Released by Chargers (September 4, 1995). ... Re-signed by Chargers (March 11, 1996). ... Claimed on waivers by Philadelphia Eagles (August 20, 1996). ... Released by Eagles (August 30, 1996). ... Re-signed by Eagles to practice squad (September 2, 1996). ... Traded by Eagles to Baltimore Ravens for seventh-round pick in 1999 draft (August 24, 1997).
PLAYING EXPERIENCE: Baltimore NFL, 1997. ... Games/Games started: 15/8.

CENTERS, LARRY   RB   CARDINALS

PERSONAL: Born June 1, 1968, in Tatum, Texas. ... 6-0/225. ... Full name: Larry E. Centers.
HIGH SCHOOL: Tatum (Texas).
COLLEGE: Stephen F. Austin State.
TRANSACTIONS/CAREER NOTES: Selected by Phoenix Cardinals in fifth round (115th pick overall) of 1990 NFL draft. ... Signed by Cardinals (July 23, 1990). ... On injured reserve with broken foot (September 11-October 30, 1991). ... Granted free agency (February 1, 1992). ... Re-signed by Cardinals (July 23, 1992). ... Granted unconditional free agency (February 17, 1994). ... Re-signed by Cardinals (March 15, 1994). ... Cardinals franchise renamed Arizona Cardinals for 1994 season. ... Granted unconditional free agency (February 14, 1997). ... Re-signed by Cardinals (March 14, 1997).
HONORS: Played in Pro Bowl (1995 and 1996 seasons).
PRO STATISTICS: 1991—Returned five punts for 30 yards and recovered two fumbles. 1993—Recovered two fumbles. 1994—Recovered two fumbles for 27 yards. 1995—Had only pass attempt intercepted and recovered one fumble. 1996—Recovered one fumble.
SINGLE GAME HIGHS (regular season): Attempts—15 (September 4, 1994, vs. Los Angeles Rams); yards—62 (November 26, 1995, vs. Atlanta); and rushing touchdowns—2 (December 4, 1994, vs. Houston).
STATISTICAL PLATEAUS: 100-yard receiving games: 1995 (2), 1996 (1). Total: 3.

			RUSHING				RECEIVING				KICKOFF RETURNS				TOTALS			
Year Team	G	GS	Att.	Yds.	Avg.	TD	No.	Yds.	Avg.	TD	No.	Yds.	Avg.	TD	TD	2pt.	Pts.	Fum.
1990—Phoenix NFL	6	0	0	0	0	0	0	0	...	0	16	272	17.0	0	0	...	0	1
1991—Phoenix NFL	9	2	14	44	3.1	0	19	176	9.3	0	16	330	20.6	0	0	...	0	4
1992—Phoenix NFL	16	1	37	139	3.8	0	50	417	8.3	2	0	0	...	0	2	...	12	1
1993—Phoenix NFL	16	9	25	152	6.1	0	66	603	9.1	3	0	0	...	0	3	...	18	1
1994—Arizona NFL	16	5	115	336	2.9	5	77	647	8.4	2	0	0	...	0	7	0	42	2
1995—Arizona NFL	16	10	78	254	3.3	2	101	962	9.5	2	1	15	15.0	0	4	0	24	2
1996—Arizona NFL	16	14	116	425	3.7	2	99	766	7.7	7	0	0	...	0	9	0	54	1
1997—Arizona NFL	15	14	101	276	2.7	1	54	409	7.6	1	0	0	...	0	2	0	12	1
Pro totals (8 years)	110	55	486	1626	3.3	10	466	3980	8.5	17	33	617	18.7	0	27	0	162	13

CHALENSKI, MIKE   DE   DOLPHINS

PERSONAL: Born January 28, 1970, in Elizabeth, N.J. ... 6-5/280.
HIGH SCHOOL: David Brearley Regional (Kenilworth, N.J.).
COLLEGE: Pittsburgh, then UCLA.
TRANSACTIONS/CAREER NOTES: Signed as non-drafted free agent by Philadelphia Eagles (April 30, 1993). ... On injured reserve with knee injury (August 23, 1994-entire season). ... Granted unconditional free agency (February 16, 1996). ... Signed by New York Jets (April 25, 1996). ... Granted unconditional free agency (February 14, 1997). ... Signed by Minnesota Vikings (June 9, 1997). ... Released by Vikings (August 24, 1997). ... Signed by Miami Dolphins (October 21, 1997). ... Granted unconditional free agency (February 13, 1998). ... Re-signed by Dolphins (March 23, 1998).
PLAYING EXPERIENCE: Philadelphia NFL, 1993 and 1995; New York Jets NFL, 1996; Miami NFL, 1997. ... Games/Games started: 1993 (15/0), 1995 (9/0), 1996 (15/7), 1997 (8/0). Total: 47/7.
PRO STATISTICS: 1996—Recovered one fumble.

CHAMBERLAIN, BYRON   TE   BRONCOS

PERSONAL: Born October 17, 1971, in Honolulu. ... 6-1/242.
HIGH SCHOOL: Eastern Hills (Ft. Worth, Texas).
COLLEGE: Missouri, then Wayne (Neb.) State.
TRANSACTIONS/CAREER NOTES: Selected by Denver Broncos in seventh round (222nd pick overall) of 1995 NFL draft. ... Signed by Broncos (August 27, 1995). ... Released by Broncos (August 27, 1995). ... Re-signed by Broncos to practice squad (August 28, 1995). ... Activated (November 24, 1995). ... Assigned by Broncos to Rhein Fire in 1996 World League enhancement allocation program (February 19, 1996).
CHAMPIONSHIP GAME EXPERICNCE: Member of Broncos for AFC championship game (1997 season); did not play. ... Member of Super Bowl championship team (1997 season); did not play.
PRO STATISTICS: 1996—Rushed once for four yards and returned one kickoff for eight yards. NFL: 1996—Returned three kickoffs for 49 yards. 1997—Returned one kickoff for 13 yards.
SINGLE GAME HIGHS (regular season): Receptions—5 (December 15, 1996, vs. Oakland); yards—61 (December 15, 1996, vs. Oakland); and touchdown receptions—0.

			RECEIVING				TOTALS			
Year Team	G	GS	No.	Yds.	Avg.	TD	TD	2pt.	Pts.	Fum.
1995—Denver NFL	5	0	1	11	11.0	0	0	0	0	0
1996—Rhein W.L.	...	...	58	685	11.8	8	8	0	48	...
—Denver NFL	11	0	12	129	10.8	0	0	0	0	1
1997—Denver NFL	10	0	2	18	9.0	0	0	0	0	1
W.L. totals (1 year)	...	...	58	685	11.8	8	8	0	48	...
NFL totals (3 years)	26	0	15	158	10.5	0	0	0	0	2
Pro totals (4 years)	...	...	73	843	11.5	8	8	0	48	...

CHANCEY, ROBERT   FB   CHARGERS

PERSONAL: Born September 7, 1972, in Macon, Ala. ... 6-0/260. ... Full name: Robert Dewayne Chancey.
HIGH SCHOOL: Elmore (Millbrook, Ala.).
COLLEGE: None.
TRANSACTIONS/CAREER NOTES: Signed as non-drafted free agent by San Diego Chargers (April 7, 1997). ... Released by Chargers (August 24, 1997). ... Re-signed by Chargers to practice squad (August 25, 1997). ... Activated (November 4, 1997).
PLAYING EXPERIENCE: San Diego NFL, 1997. ... Games/Games started: 6/0.

TRANSACTIONS/CAREER NOTES: Selected by Baltimore Orioles organization in sixth round of free-agent draft (June 1, 1992). ... Released by Gulf Coast Orioles, Orioles organization (September 30, 1993). ... Signed by Pittsfield, New York Mets organization (April 15, 1996). ... On Pittsfield temporarily inactive list (May 10-June 10, 1996). ... Released by Kingsport, Mets organization (July 1, 1996).

STATISTICAL NOTES: Led Gulf Coast League outfielders with seven errors (1992).

Year Team (League)	Pos.	G	AB	R	H	2B	3B	HR	RBI	Avg.	BB	SO	SB	PO	A	E	Avg.
1992— GC Orioles (GCL)........	OF	43	141	22	41	3	3	1	23	.291	7	50	13	70	5	7	.915
1993— GC Orioles (GCL)	OF	29	84	7	12	3	0	0	3	.143	4	39	3	31	3	6	.850
1996— Kingsport (Appal.)	OF	6	19	4	5	0	0	1	3	.263	2	5	1	7	0	1	.875

CHANDLER, CHRIS   QB   FALCONS

PERSONAL: Born October 12, 1965, in Everett, Wash. ... 6-4/225. ... Full name: Christopher Mark Chandler. ... Brother of Greg Chandler, catcher, San Francisco Giants organization (1978); and son-in-law of John Brodie, quarterback with San Francisco 49ers (1957-1973).

HIGH SCHOOL: Everett (Wash.).

COLLEGE: Washington (degree in economics, 1988).

TRANSACTIONS/CAREER NOTES: Selected by Indianapolis Colts in third round (76th pick overall) of 1988 NFL draft. ... Signed by Colts (July 23, 1988). ... On injured reserve with knee injury (October 3, 1989-remainder of season). ... Traded by Colts to Tampa Bay Buccaneers for first round pick (DL Steve Emtman) in 1992 draft (August 7, 1990). ... Claimed on waivers by Phoenix Cardinals (November 6, 1991). ... Granted unconditional free agency (February 17, 1994). ... Signed by Los Angeles Rams (May 6, 1994). ... Granted unconditional free agency (February 17, 1995). ... Signed by Houston Oilers (March 10, 1995). ... Traded by Oilers to Atlanta Falcons for fourth- (WR Derrick Mason) and sixth-round (traded to New Orleans) picks in 1997 draft (February 24, 1997).

HONORS: Played in Pro Bowl (1997 season).

PRO STATISTICS: 1988—Fumbled eight times and recovered five fumbles for minus six yards. 1990—Fumbled five times and recovered one fumble for minus two yards. 1991—Fumbled six times and recovered two fumbles for minus seven yards. 1992—Fumbled nine times and recovered two fumbles for minus 11 yards. 1993—Fumbled twice. 1994—Fumbled three times. 1995—Fumbled 12 times and recovered five fumbles for minus nine yards. 1996—Fumbled eight times and recovered three fumbles for minus four yards. 1997—Fumbled nine times and recovered three fumbles for minus 18 yards.

SINGLE GAME HIGHS (regular season): Attempts—47 (October 1, 1995, vs. Jacksonville); completions—28 (September 20, 1992, vs. Dallas); yards—383 (September 20, 1992, vs. Dallas); and touchdown passes—4 (September 24, 1995, vs. Cincinnati).

STATISTICAL PLATEAUS: 300-yard passing games: 1992 (1), 1995 (1). Total: 2.

MISCELLANEOUS: Regular-season record as starting NFL quarterback: 35-49 (.417).

			PASSING								RUSHING				TOTALS		
Year Team	G	GS	Att.	Cmp.	Pct.	Yds.	TD	Int.	Avg.	Rat.	Att.	Yds.	Avg.	TD	TD	2pt.	Pts.
1988—Indianapolis NFL	15	13	233	129	55.4	1619	8	12	6.95	67.2	46	139	3.0	3	3	...	18
1989—Indianapolis NFL	3	3	80	39	48.8	537	2	3	6.71	63.4	7	57	8.1	1	1	...	6
1990—Tampa Bay NFL..........	7	3	83	42	50.6	464	1	6	5.59	41.4	13	71	5.5	1	1	...	6
1991—Tampa Bay NFL..........	6	3	104	53	51.0	557	4	8	5.36	47.6	18	79	4.4	0	0	...	0
—Phoenix NFL..............	3	2	50	25	50.0	289	1	2	5.78	57.8	8	32	4.0	0	0	...	0
1992—Phoenix NFL..............	15	13	413	245	59.3	2832	15	15	6.86	77.1	36	149	4.1	1	1	...	6
1993—Phoenix NFL..............	4	2	103	52	50.5	471	3	2	4.57	64.8	3	2	0.7	0	0	...	0
1994—L.A. Rams NFL............	12	6	176	108	61.4	1352	7	2	7.68	93.8	18	61	3.4	1	1	0	6
1995—Houston NFL..............	13	13	356	225	63.2	2460	17	10	6.91	87.8	28	58	2.1	2	2	1	14
1996—Houston NFL..............	12	12	320	184	57.5	2099	16	11	6.56	79.7	28	113	4.0	0	0	0	0
1997—Atlanta NFL	14	14	342	202	59.1	2692	20	7	7.87	95.1	43	158	3.7	0	0	0	0
Pro totals (10 years)	104	84	2260	1304	57.7	15372	94	78	6.80	78.0	248	919	3.7	9	9	1	56

CHEEVER, MICHAEL   C   JAGUARS

PERSONAL: Born June 24, 1973, in Newnan, Ga. ... 6-4/295. ... Full name: Michael John Cheever.

HIGH SCHOOL: Newnan (Ga.).

COLLEGE: Georgia Tech.

TRANSACTIONS/CAREER NOTES: Selected by Jacksonville Jaguars in second round (60th pick overall) of 1996 NFL draft. ... Signed by Jaguars (May 24, 1996). ... On injured reserve with back injury (December 8, 1997-remainder of season).

PLAYING EXPERIENCE: Jacksonville NFL, 1996 and 1997. ... Games/Games started: 1996 (11/2), 1997 (6/4). Total: 17/6.

CHAMPIONSHIP GAME EXPERIENCE: Member of Jaguars for AFC championship game (1996 season); did not play.

CHERRY, JE'ROD   S   SAINTS

PERSONAL: Born May 30, 1973, in Charlotte. ... 6-1/210. ... Full name: Je'Rod L. Cherry. ... Name pronounced juh-ROD.

HIGH SCHOOL: Berkeley (Calif.).

COLLEGE: California (degree in political science, 1995).

TRANSACTIONS/CAREER NOTES: Selected by New Orleans Saints in second round (40th pick overall) of 1996 NFL draft. ... Signed by Saints (July 3, 1996).

PLAYING EXPERIENCE: New Orleans NFL, 1996 and 1997. ... Games/Games started: 1996 (13/0), 1997 (16/0). Total: 29/0.

PRO STATISTICS: 1996—Recovered one fumble.

CHERRY, MIKE   QB   GIANTS

PERSONAL: Born December 15, 1973, in Texarkana, Ark. ... 6-3/225.

HIGH SCHOOL: Arkansas (Texarkana, Ark.).

COLLEGE: Murray State.

TRANSACTIONS/CAREER NOTES: Selected by New York Giants in sixth round (171st pick overall) of 1997 NFL draft. ... Signed by Giants for 1997 season.
PLAYING EXPERIENCE: New York Giants NFL, 1997. ... Games/Games started: 1997 (1/0).
PRO STATISTICS: 1997—Rushed once for minus two yards.
SINGLE GAME HIGHS (regular season): Attempts—0; completions—0; yards—0; and touchdown passes—0.

CHMURA, MARK   TE   PACKERS

PERSONAL: Born February 22, 1969, in Deerfield, Mass. ... 6-5/253. ... Full name: Mark William Chmura. ... Name pronounced cha-MER-ah.
HIGH SCHOOL: Frontier Regional (South Deerfield, Mass.).
COLLEGE: Boston College.
TRANSACTIONS/CAREER NOTES: Selected by Green Bay Packers in sixth round (157th pick overall) of 1992 NFL draft. ... Signed by Packers (July 22, 1992). ... On injured reserve with back injury (August 24, 1992-entire season).
CHAMPIONSHIP GAME EXPERIENCE: Played in NFC championship game (1995-97 seasons). ... Member of Super Bowl championship team (1996 season). ... Played in Super Bowl XXXII (1997 season).
HONORS: Named tight end on THE SPORTING NEWS college All-America second team (1991). ... Played in Pro Bowl (1995 and 1997 seasons).
POST SEASON RECORDS: Shares Super Bowl and NFL postseason career and single-game records for most two-point conversions—1 (January 26, 1997, vs. New England).
PRO STATISTICS: 1993—Returned one kickoff for no yards and recovered one fumble.
SINGLE GAME HIGHS (regular season): Receptions—7 (December 3, 1995, vs. Cincinnati); yards—109 (December 3, 1995, vs. Cincinnati); and touchdown receptions—2 (November 23, 1997, vs. Dallas).
STATISTICAL PLATEAUS: 100-yard receiving games: 1995 (2).

			RECEIVING				TOTALS			
Year Team	G	GS	No.	Yds.	Avg.	TD	TD	2pt.	Pts.	Fum.
1992—Green Bay NFL						Did not play.				
1993—Green Bay NFL	14	0	2	13	6.5	0	0	...	0	1
1994—Green Bay NFL	14	4	14	165	11.8	0	0	0	0	0
1995—Green Bay NFL	16	15	54	679	12.6	7	7	1	44	0
1996—Green Bay NFL	13	13	28	370	13.2	0	0	0	0	0
1997—Green Bay NFL	15	14	38	417	11.0	6	6	0	36	1
Pro totals (5 years)	72	46	136	1644	12.1	13	13	1	80	2

CHREBET, WAYNE   WR   JETS

PERSONAL: Born August 14, 1973, in Garfield, N.J. ... 5-10/185. ... Name pronounced kra-BET.
HIGH SCHOOL: Garfield (N.J.).
COLLEGE: Hofstra.
TRANSACTIONS/CAREER NOTES: Signed as non-drafted free agent by New York Jets (April 25, 1995).
PRO STATISTICS: 1995—Rushed once for one yard. 1996—Recovered two fumbles. 1997—Returned one kickoff for five yards.
SINGLE GAME HIGHS (regular season): Receptions—12 (October 13, 1996, vs. Jacksonville); yards—162 (October 13, 1996, vs. Jacksonville); and touchdown receptions—2 (August 31, 1997, vs. Seattle).
STATISTICAL PLATEAUS: 100-yard receiving games: 1996 (1), 1997 (1). Total: 2.

			RECEIVING				PUNT RETURNS				TOTALS			
Year Team	G	GS	No.	Yds.	Avg.	TD	No.	Yds.	Avg.	TD	TD	2pt.	Pts.	Fum.
1995—New York Jets NFL	16	16	66	726	11.0	4	0	0	...	0	4	0	24	1
1996—New York Jets NFL	16	9	84	909	10.8	3	28	139	5.0	0	3	0	18	5
1997—New York Jets NFL	16	1	58	799	13.8	3	0	0	...	0	3	0	18	0
Pro totals (3 years)	48	26	208	2434	11.7	10	28	139	5.0	0	10	0	60	6

CHRISTIAN, BOB   RB   FALCONS

PERSONAL: Born November 14, 1968, in St. Louis. ... 5-11/230. ... Full name: Robert Douglas Christian.
HIGH SCHOOL: McCluer North (Florissant, Mo.).
COLLEGE: Northwestern.
TRANSACTIONS/CAREER NOTES: Selected by Atlanta Falcons in 12th round (310th pick overall) of 1991 NFL draft. ... Signed by Falcons (July 18, 1991). ... Released by Falcons (August 20, 1991). ... Selected by London Monarchs in 16th round (175th pick overall) of 1992 World League draft. ... Signed by San Diego Chargers (July 10, 1992). ... Released by Chargers (August 25, 1992). ... Signed by Chicago Bears to practice squad (September 8, 1992). ... Activated (December 18, 1992). ... On injured reserve with knee injury (December 2, 1994-remainder of season). ... Selected by Carolina Panthers from Bears in NFL expansion draft (February 15, 1995). ... Granted free agency (February 16, 1996). ... Re-signed by Panthers (July 19, 1996). ... On injured reserve with shoulder injury (August 25, 1996-entire season). ... Granted unconditional free agency (February 14, 1997). ... Signed by Falcons (March 6, 1997).
PRO STATISTICS: 1995—Recovered one fumble. 1997—Recovered one fumble.
SINGLE GAME HIGHS (regular season): Attempts—6 (December 3, 1995, vs. Indianapolis); yards—39 (November 26, 1995, vs. New Orleans); and rushing touchdowns—0.

			RUSHING				RECEIVING				TOTALS			
Year Team	G	GS	Att.	Yds.	Avg.	TD	No.	Yds.	Avg.	TD	TD	2pt.	Pts.	Fum.
1992—Chicago NFL	2	0	0	0	...	0	0	0	...	0	0	...	0	0
1993—Chicago NFL	14	1	8	19	2.4	0	16	160	10.0	0	0	...	0	0
1994—Chicago NFL	12	0	7	29	4.1	0	2	30	15.0	0	0	0	0	0
1995—Carolina NFL	14	12	41	158	3.9	0	29	255	8.8	1	1	1	8	1
1996—Carolina NFL						Did not play.								
1997—Atlanta NFL	16	12	7	8	1.1	0	22	154	7.0	1	1	0	6	3
Pro totals (5 years)	58	25	63	214	3.4	0	69	599	8.7	2	2	1	14	4

CHRISTIE, STEVE   K   BILLS

PERSONAL: Born November 13, 1967, in Oakville, Ontario. ... 6-0/185. ... Full name: Geoffrey Stephen Christie.
HIGH SCHOOL: Oakville (Ont.) Trafalgar.
COLLEGE: William & Mary.
TRANSACTIONS/CAREER NOTES: Signed as non-drafted free agent by Tampa Bay Buccaneers (May 8, 1990). ... Granted unconditional free agency (February 1, 1992). ... Signed by Buffalo Bills (February 5, 1992).
CHAMPIONSHIP GAME EXPERIENCE: Played in AFC championship game (1992 and 1993 seasons). ... Played in Super Bowl XXVII (1992 season) and Super Bowl XXVIII (1993 season).
POST SEASON RECORDS: Holds Super Bowl single-game record for longest field goal—54 yards (January 30, 1994, vs. Dallas). ... Shares NFL postseason single-game record for most field goals—5; and most field goals attempted—6 (January 17 1993, at Miami).
PRO STATISTICS: 1994—Recovered one fumble.

Year Team	G	GS	XPM	XPA	FGM	FGA	Lg.	50+	Pts.
1990—Tampa Bay NFL	16	0	27	27	23	27	54	2-2	96
1991—Tampa Bay NFL	16	0	22	22	15	20	49	0-0	67
1992—Buffalo NFL	16	0	43	§44	24	30	54	3-5	115
1993—Buffalo NFL	16	0	36	37	23	32	59	1-6	105
1994—Buffalo NFL	16	0	38	§38	24	28	52	2-2	110
1995—Buffalo NFL	16	0	33	35	31	40	51	2-5	126
1996—Buffalo NFL	16	0	33	33	24	29	48	0-1	105
1997—Buffalo NFL	16	0	21	21	24	30	55	1-2	93
Pro totals (8 years)	128	0	253	257	188	236	59	11-23	817

CHRISTY, JEFF   C   VIKINGS

PERSONAL: Born February 3, 1969, in Natrona Heights, Pa. ... 6-3/281. ... Full name: Jeffrey Alan Christy. ... Brother of Greg Christy, tackle with Buffalo Bills (1985).
HIGH SCHOOL: Freeport (Pa.) Area.
COLLEGE: Pittsburgh.
TRANSACTIONS/CAREER NOTES: Selected by Phoenix Cardinals in fourth round (91st pick overall) of 1992 NFL draft. ... Signed by Cardinals (July 21, 1992). ... Released by Cardinals (August 31, 1992). ... Signed by Minnesota Vikings (March 16, 1993). ... On injured reserve with ankle injury (November 26, 1997-remainder of season).
PLAYING EXPERIENCE: Minnesota NFL, 1993-1997. ... Games/Games started: 1993 (9/0), 1994 (16/16), 1995 (16/16), 1996 (16/16), 1997 (12/12). Total: 69/60.

CHRYPLEWICZ, PETE   TE   LIONS

PERSONAL: Born April 27, 1974, in Detroit. ... 6-5/253. ... Full name: Pete Gerald Chryplewicz.
HIGH SCHOOL: Sterling Heights (Detroit).
COLLEGE: Notre Dame (degree in business administration, 1996).
TRANSACTIONS/CAREER NOTES: Selected by Detroit Lions in fifth round (135th pick overall) of 1997 NFL draft. ... Signed by Lions (July 10, 1997).
SINGLE GAME HIGHS (regular season): Receptions—2 (September 21, 1997, vs. New Orleans); yards—23 (September 21, 1997, vs. New Orleans); and touchdown receptions—1 (September 28, 1997, vs. Green Bay).

Year Team	G	GS	RECEIVING				TOTALS			
			No.	Yds.	Avg.	TD	TD	2pt.	Pts.	Fum.
1997—Detroit NFL	10	0	3	27	9.0	1	1	0	6	0

CHUNG, EUGENE   G/OT

PERSONAL: Born June 14, 1969, in Prince George's County, Md. ... 6-5/311. ... Full name: Eugene Yon Chung.
HIGH SCHOOL: Oakton (Vienna, Va.).
COLLEGE: Virginia Tech (degree in hotel, restaurant and institutional management).
TRANSACTIONS/CAREER NOTES: Selected by New England Patriots in first round (13th pick overall) of 1992 NFL draft. ... Signed by Patriots (July 29, 1992). ... Selected by Jacksonville Jaguars from Patriots in NFL expansion draft (February 15, 1995). ... Granted unconditional free agency (February 16, 1996). ... Signed by San Francisco 49ers (March 20, 1996). ... Released by 49ers (August 25, 1996). ... Signed by Green Bay Packers (February 17, 1997). ... Released by Packers (August 24, 1997). ... Signed by Indianapolis Colts (August 27, 1997). ... Released by Colts (February 4, 1998).
PLAYING EXPERIENCE: New England NFL, 1992-1994; Jacksonville NFL, 1995; Indianapolis NFL, 1997. ... Games/Games started: 1992 (15/14), 1993 (16/16), 1994 (3/0), 1995 (11/0), 1997 (10/0). Total: 55/30.

CLARK, GREG   TE   49ERS

PERSONAL: Born April 7, 1972, in Bountiful, Utah. ... 6-4/251. ... Full name: Gregory Jay Clark.
HIGH SCHOOL: Mont (Centerville, Utah).
JUNIOR COLLEGE: Ricks College (Idaho).
COLLEGE: Stanford.
TRANSACTIONS/CAREER NOTES: Selected by San Francisco 49ers in third round (77th pick overall) of 1997 NFL draft. ... Signed by 49ers (July 17, 1997).
CHAMPIONSHIP GAME EXPERIENCE: Played in NFC championship game (1997 season).
SINGLE GAME HIGHS (regular season): Receptions—2 (November 16, 1997, vs. Carolina); yards—31 (October 26, 1997, vs. New Orleans); and touchdown receptions—1 (October 12, 1997, vs. St. Louis).

Year Team	G	GS	RECEIVING				TOTALS			
			No.	Yds.	Avg.	TD	TD	2pt.	Pts.	Fum.
1997—San Francisco NFL	15	4	8	96	12.0	1	1	0	6	0

CLARK, JON   OL   CARDINALS

PERSONAL: Born April 11, 1973, in Philadelphia ... 6-6/345.
HIGH SCHOOL: John Bartram (Philadelphia).
COLLEGE: Temple.
TRANSACTIONS/CAREER NOTES: Selected by Chicago Bears in sixth round (187th pick overall) of 1996 NFL draft. ... Signed by Bears (July 11, 1996). ... Released by Bears (October 7, 1997). ... Signed by New York Jets (December 8, 1997). ... Released by Jets (December 12, 1997). ... Signed by Arizona Cardinals (February 18, 1998).
PLAYING EXPERIENCE: Chicago NFL, 1996 and 1997. ... Games/Games started: 1996 (1/0), 1997 (1/0). Total: 2/0.

CLARK, REGGIE   LB   CHIEFS

PERSONAL: Born October 17, 1967, in Charlotte. ... 6-2/240. ... Full name: Reggie Boice Clark.
HIGH SCHOOL: Providence Day (Charlotte).
COLLEGE: North Carolina.
TRANSACTIONS/CAREER NOTES: Signed as non-drafted free agent by New England Patriots (April 27, 1991). ... Released by Patriots (August 26, 1991). ... Signed by Patriots to practice squad (August 28, 1991). ... Granted free agency after 1991 season. ... Re-signed by Patriots (February 1, 1992). ... Assigned by Patriots to Montreal Machine in 1992 World League enhancement allocation program (February 20, 1992). ... Released by Patriots (August 31, 1992). ... Re-signed by Patriots to practice squad (September 2, 1992). ... Released by Patriots (September 9, 1992). ... Signed by San Diego Chargers to practice squad (September 30, 1992). ... Granted free agency after 1992 season. ... Re-signed by Chargers (February 8, 1993). ... Released by Chargers (August 24, 1993). ... Signed by Pittsburgh Steelers (July 28, 1994). ... Released by Steelers (October 21, 1994). ... Signed by Jacksonville Jaguars (January 10, 1995). ... On injured reserve with knee injury (October 10, 1995-remainder of season). ... Released by Jaguars (October 1, 1996). ... Signed by Green Bay Packers (January 6, 1997). ... Released by Packers (June 2, 1997). ... Signed by Kansas City Chiefs (April 7, 1998).
PLAYING EXPERIENCE: Montreal W.L., 1992; Pittsburgh NFL, 1994; Jacksonville NFL, 1995 and 1996. ... Games/Games started: 1992 (10/4), 1994 (5/0), 1995 (5/0), 1996 (5/0). Total W.L.: 10/4. Total NFL: 15/0. Total Pro: 25/4.
PRO STATISTICS: W.L.: 1992—Credited with one sack and recovered one fumble. NFL: 1994—Recovered one fumble. 1995—Recovered one fumble.

CLARK, RICO   DB   COLTS

PERSONAL: Born June 6, 1974, in Atlanta. ... 5-10/181. ... Full name: Rico Cornell Clark.
HIGH SCHOOL: Lakeside (Atlanta).
COLLEGE: Louisville.
TRANSACTIONS/CAREER NOTES: Signed as non-drafted free agent by Indianapolis Colts (April 27, 1997). ... Released by Colts (August 18, 1997). ... Re-signed by Colts to practice squad (August 25, 1997). ... Released by Colts (October 8, 1997). ... Re-signed by Colts to practice squad (November 4, 1997). ... Activated (November 25, 1997).
PLAYING EXPERIENCE: Indianapolis NFL, 1997. ... Games/Games started: 4/2.
PRO STATISTICS: 1997—Intercepted one pass for 14 yards.

CLARK, WILLIE   CB   RAMS

PERSONAL: Born January 6, 1972, in New Haven, Conn. ... 5-10/186. ... Full name: Willie Calvin Clark.
HIGH SCHOOL: Wheatland (Calif.).
COLLEGE: Notre Dame.
TRANSACTIONS/CAREER NOTES: Selected by San Diego Chargers in third round (82nd pick overall) of 1994 NFL draft. ... Signed by Chargers (July 12, 1994). ... Granted free agency (February 14, 1997). ... Re-signed by Chargers (April 18, 1997). ... Released by Chargers (August 24, 1997). ... Traded by Baltimore Ravens to Philadelphia Eagles for undisclosed draft pick (August 27, 1997). ... Granted unconditional free agency (February 13, 1998). ... Signed by St. Louis Rams (May 6, 1998).
CHAMPIONSHIP GAME EXPERIENCE: Played in AFC championship game (1994 season). ... Played in Super Bowl XXIX (1994 season).
PRO STATISTICS: 1995—Recovered one fumble. 1996—Recovered one fumble for nine yards. 1997—Returned one kickoff for 39 yards and a touchdown.

			INTERCEPTIONS			
Year Team	G	GS	No.	Yds.	Avg.	TD
1994—San Diego NFL	6	0	0	0	...	0
1995—San Diego NFL	16	2	2	14	7.0	0
1996—San Diego NFL	16	4	2	83	41.5	1
1997—Philadelphia NFL	16	2	0	0	...	0
Pro totals (4 years)	54	8	4	97	24.3	1

CLAVELLE, SHANNON   DE

PERSONAL: Born October 12, 1973, in Lafayette, La. ... 6-2/287. ... Full name: Shannon Lynn Clavelle.
HIGH SCHOOL: O. Perry Walker (New Orleans).
COLLEGE: Colorado.
TRANSACTIONS/CAREER NOTES: Selected after junior season by Buffalo Bills in sixth round (185th pick overall) of 1995 NFL draft. ... Signed by Bills (June 27, 1995). ... Released by Bills (August 27, 1995). ... Signed by Green Bay Packers to practice squad (September 18, 1995). ... Activated (October 25, 1995). ... Released by Packers (October 22, 1997). ... Signed by Kansas City Chiefs (November 19, 1997). ... Released by Chiefs (December 5, 1997).
PLAYING EXPERIENCE: Green Bay NFL, 1995-1997. ... Games/Games started: 1995 (1/0), 1996 (8/0), 1997 (6/0). Total: 15/0.
CHAMPIONSHIP GAME EXPERIENCE: Member of Packers for NFC championship game (1995 and 1996 seasons); inactive. ... Member of Super Bowl championship team (1996 season); inactive.

CLAY, WILLIE   S   PATRIOTS

PERSONAL: Born September 5, 1970, in Pittsburgh. ... 5-10/200. ... Full name: Willie James Clay.
HIGH SCHOOL: Linsly (Wheeling, W.Va.).
COLLEGE: Georgia Tech.
TRANSACTIONS/CAREER NOTES: Selected by Detroit Lions in eighth round (221st pick overall) of 1992 NFL draft. ... Signed by Lions (July 25, 1992). ... Released by Lions (September 4, 1992). ... Re-signed by Lions to practice squad (September 8, 1992). ... Activated (November 20, 1992). ... Granted free agency (February 17, 1995). ... Re-signed by Lions (May 16, 1995). ... Granted unconditional free agency (February 16, 1996). ... Signed by New England Patriots (March 14, 1996).
CHAMPIONSHIP GAME EXPERIENCE: Played in AFC championship game (1996 season). ... Played in Super Bowl XXXI (1996 season).
HONORS: Named defensive back on THE SPORTING NEWS college All-America second team (1991).
PRO STATISTICS: 1993—Credited with one sack, returned two kickoffs for 34 yards and recovered two fumbles for 54 yards and two touchdowns. 1996—Recovered one fumble for 17 yards. 1997—Recovered two fumbles.

| | | | INTERCEPTIONS | | |
Year Team	G	GS	No.	Yds.	Avg.	TD
1992—Detroit NFL	6	0	0	0	...	0
1993—Detroit NFL	16	1	0	0	...	0
1994—Detroit NFL	16	16	3	54	18.0	1
1995—Detroit NFL	16	16	8	*173	21.6	0
1996—New England NFL	16	16	4	50	12.5	0
1997—New England NFL	16	16	6	109	18.2	1
Pro totals (6 years)	86	65	21	386	18.4	2

CLEMENTS, CHUCK   QB   JETS

PERSONAL: Born September 29, 1973, in Kingsville, Texas. ... 6-3/214.
HIGH SCHOOL: Huntsville (Texas).
COLLEGE: Houston.
TRANSACTIONS/CAREER NOTES: Selected by New York Jets in sixth round (191st pick overall) of 1997 NFL draft. ... Signed by Jets (July 17, 1997).
PLAYING EXPERIENCE: New York Jets NFL, 1997. ... Games/Games started: 1997 (1/0).
PRO STATISTICS: 1997—Rushed twice for minus three yards.
SINGLE GAME HIGHS (regular season): Attempts—0; completions—0; yards—0; and touchdown passes—0.

CLEMONS, CHARLIE   LB   RAMS

PERSONAL: Born July 4, 1972, in Griffin, Ga. ... 6-2/255. ... Full name: Charlie Fitzgerald Clemons.
HIGH SCHOOL: Griffin (Ga.).
JUNIOR COLLEGE: Northeast Oklahoma.
COLLEGE: Georgia.
TRANSACTIONS/CAREER NOTES: Signed by Winnipeg Blue Bombers of CFL (May 1994). ... Transferred to Ottawa Rough Riders (August 1995). ... Transferred to Blue Bombers (January 1996). ... Signed by St. Louis Rams (February 19, 1997). ... On injured reserve with hamstring injury (November 24, 1997-remainder of season).
PLAYING EXPERIENCE: St. Louis NFL, 1997. ... Games/Games started: 5/0.
PRO STATISTICS: CFL: 1994—Recovered one fumble. 1995—Returned one kickoff for 10 yards.

Year Team	G	GS	Sacks
1994—Winnipeg CFL	7	...	0.0
1995—Winnipeg CFL	6	...	3.0
—Ottawa CFL	7	...	3.0
1996—Ottawa CFL	14	...	6.0
1997—St. Louis NFL	5	0	0.0
CFL totals (3 years)	34	...	12.0
NFL totals (1 year)	5	0	0.0
Pro totals (4 years)	59	...	12.0

CLEMONS, DUANE   DE   VIKINGS

PERSONAL: Born May 23, 1974, in Riverside, Calif. ... 6-5/277.
HIGH SCHOOL: John W. North (Riverside, Calif.).
COLLEGE: California.
TRANSACTIONS/CAREER NOTES: Selected after junior season by Minnesota Vikings in first round (16th pick overall) of 1996 NFL draft. ... Signed by Vikings (July 25, 1996).
PRO STATISTICS: 1996—Recovered one fumble for eight yards. 1997—Recovered one fumble.

Year Team	G	GS	SACKS
1996—Minnesota NFL	13	0	0.0
1997—Minnesota NFL	13	3	7.0
Pro totals (2 years)	26	3	7.0

CLINE, TONY   TE

PERSONAL: Born November 24, 1971, in Davis, Calif. ... 6-4/247. ... Full name: Anthony Francis Cline. ... Son of Tony Cline, defensive lineman with Oakland Raiders (1970-1975) and San Francisco 49ers (1976).
HIGH SCHOOL: Davis (Calif.).
COLLEGE: Stanford.

TRANSACTIONS/CAREER NOTES: Selected by Buffalo Bills in fourth round (131st pick overall) of 1995 NFL draft. ... Signed by Bills (July 10, 1995). ... Granted free agency (February 13, 1998).
PRO STATISTICS: 1995—Returned one kickoff for 11 yards. 1997—Returned one kickoff for no yards.
SINGLE GAME HIGHS (regular season): Receptions—6 (September 1, 1996, vs. New York Giants); yards—41 (September 1, 1996, vs. New York Giants); and touchdown receptions—1 (December 22, 1996, vs. Kansas City).

			RECEIVING				TOTALS		
Year Team	G	GS	No.	Yds.	Avg.	TD	TD	2pt.	Pts.	Fum.
1995—Buffalo NFL	16	1	8	64	8.0	0	0	0	0	0
1996—Buffalo NFL	16	7	19	117	6.2	1	1	0	6	0
1997—Buffalo NFL	10	1	1	29	29.0	0	0	0	0	0
Pro totals (3 years)	42	9	28	210	7.5	1	1	0	6	0

COAKLEY, DEXTER — LB — COWBOYS

PERSONAL: Born October 20, 1972, in Charleston, S.C. ... 5-10/215. ... Full name: William Dexter Coakley.
HIGH SCHOOL: Wando (Mt. Pleasant, S.C.), then Fork Union (Va.) Military Academy.
COLLEGE: Appalachian State.
TRANSACTIONS/CAREER NOTES: Selected by Dallas Cowboys in third round (65th pick overall) of 1997 NFL draft. ... Signed by Cowboys (July 14, 1997).
PRO STATISTICS: 1997—Recovered one fumble for 16 yards and a touchdown.

			INTERCEPTIONS				SACKS
Year Team	G	GS	No.	Yds.	Avg.	TD	No.
1997—Dallas NFL	16	16	1	6	6.0	0	2.5

COATES, BEN — TE — PATRIOTS

PERSONAL: Born August 16, 1969, in Greenwood, S.C. ... 6-5/245. ... Full name: Ben Terrence Coates.
HIGH SCHOOL: Greenwood (S.C.).
COLLEGE: Livingstone College, N.C. (degree in sports management).
TRANSACTIONS/CAREER NOTES: Selected after junior season by New England Patriots in fifth round (124th pick overall) of 1991 NFL draft. ... Signed by Patriots (April 25, 1991). ... Granted free agency (February 17, 1994). ... Re-signed by Patriots (April 2, 1994).
CHAMPIONSHIP GAME EXPERIENCE: Played in AFC championship game (1996 season). ... Played in Super Bowl XXXI (1996 season).
HONORS: Named tight end on THE SPORTING NEWS NFL All-Pro team (1994 and 1995). ... Played in Pro Bowl (1994-1997 seasons).
RECORDS: Holds NFL single-season record for most receptions by tight end—96 (1994).
PRO STATISTICS: 1991—Rushed once for minus six yards and returned one kickoff for six yards. 1992—Rushed once for two yards. 1994—Rushed once for no yards and recovered two fumbles. 1997—Returned one kickoff for 20 yards.
SINGLE GAME HIGHS (regular season): Receptions—12 (November 27, 1994, vs. Indianapolis); yards—161 (September 4, 1994, vs. Miami); and touchdown receptions—3 (November 26, 1995, vs. Buffalo).
STATISTICAL PLATEAUS: 100-yard receiving games: 1993 (1), 1994 (5), 1995 (1), 1996 (1). Total: 8.

			RECEIVING				TOTALS		
Year Team	G	GS	No.	Yds.	Avg.	TD	TD	2pt.	Pts.	Fum.
1991—New England NFL	16	2	10	95	9.5	1	1	...	6	0
1992—New England NFL	16	2	20	171	8.6	3	3	...	18	1
1993—New England NFL	16	10	53	659	12.4	8	8	...	48	0
1994—New England NFL	16	16	§96	1174	12.2	7	7	0	42	2
1995—New England NFL	16	15	84	915	10.9	6	6	0	36	4
1996—New England NFL	16	15	62	682	11.0	9	9	1	56	1
1997—New England NFL	16	16	66	737	11.2	8	8	0	48	0
Pro totals (7 years)	112	76	391	4433	11.3	42	42	1	254	8

COBBINS, LYRON — LB — CARDINALS

PERSONAL: Born September 17, 1974, in Kansas City, Kan. ... 6-0/250.
HIGH SCHOOL: Wyandotte (Kansas City, Kan.).
COLLEGE: Notre Dame (degree in psychology, 1997).
TRANSACTIONS/CAREER NOTES: Signed as non-drafted free agent by Arizona Cardinals (April 21, 1997). ... Released by Cardinals (August 24, 1997). ... Re-signed by Cardinals to practice squad (August 26, 1997). ... Activated (September 1, 1997). ... Released by Cardinals (October 10, 1997). ... Re-signed by Cardinals to practice squad (October 12, 1997). ... Activated (November 1, 1997).
PLAYING EXPERIENCE: Arizona NFL, 1997. ... Games/Games started: 6/0.

COCOZZO, JOE — G — REDSKINS

PERSONAL: Born August 7, 1970, in Mechanicville, N.Y. ... 6-4/300. ... Full name: Joseph Ramond Cocozzo. ... Name pronounced cuh-COE-zoe.
HIGH SCHOOL: Mechanicville (N.Y.).
COLLEGE: Michigan (degree in communications, 1993).
TRANSACTIONS/CAREER NOTES: Selected by San Diego Chargers in third round (64th pick overall) of 1993 NFL draft. ... Signed by Chargers (July 14, 1993). ... Granted free agency (February 16, 1996). ... Re-signed by Chargers (June 14, 1996). ... Granted unconditional free agency (February 13, 1998). ... Signed by Washington Redskins (June 1, 1998).
PLAYING EXPERIENCE: San Diego NFL, 1993-1997. ... Games/Games started: 1993 (16/5), 1994 (13/13), 1995 (15/7), 1996 (16/11), 1997 (16/12). Total: 76/48.
CHAMPIONSHIP GAME EXPERIENCE: Played in AFC championship game (1994 season). ... Played in Super Bowl XXIX (1994 season).
HONORS: Named guard on THE SPORTING NEWS college All-America second team (1992).

COLEMAN, ANDRE — WR/KR — STEELERS

PERSONAL: Born September 19, 1972, in Hermitage, Pa. ... 5-9/165. ... Full name: Andre Clintonian Coleman.
HIGH SCHOOL: Hickory (Hermitage, Pa.).
COLLEGE: Kansas State.
TRANSACTIONS/CAREER NOTES: Selected by San Diego Chargers in third round (70th pick overall) of 1994 NFL draft. ... Signed by Chargers (July 12, 1994). ... Granted free agency (February 14, 1997). ... Re-signed by Chargers (June 2, 1997). ... Released by Chargers (August 19, 1997). ... Signed by Seattle Seahawks (August 26, 1997). ... Released by Seahawks (October 1, 1997). ... Signed by Pittsburgh Steelers (October 14, 1997).
CHAMPIONSHIP GAME EXPERIENCE: Played in AFC championship game (1994 and 1997 seasons). ... Played in Super Bowl XXIX (1994 season).
POST SEASON RECORDS: Shares Super Bowl and NFL postseason career and single-game records for most touchdowns by kickoff return—1. ... Holds Super Bowl and NFL postseason single-game records for most kickoff returns—8; and most yards by kickoff returns—244 (January 29, 1995, vs. San Francisco. ... Shares Super Bowl and NFL postseason single-game records for most yards by combined kick returns—244 (January 29, 1995, vs. San Francisco).
PRO STATISTICS: 1994—Recovered one fumble. 1995—Recovered three fumbles. 1996—Recovered three fumbles.
SINGLE GAME HIGHS (regular season): Receptions—5 (September 15, 1996, vs. Green Bay); yards—70 (September 8, 1996, vs. Cincinnati); and touchdown receptions—1 (December 14, 1996, vs. Chicago).

Year Team	G	GS	RECEIVING No.	Yds.	Avg.	TD	PUNT RETURNS No.	Yds.	Avg.	TD	KICKOFF RETURNS No.	Yds.	Avg.	TD	TOTALS TD	2pt.	Pts.	Fum.
1994—San Diego NFL	13	0	0	0	...	0	0	0	...	0	§49	§1293	26.4	▲2	2	0	12	3
1995—San Diego NFL	15	0	4	78	19.5	0	28	326	§11.6	†1	62	§1411	22.8	†2	3	0	18	10
1996—San Diego NFL	16	10	36	486	13.5	2	0	0	...	0	§55	1210	22.0	0	2	0	12	4
1997—Seattle NFL	2	0	0	0	...	0	0	0	...	0	3	65	21.7	0	0	0	0	1
—Pittsburgh NFL	8	0	0	0	...	0	5	5	1.0	0	24	487	20.3	0	0	0	0	1
Pro totals (4 years)	54	10	40	564	14.1	2	33	331	10.0	1	193	4466	23.1	4	7	0	42	19

COLEMAN, BEN — G/OT — JAGUARS

PERSONAL: Born May 18, 1971, in South Hill, Va. ... 6-5/627. ... Full name: Benjamin Leon Coleman.
HIGH SCHOOL: Park View Senior (South Hill, Va.).
COLLEGE: Wake Forest.
TRANSACTIONS/CAREER NOTES: Selected by Phoenix Cardinals in second round (32nd pick overall) of 1993 NFL draft. ... Signed by Cardinals (July 6, 1993). ... Cardinals franchise renamed Arizona Cardinals for 1994 season. ... Claimed on waivers by Jacksonville Jaguars (September 27, 1995). ... Granted free agency (February 16, 1996). ... Re-signed by Jaguars (June 6, 1996). ... Granted unconditional free agency (February 14, 1997). ... Re-signed by Jaguars (March 3, 1997).
PLAYING EXPERIENCE: Phoenix NFL, 1993; Arizona NFL, 1994; Arizona (3)-Jacksonville (10) NFL, 1995; Jacksonville NFL, 1996 and 1997. ... Games/Games started: 1993 (12/0), 1994 (15/13), 1995 (Ariz.-3/0; Jack.-10/5; Total: 13/5), 1996 (16/16), 1997 (16/16). Total: 72/50.
CHAMPIONSHIP GAME EXPERIENCE: Played in AFC championship game (1996 season).
PRO STATISTICS: 1995—Recovered one fumble.

COLEMAN, MARCO — DE — CHARGERS

PERSONAL: Born December 18, 1969, in Dayton, Ohio. ... 6-3/267. ... Full name: Marco Darnell Coleman.
HIGH SCHOOL: Patterson Co-op (Dayton, Ohio).
COLLEGE: Georgia Tech.
TRANSACTIONS/CAREER NOTES: Selected after junior season by Miami Dolphins in first round (12th pick overall) of 1992 NFL draft. ... Signed by Dolphins (August 1, 1992). ... Designated by Dolphins as transition player (February 25, 1993). ... Tendered offer sheet by San Diego Chargers (February 28, 1996). ... Dolphins declined to match offer (March 7, 1996).
CHAMPIONSHIP GAME EXPERIENCE: Played in AFC championship game (1992 season).
HONORS: Named linebacker on THE SPORTING NEWS college All-America second team (1991).
PRO STATISTICS: 1997—Intercepted one pass for two yards.

Year Team	G	GS	SACKS
1992—Miami NFL	16	15	6.0
1993—Miami NFL	16	15	5.5
1994—Miami NFL	16	16	6.0
1995—Miami NFL	16	16	6.5
1996—San Diego NFL	16	15	4.0
1997—San Diego NFL	16	16	2.0
Pro totals (6 years)	95	93	30.0

COLEMAN, MARCUS — S — JETS

PERSONAL: Born May 24, 1974, in Dallas. ... 6-2/210.
HIGH SCHOOL: Lake Highlands (Dallas).
COLLEGE: Texas Tech.
TRANSACTIONS/CAREER NOTES: Selected by New York Jets in fifth round (133rd pick overall) of 1996 NFL draft. ... Signed by Jets (July 11, 1996).
PRO STATISTICS: 1997—Recovered one fumble.

Year Team	G	GS	INTERCEPTIONS No.	Yds.	Avg.	TD
1996—New York Jets NFL	13	4	1	23	23.0	0
1997—New York Jets NFL	16	2	1	24	24.0	0
Pro totals (2 years)	29	6	2	47	23.5	0

COLINET, STALIN   DE   VIKINGS

PERSONAL: Born July 19, 1974, in Bronx, N.Y. ... 6-6/274.
HIGH SCHOOL: Cardinal Hayes (Bronx, N.Y.).
COLLEGE: Boston College (degree in sociology, 1996).
TRANSACTIONS/CAREER NOTES: Selected by Minnesota Vikings in third round (78th pick overall) of 1997 NFL draft. ... Signed by Vikings (June 30, 1997).
PLAYING EXPERIENCE: Minnesota NFL, 1997. ... Games/Games started: 10/2.

COLLINS, ANDRE   LB   BEARS

PERSONAL: Born May 4, 1968, in Riverside, N.J. ... 6-1/231. ... Full name: Andre Pierre Collins.
HIGH SCHOOL: Cinnaminson (N.J.).
COLLEGE: Penn State (degree in health planning and administration, 1991).
TRANSACTIONS/CAREER NOTES: Selected by Washington Redskins in second round (46th pick overall) of 1990 NFL draft. ... Signed by Redskins (July 22, 1990). ... Granted free agency (March 1, 1993). ... Re-signed by Redskins for 1993 season. ... Released by Redskins (April 11, 1995). ... Signed by Cincinnati Bengals (May 7, 1995). ... Granted free agency (February 16, 1996). ... Re-signed by Bengals (August 22, 1996). ... Granted free agency (February 14, 1997). ... Re-signed by Bengals (July 2, 1997). ... Granted unconditional free agency (February 13, 1998). ... Signed by Chicago Bears (May 27, 1998).
CHAMPIONSHIP GAME EXPERIENCE: Played in NFC championship game (1991 season). ... Member of Super Bowl championship team (1991 season).
HONORS: Named inside linebacker on THE SPORTING NEWS college All-America second team (1989).
PRO STATISTICS: 1991—Fumbled once. 1992—Recovered one fumble for 40 yards. 1994—Returned one kickoff for no yards and recovered one fumble for 16 yards. 1995—Returned one kickoff for minus three yards. 1997—Recovered one fumble.

				INTERCEPTIONS			SACKS
Year Team	G	GS	No.	Yds.	Avg.	TD	No.
1990—Washington NFL	16	16	0	0	...	0	6.0
1991—Washington NFL	16	16	2	33	16.5	∞1	3.0
1992—Washington NFL	14	14	1	59	59.0	0	2.0
1993—Washington NFL	13	13	1	5	5.0	0	6.0
1994—Washington NFL	16	16	4	150	37.5	2	1.5
1995—Cincinnati NFL	16	6	2	3	1.5	0	4.0
1996—Cincinnati NFL	14	0	0	0	...	0	0.0
1997—Cincinnati NFL	16	0	0	0	...	0	3.0
Pro totals (8 years)	121	81	10	250	25.0	3	25.5

COLLINS, CALVIN   C   FALCONS

PERSONAL: Born January 5, 1974, in Beaumont, Texas. ... 6-2/307. ... Full name: Calvin Lewis Collins.
HIGH SCHOOL: West Brook (Beaumont, Texas).
COLLEGE: Texas A&M.
TRANSACTIONS/CAREER NOTES: Selected by Atlanta Falcons in sixth round (180th pick overall) of 1997 NFL draft. ... Signed by Falcons (June 22, 1997).
PLAYING EXPERIENCE: Atlanta NFL, 1997. ... Games/Games started: 15/13.

COLLINS, KERRY   QB   PANTHERS

PERSONAL: Born December 30, 1972, in West Lawn, Pa. ... 6-5/240. ... Full name: Kerry Michael Collins.
HIGH SCHOOL: Wilson-West Lawn (Pa.).
COLLEGE: Penn State.
TRANSACTIONS/CAREER NOTES: Selected by Carolina Panthers in first round (fifth pick overall) of 1995 NFL draft. ... Signed by Panthers (July 17, 1995). ... Granted free agency (February 13, 1998).
CHAMPIONSHIP GAME EXPERIENCE: Played in NFC championship game (1996 season).
HONORS: Maxwell Award winner (1994). ... Davey O'Brien Award winner (1994). ... Named quarterback on THE SPORTING NEWS college All-America first team (1994). ... Played in Pro Bowl (1996 season).
PRO STATISTICS: 1995—Fumbled 13 times and recovered four fumbles for minus 15 yards. 1996—Fumbled six times and recovered one fumble. 1997—Fumbled eight times and recovered two fumbles for minus 14 yards.
SINGLE GAME HIGHS (regular season): Attempts—47 (September 21, 1997, vs. Kansas City); completions—26 (December 15, 1996, vs. Baltimore); yards—335 (November 26, 1995, vs. New Orleans); and touchdown passes—3 (December 8, 1996, vs. San Francisco).
STATISTICAL PLATEAUS: 300-yard passing games: 1995 (2), 1996 (1), 1997 (1). Total: 4.
MISCELLANEOUS: Selected by Detroit Tigers organization in 26th round of free-agent draft (June 4, 1990); did not sign. ... Selected by Toronto Blue Jays organization in 58th round of free-agent draft (June 4, 1994); did not sign. ... Regular-season record as starting NFL quarterback: 22-16 (.579). ... Postseason record as starting NFL quarterback: 1-1 (.500). ... Holds Carolina Panthers all-time records for most yards passing (7,295) and most touchdown passes (39).

					PASSING						RUSHING				TOTALS		
Year Team	G	GS	Att.	Cmp.	Pct.	Yds.	TD	Int.	Avg.	Rat.	Att.	Yds.	Avg.	TD	TD	2pt.	Pts.
1995—Carolina NFL	15	13	433	214	49.4	2717	14	19	6.27	61.9	42	74	1.8	3	3	0	18
1996—Carolina NFL	13	12	364	204	56.0	2454	14	9	6.74	79.4	32	38	1.2	0	0	1	2
1997—Carolina NFL	13	13	381	200	52.5	2124	11	*21	5.57	55.7	26	65	2.5	1	1	0	0
Pro totals (3 years)	41	38	1178	618	52.5	7295	39	49	6.19	65.3	100	177	1.8	4	4	1	26

COLLINS, MARK   CB   SEAHAWKS

PERSONAL: Born January 16, 1964, in San Bernardino, Calif. ... 5-10/205. ... Full name: Mark Anthony Collins.
HIGH SCHOOL: Pacific (San Bernardino, Calif.).
COLLEGE: Cal State Fullerton.
TRANSACTIONS/CAREER NOTES: Selected by New York Giants in second round (44th pick overall) of 1986 NFL draft. ... Signed by Giants (July 30, 1986). ... On injured reserve with back injury (December 23, 1987-remainder of season). ... On injured reserve with pulled groin (December 3, 1988-remainder of season). ... On injured reserve with sprained ankle (September 19-October 19, 1990). ... Granted free agency (February 1, 1992). ... Re-signed by Giants (August 7, 1992). ... On injured reserve with rib injury (December 24, 1992-remainder of season). ... Granted unconditional free agency (February 17, 1994). ... Signed by Kansas City Chiefs (April 26, 1994). ... Released by Chiefs (May 9, 1997). ... Signed by Green Bay Packers (November 27, 1997). ... Granted unconditional free agency (February 13, 1998). ... Signed by Seattle Seahawks (April 21, 1998).
CHAMPIONSHIP GAME EXPERIENCE: Played in NFC championship game (1986, 1990 and 1997 seasons). ... Member of Super Bowl championship team (1986 and 1990 seasons). ... Played in Super Bowl XXXII (1997 season).
HONORS: Named defensive back on THE SPORTING NEWS college All-America first team (1985).
PRO STATISTICS: 1986—Returned three punts for 11 yards and recovered three fumbles for five yards. 1988—Credited with one safety. 1989—Recovered two fumbles for eight yards. 1991—Recovered two fumbles. 1994—Recovered two fumbles. 1995—Recovered one fumble for 34 yards and a touchdown. 1996—Recovered one fumble.

			INTERCEPTIONS				SACKS	KICKOFF RETURNS				TOTALS			
Year Team	G	GS	No.	Yds.	Avg.	TD	No.	No.	Yds.	Avg.	TD	TD	2pt.	Pts.	Fum.
1986—New York Giants NFL	15	9	1	0	0.0	0	0.0	11	204	18.5	0	0	...	0	2
1987—New York Giants NFL	11	11	2	28	14.0	0	1.5	0	0	...	0	0	...	0	0
1988—New York Giants NFL	11	11	1	13	13.0	0	0.0	4	67	16.8	0	0	...	2	0
1989—New York Giants NFL	16	16	2	12	6.0	0	1.0	1	0	0.0	0	0	...	0	0
1990—New York Giants NFL	13	12	2	0	0.0	0	0.0	0	0	...	0	0	...	0	0
1991—New York Giants NFL	16	15	4	77	19.3	0	0.0	0	0	...	0	0	...	0	0
1992—New York Giants NFL	14	14	1	0	0.0	0	0.0	0	0	...	0	0	...	0	0
1993—New York Giants NFL	16	16	4	77	19.3	1	1.0	0	0	...	0	1	...	6	0
1994—Kansas City NFL	14	13	2	83	41.5	1	2.0	0	0	...	0	1	0	6	0
1995—Kansas City NFL	16	15	1	8	8.0	0	0.0	0	0	...	0	1	0	6	1
1996—Kansas City NFL	16	15	6	45	7.5	0	1.0	0	0	...	0	0	...	0	0
1997—Green Bay NFL	1	0	0	0		0	0.0	0	0	...	0	0	...	0	0
Pro totals (12 years)	159	147	26	343	13.2	2	6.5	16	271	16.9	0	3	0	20	3

COLLINS, TODD   QB   BILLS

PERSONAL: Born November 5, 1971, in Walpole, Mass. ... 6-4/224.
HIGH SCHOOL: Walpole (Mass.).
COLLEGE: Michigan.
TRANSACTIONS/CAREER NOTES: Selected by Buffalo Bills in second round (45th pick overall) of 1995 NFL draft. ... Signed by Bills (July 10, 1995).
PRO STATISTICS: 1996—Fumbled three times. 1997—Fumbled 10 times for minus 30 yards.
SINGLE GAME HIGHS (regular season): Attempts—44 (October 6, 1996, vs. Indianapolis); completions—25 (November 23, 1997, vs. Tennessee); yards—309 (October 6, 1996, vs. Indianapolis); and touchdown passes—3 (September 7, 1997, vs. New York Jets).
STATISTICAL PLATEAUS: 300-yard passing games: 1996 (1).
MISCELLANEOUS: Regular-season record as starting NFL quarterback: 7-10 (.412).

			PASSING								RUSHING				TOTALS		
Year Team	G	GS	Att.	Cmp.	Pct.	Yds.	TD	Int.	Avg.	Rat.	Att.	Yds.	Avg.	TD	TD	2pt.	Pts.
1995—Buffalo NFL	7	1	29	14	48.3	112	0	1	3.86	44.0	9	23	2.6	0	0	0	0
1996—Buffalo NFL	7	3	99	55	55.6	739	4	5	7.46	71.9	21	43	2.0	0	0	0	0
1997—Buffalo NFL	14	13	391	215	55.0	2367	12	13	6.05	69.5	30	77	2.6	0	0	0	0
Pro totals (3 years)	28	17	519	284	54.7	3218	16	19	6.20	68.5	60	143	2.4	0	0	0	0

COLLINS, TODD   LB   PATRIOTS

PERSONAL: Born May 27, 1970, in New Market, Tenn. ... 6-2/248. ... Full name: Todd Franklin Collins.
HIGH SCHOOL: Jefferson County (Dandridge, Tenn.).
COLLEGE: Georgia (did not play football), then Tennessee (did not play football), then Carson-Newman College (Tenn.).
TRANSACTIONS/CAREER NOTES: Selected after junior season by New England Patriots in third round (64th pick overall) of 1992 NFL draft. ... Signed by Patriots (July 23, 1992). ... On injured reserve with neck injury (October 16-November 13, 1992); on practice squad (November 11-13, 1992). ... On injured reserve with knee injury (November 15, 1994-remainder of season). ... Granted free agency (February 17, 1995). ... Re-signed by Patriots (April 20, 1995). ... Placed on reserved/retired list (July 21, 1995-April 16, 1996). ... Granted unconditional free agency (February 14, 1997). ... Re-signed by Patriots (April 4, 1997).
PLAYING EXPERIENCE: New England NFL, 1992-1994, 1996 and 1997. ... Games/Games started: 1992 (10/0), 1993 (16/12), 1994 (7/7), 1996 (16/9), 1997 (15/15). Total: 64/43.
CHAMPIONSHIP GAME EXPERIENCE: Played in AFC championship game (1996 season). ... Played in Super Bowl XXXI (1996 season).
PRO STATISTICS: 1992—Recovered two fumbles. 1993—Credited with one sack, intercepted one pass for eight yards and recovered one fumble for two yards. 1996—Intercepted one pass for seven yards. 1997—Credited with 1 1/2 sacks.

COLLONS, FERRIC   DE   PATRIOTS

PERSONAL: Born December 4, 1969, in Scott Air Force Base (Belleville, Ill.). ... 6-6/285. ... Full name: Ferric Jason Collons.
HIGH SCHOOL: Jesuit (Carmichael, Calif.).
COLLEGE: California.

TRANSACTIONS/CAREER NOTES: Signed as non-drafted free agent by Los Angeles Raiders (April 1992). ... Released by Raiders (August 31, 1992). ... Re-signed by Raiders to practice squad (September 2, 1992). ... Inactive for all 16 games (1993). ... Released by Raiders (August 23, 1994). ... Signed by Jacksonville Jaguars (December 15, 1994). ... Released by Jaguars (May 1, 1995). ... Signed by Green Bay Packers (May 22, 1995). ... Traded by Packers to New England Patriots for past considerations (August 27, 1995). ... Granted free agency (February 14, 1997). ... Tendered offer sheet by Philadelphia Eagles (April 14, 1997). ... Offer matched by Patriots (April 18, 1997). ... On injured reserve with shoulder injury (October 30, 1997-remainder of season).

CHAMPIONSHIP GAME EXPERIENCE: Played in AFC championship game (1996 season). ... Played in Super Bowl XXXI (1996 season).

PRO STATISTICS: 1997—Recovered one fumble for five yards.

Year Team	G	GS	SACKS
1992—Los Angeles NFL	Did not play.		
1993—Los Angeles NFL	Did not play.		
1994—Jacksonville NFL	Did not play.		
1995—New England NFL	16	4	4.0
1996—New England NFL	15	5	0.5
1997—New England NFL	6	5	1.0
Pro totals (3 years)	37	14	5.5

COLMAN, DOUG — LB — GIANTS

PERSONAL: Born June 4, 1973, in Somers Point, N.J. ... 6-2/250.
HIGH SCHOOL: Ocean City (N.J.).
COLLEGE: Nebraska.
TRANSACTIONS/CAREER NOTES: Selected by New York Giants in sixth round (171st pick overall) of 1996 NFL draft. ... Signed by Giants (June 18, 1996).
PLAYING EXPERIENCE: New York Giants NFL, 1996 and 1997. ... Games/Games started: 1996 (13/0), 1997 (14/0). Total: 27/0.

COLON, HARRY — S

PERSONAL: Born February 14, 1969, in Kansas City, Kan. ... 6-0/203.
HIGH SCHOOL: Washington (Kansas City, Kan.).
COLLEGE: Missouri.
TRANSACTIONS/CAREER NOTES: Selected by New England Patriots in eighth round (196th pick overall) of 1991 NFL draft. ... Signed by Patriots (July 12, 1991). ... Granted unconditional free agency (February 1, 1992). ... Signed by Detroit Lions (March 30, 1992). ... Granted free agency (February 15, 1994). ... Re-signed by Lions (July 20, 1994). ... Selected by Jacksonville Jaguars from Lions in NFL expansion draft (February 15, 1995). ... Released by Jaguars (April 16, 1996). ... Signed by Lions (March 19, 1997). ... Released by Lions (June 20, 1997). ... Re-signed by Lions (August 12, 1997). ... On injured reserve with neck injury (October 21, 1997-remainder of season). ... Granted unconditional free agency (February 13, 1998).

PRO STATISTICS: 1991—Recovered two fumbles for minus eight yards. 1992—Recovered two fumbles. 1993—Credited with a sack.

			INTERCEPTIONS			
Year Team	G	GS	No.	Yds.	Avg.	TD
1991—New England NFL	16	...	0	0	...	0
1992—Detroit NFL	16	...	0	0	...	0
1993—Detroit NFL	15	11	2	28	14.0	0
1994—Detroit NFL	16	0	1	3	3.0	0
1995—Jacksonville NFL	16	16	3	46	15.3	0
1996—			Did not play.			
1997—Detroit NFL	8	4	0	0	...	0
Pro totals (6 years)	87	31	6	77	12.8	0

COMPTON, MIKE — G — LIONS

PERSONAL: Born September 18, 1970, in Richlands, Va. ... 6-6/297. ... Full name: Michael Eugene Compton.
HIGH SCHOOL: Richlands (Va.).
COLLEGE: West Virginia.
TRANSACTIONS/CAREER NOTES: Selected by Detroit Lions in third round (68th pick overall) of 1993 NFL draft. ... Signed by Lions (June 4, 1993).
PLAYING EXPERIENCE: Detroit NFL, 1993-1997. ... Games/Games started: 1993 (8/0), 1994 (2/0), 1995 (16/8), 1996 (15/15), 1997 (16/16). Total: 57/39.
HONORS: Named center on THE SPORTING NEWS college All-America first team (1992).
PRO STATISTICS: 1996—Fumbled once.

CONATY, BILLY — C — BILLS

PERSONAL: Born March 8, 1973, in Baltimore. ... 6-2/306. ... Full name: William B. Conaty. ... Name pronounced con-ah-TEE.
HIGH SCHOOL: Camden (N.J.) Catholic, then Milford (Conn.) Academy.
COLLEGE: Virginia Tech.
TRANSACTIONS/CAREER NOTES: Signed as non-drafted free agent by Buffalo Bills (April 25, 1997). ... Released by Bills (August 24, 1997). ... Re-signed by Bills to practice squad (August 26, 1997). ... Activated (September 6, 1997). ... Released by Bills (September 22, 1997). ... Re-signed by Bills to practice squad (September 24, 1997).
PLAYING EXPERIENCE: Buffalo NFL, 1997. ... Games/Games started: 1/0.
HONORS: Named center on THE SPORTING NEWS college All-America first team (1996).

CONLEY, STEVEN   LB   STEELERS

PERSONAL: Born January 18, 1972, in Chicago. ... 6-5/235.
HIGH SCHOOL: Luther South (Chicago).
COLLEGE: Arkansas.
TRANSACTIONS/CAREER NOTES: Selected by Pittsburgh Steelers in third round (72nd pick overall) of 1996 NFL draft. ... Signed by Steelers (July 12, 1996).
CHAMPIONSHIP GAME EXPERIENCE: Played in AFC championship game (1997 season).
PRO STATISTICS: 1997—Intercepted one pass for minus three yards.

Year Team	G	GS	SACKS
1996—Pittsburgh NFL	2	0	0.0
1997—Pittsburgh NFL	16	0	4.0
Pro totals (2 years)	18	0	4.0

CONNELL, ALBERT   WR   REDSKINS

PERSONAL: Born May 13, 1974, in Fort Lauderdale ... 6-0/179 Full name: Albert Gene Anthony Connell.
HIGH SCHOOL: Piper (Fort Lauderdale).
JUNIOR COLLEGE: Trinity Valley Community College (Texas).
COLLEGE: Texas A&M.
TRANSACTIONS/CAREER NOTES: Selected by Washington Redskins in fourth round (115th pick overall) of 1997 NFL draft. ... Signed by Redskins (May 28, 1997).
PRO STATISTICS: 1997—Rushed once for three yards.
SINGLE GAME HIGHS (regular season): Receptions—5 (December 13, 1997, vs. New York Giants); yards—89 (December 13, 1997, vs. New York Giants); and touchdown receptions—1 (December 13, 1997, vs. New York Giants).

Year Team	G	GS	RECEIVING				TOTALS			
			No.	Yds.	Avg.	TD	TD	2pt.	Pts.	Fum.
1997—Washington NFL	5	1	9	138	15.3	2	2	0	12	0

CONNER, DARION   LB

PERSONAL: Born September 28, 1967, in Macon, Ga. ... 6-2/250.
HIGH SCHOOL: Noxubee County (Macon, Ga.).
COLLEGE: Jackson State.
TRANSACTIONS/CAREER NOTES: Selected by Atlanta Falcons in second round (27th pick overall) of 1990 NFL draft. ... Signed by Falcons (July 12, 1990). ... Granted free agency (March 1, 1993). ... Re-signed by Falcons (August 13, 1993). ... Granted unconditional free agency (February 17, 1994). ... Signed by New Orleans Saints (July 18, 1994). ... Granted unconditional free agency (February 17, 1995). ... Signed by Carolina Panthers (April 6, 1995). ... Granted free agency (February 16, 1996). ... Re-signed by Panthers (July 17, 1996). ... Released by Panthers (August 27, 1996). ... Signed by Philadelphia Eagles (September 18, 1996). ... Granted unconditional free agency (February 14, 1997). ... Re-signed by Eagles (July 16, 1997). ... Granted unconditional free agency (February 13, 1998).
PRO STATISTICS: 1991—Fumbled once and recovered one fumble for five yards. 1994—Intercepted one pass for 58 yards and recovered one fumble.

Year Team	G	GS	SACKS
1990—Atlanta NFL	16	7	2.0
1991—Atlanta NFL	15	14	3.5
1992—Atlanta NFL	16	16	7.0
1993—Atlanta NFL	14	10	1.5
1994—New Orleans NFL	16	13	10.5
1995—Carolina NFL	16	16	7.0
1996—Philadelphia NFL	7	0	0.0
1997—Philadelphia NFL	14	0	1.5
Pro totals (8 years)	114	76	33.0

CONRAD, J.R.   OT   JETS

PERSONAL: Born February 2, 1974, in Fairland, Okla. ... 6-4/300. ... Full name: James Robert Conrad.
HIGH SCHOOL: Fairland (Okla.).
COLLEGE: Oklahoma.
TRANSACTIONS/CAREER NOTES: Selected by New England Patriots in seventh round (247th pick overall) of 1996 NFL draft. ... Signed by Patriots (July 17, 1996). ... Released by Patriots (August 25, 1996). ... Re-signed by Patriots (February 27, 1997). ... Released by Patriots (August 24, 1997). ... Signed by New York Jets to practice squad (September 10, 1997). ... Activated (September 20, 1997).
PLAYING EXPERIENCE: New York Jets NFL, 1997. ... Games/Games started: 12/1.

CONWAY, BRETT   K   PACKERS

PERSONAL: Born March 8, 1975, in Atlanta. ... 6-2/192. ... Full name: Brett Alan Conway.
HIGH SCHOOL: Parkview (Lilburn, Ga.).
COLLEGE: Penn State.
TRANSACTIONS/CAREER NOTES: Selected by Green Bay Packers in third round (90th pick overall) of 1997 NFL draft. ... Signed by Packers (July 8, 1997). ... On injured reserve with thigh injury (September 3, 1997-entire season).

Year Team	G	GS	KICKING						
			XPM	XPA	FGM	FGA	Lg.	50+	Pts.
1997—Green Bay NFL					Did not play.				

CONWAY, CURTIS   WR   BEARS

PERSONAL: Born March 13, 1971, in Los Angeles. ... 6-0/194. ... Full name: Curtis LaMont Conway.
HIGH SCHOOL: Hawthorne (Calif.).
JUNIOR COLLEGE: El Camino College (Calif.).
COLLEGE: Southern California.
TRANSACTIONS/CAREER NOTES: Selected after junior season by Chicago Bears in first round (seventh pick overall) of 1993 NFL draft. ... Signed by Bears (May 24, 1993). ... Granted free agency (February 16, 1996). ... Re-signed by Bears (March 4, 1996).
HONORS: Named kick returner on THE SPORTING NEWS college All-America second team (1992).
PRO STATISTICS: 1993—Fumbled once. 1994—Attempted one pass with one completion for 23 yards and a touchdown, fumbled twice and recovered one fumble. 1994—Returned eight punts for 63 yards. 1995—Attempted one pass without a completion. 1996—Attempted one pass with one completion for 33 yards and a touchdown. 1997—Attempted one pass without a completion.
SINGLE GAME HIGHS (regular season): Receptions—9 (December 22, 1996, vs. Tampa Bay); yards—148 (September 12, 1994, vs. Philadelphia); and touchdown receptions—3 (October 15, 1995, vs. Jacksonville).
STATISTICAL PLATEAUS: 100-yard receiving games: 1994 (1), 1995 (3), 1996 (4), 1997 (3). Total: 11.

			RUSHING				RECEIVING				KICKOFF RETURNS				TOTALS			
Year Team	G	GS	Att.	Yds.	Avg.	TD	No.	Yds.	Avg.	TD	No.	Yds.	Avg.	TD	TD	2pt.	Pts.	Fum.
1993—Chicago NFL	16	7	5	44	8.8	0	19	231	12.2	2	21	450	21.4	0	2	...	12	1
1994—Chicago NFL	13	12	6	31	5.2	0	39	546	14.0	2	10	228	22.8	0	2	1	14	2
1995—Chicago NFL	16	16	5	77	15.4	0	62	1037	16.7	12	0	0	...	0	12	0	72	0
1996—Chicago NFL	16	16	8	50	6.3	0	81	1049	13.0	7	0	0	...	0	7	0	42	1
1997—Chicago NFL	7	7	3	17	5.7	0	30	476	15.9	1	0	0	...	0	1	0	6	0
Pro totals (5 years)	68	58	27	219	8.1	0	231	3339	14.5	24	31	678	21.9	0	24	1	146	4

CONWELL, ERNIE   TE   RAMS

PERSONAL: Born August 17, 1972, in Renton, Wash. ... 6-1/265. ... Full name: Ernest Harold Conwell.
HIGH SCHOOL: Kentwood (Kent, Wash.).
COLLEGE: Washington.
TRANSACTIONS/CAREER NOTES: Selected by St. Louis Rams in second round (59th pick overall) of 1996 NFL draft. ... Signed by Rams (June 25, 1996).
PRO STATISTICS: 1996—Recovered one fumble. 1997—Recovered one fumble.
SINGLE GAME HIGHS (regular season): Receptions—5 (November 16, 1997, vs. Atlanta); yards—75 (November 23, 1997, vs. Carolina); and touchdown receptions—1 (November 23, 1997, vs. Carolina).

			RECEIVING				TOTALS			
Year Team	G	GS	No.	Yds.	Avg.	TD	TD	2pt.	Pts.	Fum.
1996—St. Louis NFL	10	8	15	164	10.9	0	0	0	0	0
1997—St. Louis NFL	16	16	38	404	10.6	4	4	0	24	0
Pro totals (2 years)	26	24	53	568	10.7	4	4	0	24	0

COOK, ANTHONY   DL   OILERS

PERSONAL: Born May 30, 1972, in Bennettsville, S.C. ... 6-3/290. ... Full name: Anthony Andrew Cook.
HIGH SCHOOL: Marlboro County (Bennettsville, S.C.).
COLLEGE: South Carolina State.
TRANSACTIONS/CAREER NOTES: Selected by Houston Oilers in second round (35th pick overall) of 1995 NFL draft. ... Signed by Oilers (July 20, 1995). ... Oilers franchise moved to Tennessee for 1997 season.
PRO STATISTICS: 1997—Recovered two fumbles.

Year Team	G	GS	SACKS
1995—Houston NFL	11	5	4.5
1996—Houston NFL	12	11	7.5
1997—Tennessee NFL	16	16	0.0
Pro totals (3 years)	39	32	12.0

COOK, TOI   CB

PERSONAL: Born December 3, 1964, in Chicago. ... 5-11/188. ... Full name: Toi Fitzgerald Cook. ... Name pronounced TOY.
HIGH SCHOOL: Montclair (Calif.).
COLLEGE: Stanford.
TRANSACTIONS/CAREER NOTES: Selected by New Orleans Saints in eighth round (207th pick overall) of 1987 NFL draft. ... Signed by Saints (July 24, 1987). ... Granted free agency (February 1, 1990). ... Re-signed by Saints (August 13, 1990). ... On injured reserve with forearm injury (December 9, 1991-remainder of season). ... Granted free agency (February 1, 1992). ... Re-signed by Saints (August 24, 1992). ... Granted roster exemption (August 24-September 5, 1992). ... Granted unconditional free agency (February 17, 1994). ... Signed by San Francisco 49ers (August 22, 1994). ... Granted unconditional free agency (February 17, 1995). ... Re-signed by 49ers (August 19, 1995). ... On injured reserve with shoulder injury (September 27, 1995-remainder of season). ... Granted unconditional free agency (February 16, 1996). ... Signed by Denver Broncos (April 17, 1996). ... Released by Broncos (August 18, 1996). ... Signed by Carolina Panthers (August 21, 1996). ... Granted unconditional free agency (February 14, 1997). ... Re-signed by Panthers (July 31, 1997). ... Granted unconditional free agency (February 13, 1998).
CHAMPIONSHIP GAME EXPERIENCE: Played in NFC championship game (1994 and 1996 seasons). ... Member of Super Bowl championship team (1994 season).
PRO STATISTICS: 1987—Returned one punt for three yards. 1909—Caught one pass for eight yards and fumbled once. 1993—Recovered three fumbles. 1996—Recovered one fumble for three yards.
MISCELLANEOUS: Selected by Minnesota Twins organization in 38th round of free-agent baseball draft (June 2, 1987); did not sign.

Year Team	G	GS	INTERCEPTIONS No.	Yds.	Avg.	TD	SACKS No.
1987—New Orleans NFL	7	0	0	0	...	0	0.0
1988—New Orleans NFL	16	0	1	0	0.0	0	0.0
1989—New Orleans NFL	16	14	3	81	27.0	∞1	1.0
1990—New Orleans NFL	16	16	2	55	27.5	0	1.0
1991—New Orleans NFL	14	14	3	54	18.0	0	0.0
1992—New Orleans NFL	16	15	6	90	15.0	1	1.0
1993—New Orleans NFL	16	16	1	0	0.0	0	1.0
1994—San Francisco NFL	16	2	1	18	18.0	0	0.0
1995—San Francisco NFL	2	0	0	0	...	0	0.0
1996—Carolina NFL	15	1	3	28	9.3	0	4.0
1997—Carolina NFL	16	0	0	0	...	0	1.0
Pro totals (11 years)	150	78	20	326	16.3	2	9.0

COONS, ROBERT   TE

PERSONAL: Born September 18, 1969, in Brea, Calif. ... 6-5/249. ... Full name: Robert Allen Coons.
HIGH SCHOOL: El Dorado (Calif.).
JUNIOR COLLEGE: Fullerton (Calif.) Junior College.
COLLEGE: Pittsburgh.
TRANSACTIONS/CAREER NOTES: Signed as non-drafted free agent by Miami Dolphins (April 29, 1993). ... Released by Dolphins (August 30, 1993). ... Re-signed by Dolphins to practice squad (August 31, 1993). ... Released by Dolphins (November 10, 1993). ... Re-signed by Dolphins to practice squad (November 18, 1993). ... On injured reserve (August 29-November 23, 1994). ... Released by Dolphins (November 23, 1994). ... Signed by Buffalo Bills (April 19, 1995). ... Granted free agency (February 14, 1997). ... Re-signed by Bills (June 12, 1997). ... Granted unconditional free agency (February 13, 1998).
PLAYING EXPERIENCE: Buffalo NFL, 1995-1997. ... Games/Games started: 1995 (4/0), 1996 (16/0), 1997 (12/0). Total: 32/0.
PRO STATISTICS: 1995—Caught three passes for 28 yards. 1996—Caught one pass for 12 yards. 1997—Returned one kickoff for 12 yards.
SINGLE GAME HIGHS (regular season): Receptions—3 (December 24, 1995, vs. Houston); yards—28 (December 24, 1995, vs. Houston); and touchdown receptions—0.

COPELAND, HORACE   WR   BUCCANEERS

PERSONAL: Born January 2, 1971, in Orlando. ... 6-3/208. ... Full name: Horace Nathaniel Copeland.
HIGH SCHOOL: Maynard Evans (Orlando).
COLLEGE: Miami, Fla (degree in criminal justice, 1992).
TRANSACTIONS/CAREER NOTES: Selected by Tampa Bay Buccaneers in fourth round (104th pick overall) of 1993 NFL draft. ... Signed by Buccaneers (June 22, 1993). ... On injured reserve with knee injury (August 18, 1996-entire season).
PRO STATISTICS: 1993—Rushed three times for 34 yards.
SINGLE GAME HIGHS (regular season): Receptions—8 (December 10, 1995, vs. Green Bay); yards—155 (September 3, 1995, vs. Philadelphia); and touchdown receptions—2 (October 31, 1993, vs. Atlanta).
STATISTICAL PLATEAUS: 100-yard receiving games: 1993 (2), 1995 (2), 1997 (1). Total: 5.

Year Team	G	GS	RECEIVING No.	Yds.	Avg.	TD	TOTALS TD	2pt.	Pts.	Fum.
1993—Tampa Bay NFL	14	8	30	633	21.1	4	4	...	24	0
1994—Tampa Bay NFL	16	2	17	308	18.1	0	0	1	2	0
1995—Tampa Bay NFL	15	7	35	605	17.3	2	2	0	12	0
1996—Tampa Bay NFL					Did not play.					
1997—Tampa Bay NFL	13	11	33	431	13.1	1	1	0	6	3
Pro totals (4 years)	58	28	115	1977	17.2	7	7	1	44	3

COPELAND, JOHN   DE   BENGALS

PERSONAL: Born September 20, 1970, in Lanett, Ala. ... 6-3/280.
HIGH SCHOOL: Valley (Ala.).
JUNIOR COLLEGE: Hinds Community College (Miss.).
COLLEGE: Alabama.
TRANSACTIONS/CAREER NOTES: Selected by Cincinnati Bengals in first round (fifth pick overall) of 1993 NFL draft. ... Signed by Bengals (August 13, 1993). ... Granted unconditional free agency (February 13, 1998). ... Re-signed by Bengals (February 20, 1998).
HONORS: Named defensive lineman on THE SPORTING NEWS college All-America first team (1992).
PRO STATISTICS: 1997—Recovered two fumbles for 25 yards and one touchdown.

Year Team	G	GS	SACKS
1993—Cincinnati NFL	14	14	3.0
1994—Cincinnati NFL	12	12	1.0
1995—Cincinnati NFL	16	16	9.0
1996—Cincinnati NFL	13	13	3.0
1997—Cincinnati NFL	15	15	3.0
Pro totals (5 years)	70	70	19.0

COPELAND, RUSSELL   WR   EAGLES

PERSONAL: Born November 4, 1971, in Tupelo, Miss. ... 6-0/200. ... Full name: Russell S. Copeland.
HIGH SCHOOL: Tupelo (Miss.).
COLLEGE: Memphis State.

TRANSACTIONS/CAREER NOTES: Selected after junior season by Buffalo Bills in fourth round (111th pick overall) of 1993 NFL draft. ... Signed by Bills (July 12, 1993). ... Granted free agency (February 16, 1996). ... Re-signed by Bills (June 5, 1996). ... Granted unconditional free agency (February 14, 1997). ... Signed by Philadelphia Eagles (June 2, 1997). ... Released by Eagles (August 24, 1997). ... Re-signed by Eagles (November 4, 1997). ... Active for one game (1997); did not play.

CHAMPIONSHIP GAME EXPERIENCE: Played in AFC championship game (1993 season). ... Played in Super Bowl XXVIII (1993 season).

PRO STATISTICS: 1994—Rushed once for minus seven yards. 1995—Rushed once for minus one yard and recovered one fumble. 1996—Recovered one fumble.

SINGLE GAME HIGHS (regular season): Receptions—6 (September 3, 1995, vs. Denver); yards—112 (September 10, 1995, vs. Carolina); and touchdown receptions—1 (September 10, 1995, vs. Carolina).

STATISTICAL PLATEAUS: 100-yard receiving games: 1995 (1).

			RECEIVING				PUNT RETURNS				KICKOFF RETURNS				TOTALS			
Year Team	G	GS	No.	Yds.	Avg.	TD	No.	Yds.	Avg.	TD	No.	Yds.	Avg.	TD	TD	2pt.	Pts.	Fum.
1993—Buffalo NFL	16	2	13	242	18.6	0	31	274	8.8	1	24	436	18.2	0	1	...	6	1
1994—Buffalo NFL	15	4	21	255	12.1	1	1	11	11.0	0	12	232	19.3	0	1	0	6	0
1995—Buffalo NFL	16	15	42	646	15.4	1	2	8	4.0	0	0	0	...	0	1	0	6	1
1996—Buffalo NFL	11	0	7	85	12.1	0	14	119	8.5	0	6	136	22.7	0	0	0	0	2
1997—Philadelphia NFL									Did not play.									
Pro totals (4 years)	58	21	83	1228	14.8	2	48	412	8.6	1	42	804	19.1	0	3	0	18	4

CORYATT, QUENTIN   LB   COLTS

PERSONAL: Born August 1, 1970, in St. Croix, Virgin Islands. ... 6-3/250. ... Full name: Quentin John Coryatt.

HIGH SCHOOL: Robert E. Lee (Baytown, Texas).

COLLEGE: Texas A&M.

TRANSACTIONS/CAREER NOTES: Selected by Indianapolis Colts in first round (second pick overall) of 1992 NFL draft. ... Signed by Colts (April 24, 1992). ... On injured reserve with displaced wrist bone (October 27, 1992-remainder of season). ... Designated by Colts as transition player (February 25, 1993). ... Tendered offer sheet by Jacksonville Jaguars (February 22, 1996). ... Offer matched by Colts (February 28, 1996). ... On injured reserve with pectoral injury (December 11, 1996-remainder of season).

CHAMPIONSHIP GAME EXPERIENCE: Played in AFC championship game (1995 season).

PRO STATISTICS: 1992—Recovered one fumble. 1994—Recovered one fumble for 78 yards and a touchdown. 1995—Intercepted one pass for six yards and recovered three fumbles. 1996—Recovered two fumbles for seven yards. 1997—Intercepted two passes for three yards.

Year Team	G	GS	SACKS
1992—Indianapolis NFL	7	7	2.0
1993—Indianapolis NFL	16	16	1.0
1994—Indianapolis NFL	16	16	1.0
1995—Indianapolis NFL	16	16	2.5
1996—Indianapolis NFL	8	7	0.0
1997—Indianapolis NFL	15	15	2.0
Pro totals (6 years)	78	77	8.5

COTA, CHAD   S   SAINTS

PERSONAL: Born August 13, 1971, in Ashland, Ore. ... 6-1/198. ... Full name: Chad Garrett Cota.

HIGH SCHOOL: Ashland (Ore.).

COLLEGE: Oregon.

TRANSACTIONS/CAREER NOTES: Selected by Carolina Panthers in seventh round (209th pick overall) of 1995 NFL draft. ... Signed by Panthers (July 14, 1995). ... Granted free agency (February 13, 1998). ... Tendered offer sheet by New Orleans Saints (March 11, 1998). ... Panthers declined to match offer (March 18, 1998).

CHAMPIONSHIP GAME EXPERIENCE: Played in NFC championship game (1996 season).

PRO STATISTICS: 1995—Recovered one fumble. 1996—Credited with one sack, fumbled once and recovered one fumble. 1997—Credited with one sack and recovered one fumble.

			INTERCEPTIONS			
Year Team	G	GS	No.	Yds.	Avg.	TD
1995—Carolina NFL	16	0	0	0	...	0
1996—Carolina NFL	16	2	5	63	12.6	0
1997—Carolina NFL	16	16	2	28	14.0	0
Pro totals (3 years)	48	18	7	91	13.0	0

COTHRAN, JEFF   FB   EAGLES

PERSONAL: Born June 28, 1971, in Middletown, Ohio. ... 6-1/249.

HIGH SCHOOL: Middletown (Ohio).

COLLEGE: Ohio State.

TRANSACTIONS/CAREER NOTES: Selected by Cincinnati Bengals in third round (66th pick overall) of 1994 NFL draft. ... Signed by Bengals (July 19, 1994). ... Granted free agency (February 14, 1997). ... Re-signed by Bengals (April 23, 1997). ... Released by Bengals (August 5, 1997). ... Signed by Eagles (April 9, 1998).

PRO STATISTICS: 1996—Returned one kickoff for 11 yards.

SINGLE GAME HIGHS (regular season): Attempts—7 (December 11, 1994, vs. New York Giants); yards—25 (October 6, 1996, vs. Houston); and rushing touchdowns—1 (October 6, 1996, vs. Houston).

			RUSHING				RECEIVING				TOTALS			
Year Team	G	GS	Att.	Yds.	Avg.	TD	No.	Yds.	Avg.	TD	TD	2pt.	Pts.	Fum.
1994—Cincinnati NFL	14	4	26	85	3.3	0	4	24	6.0	1	1	0	6	0
1995—Cincinnati NFL	15	13	16	62	3.9	0	8	44	5.5	0	0	0	0	1
1996—Cincinnati NFL	11	11	15	44	2.9	1	7	49	7.0	0	1	0	6	0
1997—						Did not play.								
Pro totals (3 years)	40	28	57	191	3.4	1	19	117	6.2	1	2	0	12	1

COTTON, KENYON — FB — RAVENS

PERSONAL: Born February 23, 1974, in Bossier City, La. ... 6-0/255. ... Full name: Timothy Kenyon Cotton.
HIGH SCHOOL: Minden (La.).
COLLEGE: Southwestern Louisiana.
TRANSACTIONS/CAREER NOTES: Signed as non-drafted free agent by Baltimore Ravens (April 25, 1997).
PLAYING EXPERIENCE: Baltimore NFL, 1997. ... Games/Games started: 16/0.
PRO STATISTICS: 1997—Rushed twice for two yards and one touchdown.
SINGLE GAME HIGHS (regular season): Attempts—1 (December 14, 1997, vs. Tennessee); yards—1 (December 14, 1997, vs. Tennessee); and rushing touchdowns—1 (November 30, 1997, vs. Jacksonville).

COUSIN, TERRY — CB — BEARS

PERSONAL: Born March 11, 1975 ... 5-9/182. ... Full name: Terry Sean Cousin.
HIGH SCHOOL: Miami Beach.
COLLEGE: South Carolina.
TRANSACTIONS/CAREER NOTES: Signed as non-drafted free agent by Chicago Bears (April 25, 1997). ... Released by Bears (August 24, 1997). ... Re-signed by Bears to practice squad (August 26, 1997). ... Activated (October 25, 1997). ... Released by Bears (October 28, 1997). ... Re-signed by Bears to practice squad (October 30, 1997). ... Activated (November 15, 1997).
PLAYING EXPERIENCE: Chicago NFL, 1997. ... Games/Games started: 6/0.

COVINGTON, DAMIEN — LB

PERSONAL: Born December 4, 1972, in Berlin, N.J. ... 5-11/236.
HIGH SCHOOL: Overbrook (Berlin, N.J.).
COLLEGE: North Carolina State.
TRANSACTIONS/CAREER NOTES: Selected by Buffalo Bills in third round (96th pick overall) of 1995 NFL draft. ... Signed by Bills (July 5, 1995). ... Granted free agency (February 13, 1998).
PLAYING EXPERIENCE: Buffalo NFL, 1995-1997. ... Games/Games started: 1995 (12/1), 1996 (9/2), 1997 (8/8). Total: 29/11.
PRO STATISTICS: 1997—Intercepted one pass for six yards and credited with $1/2$ sack.

COX, BRYAN — LB

PERSONAL: Born February 17, 1968, in St. Louis. ... 6-4/250. ... Full name: Bryan Keith Cox.
HIGH SCHOOL: East St. Louis (Ill.) Senior.
COLLEGE: Western Illinois (bachelor of science degree in mass communications).
TRANSACTIONS/CAREER NOTES: Selected by Miami Dolphins in fifth round (113th pick overall) of 1991 NFL draft. ... Signed by Dolphins (July 11, 1991). ... On injured reserve with sprained ankle (October 5-November 2, 1991). ... Granted unconditional free agency (February 16, 1996). ... Signed by Chicago Bears (February 20, 1996). ... On injured reserve with thumb injury (November 5, 1996-remainder of season). ... Released by Bears (June 2, 1998).
CHAMPIONSHIP GAME EXPERIENCE: Played in AFC championship game (1992 season).
HONORS: Played in Pro Bowl (1992, 1994 and 1995 seasons).
PRO STATISTICS: 1992—Recovered one fumble. 1993—Recovered four fumbles for one yard. 1995—Recovered one fumble. 1996—Recovered three fumbles, including one in end zone for a touchdown. 1997—Recovered one fumble.

Year Team	G	GS	INTERCEPTIONS No.	Yds.	Avg.	TD	SACKS No.
1991—Miami NFL	13	13	0	0	...	0	2.0
1992—Miami NFL	16	16	1	0	0.0	0	14.0
1993—Miami NFL	16	16	1	26	26.0	0	5.0
1994—Miami NFL	16	16	0	0	...	0	3.0
1995—Miami NFL	16	16	1	12	12.0	0	7.5
1996—Chicago NFL	9	9	0	0	...	0	3.0
1997—Chicago NFL	16	15	0	0	...	0	5.0
Pro totals (7 years)	102	101	3	38	12.7	0	39.5

COX, RON — LB

PERSONAL: Born February 27, 1968, in Fresno, Calif. ... 6-2/235. ... Full name: Ron E. Cox.
HIGH SCHOOL: Washington Union (Fresno, Calif.).
COLLEGE: Fresno State.
TRANSACTIONS/CAREER NOTES: Selected after junior season by Chicago Bears in second round (33rd pick overall) of 1990 NFL draft. ... Signed by Bears (July 25, 1990). ... On injured reserve with knee injury (September 25-October 31, 1991). ... On injured reserve with knee injury (November 27, 1991-remainder of season). ... Granted unconditional free agency (February 17, 1994). ... Re-signed by Bears (May 16, 1994). ... Granted free agency (February 16, 1996). ... Tendered offer sheet by Green Bay Packers (March 29, 1996). ... Bears declined to match offer (April 4, 1996). ... Released by Packers (June 2, 1997). ... Signed by Bears (July 11, 1997). ... Granted unconditional free agency (February 13, 1998).
CHAMPIONSHIP GAME EXPERIENCE: Played in NFC championship game (1996 season). ... Member of Super Bowl championship team (1996 season).
HONORS: Named outside linebacker on THE SPORTING NEWS college All-America second team (1989).
PRO STATISTICS: 1992—Recovered one fumble. 1993—Recovered one fumble. 1995—Intercepted one pass for one yard.

Year Team	G	GS	SACKS
1990—Chicago NFL	13	0	3.0
1991—Chicago NFL	6	0	1.0
1992—Chicago NFL	16	3	1.0
1993—Chicago NFL	16	2	2.0

Year Team	G	GS	SACKS
1994—Chicago NFL	15	3	0.0
1995—Chicago NFL	16	13	0.0
1996—Green Bay NFL	16	1	0.0
1997—Chicago NFL	15	13	1.0
Pro totals (8 years)	113	35	8.0

CRAFTS, JERRY   OT/G   EAGLES

PERSONAL: Born January 6, 1968, in Tulsa, Okla. ... 6-5/334. ... Full name: Jerry Wayne Crafts.
HIGH SCHOOL: Metro Christian Academy (Tulsa, Okla.).
COLLEGE: Oklahoma, then Louisville.
TRANSACTIONS/CAREER NOTES: Selected by Indianapolis Colts in 11th round (293rd pick overall) of 1991 NFL draft. ... Signed by Colts (July 13, 1991). ... Released by Colts (August 16, 1991). ... Selected by Orlando Thunder in 16th round (170th pick overall) of 1992 World League draft. ... Signed by Buffalo Bills (July 7, 1992). ... On injured reserve with knee injury (October 26, 1992-remainder of season). ... Granted unconditional free agency (February 17, 1995). ... Signed by Green Bay Packers (March 17, 1995). ... Released by Packers (August 21, 1995). ... Selected by Amsterdam Admirals in 1996 World League draft (February 22, 1996). ... Signed by Philadelphia Eagles (July 8, 1997). ... Granted unconditional free agency (February 13, 1998). ... Re-signed by Eagles (February 19, 1998).
PLAYING EXPERIENCE: Orlando W.L., 1992; Buffalo NFL, 1992-1994; Amsterdam W.L., 1996; Philadelphia NFL, 1997. ... Games/Games started: 1992 (W.L.-9/9, NFL-6/0, Total: 15/9), 1993 (16/0), 1994 (16/7), 1996 (games played unavailable), 1997 (15/6). Total NFL: 38/13. Total Pro: 62/22.
CHAMPIONSHIP GAME EXPERIENCE: Played in AFC championship game (1993 season). ... Played in Super Bowl XXVIII (1993 season).
PRO STATISTICS: 1994—Recovered two fumbles. W.L. 1996—Returned one punt for five yards.

CRAVER, AARON   RB   SAINTS

PERSONAL: Born December 18, 1968, in Los Angeles. ... 6-0/220. ... Full name: Aaron LeRenze Craver.
HIGH SCHOOL: Compton (Calif.).
JUNIOR COLLEGE: El Camino College (Calif.).
COLLEGE: Fresno State.
TRANSACTIONS/CAREER NOTES: Selected by Miami Dolphins in third round (60th pick overall) of 1991 NFL draft. ... Signed by Dolphins (July 23, 1991). ... On injured reserve with pulled hamstring (October 21-December 12, 1992). ... On practice squad (December 12, 1992-January 9, 1993). ... On injured reserve with knee injury (August 23, 1993-entire season). ... Granted free agency (February 17, 1994). ... Re-signed by Dolphins (May 31, 1994). ... Released by Dolphins (August 28, 1994). ... Re-signed by Dolphins (September 26, 1994). ... Released by Dolphins (October 4, 1994). ... Re-signed by Dolphins (November 9, 1994). ... Granted unconditional free agency (February 17, 1995). ... Signed by Denver Broncos (March 9, 1995). ... Granted unconditional free agency (February 14, 1997). ... Signed by San Diego Chargers (April 24, 1997). ... Granted unconditional free agency (February 13, 1998). ... Signed by New Orleans Saints (April 16, 1998).
CHAMPIONSHIP GAME EXPERIENCE: Played in AFC championship game (1992 season).
PRO STATISTICS: 1991—Recovered two fumbles. 1994—Recovered one fumble. 1995—Recovered one fumble. 1996—Attempted one pass without a completion. 1997—Recovered one fumble.
SINGLE GAME HIGHS (regular season): Attempts—20 (December 24, 1995, vs. Oakland); yards—108 (December 24, 1995, vs. Oakland); and rushing touchdowns—1 (December 15, 1996, vs. Oakland).
STATISTICAL PLATEAUS: 100-yard rushing games: 1995 (1).

			RUSHING				RECEIVING				KICKOFF RETURNS				TOTALS			
Year Team	G	GS	Att.	Yds.	Avg.	TD	No.	Yds.	Avg.	TD	No.	Yds.	Avg.	TD	TD 2pt.	Pts.	Fum.
1991—Miami NFL	14	0	20	58	2.9	1	8	67	8.4	0	32	615	19.2	0	1 ...	6	2
1992—Miami NFL	6	0	3	9	3.0	0	0	0	...	0	8	174	21.8	0	0 ...	0	0
1993—Miami NFL									Did not play.								
1994—Miami NFL	8	0	6	43	7.2	0	24	237	9.9	0	0	0	...	0	0 1	2	1
1995—Denver NFL	16	10	73	333	4.6	5	43	369	8.6	1	7	50	7.1	0	6 0	36	1
1996—Denver NFL	15	15	59	232	3.9	2	39	297	7.6	1	0	0	...	0	3 0	18	1
1997—San Diego NFL	15	5	20	71	3.6	0	4	26	6.5	0	3	68	22.7	0	0 0	0	0
Pro totals (6 years)	74	30	181	746	4.1	8	118	996	8.4	2	50	907	18.1	0	10 1	62	5

CRAWFORD, KEITH   WR   FALCONS

PERSONAL: Born November 21, 1970, in Palestine, Texas. ... 6-2/195. ... Full name: Keith L. Crawford.
HIGH SCHOOL: Westwood (Palestine, Texas).
COLLEGE: Howard Payne (Texas).
TRANSACTIONS/CAREER NOTES: Signed as non-drafted free agent by New York Giants (May 1, 1993). ... Released by Giants (October 7, 1993). ... Re-signed by Giants to practice squad (October 8, 1993). ... Activated (October 20, 1993). ... Released by Giants (August 22, 1994). ... Signed by Green Bay Packers (October 28, 1994). ... Released by Packers (November 22, 1994). ... Re-signed by Packers (December 27, 1994). ... Claimed on waivers by St. Louis Rams (August 26, 1996). ... Granted free agency (February 14, 1997). ... Signed by St. Louis Rams (May 20, 1997). ... Granted unconditional free agency (February 13, 1998). ... Signed by Atlanta Falcons (March 16, 1998).
CHAMPIONSHIP GAME EXPERIENCE: Played in NFC championship game (1995 season).
PRO STATISTICS: 1996—Returned four kickoffs for 47 yards. 1997—Rushed twice for 32 yards and recovered one fumble.
SINGLE GAME HIGHS (regular season): Receptions—4 (October 26, 1997, vs. Kansas City); yards—86 (October 12, 1997, vs. San Francisco); and touchdown receptions—0.

			RECEIVING				TOTALS			
Year Team	G	GS	No.	Yds.	Avg.	TD	TD	2pt.	Pts.	Fum.
1993—New York Giants NFL	7	0	1	6	6.0	0	0	...	0	0
1994—Green Bay NFL					Did not play.					
1995—Green Bay NFL	13	0	0	0	...	0	0	0	0	0
1996—St. Louis NFL	16	0	0	0	...	0	0	0	0	0
1997—St. Louis NFL	15	2	11	232	21.1	0	0	0	0	0
Pro totals (4 years)	51	2	12	238	19.8	0	0	0	0	0

CRAWFORD, MIKE LB DOLPHINS

PERSONAL: Born October 29, 1974, in Reno, Nev. ... 6-1/238. ... Full name: Michael Joseph Crawford.
HIGH SCHOOL: George Whittell (Zephyr Cove, Nev.).
COLLEGE: Nevada.
TRANSACTIONS/CAREER NOTES: Selected by Miami Dolphins in sixth round (173rd pick overall) of 1997 NFL draft. ... Signed by Dolphins (June 10, 1997). ... Released by Dolphins (September 6, 1997). ... Re-signed by Dolphins to practice squad (September 9, 1997). ... Activated (October 1, 1997).
PLAYING EXPERIENCE: Miami NFL, 1997. ... Games/Games started: 7/0.

CRAWFORD, VERNON LB PATRIOTS

PERSONAL: Born June 25, 1974, in Texas City, Texas ... 6-3/245. ... Full name: Vernon Dean Crawford Jr.
HIGH SCHOOL: Texas City (Texas).
JUNIOR COLLEGE: San Francisco City College.
COLLEGE: Florida State.
TRANSACTIONS/CAREER NOTES: Selected by New England Patriots in fifth round (159th pick overall) of 1997 NFL draft. ... Signed by Patriots (June 19, 1997).
PRO STATISTICS: 1997—Recovered one fumble.
PLAYING EXPERIENCE: New England NFL, 1997. ... Games/Games started: 16/0.

C CRISWELL, JEFF OT CHIEFS

PERSONAL: Born March 7, 1964, in Grinnell, Iowa. ... 6-7/294. ... Full name: Jeffrey L. Criswell.
HIGH SCHOOL: Lynnville-Sully (Sully, Iowa).
COLLEGE: Graceland College, Iowa (degree in physical education, health and secondary education).
TRANSACTIONS/CAREER NOTES: Signed as free-agent replacement player by Indianapolis Colts (September 26, 1987). ... Released by Colts (October 19, 1987). ... Signed by New York Jets (May 3, 1988). ... On injured reserve with foot injury (December 24, 1992-remainder of season). ... Granted unconditional free agency (February 17, 1995). ... Signed by Kansas City Chiefs (March 9, 1995).
PLAYING EXPERIENCE: Indianapolis NFL, 1987; New York Jets NFL, 1988-1994; Kansas City NFL, 1995-1997. ... Games/Games started: 1987 (3/3), 1988 (15/12), 1989 (16/16), 1990 (16/16), 1991 (16/16), 1992 (14/13), 1993 (16/16), 1994 (15/15), 1995 (15/4), 1996 (15/5), 1997 (16/16). Total: 157/132.
PRO STATISTICS: 1989—Recovered one fumble. 1990—Recovered one fumble. 1994—Recovered one fumble.

CRITTENDEN, RAY WR

PERSONAL: Born March 1, 1970, in Washington, D.C. ... 6-1/188. ... Full name: Raymond C. Crittenden.
HIGH SCHOOL: Annandale (Va.).
COLLEGE: Virginia Tech.
TRANSACTIONS/CAREER NOTES: Signed as non-drafted free agent by New England Patriots (May 20, 1993). ... Released by Patriots (August 22, 1995). ... Claimed on waivers by Carolina Panthers (August 24, 1995); released after failing physical. ... Re-signed by Panthers (January 18, 1996). ... Released by Panthers (August 19, 1996). ... Signed by San Diego Chargers (July 11, 1997). ... Granted free agency (February 13, 1998).
PRO STATISTICS: 1993—Rushed once for minus three yards. 1994—Recovered one fumble.

			RECEIVING			PUNT RETURNS				KICKOFF RETURNS				TOTALS			
Year Team	G	GS	No.	Yds.	Avg.	TD	No.	Yds.	Avg.	TD	No.	Yds.	Avg.	TD	TD	2pt.	Pts. Fum.
1993—New England NFL........	16	2	16	293	18.3	1	2	37	18.5	0	23	478	20.8	0	1	...	6	0
1994—New England NFL........	16	2	28	379	13.5	3	19	155	8.2	0	24	460	19.2	0	3	0	18	1
1995—									Did not play.									
1996—									Did not play.									
1997—San Diego NFL...........	2	0	0	0	...	0	0	0	0	0	0	0	...	0	0	0	0	0
Pro totals (3 years)	34	4	44	672	15.3	4	21	192	9.1	0	47	938	20.0	0	4	0	24	1

CROCKETT, HENRI LB FALCONS

PERSONAL: Born October 28, 1974, in Pompano Beach, Fla. ... 6-2/251. ... Full name: Henri W. Crockett. ... Brother of Zack Crockett, fullback, Indianapolis Colts.
HIGH SCHOOL: Ely (Pompano Beach, Fla.).
COLLEGE: Florida State (degree in criminology, 1996).
TRANSACTIONS/CAREER NOTES: Selected by Atlanta Falcons in fourth round (100th pick overall) of 1997 NFL draft. ... Signed by Falcons (July 14, 1997).
PRO STATISTICS: 1997—Recovered one fumble.

Year Team	G	GS	SACKS
1997—Atlanta NFL..	16	10	2.0

CROCKETT, RAY CB BRONCOS

PERSONAL: Born January 5, 1967, in Dallas. ... 5-10/184. ... Full name: Donald Ray Crockett.
HIGH SCHOOL: Duncanville (Texas).
COLLEGE: Baylor.
TRANSACTIONS/CAREER NOTES: Selected by Detroit Lions in fourth round (86th pick overall) of 1989 NFL draft. ... Signed by Lions (July 18, 1989). ... Granted unconditional free agency (February 17, 1994). ... Signed by Denver Broncos (March 9, 1994).
CHAMPIONSHIP GAME EXPERIENCE: Played in NFC championship game (1991 season). ... Played in AFC championship game (1997 season). ... Member of Super Bowl championship team (1997 season).

PRO STATISTICS: 1989—Returned one kickoff for eight yards and recovered one fumble. 1990—Recovered two fumbles for 22 yards and a touchdown. 1992—Recovered one fumble for 15 yards. 1993—Recovered one fumble. 1994—Recovered two fumbles for 43 yards. 1995— Ran four yards with lateral from punt return and recovered one fumble for 50 yards and a touchdown.

				INTERCEPTIONS				SACKS
Year	Team	G	GS	No.	Yds.	Avg.	TD	No.
1989—Detroit NFL		16	0	1	5	5.0	0	0.0
1990—Detroit NFL		16	6	3	17	5.7	0	1.0
1991—Detroit NFL		16	16	∞6	141	23.5	∞1	1.0
1992—Detroit NFL		15	15	4	50	12.5	0	1.0
1993—Detroit NFL		16	16	2	31	15.5	0	1.0
1994—Denver NFL		14	14	2	6	3.0	0	0.0
1995—Denver NFL		16	16	0	0	...	0	3.0
1996—Denver NFL		15	15	2	34	17.0	0	4.0
1997—Denver NFL		16	16	4	18	4.5	0	0.0
Pro totals (9 years)		140	114	24	302	12.6	1	11.0

CROCKETT, ZACK   FB   COLTS

PERSONAL: Born December 2, 1972, in Pompano Beach, Fla. ... 6-2/246. ... Brother of Henri Crockett, linebacker, Atlanta Falcons.
HIGH SCHOOL: Ely (Pompano Beach, Fla.).
JUNIOR COLLEGE: Hinds Community College (Miss.).
COLLEGE: Florida State.
TRANSACTIONS/CAREER NOTES: Selected by Indianapolis Colts in third round (79th pick overall) of 1995 NFL draft. ... Signed by Colts (July 21, 1995). ... On injured reserve with knee injury (October 22, 1996-remainder of season). ... Granted free agency (February 13, 1998).
CHAMPIONSHIP GAME EXPERIENCE: Played in AFC championship game (1995 season).
SINGLE GAME HIGHS (regular season): Attempts—15 (December 7, 1997, vs. New York Jets); yards—81 (November 2, 1997, vs. Tampa Bay); and rushing touchdowns—1 (December 7, 1997, vs. New York Jets).

				RUSHING				RECEIVING				TOTALS			
Year	Team	G	GS	Att.	Yds.	Avg.	TD	No.	Yds.	Avg.	TD	TD	2pt.	Pts.	Fum.
1995—Indianapolis NFL		16	0	1	0	0.0	0	2	35	17.5	0	0	0	0	0
1996—Indianapolis NFL		5	5	31	164	5.3	0	11	96	8.7	1	1	0	6	2
1997—Indianapolis NFL		16	12	95	300	3.2	1	15	112	7.5	0	1	0	6	3
Pro totals (3 years)		37	17	127	464	3.7	1	28	243	8.7	1	2	0	12	5

CROSS, HOWARD   TE   GIANTS

PERSONAL: Born August 8, 1967, in Huntsville, Ala. ... 6-5/270. ... Full name: Howard E. Cross.
HIGH SCHOOL: New Hope (Ala.).
COLLEGE: Alabama.
TRANSACTIONS/CAREER NOTES: Selected by New York Giants in sixth round (158th pick overall) of 1989 NFL draft. ... Signed by Giants (July 24, 1989). ... Granted free agency (February 1, 1991). ... Re-signed by Giants (July 24, 1991). ... Granted free agency (March 1, 1993). ... Re-signed by Giants (July 16, 1993). ... Designated by Giants as transition player (February 15, 1994).
CHAMPIONSHIP GAME EXPERIENCE: Played in NFC championship game (1990 season). ... Member of Super Bowl championship team (1990 season).
PRO STATISTICS: 1992—Recovered one fumble. 1993—Recovered one fumble. 1994—Recovered one fumble. 1997—Recovered one fumble.
SINGLE GAME HIGHS (regular season): Receptions—6 (September 13, 1992, vs. Dallas); yards—77 (September 13, 1992, vs. Dallas); and touchdown receptions—2 (September 11, 1994, vs. Arizona).

				RECEIVING				KICKOFF RETURNS				TOTALS			
Year	Team	G	GS	No.	Yds.	Avg.	TD	No.	Yds.	Avg.	TD	TD	2pt.	Pts.	Fum.
1989—New York Giants NFL		16	4	6	107	17.8	1	0	0	...	0	1	...	6	1
1990—New York Giants NFL		16	8	8	106	13.3	0	1	10	10.0	0	0	...	0	0
1991—New York Giants NFL		16	16	20	283	14.2	2	1	11	11.0	0	2	...	12	1
1992—New York Giants NFL		16	16	27	357	13.2	2	0	0	...	0	2		12	2
1993—New York Giants NFL		16	16	21	272	13.0	5	2	15	7.5	0	5	...	30	0
1994—New York Giants NFL		16	16	31	364	11.7	4	0	0	...	0	4	0	24	0
1995—New York Giants NFL		15	15	18	197	10.9	0	0	0	...	0	0	0	0	0
1996—New York Giants NFL		16	16	22	178	8.1	1	0	0	...	0	1	0	6	1
1997—New York Giants NFL		16	16	21	150	7.1	2	0	0	...	0	2	0	12	1
Pro totals (9 years)		143	123	174	2014	11.6	17	4	36	9.0	0	17	0	102	6

CRUMPLER, CARLESTER   TE   SEAHAWKS

PERSONAL: Born September 5, 1971, in Greenville, N.C. ... 6-6/260. ... Full name: Carlester Crumpler Jr.
HIGH SCHOOL: Greenville (N.C.).
COLLEGE: East Carolina.
TRANSACTIONS/CAREER NOTES: Selected by Seattle Seahawks in seventh round (202nd pick overall) of 1994 NFL draft. ... Signed by Seahawks (July 6, 1994). ... Granted unconditional free agency (February 13, 1998). ... Re-signed by Seahawks (April 21, 1998).
HONORS: Named tight end on THE SPORTING NEWS college All-America second team (1993).
SINGLE GAME HIGHS (regular season): Receptions—6 (December 15, 1996, vs. Jacksonville); yards—59 (October 29, 1995, vs. Arizona); and touchdown receptions—1 (September 7, 1997, vs. Denver).

				RECEIVING				TOTALS			
Year	Team	G	GS	No.	Yds.	Avg.	TD	TD	2pt.	Pts.	Fum.
1994—Seattle NFL		9	4	2	19	9.5	0	0	0	0	0
1995—Seattle NFL		16	7	23	254	11.0	1	1	0	6	1
1996—Seattle NFL		16	7	26	268	9.9	0	0	0	0	1
1997—Seattle NFL		15	12	31	361	11.6	1	1	0	6	0
Pro totals (4 years)		56	30	82	892	10.9	2	2	0	12	2

CULLORS, DERRICK   RB   PATRIOTS

PERSONAL: Born December 26, 1972, in Dallas. ... 5-11/205. ... Full name: Derrick Shane Cullors.
HIGH SCHOOL: Lake Highlands (Texas).
COLLEGE: Texas Christian, then Murray State.
TRANSACTIONS/CAREER NOTES: Signed as non-drafted free agent by Baltimore Ravens prior to 1996 season. ... Released by Ravens (August 25, 1996). ... Signed by New England Patriots to practice squad (September 18, 1996). ... Inactive for 16 games (1996).
SINGLE GAME HIGHS (regular season): Attempts—10 (December 22, 1997, vs. Miami); yards—41 (November 16, 1997, vs. Tampa Bay); and rushing touchdowns—0.

			RUSHING				RECEIVING				KICKOFF RETURNS				TOTALS		
Year—Team	G	GS	Att.	Yds.	Avg.	TD	No.	Yds.	Avg.	TD	No.	Yds.	Avg.	TD	TD	2pt.	Pts. Fum.
1997—New England NFL........	15	1	22	101	4.6	0	2	8	4.0	0	15	386	25.7	▲1	1	0	6 3

CULPEPPER, BRAD   DT   BUCCANEERS

PERSONAL: Born May 8, 1969, in Tallahassee, Fla. ... 6-1/275. ... Full name: John Broward Culpepper.
HIGH SCHOOL: Leon (Tallahassee, Fla.).
COLLEGE: Florida (degree in history).
TRANSACTIONS/CAREER NOTES: Selected by Minnesota Vikings in 10th round (264th pick overall) of 1992 NFL draft. ... Signed by Vikings (July 20, 1992). ... On injured reserve with toe injury (November 23, 1992-remainder of season). ... Claimed on waivers by Tampa Bay Buccaneers (August 30, 1994).
HONORS: Named defensive lineman on THE SPORTING NEWS college All-America first team (1991).
PRO STATISTICS: 1994—Returned two kickoffs for 30 yards and recovered one fumble. 1995—Recovered one fumble for 12 yards.

Year—Team	G	GS	SACKS
1992—Minnesota NFL	11	2	0.0
1993—Minnesota NFL	15	0	0.0
1994—Tampa Bay NFL	16	15	4.0
1995—Tampa Bay NFL	16	4	4.0
1996—Tampa Bay NFL	13	13	1.5
1997—Tampa Bay NFL	16	16	8.5
Pro totals (6 years)	87	50	18.0

CUNNINGHAM, RANDALL   QB   VIKINGS

PERSONAL: Born March 27, 1963, in Santa Barbara, Calif. ... 6-4/214. ... Brother of Sam Cunningham, running back with New England Patriots (1973-1979 and 1981).
HIGH SCHOOL: Santa Barbara (Calif.).
COLLEGE: UNLV.
TRANSACTIONS/CAREER NOTES: Selected by Arizona Outlaws in 1985 USFL territorial draft. ... Selected by Philadelphia Eagles in second round (37th pick overall) of 1985 NFL draft. ... Signed by Eagles (July 22, 1985). ... On injured reserve with knee injury (September 3, 1991-remainder of season). ... Granted unconditional free agency (February 16, 1996). ... On retired list (August 30, 1996-April 15, 1997). ... Signed by Minnesota Vikings (April 15, 1997). ... Granted unconditional free agency (February 13, 1998). ... Re-signed by Vikings (March 22, 1998).
HONORS: Named punter on THE SPORTING NEWS college All-America first team (1984). ... Played in Pro Bowl (1988-1990 seasons). ... Named Outstanding Player of Pro Bowl (1988 season).
RECORDS: Holds NFL single-season record for most times sacked—72 (1986). ... Shares NFL single-game records for most own fumbles recovered—4 (November 30, 1986, OT, at Los Angeles Raiders); and most own and opponents' fumbles recovered—4 (November 30, 1986, OT, at Los Angeles Raiders).
PRO STATISTICS: 1985—Fumbled three times. 1986—Punted twice for 54 yards, fumbled seven times and recovered four fumbles. 1987—Caught one pass for minus three yards, led league with 12 fumbles and recovered six fumbles for minus seven yards. 1988—Punted three times for 167 yards, led league with 12 fumbles and recovered six fumbles. 1989—Punted six times for 319 yards, fumbled 17 times and recovered four fumbles for minus four yards. 1990—Fumbled nine times and recovered three fumbles for minus four yards. 1992—Led league with 13 fumbles and recovered three fumbles. 1993—Fumbled three times. 1994—Punted once for 80 yards, fumbled 10 times and recovered two fumbles for minus 15 yards. 1995—Fumbled three times and recovered one fumble for minus five yards. 1997—Fumbled four times and recovered two fumbles.
STATISTICAL PLATEAUS: 300-yard passing games: 1987 (1), 1988 (2), 1989 (3), 1992 (1), 1993 (1), 1994 (4). Total: 12. ... 100-yard rushing games: 1986 (1), 1990 (1), 1992 (1). Total: 3.
MISCELLANEOUS: Regular-season record as starting NFL quarterback: 64-45-1 (.586). ... Postseason record as starting NFL quarterback: 2-5 (.286).

			PASSING								RUSHING				TOTALS		
Year—Team	G	GS	Att.	Cmp.	Pct.	Yds.	TD	Int.	Avg.	Rat.	Att.	Yds.	Avg.	TD	TD	2pt.	Pts.
1985—Philadelphia NFL.........	6	4	81	34	42.0	548	1	8	6.77	29.8	29	205	7.1	0	0	...	0
1986—Philadelphia NFL.........	15	5	209	111	53.1	1391	8	7	6.66	72.9	66	540	8.2	5	5	...	30
1987—Philadelphia NFL.........	12	12	406	223	54.9	2786	23	12	6.86	83.0	76	505	6.6	3	3	...	18
1988—Philadelphia NFL.........	16	16	‡560	301	53.8	3808	24	16	6.80	77.6	93	624	*6.7	6	6	...	36
1989—Philadelphia NFL.........	16	16	532	290	54.5	3400	21	15	6.39	75.5	104	621	*6.0	4	4	...	24
1990—Philadelphia NFL.........	16	16	465	271	58.3	3466	‡30	13	7.45	91.6	118	942	*8.0	5	5	...	30
1991—Philadelphia NFL.........	1	1	4	1	25.0	19	0	0	4.75	46.9	0	0	...	0	0	...	0
1992—Philadelphia NFL.........	15	15	384	233	60.7	2775	19	11	7.23	87.3	87	549	6.3	5	5	...	30
1993—Philadelphia NFL.........	4	4	110	76	69.1	850	5	5	7.73	88.1	18	110	6.1	1	1	...	6
1994—Philadelphia NFL.........	14	14	490	265	54.1	3229	16	13	6.59	74.4	65	288	4.4	3	3	0	18
1995—Philadelphia NFL.........	7	4	121	69	57.0	605	3	5	5.00	61.5	21	98	4.7	0	0	0	0
1996—							Did not play.										
1997—Minnesota NFL............	6	3	88	44	50.0	501	6	4	5.69	71.3	19	127	6.7	0	0	0	0
Pro totals (12 years)	128	110	3450	1918	55.6	23378	156	109	6.78	78.6	696	4609	6.6	32	32	0	192

CUNNINGHAM, RICHIE   K   COWBOYS

PERSONAL: Born August 18, 1970, in Terrebonne, La. ... 5-10/167. ... Full name: Richard Anthony Cunningham.
HIGH SCHOOL: Terrebonne (La.).
COLLEGE: Southwestern Louisiana (degree in marketing).
TRANSACTIONS/CAREER NOTES: Signed as non-drafted free agent by Dallas Cowboys (May 2, 1994). ... Released by Cowboys (August 17, 1994). ... Signed by Green Bay Packers (April 22, 1996). ... Released by Packers (August 19, 1996). ... Signed by Cowboys (April 15, 1997).
HONORS: Named kicker on THE SPORTING NEWS NFL All-Pro team (1997).

					KICKING				
Year Team	G	GS	XPM	XPA	FGM	FGA	Lg.	50+	Pts.
1997—Dallas NFL	16	0	24	24	*34	∞37	53	1-1	‡126

CUNNINGHAM, RICK   OT   RAIDERS

PERSONAL: Born January 4, 1967, in Los Angeles. ... 6-6/307. ... Full name: Patrick Dante Ross Cunningham.
HIGH SCHOOL: Beverly Hills (Calif.).
JUNIOR COLLEGE: Sacramento (Calif.) Community College.
COLLEGE: Texas A&M.
TRANSACTIONS/CAREER NOTES: Selected by Indianapolis Colts in fourth round (106th pick overall) of 1990 NFL draft. ... Signed by Colts (July 17, 1990). ... Released by Colts (August 26, 1991). ... Selected by Orlando Thunder in third round (28th pick overall) of 1992 World League draft. ... Signed by Phoenix Cardinals (June 16, 1992). ... On injured reserve with forearm injury (December 4, 1992-remainder of season). ... Cardinals franchise renamed Arizona Cardinals for 1994 season. ... Granted unconditional free agency (February 17, 1995). ... Signed by Minnesota Vikings (April 3, 1995). ... Granted unconditional free agency (February 16, 1996). ... Signed by Oakland Raiders (July 24, 1996).
PLAYING EXPERIENCE: Indianapolis NFL, 1990; Orlando W.L., 1992; Phoenix NFL, 1992 and 1993; Arizona NFL, 1994; Minnesota NFL, 1995; Oakland NFL, 1996 and 1997. ... Games/Games started: 1990 (2/0), 1992 (W.L.-10/10, NFL-8/6, Total: 18/16), 1993 (16/16), 1994 (11/10), 1995 (11/1), 1996 (13/0), 1997 (7/0). Total W.L.: 10/10. Total NFL: 68/33. Total Pro: 78/43.
HONORS: Named offensive tackle on All-World League team (1992).
PRO STATISTICS: W.L.: 1992—Recovered one fumble. NFL: 1993—Recovered one fumble. 1995—Recovered one fumble. 1996—Caught one pass for three yards and a touchdown.

CURRY, ERIC   DE   PACKERS

PERSONAL: Born February 3, 1970, in Thomasville, Ga. ... 6-6/275. ... Full name: Eric Felece Curry. ... Cousin of William Andrews, running back with Atlanta Falcons (1979-1983 and 1986); cousin of Lomas Brown, offensive tackle, Arizona Cardinals; and cousin of Guy McIntyre, guard with three NFL teams (1984-1996).
HIGH SCHOOL: Thomasville (Ga.).
COLLEGE: Alabama (degree in criminal justice, 1992).
TRANSACTIONS/CAREER NOTES: Selected by Tampa Bay Buccaneers in first round (sixth pick overall) of 1993 NFL draft. ... Signed by Buccaneers (August 16, 1993). ... Designated by Buccaneers as transition player (February 15, 1994). ... Released by Buccaneers (August 23, 1997). ... Re-signed by Buccaneers (August 25, 1997). ... Granted unconditional free agency (February 13, 1998). ... Signed by Green Bay Packers (April 1, 1998).
HONORS: Named defensive lineman on THE SPORTING NEWS college All-America first team (1992).
PRO STATISTICS: Recovered one fumble. 1995—Recovered one fumble.

Year Team	G	GS	SACKS
1993—Tampa Bay NFL	10	10	5.0
1994—Tampa Bay NFL	15	14	3.0
1995—Tampa Bay NFL	16	16	2.0
1996—Tampa Bay NFL	12	3	2.0
1997—Tampa Bay NFL	6	1	0.0
Pro totals (5 years)	59	44	12.0

CURTIS, CANUTE   LB   BENGALS

PERSONAL: Born August 4, 1974, in Amityville, N.Y. ... 6-2/256. ... Name pronounced kuh-NOOT.
HIGH SCHOOL: Farmingdale (N.Y.).
COLLEGE: West Virginia.
TRANSACTIONS/CAREER NOTES: Selected by Cincinnati Bengals in sixth round (176th pick overall) of 1997 NFL draft. ... Signed by Bengals (July 11, 1997). ... Released by Bengals (August 24, 1997). ... Re-signed by Bengals to practice squad (August 26, 1997). ... Activated (October 21, 1997).
HONORS: Named outside linebacker on THE SPORTING NEWS college All-America first team (1996).
PLAYING EXPERIENCE: Cincinnati NFL, 1997. ... Games/Games started: 3/0.

DAFNEY, BERNARD   OL

PERSONAL: Born November 1, 1968, in Los Angeles. ... 6-5/335. ... Full name: Bernard Eugene Dafney.
HIGH SCHOOL: John C. Fremont (Los Angeles).
JUNIOR COLLEGE: Los Angeles Southwest Community College.
COLLEGE: Tennessee.
TRANSACTIONS/CAREER NOTES: Selected by Houston Oilers in ninth round (247th pick overall) of 1992 NFL draft. ... Signed by Oilers (July 9, 1992). ... Released by Oilers (August 31, 1992). ... Signed by Minnesota Vikings to practice squad (September 9, 1992). ... Activated (October 29, 1992). ... Released by Vikings (August 31, 1995). ... Signed by Arizona Cardinals (September 15, 1995). ... Granted unconditional free agency (February 16, 1996). ... Signed by Pittsburgh Steelers (April 10, 1996). ... Traded by Steelers to Baltimore Ravens for seventh-round draft pick (traded to Atlanta) in 1998 draft (August 24, 1997). ... Released by Ravens (November 26, 1997).

C
D

PLAYING EXPERIENCE: Minnesota NFL, 1992-1994; Arizona NFL, 1995; Pittsburgh NFL, 1996; Baltimore NFL, 1997. ... Games/Games started: 1992 (2/0), 1993 (16/4), 1994 (16/16), 1995 (11/8), 1996 (14/1), 1997 (2/0). Total: 61/29.
PRO STATISTICS: 1994—Recovered one fumble.

DAHL, BOB   G

PERSONAL: Born January 15, 1968, in Chicago. ... 6-5/319. ... Full name: Robert Allen Dahl.
HIGH SCHOOL: Chagrin Falls (Ohio).
COLLEGE: Notre Dame.
TRANSACTIONS/CAREER NOTES: Selected by Cincinnati Bengals in third round (72nd pick overall) of 1991 NFL draft. ... Signed by Bengals (July 15, 1991). ... Released by Bengals (August 26, 1991). ... Re-signed by Bengals to practice squad (August 28, 1991). ... Released by Bengals (November 12, 1991). ... Signed by Cleveland Browns (March 3, 1992). ... Granted free agency (September 11, 1992). ... Re-signed by Browns to practice squad (September 16, 1992). ... Activated (October 31, 1992). ... Granted free agency by Browns after 1995 season. ... Signed by Washington Redskins (March 4, 1996). ... Granted unconditional free agency (February 13, 1998).
PLAYING EXPERIENCE: Cleveland NFL, 1992-1995; Washington NFL, 1996 and 1997. ... Games/Games started: 1992 (9/9), 1993 (16/16), 1994 (15/15), 1995 (16/16), 1996 (15/15), 1997 (11/9). Total: 82/80.
PRO STATISTICS: 1993—Recovered one fumble. 1996—Recovered one fumble. 1997—Recovered one fumble.

DALMAN, CHRIS   G/C   49ERS

PERSONAL: Born March 15, 1970, in Salinas, Calif. ... 6-3/297. ... Full name: Chris William Dalman.
HIGH SCHOOL: Palma (Salinas, Calif.).
COLLEGE: Stanford (degree in political science, 1992).
TRANSACTIONS/CAREER NOTES: Selected by San Francisco 49ers in sixth round (166th pick overall) of 1993 NFL draft. ... Signed by 49ers (June 24, 1993). ... Granted unconditional free agency (February 14, 1997). ... Re-signed by 49ers (April 25, 1997).
PLAYING EXPERIENCE: San Francisco NFL, 1993-1997. ... Games/Games started: 1993 (15/0), 1994 (16/4), 1995 (15/1), 1996 (16/16), 1997 (13/13). Total: 75/34.
CHAMPIONSHIP GAME EXPERIENCE: Played in NFC championship game (1993, 1994 and 1997 seasons). ... Member of Super Bowl championship team (1994 season).
PRO STATISTICS: 1993—Recovered one fumble. 1994—Fumbled once. 1995—Caught one pass for minus one yard, returned three kickoffs for 29 yards and recovered one fumble. 1997—Recovered one fumble.

DALUISO, BRAD   K   GIANTS

PERSONAL: Born December 31, 1967, in San Diego. ... 6-2/215. ... Full name: Bradley William Daluiso. ... Name pronounced DOLL-uh-WEE-so.
HIGH SCHOOL: Valhalla (El Cajon, Calif.).
JUNIOR COLLEGE: Grossmont (Calif.) College.
COLLEGE: San Diego State, then UCLA.
TRANSACTIONS/CAREER NOTES: Signed as non-drafted free agent by Green Bay Packers (May 2, 1991). ... Traded by Packers to Atlanta Falcons for an undisclosed pick in 1992 draft (August 26, 1991). ... Claimed on waivers by Buffalo Bills (September 10, 1991). ... Granted unconditional free agency (February 1, 1992). ... Signed by Dallas Cowboys (February 18, 1992). ... Claimed on waivers by Denver Broncos (September 1, 1992). ... Released by Broncos (August 23, 1993). ... Signed by New York Giants (September 1, 1993). ... Granted free agency (February 17, 1994). ... Re-signed by Giants (June 21, 1994). ... Granted unconditional free agency (February 17, 1995). ... Re-signed by Giants (February 22, 1995). ... Granted unconditional free agency (February 13, 1998). ... Re-signed by Giants (February 13, 1998).
CHAMPIONSHIP GAME EXPERIENCE: Played in AFC championship game (1991 season). ... Played in Super Bowl XXVI (1991 season).
PRO STATISTICS: 1992—Punted 10 times for 467 yards.

| | | | | KICKING | | | | | |
Year Team	G	GS	XPM	XPA	FGM	FGA	Lg.	50+	Pts.
1991—Atlanta NFL	2	0	2	2	2	3	23	0-0	8
—Buffalo NFL	14	0	0	0	0	0	...	0-0	0
1992—Denver NFL	16	0	0	0	0	1	0	0-1	0
1993—New York Giants NFL	15	0	0	0	1	3	54	1-3	3
1994—New York Giants NFL	16	0	5	5	11	11	52	1-1	38
1995—New York Giants NFL	16	0	28	28	20	28	51	2-2	88
1996—New York Giants NFL	16	0	22	22	24	27	46	0-0	94
1997—New York Giants NFL	16	0	27	29	22	32	52	1-4	93
Pro totals (7 years)	111	0	84	86	80	105	54	5-11	324

DANIEL, EUGENE   DB

PERSONAL: Born May 4, 1961, in Baton Rouge, La. ... 5-11/178. ... Full name: Eugene Daniel Jr.
HIGH SCHOOL: Robert E. Lee (Baton Rouge, La.).
COLLEGE: Louisiana State (degree in marketing, 1984).
TRANSACTIONS/CAREER NOTES: Selected by New Orleans Breakers in 1984 USFL territorial draft. ... Selected by Indianapolis Colts in eighth round (205th pick overall) of 1984 NFL draft. ... Signed by Colts (June 21, 1984). ... Granted free agency (February 1, 1991). ... Re-signed by Colts (July 25, 1991). ... Granted unconditional free agency (February 17, 1994). ... Re-signed by Colts (March 9, 1994). ... Granted free agency (February 14, 1997). ... Signed by Baltimore Ravens (September 17, 1997). ... Granted unconditional free agency (February 13, 1998).
CHAMPIONSHIP GAME EXPERIENCE: Played in AFC championship game (1995 season).
PRO STATISTICS: 1985—Returned one punt for six yards, fumbled once and recovered three fumbles for 25 yards. 1986—Returned blocked punt 13 yards for a touchdown and recovered one fumble. 1989—Recovered one fumble for five yards. 1990—Returned one punt for no yards. 1992—Credited with two sacks. 1996—Recovered one fumble.

Year Team	G	GS	INTERCEPTIONS No.	Yds.	Avg.	TD
1984—Indianapolis NFL	15	13	6	25	4.2	0
1985—Indianapolis NFL	16	16	▲8	53	6.6	0
1986—Indianapolis NFL	15	15	3	11	3.7	0
1987—Indianapolis NFL	12	11	2	34	17.0	0
1988—Indianapolis NFL	16	15	2	44	22.0	1
1989—Indianapolis NFL	15	14	1	34	34.0	0
1990—Indianapolis NFL	15	15	0	0	...	0
1991—Indianapolis NFL	16	16	3	22	7.3	0
1992—Indianapolis NFL	14	13	1	0	0.0	0
1993—Indianapolis NFL	16	16	1	17	17.0	0
1994—Indianapolis NFL	16	15	2	6	3.0	0
1995—Indianapolis NFL	16	16	3	142	47.3	▲1
1996—Indianapolis NFL	16	9	3	35	11.7	1
1997—Baltimore NFL	9	6	3	60	20.0	0
Pro totals (14 years)	207	190	38	483	12.7	3

DANIELS, JEROME   OT   CARDINALS

PERSONAL: Born September 13, 1974, in Hartford, Conn. ... 6-5/350. ... Full name: Jerome Alvonne Daniels.
HIGH SCHOOL: Bloomfield (Conn.).
COLLEGE: Northeastern.
TRANSACTIONS/CAREER NOTES: Selected by Miami Dolphins in fourth round (121st pick overall) of 1997 NFL draft. ... Signed by Dolphins (June 10, 1997). ... Released by Dolphins (August 18, 1997). ... Claimed on waivers by Baltimore Ravens (August 19, 1997). ... Released by Ravens (August 24, 1997). ... Re-signed by Ravens to practice squad (August 26, 1997). ... Signed by Arizona Cardinals off Ravens practice squad (November 28, 1997). ... Inactive for four games (1997).

DANIELS, LESHUN   G   VIKINGS

PERSONAL: Born May 30, 1974, in Warren, Ohio. ... 6-1/304.
HIGH SCHOOL: Harding (Warren, Ohio).
COLLEGE: Ohio State.
TRANSACTIONS/CAREER NOTES: Signed as non-drafted free agent by Minnesota Vikings (April 25, 1997). ... Released by Vikings (August 24, 1997). ... Re-signed by Vikings to practice squad (August 25, 1997). ... Activated (November 13, 1997).
PLAYING EXPERIENCE: Minnesota NFL, 1997. ... Games/Games started: 1/0.

D

DANIELS, PHILLIP   DE   SEAHAWKS

PERSONAL: Born March 4, 1973, in Donalsonville, Ga. ... 6-5/263. ... Full name: Phillip Bernard Daniels.
HIGH SCHOOL: Seminole County (Ga.).
COLLEGE: Georgia.
TRANSACTIONS/CAREER NOTES: Selected by Seattle Seahawks in fourth round (99th pick overall) of 1996 NFL draft. ... Signed by Seahawks (July 17, 1996).
PRO STATISTICS: 1996—Recovered one fumble. 1997—Returned one kickoff for minus two yards and fumbled once.

Year Team	G	GS	SACKS
1996—Seattle NFL	15	0	2.0
1997—Seattle NFL	13	10	4.0
Pro totals (2 years)	28	10	6.0

DAR DAR, KIRBY   WR   DOLPHINS

PERSONAL: Born March 27, 1972, in Morgan City, La. ... 5-9/188. ... Full name: Kirby David Dar Dar.
HIGH SCHOOL: Thomas Jefferson (Tampa).
COLLEGE: Syracuse.
TRANSACTIONS/CAREER NOTES: Signed as non-drafted free agent by Miami Dolphins (April 27, 1995). ... Released by Dolphins (August 22, 1995). ... Re-signed by Dolphins to practice squad (August 30, 1995). ... Activated (December 23, 1995). ... Released by Dolphins (August 20, 1996). ... Re-signed by Dolphins (August 24, 1996). ... On injured reserve with knee injury (August 18, 1997-entire season).
PLAYING EXPERIENCE: Miami NFL, 1995 and 1996. ... Games/Games started: 1995 (1/0), 1996 (11/0). Total: 12/0.
PRO STATISTICS: 1995—Returned one kickoff for 22 yards. 1996—Returned seven kickoffs for 132 yards.
SINGLE GAME HIGHS (regular season): Receptions—0; yards—0; and touchdown receptions—0.

DARBY, MATT   S

PERSONAL: Born November 19, 1968, in Virginia Beach, Va. ... 6-2/203. ... Full name: Matthew Lamont Darby.
HIGH SCHOOL: Green Run (Virginia Beach, Va.).
COLLEGE: UCLA.
TRANSACTIONS/CAREER NOTES: Selected by Buffalo Bills in fifth round (139th pick overall) of 1992 NFL draft. ... Signed by Bills (July 22, 1992). ... Released by Bills (February 16, 1996). ... Signed by Arizona Cardinals (April 9, 1996). ... Granted free agency (February 14, 1997). ... Re-signed by Cardinals (July 9, 1997). ... Granted unconditional free agency (February 13, 1998).
CHAMPIONSHIP GAME EXPERIENCE: Played in AFC championship game (1992 and 1993 seasons). ... Played in Super Bowl XXVII (1992 season) and Super Bowl XXVIII (1993 season).
HONORS: Named defensive back on THE SPORTING NEWS college All-America second team (1991).
PRO STATISTICS: 1992—Recovered one fumble. 1993—Recovered one fumble. 1996—Recovered one fumble. 1997—Recovered two fumbles.

Year Team	G	GS	INTERCEPTIONS No.	Yds.	Avg.	TD
1992—Buffalo NFL	16	1	0	0	...	0
1993—Buffalo NFL	16	3	2	32	16.0	0
1994—Buffalo NFL	16	16	4	20	5.0	0
1995—Buffalo NFL	7	3	2	37	18.5	0
1996—Arizona NFL	15	15	0	0	...	0
1997—Arizona NFL	11	7	0	0	...	0
Pro totals (6 years)	81	45	8	89	11.1	0

DARKINS, CHRIS — RB — PACKERS

PERSONAL: Born April 30, 1974, in Houston. ... 6-0/210.
HIGH SCHOOL: Strake Jesuit College Prep (Houston).
COLLEGE: Minnesota.
TRANSACTIONS/CAREER NOTES: Selected by Green Bay Packers in fourth round (123rd pick overall) of 1996 NFL draft. ... Signed by Packers (July 17, 1996). ... On injured reserve with shoulder injury (August 19, 1996-entire season).
CHAMPIONSHIP GAME EXPERIENCE: Played in NFC championship game (1997 season). ... Played in Super Bowl XXXII (1997 season).
PLAYING EXPERIENCE: Green Bay NFL, 1997. ... Games/Games started: 14/0.
PRO STATISTICS: 1997—Returned four kickoffs for 68 yards.
SINGLE GAME HIGHS (regular season): Attempts—0; yards—0; and rushing touchdowns—0.

DARLING, JAMES — LB — EAGLES

PERSONAL: Born December 29, 1974, in Kettle Falls, Wash. ... 6-0/250. ... Full name: James V. Darling.
HIGH SCHOOL: Kettle Falls (Wash.).
COLLEGE: Washington State.
TRANSACTIONS/CAREER NOTES: Selected by Philadelphia Eagles in second round (57th pick overall) of 1997 NFL draft. ... Signed by Eagles (July 16, 1997).
PLAYING EXPERIENCE: Philadelphia NFL, 1997. ... Games/Games started: 16/6.
HONORS: Named inside linebacker on THE SPORTING NEWS college All-America second team (1996).

DAVEY, DON — DT — JAGUARS

PERSONAL: Born April 8, 1968, in Scottsville, N.Y. ... 6-4/270. ... Full name: Donald Vincent Davey.
HIGH SCHOOL: Lincoln (Manitowoc, Wis.).
COLLEGE: Wisconsin (bachelor's and master's degree in mechanical engineering).
TRANSACTIONS/CAREER NOTES: Selected by Green Bay Packers in third round (67th pick overall) of 1991 NFL draft. ... Signed by Packers (June 14, 1991). ... Released by Packers (September 16, 1992). ... Re-signed by Packers (November 12, 1992). ... Granted free agency (February 17, 1994). ... Re-signed by Packers (April 11, 1994). ... Granted unconditional free agency (February 17, 1995). ... Signed by Jacksonville Jaguars (February 28, 1995). ... On injured reserve with knee injury (November 11, 1997-remainder of season).
PLAYING EXPERIENCE: Green Bay NFL, 1991-1994; Jacksonville NFL, 1995-1997. ... Games/Games started: 1991 (16/0), 1992 (9/0), 1993 (9/0), 1994 (16/2), 1995 (16/16), 1996 (16/12), 1997 (10/10). Total: 92/40.
CHAMPIONSHIP GAME EXPERIENCE: Played in AFC championship game (1996 season).
PRO STATISTICS: 1991—Returned one kickoff for eight yards. 1992—Returned one kickoff for eight yards. 1994—Credited with 1½ sacks and returned one kickoff for six yards. 1995—Credited with three sacks. 1996—Recovered one fumble. 1997—Credited with three sacks.

DAVIDDS-GARRIDO, NORBERTO — OT — PANTHERS

PERSONAL: Born October 4, 1972, in La Puenta, Calif. ... 6-6/313. ... Formerly known as Norberto Garrido. ... Name pronounced No-BURR-toe DAY-vids Gah-REE-do.
HIGH SCHOOL: Workman (La Puenta, Calif.).
COLLEGE: Southern California.
TRANSACTIONS/CAREER NOTES: Selected by Carolina Panthers in fourth round (106th pick overall) of 1996 NFL draft. ... Signed by Panthers (June 17, 1996). ... On injured reserve with ankle injury (December 15, 1997-remainder of season).
PLAYING EXPERIENCE: Carolina NFL, 1996 and 1997. ... Games: 1996 (12/8), 1997 (15/15). Total: 27/23.
CHAMPIONSHIP GAME EXPERIENCE: Played in NFC championship game (1996 season).

DAVIS, ANTHONY — LB — CHIEFS

PERSONAL: Born March 7, 1969, in Pasco, Wash. ... 6-0/235. ... Full name: Anthony D. Davis.
HIGH SCHOOL: Pasco (Wash.).
JUNIOR COLLEGE: Spokane Falls Community College (Wash.).
COLLEGE: Utah.
TRANSACTIONS/CAREER NOTES: Selected by Houston Oilers in 11th round (301st pick overall) of 1992 NFL draft. ... Signed by Oilers prior to 1992 season. ... Released by Oilers (August 24, 1992). ... Re-signed by Oilers to practice squad (September 2, 1992). ... Released by Oilers (October 6, 1992). ... Signed by Seattle Seahawks to practice squad (December 9, 1992). ... Released by Seahawks (August 30, 1993). ... Re-signed by Seahawks to practice squad (September 1, 1993). ... Activated (October 11, 1993). ... Released by Seahawks (August 22, 1994). ... Signed by Kansas City Chiefs (November 24, 1994).
PRO STATISTICS: 1997—Recovered one fumble for two yards.

			INTERCEPTIONS				SACKS
Year Team	G	GS	No.	Yds.	Avg.	TD	No.
1993—Seattle NFL	10	0	0	0	...	0	0.0
1994—Kansas City NFL	5	0	0	0	...	0	0.0
1995—Kansas City NFL	16	2	1	11	11.0	0	2.0
1996—Kansas City NFL	16	15	2	37	18.5	0	2.5
1997—Kansas City NFL	15	15	0	0	...	0	3.5
Pro totals (5 years)	62	32	3	48	16.0	0	8.0

DAVIS, ANTONE — OT

PERSONAL: Born February 28, 1967, in Sweetwater, Tenn. ... 6-4/330. ... Full name: Antone Eugene Davis.
HIGH SCHOOL: Peach County (Fort Valley, Ga.).
COLLEGE: Tennessee (degree in city planning).
TRANSACTIONS/CAREER NOTES: Selected by Philadelphia Eagles in first round (ninth pick overall) of 1991 NFL draft. ... Signed by Eagles (August 5, 1991). ... Granted unconditional free agency (February 16, 1996). ... Signed by Atlanta Falcons (May 9, 1996). ... Released by Falcons (February 13, 1998).
PLAYING EXPERIENCE: Philadelphia NFL, 1991-1995; Atlanta NFL, 1996 and 1997. ... Games/Games started: 1991 (16/15), 1992 (15/15), 1993 (16/16), 1994 (16/14), 1995 (15/14), 1996 (16/10), 1997 (3/3). Total: 97/87.
HONORS: Named offensive tackle on THE SPORTING NEWS college All-America first team (1990).
PRO STATISTICS: 1997—Recovered one fumble.

DAVIS, BILLY — WR — COWBOYS

PERSONAL: Born July 6, 1972, in El Paso, Texas. ... 6-1/205. ... Full name: William Augusta Davis III.
HIGH SCHOOL: Irvin (El Paso, Texas).
COLLEGE: Pittsburgh.
TRANSACTIONS/CAREER NOTES: Signed as non-drafted free agent by Dallas Cowboys (April 27, 1995). ... Granted free agency (February 13, 1998). ... Re-signed by Cowboys (February 27, 1998).
PLAYING EXPERIENCE: Dallas NFL, 1995-1997. ... Games/Games started: 1995 (16/0), 1996 (13/0), 1997 (16/0). Total: 45/0.
CHAMPIONSHIP GAME EXPERIENCE: Played in NFC championship game (1995 season). ... Member of Super Bowl championship team (1995 season).
PRO STATISTICS: 1997—Caught three passes for 33 yards.
SINGLE GAME HIGHS (regular season): Receptions—1 (November 16, 1997, vs. Washington); yards—12 (November 16, 1997, vs. Washington); and touchdown receptions—0.

DAVIS, DON — LB — SAINTS

PERSONAL: Born December 17, 1972, in Olathe, Kan. ... 6-1/240.
HIGH SCHOOL: Olathe (Kan.).
COLLEGE: Kansas.
TRANSACTIONS/CAREER NOTES: Signed as non-drafted free agent by Kansas City Chiefs (January 9, 1996). ... Released by Chiefs (August 20, 1996). ... Signed by New Orleans Saints to practice squad (August 27, 1996). ... Activated (October 4, 1996). ... On injured reserve with wrist injury (November 19, 1997-remainder of season).
PLAYING EXPERIENCE: New Orleans NFL, 1996 and 1997. ... Games/Games started: 1996 (11/0), 1997 (11/0). Total: 22/0.
PRO STATISTICS: 1996—Recovered one fumble.

DAVIS, ERIC — CB — PANTHERS

PERSONAL: Born January 26, 1968, in Anniston, Ala. ... 5-11/185. ... Full name: Eric Wayne Davis.
HIGH SCHOOL: Anniston (Ala.).
COLLEGE: Jacksonville (Ala.) State.
TRANSACTIONS/CAREER NOTES: Selected by San Francisco 49ers in second round (53rd pick overall) of 1990 NFL draft. ... Signed by 49ers (July 28, 1990). ... On injured reserve with shoulder injury (September 11, 1991-remainder of season). ... Granted free agency (March 1, 1993). ... Re-signed by 49ers (July 20, 1993). ... Granted unconditional free agency (February 16, 1996). ... Signed by Carolina Panthers (February 21, 1996).
CHAMPIONSHIP GAME EXPERIENCE: Played in NFC championship game (1990, 1992-1994 and 1996 seasons). ... Member of Super Bowl championship team (1994 season).
HONORS: Played in Pro Bowl (1995 and 1996 seasons).
POST SEASON RECORDS: Shares NFL postseason career record for most consecutive games with one or more interception—3.
PRO STATISTICS: 1990—Returned five punts for 38 yards and recovered one fumble for 34 yards. 1992—Recovered two fumbles. 1993—Recovered one fumble for 47 yards and a touchdown. 1994—Recovered two fumbles. 1995—Credited with one sack. 1997—Recovered one fumble for two yards.
MISCELLANEOUS: Holds Carolina Panthers all-time record for most interceptions (10).

			INTERCEPTIONS			
Year Team	G	GS	No.	Yds.	Avg.	TD
1990—San Francisco NFL	16	0	1	13	13.0	0
1991—San Francisco NFL	2	2	0	0	...	0
1992—San Francisco NFL	16	16	3	52	17.3	0
1993—San Francisco NFL	16	16	4	45	11.3	1
1994—San Francisco NFL	16	16	1	8	8.0	0
1995—San Francisco NFL	15	15	3	84	28.0	1
1996—Carolina NFL	16	16	5	57	11.4	0
1997—Carolina NFL	14	14	5	25	5.0	0
Pro totals (8 years)	111	95	22	284	12.9	2

D

DAVIS, GREG   K   RAIDERS

PERSONAL: Born October 29, 1965, in Rome, Ga. ... 6-0/205. ... Full name: Gregory Brian Davis.
HIGH SCHOOL: Lakeside (Atlanta).
COLLEGE: The Citadel (degree in physical education, 1987).
TRANSACTIONS/CAREER NOTES: Selected by Tampa Bay Buccaneers in ninth round (246th pick overall) of 1987 NFL draft. ... Signed by Buccaneers (July 18, 1987). ... Released by Buccaneers (September 7, 1987). ... Signed as replacement player by Atlanta Falcons (September 24, 1987). ... Claimed on waivers by Buccaneers (October 20, 1987). ... Released by Buccaneers (November 2, 1987). ... Signed by Falcons (December 24, 1987). ... Granted unconditional free agency (February 1, 1989). ... Signed by New England Patriots (March 9, 1989). ... Released by Patriots (November 8, 1989). ... Signed by Falcons (November 15, 1989). ... Granted unconditional free agency (February 1, 1991). ... Signed by Phoenix Cardinals (February 21, 1991). ... Granted unconditional free agency (March 1, 1993). ... Re-signed by Cardinals (July 15, 1993). ... Cardinals franchise renamed Arizona Cardinals for 1994 season. ... Released by Cardinals (November 5, 1996). ... Signed by Minnesota Vikings (April 11, 1997). ... Released by Vikings (September 24, 1997). ... Signed by San Diego Chargers (September 24, 1997). ... Granted unconditional free agency (February 13, 1998). ... Signed by Oakland Raiders (June 16, 1998).

| | | | | | | KICKING | | | |
Year—Team	G	GS	XPM	XPA	FGM	FGA	Lg.	50+	Pts.
1987—Atlanta NFL	3	0	6	6	3	4	42	0-0	15
1988—Atlanta NFL	16	0	25	27	19	30	52	1-4	82
1989—New England NFL	9	0	13	16	16	23	52	2-2	61
—Atlanta NFL	6	0	12	12	7	11	47	0-0	33
1990—Atlanta NFL	16	0	40	40	22	33	53	2-5	106
1991—Phoenix NFL	16	0	19	19	21	30	52	3-7	82
1992—Phoenix NFL	16	0	28	28	13	26	49	0-3	67
1993—Phoenix NFL	16	0	37	37	21	28	55	4-5	100
1994—Arizona NFL	14	0	17	17	20	26	51	1-4	77
1995—Arizona NFL	16	0	19	19	30	‡39	55	1-6	109
1996—Arizona NFL	9	0	12	12	9	14	49	0-0	39
1997—Minnesota NFL	4	0	10	10	7	10	43	0-0	31
—San Diego NFL	12	0	21	22	19	24	45	0-0	78
Pro totals (11 years)	153	0	259	265	207	298	55	14-36	880

DAVIS, ISAAC   G

PERSONAL: Born April 8, 1972, in Malvern, Ark. ... 6-3/320. ... Full name: John Isaac Davis. ... Cousin of Keith Traylor, defensive tackle, Denver Broncos.
HIGH SCHOOL: Malvern (Ark.).
COLLEGE: Arkansas.
TRANSACTIONS/CAREER NOTES: Selected by San Diego Chargers in second round (43rd pick overall) of 1994 NFL draft. ... Signed by Chargers (July 13, 1994). ... Granted free agency (February 14, 1997). ... Re-signed by Chargers (July 17, 1997). ... Released by Chargers (November 25, 1997). ... Signed by New Orleans Saints (November 26, 1997). ... Granted unconditional free agency (February 13, 1998). ... Re-signed by Saints (March 3, 1998).
PLAYING EXPERIENCE: San Diego NFL, 1994-1996; San Diego (12)-New Orleans (3) NFL, 1997. ... Games/Games started: 1994 (13/2), 1995 (16/10), 1996 (14/5), 1997 (S.D.-12/12; N.O.-3/2; Total:15/14). Total: 58/31.
CHAMPIONSHIP GAME EXPERIENCE: Played in AFC championship game (1994 season). ... Played in Super Bowl XXIX (1994 season).

DAVIS, JOHN   TE   BUCCANEERS

PERSONAL: Born May 14, 1973 ... 6-4/257.
HIGH SCHOOL: Jasper (Texas).
JUNIOR COLLEGE: Cisco (Texas) Junior College.
COLLEGE: Emporia State.
TRANSACTIONS/CAREER NOTES: Selected by Dallas Cowboys in fifth round of 1994 supplemental draft. ... Signed by Cowboys prior to 1994 season. ... Released by Cowboys (August 28, 1994). ... Re-signed by Cowboys to practice squad (August 20, 1994). ... On injured reserve with ankle injury (prior to 1995 season-October 1995). ... Released by Cowboys (October 1995). ... Signed by New Orleans Saints (June 3, 1996). ... Released by Saints (August 12, 1996). ... Signed by Tampa Bay Buccaneers (January 20, 1997).
SINGLE GAME HIGHS (regular season): Receptions—1 (December 21, 1997, vs. Chicago); yards—16 (December 21, 1997, vs. Chicago); and touchdown receptions—0.

| | | | RECEIVING | | | TOTALS | | | |
Year—Team	G	GS	No.	Yds.	Avg.	TD	TD	2pt.	Pts.	Fum.
1997—Tampa Bay NFL	8	2	3	35	11.7	0	0	0	0	0

DAVIS, NATHAN   DE   FALCONS

PERSONAL: Born February 6, 1974, in Hartford, Conn. ... 6-5/312. ... Full name: Nathan Michael Davis. ... Cousin of Barry Larkin, shortstop, Cincinnati Reds.
HIGH SCHOOL: Richmond (Ind.).
COLLEGE: Indiana.
TRANSACTIONS/CAREER NOTES: Selected by Atlanta Falcons in second round (32nd pick overall) of 1997 NFL draft. ... Signed by Falcons (July 14, 1997).
PLAYING EXPERIENCE: Atlanta NFL, 1997. ... Games/Games started: 2/0.

DAVIS, REUBEN   DT   CHARGERS

PERSONAL: Born May 7, 1965, in Greensboro, N.C. ... 6-5/320. ... Full name: Reuben Cordell Davis.
HIGH SCHOOL: Grimsley (Greensboro, N.C.).
COLLEGE: North Carolina (degree in journalism and mass communications, 1988).

TRANSACTIONS/CAREER NOTES: Selected by Tampa Bay Buccaneers in ninth round (225th pick overall) of 1988 NFL draft. ... Signed by Buccaneers (July 6, 1988). ... Granted free agency (February 1, 1990). ... Re-signed by Buccaneers (July 22, 1990). ... On injured reserve with knee injury (December 3, 1991-remainder of season). ... Granted free agency (February 1, 1992). ... Re-signed by Buccaneers (August 20, 1992). ... Granted roster exemption (August 20-28, 1992). ... Traded by Buccaneers to Phoenix Cardinals for third-round pick (traded to San Diego) in 1993 draft (October 12, 1992). ... Granted unconditional free agency (February 17, 1994). ... Signed by San Diego Chargers (March 18, 1994). ... Granted unconditional free agency (February 14, 1997). ... Re-signed by Chargers (March 18, 1997). ... On injured reserve with Achilles' tendon injury (August 24, 1997-entire season).
CHAMPIONSHIP GAME EXPERIENCE: Played in AFC championship game (1994 season). ... Played in Super Bowl XXIX (1994 season).
POST SEASON RECORDS: Shares NFL postseason single-game record for most safeties—1 (January 8, 1995, vs. Miami).
PRO STATISTICS: 1989—Intercepted one pass for 13 yards and recovered two fumbles. 1990—Recovered one fumble. 1993—Recovered one fumble. 1994—Recovered one fumble. 1996—Recovered one fumble.

Year Team	G	GS	SACKS
1988—Tampa Bay NFL	16	13	3.0
1989—Tampa Bay NFL	16	15	3.0
1990—Tampa Bay NFL	16	16	1.0
1991—Tampa Bay NFL	12	11	3.5
1992—Tampa Bay NFL	5	0	0.0
—Phoenix NFL	11	5	2.0
1993—Phoenix NFL	16	15	1.0
1994—San Diego NFL	16	16	0.5
1995—San Diego NFL	16	16	3.5
1996—San Diego NFL	15	15	3.0
Pro totals (9 years)	139	122	20.5

DAVIS, ROBERT　　　C　　　PACKERS

PERSONAL: Born December 10, 1968, in Washington, D.C. ... 6-3/288. ... Full name: Robert Emmett Davis.
HIGH SCHOOL: Eleanor Roosevelt (District Heights, Md.).
COLLEGE: Shippensburg, Pa. (degree in criminal justice/law enforcement).
TRANSACTIONS/CAREER NOTES: Signed as non-drafted free agent by New York Jets (April 27, 1993). ... Released by Jets (August 24, 1993). ... Re-signed by Jets (April 29, 1994). ... Released by Jets (August 22, 1994). ... Signed as free agent by Baltimore Stallions of CFL (April 1995). ... Signed by Kansas City Chiefs prior to 1996 season. ... Released by Chiefs (August 20, 1996). ... Signed by Chicago Bears (August 28, 1996). ... Released by Bears (August 27, 1997). ... Signed by Green Bay Packers (November 4, 1997).
PLAYING EXPERIENCE: Baltimore CFL, 1995; Chicago NFL, 1996; Green Bay NFL, 1997. ... Games/Games started: 1995 (18/0), 1996 (16/0), 1997 (7/0). Total CFL: 18/0. Total NFL: 23/0. Total Pro: 41/0.
CHAMPIONSHIP GAME EXPERIENCE: Played in NFC championship game (1997 season). ... Played in Super Bowl XXXII (1997 season).

DAVIS, SCOTT　　　G

PERSONAL: Born January 29, 1970, in Glenwood, Iowa. ... 6-3/292.
HIGH SCHOOL: Glenwood (Iowa).
COLLEGE: Iowa.
TRANSACTIONS/CAREER NOTES: Selected by New York Giants in sixth round (150th pick overall) of 1993 NFL draft. ... Signed by Giants (July 19, 1993). ... On injured reserve with knee injury (August 22, 1995-entire season). ... Active for two games (1996), did not play. ... Granted unconditional free agency (February 14, 1997). ... Signed by Atlanta Falcons (June 16, 1997). ... On suspended list for violating league substance abuse policy (September 12-October 13, 1997). ... Released by Falcons (December 8, 1997).
PLAYING EXPERIENCE: New York Giants NFL, 1993 and 1994; Atlanta NFL, 1997. ... Games/Games started: 1993 (4/0), 1994 (15/4), 1997 (3/2). Total: 22/6.

DAVIS, STEPHEN　　　RB　　　REDSKINS

PERSONAL: Born March 1, 1974, in Spartanburg, S.C. ... 6-0/234.
HIGH SCHOOL: Spartanburg (S.C.).
COLLEGE: Auburn.
TRANSACTIONS/CAREER NOTES: Selected by Washington Redskins in fourth round (102nd pick overall) of 1996 NFL draft. ... Signed by Redskins (July 16, 1996).
PRO STATISTICS: 1997—Returned three kickoffs for 62 yards and recovered one fumble.
SINGLE GAME HIGHS (regular season): Attempts—22 (October 13, 1997, vs. Dallas); yards—94 (October 13, 1997, vs. Dallas); and rushing touchdowns—2 (October 13, 1997, vs. Dallas).

Year Team	G	GS	RUSHING				RECEIVING				TOTALS			
			Att.	Yds.	Avg.	TD	No.	Yds.	Avg.	TD	TD	2pt.	Pts.	Fum.
1996—Washington NFL	12	0	23	139	6.0	2	0	0	...	0	2	0	12	0
1997—Washington NFL	14	6	141	567	4.0	3	18	134	7.4	0	3	0	18	1
Pro totals (2 years)	26	6	164	706	4.3	5	18	134	7.4	0	5	0	30	1

DAVIS, TERRELL　　　RB　　　BRONCOS

PERSONAL: Born October 28, 1972, in San Diego. ... 5-11/210.
HIGH SCHOOL: Abraham Lincoln Prep (San Diego).
COLLEGE: Long Beach State, then Georgia.
TRANSACTIONS/CAREER NOTES: Selected by Denver Broncos in sixth round (196th pick overall) of 1995 NFL draft. ... Signed by Broncos (June 30, 1995).
CHAMPIONSHIP GAME EXPERIENCE: Played in AFC championship game (1997 season). ... Member of Super Bowl championship team (1997 season).

HONORS: Named running back on THE SPORTING NEWS NFL All-Pro team (1996 and 1997). ... Played in Pro Bowl (1996 and 1997 seasons). ... Named Most Valuable Player of Super Bowl XXXII (1997 season).

POST SEASON RECORDS: Holds Super Bowl single-game record for most rushing touchdowns—3 (January 25, 1998, vs. Green Bay). ... Shares Super Bowl single-game records for most points—18; and most touchdowns—3 (January 25, 1998, vs. Green Bay). ... Holds NFL postseason career record for highest average gain—5.33.

PRO STATISTICS: 1995—Recovered one fumble. 1996—Recovered two fumbles. 1997—Recovered two fumbles for minus seven yards.

SINGLE GAME HIGHS (regular season): Attempts—42 (October 26, 1997, vs. Buffalo); yards—215 (September 21, 1997, vs. Cincinnati); and rushing touchdowns—3 (November 24, 1997, vs. Oakland).

STATISTICAL PLATEAUS: 100-yard rushing games: 1995 (3), 1996 (6), 1997 (10). Total: 19.

			RUSHING				RECEIVING				TOTALS			
Year Team	G	GS	Att.	Yds.	Avg.	TD	No.	Yds.	Avg.	TD	TD	2pt.	Pts.	Fum.
1995—Denver NFL	14	14	237	1117	§4.7	7	49	367	7.5	1	8	0	48	5
1996—Denver NFL	16	16	§345	§1538	4.5	13	36	310	8.6	2	15	0	90	5
1997—Denver NFL	15	15	369	§1750	4.7	†15	42	287	6.8	0	15	3	†96	4
Pro totals (3 years)	45	45	951	4405	4.6	35	127	964	7.6	3	38	3	234	14

DAVIS, TRAVIS   S   JAGUARS

PERSONAL: Born January 10, 1973, in Harbor City, Calif. ... 6-0/204. ... Full name: Travis H. Davis.

HIGH SCHOOL: Banning (Wilmington, Calif.).

COLLEGE: Notre Dame.

TRANSACTIONS/CAREER NOTES: Selected by New Orleans Saints in seventh round (242nd pick overall) of 1995 NFL draft. ... Signed by Saints (July 14, 1995). ... Released by Saints (September 5, 1995). ... Re-signed by Saints to practice squad (September 6, 1995). ... Signed by Jacksonville Jaguars off Saints practice squad (October 17, 1995). ... Granted free agency (February 13, 1998). ... Re-signed by Jaguars (June 12, 1998).

CHAMPIONSHIP GAME EXPERIENCE: Played in AFC championship game (1996 season).

PRO STATISTICS: 1995—Recovered one fumble. 1996—Recovered two fumbles. 1997—Credited with two sacks, returned one kickoff for nine yards and recovered three fumbles for 10 yards.

			INTERCEPTIONS			
Year Team	G	GS	No.	Yds.	Avg.	TD
1995—Jacksonville NFL	9	5	0	0	...	0
1996—Jacksonville NFL	16	7	2	0	0.0	0
1997—Jacksonville NFL	16	16	1	23	23.0	0
Pro totals (3 years)	41	28	3	23	7.7	0

DAVIS, TROY   RB   SAINTS

PERSONAL: Born September 14, 1975, in Miami. ... 5-7/191.

HIGH SCHOOL: Southridge (Miami).

COLLEGE: Iowa State.

TRANSACTIONS/CAREER NOTES: Selected after junior season by New Orleans Saints in third round (62nd pick overall) of 1997 NFL draft. ... Signed by Saints (June 13, 1997).

HONORS: Named running back on THE SPORTING NEWS college All-America first team (1995 and 1996).

SINGLE GAME HIGHS (regular season): Attempts—12 (October 19, 1997, vs. Carolina); yards—45 (October 19, 1997, vs. Carolina); and rushing touchdowns—0.

			RUSHING				RECEIVING				KICKOFF RETURNS				TOTALS			
Year Team	G	GS	Att.	Yds.	Avg.	TD	No.	Yds.	Avg.	TD	No.	Yds.	Avg.	TD	TD	2pt.	Pts.	Fum.
1997—New Orleans NFL	16	7	75	271	3.6	0	13	85	6.5	0	9	173	19.2	0	0	0	0	3

DAVIS, TYREE   WR   SEAHAWKS

PERSONAL: Born September 23, 1970, in Altheimer, Ark. ... 5-9/175. ... Brother of Willie Davis, wide receiver, Tennessee Oilers.

HIGH SCHOOL: Altheimer (Ark.).

COLLEGE: Central Arkansas.

TRANSACTIONS/CAREER NOTES: Selected by Tampa Bay Buccaneers in seventh round (176th pick overall) of 1993 NFL draft. ... Signed by Buccaneers (June 22, 1993). ... Released by Buccaneers (August 24, 1993). ... Re-signed by Buccaneers to practice squad (August 31, 1993). ... Granted free agency (January 10, 1994). ... Re-signed by Buccaneers (March 29, 1994). ... Released by Buccaneers (August 28, 1994). ... Re-signed by Buccaneers to practice squad (August 30, 1994). ... Activated (December 16, 1994). ... Assigned by Buccaneers to Barcelona Dragons in 1995 World League enhancement allocation program (February 20, 1995). ... Released by Buccaneers (October 17, 1995). ... Signed by Cincinnati Bengals (February 22, 1996). ... Released by Bengals (August 19, 1996). ... Signed by Seattle Seahawks (July 15, 1997).

PRO STATISTICS: 1997—Recovered one fumble.

SINGLE GAME HIGHS (regular season): Receptions—2 (September 21, 1997, vs. San Diego); yards—48 (September 21, 1997, vs. San Diego); and touchdown receptions—0.

			RECEIVING				PUNT RETURNS				KICKOFF RETURNS				TOTALS			
Year Team	G	GS	No.	Yds.	Avg.	TD	No.	Yds.	Avg.	TD	No.	Yds.	Avg.	TD	TD	2pt.	Pts.	Fum.
1995—Barcelona W.L.	...	...	56	855	15.3	6	18	143	7.9	0	13	286	22.0	0	6	0	36	0
—Cincinnati NFL	1	0	0	0	...	0	0	0	...	0	0	0	...	0	0	0	0	0
—Tampa Bay NFL	1	0	0	0	...	0	0	0	...	0	0	0	...	0	0	0	0	0
1997—Barcelona W.L.	10	7	43	738	17.2	6	29	351	12.1	1	7	92	13.1	0	7	0	42	0
—Seattle NFL	13	1	2	48	24.0	0	16	104	6.5	0	2	25	12.5	0	0	0	0	1
W.L. totals (2 years)	...	...	99	1593	16.1	12	47	494	10.5	1	20	378	18.9	0	13	0	78	0
NFL totals (2 years)	15	1	2	48	24.0	0	16	104	6.5	0	2	25	12.5	0	0	0	0	1
Pro totals (4 years)	...	...	101	1641	16.2	12	63	598	9.5	1	22	403	18.3	0	13	0	78	1

DAVIS, TYRONE — TE — PACKERS

PERSONAL: Born June 30, 1972, in Halifax, Va. ... 6-4/245.
HIGH SCHOOL: Halifax (Va.), then Fork Union (Va.) Military Academy.
COLLEGE: Virginia.
TRANSACTIONS/CAREER NOTES: Selected by New York Jets in fourth round (107th pick overall) of 1995 NFL draft. ... Signed by Jets (June 14, 1995). ... Released by Jets (September 13, 1995). ... Re-signed by Jets to practice squad (September 15, 1995). ... Activated (December 11, 1995). ... Granted free agency (February 14, 1997). ... Re-signed by Jets for 1997 season. ... Traded by Jets to Green Bay Packers for past considerations (August 25, 1997). ... Released by Packers (September 25, 1997). ... Re-signed by Packers (September 29, 1997). ... Released by Packers following 1997 season. ... Re-signed by Packers (March 23, 1998)
CHAMPIONSHIP GAME EXPERIENCE: Played in NFC championship game (1997 season). ... Played in Super Bowl XXXII (1997 season).
PRO STATISTICS: 1997—Recovered fumble in end zone for touchdown.
SINGLE GAME HIGHS (regular season): Receptions—1 (December 20, 1997, vs. Buffalo); yards—26 (November 2, 1997, vs. Detroit); and touchdown receptions—1 (December 20, 1997, vs. Buffalo).

| | | | RECEIVING | | | | TOTALS | | |
Year Team	G	GS	No.	Yds.	Avg.	TD	TD	2pt.	Pts.	Fum.
1995—New York Jets NFL	4	0	1	9	9.0	0	0	0	0	0
1996—New York Jets NFL	2	0	1	6	6.0	0	0	0	0	0
1997—Green Bay NFL	13	0	2	28	14.0	1	2	0	12	0
Pro totals (3 years)	19	0	4	43	10.8	1	2	0	12	0

DAVIS, WENDELL — CB — COWBOYS

PERSONAL: Born June 27, 1973, in Wichita, Kan. ... 5-10/183.
HIGH SCHOOL: North (Wichita, Kan.).
JUNIOR COLLEGE: Coffeyville (Kan.) Community College.
COLLEGE: Oklahoma.
TRANSACTIONS/CAREER NOTES: Selected by Dallas Cowboys in sixth round (207th pick overall) of 1996 NFL draft. ... Signed by Cowboys (July 15, 1996). ... Released by Cowboys (August 27, 1996). ... Re-signed by Cowboys to practice squad (August 28, 1996). ... Activated (September 6, 1996).
PLAYING EXPERIENCE: Dallas NFL, 1996 and 1997. ... Games/Games started: 1996 (13/0), 1997 (15/0). Total: 28/0.
PRO STATISTICS: 1997—Recovered two fumbles.

DAVIS, WILLIE — WR — OILERS

PERSONAL: Born October 10, 1967, in Little Rock, Ark. ... 6-0/182. ... Full name: Willie Clark Davis. ... Brother of Tyree Davis, wide receiver, Seattle Seahawks.
HIGH SCHOOL: Altheimer (Ark.).
COLLEGE: Central Arkansas.
TRANSACTIONS/CAREER NOTES: Signed as non-drafted free agent by Kansas City Chiefs (May 2, 1990). ... Released by Chiefs (September 3, 1990). ... Re-signed by Chiefs to practice squad (1990). ... Released by Chiefs (August 26, 1991). ... Re-signed by Chiefs to practice squad (August 28, 1991). ... Activated (November 23, 1991). ... Moved to practice squad (November 26, 1991). ... Assigned by Chiefs to Orlando Thunder in 1992 World League enhancement allocation program (February 20, 1992). ... Granted unconditional free agency (February 16, 1996). ... Signed by Houston Oilers (March 26, 1996). ... Oilers franchise moved to Tennessee for 1997 season.
CHAMPIONSHIP GAME EXPERIENCE: Played in AFC championship game (1993 season).
PRO STATISTICS: W.L.: 1992—Recovered one fumble and rushed once for 12 yards. NFL: 1992—Rushed once for minus 11 yards. 1996— Rushed once for 15 yards. 1997—Attempted one pass with one completion for 22 yards and a touchdown.
SINGLE GAME HIGHS (regular season): Receptions—7 (October 17, 1994, vs. Denver); yards—167 (October 11, 1992, vs. Philadelphia); and touchdown receptions—2 (October 12, 1997, vs. Cincinnati).
STATISTICAL PLATEAUS: 100-yard receiving games: 1992 (3), 1993 (2), 1994 (2), 1995 (1). Total: 8.

| | | | RECEIVING | | | | TOTALS | | |
Year Team	G	GS	No.	Yds.	Avg.	TD	TD	2pt.	Pts.	Fum.
1991—Kansas City NFL	1	0	0	0	...	0	0	...	0	0
1992—Orlando W.L.	6	3	20	242	12.1	1	1	...	6	0
—Kansas City NFL	16	14	36	756	*21.0	3	3	...	18	0
1993—Kansas City NFL	16	15	52	909	17.5	7	7	...	42	0
1994—Kansas City NFL	14	13	51	822	16.1	5	5	1	32	1
1995—Kansas City NFL	16	16	33	527	16.0	5	5	0	30	0
1996—Houston NFL	16	14	39	464	11.9	6	6	0	36	1
1997—Tennessee NFL	16	15	43	564	13.1	4	4	0	24	0
W.L. totals (1 year)	6	3	20	242	12.1	1	1	0	6	0
NFL totals (7 years)	95	87	254	4042	15.9	30	30	1	182	2
Pro totals (8 years)	101	90	274	4284	15.6	31	31	1	188	2

DAVISON, JERONE — RB

PERSONAL: Born September 16, 1970, in Picayne, Miss. ... 6-1/225. ... Full name: Jerone Lamar Davison.
HIGH SCHOOL: Picayne (Miss.).
JUNIOR COLLEGE: Solano Community College (Calif.).
COLLEGE: Arizona State.
TRANSACTIONS/CAREER NOTES: Signed as non-drafted free agent by Los Angeles Rams prior to 1993 season. ... Released by Rams (July 24, 1993). ... Played for Sacramento Gold Miners of CFL (1994). ... Signed by San Francisco 49ers (July 28, 1994). ... Released by 49ers (August 2, 1994). ... Re-signed by 49ers (May 25, 1995). ... Released by 49ers (July 24, 1995). ... Re-signed by 49ers to practice squad (October 16, 1995). ... Released by 49ers (November 14, 1995). ... Played for Rhein Fire of World League (1996). ... Signed by Oakland Raiders for 1996 season. ... Released by Raiders (August 20, 1996). ... Re-signed by Raiders (August 27, 1996). ... Granted free agency (February 13, 1998).
SINGLE GAME HIGHS (regular season): Attempts—2 (December 7, 1997, vs. Kansas City); yards—4 (December 7, 1997, vs. Kansas City); and rushing touchdowns—0.

Year Team	G	GS	RUSHING Att.	Yds.	Avg.	TD	RECEIVING No.	Yds.	Avg.	TD	TOTALS TD	2pt.	Pts.	Fum.
1993—							Did not play.							
1994—Sacramento CFL	2	...	3	1	0.3	0	0	0	...	0	0	0	0	0
1995—San Francisco NFL							Did not play.							
1996—Rhein W.L.	...	...	55	224	4.1	0	28	172	6.1	0	0	0	0	...
—Oakland NFL	2	0	0	0	...	0	4	21	5.3	0	0	0	0	0
1997—Oakland NFL	8	1	2	4	2.0	0	2	34	17.0	0	0	0	0	0
CFL totals (1 year)	2	...	3	1	0.3	0	0	0		0	0	0	0	0
W.L. totals (1 year)	...	...	55	224	4.1	0	28	172	6.1	0	0	0	0	...
NFL totals (2 years)	10	1	2	4	2.0	0	6	55	9.2	0	0	0	0	0
Pro totals (3 years)	...	...	60	229	3.8	0	34	227	6.7	0	0	0	0	0

DAWKINS, BRIAN — S — EAGLES

PERSONAL: Born October 13, 1973, in Jacksonville. ... 5-11/190.
HIGH SCHOOL: Raines (Jacksonville).
COLLEGE: Clemson.
TRANSACTIONS/CAREER NOTES: Selected by Philadelphia Eagles in second round (61st pick overall) of 1996 NFL draft. ... Signed by Eagles (July 17, 1996).
HONORS: Named defensive back on THE SPORTING NEWS college All-America second team (1995).
PRO STATISTICS: 1996—Recovered two fumbles for 23 yards.

Year Team	G	GS	INTERCEPTIONS No.	Yds.	Avg.	TD	SACKS No.
1996—Philadelphia NFL	14	13	3	41	13.7	0	1.0
1997—Philadelphia NFL	15	15	3	76	25.3	1	0.0
Pro totals (2 years)	29	28	6	117	19.5	1	1.0

DAWKINS, SEAN — WR — SAINTS

PERSONAL: Born February 3, 1971, in Red Bank, N.J. ... 6-4/215. ... Full name: Sean Russell Dawkins.
HIGH SCHOOL: Homestead (Cupertino, Calif.).
COLLEGE: California.
TRANSACTIONS/CAREER NOTES: Selected after junior season by Indianapolis Colts in first round (16th pick overall) of 1993 NFL draft. ... Signed by Colts (August 4, 1993). ... Granted unconditional free agency (February 13, 1998). ... Signed by New Orleans Saints (April 30, 1998).
CHAMPIONSHIP GAME EXPERIENCE: Played in AFC championship game (1995 season).
HONORS: Named wide receiver on THE SPORTING NEWS college All-America first team (1992).
SINGLE GAME HIGHS (regular season): Receptions—8 (October 20, 1996, vs. New England); yards—144 (October 10, 1993, vs. Dallas); and touchdown receptions—1 (November 30, 1997, vs. New England).
STATISTICAL PLATEAUS: 100-yard receiving games: 1993 (1), 1994 (1), 1995 (2), 1997 (1). Total: 5.

Year Team	G	GS	RECEIVING No.	Yds.	Avg.	TD	TOTALS TD	2pt.	Pts.	Fum.
1993—Indianapolis NFL	16	7	26	430	16.5	1	1	...	6	0
1994—Indianapolis NFL	16	16	51	742	14.5	5	5	0	30	1
1995—Indianapolis NFL	16	13	52	784	15.1	3	3	0	18	1
1996—Indianapolis NFL	15	14	54	751	13.9	1	1	0	6	1
1997—Indianapolis NFL	14	12	68	804	11.8	2	2	0	12	0
Pro totals (5 years)	77	62	251	3511	14.0	12	12	0	72	3

DAWSON, DERMONTTI — C — STEELERS

PERSONAL: Born June 17, 1965, in Lexington, Ky. ... 6-2/288. ... Full name: Dermontti Farra Dawson. ... Cousin of Marc Logan, running back with Cincinnati Bengals (1987-88), Miami Dolphins (1989-91), San Francisco 49ers (1992-94) and Washington Redskins (1995-97); and cousin of George Adams, running back with New York Giants (1985-1989) and New England Patriots (1990-1991).
HIGH SCHOOL: Bryan Station (Lexington, Ky.).
COLLEGE: Kentucky (degree in education, 1988).
TRANSACTIONS/CAREER NOTES: Selected by Pittsburgh Steelers in second round (44th pick overall) of 1988 NFL draft. ... Signed by Steelers (August 1, 1988). ... On injured reserve with knee injury (September 26-November 26, 1988). ... Designated by Steelers as transition player (February 25, 1993).
PLAYING EXPERIENCE: Pittsburgh NFL, 1988-1997. ... Games: 1988 (8/5), 1989 (16/16), 1990 (16/16), 1991 (16/16), 1992 (16/16), 1993 (16/16), 1994 (16/16), 1995 (16/16), 1996 (16/16), 1997 (16/16). Total: 152/149.
CHAMPIONSHIP GAME EXPERIENCE: Played in AFC championship game (1994, 1995 and 1997 seasons). ... Played in Super Bowl XXX (1995 season).
HONORS: Played in Pro Bowl (1992-1997 seasons). ... Named center on THE SPORTING NEWS NFL All-Pro team (1994-1997).
PRO STATISTICS: 1991—Fumbled twice and recovered one fumble for two yards. 1993—Fumbled once.

DAWSON, LAKE — WR

PERSONAL: Born January 2, 1972, in Boston. ... 6-1/200.
HIGH SCHOOL: Federal Way (Wash.).
COLLEGE: Notre Dame (degree in telecommunications).
TRANSACTIONS/CAREER NOTES: Selected by Kansas City Chiefs in third round (92nd pick overall) of 1994 NFL draft. ... Signed by Chiefs (May 5, 1994). ... On injured reserve with knee injury (September 24, 1996-remainder of season). ... Granted free agency (February 14, 1997). ... Re-signed by Chiefs (June 11, 1997). ... Granted unconditional free agency (February 13, 1998).
PRO STATISTICS: 1994—Rushed three times for 24 yards. 1995—Rushed once for minus nine yards.

Year	Team	G	GS	No.	Yds.	Avg.	TD	TD	2pt.	Pts.	Fum.
					RECEIVING					TOTALS	
1994—Kansas City NFL		12	6	37	537	14.5	2	2	0	12	1
1995—Kansas City NFL		16	9	40	513	12.8	5	5	0	30	0
1996—Kansas City NFL		4	0	5	83	16.6	1	1	0	6	0
1997—Kansas City NFL		11	11	21	273	13.0	2	2	0	12	0
Pro totals (4 years)		43	26	103	1406	13.7	10	10	0	60	1

DAY, TERRY   DE   JETS

PERSONAL: Born September 18, 1974, in Pickens, Miss. ... 6-4/280. ... Full name: Terry Lee Day.
HIGH SCHOOL: Williams-Sullivan (Durant, Miss.).
JUNIOR COLLEGE: Holmes (Miss.) Community College.
COLLEGE: Mississippi State.
TRANSACTIONS/CAREER NOTES: Selected by New York Jets in fourth round (102nd pick overall) of 1997 NFL draft. ... Signed by Jets (July 17, 1997).
PLAYING EXPERIENCE: New York Jets NFL, 1997. ... Games/Games started: 1/0.

DEESE, DERRICK   G   49ERS

PERSONAL: Born May 17, 1970, in Culver City, Calif. ... 6-3/289.
HIGH SCHOOL: Culver City (Calif.).
JUNIOR COLLEGE: El Camino Junior College (Calif.).
COLLEGE: Southern California.
TRANSACTIONS/CAREER NOTES: Signed as non-drafted free agent by San Francisco 49ers (May 8, 1992). ... On injured reserve with elbow injury (August 4, 1992-entire season). ... On inactive list for six games (1993). ... On injured reserve with broken wrist (October 23, 1993-remainder of season). ... Granted free agency (February 17, 1995). ... Tendered offer sheet by St. Louis Rams (April 20, 1995). ... Offer matched by 49ers (April 21, 1995). ... Granted unconditional free agency (February 16, 1996). ... Re-signed by 49ers (June 4, 1996). ... Granted unconditional free agency (February 14, 1997). ... Re-signed by 49ers (April 22, 1997).
PLAYING EXPERIENCE: San Francisco NFL, 1994-1997. ... Games/Games started: 1994 (16/15), 1995 (2/2), 1996 (16/0), 1997 (16/13). Total: 50/30.
CHAMPIONSHIP GAME EXPERIENCE: Played in NFC championship game (1994 and 1997 seasons). ... Member of Super Bowl championship team (1994 season).
PRO STATISTICS: 1996—Returned two kickoffs for 20 yards. 1997—Recovered one fumble.

DEL GRECO, AL   K   OILERS

PERSONAL: Born March 2, 1962, in Providence, R.I. ... 5-10/202. ... Full name: Albert Louis Del Greco Jr.
HIGH SCHOOL: Coral Gables (Fla.).
COLLEGE: Auburn.
TRANSACTIONS/CAREER NOTES: Signed as non-drafted free agent by Miami Dolphins (May 17, 1984). ... Released by Dolphins (August 27, 1984). ... Signed by Green Bay Packers (October 17, 1984). ... Released by Packers (November 25, 1987). ... Signed by St. Louis Cardinals (December 8, 1987). ... Cardinals franchise moved to Phoenix (March 15, 1988). ... Granted unconditional free agency (February 1-April 1, 1991). ... Re-signed by Cardinals (July 1, 1991). ... Released by Cardinals (August 19, 1991). ... Signed by Houston Oilers (November 5, 1991). ... Granted unconditional free agency (February 1-April 1, 1992). ... Re-signed by Oilers for 1992 season. ... Granted unconditional free agency (February 1, 1995). ... Re-signed by Oilers (June 2, 1995). ... Oilers franchise moved to Tennessee for 1997 season.
PRO STATISTICS: 1988—Rushed once for eight yards. 1990—Recovered one fumble. 1995—Punted once for 15 yards. 1997—Punted once for 32 yards.

Year	Team	G	GS	XPM	XPA	FGM	FGA	Lg.	50+	Pts.
						KICKING				
1984—Green Bay NFL		9	0	34	34	9	12	45	0-1	61
1985—Green Bay NFL		16	0	38	40	19	26	46	0-1	95
1986—Green Bay NFL		16	0	29	29	17	27	50	2-4	80
1987—Green Bay NFL		5	0	11	11	5	10	47	0-0	26
—St. Louis NFL		3	0	8	9	4	5	37	0-0	20
1988—Phoenix NFL		16	0	42	44	12	21	51	1-2	78
1989—Phoenix NFL		16	0	28	29	18	26	50	1-2	82
1990—Phoenix NFL		16	0	31	31	17	27	50	2-6	82
1991—Houston NFL		7	0	16	16	10	13	52	1-1	46
1992—Houston NFL		16	0	41	41	21	27	54	1-1	104
1993—Houston NFL		16	0	39	40	29	34	52	4-7	126
1994—Houston NFL		16	0	18	18	16	20	50	1-3	66
1995—Houston NFL		16	0	33	33	27	31	53	3-5	114
1996—Houston NFL		16	0	35	35	32	38	56	1-3	131
1997—Tennessee NFL		16	0	32	32	27	35	52	2-2	113
Pro totals (14 years)		200	0	435	442	263	352	56	19-38	1224

DELLENBACH, JEFF   C/G

PERSONAL: Born February 14, 1963, in Wausau, Wis. ... 6-6/300. ... Full name: Jeffrey Alan Dellenbach. ... Name pronounced del-en-BOK.
HIGH SCHOOL: East (Wausau, Wis.).
COLLEGE: Wisconsin.

D

TRANSACTIONS/CAREER NOTES: Selected by Jacksonville Bulls in 1985 USFL territorial draft. ... Selected by Miami Dolphins in fourth round (111th pick overall) of 1985 NFL draft. ... Signed by Dolphins (July 15, 1985). ... Granted free agency (February 1, 1990). ... Re-signed by Dolphins (August 30, 1990). ... Granted roster exemption (August 30-September 8, 1990). ... Granted free agency (February 1, 1992). ... Re-signed by Dolphins (May 4, 1992). ... Granted unconditional free agency (February 17, 1995). ... Signed by New England Patriots (March 6, 1995). ... Released by Patriots (September 10, 1996). ... Signed by Green Bay Packers (December 3, 1996). ... Granted unconditional free agency (February 14, 1997). ... Re-signed by Packers (July 25, 1997).
PLAYING EXPERIENCE: Miami NFL, 1985-1994; New England NFL, 1995; New England (2)-Green Bay (3) NFL, 1996; Green Bay NFL, 1997. ... Games/Games started: 1985 (11/1), 1986 (13/6), 1987 (11/6), 1988 (16/16), 1989 (16/16), 1990 (15/0), 1991 (15/2), 1992 (16/8), 1993 (16/16), 1994 (16/16), 1995 (15/5), 1996 (N.E.-2/0; G.B.-3/0; Total: 5/0), 1997 (13/5). Total: 178/97.
CHAMPIONSHIP GAME EXPERIENCE: Played in AFC championship game (1985 and 1992 seasons). ... Played in NFC championship game (1996 season). ... Member of Super Bowl championship team (1996 season). ... Member of Packers for NFC championship game (1997 season); did not play. ... Member of Packers for Super Bowl XXXII (1997 season); did not play.
PRO STATISTICS: 1987—Fumbled once for minus 13 yards. 1988—Fumbled once for minus nine yards. 1991—Returned one kickoff for no yards. 1992—Recovered one fumble. 1993—Fumbled once and recovered one fumble for minus six yards. 1994—Fumbled once.

DeLONG, GREG   TE   VIKINGS

PERSONAL: Born April 3, 1973, in Orefield, Pa. ... 6-4/247. ... Full name: Gregory A. DeLong.
HIGH SCHOOL: Parkland Senior (Orefield, Pa.).
COLLEGE: North Carolina.
TRANSACTIONS/CAREER NOTES: Signed as non-drafted free agent by Cleveland Browns (May 2, 1995). ... Released by Browns (August 21, 1995). ... Signed by Minnesota Vikings to practice squad (August 28, 1995). ... Activated (November 15, 1995). ... Granted free agency (February 13, 1998).
PRO STATISTICS: 1996—Returned one kickoff for three yards and recovered one fumble.
SINGLE GAME HIGHS (regular season): Receptions—4 (December 18, 1995, vs. San Francisco); yards—26 (December 18, 1995, vs. San Francisco); and touchdown receptions—0.

				RECEIVING				TOTALS		
Year Team	G	GS	No.	Yds.	Avg.	TD	TD	2pt.	Pts.	Fum.
1995—Minnesota NFL	2	2	6	38	6.3	0	0	0	0	0
1996—Minnesota NFL	16	8	8	34	4.3	0	0	0	0	0
1997—Minnesota NFL	16	3	8	75	9.4	0	0	0	0	1
Pro totals (3 years)	34	13	22	147	6.7	0	0	0	0	1

DeMARCO, BRIAN   G   JAGUARS

PERSONAL: Born April 9, 1972, in Berea, Ohio. ... 6-7/329. ... Full name: Brian Thomas DeMarco.
HIGH SCHOOL: Admiral King (Lorain, Ohio).
COLLEGE: Michigan State.
TRANSACTIONS/CAREER NOTES: Selected by Jacksonville Jaguars in second round (40th pick overall) of 1995 NFL draft. ... Signed by Jaguars (June 1, 1995).
PLAYING EXPERIENCE: Jacksonville NFL, 1995-1997. ... Games/Games started: 1995 (16/16), 1996 (10/9), 1997 (14/5). Total: 40/30.
CHAMPIONSHIP GAME EXPERIENCE: Played in AFC championship game (1996 season).

DENSON, DAMON   G   PATRIOTS

PERSONAL: Born February 8, 1975, in Pittsburgh. ... 6-3/305. ... Full name: Damon Michael Denson.
HIGH SCHOOL: Baldwin (Pittsburgh).
COLLEGE: Michigan.
TRANSACTIONS/CAREER NOTES: Selected by New England Patriots in fourth round (97th pick overall) of 1997 NFL draft. ... Signed by Patriots (July 16, 1997).
PLAYING EXPERIENCE: New England NFL, 1997. ... Games/Games started: 2/0.

DENT, RICHARD   DE

PERSONAL: Born December 13, 1960, in Atlanta. ... 6-5/265. ... Full name: Richard Lamar Dent. ... Cousin of Vince Marrow, tight end with Buffalo Bills (1994).
HIGH SCHOOL: Murphy (Atlanta).
COLLEGE: Tennessee State.
TRANSACTIONS/CAREER NOTES: Selected by Philadelphia Stars in eighth round (89th pick overall) of 1983 USFL draft. ... Selected by Chicago Bears in eighth round (203rd pick overall) of 1983 NFL draft. ... Signed by Bears (May 12, 1983). ... On non-football injury list for substance abuse (September 8, 1988). ... Activated (September 9, 1988). ... On injured reserve with fractured fibula (November 29, 1988-remainder of season). ... Released by Bears (April 27, 1994). ... Signed by San Francisco 49ers (June 9, 1994). ... Released by 49ers (February 14, 1995). ... Signed by Bears (September 18, 1995). ... Released by Bears (October 24, 1995). ... Signed by Indianapolis Colts (July 26, 1996). ... Granted unconditional free agency (February 14, 1997). ... Signed by Philadelphia Eagles (September 2, 1997). ... Granted unconditional free agency (February 13, 1998).
CHAMPIONSHIP GAME EXPERIENCE: Played in NFC championship game (1984 and 1985 seasons). ... Member of Super Bowl championship team (1985 and 1994 seasons). ... Member of 49ers for NFC championship game (1994 season); inactive.
HONORS: Played in Pro Bowl (1984, 1985, 1990 and 1993 seasons). ... Named Most Valuable Player of Super Bowl XX (1985 season).
POST SEASON RECORDS: Shares NFL postseason single-game record for most sacks—3 1/2 (January 5, 1986, vs. New York Giants).
PRO STATISTICS: 1984—Recovered one fumble. 1985—Recovered two fumbles. 1987—Recovered two fumbles for 11 yards. 1988—Recovered one fumble. 1989—Recovered two fumbles. 1990—Recovered three fumbles for 45 yards and one touchdown. 1991—Recovered one fumble. 1992—Recovered one fumble.
MISCELLANEOUS: Holds Chicago Bears all-time record for most sacks (124.5).

| Year Team | G | GS | INTERCEPTIONS | | | | SACKS |
			No.	Yds.	Avg.	TD	No.
1983—Chicago NFL	16	3	0	0	...	0	3.0
1984—Chicago NFL	16	10	0	0	...	0	‡17.5
1985—Chicago NFL	16	16	2	10	5.0	1	*17.0
1986—Chicago NFL	15	13	0	0	...	0	11.5
1987—Chicago NFL	12	12	0	0	...	0	12.5
1988—Chicago NFL	13	12	0	0	...	0	10.5
1989—Chicago NFL	15	15	1	30	30.0	0	9.0
1990—Chicago NFL	16	16	3	21	7.0	0	12.0
1991—Chicago NFL	16	16	1	4	4.0	0	10.5
1992—Chicago NFL	16	16	0	0	...	0	8.5
1993—Chicago NFL	16	16	1	24	24.0	0	12.5
1994—San Francisco NFL	2	2	0	0	...	0	2.0
1995—Chicago NFL	3	1	0	0	...	0	0.0
1996—Indianapolis NFL	16	1	0	0	...	0	6.5
1997—Philadelphia NFL	15	0	0	0	...	0	4.5
Pro totals (15 years)	203	149	8	89	11.1	1	137.5

DeRAMUS, LEE   WR   PACKERS

PERSONAL: Born August 24, 1972, in Sicklerville, N.J. ... 6-1/205. ... Full name: Lee Collins DeRamus.
HIGH SCHOOL: Edgewood Regional (Atco, N.J.).
COLLEGE: Wisconsin.
TRANSACTIONS/CAREER NOTES: Selected after junior season by New Orleans Saints in sixth round (184th pick overall) of 1995 NFL draft. ... Signed by Saints (July 14, 1995). ... On reserve/non-football injury list with broken leg (August 22-October 30, 1995). ... Activated (October 30, 1995). ... Released by Saints (August 18, 1997). ... Signed by Green Bay Packers (March 17, 1998).
PRO STATISTICS: 1996—Rushed once for two yards.
SINGLE GAME HIGHS (regular season): Receptions—4 (December 16, 1995, vs. Green Bay); yards—56 (December 16, 1995, vs. Green Bay); and touchdown receptions—1 (October 13, 1996, vs. Chicago).

| Year Team | G | GS | RECEIVING | | | | TOTALS | | | |
			No.	Yds.	Avg.	TD	TD	2pt.	Pts.	Fum.
1995—New Orleans NFL	8	0	6	76	12.7	0	0	0	0	0
1996—New Orleans NFL	15	4	15	182	12.1	1	1	0	6	0
1997—					Did not play.					
Pro totals (2 years)	23	4	21	258	12.3	1	1	0	6	0

DETMER, TY   QB   49ERS

PERSONAL: Born October 30, 1967, in San Marcos, Texas. ... 6-0/194. ... Full name: Ty Hubert Detmer. ... Brother of Koy Detmer, quarterback, Philadelphia Eagles.
HIGH SCHOOL: Southwest (San Antonio).
COLLEGE: Brigham Young (degree in recreation administration).
TRANSACTIONS/CAREER NOTES: Selected by Green Bay Packers in ninth round (230th pick overall) of 1992 NFL draft. ... Signed by Packers (July 22, 1992). ... Active for two games (1992); did not play. ... Active for five games (1995); did not play. ... On injured reserve with thumb injury (November 8, 1995-remainder of season). ... Granted unconditional free agency (February 16, 1996). ... Signed by Philadelphia Eagles (March 1, 1996). ... Granted unconditional free agency (February 13, 1998). ... Signed by San Francisco 49ers (March 1, 1998).
HONORS: Heisman Trophy winner (1990). ... Maxwell Award winner (1990). ... Davey O'Brien Award winner (1990 and 1991). ... Named quarterback on THE SPORTING NEWS college All-America first team (1990 and 1991).
PRO STATISTICS: 1995—Fumbled once and recovered one fumble. 1996—Fumbled seven times and recovered one fumble. 1997—Fumbled six times and recovered one fumble for minus two yards.
SINGLE GAME HIGHS (regular season): Attempts—45 (September 28, 1997, vs. Minnesota); completions—28 (September 28, 1997, vs. Minnesota); yards—342 (October 27, 1996, vs. Carolina); and touchdown passes—4 (October 20, 1996, vs. Miami).
STATISTICAL PLATEAUS: 300-yard passing games: 1996 (3).
MISCELLANEOUS: Regular-season record as starting NFL quarterback: 9-9 (.500). ... Postseason record as starting NFL quarterback: 0-1.

| Year Team | G | GS | PASSING | | | | | | | | RUSHING | | | | TOTALS | | |
			Att.	Cmp.	Pct.	Yds.	TD	Int.	Avg.	Rat.	Att.	Yds.	Avg.	TD	TD	2pt.	Pts.
1992—Green Bay NFL							Did not play.										
1993—Green Bay NFL	3	0	5	3	60.0	26	0	0	5.20	73.8	1	-2	-2.0	0	0	...	0
1994—Green Bay NFL							Did not play.										
1995—Green Bay NFL	4	0	16	8	50.0	81	1	1	5.06	59.6	3	3	1.0	0	0	0	0
1996—Philadelphia NFL	13	11	401	238	59.4	2911	15	13	7.26	80.8	31	59	1.9	1	1	0	6
1997—Philadelphia NFL	8	7	244	134	54.9	1567	7	6	6.42	73.9	14	46	3.3	1	1	0	6
Pro totals (4 years)	28	18	666	383	57.5	4585	23	20	6.88	77.7	49	106	2.2	2	2	0	12

DEVINE, KEVIN   CB   JAGUARS

PERSONAL: Born December 11, 1974, in Jackson, Miss. ... 5-9/177. ... Full name: Kevin L. Devine.
HIGH SCHOOL: West Nogales (West Covina, Calif.).
COLLEGE: California.
TRANSACTIONS/CAREER NOTES: Signed as non-drafted free agent by Jacksonville Jaguars (April 21, 1997). ... Assigned by Jaguars to Amsterdam Admirals in 1998 NFL Europe enhancement allocation program (February 18, 1998).
PLAYING EXPERIENCE: Jacksonville NFL, 1997. ... Games/Games started: 12/0.

DEVLIN, MIKE C CARDINALS

PERSONAL: Born November 16, 1969, in Marlton, N.J. ... 6-2/318. ... Full name: Michael R. Devlin. ... Cousin of Joe Devlin, offensive tackle/guard with Buffalo Bills (1976-1982 and 1984-1989).
HIGH SCHOOL: Cherokee (Marlton, N.J.).
COLLEGE: Iowa.
TRANSACTIONS/CAREER NOTES: Selected by Buffalo Bills in fifth round (136th pick overall) of 1993 NFL draft. ... Signed by Bills (July 12, 1993). ... Granted unconditional free agency (February 16, 1996). ... Signed by Arizona Cardinals (March 8, 1996). ... Granted unconditional free agency (February 14, 1997). ... Re-signed by Cardinals (February 25, 1997).
PLAYING EXPERIENCE: Buffalo NFL, 1993-1995; Arizona NFL, 1996 and 1997. ... Games/Games started: 1993 (12/0), 1994 (16/0), 1995 (16/0), 1996 (11/11), 1997 (15/13). Total: 70/24.
CHAMPIONSHIP GAME EXPERIENCE: Played in AFC championship game (1993 season). ... Played in Super Bowl XXVIII (1993 season).
PRO STATISTICS: 1997—Recovered one fumble.

DEXTER, JAMES OT CARDINALS

PERSONAL: Born March 3, 1973, in Springfield, Va. ... 6-7/319.
HIGH SCHOOL: West Springfield (Va.).
COLLEGE: South Carolina.
TRANSACTIONS/CAREER NOTES: Selected by Arizona Cardinals in fifth round (137th pick overall) of 1996 NFL draft. ... Signed by Cardinals (July 21, 1996).
PLAYING EXPERIENCE: Arizona NFL, 1996 and 1997. ... Games/Games started: 1996 (6/1), 1997 (10/9). Total: 16/10.

DIAZ, JORGE G BUCCANEERS

PERSONAL: Born November 15, 1973 in New York. ... 6-4/308.
HIGH SCHOOL: Katy (Texas).
JUNIOR COLLEGE: Kilgore (Texas).
COLLEGE: Texas A&M-Kingsville.
TRANSACTIONS/CAREER NOTES: Signed as a non-drafted free agent by Tampa Bay Buccaneers (April 23, 1996).
PLAYING EXPERIENCE: Tampa Bay NFL, 1996 and 1997. ... Games/Games started: 1996 (11/6), 1997 (16/16). Total: 27/22.
PRO STATISTICS: 1997—Recovered one fumble.

DIAZ-INFANTE, DAVID OL BRONCOS

PERSONAL: Born March 31, 1964, in San Jose, Calif. ... 6-3/296. ... Full name: Gustavo David Mienez Diaz-Infante.
HIGH SCHOOL: Bellarmine Prep (San Jose, Calif.).
COLLEGE: San Jose State.
TRANSACTIONS/CAREER NOTES: Signed as non-drafted free agent by San Diego Chargers prior to 1987 season. ... Released by Chargers prior to 1987 season. ... Re-signed by Chargers as replacement player for 1987 season. ... Released by Chargers (October 1987). ... Signed by Los Angeles Rams for 1988 season. ... Released by Rams prior to 1988 season. ... Re-signed by Rams for 1989 season. ... Released by Rams prior to 1989 season. ... Selected by Franfurt Galaxy in third round (fourth offensive lineman) of 1991 WLAF positional draft. ... Signed by Galaxy (January 11, 1991). ... Signed by San Francisco 49ers (May 25, 1993). ... Released by 49ers (August 22, 1993). ... Signed by Sacramento Gold Miners of CFL (September 1993). ... Signed by Denver Broncos (March 30, 1995). ... Released by Broncos (August 27, 1995). ... Re-signed by Broncos to practice squad (August 28, 1995).
PLAYING EXPERIENCE: San Diego NFL, 1987; Frankfurt WL, 1991 and 1992; Sacramento CFL, 1993 and 1994; Denver NFL, 1996 and 1997. ... Games/Games started: 1987 (3/0; replacement games), 1991, 1992 and 1994 games played unavailable, 1993 (8/-), 1996 (9/2), 1997 (16/7). Total NFL: 28/9; including 3/0 as replacement player.
CHAMPIONSHIP GAME EXPERIENCE: Played in AFC championship game (1997 season). ... Member of Super Bowl championship team (1997 season).

DILFER, TRENT QB BUCCANEERS

PERSONAL: Born March 13, 1972, in Santa Cruz, Calif. ... 6-4/234. ... Full name: Trent Farris Dilfer.
HIGH SCHOOL: Aptos (Calif.).
COLLEGE: Fresno State.
TRANSACTIONS/CAREER NOTES: Selected after junior season by Tampa Bay Buccaneers in first round (sixth pick overall) of 1994 NFL draft. ... Signed by Buccaneers (August 3, 1994).
HONORS: Played in Pro Bowl (1997 season).
PRO STATISTICS: 1994—Fumbled twice. 1995—Fumbled 13 times and recovered one fumble for minus nine yards. 1996—Fumbled 10 times and recovered four fumbles for minus four yards. 1997—Fumbled nine times and recovered three fumbles for minus 22 yards.
SINGLE GAME HIGHS (regular season): Attempts—48 (November 26, 1995, vs. Green Bay); completions—30 (November 17, 1996, vs. San Diego); yards—327 (November 17, 1996, vs. San Diego); and touchdown passes—4 (September 21, 1997, vs. Miami).
STATISTICAL PLATEAUS: 300-yard passing games: 1995 (1), 1996 (1). Total: 2.
MISCELLANEOUS: Regular-season record as starting NFL quarterback: 23-27 (.460). ... Postseason record as starting NFL quarterback: 1-1 (.500).

Year Team	G	GS	Att.	Cmp.	Pct.	Yds.	TD	Int.	Avg.	Rat.	Att.	Yds.	Avg.	TD	TD	2pt.	Pts.
						PASSING						RUSHING				TOTALS	
1994—Tampa Bay NFL	5	2	82	38	46.3	433	1	6	5.28	36.3	2	27	13.5	0	0	0	0
1995—Tampa Bay NFL	16	16	415	224	54.0	2774	4	18	6.68	60.1	23	115	5.0	2	2	0	12
1996—Tampa Bay NFL	16	16	482	267	55.4	2859	12	19	5.93	64.8	32	124	3.9	0	0	0	0
1997—Tampa Bay NFL	16	16	386	217	56.2	2555	21	11	6.62	82.8	33	99	3.0	1	1	0	6
Pro totals (4 years)	53	50	1365	746	54.7	8621	38	54	6.32	66.7	90	365	4.1	3	3	0	18

DILGER, KEN — TE — COLTS

PERSONAL: Born February 2, 1971, in Mariah Hill, Ind. ... 6-5/259. ... Full name: Kenneth Ray Dilger.
HIGH SCHOOL: Heritage Hills (Lincoln City, Ind.).
COLLEGE: Illinois.
TRANSACTIONS/CAREER NOTES: Selected by Indianapolis Colts in second round (48th pick overall) of 1995 NFL draft. ... Signed by Colts (July 15, 1995).
CHAMPIONSHIP GAME EXPERIENCE: Played in AFC championship game (1995 season).
SINGLE GAME HIGHS (regular season): Receptions—7 (September 8, 1996, vs. New York Jets); yards—156 (September 8, 1996, vs. New York Jets); and touchdown receptions—3 (December 14, 1997, vs. Miami).
STATISTICAL PLATEAUS: 100-yard receiving games: 1995 (1), 1996 (1), 1997 (1). Total: 3.

			RECEIVING				TOTALS		
Year Team	G	GS	No.	Yds.	Avg.	TD	TD	2pt.	Pts.	Fum.
1995—Indianapolis NFL	16	13	42	635	15.1	4	4	0	24	0
1996—Indianapolis NFL	16	16	42	503	12.0	4	4	0	24	1
1997—Indianapolis NFL	14	14	27	380	14.1	3	3	0	18	0
Pro totals (3 years)	46	43	111	1518	13.7	11	11	0	66	1

DILL, SCOTT — OT/G

PERSONAL: Born April 5, 1966, in Birmingham, Ala. ... 6-5/294. ... Full name: Gerald Scott Dill.
HIGH SCHOOL: W.A. Berry (Birmingham, Ala.).
COLLEGE: Memphis State.
TRANSACTIONS/CAREER NOTES: Selected by Phoenix Cardinals in ninth round (233rd pick overall) of 1988 NFL draft. ... Signed by Cardinals (July 13, 1988). ... Granted unconditional free agency (February 1, 1990). ... Signed by Tampa Bay Buccaneers (March 16, 1990). ... On injured reserve with back injury (October 19, 1990-remainder of season). ... Granted unconditional free agency (February 1-April 1, 1991). ... Re-signed by Buccaneers for 1991 season. ... Granted free agency (February 1, 1992). ... Re-signed by Buccaneers (July 23, 1992). ... On injured reserve with foot injury (September 1-November 13, 1992). ... Granted unconditional free agency (February 17, 1995). ... Re-signed by Buccaneers (February 17, 1995). ... Released by Buccaneers (June 28, 1996). ... Re-signed by Buccaneers (July 19, 1996). ... Released by Buccaneers (August 12, 1996). ... Signed by Minnesota Vikings (August 16, 1996). ... Granted unconditional free agency (February 14, 1997). ... Re-signed by Vikings (April 3, 1997). ... On injured reserve with back injury (December 11, 1997-remainder of season). ... Granted unconditional free agency (February 13, 1998).
PLAYING EXPERIENCE: Phoenix NFL, 1988 and 1989; Tampa Bay NFL, 1990-1995; Minnesota NFL, 1996 and 1997. ... Games/Games started: 1988 (13/0), 1989 (16/0), 1990 (3/2), 1991 (8/0), 1992 (4/0), 1993 (16/16), 1994 (16/16), 1995 (12/12), 1996 (9/1), 1997 (13/5). Total: 110/52.
PRO STATISTICS: 1989—Recovered one fumble. 1993—Recovered one fumble.

DILLON, COREY — RB — BENGALS

PERSONAL: Born October 24, 1975, in Seattle. ... 6-1/220.
HIGH SCHOOL: Franklin (Seattle).
JUNIOR COLLEGE: Garden City (Kan.) Community College, then Dixie (Utah) College.
COLLEGE: Washington.
TRANSACTIONS/CAREER NOTES: Selected after junior season by Cincinnati Bengals in second round (43rd pick overall) of 1997 NFL draft. ... Signed by Bengals (July 21, 1997).
HONORS: Named running back on THE SPORTING NEWS college All-America second team (1996).
PRO STATISTICS: 1997—Recovered one fumble for four yards.
SINGLE GAME HIGHS (regular season): Attempts—39 (December 4, 1997, vs. Tennessee); yards—246 (December 4, 1997, vs. Tennessee); and rushing touchdowns—4 (December 4, 1997, vs. Tennessee).
STATISTICAL PLATEAUS: 100-yard rushing games: 1997 (4).
MISCELLANEOUS: Selected by San Diego Padres organization in 34th round of free-agent draft (June 3, 1993); did not sign.

			RUSHING				RECEIVING				KICKOFF RETURNS				TOTALS			
Year Team	G	GS	Att.	Yds.	Avg.	TD	No.	Yds.	Avg.	TD	No.	Yds.	Avg.	TD	TD	2pt.	Pts.	Fum.
1997—Cincinnati NFL	16	6	233	1129	4.8	10	27	259	9.6	0	6	182	30.3	0	10	0	60	1

DIMRY, CHARLES — CB — CHARGERS

PERSONAL: Born January 31, 1966, in San Diego. ... 6-0/176. ... Full name: Charles Louis Dimry III.
HIGH SCHOOL: Oceanside (Calif.).
COLLEGE: UNLV.
TRANSACTIONS/CAREER NOTES: Selected by Atlanta Falcons in fifth round (110th pick overall) of 1988 NFL draft. ... Signed by Falcons (July 16, 1988). ... Granted unconditional free agency (February 1, 1991). ... Signed by Denver Broncos (March 28, 1991). ... Granted unconditional free agency (February 17, 1994). ... Signed by Tampa Bay Buccaneers (May 23, 1994). ... Released by Buccaneers (July 20, 1997). ... Signed by Philadelphia Eagles (July 29, 1997). ... Granted unconditional free agency (February 13, 1998). ... Signed by San Diego Chargers (June 10, 1998).
CHAMPIONSHIP GAME EXPERIENCE: Played in AFC championship game (1991 season).
PRO STATISTICS: 1989—Credited with one sack. 1991—Recovered one fumble. 1992—Returned one punt for four yards. 1994—Recovered one fumble. 1995—Recovered two fumbles. 1996—Recovered one fumble. 1997—Fumbled once and recovered two fumbles for 34 yards.

			INTERCEPTIONS			
Year Team	G	GS	No.	Yds.	Avg.	TD
1988—Atlanta NFL	16	1	0	0	...	0
1989—Atlanta NFL	16	4	2	72	36.0	0
1990—Atlanta NFL	16	12	3	16	5.3	0
1991—Denver NFL	16	1	3	35	11.7	1
1992—Denver NFL	16	6	1	2	2.0	0

Year Team	G	GS	No.	Yds.	Avg.	TD
			INTERCEPTIONS			
1993—Denver NFL	12	11	1	0	0.0	0
1994—Tampa Bay NFL	16	16	1	0	0.0	0
1995—Tampa Bay NFL	16	16	1	0	0.0	0
1996—Tampa Bay NFL	16	7	2	1	0.5	0
1997—Philadelphia NFL	15	9	2	25	12.5	0
Pro totals (10 years)	155	83	16	151	9.4	1

DINGLE, NATE LB

PERSONAL: Born July 23, 1971, in Wells, Maine. ... 6-2/242. ... Full name: Nathan Hunter Dingle.
HIGH SCHOOL: Wells (Maine).
COLLEGE: Cincinnati.
TRANSACTIONS/CAREER NOTES: Signed as non-drafted free agent by Washington Redskins (April 28, 1994). ... Released by Redskins (August 15, 1994). ... Signed by San Diego Chargers (June 29, 1995). ... Released by Chargers (August 28, 1995). ... Signed by Philadelphia Eagles to practice squad (September 8, 1995). ... Activated (September 17, 1995). ... Released by Eagles (October 31, 1995). ... Re-signed by Eagles to practice squad (November 1, 1995). ... Activated (December 1, 1995)   Returned to practice squad (December 22, 1995). ... Granted free agency after 1995 season. ... Signed by Kansas City Chiefs (April 1996). ... Released by Chiefs (August 20, 1996). ... Signed by Jacksonville Jaguars (October 15, 1996). ... On injured reserve with Achilles' tendon injury (November 26, 1996-remainder of season). ... Signed by St. Louis Rams (April 1, 1997). ... Released by Rams (November 4, 1997).
PLAYING EXPERIENCE: Philadelphia NFL, 1995; Jacksonville NFL, 1996; St. Louis NFL, 1997. ... Games/Games started: 1995 (6/0), 1996 (2/0), 1997 (9/0). Total: 17/0.

DISHMAN, CHRIS G CARDINALS

PERSONAL: Born February 27, 1974, in Cozad, Neb. ... 6-3/320.
HIGH SCHOOL: Cozad (Neb.).
COLLEGE: Nebraska.
TRANSACTIONS/CAREER NOTES: Selected by Arizona Cardinals in fourth round (106th pick overall) of 1997 NFL draft. ... Signed by Cardinals (July 9, 1997).
PLAYING EXPERIENCE: Arizona NFL, 1997. ... Games/Games started: 8/0.

D

DISHMAN, CRIS CB REDSKINS

PERSONAL: Born August 13, 1965, in Louisville, Ky. ... 6-0/195. ... Full name: Cris Edward Dishman.
HIGH SCHOOL: DeSales (Louisville, Ky.).
COLLEGE: Purdue.
TRANSACTIONS/CAREER NOTES: Selected by Houston Oilers in fifth round (125th pick overall) of 1988 NFL draft. ... Signed by Oilers (July 15, 1988). ... Granted free agency (February 1, 1991). ... Re-signed by Oilers (August 18, 1991). ... Granted free agency (February 1, 1992). ... Re-signed by Oilers (September 10, 1992). ... Designated by Oilers as transition player (February 15, 1994). ... Free agency status changed by Oilers from transitional to franchise player (February 15, 1996). ... Granted unconditional free agency (February 14, 1997). ... Signed by Washington Redskins (April 5, 1997).
HONORS: Played in Pro Bowl (1991 and 1997 seasons).
PRO STATISTICS: 1988—Returned blocked punt 10 yards for a touchdown and recovered one fumble. 1989—Returned blocked punt seven yards for a touchdown and recovered one fumble. 1991—Recovered three fumbles for 19 yards and one touchdown. 1993—Recovered two fumbles for 69 yards and one touchdown. 1994—Returned one punt for no yards and recovered one fumble for 29 yards. 1995—Recovered two fumbles for 15 yards. 1996—Recovered two fumbles. 1997—Credited with 1 1/2 sacks and recovered one fumble.

Year Team	G	GS	No.	Yds.	Avg.	TD
			INTERCEPTIONS			
1988—Houston NFL	15	2	0	0	...	0
1989—Houston NFL	16	0	4	31	7.8	0
1990—Houston NFL	16	14	4	50	12.5	0
1991—Houston NFL	15	15	6	61	10.2	0
1992—Houston NFL	15	15	3	34	11.3	0
1993—Houston NFL	16	16	6	74	12.3	0
1994—Houston NFL	16	16	4	74	18.5	1
1995—Houston NFL	15	15	3	17	5.7	0
1996—Houston NFL	16	16	1	7	7.0	0
1997—Washington NFL	16	15	4	47	11.8	1
Pro totals (10 years)	156	124	35	395	11.3	2

DIXON, DAVID G/OT VIKINGS

PERSONAL: Born January 5, 1969, in Auckland, New Zealand. ... 6-5/352. ... Full name: David Tukatahi Dixon.
HIGH SCHOOL: Pukekohe (New Zealand).
JUNIOR COLLEGE: Ricks Junior College (Idaho).
COLLEGE: Arizona State.
TRANSACTIONS/CAREER NOTES: Signed as non-drafted free agent by Minnesota Vikings to practice squad (October 20, 1992). ... Granted free agency after 1992 season. ... Re-signed by Vikings (February 23, 1993). ... Released by Vikings (August 23, 1993). ... Signed by Dallas Cowboys to practice squad (September 8, 1993). ... Granted free agency after 1993 season. ... Signed by Vikings (July 12, 1994). ... Granted free agency (February 14, 1997). ... Re-signed by Vikings (May 1, 1997). ... Granted unconditional free agency (February 13, 1998). ... Re-signed by Vikings (February 17, 1998).
PLAYING EXPERIENCE: Minnesota NFL, 1994-1997. ... Games/Games started: 1994 (1/0), 1995 (15/6), 1996 (13/6), 1997 (13/13). Total: 42/25.

DIXON, ERNEST   LB   PANTHERS

PERSONAL: Born October 17, 1971, in Fort Mill, S.C. ... 6-1/240. ... Full name: Ernest James Dixon.

HIGH SCHOOL: Fort Mill (S.C.).

COLLEGE: South Carolina.

TRANSACTIONS/CAREER NOTES: Signed as non-drafted free agent by New Orleans Saints (April 28, 1994). ... Granted unconditional free agency (February 14, 1997). ... Re-signed by Saints (June 2, 1997). ... Granted unconditional free agency (February 13, 1998). ... Signed by Carolina Panthers (February 19, 1998).

PRO STATISTICS: 1995—Fumbled once. 1996—Recovered one fumble for 22 yards.

Year Team	G	GS	INTERCEPTIONS No.	Yds.	Avg.	TD	SACKS No.
1994—New Orleans NFL	15	1	0	0	...	0	0.0
1995—New Orleans NFL	16	5	2	17	8.5	0	4.0
1996—New Orleans NFL	16	0	0	0	...	0	0.0
1997—New Orleans NFL	15	0	0	0	...	0	0.5
Pro totals (4 years)	62	6	2	17	8.5	0	4.5

DIXON, GERALD   LB   CHARGERS

PERSONAL: Born June 20, 1969, in Charlotte. ... 6-3/250. ... Full name: Gerald Scott Dixon.

HIGH SCHOOL: Rock Hill (S.C.).

COLLEGE: South Carolina.

TRANSACTIONS/CAREER NOTES: Selected by Cleveland Browns in third round (78th pick overall) of 1992 NFL draft. ... Signed by Browns (July 15, 1992). ... On injured reserve with ankle injury (September 2, 1992-entire season). ... Granted free agency (February 17, 1995). ... Re-signed by Browns for 1995 season. ... Granted unconditional free agency (February 16, 1996). ... Signed by Cincinnati Bengals (March 14, 1996). ... Granted unconditional free agency (February 13, 1998). ... Signed by San Diego Chargers (March 24, 1998).

PRO STATISTICS: 1995—Intercepted two passes for 48 yards and one touchdown, returned one kickoff for 10 yards and recovered one fumble.

Year Team	G	GS	SACKS
1992—Cleveland NFL	Did not play.		
1993—Cleveland NFL	11	0	0.0
1994—Cleveland NFL	16	0	1.0
1995—Cleveland NFL	16	9	0.0
1996—Cincinnati NFL	16	1	0.0
1997—Cincinnati NFL	15	12	8.5
Pro totals (5 years)	74	22	9.5

DIXON, RONNIE   DL   JETS

PERSONAL: Born May 10, 1971, in Clinton, N.C. ... 6-3/310. ... Full name: Ronnie Christopher Dixon.

HIGH SCHOOL: Clinton (N.C.).

COLLEGE: Cincinnati.

TRANSACTIONS/CAREER NOTES: Selected by New Orleans Saints in sixth round (165th pick overall) of 1993 NFL draft. ... Signed by Saints (July 2, 1993). ... Released by Saints (August 30, 1993). ... Re-signed by Saints (August 31, 1993). ... Released by Saints (August 22, 1994). ... Selected by Frankfurt Galaxy in 17th round (98th pick overall) of 1995 World League Draft. ... Signed by Cleveland Browns for 1995 season. ... Traded by Browns to Philadelphia Eagles for seventh-round pick (QB Jon Stark) in 1996 draft (August 21, 1995). ... Traded by Eagles to New York Jets for seventh-round pick (QB Koy Detmer) in 1997 draft (April 18, 1997). ... Released by Jets (October 24, 1997). ... Re-signed by Jets (October 29, 1997). ... Released by Jets (November 22, 1997). ... Re-signed by Jets (November 27, 1997). ... Released by Jets (December 8, 1997). ... Re-signed by Jets (December 15, 1997).

PLAYING EXPERIENCE: New Orleans NFL, 1993; Philadelphia NFL, 1995 and 1996; New York Jets NFL, 1997. ... Games/Games started: 1993 (2/0), 1995 (16/10), 1996 (16/4), 1997 (6/3). Total: 40/17

DODGE, DEDRICK   S

PERSONAL: Born June 14, 1967, in Neptune, N.J. ... 6-2/187. ... Full name: Dedrick Allen Dodge. ... Name pronounced DEAD-rik.

HIGH SCHOOL: East Brunswick (N.J.) and Mulberry (Fla.).

COLLEGE: Florida State (degree in criminology).

TRANSACTIONS/CAREER NOTES: Signed as non-drafted free agent by Seattle Seahawks (May 1, 1990). ... Released by Seahawks (August 29, 1990). ... Signed by WLAF (January 31, 1991). ... Selected by London Monarchs in fourth round (40th defensive back) of 1991 WLAF positional draft. ... Signed by Seahawks (August 13, 1991). ... Released by Seahawks (August 26, 1991). ... Re-signed by Seahawks to practice squad (August 28, 1991). ... Activated (October 5, 1991). ... Assigned by Seahawks to Monarchs in 1992 World League enhancement allocation program (February 20, 1992). ... On injured reserve with knee injury (December 19, 1992-remainder of season). ... Granted free agency (March 1, 1993). ... Re-signed by Seahawks (July 2, 1993). ... Released by Seahawks (August 30, 1993). ... Signed by San Francisco 49ers (June 1, 1994). ... Granted unconditional free agency (February 17, 1995). ... Re-signed by 49ers (April 13, 1995). ... Released by 49ers (February 3, 1997). ... Signed by Denver Broncos (February 25, 1997). ... Released by Broncos (June 17, 1998).

CHAMPIONSHIP GAME EXPERIENCE: Played in NFC championship game (1994 season). ... Member of Super Bowl championship team (1994 and 1997 seasons). ... Played in AFC championship game (1997 season).

HONORS: Named strong safety on All-World League team (1992).

PRO STATISTICS: W.L.: 1991—Recovered one fumble. NFL: 1992—Credited with a sack. 1997—Recovered one fumble.

Year Team	G	GS	INTERCEPTIONS No.	Yds.	Avg.	TD
1991—London W.L.	10	...	6	202	33.7	*2
—Seattle NFL	11	0	0	0	...	0
1992—London W.L.	10	10	3	35	11.7	0
—Seattle NFL	14	0	1	13	13.0	0

Year Team	G	GS	INTERCEPTIONS No.	Yds.	Avg.	TD
1993—			Did not play.			
1994—San Francisco NFL	15	0	0	0	...	0
1995—San Francisco NFL	16	0	1	13	13.0	0
1996—San Francisco NFL	16	3	3	27	9.0	0
1997—Denver NFL	16	1	0	0	...	0
W.L. totals (2 years)	20	...	9	237	26.3	2
NFL totals (6 years)	88	4	5	53	10.6	0
Pro totals (8 years)	108	...	14	290	20.7	2

DOERING, CHRIS — WR — BENGALS

PERSONAL: Born May 19, 1973, in Gainesville, Fla. ... 6-4/195. ... Full name: Christopher Paul Doering. ... Name pronounced DOOR-ing.
HIGH SCHOOL: P.K. Yonge (Gainesville, Fla.).
COLLEGE: Florida.
TRANSACTIONS/CAREER NOTES: Selected by Jacksonville Jaguars in sixth round (185th pick overall) of 1996 NFL draft. ... Signed by Jaguars (June 5, 1996). ... Claimed on waivers by New York Jets (August 20, 1996). ... Released by Jets (August 25, 1996). ... Signed by Indianapolis Colts to practice squad (August 27, 1996). ... Activated (December 20, 1996). ... Released by Colts (August 24, 1997). ... Re-signed by Colts to practice squad (August 25, 1997). ... Activated (December 5, 1997). ... Claimed on waivers by Cincinnati Bengals (February 25, 1998).
PLAYING EXPERIENCE: Indianapolis NFL, 1996 and 1997. ... Games/Games started: 1996 (1/0), 1997 (2/0). Total: 3/0.
PRO STATISTICS: 1996—Caught one pass for 10 yards. 1997—Caught two passes for 12 yards.
SINGLE GAME HIGHS (regular season): Receptions—2 (December 21, 1997, vs. Minnesota); yards—12 (December 21, 1997, vs. Minnesota); and touchdown receptions—0.

DOLEMAN, CHRIS — DE — 49ERS

PERSONAL: Born October 16, 1961, in Indianapolis. ... 6-5/289. ... Full name: Christopher John Doleman.
HIGH SCHOOL: Valley Forge Military Academy (Wayne, Pa.), then William Penn (York, Pa.).
COLLEGE: Pittsburgh.
TRANSACTIONS/CAREER NOTES: Selected by Baltimore Stars in 1985 USFL territorial draft. ... Selected by Minnesota Vikings in first round (fourth pick overall) of 1985 NFL draft. ... Signed by Vikings (August 8, 1985). ... Granted free agency (February 1, 1991). ... Re-signed by Vikings (July 25, 1991). ... Traded by Vikings with second-round pick (WR Bert Emanuel) in 1994 draft to Atlanta Falcons for second-round pick (RB/WR/KR David Palmer) in 1994 draft and first-round pick (DE Derrick Alexander) in 1995 draft (April 24, 1994). ... Granted unconditional free agency (February 16, 1996). ... Signed by San Francisco 49ers (March 14, 1996).
CHAMPIONSHIP GAME EXPERIENCE: Played in NFC championship game (1987 and 1997 seasons).
HONORS: Played in Pro Bowl (1987-1990, 1992, 1993, 1995 and 1997 seasons). ... Named defensive end on THE SPORTING NEWS NFL All-Pro team (1989 and 1992).
PRO STATISTICS: 1985—Recovered three fumbles. 1989—Recovered five fumbles for seven yards. 1990—Credited with one safety. 1991—Recovered two fumbles for seven yards. 1992—Credited with one safety and recovered three fumbles. 1993—Recovered one fumble. 1995—Recovered two fumbles. 1996—Recovered three fumbles for 13 yards (including one in end zone for a touchdown). 1997—Recovered one fumble.

Year Team	G	GS	INTERCEPTIONS No.	Yds.	Avg.	TD	SACKS No.
1985—Minnesota NFL	16	13	1	5	5.0	0	0.5
1986—Minnesota NFL	16	9	1	59	59.0	1	3.0
1987—Minnesota NFL	12	12	0	0	...	0	11.0
1988—Minnesota NFL	16	16	0	0	...	0	8.0
1989—Minnesota NFL	16	16	0	0	...	0	*21.0
1990—Minnesota NFL	16	16	1	30	30.0	0	11.0
1991—Minnesota NFL	16	16	0	0	...	0	7.0
1992—Minnesota NFL	16	16	1	27	27.0	1	14.5
1993—Minnesota NFL	16	16	1	-3	-3.0	0	12.5
1994—Atlanta NFL	14	7	1	2	2.0	0	7.0
1995—Atlanta NFL	16	16	0	0	...	0	9.0
1996—San Francisco NFL	16	16	2	1	0.5	0	11.0
1997—San Francisco NFL	16	16	0	0	...	0	12.0
Pro totals (13 years)	202	185	8	121	15.1	2	127.5

DONNALLEY, KEVIN — G — DOLPHINS

PERSONAL: Born June 10, 1968, in St. Louis. ... 6-5/305. ... Full name: Kevin Thomas Donnalley. ... Brother of Rick Donnalley, center with three NFL teams (1982-1987).
HIGH SCHOOL: Athens Drive Senior (Raleigh, N.C.).
COLLEGE: Davidson, then North Carolina (degree in economics).
TRANSACTIONS/CAREER NOTES: Selected by Houston Oilers in third round (79th pick overall) of 1991 NFL draft. ... Signed by Oilers (July 10, 1991). ... Granted free agency (February 17, 1994). ... Tendered offer sheet by Los Angeles Rams (March 17, 1994). ... Offer matched by Oilers (March 23, 1994). ... Oilers franchise moved to Tennessee for 1997 season. ... Granted unconditional free agency (February 13, 1998). ... Signed by Miami Dolphins (February 17, 1998).
PLAYING EXPERIENCE: Houston NFL, 1991-1996; Tennessee NFL, 1997. ... Games/Games started: 1991 (16/0), 1992 (16/2), 1993 (16/6), 1994 (13/11), 1995 (16/16), 1996 (16/16), 1997 (16/16). Total: 109/67.
PRO STATISTICS: 1995—Recovered one fumble.

DORSETT, ANTHONY   CB   OILERS

PERSONAL: Born September 14, 1973, in Aliquippa, Pa. ... 5-11/203. ... Full name: Anthony Drew Dorsett Jr. ... Son of Tony Dorsett, Hall of Fame running back with Dallas Cowboys (1977-1987) and Denver Broncos (1988).
HIGH SCHOOL: Richland (Dallas), then J.J. Pearce (Dallas).
COLLEGE: Pittsburgh.
TRANSACTIONS/CAREER NOTES: Selected by Houston Oilers in sixth round (177th pick overall) of 1996 NFL draft. ... Signed by Oilers (June 21, 1996). ... Assigned by Oilers to Barcelona Dragons in 1997 World League enhancement allocation program (February 19, 1997). ... Oilers franchise moved to Tennessee for 1997 season.
PLAYING EXPERIENCE: Houston NFL, 1996; Tennessee NFL, 1997. ... Games/Games started: 1996 (8/0), 1997 (16/0). Total: 24/0.

DORSETT, MATTHEW   CB   CHIEFS

PERSONAL: Born August 23, 1973, in New Orleans. ... 5-11/190. ... Full name: Matthew Herbert Dorsett.
HIGH SCHOOL: Eleanor McMain (New Orleans).
COLLEGE: Southern (La.).
TRANSACTIONS/CAREER NOTES: Signed as non-drafted free agent by Green Bay Packers (April 27, 1995). ... On injured reserve with knee injury (August 19, 1996-entire season). ... Released by Packers after 1996 season. ... Re-signed by Packers (July 7, 1997). ... Released by Packers (July 18, 1997). ... Signed by Kansas City Chiefs (April 7, 1998).
PLAYING EXPERIENCE: Green Bay NFL, 1995. ... Games: 1995 (10/0).
CHAMPIONSHIP GAME EXPERIENCE: Member of Packers for NFC championship game (1995 season); inactive.

DOTSON, DEWAYNE   FB

PERSONAL: Born June 10, 1971, in Hendersonville, Tenn. ... 6-1/256. ... Full name: Jack Dewayne Dotson.
HIGH SCHOOL: Hendersonville (Tenn.).
COLLEGE: Tennessee, then Mississippi.
TRANSACTIONS/CAREER NOTES: Selected by Dallas Cowboys in fourth round (131st pick overall) of 1994 NFL draft. ... Signed by Cowboys (July 15, 1994). ... Released by Cowboys (August 27, 1994). ... Signed by Miami Dolphins to practice squad (September 7, 1994). ... Released by Dolphins (September 28, 1994). ... Re-signed by Dolphins to practice squad (October 5, 1994). ... Activated (December 31, 1994). ... Released by Dolphins (August 20, 1996). ... Re-signed by Dolphins (June 2, 1997). ... Released by Dolphins (November 18, 1997).
PLAYING EXPERIENCE: Miami NFL, 1995; Miami NFL, 1997. ... Games/Games started: 1995 (15/0), 1997 (10/2). Total: 25/2.
PRO STATISTICS: 1995—Recovered one fumble. 1997—Caught one pass for four yards.
SINGLE GAME HIGHS (regular season): Attempts—0; yards—0; and rushing touchdowns—0.

DOTSON, EARL   OT   PACKERS

PERSONAL: Born December 17, 1970, in Beaumont, Texas. ... 6-4/315. ... Full name: Earl Christopher Dotson.
HIGH SCHOOL: West Brook (Beaumont, Texas).
JUNIOR COLLEGE: Tyler (Texas) Junior College.
COLLEGE: Texas A&I.
TRANSACTIONS/CAREER NOTES: Selected by Green Bay Packers in third round (81st pick overall) of 1993 NFL draft. ... Signed by Packers (June 14, 1993).
PLAYING EXPERIENCE: Green Bay NFL, 1993-1997. ... Games/Games started: 1993 (13/0), 1994 (4/0), 1995 (16/16), 1996 (15/15), 1997 (13/13). Total: 61/44.
CHAMPIONSHIP GAME EXPERIENCE: Played in NFC championship game (1995-97 seasons). ... Member of Super Bowl championship team (1996 season). ... Played in Super Bowl XXXII (1997 season).
PRO STATISTICS: 1996—Recovered one fumble. 1997—Recovered one fumble.

DOTSON, SANTANA   DT   PACKERS

PERSONAL: Born December 19, 1969, in New Orleans. ... 6-5/285. ... Full name: Santana N. Dotson. ... Son of Alphonse Dotson, defensive tackle with three NFL teams (1965, 1966, and 1968-1970).
HIGH SCHOOL: Jack Yates (Houston).
COLLEGE: Baylor.
TRANSACTIONS/CAREER NOTES: Selected by Tampa Bay Buccaneers in fifth round (132nd pick overall) of 1992 NFL draft. ... Signed by Buccaneers (July 7, 1992). ... Granted free agency (February 17, 1995). ... Re-signed by Buccaneers (June 14, 1995). ... Granted unconditional free agency (February 16, 1996). ... Signed by Green Bay Packers (March 7, 1996).
CHAMPIONSHIP GAME EXPERIENCE: Played in NFC championship game (1996 and 1997 seasons). ... Member of Super Bowl championship team (1996 season). ... Played in Super Bowl XXXII (1997 season).
HONORS: Named defensive lineman on THE SPORTING NEWS college All-America first team (1991). ... Named NFL Rookie of the Year by THE SPORTING NEWS (1992).
PRO STATISTICS: 1992—Recovered two fumbles for 42 yards and one touchdown. 1995—Recovered two fumbles. 1996—Recovered one fumble for eight yards.

Year Team	G	GS	SACKS
1992—Tampa Bay NFL	16	16	10.0
1993—Tampa Bay NFL	16	13	5.0
1994—Tampa Bay NFL	16	9	3.0
1995—Tampa Bay NFL	16	8	5.0
1996—Green Bay NFL	16	16	6.5
1997—Green Bay NFL	16	16	5.5
Pro totals (6 years)	96	77	34.0

DOUGLAS, HUGH — DE/LB — EAGLES

PERSONAL: Born August 23, 1971, in Mansfield, Ohio. ... 6-2/280.
HIGH SCHOOL: Mansfield (Ohio).
COLLEGE: Central State (Ohio).
TRANSACTIONS/CAREER NOTES: Selected after junior season by New York Jets in first round (16th pick overall) of 1995 NFL draft. ... Signed by Jets (June 8, 1995). ... Traded by Jets to Philadelphia Eagles for second-(traded to Pittsburgh) and fifth-round (LB Casey Dailey) picks in 1998 draft (March 13, 1998).
PRO STATISTICS: 1995—Recovered two fumbles. 1996—Recovered three fumbles for 64 yards and a touchdown.

Year Team	G	GS	SACKS
1995—New York Jets NFL	15	3	10.0
1996—New York Jets NFL	10	10	8.0
1997—New York Jets NFL	15	15	4.0
Pro totals (3 years)	40	28	22.0

DOUGLAS, OMAR — WR

PERSONAL: Born June 3, 1972, in New Orleans. ... 5-10/180.
HIGH SCHOOL: Isidore Newman (New Orleans).
COLLEGE: Minnesota.
TRANSACTIONS/CAREER NOTES: Signed as non-drafted free agent by New York Giants (April 29, 1994). ... On injured reserve with thumb injury (November 13, 1996-remainder of season). ... Granted free agency (February 14, 1997). ... On injured reserve with knee injury (August 18, 1997-entire season). ... Granted unconditional free agency (February 13, 1998).
PLAYING EXPERIENCE: New York Giants NFL, 1994-1996. ... Games/Games started: 1994 (6/0), 1995 (8/1), 1996 (4/0). Total: 18/1.
PRO STATISTICS: 1995—Caught two passes for 15 yards, returned one kickoff for 13 yards, fumbled once and recovered two fumbles for 41 yards and a touchdown. 1996—Caught one pass for eight yards and returned one kickoff for 11 yards.
SINGLE GAME HIGHS (regular season): Receptions—1 (November 3, 1996, vs. Arizona); yards—11 (November 26, 1995, vs. Chicago); and touchdown receptions—0.

DOUTHARD, TY — FB — BENGALS

PERSONAL: Born May 27, 1973, in Cincinnati. ... 6-1/214. ... Full name: Talib Douthard.
HIGH SCHOOL: LaSalle (Cincinnati).
COLLEGE: Illinois.
TRANSACTIONS/CAREER NOTES: Signed as non-drafted free agent by Cincinnati Bengals (April 25, 1997). ... Released by Bengals (August 24, 1997). ... Re-signed by Bengals to practice squad (August 26, 1997). ... Activated (December 1, 1997).
PLAYING EXPERIENCE: Cincinnati NFL, 1997. ... Games/Games started: 1/0.
SINGLE GAME HIGHS (regular season): Attempts—0; yards—0; and rushing touchdowns—0.

DOWDELL, MARCUS — WR/KR — CHIEFS

PERSONAL: Born May 22, 1970, in Birmingham, Ala. ... 5-10/179. ... Full name: Marcus L. Dowdell.
HIGH SCHOOL: Banks (Birmingham, Ala.).
COLLEGE: Tennessee State.
TRANSACTIONS/CAREER NOTES: Selected by New Orleans Saints in 10th round (276th pick overall) of 1992 NFL draft. ... Signed by Saints (July 21, 1992). ... Released by Saints (August 31, 1992). ... Re-signed by Saints to practice squad (September 2, 1992). ... Activated (October 10, 1992). ... Released by Saints (November 10, 1992). ... Re-signed by Saints to practice squad (November 12, 1992). ... Released by Saints (August 30, 1993). ... Re-signed by Saints (August 31, 1993). ... Released by Saints (August 23, 1994). ... Signed by Sacramento Gold Miners of CFL (September 1994). ... Transferred to Winnipeg Blue Bombers of CFL (November 1994). ... Signed by Arizona Cardinals (August 7, 1995). ... Released by Cardinals after 1995 season. ... Re-signed by Cardinals (April 25, 1996). ... Granted free agency (February 14, 1997). ... Re-signed by Cardinals for 1997 season. ... Released by Cardinals (April 10, 1997). ... Signed by Kansas City Chiefs (April 7, 1998).
PRO STATISTICS: NFL: 1992—Recovered three fumbles. 1995—Recovered one fumble. 1996—Returned five kickoffs for 122 yards. CFL: 1995—Returned three kickoffs for 35 yards.
SINGLE GAME HIGHS (regular season): Receptions—4 (October 1, 1995, vs. Kansas City); yards—92 (November 10, 1996, vs. Washington); and touchdown receptions—1 (November 24, 1996, vs. Philadelphia).

			RECEIVING				PUNT RETURNS				TOTALS			
Year Team	G	GS	No.	Yds.	Avg.	TD	No.	Yds.	Avg.	TD	TD	2pt.	Pts.	Fum.
1992—New Orleans NFL	4	0	1	6	6.0	0	12	37	3.1	0	0	...	0	4
1993—New Orleans NFL	9	1	6	46	7.7	1	0	0	...	0	1	...	6	1
1994—Sacramento CFL	7	...	19	268	14.1	1	...	...	...	...	...	0	...	...
1995—Winnipeg CFL	2	...	0	0	...	0	3	15	5.0	0	0	0	0	1
—Arizona NFL	13	0	10	96	9.6	0	1	0	0.0	0	0	0	0	1
1996—Arizona NFL	15	0	20	318	15.9	2	34	297	8.7	0	2	0	12	6
1997—							Did not play.							
CFL totals (2 years)	9	...	19	268	14.1	1	3	15	5.0	0	0	0	0	1
NFL totals (4 years)	41	1	37	466	12.6	3	47	334	7.1	0	3	0	18	12
Pro totals (6 years)	50	...	56	734	13.1	4	50	349	7.0	0	3	0	18	13

DOWDEN, COREY — DB

PERSONAL: Born October 18, 1968, in New Orleans. ... 5-11/190.
HIGH SCHOOL: John McDonogh (New Orleans).
COLLEGE: Tulane.

TRANSACTIONS/CAREER NOTES: Played with Tampa Bay Storm of Arena League (1992-1995). ... Signed by Ottawa Rough Riders of CFL for 1994 season. ... Signed by New Orleans Saints (February 26, 1996). ... Released by Saints (August 20, 1996). ... Signed by Green Bay Packers (August 21, 1996). ... Released by Packers (November 8, 1996). ... Signed by Baltimore Ravens (December 4, 1996). ... Released by Ravens after 1996 season. ... Signed by San Francisco 49ers (April 4, 1997). ... Released by 49ers (July 29, 1997). ... Signed by Chicago Bears (July 31, 1997). ... Released by Bears (September 9, 1997).
PLAYING EXPERIENCE: Ottawa CFL, 1994; Green Bay (9)-Baltimore (3) NFL, 1996; Chicago NFL, 1997. ... Games/Games started: CFL: 1994 (games played unavailable); NFL: 1996 (G.B.-9/0; Balt.- 3/0; Total: 12/0), 1997 (2/0). Total NFL: 14/0.

DOWNS, GARY — RB — FALCONS

PERSONAL: Born June 6, 1972, in Columbus, Ga. ... 6-1/212. ... Full name: Gary McLinton Downs.
HIGH SCHOOL: William H. Spencer (Columbus, Ga.).
COLLEGE: North Carolina State.
TRANSACTIONS/CAREER NOTES: Selected by New York Giants in third round (95th pick overall) of 1994 NFL draft. ... Signed by Giants (July 19, 1994). ... Released by Giants (August 27, 1995). ... Signed by Denver Broncos (August 28, 1995). ... Released by Broncos (August 28, 1996). ... Signed by Giants (October 31, 1996). ... Granted unconditional free agency (February 14, 1997). ... Signed by Atlanta Falcons (March 17, 1997). ... Granted unconditional free agency (February 13, 1998). ... Re-signed by Falcons (March 13, 1998).
PRO STATISTICS: 1996—Recovered one fumble.
SINGLE GAME HIGHS (regular season): Attempts—22 (December 21, 1996, vs. New England); yards—52 (December 21, 1996, vs. New England); and rushing touchdowns—0.

			RUSHING				RECEIVING				TOTALS		
Year Team	G	GS	Att.	Yds.	Avg.	TD	No.	Yds.	Avg.	TD	TD	2pt.	Pts.	Fum.
1994—New York Giants NFL	14	0	15	51	3.4	0	2	15	7.5	0	0	0	0	1
1995—Denver NFL	1	0	0	0	...	0	0	0	...	0	0	0	0	0
1996—New York Giants NFL	6	1	29	94	3.2	0	3	20	6.7	0	0	0	0	1
1997—Atlanta NFL	16	0	0	0	...	0	0	0	...	0	0	0	0	0
Pro totals (4 years)	37	1	44	145	3.3	0	5	35	7.0	0	0	0	0	2

DRAKE, JERRY — DL — CARDINALS

PERSONAL: Born July 9, 1969, in Kingston, N.Y. ... 6-5/310.
HIGH SCHOOL: Kingston (N.Y.).
JUNIOR COLLEGE: Ulster Community College (N.Y.).
COLLEGE: Hastings (Neb.) College.
TRANSACTIONS/CAREER NOTES: Signed as non-drafted free agent by Arizona Cardinals (May 2, 1995). ... Released by Cardinals (August 21, 1995). ... Re-signed by Cardinals to practice squad (August 30, 1995). ... Activated (November 24, 1995). ... Assigned by Cardinals to London Monarchs in 1996 World League enhancement allocation program (February 19, 1996). ... On injured reserve with neck injury (August 19, 1997-entire season).
PLAYING EXPERIENCE: Arizona NFL, 1995 and 1996; London W.L., 1996. ... Games/Games started: 1995 (2/0), 1996 (W.L.-10/10; NFL-11/0; Total 21/10). Total: W.L.: 10/10. Total NFL: 13/0. Total Pro: 23/10.
PRO STATISTICS: W.L.: 1996—Credited with eight sacks.

DRAKE, TROY — OT — REDSKINS

PERSONAL: Born May 15, 1972, in Rockford, Ill. ... 6-6/305.
HIGH SCHOOL: Byron (Ill.).
COLLEGE: Indiana.
TRANSACTIONS/CAREER NOTES: Signed as non-drafted free agent by Philadelphia Eagles (April 26, 1995). ... Released by Eagles (October 23, 1995). ... Re-signed by Eagles to practice squad (October 25, 1995). ... Activated (November 12, 1995). ... Released by Eagles (November 14, 1995). ... Re-signed by Eagles to practice squad (November 15, 1995). ... Granted free agency (February 13, 1998). ... Re-signed by Redskins (April 6, 1998).
PLAYING EXPERIENCE: Philadelphia NFL, 1995-1997. ... Games/Games started: 1995 (1/0), 1996 (11/0), 1997 (9/2). Total: 21/2.

DRAKEFORD, TYRONNE — CB — SAINTS

PERSONAL: Born June 21, 1971, in Camden, S.C. ... 5-9/185. ... Full name: Tyronne James Drakeford.
HIGH SCHOOL: Camden (S.C.) County.
COLLEGE: Virginia Tech.
TRANSACTIONS/CAREER NOTES: Selected by San Francisco 49ers in second round (62nd pick overall) of 1994 NFL draft. ... Signed by 49ers (July 20, 1994). ... Granted free agency (February 14, 1997). ... Re-signed by 49ers (April 8, 1997). ... Granted unconditional free agency (February 13, 1998). ... Signed by New Orleans Saints (February 19, 1998).
CHAMPIONSHIP GAME EXPERIENCE: Played in NFC championship game (1994 and 1997 seasons). ... Member of Super Bowl championship team (1994 season).
PRO STATISTICS: 1995—Fumbled once and recovered one fumble for 12 yards. 1996—Recovered one fumble for eight yards. 1997—Returned one kickoff for 24 yards.

			INTERCEPTIONS				SACKS
Year Team	G	GS	No.	Yds.	Avg.	TD	No.
1994—San Francisco NFL	13	0	1	6	6.0	0	0.0
1995—San Francisco NFL	16	2	5	54	10.8	0	1.0
1996—San Francisco NFL	16	16	1	11	11.0	0	2.0
1997—San Francisco NFL	16	2	5	15	3.0	0	0.0
Pro totals (4 years)	61	20	12	86	7.2	0	3.0

DRAYTON, TROY   TE   DOLPHINS

PERSONAL: Born June 29, 1970, in Harrisburg, Pa. ... 6-3/265. ... Full name: Troy Anthony Drayton. ... Cousin of Kevin Mitchell, linebacker, New Orleans Saints.
HIGH SCHOOL: Highspire (Steelton, Pa.).
COLLEGE: Penn State.
TRANSACTIONS/CAREER NOTES: Selected by Los Angeles Rams in second round (39th pick overall) of 1993 NFL draft. ... Signed by Rams (July 20, 1993). ... Rams franchise moved to St. Louis (April 12, 1995). ... Granted free agency (February 16, 1996). ... Re-signed by Rams (April 17, 1996). ... Traded by Rams to Miami Dolphins for OT Bill Milner (October 1, 1996).
PRO STATISTICS: 1993—Rushed once for seven yards and returned one kickoff for minus 15 yards. 1994—Rushed once for four yards. 1996—Recovered one fumble.
SINGLE GAME HIGHS (regular season): Receptions—8 (November 19, 1995, vs. Atlanta); yards—106 (September 24, 1995, vs. Chicago); and touchdown receptions—2 (December 7, 1997, vs. Detroit).
STATISTICAL PLATEAUS: 100-yard receiving games: 1995 (1).

| | | | RECEIVING | | | | TOTALS | | | |
Year Team	G	GS	No.	Yds.	Avg.	TD	TD	2pt.	Pts.	Fum.
1993—Los Angeles Rams NFL	16	2	27	319	11.8	4	4	...	24	1
1994—Los Angeles Rams NFL	16	16	32	276	8.6	6	6	0	36	0
1995—St. Louis NFL	16	16	47	458	9.7	4	4	0	24	2
1996—St. Louis NFL	3	3	2	11	5.5	0	0	0	0	0
—Miami NFL	10	10	26	320	12.3	0	0	1	2	0
1997—Miami NFL	16	15	39	558	14.3	4	4	0	24	0
Pro totals (5 years)	77	62	173	1942	11.2	18	18	1	110	3

DRONETT, SHANE   DE   FALCONS

PERSONAL: Born January 12, 1971, in Orange, Texas. ... 6-6/288.
HIGH SCHOOL: Bridge City (Texas).
COLLEGE: Texas.
TRANSACTIONS/CAREER NOTES: Selected after junior season by Denver Broncos in second round (54th pick overall) of 1992 NFL draft. ... Signed by Broncos (July 15, 1992). ... Granted free agency (February 17, 1995). ... Re-signed by Broncos (May 12, 1995). ... Granted unconditional free agency (February 16, 1996). ... Signed by Atlanta Falcons (April 9, 1996). ... Released by Falcons (October 7, 1996). ... Granted unconditional free agency (February 14, 1997). ... Re-signed by Lions for 1997 season. ... Released by Lions (August 24, 1997). ... Signed by Falcons (August 27, 1997). ... Granted unconditional free agency (February 13, 1998). ... Re-signed by Falcons (February 20, 1998).
PRO STATISTICS: 1992—Recovered two fumbles for minus five yards.

| | | | INTERCEPTIONS | | | | SACKS |
Year Team	G	GS	No.	Yds.	Avg.	TD	No.
1992—Denver NFL	16	2	0	0	...	0	6.5
1993—Denver NFL	16	16	2	13	6.5	0	7.0
1994—Denver NFL	16	15	0	0	...	0	6.0
1995—Denver NFL	13	2	0	0	...	0	2.0
1996—Atlanta NFL	5	0	0	0	...	0	0.0
—Detroit NFL	7	0	0	0	...	0	0.0
1997—Atlanta NFL	16	1	0	0	...	0	3.0
Pro totals (6 years)	89	36	2	13	6.5	0	24.5

DRUCKENMILLER, JIM   QB   49ERS

PERSONAL: Born September 19, 1972, in Allentown, Pa. ... 6-4/241. ... Full name: James Davis Druckenmiller Jr.
HIGH SCHOOL: Northhampton (Pa.), then Fork Union (Va.) Military.
COLLEGE: Virginia Tech.
TRANSACTIONS/CAREER NOTES: Selected by San Francisco 49ers in first round (26th pick overall) of 1997 NFL draft. ... Signed by 49ers (July 31, 1997).
CHAMPIONSHIP GAME EXPERIENCE: Member of 49ers for NFC championship game (1997 season); inactive.
SINGLE GAME HIGHS (regular season): Attempts—28 (September 7, 1997, vs. St. Louis); completions—10 (September 7, 1997, vs. St. Louis); yards—102 (September 7, 1997, vs. St. Louis); and touchdowns—1 (September 7, 1997, vs. St. Louis).
MISCELLANEOUS: Regular-season record as starting NFL quarterback: 1-0.

| | | | PASSING | | | | | | | RUSHING | | | | TOTALS | | |
Year Team	G	GS	Att.	Cmp.	Pct.	Yds.	TD	Int.	Avg.	Rat.	Att.	Yds.	Avg.	TD	TD	2pt.	Pts.
1997—San Francisco NFL	4	1	52	21	40.4	239	1	4	4.60	29.2	10	-6	-0.6	0	0	0	0

DUDLEY, RICKEY   TE   RAIDERS

PERSONAL: Born July 15, 1972, in Henderson, Texas. ... 6-6/250.
HIGH SCHOOL: Henderson (Texas).
COLLEGE: Ohio State.
TRANSACTIONS/CAREER NOTES: Selected by Oakland Raiders in first round (ninth pick overall) of 1996 NFL draft. ... Signed by Raiders (July 12, 1996).
SINGLE GAME HIGHS (regular season): Receptions—6 (October 5, 1997, vs. San Diego); yards—116 (November 9, 1997, vs. New Orleans); and touchdown receptions—2 (September 28, 1997, vs. St. Louis).
STATISTICAL PLATEAUS: 100-yard receiving games: 1997 (2).
MISCELLANEOUS: Member of Ohio State basketball team (1991-92 through 1993-94).

| | | | RECEIVING | | | | TOTALS | | | |
Year Team	G	GS	No.	Yds.	Avg.	TD	TD	2pt.	Pts.	Fum.
1996—Oakland NFL	16	15	34	386	11.4	4	4	0	24	1
1997—Oakland NFL	16	16	48	787	16.4	7	7	0	42	0
Pro totals (2 years)	32	31	82	1173	14.3	11	11	0	66	1

DUFF, JAMAL   DE   REDSKINS

PERSONAL: Born March 11, 1972, in Columbus, Ohio. ... 6-7/285. ... Full name: Jamal Edwin Duff. ... Brother of John Duff, tight end with Dallas Cowboys (1989), Los Angeles Raiders (1993-1994) and Philadelphia Eagles (1997).
HIGH SCHOOL: Foothill (Tustin, Calif.).
COLLEGE: San Diego State.
TRANSACTIONS/CAREER NOTES: Selected by New York Giants in sixth round (204th pick overall) of 1995 NFL draft. ... Signed by Giants (July 23, 1995). ... On injured reserve with foot injury (August 26, 1996-entire season). ... On physically unable to perform list with ankle injury (July 19-August 20, 1997). ... Claimed on waivers by Washington Redskins (August 20, 1997). ... Granted free agency (February 13, 1998). ... Re-signed by Redskins (May 7, 1998).

Year Team	G	GS	SACKS
1995—New York Giants NFL	15	2	4.0
1996—New York Giants NFL	Did not play.		
1997—Washington NFL	13	5	2.0
Pro totals (2 years)	28	7	6.0

DUFFY, ROGER   G/C   STEELERS

PERSONAL: Born July 16, 1967, in Pittsburgh. ... 6-3/305. ... Full name: Roger Thomas Duffy.
HIGH SCHOOL: Canton (Ohio) Central Catholic.
COLLEGE: Penn State (degree in communications, 1990).
TRANSACTIONS/CAREER NOTES: Selected by New York Jets in eighth round (196th pick overall) of 1990 NFL draft. ... Signed by Jets (July 18, 1990). ... Granted free agency (February 1, 1992). ... Re-signed by Jets (May 15, 1992). ... Granted unconditional free agency (February 17, 1994). ... Re-signed by Jets (March 2, 1994). ... Granted unconditional free agency (February 16, 1996). ... Re-signed by Jets (April 1, 1996). ... Granted unconditional free agency (February 13, 1998). ... Signed by Pittsburgh Steelers (March 13, 1998).
PLAYING EXPERIENCE: New York Jets NFL, 1990-1997. ... Games/Games started: 1990 (16/2), 1991 (12/0), 1992 (16/6), 1993 (16/1), 1994 (16/14), 1995 (16/16), 1996 (16/16), 1997 (15/15). Total: 123/70.
PRO STATISTICS: 1991—Returned one kickoff for eight yards. 1992—Returned one kickoff for seven yards and recovered one fumble. 1993—Recovered one fumble. 1995—Recovered two fumbles. 1996—Recovered one fumble. 1997—Fumbled twice and recovered one fumble for minus 22 yards.

DULANEY, MIKE   FB   PANTHERS

D

PERSONAL: Born September 9, 1970, in Kingsport, Tenn. ... 6-0/245. ... Full name: Michael Wayne Dulaney. ... Formerly known as Mike Faulkerson.
HIGH SCHOOL: Dobyns-Bennett (Kingsport, Tenn.).
COLLEGE: North Carolina.
TRANSACTIONS/CAREER NOTES: Played in Arena Football League with Albany Firebirds (1995). ... Signed as free agent by Chicago Bears (July 17, 1995). ... Released by Bears (August 27, 1995). ... Re-signed by Bears to practice squad (August 29, 1995). ... Activated (September 22, 1995). ... Released by Bears (September 25, 1995). ... Re-signed by Bears to practice squad (September 27, 1995). ... Activated (November 29, 1995). ... Released by Bears (August 24, 1997). ... Re-signed by Bears (October 28, 1997). ... Released by Bears after 1997 season. ... Signed by Carolina Panthers (March 24, 1998).
PLAYING EXPERIENCE: Chicago NFL, 1995-1997. ... Games/Games started: 1995 (5/1), 1996 (16/0), 1997 (7/0). Total: 28/1.
PRO STATISTICS: 1995—Caught two passes for 22 yards. 1996—Caught one pass for one yard and a touchdown and returned four kickoffs for 63 yards. 1997—Returned one punt for no yards and fumbled once.

DUMAS, MIKE   S   CHARGERS

PERSONAL: Born March 18, 1969, in Grand Rapids, Mich. ... 6-0/202. ... Full name: Michael Dion Dumas.
HIGH SCHOOL: Lowell (Mich.).
COLLEGE: Indiana.
TRANSACTIONS/CAREER NOTES: Selected by Houston Oilers in second round (28th pick overall) of 1991 NFL draft. ... Signed by Oilers (August 12, 1991). ... On injured reserve with Achilles' tendon injury (August 23, 1993-entire season). ... Granted free agency (February 17, 1994). ... Re-signed by Oilers (June 1994). ... Released by Oilers (July 14, 1994). ... Signed by Buffalo Bills (July 25, 1994). ... Granted unconditional free agency (February 17, 1995). ... Signed by Jacksonville Jaguars (April 24, 1995). ... Released by Jaguars (April 24, 1996). ... Signed by San Diego Chargers (March 4, 1997). ... Granted unconditional free agency (February 13, 1998). ... Re-signed by Chargers (February 20, 1998).
HONORS: Named defensive back on THE SPORTING NEWS college All-America second team (1990).
PRO STATISTICS: 1991—Recovered three fumbles for 19 yards and one touchdown. 1992—Recovered one fumble. 1994—Recovered two fumbles for 40 yards. 1995—Recovered two fumbles. 1997—Credited with one sack and recovered one fumble.

			INTERCEPTIONS			
Year Team	G	GS	No.	Yds.	Avg.	TD
1991—Houston NFL	13	0	1	19	19.0	0
1992—Houston NFL	16	1	1	0	0.0	0
1993—Houston NFL	Did not play.					
1994—Buffalo NFL	14	0	0	0		0
1995—Jacksonville NFL	14	8	1	0	0.0	0
1996—	Did not play.					
1997—San Diego NFL	16	15	1	0	0.0	0
Pro totals (5 years)	73	24	4	19	4.8	0

DUMAS, TROY   LB   RAMS

PERSONAL: Born September 30, 1972, in Riverside, Calif. ... 6-3/242.
HIGH SCHOOL: Cheyenne (Wyo.) East.
COLLEGE: Nebraska.

TRANSACTIONS/CAREER NOTES: Selected by Kansas City Chiefs in third round (97th pick overall) of 1995 NFL draft. ... Signed by Chiefs (June 7, 1995). ... On injured reserve with knee injury (August 22, 1995-entire season). ... Released by Chiefs (November 19, 1997). ... Signed by St. Louis Rams (November 24, 1997). ... Granted free agency (February 13, 1998). ... Re-signed by Rams (Aprils 24, 1998).
PLAYING EXPERIENCE: Kansas City NFL, 1996; Kansas City (8)-St. Louis (2) NFL, 1997. ... Games/Games started: 1996 (6/0), 1997 (K.C.-8/0; S.L.-2/0; Total: 10/0). Total: 16/0.
PRO STATISTICS: 1997—Credited with one sack.

DUNN, DAVID — WR/KR — BENGALS

PERSONAL: Born June 10, 1972, in San Diego. ... 6-3/220.
HIGH SCHOOL: Morse (San Diego).
JUNIOR COLLEGE: Bakersfield (Calif.) College.
COLLEGE: Fresno State.
TRANSACTIONS/CAREER NOTES: Selected by Cincinnati Bengals in fifth round (139th pick overall) of 1995 NFL draft. ... Signed by Bengals (July 31, 1995). ... Granted free agency (February 13, 1998). ... Re-signed by Bengals (April 23, 1998).
HONORS: Named kick returner on THE SPORTING NEWS college All-America second team (1994).
PRO STATISTICS: 1995—Rushed once for minus 13 yards. 1996—Returned seven punts for 54 yards. 1997—Recovered one fumble.
SINGLE GAME HIGHS (regular season): Receptions—7 (December 15, 1996, vs. Houston); yards—95 (December 15, 1996, vs. Houston); and touchdown receptions—1 (December 14, 1997, vs. Dallas).

Year Team	G	GS	RECEIVING				KICKOFF RETURNS				TOTALS			
			No.	Yds.	Avg.	TD	No.	Yds.	Avg.	TD	TD	2pt.	Pts.	Fum.
1995—Cincinnati NFL	16	0	17	209	12.3	1	50	1092	21.8	0	1	0	6	2
1996—Cincinnati NFL	16	0	32	509	15.9	1	35	782	22.3	▲1	3	0	18	1
1997—Cincinnati NFL	14	5	27	414	15.3	2	19	487	25.6	0	2	0	12	1
Pro totals (3 years)	46	5	76	1132	14.9	4	104	2361	22.7	1	6	0	36	4

DUNN, JASON — TE — EAGLES

PERSONAL: Born November 15, 1973, in Harrodsburg, Ky. ... 6-4/257.
HIGH SCHOOL: Harrodsburg (Ky.).
COLLEGE: Eastern Kentucky.
TRANSACTIONS/CAREER NOTES: Selected by Philadelphia Eagles in second round (54th pick overall) of 1996 NFL draft. ... Signed by Eagles (July 17, 1996).
PRO STATISTICS: 1996—Recovered one fumble. 1997—Returned two kickoffs for 32 yards.
SINGLE GAME HIGHS (regular season): Receptions—3 (December 1, 1996, vs. New York Giants); yards—58 (September 22, 1996, vs. Atlanta); and touchdown receptions—1 (December 21, 1997, vs. Washington).

Year Team	G	GS	RECEIVING				TOTALS			
			No.	Yds.	Avg.	TD	TD	2pt.	Pts.	Fum.
1996—Philadelphia NFL	16	12	15	332	22.1	2	2	0	12	0
1997—Philadelphia NFL	15	4	7	93	13.3	2	2	0	12	0
Pro totals (2 years)	31	16	22	425	19.3	4	4	0	24	0

DUNN, WARRICK — RB — BUCCANEERS

PERSONAL: Born January 5, 1975, in Baton Rouge, La. ... 5-8/176.
HIGH SCHOOL: Catholic (Baton Rouge, La.).
COLLEGE: Florida State.
TRANSACTIONS/CAREER NOTES: Selected by Tampa Bay Buccaneers in first round (12th pick overall) of 1997 NFL draft. ... Signed by Buccaneers (July 24, 1997).
HONORS: Named NFL Rookie of the Year by THE SPORTING NEWS (1997). ... Played in Pro Bowl (1997 season).
PRO STATISTICS: 1997—Returned five punts for 48 yards and recovered four fumbles.
SINGLE GAME HIGHS (regular season): Attempts—24 (November 30, 1997, vs. New York Giants); yards—130 (September 7, 1997, vs. Detroit); and rushing touchdowns—1 (November 9, 1997, vs. Atlanta).
STATISTICAL PLATEAUS: 100-yard rushing games: 1997 (5). ... 100-yard receiving games: 1997 (1).

Year Team	G	GS	RUSHING				RECEIVING				KICKOFF RETURNS				TOTALS			
			Att.	Yds.	Avg.	TD	No.	Yds.	Avg.	TD	No.	Yds.	Avg.	TD	TD	2pt.	Pts.	Fum.
1997—Tampa Bay NFL	16	10	224	978	4.4	4	39	462	11.8	3	6	129	21.5	0	7	0	42	4

DYE, ERNEST — G

PERSONAL: Born July 15, 1971, in Greenwood, S.C. ... 6-5/333. ... Full name: Ernest Thaddius Dye.
HIGH SCHOOL: Greenwood (S.C.).
JUNIOR COLLEGE: Itawamba (Miss.) Junior College.
COLLEGE: South Carolina.
TRANSACTIONS/CAREER NOTES: Selected by Phoenix Cardinals in first round (18th pick overall) of 1993 NFL draft. ... Signed by Cardinals (July 23, 1993). ... Cardinals franchise renamed Arizona Cardinals for 1994 season. ... On injured reserve with ankle injury (December 11, 1996-remainder of season). ... Granted unconditional free agency (February 14, 1997). ... Signed by St. Louis Rams (May 30, 1997). ... Granted unconditional free agency (February 13, 1998).
PLAYING EXPERIENCE: Phoenix NFL, 1993; Arizona NFL, 1994-1996; St. Louis NFL, 1997. ... Games/Games started: 1993 (7/1), 1994 (16/16), 1995 (6/6), 1996 (8/0), 1997 (13/0). Total: 50/23.
PRO STATISTICS: 1994—Recovered one fumble.

PERSONAL: Born April 13, 1965, in West Hempstead, N.Y. ... 6-0/190. ... Full name: Quinn Remar Early.

HIGH SCHOOL: Great Neck (N.Y.).

COLLEGE: Iowa (degree in art, 1988).

TRANSACTIONS/CAREER NOTES: Selected by San Diego Chargers in third round (60th pick overall) of 1988 NFL draft. ... Signed by Chargers (July 11, 1988). ... On injured reserve with knee injury (October 21-December 13, 1989). ... On developmental squad (December 14-15, 1989). ... Activated (December 16, 1989). ... Granted unconditional free agency (February 1, 1991). ... Signed by New Orleans Saints (April 1, 1991). ... Granted unconditional free agency (February 16, 1996). ... Signed by Buffalo Bills (March 8, 1996).

PRO STATISTICS: 1991—Returned nine kickoffs for 168 yards.

SINGLE GAME HIGHS (regular season): Receptions—9 (November 19, 1995, vs. Minnesota); yards—150 (November 19, 1995, vs. Minnesota); and touchdown receptions—2 (November 23, 1997, vs. Tennessee).

STATISTICAL PLATEAUS: 100-yard receiving games: 1991 (1), 1994 (1), 1995 (2), 1996 (2), 1997 (2). Total: 8.

			RUSHING				RECEIVING				TOTALS			
Year Team	G	GS	Att.	Yds.	Avg.	TD	No.	Yds.	Avg.	TD	TD	2pt.	Pts.	Fum.
1988—San Diego NFL	16	10	7	63	9.0	0	29	375	12.9	4	4	...	24	1
1989—San Diego NFL	6	3	1	19	19.0	0	11	126	11.5	0	0	...	0	0
1990—San Diego NFL	14	4	0	0	...	0	15	238	15.9	1	1	...	6	0
1991—New Orleans NFL	15	12	3	13	4.3	0	32	541	16.9	2	2	...	12	2
1992—New Orleans NFL	16	16	3	-1	-0.3	0	30	566	18.9	5	5	...	30	0
1993—New Orleans NFL	16	15	2	32	16.0	0	45	670	14.9	6	6	...	36	1
1994—New Orleans NFL	16	13	2	10	5.0	0	82	894	10.9	4	4	0	24	0
1995—New Orleans NFL	16	15	2	-3	-1.5	0	81	1087	13.4	8	8	0	48	1
1996—Buffalo NFL	16	13	3	39	13.0	0	50	798	16.0	4	4	1	26	0
1997—Buffalo NFL	16	16	0	0	...	0	60	853	14.2	5	5	0	30	0
Pro totals (10 years)	147	117	23	172	7.5	0	435	6148	14.1	39	39	1	236	5

PERSONAL: Born April 4, 1972, in Exeter, N.H. ... 6-5/300. ... Full name: Chad Everett Eaton.

HIGH SCHOOL: Rogers (Puyallup, Wash.).

COLLEGE: Washington State.

TRANSACTIONS/CAREER NOTES: Selected by Arizona Cardinals in seventh round (241st pick overall) of 1995 NFL draft. ... Signed by Cardinals (July 24, 1995). ... Released by Cardinals (August 14, 1995). ... Signed by New York Jets (August 15, 1995). ... Released by Jets (August 27, 1995). ... Signed by Cleveland Browns to practice squad (September 28, 1995). ... Activated (December 15, 1995). ... Browns franchise moved to Baltimore and renamed Ravens for 1996 season (March 11, 1996). ... Released by Ravens (August 19, 1996). ... Signed by New England Patriots to practice squad (August 27, 1996). ... Activated (November 28, 1996).

PLAYING EXPERIENCE: New England NFL, 1996 and 1997. ... Games/Games started: 1996 (4/0), 1997 (16/1). Total: 20/1.

CHAMPIONSHIP GAME EXPERIENCE: Played in AFC championship game (1996 season). ... Played in Super Bowl XXXI (1996 season).

HONORS: Named defensive lineman on THE SPORTING NEWS college All-America second team (1994).

PRO STATISTICS: 1996—Credited with one sack. 1997—Credited with one sack.

E

PERSONAL: Born May 26, 1966, in Casa Grande, Ariz. ... 5-10/197.

HIGH SCHOOL: Union (Casa Grande, Ariz.).

COLLEGE: New Mexico Highlands.

TRANSACTIONS/CAREER NOTES: Signed as non-drafted free agent by Philadelphia Eagles (July 7, 1989). ... Released by Eagles (September 5, 1989). ... Re-signed by Eagles to developmental squad (September 6, 1989). ... Activated (October 20, 1989). ... On injured reserve with knee injury (September 4-October 1, 1990). ... On practice squad (October 1-30, 1990). ... Released by Eagles (October 30, 1990). ... Re-signed by Eagles (October 31, 1990). ... Released by Eagles (December 12, 1990). ... Signed by Phoenix Cardinals (May 1991). ... Released by Cardinals (August 26, 1991). ... Re-signed by Cardinals (September 18, 1991). ... Granted unconditional free agency (February 1-April 1, 1992). ... Re-signed by Cardinals for 1992 season. ... Granted unconditional free agency (February 17, 1994). ... Re-signed by Cardinals (April 14, 1994). ... Cardinals franchise renamed Arizona Cardinals for 1994 season. ... On injured reserve with knee injury (August 12, 1994-entire season). ... Granted unconditional free agency (February 14, 1997). ... Re-signed by Cardinals (July 8, 1997). ... Granted unconditional free agency (February 13, 1998). ... Re-signed by Cardinals (April 21, 1998).

PRO STATISTICS: 1989—Recovered one fumble. 1995—Recovered one fumble. 1996—Rushed once for minus eight yards and recovered one fumble. 1997—Recovered one fumble.

SINGLE GAME HIGHS (regular season): Receptions—5 (November 10, 1996, vs. Washington); yards—112 (October 24, 1993, vs. San Francisco); and touchdown receptions—1 (November 10, 1996, vs. Washington).

STATISTICAL PLATEAUS: 100-yard receiving games: 1993 (1).

			RECEIVING				PUNT RETURNS				KICKOFF RETURNS				TOTALS			
Year Team	G	GS	No.	Yds.	Avg.	TD	No.	Yds.	Avg.	TD	No.	Yds.	Avg.	TD	TD	2pt.	Pts.	Fum.
1989—Philadelphia NFL	9	0	2	74	37.0	0	7	64	9.1	0	3	23	7.7	0	0	...	0	2
1990—Philadelphia NFL	5	0	0	0	...	0	8	60	7.5	0	3	36	12.0	0	0	...	0	2
1991—Phoenix NFL	13	0	0	0	...	0	1	7	7.0	0	13	261	20.1	0	0	...	0	0
1992—Phoenix NFL	16	0	14	147	10.5	1	0	0	...	0	8	143	17.9	0	1	...	6	0
1993—Phoenix NFL	16	0	13	326	25.1	1	3	12	4.0	0	3	51	17.0	0	1	...	6	0
1994—Arizona NFL									Did not play.									
1995—Arizona NFL	15	0	29	417	14.4	2	18	131	7.3	0	3	50	16.7	0	2	0	12	0
1996—Arizona NFL	16	1	29	311	10.7	1	5	46	9.2	0	0	0	...	0	1	0	6	1
1997—Arizona NFL	16	1	20	203	10.2	0	1	-1	-1.0	0	0	0	...	0	0	0	0	0
Pro totals (8 years)	106	2	107	1478	13.8	5	43	319	7.4	0	33	564	17.1	0	5	0	30	5

EDWARDS, ANTONIO   DE

PERSONAL: Born March 10, 1970, in Moultrie, Ga. ... 6-3/271.
HIGH SCHOOL: Colquitt County (Moultrie, Ga.).
COLLEGE: Valdosta (Ga.) State.
TRANSACTIONS/CAREER NOTES: Selected by Seattle Seahawks in eighth round (204th pick overall) of 1993 NFL draft. ... Signed by Seahawks (July 14, 1993). ... Released by Seahawks (August 5, 1997). ... Re-signed by Seahawks (September 23, 1997). ... Released by Seahawks (October 20, 1997). ... Signed by New York Giants (December 2, 1997). ... Granted unconditional free agency (February 13, 1998).
PRO STATISTICS: 1993—Credited with one safety. 1995—Recovered one fumble for 83 yards and a touchdown.

Year Team	G	GS	SACKS
1993—Seattle NFL	9	0	3.0
1994—Seattle NFL	15	14	2.5
1995—Seattle NFL	13	8	5.5
1996—Seattle NFL	12	3	2.0
1997—Seattle NFL	1	0	0.0
—New York Giants NFL	3	0	0.0
Pro totals (5 years)	53	25	13.0

EDWARDS, DIXON   LB   VIKINGS

PERSONAL: Born March 25, 1968, in Cincinnati. ... 6-1/237. ... Full name: Dixon Voldean Edwards III.
HIGH SCHOOL: Aiken (Cincinnati).
COLLEGE: Michigan State.
TRANSACTIONS/CAREER NOTES: Selected by Dallas Cowboys in second round (37th pick overall) of 1991 NFL draft. ... Signed by Cowboys (April 22, 1991). ... On injured reserve with hamstring injury (August 27-September 25, 1991). ... Granted unconditional free agency (February 16, 1996). ... Signed by Minnesota Vikings (February 26, 1996).
CHAMPIONSHIP GAME EXPERIENCE: Played in NFC championship game (1992-1995 seasons). ... Member of Super Bowl championship team (1992, 1993 and 1995 seasons).
PRO STATISTICS: 1991—Intercepted one pass for 36 yards and a touchdown. 1992—Returned one kickoff for no yards. 1993—Recovered one fumble. 1994—Recovered one fumble for 21 yards. 1996—Intercepted one pass for 18 yards. 1997—Recovered one fumble.

Year Team	G	GS	SACKS
1991—Dallas NFL	11	1	0.0
1992—Dallas NFL	16	1	0.0
1993—Dallas NFL	16	15	1.5
1994—Dallas NFL	16	15	1.0
1995—Dallas NFL	15	15	0.0
1996—Minnesota NFL	14	13	3.5
1997—Minnesota NFL	16	16	1.5
Pro totals (7 years)	104	76	7.5

EDWARDS, DONNIE   LB   CHIEFS

PERSONAL: Born April 6, 1973, in San Diego ... 6-2/236. ... Full name: Donald Lewis Edwards.
HIGH SCHOOL: Chula Vista (San Diego).
COLLEGE: UCLA.
TRANSACTIONS/CAREER NOTES: Selected by Kansas City Chiefs in fourth round (98th pick overall) of 1996 NFL draft. ... Played with Barcelona Dragons of World League for 1996 season. ... Signed by Chiefs (July 24, 1996).
PRO STATISTICS: 1997—Credited with 2$\frac{1}{2}$ sacks and recovered one fumble.

Year Team	G	GS	INTERCEPTIONS No.	Yds.	Avg.	TD
1996—Barcelona W.L.	...	...	0	0	...	0
—Kansas City NFL	15	1	1	22	22.0	0
1997—Kansas City NFL	16	16	2	15	7.5	0
W.L. totals (1 year)	...	...	0	0	...	0
NFL totals (2 years)	31	17	3	37	12.3	0
Pro totals (3 years)	...	...	3	37	12.3	0

EDWARDS, MARC   FB   49ERS

PERSONAL: Born November 17, 1974, in Cincinnati. ... 6-0/229. ... Full name: Marc Anthony Edwards.
HIGH SCHOOL: Norwood (Ohio).
COLLEGE: Notre Dame.
TRANSACTIONS/CAREER NOTES: Selected by San Francisco 49ers in second round (55th pick overall) of 1997 NFL draft. ... Signed by 49ers (July 23, 1997).
CHAMPIONSHIP GAME EXPERIENCE: Played in NFC championship game (1997 season).
PRO STATISTICS: 1997—Returned one kickoff for 30 yards.
SINGLE GAME HIGHS (regular season): Attempts—3 (December 21, 1997, vs. Seattle); yards—12 (December 21, 1997, vs. Seattle); and rushing touchdowns—0.

Year Team	G	GS	RUSHING Att.	Yds.	Avg.	TD	RECEIVING No.	Yds.	Avg.	TD	TOTALS TD	2pt.	Pts.	Fum.
1997—San Francisco NFL	15	1	5	17	3.4	0	6	48	8.0	0	0	0	0	0

EL-MASHTOUB, HICHAM   C/G   CHIEFS

PERSONAL: Born May 11, 1972, in Lebanon. ... 6-2/300. ... Name pronounced EE-shum el-mash-toob.
HIGH SCHOOL: Polyvalente Georges-Vanier (Montreal).
COLLEGE: Arizona.
TRANSACTIONS/CAREER NOTES: Selected by Edmonton Eskimos in first round (fifth pick overall) of 1995 CFL draft. ... Selected by Houston Oilers in sixth round (174th pick overall) of 1995 NFL draft. ... Signed by Oilers (July 20, 1995). ... Oilers franchise moved to Tennessee for 1997 season. ... Released by Oilers (August 27, 1997). ... Signed by Kansas City Chiefs (April 7, 1998).
PLAYING EXPERIENCE: Houston NFL, 1995 and 1996. ... Games/Games started: 1995 (2/0), 1996 (1/0). Total: 3/0.

ELAM, JASON   K   BRONCOS

PERSONAL: Born March 8, 1970, in Fort Walton Beach, Fla. ... 5-11/200.
HIGH SCHOOL: Brookwood (Snellville, Ga.).
COLLEGE: Hawaii.
TRANSACTIONS/CAREER NOTES: Selected by Denver Broncos in third round (70th pick overall) of 1993 NFL draft. ... Signed by Broncos (July 12, 1993).
CHAMPIONSHIP GAME EXPERIENCE: Played in AFC championship game (1997 season). ... Member of Super Bowl championship team (1997 season).
HONORS: Named kicker on THE SPORTING NEWS college All-America second team (1989 and 1991). ... Played in Pro Bowl (1995 season).
PRO STATISTICS: 1995—Punted once for 17 yards.

					KICKING				
Year Team	G	GS	XPM	XPA	FGM	FGA	Lg.	50+	Pts.
1993—Denver NFL	16	0	41	42	26	35	54	4-6	119
1994—Denver NFL	16	0	29	29	30	37	54	1-3	119
1995—Denver NFL	16	0	39	39	31	38	56	5-7	132
1996—Denver NFL	16	0	§46	§46	21	28	51	1-3	109
1997—Denver NFL	15	0	§46	§46	26	36	53	3-5	124
Pro totals (5 years)	79	0	201	202	134	174	56	14-24	603

ELLARD, HENRY   WR

PERSONAL: Born July 21, 1961, in Fresno, Calif. ... 5-11/188. ... Full name: Henry Austin Ellard. ... Name pronounced EL-lard.
HIGH SCHOOL: Hoover (Fresno, Calif.).
COLLEGE: Fresno State.
TRANSACTIONS/CAREER NOTES: Selected by Oakland Invaders in 1983 USFL territorial draft. ... Selected by Los Angeles Rams in second round (32nd pick overall) of 1983 NFL draft. ... Signed by Rams (July 22, 1983). ... Granted free agency (February 1, 1986). ... Re-signed by Rams (October 22, 1986). ... Granted roster exemption (October 22-25, 1986). ... Granted unconditional free agency (February 17, 1994). ... Signed by Washington Redskins (April 13, 1994). ... Granted unconditional free agency (February 16, 1996). ... Re-signed by Redskins (February 17, 1996). ... Granted unconditional free agency (February 13, 1998).
CHAMPIONSHIP GAME EXPERIENCE: Played in NFC championship game (1985 and 1989 seasons).
HONORS: Named punt returner on THE SPORTING NEWS NFL All-Pro team (1984 and 1985). ... Played in Pro Bowl (1984, 1988 and 1989 seasons). ... Named wide receiver on THE SPORTING NEWS NFL All-Pro team (1988).
PRO STATISTICS: 1983—Fumbled twice and recovered two fumbles. 1984—Fumbled four times and recovered two fumbles. 1985—Fumbled three times and recovered five fumbles. 1986—Fumbled three times and recovered one fumble. 1987—Fumbled three times and recovered one fumble. 1988—Fumbled three times. 1990—Fumbled four times. 1991—Fumbled once and recovered one fumble. 1994—Fumbled once. 1995—Fumbled once.
SINGLE GAME HIGHS (regular season): Receptions—12 (September 17, 1989, vs. Indianapolis); yards—230 (September 17, 1989, vs. Indianapolis); touchdown receptions—3 (September 17, 1989, vs. Indianapolis).
STATISTICAL PLATEAUS: 100-yard receiving games: 1985 (2), 1986 (2), 1987 (1), 1988 (5), 1989 (5), 1990 (6), 1991 (1), 1993 (3), 1994 (5), 1995 (3), 1996 (3). Total: 36
MISCELLANEOUS: Holds Rams franchise all-time records for most receptions (593) and most yards receiving (9,761).

			RUSHING				RECEIVING				PUNT RETURNS				KICKOFF RETURNS				TOTALS		
Year Team	G	GS	Att.	Yds.	Avg.	TD	No.	Yds.	Avg.	TD	No.	Yds.	Avg.	TD	No.	Yds.	Avg.	TD	TD	2pt.	Pts.
1983—LA Rams NFL	12	0	3	7	2.3	0	16	268	16.8	0	16	217*13.6		†1	15	314	20.9	0	1	...	6
1984—LA Rams NFL	16	16	3	-5	-1.7	0	34	622	18.3	6	30	403‡13.4		*2	2	24	12.0	0	8	...	48
1985—LA Rams NFL	16	16	3	8	2.7	0	54	811	15.0	5	37	‡501‡13.5		1	0	0	...	0	6	...	36
1986—LA Rams NFL	9	8	1	-15	-15.0	0	34	447	13.1	4	14	127	9.1	0	1	18	18.0	0	4	...	24
1987—LA Rams NFL	12	12	1	4	4.0	0	51	799	15.7	3	15	107	7.1	0	1	8	8.0	0	3	...	18
1988—LA Rams NFL	16	16	1	7	7.0	0	‡86	*1414	16.4	10	17	119	7.0	0	0	0	...	0	10	...	60
1989—LA Rams NFL	14	12	2	10	5.0	0	70	1382	19.7	8	2	20	10.0	0	0	0	...	0	8	...	48
1990—LA Rams NFL	15	15	2	21	10.5	0	76	1294	17.0	4	2	15	7.5	0	0	0	...	0	4	...	24
1991—LA Rams NFL	16	16	0	0	...	0	64	1052	16.4	3	0	0	...	0	0	0	...	0	3	...	18
1992—LA Rams NFL	16	15	0	0	...	0	47	727	15.5	3	0	0	...	0	0	0	...	0	3	...	18
1993—LA Rams NFL	16	16	2	18	9.0	0	61	945	15.5	2	2	18	9.0	0	0	0	...	0	2	...	12
1994—Wash. NFL	16	16	1	-5	-5.0	0	74	1397	18.9	6	0	0	...	0	0	0	...	0	6	0	36
1995—Wash. NFL	15	15	0	0	...	0	56	1005	17.9	5	0	0	...	0	0	0	...	0	5	0	30
1996—Wash. NFL	16	16	0	0	...	0	52	1014	*19.5	2	0	0	...	0	0	0	...	0	2	0	12
1997—Wash. NFL	16	11	0	0	...	0	32	485	15.2	4	0	0	...	0	0	0	...	0	4	0	24
Pro totals (15 years)	221	200	19	50	2.6	0	807	13662	16.9	65	135	1527	11.3	4	19	364	19.2	0	69	0	414

ELLIOTT, JUMBO   OT   JETS

PERSONAL: Born April 1, 1965, in Lake Ronkonkoma, N.Y. ... 6-7/308. ... Full name: John Elliott.
HIGH SCHOOL: Sachem (Lake Ronkonkoma, N.Y.).
COLLEGE: Michigan (received undergraduate degree, 1988).

TRANSACTIONS/CAREER NOTES: Selected by New York Giants in second round (36th pick overall) of 1988 NFL draft. ... Signed by Giants (July 18, 1988). ... Granted free agency (February 1, 1991). ... Re-signed by Giants (August 22, 1991). ... Designated by Giants as franchise player (February 25, 1993). ... On injured reserve (January 7, 1994-remainder of 1993 playoffs). ... Granted unconditional free agency (February 16, 1996). ... Signed by New York Jets (February 24, 1996). ... On injured reserve with ankle injury (December 1, 1997-remainder of season).

PLAYING EXPERIENCE: New York Giants NFL, 1988-1995; New York Jets NFL, 1996 and 1997. ... Games/Games started: 1988 (16/5), 1989 (13/11), 1990 (8/8), 1991 (16/16), 1992 (16/16), 1993 (11/11), 1994 (16/15), 1995 (16/16), 1996 (14/14), 1997 (13/13). Total: 139/125.

CHAMPIONSHIP GAME EXPERIENCE: Played in NFC championship game (1990 season). ... Member of Super Bowl championship team (1990 season).

HONORS: Played in Pro Bowl (1993 season).

PRO STATISTICS: 1988—Recovered one fumble.

ELLIOTT, MATT C/G FALCONS

PERSONAL: Born October 1, 1968, in Carmel, Ind. ... 6-3/295. ... Full name: Eric Matthew Elliott.
HIGH SCHOOL: Carmel (Ind.).
COLLEGE: Michigan.
TRANSACTIONS/CAREER NOTES: Selected by Washington Redskins in 12th round (336th pick overall) of 1992 NFL draft. ... Signed by Redskins for 1992 season. ... On injured reserve (August 20, 1993-remainder of season). ... Released by Redskins (August 23, 1994). ... Signed by Carolina Panthers (January 10, 1995). ... Granted free agency (February 16, 1996). ... Re-signed by Panthers (May 10, 1996). ... Granted unconditional free agency (February 14, 1997). ... Re-signed by Panthers (April 1, 1997). ... Granted unconditional free agency (February 13, 1998). ... Signed by Atlanta Falcons (March 16, 1998).
PLAYING EXPERIENCE: Washington NFL, 1992; Carolina NFL, 1995-1997. ... Games/Games started: 1992 (16/2), 1995 (15/14), 1996 (16/12), 1997 (16/6). Total: 63/34.
CHAMPIONSHIP GAME EXPERIENCE: Played in NFC championship game (1996 season).
PRO STATISTICS: 1996—Recovered one fumble.

ELLIS, ED OT PATRIOTS

PERSONAL: Born October 13, 1975, in Hamden, Conn. ... 6-7/340. ... Full name: Edward Ellis.
HIGH SCHOOL: Hamden (Conn.).
COLLEGE: Buffalo.
TRANSACTIONS/CAREER NOTES: Selected by New England Patriots in fourth round (125th pick overall) of 1997 NFL draft. ... Signed by Patriots (June 19, 1997).
PLAYING EXPERIENCE: New England NFL, 1997. ... Games/Games started: 1/0.

ELLISON, JERRY RB BUCCANEERS

PERSONAL: Born December 20, 1971, in Augusta, Ga. ... 5-10/204. ... Full name: Jerry Ernest Ellison.
HIGH SCHOOL: Glenn Hills (Augusta, Ga.).
COLLEGE: UT-Chattanooga.
TRANSACTIONS/CAREER NOTES: Signed as non-drafted free agent by Tampa Bay Buccaneers (May 5, 1994). ... Released by Buccaneers (August 23, 1994). ... Re-signed by Buccaneers to practice squad (September 7, 1994). ... Released by Buccaneers (September 12, 1994). ... Re-signed by Buccaneers to practice squad (September 27, 1994). ... Granted free agency (February 13, 1998). ... Re-signed by Buccaneers (May 6, 1998).
PRO STATISTICS: 1995—Recovered one fumble. 1996—Recovered one fumble. 1997—Recovered one fumble.
SINGLE GAME HIGHS (regular season): Attempts—8 (September 8, 1996, vs. Detroit); yards—91 (December 23, 1995, vs. Detroit); and rushing touchdowns—2 (November 12, 1995, vs. Detroit).

			RUSHING				RECEIVING				KICKOFF RETURNS				TOTALS		
Year Team	G	GS	Att.	Yds.	Avg.	TD	No.	Yds.	Avg.	TD	No.	Yds.	Avg.	TD	TD	2pt.	Pts. Fum.
1995—Tampa Bay NFL	16	3	26	218	8.4	5	7	44	6.3	0	15	261	17.4	0	5	0	30	0
1996—Tampa Bay NFL	16	2	35	106	3.0	0	18	208	11.6	0	0	0	...	0	0	0	0	2
1997—Tampa Bay NFL	16	0	2	10	5.0	0	1	8	8.0	0	2	61	30.5	0	0	0	0	0
Pro totals (3 years)	48	5	63	334	5.3	5	26	260	10.0	0	17	322	18.9	0	5	0	30	2

ELLISS, LUTHER DT LIONS

PERSONAL: Born March 22, 1973, in Mancos, Colo. ... 6-5/291.
HIGH SCHOOL: Mancos (Colo.).
COLLEGE: Utah.
TRANSACTIONS/CAREER NOTES: Selected by Detroit Lions in first round (20th pick overall) of 1995 NFL draft. ... Signed by Lions (July 19, 1995).
HONORS: Named defensive lineman on THE SPORTING NEWS college All-America first team (1994).
PRO STATISTICS: 1997—Recovered two fumbles.

Year Team	G	GS	SACKS
1995—Detroit NFL	16	16	0.0
1996—Detroit NFL	14	14	6.5
1997—Detroit NFL	16	16	8.5
Pro totals (3 years)	46	46	15.0

ELLSWORTH, PERCY S GIANTS

PERSONAL: Born October 19, 1974, in Drewryville, Va. ... 6-2/220.
HIGH SCHOOL: Southhampton (Drewryville, Va.).
COLLEGE: Virginia.

E

TRANSACTIONS/CAREER NOTES: Signed as non-drafted free agent by New York Giants (April 27, 1996).
PRO STATISTICS: 1996—Recovered one fumble. 1997—Recovered two fumbles for 24 yards.

				INTERCEPTIONS		
Year Team	G	GS	No.	Yds.	Avg.	TD
1996—New York Giants NFL	14	4	3	62	20.7	0
1997—New York Giants NFL	16	1	4	40	10.0	0
Pro totals (2 years)	30	5	7	102	14.6	0

ELWAY, JOHN   QB   BRONCOS

PERSONAL: Born June 28, 1960, in Port Angeles, Wash. ... 6-3/215. ... Full name: John Albert Elway. ... Son of Jack Elway, director of pro scouting, Denver Broncos.
HIGH SCHOOL: Granada Hills (Calif.).
COLLEGE: Stanford (degree in economics, 1983).
TRANSACTIONS/CAREER NOTES: Selected by Oakland Invaders in 1983 USFL territorial draft. ... Selected by Baltimore Colts in first round (first pick overall) of 1983 NFL draft. ... Rights traded by Colts to Denver Broncos for QB Mark Herrmann, rights to OL Chris Hinton and first-round pick (G Ron Solt) in 1984 draft (May 2, 1983). ... Signed by Broncos (May 2, 1983).
CHAMPIONSHIP GAME EXPERIENCE: Played in AFC championship game (1986, 1987, 1989, 1991 and 1997 seasons). ... Played in Super Bowl XXI (1986 season), Super Bowl XXII (1987 season) and Super Bowl XXIV (1989 season). ... Member of Super Bowl championship team (1997 season).
HONORS: Named quarterback on THE SPORTING NEWS college All-America first team (1980 and 1982). ... Played in Pro Bowl (1986, 1987, 1993 and 1994 seasons). ... Named quarterback on THE SPORTING NEWS NFL All-Pro team (1987). ... Named to play in Pro Bowl (1989 season); replaced by Dave Krieg due to injury. ... Named to play in Pro Bowl as replacement for Dan Marino (1991); replaced by Ken O'Brien due to injury. ... Named to play in Pro Bowl (1996 season); replaced by Mark Brunell due to injury. ... Named to play in Pro Bowl (1997 season); replaced by Warren Moon due to injury.
RECORDS: Holds NFL career record for most wins as a starting quarterback—126. ... Shares NFL record for most seasons with 3,000 or more yards passing—12.
POST SEASON RECORDS: Holds Super Bowl record for oldest player to score a touchdown—37 (January 25, 1998, vs. Green Bay). ... Shares Super Bowl career records for most fumbles recovered—2; and most passes intercepted—7.
PRO STATISTICS: 1983—Fumbled six times and recovered three fumbles. 1984—Fumbled 14 times and recovered five fumbles for minus 10 yards. 1985—Fumbled seven times and recovered two fumbles for minus 35 yards. 1986—Caught one pass for 23 yards and a touchdown, fumbled eight times and recovered one fumble for minus 13 yards. 1987—Punted once for 31 yards and fumbled twice. 1988—Punted three times for 117 yards, fumbled seven times and recovered five fumbles for minus nine yards. 1989—Punted once for 34 yards, fumbled nine times and recovered two fumbles for minus four yards. 1990—Punted once for 37 yards, fumbled eight times and recovered one fumble for minus three yards. 1991—Caught one pass for 24 yards, punted once for 34 yards, led league with 12 fumbles and recovered two fumbles. 1992—Fumbled 12 times and recovered one fumble. 1993—Fumbled eight times and recovered five fumbles for minus five yards. 1994—Fumbled 11 times and recovered two fumbles for minus five yards. 1995—Fumbled nine times and recovered one fumble for minus seven yards. 1996—Fumbled six times and recovered two fumbles for minus four yards. 1997—Fumbled 11 times and recovered one fumble for minus 21 yards.
SINGLE GAME HIGHS (regular season): Attempts—59 (October 10, 1993, vs. Green Bay); completions—36 (September 4, 1994, vs. San Diego); yards—432 (December 20, 1985, vs. Seattle); and touchdown passes—5 (November 18, 1984, vs. Minnesota).
STATISTICAL PLATEAUS: 300-yard passing games: 1983 (1), 1984 (1), 1985 (3), 1986 (2), 1987 (4), 1988 (1), 1989 (1), 1990 (2), 1991 (1), 1992 (1), 1993 (3), 1994 (4), 1995 (5), 1996 (4), 1997 (1). Total: 34.
MISCELLANEOUS: Regular-season record as starting NFL quarterback: 138-80-1 (.632). ... Postseason record as starting NFL quarterback: 11-7 (.611). ... Holds Denver Broncos all-time records for most yards passing (48,669) and most touchdown passes (278).

				PASSING							RUSHING				TOTALS		
Year Team	G	GS	Att.	Cmp.	Pct.	Yds.	TD	Int.	Avg.	Rat.	Att.	Yds.	Avg.	TD	TD	2pt.	Pts.
1983—Denver NFL	11	10	259	123	47.5	1663	7	14	6.42	54.9	28	146	5.2	1	1	...	6
1984—Denver NFL	15	14	380	214	56.3	2598	18	15	6.84	76.8	56	237	4.2	1	1	...	6
1985—Denver NFL	16	16	*605	327	54.0	3891	22	§23	6.43	70.2	51	253	5.0	0	0	...	0
1986—Denver NFL	16	16	504	280	55.6	3485	19	13	6.91	79.0	52	257	4.9	1	2	...	12
1987—Denver NFL	12	12	410	224	54.6	3198	19	12	§7.80	83.4	66	304	4.6	4	4	...	24
1988—Denver NFL	15	15	496	274	55.2	3309	17	19	6.67	71.4	54	234	4.3	1	1	...	6
1989—Denver NFL	15	15	416	223	53.6	3051	18	18	7.33	73.7	48	244	5.1	3	3	...	18
1990—Denver NFL	16	16	502	294	58.6	3526	15	14	7.02	78.5	50	258	5.2	3	3	...	18
1991—Denver NFL	16	16	451	242	53.7	3253	13	12	7.21	75.4	55	255	4.6	6	6	...	36
1992—Denver NFL	12	12	316	174	55.1	2242	10	17	7.09	65.7	34	94	2.8	2	2	...	12
1993—Denver NFL	16	16	*551	*348	§63.2	*4030	§25	10	7.31	§92.8	44	153	3.5	0	0	...	0
1994—Denver NFL	14	14	494	307	62.1	3490	16	10	7.06	85.7	58	235	4.1	4	4	0	24
1995—Denver NFL	16	16	542	316	58.3	§3970	26	14	7.32	86.4	41	176	4.3	1	1	1	8
1996—Denver NFL	15	15	466	287	61.6	3328	26	14	7.14	§89.2	50	249	5.0	4	4	0	24
1997—Denver NFL	16	16	502	280	55.8	3635	27	11	7.24	87.5	50	218	4.4	1	1	...	6
Pro totals (15 years)	221	219	6894	3913	56.8	48669	278	216	7.06	79.2	737	3313	4.5	32	33	1	200

RECORD AS BASEBALL PLAYER

TRANSACTIONS//CAREER NOTES: Threw right, batted left. ... Selected by Kansas City Royals organization in 18th round of free-agent draft (June 5, 1979); did not sign. ... Selected by New York Yankees organization in second round of free-agent draft (June 8, 1981). ... On temporary inactive list (August 2-September 13, 1982). ... On suspended list (April 8-18, 1983). ... Placed on restricted list (April 18, 1983).

					BATTING								FIELDING			
Year Team (League)	Pos.	G	AB	R	H	2B	3B	HR	RBI	Avg.	BB	SO	SB	PO	A	E	Avg.
1982—Oneonta (NYP)	OF	42	151	26	48	6	2	4	25	.318	28	25	13	69	8	0	1.000

EMANUEL, BERT   WR   BUCCANEERS

PERSONAL: Born October 28, 1970, in Kansas City, Mo. ... 5-10/180. ... Full name: Bert Tyrone Emanuel.
HIGH SCHOOL: Langham Creek (Houston).
COLLEGE: Rice.

TRANSACTIONS/CAREER NOTES: Selected by Atlanta Falcons in second round (45th pick overall) of 1994 NFL draft. ... Signed by Falcons (July 11, 1994). ... Granted free agency (February 14, 1997). ... Re-signed by Falcons (July 16, 1997). ... Designated by Falcons as transition player (February 13, 1998). ... Tendered offer sheet by Tampa Bay Buccaneers (April 9, 1998). ... Falcons declined to match offer (April 14, 1998).
PRO STATISTICS: 1994—Rushed twice for four yards and had only pass attempt intercepted. 1995—Rushed once for no yards. 1997—Recovered two fumbles.
SINGLE GAME HIGHS (regular season): Receptions—9 (December 15, 1996, vs. St. Louis); yards—173 (December 15, 1996, vs. St. Louis); and touchdown receptions—2 (November 2, 1997, vs. St. Louis).
STATISTICAL PLATEAUS: 100-yard receiving games: 1994 (1), 1995 (4), 1996 (3), 1997 (1). Total: 9.
MISCELLANEOUS: Selected by Toronto Blue Jays organization in 75th round of free-agent baseball draft (June 5, 1989); did not sign. ... Selected by Pittsburgh Pirates organization in 49th round of free-agent baseball draft (June 1, 1992); did not sign.

				RECEIVING					TOTALS		
Year Team	G	GS	No.	Yds.	Avg.	TD	TD	2pt.	Pts.	Fum.
1994—Atlanta NFL	16	16	46	649	14.1	4	4	0	24	0
1995—Atlanta NFL	16	16	74	1039	14.0	5	5	0	30	2
1996—Atlanta NFL	14	13	75	921	12.3	6	6	0	36	0
1997—Atlanta NFL	16	16	65	991	15.2	9	9	0	54	2
Pro totals (4 years)	62	61	260	3600	13.8	24	24	0	144	4

EMANUEL, CHARLES   S   EAGLES

PERSONAL: Born June 3, 1973, in Indiantown, Fla. ... 6-0/196. ... Cousin of Cleveland Gary, running back with Los Angeles Rams (1989-93) and Miami Dolphins (1994).
HIGH SCHOOL: South Fork (Stuart, Fla.).
COLLEGE: West Virginia.
TRANSACTIONS/CAREER NOTES: Signed as non-drafted free agent by Minnesota Vikings (April 25, 1997). ... Released by Vikings (September 12, 1997). ... Signed by Philadelphia Eagles (September 17, 1997). ... On injured reserve with leg injury (October 29, 1997-remainder of season).
PLAYING EXPERIENCE: Philadelphia NFL, 1997. ... Games/Games started: 5/1.

EMMONS, CARLOS   LB   STEELERS

PERSONAL: Born September 3, 1973, in Greenwood, Miss. ... 6-5/246.
HIGH SCHOOL: Greenwood (Miss.).
COLLEGE: Arkansas State.
TRANSACTIONS/CAREER NOTES: Selected by Pittsburgh Steelers in seventh round (242nd pick overall) of 1996 NFL draft. ... Signed by Steelers (July 16, 1996).
CHAMPIONSHIP GAME EXPERIENCE: Played in AFC championship game (1997 season).
PRO STATISTICS: 1996—Recovered one fumble.

Year Team	G	GS	SACKS
1996—Pittsburgh NFL	15	0	2.5
1997—Pittsburgh NFL	5	0	0.0
Pro totals (2 years)	20	0	2.5

E

EMTMAN, STEVE   DE

PERSONAL: Born April 16, 1970, in Spokane, Wash. ... 6-4/284. ... Full name: Steven Charles Emtman.
HIGH SCHOOL: Cheney (Wash.).
COLLEGE: Washington.
TRANSACTIONS/CAREER NOTES: Selected after junior season by Indianapolis Colts in first round (first pick overall) of 1992 NFL draft. ... Signed by Colts (April 25, 1992). ... On injured reserve with knee injury (November 11, 1992-remainder of season). ... Designated by Colts as transition player (February 25, 1993). ... On injured reserve with knee injury (October 12, 1993-remainder of season). ... Released by Colts (July 15, 1995). ... Signed by Miami Dolphins (July 27, 1995). ... Released by Dolphins (February 13, 1997). ... Signed by San Francisco 49ers (July 21, 1997). ... Released by 49ers (August 24, 1997). ... Signed by Washington Redskins (November 25, 1997). ... Granted unconditional free agency (February 13, 1998).
HONORS: Named defensive lineman on THE SPORTING NEWS college All-America second team (1990). ... Lombardi Award winner (1991). ... Outland Trophy winner (1991). ... Named defensive lineman on THE SPORTING NEWS college All-America first team (1991).
PRO STATISTICS: 1992—Intercepted one pass for 90 yards and a touchdown. 1994—Recovered one fumble. 1995—Recovered one fumble. 1996—Recovered one fumble.

Year Team	G	GS	SACKS
1992—Indianapolis NFL	9	9	3.0
1993—Indianapolis NFL	5	5	1.0
1994—Indianapolis NFL	4	0	1.0
1995—Miami NFL	16	1	1.0
1996—Miami NFL	13	4	2.0
1997—Washington NFL	3	0	0.0
Pro totals (6 years)	50	19	8.0

ENGEL, GREG   C   CHARGERS

PERSONAL: Born January 18, 1971, in Davenport, Iowa. ... 6-3/285. ... Full name: Gregory Allen Engel.
HIGH SCHOOL: Bloomington (Ill.).
COLLEGE: Illinois.
TRANSACTIONS/CAREER NOTES: Signed as non-drafted free agent by San Diego Chargers (April 28, 1994). ... Inactive for 16 games (1994). ... Granted free agency (February 14, 1997). ... Re-signed by Chargers prior to 1997 season. ... Granted unconditional free agency (February 13, 1998). ... Re-signed by Chargers (February 13, 1998).
PLAYING EXPERIENCE: San Diego NFL, 1995-1997. ... Games/Games started: 1995 (10/0), 1996 (12/9), 1997 (9/0). Total: 31/9.
PRO STATISTICS: 1995—Ran one yard with lateral from kickoff return.

ENGLAND, ERIC DE OILERS

PERSONAL: Born April 25, 1971, in Fort Wayne, Ind. ... 6-3/273. ... Full name: Eric Jevon England.
HIGH SCHOOL: Willowridge (Sugar Land, Texas).
COLLEGE: Texas A&M.
TRANSACTIONS/CAREER NOTES: Selected by Arizona Cardinals in third round (89th pick overall) of 1994 NFL draft. ... Signed by Cardinals (July 30, 1994). ... Released by Cardinals (August 24, 1997). ... Signed by Tennessee Oilers (November 20, 1997). ... Inactive for five games (1997). ... Granted free agency (February 13, 1998).
PLAYING EXPERIENCE: Arizona NFL, 1994-1996. ... Games/Games started: 1994 (11/1), 1995 (15/0), 1996 (11/1). Total: 37/2.
PRO STATISTICS: 1995—Recovered two fumbles.

ENGLER, DEREK C GIANTS

PERSONAL: Born July 11, 1974, in St. Paul, Minn. ... 6-5/300.
HIGH SCHOOL: Crestin-Derham Hall (St. Paul, Minn.).
COLLEGE: Wisconsin.
TRANSACTIONS/CAREER NOTES: Signed as non-drafted free agent by New York Giants (April 28, 1997).
PLAYING EXPERIENCE: New York Giants NFL, 1997. ... Games/Games started: 5/5.
PRO STATISTICS: 1997—Fumbled once for minus two yards.

ENGRAM, BOBBY WR BEARS

PERSONAL: Born January 7, 1973, in Camden, S.C. ... 5-10/192. ... Full name: Simon Engram III.
HIGH SCHOOL: Camden (S.C.).
COLLEGE: Penn State.
TRANSACTIONS/CAREER NOTES: Selected by Chicago Bears in second round (52nd pick overall) of 1996 NFL draft. ... Signed by Bears (July 17, 1996).
HONORS: Named wide receiver on THE SPORTING NEWS college All-America second team (1994 and 1995).
PRO STATISTICS: 1997—Recovered one fumble.
SINGLE GAME HIGHS (regular season): Receptions—8 (October 27, 1997, vs. Miami); yards—63 (October 27, 1997, vs. Miami); and touchdown receptions—2 (December 1, 1996, vs. Green Bay).

			RECEIVING				PUNT RETURNS				KICKOFF RETURNS				TOTALS			
Year Team	G	GS	No.	Yds.	Avg.	TD	No.	Yds.	Avg.	TD	No.	Yds.	Avg.	TD	TD	2pt.	Pts.	Fum.
1996—Chicago NFL	16	2	33	389	11.8	6	31	282	9.1	0	25	580	23.2	0	6	0	36	2
1997—Chicago NFL	11	11	45	399	8.9	2	1	4	4.0	0	2	27	13.5	0	2	1	14	1
Pro totals (2 years)	27	13	78	788	10.1	8	32	286	8.9	0	27	607	22.5	0	8	1	50	3

ERICKSON, CRAIG QB DOLPHINS

PERSONAL: Born May 17, 1969, in Boynton Beach, Fla. ... 6-2/210. ... Full name: Craig Neil Erickson.
HIGH SCHOOL: Cardinal Newman (West Palm Beach, Fla.).
COLLEGE: Miami, Fla (degree in business).
TRANSACTIONS/CAREER NOTES: Selected by Philadelphia Eagles in fifth round (131st pick overall) of 1991 NFL draft; did not sign. ... Selected by Tampa Bay Buccaneers in fourth round (86th pick overall) of 1992 NFL draft. ... Signed by Buccaneers (July 10, 1992). ... Granted free agency (February 17, 1995). ... Re-signed by Buccaneers (April 26, 1995). ... Traded by Buccaneers to Indianapolis Colts for first-round (DT Marcus Jones) and conditional fourth-round picks in 1996 draft (April 26, 1995). ... Released by Colts (August 25, 1996). ... Signed by Miami Dolphins (September 2, 1996). ... Granted unconditional free agency (February 13, 1998). ... Re-signed by Dolphins (March 5, 1998).
CHAMPIONSHIP GAME EXPERIENCE: Member of Colts for AFC championship game (1995 season); did not play.
PRO STATISTICS: 1993—Fumbled nine times and recovered six fumbles for minus two yards. 1994—Fumbled six times and recovered one fumble for minus one yard. 1995—Fumbled twice for minus four yards. 1996—Fumbled four times and recovered three fumbles for minus three yards. 1997—Fumbled twice and recovered two fumbles for minus 13 yards.
SINGLE GAME HIGHS (regular season): Attempts—41 (January 2, 1994, vs. San Diego); completions—22 (November 20, 1994, vs. Seattle); yards—318 (October 31, 1993, vs. Atlanta); and touchdown passes—4 (October 31, 1993, vs. Atlanta).
STATISTICAL PLATEAUS: 300-yard passing games: 1993 (1), 1994 (1). Total: 2.
MISCELLANEOUS: Graduate assistant football coach, University of Georgia (1991). ... Regular-season record as starting NFL quarterback: 14-21 (.400).

			PASSING								RUSHING				TOTALS		
Year Team	G	GS	Att.	Cmp.	Pct.	Yds.	TD	Int.	Avg.	Rat.	Att.	Yds.	Avg.	TD	TD	2pt.	Pts.
1992—Tampa Bay NFL	6	0	26	15	57.7	121	0	0	4.65	69.6	1	-1	-1.0	0	0	...	0
1993—Tampa Bay NFL	16	15	457	233	51.0	3054	18	21	6.68	66.4	26	96	3.7	0	0	...	0
1994—Tampa Bay NFL	15	15	399	225	56.4	2919	16	10	7.32	82.5	26	68	2.6	1	1	0	6
1995—Indianapolis NFL	6	3	83	50	60.2	586	3	3	7.06	73.7	9	14	1.6	0	0	0	0
1996—Miami NFL	7	3	99	55	55.6	780	4	2	7.88	86.3	11	16	1.5	0	0	0	0
1997—Miami NFL	2	0	28	13	46.4	165	0	1	5.89	50.4	4	8	2.0	0	0	0	0
Pro totals (6 years)	52	36	1092	591	54.1	7625	41	38	6.98	74.3	77	201	2.6	1	1	0	6

ESIASON, BOOMER QB

PERSONAL: Born April 17, 1961, in West Islip, N.Y. ... 6-5/224. ... Full name: Norman Julius Esiason.
HIGH SCHOOL: East Islip (Islip Terrace, N.Y.).
COLLEGE: Maryland.
TRANSACTIONS/CAREER NOTES: Selected by Washington Federals in 1984 USFL territorial draft. ... Selected by Cincinnati Bengals in second round (38th pick overall) of 1984 NFL draft. ... Signed by Bengals (June 19, 1984). ... Traded by Bengals to New York Jets for third-round pick (DT Ty Parten) in 1993 draft (March 17, 1993). ... Granted unconditional free agency (February 16, 1996). ... Signed by Arizona Cardinals (April 8, 1996). ... Released by Cardinals (March 17, 1997). ... Signed by Bengals (April 5, 1997). ... Announced retirement (January 16, 1998).

CHAMPIONSHIP GAME EXPERIENCE: Played in AFC championship game (1988 season). ... Played in Super Bowl XXIII (1988 season).

HONORS: Named quarterback on The Sporting News college All-America second team (1983). ... Played in Pro Bowl (1986 and 1993 seasons). ... Named NFL Player of the Year by The Sporting News (1988). ... Named quarterback on The Sporting News NFL All-Pro team (1988). ... Named to play in Pro Bowl (1988 season); replaced by Jim Kelly due to injury. ... Named to play in Pro Bowl (1989 season); replaced by John Elway due to injury.

PRO STATISTICS: 1984—Fumbled four times and recovered two fumbles for minus two yards. 1985—Fumbled nine times and recovered four fumbles for minus five yards. 1986—Punted once for 31 yards, fumbled 12 times and recovered five fumbles for minus 10 yards. 1987—Punted twice for 68 yards, fumbled 10 times and recovered four fumbles for minus eight yards. 1988—Punted once for 21 yards, fumbled five times and recovered four fumbles. 1989—Fumbled eight times and recovered two fumbles for minus four yards. 1990—Fumbled 11 times and recovered two fumbles for minus 23 yards. 1991—Fumbled 10 times and recovered three fumbles for minus five yards. 1992—Fumbled 12 times. 1993—Caught one pass for minus eight yards, fumbled 13 times and recovered five fumbles for minus 10 yards. 1994—Fumbled 11 times and recovered three fumbles for minus 11 yards. 1995—Fumbled 12 times and recovered four fumbles for minus 27 yards. 1996—Fumbled five times and recovered one fumble for minus eight yards. 1997—Fumbled once.

SINGLE GAME HIGHS (regular season): Attempts—59 (November 10, 1996, vs. Washington); completions—35 (November 10, 1996, vs. Washington); yards—522 (November 10, 1996, vs. Washington); and touchdown passes—5 (October 29, 1989, vs. Tampa Bay).

STATISTICAL PLATEAUS: 300-yard passing games: 1985 (4), 1986 (3), 1987 (5), 1988 (3), 1989 (4), 1990 (1), 1991 (2), 1993 (2), 1994 (1), 1995 (1), 1996 (2), 1997 (1). Total: 29.

MISCELLANEOUS: Regular-season record as starting NFL quarterback: 80-93 (.462). Postseason record as starting NFL quarterback: 3-2 (.600).

					PASSING							RUSHING				TOTALS	
Year Team	G	GS	Att.	Cmp.	Pct.	Yds.	TD	Int.	Avg.	Rat.	Att.	Yds.	Avg.	TD	TD	2pt.	Pts.
1984—Cincinnati NFL............	10	4	102	51	50.0	530	3	3	5.20	62.9	19	63	3.3	2	2	...	12
1985—Cincinnati NFL............	15	14	431	251	58.2	3443	27	12	7.99	93.2	33	79	2.4	1	1	...	6
1986—Cincinnati NFL............	16	16	469	273	58.2	3959	24	17	*8.44	87.7	44	146	3.3	1	1	...	6
1987—Cincinnati NFL............	12	12	440	240	54.5	§3321	16	▲19	7.55	73.1	52	241	4.6	0	0	...	0
1988—Cincinnati NFL............	16	16	388	223	57.5	3572	▲28	14	*9.21	*97.4	43	248	5.8	1	1	...	6
1989—Cincinnati NFL............	16	15	455	258	56.7	3525	§28	11	7.75	§92.1	47	278	5.9	0	0	...	0
1990—Cincinnati NFL............	16	16	402	224	55.7	3031	24	*22	7.54	77.0	49	157	3.2	0	0	...	0
1991—Cincinnati NFL............	14	14	413	233	56.4	2883	13	16	6.98	72.5	24	66	2.8	0	0	...	0
1992—Cincinnati NFL............	12	11	278	144	51.8	1407	11	15	5.06	57.0	21	66	3.1	0	0	...	0
1993—New York Jets NFL......	16	16	473	288	60.9	3421	16	11	7.23	84.5	45	118	2.6	1	1	...	6
1994—New York Jets NFL......	15	14	440	255	58.0	2782	17	13	6.32	77.3	28	59	2.1	0	0	...	0
1995—New York Jets NFL......	12	12	389	221	56.8	2275	16	15	5.85	71.4	19	14	0.7	0	0	0	0
1996—Arizona NFL	10	8	339	190	56.0	2293	11	14	6.76	70.6	15	52	3.5	1	6	1	8
1997—Cincinnati NFL............	7	5	186	118	63.4	1478	13	2	7.95	106.9	8	11	1.4	0	0	0	0
Pro totals (14 years)............	187	173	5205	2969	57.0	37920	247	184	7.29	81.1	447	1598	3.6	7	12	1	44

ETHRIDGE, RAY — WR

PERSONAL: Born December 12, 1968, in San Diego. ... 5-10/180. ... Full name: Raymond Arthur Ethridge Jr.

HIGH SCHOOL: Crawford (San Diego).

COLLEGE: Pasadena (Calif.) City College.

TRANSACTIONS/CAREER NOTES: Signed as non-drafted free agent by B.C. Lions of CFL (June 1991). ... Released by Lions (September 1991). ... Selected by San Diego Chargers in third round (63rd pick overall) of 1992 NFL draft. ... On reserve/physically unable to perform list with hamstring injury (July 16, 1992-February 1, 1993). ... On injured reserve (August 24-September 1, 1993). ... Released by Chargers (September 1, 1993). ... Signed by Cleveland Browns for 1995 season. ... Traded by Browns to Carolina Panthers for undisclosed draft pick (August 21, 1995). ... Released by Panthers (August 29, 1995). ... Signed by Browns to practice squad (September 6, 1995). ... Activated (December 22, 1995). ... Browns franchise moved to Baltimore and renamed Ravens for 1996 season (March 11, 1996). ... On injured reserve with hand and wrist injury (October 13, 1997-remainder of season). ... Released by Ravens (February 13, 1998).

PRO STATISTICS: 1996—Recovered one fumble. 1997—Fumbled twice.

SINGLE GAME HIGHS (regular season): Receptions—1 (December 22, 1996, vs. Houston); yards—15 (December 22, 1996, vs. Houston); and touchdown receptions—0.

			RUSHING				RECEIVING				PUNT RETURNS				KICKOFF RETURNS				TOTALS		
Year Team	G	GS	Att.	Yds.	Avg.	TD	No.	Yds.	Avg.	TD	No.	Yds.	Avg.	TD	No.	Yds.	Avg.	TD	TD	2pt.	Pts.
1991—Brit. Col. CFL.......	6	...	1	-8	-8.0	0	18	200	11.1	1	8	75	9.4	0	16	402	25.1	1	2	...	12
1992—San Diego NFL							Did not play.														
1993—							Did not play.														
1994—							Did not play.														
1995—							Did not play.														
1996—Baltimore NFL.....	14	1	0	0	...	0	2	24	12.0	0	1	3	3.0	0	8	171	21.4	0	0	0	0
1997—Baltimore NFL.....	2	0	0	0	...	0	0	0	...	0	5	21	4.2	0	2	37	18.5	0	0	0	0
CFL totals (1 year)........	6	...	1	-8	-8.0	0	18	200	11.1	1	8	75	9.4	0	16	402	25.1	1	2	0	12
NFL totals (2 years).......	16	1	0	0	...	0	2	24	12.0	0	6	24	4.0	0	10	208	20.8	0	0	0	0
Pro totals (3 years)........	22	1	1	-8	-8.0	0	20	224	11.2	1	14	99	7.1	0	26	610	23.5	1	2	0	12

EVANS, CHUCK — FB — VIKINGS

PERSONAL: Born April 16, 1967, in Augusta, Ga. ... 6-1/243. ... Full name: Charles Evans Jr.

HIGH SCHOOL: Glenn Hills (Augusta, Ga.).

COLLEGE: Clark Atlanta (Ga.).

TRANSACTIONS/CAREER NOTES: Selected by Minnesota Vikings in 11th round (295th pick overall) of 1992 NFL draft. ... Signed by Vikings (June 10, 1992). ... Released by Vikings (August 31, 1992). ... Re-signed by Vikings (February 10, 1993). ... On injured reserve with wrist injury (October 11, 1993-remainder of season). ... Granted free agency (February 16, 1996). ... Re-signed by Vikings (May 9, 1996). ... Granted unconditional free agency (February 14, 1997). ... Re-signed by Vikings (April 11, 1997).

PRO STATISTICS: 1993—Returned one kickoff for 11 yards. 1994—Returned one kickoff for four yards. 1997—Recovered one fumble.

SINGLE GAME HIGHS (regular season): Attempts—10 (December 9, 1995, vs. Cleveland); yards—50 (November 9, 1997, vs. Chicago); and rushing touchdowns—1 (November 9, 1997, vs. Chicago).

			RUSHING				RECEIVING				TOTALS			
Year Team	G	GS	Att.	Yds.	Avg.	TD	No.	Yds.	Avg.	TD	TD	2pt.	Pts.	Fum.
1992—							Did not play.							
1993—Minnesota NFL	3	0	14	32	2.3	0	4	39	9.8	0	0	...	0	0
1994—Minnesota NFL	14	0	6	20	3.3	0	1	2	2.0	0	0	0	0	0
1995—Minnesota NFL	16	7	19	59	3.1	1	18	119	6.6	1	2	0	12	0
1996—Minnesota NFL	16	6	13	29	2.2	0	22	135	6.1	0	0	0	0	0
1997—Minnesota NFL	16	13	43	157	3.7	2	21	152	7.2	0	2	1	14	0
Pro totals (5 years)	65	26	95	297	3.1	3	66	447	6.8	1	4	1	26	0

EVANS, DOUG — CB — PANTHERS

PERSONAL: Born May 13, 1970, in Shreveport, La. ... 6-1/190. ... Full name: Douglas Edwards Evans. ... Brother of Bobby Evans, safety with Winnipeg of the CFL (1990-1994).
HIGH SCHOOL: Haynesville (La.).
COLLEGE: Louisiana Tech (degree in finance).
TRANSACTIONS/CAREER NOTES: Selected by Green Bay Packers in sixth round (141st pick overall) of 1993 NFL draft. ... Signed by Packers (July 9, 1993). ... Granted unconditional free agency (February 13, 1998). ... Signed by Carolina Panthers (February 18, 1998).
CHAMPIONSHIP GAME EXPERIENCE: Played in NFC championship game (1995-97 seasons). ... Member of Super Bowl championship team (1996 season). ... Played in Super Bowl XXXII (1997 season).
PRO STATISTICS: 1993—Recovered two fumbles. 1994—Recovered one fumble for three yards. 1995—Returned one punt for no yards and fumbled once. 1996—Fumbled once and recovered one fumble for two yards.

			INTERCEPTIONS				SACKS
Year Team	G	GS	No.	Yds.	Avg.	TD	No.
1993—Green Bay NFL	16	0	1	0	0.0	0	0.0
1994—Green Bay NFL	16	15	1	0	0.0	0	1.0
1995—Green Bay NFL	16	16	2	24	12.0	0	1.0
1996—Green Bay NFL	16	16	5	102	20.4	1	3.0
1997—Green Bay NFL	15	15	3	33	11.0	0	1.0
Pro totals (5 years)	79	62	12	159	13.3	1	6.0

EVANS, JOSH — DL — OILERS

PERSONAL: Born September 6, 1972, in Langdale, Ala. ... 6-0/275. ... Full name: Mijoshki Antwon Evans.
HIGH SCHOOL: Lanett (Ala.).
COLLEGE: Alabama-Birmingham.
TRANSACTIONS/CAREER NOTES: Signed as non-drafted free agent by Dallas Cowboys (April 27, 1995). ... Released by Cowboys (August 22, 1995). ... Signed by Houston Oilers to practice squad (September 1, 1995). ... Activated (November 10, 1995). ... On injured reserve with knee injury (November 29, 1996-remainder of season). ... Oilers franchise moved to Tennessee for 1997 season. ... Granted free agency (February 13, 1998).
PLAYING EXPERIENCE: Houston NFL, 1995 and 1996; Tennessee NFL, 1997. ... Games/Games started: 1995 (7/0), 1996 (8/0), 1997 (15/0). Total: 30/0.
PRO STATISTICS: 1997—Credited with two sacks and recovered one fumble.

EVANS, LEOMONT — S — REDSKINS

PERSONAL: Born July 12, 1974, in Abbeville, S.C. ... 6-1/202.
HIGH SCHOOL: Abbeville (S.C.).
COLLEGE: Clemson.
TRANSACTIONS/CAREER NOTES: Selected by Washington Redskins in fifth round (138th pick overall) of 1996 NFL draft. ... Signed by Redskins (June 4, 1996)
PLAYING EXPERIENCE: Washington NFL, 1996 and 1997. ... Games/Games started: 1996 (12/0), 1997 (16/0). Total: 28/0.
PRO STATISTICS: 1997—Recovered one fumble.

EVERETT, JIM — QB

PERSONAL: Born January 3, 1963, in Emporia, Kan. ... 6-5/212. ... Full name: James Samuel Everett III.
HIGH SCHOOL: Eldorado (Albuquerque, N.M.).
COLLEGE: Purdue (degree in finance, 1986).
TRANSACTIONS/CAREER NOTES: Selected by Houston Oilers in first round (third pick overall) of 1986 NFL draft. ... Selected by Memphis Showboats in first round (fourth pick overall) of 1986 USFL draft. ... NFL rights traded by Oilers to Los Angeles Rams for G Kent Hill, DE William Fuller, first-round (WR Haywood Jeffires) and fifth-round (RB Spencer Tillman) picks in 1987 draft and first-round pick (traded to Rams) in 1988 draft (September 18, 1986). ... Signed by Rams (September 25, 1986). ... Granted roster exemption (September 25-30, 1986). ... Crossed picket line during players strike (October 14, 1987). ... Designated by Rams as transition player (February 25, 1993). ... Traded by Rams to New Orleans Saints for seventh-round pick (CB Herman O'Berry) in 1995 draft (March 18, 1994). ... Released by Saints (May 15, 1997). ... Signed by San Diego Chargers (June 3, 1997). ... On injured reserve with elbow injury (November 14, 1997-remainder of season). ... Granted unconditional free agency (February 13, 1998).
CHAMPIONSHIP GAME EXPERIENCE: Played in NFC championship game (1989 season).
HONORS: Named to play in Pro Bowl (1989 season); replaced by Randall Cunningham due to injury. ... Played in Pro Bowl (1990 season).
PRO STATISTICS: 1986—Fumbled twice. 1987—Fumbled twice and recovered one fumble. 1988—Fumbled seven times. 1989—Fumbled four times and recovered four fumbles for minus one yard. 1990—Fumbled four times. 1991—Led league with 12 fumbles and recovered one fumble for minus four yards. 1992—Fumbled five times. 1993—Fumbled seven times and recovered one fumble for minus one yard. 1994—Fumbled three times. 1995—Fumbled six times for minus six yards. 1996—Fumbled 10 times and recovered one fumble for minus nine yards. 1997—Fumbled twice and recovered one fumble for minus eight yards.

SINGLE GAME HIGHS (regular season): Attempts—55 (September 25, 1994, vs. San Francisco); completions—31 (December 10, 1995, vs. Atlanta); yards—454 (November 26, 1989, vs. New Orleans); and touchdown passes—5 (September 25, 1988, vs. New York Giants).
STATISTICAL PLATEAUS: 300-yard passing games: 1987 (1), 1988 (5), 1989 (4), 1990 (4), 1991 (4), 1992 (1), 1993 (1), 1994 (2), 1995 (2). Total: 24.
MISCELLANEOUS: Regular-season record as starting NFL quarterback: 64-89 (.418). ... Postseason record as starting NFL quarterback: 2-3 (.400). ... Holds Rams franchise all-time record for most yards passing (23,758).

			PASSING								RUSHING				TOTALS		
Year Team	G	GS	Att.	Cmp.	Pct.	Yds.	TD	Int.	Avg.	Rat.	Att.	Yds.	Avg.	TD	TD	2pt	Pts.
1986—L.A. Rams NFL...........	6	5	147	73	49.7	1018	8	8	6.93	67.8	16	46	2.9	1	1	...	6
1987—L.A. Rams NFL...........	11	11	302	162	53.6	2064	10	13	6.83	68.4	18	83	4.6	1	1	...	6
1988—L.A. Rams NFL...........	16	16	517	‡308	59.6	‡3964	*31	18	7.67	89.2	34	104	3.1	0	0	...	0
1989—L.A. Rams NFL...........	16	16	518	304	58.7	4310	*29	17	8.32	90.6	25	31	1.2	1	1	...	6
1990—L.A. Rams NFL...........	16	16	‡554	307	55.4	‡3989	23	17	7.20	79.3	20	31	1.6	1	1	...	6
1991—L.A. Rams NFL...........	16	16	‡490	‡277	56.5	3438	11	‡20	7.02	68.9	27	44	1.6	0	0	...	0
1992—L.A. Rams NFL...........	16	16	475	281	59.2	3323	22	‡18	7.00	80.2	32	133	4.2	0	0	...	0
1993—L.A. Rams NFL...........	10	9	274	135	49.3	1652	8	12	6.03	59.7	19	38	2.0	0	0	...	0
1994—New Orleans NFL	16	16	540	346	64.1	3855	22	18	7.14	84.9	15	35	2.3	0	0	0	0
1995—New Orleans NFL	16	16	567	345	60.8	3970	26	14	7.00	87.0	24	42	1.8	0	0	0	0
1996—New Orleans NFL	15	15	464	267	57.5	2797	12	16	6.03	69.4	22	3	0.1	0	0	0	0
1997—San Diego NFL...........	4	1	75	36	48.0	457	1	4	6.09	49.7	5	6	1.2	0	0	0	0
Pro totals (12 years)	158	153	4923	2841	57.7	34837	203	175	7.08	78.6	257	596	2.3	4	4	0	24

EVERITT, STEVE   C   EAGLES

PERSONAL: Born August 21, 1970, in Miami. ... 6-5/290. ... Full name: Steven Michael Everitt.
HIGH SCHOOL: Southridge (Miami).
COLLEGE: Michigan (degree in fine arts, 1993).
TRANSACTIONS/CAREER NOTES: Selected by Cleveland Browns in first round (14th pick overall) of 1993 NFL draft. ... Signed by Browns (July 15, 1993). ... Designated by Browns as transition player (February 15, 1994). ... Browns franchise moved to Baltimore and renamed Ravens for 1996 season (March 11, 1996). ... Free agency status changed by Ravens from transitional to unconditional (February 14, 1997). ... Signed by Philadelphia Eagles (March 6, 1997).
PLAYING EXPERIENCE: Cleveland NFL, 1993-1995; Baltimore NFL, 1996; Philadelphia NFL, 1997. ... Games/Games started: 1993 (16/16), 1994 (15/15), 1995 (15/14), 1996 (8/7), 1997 (16/16). Total: 70/68.
HONORS: Named center on THE SPORTING NEWS college All-America second team (1992).
PRO STATISTICS: 1993—Recovered two fumbles. 1995—Recovered one fumble. 1997—Recovered one fumble.

FANN, CHAD   TE   49ERS

PERSONAL: Born June 7, 1970, in Jacksonville. ... 6-3/250. ... Full name: Chad Fitzgerald Fann.
HIGH SCHOOL: Ribault (Jacksonville).
COLLEGE: Mississippi, then Florida A&M.
TRANSACTIONS/CAREER NOTES: Signed as non-drafted free agent by Phoenix Cardinals (April 28, 1993). ... Released by Cardinals (August 23, 1993). ... Re-signed by Cardinals to practice squad (October 24, 1993). ... Activated (November 4, 1993). ... Cardinals franchise renamed Arizona Cardinals for 1994 season. ... Granted free agency (February 16, 1996). ... Signed by San Francisco 49ers (June 11, 1996). ... Released by 49ers (August 21, 1996). ... Re-signed by 49ers (January 29, 1997). ... Granted unconditional free agency (February 13, 1998). ... Re-signed by 49ers (June 1, 1998).
CHAMPIONSHIP GAME EXPERIENCE: Played in NFC championship game (1997 season).
PRO STATISTICS: 1997—Returned one kickoff for no yards.
SINGLE GAME HIGHS (regular season): Receptions—6 (November 27, 1994, vs. Chicago); yards—50 (December 21, 1997, vs. Seattle); and touchdown receptions—0.

			RECEIVING				TOTALS			
Year Team	G	GS	No.	Yds.	Avg.	TD	TD	2pt.	Pts.	Fum.
1993—Phoenix NFL...	1	0	0	0	...	0	0	...	0	0
1994—Arizona NFL...	16	9	12	96	8.0	0	0	0	0	1
1995—Arizona NFL...	16	3	5	41	8.2	0	0	0	0	1
1996—					Did not play.					
1997—San Francisco NFL...	11	0	5	78	15.6	0	0	0	0	0
Pro totals (4 years)	44	12	22	215	9.8	0	0	0	0	2

FARMER, RAY   LB   EAGLES

PERSONAL: Born July 1, 1974, in White Plains, N.Y. ... 6-3/225.
HIGH SCHOOL: Glenn (Kernersville, N.C.).
COLLEGE: Duke.
TRANSACTIONS/CAREER NOTES: Selected by Philadelphia Eagles in fourth round (121st pick overall) of 1996 NFL draft. ... Signed by Eagles (June 20, 1996).
PRO STATISTICS: 1996—Fumbled once and recovered three fumbles for 10 yards. 1997—Recovered one fumble.
MISCELLANEOUS: Selected by Seattle Mariners in 26th round of free-agent draft (June 1, 1992); did not sign.

			INTERCEPTIONS				SACKS
Year Team	G	GS	No.	Yds.	Avg.	TD	No.
1996—Philadelphia NFL	16	11	1	0	0.0	0	1.0
1997—Philadelphia NFL	14	5	0	0	...	0	1.0
Pro totals (2 years)	30	16	1	0	0.0	0	2.0

FARQUHAR, JOHN TE SAINTS

PERSONAL: Born March 22, 1972, in Stanford, Calif. ... 6-6/278. ... Name pronounced far-QUAR.
HIGH SCHOOL: Menlo (Ca.).
COLLEGE: Duke.
TRANSACTIONS/CAREER NOTES: Signed as non-drafted free agent by Denver Broncos (April 28, 1995). ... Released by Broncos (May 25, 1995). ... Signed by Pittsburgh Steelers (February 29, 1996). ... Released by Steelers (August 24, 1996). ... Re-signed by Steelers to practice squad (August 27, 1996). ... Released by Steelers (October 23, 1996). ... Signed by Tampa Bay Buccaneers (October 23, 1996). ... Released by Buccaneers (November 12, 1996). ... Re-signed by Steelers to practice squad (November 18, 1996). ... Activated (November 29, 1996). ... Released by Steelers (August 23, 1997). ... Signed by New Orleans Saints (September 8, 1997).
SINGLE GAME HIGHS (regular season): Receptions—4 (October 12, 1997, vs. Atlanta); yards—82 (September 28, 1997, vs. New York Giants); and touchdown receptions—1 (December 14, 1997, vs. Arizona).

			RECEIVING					TOTALS		
Year Team	G	GS	No.	Yds.	Avg.	TD	TD	2pt.	Pts.	Fum.
1996—Tampa Bay NFL	1	0	0	0	...	0	0	0	0	0
—Pittsburgh NFL	4	0	0	0	...	0	0	0	0	0
1997—New Orleans NFL	12	8	17	253	14.9	1	1	0	6	0
Pro totals (2 years)	17	8	17	253	14.9	1	1	0	6	0

FARR, D'MARCO DT RAMS

PERSONAL: Born June 9, 1971, in San Pablo, Calif. ... 6-1/280. ... Full name: D'Marco Marcellus Farr. ... Cousin of Mel Farr Sr., running back, Detroit Lions (1967-1973); cousin of Mel Farr Jr., running back with Los Angeles Rams (1989) and Sacramento Surge of World League (1991); and cousin of Mike Farr, wide receiver with Detroit Lions (1990-1992).
HIGH SCHOOL: John F. Kennedy (Richmond, Calif.).
COLLEGE: Washington.
TRANSACTIONS/CAREER NOTES: Signed as non-drafted free agent by Los Angeles Rams (May 4, 1994). ... On injured reserve with dislocated left elbow (December 7, 1994-remainder of season). ... Rams franchise moved to St. Louis (April 12, 1995).
PRO STATISTICS: 1994—Returned one kickoff for 16 yards. 1995—Intercepted one pass for five yards. 1996—Intercepted one pass for five yards. 1997—Intercepted one pass for 22 yards and recovered two fumbles.

Year Team	G	GS	SACKS
1994—Los Angeles Rams NFL	10	3	1.0
1995—St. Louis NFL	16	16	11.5
1996—St. Louis NFL	16	16	4.5
1997—St. Louis NFL	16	16	3.0
Pro totals (4 years)	58	51	20.0

FARRIOR, JAMES LB JETS

PERSONAL: Born January 6, 1975, in Ettrick, Va. ... 6-2/240. ... Full name: James Alfred Farrior.
HIGH SCHOOL: Matoaca (Ettrick, Va.).
COLLEGE: Virginia.
TRANSACTIONS/CAREER NOTES: Selected by New York Jets in first round (eighth pick overall) of 1997 NFL draft. ... Signed by Jets (July 20, 1997).

Year Team	G	GS	SACKS
1997—New York Jets NFL	16	15	1.5

FAULK, MARSHALL RB COLTS

F

PERSONAL: Born February 26, 1973, in New Orleans. ... 5-10/211. ... Full name: Marshall William Faulk.
HIGH SCHOOL: George Washington Carver (New Orleans).
COLLEGE: San Diego State.
TRANSACTIONS/CAREER NOTES: Selected after junior season by Indianapolis Colts in first round (second pick overall) of 1994 NFL draft. ... Signed by Colts (July 24, 1994).
CHAMPIONSHIP GAME EXPERIENCE: Member of Colts for AFC championship game (1995 season); inactive.
HONORS: Named running back on THE SPORTING NEWS college All-America first team (1991-1993). ... Named NFL Rookie of the Year by THE SPORTING NEWS (1994). ... Played in Pro Bowl (1994 and 1995 seasons). ... Named Outstanding Player of Pro Bowl (1994 season).
PRO STATISTICS: 1994—Recovered one fumble. 1995—Recovered one fumble. 1997—Recovered one fumble.
SINGLE GAME HIGHS (regular season): Attempts—27 (December 4, 1994, vs. Seattle); yards—177 (October 1, 1995, vs. St. Louis); and rushing touchdowns—3 (October 1, 1995, vs. St. Louis).
STATISTICAL PLATEAUS: 100-yard rushing games: 1994 (4), 1995 (1), 1996 (1), 1997 (4). Total: 10. ... 100-yard receiving games: 1994 (1).

			RUSHING				RECEIVING				TOTALS			
Year Team	G	GS	Att.	Yds.	Avg.	TD	No.	Yds.	Avg.	TD	TD	2pt.	Pts.	Fum.
1994—Indianapolis NFL	16	16	314	1282	4.1	11	52	522	10.0	1	▲12	0	72	5
1995—Indianapolis NFL	16	16	289	1078	3.7	11	56	475	8.5	3	14	0	84	8
1996—Indianapolis NFL	13	13	198	587	3.0	7	56	428	7.6	0	7	0	42	2
1997—Indianapolis NFL	16	16	264	1054	4.0	7	47	471	10.0	1	8	0	48	5
Pro totals (4 years)	61	61	1065	4001	3.8	36	211	1896	9.0	5	41	0	246	20

FAURIA, CHRISTIAN TE SEAHAWKS

PERSONAL: Born September 22, 1971, in Harbor City, Calif. ... 6-4/245. ... Name pronounced FOUR-ee-a.
HIGH SCHOOL: Crespi Carmelite (Encino, Calif.).
COLLEGE: Colorado.

TRANSACTIONS/CAREER NOTES: Selected by Seattle Seahawks in second round (39th pick overall) of 1995 NFL draft. ... Signed by Seahawks (July 17, 1995). ... Granted free agency (February 13, 1998). ... Re-signed by Seahawks (April 20, 1998).
PRO STATISTICS: 1996—Returned one kickoff for eight yards.
SINGLE GAME HIGHS (regular season): Receptions—4 (September 8, 1996, vs. Denver); yards—53 (September 8, 1996, vs. Denver); and touchdown receptions—1 (September 8, 1996, vs. Denver).

				RECEIVING				TOTALS		
Year Team	G	GS	No.	Yds.	Avg.	TD	TD	2pt.	Pts.	Fum.
1995—Seattle NFL	14	9	17	181	10.6	1	1	0	6	0
1996—Seattle NFL	10	9	18	214	11.9	1	1	0	6	0
1997—Seattle NFL	16	3	10	110	11.0	0	0	0	0	0
Pro totals (3 years)	40	21	45	505	11.2	2	2	0	12	0

FAVRE, BRETT   QB   PACKERS

PERSONAL: Born October 10, 1969, in Pass Christian, Miss. ... 6-2/225. ... Full name: Brett Lorenzo Favre. ... Name pronounced FAHRV.
HIGH SCHOOL: Hancock North Central (Pass Christian, Miss.).
COLLEGE: Southern Mississippi.
TRANSACTIONS/CAREER NOTES: Selected by Atlanta Falcons in second round (33rd pick overall) of 1991 NFL draft. ... Signed by Falcons (July 18, 1991). ... Traded by Falcons to Green Bay Packers for first-round pick (OT Bob Whitfield) in 1992 draft (February 11, 1992). ... Granted free agency (February 17, 1994). ... Re-signed by Packers (July 14, 1994).
CHAMPIONSHIP GAME EXPERIENCE: Played in NFC championship game (1995-97 seasons). ... Member of Super Bowl championship team (1996 season). ... Played in Super Bowl XXXII (1997 season).
HONORS: Played in Pro Bowl (1992, 1993, 1995 and 1996 seasons). ... Named NFL Player of the Year by The Sporting News (1995 and 1996). ... Named quarterback on The Sporting News NFL All-Pro team (1995-97). ... Named to play in Pro Bowl (1997 season); replaced by Chris Chandler due to injury.
RECORDS: Shares NFL record for longest pass completion (to Robert Brooks)—99 yards, touchdown (September 11, 1995, at Chicago).
POST SEASON RECORDS: Holds Super Bowl record for longest pass completion (to Antonio Freeman)—81 yards (January 26, 1997, vs. New England).
PRO STATISTICS: 1992—Caught one pass for minus seven yards, fumbled 12 times and recovered three fumbles for minus 12 yards. 1993—Fumbled 12 times and recovered two fumbles for minus one yard. 1994—Fumbled seven times and recovered one fumble for minus two yards. 1995—Fumbled eight times. 1996—Fumbled 11 times and recovered five fumbles for minus 10 yards. 1997—Fumbled seven times and recovered one fumble for minus 10 yards.
SINGLE GAME HIGHS (regular season): Attempts—61 (October 14, 1996, vs. San Francisco); completions—36 (December 5, 1993, vs. Chicago); yards—402 (December 5, 1993, vs. Chicago); and touchdown passes—5 (September 21, 1997, vs. Minnesota).
STATISTICAL PLATEAUS: 300-yard passing games: 1993 (1), 1994 (4), 1995 (7), 1996 (2), 1997 (2). Total: 16.
MISCELLANEOUS: Regular-season record as starting NFL quarterback: 63-30 (.677). Postseason record as starting NFL quarterback: 9-4 (.692). ... Holds Green Bay Packers all-time record for most touchdown passes (182).

					PASSING						RUSHING				TOTALS		
Year Team	G	GS	Att.	Cmp.	Pct.	Yds.	TD	Int.	Avg.	Rat.	Att.	Yds.	Avg.	TD	TD	2pt.	Pts.
1991—Atlanta NFL	2	0	5	0	0.0	0	0	2	...	0.0	0	0	...	0	0	...	0
1992—Green Bay NFL	15	13	471	∞302	64.1	3227	18	13	6.85	85.3	47	198	4.2	1	1	...	6
1993—Green Bay NFL	16	16	‡522	‡318	60.9	3303	19	*24	6.33	72.2	58	216	3.7	1	1	...	6
1994—Green Bay NFL	16	16	582	363	62.4	3882	33	14	6.67	90.7	42	202	4.8	2	2	0	12
1995—Green Bay NFL	16	16	570	359	63.0	*4413	*38	13	‡7.74	‡99.5	39	181	4.6	3	3	0	18
1996—Green Bay NFL	16	16	‡543	‡325	59.9	‡3899	*39	13	7.18	95.8	49	136	2.8	2	2	0	12
1997—Green Bay NFL	16	16	513	‡304	59.3	‡3867	*35	16	7.54	92.6	58	187	3.2	1	1	0	6
Pro totals (7 years)	97	93	3206	1971	61.5	22591	182	95	7.05	89.3	293	1120	3.8	10	10	0	60

FEAGLES, JEFF   P   SEAHAWKS

PERSONAL: Born March 7, 1966, in Scottsdale, Ariz. ... 6-1/207. ... Full name: Jeffrey Allan Feagles.
HIGH SCHOOL: Gerard Catholic (Phoenix).
JUNIOR COLLEGE: Scottsdale (Ariz.) Community College.
COLLEGE: Miami, Fla. (degree in business administration, 1988).
TRANSACTIONS/CAREER NOTES: Signed as non-drafted free agent by New England Patriots (May 1, 1988). ... Claimed on waivers by Philadelphia Eagles (June 5, 1990). ... Granted unconditional free agency (February 1-April 1, 1992). ... Re-signed by Eagles for 1992 season. ... Granted unconditional free agency (February 17, 1994). ... Signed by Phoenix Cardinals (March 2, 1994). ... Cardinals franchise renamed Arizona Cardinals for 1994 season. ... Granted unconditional free agency (February 13, 1998). ... Signed by Seattle Seahawks (March 4, 1998).
HONORS: Played in Pro Bowl (1995 season).
PRO STATISTICS: 1988—Rushed once for no yards and recovered one fumble. 1989—Attempted two passes without a completion, fumbled once and recovered one fumble. 1990—Rushed twice for three yards and attempted one pass without a completion. 1991—Rushed three times for minus one yard, fumbled once and recovered one fumble. 1993—Rushed twice for six yards and recovered one fumble. 1994—Rushed twice for eight yards. 1995—Rushed twice for four yards and fumbled once for minus 22 yards. 1996—Rushed once for no yards and fumbled once for minus seven yards. 1997—Fumbled once and recovered one fumble.

				PUNTING				
Year Team	G	GS	No.	Yds.	Avg.	Net avg.	In. 20	Blk.
1988—New England NFL	16	0	▲91	3482	38.3	34.1	24	0
1989—New England NFL	16	0	63	2392	38.0	31.3	13	1
1990—Philadelphia NFL	16	0	72	3026	42.0	35.5	20	2
1991—Philadelphia NFL	16	0	*87	3640	41.8	34.0	*29	1
1992—Philadelphia NFL	16	0	‡82	‡3459	42.2	36.8	‡26	0
1993—Philadelphia NFL	16	0	83	3323	40.0	35.2	*31	0
1994—Arizona NFL	16	0	*98	‡3997	40.8	36.0	‡33	0
1995—Arizona NFL	16	0	72	3150	43.8	‡38.2	20	0
1996—Arizona NFL	16	0	76	3328	43.8	36.3	23	1
1997—Arizona NFL	16	0	91	4028	44.3	36.8	24	1
Pro totals (10 years)	160	0	815	33825	41.5	35.5	243	6

F

FENNER, DERRICK — RB

PERSONAL: Born April 6, 1967, in Washington, D.C. ... 6-3/230. ... Full name: Derrick Steven Fenner.
HIGH SCHOOL: Oxon Hill (Md.).
COLLEGE: North Carolina, then Gardner-Webb College, N.C. (did not play football).
TRANSACTIONS/CAREER NOTES: Selected after sophomore season by Seattle Seahawks in 10th round (268th pick overall) of 1989 NFL draft. ... Signed by Seahawks (July 22, 1989). ... Granted free agency (February 1, 1991). ... Re-signed by Seahawks (August 4, 1991). ... Granted unconditional free agency (February 1, 1992). ... Signed by Cincinnati Bengals (March 24, 1992). ... Granted free agency (March 1, 1993). ... Tendered offer sheet by New York Jets (April 17, 1993). ... Offer matched by Bengals (April 24, 1993). ... Granted unconditional free agency (February 17, 1995). ... Signed by Los Angeles Raiders (March 27, 1995). ... Raiders franchise moved to Oakland (July 21, 1995). ... Released by Raiders (February 14, 1997). ... Re-signed by Raiders (July 17, 1997). ... Granted unconditional free agency (February 13, 1998).
PRO STATISTICS: 1990—Recovered one fumble. 1992—Returned two kickoffs for 38 yards and recovered one fumble. 1993—Recovered two fumbles. 1994—Recovered one fumble. 1995—Recovered two fumbles.
SINGLE GAME HIGHS (regular season): Attempts—22 (September 23, 1990, vs. Denver); yards—144 (September 23, 1990, vs. Denver); and rushing touchdowns—3 (September 23, 1990, vs. Denver).
STATISTICAL PLATEAUS: 100-yard rushing games: 1990 (2).

			RUSHING				RECEIVING				TOTALS			
Year Team	G	GS	Att.	Yds.	Avg.	TD	No.	Yds.	Avg.	TD	TD	2pt.	Pts.	Fum.
1989—Seattle NFL	5	1	11	41	3.7	1	3	23	7.7	0	1	...	6	0
1990—Seattle NFL	16	15	215	859	4.0	†14	17	143	8.4	1	§15	...	90	3
1991—Seattle NFL	11	7	91	267	2.9	4	11	72	6.5	0	4	...	24	2
1992—Cincinnati NFL	16	1	112	500	4.5	7	7	41	5.9	1	8	...	48	1
1993—Cincinnati NFL	15	14	121	482	4.0	1	48	427	8.9	0	1	...	6	1
1994—Cincinnati NFL	16	13	141	468	3.3	1	36	276	7.7	1	2	0	12	6
1995—Oakland NFL	16	13	39	110	2.8	0	35	252	7.2	3	3	0	18	2
1996—Oakland NFL	16	11	67	245	3.7	4	31	252	8.1	4	8	0	48	0
1997—Oakland NFL	9	7	7	24	3.4	0	14	92	6.6	0	0	0	0	1
Pro totals (9 years)	120	82	804	2996	3.7	32	202	1578	7.8	10	42	0	252	16

FERGUSON, JASON — DT — JETS

PERSONAL: Born November 28, 1974, in Nettleton, Miss. ... 6-3/300. ... Full name: Jason O. Ferguson.
HIGH SCHOOL: Nettleton (Miss.).
JUNIOR COLLEGE: Itawamba Junior College (Miss.).
COLLEGE: Georgia.
TRANSACTIONS/CAREER NOTES: Selected by New York Jets in seventh round (229th pick overall) of 1997 NFL draft. ... Signed by Jets (April 30, 1997).
PRO STATISTICS: 1997—Returned one kickoff for one yard.

Year Team	G	GS	SACKS
1997—New York Jets NFL	13	1	3.5

FIELDS, MARK — LB — SAINTS

PERSONAL: Born November 9, 1972, in Los Angeles. ... 6-2/244. ... Full name: Mark Lee Fields.
HIGH SCHOOL: Washington (Cerritos, Calif.).
JUNIOR COLLEGE: Los Angeles Southwest College.
COLLEGE: Washington State.
TRANSACTIONS/CAREER NOTES: Selected by New Orleans Saints in first round (13th pick overall) of 1995 NFL draft. ... Signed by Saints (July 20, 1995).
PRO STATISTICS: 1996—Recovered one fumble for 20 yards. 1997—Recovered two fumbles for 28 yards and one touchdown.

Year Team	G	GS	SACKS
1995—New Orleans NFL	16	3	1.0
1996—New Orleans NFL	16	15	2.0
1997—New Orleans NFL	16	15	8.0
Pro totals (3 years)	48	33	11.0

F

FIGURES, DEON — CB — JAGUARS

PERSONAL: Born January 10, 1970, in Bellflower, Calif. ... 6-0/195. ... Full name: Deon Juniel Figures.
HIGH SCHOOL: Serra (Compton, Calif.).
COLLEGE: Colorado.
TRANSACTIONS/CAREER NOTES: Selected by Pittsburgh Steelers in first round (23rd pick overall) of 1993 NFL draft. ... Signed by Steelers (July 21, 1993). ... Granted unconditional free agency (February 14, 1997). ... Signed by Jacksonville Jaguars (March 5, 1997).
CHAMPIONSHIP GAME EXPERIENCE: Played in AFC championship game (1994 and 1995 seasons). ... Played in Super Bowl XXX (1995 season).
HONORS: Jim Thorpe Award winner (1992). ... Named defensive back on THE SPORTING NEWS college All-America first team (1992).
PRO STATISTICS: 1993—Returned five punts for 15 yards and recovered two fumbles for six yards. 1994—Credited with one sack and recovered one fumble. 1996—Recovered one fumble.
MISCELLANEOUS: Shares Jacksonville Jaguars all-time record for most interceptions (5).

			INTERCEPTIONS			
Year Team	G	GS	No.	Yds.	Avg.	TD
1993—Pittsburgh NFL	15	4	1	78	78.0	0
1994—Pittsburgh NFL	16	15	0	0	...	0
1995—Pittsburgh NFL	14	1	0	0	...	0
1996—Pittsburgh NFL	16	3	2	13	6.5	0
1997—Jacksonville NFL	16	12	5	48	9.6	0
Pro totals (5 years)	77	35	8	139	17.4	0

FINA, JOHN   OT   BILLS

PERSONAL: Born March 11, 1969, in Rochester, Minn. ... 6-4/285. ... Full name: John Joseph Fina. ... Name pronounced FEE-nuh.
HIGH SCHOOL: Salpointe Catholic (Tucson, Ariz.).
COLLEGE: Arizona.
TRANSACTIONS/CAREER NOTES: Selected by Buffalo Bills in first round (27th pick overall) of 1992 NFL draft. ... Signed by Bills (July 21, 1992). ... Designated by Bills as franchise player (February 16, 1996).
PLAYING EXPERIENCE: Buffalo NFL, 1992-1997. ... Games/Games started: 1992 (16/0), 1993 (16/16), 1994 (12/12), 1995 (16/16), 1996 (15/15), 1997 (16/16). Total: 91/75.
CHAMPIONSHIP GAME EXPERIENCE: Played in AFC championship game (1992 and 1993 seasons). ... Played in Super Bowl XXVII (1992 season) and Super Bowl XXVIII (1993 season).
PRO STATISTICS: 1992—Caught one pass for one yard and a touchdown. 1993—Rushed once for minus two yards. 1996—Recovered two fumbles for minus one yard. 1997—Recovered one fumble.

FINKES, MATT   DE   JETS

PERSONAL: Born February 12, 1975, in Piqua, Ohio. ... 6-3/260.
HIGH SCHOOL: Piqua (Ohio).
COLLEGE: Ohio State.
TRANSACTIONS/CAREER NOTES: Selected by Carolina Panthers in sixth round (189th pick overall) of 1997 NFL draft. ... Signed by Panthers (July 18, 1997). ... Claimed on waivers by New York Jets (August 25, 1997).
PLAYING EXPERIENCE: New York Jets NFL, 1997. ... Games: 8/0.

FISK, JASON   DT   VIKINGS

PERSONAL: Born September 4, 1972, in Davis, Calif. ... 6-3/295.
HIGH SCHOOL: Davis (Calif.).
COLLEGE: Stanford.
TRANSACTIONS/CAREER NOTES: Selected by Minnesota Vikings in seventh round (243rd pick overall) of 1995 NFL draft. ... Signed by Vikings (July 24, 1995).
PRO STATISTICS: 1996—Intercepted one pass for no yards and recovered one fumble. 1997—Intercepted one pass for one yard and recovered one fumble.

Year Team	G	GS	SACKS
1995—Minnesota NFL	8	0	0.0
1996—Minnesota NFL	16	6	1.0
1997—Minnesota NFL	16	10	3.0
Pro totals (3 years)	40	16	4.0

FLANAGAN, MIKE   C   PACKERS

PERSONAL: Born November 10, 1973, in Washington, D.C. ... 6-5/290. ... Full name: Michael Christopher Flanagan.
HIGH SCHOOL: Rio Americano (Sacramento).
COLLEGE: UCLA.
TRANSACTIONS/CAREER NOTES: Selected by Green Bay Packers in third round (90th pick overall) of 1996 NFL draft. ... Signed by Packers (July 17, 1996). ... On injured reserve with leg injury (August 19, 1996-entire season). ... On physically unable to perform list with ankle injury (August 19, 1997-entire season).

F

FLANIGAN, JIM   DT   BEARS

PERSONAL: Born August 27, 1971, in Green Bay. ... 6-2/286. ... Full name: James Michael Flanigan.
HIGH SCHOOL: Southern Door (Brussels, Wis.).
COLLEGE: Notre Dame.
TRANSACTIONS/CAREER NOTES: Selected by Chicago Bears in third round (74th pick overall) of 1994 NFL draft. ... Signed by Bears (July 14, 1994). ... Granted free agency (February 14, 1997). ... Re-signed by Bears (June 1, 1997). ... Granted unconditional free agency (February 13, 1998). ... Re-signed by Bears (February 13, 1998).
PRO STATISTICS: 1994—Returned two kickoffs for 26 yards. 1995—Rushed once for no yards, caught two passes for six yards and two touchdowns and recovered one fumble. 1996—Caught one pass for one yard and a touchdown. 1997—Recovered three fumbles for three yards and credited with one two-point conversion.

Year Team	G	GS	SACKS
1994—Chicago NFL	14	0	0.0
1995—Chicago NFL	16	12	11.0
1996—Chicago NFL	14	14	5.0
1997—Chicago NFL	16	16	6.0
Pro totals (4 years)	60	42	22.0

FLANNERY, JOHN   G/C   RAMS

PERSONAL: Born January 13, 1969, in Pottsville, Pa. ... 6-3/304. ... Full name: John Joseph Flannery.
HIGH SCHOOL: Pottsville (Pa.) Area.
COLLEGE: Syracuse (degree in political science, 1991).

TRANSACTIONS/CAREER NOTES: Selected by Houston Oilers in second round (44th pick overall) of 1991 NFL draft. ... Signed by Oilers (July 21, 1991). ... On injured reserve with knee injury (August 23, 1993-entire season). ... Released by Oilers (August 8, 1995). ... Signed by Dallas Cowboys (October 3, 1996). ... Granted unconditional free agency (February 13, 1998). ... Signed by St. Louis Rams (April 1, 1998).
PLAYING EXPERIENCE: Houston NFL, 1991, 1992 and 1994; Dallas NFL, 1996 and 1997. ... Games/Games started: 1991 (16/9), 1992 (15/2), 1994 (16/16), 1996 (1/0), 1997 (16/4). Total: 64/31.
HONORS: Named center on THE SPORTING NEWS college All-America first team (1990).
PRO STATISTICS: 1991—Returned one kickoff for no yards and recovered one fumble. 1992—Returned one kickoff for 12 yards and recovered two fumbles. 1994—Recovered two fumbles.

FLETCHER, TERRELL — RB — CHARGERS

PERSONAL: Born September 14, 1973, in St. Louis. ... 5-8/196. ... Full name: Terrell Antoine Fletcher.
HIGH SCHOOL: Hazelwood East (St. Louis).
COLLEGE: Wisconsin.
TRANSACTIONS/CAREER NOTES: Selected by San Diego Chargers in second round (51st pick overall) of 1995 NFL draft. ... Signed by Chargers (July 12, 1995). ... On injured reserve with knee injury (December 17, 1997-remainder of season). ... Granted free agency (February 13, 1998).
PRO STATISTICS: 1995—Fumbled twice and recovered two fumbles. 1996—Fumbled once and recovered one fumble. 1997—Fumbled four times.
SINGLE GAME HIGHS (regular season): Attempts—17 (December 14, 1996, vs. Chicago); yards—57 (October 22, 1995, vs. Seattle); and rushing touchdowns—1 (December 3, 1995, vs. Cleveland).

			RUSHING				RECEIVING				PUNT RETURNS				KICKOFF RETURNS				TOTALS		
Year Team	G	GS	Att.	Yds.	Avg.	TD	No.	Yds.	Avg.	TD	No.	Yds.	Avg.	TD	No.	Yds.	Avg.	TD	TD	2pt.	Pts.
1995—San Diego NFL....	16	0	26	140	5.4	1	3	26	8.7	0	3	12	4.0	0	4	65	16.3	0	1	0	6
1996—San Diego NFL....	16	0	77	282	3.7	0	61	476	7.8	2	0	0	...	0	0	0	...	0	2	0	12
1997—San Diego NFL....	13	1	51	161	3.2	0	39	292	7.5	0	0	0	...	0	0	0	...	0	0	0	0
Pro totals (3 years)........	45	1	154	583	3.8	1	103	794	7.7	2	3	12	4.0	0	4	65	16.3	0	3	0	18

FLOWERS, LETHON — CB — STEELERS

PERSONAL: Born January 14, 1973, in Columbia, S.C. ... 6-0/213. ... Full name: Lethon Flowers III. ... Name pronounced LEE-thon.
HIGH SCHOOL: Spring Valley (Columbia, S.C.).
COLLEGE: Georgia Tech.
TRANSACTIONS/CAREER NOTES: Selected by Pittsburgh Steelers in fifth round (151st pick overall) of 1995 NFL draft. ... Signed by Steelers (July 18, 1995). ... Granted free agency (February 13, 1998). ... Re-signed by Steelers (June 9, 1998).
PLAYING EXPERIENCE: Pittsburgh NFL, 1995-1997. ... Games/Games started: 1995 (10/0), 1996 (16/0), 1997 (10/0). Total: 36/0.
CHAMPIONSHIP GAME EXPERIENCE: Played in AFC championship game (1995 and 1997 seasons). ... Played in Super Bowl XXX (1995 season).
PRO STATISTICS: 1997—Recovered one fumble.

FLOYD, MALCOLM — WR

PERSONAL: Born December 29, 1972, in San Francisco. ... 6-0/194. ... Formerly known as Malcolm Seabron.
HIGH SCHOOL: C.K. McClatchy (Sacramento).
COLLEGE: Fresno State.
TRANSACTIONS/CAREER NOTES: Selected by Houston Oilers in third round (101st pick overall) of 1994 NFL draft. ... Signed by Oilers (June 17, 1994). ... Oilers franchise moved to Tennessee for 1997 season. ... Released by Oilers (September 5, 1997). ... Signed by St. Louis Rams (September 30, 1997). ... On injured reserve with heel injury (December 13, 1997-remainder of season). ... Granted unconditional free agency (February 13, 1998).
PRO STATISTICS: 1997—Returned four punts for 15 yards.

			RECEIVING				TOTALS			
Year Team	G	GS	No.	Yds.	Avg.	TD	TD	2pt.	Pts.	Fum.
1994—Houston NFL	13	0	0	0	...	0	0	0	0	0
1995—Houston NFL	15	1	12	167	13.9	1	1	0	6	0
1996—Houston NFL	16	0	10	145	14.5	1	1	0	6	0
1997—Tennessee NFL	1	0	0	0	...	0	0	0	0	0
—St. Louis NFL................................	4	0	4	39	9.8	0	0	0	0	0
Pro totals (4 years)	49	1	26	351	13.5	2	2	0	12	0

FLOYD, WILLIAM — FB — PANTHERS

PERSONAL: Born February 17, 1972, in St. Petersburg, Fla. ... 6-1/230. ... Full name: William Ali Floyd.
HIGH SCHOOL: Lakewood Senior (St. Petersburg, Fla.).
COLLEGE: Florida State.
TRANSACTIONS/CAREER NOTES: Selected after junior season by San Francisco 49ers in first round (28th pick overall) of 1994 NFL draft. ... Signed by 49ers (July 28, 1994). ... On injured reserve with knee injury (October 31, 1995-remainder of season). ... On physically unable to perform list (August 20-October 12, 1996). ... Granted unconditional free agency (February 13, 1998). ... Signed by Carolina Panthers (March 6, 1998).
CHAMPIONSHIP GAME EXPERIENCE: Played in NFC championship game (1994 and 1997 seasons). ... Member of Super Bowl championship team (1994 season).
POST SEASON RECORDS: Holds postseason single-game record for most touchdowns by rookie—3 (January 7, 1995, vs Chicago).
PRO STATISTICS: 1996—Recovered one fumble.
SINGLE GAME HIGHS (regular season): Attempts—12 (October 1, 1995, vs. New York Giants); yards—61 (December 4, 1994, vs. Atlanta); and rushing touchdowns—2 (December 17, 1994, vs. Denver).

Year Team	G	GS	RUSHING				RECEIVING				TOTALS			
			Att.	Yds.	Avg.	TD	No.	Yds.	Avg.	TD	TD	2pt.	Pts.	Fum.
1994—San Francisco NFL	16	11	87	305	3.5	6	19	145	7.6	0	6	0	36	0
1995—San Francisco NFL	8	8	64	237	3.7	2	47	348	7.4	1	3	0	18	1
1996—San Francisco NFL	9	8	47	186	4.0	2	26	197	7.6	1	3	0	18	4
1997—San Francisco NFL	15	15	78	231	3.0	3	37	321	8.7	1	4	0	24	2
Pro totals (4 years)	48	42	276	959	3.5	13	129	1011	7.8	3	16	0	96	7

FLUTIE, DOUG   QB   BILLS

PERSONAL: Born October 23, 1962, in Manchester, Md. ... 5-10/175. ... Full name: Douglas Richard Flutie.
HIGH SCHOOL: Natick (Mass.).
COLLEGE: Boston College.
TRANSACTIONS/CAREER NOTES: Selected by New Jersey Generals in 1985 USFL territorial draft. ... Signed by Generals (February 4, 1985). ... Granted roster exemption (February 4-14, 1985). ... Activated (February 15, 1985). ... On developmental squad for three games with Generals (1985). ... Selected by Los Angeles Rams in 11th round (285th pick overall) of 1985 NFL draft. ... On developmental squad (June 10, 1995-remainder of season). ... Rights traded by Rams with fourth-round pick in 1987 draft to Chicago Bears for third- and sixth-round picks in 1987 draft (October 14, 1986). ... Signed by Bears (October 21, 1986). ... Granted roster exemption (October 21-November 3, 1986). ... Activated (November 4, 1986). ... Crossed picket line during players strike (October 13, 1987). ... Traded by Bears to New England Patriots for eighth-round pick in 1988 draft (October 13, 1987). ... Released by Patriots after 1989 season. ... Signed by B.C. Lions of CFL (June 1990). ... Granted free agency (February 1992). ... Signed by Calgary Stampeders of CFL (March 1992). ... Rights assigned to Toronto Argonauts of CFL (March 15, 1996). ... Signed by Buffalo Bills (January 16, 1998).
CHAMPIONSHIP GAME EXPERIENCE: Member of CFL championship team (1992 and 1996). ... Named Most Valuable Player of Grey Cup, CFL championship game (1992 and 1996). ... Played in Grey Cup (1993).
HONORS: Heisman Trophy winner (1984). ... Named College Football Player of the Year by THE SPORTING NEWS (1984). ... Named quarterback on THE SPORTING NEWS college All-America first team (1984).
PRO STATISTICS: USFL: 1985—Recovered two fumbles. NFL: 1986—Recovered two fumbles and fumbled three times for minus four yards. 1987—Recovered one fumble. 1988—Fumbled three times. 1989—Fumbled once. CFL: 1990—Fumbled six times. 1991—Fumbled seven times. 1992—Fumbled five times. 1993—Caught one pass for 11 yards and fumbled five times. 1994—Fumbled eight times. 1995—Fumbled twice. 1996—Fumbled once. 1997—Fumbled three times.
MISCELLANEOUS: Regular-season record as starting NFL quarterback: (9-5). ... Postseason record as starting NFL quarterback: 0-1.

Year Team	G	GS	PASSING								RUSHING				TOTALS		
			Att.	Cmp.	Pct.	Yds.	TD	Int.	Avg.	Rat.	Att.	Yds.	Avg.	TD	TD	2pt.	Pts.
1985—New Jersey USFL	15	...	281	134	47.7	2109	13	14	7.51	67.8	65	465	7.2	6	6	...	36
1986—Chicago NFL	4	1	46	23	50.0	361	3	2	7.85	80.1	9	36	4.0	1	1	...	6
1987—Chicago NFL						Did not play.											
—New England NFL	1	1	25	15	60.0	199	1	0	7.96	98.6	6	43	7.2	0	0	...	0
1988—New England NFL	11	9	179	92	51.4	1150	8	10	6.42	63.3	38	179	4.7	1	1	...	6
1989—New England NFL	5	3	91	36	39.6	493	2	4	5.42	46.6	16	87	5.4	0	0	...	0
1990—British Columbia CFL	16	...	392	207	52.8	2960	16	19	7.55	71.0	79	662	8.4	3	3	0	18
1991—British Columbia CFL	18	...	730	466	63.8	6619	38	24	9.07	96.7	120	610	5.1	14	14	1	86
1992—Calgary CFL	18	...	688	396	57.6	5945	32	30	8.64	83.4	96	669	7.0	11	11	0	66
1993—Calgary CFL	18	...	703	416	59.2	6092	44	17	8.67	98.3	74	373	5.0	11	11	0	66
1994—Calgary CFL	18	...	659	403	61.2	5726	48	19	8.69	101.5	96	760	7.9	8	8	0	48
1995—Calgary CFL	12	...	332	223	67.2	2788	16	5	8.40	102.8	46	288	6.3	5	5	0	30
1996—Toronto CFL	18	...	677	434	64.1	5720	29	17	8.45	94.5	101	756	7.5	9	9	0	54
1997—Toronto CFL	18	...	673	430	63.9	5505	47	24	8.18	97.8	92	542	5.9	9	9	0	54
USFL totals (1 year)	15	...	281	134	47.7	2109	13	14	7.51	67.8	65	465	7.2	6	6	...	36
CFL totals (8 years)	136	...	4854	2975	61.3	41355	270	155	8.52	93.9	704	4660	6.6	70	70	1	422
NFL totals (4 years)	21	14	341	166	48.7	2203	14	16	6.46	63.7	69	345	5.0	2	2	...	12
Pro totals (13 years)	173	...	5476	3275	59.8	45667	297	185	8.34	90.7	838	5470	6.5	78	78	...	470

F

FOGLE, DESHAWN   LB   EAGLES

PERSONAL: Born April 1, 1975, in Brooklyn, N.Y. ... 6-1/220.
HIGH SCHOOL: Chapman (Kan.).
COLLEGE: Kansas State.
TRANSACTIONS/CAREER NOTES: Signed as non-drafted free agent by Philadelphia Eagles (April 22, 1997). ... Released by Eagles (August 24, 1997). ... Re-signed by Eagles to practice squad (August 27, 1997). ... Activated (August 29, 1997). ... Released by Eagles (September 2, 1997). ... Re-signed by Eagles to practice squad (September 4, 1997). ... Activated (November 4, 1997). ... Released by Eagles (December 2, 1997). ... Re-signed by Eagles to practice squad (December 3, 1997). ... Activated (December 10, 1997).
PLAYING EXPERIENCE: Philadelphia NFL, 1997. ... Games/Games started: 5/0.

FOLAU, SPENCER   OT   RAVENS

PERSONAL: Born April 5, 1973, in Nuk 'Alofa, Tonga, Samoan Islands. ... 6-5/300.
HIGH SCHOOL: Sequoia (Redwood City, Calif.).
COLLEGE: Idaho.
TRANSACTIONS/CAREER NOTES: Signed as non-drafted free agent by Baltimore Ravens for 1996 season. ... Released by Ravens (August 25, 1996). ... Re-signed by Ravens to practice squad (October 29, 1996).
PLAYING EXPERIENCE: Baltimore NFL, 1997. ... Games/Games started: 10/0.

FOLEY, GLENN   QB   JETS

PERSONAL: Born October 10, 1970, in Cherry Hill, N.J. ... 6-2/210. ... Full name: Glenn Edward Foley.
HIGH SCHOOL: Cherry Hill (N.J.) East.
COLLEGE: Boston College.
TRANSACTIONS/CAREER NOTES: Selected by New York Jets in seventh round (208th pick overall) of 1994 NFL draft. ... Signed by Jets (June 21, 1994). ... On injured reserve with shoulder injury (November 8, 1995-remainder of season). ... On physically unable to perform list with knee injury (July 18-21, 1997).
PRO STATISTICS: 1995—Caught one pass for minus nine yards. 1996—Fumbled once for minus four yards. 1997—Fumbled once.
SINGLE GAME HIGHS (regular season): Attempts—48 (November 9, 1997, vs. Miami); completions—25 (November 9, 1997, vs. Miami; yards—322 (November 9, 1997, vs. Miami); and touchdown passes—1 (November 16, 1997, vs. Chicago).
STATISTICAL PLATEAUS: 300-yard passing games: 1997 (1).
MISCELLANEOUS: Regular-season record as starting NFL quarterback: 1-4 (.200).

			PASSING								RUSHING				TOTALS		
Year Team	G	GS	Att.	Cmp.	Pct.	Yds.	TD	Int.	Avg.	Rat.	Att.	Yds.	Avg.	TD	TD	2pt.	Pts.
1994—New York Jets NFL......	1	0	8	5	62.5	45	0	1	5.63	38.0	0	0	...	0	0	0	0
1995—New York Jets NFL......	1	0	29	16	55.2	128	0	1	4.41	52.1	1	9	9.0	0	0	0	0
1996—New York Jets NFL......	5	3	110	54	49.1	559	3	7	5.08	46.7	7	40	5.7	0	0	0	0
1997—New York Jets NFL......	6	2	97	56	57.7	705	3	1	7.27	86.5	3	-5	-1.7	0	0	0	0
Pro totals (4 years)...............	13	5	244	131	53.7	1437	6	10	5.89	62.5	11	44	4.0	0	0	0	0

FOLSTON, JAMES   DE   RAIDERS

PERSONAL: Born August 14, 1971, in Cocoa, Fla. ... 6-3/235. ... Full name: James Edward Folston.
HIGH SCHOOL: Cocoa (Fla.).
COLLEGE: Northeast Louisiana.
TRANSACTIONS/CAREER NOTES: Selected by Los Angeles Raiders in second round (52nd pick overall) of 1994 NFL draft. ... Signed by Raiders (July 13, 1994). ... Raiders franchise moved to Oakland (July 21, 1995). ... Granted free agency (February 14, 1997).
PLAYING EXPERIENCE: Los Angeles Raiders NFL, 1994; Oakland NFL, 1995-1997. ... Games/Games started: 1994 (7/0), 1995 (15/0), 1996 (12/0), 1997 (16/7). Total: 50/7.
PRO STATISTICS: 1997—Recovered one fumble.

FONTENOT, AL   DE   COLTS

PERSONAL: Born September 17, 1970, in Houston. ... 6-4/287. ... Full name: Albert Paul Fontenot. ... Name pronounced FAHN-tuh-no.
HIGH SCHOOL: Jack Yates (Houston).
JUNIOR COLLEGE: Navarro College (Texas).
COLLEGE: Baylor.
TRANSACTIONS/CAREER NOTES: Selected by Chicago Bears in fourth round (112th pick overall) of 1993 NFL draft. ... Signed by Bears (July 16, 1993). ... Granted free agency (February 16, 1996). ... Re-signed by Bears (April 18, 1996). ... Granted unconditional free agency (February 14, 1997). ... Signed by Indianapolis Colts (April 3, 1997).
PRO STATISTICS: 1993—Returned one kickoff for eight yards. 1995—Credited with one safety and recovered one fumble. 1997—Recovered three fumbles for 35 yards and one touchdown.

Year Team	G	GS	SACKS
1993—Chicago NFL	16	0	1.0
1994—Chicago NFL	16	8	4.0
1995—Chicago NFL	13	5	2.5
1996—Chicago NFL	16	15	4.5
1997—Indianapolis NFL	16	16	4.5
Pro totals (5 years)...............	77	44	16.5

FONTENOT, JERRY   C   SAINTS

PERSONAL: Born November 21, 1966, in Lafayette, La. ... 6-3/300. ... Full name: Jerry Paul Fontenot. ... Name pronounced FAHN-tuh-no.
HIGH SCHOOL: Lafayette (La.).
COLLEGE: Texas A&M.
TRANSACTIONS/CAREER NOTES: Selected by Chicago Bears in third round (65th pick overall) of 1989 NFL draft. ... Signed by Bears (July 27, 1989). ... Granted free agency (March 1, 1993). ... Re-signed by Bears (June 16, 1993). ... Granted free agency (February 16, 1996). ... Re-signed by Bears (July 10, 1996). ... Granted unconditional free agency (February 14, 1997). ... Signed by New Orleans Saints (May 28, 1997).
PLAYING EXPERIENCE: Chicago NFL, 1989-1996; New Orleans NFL, 1997. ... Games/Games started: 1989 (16/0), 1990 (16/2), 1991 (16/7), 1992 (16/16), 1993 (16/16), 1994 (16/16), 1995 (16/16), 1996 (16/16), 1997 (16/16). Total: 144/105.
PRO STATISTICS: 1989—Recovered one fumble. 1990—Fumbled once. 1992—Fumbled once for minus two yards. 1993—Recovered one fumble. 1997—Fumbled three times.

FOOTMAN, DAN   DE   COLTS

PERSONAL: Born January 13, 1969, in Tampa. ... 6-5/290. ... Full name: Dan Ellis Footman.
HIGH SCHOOL: Hillsborough (Tampa).
COLLEGE: Florida State.
TRANSACTIONS/CAREER NOTES: Selected by Cleveland Browns in second round (42nd pick overall) of 1993 NFL draft. ... Signed by Browns (July 15, 1993). ... Granted free agency (February 16, 1996). ... Browns franchise moved to Baltimore and renamed Ravens for 1996 season (March 11, 1996). ... Signed by Ravens (April 3, 1996). ... Released by Ravens (June 2, 1997). ... Signed by Indianapolis Colts (June 20, 1997).
PRO STATISTICS: 1995—Recovered one fumble. 1997—Recovered two fumbles for 14 yards.

F

Year Team	G	GS	SACKS
1993—Cleveland NFL	8	0	1.0
1994—Cleveland NFL	16	2	2.5
1995—Cleveland NFL	16	16	5.0
1996—Baltimore NFL	10	8	0.5
1997—Indianapolis NFL	16	10	10.5
Pro totals (5 years)	66	36	19.5

FORBES, MARLON   S   BEARS

PERSONAL: Born December 25, 1971, in Long Island, N.Y. ... 6-1/215.
HIGH SCHOOL: Central Islip (Long Island, N.Y.).
COLLEGE: Penn State.
TRANSACTIONS/CAREER NOTES: Signed as non-drafted free agent by Chicago Bears (December 1, 1995). ... Re-signed by Bears (February 12, 1996). ... Released by Bears (August 27, 1996). ... Released by Bears (September 3, 1996). ... Re-signed by Bears to practice squad (September 4, 1996). ... Activated (September 9, 1996).
PLAYING EXPERIENCE: Chicago NFL, 1996 and 1997. ... Games/Games started: 1996 (15/0), 1997 (16/1). Total: 31/1.
PRO STATISTICS: 1996—Recovered one fumble.

FORD, COLE   K   RAIDERS

PERSONAL: Born December 31, 1972, in Tucson, Ariz. ... 6-2/195.
HIGH SCHOOL: Sabino (Tucson, Ariz.).
COLLEGE: Southern California.
TRANSACTIONS/CAREER NOTES: Selected by Pittsburgh Steelers in seventh round (247th pick overall) of 1995 NFL draft. ... Signed by Steelers (July 17, 1995). ... Released by Steelers (August 15, 1995). ... Signed by Oakland Raiders to practice squad (August 31, 1995). ... Activated (September 2, 1995). ... Released by Raiders (September 5, 1995). ... Re-signed by Raiders to practice squad (September 6, 1995). ... Activated (September 9, 1995). ... Granted free agency (February 13, 1998). ... Re-signed by Raiders (April 28, 1998).

Year Team	G	GS	KICKING						
			XPM	XPA	FGM	FGA	Lg.	50+	Pts.
1995—Oakland NFL	5	0	17	18	8	9	46	0-1	41
1996—Oakland NFL	16	0	36	36	24	31	47	0-1	108
1997—Oakland NFL	16	0	33	35	13	22	53	1-1	72
Pro totals (3 years)	37	0	86	89	45	62	53	1-3	221

FORD, HENRY   DE   OILERS

PERSONAL: Born October 30, 1971, in Fort Worth, Texas. ... 6-3/292.
HIGH SCHOOL: Trimble Technical (Fort Worth, Texas).
COLLEGE: Arkansas.
TRANSACTIONS/CAREER NOTES: Selected by Houston Oilers in first round (26th pick overall) of 1994 NFL draft. ... Signed by Oilers (June 16, 1994). ... Oilers franchise moved to Tennessee for 1997 season. ... Granted unconditional free agency (February 13, 1998). ... Re-signed by Oilers (March 2, 1998).
PRO STATISTICS: 1997—Recovered two fumbles for 13 yards.

Year Team	G	GS	SACKS
1994—Houston NFL	11	0	0.0
1995—Houston NFL	16	16	4.5
1996—Houston NFL	15	14	1.0
1997—Tennessee NFL	16	16	5.0
Pro totals (4 years)	58	46	10.5

F

FORDHAM, TODD   G/OT   JAGUARS

PERSONAL: Born October 9, 1973, in Atlanta. ... 6-5/303. ... Full name: Lindsey Todd Fordham. ... Nickname: Earl.
HIGH SCHOOL: Tift County (Tifton, Ga.).
COLLEGE: Florida State.
TRANSACTIONS/CAREER NOTES: Signed as non-drafted free agent by Jacksonville Jaguars (April 21, 1997). ... Released by Jaguars (August 24, 1997). ... Re-signed by Jaguars to practice squad (August 25, 1997). ... Activated (September 23, 1997).
PLAYING EXPERIENCE: Jacksonville NFL, 1997. ... Games/Games started: 1/0.

FORTIN, ROMAN   C/G   CHARGERS

PERSONAL: Born February 26, 1967, in Columbus, Ohio. ... 6-5/297. ... Full name: Roman Brian Fortin.
HIGH SCHOOL: Ventura (Calif.).
COLLEGE: Oregon, then San Diego State.
TRANSACTIONS/CAREER NOTES: Selected by Detroit Lions in eighth round (203rd pick overall) of 1990 NFL draft. ... On injured reserve (September 5, 1990-entire season). ... Granted unconditional free agency (February 1, 1992). ... Signed by Atlanta Falcons (March 31, 1992). ... Granted unconditional free agency (February 17, 1994). ... Re-signed by Falcons (February 24, 1994). ... Granted unconditional free agency (February 16, 1996). ... Re-signed by Falcons (February 20, 1996). ... Released by Falcons (February 13, 1998). ... Signed by San Diego Chargers (March 17, 1998).
PLAYING EXPERIENCE: Detroit NFL, 1991; Atlanta NFL, 1992-1997. ... Games/Games started: 1991 (16/2), 1992 (16/1), 1993 (16/1), 1994 (16/16), 1995 (16/16), 1996 (16/16), 1997 (3/3). Total: 99/55.
CHAMPIONSHIP GAME EXPERIENCE: Played in NFC championship game (1991 season).
PRO STATISTICS: 1991—Caught one pass for four yards. 1992—Returned one kickoff for five yards and recovered one fumble. 1995—Fumbled twice for minus six yards. 1996—Recovered two fumbles.

FOUNTAINE, JAMAL   DE   FALCONS

PERSONAL: Born January 29, 1971, in San Francisco. ... 6-3/240.
HIGH SCHOOL: Abraham Lincoln (San Francisco).
COLLEGE: Washington.
TRANSACTIONS/CAREER NOTES: Signed as non-drafted free agent by San Francisco 49ers (May 4, 1994). ... Released by 49ers (August 23, 1994). ... Re-signed by 49ers (August 31, 1994). ... Claimed on waivers by Carolina Panthers (November 15, 1995). ... Signed by Carolina Panthers (April 12, 1996). ... On injured reserve with knee injury (August 20-October 30, 1996). ... Released by Panthers (October 30, 1996). ... Signed by Atlanta Falcons (January 8, 1997). ... Released by Falcons (August 18, 1997). ... Re-signed by Falcons (September 24, 1997). ... Granted free agency (February 13, 1998).
PLAYING EXPERIENCE: San Francisco NFL, 1995; Atlanta NFL, 1997. ... Games/Games started: 1995 (7/0), 1997 (3/0). Total: 10/0.
PRO STATISTICS: 1995—Credited with one sack.

FOX, MIKE   DE   PANTHERS

PERSONAL: Born August 5, 1967, in Akron, Ohio. ... 6-8/295. ... Full name: Michael James Fox.
HIGH SCHOOL: Akron (Ohio) North.
COLLEGE: West Virginia.
TRANSACTIONS/CAREER NOTES: Selected by New York Giants in second round (51st pick overall) of 1990 NFL draft. ... Signed by Giants (July 31, 1990). ... Granted free agency (March 1, 1993). ... Re-signed by Giants (August 13, 1993). ... Granted unconditional free agency (February 17, 1995). ... Signed by Carolina Panthers (February 20, 1995).
CHAMPIONSHIP GAME EXPERIENCE: Played in NFC championship game (1990 and 1996 seasons). ... Member of Super Bowl championship team (1990 season).
PRO STATISTICS: 1993—Recovered one fumble for two yards.

Year Team	G	GS	SACKS
1990—New York Giants NFL	16	0	1.5
1991—New York Giants NFL	15	5	0.0
1992—New York Giants NFL	16	4	2.5
1993—New York Giants NFL	16	16	4.5
1994—New York Giants NFL	16	16	1.0
1995—Carolina NFL	16	16	4.5
1996—Carolina NFL	11	11	2.0
1997—Carolina NFL	11	9	0.0
Pro totals (8 years)	117	77	16.0

FRANCIS, JAMES   LB   BENGALS

PERSONAL: Born August 4, 1968, in Houston. ... 6-5/257. ... Brother of Ron Francis, cornerback with Dallas Cowboys (1987-1990).
HIGH SCHOOL: La Marque (Texas).
COLLEGE: Baylor.
TRANSACTIONS/CAREER NOTES: Selected by Cincinnati Bengals in first round (12th pick overall) of 1990 NFL draft. ... Signed by Bengals (July 19, 1990). ... On injured reserve with knee injury (December 26, 1992-remainder of season). ... Designated by Bengals as transition player (February 25, 1993). ... On injured reserve with broken leg (November 22, 1995-remainder of season).
HONORS: Named special-teams player on THE SPORTING NEWS college All-America first team (1989).
PRO STATISTICS: 1990—Credited with one safety. 1991—Recovered one fumble. 1992—Recovered two fumbles for three yards. 1993—Recovered one fumble. 1996—Recovered three fumbles. 1997—Recovered one fumble.

Year Team	G	GS	INTERCEPTIONS No.	INTERCEPTIONS Yds.	INTERCEPTIONS Avg.	INTERCEPTIONS TD	SACKS No.
1990—Cincinnati NFL	16	16	1	17	17.0	▲1	8.0
1991—Cincinnati NFL	16	16	1	0	0.0	0	3.0
1992—Cincinnati NFL	14	13	3	108	36.0	1	6.0
1993—Cincinnati NFL	14	12	2	12	6.0	0	2.0
1994—Cincinnati NFL	16	16	0	0	...	0	4.5
1995—Cincinnati NFL	11	11	0	0	...	0	3.0
1996—Cincinnati NFL	16	15	3	61	20.3	1	3.0
1997—Cincinnati NFL	16	16	1	7	7.0	0	3.5
Pro totals (8 years)	119	115	11	205	18.6	3	33.0

FRASE, PAUL   DE/DT   PACKERS

PERSONAL: Born May 5, 1965, in Elmira, N.Y. ... 6-5/267. ... Full name: Paul Miles Frase. ... Name pronounced FRAZE.
HIGH SCHOOL: Spaulding (Rochester, N.H.).
COLLEGE: Syracuse (degree in psychology).
TRANSACTIONS/CAREER NOTES: Selected by New York Jets in sixth round (146th pick overall) of 1988 NFL draft. ... Signed by Jets (June 21, 1988). ... On reserve/non-football illness list with hyperthyroidism (August 27, 1990-entire season). ... Granted unconditional free agency (February 1-April 1, 1991). ... Re-signed by Jets for 1991 season. ... Granted free agency (February 1, 1992). ... Re-signed by Jets (July 13, 1992). ... Granted free agency (March 1, 1993). ... Re-signed by Jets (April 12, 1993). ... Granted unconditional free agency (February 17, 1994). ... Re-signed by Jets (April 6, 1994). ... Selected by Jacksonville Jaguars from Jets in NFL expansion draft (February 15, 1995). ... Granted unconditional free agency (February 14, 1997). ... Re-signed by Jaguars (April 28, 1997). ... Traded by Jaguars to Green Bay Packers for sixth-round pick (RB Kevin McLeod) in 1998 draft (August 24, 1997). ... Granted unconditional free agency (February 13, 1998). ... Re-signed by Packers (April 24, 1998).
CHAMPIONSHIP GAME EXPERIENCE: Played in AFC championship game (1986 season). ... Played in NFC championship game (1997 season). ... Member of Packers for Super Bowl XXXII (1997 season); inactive.
PRO STATISTICS: 1991—Fumbled once. 1993—Recovered two fumbles. 1994—Recovered one fumble.

Year Team	G	GS	SACKS
1988—New York Jets NFL	16	7	1.0
1989—New York Jets NFL	16	14	2.0
1990—New York Jets NFL	Did not play.		
1991—New York Jets NFL	16	2	0.0
1992—New York Jets NFL	16	12	5.0
1993—New York Jets NFL	16	4	1.0
1994—New York Jets NFL	16	5	1.0
1995—Jacksonville NFL	9	5	1.0
1996—Jacksonville NFL	14	0	0.0
1997—Green Bay NFL	9	0	0.0
Pro totals (9 years)	128	49	11.0

FREDERICK, MIKE — DE — RAVENS

PERSONAL: Born August 6, 1972, in Abington, Pa. ... 6-5/280. ... Full name: Thomas Michael Frederick.
HIGH SCHOOL: Neshaminy (Langhorne, Pa.).
COLLEGE: Virginia (degree in management).
TRANSACTIONS/CAREER NOTES: Selected by Cleveland Browns in third round (94th pick overall) of 1995 NFL draft. ... Signed by Browns (July 14, 1995). ... Browns franchise moved to Baltimore and renamed Ravens for 1996 season (March 11, 1996). ... Granted free agency (February 13, 1998).
PLAYING EXPERIENCE: Cleveland NFL, 1995; Baltimore NFL, 1996 and 1997. ... Games/Games started: 1995 (16/0), 1996 (16/11), 1997 (16/1). Total: 48/12.
PRO STATISTICS: 1995—Credited with one sack and returned two kickoffs for 16 yards. 1996—Ran minus one yard with lateral from kickoff return. 1997—Recovered one fumble.

FREDRICKSON, ROB — LB — LIONS

PERSONAL: Born May 13, 1971, in Saint Joseph, Mich. ... 6-4/240. ... Full name: Robert J. Fredrickson.
HIGH SCHOOL: Saint Joseph (Mich.) Senior.
COLLEGE: Michigan State.
TRANSACTIONS/CAREER NOTES: Selected by Los Angeles Raiders in first round (22nd pick overall) of 1994 NFL draft. ... Signed by Raiders (July 19, 1994). ... Raiders franchise moved to Oakland (July 21, 1995). ... On injured reserve with shoulder injury (November 20, 1996-remainder of season). ... Traded by Raiders to Detroit Lions for fourth-round pick (traded to Washington) in 1998 draft (March 25, 1998).
PLAYING EXPERIENCE: Los Angeles Raiders NFL, 1994; Oakland NFL, 1995-1997. ... Games/Games started: 1994 (16/12), 1995 (16/15), 1996 (10/10), 1997 (16/13). Total: 58/50.
PRO STATISTICS: 1994—Credited with three sacks. 1995—Intercepted one pass for 14 yards and recovered four fumbles for 35 yards and one touchdown. 1997—Credited with two sacks.

FREEMAN, ANTONIO — WR — PACKERS

PERSONAL: Born May 27, 1972, in Baltimore. ... 6-1/194. ... Full name: Antonio Michael Freeman.
HIGH SCHOOL: Baltimore Polytechnic.
COLLEGE: Virginia Tech.
TRANSACTIONS/CAREER NOTES: Selected by Green Bay Packers in third round (90th pick overall) of 1995 NFL draft. ... Signed by Packers (June 22, 1995). ... Granted free agency (February 13, 1998). ... Re-signed by Packers (February 20, 1998).
CHAMPIONSHIP GAME EXPERIENCE: Played in NFC championship game (1995-97 seasons). ... Member of Super Bowl championship team (1996 season). ... Played in Super Bowl XXXII (1997 season).
POST SEASON RECORDS: Holds Super Bowl record for longest pass reception (from Brett Favre)—81 yards (January 26, 1997, vs. New England). ... Shares NFL postseason record for most touchdowns by punt return—1 ... (December 31, 1995, vs. Atlanta).
PRO STATISTICS: 1995—Recovered four fumbles. 1996—Recovered one fumble for 14 yards. 1997—Rushed once for 14 yards.
SINGLE GAME HIGHS (regular season): Receptions—10 (December 14, 1997, vs. Carolina); yards—175 (December 8, 1996, vs. Denver); and touchdown receptions—3 (December 8, 1996, vs. Denver).
STATISTICAL PLATEAUS: 100-yard receiving games: 1996 (4), 1997 (3). Total: 7.

Year Team	G	GS	RECEIVING No.	RECEIVING Yds.	RECEIVING Avg.	RECEIVING TD	PUNT RETURNS No.	PUNT RETURNS Yds.	PUNT RETURNS Avg.	PUNT RETURNS TD	KICKOFF RETURNS No.	KICKOFF RETURNS Yds.	KICKOFF RETURNS Avg.	KICKOFF RETURNS TD	TOTALS TD	TOTALS 2pt.	TOTALS Pts.	TOTALS Fum.
1995—Green Bay NFL	11	0	8	106	13.3	1	37	292	7.9	0	24	556	23.2	0	1	0	6	7
1996—Green Bay NFL	12	12	56	933	16.7	9	0	0	...	0	1	16	16.0	0	9	0	54	3
1997—Green Bay NFL	16	16	81	1243	15.3	12	0	0	...	0	0	0	...	0	12	0	72	1
Pro totals (3 years)	39	28	145	2282	15.7	22	37	292	7.9	0	25	572	22.9	0	22	0	132	11

FREROTTE, GUS — QB — REDSKINS

PERSONAL: Born July 31, 1971, in Kittanning, Pa. ... 6-2/240. ... Full name: Gustave Joseph Frerotte.
HIGH SCHOOL: Ford City (Pa.) Junior-Senior.
COLLEGE: Tulsa.
TRANSACTIONS/CAREER NOTES: Selected by Washington Redskins in seventh round (197th pick overall) of 1994 NFL draft. ... Signed by Redskins (July 19, 1994). ... Granted free agency (February 14, 1997). ... Re-signed by Redskins (July 18, 1997). ... On injured reserve with hip injury (December 2, 1997-remainder of season).
HONORS: Played in Pro Bowl (1996 season).
PRO STATISTICS: 1994—Fumbled four times and recovered two fumbles for minus four yards. 1995—Fumbled seven times and recovered four fumbles for minus 16 yards. 1996—Fumbled 12 times and recovered one fumble for minus 12 yards. 1997—Fumbled eight times and recovered two fumbles for minus 16 yards.
SINGLE GAME HIGHS (regular season): Attempts—45 (November 30, 1997, vs. St. Louis); completions—22 (December 22, 1996, vs. Dallas); yards—346 (December 22, 1996, vs. Dallas); and touchdown passes—3 (September 28, 1997, vs. Jacksonville).

STATISTICAL PLATEAUS: 300-yard passing games: 1995 (1), 1996 (1). Total: 2.
MISCELLANEOUS: Regular-season record as starting NFL quarterback: 19-24-1 (.443).

			PASSING								RUSHING				TOTALS		
Year Team	G	GS	Att.	Cmp.	Pct.	Yds.	TD	Int.	Avg.	Rat.	Att.	Yds.	Avg.	TD	TD	2pt.	Pts.
1994—Washington NFL	4	4	100	46	46.0	600	5	5	6.00	61.3	4	1	0.3	0	0	0	0
1995—Washington NFL	16	11	396	199	50.3	2751	13	13	6.95	70.2	22	16	0.7	1	1	0	6
1996—Washington NFL	16	16	470	270	57.4	3453	12	11	7.35	79.3	28	16	0.6	0	0	0	0
1997—Washington NFL	13	13	402	204	50.7	2682	17	12	6.67	73.8	24	65	2.7	2	2	0	12
Pro totals (4 years)	49	44	1368	719	52.6	9486	47	41	6.93	73.7	78	98	1.3	3	3	0	18

FRIESZ, JOHN — QB — SEAHAWKS

PERSONAL: Born May 19, 1967, in Missoula, Mont. ... 6-4/223. ... Full name: John Melvin Friesz. ... Name pronounced FREEZE.
HIGH SCHOOL: Coeur D'Alene (Idaho).
COLLEGE: Idaho.
TRANSACTIONS/CAREER NOTES: Selected by San Diego Chargers in sixth round (138th pick overall) of 1990 NFL draft. ... Signed by Chargers (July 20, 1990). ... On injured reserve with elbow injury (September 4-October 3, 1990). ... On practice squad (October 3-December 28, 1990). ... Granted free agency (February 1, 1992). ... Re-signed by Chargers (July 27, 1992). ... On injured reserve with knee injury (August 25, 1992-entire season). ... Granted unconditional free agency (February 17, 1994). ... Signed by Washington Redskins (April 18, 1994). ... Granted unconditional free agency (February 17, 1995). ... Signed by Seattle Seahawks (March 17, 1995).
HONORS: Walter Payton Award winner (1989).
PRO STATISTICS: 1991—Fumbled 10 times and recovered two fumbles for minus 21 yards. 1993—Fumbled twice and recovered one fumble for minus three yards. 1994—Fumbled twice and recovered one fumble. 1995—Fumbled twice and recovered one fumble for minus three yards. 1996—Fumbled seven times and recovered two fumbles for minus six yards. 1997—Fumbled once and recovered one fumble for minus two yards.
SINGLE GAME HIGHS (regular season): Attempts—54 (October 20, 1991, vs. Cleveland); completions—33 (October 20, 1991, vs. Cleveland); yards—381 (September 18, 1994, vs. New York Giants); and touchdown passes—4 (September 11, 1994, vs. New Orleans).
STATISTICAL PLATEAUS: 300-yard passing games: 1991 (2), 1994 (1), 1996 (1). Total: 4.
MISCELLANEOUS: Regular-season record as starting NFL quarterback: 12-25 (.324).

			PASSING								RUSHING				TOTALS		
Year Team	G	GS	Att.	Cmp.	Pct.	Yds.	TD	Int.	Avg.	Rat.	Att.	Yds.	Avg.	TD	TD	2pt.	Pts.
1990—San Diego NFL	1	1	22	11	50.0	98	1	1	4.45	58.5	1	3	3.0	0	0	...	0
1991—San Diego NFL	16	16	487	262	53.8	2896	12	15	5.95	67.1	10	18	1.8	0	0	...	0
1992—San Diego NFL								Did not play.										
1993—San Diego NFL	12	6	238	128	53.8	1402	6	4	5.89	72.8	10	3	0.3	0	0	0	0
1994—Washington NFL	16	4	180	105	58.3	1266	10	9	7.03	77.7	1	1	1.0	0	0	0	0
1995—Seattle NFL	6	3	120	64	53.3	795	6	3	6.63	80.4	11	0	0.0	0	0	0	0
1996—Seattle NFL	8	6	211	120	56.9	1629	8	4	7.72	86.4	12	1	0.1	0	0	0	0
1997—Seattle NFL	2	1	36	15	41.7	138	0	3	3.83	18.1	1	0	0.0	0	0	0	0
Pro totals (7 years)	61	37	1294	705	54.5	8224	43	39	6.36	72.5	46	26	0.6	0	0	0	0

FRISCH, DAVID — TE — REDSKINS

PERSONAL: Born June 22, 1970, in Kirkwood, Mo. ... 6-7/260. ... Full name: David Joseph Frisch.
HIGH SCHOOL: Northwest (House Springs, Mo.).
JUNIOR COLLEGE: Iowa Central Community College.
COLLEGE: Missouri, then Colorado State.
TRANSACTIONS/CAREER NOTES: Signed as non-drafted free agent by Cincinnati Bengals (April 27, 1993). ... Released by Bengals (August 20, 1995). ... Signed by New England Patriots (October 25, 1995). ... Released by Patriots (December 19, 1995). ... Signed by Minnesota Vikings (February 13, 1996). ... Granted unconditional free agency (February 14, 1997). ... Re-signed by Vikings (April 15, 1997). ... Released by Vikings (August 19, 1997). ... Signed by Washington Redskins (November 19, 1997). ... Released by Redskins (November 25, 1997). ... Re-signed by Redskins (December 9, 1997). ... Granted unconditional free agency (February 13, 1998). ... Re-signed by Redskins (March 19, 1998).
PLAYING EXPERIENCE: Cincinnati NFL, 1993 and 1994; New England NFL, 1995; Minnesota NFL, 1996; Washington NFL, 1997. ... Games/Games started: 1993 (11/2), 1994 (16/0), 1995 (2/0), 1996 (10/1), 1997 (2/0). Total: 41/3.
PRO STATISTICS: 1993—Caught six passes for 43 yards. 1995—Returned one kickoff for eight yards. 1996—Caught three passes for 27 yards and a touchdown.
SINGLE GAME HIGHS (regular season): Receptions—2 (December 5, 1993, vs. San Francisco); yards—21 (November 24, 1996, vs. Denver); and touchdown receptions—1 (September 8, 1996, vs. Atlanta).

FRYAR, IRVING — WR — EAGLES

PERSONAL: Born September 28, 1962, in Mount Holly, N.J. ... 6-0/200. ... Full name: Irving Dale Fryar.
HIGH SCHOOL: Rancocas Valley Regional (Mount Holly, N.J.).
COLLEGE: Nebraska.
TRANSACTIONS/CAREER NOTES: Selected by Chicago Blitz in first round (third pick overall) of 1984 USFL draft. ... Signed by New England Patriots (April 11, 1984). ... Selected officially by Patriots in first round (first pick overall) of 1984 NFL draft. ... Traded by Patriots to Miami Dolphins for second-round pick (OL Todd Rucci) in 1993 draft and third-round pick (C Joe Burch) in 1994 draft (April 1, 1993). ... Granted unconditional free agency (February 16, 1996). ... Signed by Philadelphia Eagles (March 19, 1996).
CHAMPIONSHIP GAME EXPERIENCE: Played in Super Bowl XX (1985 season).
HONORS: Named wide receiver on THE SPORTING NEWS college All-America first team (1983). ... Played in Pro Bowl (1985, 1993, 1994, 1996 and 1997 seasons).
PRO STATISTICS: 1984—Fumbled four times and recovered one fumble. 1985—Fumbled four times. 1986—Fumbled four times and recovered one fumble. 1987—Fumbled twice. 1988—Fumbled twice. 1989—Fumbled twice. 1990—Fumbled once and recovered one fumble. 1991—Attempted one pass without a completion and fumbled twice. 1994—Ran two yards with lateral from reception for a touchdown and recovered one fumble for seven yards. 1997—Fumbled once.

F

SINGLE GAME HIGHS (regular season): Receptions—10 (October 12, 1997, vs. Jacksonville); yards—211 (September 4, 1994, vs. New England); and touchdown receptions—4 (October 20, 1996, vs. Miami).
STATISTICAL PLATEAUS: 100-yard receiving games: 1985 (1), 1986 (2), 1987 (1), 1988 (1), 1989 (1), 1990 (1), 1991 (3), 1992 (2), 1993 (2), 1994 (6), 1995 (2), 1996 (4), 1997 (6). Total: 32.

Year Team	G	GS	RUSHING				RECEIVING				PUNT RETURNS				KICKOFF RETURNS				TOTALS		
			Att.	Yds.	Avg.	TD	No.	Yds.	Avg.	TD	No.	Yds.	Avg.	TD	No.	Yds.	Avg.	TD	TD	2pt.	Pts.
1984—New England NFL	14	2	2	-11	-5.5	0	11	164	14.9	1	36	347	9.6	0	5	95	19.0	0	1	...	6
1985—New England NFL	16	14	7	27	3.9	1	39	670	17.2	7	37	520*14.1	*2	3	39	13.0	0	10	...	60
1986—New England NFL	14	13	4	80	20.0	0	43	737	17.1	6	35	366	10.5	▲1	10	192	19.2	0	7	...	42
1987—New England NFL	12	12	9	52	5.8	0	31	467	15.1	5	18	174	9.7	0	6	119	19.8	0	5	...	30
1988—New England NFL	15	14	6	12	2.0	0	33	490	14.8	5	38	398	10.5	0	1	3	3.0	0	5	...	30
1989—New England NFL	11	5	2	15	7.5	0	29	537	18.5	3	12	107	8.9	0	1	47	47.0	0	3	...	18
1990—New England NFL	16	15	0	0	...	0	54	856	15.9	4	28	133	4.8	0	0	0	...	0	4	...	24
1991—New England NFL	16	15	2	11	5.5	0	68	1014	14.9	3	2	10	5.0	0	0	0	...	0	3	...	18
1992—New England NFL	15	14	1	6	6.0	0	55	791	14.4	4	0	0	...	0	0	0	...	0	4	...	24
1993—Miami NFL	16	16	3	-4	-1.3	0	64	1010	15.8	5	0	0	...	0	1	10	10.0	0	5	...	30
1994—Miami NFL	16	16	0	0	...	0	73	1270	17.4	7	0	0	...	0	0	0	...	0	7	2	46
1995—Miami NFL	16	16	0	0	...	0	62	910	14.7	8	0	0	...	0	0	0	...	0	8	0	48
1996—Philadelphia NFL	16	16	1	-4	-4.0	0	88	1195	13.6	11	0	0	...	0	0	0	...	0	11	0	66
1997—Philadelphia NFL	16	16	0	0	...	0	86	1316	15.3	6	0	0	...	0	0	0	...	0	6	0	36
Pro totals (14 years)	209	184	37	184	5.0	1	736	11427	15.5	75	206	2055	10.0	3	27	505	18.7	0	79	2	478

FULLER, COREY   CB   VIKINGS

PERSONAL: Born May 1, 1971, in Tallahassee, Fla. ... 5-10/206.
HIGH SCHOOL: James S. Rickards (Tallahassee, Fla.).
COLLEGE: Florida State.
TRANSACTIONS/CAREER NOTES: Selected by Minnesota Vikings in second round (55th pick overall) of 1995 NFL draft. ... Signed by Vikings (July 24, 1995).
PRO STATISTICS: 1995—Credited with 1/2 sack and recovered one fumble for 12 yards and a touchdown.

Year Team	G	GS	INTERCEPTIONS			
			No.	Yds.	Avg.	TD
1995—Minnesota NFL	16	11	1	0	0.0	0
1996—Minnesota NFL	16	14	3	3	1.0	0
1997—Minnesota NFL	16	16	2	24	12.0	0
Pro totals (3 years)	48	41	6	27	4.5	0

FULLER, RANDY   CB   FALCONS

PERSONAL: Born June 2, 1970, in Columbus, Ga. ... 5-10/175. ... Full name: Randy Lamar Fuller.
HIGH SCHOOL: William H. Spencer (Columbus, Ga.).
COLLEGE: Tennessee State.
TRANSACTIONS/CAREER NOTES: Selected by Denver Broncos in fourth round (123rd pick overall) of 1994 NFL draft. ... Signed by Broncos (July 22, 1994). ... Released by Broncos (August 22, 1995). ... Signed by Pittsburgh Steelers (September 12, 1995). ... Granted free agency (February 14, 1997). ... Re-signed by Steelers prior to 1997 season. ... Granted unconditional free agency (February 13, 1998). ... Signed by Atlanta Falcons (March 19, 1998).
PLAYING EXPERIENCE: Denver NFL, 1994; Pittsburgh NFL, 1995-1997. ... Games/Games started: 1994 (10/1), 1995 (13/0), 1996 (14/1), 1997 (12/3). Total: 49/5.
CHAMPIONSHIP GAME EXPERIENCE: Played in AFC championship game (1995 and 1997 seasons). ... Played in Super Bowl XXX (1995 season).
PRO STATISTICS: 1996—Intercepted one pass for no yards. 1997—Credited with one sack.

F

FULLER, WILLIAM   DE   CHARGERS

PERSONAL: Born March 8, 1962, in Norfolk, Va. ... 6-3/280. ... Full name: William Henry Fuller Jr.
HIGH SCHOOL: Indian River (Chesapeake, Va.).
COLLEGE: North Carolina.
TRANSACTIONS/CAREER NOTES: Selected by Philadelphia Stars in 1984 USFL territorial draft. ... Signed by Stars (February 6, 1984). ... On injured reserve with fractured ankle (May 18-June 23, 1984). ... Selected by Los Angeles Rams in first round (21st pick overall) of 1984 NFL supplemental draft. ... Stars franchise moved to Baltimore (November 1, 1984). ... Granted free agency when USFL suspended operations (August 7, 1986). ... Signed by Rams (September 10, 1986). ... Traded by Rams with G Kent Hill, first-round (WR Haywood Jeffires) and fifth-round (RB Spencer Tillman) picks in 1987 draft and first-round pick (traded to Los Angeles Raiders) in 1988 draft to Houston Oilers for rights to QB Jim Everett (September 18, 1986). ... Granted roster exemption (September 18-22, 1986). ... Granted free agency (February 1, 1992). ... Re-signed by Oilers (September 11, 1992). ... Granted unconditional free agency (February 17, 1994). ... Signed by Philadelphia Eagles (March 31, 1994). ... Granted unconditional free agency (February 14, 1997). ... Signed by San Diego Chargers (April 14, 1997).
CHAMPIONSHIP GAME EXPERIENCE: Played in USFL championship game (1984 and 1985 seasons).
HONORS: Named defensive tackle on THE SPORTING NEWS college All-America first team (1983). ... Named defensive end on THE SPORTING NEWS USFL All-Star team (1985). ... Played in Pro Bowl (1991 and 1994-1996 seasons).
PRO STATISTICS: USFL: 1984—Recovered one fumble. 1985—Intercepted one pass for 35 yards and recovered four fumbles for 17 yards. NFL: 1987—Returned one kickoff for no yards and recovered one fumble. 1988—Intercepted one pass for nine yards. 1990—Recovered one fumble. 1991—Recovered two fumbles for three yards. 1992—Recovered one fumble for 10 yards and a touchdown. 1994—Credited with one safety and recovered one fumble. 1995—Recovered one fumble. 1996—Recovered one fumble. 1997—Intercepted one pass for no yards.

Year Team	G	GS	SACKS
1984—Philadelphia USFL	13	12	2.0
1985—Baltimore USFL	18	...	8.5
1986—Houston NFL	13	0	1.0
1987—Houston NFL	12	1	2.0
1988—Houston NFL	16	15	8.5
1989—Houston NFL	15	8	6.5
1990—Houston NFL	16	16	8.0
1991—Houston NFL	16	16	§15.0
1992—Houston NFL	15	14	8.0
1993—Houston NFL	16	16	10.0
1994—Philadelphia NFL	16	16	9.5
1995—Philadelphia NFL	14	13	∞13.0
1996—Philadelphia NFL	16	16	13.0
1997—San Diego NFL	16	16	3.0
USFL totals (2 years)	31	...	10.5
NFL totals (12 years)	181	147	97.5
Pro totals (14 years)	212	...	108.0

FURRER, WILL   QB   RAMS

PERSONAL: Born February 5, 1968, in Danville, Pa. ... 6-3/215. ... Full name: William Mason Furrer.
HIGH SCHOOL: Pullman (Wash.) and Fork Union (Va.) Military Academy.
COLLEGE: Virginia Tech.
TRANSACTIONS/CAREER NOTES: Selected by Chicago Bears in fourth round (107th pick overall) of 1992 NFL draft. ... Signed by Bears (July 23, 1992). ... Claimed on waivers by Phoenix Cardinals (August 31, 1993). ... Cardinals franchise renamed Arizona Cardinals for 1994 season. ... Released by Cardinals (August 22, 1994). ... Signed by Denver Broncos (August 24, 1994). ... Granted unconditional free agency (February 17, 1995). ... Assigned by Broncos to Amsterdam Admirals in 1995 World League enhancement allocation program (February 20, 1995). ... Signed by Houston Oilers (July 21, 1995). ... Released by Oilers (February 15, 1996). ... Signed by St. Louis Rams (February 24, 1997). ... Inactive for 16 games (1997). ... Granted unconditional free agency (February 13, 1998). ... Re-signed by Rams (March 10, 1998).
PRO STATISTICS: 1992—Fumbled once. 1995—Fumbled three times.
MISCELLANEOUS: Regular-season record as starting NFL quarterback: 0-2.

			PASSING						RUSHING				TOTALS		
Year Team	G	GS	Att.	Cmp.	Pct.	Yds.	TD	Int.	Avg.	Rat.	Att.	Yds.	Avg.	TD	TD	2pt.	Pts.
1992—Chicago NFL	2	1	25	9	36.0	89	0	3	3.56	7.3	0	0	...	0	0	...	0
1993—Arizona NFL							Did not play.									
1994—Denver NFL							Did not play.									
1995—Amsterdam W.L.	...	...	85	51	60.0	542	4	2	6.38	84.5	14	32	2.3	1	1	0	6
—Houston NFL	7	1	99	48	48.5	483	2	7	4.88	40.1	8	20	2.5	0	0	0	0
1996—Amsterdam W.L.	...	...	368	206	56.0	2689	20	13	7.31	82.6	26	189	7.3	1	1	0	6
1997—St. Louis NFL							Did not play.									
W.L. totals (2 years)	...	...	453	257	56.7	3231	24	15	7.13	82.9	40	221	5.5	2	2	0	12
NFL totals (3 years)	9	2	124	57	46.0	572	2	10	4.61	31.4	8	20	2.5	0	0	0	0
Pro totals (5 years)	...	...	577	314	54.4	3803	26	25	6.59	71.9	48	241	5.0	2	2	0	12

GAINES, WILLIAM   DT

PERSONAL: Born June 20, 1971, in Jackson, Miss. ... 6-5/318. ... Full name: William Albert Gaines.
HIGH SCHOOL: Lanier (Jackson, Miss.).
COLLEGE: Florida.
TRANSACTIONS/CAREER NOTES: Selected by Miami Dolphins in fifth round (147th pick overall) of 1994 NFL draft. ... Signed by Dolphins (July 11, 1994). ... Claimed on waivers by Washington Redskins (August 28, 1995). ... Granted free agency (February 14, 1997). ... Re-signed by Redskins (May 5, 1997). ... Granted unconditional free agency (February 13, 1998).
PLAYING EXPERIENCE: Miami NFL, 1994; Washington NFL, 1995-1997. ... Games/Games started: 1994 (7/0), 1995 (15/11), 1996 (16/6), 1997 (13/7). Total: 51/24.
PRO STATISTICS: 1995—Credited with two sacks.

GAITER, TONY   WR   PATRIOTS

PERSONAL: Born July 15, 1974, in Miami. ... 5-8/170. ... Full name: Tony Gaiter Jr.
HIGH SCHOOL: Killian (Miami).
JUNIOR COLLEGE: San Bernardino (Calif.) Valley.
COLLEGE: Miami (Fla.).
TRANSACTIONS/CAREER NOTES: Selected by New England Patriots in sixth round (192nd pick overall) of 1997 NFL draft. ... Signed by Patriots (July 16, 1997). ... Released by Patriots (August 24, 1997). ... Re-signed by Patriots to practice squad (August 26, 1997). ... Activated (November 28, 1997).
PLAYING EXPERIENCE: New England NFL, 1997. ... Games/Games started: 1/0.
SINGLE GAME HIGHS (regular season): Receptions—0; yards—0; and touchdown receptions—0.

GALBRAITH, SCOTT   TE

PERSONAL: Born January 7, 1967, in Sacramento. ... 6-2/254. ... Full name: Alan Scott Galbraith. ... Name pronounced GAL-breath.
HIGH SCHOOL: Highlands (North Highlands, Calif.).
COLLEGE: Southern California.

F
G

TRANSACTIONS/CAREER NOTES: Selected by Cleveland Browns in seventh round (178th pick overall) of 1990 NFL draft. ... Signed by Browns (July 17, 1990). ... Granted free agency (February 1, 1992). ... Re-signed by Browns (August 30, 1992). ... Granted free agency (March 1, 1993). ... Re-signed by Browns (July 24, 1993). ... Released by Browns (August 30, 1993). ... Signed by Dallas Cowboys (November 11, 1993). ... Granted unconditional free agency (February 17, 1995). ... Signed by Washington Redskins (May 16, 1995). ... Granted unconditional free agency (February 16, 1996). ... Re-signed by Redskins (April 17, 1996). ... Released by Redskins (June 4, 1997). ... Signed by Cowboys (July 16, 1997). ... Granted unconditional free agency (February 13, 1998).

CHAMPIONSHIP GAME EXPERIENCE: Played in NFC championship game (1993 and 1994 seasons). ... Member of Super Bowl championship team (1993 season).

PRO STATISTICS: 1990—Returned three kickoffs for 16 yards and recovered one fumble. 1991—Returned two kickoffs for 13 yards and recovered one fumble. 1997—Returned two kickoffs for 24 yards.

SINGLE GAME HIGHS (regular season): Receptions—4 (December 15, 1991, vs. Houston); yards—60 (December 9, 1990, vs. Houston); and touchdown receptions—1 (September 22, 1996, vs. St. Louis).

Year Team	G	GS	RECEIVING				TOTALS			
			No.	Yds.	Avg.	TD	TD	2pt.	Pts.	Fum.
1990—Cleveland NFL	16	1	4	62	15.5	0	0	...	0	0
1991—Cleveland NFL	16	13	27	328	12.1	0	0	...	0	0
1992—Cleveland NFL	14	2	4	63	15.8	1	1	...	6	0
1993—Dallas NFL	7	0	1	1	1.0	1	1	...	6	0
1994—Dallas NFL	16	2	4	31	7.8	0	0	0	0	0
1995—Washington NFL	16	16	10	80	8.0	2	2	0	12	0
1996—Washington NFL	16	6	8	89	11.1	2	2	0	12	0
1997—Dallas NFL	16	0	2	16	8.0	0	0	0	0	0
Pro totals (8 years)	117	40	60	670	11.2	6	6	0	36	0

GALLERY, NICK   P   JETS

PERSONAL: Born February 15, 1975, in Manchester, Iowa. ... 6-4/239. ... Full name: Nick Patrick Gallery.
HIGH SCHOOL: East Buchanan (Winthrop, Iowa).
COLLEGE: Iowa.
TRANSACTIONS/CAREER NOTES: Signed as a non-drafted free agent by Kansas City Chiefs (August 26, 1997). ... Released by Chiefs (August 12, 1997). ... Signed by New York Jets to practice squad (October 20, 1997).

GALLOWAY, JOEY   WR   SEAHAWKS

PERSONAL: Born November 20, 1971, in Bellaire, Ohio. ... 5-11/188.
HIGH SCHOOL: Bellaire (Ohio).
COLLEGE: Ohio State.
TRANSACTIONS/CAREER NOTES: Selected by Seattle Seahawks in first round (eighth pick overall) of 1995 NFL draft. ... Signed by Seahawks (July 20, 1995).
PRO STATISTICS: 1995—Fumbled once. 1996—Fumbled twice. 1997—Fumbled once and recovered one fumble.
SINGLE GAME HIGHS (regular season): Receptions—8 (November 2, 1997, vs. Denver); yards—137 (October 6, 1996, vs. Miami); and touchdown receptions—3 (October 26, 1997, vs. Oakland).
STATISTICAL PLATEAUS: 100-yard receiving games: 1995 (3), 1996 (2), 1997 (3). Total: 8.

Year Team	G	GS	RUSHING				RECEIVING				PUNT RETURNS				KICKOFF RETURNS				TOTALS		
			Att.	Yds.	Avg.	TD	No.	Yds.	Avg.	TD	No.	Yds.	Avg.	TD	No.	Yds.	Avg.	TD	TD	2pt.	Pts.
1995—Seattle NFL	16	16	11	154	14.0	1	67	1039	15.5	7	36	360	10.0	†1	2	30	15.0	0	9	0	54
1996—Seattle NFL	16	16	15	127	8.5	0	57	987	17.3	7	15	158	10.5	s1	0	0	...	0	8	0	48
1997—Seattle NFL	15	15	9	72	8.0	0	72	1049	14.6	12	0	0	...	0	0	0	...	0	12	0	72
Pro totals (3 years)	47	47	35	353	10.1	1	196	3075	15.7	26	51	518	10.2	2	2	30	15.0	0	29	0	174

GALLOWAY, MITCHELL   WR   BILLS

PERSONAL: Born October 8, 1974 ... 5-8/178.
HIGH SCHOOL: Marlboro County (S.C.).
COLLEGE: East Carolina.
TRANSACTIONS/CAREER NOTES: Signed as non-drafted free agent by Buffalo Bills (April 25, 1997). ... Released by Bills (August 24, 1997). ... Resigned by Bills to practice squad (August 26, 1997). ... Activated (September 20, 1997). ... Released by Bills (October 5, 1997). ... Re-signed by Bills to practice squad (October 7, 1997). ... Activated (December 12, 1997). ... Assigned by Bills to Frankfurt Galaxy in 1998 NFL Europe enhancement allocation program (February 18, 1998).
PLAYING EXPERIENCE: Buffalo NFL, 1997. ... Games/Games started: 3/0.
PRO STATISTICS: 1997—Returned six kickoffs for 130 yards, returned two punts for 15 yards and fumbled once.

G

GALYON, SCOTT   LB   GIANTS

PERSONAL: Born March 23, 1974, in Seymour, Tenn. ... 6-2/245.
HIGH SCHOOL: Seymour (Tenn.).
COLLEGE: Tennessee (degree in education business marketing, 1996).
TRANSACTIONS/CAREER NOTES: Selected by New York Giants in sixth round (182nd pick overall) of 1996 NFL draft. ... Signed by Giants (July 17, 1996).
PLAYING EXPERIENCE: New York Giants NFL, 1996 and 1997. ... Games/Games started: 1996 (16/0), 1997 (16/0). Total: 32/0.
PRO STATISTICS: 1997—Credited with three sacks.

GAMBLE, DAVID — WR — BRONCOS

PERSONAL: Born June 14, 1971, in Albany, N.Y. ... 6-1/190.
COLLEGE: New Hampshire.
TRANSACTIONS/CAREER NOTES: Signed as non-drafted free agent by Philadelphia Eagles (April 1994). ... Released by Eagles (August 1994). ... Signed by Sacramento Gold Miners of CFL (September 1994). ... Gold Miners franchise moved to San Antonio and renamed Texans for 1995 season. ... Granted free agency (February 16, 1996). ... Signed by Denver Broncos (April 10. 1996). ... Released by Broncos (August 20, 1996). ... Re-signed by Broncos (April 7, 1997). ... Released by Broncos (August 18, 1997). ... Re-signed by Broncos to practice squad (September 9, 1997). ... Activated (November 18, 1997). ... Released by Broncos (December 8, 1997). ... Re-signed by Broncos to practice squad (December 9, 1997).
PLAYING EXPERIENCE: Denver NFL, 1997. ... Games/Games started: 2/0.
SINGLE GAME HIGHS (regular season): Receptions—0; yards—0; and touchdown receptions—0.

GAMMON, KENDALL — C — SAINTS

PERSONAL: Born October 23, 1968, in Wichita, Kan. ... 6-4/288. ... Full name: Kendall Robert Gammon.
HIGH SCHOOL: Rose Hill (Kan.).
COLLEGE: Pittsburg (Kan.) State.
TRANSACTIONS/CAREER NOTES: Selected by Pittsburgh Steelers in 11th round (291st pick overall) of 1992 NFL draft. ... Signed by Steelers (July 14, 1992). ... Released by Steelers (August 30, 1993). ... Re-signed by Steelers (August 31, 1993). ... Granted unconditional free agency (February 17, 1995). ... Re-signed by Steelers (May 8, 1995). ... Released by Steelers (August 26, 1996). ... Signed by New Orleans Saints (August 28, 1996).
PLAYING EXPERIENCE: Pittsburgh NFL, 1992-1995; New Orleans NFL, 1996 and 1997. ... Games/Games started: 1992 (16/0), 1993 (16/0), 1994 (16/0), 1995 (16/0), 1996 (16/0), 1997 (16/0). Total: 96/0.
CHAMPIONSHIP GAME EXPERIENCE: Played in AFC championship game (1994 and 1995 seasons). ... Played in Super Bowl XXX (1995 season).

GANDY, WAYNE — OT — RAMS

PERSONAL: Born February 10, 1971, in Haines City, Fla. ... 6-4/310. ... Full name: Wayne Lamar Gandy.
HIGH SCHOOL: Haines City (Fla.).
COLLEGE: Auburn.
TRANSACTIONS/CAREER NOTES: Selected by Los Angeles Rams in first round (15th pick overall) of 1994 NFL draft. ... Signed by Rams (July 23, 1994). ... Rams franchise moved to St. Louis (April 12, 1995).
PLAYING EXPERIENCE: Los Angeles Rams NFL, 1994; St. Louis NFL, 1995-1997. ... Games/Games started: 1994 (16/9), 1995 (16/16), 1996 (16/16), 1997 (16/16). Total: 64/57.
HONORS: Named offensive lineman on THE SPORTING NEWS college All-America first team (1993).

GANNON, RICH — QB — CHIEFS

PERSONAL: Born December 20, 1965, in Philadelphia. ... 6-3/210. ... Full name: Richard Joseph Gannon.
HIGH SCHOOL: St. Joseph's Prep (Philadelphia).
COLLEGE: Delaware (degree in criminal justice, 1987).
TRANSACTIONS/CAREER NOTES: Selected by New England Patriots in fourth round (98th pick overall) of 1987 NFL draft. ... Rights traded by Patriots to Minnesota Vikings for fourth-round (WR Sammy Martin) and 11th-round (traded) picks in 1988 draft (May 6, 1987). ... Signed by Vikings (July 30, 1987). ... Active for 13 games (1989); did not play. ... Granted free agency (February 1, 1990). ... Re-signed by Vikings (July 30, 1990). ... Granted free agency (February 1, 1991). ... Re-signed by Vikings (July 25, 1991). ... Granted free agency (February 1, 1992). ... Re-signed by Vikings (August 8, 1992). ... Traded by Vikings to Washington Redskins for conditional draft pick (August 20, 1993). ... Granted unconditional free agency (February 17, 1994). ... Signed by Kansas City Chiefs (March 29, 1995). ... Released by Chiefs (February 15, 1996). ... Re-signed by Chiefs (April 3, 1996).
CHAMPIONSHIP GAME EXPERIENCE: Member of Vikings for NFC championship game (1987 season); did not play.
PRO STATISTICS: 1990—Recovered six fumbles for minus three yards. 1991—Caught one pass for no yards. 1993—Recovered one fumble. 1996—Fumbled once. 1997—Fumbled five times.
SINGLE GAME HIGHS (regular season): Attempts—63 (October 20, 1991, vs. New England); completions—35 (October 20, 1991, vs. New England); yards—318 (September 27, 1992, vs. Cincinnati); and touchdown passes—4 (September 27, 1992, vs. Cincinnati).
STATISTICAL PLATEAUS: 300-yard passing games: 1991 (1), 1992 (1), 1997 (1). Total: 3.
MISCELLANEOUS: Regular-season record as starting NFL quarterback: 26-22 (.542).

Year Team	G	GS	PASSING								RUSHING				TOTALS		
			Att.	Cmp.	Pct.	Yds.	TD	Int.	Avg.	Rat.	Att.	Yds.	Avg.	TD	TD	2pt.	Pts.
1987—Minnesota NFL	4	0	6	2	33.3	18	0	1	3.00	2.8	0	0	...	0	0	...	0
1988—Minnesota NFL	3	0	15	7	46.7	90	0	0	6.00	66.0	4	29	7.3	0	0	...	0
1989—Minnesota NFL							Did not play.										
1990—Minnesota NFL	14	12	349	182	52.1	2278	16	16	6.53	68.9	52	268	5.2	1	1	...	6
1991—Minnesota NFL	15	11	354	211	59.6	2166	12	6	6.12	81.5	43	236	5.5	2	2	...	12
1992—Minnesota NFL	12	12	279	159	57.0	1905	12	13	6.83	72.9	45	187	4.2	0	0	...	0
1993—Washington NFL	8	4	125	74	59.2	704	3	7	5.63	59.6	21	88	4.2	1	1	...	6
1994—							Did not play.										
1995—Kansas City NFL	2	0	11	7	63.6	57	0	0	5.18	76.7	8	25	3.1	1	0	0	0
1996—Kansas City NFL	4	3	90	54	60.0	491	6	1	5.46	92.4	12	81	6.8	0	0	0	0
1997—Kansas City NFL	9	6	175	98	56.0	1144	7	4	6.54	79.8	33	109	3.3	2	2	0	12
Pro totals (9 years)	71	48	1404	794	56.6	8853	56	48	6.31	74.5	218	1023	4.7	7	0	0	36

G

GANT, KENNETH   S

PERSONAL: Born April 18, 1967, in Lakeland, Fla. ... 5-11/203. ... Full name: Kenneth Dwayne Gant.
HIGH SCHOOL: Kathleen (Lakeland, Fla.).
COLLEGE: Albany (Ga.) State.
TRANSACTIONS/CAREER NOTES: Selected by Dallas Cowboys in ninth round (221st pick overall) of 1990 NFL draft. ... Signed by Cowboys (July 18, 1990). ... On injured reserve with hamstring injury (September 6-October 1, 1990). ... Granted free agency (March 1, 1993). ... Re-signed by Cowboys (April 23, 1993). ... Granted unconditional free agency (February 17, 1995). ... Signed by Tampa Bay Buccaneers (March 24, 1995). ... Released by Buccaneers (November 28, 1997). ... Re-signed by Buccaneers (December 23, 1997). ... Granted unconditional free agency (February 13, 1998).
CHAMPIONSHIP GAME EXPERIENCE: Played in NFC championship game (1992-1994 seasons). ... Member of Super Bowl championship team (1992 and 1993 seasons).
PRO STATISTICS: 1991—Returned six kickoffs for 114 yards and recovered one fumble. 1992—Credited with three sacks and recovered one fumble. 1993—Returned one kickoff for 18 yards. 1995—Recovered one fumble for 13 yards.

			INTERCEPTIONS			
Year Team	G	GS	No.	Yds.	Avg.	TD
1990—Dallas NFL	12	0	1	26	26.0	0
1991—Dallas NFL	16	1	1	0	0.0	0
1992—Dallas NFL	16	4	3	19	6.3	0
1993—Dallas NFL	12	1	1	0	0.0	0
1994—Dallas NFL	16	0	1	0	0.0	0
1995—Tampa Bay NFL	16	3	0	0	...	0
1996—Tampa Bay NFL	16	0	0	0	...	0
1997—Tampa Bay NFL	9	0	0	0	...	0
Pro totals (8 years)	113	9	7	45	6.4	0

GARCIA, FRANK   C   PANTHERS

PERSONAL: Born January 28, 1972, in Phoenix. ... 6-1/295. ... Full name: Frank Christopher Garcia.
HIGH SCHOOL: Maryvale (Phoenix).
COLLEGE: Washington.
TRANSACTIONS/CAREER NOTES: Selected by Carolina Panthers in fourth round (132nd pick overall) of 1995 NFL draft. ... Signed by Panthers (July 14, 1995). ... Granted free agency (February 13, 1998). ... Re-signed by Panthers (March 12, 1998).
PLAYING EXPERIENCE: Carolina NFL, 1995-1997. ... Games/Games started: 1995 (15/14), 1996 (14/8), 1997 (16/16). Total: 45/38.
CHAMPIONSHIP GAME EXPERIENCE: Played in NFC championship game (1996 season).
PRO STATISTICS: 1995—Fumbled once and recovered one fumble for 10 yards. 1996—Recovered two fumbles. 1997—Returned one kickoff for 11 yards.

GARDENER, DARYL   DT   DOLPHINS

PERSONAL: Born February 25, 1973, in Lawton, Okla. ... 6-6/315. ... Full name: Daryl Ronald Gardener.
HIGH SCHOOL: Lawton (Okla.).
COLLEGE: Baylor.
TRANSACTIONS/CAREER NOTES: Selected by Miami Dolphins in first round (20th pick overall) of 1996 NFL draft. ... Signed by Dolphins (June 6, 1996).
PRO STATISTICS: 1996—Recovered one fumble. 1997—Recovered one fumble.

Year Team	G	GS	SACKS
1996—Miami NFL	16	12	1.0
1997—Miami NFL	16	16	1.5
Pro totals (2 years)	32	28	2.5

GARDNER, CARWELL   FB

PERSONAL: Born November 27, 1966, in Louisville, Ky. ... 6-2/240. ... Full name: Carwell Ernest Gardner. ... Brother of Donnie Gardner, defensive lineman with San Antonio Riders of World League (1991) and Miami Dolphins (1991).
HIGH SCHOOL: Trinity High School for Boys (Louisville, Ky.).
COLLEGE: Kentucky, then Louisville.
TRANSACTIONS/CAREER NOTES: Selected by Buffalo Bills in second round (42nd pick overall) of 1990 NFL draft. ... Signed by Bills (July 28, 1990). ... On injured reserve with knee injury (September 4-November 3, 1990). ... Granted free agency (March 1, 1993). ... Re-signed by Bills (May 21, 1993). ... Granted unconditional free agency (February 17, 1995). ... Re-signed by Bills (April 21, 1995). ... Released by Bills (February 16, 1996). ... Signed by Baltimore Ravens (July 20, 1996). ... Granted unconditional free agency (February 14, 1997). ... Signed by San Diego Chargers (April 11, 1997). ... Released by Chargers (November 4, 1997).
CHAMPIONSHIP GAME EXPERIENCE: Played in AFC championship game (1990-1993 seasons). ... Played in Super Bowl XXV (1990 season), Super Bowl XXVI (1991 season), Super Bowl XXVII (1992 season) and Super Bowl XXVIII (1993 season).
PRO STATISTICS: 1991—Recovered three fumbles and returned one kickoff for 10 yards. 1992—Recovered two fumbles. 1994—Returned one kickoff for six yards. 1995—Recovered two fumbles (including one in end zone for touchdown).
SINGLE GAME HIGHS (regular season): Attempts—8 (November 22, 1992, vs. Atlanta); rushing yards—50 (October 6, 1996, vs. New England); and rushing touchdowns—2 (December 4, 1994, vs. Miami).

			RUSHING				RECEIVING				TOTALS			
Year Team	G	GS	Att.	Yds.	Avg.	TD	No.	Yds.	Avg.	TD	TD	2pt.	Pts.	Fum.
1990—Buffalo NFL	7	0	15	41	2.7	0	0	0	...	0	0	...	0	0
1991—Buffalo NFL	16	5	42	146	3.5	4	3	20	6.7	0	4	...	24	4
1992—Buffalo NFL	16	7	40	166	4.2	2	7	67	9.6	0	2	...	12	0
1993—Buffalo NFL	13	2	20	56	2.8	0	4	50	12.5	1	1	...	6	1
1994—Buffalo NFL	16	7	41	135	3.3	4	11	89	8.1	0	4	0	24	1
1995—Buffalo NFL	15	4	20	77	3.9	0	2	17	8.5	0	1	1	8	0
1996—Baltimore NFL	13	3	26	108	4.2	0	7	28	4.0	0	0	1	2	0
1997—San Diego NFL	5	2	7	20	2.9	0	2	10	5.0	0	0	0	0	0
Pro totals (8 years)	101	30	211	749	3.5	10	36	281	7.8	1	12	2	76	6

GARDOCKI, CHRIS — P — COLTS

PERSONAL: Born February 7, 1970, in Stone Mountain, Ga. ... 6-1/200. ... Full name: Christopher Allen Gardocki.
HIGH SCHOOL: Redan (Stone Mountain, Ga.).
COLLEGE: Clemson.
TRANSACTIONS/CAREER NOTES: Selected after junior season by Chicago Bears in third round (78th pick overall) of 1991 NFL draft. ... Signed by Bears (June 24, 1991). ... On injured reserve with groin injury (August 27-November 27, 1991). ... Granted unconditional free agency (February 17, 1995). ... Signed by Indianapolis Colts (February 24, 1995).
CHAMPIONSHIP GAME EXPERIENCE: Played in AFC championship game (1995 season).
HONORS: Named kicker on THE SPORTING NEWS college All-America second team (1990). ... Named punter on THE SPORTING NEWS NFL All-Pro team (1996). ... Played in Pro Bowl (1996 season).
PRO STATISTICS: 1992—Attempted three passes with one completion for 43 yards and recovered one fumble. 1993—Attempted two passes without a completion, fumbled once and recovered one fumble. 1995—Attempted one pass without a completion.

				PUNTING				
Year Team	G	GS	No.	Yds.	Avg.	Net avg.	In. 20	Blk.
1991—Chicago NFL	4	0	0	0	...	...	0	0
1992—Chicago NFL	16	0	79	3393	42.9	36.2	19	0
1993—Chicago NFL	16	0	80	3080	38.5	36.6	28	0
1994—Chicago NFL	16	0	76	2871	37.8	32.3	23	0
1995—Indianapolis NFL	16	0	63	2681	42.6	33.3	16	0
1996—Indianapolis NFL	16	0	68	3105	45.7	§39.0	23	0
1997—Indianapolis NFL	16	0	67	3034	45.3	36.2	18	0
Pro totals (7 years)	100	0	433	18164	41.9	35.6	127	0

GARNER, CHARLIE — RB — EAGLES

PERSONAL: Born February 13, 1972, in Falls Church, Va. ... 5-9/187.
HIGH SCHOOL: J. E. B. Stuart (Falls Church, Va.).
COLLEGE: Tennessee.
TRANSACTIONS/CAREER NOTES: Selected by Philadelphia Eagles in second round (42nd pick overall) of 1994 NFL draft. ... Signed by Eagles (July 18, 1994). ... Granted free agency (February 14, 1997). ... Re-signed by Eagles (June 16, 1997). ... Granted unconditional free agency (February 13, 1998). ... Re-signed by Eagles (February 23, 1998).
SINGLE GAME HIGHS (regular season): Attempts—28 (October 9, 1994, vs. Washington); yards—122 (October 9, 1994, vs. Washington); and rushing touchdowns—3 (October 8, 1995, vs. Washington).
STATISTICAL PLATEAUS: 100-yard rushing games: 1994 (2), 1995 (1), 1997 (1). Total: 4.

			RUSHING				RECEIVING				KICKOFF RETURNS				TOTALS			
Year Team	G	GS	Att.	Yds.	Avg.	TD	No.	Yds.	Avg.	TD	No.	Yds.	Avg.	TD	TD	2pt.	Pts.	Fum.
1994—Philadelphia NFL	10	8	109	399	3.7	3	8	74	9.3	0	0	0	...	0	3	0	18	3
1995—Philadelphia NFL	15	2	108	588	*5.4	6	10	61	6.1	0	29	590	20.3	0	6	0	36	2
1996—Philadelphia NFL	15	1	66	346	5.2	1	14	92	6.6	0	6	117	19.5	0	1	0	6	1
1997—Philadelphia NFL	16	2	116	547	4.7	3	24	225	9.4	0	0	0	...	0	0	0	0	1
Pro totals (4 years)	56	13	399	1880	4.7	13	56	452	8.1	0	35	707	20.2	0	10	0	60	7

GARNES, SAM — S — GIANTS

PERSONAL: Born July 12, 1974, in Bronx, N.Y. ... 6-3/220.
HIGH SCHOOL: DeWitt Clinton (Bronx, N.Y.).
COLLEGE: Cincinnati.
TRANSACTIONS/CAREER NOTES: Selected by New York Giants in fifth round (136th pick overall) of 1997 NFL draft. ... Signed prior to 1997 season.

			INTERCEPTIONS			
Year Team	G	GS	No.	Yds.	Avg.	TD
1997—New York Giants NFL	16	15	1	95	95.0	1

GARRETT, JASON — QB — COWBOYS

PERSONAL: Born March 28, 1966, in Abington, Pa. ... 6-2/195. ... Full name: Jason Calvin Garrett. ... Son of Jim Garrett, scout, Dallas Cowboys; brother of John Garrett, wide receiver with Cincinnati Bengals (1989) and San Antonio Riders of World League (1991); and brother of Judd Garrett, running back with London of World League (1991-1992).
HIGH SCHOOL: University (Hunting Valley, Ohio).
COLLEGE: Princeton (degree in history).
TRANSACTIONS/CAREER NOTES: Signed as non-drafted free agent by New Orleans Saints (April 1989). ... Released by Saints (August 30, 1989). ... Re-signed by Saints to developmental squad (September 6, 1989). ... Released by Saints (December 29, 1989). ... Re-signed by Saints for 1990 season. ... Released by Saints (September 3, 1990). ... Signed by WLAF (January 3, 1991). ... Selected by San Antonio Riders in first round (seventh quarterback) of 1991 WLAF positional draft. ... Signed by Ottawa Rough Riders of CFL (1991). ... Released by San Antonio Riders (March 3, 1992). ... Signed by Dallas Cowboys (March 23, 1992). ... Released by Cowboys (August 31, 1992). ... Re-signed by Cowboys to practice squad (September 1, 1992). ... Granted unconditional free agency (February 16, 1996). ... Re-signed by Cowboys (April 3, 1996). ... Granted unconditional free agency (February 14, 1997). ... Re-signed by Cowboys (April 8, 1997).
CHAMPIONSHIP GAME EXPERIENCE: Member of Cowboys for NFC championship game (1993-1995 seasons); inactive. ... Member of Super Bowl championship team (1993 and 1995 seasons).
PRO STATISTICS: W.L.: 1991—Fumbled twice. CFL: 1991—Fumbled once. NFL: 1993—Fumbled once. 1994—Recovered one fumble.
SINGLE GAME HIGHS (regular season): Attempts—26 (November 24, 1994, vs. Green Bay); completions—15 (November 24, 1994, vs. Green Bay); yards—311 (November 24, 1994, vs. Green Bay); and touchdown passes—2 (November 24, 1994, vs. Green Bay).
STATISTICAL PLATEAUS: 300-yard passing games: 1994 (1).
MISCELLANEOUS: Regular-season record as starting NFL quarterback: 2-0.

G

Year Team	G	GS	PASSING Att.	Cmp.	Pct.	Yds.	TD	Int.	Avg.	Rat.	RUSHING Att.	Yds.	Avg.	TD	TOTALS TD	2pt.	Pts.
1991—San Antonio W.L.	5	3	113	66	58.4	609	3	3	5.39	71.0	7	7	1.0	0	0	...	0
—Ottawa CFL	13	...	3	2	66.7	28	0	0	9.33	96.5	0	0	...	0	0	...	0
1992—Dallas NFL						Did not play.											
1993—Dallas NFL	5	1	19	9	47.4	61	0	0	3.21	54.9	8	-8	-1.0	0	0	...	0
1994—Dallas NFL	2	1	31	16	51.6	315	2	1	10.16	95.5	3	-2	-0.7	0	0	0	0
1995—Dallas NFL	1	0	5	4	80.0	46	1	0	9.20	144.6	1	-1	-1.0	0	0	0	0
1996—Dallas NFL	1	0	3	3	100.0	44	0	0	14.67	118.8	0	0	...	0	0	0	0
1997—Dallas NFL	1	0	14	10	71.4	56	0	0	4.00	78.3	0	0	...	0	0	0	0
W.L. totals (1 year)	5	3	113	66	58.4	609	3	3	5.39	71.0	7	7	1.0	0	0	0	0
CFL totals (1 year)	13	...	3	2	66.7	28	0	0	9.33	96.5	0	0	...	0	0	0	0
NFL totals (5 years)	10	2	72	42	58.3	522	3	1	7.25	89.0	12	-11	-0.9	0	0	0	0
Pro totals (7 years)	28	...	188	110	58.5	1159	6	4	6.16	78.3	19	-4	-0.2	0	0	0	0

GASH, SAM   FB   BILLS

PERSONAL: Born March 7, 1969, in Hendersonville, N.C. ... 6-0/235. ... Full name: Samuel Lee Gash Jr.. ... Cousin of Thane Gash, safety with Cleveland Browns (1988-1990) and San Francisco 49ers (1992).
HIGH SCHOOL: Hendersonville (N.C.).
COLLEGE: Penn State (degree in liberal arts).
TRANSACTIONS/CAREER NOTES: Selected by New England Patriots in eighth round (205th pick overall) of 1992 NFL draft. ... Signed by Patriots (June 10, 1992). ... Granted free agency (February 17, 1995). ... Re-signed by Patriots (May 5, 1995). ... On injured reserve with knee injury (December 10, 1996-remainder of season). ... Granted unconditional free agency (February 13, 1998). ... Signed by Buffalo Bills (March 5, 1998).
PRO STATISTICS: 1992—Recovered two fumbles. 1994—Returned one kickoff for nine yards and recovered one fumble.
SINGLE GAME HIGHS (regular season): Attempts—15 (December 18, 1994, vs. Buffalo); yards—56 (December 18, 1994, vs. Buffalo); and rushing touchdowns—1 (September 19, 1993, vs. Seattle).

Year Team	G	GS	RUSHING Att.	Yds.	Avg.	TD	RECEIVING No.	Yds.	Avg.	TD	TOTALS TD	2pt.	Pts.	Fum.
1992—New England NFL	15	0	5	7	1.4	1	0	0	...	0	1	...	6	1
1993—New England NFL	15	4	48	149	3.1	1	14	93	6.6	0	1	...	6	1
1994—New England NFL	13	6	30	86	2.9	0	9	61	6.8	0	0	0	0	1
1995—New England NFL	15	12	8	24	3.0	0	26	242	9.3	1	1	0	6	0
1996—New England NFL	14	9	8	15	1.9	0	33	276	8.4	2	2	1	14	0
1997—New England NFL	16	5	6	10	1.7	0	22	154	7.0	3	3	0	18	0
Pro totals (6 years)	88	36	105	291	2.8	2	104	826	7.9	6	8	1	50	3

GASKINS, PERCELL   LB   PANTHERS

PERSONAL: Born April 25, 1972, in Daytona Beach, Fla. ... 6-0/230. ... Full name: Percell McGahee Gaskins.
HIGH SCHOOL: Seabreeze (Ormand Beach, Fla.).
COLLEGE: Northwestern Oklahoma State, then Kansas State.
TRANSACTIONS/CAREER NOTES: Selected by St. Louis Rams in fourth round (105th pick overall) of 1996 NFL draft. ... Signed by Rams (July 9, 1996). ... Claimed on waivers by Carolina Panthers (August 25, 1997).
PLAYING EXPERIENCE: St. Louis NFL, 1996; Carolina NFL, 1997. ... Games/Games started: 1996 (15/1), 1997 (12/0). Total: 27/1.
PRO STATISTICS: 1996—Recovered one fumble.
MISCELLANEOUS: Won NCAA indoor high jump championship (1993).

GEDNEY, CHRIS   TE   CARDINALS

PERSONAL: Born August 9, 1970, in Liverpool, N.Y. ... 6-5/250. ... Full name: Christopher Joseph Gedney.
HIGH SCHOOL: Liverpool (N.Y.).
COLLEGE: Syracuse.
TRANSACTIONS/CAREER NOTES: Selected by Chicago Bears in third round (61st pick overall) of 1993 NFL draft. ... Signed by Bears (June 16, 1994). ... On injured reserve with broken right fibula (October 24, 1994-remainder of season). ... Granted free agency (February 16, 1996). ... Re-signed by Bears (March 29, 1996). ... On injured reserve with ankle injury (September 20, 1996-entire season). ... Granted unconditional free agency (February 14, 1997). ... Signed by Arizona Cardinals (February 28, 1997). ... Granted unconditional free agency (February 13, 1998). ... Re-signed by Cardinals (February 24, 1998).
HONORS: Named tight end on THE SPORTING NEWS college All-America first team (1992).
PRO STATISTICS: 1997—Rushed once for 15 yards and returned two kickoffs for 26 yards.
SINGLE GAME HIGHS (regular season): Receptions—6 (October 25, 1993, vs. Minnesota); yards—69 (October 25, 1993, vs. Minnesota); and touchdown receptions—2 (September 4, 1994, vs. Tampa Bay).

G

Year Team	G	GS	RECEIVING No.	Yds.	Avg.	TD	TOTALS TD	2pt.	Pts.	Fum.
1993—Chicago NFL	7	4	10	98	9.8	0	0	...	0	1
1994—Chicago NFL	7	7	13	157	12.1	3	3	0	18	1
1995—Chicago NFL	14	1	5	52	10.4	0	0	0	0	0
1996—					Did not play.					
1997—Arizona NFL	16	3	23	261	11.3	4	4	0	24	1
Pro totals (4 years)	44	15	51	568	11.1	7	7	0	42	3

GEORGE, EDDIE   RB   OILERS

PERSONAL: Born September 24, 1973, in Philadelphia. ... 6-3/238. ... Full name: Edward Nathan George.
HIGH SCHOOL: Abington (Philadelphia), then Fork Union (Va.) Military Academy.

COLLEGE: Ohio State.
TRANSACTIONS/CAREER NOTES: Selected by Houston Oilers in first round (14th pick overall) of 1996 NFL draft. ... Signed by Oilers (July 20, 1996). ... Oilers franchise moved to Tennessee for 1997 season.
HONORS: Heisman Trophy winner (1995). ... Maxwell Award winner (1995). ... Doak Walker Award winner (1995). ... Named running back on THE SPORTING NEWS college All-America first team (1995). ... Named NFL Rookie of the Year by THE SPORTING NEWS (1996). ... Played in Pro Bowl (1997 season).
PRO STATISTICS: 1996—Recovered one fumble.
SINGLE GAME HIGHS (regular season): Attempts—35 (August 31, 1997, vs. Oakland); yards—216 (August 31, 1997, vs. Oakland); and rushing touchdowns—2 (October 19, 1997, vs. Washington).
STATISTICAL PLATEAUS: 100-yard rushing games: 1996 (4), 1997 (8). Total: 12.

				RUSHING				RECEIVING				TOTALS		
Year Team	G	GS	Att.	Yds.	Avg.	TD	No.	Yds.	Avg.	TD	TD	2pt.	Pts.	Fum.
1996—Houston NFL	16	16	335	1368	4.1	8	23	182	7.9	0	8	0	48	3
1997—Tennessee NFL	16	16	357	1399	3.9	6	7	44	6.3	1	7	1	44	4
Pro totals (2 years)	32	32	692	2767	4.0	14	30	226	7.5	1	15	1	92	7

GEORGE, JEFF   QB   RAIDERS

PERSONAL: Born December 8, 1967, in Indianapolis. ... 6-4/215. ... Full name: Jeffrey Scott George.
HIGH SCHOOL: Warren Central (Indianapolis).
COLLEGE: Purdue, then Illinois (degree in speech communications, 1991).
TRANSACTIONS/CAREER NOTES: Signed after junior season by Indianapolis Colts (April 20, 1990). ... Selected officially by Colts in first round (first pick overall) of 1990 NFL draft. ... On reserve/did not report list (July 23-August 20, 1993). ... Traded by Colts to Atlanta Falcons for first- (LB Trev Alberts) and third-round (OT Jason Mathews) picks in 1994 draft and a first-round pick (WR Marvin Harrison) in 1996 draft (March 24, 1994). ... Designated by Falcons as transition player (February 16, 1996). ... Released by Falcons (October 22, 1996). ... Signed by Oakland Raiders (February 15, 1997).
PRO STATISTICS: 1990—Fumbled four times and recovered two fumbles. 1991—Fumbled eight times and recovered two fumbles for minus four yards. 1992—Fumbled six times and recovered one fumble for minus two yards. 1993—Fumbled four times. 1994—Led league with 12 fumbles and recovered six fumbles for minus 12 yards. 1995—Fumbled six times and recovered two fumbles for minus 15 yards. 1996—Fumbled three times and recovered two fumbles for minus 24 yards. 1997—Fumbled seven times and recovered three fumbles for minus 14 yards.
SINGLE GAME HIGHS (regular season): Attempts—59 (November 7, 1993, vs. Washington); completions—37 (November 7, 1993, vs. Washington); yards—386 (September 17, 1995, vs. New Orleans); and touchdown passes—4 (September 28, 1997, vs. St. Louis).
STATISTICAL PLATEAUS: 300-yard passing games: 1991 (2), 1992 (3), 1993 (2), 1994 (2), 1995 (3), 1997 (2). Total: 14.
MISCELLANEOUS: Regular-season record as starting NFL quarterback: 34-66 (.340). ... Postseason record as starting NFL quarterback: 0-1.

						PASSING					RUSHING				TOTALS		
Year Team	G	GS	Att.	Cmp.	Pct.	Yds.	TD	Int.	Avg.	Rat.	Att.	Yds.	Avg.	TD	TD	2pt.	Pts.
1990—Indianapolis NFL	13	12	334	181	54.2	2152	16	13	6.44	73.8	11	2	0.2	1	1	...	6
1991—Indianapolis NFL	16	16	485	292	60.2	2910	10	12	6.00	73.8	16	36	2.3	0	0	...	0
1992—Indianapolis NFL	10	10	306	167	54.6	1963	7	15	6.42	61.5	14	26	1.9	1	1	...	6
1993—Indianapolis NFL	13	11	407	234	57.5	2526	8	6	6.21	76.3	13	39	3.0	0	0	...	0
1994—Atlanta NFL	16	16	524	322	61.5	3734	23	18	7.13	83.3	30	66	2.2	0	0	0	0
1995—Atlanta NFL	16	16	557	336	60.3	4143	24	11	7.44	89.5	27	17	0.6	0	0	0	0
1996—Atlanta NFL	3	3	99	56	56.6	698	3	3	7.05	76.1	5	10	2.0	0	0	0	0
1997—Oakland NFL	16	16	521	290	55.7	*3917	§29	9	7.52	91.2	17	44	2.6	0	0	0	0
Pro totals (8 years)	103	100	3233	1878	58.1	22043	120	87	6.82	80.1	133	240	1.8	2	2	0	12

GEORGE, RON   LB   CHIEFS

PERSONAL: Born March 20, 1970, in Heidelberg, West Germany. ... 6-2/236. ... Full name: Ronald L. George.
HIGH SCHOOL: Heidelberg (West Germany) American.
COLLEGE: Air Force, then Stanford (degree in economics, 1992).
TRANSACTIONS/CAREER NOTES: Selected by Atlanta Falcons in fifth round (121st pick overall) of 1993 NFL draft. ... Signed by Falcons (June 4, 1993). ... Granted free agency (February 16, 1996). ... Re-signed by Falcons (June 12, 1996). ... Granted unconditional free agency (February 14, 1997). ... Signed by Minnesota Vikings (June 9, 1997). ... Released by Vikings (February 2, 1998). ... Signed by Kansas City Chiefs (April 6, 1998).
PLAYING EXPERIENCE: Atlanta NFL, 1993-1996; Minnesota NFL, 1997. ... Games/Games started: 1993 (12/4), 1994 (16/9), 1995 (16/0), 1996 (16/15), 1997 (16/0). Total: 76/28.
HONORS: Named linebacker on THE SPORTING NEWS college All-America second team (1992).
PRO STATISTICS: 1993—Credited with one sack. 1994—Recovered one fumble. 1995—Returned three kickoffs for 45 yards. 1996—Credited with two sacks and recovered three fumbles for 14 yards. 1997—Returned one kickoff for 10 yards.

GEORGE, SPENCER   RB   OILERS

PERSONAL: Born October 28, 1973, in Beaumont, Texas. ... 5-9/202. ... Full name: Spencer James George.
HIGH SCHOOL: Hamshire-Fannett (Hamshire, Texas).
COLLEGE: Rice.
TRANSACTIONS/CAREER NOTES: Signed as non-drafted free agent by Tennessee Oilers (May 5, 1997). ... Released by Oilers (August 25, 1997). ... Re-signed by Oilers to practice squad (August 28, 1997). ... Activated (November 18, 1997).
PLAYING EXPERIENCE: Tennessee NFL, 1997. ... Games/Games started: 5/0.
SINGLE GAME HIGHS (regular season): Attempts—0; yards—0; and rushing touchdowns—0.

G

GERAK, JOHN G

PERSONAL: Born January 6, 1970, in Youngstown, Ohio. ... 6-3/300. ... Full name: John Matthew Gerak.
HIGH SCHOOL: Struthers (Ohio).
COLLEGE: Penn State.
TRANSACTIONS/CAREER NOTES: Selected by Minnesota Vikings in third round (57th pick overall) of 1993 NFL draft. ... Signed by Vikings (July 17, 1993). ... Granted unconditional free agency (February 14, 1997). ... Signed by St. Louis Rams (April 18, 1997). ... Released by Rams (June 16, 1998).
PLAYING EXPERIENCE: Minnesota NFL, 1993-1996; St. Louis NFL, 1997. ... Games/Games started: 1993 (4/0), 1994 (13/3), 1995 (15/6), 1996 (14/10), 1997 (16/16). Total: 62/35.
PRO STATISTICS: 1995—Caught one pass for three yards and returned one kickoff for 19 yards. 1996—Returned one kickoff for 13 yards and recovered one fumble.

GIBSON, OLIVER DT STEELERS

PERSONAL: Born March 15, 1972, in Chicago. ... 6-3/298. ... Full name: Oliver Donnovan Gibson. ... Cousin of Godfrey Myles, linebacker with Denver Broncos (1991-1997).
HIGH SCHOOL: Romeoville (Ill.).
COLLEGE: Notre Dame (degree in economics, 1994).
TRANSACTIONS/CAREER NOTES: Selected by Pittsburgh Steelers in fourth round (120th pick overall) of 1995 NFL draft. ... Signed by Steelers (July 18, 1995). ... Granted free agency (February 13, 1998). ... Re-signed by Steelers (June 9, 1998).
PLAYING EXPERIENCE: Pittsburgh NFL, 1995-1997. ... Games/Games started: 1995 (12/0), 1996 (16/0), 1997 (16/0). Total: 44/0.
CHAMPIONSHIP GAME EXPERIENCE: Member of Steelers for AFC championship game (1995 season); inactive. ... Played in AFC championship game (1997 season).
PRO STATISTICS: 1995—Returned one kickoff for 10 yards. 1996—Credited with 2 1/2 sacks. 1997—Credited with one sack and recovered one fumble.

GILBERT, SEAN DT PANTHERS

PERSONAL: Born April 10, 1970, in Aliquippa, Pa. ... 6-5/318.
HIGH SCHOOL: Aliquippa (Pa.).
COLLEGE: Pittsburgh.
TRANSACTIONS/CAREER NOTES: Selected after junior season by Los Angeles Rams in first round (third pick overall) of 1992 NFL draft. ... Signed by Rams (July 28, 1992). ... Designated by Rams as transition player (February 25, 1993). ... Rams franchise moved to St. Louis (April 12, 1995). ... Traded by Rams to Washington Redskins for first-round pick (RB Lawrence Phillips) in 1996 draft (April 8, 1996). ... Designated by Redskins as franchise player (February 12, 1997). Designated by Redskins as franchise player (February 13, 1998). ... Tendered offer sheet by Carolina Panthers (March 24, 1998). ... Redskins declined to match offer (April 21, 1998).
HONORS: Played in Pro Bowl (1993 season).
PRO STATISTICS: 1992—Recovered one fumble. 1994—Credited with one safety. 1995—Recovered one fumble.

Year Team	G	GS	SACKS
1992—Los Angeles Rams NFL	16	16	5.0
1993—Los Angeles Rams NFL	16	16	10.5
1994—Los Angeles Rams NFL	14	14	3.0
1995—St. Louis NFL	14	14	5.5
1996—Washington NFL	16	16	3.0
1997—Washington NFL	Did not play.		
Pro totals (5 years)	76	76	27.0

GILDON, JASON LB STEELERS

PERSONAL: Born July 31, 1972, in Altus, Okla. ... 6-3/245. ... Full name: Jason Larue Gildon. ... Related to Wendall Gaines, defensive end with Arizona Cardinals (1995), Green Bay Packers (1996), St. Louis Rams (1997).
HIGH SCHOOL: Altus (Okla.).
COLLEGE: Oklahoma State.
TRANSACTIONS/CAREER NOTES: Selected by Pittsburgh Steelers in third round (88th pick overall) of 1994 NFL draft. ... Signed by Steelers (July 15, 1994). ... Granted free agency (February 14, 1997). ... Re-signed by Steelers (July 21, 1997). ... Granted unconditional free agency (February 13, 1998). ... Re-signed by Steelers (April 7, 1998).
CHAMPIONSHIP GAME EXPERIENCE: Played in AFC championship game (1994, 1995 and 1997 seasons). ... Played in Super Bowl XXX (1995 season).
PRO STATISTICS: 1995—Recovered one fumble. 1997—Recovered two fumbles for 32 yards and one touchdown.

Year Team	G	GS	SACKS
1994—Pittsburgh NFL	16	1	2.0
1995—Pittsburgh NFL	16	0	3.0
1996—Pittsburgh NFL	14	13	7.0
1997—Pittsburgh NFL	16	16	5.0
Pro totals (4 years)	62	30	17.0

GISLER, MIKE G/C JETS

PERSONAL: Born August 26, 1969, in Runge, Texas. ... 6-4/295. ... Full name: Michael Gisler.
HIGH SCHOOL: Runge (Texas).
COLLEGE: Houston.

G

TRANSACTIONS/CAREER NOTES: Selected by New Orleans Saints in 11th round (303rd pick overall) of 1992 NFL draft. ... Signed by Saints (July 15, 1992). ... Released by Saints (August 31, 1992). ... Re-signed by Saints to practice squad (September 2, 1992). ... Released by Saints (September 7, 1992). ... Signed by Houston Oilers to practice squad (September 9, 1992-remainder of season). ... Granted free agency after 1992 season. ... Signed by New England Patriots (March 3, 1993). ... Granted free agency (February 16, 1996). ... Re-signed by Patriots (May 20, 1996). ... Released by Patriots (August 25, 1996). ... Re-signed by Patriots (September 10, 1996). ... Granted unconditional free agency (February 14, 1997). ... Re-signed by Patriots (April 22, 1997). ... Granted unconditional free agency (February 13, 1998). ... Signed by New York Jets (February 18, 1998).

PLAYING EXPERIENCE: New England NFL, 1993-1997. ... Games/Games started: 1993 (12/0), 1994 (15/5), 1995 (16/0), 1996 (14/0), 1997 (16/2). Total: 73/7.

CHAMPIONSHIP GAME EXPERIENCE: Played in AFC championship game (1996 season). ... Played in Super Bowl XXXI (1996 season).

PRO STATISTICS: 1995—Returned two kickoffs for 19 yards and fumbled once. 1996—Returned one kickoff for nine yards.

GLENN, AARON — CB/KR — JETS

PERSONAL: Born July 16, 1972, in Humble, Texas. ... 5-9/185. ... Full name: Aaron DeVon Glenn.
HIGH SCHOOL: Nimitz (Houston).
COLLEGE: Texas A&M.
TRANSACTIONS/CAREER NOTES: Selected by New York Jets in first round (12th pick overall) of 1994 NFL draft. ... Signed by Jets (July 21, 1994).
HONORS: Named defensive back on THE SPORTING NEWS college All-America first team (1993). ... Played in Pro Bowl (1997 season).
PRO STATISTICS: 1994—Recovered one fumble. 1995—Recovered one fumble.

		INTERCEPTIONS				KICKOFF RETURNS				TOTALS			
Year Team	G	GS	No.	Yds.	Avg.	TD	No.	Yds.	Avg.	TD	TD	2pt.	Pts.	Fum.
1994—New York Jets NFL	15	15	0	0	...	0	27	582	21.6	0	0	0	0	2
1995—New York Jets NFL	16	16	1	17	17.0	0	1	12	12.0	0	0	0	0	0
1996—New York Jets NFL	16	16	4	113	28.3	†2	1	6	6.0	0	2	0	12	0
1997—New York Jets NFL	16	16	1	5	5.0	0	28	741	§26.5	▲1	1	0	6	1
Pro totals (4 years)	63	63	6	135	22.5	2	57	1341	23.5	1	3	0	18	3

GLENN, TARIK — OT — COLTS

PERSONAL: Born May 25, 1976, in Cleveland. ... 6-5/335.
HIGH SCHOOL: Bishop O'Dowd (Oakland).
COLLEGE: California.
TRANSACTIONS/CAREER NOTES: Selected by Indianapolis Colts in first round (19th pick overall) of 1997 NFL draft. ... Signed by Colts (August 11, 1997).
PLAYING EXPERIENCE: Indianapolis NFL, 1997. ... Games/Games started: 16/16.
HONORS: Named offensive tackle on THE SPORTING NEWS college All-America second team (1996).
PRO STATISTICS: 1997—Caught one pass for three yards and recovered one fumble.

GLENN, TERRY — WR — PATRIOTS

PERSONAL: Born July 23, 1974, in Columbus, Ohio. ... 5-11/185.
HIGH SCHOOL: Brookhaven (Columbus, Ohio).
COLLEGE: Ohio State.
TRANSACTIONS/CAREER NOTES: Selected after junior season by New England Patriots in the first round (seventh pick overall) of 1996 NFL draft. ... Signed by Patriots (July 12, 1996).
CHAMPIONSHIP GAME EXPERIENCE: Played in AFC championship game (1996 season). ... Played in Super Bowl XXXI (1996 season).
HONORS: Fred Biletnikoff Award winner (1995). ... Named wide receiver on THE SPORTING NEWS college All-America first team (1995).
RECORDS: Holds NFL single-season record for most receptions by a rookie—90 (1996).
SINGLE GAME HIGHS (regular season): Receptions—10 (November 3, 1996, vs. Miami); yards—163 (October 27, 1997, vs. Green Bay); and touchdown receptions—1 (November 2, 1997, vs. Minnesota).
STATISTICAL PLATEAUS: 100-yard receiving games: 1996 (2), 1997 (1). Total: 3.

		RUSHING				RECEIVING				TOTALS			
Year Team	G	GS	Att.	Yds.	Avg.	TD	No.	Yds.	Avg.	TD	TD	2pt.	Pts.	Fum.
1996—New England NFL	15	15	5	42	8.4	0	90	1132	12.6	6	6	0	36	1
1997—New England NFL	9	9	0	0	...	0	27	431	16.0	2	2	0	12	1
Pro totals (2 years)	24	24	5	42	8.4	0	117	1563	13.4	8	8	0	48	2

GLOVER, ANDREW — TE — VIKINGS

G

PERSONAL: Born August 12, 1967, in New Orleans. ... 6-6/253. ... Full name: Andrew Lee Glover.
HIGH SCHOOL: East Ascension (Gonzales, La.).
COLLEGE: Grambling State (degree in criminal justice).
TRANSACTIONS/CAREER NOTES: Selected by Los Angeles Raiders in 10th round (274th pick overall) of 1991 NFL draft. ... Signed by Raiders (1991). ... On injured reserve with knee injury (December 27, 1993-remainder of season). ... Raiders franchise moved to Oakland (July 21, 1995). ... Granted unconditional free agency (February 16, 1996). ... Re-signed by Raiders (May 24, 1996). ... Granted unconditional free agency (February 14, 1997). ... Signed by Minnesota Vikings (July 28, 1997). ... Granted unconditional free agency (February 13, 1998). ... Re-signed by Vikings (February 19, 1998).
PRO STATISTICS: 1992—Recovered one fumble.
SINGLE GAME HIGHS (regular season): Receptions—6 (October 5, 1997, vs. Arizona); yards—86 (October 5, 1997, vs. Arizona); and touchdown receptions—1 (December 21, 1997, vs. Indianapolis).

Year Team		G	GS	RECEIVING				TOTALS			
				No.	Yds.	Avg.	TD	TD	2pt.	Pts.	Fum.
1991—Los Angeles Raiders NFL		16	1	5	45	9.0	3	3	...	18	0
1992—Los Angeles Raiders NFL		16	2	15	178	11.9	1	1	...	6	1
1993—Los Angeles Raiders NFL		15	0	4	55	13.8	1	1	...	6	0
1994—Los Angeles Raiders NFL		16	16	33	371	11.2	2	2	0	12	0
1995—Oakland NFL		16	7	26	220	8.5	3	3	0	18	0
1996—Oakland NFL		14	4	9	101	11.2	1	1	0	6	0
1997—Minnesota NFL		13	11	32	378	11.8	3	3	0	18	0
Pro totals (7 years)		106	41	124	1348	10.9	14	14	0	84	1

GLOVER, KEVIN　　　　　C　　　　　SEAHAWKS

PERSONAL: Born June 17, 1963, in Washington, D.C. ... 6-2/282. ... Full name: Kevin Bernard Glover.
HIGH SCHOOL: Largo (Md.).
COLLEGE: Maryland.
TRANSACTIONS/CAREER NOTES: Selected by Tampa Bay Bandits in 1985 USFL territorial draft. ... Selected by Detroit Lions in second round (34th pick overall) of 1985 NFL draft. ... Signed by Lions (July 23, 1985). ... On injured reserve with knee injury (December 7, 1985-remainder of season). ... On injured reserve with knee injury (September 29-December 20, 1986). ... Granted free agency (February 1, 1992). ... Re-signed by Lions (August 25, 1992). ... On injured reserve with ankle injury (October 27, 1992-remainder of season). ... Designated by Lions as franchise player (February 16, 1996). ... Granted unconditional free agency (February 13, 1998). ... Signed by Seattle Seahawks (February 21, 1998).
PLAYING EXPERIENCE: Detroit NFL, 1985-1997. ... Games/Games started: 1985 (10/0), 1986 (4/1), 1987 (12/9), 1988 (16/16), 1989 (16/16), 1990 (16/16), 1991 (16/16), 1992 (7/7), 1993 (16/16), 1994 (16/16), 1995 (16/16), 1996 (16/16), 1997 (16/16). Total: 177/161.
CHAMPIONSHIP GAME EXPERIENCE: Played in NFC championship game (1991 season).
HONORS: Named center on THE SPORTING NEWS college All-America first team (1984). ... Played in Pro Bowl (1995-1997 seasons).
PRO STATISTICS: 1987—Returned one kickoff for 19 yards. 1988—Recovered two fumbles. 1990—Recovered one fumble. 1992—Recovered one fumble. 1995—Fumbled twice and recovered one fumble for minus 14 yards. 1996—Recovered two fumbles. 1997—Recovered one fumble.

GLOVER, La'ROI　　　　　DT　　　　　SAINTS

PERSONAL: Born July 4, 1974, in San Diego. ... 6-1/285. ... Full name: La'Roi Damon Glover. ... Name pronounced la-ROY.
HIGH SCHOOL: Point Loma (San Diego).
COLLEGE: San Diego State.
TRANSACTIONS/CAREER NOTES: Selected by Oakland Raiders in fifth round (166th pick overall) of 1996 NFL draft. ... Signed by Raiders (July 12, 1996). ... Assigned by Raiders to Barcelona Dragons in 1997 World League enhancement allocation program (February 19, 1997). ... Claimed on waivers by New Orleans Saints (August 25, 1997).
PRO STATISTICS: 1997—Recovered one fumble.

Year Team	G	GS	SACKS
1996—Oakland NFL	2	0	0.0
1997—Barcelona W.L.	...	...	6.5
—New Orleans NFL	15	2	6.5
W.L. totals (1 year)	...	...	6.5
NFL totals (2 years)	17	2	6.5
Pro totals (3 years)	...	...	13.0

GODFREY, RANDALL　　　　　LB　　　　　COWBOYS

PERSONAL: Born April 6, 1973, in Valdosta, Ga. ... 6-2/237. ... Full name: Randall Euralentris Godfrey.
HIGH SCHOOL: Lowndes County (Valdosta, Ga.).
COLLEGE: Georgia.
TRANSACTIONS/CAREER NOTES: Selected by Dallas Cowboys in second round (49th pick overall) of 1996 NFL draft. ... Signed by Cowboys (July 17, 1996).
PLAYING EXPERIENCE: Dallas NFL, 1996 and 1997. ... Games/Games started: 1996 (16/6), 1997 (16/16). Total: 32/32.
PRO STATISTICS: 1997—Credited with one sack and recovered one fumble.

GOEAS, LEO　　　　　C/G　　　　　BRONCOS

G

PERSONAL: Born August 15, 1966, in Honolulu. ... 6-4/300. ... Full name: Leo Douglas Goeas. ... Name pronounced GO-az.
HIGH SCHOOL: Kamehameha (Honolulu).
COLLEGE: Hawaii.
TRANSACTIONS/CAREER NOTES: Selected by San Diego Chargers in third round (60th pick overall) of 1990 NFL draft. ... Signed by Chargers (July 19, 1990). ... Granted free agency (February 1, 1992). ... Re-signed by Chargers (July 24, 1992). ... Granted free agency (March 1, 1993). ... Re-signed by Chargers (April 15, 1993). ... Traded by Chargers to Los Angeles Rams for fourth-round pick in 1993 draft (April 15, 1993). ... Rams franchise moved to St. Louis (April 12, 1995). ... Granted unconditional free agency (February 16, 1996). ... Re-signed by Rams (June 21, 1996). ... Granted unconditional free agency (February 14, 1997). ... Signed by Baltimore Ravens (March 20, 1997). ... On injured reserve with chest injury (December 10, 1997-remainder of season). ... Released by Ravens after 1997 season. ... Signed by Denver Broncos (April 1, 1998).
PLAYING EXPERIENCE: San Diego NFL, 1990-1992; Los Angeles Rams NFL, 1993 and 1994; St. Louis NFL, 1995 and 1996; Baltimore NFL, 1997. ... Games/Games started: 1990 (15/9), 1991 (9/4), 1992 (16/5), 1993 (16/16), 1994 (13/13), 1995 (15/14), 1996 (16/13), 1997 (11/7). Total: 111/81.
PRO STATISTICS: 1990—Recovered one fumble. 1992—Recovered one fumble. 1994—Recovered one fumble. 1996—Recovered one fumble.

GOGAN, KEVIN G 49ERS

PERSONAL: Born November 2, 1964, in Pacifica, Calif. ... 6-7/330. ... Full name: Kevin Patrick Gogan.
HIGH SCHOOL: Sacred Heart (San Francisco).
COLLEGE: Washington (degree in sociology, 1987).
TRANSACTIONS/CAREER NOTES: Selected by Dallas Cowboys in eighth round (206th pick overall) of 1987 NFL draft. ... Signed by Cowboys (July 18, 1987). ... On non-football injury list with substance abuse problem (August 5-31, 1988). ... Granted roster exemption (August 31-September 5, 1988). ... Granted unconditional free agency (February 17, 1994). ... Signed by Los Angeles Raiders (April 18, 1994). ... Raiders franchise moved to Oakland (July 21, 1995). ... Granted unconditional free agency (February 14, 1997). ... Signed by San Francisco 49ers (February 25, 1997).
PLAYING EXPERIENCE: Dallas NFL, 1987-1993; Los Angeles Raiders NFL, 1994; Oakland NFL, 1995 and 1996; San Francisco NFL, 1997. ... Games/Games started: 1987 (11/10), 1988 (15/15), 1989 (13/13), 1990 (16/4), 1991 (16/16), 1992 (16/1), 1993 (16/16), 1994 (16/16), 1995 (16/16), 1996 (16/16), 1997 (16/16). Total: 167/139.
CHAMPIONSHIP GAME EXPERIENCE: Played in NFC championship game (1992, 1993 and 1997 seasons). ... Member of Super Bowl championship team (1992 and 1993 seasons).
HONORS: Played in Pro Bowl (1994 and 1997 seasons).
PRO STATISTICS: 1987—Recovered one fumble. 1990—Recovered one fumble. 1996—Recovered one fumble.

GONZALEZ, TONY TE CHIEFS

PERSONAL: Born February 27, 1976, in Torrance, Calif. ... 6-4/244. ... Full name: Anthony Gonzalez.
HIGH SCHOOL: Huntington Beach (Calif.).
COLLEGE: California.
TRANSACTIONS/CAREER NOTES: Selected by Kansas City Chiefs in first round (13th pick overall) of 1997 NFL draft. ... Signed by Chiefs (July 29, 1997).
HONORS: Named tight end on THE SPORTING NEWS college All-America first team (1996).
SINGLE GAME HIGHS (regular season): Receptions—7 (November 9, 1997, vs. Jacksonville); yards—69 (November 9, 1997, vs. Jacksonville); and touchdown receptions—1 (November 30, 1997, vs. San Francisco).

			RECEIVING				TOTALS		
Year Team	G	GS	No.	Yds.	Avg.	TD	TD	2pt.	Pts.	Fum.
1997—Kansas City NFL	16	0	33	368	11.2	2	2	1	14	0

GOOCH, JEFF LB BUCCANEERS

PERSONAL: Born October 31, 1974, in Nashville. ... 5-11/224.
HIGH SCHOOL: Overton (Nashville).
COLLEGE: Austin Peay.
TRANSACTIONS/CAREER NOTES: Signed as non-drafted free agent by Tampa Bay Buccaneers (April 23, 1996). ... On injured reserve with knee injury (December 17, 1996-remainder of season).
PLAYING EXPERIENCE: Tampa Bay NFL, 1996 and 1997. ... Games/Games started: 1996 (15/0), 1997 (14/5). Total: 29/5.
PRO STATISTICS: 1996—Recovered one fumble.

GOODWIN, HUNTER TE VIKINGS

PERSONAL: Born October 10, 1972, in Bellville, Texas. ... 6-5/273. ... Full name: Robert Hunter Goodwin.
HIGH SCHOOL: Bellville (Texas).
COLLEGE: Texas A&M-Kingsville, then Texas A&M.
TRANSACTIONS/CAREER NOTES: Selected by Minnesota Vikings in fourth round (97th pick overall) of 1996 NFL draft. ... Signed by Vikings (July 20, 1996).
SINGLE GAME HIGHS (regular season): Receptions—2 (September 7, 1997, vs. Chicago); yards—24 (December 1, 1996, vs. Arizona); and touchdown receptions—0.

			RECEIVING				TOTALS		
Year Team	G	GS	No.	Yds.	Avg.	TD	TD	2pt.	Pts.	Fum.
1996—Minnesota NFL	9	6	1	24	24.0	0	0	0	0	0
1997—Minnesota NFL	16	5	7	61	8.7	0	0	0	0	0
Pro totals (2 years)	25	11	8	85	10.6	0	0	0	0	0

GORDON, DARRIEN CB BRONCOS G

PERSONAL: Born November 14, 1970, in Shawnee, Okla. ... 5-11/178. ... Full name: Darrien X. Jamal Gordon.
HIGH SCHOOL: Shawnee (Okla.).
COLLEGE: Stanford.
TRANSACTIONS/CAREER NOTES: Selected by San Diego Chargers in first round (22nd pick overall) of 1993 NFL draft. ... Signed by Chargers (July 16, 1993). ... Inactive for 16 games due to shoulder injury (1995 season). ... Granted unconditional free agency (February 14, 1997). ... Signed by Denver Broncos (April 30, 1997).
CHAMPIONSHIP GAME EXPERIENCE: Played in AFC championship game (1994 and 1997 seasons). ... Played in Super Bowl XXIX (1994 season). ... Member of Super Bowl championship team (1997 season).
HONORS: Named punt returner on THE SPORTING NEWS NFL All-Pro team (1997).
RECORDS: Shares NFL single-game records for most touchdowns by punt return—2; and most touchdowns by combined kick return—2 (November 9, 1997, vs. Carolina).
PRO STATISTICS: 1993—Recovered two fumbles for minus two yards. 1994—Recovered three fumbles for 15 yards. 1996—Credited with two sacks. 1997—Credited with two sacks and recovered four fumbles.

Year Team	G	GS	INTERCEPTIONS				PUNT RETURNS				TOTALS			
			No.	Yds.	Avg.	TD	No.	Yds.	Avg.	TD	TD	2pt.	Pts.	Fum.
1993—San Diego NFL	16	7	1	3	3.0	0	31	395	12.7	0	0	...	0	4
1994—San Diego NFL	16	16	4	32	8.0	0	36	475	§13.2	†2	2	0	12	2
1995—San Diego NFL							Did not play.							
1996—San Diego NFL	16	6	2	55	27.5	0	36	537	§14.9	§1	1	0	6	3
1997—Denver NFL	16	16	4	64	16.0	1	40	543	13.6	†3	4	0	24	3
Pro totals (4 years)	64	45	11	154	14.0	1	143	1950	13.6	6	7	0	42	12

GORDON, DWAYNE — LB — JETS

PERSONAL: Born November 2, 1969, in White Plains, N.Y. ... 6-1/240. ... Full name: Dwayne K. Gordon.
HIGH SCHOOL: Arlington North (LaGrangeville, N.Y.).
COLLEGE: New Hampshire.
TRANSACTIONS/CAREER NOTES: Selected by Miami Dolphins in eighth round (218th pick overall) of 1993 NFL draft. ... Released by Dolphins (July 12, 1993). ... Signed by Atlanta Falcons (July 19, 1993). ... Released by Falcons (August 27, 1995). ... Signed by San Diego Chargers (August 28, 1995). ... Granted free agency (February 16, 1996). ... Re-signed by Chargers (June 14, 1996). ... Granted unconditional free agency (February 17, 1997). ... Signed by New York Jets (June 4, 1997).
PLAYING EXPERIENCE: Atlanta NFL, 1993 and 1994; San Diego NFL, 1995 and 1996; New York Jets NFL, 1997. ... Games/Games started: 1993 (5/0), 1994 (16/0), 1995 (16/3), 1996 (13/0), 1997 (16/8). Total: 66/11.
PRO STATISTICS: 1993—Fumbled once. 1995—Credited with one sack and recovered one fumble. 1997—Credited with one sack.

GOUVEIA, KURT — LB — CHARGERS

PERSONAL: Born September 14, 1964, in Honolulu. ... 6-1/240. ... Full name: Kurt Keola Gouveia. ... Name pronounced goo-VAY-uh.
HIGH SCHOOL: Waianae (Hawaii).
COLLEGE: Brigham Young.
TRANSACTIONS/CAREER NOTES: Selected by Washington Redskins in eighth round (213th pick overall) of 1986 NFL draft. ... Signed by Redskins (July 18, 1986). ... On injured reserve with knee injury (August 25, 1986-entire season). ... Granted unconditional free agency (March 1, 1993). ... Re-signed by Redskins for 1993 season. ... Granted free agency (February 17, 1995). ... Signed by Philadelphia Eagles (April 23, 1995). ... Granted unconditional free agency (February 16, 1996). ... Signed by San Diego Chargers (February 27, 1996). ... On injured reserve with neck injury (October 22, 1997-remainder of season).
CHAMPIONSHIP GAME EXPERIENCE: Played in NFC championship game (1987 and 1991 seasons). ... Member of Super Bowl championship team (1987 and 1991 seasons).
POST SEASON RECORDS: Shares NFL postseason career record for most consecutive games with one or more interception—3.
PRO STATISTICS: 1990—Recovered one fumble for 39 yards and a touchdown. 1995—Recovered one fumble.

Year Team	G	GS	INTERCEPTIONS				SACKS	KICKOFF RETURNS				TOTALS			
			No.	Yds.	Avg.	TD	No.	No.	Yds.	Avg.	TD	TD	2pt.	Pts.	Fum.
1986—Washington NFL								Did not play.							
1987—Washington NFL	11	1	0	0	...	0	0.0	0	0	...	0	0	...	0	0
1988—Washington NFL	16	0	0	0	...	0	0.0	0	0	...	0	0	...	0	0
1989—Washington NFL	15	1	1	1	1.0	0	0.0	1	0	0.0	0	0	...	0	0
1990—Washington NFL	16	7	0	0	...	0	1.0	2	23	11.5	0	1	...	6	0
1991—Washington NFL	14	1	1	22	22.0	0	0.0	3	12	4.0	0	0	...	0	0
1992—Washington NFL	16	14	3	43	14.3	0	1.0	1	7	7.0	0	0	...	0	0
1993—Washington NFL	16	16	1	59	59.0	1	1.5	0	0	...	0	1	...	6	0
1994—Washington NFL	14	1	1	7	7.0	0	0.0	0	0	...	0	0	0	0	0
1995—Philadelphia NFL	16	16	1	20	20.0	0	0.0	0	0	...	0	0	0	0	0
1996—San Diego NFL	16	16	3	41	13.7	0	1.0	0	0	...	0	0	0	0	0
1997—San Diego NFL	7	6	1	0	0.0	0	0.0	0	0	...	0	0	0	0	0
Pro totals (11 years)	157	79	12	193	16.1	1	4.5	7	42	6.0	0	2	0	12	0

GOWIN, TOBY — P — COWBOYS

PERSONAL: Born March 30, 1975, in Jacksonville, Texas. ... 5-10/167.
HIGH SCHOOL: Jacksonville (Texas).
COLLEGE: North Texas.
TRANSACTIONS/CAREER NOTES: Signed as non-drafted free agent by Dallas Cowboys (April 24, 1997).

Year Team	G	GS	PUNTING						KICKING						
			No.	Yds.	Avg.	Net avg.	In. 20	Blk.	XPM	XPA	FGM	FGA	Lg.	50+	Pts.
1997—Dallas NFL	16	0	86	3592	41.8	35.4	26	0	0	0	0	1	0	0-1	0

GRAGG, SCOTT — OT — GIANTS

PERSONAL: Born February 28, 1972, in Altus, Okla. ... 6-8/325.
HIGH SCHOOL: Silverton (Ore.) Union.
COLLEGE: Montana.
TRANSACTIONS/CAREER NOTES: Selected by New York Giants in second round (54th pick overall) of 1995 NFL draft. ... Signed by Giants (July 23, 1995). ... Granted free agency (February 13, 1998).
PLAYING EXPERIENCE: New York Giants NFL, 1995-1997. ... Games/Games started: 1995 (13/0), 1996 (16/16), 1997 (16/16). Total: 45/32.
PRO STATISTICS: 1997—Recovered one fumble.

G

GRAHAM, AARON   C   CARDINALS

PERSONAL: Born May 22, 1973, in Las Vegas, N.M. ... 6-4/293.
HIGH SCHOOL: Denton (Texas).
COLLEGE: Nebraska.
TRANSACTIONS/CAREER NOTES: Selected by Arizona Cardinals in fourth round (112th pick overall) of 1996 NFL draft. ... Signed by Cardinals for 1996 season.
PLAYING EXPERIENCE: Arizona NFL, 1996 and 1997. ... Games/Games started: 1996 (16/7), 1997 (16/4). Total: 32/11.
PRO STATISTICS: 1997—Recovered one fumble.

GRAHAM, DERRICK   G   RAIDERS

PERSONAL: Born March 18, 1967, in Groveland, Fla. ... 6-4/315. ... Full name: Deltrice Andrew Graham.
HIGH SCHOOL: Groveland (Fla.).
COLLEGE: Appalachian State (degree in criminal justice).
TRANSACTIONS/CAREER NOTES: Selected by Kansas City Chiefs in fifth round (124th pick overall) of 1990 NFL draft. ... Signed by Chiefs (July 28, 1990). ... On injured reserve with ankle injury (November 3, 1990-remainder of season). ... On injured reserve with knee injury (September 16, 1992-remainder of season). ... Granted unconditional free agency (February 17, 1995). ... Signed by Carolina Panthers (February 21, 1995). ... Released by Panthers (February 14, 1996). ... Signed by Seattle Seahawks (February 29, 1996). ... Granted unconditional free agency (February 13, 1998). ... Signed by Oakland Raiders (June 13, 1998).
PLAYING EXPERIENCE: Kansas City NFL, 1990-1994; Carolina NFL, 1995; Seattle NFL, 1996 and 1997. ... Games/Games started: 1990 (6/0), 1991 (16/1), 1992 (2/2), 1993 (11/2), 1994 (16/11), 1995 (11/7), 1996 (16/16), 1997 (9/9). Total: 87/48.
CHAMPIONSHIP GAME EXPERIENCE: Played in AFC championship game (1993 season).

GRAHAM, JAY   RB   RAVENS

PERSONAL: Born July 14, 1975, in Concord, N.C. ... 5-11/220. ... Full name: Herman Jason Graham.
HIGH SCHOOL: Concord (N.C.).
COLLEGE: Tennessee.
TRANSACTIONS/CAREER NOTES: Selected by Baltimore Ravens in third round (64th pick overall) of 1997 NFL draft. ... Signed by Ravens (June 19, 1997).
PRO STATISTICS: 1997—Returned six kickoffs for 115 yards and recovered one fumble.
SINGLE GAME HIGHS (regular season): Attempts—35 (November 16, 1997, vs. Philadelphia); yards—154 (November 16, 1997, vs. Philadelphia); and rushing touchdowns—1 (September 14, 1997, vs. New York Giants).
STATISTICAL PLATEAUS: 100-yard rushing games: 1997 (1).

			RUSHING				RECEIVING				TOTALS			
Year Team	G	GS	Att.	Yds.	Avg.	TD	No.	Yds.	Avg.	TD	TD	2pt.	Pts.	Fum.
1997—Baltimore NFL	13	3	81	299	3.7	2	12	51	4.3	0	2	0	12	2

GRAHAM, JEFF   WR   EAGLES

PERSONAL: Born February 14, 1969, in Dayton, Ohio. ... 6-2/206. ... Full name: Jeff Todd Graham.
HIGH SCHOOL: Alter (Kettering, Ohio).
COLLEGE: Ohio State.
TRANSACTIONS/CAREER NOTES: Selected by Pittsburgh Steelers in second round (46th pick overall) of 1991 NFL draft. ... Signed by Steelers (August 3, 1991). ... Traded by Steelers to Chicago Bears for fifth-round pick (DB Lethon Flowers) in 1995 draft (April 29, 1994). ... Granted unconditional free agency (February 16, 1996). ... Signed by New York Jets (March 14, 1996). ... Traded by Jets to Philadelphia Eagles for sixth-round pick (DE Eric Ogbogu) in 1998 draft (April 19, 1998).
PRO STATISTICS: 1991—Returned three kickoffs for 48 yards. 1994—Recovered one fumble. 1995—Returned one kickoff for 12 yards. 1997—Recovered one fumble.
SINGLE GAME HIGHS (regular season): Receptions—9 (November 17, 1996, vs. Indianapolis); yards—192 (December 19, 1993, vs. Houston); and touchdown receptions—3 (November 17, 1996, vs. Indianapolis).
STATISTICAL PLATEAUS: 100-yard receiving games: 1992 (2), 1993 (2), 1994 (2), 1995 (7), 1996 (3), 1997 (1). Total: 17.

			RECEIVING				PUNT RETURNS				TOTALS			
Year Team	G	GS	No.	Yds.	Avg.	TD	No.	Yds.	Avg.	TD	TD	2pt.	Pts.	Fum.
1991—Pittsburgh NFL	13	1	2	21	10.5	0	8	46	5.8	0	0	...	0	0
1992—Pittsburgh NFL	14	10	49	711	14.5	1	0	0	...	0	1	...	6	0
1993—Pittsburgh NFL	15	12	38	579	15.2	0	0	0	...	0	0	...	0	0
1994—Chicago NFL	16	15	68	944	13.9	4	15	140	9.3	1	5	1	32	1
1995—Chicago NFL	16	16	82	1301	15.9	4	23	183	8.0	0	4	0	24	3
1996—New York Jets NFL	11	9	50	788	15.8	6	0	0	...	0	6	0	36	0
1997—New York Jets NFL	16	16	42	542	12.9	2	0	0	...	0	2	0	12	0
Pro totals (7 years)	101	79	331	4886	14.8	17	46	369	8.0	1	18	1	110	4

GRAHAM, KENT   QB   GIANTS

PERSONAL: Born November 1, 1968, in Winfield, Ill. ... 6-5/246. ... Full name: Kent Douglas Graham.
HIGH SCHOOL: Wheaton (Ill.) North.
COLLEGE: Notre Dame, then Ohio State.
TRANSACTIONS/CAREER NOTES: Selected by New York Giants in eighth round (211th pick overall) of 1992 NFL draft. ... Signed by Giants (July 21, 1992). ... On injured reserve with elbow injury (September 18-October 14, 1992). ... Granted free agency (February 17, 1995). ... Re-signed by Giants (July 1995). ... Released by Giants (August 30, 1995). ... Signed by Detroit Lions (September 5, 1995). ... Granted unconditional free agency (February 16, 1996). ... Signed by Arizona Cardinals (March 7, 1996). ... Granted unconditional free agency (February 13, 1998). ... Signed by New York Giants (February 17, 1998).

PRO STATISTICS: 1992—Fumbled once and recovered one fumble. 1994—Fumbled twice and recovered one fumble. 1996—Fumbled five times. 1997—Fumbled five times.

SINGLE GAME HIGHS (regular season): Attempts—58 (September 29, 1996, vs. St. Louis); completions—37 (September 29, 1996, vs. St. Louis); yards—366 (September 29, 1996, vs. St. Louis); and touchdown passes—4 (September 29, 1996, vs. St. Louis).

STATISTICAL PLATEAUS: 300-yard passing games: 1996 (1), 1997 (1). Total: 2.

MISCELLANEOUS: Regular-season record as starting NFL quarterback: 5-13 (.278).

Year Team	G	GS	PASSING Att	Cmp	Pct	Yds	TD	Int	Avg	Rat	RUSHING Att	Yds	Avg	TD	TOTALS TD	2pt	Pts
1992—N.Y. Giants NFL	6	3	97	42	43.3	470	1	4	4.85	44.6	6	36	6.0	0	0	...	0
1993—N.Y. Giants NFL	9	0	22	8	36.4	79	0	0	3.59	47.3	2	-3	-1.5	0	0	...	0
1994—N.Y. Giants NFL	13	1	53	24	45.3	295	3	2	5.57	66.2	2	11	5.5	0	0	0	0
1995—Detroit NFL	2	0	0	0	...	0	0	0	...	...	0	0	...	0	0	0	0
1996—Arizona NFL	10	8	274	146	53.3	1624	12	7	5.93	75.1	21	87	4.1	0	0	0	0
1997—Arizona NFL	8	6	250	130	52.0	1408	4	5	5.63	65.9	13	23	1.8	2	2	0	12
Pro totals (6 years)	48	18	696	350	50.3	3876	20	18	5.57	66.0	44	154	3.5	2	2	0	12

GRAHAM, SCOTTIE　　RB　　VIKINGS

PERSONAL: Born March 28, 1969, in Long Beach, N.Y. ... 5-9/222. ... Full name: James Otis Graham.

HIGH SCHOOL: Long Beach (N.Y.).

COLLEGE: Ohio State (degree in recreation education).

TRANSACTIONS/CAREER NOTES: Selected by Pittsburgh Steelers in seventh round (188th pick overall) of 1992 NFL draft. ... Signed by Steelers (July 16, 1992). ... Released by Steelers (August 31, 1992). ... Re-signed by Steelers to practice squad (September 1, 1992). ... Signed by New York Jets off Steelers practice squad (December 15, 1992). ... Released by Jets (August 23, 1993). ... Signed by Minnesota Vikings to practice squad (September 29, 1993). ... Activated (November 9, 1993). ... Granted free agency (February 16, 1996). ... Re-signed by Vikings (July 16, 1996). ... Granted unconditional free agency (February 14, 1997). ... Signed by Cincinnati Bengals (April 16, 1997). ... On injured reserve with knee injury (November 17, 1997-remainder of season). ... Released by Bengals (April 20, 1998). ... Signed by Vikings (June 16, 1998).

PRO STATISTICS: 1993—Returned one kickoff for 16 yards.

SINGLE GAME HIGHS (regular season): Attempts—33 (December 26, 1993, vs. Kansas City); yards—166 (December 26, 1993, vs. Kansas City); and rushing touchdowns—1 (December 3, 1995, vs. Tampa Bay).

STATISTICAL PLATEAUS: 100-yard rushing games: 1993 (2), 1995 (1). Total: 3.

Year Team	G	GS	RUSHING Att	Yds	Avg	TD	RECEIVING No.	Yds	Avg	TD	TOTALS TD	2pt	Pts.	Fum.
1992—New York Jets NFL	2	0	14	29	2.1	0	0	0	...	0	1	...	6	0
1993—Minnesota NFL	7	3	118	488	4.1	3	7	46	6.6	0	3	...	18	0
1994—Minnesota NFL	16	0	64	207	3.2	2	1	1	1.0	0	2	0	12	0
1995—Minnesota NFL	16	6	110	406	3.7	2	4	30	7.5	0	2	0	12	0
1996—Minnesota NFL	11	0	57	138	2.4	0	7	48	6.9	0	0	0	0	0
1997—Cincinnati NFL	5	0	1	-1	-1.0	0	1	1	1.0	0	0	0	0	0
Pro totals (6 years)	57	9	364	1267	3.5	7	20	126	6.3	0	8	0	48	0

GRANT, STEPHEN　　LB

PERSONAL: Born December 23, 1969, in Miami. ... 6-0/244. ... Full name: Stephen Mitchell Grant.

HIGH SCHOOL: Miami Southridge.

COLLEGE: West Virginia.

TRANSACTIONS/CAREER NOTES: Selected by Indianapolis Colts in 10th round (253rd pick overall) of 1992 NFL draft. ... Signed by Colts (July 17, 1992). ... Granted free agency (February 17, 1995). ... Re-signed by Colts (May 31, 1995). ... Released by Colts (March 18, 1998).

PLAYING EXPERIENCE: Indianapolis NFL, 1992-1997. ... Games/Games started: 1992 (16/0), 1993 (16/0), 1994 (16/12), 1995 (15/15), 1996 (11/11), 1997 (9/9). Total: 83/47.

CHAMPIONSHIP GAME EXPERIENCE: Played in AFC championship game (1995 season).

PRO STATISTICS: 1994—Recovered one fumble for two yards. 1995—Credited with two sacks, intercepted one pass for nine yards and recovered three fumbles for two yards. 1996—Credited with one sack and recovered one fumble. 1997—Recovered one fumble.

GRANVILLE, BILLY　　LB　　BENGALS

G

PERSONAL: Born March 11, 1974, in Lawrenceville, N.J. ... 6-3/252.

HIGH SCHOOL: Lawrenceville (N.J.).

COLLEGE: Duke (degree in sociology, 1997).

TRANSACTIONS/CAREER NOTES: Signed as non-drafted free agent by Cincinnati Bengals (April 25, 1997).

PLAYING EXPERIENCE: Cincinnati NFL, 1997. ... Games/Games started: 12/4.

GRASMANIS, PAUL　　DT　　BEARS

PERSONAL: Born August 2, 1974, in Grand Rapids, Mich. ... 6-2/298. ... Full name: Paul Ryan Grasmanis.

HIGH SCHOOL: Jenison (Mich.).

COLLEGE: Notre Dame.

TRANSACTIONS/CAREER NOTES: Selected by Chicago Bears in fourth round (116th pick overall) of 1996 NFL draft. ... Signed by Bears (June 13, 1996).

PLAYING EXPERIENCE: Chicago NFL, 1996 and 1997. ... Games/Games started: 1996 (14/3), 1997 (16/0). Total: 30/3.

PRO STATISTICS: 1997—Credited with 1/2 sack and recovered one fumble.

GRAY, CARLTON   CB   COLTS

PERSONAL: Born June 26, 1971, in Cincinnati. ... 6-0/200. ... Full name: Carlton Patrick Gray.
HIGH SCHOOL: Forest Park (Cincinnati).
COLLEGE: UCLA.
TRANSACTIONS/CAREER NOTES: Selected by Seattle Seahawks in second round (30th pick overall) of 1993 NFL draft. ... Signed by Seahawks (July 22, 1993). ... On injured reserve with forearm injury (November 23, 1994-remainder of season). ... Granted free agency (February 16, 1996). ... Re-signed by Seahawks (February 16, 1996). ... Granted unconditional free agency (February 14, 1997). ... Signed by Indianapolis Colts (March 3, 1997).
HONORS: Named defensive back on THE SPORTING NEWS college All-America first team (1992).
PRO STATISTICS: 1993—Credited with one sack. 1995—Fumbled once. 1996—Ran three yards with lateral from interception return and recovered one fumble for 62 yards.

				INTERCEPTIONS		
Year Team	G	GS	No.	Yds.	Avg.	TD
1993—Seattle NFL	10	2	3	33	11.0	0
1994—Seattle NFL	11	11	2	0	0.0	0
1995—Seattle NFL	16	16	4	45	11.3	0
1996—Seattle NFL	16	16	0	3	...	0
1997—Indianapolis NFL	15	13	2	0	0.0	0
Pro totals (5 years)	68	58	11	81	7.4	0

GRAY, CHRIS   G   SEAHAWKS

PERSONAL: Born June 19, 1970, in Birmingham, Ala. ... 6-4/305. ... Full name: Christopher William Gray.
HIGH SCHOOL: Homewood (Ala.).
COLLEGE: Auburn (degree in marketing).
TRANSACTIONS/CAREER NOTES: Selected by Miami Dolphins in fifth round (132nd pick overall) of 1993 NFL draft. ... Signed by Dolphins (July 12, 1993). ... On injured reserve with ankle injury (November 15, 1995-remainder of season). ... On injured reserve with broken leg (November 19, 1996-remainder of season). ... Released by Dolphins (August 12, 1997). ... Signed by Chicago Bears (September 9, 1997). ... Granted unconditional free agency (February 13, 1998). ... Signed by Seattle Seahawks (February 20, 1998).
PLAYING EXPERIENCE: Miami NFL, 1993-1996; Chicago NFL, 1997. ... Games/Games started: 1993 (5/0), 1994 (16/2), 1995 (10/10), 1996 (11/11), 1997 (8/2). Total: 50/25.
PRO STATISTICS: 1994—Recovered one fumble.

GRAY, DERWIN   DB   PANTHERS

PERSONAL: Born April 9, 1971, in San Antonio. ... 5-11/210. ... Full name: Derwin Lamont Gray.
HIGH SCHOOL: Judson (Converse, Texas).
COLLEGE: Brigham Young.
TRANSACTIONS/CAREER NOTES: Selected by Indianapolis Colts in fourth round (92nd pick overall) of 1993 NFL draft. ... Signed by Colts (July 20, 1993). ... Granted free agency (February 16, 1996). ... Re-signed by Colts (July 16, 1996). ... Granted unconditional free agency (February 13, 1998). ... Signed by Carolina Panthers (April 15, 1998).
PLAYING EXPERIENCE: Indianapolis NFL, 1993-1997. ... Games/Games started: 1993 (11/0), 1994 (16/2), 1995 (16/0), 1996 (10/1), 1997 (11/0). Total: 64/3.
CHAMPIONSHIP GAME EXPERIENCE: Played in AFC championship game (1995 season).
PRO STATISTICS: 1993—Recovered one fumble. 1994—Ran four yards with lateral from kickoff return. 1995—Intercepted one pass for 10 yards and recovered one fumble.

GRAY, MEL   KR

PERSONAL: Born March 16, 1961, in Williamsburg, Va. ... 5-9/171.
HIGH SCHOOL: Lafayette (Williamsburg, Va.).
JUNIOR COLLEGE: Coffeyville (Kan.) Community College.
COLLEGE: Purdue.
TRANSACTIONS/CAREER NOTES: Selected by Chicago Blitz in seventh round (132nd pick overall) of 1984 USFL draft. ... USFL rights traded by Blitz to Los Angeles Express for WR Kris Haines (February 11, 1984). ... Signed by Express (February 16, 1984). ... On developmental squad for four games (February 24-March 9 and May 26-June 9, 1984). ... Selected by New Orleans Saints in second round (42nd pick overall) of 1984 NFL supplemental draft. ... Traded by Express with DB Dwight Drane, DB John Warren, DB Troy West, G Wayne Jones, LB Howard Carson and TE Ken O'Neal to Arizona Outlaws for past considerations (August 1, 1985). ... Granted free agency when USFL suspended operations (August 7, 1986). ... Signed by Saints (August 18, 1986). ... Granted roster exemption (August 18-29, 1986). ... Granted unconditional free agency (February 1, 1989). ... Signed by Detroit Lions (March 1, 1989). ... Granted free agency (February 1, 1992). ... Re-signed by Lions (1992). ... On injured reserve with knee injury (December 22, 1992-remainder of season). ... Granted unconditional free agency (February 17, 1994). ... Re-signed by Lions (April 29, 1994). ... Granted unconditional free agency (February 17, 1995). ... Signed by Houston Oilers (March 3, 1995). ... Released by Oilers (July 20, 1996). ... Re-signed by Oilers (July 23, 1996). ... Oilers franchise moved to Tennessee for 1997 season. ... Released by Oilers (November 18, 1997). ... Signed by Philadelphia Eagles (December 2, 1997). ... Granted unconditional free agency (February 13, 1998).
CHAMPIONSHIP GAME EXPERIENCE: Played in NFC championship game (1991 season).
HONORS: Named kick returner on THE SPORTING NEWS NFL All-Pro team (1986, 1990, 1991, 1993 and 1994). ... Named punt returner on THE SPORTING NEWS NFL All-Pro team (1987, 1991 and 1992). ... Played in Pro Bowl (1990, 1991 and 1994 seasons). ... Named to play in Pro Bowl (1992 season); replaced by Johnny Bailey due to injury.
RECORDS: Holds NFL career records for most kickoff returns—421; most yards by kickoff return 10,250; most combined kick returns—664; and most yards by combined kick return—12,810. ... Shares NFL career records for most touchdowns by kickoff return—6; and most touchdowns by combined kick return—9.

G

PRO STATISTICS: USFL: 1984—Attempted one pass with one completion for 29 yards, fumbled 10 times and recovered two fumbles. 1985—Fumbled seven times and recovered one fumble. NFL: 1987—Fumbled three times and recovered one fumble. 1988—Fumbled five times and recovered two fumbles. 1990—Fumbled four times and recovered three fumbles. 1991—Fumbled three times and recovered two fumbles. 1993—Fumbled three times. 1994—Fumbled three times and recovered two fumbles for 13 yards. 1995—Fumbled five times and recovered one fumble. 1996—Fumbled four times. 1997—Fumbled once.
SINGLE GAME HIGHS (regular season): Receptions—2 (September 8, 1991, vs. Green Bay); yards—45 (November 16, 1986, vs. St. Louis); and touchdown receptions—0.

			RUSHING				RECEIVING				PUNT RETURNS				KICKOFF RETURNS				TOTALS		
Year Team	G	GS	Att.	Yds.	Avg.	TD	No.	Yds.	Avg.	TD	No.	Yds.	Avg.	TD	No.	Yds.	Avg.	TD	TD	2pt.	Pts.
1984—LA USFL	15	6	133	625	4.7	3	27	288	10.7	1	0	0	...	0	20	332	16.6	0	4	...	24
1985—LA USFL	16	...	125	526	4.2	1	20	101	5.1	0	0	0	...	0	11	203	18.5	0	1	...	6
1986—New Orleans NFL	16	0	6	29	4.8	0	2	45	22.5	0	0	0	...	0	31	866	27.9	*1	1	...	6
1987—New Orleans NFL	12	1	8	37	4.6	1	6	30	5.0	0	24	352	*14.7	0	30	636	21.2	0	1	...	6
1988—New Orleans NFL	14	0	0	0	...	0	0	0	...	0	25	305	12.2	†1	32	670	20.9	0	0	...	0
1989—Detroit NFL	10	1	3	22	7.3	0	2	47	23.5	0	11	76	6.9	0	24	640	‡26.7	0	0	...	0
1990—Detroit NFL	16	0	0	0	...	0	0	0	...	0	34	361	10.6	0	41	939	22.9	0	0	...	0
1991—Detroit NFL	16	0	2	11	5.5	0	3	42	14.0	0	25	385	*15.4	1	36	*929	*25.8	0	1	...	6
1992—Detroit NFL	15	0	0	0	...	0	0	0	...	0	18	175	9.7	1	*42	1006	24.0	1	2	...	12
1993—Detroit NFL	11	0	0	0	...	0	0	0	...	0	23	197	8.6	0	28	688	24.6	†1	1	...	6
1994—Detroit NFL	16	0	0	0	...	0	0	0	...	0	21	233	11.1	0	45	1276	*28.4	*3	3	0	18
1995—Houston NFL	15	0	0	0	...	0	0	0	...	0	30	303	10.1	0	53	1183	22.3	0	0	0	0
1996—Houston NFL	14	0	0	0	...	0	0	0	...	0	22	205	9.3	0	50	§1224	24.5	0	0	0	0
1997—Tennessee NFL	11	0	0	0	...	0	0	0	...	0	17	144	8.5	0	8	185	23.1	0	0	0	0
—Philadelphia NFL	3	0	0	0	...	0	0	0	...	0	2	17	8.5	0	1	8	8.0	0	0	0	0
USFL totals (2 years)	31	...	258	1151	4.5	4	47	389	8.3	1	0	0	...	0	31	535	17.3	0	5	0	30
NFL totals (12 years)	169	2	19	99	5.2	1	13	164	12.6	0	252	2753	10.9	3	421	10250	24.3	6	9	0	54
Pro totals (14 years)	200	...	277	1250	4.5	5	60	553	9.2	1	252	2753	10.9	3	452	10785	23.9	6	14	0	84

GRAY, TORRIAN   DB   VIKINGS

PERSONAL: Born March 18, 1974, in Bartow, Fla. ... 6-0/198. ... Full name: Torrian Deshon Gray.
HIGH SCHOOL: Kathleen (Lakeland, Fla.).
COLLEGE: Virginia Tech.
TRANSACTIONS/CAREER NOTES: Selected by Minnesota Vikings in second round (49th pick overall) of 1997 NFL draft. ... Signed by Vikings (June 5, 1997).
PLAYING EXPERIENCE: Minnesota NFL, 1997. ... Games/Games started: 16/3.

GRAZIANI, TONY   QB   FALCONS

PERSONAL: Born December 23, 1973, in Las Vegas. ... 6-2/195. ... Full name: Anthony Robert Graziani.
HIGH SCHOOL: Downey (Modesto, Calif.).
COLLEGE: Oregon.
TRANSACTIONS/CAREER NOTES: Selected by Atlanta Falcons in seventh round (204th pick overall) of 1997 NFL draft.
SINGLE GAME HIGHS (regular season): Attempts—18 (October 26, 1997, vs. Carolina); completions—4 (October 26, 1997, vs. Carolina); yards—24 (October 26, 1997, vs. Carolina); and touchdown passes—0.
MISCELLANEOUS: Regular-season record as starting NFL quarterback: 0-1.

			PASSING								RUSHING				TOTALS		
Year Team	G	GS	Att.	Cmp.	Pct.	Yds.	TD	Int.	Avg.	Rat.	Att.	Yds.	Avg.	TD	TD	2pt.	Pts.
1997—Atlanta NFL	3	1	23	7	30.4	41	0	2	1.78	3.7	3	19	6.3	0	0	0	0

GRBAC, ELVIS   QB   CHIEFS

G

PERSONAL: Born August 13, 1970, in Cleveland. ... 6-5/232.
HIGH SCHOOL: St. Joseph (Cleveland).
COLLEGE: Michigan (degree in communications, 1993).
TRANSACTIONS/CAREER NOTES: Selected by San Francisco 49ers in eighth round (219th pick overall) of 1993 NFL draft. ... Signed by 49ers (July 13, 1993). ... Granted unconditional free agency (February 14, 1997). ... Signed by Kansas City Chiefs (March 17, 1997).
CHAMPIONSHIP GAME EXPERIENCE: Member of 49ers for NFC championship game (1993 season); inactive. ... Member of 49ers for NFC championship game (1994 season); did not play. ... Member of Super Bowl championship team (1994 season).
PRO STATISTICS: 1994—Fumbled five times. 1995—Fumbled twice and recovered two fumbles for minus one yard. 1997—Fumbled once.
SINGLE GAME HIGHS (regular season): Attempts—42 (October 29, 1995, vs. New Orleans); completions—31 (November 20, 1995, vs. Miami); yards—382 (November 20, 1995, vs. Miami); and touchdown passes—4 (November 20, 1995, vs. Miami).
STATISTICAL PLATEAUS: 300-yard passing games: 1995 (3), 1997 (1). Total: 4.
MISCELLANEOUS: Regular-season record as starting NFL quarterback: 14-5 (.737). ... Postseason record as starting NFL quarterback: 0-1.

			PASSING								RUSHING				TOTALS		
Year Team	G	GS	Att.	Cmp.	Pct.	Yds.	TD	Int.	Avg.	Rat.	Att.	Yds.	Avg.	TD	TD	2pt.	Pts.
1993—San Francisco NFL						Did not play.											
1994—San Francisco NFL	11	0	50	35	70.0	393	2	1	7.86	98.2	13	1	0.1	0	0	0	0
1995—San Francisco NFL	16	5	183	127	69.4	1469	8	5	8.03	96.6	20	33	1.7	2	0	0	0
1996—San Francisco NFL	15	4	197	122	61.9	1236	8	10	6.27	72.2	23	21	0.9	2	2	0	12
1997—Kansas City NFL	10	10	314	179	57.0	1943	11	6	6.19	79.1	30	168	5.6	1	1	0	6
Pro totals (4 years)	52	19	744	463	62.2	5041	29	22	6.78	82.8	86	223	2.6	5	3	0	18

PERSONAL: Born July 30, 1972 ... 6-2/285. ... Full name: Paul Domero Greeley.
HIGH SCHOOL: Wilkes-Barre (Pa.) Coughlin.
COLLEGE: Penn State.
TRANSACTIONS/CAREER NOTES: Signed as non-drafted free agent by Chicago Bears (April 26, 1995). ... Released by Bears (August 22, 1995). ... Signed by Carolina Panthers (April 24, 1996). ... Released by Panthers (August 19, 1996). ... Re-signed by Panthers (September 4, 1996). ... Released by Panthers (September 24, 1996). ... Re-signed by Panthers (October 31, 1996). ... Released by Panthers (November 28, 1996). ... Re-signed by Panthers to practice squad (November 29, 1996).
PLAYING EXPERIENCE: Carolina NFL, 1997. ... Games/Games started: 6/0.

PERSONAL: Born February 15, 1960, in Houston. ... 5-8/184.
HIGH SCHOOL: Jesse H. Jones Senior (Houston).
COLLEGE: Texas A&I.
TRANSACTIONS/CAREER NOTES: Selected by Denver Gold in 10th round (112th pick overall) of 1983 USFL draft. ... Selected by Washington Redskins in first round (28th pick overall) of 1983 NFL draft. ... Signed by Redskins (June 10, 1983). ... On injured reserve with broken hand (December 13, 1988-remainder of season). ... On injured reserve with broken bone in wrist (October 24, 1989-remainder of season). ... Granted free agency (February 1, 1992). ... Re-signed by Redskins (August 25, 1992). ... On injured reserve with broken forearm (September 16-November 23, 1992). ... Granted unconditional free agency (February 17, 1995). ... Re-signed by Redskins (March 10, 1995). ... Granted unconditional free agency (February 14, 1997). ... Re-signed by Redskins (April 25, 1997).
CHAMPIONSHIP GAME EXPERIENCE: Played in NFC championship game (1983, 1986, 1987 and 1991 seasons). ... Played in Super Bowl XVIII (1983 season). ... Member of Super Bowl championship team (1987 and 1991 seasons).
HONORS: Played in Pro Bowl (1984, 1986, 1987, 1990, 1991, 1996 and 1997 seasons). ... Named cornerback on THE SPORTING NEWS NFL All-Pro team (1991).
POST SEASON RECORDS: Shares NFL postseason career record for most touchdowns by punt return—1 (January 10, 1988, at Chicago).
PRO STATISTICS: 1983—Recovered one fumble. 1985—Rushed once for six yards and recovered one fumble. 1986—Recovered one fumble. 1987—Recovered one fumble for 26 yards and a touchdown. 1988—Credited with one sack and recovered one fumble. 1989—Recovered one fumble. 1993—Recovered one fumble for 78 yards and a touchdown. 1996—Recovered one fumble for 15 yards. 1997—Returned one kickoff for nine yards.
MISCELLANEOUS: Holds Washington Redskins all-time record for most interceptions (44).

			INTERCEPTIONS				PUNT RETURNS				TOTALS			
Year Team	G	GS	No.	Yds.	Avg.	TD	No.	Yds.	Avg.	TD	TD	2pt.	Pts.	Fum.
1983—Washington NFL	16	16	2	7	3.5	0	4	29	7.3	0	0	...	0	1
1984—Washington NFL	16	16	5	91	18.2	1	2	13	6.5	0	1	...	6	0
1985—Washington NFL	16	16	2	0	0.0	0	16	214	13.4	0	0	...	0	2
1986—Washington NFL	16	15	5	9	1.8	0	12	120	10.0	0	0	...	0	1
1987—Washington NFL	12	12	3	65	21.7	0	5	53	10.6	0	1	...	6	0
1988—Washington NFL	15	15	1	12	12.0	0	9	103	11.4	0	0	...	0	1
1989—Washington NFL	7	7	2	0	0.0	0	1	11	11.0	0	0	...	0	1
1990—Washington NFL	16	16	4	20	5.0	1	1	6	6.0	0	1	...	6	0
1991—Washington NFL	16	16	5	47	9.4	0	0	0	...	0	0	...	0	0
1992—Washington NFL	8	7	1	15	15.0	0	0	0	...	0	0	...	0	0
1993—Washington NFL	16	16	4	10	2.5	0	1	27	27.0	0	1	...	6	0
1994—Washington NFL	16	16	3	32	10.7	1	0	0	...	0	1	0	6	0
1995—Washington NFL	16	16	3	42	14.0	1	0	0	...	0	1	0	6	0
1996—Washington NFL	16	16	3	84	28.0	1	0	0	...	0	1	0	6	0
1997—Washington NFL	16	16	1	83	83.0	1	0	0	...	0	1	0	6	0
Pro totals (15 years)	218	216	44	517	11.8	6	51	576	11.3	0	8	0	48	6

PERSONAL: Born June 22, 1967, in Savannah, Ga. ... 6-5/285. ... Full name: Bernard Eric Green.
HIGH SCHOOL: A.E. Beach (Savannah, Ga.).
COLLEGE: Liberty, Va. (degree in finance, 1991).
TRANSACTIONS/CAREER NOTES: Selected by Pittsburgh Steelers in first round (21st pick overall) of 1990 NFL draft. ... Signed by Steelers (September 10, 1990). ... Granted roster exemption (September 10-24, 1990). ... On injured reserve with ankle injury (November 23, 1991-remainder of season). ... On injured reserve with shoulder injury (September 9-October 5, 1992). ... On practice squad (October 5-10, 1992). ... On reserve/suspended list for substance abuse (November 9-December 21, 1992). ... Granted roster exemption (December 21-27, 1992). ... Designated by Steelers as franchise player (February 15, 1994). ... Free agency status changed by Steelers from franchise to unconditional (February 15, 1995). ... Signed by Miami Dolphins (March 10, 1995). ... Released by Dolphins (July 9, 1996). ... Signed by Baltimore Ravens (September 24, 1996). ... Granted unconditional free agency (February 14, 1997). ... Re-signed by Ravens (July 18, 1997). ... Granted unconditional free agency (February 13, 1998). ... Re-signed by Ravens (February 18, 1998).
CHAMPIONSHIP GAME EXPERIENCE: Played in AFC championship game (1994 season).
HONORS: Played in Pro Bowl (1993 and 1994 seasons).
PRO STATISTICS: 1990—Returned one kickoff for 16 yards and recovered one fumble.
SINGLE GAME HIGHS (regular season): Receptions—9 (November 2, 1997, vs. New York Jets); yards—158 (September 22, 1991, vs. Philadelphia); and touchdown receptions—3 (October 14, 1990, vs. Denver).
STATISTICAL PLATEAUS: 100-yard receiving games: 1990 (1), 1991 (1), 1993 (2). Total: 4.

			RECEIVING				TOTALS			
Year Team	G	GS	No.	Yds.	Avg.	TD	TD	2pt.	Pts.	Fum.
1990—Pittsburgh NFL	13	7	34	387	11.4	7	7	...	42	1
1991—Pittsburgh NFL	11	11	41	582	14.2	6	6	...	36	2

G

Year Team	G	GS	RECEIVING No.	Yds.	Avg.	TD	TOTALS TD	2pt.	Pts.	Fum.
1992—Pittsburgh NFL	7	5	14	152	10.9	2	2	...	12	0
1993—Pittsburgh NFL	16	16	63	942	15.0	5	5	...	30	3
1994—Pittsburgh NFL	15	14	46	618	13.4	4	4	0	24	2
1995—Miami NFL	14	14	43	499	11.6	3	3	1	20	0
1996—Baltimore NFL	6	3	15	150	10.0	1	0	0	0	0
1997—Baltimore NFL	16	15	65	601	9.2	5	5	0	30	1
Pro totals (8 years)	98	85	321	3931	12.2	33	32	1	194	9

GREEN, HAROLD · RB · FALCONS

PERSONAL: Born January 29, 1968, in Ladson, S.C. ... 6-2/222. ... Full name: Harold Green Jr.
HIGH SCHOOL: Stratford (Goose Creek, S.C.).
COLLEGE: South Carolina.
TRANSACTIONS/CAREER NOTES: Selected by Cincinnati Bengals in second round (38th pick overall) of 1990 NFL draft. ... Signed by Bengals (August 1, 1990). ... Designated by Bengals as transition player (February 25, 1993). ... Free agency status changed by Bengals from transitional to unconditional (February 16, 1996). ... Signed by St. Louis Rams (July 10, 1996). ... Granted unconditional free agency (February 14, 1997). ... Signed by Atlanta Falcons (June 16, 1997). ... Granted unconditional free agency (February 13, 1998). ... Re-signed by Falcons (February 27, 1998).
HONORS: Played in Pro Bowl (1992 season).
PRO STATISTICS: 1990—Recovered two fumbles. 1991—Returned four kickoffs for 66 yards. 1992—Recovered one fumble. 1994—Returned five kickoffs for 113 yards and recovered one fumble. 1995—Recovered one fumble. 1996—Recovered one fumble. 1997—Returned one kickoff for 23 yards and recovered one fumble.
SINGLE GAME HIGHS (regular season): Attempts—31 (December 20, 1992, vs. New England); yards—190 (December 20, 1992, vs. New England); and rushing touchdowns—2 (November 10, 1996, vs. Atlanta).
STATISTICAL PLATEAUS: 100-yard rushing games: 1991 (3), 1992 (5), 1996 (1). Total: 9.

Year Team	G	GS	RUSHING Att.	Yds.	Avg.	TD	RECEIVING No.	Yds.	Avg.	TD	TOTALS TD	2pt.	Pts.	Fum.
1990—Cincinnati NFL	12	9	83	353	4.3	1	12	90	7.5	1	2	...	12	2
1991—Cincinnati NFL	14	10	158	731	4.6	2	16	136	8.5	0	2	...	12	2
1992—Cincinnati NFL	16	15	265	1170	4.4	2	41	214	5.2	0	2	...	12	1
1993—Cincinnati NFL	15	15	215	589	2.7	0	22	115	5.2	0	0	...	0	3
1994—Cincinnati NFL	14	11	76	223	2.9	1	27	267	9.9	1	2	0	12	1
1995—Cincinnati NFL	15	15	171	661	3.9	2	27	182	6.7	1	3	0	18	2
1996—St. Louis NFL	16	5	127	523	4.1	4	37	246	6.6	1	5	1	32	2
1997—Atlanta NFL	16	1	36	78	2.2	1	29	360	12.4	0	1	0	6	0
Pro totals (8 years)	118	81	1131	4328	3.8	13	211	1610	7.6	4	17	1	104	13

GREEN, ROBERT · RB

PERSONAL: Born September 10, 1970, in Washington, D.C. ... 5-8/212. ... Full name: Robert David Green.
HIGH SCHOOL: Friendly (Md.) Senior.
COLLEGE: William & Mary.
TRANSACTIONS/CAREER NOTES: Signed as non-drafted free agent by Washington Redskins for 1992 season. ... Claimed on waivers by Chicago Bears (August 31, 1993). ... On injured reserve with broken leg (December 5, 1995-remainder of season). ... Released by Bears (March 31, 1997). ... Signed by Minnesota Vikings (July 15, 1997). ... Granted unconditional free agency (February 13, 1998).
PRO STATISTICS: 1994—Recovered one fumble. 1995—Recovered one fumble. 1996—Recovered three fumbles. 1997—Recovered one fumble.
SINGLE GAME HIGHS (regular season): Attempts—20 (September 8, 1996, vs. Washington); yards—106 (September 8, 1996, vs. Washington); and rushing touchdowns—1 (December 4, 1995, vs. Detroit).
STATISTICAL PLATEAUS: 100-yard rushing games: 1996 (1).

Year Team	G	GS	RUSHING Att.	Yds.	Avg.	TD	RECEIVING No.	Yds.	Avg.	TD	KICKOFF RETURNS No.	Yds.	Avg.	TD	TOTALS TD	2pt.	Pts.	Fum.
1992—Washington NFL	15	0	8	46	5.8	0	1	5	5.0	0	1	9	9.0	0	0	...	0	0
1993—Chicago NFL	16	0	15	29	1.9	0	13	63	4.8	0	9	141	15.7	0	0	...	0	0
1994—Chicago NFL	15	0	25	122	4.9	0	24	199	8.3	2	6	77	12.8	0	2	0	12	1
1995—Chicago NFL	12	3	107	570	5.3	3	28	246	8.8	0	3	29	9.7	0	3	0	18	2
1996—Chicago NFL	10	3	60	249	4.2	0	13	78	6.0	0	0	0	...	0	0	0	0	3
1997—Minnesota NFL	3	1	6	22	3.7	0	1	5	5.0	0	0	0	...	0	0	0	0	0
Pro totals (6 years)	71	7	221	1038	4.7	3	80	596	7.5	2	19	256	13.5	0	5	0	30	6

G

GREEN, TRENT · QB · REDSKINS

PERSONAL: Born July 9, 1970 ... 6-3/215. ... Full name: Trent Jason Green.
HIGH SCHOOL: Vianney (St. Louis).
COLLEGE: Indiana.
TRANSACTIONS/CAREER NOTES: Selected by San Diego Chargers in eighth round (222nd pick overall) of 1993 NFL draft. ... Signed by Chargers (July 15, 1993). ... Inactive for all 16 games (1993). ... Released by Chargers (August 22, 1994). ... Signed by B.C. Lions of CFL (1995). ... Signed by Washington Redskins (April 5, 1995). ... Inactive for all 16 games (1995). ... Inactive for all 16 games (1996). ... Granted free agency (February 14, 1997).
PLAYING EXPERIENCE: Washington NFL, 1997. ... Games/Games started: 1/0.
PRO STATISTICS: 1997—Attempted one pass without a completion.
SINGLE GAME HIGHS (regular season): Attempts—1 (December 21, 1997, vs. Philadelphia); completions—0; yards—0; and touchdown passes—0.

GREEN, VICTOR   S   JETS

PERSONAL: Born December 8, 1969, in Americus, Ga. ... 5-11/205. ... Full name: Victor Bernard Green. ... Cousin of Tommy Sims, defensive back with Indianapolis Colts (1986).
HIGH SCHOOL: Americus (Ga.).
JUNIOR COLLEGE: Copiah-Lincoln (Miss.) Junior College.
COLLEGE: Akron (degree in criminal justice, 1993).
TRANSACTIONS/CAREER NOTES: Signed as non-drafted free agent by New York Jets (April 29, 1993). ... Released by Jets (August 30, 1993). ... Re-signed by Jets to practice squad (September 1, 1993). ... Activated (September 28, 1993).
PRO STATISTICS: 1994—Recovered one fumble. 1995—Recovered one fumble. 1996—Recovered three fumbles.

			INTERCEPTIONS			SACKS
Year Team	G	GS	No.	Yds.	Avg.	TD	No.
1993—New York Jets NFL	11	0	0	0	...	0	0.0
1994—New York Jets NFL	16	0	0	0	...	0	1.0
1995—New York Jets NFL	16	12	1	2	2.0	0	2.0
1996—New York Jets NFL	16	16	2	27	13.5	0	2.0
1997—New York Jets NFL	16	16	3	89	29.7	0	1.0
Pro totals (5 years)	75	44	6	118	19.7	0	6.0

GREEN, WILLIE   WR   BRONCOS

PERSONAL: Born April 2, 1966, in Athens, Ga. ... 6-4/191. ... Full name: Willie Aaron Green.
HIGH SCHOOL: Clarke Central (Athens, Ga.), then Tennessee Military Academy.
COLLEGE: Mississippi.
TRANSACTIONS/CAREER NOTES: Selected by Detroit Lions in eighth round (194th pick overall) of 1990 NFL draft. ... On injured reserve with shoulder injury (September 5, 1990-entire season). ... Granted free agency (February 1, 1992). ... Re-signed by Lions (August 11, 1992). ... On suspended list (December 7-14, 1992). ... Released by Lions (June 9, 1994). ... Signed by Tampa Bay Buccaneers (July 5, 1994). ... Released by Buccaneers (October 11, 1994). ... Signed by Carolina Panthers (December 15, 1994). ... Granted unconditional free agency (February 14, 1997). ... Signed by Denver Broncos (March 21, 1997).
CHAMPIONSHIP GAME EXPERIENCE: Played in NFC championship game (1991 and 1996 seasons). ... Played in AFC championship game (1997 season). ... Member of Super Bowl championship team (1997 season).
PRO STATISTICS: 1996—Rushed once for one yard.
SINGLE GAME HIGHS (regular season): Receptions—9 (November 3, 1996, vs. Atlanta); yards—157 (December 8, 1996, vs. San Francisco); and touchdown receptions—2 (November 24, 1996, vs. Houston).
STATISTICAL PLATEAUS: 100-yard receiving games: 1992 (2), 1993 (1), 1995 (4), 1996 (1). Total: 8.

			RECEIVING				TOTALS			
Year Team	G	GS	No.	Yds.	Avg.	TD	TD	2pt.	Pts.	Fum.
1990—Detroit NFL						Did not play.				
1991—Detroit NFL	16	15	39	592	15.2	7	7	...	42	0
1992—Detroit NFL	15	13	33	586	17.8	5	5	...	30	1
1993—Detroit NFL	16	6	28	462	16.5	2	2	...	12	0
1994—Tampa Bay NFL	5	0	9	150	16.7	0	0	0	0	0
1995—Carolina NFL	16	7	47	‡882	18.8	6	6	0	36	1
1996—Carolina NFL	15	10	46	614	13.3	3	3	0	18	0
1997—Denver NFL	16	1	19	240	12.6	2	2	0	12	0
Pro totals (7 years)	99	52	221	3526	16.0	25	25	0	150	2

GREEN, YATIL   WR   DOLPHINS

PERSONAL: Born November 25, 1973, in Lake City, Fla. ... 6-2/200.
HIGH SCHOOL: Columbia (Lake City, Fla.).
COLLEGE: Miami (Fla.).
TRANSACTIONS/CAREER NOTES: Selected by Miami Dolphins in first round (15th pick overall) of 1997 NFL draft. ... Signed by Dolphins (June 13, 1997). ... On injured reserve with knee injury (August 18, 1997-entire season).

GREENE, KEVIN   LB   PANTHERS

PERSONAL: Born July 31, 1962, in New York. ... 6-3/247. ... Full name: Kevin Darwin Greene.
HIGH SCHOOL: South (Granite City, Ill.).
COLLEGE: Auburn.
TRANSACTIONS/CAREER NOTES: Selected by Birmingham Stallions in 1985 USFL territorial draft. ... Selected by Los Angeles Rams in fifth round (113th pick overall) of 1985 NFL draft. ... Signed by Rams (July 12, 1985). ... Crossed picket line during players strike (October 14, 1987). ... Granted free agency (February 1, 1990). ... Re-signed by Rams (September 1, 1990). ... Granted roster exemption (September 1-7, 1990). ... Granted unconditional free agency (March 1, 1993). ... Signed by Pittsburgh Steelers (April 3, 1993). ... Granted unconditional free agency (February 16, 1996). ... Signed by Carolina Panthers (May 3, 1996). ... On reserve/did not report list (July 21-August 25, 1997). ... Released by Panthers (August 25, 1997). ... Signed by San Francisco 49ers (August 28, 1997). ... Released by 49ers (February 13, 1998). ... Signed by Panthers (February 27, 1998).
CHAMPIONSHIP GAME EXPERIENCE: Played in NFC championship game (1985, 1989, 1996 and 1997 seasons). ... Played in AFC championship game (1994 and 1995 seasons). ... Played in Super Bowl XXX (1995 season).
HONORS: Named outside linebacker on THE SPORTING NEWS NFL All-Pro team (1989 and 1994). ... Played in Pro Bowl (1989 and 1994-1996 seasons).
PRO STATISTICS: 1986—Recovered one fumble for 13 yards. 1987—Intercepted one pass for 25 yards. 1988—Credited with a safety and intercepted one pass for 10 yards. 1989—Recovered two fumbles. 1990—Recovered four fumbles. 1991—Credited with one safety. 1992—Credited with one safety and recovered four fumbles for two yards. 1993—Recovered three fumbles for five yards. 1994—Recovered three fumbles. 1995—Intercepted one pass for no yards. 1996—Recovered three fumbles for 66 yards and a touchdown. 1997—Recovered two fumbles for 40 yards and one touchdown.

G

Year Team	G	GS	SACKS
1985—Los Angeles Rams NFL	15	0	0.0
1986—Los Angeles Rams NFL	16	0	7.0
1987—Los Angeles Rams NFL	9	0	6.5
1988—Los Angeles Rams NFL	16	14	16.5
1989—Los Angeles Rams NFL	16	16	16.5
1990—Los Angeles Rams NFL	15	16	13.0
1991—Los Angeles Rams NFL	16	16	3.0
1992—Los Angeles Rams NFL	16	16	10.0
1993—Pittsburgh NFL	16	16	12.5
1994—Pittsburgh NFL	16	16	*14.0
1995—Pittsburgh NFL	16	16	9.0
1996—Carolina NFL	16	16	*14.5
1997—San Francisco NFL	14	4	10.5
Pro totals (13 years)	197	145	133.0

GREENE, SCOTT FB PANTHERS

PERSONAL: Born June 1, 1972, in Honeoye, N.Y. ... 5-11/225.
HIGH SCHOOL: Canandaigua (N.Y.) Academy.
COLLEGE: Michigan State.
TRANSACTIONS/CAREER NOTES: Selected by Carolina Panthers in sixth round (193rd pick overall) of 1996 NFL draft. ... Signed by Panthers (July 17, 1996). ... Released by Panthers (August 21, 1996). ... Re-signed by Panthers to practice squad (August 27, 1996).
CHAMPIONSHIP GAME EXPERIENCE: Played in NFC championship game (1996 season).
PRO STATISTICS: 1996—Returned two kickoffs for 10 yards. 1997—Returned three kickoffs for 18 yards.
SINGLE GAME HIGHS (regular season): Attempts—7 (November 30, 1997, vs. New Orleans); yards—30 (November 30, 1997, vs. New Orleans); and rushing touchdowns—1 (November 1, 1997, vs. Oakland).

			RUSHING				RECEIVING				TOTALS			
Year Team	G	GS	Att.	Yds.	Avg.	TD	No.	Yds.	Avg.	TD	TD	2pt.	Pts.	Fum.
1996—Carolina NFL	8	0	0	0	...	0	2	7	3.5	1	1	0	6	0
1997—Carolina NFL	16	14	45	157	3.5	1	40	277	6.9	1	2	0	12	1
Pro totals (2 years)	24	14	45	157	3.5	1	42	284	6.8	2	3	0	18	1

GREER, DONOVAN CB SAINTS

PERSONAL: Born September 11, 1974, in Houston. ... 5-9/178.
HIGH SCHOOL: Elsik (Alief, Texas).
COLLEGE: Texas A&M.
TRANSACTIONS/CAREER NOTES: Signed as non-drafted free agent by New Orleans Saints (April 25, 1997). ... Released by Saints (August 24, 1997). ... Signed by Atlanta Falcons (August 26, 1997). ... Released by Falcons (September 3, 1997). ... Signed by Saints to practice squad (September 4, 1997). ... Activated (November 15, 1997).
PLAYING EXPERIENCE: Atlanta (1)-New Orleans (6) NFL, 1997. ... Games/Games started: 1997 (Atl.-1/0; N.O.-6/1; Total: 7/1).

GRIER, MARRIO RB PATRIOTS

PERSONAL: Born December 5, 1971, in Charlotte, N.C. ... 5-10/229. ... Full name: Marrio Darnell Grier.
HIGH SCHOOL: Independence (Charlotte, N.C.).
COLLEGE: Clemson, then Tennessee-Chattanooga.
TRANSACTIONS/CAREER NOTES: Selected by New England Patriots in sixth round (195th pick overall) of 1996 NFL draft. ... Signed by Patriots (July 9, 1996).
CHAMPIONSHIP GAME EXPERIENCE: Played in AFC championship game (1996 season). ... Played in Super Bowl XXXI (1996 season).
PRO STATISTICS: 1996—Attempted one pass without a completion and recovered one fumble for four yards.
SINGLE GAME HIGHS (regular season): Attempts—12 (December 1, 1996, vs. San Diego); yards—35 (November 24, 1996, vs. Indianapolis); and rushing touchdowns—1 (December 22, 1997, vs. Miami).

			RUSHING				RECEIVING				TOTALS			
Year Team	G	GS	Att.	Yds.	Avg.	TD	No.	Yds.	Avg.	TD	TD	2pt.	Pts.	Fum.
1996—New England NFL	16	0	27	105	3.9	1	1	8	8.0	0	1	0	6	0
1997—New England NFL	16	0	33	75	2.3	1	0	0	...	0	1	0	6	0
Pro totals (2 years)	32	0	60	180	3.0	2	1	8	8.0	0	2	0	12	0

G

GRIFFITH, HOWARD FB BRONCOS

PERSONAL: Born November 17, 1967, in Chicago. ... 6-0/232. ... Full name: Howard Thomas Griffith.
HIGH SCHOOL: Percy L. Julian (Chicago).
COLLEGE: Illinois.
TRANSACTIONS/CAREER NOTES: Selected by Indianapolis Colts in ninth round (237th pick overall) of 1991 NFL draft. ... Signed by Colts (July 12, 1991). ... Released by Colts (August 26, 1991). ... Signed by Buffalo Bills to practice squad (September 4, 1991). ... Released by Bills (August 31, 1992). ... Re-signed by Bills to practice squad (September 2, 1992). ... Released by Bills (October 21, 1992). ... Signed by San Diego Chargers to practice squad (October 23, 1992). ... Released by Chargers (October 28, 1992). ... Re-signed by Chargers to practice squad (October 30, 1992). ... Released by Chargers (December 9, 1992). ... Re-signed by Chargers to practice squad (December 14, 1992). ... Released by Chargers (August 30, 1993). ... Signed by Los Angeles Rams (September 2, 1993). ... Selected by Carolina Panthers from Rams in NFL expansion draft (February 15, 1995). ... Granted free agency (February 16, 1996). ... Re-signed by Panthers (July 20, 1996). ... Granted unconditional free agency (February 14, 1997). ... Signed by Denver Broncos (February 18, 1997).
CHAMPIONSHIP GAME EXPERIENCE: Played in NFC championship game (1996 season). ... Played in AFC championship game (1997 season). ... Member of Super Bowl championship team (1997 season).

PRO STATISTICS: 1995—Recovered one fumble. 1996—Recovered one fumble. 1997—Recovered one fumble.

SINGLE GAME HIGHS (regular season): Attempts—25 (November 19, 1995, vs. Arizona); yards—88 (November 19, 1995, vs. Arizona); and rushing touchdowns—1 (December 1, 1996, vs. Tampa Bay).

Year Team	G	GS	RUSHING Att.	Yds.	Avg.	TD	RECEIVING No.	Yds.	Avg.	TD	KICKOFF RETURNS No.	Yds.	Avg.	TD	TOTALS TD	2pt.	Pts.	Fum.
1991—Buffalo NFL								Did not play.										
1992—San Diego NFL								Did not play.										
1993—LA Rams NFL	15	0	0	0	...	0	0	0	...	0	8	169	21.1	0	0	...	0	0
1994—LA Rams NFL	16	10	9	30	3.3	0	16	113	7.1	1	2	35	17.5	0	1	0	6	0
1995—Carolina NFL	15	7	65	197	3.0	1	11	63	5.7	1	0	0	...	0	2	0	12	1
1996—Carolina NFL	16	14	12	7	0.6	1	27	223	8.3	1	0	0	...	0	2	0	12	1
1997—Denver NFL	15	13	9	34	3.8	0	11	55	5.0	0	0	0	...	0	0	0	0	0
Pro totals (5 years)	77	44	95	268	2.8	2	65	454	7.0	3	10	204	20.4	0	5	0	30	2

GRIFFITH, RICH   TE   JAGUARS

PERSONAL: Born July 31, 1969, in Tucson, Ariz. ... 6-5/256. ... Full name: Richard Pope Griffith.
HIGH SCHOOL: Catalina (Tucson, Ariz.).
COLLEGE: Arizona.
TRANSACTIONS/CAREER NOTES: Selected by New England Patriots in fifth round (138th pick overall) of 1993 NFL draft. ... Signed by Patriots (July 16, 1993). ... Released by Patriots (August 20, 1994). ... Signed by Jacksonville Jaguars (January 6, 1995). ... Granted free agency (February 14, 1997). ... Re-signed by Jaguars (April 15, 1997). ... Granted unconditional free agency (February 13, 1998). ... Re-signed by Jaguars (February 17, 1998).
CHAMPIONSHIP GAME EXPERIENCE: Played in AFC championship game (1996 season).
PRO STATISTICS: 1995—Returned one kickoff for nine yards. 1996—Returned two kickoffs for 24 yards and recovered one fumble.
SINGLE GAME HIGHS (regular season): Receptions—4 (December 10, 1995, vs. Indianapolis); yards—54 (December 10, 1995, vs. Indianapolis); and touchdown receptions—0.

Year Team	G	GS	RECEIVING No.	Yds.	Avg.	TD	TOTALS TD	2pt.	Pts.	Fum.
1993—New England NFL	3	0	0	0	...	0	0	...	0	0
1994—					Did not play.					
1995—Jacksonville NFL	16	15	16	243	15.2	0	0	0	0	0
1996—Jacksonville NFL	16	2	5	53	10.6	0	0	0	0	0
1997—Jacksonville NFL	16	1	0	0	...	0	0	0	0	0
Pro totals (4 years)	51	18	21	296	14.1	0	0	0	0	0

GRIFFITH, ROBERT   S   VIKINGS

PERSONAL: Born November 30, 1970, in Lonham, Md. ... 5-11/198. ... Full name: Robert Otis Griffith.
HIGH SCHOOL: Mount Miguel (Spring Valley, Calif.).
COLLEGE: San Diego State.
TRANSACTIONS/CAREER NOTES: Signed by Sacramento Gold Miners of CFL to practice squad (August 8, 1993). ... Granted free agency after 1993 season. ... Signed by Minnesota Vikings (April 21, 1994). ... Granted free agency (February 14, 1997). ... Re-signed by Vikings (May 7, 1997).
PRO STATISTICS: 1996—Fumbled once.

Year Team	G	GS	INTERCEPTIONS No.	Yds.	Avg.	TD	SACKS No.
1994—Minnesota NFL	15	0	0	0	...	0	0.0
1995—Minnesota NFL	16	0	0	0	...	0	0.5
1996—Minnesota NFL	14	14	4	67	16.8	0	2.0
1997—Minnesota NFL	16	16	2	26	13.0	0	0.0
Pro totals (4 years)	61	30	6	93	15.5	0	2.5

GROCE, CLIF   RB   COLTS

PERSONAL: Born July 30, 1972, in College Station, Texas. ... 5-11/245. ... Full name: Clifton Allen Groce.
HIGH SCHOOL: A&M Consolidated (College Station, Texas).
COLLEGE: Texas A&M.
TRANSACTIONS/CAREER NOTES: Signed as non-drafted free agent by Indianapolis Colts (April 27, 1995). ... Released by Colts (August 22, 1995). ... Re-signed by Colts to practice squad (August 28, 1995). ... Activated (December 7, 1995).
CHAMPIONSHIP GAME EXPERIENCE: Played in AFC championship game (1995 season).
PRO STATISTICS: 1996—Returned one kickoff for 18 yards and recovered one fumble. 1997—Returned one kickoff for 15 yards.
SINGLE GAME HIGHS (regular season): Attempts—11 (October 13, 1996, vs. Baltimore); yards—55 (October 13, 196, vs. Baltimore); and rushing touchdowns—0.

G

Year Team	G	GS	RUSHING Att.	Yds.	Avg.	TD	RECEIVING No.	Yds.	Avg.	TD	TOTALS TD	2pt.	Pts.	Fum.
1995—Indianapolis NFL	1	0	0	0	...	0	0	0	...	0	0	0	0	0
1996—Indianapolis NFL	15	8	46	184	4.0	0	13	106	8.2	0	0	0	0	2
1997—Indianapolis NFL	7	0	10	66	6.6	0	0	0	...	0	0	0	0	0
Pro totals (3 years)	23	8	56	250	4.5	0	13	106	8.2	0	0	0	0	2

GRUBER, PAUL   OT   BUCCANEERS

PERSONAL: Born February 24, 1965, in Madison, Wis. ... 6-5/292. ... Full name: Paul Blake Gruber.
HIGH SCHOOL: Sauk Prairie (Prairie du Sac, Wis.).
COLLEGE: Wisconsin (degree in communication arts, 1988).

TRANSACTIONS/CAREER NOTES: Selected by Tampa Bay Buccaneers in first round (fourth pick overall) of 1988 NFL draft. ... Signed by Buccaneers (August 7, 1988). ... Designated by Buccaneers as franchise player (February 25, 1993). ... Re-signed by Buccaneers (October 20, 1993). ... Granted roster exemption (October 20-23, 1993).

PLAYING EXPERIENCE: Tampa Bay NFL, 1988-1997. ... Games/Games started: 1988 (16/16), 1989 (16/16), 1990 (16/16), 1991 (16/16), 1992 (16/16), 1993 (10/10), 1994 (16/16), 1995 (16/16), 1996 (13/13), 1997 (16/16). Total: 151/151.

HONORS: Named offensive tackle on THE SPORTING NEWS college All-America first team (1987).

PRO STATISTICS: 1988—Recovered two fumbles. 1990—Recovered one fumble. 1991—Recovered one fumble. 1992—Recovered one fumble. 1994—Recovered one fumble. 1995—Recovered two fumbles. 1997—Recovered one fumble.

GRUNHARD, TIM — C — CHIEFS

PERSONAL: Born May 17, 1968, in Chicago. ... 6-2/307. ... Full name: Timothy Gerard Grunhard.

HIGH SCHOOL: St. Laurence (Burbank, Ill.).

COLLEGE: Notre Dame (degree in political science).

TRANSACTIONS/CAREER NOTES: Selected by Kansas City Chiefs in second round (40th pick overall) of 1990 NFL draft. ... Signed by Chiefs (July 22, 1990).

PLAYING EXPERIENCE: Kansas City NFL, 1990-1997. ... Games/Games started: 1990 (14/9), 1991 (16/16), 1992 (12/12), 1993 (16/16), 1994 (16/16), 1995 (16/16), 1996 (16/16), 1997 (16/16). Total: 122/117.

CHAMPIONSHIP GAME EXPERIENCE: Played in AFC championship game (1993 season).

PRO STATISTICS: 1991—Recovered one fumble. 1992—Recovered two fumbles. 1993—Fumbled once. 1995—Recovered one fumble. 1996—Recovered one fumble. 1997—Recovered one fumble.

GRUTTADAURIA, MIKE — C — RAMS

PERSONAL: Born December 6, 1972, in Fort Lauderdale. ... 6-4/297. ... Full name: Michael Jason Gruttadauria.

HIGH SCHOOL: Tarpon Springs (Fla.).

COLLEGE: Central Florida.

TRANSACTIONS/CAREER NOTES: Signed as non-drafted free agent by Dallas Cowboys (April 26, 1995). ... Released by Cowboys (August 22, 1995). ... Signed by St. Louis Rams (February 9, 1996).

PLAYING EXPERIENCE: St. Louis NFL, 1996 and 1997. ... Games/Games started: 1996 (9/3), 1997 (14/14). Total: 23/17.

PRO STATISTICS: 1997—Caught one pass for no yards.

GULIFORD, ERIC — WR — SAINTS

PERSONAL: Born October 25, 1969, in Kansas City, Kan. ... 5-8/165. ... Full name: Eric Andre Guliford.

HIGH SCHOOL: Peoria (Ariz.).

COLLEGE: Arizona State.

TRANSACTIONS/CAREER NOTES: Signed as non-drafted free agent by Minnesota Vikings (May 3, 1993). ... Selected by Carolina Panthers from Vikings in NFL expansion draft (February 15, 1995). ... On injured reserve with hamstring injury (December 13, 1995-remainder of season). ... Granted unconditional free agency (February 16, 1996). ... Signed by Winnipeg Blue Bombers of CFL (May 26, 1996). ... Released by Blue Bombers (November 23, 1996). ... Signed by New Orleans Saints (May 19, 1997).

PRO STATISTICS: 1995—Attempted two passes with one completion for 46 yards and an interception, rushed twice for two yards and recovered one fumble. 1997—Rushed once for minus two yards and recovered one fumble.

SINGLE GAME HIGHS (regular season): Receptions—7 (October 29, 1995, vs. New England); yards— 94 (October 29, 1995, vs. New England); and touchdown receptions—1 (December 14, 1997, vs. Arizona).

			RECEIVING				PUNT RETURNS				KICKOFF RETURNS				TOTALS			
Year Team	G	GS	No.	Yds.	Avg.	TD	No.	Yds.	Avg.	TD	No.	Yds.	Avg.	TD	TD	2pt.	Pts.	Fum.
1993—Minnesota NFL	10	0	1	45	45.0	0	29	212	7.3	0	5	101	20.2	0	0	...	0	1
1994—Minnesota NFL	7	1	0	0	...	0	5	14	2.8	0	0	0	...	0	0	0	0	1
1995—Carolina NFL	14	9	29	444	15.3	1	43	‡475	11.0	†1	0	0	...	0	2	0	12	1
1996—Winnipeg CFL	11	...	47	758	16.1	3	44	546	12.4	0	31	634	20.5	0	3	0	18	4
1997—New Orleans NFL	16	2	27	362	13.4	1	47	498	10.6	0	43	1128	26.2	1	2	0	12	2
CFL totals (1 year)	11		47	758	16.1	3	44	546	12.4	0	31	634	20.5	0	3	0	18	4
NFL totals (4 years)	47	12	57	851	14.9	2	124	1199	9.7	1	48	1229	25.6	4	4	0	24	5
Pro totals (5 years)	58	...	104	1609	15.5	5	168	1745	10.4	1	79	1863	23.6	1	7	0	42	9

GUYNES, THOMAS — OT — CARDINALS

PERSONAL: Born September 9, 1974, in Marion, Ind. ... 6-5/330.

HIGH SCHOOL: McNamara (Kankakee, Ill.).

COLLEGE: Michigan (degree in sports management and communications, 1997).

TRANSACTIONS/CAREER NOTES: Signed as non-drafted free agent by Arizona Cardinals (April 21, 1997).

PLAYING EXPERIENCE: Arizona NFL, 1997. ... Games/Games started: 4/0.

HABIB, BRIAN — G — SEAHAWKS

G
H

PERSONAL: Born December 2, 1964, in Ellensburg, Wash. ... 6-7/299. ... Full name: Brian Richard Habib.

HIGH SCHOOL: Ellensburg (Wash.).

COLLEGE: Washington.

TRANSACTIONS/CAREER NOTES: Selected by Minnesota Vikings in 10th round (264th pick overall) of 1988 NFL draft. ... Signed by Vikings (July 19, 1988). ... On injured reserve with shoulder injury (September 3-December 24, 1988). ... Granted free agency (February 1, 1991). ... Re-signed by Vikings (July 18, 1991). ... Granted free agency (February 1, 1992). ... Re-signed by Vikings (July 24, 1992). ... Granted unconditional free agency (March 1, 1993). ... Signed by Denver Broncos (March 8, 1993). ... Granted unconditional free agency (February 13, 1998). ... Signed by Seattle Seahawks (March 6, 1998).

PLAYING EXPERIENCE: Minnesota NFL, 1989-1992; Denver NFL, 1993-1997. ... Games/Games started: 1989 (16/0), 1990 (16/0), 1991 (16/8), 1992 (16/15), 1993 (16/16), 1994 (16/16), 1995 (16/16), 1996 (16/16), 1997 (14/14). Total: 142/101.
CHAMPIONSHIP GAME EXPERIENCE: Played in AFC championship game (1997 season). ... Member of Super Bowl championship team (1997 season).
PRO STATISTICS: 1994—Recovered one fumble.

HAGER, BRITT — LB

PERSONAL: Born February 20, 1966, in Odessa, Texas. ... 6-1/225. ... Full name: Britt Harley Hager. ... Name pronounced HAY-ghurr.
HIGH SCHOOL: Permian (Odessa, Texas).
COLLEGE: Texas.
TRANSACTIONS/CAREER NOTES: Selected by Philadelphia Eagles in third round (81st pick overall) of 1989 NFL draft. ... Signed by Eagles (August 7, 1989). ... Granted free agency (February 1, 1992). ... Re-signed by Eagles (August 11, 1992). ... On injured reserve with back injury (November 18, 1992-remainder of season). ... Granted free agency (March 1, 1993). ... Re-signed by Eagles (July 21, 1993). ... Granted unconditional free agency (February 17, 1995). ... Signed by Denver Broncos (March 6, 1995). ... Released by Broncos (February 14, 1997). ... Signed by St. Louis Rams (May 26, 1997). ... Granted unconditional free agency (February 13, 1998).
PRO STATISTICS: 1989—Recovered two fumbles for nine yards. 1990—Returned one kickoff for no yards. 1991—Recovered one fumble. 1994—Recovered one fumble.

Year Team	G	GS	INTERCEPTIONS No.	Yds.	Avg.	TD	SACKS No.
1989—Philadelphia NFL	16	0	0	0	...	0	0.0
1990—Philadelphia NFL	16	1	0	0	...	0	0.0
1991—Philadelphia NFL	10	0	0	0	...	0	0.0
1992—Philadelphia NFL	10	0	0	0	...	0	0.0
1993—Philadelphia NFL	16	7	1	19	19.0	0	1.0
1994—Philadelphia NFL	16	5	1	0	0.0	0	1.0
1995—Denver NFL	16	5	1	19	19.0	0	0.0
1996—Denver NFL	2	0	0	0	...	0	0.0
1997—St. Louis NFL	13	0	0	0	...	0	0.0
Pro totals (9 years)	115	18	3	38	12.7	0	2.0

HAGOOD, JAY — OT — JETS

PERSONAL: Born August 9, 1973, in Easley, S.C. ... 6-4/306.
HIGH SCHOOL: Easley (S.C.), then Fork Union (Va.) Military Academy.
COLLEGE: Virginia Tech.
TRANSACTIONS/CAREER NOTES: Signed as non-drafted free agent by New York Jets (April 25, 1997).
PLAYING EXPERIENCE: New York Jets NFL, 1997. ... Games/Games started: 2/0.

HALAPIN, MIKE — DT — OILERS

PERSONAL: Born July 1, 1973, in New Kinsington, Pa. ... 6-4/283.
HIGH SCHOOL: Kiski (Saltsburg, Penn.).
COLLEGE: Pittsburgh.
TRANSACTIONS/CAREER NOTES: Signed as non-drafted free agent by Houston Oilers (April 23, 1996). ... Oilers franchise moved to Tennessee for 1997 season. ... On injured reserve with shoulder injury (November 21, 1997-remainder of season).
PLAYING EXPERIENCE: Houston NFL, 1996; Tennessee NFL, 1997. ... Games/Games started: 1996 (9/0), 1997 (3/1). Total: 12/1.

HALL, DANA — S

PERSONAL: Born July 8, 1969, in Bellflower, Calif. ... 6-2/209. ... Full name: Dana Eric Hall.
HIGH SCHOOL: Genesha (Pomona, Calif.).
COLLEGE: Washington (degree in political science, 1992).
TRANSACTIONS/CAREER NOTES: Selected by San Francisco 49ers in first round (18th pick overall) of 1992 NFL draft. ... Signed by 49ers (July 20, 1992). ... Granted unconditional free agency (February 17, 1995). ... Signed by Cleveland Browns (April 28, 1995). ... Granted unconditional free agency (February 16, 1996). ... Signed by Jacksonville Jaguars (March 13, 1996). ... Released by Jaguars (February 17, 1998).
CHAMPIONSHIP GAME EXPERIENCE: Played in NFC championship game (1992-1994 seasons). ... Member of Super Bowl championship team (1994 season). ... Played in AFC championship game (1996 season).
PRO STATISTICS: 1992—Credited with one sack and recovered one fumble. 1995—Credited with one sack. 1996—Recovered two fumbles. 1997—Caught one pass for 22 yards.

Year Team	G	GS	INTERCEPTIONS No.	Yds.	Avg.	TD
1992—San Francisco NFL	15	15	2	34	17.0	0
1993—San Francisco NFL	13	7	0	0	...	0
1994—San Francisco NFL	16	4	2	0	0.0	0
1995—Cleveland NFL	15	2	2	41	20.5	0
1996—Jacksonville NFL	16	10	1	20	20.0	0
1997—Jacksonville NFL	16	0	0	0	...	0
Pro totals (6 years)	91	38	7	95	13.6	0

HALL, JOHN — K — JETS

PERSONAL: Born March 17, 1974, in Port Charlotte, Fla. ... 6-3/223.
HIGH SCHOOL: Port Charlotte (Fla.).
COLLEGE: Wisconsin.

H

TRANSACTIONS/CAREER NOTES: Signed as non-drafted free agent by New York Jets (April 25, 1997).
PRO STATISTICS: 1997—Punted three times for 144 yards.

				KICKING						
Year Team	G	GS	XPM	XPA	FGM	FGA	Lg.	50+	Pts.
1997—New York Jets NFL..............................	16	0	36	36	28	†41	55	4-6	120

HALL, LEMANSKI   LB   OILERS

PERSONAL: Born November 24, 1970, in Valley, Ala. ... 6-0/230.
HIGH SCHOOL: Valley (Ala.).
COLLEGE: Alabama.
TRANSACTIONS/CAREER NOTES: Selected by Houston Oilers in seventh round (220th pick overall) of 1994 NFL draft. ... Signed by Oilers (June 20, 1994). ... Released by Oilers (August 28, 1994). ... Re-signed by Oilers to practice squad (August 30, 1994). ... Activated (December 23, 1994); did not play. ... Assigned by Oilers to Frankfurt Galaxy in 1995 World League enhancement allocation program (February 20, 1995). ... Assigned by Oilers to Amsterdam Admirals in 1996 World League enhancement allocation program (February 19, 1996). ... Oilers franchise moved to Tennessee for 1997 season. ... Granted free agency (February 13, 1998).
PLAYING EXPERIENCE: Houston NFL, 1995 and 1996; Tennessee NFL, 1997. ... Games/Games started: 1995 (12/0), 1996 (3/0), 1997 (16/2). Total: 31/2.
PRO STATISTICS: 1997—Credited with two sacks.

HALL, RHETT   DT   EAGLES

PERSONAL: Born December 5, 1968, in San Jose, Calif. ... 6-2/276. ... Full name: Rhett Floyd Hall.
HIGH SCHOOL: Live Oak (Morgan Hill, Calif.).
JUNIOR COLLEGE: Gavilan College (Calif.).
COLLEGE: California (degree in social sciences).
TRANSACTIONS/CAREER NOTES: Selected by Tampa Bay Buccaneers in sixth round (147th pick overall) of 1991 NFL draft. ... Signed by Buccaneers (July 18, 1991). ... Released by Buccaneers (August 31, 1992). ... Re-signed by Buccaneers (September 1, 1992). ... Released by Buccaneers (September 2, 1992). ... Re-signed by Buccaneers (September 4, 1992). ... Released by Buccaneers (September 23, 1992). ... Re-signed by Buccaneers (December 9, 1992). ... Released by Buccaneers (August 30, 1993). ... Re-signed by Buccaneers (August 31, 1993). ... Released by Buccaneers (September 11, 1993). ... Re-signed by Buccaneers (November 23, 1993). ... Granted free agency (February 17, 1994). ... Signed by San Francisco 49ers (June 1, 1994). ... Released by 49ers (September 7, 1994). ... Re-signed by 49ers (September 14, 1994). ... Granted unconditional free agency (February 17, 1995). ... Signed by Philadelphia Eagles (March 9, 1995). ... Designated by Eagles as transition player (February 13, 1998). ... Re-signed by Eagles (June 8, 1998).
CHAMPIONSHIP GAME EXPERIENCE: Played in NFC championship game (1994 season). ... Member of Super Bowl championship team (1994 season).
PRO STATISTICS: 1994—Recovered one fumble. 1996—Recovered two fumbles for 32 yards and a touchdown. 1997—Intercepted one pass for 39 yards.

Year Team	G	GS	SACKS
1991—Tampa Bay NFL...	16	0	1.0
1992—Tampa Bay NFL...	4	0	0.0
1993—Tampa Bay NFL...	1	0	0.0
1994—San Francisco NFL...	12	2	4.0
1995—Philadelphia NFL..	3	1	1.0
1996—Philadelphia NFL..	16	16	4.5
1997—Philadelphia NFL..	15	15	8.0
Pro totals (7 years)...	67	34	18.5

HALL, TIM   RB   RAIDERS

PERSONAL: Born February 15, 1974, in Kansas City, Mo. ... 5-11/218.
HIGH SCHOOL: Northeast (Kansas City, Mo.).
JUNIOR COLLEGE: Kemper Military Junior College (Mo.).
COLLEGE: Robert Morris.
TRANSACTIONS/CAREER NOTES: Selected by Oakland Raiders in sixth round (183rd pick overall) of 1996 NFL draft. ... Signed by Raiders (July 18, 1996).
PRO STATISTICS: 1997—Caught one pass for nine yards.
SINGLE GAME HIGHS (regular season): Attempts—7 (November 16, 1997, vs. San Diego); yards—31 (November 24, 1997, vs. Denver); and rushing touchdowns—0.

			RUSHING				KICKOFF RETURNS				TOTALS			
Year Team	G	GS	Att.	Yds.	Avg.	TD	No.	Yds.	Avg.	TD	TD	2pt.	Pts.	Fum.
1996—Oakland NFL	2	0	3	7	2.3	0	0	0	...	0	0	0	0	0
1997—Oakland NFL	16	0	23	120	5.2	0	9	182	20.2	0	0	0	0	0
Pro totals (2 years).........................	18	0	26	127	4.9	0	9	182	20.2	0	0	0	0	0

HALL, TRAVIS   DL   FALCONS

H

PERSONAL: Born August 3, 1972, in Kenai, Alaska. ... 6-5/288.
HIGH SCHOOL: West Jordan (Utah).
COLLEGE: Brigham Young.
TRANSACTIONS/CAREER NOTES: Selected by Atlanta Falcons in sixth round (181st pick overall) of 1995 NFL draft. ... Signed by Falcons (June 30, 1995).
PRO STATISTICS: 1996—Recovered one fumble. 1997—Recovered one fumble.

Year Team	G	GS	SACKS
1995—Atlanta NFL	1	0	0.0
1996—Atlanta NFL	14	13	6.0
1997—Atlanta NFL	16	16	10.5
Pro totals (3 years)	31	29	16.5

HALLOCK, TY — FB — BEARS

PERSONAL: Born April 30, 1971, in Grand Rapids, Mich. ... 6-2/256. ... Full name: Ty Edward Hallock.
HIGH SCHOOL: Greenville (Mich.).
COLLEGE: Michigan State.
TRANSACTIONS/CAREER NOTES: Selected by Detroit Lions in seventh round (174th pick overall) of 1993 NFL draft. ... Signed by Lions (July 15, 1993). ... Released by Lions (August 30, 1993). ... Re-signed by Lions to practice squad (August 31, 1993). ... Activated (September 3, 1993). ... Traded by Lions to Jacksonville Jaguars for CB Corey Raymond (May 30, 1995). ... On reserve/retired list (July 10, 1995-February 12, 1996). ... Granted free agency (February 14, 1997). ... Re-signed by Jaguars (June 9, 1997). ... Granted unconditional free agency (February 13, 1998). ... Signed by Chicago Bears (February 16, 1998).
CHAMPIONSHIP GAME EXPERIENCE: Played in AFC championship game (1996 season).
PRO STATISTICS: 1993—Returned one kickoff for 11 yards. 1997—Rushed four times for 21 yards and returned one kickoff for six yards.
SINGLE GAME HIGHS (regular season): Attempts—2 (October 12, 1997, vs. Philadelphia); yards—11 (November 24, 1997, vs. Philadelphia); and rushing touchdowns—0.

Year Team	G	GS	RECEIVING No.	RECEIVING Yds.	RECEIVING Avg.	RECEIVING TD	TOTALS TD	TOTALS 2pt.	TOTALS Pts.	Fum.
1993—Detroit NFL	16	4	8	88	11.0	2	2	...	12	0
1994—Detroit NFL	15	10	7	75	10.7	0	0	0	0	0
1995—Jacksonville NFL					Did not play.					
1996—Jacksonville NFL	7	0	1	5	5.0	0	0	0	0	0
1997—Jacksonville NFL	15	8	18	131	7.3	1	1	0	6	0
Pro totals (4 years)	53	22	34	299	8.8	3	3	0	18	0

HAMILTON, BOBBY — DE — JETS

PERSONAL: Born January 7, 1971, in Columbia, Miss. ... 6-5/280.
HIGH SCHOOL: East Marion (Columbia, Miss.).
COLLEGE: Southern Mississippi.
TRANSACTIONS/CAREER NOTES: Signed as non-drafted free agent by Seattle Seahawks (April 19, 1994). ... On injured reserve with knee injury (August 17, 1994-entire season). ... Assigned by Seahawks to Amsterdam Admirals in 1995 World League enhancement allocation draft. ... Released by Seahawks (August 15, 1996). ... Signed by New York Jets (August 17, 1996). ... Released by Jets (August 24, 1996). ... Re-signed by Jets to practice squad (August 26, 1996). ... Activated (September 4, 1996).
PRO STATISTICS: 1996—Recovered one fumble for seven yards. 1997—Returned one kickoff for no yards.

Year Team	G	GS	SACKS
1994—Seattle NFL		Did not play.	
1995—Amsterdam W.L.	10	9	5.0
1996—Amsterdam W.L.	...	...	5.0
—New York Jets NFL	15	11	4.5
1997—New York Jets NFL	16	0	1.0
W.L. totals (2 years)	...	...	10.0
NFL totals (2 years)	31	11	5.5
Pro totals (4 years)	...	...	15.5

HAMILTON, CONRAD — CB — GIANTS

PERSONAL: Born November 5, 1974, in Alamogordo, N.M. ... 5-10/195.
HIGH SCHOOL: Alamogordo (N.M.).
JUNIOR COLLEGE: New Mexico Military Institute.
COLLEGE: Eastern New Mexico.
TRANSACTIONS/CAREER NOTES: Selected by New York Giants in seventh round (214th pick overall) of 1996 NFL draft. ... Signed by Giants (July 18, 1996).

Year Team	G	GS	INTERCEPTIONS No.	INTERCEPTIONS Yds.	INTERCEPTIONS Avg.	INTERCEPTIONS TD	KICKOFF RETURNS No.	KICKOFF RETURNS Yds.	KICKOFF RETURNS Avg.	KICKOFF RETURNS TD	TOTALS TD	TOTALS 2pt.	TOTALS Pts.	Fum.
1996—New York Giants NFL	15	1	1	29	29.0	0	19	382	20.1	0	0	0	0	0
1997—New York Giants NFL	14	0	1	18	18.0	0	0	0	...	0	0	0	0	0
Pro totals (2 years)	29	1	2	47	23.5	0	19	382	20.1	0	0	0	0	0

HAMILTON, JAMES — LB — JAGUARS

PERSONAL: Born April 17, 1974, in Hamlet, N.C. ... 6-5/238. ... Full name: James Samuel Hamilton.
HIGH SCHOOL: Richmond County (Hamlet, N.C.).
COLLEGE: North Carolina.
TRANSACTIONS/CAREER NOTES: Selected by Jacksonville Jaguars in third round (79th pick overall) of 1997 NFL draft. ... Signed by Jaguars (May 23, 1997).

Year Team	G	GS	SACKS
1997—Jacksonville NFL	9	0	1.0

H

HAMILTON, KEITH — DT — GIANTS

PERSONAL: Born May 25, 1971, in Paterson, N.J. ... 6-6/295. ... Full name: Keith Lamarr Hamilton.
HIGH SCHOOL: Heritage (Lynchburg, Va.).
COLLEGE: Pittsburgh.
TRANSACTIONS/CAREER NOTES: Selected after junior season by New York Giants in fourth round (99th pick overall) of 1992 NFL draft. ... Signed by Giants (July 21, 1992).
PRO STATISTICS: 1992—Recovered one fumble for four yards. 1993—Credited with a safety and recovered one fumble for 10 yards. 1994—Recovered three fumbles. 1995—Fumbled once and recovered three fumbles for 87 yards. 1997—Recovered three fumbles.

Year Team	G	GS	SACKS
1992—New York Giants NFL	16	0	3.5
1993—New York Giants NFL	16	16	11.5
1994—New York Giants NFL	15	15	6.5
1995—New York Giants NFL	14	14	2.0
1996—New York Giants NFL	14	14	3.0
1997—New York Giants NFL	16	16	8.0
Pro totals (6 years)	91	75	34.5

HAMILTON, MICHAEL — LB — CHARGERS

PERSONAL: Born December 3, 1973, in Greenville, S.C. ... 6-2/244. ... Full name: Michael Antonio Hamilton.
HIGH SCHOOL: Southside (Greenville, S.C.).
COLLEGE: North Carolina A&T.
TRANSACTIONS/CAREER NOTES: Selected by San Diego Chargers in third round (74th pick overall) of 1997 NFL draft. ... Signed by Chargers (June 11, 1997). ... Released by Chargers (September 2, 1997). ... Re-signed by Chargers to practice squad (September 3, 1997). ... Activated (November 4, 1997).
PLAYING EXPERIENCE: San Diego NFL, 1997. ... Games/Games started: 6/0.

HAMILTON, RUFFIN — LB — FALCONS

PERSONAL: Born March 2, 1971, in Detroit. ... 6-1/238. ... Full name: Ruffin Hamilton III.
HIGH SCHOOL: Northeast (Zachary, La.).
COLLEGE: Tulane.
TRANSACTIONS/CAREER NOTES: Selected by Green Bay Packers in sixth round (175th pick overall) of 1994 NFL draft. ... Signed by Packers (July 19, 1994). ... Released by Packers (October 6, 1994). ... Re-signed by Packers to practice squad (October 7, 1994). ... Activated (December 6, 1994). ... Released by Packers (August 27, 1995). ... Signed by Atlanta Falcons (January 30, 1996). ... Released by Falcons (August 25, 1996). ... Re-signed by Falcons (February 13, 1997).
PLAYING EXPERIENCE: Green Bay NFL, 1994; Atlanta NFL, 1997. ... Games/Games started: 1994 (5/0), 1997 (13/0). Total: 18/0.

HAMPTON, RODNEY — RB

PERSONAL: Born April 3, 1969, in Houston. ... 5-11/230.
HIGH SCHOOL: Kashmere Senior (Houston).
COLLEGE: Georgia.
TRANSACTIONS/CAREER NOTES: Selected after junior season by New York Giants in first round (24th pick overall) of 1990 NFL draft. ... Signed by Giants (July 26, 1990). ... Deactivated for NFC championship game and Super Bowl XXV after 1990 season due to broken leg (January 1991). ... Designated by Giants as transition player (February 16, 1996). ... Tendered offer sheet by San Francisco 49ers (March 2, 1996). ... Offer matched by Giants (March 4, 1996). ... Released by Giants (April 21, 1998).
HONORS: Played in Pro Bowl (1992 and 1993 seasons).
PRO STATISTICS: 1991—Recovered one fumble. 1992—Recovered two fumbles. 1993—Recovered one fumble. 1994—Recovered one fumble. 1995—Recovered one fumble. 1996—Recovered one fumble.
SINGLE GAME HIGHS (regular season): Attempts—41 (September 19, 1993, vs. Los Angeles Rams); yards—187 (December 17, 1995, vs. Dallas); and rushing touchdowns—4 (September 24, 1995, vs. New Orleans).
STATISTICAL PLATEAUS: 100-yard rushing games: 1990 (1), 1991 (3), 1992 (2), 1993 (5), 1994 (4), 1995 (2). Total: 17.
MISCELLANEOUS: Holds New York Giants all-time record for most yards rushing (6,897) and most rushing touchdowns (49).

			RUSHING				RECEIVING				KICKOFF RETURNS				TOTALS			
Year Team	G	GS	Att.	Yds.	Avg.	TD	No.	Yds.	Avg.	TD	No.	Yds.	Avg.	TD	TD	2pt.	Pts.	Fum.
1990—New York Giants NFL	15	2	109	455	4.2	2	32	274	8.6	2	20	340	17.0	0	4	...	24	2
1991—New York Giants NFL	14	14	256	1059	4.1	10	43	283	6.6	0	10	204	20.4	0	10	...	60	5
1992—New York Giants NFL	16	16	257	1141	4.4	14	28	215	7.7	0	0	0	...	0	14	...	84	1
1993—New York Giants NFL	12	10	292	1077	3.7	5	18	210	11.7	0	0	0	...	0	5	...	30	2
1994—New York Giants NFL	14	13	327	1075	3.3	6	14	103	7.4	0	0	0	...	0	6	1	38	0
1995—New York Giants NFL	16	15	306	1182	3.9	10	24	142	5.9	0	0	0	...	0	10	1	62	5
1996—New York Giants NFL	15	15	254	827	3.3	1	15	82	5.5	0	0	0	...	0	1	0	6	3
1997—New York Giants NFL	2	0	23	81	3.5	1	0	0	...	0	0	0	...	0	1	0	6	0
Pro totals (8 years)	104	85	1824	6897	3.8	49	174	1309	7.5	2	30	544	18.1	0	51	2	310	18

HAND, NORMAN — DT — CHARGERS

PERSONAL: Born September 4, 1972, in Walterboro, S.C. ... 6-3/313. ... Full name: Norman L. Hand.
HIGH SCHOOL: Walterboro (S.C.).
COLLEGE: Mississippi.

TRANSACTIONS/CAREER NOTES: Selected by Miami Dolphins in fifth round (158th pick overall) of 1995 NFL draft. ... Signed by Dolphins (May 17, 1995). ... Inactive for 16 games (1995). ... Claimed on waivers by San Diego Chargers (August 25, 1997). ... Granted free agency (February 13, 1998).
PLAYING EXPERIENCE: Miami NFL, 1996; San Diego NFL, 1997. ... Games/Games started: 1996 (9/0), 1997 (15/1). Total: 24/1.
PRO STATISTICS: 1997—Credited with one sack.

HANKS, BEN — LB — LIONS

PERSONAL: Born July 31, 1972, in Miami. ... 6-2/222. ... Full name: Benjamin Hanks.
HIGH SCHOOL: Miami Senior.
COLLEGE: Florida (degree in recreation/parks and tourism).
TRANSACTIONS/CAREER NOTES: Signed as non-drafted free agent by Minnesota Vikings (April 22, 1996). ... On injured reserve with ankle injury (December 20, 1996-remainder of season). ... Claimed on waivers by Detroit Lions (August 25, 1997). ... Released by Lions (September 30, 1997). ... Re-signed by Lions (December 23, 1997). ... Released by Lions after 1997 season ... Re-signed by Lions (March 26, 1998).
PLAYING EXPERIENCE: Minnesota NFL, 1996; Detroit NFL, 1997. ... Games/Games started: 1996 (12/0), 1997 (2/0). Total: 14/0.

HANKS, MERTON — S — 49ERS

PERSONAL: Born March 12, 1968, in Dallas. ... 6-2/181. ... Full name: Merton Edward Hanks.
HIGH SCHOOL: Lake Highlands (Dallas).
COLLEGE: Iowa (degree in liberal arts, 1990).
TRANSACTIONS/CAREER NOTES: Selected by San Francisco 49ers in fifth round (122nd pick overall) of 1991 NFL draft. ... Signed by 49ers (July 10, 1991).
CHAMPIONSHIP GAME EXPERIENCE: Played in NFC championship game (1992-1994 and 1997 seasons). ... Member of Super Bowl championship team (1994 season).
HONORS: Named free safety on THE SPORTING NEWS NFL All-Pro team (1994 and 1995). ... Played in Pro Bowl (1994-1997 seasons).
PRO STATISTICS: 1991—Recovered two fumbles. 1992—Returned one punt for 48 yards. 1993—Recovered one fumble. 1994—Credited with 1/2 sack, fumbled once and recovered two fumbles. 1995—Returned one punt for no yards and recovered two fumbles for 69 yards and one touchdown. 1997—Recovered two fumbles for 38 yards and one touchdown.

| | | | INTERCEPTIONS | | | |
Year Team	G	GS	No.	Yds.	Avg.	TD
1991—San Francisco NFL	13	8	0	0	...	0
1992—San Francisco NFL	16	5	2	5	2.5	0
1993—San Francisco NFL	16	14	3	104	34.7	1
1994—San Francisco NFL	16	16	7	93	13.3	0
1995—San Francisco NFL	16	16	5	31	6.2	0
1996—San Francisco NFL	16	16	4	7	1.8	0
1997—San Francisco NFL	16	16	6	103	17.2	1
Pro totals (7 years)	109	91	27	343	12.7	2

HANSEN, BRIAN — P — JETS

PERSONAL: Born October 26, 1960, in Hawarden, Iowa. ... 6-4/215. ... Full name: Brian Dean Hansen.
HIGH SCHOOL: West Sioux Community (Hawarden, Iowa).
COLLEGE: Sioux Falls (S.D.) College.
TRANSACTIONS/CAREER NOTES: Selected by New Orleans Saints in ninth round (237th pick overall) of 1984 NFL draft. ... Released by Saints (September 5, 1989). ... Signed by New England Patriots (May 3, 1990). ... Granted unconditional free agency (February 1, 1991). ... Signed by Cleveland Browns (April 1, 1991). ... Granted unconditional free agency (February 1-April 1, 1992). ... Re-signed by Browns for 1992 season. ... Granted unconditional free agency (February 17, 1994). ... Signed by New York Jets (April 19, 1994). ... Released by Jets (August 25, 1997). ... Re-signed by Jets (August 27, 1997).
HONORS: Played in Pro Bowl (1984 season).
PRO STATISTICS: 1984—Rushed twice for minus 27 yards. 1985—Attempted one pass with one completion for eight yards. 1986—Rushed once for no yards, fumbled once and recovered one fumble. 1987—Rushed twice for minus six yards. 1988—Rushed once for 10 yards. 1990—Rushed once for no yards, fumbled once and recovered two fumbles for minus 18 yards. 1991—Attempted one pass with one completion for 11 yards and a touchdown, rushed twice for minus three yards and recovered one fumble. 1992—Fumbled once and recovered one fumble. 1996—Rushed once for one yard. 1997—Attempted one pass with one completion for 26 yards.

| | | | PUNTING | | | | | |
Year Team	G	GS	No.	Yds.	Avg.	Net avg.	In. 20	Blk.
1984—New Orleans NFL	16	0	69	3020	43.8	33.2	9	1
1985—New Orleans NFL	16	0	89	3763	42.3	36.5	14	0
1986—New Orleans NFL	16	0	81	3456	42.7	36.6	17	1
1987—New Orleans NFL	12	0	52	2104	40.5	35.6	19	0
1988—New Orleans NFL	16	0	72	2913	40.5	34.2	19	1
1989—				Did not play.				
1990—New England NFL	16	0	*90	*3752	41.7	33.6	18	2
1991—Cleveland NFL	16	0	80	3397	42.5	36.1	20	0
1992—Cleveland NFL	16	0	74	3083	41.7	36.1	28	1
1993—Cleveland NFL	16	0	82	3632	44.3	35.6	15	2
1994—New York Jets NFL	16	0	84	3534	42.1	36.1	25	0
1995—New York Jets NFL	16	0	*99	*4090	41.3	31.8	23	1
1996—New York Jets NFL	16	0	74	3293	44.5	36.5	13	0
1997—New York Jets NFL	15	0	71	3068	43.2	35.3	20	1
Pro totals (13 years)	203	0	1017	43105	42.4	35.1	240	10

H

HANSEN, PHIL DE BILLS

PERSONAL: Born May 20, 1968, in Ellendale, N.D. ... 6-5/278. ... Full name: Phillip Allen Hansen.
HIGH SCHOOL: Oakes (N.D.).
COLLEGE: North Dakota State (degree in agricultural economics).
TRANSACTIONS/CAREER NOTES: Selected by Buffalo Bills in second round (54th pick overall) of 1991 NFL draft. ... Signed by Bills (July 10, 1991). ... Granted free agency (February 17, 1994). ... Re-signed by Bills (April 29, 1994).
CHAMPIONSHIP GAME EXPERIENCE: Played in AFC championship game (1991-1993 seasons). ... Played in Super Bowl XXVI (1991 season), Super Bowl XXVII (1992 season) and Super Bowl XXVIII (1993 season).
PRO STATISTICS: 1991—Recovered one fumble. 1995—Recovered one fumble. 1996—Recovered two fumbles. 1997—Credited with a safety.

Year Team	G	GS	SACKS
1991—Buffalo NFL	14	10	2.0
1992—Buffalo NFL	16	16	8.0
1993—Buffalo NFL	11	9	3.5
1994—Buffalo NFL	16	16	5.5
1995—Buffalo NFL	16	16	10.0
1996—Buffalo NFL	16	16	8.0
1997—Buffalo NFL	16	16	6.0
Pro totals (7 years)	105	99	43.0

HANSHAW, TIM G 49ERS

PERSONAL: Born April 27, 1970, in Spokane, Wash. ... 6-5/302.
HIGH SCHOOL: West Valley (Spokane, Wash.).
COLLEGE: Brigham Young.
TRANSACTIONS/CAREER NOTES: Selected by San Francisco 49ers in fourth round (127th pick overall) of 1995 NFL draft. ... Signed by 49ers (July 17, 1995). ... Inactive for 16 games (1995). ... Released by 49ers (October 22, 1996). ... Re-signed by 49ers (October 30, 1996). ... Released by 49ers (November 15, 1996). ... Re-signed by 49ers (November 25, 1996). ... Inactive for 12 games (1996). ... Granted free agency (February 13, 1998).
PLAYING EXPERIENCE: San Francisco NFL, 1997. ... Games/Games started: 13/3.
CHAMPIONSHIP GAME EXPERIENCE: Played in NFC championship game (1997 season).

HANSON, JASON K LIONS

PERSONAL: Born June 17, 1970, in Spokane, Wash. ... 5-11/183. ... Full name: Jason Douglas Hanson.
HIGH SCHOOL: Mead (Spokane, Wash.).
COLLEGE: Washington State (bachelor of science degree).
TRANSACTIONS/CAREER NOTES: Selected by Detroit Lions in second round (56th pick overall) of 1992 NFL draft. ... Signed by Lions (July 23, 1992). ... Designated by Lions as transition player (February 15, 1994).
HONORS: Named kicker on THE SPORTING NEWS college All-America first team (1989). ... Named kicker on THE SPORTING NEWS NFL All-Pro team (1993). ... Played in Pro Bowl (1997 season).
PRO STATISTICS: 1995—Punted once for 34 yards. 1996—Punted once for 24 yards.

			KICKING						
Year Team	G	GS	XPM	XPA	FGM	FGA	Lg.	50+	Pts.
1992—Detroit NFL	16	0	30	30	21	26	52	2-5	93
1993—Detroit NFL	16	0	28	28	‡34	‡43	53	3-7	‡130
1994—Detroit NFL	16	0	39	40	18	27	49	0-5	93
1995—Detroit NFL	16	0	*48	†48	28	34	56	1-1	132
1996—Detroit NFL	16	0	36	36	12	17	51	1-3	72
1997—Detroit NFL	16	0	39	40	26	29	55	3-5	117
Pro totals (6 years)	96	0	220	222	139	176	56	10-26	637

HANSPARD, BYRON RB FALCONS

PERSONAL: Born January 23, 1976, in Dallas. ... 5-10/198. ... Cousin of Essex Johnson, running back with Cincinnati Bengals (1968-75).
HIGH SCHOOL: DeSoto (Texas).
COLLEGE: Texas Tech.
TRANSACTIONS/CAREER NOTES: Selected by Atlanta Falcons in second round (41st pick overall) of 1997 NFL draft. ... Signed by Falcons (July 14, 1997).
HONORS: Doak Walker Award winner (1996). ... Named running back on THE SPORTING NEWS college All-America first team (1996).
PRO STATISTICS: 1997—Recovered two fumbles.
SINGLE GAME HIGHS (regular season): Attempts—8 (September 28, 1997, vs. Denver); yards—84 (September 14, 1997, vs. Oakland); and rushing touchdowns—0.

			RUSHING				RECEIVING				KICKOFF RETURNS				TOTALS			
Year Team	G	GS	Att.	Yds.	Avg.	TD	No.	Yds.	Avg.	TD	No.	Yds.	Avg.	TD	TD	2pt.	Pts.	Fum.
1997—Atlanta NFL	16	0	53	335	6.3	0	6	53	8.8	1	40	987	24.7	*2	3	0	18	3

H

HAPE, PATRICK TE BUCCANEERS

PERSONAL: Born June 6, 1974, in Killen, Ala. ... 6-4/256.
HIGH SCHOOL: Brooks (Killen, Ala.).
COLLEGE: Alabama.

TRANSACTIONS/CAREER NOTES: Selected by Tampa Bay Buccaneers in fifth round (137th pick overall) of 1997 NFL draft. ... Signed by Buccaneers (July 20, 1997).
PRO STATISTICS: 1997—Rushed once for one yard.
SINGLE GAME HIGHS (regular season): Receptions—1 (November 9, 1997, vs. Atlanta); yards—13 (October 5, 1997, vs. Green Bay); and touchdown receptions—1 (September 7, 1997, vs. Detroit).

			RECEIVING				TOTALS		
Year Team	G	GS	No.	Yds.	Avg.	TD	TD	2pt.	Pts.	Fum.
1997—Tampa Bay NFL	14	3	4	22	5.5	1	1	0	6	1

HARBAUGH, JIM   QB   RAVENS

PERSONAL: Born December 23, 1963, in Toledo, Ohio. ... 6-3/215. ... Full name: James Joseph Harbaugh. ... Son of Jack Harbaugh, head coach, Western Kentucky University; and cousin of Mike Gottfried, ESPN college football analyst; and former head coach, Murray State University, University of Cincinnati, University of Kansas and University of Pittsburgh.
HIGH SCHOOL: Pioneer (Ann Arbor, Mich.), then Palo Alto (Calif.).
COLLEGE: Michigan (degree in communications, 1987).
TRANSACTIONS/CAREER NOTES: Selected by Chicago Bears in first round (26th pick overall) of 1987 NFL draft. ... Signed by Bears (August 3, 1987). ... On injured reserve with separated shoulder (December 19, 1990-remainder of season). ... Granted free agency (February 1, 1991). ... Re-signed by Bears (July 22, 1991). ... Granted unconditional free agency (March 1, 1993). ... Re-signed by Bears (March 19, 1993). ... Released by Bears (March 16, 1994). ... Signed by Indianapolis Colts (April 7, 1994). ... Designated by Colts as franchise player (February 16, 1996). ... Traded by Colts with fourth-round (traded to Indianapolis) pick in 1998 draft to Baltimore Ravens for third- (WR E.G. Green) and fourth-round (traded back to Baltimore) picks in 1998 draft (February 14, 1998).
CHAMPIONSHIP GAME EXPERIENCE: Member of Bears for NFC championship game (1988 season); did not play. ... Played in AFC championship game (1995 season).
HONORS: Played in Pro Bowl (1995 season).
PRO STATISTICS: 1988—Fumbled once. 1989—Fumbled twice. 1990—Fumbled eight times and recovered three fumbles for minus four yards. 1991—Fumbled six times. 1992—Fumbled six times and recovered three fumbles. 1993—Caught one pass for one yard, led league with 15 fumbles and recovered four fumbles for minus one yard. 1994—Fumbled once. 1995—Caught one pass for minus nine yards, fumbled four times and recovered one fumble for minus 20 yards. 1996—Fumbled eight times and recovered four fumbles for minus three yards. 1997—Fumbled four times and recovered one fumble.
SINGLE GAME HIGHS (regular season): Attempts—47 (November 28, 1991, vs. Detroit); completions—30 (September 7, 1997, vs. New England); yards—319 (October 8, 1995, vs. Miami); and touchdown passes—4 (December 14, 1997, vs. Miami).
STATISTICAL PLATEAUS: 300-yard passing games: 1991 (1), 1992 (1), 1995 (1), 1997 (1). Total: 4.
MISCELLANEOUS: Regular-season record as starting NFL quarterback: 55-56 (.495). ... Postseason record as starting NFL quarterback: 2-3 (.400).

			PASSING								RUSHING				TOTALS		
Year Team	G	GS	Att.	Cmp.	Pct.	Yds.	TD	Int.	Avg.	Rat.	Att.	Yds.	Avg.	TD	TD	2pt.	Pts.
1987—Chicago NFL................	6	0	11	8	72.7	62	0	0	5.64	86.2	4	15	3.8	0	0	...	0
1988—Chicago NFL................	10	2	97	47	48.5	514	0	2	5.30	55.9	19	110	5.8	1	1	...	6
1989—Chicago NFL................	12	5	178	111	62.4	1204	5	9	6.76	70.5	45	276	6.1	3	3	...	18
1990—Chicago NFL................	14	14	312	180	57.7	2178	10	6	6.98	81.9	51	321	6.3	4	4	...	24
1991—Chicago NFL................	16	16	478	275	57.5	3121	15	16	6.53	73.7	70	338	4.8	2	2	...	12
1992—Chicago NFL................	16	13	358	202	56.4	2486	13	12	6.94	76.2	47	272	5.8	1	1	...	6
1993—Chicago NFL................	15	15	325	200	61.5	2002	7	11	6.16	72.1	60	277	4.6	4	4	...	24
1994—Indianapolis NFL........	12	9	202	125	61.9	1440	9	6	7.13	85.8	39	223	5.7	0	0	0	0
1995—Indianapolis NFL........	15	12	314	200	63.7	2575	17	5	*8.20	*100.7	52	235	4.5	2	2	0	12
1996—Indianapolis NFL........	14	14	405	232	57.3	2630	13	11	6.49	76.3	48	192	4.0	1	1	0	6
1997—Indianapolis NFL........	12	11	309	189	§61.2	2060	10	4	6.67	86.2	36	206	5.7	0	0	0	0
Pro totals (11 years).............	142	111	2989	1769	59.2	20272	99	82	6.78	79.3	471	2465	5.2	18	18	0	108

HARDIN, STEVE   G   COLTS

PERSONAL: Born December 30, 1971, in Bellevue, Wash   6-6/334. ... Full name: Steven John Hardin.
HIGH SCHOOL: Snohomish (Wash.).
COLLEGE: Oregon.
TRANSACTIONS/CAREER NOTES: Signed as non-drafted free agent by Indianapolis Colts (April 27, 1995). ... On reserve/left squad list (August 16, 1995-February 8, 1996). ... Released by Colts (October 15, 1996). ... Re-signed by Colts to practice squad (October 29, 1996). ... Released by Colts (November 26, 1996). ... Re-signed by Colts to practice squad (December 9, 1996). ... Released by Colts (August 24, 1997). ... Re-signed by Colts (February 19, 1998).
PLAYING EXPERIENCE: Indianapolis NFL, 1996. ... Games/Games started: 1/0.

HARDY, DARRYL   LB   SEAHAWKS

PERSONAL: Born November 22, 1968, in Cincinnati. ... 6-2/230. ... Full name: Darryl Gerrod Hardy.
HIGH SCHOOL: Princeton (Cincinnati).
COLLEGE: Tennessee.
TRANSACTIONS/CAREER NOTES: Selected by Atlanta Falcons in 10th round (270th pick overall) of 1992 NFL draft. ... Released by Falcons (August 31, 1992). ... Re-signed by Falcons to practice squad (September 2, 1992). ... Released by Falcons (August 24, 1993). ... Signed by Dallas Cowboys (July 16, 1994). ... Claimed on waivers by Arizona Cardinals (August 4, 1994). ... Released by Cardinals (August 27, 1994). ... Re-signed by Cardinals to practice squad (August 30, 1994). ... Activated (December 24, 1994); did not play. ... Claimed on waivers by Dallas Cowboys (October 3, 1995). ... Released by Cowboys (August 20, 1996). ... Re-signed by Cowboys (June 6, 1997). ... Claimed on waivers by Seatle Seahawks (December 10, 1997).
PLAYING EXPERIENCE: Arizona (4)-Dallas (5) NFL, 1995; Dallas (12)-Seattle (2) NFL, 1997. ... Games/Games started: 1995 (Ari.-4/0; Dal.-5/0; Total: 9/0), 1997 (Dal.-12/0; Sea.-2/0; Total: 14/0), Total: 23/0.
CHAMPIONSHIP GAME EXPERIENCE: Member of Cowboys for NFC championship game (1995 season); inactive.

H

HARDY, KEVIN — LB — JAGUARS

PERSONAL: Born July 24, 1973, in Evansville, Ind. ... 6-4/249. ... Full name: Kevin Lamont Hardy.
HIGH SCHOOL: Harrison (Evansville, Ind.).
COLLEGE: Illinois (degree in marketing, 1995).
TRANSACTIONS/CAREER NOTES: Selected by Jacksonville Jaguars in first round (second pick overall) of 1996 NFL draft. ... Signed by Jaguars (July 17, 1996).
CHAMPIONSHIP GAME EXPERIENCE: Played in AFC championship game (1996 season).
HONORS: Butkus Award winner (1995). ... Named linebacker on THE SPORTING NEWS college All-America first team (1995).
PRO STATISTICS: 1996—Recovered one fumble for 13 yards.

| | | | INTERCEPTIONS | | | | SACKS |
Year Team	G	GS	No.	Yds.	Avg.	TD	No.
1996—Jacksonville NFL	16	15	2	19	9.5	0	5.5
1997—Jacksonville NFL	13	11	0	0	...	0	2.5
Pro totals (2 years)	29	26	2	19	9.5	0	8.0

HARLOW, PAT — OT — RAIDERS

PERSONAL: Born March 16, 1969, in Norco, Calif. ... 6-6/290. ... Full name: Patrick Christopher Harlow.
HIGH SCHOOL: Norco (Calif.).
COLLEGE: Southern California (degree in public administration).
TRANSACTIONS/CAREER NOTES: Selected by New England Patriots in first round (11th pick overall) of 1991 NFL draft. ... Signed by Patriots (July 15, 1991). ... Granted free agency (February 17, 1994). ... Re-signed by Patriots (April 2, 1994). ... Traded by Patriots to Oakland Raiders for second-round pick (traded to Oakland) in 1996 NFL draft (April 17, 1996).
PLAYING EXPERIENCE: New England NFL, 1991-1995; Oakland NFL, 1996 and 1997. ... Games/Games started: 1991 (16/16), 1992 (16/16), 1993 (16/16), 1994 (16/16), 1995 (10/0), 1996 (10/9), 1997 (16/16). Total: 100/89.

HARMON, ANDY — DT

PERSONAL: Born April 6, 1969, in Centerville, Ohio ... 6-4/278. ... Full name: Andrew Phillip Harmon.
HIGH SCHOOL: Centerville (Ohio).
COLLEGE: Kent.
TRANSACTIONS/CAREER NOTES: Selected by Philadelphia Eagles in sixth round (157th pick overall) of 1991 NFL draft. ... Signed by Eagles (July 12, 1991). ... On injured reserve with knee injury (December 10, 1996-remainder of season). ... Released by Eagles (October 6, 1997).
PRO STATISTICS: 1992—Recovered one fumble. 1993—Recovered two fumbles. 1994—Intercepted one pass for no yards and recovered two fumbles. 1995—Recovered one fumble.

Year Team	G	GS	SACKS
1991—Philadelphia NFL	16	0	0.0
1992—Philadelphia NFL	16	13	7.0
1993—Philadelphia NFL	16	15	11.5
1994—Philadelphia NFL	16	16	9.0
1995—Philadelphia NFL	15	15	11.0
1996—Philadelphia NFL	2	2	1.0
1997—Philadelphia NFL	5	0	0.0
Pro totals (7 years)	86	61	39.5

HARMON, RONNIE — RB — BEARS

PERSONAL: Born May 7, 1964, in Queens, N.Y. ... 5-11/195. ... Full name: Ronnie Keith Harmon. ... Brother of Derrick Harmon, running back with San Francisco 49ers (1984-1986); and brother of Kevin Harmon, running back with Seattle Seahawks (1988 and 1989).
HIGH SCHOOL: Bayside (Queens, N.Y.).
COLLEGE: Iowa.
TRANSACTIONS/CAREER NOTES: Selected by Buffalo Bills in first round (16th pick overall) of 1986 NFL draft. ... Signed by Bills (August 13, 1986). ... Granted roster exemption (August 13-25, 1986). ... Granted unconditional free agency (February 1, 1990). ... Signed by San Diego Chargers (March 23, 1990). ... Designated by Chargers as transition player (February 25, 1993). ... Free agency status changed by Chargers from transitional to unconditional (February 16, 1996). ... Signed by Houston Oilers (May 10, 1996). ... Oilers franchise moved to Tennessee for 1997 season. ... Released by Oilers (November 18, 1997). ... Signed by Chicago Bears (December 9, 1997).
CHAMPIONSHIP GAME EXPERIENCE: Played in AFC championship game (1988 and 1994 seasons). ... Played in Super Bowl XXIX (1994 season).
HONORS: Named running back on THE SPORTING NEWS college All-America second team (1984). ... Played in Pro Bowl (1992 season).
PRO STATISTICS: 1992—Recovered two fumbles. 1994—Recovered one fumble.
SINGLE GAME HIGHS (regular season): Attempts—23 (November 29, 1987, vs. Miami); yards—119 (November 29, 1987, vs. Miami); and rushing touchdowns—2 (December 6, 1987, vs. Los Angeles Raiders).
STATISTICAL PLATEAUS: 100-yard rushing games: 1987 (1). ... 100-yard receiving games: 1990 (1), 1996 (1). Total: 2.

| | | | RUSHING | | | | RECEIVING | | | | KICKOFF RETURNS | | | | TOTALS | | | |
Year Team	G	GS	Att.	Yds.	Avg.	TD	No.	Yds.	Avg.	TD	No.	Yds.	Avg.	TD	TD	2pt.	Pts.	Fum.
1986—Buffalo NFL	14	2	54	172	3.2	0	22	185	8.4	1	18	321	17.8	0	1	...	6	2
1987—Buffalo NFL	12	10	116	485	4.2	2	56	477	8.5	2	1	30	30.0	0	4	...	24	2
1988—Buffalo NFL	16	1	57	212	3.7	1	37	427	11.5	3	11	249	22.6	0	4	...	24	2
1989—Buffalo NFL	15	2	17	99	5.8	0	29	363	12.5	4	18	409	22.7	0	4	...	24	2
1990—San Diego NFL	16	2	66	363	5.5	0	46	511	11.1	2	0	0	...	0	2	...	12	1
1991—San Diego NFL	16	0	89	544	6.1	1	59	555	9.4	1	2	25	12.5	0	2	...	12	2
1992—San Diego NFL	16	2	55	235	4.3	3	79	914	11.6	1	7	96	13.7	0	4	...	24	4
1993—San Diego NFL	16	1	46	216	4.7	0	73	671	9.2	2	1	18	18.0	0	2	...	12	0

H

			RUSHING				RECEIVING				KICKOFF RETURNS				TOTALS			
Year Team	G	GS	Att.	Yds.	Avg.	TD	No.	Yds.	Avg.	TD	No.	Yds.	Avg.	TD	TD	2pt.	Pts.	Fum.
1994—San Diego NFL	16	0	25	94	3.8	1	58	615	10.6	1	9	157	17.4	0	2	3	18	0
1995—San Diego NFL	16	1	51	187	3.7	1	63	673	10.7	5	4	25	6.3	0	6	0	36	1
1996—Houston NFL	16	6	29	131	4.5	1	42	488	11.6	2	4	69	17.3	0	3	0	18	0
1997—Tennessee NFL	11	0	8	30	3.8	0	16	189	11.8	0	1	16	16.0	0	0	0	0	0
—Chicago NFL	1	0	2	6	3.0	0	2	8	4.0	0	0	0	...	0	0	0	0	0
Pro totals (12 years)	181	27	615	2774	4.5	10	582	6076	10.4	24	76	1415	18.6	0	34	3	210	16

HARPER, ALVIN　　　　WR　　　　SAINTS

PERSONAL: Born July 6, 1968, in Lake Wells, Fla. ... 6-4/218. ... Full name: Alvin Craig Harper.

HIGH SCHOOL: Frostproof (Fla.).

COLLEGE: Tennessee (degree in psychology).

TRANSACTIONS/CAREER NOTES: Selected by Dallas Cowboys in first round (12th pick overall) of 1991 NFL draft. ... Signed by Cowboys (April 22, 1991). ... Granted free agency (February 17, 1994). ... Re-signed by Cowboys (June 1, 1994). ... Granted unconditional free agency (February 17, 1995). ... Signed by Tampa Bay Buccaneers (March 8, 1995). ... Released by Buccaneers (June 10, 1997). ... Signed by Washington Redskins (June 11, 1997). ... Claimed on waivers by New Orleans Saints (December 2, 1997).

CHAMPIONSHIP GAME EXPERIENCE: Played in NFC championship game (1992-1994 seasons). ... Member of Super Bowl championship team (1992 and 1993 seasons).

POST SEASON RECORDS: Holds NFL postseason career records for highest average gain (minimum 20 receptions)—27.3; and longest reception (from Troy Aikman)—94 yards (January 8, 1995, vs. Green Bay).

PRO STATISTICS: 1992—Rushed once for 15 yards and intercepted one pass for one yard. 1993—Attempted one pass with one completion for 46 yards.

SINGLE GAME HIGHS (regular season): Receptions—6 (November 26, 1995, vs. Green Bay); yards—140 (September 6, 1993, vs. Washington); and touchdown receptions—2 (November 7, 1993, vs. New York Giants).

STATISTICAL PLATEAUS: 100-yard receiving games: 1991 (1), 1993 (2), 1994 (3), 1995 (1). Total: 7.

			RECEIVING				TOTALS			
Year Team	G	GS	No.	Yds.	Avg.	TD	TD	2pt.	Pts.	Fum.
1991—Dallas NFL	15	5	20	326	16.3	1	1	...	6	0
1992—Dallas NFL	16	13	35	562	16.1	4	4	...	24	1
1993—Dallas NFL	16	15	36	777	‡21.6	5	5	...	30	1
1994—Dallas NFL	16	14	33	821	*24.9	8	8	0	48	2
1995—Tampa Bay NFL	13	13	46	633	13.8	2	2	0	12	0
1996—Tampa Bay NFL	12	7	19	289	15.2	1	1	0	6	1
1997—Washington NFL	12	0	2	65	32.5	0	0	0	0	0
Pro totals (7 years)	100	67	191	3473	18.2	21	21	0	126	5

HARPER, DWAYNE　　　　CB　　　　CHARGERS

PERSONAL: Born March 29, 1966, in Orangeburg, S.C. ... 5-11/175. ... Full name: Dwayne Anthony Harper.

HIGH SCHOOL: Orangeburg (S.C.)-Wilkinson.

COLLEGE: South Carolina State.

TRANSACTIONS/CAREER NOTES: Selected by Seattle Seahawks in 11th round (299th pick overall) of 1988 NFL draft. ... Signed by Seahawks (July 16, 1988). ... Granted free agency (February 1, 1992). ... Re-signed by Seahawks (August 10, 1992). ... Granted unconditional free agency (February 17, 1994). ... Signed by San Diego Chargers (March 3, 1994). ... Granted unconditional free agency (February 14, 1997). ... Re-signed by Chargers (February 16, 1997). ... On injured reserve with hamstring injury (December 17, 1997-remainder of season).

CHAMPIONSHIP GAME EXPERIENCE: Played in AFC championship game (1994 season). ... Played in Super Bowl XXIX (1994 season).

PRO STATISTICS: 1988—Credited with a sack and recovered one fumble. 1989—Recovered one fumble. 1991—Returned one punt for five yards. 1992—Fumbled once and recovered two fumbles for 52 yards and a touchdown. 1993—Recovered one fumble. 1995—Recovered one fumble for one yard. 1997—Recovered one fumble.

			INTERCEPTIONS			
Year Team	G	GS	No.	Yds.	Avg.	TD
1988—Seattle NFL	16	1	0	0	...	0
1989—Seattle NFL	16	13	2	15	7.5	0
1990—Seattle NFL	16	16	3	69	23.0	0
1991—Seattle NFL	16	16	4	84	21.0	0
1992—Seattle NFL	16	16	3	74	24.7	0
1993—Seattle NFL	14	14	1	0	0.0	0
1994—San Diego NFL	16	16	3	28	9.3	0
1995—San Diego NFL	16	16	4	12	3.0	0
1996—San Diego NFL	6	6	1	0	0.0	0
1997—San Diego NFL	12	12	2	43	21.5	0
Pro totals (10 years)	144	126	23	325	14.1	0

HARPER, ROGER　　　　S　　　　PACKERS

PERSONAL: Born October 26, 1970, in Columbus, Ohio. ... 6-2/223. ... Full name: Roger M. Harper.

HIGH SCHOOL: Independence (Columbus, Ohio).

COLLEGE: Ohio State.

TRANSACTIONS/CAREER NOTES: Selected after junior season by Atlanta Falcons in second round (38th pick overall) of 1993 NFL draft. ... Signed by Falcons (July 23, 1993). ... On injured reserve with arm injury (November 16, 1994-remainder of season). ... Granted free agency (February 16, 1996). ... Re-signed by Falcons (April 1996). ... Traded by Falcons to Dallas Cowboys for fourth-(DB Juran Bolden) and fifth-round (DE Gary Bandy) picks in 1996 draft (April 19, 1996). ... Released by Cowboys (August 17, 1997). ... Signed by Green Bay Packers (February 24, 1998).

PRO STATISTICS: 1993—Fumbled once and recovered one fumble.

H

Year Team	G	GS	INTERCEPTIONS No.	Yds.	Avg.	TD	SACKS No.
1993—Atlanta NFL	16	12	0	0	...	0	0.0
1994—Atlanta NFL	10	10	1	22	22.0	0	1.0
1995—Atlanta NFL	16	12	1	0	0.0	0	0.0
1996—Dallas NFL	14	0	2	30	15.0	0	0.0
1997—				Did not play.			
Pro totals (4 years)	56	34	4	52	13.0	0	1.0

HARRIS, ANTHONY — LB — DOLPHINS

PERSONAL: Born January 25, 1973, in Fort Pierce, Fla. ... 6-1/235. ... Full name: Anthony Jerrod Harris.
HIGH SCHOOL: Westwood (Fort Pierce, Fla.).
COLLEGE: Auburn.
TRANSACTIONS/CAREER NOTES: Signed as non-drafted free agent by Miami Dolphins (April 21, 1996).
PLAYING EXPERIENCE: Miami NFL, 1996 and 1997. ... Games/Games started: 1996 (7/3), 1997 (16/16). Total: 23/19.
PRO STATISTICS: 1996—Recovered one fumble. 1997—Returned one kickoff for no yards and credited with one sack.

HARRIS, BERNARDO — LB — PACKERS

PERSONAL: Born October 15, 1971, in Chapel Hill, N.C. ... 6-2/247. ... Full name: Bernardo Jamaine Harris.
HIGH SCHOOL: Chapel Hill (N.C.).
COLLEGE: North Carolina.
TRANSACTIONS/CAREER NOTES: Signed as non-drafted free agent by Kansas City Chiefs (June 2, 1994). ... Released by Chiefs (August 2, 1994). ... Signed by Green Bay Packers (January 20, 1995).
PLAYING EXPERIENCE: Green Bay NFL, 1995-1997. ... Games/Games started: 1995 (11/0), 1996 (16/0), 1997 (16/16). Total: 43/16.
CHAMPIONSHIP GAME EXPERIENCE: Played in NFC championship game (1995-97 seasons). ... Member of Super Bowl championship team (1996 season). ... Played in Super Bowl XXXII (1997 season).
PRO STATISTICS: 1997—Intercepted one pass for no yards and credited with one sack.

HARRIS, COREY — CB — DOLPHINS

PERSONAL: Born October 25, 1969, in Indianapolis. ... 5-11/205. ... Full name: Corey Lamont Harris.
HIGH SCHOOL: Ben Davis (Indianapolis).
COLLEGE: Vanderbilt (degree in human resources).
TRANSACTIONS/CAREER NOTES: Selected by Houston Oilers in third round (77th pick overall) of 1992 NFL draft. ... Signed by Oilers (August 5, 1992). ... Claimed on waivers by Green Bay Packers (October 14, 1992). ... Granted free agency (February 17, 1995). ... Tendered offer sheet by Seattle Seahawks (March 3, 1995). ... Packers declined to match offer (March 10, 1995). ... Granted unconditional free agency (February 14, 1997). ... Signed by Miami Dolphins (March 17, 1997).
PRO STATISTICS: 1992—Rushed twice for 10 yards. 1993—Caught two passes for 11 yards. 1994—Recovered one fumble. 1995—Recovered one fumble for 57 yards and a touchdown. 1996—Credited with one sack and recovered three fumbles for 28 yards.
MISCELLANEOUS: Played wide receiver (1992 and 1993).

Year Team	G	GS	INTERCEPTIONS No.	Yds.	Avg.	TD	PUNT RETURNS No.	Yds.	Avg.	TD	KICKOFF RETURNS No.	Yds.	Avg.	TD	TOTALS TD	2pt.	Pts.	Fum.
1992—Houston NFL	5	0	0	0	...	0	6	17	2.8	0	0	0	...	0	0	...	0	0
—Green Bay NFL	10	0	0	0	...	0	0	0	...	0	33	691	20.9	0	0	...	0	0
1993—Green Bay NFL	11	0	0	0	...	0	0	0	...	0	16	482	30.1	0	0	...	0	0
1994—Green Bay NFL	16	2	0	0	...	0	0	0	...	0	29	618	21.3	0	0	0	0	1
1995—Seattle NFL	16	16	3	-5	-1.7	0	0	0	...	0	19	397	20.9	0	1	0	6	0
1996—Seattle NFL	16	16	1	25	25.0	0	0	0	...	0	7	166	23.7	0	0	0	0	0
1997—Miami NFL	16	7	0	0	...	0	0	0	...	0	11	224	20.4	0	0	0	0	0
Pro totals (6 years)	90	41	4	20	5.0	0	6	17	2.8	0	115	2578	22.4	0	1	0	6	1

HARRIS, DERRICK — RB — RAMS

PERSONAL: Born September 18, 1972, in Willowridge, Texas ... 6-0/252. ... Full name: Sidney Derrick Harris.
HIGH SCHOOL: Willowridge (Texas).
COLLEGE: Miami (Fla.).
TRANSACTIONS/CAREER NOTES: Selected by St. Louis Rams in sixth round (175th pick overall) of 1996 NFL draft. ... Signed by Rams (July 9, 1996). ... Active for one game (1997); did not play.
PRO STATISTICS: 1996—Recovered one fumble.
SINGLE GAME HIGHS (regular season): Attempts—1 (October 6, 1996, vs. San Francisco); yards—3 (September 8, 1996, vs. San Francisco); and rushing touchdowns—0.

Year Team	G	GS	RUSHING Att.	Yds.	Avg.	TD	RECEIVING No.	Yds.	Avg.	TD	TOTALS TD	2pt.	Pts.	Fum.
1996—St. Louis NFL	11	6	3	5	1.7	0	4	17	4.3	0	0	0	0	0
1997—St. Louis NFL							Did not play.							

H

HARRIS, JACKIE — TE — OILERS

PERSONAL: Born January 4, 1968, in Pine Bluff, Ark. ... 6-4/254. ... Full name: Jackie Bernard Harris.
HIGH SCHOOL: Pine Bluff (Ark.).
COLLEGE: Northeast Louisiana.

TRANSACTIONS/CAREER NOTES: Selected by Green Bay Packers in fourth round (102nd pick overall) of 1990 NFL draft. ... Signed by Packers (July 22, 1990). ... Granted free agency (February 1, 1992). ... Re-signed by Packers (August 14, 1992). ... Designated by Packers as transition player (February 25, 1993). ... Tendered offer sheet by Tampa Bay Buccaneers (June 15, 1994). ... Packers declined to match offer (June 22, 1994). ... On injured reserve with shoulder injury (November 22, 1994-remainder of season). ... On injured reserve with hernia (January 2, 1998-remainder of 1997 playoffs). ... Granted unconditional free agency (February 13, 1998). ... Signed by Tennessee Oilers (March 11, 1998).

PRO STATISTICS: 1991—Rushed once for one yard and recovered one fumble.

SINGLE GAME HIGHS (regular season): Receptions—10 (November 26, 1995, vs. Green Bay); yards—128 (October 10, 1993, vs. Denver); and touchdown receptions—1 (September 14, 1997, vs. Minnesota).

STATISTICAL PLATEAUS: 100-yard receiving games: 1993 (1), 1995 (2). Total: 3.

				RECEIVING			TOTALS			
Year Team	G	GS	No.	Yds.	Avg.	TD	TD	2pt.	Pts.	Fum.
1990—Green Bay NFL	16	3	12	157	13.1	0	0	...	0	0
1991—Green Bay NFL	16	6	24	264	11.0	3	3	...	18	1
1992—Green Bay NFL	16	11	55	595	10.8	2	2	...	12	1
1993—Green Bay NFL	12	12	42	604	14.4	4	4	...	24	0
1994—Tampa Bay NFL	9	9	26	337	13.0	3	3	1	20	0
1995—Tampa Bay NFL	16	16	62	751	12.1	1	1	0	6	2
1996—Tampa Bay NFL	13	12	30	349	11.6	1	1	1	8	1
1997—Tampa Bay NFL	12	11	19	197	10.4	1	1	0	6	0
Pro totals (8 years)	110	80	270	3254	12.1	15	15	2	94	5

HARRIS, JON — DE — EAGLES

PERSONAL: Born June 9, 1974, in Inwood, N.Y. ... 6-7/280. ... Full name: Jonathon Cecil Harris.

HIGH SCHOOL: Kellenberg (Inwood, N.Y.).

COLLEGE: Virginia (degree in psychology, 1996).

TRANSACTIONS/CAREER NOTES: Selected by Philadelphia Eagles in first round (25th pick overall) of 1997 NFL draft. ... Signed by Eagles (June 10, 1997).

Year Team	G	GS	SACKS
1997—Philadelphia NFL	8	4	1.0

HARRIS, KENNY — S — CARDINALS

PERSONAL: Born April 27, 1975, in Durham, N.C. ... 6-1/203.

HIGH SCHOOL: Northern Durham (N.C.).

COLLEGE: North Carolina State.

TRANSACTIONS/CAREER NOTES: Signed as non-drafted free agent by Arizona Cardinals (April 21, 1997). ... Released by Cardinals (August 24, 1997). ... Re-signed by Cardinals to practice squad (August 26, 1997). ... Activated (October 6, 1997).

PLAYING EXPERIENCE: Arizona NFL, 1997. ... Games/Games started: 11/0.

HARRIS, MARK — WR — 49ERS

PERSONAL: Born April 28, 1970, in Clovis, N.M ... 6-4/201.

HIGH SCHOOL: Box Elder (Utah).

JUNIOR COLLEGE: Ricks College (Idaho).

COLLEGE: Stanford.

TRANSACTIONS/CAREER NOTES: Signed as non-drafted free agent by Dallas Cowboys (April, 25, 1996). ... Released by Cowboys (July 30, 1996). ... Signed by San Francisco 49ers (August 8, 1996). ... Released by 49ers (August 20, 1996). ... Re-signed by 49ers to practice squad (August 26, 1996). ... Activated (October 21, 1996). ... Released by 49ers (October 22, 1996). ... Re-signed by 49ers to practice squad (October 23, 1996).

PLAYING EXPERIENCE: San Francisco NFL, 1996 and 1997. ... Games/Games started: 1996 (1/0), 1997 (10/0). Total: 11/0.

CHAMPIONSHIP GAME EXPERIENCE: Member of 49ers for NFC championship game (1997 season); inactive.

PRO STATISTICS: 1997—Caught five passes for 53 yards.

SINGLE GAME HIGHS (regular season): Receptions—2 (October 12, 1997, vs. St. Louis); yards—25 (October 12, 1997, vs. St. Louis); and touchdown receptions—0.

HARRIS, RAYMONT — RB

PERSONAL: Born December 23, 1970, in Lorain, Ohio. ... 6-0/225. ... Full name: Raymont LeShawn Harris.

HIGH SCHOOL: Admiral King (Lorain, Ohio).

COLLEGE: Ohio State.

TRANSACTIONS/CAREER NOTES: Selected by Chicago Bears in fourth round (114th pick overall) of 1994 NFL draft. ... Signed by Bears (June 21, 1994). ... On injured reserve with broken collarbone (November 29, 1995-remainder of season). ... Granted free agency (February 14, 1997). ... On injured reserve with ankle injury (December 9, 1997-remainder of season). ... Designated by Bears as transition player (February 12, 1998). ... Free agency status changed from transitional to unconditional (April 20, 1998).

PRO STATISTICS: 1994—Returned one kickoff for 18 yards and recovered three fumbles.

SINGLE GAME HIGHS (regular season): Attempts—33 (November 23, 1997, vs. Tampa Bay); yards—122 (September 1, 1997, vs. Green Bay); and rushing touchdowns—2 (September 1, 1997, vs. Green Bay).

STATISTICAL PLATEAUS: 100-yard rushing games: 1996 (3), 1997 (5). Total: 8. ... 100-yard receiving games: 1996 (1).

H

Year Team	G	GS	RUSHING				RECEIVING				TOTALS			
			Att.	Yds.	Avg.	TD	No.	Yds.	Avg.	TD	TD	2pt.	Pts.	Fum.
1994—Chicago NFL	16	11	123	464	3.8	1	39	236	6.1	0	1	0	6	1
1995—Chicago NFL	2	1	0	0	...	0	1	4	4.0	0	0	0	0	0
1996—Chicago NFL	12	10	194	748	3.9	4	32	296	9.3	0	5	0	30	3
1997—Chicago NFL	13	13	275	1033	3.8	10	28	115	4.1	0	10	0	60	1
Pro totals (4 years)	43	35	592	2245	3.8	15	100	651	6.5	1	16	0	96	5

HARRIS, ROBERT DT GIANTS

PERSONAL: Born June 13, 1969, in Riviera Beach, Fla. ... 6-4/295. ... Full name: Robert Lee Harris.

HIGH SCHOOL: Sun Coast (Riviera Beach, Fla.).

COLLEGE: Southern (La.).

TRANSACTIONS/CAREER NOTES: Selected by Minnesota Vikings in second round (39th pick overall) of 1992 NFL draft. ... Signed by Vikings (July 20, 1992). ... On injured reserve with knee injury (September 30-November 12, 1992). ... Granted free agency (February 17, 1995). ... Tendered offer sheet by New York Giants (March 13, 1995). ... Vikings declined to match offer (March 20, 1995).

PRO STATISTICS: 1995—Recovered two fumbles for five yards. 1997—Recovered two fumbles.

Year Team	G	GS	SACKS
1992—Minnesota NFL	7	0	0.0
1993—Minnesota NFL	16	0	1.0
1994—Minnesota NFL	11	1	2.0
1995—New York Giants NFL	15	15	5.0
1996—New York Giants NFL	16	16	4.5
1997—New York Giants NFL	16	16	10.0
Pro totals (6 years)	81	48	22.5

HARRIS, RONNIE WR SEAHAWKS

PERSONAL: Born June 4, 1970, in Granada Hills, Calif. ... 5-11/179. ... Full name: Ronnie James Harris.

HIGH SCHOOL: Valley Christian (San Jose, Calif.).

COLLEGE: Oregon.

TRANSACTIONS/CAREER NOTES: Signed as non-drafted free agent by New England Patriots (April 30, 1993). ... Released by Patriots (August 23, 1993). ... Re-signed by Patriots to practice squad (August 31, 1993). ... Activated (December 3, 1993). ... Released by Patriots (August 20, 1994). ... Re-signed by Patriots to practice squad (August 30, 1994). ... Activated (October 15, 1994). ... Released by Patriots (October 19, 1994). ... Re-signed by Patriots to practice squad (October 19, 1994). ... Released by Patriots (November 23, 1994). ... Signed by Seattle Seahawks to practice squad (November 29, 1994). ... Activated (December 11, 1994). ... Granted free agency (February 13, 1998).

RECORDS: Shares NFL single-game record for most combined kick returns—13 (December 5, 1993, at Pittsburgh).

PRO STATISTICS: 1993—Recovered one fumble. 1997—Recovered two fumbles.

SINGLE GAME HIGHS (regular season): Receptions—2 (September 14, 1997, vs. Indianapolis); yards—38 (September 14, 1997, vs. Indianapolis); and touchdown receptions—0.

Year Team	G	GS	RECEIVING				PUNT RETURNS				KICKOFF RETURNS				TOTALS			
			No.	Yds.	Avg.	TD	No.	Yds.	Avg.	TD	No.	Yds.	Avg.	TD	TD	2pt.	Pts.	Fum.
1993—New England NFL	5	0	0	0	...	0	23	201	8.7	0	6	90	15.0	0	0	...	0	2
1994—New England NFL	1	0	1	11	11.0	0	3	26	8.7	0	0	0	...	0	0	0	0	1
—Seattle NFL	1	0	0	0	...	0	0	0	...	0	0	0	...	0	0	0	0	0
1995—Seattle NFL	13	0	0	0	...	0	3	23	7.7	0	1	29	29.0	0	0	0	0	0
1996—Seattle NFL	15	0	2	26	13.0	0	19	194	10.2	0	12	240	20.0	0	0	0	0	0
1997—Seattle NFL	13	0	4	81	20.3	0	21	144	6.9	0	14	318	22.7	0	0	0	0	4
Pro totals (5 years)	48	0	7	118	16.9	0	69	588	8.5	0	33	677	20.5	0	0	0	0	7

HARRIS, SEAN LB BEARS

PERSONAL: Born February 25, 1972, in Tucson, Ariz. ... 6-3/248. ... Full name: Sean Eugene Harris.

HIGH SCHOOL: Tucson (Ariz.).

COLLEGE: Arizona.

TRANSACTIONS/CAREER NOTES: Selected by Chicago Bears in third round (83rd pick overall) of 1995 NFL draft. ... Signed by Bears (July 18, 1995). ... Granted free agency (February 13, 1998). ... Re-signed by Bears (May 12, 1998).

PLAYING EXPERIENCE: Chicago NFL, 1995-1997. ... Games/Games started: 1995 (11/0), 1996 (15/0), 1997 (11/1). Total: 37/1.

HARRIS, WALT CB BEARS

PERSONAL: Born August 10, 1974, in LaGrange, Ga. ... 5-11/195. ... Full name: Walter Lee Harris.

HIGH SCHOOL: LaGrange (Ga.).

COLLEGE: Mississippi State.

TRANSACTIONS/CAREER NOTES: Selected by Chicago Bears in first round (13th pick overall) of 1996 NFL draft. ... Signed by Bears (July 11, 1996).

PRO STATISTICS: 1996—Recovered two fumbles for eight yards. 1997—Fumbled once and recovered one fumble.

Year Team	G	GS	INTERCEPTIONS			
			No.	Yds.	Avg.	TD
1996—Chicago NFL	15	13	2	0	0.0	0
1997—Chicago NFL	16	16	5	30	6.0	0
Pro totals (2 years)	31	29	7	30	4.3	0

H

HARRISON, CHRIS   G   LIONS

PERSONAL: Born February 25, 1972, in Washington, D.C. ... 6-3/290. ... Full name: Christopher Allen Harrison.
HIGH SCHOOL: St. John's (Washington, D.C.).
COLLEGE: Virginia.
TRANSACTIONS/CAREER NOTES: Signed as non-drafted free agent by Detroit Lions (April 26, 1996). ... On injured reserve with knee injury (October 7, 1997-remainder of season). ... Released by Lions after 1997 season. ... Re-signed by Lions (March 13, 1998).
PLAYING EXPERIENCE: Detroit NFL, 1996. ... Games/Games started: 2/0.

HARRISON, MARTIN   DE

PERSONAL: Born September 20, 1967, in Livermore, Calif. ... 6-5/251. ... Full name: Martin Allen Harrison.
HIGH SCHOOL: Newport (Bellevue, Wash.).
COLLEGE: Washington (degree in sociology, 1990).
TRANSACTIONS/CAREER NOTES: Selected by San Francisco 49ers in 10th round (276th pick overall) of 1990 NFL draft. ... Signed by 49ers (July 18, 1990). ... On injured reserve with shoulder injury (September 18-December 13, 1990). ... Released by 49ers (December 13, 1990). ... Re-signed by 49ers (1991). ... Released by 49ers (August 26, 1991). ... Re-signed by 49ers to practice squad (August 28, 1991). ... Granted free agency after 1991 season. ... Re-signed by 49ers (March 25, 1992). ... Released by 49ers (August 31, 1992). ... Re-signed by 49ers (September 1, 1992). ... Granted unconditional free agency (February 17, 1994). ... Re-signed by 49ers (June 1, 1994). ... Released by 49ers (August 27, 1994). ... Signed by Minnesota Vikings (September 12, 1994). ... Granted unconditional free agency (February 17, 1995). ... Re-signed by Vikings (March 27, 1995). ... Granted unconditional free agency (February 16, 1996). ... Re-signed by Vikings (March 20, 1996). ... Granted unconditional free agency (February 14, 1997). ... Signed by Seattle Seahawks (June 9, 1997). ... Released by Seahawks after 1997 season.
CHAMPIONSHIP GAME EXPERIENCE: Played in NFC championship game (1992 season). ... Member of 49ers for NFC championship game (1993 season); inactive.
PRO STATISTICS: 1995—Intercepted one pass for 15 yards. 1997—Recovered one fumble.

Year Team	G	GS	SACKS
1990—San Francisco NFL	2	0	0.0
1991—San Francisco NFL	Did not play.		
1992—San Francisco NFL	16	1	3.5
1993—San Francisco NFL	11	1	6.0
1994—Minnesota NFL	13	0	0.0
1995—Minnesota NFL	11	0	4.5
1996—Minnesota NFL	16	8	7.0
1997—Seattle NFL	8	0	0.0
Pro totals (7 years)	77	10	21.0

HARRISON, MARVIN   WR   COLTS

PERSONAL: Born August 25, 1972, in Philadelphia. ... 6-0/181. ... Full name: Marvin Daniel Harrison.
HIGH SCHOOL: Roman Catholic (Philadelphia).
COLLEGE: Syracuse.
TRANSACTIONS/CAREER NOTES: Selected by Indianapolis Colts in first round (19th pick overall) of 1996 NFL draft. ... Signed by Colts (July 8, 1996).
HONORS: Named kick returner on THE SPORTING NEWS All-America first team (1995).
PRO STATISTICS: 1996—Rushed three times for 15 yards. 1997—Recovered one fumble for five yards.
SINGLE GAME HIGHS (regular season): Receptions—9 (September 7, 1997, vs. New England); yards—106 (December 5, 1996, vs. Philadelphia); and touchdown receptions—3 (December 15, 1996, vs. Kansas City).
STATISTICAL PLATEAUS: 100-yard receiving games: 1996 (2).

Year Team	G	GS	RECEIVING				PUNT RETURNS				TOTALS			
			No.	Yds.	Avg.	TD	No.	Yds.	Avg.	TD	TD	2pt.	Pts.	Fum.
1996—Indianapolis NFL	16	15	64	836	13.1	8	18	177	9.8	0	8	0	48	1
1997—Indianapolis NFL	16	15	73	866	11.9	6	0	0	...	0	6	2	40	2
Pro totals (2 years)	32	30	137	1702	12.4	14	18	177	9.8	0	14	2	88	3

HARRISON, NOLAN   DE   STEELERS

PERSONAL: Born January 25, 1969, in Chicago. ... 6-5/280. ... Full name: Nolan Harrison III.
HIGH SCHOOL: Homewood-Flossmoor (Ill.).
COLLEGE: Indiana (degree in criminal justice, 1991).
TRANSACTIONS/CAREER NOTES: Selected by Los Angeles Raiders in sixth round (146th pick overall) of 1991 NFL draft. ... Signed by Raiders (1991). ... Raiders franchise moved to Oakland (July 21, 1995). ... Released by Raiders after 1996 season. ... Signed by Pittsburgh Steelers (May 20, 1997).
CHAMPIONSHIP GAME EXPERIENCE: Played in AFC championship game (1997 season).
PRO STATISTICS: 1992—Credited with a safety. 1993—Recovered one fumble for five yards. 1994—Recovered two fumbles.

Year Team	G	GS	SACKS
1991—Los Angeles Raiders NFL	14	3	1.0
1992—Los Angeles Raiders NFL	14	14	2.5
1993—Los Angeles Raiders NFL	16	14	3.0
1994—Los Angeles Raiders NFL	16	16	5.0
1995—Oakland NFL	7	6	0.0
1996—Oakland NFL	15	2	2.0
1997—Pittsburgh NFL	16	16	4.0
Pro totals (7 years)	98	71	17.5

H

HARRISON, RODNEY   S   CHARGERS

PERSONAL: Born December 15, 1972, in Markham, Ill. ... 6-0/201. ... Full name: Rodney Scott Harrison.
HIGH SCHOOL: Marian Catholic (Chicago Heights, Ill.).
COLLEGE: Western Illinois.
TRANSACTIONS/CAREER NOTES: Selected after junior season by San Diego Chargers in fifth round (145th pick overall) of 1994 NFL draft. ... Signed by Chargers (June 29, 1994).
CHAMPIONSHIP GAME EXPERIENCE: Played in AFC championship game (1994 season). ... Played in Super Bowl XXIX (1994 season).
PRO STATISTICS: 1994—Recovered one fumble. 1996—Returned one kickoff for 10 yards, credited with one sack, fumbled once and recovered two fumbles for four yards. 1997—Returned one punt for no yards, returned one kickoff for 40 yards and a touchdown, credited with four sacks and recovered three fumbles for no yards and one touchdown.

			INTERCEPTIONS			
Year Team	G	GS	No.	Yds.	Avg.	TD
1994—San Diego NFL	15	0	0	0	...	0
1995—San Diego NFL	11	0	5	22	4.4	0
1996—San Diego NFL	16	16	5	56	11.2	0
1997—San Diego NFL	16	16	2	75	37.5	1
Pro totals (4 years)	58	32	12	153	12.8	1

HARTINGS, JEFF   G   LIONS

PERSONAL: Born September 7, 1972, in Henry, Ohio. ... 6-3/283. ... Full name: Jeffrey Allen Hartings.
HIGH SCHOOL: St. Henry (Ohio).
COLLEGE: Penn State.
TRANSACTIONS/CAREER NOTES: Selected by Detroit Lions in first round (23rd pick overall) of 1996 NFL draft. ... Signed by Lions (September 27, 1996).
PLAYING EXPERIENCE: Detroit NFL, 1996 and 1997. ... Games/Games started: 1996 (11/10), 1997 (16/16). Total: 27/26.
HONORS: Named offensive lineman on THE SPORTING NEWS college All-America second team (1994). ... Named offensive lineman on THE SPORTING NEWS college All-America first team (1995).
PRO STATISTICS: 1996—Recovered one fumble.

HARTLEY, FRANK   TE   CHARGERS

PERSONAL: Born December 15, 1967, in Chicago. ... 6-2/268.
HIGH SCHOOL: Bogan (Chicago).
COLLEGE: Illinois (degree in political science).
TRANSACTIONS/CAREER NOTES: Signed as non-drafted free agent by Los Angeles Rams to practice squad (December 4, 1991). ... Released by Rams (August 31, 1992). ... Signed by San Francisco 49ers to practice squad (September 23, 1992). ... Released by 49ers (October 5, 1992). ... Signed by Atlanta Falcons (May 26, 1993). ... Released by Falcons (August 30, 1993). ... Signed by Cleveland Browns (February 21, 1994). ... Released by Browns (August 23, 1994). ... Re-signed by Browns (October 10, 1994). ... Browns franchise moved to Baltimore and renamed Ravens for 1996 season (March 11, 1996). ... Granted unconditional free agency (February 14, 1997). ... Signed by San Diego Chargers (June 3, 1997). ... Granted unconditional free agency (February 13, 1998). ... Re-signed by Chargers (March 6, 1998).
PRO STATISTICS: 1995—Recovered one fumble.
SINGLE GAME HIGHS (regular season): Receptions—4 (December 14, 1997, vs. Kansas City); yards—54 (December 14, 1997, vs. Kansas City); and touchdown receptions—1 (October 26, 1997, vs. Indianapolis).

			RECEIVING					TOTALS		
Year Team	G	GS	No.	Yds.	Avg.	TD	TD	2pt.	Pts.	Fum.
1994—Cleveland NFL	10	5	3	13	4.3	1	1	0	6	0
1995—Cleveland NFL	15	13	11	137	12.5	1	1	0	6	1
1996—Baltimore NFL	8	0	0	0	...	0	0	0	0	0
1997—San Diego NFL	16	16	19	246	12.9	1	1	0	6	0
Pro totals (4 years)	49	34	33	396	12.0	3	3	0	18	1

HARVEY, KEN   LB   REDSKINS

PERSONAL: Born May 6, 1965, in Austin, Texas. ... 6-2/237. ... Full name: Kenneth Ray Harvey.
HIGH SCHOOL: Lanier (Austin, Texas).
JUNIOR COLLEGE: Laney College (Calif.).
COLLEGE: California.
TRANSACTIONS/CAREER NOTES: Selected by Phoenix Cardinals in first round (12th pick overall) of 1988 NFL draft. ... Signed by Cardinals (June 17, 1988). ... Granted free agency (February 1, 1992). ... Re-signed by Cardinals (July 28, 1992). ... On injured reserve with knee injury (November 18, 1992-remainder of season). ... Designated by Cardinals as transition player (February 25, 1993). ... Free agency status changed by Cardinals from transitional to unconditional (February 17, 1994). ... Signed by Washington Redskins (March 5, 1994). ... Granted unconditional free agency (February 13, 1998). ... Re-signed by Redskins (February 13, 1998).
HONORS: Played in Pro Bowl (1994-1996 seasons). ... Named to play in Pro Bowl (1997 season); replaced by Lee Woodall due to injury.
PRO STATISTICS: 1988—Credited with one safety. 1990—Recovered one fumble. 1991—Recovered two fumbles. 1992—Recovered two fumbles. 1994—Recovered one fumble. 1995—Recovered two fumbles. 1996—Intercepted one pass for two yards, fumbled once and recovered two fumbles.

Year Team	G	GS	SACKS
1988—Phoenix NFL	16	0	6.0
1989—Phoenix NFL	16	16	7.0
1990—Phoenix NFL	16	16	10.0
1991—Phoenix NFL	16	16	9.0

H

Year Team	G	GS	SACKS
1992—Phoenix NFL	10	10	6.0
1993—Phoenix NFL	16	6	9.5
1994—Washington NFL	16	16	∞13.5
1995—Washington NFL	16	16	7.5
1996—Washington NFL	16	16	9.0
1997—Washington NFL	15	14	9.5
Pro totals (10 years)	153	126	87.0

HARVEY, RICHARD — LB — SAINTS

PERSONAL: Born September 11, 1966, in Pascagoula, Miss. ... 6-1/242. ... Full name: Richard Clemont Harvey. ... Son of Richard Harvey Sr., defensive back with Philadelphia Eagles and New Orleans Saints (1970 and 1971).
HIGH SCHOOL: Pascagoula (Miss.).
COLLEGE: Tulane.
TRANSACTIONS/CAREER NOTES: Selected by Buffalo Bills in 11th round (305th pick overall) of 1989 NFL draft. ... On injured reserve with shoulder injury (September 4, 1989-entire season). ... Granted unconditional free agency (February 1, 1990). ... Signed by New England Patriots (March 23, 1990). ... Released by Patriots (September 2, 1991). ... Signed by Bills (February 3, 1992). ... Selected by Ohio Glory in first round of 1992 World League supplemental draft. ... Granted unconditional free agency (February 17, 1994). ... Signed by Denver Broncos (May 9, 1994). ... Granted unconditional free agency (February 17, 1995). ... Signed by New Orleans Saints (April 3, 1995). ... Granted unconditional free agency (February 14, 1997). ... Re-signed by Saints (May 1, 1997). ... On injured reserve with foot injury (December 20, 1997-remainder of season). ... Granted unconditional free agency (February 13, 1998). ... Re-signed by Saints (March 2, 1998).
CHAMPIONSHIP GAME EXPERIENCE: Member of Bills for AFC championship game (1992 season); inactive. ... Member of Bills for Super Bowl XXVII (1992 season); inactive. ... Played in AFC championship game (1993 season). ... Played in Super Bowl XXVIII (1993 season).
PRO STATISTICS: 1992—Recovered one fumble. 1994—Recovered one fumble. 1997—Intercepted one pass for seven yards and recovered one fumble.

Year Team	G	GS	SACKS
1990—New England NFL	16	9	0.0
1991—New England NFL	1	0	0.0
1992—Buffalo NFL	12	0	0.0
1993—Buffalo NFL	15	0	0.0
1994—Denver NFL	16	1	0.0
1995—New Orleans NFL	16	14	2.0
1996—New Orleans NFL	14	7	2.0
1997—New Orleans NFL	14	13	3.0
Pro totals (8 years)	104	44	7.0

HASSELBACH, HARALD — DE — BRONCOS

PERSONAL: Born September 22, 1967, in Amsterdam, Holland. ... 6-6/284.
HIGH SCHOOL: South Delta (Delta, B.C.).
COLLEGE: Washington.
TRANSACTIONS/CAREER NOTES: Selected by Calgary Stampeders in fifth round (34th pick overall) of 1989 CFL draft. ... Granted free agency after 1993 season. ... Signed by Denver Broncos (April 11, 1994).
CHAMPIONSHIP GAME EXPERIENCE: Played in Grey Cup, CFL championship game (1992). ... Played in AFC championship game (1997 season). ... Member of Super Bowl championship team (1997 season).
PRO STATISTICS: CFL: 1992—Recovered two fumbles. 1993—Recovered four fumbles for 16 yards, intercepted one pass for no yards and fumbled once. NFL: 1995—Recovered four fumbles.

Year Team	G	GS	SACKS
1990—Calgary CFL	3	...	0.0
1991—Calgary CFL	11	...	3.0
1992—Calgary CFL	18	...	4.0
1993—Calgary CFL	18	...	7.0
1994—Denver NFL	16	9	2.0
1995—Denver NFL	16	10	4.0
1996—Denver NFL	16	1	2.0
1997—Denver NFL	16	3	1.5
CFL totals (4 years)	50	...	14.0
NFL totals (4 years)	64	23	9.5
Pro totals (8 years)	114	...	23.5

HASTINGS, ANDRE — WR — SAINTS

PERSONAL: Born November 7, 1970, in Macon, Ga. ... 6-1/190. ... Full name: Andre Orlando Hastings.
HIGH SCHOOL: Morrow (Ga.).
COLLEGE: Georgia.
TRANSACTIONS/CAREER NOTES: Selected after junior season by Pittsburgh Steelers in third round (76th pick overall) of 1993 NFL draft. ... Signed by Steelers (July 18, 1993). ... Granted free agency (February 16, 1996). ... Re-signed by Steelers (August 9, 1996). ... Granted unconditional free agency (February 14, 1997). ... Signed by New Orleans Saints (May 28, 1997). ... Released by Saints (February 13, 1998). ... Re-signed by Saints (March 6, 1998).
CHAMPIONSHIP GAME EXPERIENCE: Played in AFC championship game (1994 and 1995 seasons). ... Played in Super Bowl XXX (1995 season).
PRO STATISTICS: 1995—Rushed once for 14 yards. 1996—Rushed four times for 71 yards and recovered one fumble. 1997—Rushed four times for 35 yards and returned one punt for minus two yards.
SINGLE GAME HIGHS (regular season): Receptions—10 (September 18, 1995, vs. Miami); yards—120 (December 7, 1997, vs. St. Louis); and touchdown receptions—2 (December 1, 1996, vs. Baltimore).
STATISTICAL PLATEAUS: 100-yard receiving games: 1997 (1).

H

Year Team	G	GS	RECEIVING No.	Yds.	Avg.	TD	KICKOFF RETURNS No.	Yds.	Avg.	TD	TOTALS TD	2pt.	Pts.	Fum.
1993—Pittsburgh NFL	6	0	3	44	14.7	0	12	177	14.8	0	0	...	0	0
1994—Pittsburgh NFL	16	8	20	281	14.1	2	0	0	...	0	2	0	12	0
1995—Pittsburgh NFL	16	0	48	502	10.5	1	0	0	...	0	2	0	12	1
1996—Pittsburgh NFL	16	10	72	739	10.3	6	1	42	42.0	0	6	0	36	3
1997—New Orleans NFL	16	16	48	722	15.0	5	0	0	...	0	5	1	32	1
Pro totals (5 years)	70	34	191	2288	12.0	14	13	219	16.8	0	15	1	92	5

HASTY, JAMES — CB — CHIEFS

PERSONAL: Born May 23, 1965, in Seattle. ... 6-0/208. ... Full name: James Edward Hasty.
HIGH SCHOOL: Franklin (Seattle).
COLLEGE: Central Washington, then Washington State (degree in liberal arts and business, 1988).
TRANSACTIONS/CAREER NOTES: Selected by New York Jets in third round (74th pick overall) of 1988 NFL draft. ... Signed by Jets (July 12, 1988). ... Designated by Jets as transition player (February 25, 1993). ... Tendered offer sheet by Cincinnati Bengals (April 29, 1993). ... Offer matched by Jets (May 4, 1993). ... Granted unconditional free agency (February 17, 1995). ... Signed by Kansas City Chiefs (March 29, 1995). ... On reserve/did not report list (July 20-August 3, 1997). ... Granted unconditional free agency (February 13, 1998). ... Re-signed by Chiefs (February 17, 1998).
HONORS: Played in Pro Bowl (1997 season).
PRO STATISTICS: 1988—Recovered three fumbles for 35 yards. 1989—Fumbled once and recovered two fumbles for two yards. 1990—Returned one punt for no yards, fumbled once and recovered three fumbles. 1991—Recovered four fumbles for seven yards. 1992—Recovered two fumbles. 1993—Recovered two fumbles for 28 yards. 1994—Recovered two fumbles. 1995—Recovered one fumble for 20 yards. 1996—Recovered one fumble for 80 yards and a touchdown. 1997—Recovered one fumble.

Year Team	G	GS	INTERCEPTIONS No.	Yds.	Avg.	TD	SACKS No.
1988—New York Jets NFL	15	15	5	20	4.0	0	1.0
1989—New York Jets NFL	16	16	5	62	12.4	1	0.0
1990—New York Jets NFL	16	16	2	0	0.0	0	0.0
1991—New York Jets NFL	16	16	3	39	13.0	0	0.0
1992—New York Jets NFL	16	16	2	18	9.0	0	0.0
1993—New York Jets NFL	16	16	2	22	11.0	0	0.0
1994—New York Jets NFL	16	16	5	90	18.0	0	3.0
1995—Kansas City NFL	16	16	3	89	29.7	▲1	0.0
1996—Kansas City NFL	15	14	0	0	...	0	1.0
1997—Kansas City NFL	16	15	3	22	7.3	0	2.0
Pro totals (10 years)	158	156	30	362	12.1	2	7.0

HATCHETTE, MATTHEW — WR — VIKINGS

PERSONAL: Born May 1, 1974, in Cleveland. ... 6-2/195. ... Full name: Matthew Isaac Hatchette.
HIGH SCHOOL: Jefferson (Cleveland).
COLLEGE: Langston.
TRANSACTIONS/CAREER NOTES: Selected by Minnesota Vikings in seventh round (235th pick overall) of 1997 NFL draft. ... Signed by Vikings (June 20, 1997).
SINGLE GAME HIGHS (regular season): Receptions—1 (December 7, 1997, vs. San Francisco); yards—38 (October 12, 1997, vs. Carolina); and touchdown receptions—0.

Year Team	G	GS	RECEIVING No.	Yds.	Avg.	TD	TOTALS TD	2pt.	Pts.	Fum.
1997—Minnesota NFL	16	0	3	54	18.0	0	0	0	0	0

HAUCK, TIM — S

PERSONAL: Born December 20, 1966, in Butte, Mont. ... 5-10/185. ... Full name: Timothy Christian Hauck. ... Name pronounced HOWK.
HIGH SCHOOL: Sweet Grass County (Big Timber, Mont.).
COLLEGE: Pacific (Ore.), then Montana.
TRANSACTIONS/CAREER NOTES: Signed as non-drafted free agent by New England Patriots (May 1, 1990). ... Released by Patriots (August 26, 1990). ... Signed by Patriots to practice squad (October 1, 1990). ... Activated (October 27, 1990). ... Granted unconditional free agency (February 1, 1991). ... Signed by Green Bay Packers (April 1, 1991). ... Granted unconditional free agency (February 1-April 1, 1992). ... Re-signed by Packers for 1992 season. ... Granted free agency (March 1, 1993). ... Re-signed by Packers (July 13, 1993). ... Granted unconditional free agency (February 17, 1994). ... Re-signed by Packers (July 20, 1994). ... Granted unconditional free agency (February 17, 1995). ... Signed by Denver Broncos (March 6, 1995). ... Granted unconditional free agency (February 14, 1997). ... Signed by Seattle Seahawks (June 2, 1997). ... Granted unconditional free agency (February 13, 1998).
PLAYING EXPERIENCE: New England NFL, 1990; Green Bay NFL, 1991-1994; Denver NFL, 1995 and 1996; Seattle NFL, 1997. ... Games/Games started: 1990 (10/0), 1991 (16/0), 1992 (16/0), 1993 (13/0), 1994 (13/3), 1995 (16/0), 1996 (16/0), 1997 (16/0). Total: 116/3.
PRO STATISTICS: 1991—Recovered one fumble. 1992—Returned one punt for two yards. 1993—Recovered one fumble. 1997—Recovered one fumble for eight yards.

HAWKINS, COURTNEY — WR — STEELERS

H

PERSONAL: Born December 12, 1969, in Flint, Mich. ... 5-9/183. ... Full name: Courtney Tyrone Hawkins Jr. ... Cousin of Roy Marble, guard/forward with Atlanta Hawks and Denver Nuggets of NBA (1990-91 and 1993-94).
HIGH SCHOOL: Beecher (Flint, Mich.).
COLLEGE: Michigan State.

TRANSACTIONS/CAREER NOTES: Selected by Tampa Bay Buccaneers in second round (44th pick overall) of 1992 NFL draft. ... Signed by Buccaneers (July 16, 1992). ... On injured reserve with knee injury (December 16, 1994-remainder of season). ... Granted free agency (February 17, 1995). ... Re-signed by Buccaneers (July 21, 1995). ... Granted unconditional free agency (February 16, 1996). ... Re-signed by Buccaneers (April 27, 1996). ... Granted free agency (February 14, 1997). ... Signed by Pittsburgh Steelers (June 2, 1997).

CHAMPIONSHIP GAME EXPERIENCE: Played in AFC championship game (1997 season).

PRO STATISTICS: 1992—Returned nine kickoffs for 118 yards and recovered one fumble. 1995—Rushed four times for five yards. 1996—Rushed once for minus 13 yards.

SINGLE GAME HIGHS (regular season): Receptions—8 (September 8, 1996, vs. Detroit); yards—112 (December 5, 1993, vs. Washington); and touchdown receptions—2 (November 20, 1994, vs. Seattle).

STATISTICAL PLATEAUS: 100-yard receiving games: 1992 (1), 1993 (2), 1996 (1). Total: 4.

			RECEIVING				PUNT RETURNS				TOTALS		
Year Team	G	GS	No.	Yds.	Avg.	TD	No.	Yds.	Avg.	TD	TD	2pt.	Pts.	Fum.
1992—Tampa Bay NFL	16	5	20	336	16.8	2	13	53	4.1	0	2	...	12	2
1993—Tampa Bay NFL	16	12	62	933	15.0	5	15	166	11.1	0	5	...	30	2
1994—Tampa Bay NFL	13	12	37	438	11.8	5	5	28	5.6	0	5	0	30	0
1995—Tampa Bay NFL	16	3	41	493	12.0	0	0	0	...	0	0	0	0	1
1996—Tampa Bay NFL	16	16	46	544	11.8	1	1	-1	-1.0	0	1	0	6	1
1997—Pittsburgh NFL	15	3	45	555	12.3	3	4	68	17.0	0	3	0	18	1
Pro totals (6 years)	92	51	251	3299	13.1	16	38	314	8.3	0	16	0	96	7

HAYDEN, AARON   RB   PACKERS

PERSONAL: Born April 13, 1973, in Detroit. ... 6-0/216. ... Full name: Aaron Chautezz Hayden. ... Name pronounced HEY-den.

HIGH SCHOOL: Mumford (Detroit).

COLLEGE: Tennessee.

TRANSACTIONS/CAREER NOTES: Selected by San Diego Chargers in fourth round (104th pick overall) of 1995 NFL draft. ... Signed by Chargers (July 17, 1995). ... On physically unable to perform list with leg injury (August 22-November 10, 1995). ... Claimed on waivers by Green Bay Packers (July 10, 1997). ... Granted free agency (February 13, 1998).

CHAMPIONSHIP GAME EXPERIENCE: Played in NFC championship game (1997 season). ... Played in Super Bowl XXXII (1997 season).

PRO STATISTICS: 1996—Recovered one fumble. 1997—Returned six kickoffs for 141 yards.

SINGLE GAME HIGHS (regular season): Attempts—32 (December 3, 1995, vs. Cleveland); yards—127 (December 3, 1995, vs. Cleveland); and rushing touchdowns—2 (December 3, 1995, vs. Cleveland).

STATISTICAL PLATEAUS: 100-yard rushing games: 1995 (1).

			RUSHING				RECEIVING				TOTALS		
Year Team	G	GS	Att.	Yds.	Avg.	TD	No.	Yds.	Avg.	TD	TD	2pt.	Pts.	Fum.
1995—San Diego NFL	7	4	128	470	3.7	3	5	53	10.6	0	3	0	18	0
1996—San Diego NFL	11	0	55	166	3.0	0	1	10	10.0	0	0	0	0	1
1997—Green Bay NFL	14	0	32	148	4.6	1	2	11	5.5	0	1	0	6	0
Pro totals (3 years)	32	4	215	784	3.6	4	8	74	9.3	0	4	0	24	1

HAYES, CHRIS   S   JETS

PERSONAL: Born May 7, 1972, in San Bernardino, Calif. ... 6-0/200.

HIGH SCHOOL: San Gorgonio (San Bernardino, Calif.).

COLLEGE: Washington State.

TRANSACTIONS/CAREER NOTES: Selected by New York Jets in seventh round (210th pick overall) of 1996 NFL draft. ... Signed by Jets (June 26, 1996). ... Released by Jets (August 19, 1996). ... Signed by Washington Redskins to practice squad (September 11, 1996). ... Released by Redskins (October 2, 1996). ... Signed by Green Bay Packers to practice squad (October 4, 1996). ... Activated (December 9, 1996). ... Traded by Packers to Jets for CB Carl Greenwood (June 5, 1997).

PLAYING EXPERIENCE: Green Bay NFL, 1996; New York Jets NFL, 1997. ... Games/Games started: 1996 (2/0), 1997 (16/0). Total: 18/0.

CHAMPIONSHIP GAME EXPERIENCE: Played in NFC championship game (1996 season). ... Member of Super Bowl championship team (1996 season).

HAYES, MERCURY   WR   FALCONS

PERSONAL: Born January 1, 1973, in Houston. ... 5-11/195. ... Full name: Mercury W. Hayes.

HIGH SCHOOL: Washington (Houston).

COLLEGE: Michigan.

TRANSACTIONS/CAREER NOTES: Selected by New Orleans Saints in fifth round (136th pick overall) of 1996 NFL draft. ... Signed by Saints (July 11, 1996). ... Released by Saints (September 27, 1997). ... Signed by Atlanta Falcons (October 27, 1997).

PRO STATISTICS: 1996—Rushed twice for seven yards and returned two kickoffs for 30 yards.

SINGLE GAME HIGHS (regular season): Receptions—2 (December 1, 1996, vs. St. Louis); yards—60 (December 1, 1996, vs. St. Louis); and touchdown receptions—0.

			RECEIVING				TOTALS		
Year Team	G	GS	No.	Yds.	Avg.	TD	TD	2pt.	Pts.	Fum.
1996—New Orleans NFL	7	0	4	101	25.3	0	0	0	0	1
1997—New Orleans NFL	4	0	0	0	...	0	0	0	0	0
—Atlanta NFL	2	0	0	0	...	0	0	0	0	0
Pro totals (2 years)	13	0	4	101	25.3	0	0	0	0	1

HAYNES, MICHAEL   WR

PERSONAL: Born December 24, 1965, in New Orleans. ... 6-0/184. ... Full name: Michael David Haynes.

HIGH SCHOOL: Joseph S. Clark (New Orleans).

H

JUNIOR COLLEGE: Eastern Arizona Junior College.

COLLEGE: Northern Arizona.

TRANSACTIONS/CAREER NOTES: Selected by Atlanta Falcons in seventh round (166th pick overall) of 1988 NFL draft. ... Signed by Falcons (July 18, 1988). ... Designated by Falcons as transition player (February 17, 1994). ... Tendered offer sheet by New Orleans Saints (March 7, 1994). ... Falcons declined to match offer (March 14, 1994). ... Released by Saints (May 28, 1997). ... Signed by Falcons (June 7, 1997). ... Released by Falcons (February 13, 1998).

PRO STATISTICS: 1988—Returned six kickoffs for 113 yards. 1989—Rushed four times for 35 yards. 1994—Rushed four times for 43 yards.

SINGLE GAME HIGHS (regular season): Receptions—8 (October 9, 1994, vs. Chicago); yards—190 (December 17, 1989, vs. Washington); and touchdown receptions—2 (October 15, 1995, vs. Miami).

STATISTICAL PLATEAUS: 100-yard receiving games: 1989 (1), 1991 (5), 1992 (2), 1993 (1), 1996 (2). Total: 11.

			RECEIVING				TOTALS			
Year Team	G	GS	No.	Yds.	Avg.	TD	TD	2pt.	Pts.	Fum.
1988—Atlanta NFL	15	5	13	232	17.8	4	4	...	24	1
1989—Atlanta NFL	13	11	40	681	17.0	4	4	...	24	0
1990—Atlanta NFL	13	10	31	445	14.4	0	0	...	0	0
1991—Atlanta NFL	16	16	50	1122	*22.4	11	11	...	66	0
1992—Atlanta NFL	14	14	48	808	16.8	10	10	...	60	0
1993—Atlanta NFL	16	16	72	778	10.8	4	4	...	24	1
1994—New Orleans NFL	16	16	77	985	12.8	5	5	0	30	1
1995—New Orleans NFL	16	15	41	597	14.6	4	4	0	24	0
1996—New Orleans NFL	16	10	44	786	17.9	4	4	1	26	1
1997—Atlanta NFL	12	0	12	154	12.8	1	1	0	6	0
Pro totals (10 years)	147	113	428	6588	15.4	47	47	1	284	4

HEARST, GARRISON RB 49ERS

PERSONAL: Born January 4, 1971, in Lincolnton, Ga. ... 5-11/219. ... Full name: Gerald Garrison Hearst.

HIGH SCHOOL: Lincoln County (Lincolnton, Ga.).

COLLEGE: Georgia.

TRANSACTIONS/CAREER NOTES: Selected after junior season by Phoenix Cardinals in first round (third pick overall) of 1993 NFL draft. ... Signed by Cardinals (August 28, 1993). ... On injured reserve with knee injury (November 4, 1993-remainder of season). ... Cardinals franchise renamed Arizona Cardinals for 1994 season. ... On physically unable to perform list with knee injury (August 23-October 13, 1994). ... Granted free agency (February 16, 1996). ... Re-signed by Cardinals (May 23, 1996). ... Released by Cardinals (August 20, 1996). ... Claimed on waivers by Cincinnati Bengals (August 21, 1996). ... Granted unconditional free agency (February 14, 1997). ... Signed by San Francisco 49ers (March 7, 1997).

CHAMPIONSHIP GAME EXPERIENCE: Played in NFC championship game (1997 season).

HONORS: Doak Walker Award winner (1992). ... Named running back on THE SPORTING NEWS college All-America first team (1992).

PRO STATISTICS: 1993—Had only pass attempt intercepted. 1994—Attempted one pass with one completion for 10 yards and a touchdown. 1995—Attempted two passes with one completion for 16 yards and recovered two fumbles. 1996—Recovered one fumble. 1997—Recovered two fumbles.

SINGLE GAME HIGHS (regular season): Attempts—28 (September 29, 1997, vs. Carolina); yards—141 (September 29, 1997, vs. Carolina); and rushing touchdowns—1 (November 10, 1995, vs. Philadelphia).

STATISTICAL PLATEAUS: 100-yard rushing games: 1995 (3), 1997 (3). Total: 6.

			RUSHING				RECEIVING				TOTALS			
Year Team	G	GS	Att.	Yds.	Avg.	TD	No.	Yds.	Avg.	TD	TD	2pt.	Pts.	Fum.
1993—Phoenix NFL	6	5	76	264	3.5	1	6	18	3.0	0	1	...	6	2
1994—Arizona NFL	8	0	37	169	4.6	1	6	49	8.2	0	1	0	6	0
1995—Arizona NFL	16	15	284	1070	3.8	1	29	243	8.4	1	2	0	12	12
1996—Cincinnati NFL	16	12	225	847	3.8	0	12	131	10.9	1	1	1	8	1
1997—San Francisco NFL	13	13	234	1019	4.4	4	21	194	9.2	2	6	0	36	2
Pro totals (5 years)	59	45	856	3369	3.9	7	74	635	8.6	4	11	1	68	17

HEBRON, VAUGHN RB BRONCOS

PERSONAL: Born October 7, 1970, in Baltimore. ... 5-8/198. ... Full name: Vaughn Harlen Hebron.

HIGH SCHOOL: Cardinal Gibbons (Baltimore).

COLLEGE: Virginia Tech.

TRANSACTIONS/CAREER NOTES: Signed as non-drafted free agent by Philadelphia Eagles (April 29, 1993). ... On injured reserve with knee injury (August 22, 1995-entire season). ... Granted unconditional free agency (February 16, 1996). ... Re-signed by Eagles (April 18, 1996). ... Released by Eagles (August 22, 1996). ... Signed by Denver Broncos (August 28, 1996).

CHAMPIONSHIP GAME EXPERIENCE: Played in AFC championship game (1997 season). ... Member of Super Bowl championship team (1997 season).

PRO STATISTICS: 1993—Recovered one fumble. 1996—Recovered one fumble. 1997—Recovered one fumble.

SINGLE GAME HIGHS (regular season): Attempts—16 (December 24, 1994, vs. Cincinnati); yards—73 (October 27, 1996, vs. Kansas City); and rushing touchdowns—1 (December 15, 1997, vs. San Francisco).

			RUSHING				RECEIVING				KICKOFF RETURNS				TOTALS			
Year Team	G	GS	Att.	Yds.	Avg.	TD	No.	Yds.	Avg.	TD	No.	Yds.	Avg.	TD	TD	2pt.	Pts.	Fum.
1993—Philadelphia NFL	16	4	84	297	3.5	3	11	82	7.5	0	3	35	11.7	0	3	...	18	5
1994—Philadelphia NFL	16	2	82	325	4.0	2	18	137	7.6	0	21	443	21.1	0	2	0	12	0
1995—Philadelphia NFL								Did not play.										
1996—Denver NFL	16	0	49	262	5.3	0	7	43	6.1	0	45	1099	24.4	0	0	0	0	3
1997—Denver NFL	16	1	49	222	4.5	1	3	36	12.0	0	43	1009	23.5	0	1	0	6	1
Pro totals (4 years)	64	7	264	1106	4.2	6	39	298	7.6	0	112	2586	23.1	0	6	0	36	9

H

HECK, ANDY   OT   BEARS

PERSONAL: Born January 1, 1967, in Fargo, N.D. ... 6-6/298. ... Full name: Andrew Robert Heck.
HIGH SCHOOL: W.T. Woodson (Fairfax, Va.).
COLLEGE: Notre Dame (degree in American studies, 1989).
TRANSACTIONS/CAREER NOTES: Selected by Seattle Seahawks in first round (15th pick overall) of 1989 NFL draft. ... Signed by Seahawks (July 31, 1989). ... On injured reserve with ankle injury (October 21-November 20, 1992); on practice squad (November 18-20, 1992). ... Designated by Seahawks as transition player (February 25, 1993). ... Tendered offer sheet by Chicago Bears (February 21, 1994). ... Seahawks declined to match offer (March 1, 1994).
PLAYING EXPERIENCE: Seattle NFL, 1989-1993; Chicago NFL, 1994-1997. ... Games/Games started: 1989 (16/9), 1990 (16/16), 1991 (16/16), 1992 (13/13), 1993 (16/16), 1994 (14/14), 1995 (16/16), 1996 (16/16), 1997 (16/16). Total: 139/132.
HONORS: Named offensive tackle on THE SPORTING NEWS college All-America first team (1988).
PRO STATISTICS: 1989—Recovered one fumble. 1990—Recovered one fumble. 1993—Recovered two fumbles.

HEGAMIN, GEORGE   OT/G   EAGLES

PERSONAL: Born February 14, 1973, in Camden, N.J. ... 6-7/331. ... Full name: George Russell Hegamin.
HIGH SCHOOL: Camden (N.J.).
COLLEGE: North Carolina State.
TRANSACTIONS/CAREER NOTES: Selected after junior season by Dallas Cowboys in third round (102nd pick overall) of 1994 NFL draft. ... Signed by Cowboys (July 15, 1994). ... Active for four games (1995); did not play. ... Assigned by Cowboys to Frankfurt Galaxy in 1996 World League enhancement allocation program (February 19, 1996). ... Granted unconditional free agency (February 13, 1998). ... Signed by Philadelphia Eagles (February 19, 1998).
PLAYING EXPERIENCE: Dallas NFL, 1994, 1996 and 1997. ... Games/Games started: 1994 (2/0), 1996 (16/1), 1997 (13/9). Total: 31/10.
CHAMPIONSHIP GAME EXPERIENCE: Member of Cowboys for NFC championship game (1994 season); inactive. ... Member of Cowboys for NFC championship game (1995 season); did not play. ... Member of Super Bowl championship team (1995 season).
PRO STATISTICS: 1997—Recovered one fumble.

HELLESTRAE, DALE   G/C   COWBOYS

PERSONAL: Born July 11, 1962, in Phoenix. ... 6-5/291. ... Full name: Dale Robert Hellestrae. ... Name pronounced hell-us-TRAY.
HIGH SCHOOL: Saguaro (Scottsdale, Ariz.).
COLLEGE: Southern Methodist (degree in business administration).
TRANSACTIONS/CAREER NOTES: Selected by Houston Gamblers in 1985 USFL territorial draft. ... Selected by Buffalo Bills in fourth round (112th pick overall) of 1985 NFL draft. ... Signed by Bills (July 19, 1985). ... On injured reserve with broken thumb (October 4, 1985-remainder of season). ... On injured reserve with broken wrist (September 17-November 15, 1986). ... On injured reserve with hip injury (September 1, 1987-entire season). ... Granted unconditional free agency (February 1, 1989). ... Signed by Los Angeles Raiders (February 24, 1989). ... On injured reserve with broken leg (August 29, 1989-entire season). ... Traded by Raiders to Dallas Cowboys for seventh-round pick (traded to Chicago) in 1991 draft (August 20, 1990). ... Granted unconditional free agency (February 1-April 1, 1991). ... Re-signed by Cowboys for 1991 season. ... Granted unconditional free agency (February 1-April 1, 1992). ... Re-signed by Cowboys for 1992 season. ... Released by Cowboys (August 31, 1992). ... Re-signed by Cowboys (September 2, 1992). ... Granted unconditional free agency (March 1, 1993). ... Re-signed by Cowboys (June 2, 1993). ... Released by Cowboys (August 30, 1993). ... Re-signed by Cowboys (August 31, 1993). ... Granted unconditional free agency (February 17, 1994). ... Re-signed by Cowboys (July 14, 1994). ... Granted unconditional free agency (February 16, 1996). ... Re-signed by Cowboys (April 9, 1996). ... Granted unconditional free agency (February 13, 1998). ... Re-signed by Cowboys (April 7, 1998).
PLAYING EXPERIENCE: Buffalo NFL, 1985, 1986 and 1988; Dallas NFL, 1990-1997. ... Games/Games started: 1985 (4/0), 1986 (8/0), 1988 (16/2), 1990 (16/0), 1991 (16/0), 1992 (16/0), 1993 (16/0), 1994 (16/0), 1995 (16/0), 1996 (16/0), 1997 (16/0). Total: 156/2.
CHAMPIONSHIP GAME EXPERIENCE: Played in AFC championship game (1988 season). ... Played in NFC championship game (1992-1995 seasons). ... Member of Super Bowl championship team (1992, 1993 and 1995 seasons).
PRO STATISTICS: 1986—Fumbled once for minus 14 yards.

HEMPSTEAD, HESSLEY   G   LIONS

PERSONAL: Born January 29, 1972, in Upland, Calif. ... 6-1/295.
HIGH SCHOOL: Upland (Calif.).
COLLEGE: Kansas.
TRANSACTIONS/CAREER NOTES: Selected by Detroit Lions in seventh round (228th pick overall) of 1995 NFL draft. ... Signed by Lions (July 19, 1995).
PLAYING EXPERIENCE: Detroit NFL, 1995-1997. ... Games/Games started: 1995 (2/0), 1996 (13/0), 1997 (16/1). Total: 31/1.

HEMSLEY, NATE   LB   COWBOYS

PERSONAL: Born May 15, 1974 ... 6-0/219. ... Full name: Nathaniel Richard Hemsley.
HIGH SCHOOL: Delran (N.J.).
COLLEGE: Syracuse.
TRANSACTIONS/CAREER NOTES: Signed as non-drafted free agent by Tennessee Oilers (April 23, 1997). ... Released by Oilers (August 13, 1997). ... Signed by Dallas Cowboys to practice squad (September 3, 1997). ... Activated (December 10, 1997).
PLAYING EXPERIENCE: Dallas NFL, 1997. ... Games/Games started: 2/0.

HENDERSON, JEROME   CB   JETS

PERSONAL: Born August 8, 1969, in Statesville, N.C. ... 5-10/200. ... Full name: Jerome Virgil Henderson.
HIGH SCHOOL: West Iredel (Statesville, N.C.).
COLLEGE: Clemson.

H

TRANSACTIONS/CAREER NOTES: Selected by New England Patriots in second round (41st pick overall) of 1991 NFL draft. ... Signed by Patriots (July 15, 1991). ... Released by Patriots (October 11, 1993). ... Signed by Buffalo Bills (October 15, 1993). ... Granted free agency (February 17, 1994). ... Re-signed by Bills (May 27, 1994). ... Granted unconditional free agency (February 17, 1995). ... Signed by Philadelphia Eagles (March 22, 1995). ... Released by Eagles (August 20, 1996). ... Signed by Patriots (November 5, 1996). ... Granted unconditional free agency (February 14, 1997). ... Signed by New York Jets (March 17, 1997).
CHAMPIONSHIP GAME EXPERIENCE: Member of Bills for AFC championship game (1993 season); inactive. ... Played in Super Bowl XXVIII (1993 season) and Super Bowl XXXI (1996 season). ... Played in AFC championship game (1996 season).
PRO STATISTICS: 1991—Recovered one fumble. 1995—Recovered one fumble in end zone for touchdown.

Year Team	G	GS	INTERCEPTIONS				PUNT RETURNS				TOTALS			
			No.	Yds.	Avg.	TD	No.	Yds.	Avg.	TD	TD	2pt.	Pts.	Fum.
1991—New England NFL	16	1	2	2	1.0	0	27	201	7.4	0	0	...	0	2
1992—New England NFL	16	9	3	43	14.3	0	0	0	...	0	0	...	0	0
1993—New England NFL	1	0	0	0	...	0	0	0	...	0	0	...	0	0
—Buffalo NFL	2	0	0	0	...	0	0	0	...	0	0	...	0	0
1994—Buffalo NFL	12	0	0	0	...	0	0	0	...	0	0	0	0	0
1995—Philadelphia NFL	15	0	0	0	...	0	0	0	...	0	1	0	6	0
1996—Philadelphia NFL	7	0	2	7	3.5	0	0	0	...	0	0	0	0	0
1997—New York Jets NFL	16	14	1	45	45.0	0	0	0	...	0	0	0	0	0
Pro totals (7 years)	85	24	8	97	12.1	0	27	201	7.4	0	1	0	6	2

HENDERSON, WILLIAM — FB — PACKERS

PERSONAL: Born February 19, 1971, in Chester, Va. ... 6-1/249. ... Full name: William Terrelle Henderson.
HIGH SCHOOL: Thomas Dale (Chester, Va.).
COLLEGE: North Carolina.
TRANSACTIONS/CAREER NOTES: Selected by Green Bay Packers in third round (66th pick overall) of 1995 NFL draft. ... Signed by Packers (July 17, 1995). ... Granted free agency (February 13, 1998).
CHAMPIONSHIP GAME EXPERIENCE: Played in NFC championship game (1995-97 seasons). ... Member of Super Bowl championship team (1996 season). ... Played in Super Bowl XXXII (1997 season).
PRO STATISTICS: 1996—Returned two kickoffs for 38 yards. 1997—Recovered two fumbles.
SINGLE GAME HIGHS (regular season): Attempts—6 (September 29, 1997, vs. Philadelphia); yards—40 (September 9, 1996, vs. Philadelphia); and rushing touchdowns—0.

Year Team	G	GS	RUSHING				RECEIVING				TOTALS			
			Att.	Yds.	Avg.	TD	No.	Yds.	Avg.	TD	TD	2pt.	Pts.	Fum.
1995—Green Bay NFL	15	2	7	35	5.0	0	3	21	7.0	0	0	0	0	0
1996—Green Bay NFL	16	11	39	130	3.3	0	27	203	7.5	1	1	0	6	1
1997—Green Bay NFL	16	14	31	113	3.6	0	41	367	9.0	1	1	0	6	1
Pro totals (3 years)	47	27	77	278	3.6	0	71	591	8.3	2	2	0	12	2

HENDRIX, DAVID — S

PERSONAL: Born May 29, 1972, in Jesup, Ga. ... 6-1/213. ... Full name: David Tyrone Hendrix.
HIGH SCHOOL: Meadowcreek (Norcross, Ga.).
COLLEGE: Georgia Tech.
TRANSACTIONS/CAREER NOTES: Signed as non-drafted free agent by San Diego Chargers (April 28, 1995). ... Released by Chargers (August 27, 1995). ... Re-signed by Chargers to practice squad (August 29, 1995). ... Activated (October 17, 1995). ... Released by Chargers (September 26, 1997).
PLAYING EXPERIENCE: San Diego NFL, 1995-1997. ... Games/Games started: 1995 (5/0), 1996 (14/0), 1997 (4/0). Total: 23/0.

HENLEY, JUNE — RB — RAMS

PERSONAL: Born September 4, 1975, in Columbus, Ohio. ... 5-10/226. ... Full name: Charles Henley Jr.
HIGH SCHOOL: Brookhaven (Columbus, Ohio).
COLLEGE: Kansas.
TRANSACTIONS/CAREER NOTES: Selected by Kansas City Chiefs in fifth round (163rd pick overall) of 1997 NFL draft. ... Signed by Chiefs (May 5, 1997). ... Released by Chiefs (August 24, 1997). ... Signed by St. Louis Rams to practice squad (August 25, 1997).

HENNINGS, CHAD — DT — COWBOYS

PERSONAL: Born October 20, 1965, in Elberton, Iowa. ... 6-6/291. ... Full name: Chad William Hennings.
HIGH SCHOOL: Benton Community (Van Horne, Iowa).
COLLEGE: Air Force (degree in management).
TRANSACTIONS/CAREER NOTES: Selected by Dallas Cowboys in 11th round (290th pick overall) of 1988 NFL draft. ... Signed by Cowboys (November 22, 1988). ... Served in military (1988-1992). ... Granted unconditional free agency (February 17, 1994). ... Re-signed by Cowboys (1994).
CHAMPIONSHIP GAME EXPERIENCE: Played in NFC championship game (1992, 1994 and 1995 seasons). ... Member of Cowboys for NFC championship game (1993 season); inactive. ... Member of Super Bowl championship team (1992, 1993 and 1995 seasons).
HONORS: Outland Trophy winner (1987). ... Named defensive lineman on THE SPORTING NEWS college All-America first team (1987).
PRO STATISTICS: 1993—Returned one kickoff for seven yards. 1994—Recovered one fumble. 1995—Recovered one fumble. 1996—Recovered one fumble. 1997—Recovered one fumble for four yards and a touchdown.

Year Team	G	GS	SACKS
1992—Dallas NFL	8	0	0.0
1993—Dallas NFL	13	0	0.0
1994—Dallas NFL	16	0	7.0
1995—Dallas NFL	16	7	5.5
1996—Dallas NFL	15	15	4.5
1997—Dallas NFL	11	10	4.5
Pro totals (6 years)	79	32	21.5

H

HENRY, KEVIN   DE   STEELERS

PERSONAL: Born October 23, 1968, in Mound Bayou, Miss. ... 6-4/282. ... Full name: Kevin Lerell Henry. ... Name pronounced KEE-vin.
HIGH SCHOOL: John F. Kennedy (Mound Bayou, Miss.).
COLLEGE: Mississippi State.
TRANSACTIONS/CAREER NOTES: Selected by Pittsburgh Steelers in fourth round (108th pick overall) of 1993 NFL draft. ... Signed by Steelers (July 9, 1993). ... Granted free agency (February 16, 1996). ... Re-signed by Steelers (August 2, 1996). ... Granted unconditional free agency (February 14, 1997). ... Re-signed by Steelers (April 3, 1997).
CHAMPIONSHIP GAME EXPERIENCE: Played in AFC championship game (1994, 1995 and 1997 seasons). ... Played in Super Bowl XXX (1995 season).
PRO STATISTICS: 1993—Intercepted one pass for 10 yards. 1994—Recovered one fumble. 1996—Recovered one fumble for four yards. 1997—Intercepted one pass for 36 yards and recovered two fumbles.

Year Team	G	GS	SACKS
1993—Pittsburgh NFL	12	1	1.0
1994—Pittsburgh NFL	16	5	0.0
1995—Pittsburgh NFL	13	5	2.0
1996—Pittsburgh NFL	12	10	1.5
1997—Pittsburgh NFL	16	16	4.5
Pro totals (5 years)	69	37	9.0

HENTRICH, CRAIG   P   OILERS

PERSONAL: Born May 18, 1971, in Alton, Ill. ... 6-3/200. ... Full name: Craig Anthony Hentrich. ... Name pronounced HEN-trick.
HIGH SCHOOL: Marquette (Alton, Ill.).
COLLEGE: Notre Dame.
TRANSACTIONS/CAREER NOTES: Selected by New York Jets in eighth round (200th pick overall) of 1993 NFL draft. ... Signed by Jets (July 14, 1993). ... Released by Jets (August 24, 1993). ... Signed by Green Bay Packers to practice squad (September 7, 1993). ... Activated (January 14, 1994); did not play. ... Granted unconditional free agency (February 13, 1998). ... Signed by Tennessee Oilers (February 19, 1998).
CHAMPIONSHIP GAME EXPERIENCE: Played in NFC championship game (1995-97 seasons). ... Member of Super Bowl championship team (1996 season). ... Played in Super Bowl XXXII (1997 season).
PRO STATISTICS: 1996—Attempted one pass without a completion and recovered one fumble.

| Year Team | G | GS | PUNTING | | | | | KICKING | | | | | | |
			No.	Yds.	Avg.	Net avg.	In. 20	Blk.	XPM	XPA	FGM	FGA	Lg.	50+	Pts.
1993—Green Bay NFL							Did not play.								
1994—Green Bay NFL	16	0	81	3351	41.4	35.5	24	0	0	0	0	0	...	0-0	0
1995—Green Bay NFL	16	0	65	2740	42.2	34.6	26	2	5	5	3	5	49	0-0	14
1996—Green Bay NFL	16	0	68	2886	42.4	36.2	28	0	0	0	0	0	...	0-0	0
1997—Green Bay NFL	16	0	75	3378	45.0	36.0	26	0	0	0	0	0	...	0-0	0
Pro totals (4 years)	64	0	289	12355	42.8	35.6	104	2	5	5	3	5	49	0-0	14

HERNDON, JIMMY   OT   BEARS

PERSONAL: Born August 30, 1973, in Baytown, Texas. ... 6-8/318.
HIGH SCHOOL: Lee (Baytown, Texas).
COLLEGE: Houston.
TRANSACTIONS/CAREER NOTES: Selected by Jacksonville Jaguars in fifth round (146th pick overall) of 1996 NFL draft. ... Signed by Jaguars (May 24, 1996). ... Active for eight games (1996); did not play. ... Traded by Jaguars to Chicago Bears for seventh-round pick (WR Alvis Whitted) in 1998 draft (August 24, 1997).
PLAYING EXPERIENCE: Chicago NFL, 1997. ... Games/Games started: 7/0.
CHAMPIONSHIP GAME EXPERIENCE: Member of Jaguars for AFC championship game (1996 season); inactive.

HERRING, KIM   S   RAVENS

PERSONAL: Born October 10, 1975, in Cleveland. ... 5-11/210. ... Full name: Kimani Masai Herring.
HIGH SCHOOL: Solon (Ohio).
COLLEGE: Penn State.
TRANSACTIONS/CAREER NOTES: Selected by Baltimore Ravens in second round (58th pick overall) of 1997 NFL draft. ... Signed by Ravens (July 18, 1997).
PLAYING EXPERIENCE: Baltimore NFL, 1997. ... Games/Games started: 15/4.
HONORS: Named free safety on THE SPORTING NEWS college All-America first team (1996).
PRO STATISTICS: 1997—Credited with one sack and recovered one fumble.

HERROD, JEFF   LB   COLTS

PERSONAL: Born September 29, 1966, in Birmingham, Ala. ... 6-0/249. ... Full name: Jeff Sylvester Herrod.
HIGH SCHOOL: Banks (Birmingham, Ala.).
COLLEGE: Mississippi.
TRANSACTIONS/CAREER NOTES: Selected by Indianapolis Colts in ninth round (243rd pick overall) of 1988 NFL draft. ... Signed by Colts (July 13, 1988). ... Granted free agency (February 1, 1990). ... Re-signed by Colts (September 12, 1990). ... Activated (September 14, 1990). ... Released by Colts (July 10, 1995). ... Re-signed by Colts (July 20, 1995). ... Released by Colts (June 18, 1997). ... Signed by Philadelphia Eagles (September 2, 1997). ... Granted unconditional free agency (February 13, 1998). ... Signed by Colts (February 23, 1998).

H

CHAMPIONSHIP GAME EXPERIENCE: Played in AFC championship game (1995 season).
HONORS: Named linebacker on THE SPORTING NEWS college All-America second team (1986).
PRO STATISTICS: 1991—Recovered three fumbles. 1993—Recovered one fumble in end zone for a touchdown.

Year Team	G	GS	INTERCEPTIONS No.	Yds.	Avg.	TD	SACKS No.
1988—Indianapolis NFL	16	0	0	0	...	0	1.0
1989—Indianapolis NFL	15	14	0	0	...	0	2.0
1990—Indianapolis NFL	13	13	1	12	12.0	0	4.0
1991—Indianapolis NFL	14	14	1	25	25.0	0	2.5
1992—Indianapolis NFL	16	16	1	4	4.0	0	2.0
1993—Indianapolis NFL	14	14	1	29	29.0	0	2.0
1994—Indianapolis NFL	15	15	0	0	...	0	1.0
1995—Indianapolis NFL	16	16	0	0	...	0	0.0
1996—Indianapolis NFL	14	14	1	68	68.0	1	0.0
1997—Philadelphia NFL	10	2	0	0	...	0	0.0
Pro totals (10 years)	143	118	5	138	27.6	1	14.5

HESSE, JON — LB — BRONCOS

PERSONAL: Born June 6, 1973, in Lincoln, Neb. ... 6-3/258. ... Full name: Jon Andrew Hesse.
HIGH SCHOOL: Southeast (Lincoln, Neb.).
COLLEGE: Nebraska.
TRANSACTIONS/CAREER NOTES: Selected by Jacksonville Jaguars in seventh round (221st pick overall) of 1997 NFL draft. ... Signed by Jaguars (May 23, 1997). ... Released by Jaguars (August 19, 1997). ... Signed by Green Bay Packers to practice squad (August 26, 1997). ... Signed by Denver Broncos off Packers practice squad (December 19, 1997). ... Inactive for one game (1997).
CHAMPIONSHIP GAME EXPERIENCE: Member of Broncos for AFC championship game (1997 season); inactive. ... Member of Super Bowl championship team (1997 season); inactive.

HETHERINGTON, CHRIS — RB — COLTS

PERSONAL: Born November 27, 1972, in North Branford, Conn. ... 6-3/249. ... Full name: Christopher Raymond Hetherington.
HIGH SCHOOL: Avon (Conn.) Old Farms.
COLLEGE: Yale.
TRANSACTIONS/CAREER NOTES: Signed as non-drafted free agent by Cincinnati Bengals (April 23, 1996). ... Released by Bengals (August 21, 1996). ... Re-signed by Bengals to practice squad (August 26, 1996). ... Signed by Indianapolis Colts off Bengals practice squad (October 22, 1996).
PLAYING EXPERIENCE: Indianapolis NFL, 1996 and 1997. ... Games/Games started: 1996 (6/0), 1997 (16/0). Total: 22/0.
PRO STATISTICS: 1996—Returned one kickoff for 16 yards. 1997—Returned two kickoffs for 23 yards.
SINGLE GAME HIGHS (regular season): Attempts—0; yards—0; and rushing touchdowns—0.

HEWITT, CHRIS — S — SAINTS

PERSONAL: Born July 22, 1974, in Kingston, Jamaica. ... 6-0/210.
HIGH SCHOOL: Dwight Morrow (Englewood, N.J.).
COLLEGE: Cincinnati.
TRANSACTIONS/CAREER NOTES: Signed as non-drafted free agent by New Orleans Saints (April 25, 1997). ... Released by Saints (August 18, 1997). ... Re-signed by Saints to practice squad (August 25, 1997). ... Activated (October 1, 1997).
PLAYING EXPERIENCE: New Orleans NFL, 1997. ... Games/Games started: 11/2.
PRO STATISTICS: 1997—Recovered one fumble.

HEYWARD, CRAIG — FB — RAMS

PERSONAL: Born September 26, 1966, in Passaic, N.J. ... 5-11/265. ... Full name: Craig William Heyward. ... Nickname: Ironhead.
HIGH SCHOOL: Passaic (N.J.).
COLLEGE: Pittsburgh.
TRANSACTIONS/CAREER NOTES: Selected by New Orleans Saints in first round (24th pick overall) of 1988 NFL draft. ... Signed by Saints (July 8, 1988). ... Granted free agency (February 1, 1991). ... Re-signed by Saints (July 12, 1991). ... On injured reserve with foot injury (November 6-December 11, 1991). ... On suspended list (December 11, 1991-remainder of season). ... Granted unconditional free agency (March 1, 1993). ... Signed by Chicago Bears (April 11, 1993). ... Released by Bears (April 26, 1994). ... Signed by Atlanta Falcons (June 21, 1994). ... Granted unconditional free agency (February 14, 1997). ... Signed by St. Louis Rams (March 6, 1997).
HONORS: Named running back on THE SPORTING NEWS college All-America first team (1987).
PRO STATISTICS: 1988—Recovered one fumble. 1989—Recovered one fumble. 1990—Attempted one pass without a completion. 1991—Attempted one pass with one completion for 44 yards. 1992—Returned one kickoff for 14 yards and recovered one fumble. 1993—Returned one kickoff for seven yards and recovered two fumbles. 1995—Recovered three fumbles. 1996—Returned one punt for no yards and returned one kickoff for 18 yards.
SINGLE GAME HIGHS (regular season): Attempts—25 (September 17, 1995, vs. New Orleans); yards—155 (November 11, 1990, vs. Tampa Bay); and rushing touchdowns—2 (November 12, 1995, vs. Buffalo).
STATISTICAL PLATEAUS: 100-yard rushing games: 1988 (1), 1990 (2), 1995 (3). Total: 6.

H

Year Team	G	GS	RUSHING Att.	Yds.	Avg.	TD	RECEIVING No.	Yds.	Avg.	TD	TOTALS TD	2pt.	Pts.	Fum.
1988—New Orleans NFL	11	8	74	355	4.8	1	13	105	8.1	0	1	...	6	0
1989—New Orleans NFL	16	6	49	183	3.7	1	13	69	5.3	0	1	...	6	2
1990—New Orleans NFL	16	15	129	599	4.6	4	18	121	6.7	0	4	...	24	3

Year—Team	G	GS	RUSHING				RECEIVING				TOTALS			
			Att.	Yds.	Avg.	TD	No.	Yds.	Avg.	TD	TD	2pt.	Pts.	Fum.
1991—New Orleans NFL	7	4	76	260	3.4	4	4	34	8.5	1	5	...	30	0
1992—New Orleans NFL	16	13	104	416	4.0	3	19	159	8.4	0	3	...	18	1
1993—Chicago NFL	16	14	68	206	3.0	0	16	132	8.3	0	0	...	0	1
1994—Atlanta NFL	16	11	183	779	4.3	7	32	335	10.5	1	8	0	48	5
1995—Atlanta NFL	16	16	236	1083	4.6	6	37	350	9.5	2	8	0	48	3
1996—Atlanta NFL	15	5	72	321	4.5	3	16	168	10.5	0	3	0	18	0
1997—St. Louis NFL	16	12	34	84	2.5	1	8	77	9.6	0	1	0	6	1
Pro totals (10 years)	145	104	1025	4286	4.2	30	176	1550	8.8	4	34	0	204	16

HICKMAN, KEVIN   TE   EAGLES

PERSONAL: Born August 20, 1971, in Cherry Hill, N.J. ... 6-4/258. ... Full name: Kevin J. Hickman.
HIGH SCHOOL: Holy Cross (Delran, N.J.), then Marine Military Academy (Harlingen, Texas).
COLLEGE: Navy.
TRANSACTIONS/CAREER NOTES: Selected by Detroit Lions in sixth round (186th pick overall) of 1995 NFL draft. ... Signed by Lions (July 19, 1995). ... On injured reserve with knee injury (December 21, 1995-remainder of season). ... On injured reserve with knee injury (August 20, 1996-entire season). ... Released by Lions (August 19, 1997). ... Re-signed by Lions (September 19, 1997). ... Released by Lions (October 30, 1997). ... Signed by Philadelphia Eagles (April 29, 1998).
PLAYING EXPERIENCE: Detroit NFL, 1995 and 1997. ... Games/Games started: 1995 (7/0), 1997 (4/0). Total: 11/0.
SINGLE GAME HIGHS (regular season): Receptions—0; yards—0; and touchdown receptions—0.

HICKS, KERRY   DL

PERSONAL: Born December 29, 1972, in McKay, Utah. ... 6-6/283.
HIGH SCHOOL: Highland (Salt Lake City).
COLLEGE: Colorado.
TRANSACTIONS/CAREER NOTES: Selected by Carolina Panthers in seventh round (234th pick overall) of 1996 NFL draft. ... Signed by Panthers (July 17, 1996). ... Released by Panthers (August 21, 1996). ... Signed by Kansas City Chiefs to practice squad (August 27, 1996). ... Activated (October 14, 1996). ... Inactive for four games (1996). ... On reserve/non-football injury list with illness (November 16, 1996-remainder of season). ... Released by Chiefs (September 23, 1997).
PLAYING EXPERIENCE: Kansas City NFL, 1997. ... Games/Games started: 2/0.

HICKS, MICHAEL   RB

PERSONAL: Born February 1, 1973, in Barnesville, Ga. ... 6-0/194.
HIGH SCHOOL: Robert E. Lee Institute (Thomaston, Ga.).
COLLEGE: South Carolina State.
TRANSACTIONS/CAREER NOTES: Selected by Chicago Bears in seventh round (253rd pick overall) of 1996 NFL draft. ... Signed by Bears (June 13, 1996). ... Released by Bears (August 23, 1996). ... Re-signed by Bears to practice squad (August 27, 1996). ... Activated (September 20, 1996). ... Released by Bears (October 31, 1996). ... Re-signed by Bears to practice squad (November 1, 1996). ... Assigned by Bears to Barcelona Dragons in 1997 World League enhancement allocation program (February 19, 1997). ... Released by Bears (August 24, 1997). ... Re-signed by Bears to practice squad (September 23, 1997). ... Activated (November 15, 1997). ... Released by Bears (November 18, 1997). ... Re-signed by Bears to practice squad (November 19, 1997). ... Activated (December 9, 1997). ... Granted free agency after 1997 season.
SINGLE GAME HIGHS (regular season): Attempts—9 (September 22, 1996, vs. Detroit); yards—31 (September 29, 1996, vs. Oakland); and rushing touchdowns—0.

Year—Team	G	GS	RUSHING				RECEIVING				TOTALS			
			Att.	Yds.	Avg.	TD	No.	Yds.	Avg.	TD	TD	2pt.	Pts.	Fum.
1996—Chicago NFL	4	0	27	92	3.4	0	1	-1	-1.0	0	0	0	0	1
1997—Barcelona W.L.	...	...	85	290	3.4	1	8	58	7.3	0	1	...	6	...
—Chicago NFL	2	0	4	14	3.5	0	0	0	...	0	0	0	0	0
W.L. totals (1 year)	...	...	85	290	3.4	1	8	58	7.3	0	1	...	6	...
NFL totals (2 years)	6	0	31	106	3.4	0	1	-1	-1.0	0	0	0	0	1
Pro totals (3 years)	...	...	116	396	3.4	1	9	57	6.3	0	1	...	6	...

HILES, VAN   DB   BEARS

PERSONAL: Born November 1, 1975, in Baton Rouge, La. ... 6-0/198. ... Full name: Lavanda Van Hiles.
HIGH SCHOOL: Episcopal (Baton Rouge, La.).
COLLEGE: Kentucky.
TRANSACTIONS/CAREER NOTES: Selected by Chicago Bears in fifth round (141st pick overall) of 1997 NFL draft. ... Signed by Bears (July 10, 1997).
PLAYING EXPERIENCE: Chicago NFL, 1997. ... Games/Games started: 16/1.

HILL, ERIC   LB   RAMS

PERSONAL. Born November 14, 1966, in Galveston, Texas. ... 6-2/258.
HIGH SCHOOL: Ball (Galveston, Texas).
COLLEGE: Louisiana State.

TRANSACTIONS/CAREER NOTES: Selected by Phoenix Cardinals in first round (10th pick overall) of 1989 NFL draft. ... Signed by Cardinals (August 18, 1989). ... Granted free agency (March 1, 1993). ... Re-signed by Cardinals (September 4, 1993). ... Activated (September 26, 1993). ... Designated by Cardinals as transition player (February 15, 1994). ... Cardinals franchise renamed Arizona Cardinals for 1994 season. ... Granted unconditional free agency (February 13, 1998). ... Signed by St. Louis Rams (February 25, 1998).

PRO STATISTICS: 1989—Recovered one fumble. 1991—Recovered one fumble for 85 yards and a touchdown. 1992—Fumbled once and recovered one fumble for minus two yards. 1993—Recovered one fumble.

Year Team	G	GS	SACKS
1989—Phoenix NFL	15	14	1.0
1990—Phoenix NFL	16	16	1.5
1991—Phoenix NFL	16	15	1.0
1992—Phoenix NFL	16	16	0.0
1993—Phoenix NFL	13	12	1.0
1994—Arizona NFL	16	15	1.5
1995—Arizona NFL	14	14	2.0
1996—Arizona NFL	16	16	0.0
1997—Arizona NFL	11	10	0.0
Pro totals (9 years)	133	128	8.0

HILL, GREG   RB

PERSONAL: Born February 23, 1972, in Dallas. ... 5-11/214. ... Full name: Gregory Lamonte' Hill.
HIGH SCHOOL: David W. Carter (Dallas).
COLLEGE: Texas A&M.
TRANSACTIONS/CAREER NOTES: Selected after junior season by Kansas City Chiefs in first round (25th pick overall) of 1994 NFL draft. ... Signed by Chiefs (August 2, 1994). ... Granted unconditional free agency (February 13, 1998).
HONORS: Named running back on THE SPORTING NEWS college All-America second team (1992).
SINGLE GAME HIGHS (regular season): Attempts—21 (December 24, 1995, vs. Seattle); yards—113 (December 24, 1995, vs. Seattle); and rushing touchdowns—2 (November 10, 1996, vs. Green Bay).
STATISTICAL PLATEAUS: 100-yard rushing games: 1995 (2), 1996 (2). Total: 4.

			RUSHING				RECEIVING				TOTALS			
Year Team	G	GS	Att.	Yds.	Avg.	TD	No.	Yds.	Avg.	TD	TD	2pt.	Pts.	Fum.
1994—Kansas City NFL	16	1	141	574	4.1	1	16	92	5.8	0	1	0	6	1
1995—Kansas City NFL	16	1	155	667	4.3	1	7	45	6.4	0	1	0	6	2
1996—Kansas City NFL	15	1	135	645	4.8	4	3	60	20.0	1	5	0	30	1
1997—Kansas City NFL	16	16	157	550	3.5	0	12	126	10.5	0	0	0	0	1
Pro totals (4 years)	63	19	588	2436	4.1	6	38	323	8.5	1	7	0	42	5

HILL, RANDAL   WR

PERSONAL: Born September 21, 1969, in Miami. ... 5-10/180. ... Full name: Randal Thrill Hill.
HIGH SCHOOL: Miami Killian.
COLLEGE: Miami, Fla (degree in sociology).
TRANSACTIONS/CAREER NOTES: Selected by Miami Dolphins in first round (23rd pick overall) of 1991 NFL draft. ... Signed by Dolphins (August 6, 1991). ... Traded by Dolphins to Phoenix Cardinals for first-round pick (CB Troy Vincent) in 1992 draft (September 3, 1991). ... Granted free agency (February 17, 1994). ... Cardinals franchise renamed Arizona Cardinals for 1994 season. ... Re-signed by Cardinals (June 16, 1994). ... Granted unconditional free agency (February 17, 1995). ... Signed by Dolphins (March 7, 1995). ... Granted unconditional free agency (February 16, 1996). ... Re-signed by Dolphins (February 22, 1996). ... Granted free agency (February 14, 1997). ... Signed by New Orleans Saints (May 28, 1997). ... Granted unconditional free agency (February 13, 1998).
PRO STATISTICS: 1992—Rushed once for four yards. 1997—Rushed once for 11 yards and recovered one fumble.
SINGLE GAME HIGHS (regular season): Receptions—8 (September 26, 1993, vs. Detroit); yards—124 (December 14, 1997, vs. Arizona); and touchdown receptions—2 (January 2, 1994, vs. Atlanta).
STATISTICAL PLATEAUS: 100-yard receiving games: 1992 (1), 1997 (2). Total: 3.

			RECEIVING				KICKOFF RETURNS				TOTALS			
Year Team	G	GS	No.	Yds.	Avg.	TD	No.	Yds.	Avg.	TD	TD	2pt.	Pts.	Fum.
1991—Miami NFL	1	0	0	0	...	0	1	33	33.0	0	0	...	0	0
—Phoenix NFL	15	4	43	495	11.5	1	8	113	14.1	0	1	...	6	0
1992—Phoenix NFL	16	14	58	861	14.8	3	0	0	...	0	3	...	18	2
1993—Phoenix NFL	16	8	35	519	14.8	4	0	0	...	0	4	...	24	0
1994—Arizona NFL	14	14	38	544	14.3	0	0	0	...	0	0	0	0	0
1995—Miami NFL	12	0	12	260	21.7	0	12	287	23.9	0	0	0	0	0
1996—Miami NFL	14	5	21	409	19.5	4	2	4	2.0	0	4	0	24	1
1997—New Orleans NFL	15	15	55	761	13.8	2	0	0	...	0	2	0	12	0
Pro totals (7 years)	103	60	262	3849	14.7	14	23	437	19.0	0	14	0	84	3

HILL, SEAN   S   LIONS

PERSONAL: Born August 14, 1971, in Dowagiac, Mich. ... 5-10/195. ... Full name: Sean Terrell Hill.
HIGH SCHOOL: Widefield (Security, Mich.).
COLLEGE: Montana State.
TRANSACTIONS/CAREER NOTES: Selected by Miami Dolphins in seventh round (214th pick overall) of 1994 NFL draft. ... Signed by Dolphins (July 18, 1994). ... Released by Dolphins (August 24, 1997). ... Signed by Detroit Lions (November 19, 1997). ... Released by Lions (November 26, 1997). ... Re-signed by Lions (December 2, 1997). ... Released by Lions (December 20, 1997). ... Re-signed by Lions (February 11, 1998).
PLAYING EXPERIENCE: Miami NFL, 1994-1996. ... Games/Games started: 1994 (16/1), 1995 (16/0), 1996 (12/5). Total: 44/6.
PRO STATISTICS: 1995—Returned one kickoff for 38 yards. 1996—Intercepted one pass for no yards, credited with one sack and recovered one fumble for 10 yards and a touchdown.

H

HILLIARD, IKE   WR   GIANTS

PERSONAL: Born April 5, 1976, in Patterson, La. ... 5-11/190. ... Full name: Isaac Jason Hilliard. ... Nephew of Dalton Hilliard, running back with New Orleans Saints (1986-93).
HIGH SCHOOL: Patterson (La.).
COLLEGE: Florida.
TRANSACTIONS/CAREER NOTES: Selected by New York Giants in first round (seventh pick overall) of 1997 NFL draft. ... Signed by Giants (July 19, 1997). ... On injured reserve with neck injury (September 30, 1997-remainder of season).
SINGLE GAME HIGHS (regular season): Receptions—1 (September 7, 1997, vs. Jacksonville); yards—23 (September 7, 1997, vs. Jacksonville); and touchdown receptions—0.

| | | | RECEIVING | | | | TOTALS | | | |
Year Team	G	GS	No.	Yds.	Avg.	TD	TD	2pt.	Pts.	Fum.
1997—New York Giants NFL	2	2	2	42	21.0	0	0	0	0	0

HILLIARD, RANDY   CB   BRONCOS

PERSONAL: Born February 6, 1967, in Metairie, La. ... 5-11/168.
HIGH SCHOOL: East Jefferson (Metairie, La.).
COLLEGE: Northwestern (La.) State.
TRANSACTIONS/CAREER NOTES: Selected by Cleveland Browns in sixth round (157th pick overall) of 1990 NFL draft. ... Signed by Browns (July 22, 1990). ... Granted free agency (February 1, 1992). ... Re-signed by Browns (July 28, 1992). ... Granted free agency (March 1, 1993). ... Re-signed by Browns (July 19, 1993). ... Granted unconditional free agency (February 17, 1994). ... Signed by Denver Broncos (May 16, 1994). ... Granted unconditional free agency (February 16, 1996). ... Re-signed by Broncos (February 26, 1996).
CHAMPIONSHIP GAME EXPERIENCE: Played in AFC championship game (1997 season). ... Member of Super Bowl championship team (1997 season).
PRO STATISTICS: 1991—Recovered one fumble. 1992—Recovered one fumble. 1996—Recovered one fumble.

| | | | INTERCEPTIONS | | | | SACKS |
Year Team	G	GS	No.	Yds.	Avg.	TD	No.
1990—Cleveland NFL	15	0	0	0	...	0	0.0
1991—Cleveland NFL	14	10	1	19	19.0	0	2.0
1992—Cleveland NFL	16	4	0	0	...	0	1.0
1993—Cleveland NFL	12	5	1	54	54.0	0	0.0
1994—Denver NFL	15	6	2	8	4.0	0	0.0
1995—Denver NFL	12	0	0	0	...	0	0.0
1996—Denver NFL	13	3	1	27	27.0	0	0.0
1997—Denver NFL	14	0	0	0	...	0	0.0
Pro totals (8 years)	111	28	5	108	21.6	0	3.0

HILLS, KENO   OT   SAINTS

PERSONAL: Born June 13, 1973, in Tampa. ... 6-6/305. ... Full name: Keno J. Hills. ... Name pronounced KEY-no.
HIGH SCHOOL: Tampa Tech.
COLLEGE: Kent State, then Southwestern Louisiana.
TRANSACTIONS/CAREER NOTES: Selected by New Orleans Saints in sixth round (179th pick overall) of 1996 NFL draft. ... Signed by Saints (July 13, 1996). ... On physically unable to perform list with hamstring injury (July 18, 1997-October 16, 1997).
PLAYING EXPERIENCE: New Orleans NFL, 1996 and 1997. ... Games/Games started: 1996 (1/0), 1997 (9/6). Total: 10/6.

HINTON, MARCUS   TE   SAINTS

PERSONAL: Born December 27, 1971, in Wiggins, Miss. ... 6-4/265.
HIGH SCHOOL: Stone (Wiggins, Miss.).
COLLEGE: Alcorn State.
TRANSACTIONS/CAREER NOTES: Signed as non-drafted free agent by Oakland Raiders (May 1995). ... Released by Raiders (August 26, 1995). ... Re-signed by Raiders to practice squad (August 28, 1995). ... Activated (December 9, 1995); did not play. ... Released by Raiders (August 24, 1997). ... Signed by New Orleans Saints (December 23, 1997).
PLAYING EXPERIENCE: Oakland NFL, 1996. ... Games/Games started: 2/0.

HITCHCOCK, JIMMY   CB   VIKINGS

PERSONAL: Born November 9, 1971, in Concord, N.C. ... 5-10/188. ... Full name: Jimmy Davis Hitchcock Jr.
HIGH SCHOOL: Concord (N.C.).
COLLEGE: North Carolina.
TRANSACTIONS/CAREER NOTES: Selected by New England Patriots in third round (88th pick overall) of 1995 NFL draft. ... Signed by Patriots (July 19, 1995). ... Granted free agency (February 13, 1998). ... Signed by Minnesota Vikings (April 18, 1998); Patriots received third-round pick in 1999 draft as compensation.
CHAMPIONSHIP GAME EXPERIENCE: Member of Patriots for AFC championship game (1996 season); inactive. ... Member of Patriots for Super Bowl XXXI (1996 season); inactive.

| | | | INTERCEPTIONS | | | |
Year Team	G	GS	No.	Yds.	Avg.	TD
1995—New England NFL	8	0	0	0	...	0
1996—New England NFL	13	5	2	14	7.0	0
1997—New England NFL	15	15	2	104	52.0	1
Pro totals (3 years)	36	20	4	118	29.5	1

H

PERSONAL: Born May 15, 1968, in New Orleans. ... 5-11/223.
HIGH SCHOOL: St. Augustine (New Orleans).
COLLEGE: Michigan.
TRANSACTIONS/CAREER NOTES: Selected after junior season by Cleveland Browns in second round (45th pick overall) of 1990 NFL draft. ... Signed by Browns (July 29, 1990). ... Granted free agency (March 1, 1993). ... Re-signed by Browns (1993). ... On physically unable to perform list with rib injury (July 22-24, 1995). ... On injured reserve with rib injury (December 16, 1995-remainder of season). ... Browns franchise moved to Baltimore and renamed Ravens for 1996 season (March 11, 1996). ... Released by Ravens (September 24, 1996). ... Signed by Carolina Panthers (October 1, 1996). ... Released by Panthers (October 22, 1996). ... Signed by Minnesota Vikings (November 5, 1996). ... Granted unconditional free agency (February 14, 1997). ... Re-signed by Vikings (April 3, 1997).
HONORS: Played in Pro Bowl (1994 season).
PRO STATISTICS: 1991—Recovered one fumble for four yards. 1992—Recovered one fumble. 1993—Attempted one pass without a completion.
SINGLE GAME HIGHS (regular season): Attempts—25 (December 10, 1994, vs. Dallas); yards—123 (November 6, 1994, vs. New England); and rushing touchdowns—2 (December 15, 1996, vs. Tampa Bay).
STATISTICAL PLATEAUS: 100-yard rushing games: 1994 (2), 1996 (2). Total: 4. ... 100-yard receiving games: 1991 (1).

Year—Team	G	GS	RUSHING Att.	Yds.	Avg.	TD	RECEIVING No.	Yds.	Avg.	TD	KICKOFF RETURNS No.	Yds.	Avg.	TD	TOTALS TD	2pt.	Pts.	Fum.
1990—Cleveland NFL	14	5	58	149	2.6	3	10	73	7.3	0	2	18	9.0	0	3	...	18	6
1991—Cleveland NFL	16	9	37	154	4.2	2	48	567	11.8	9	0	0	...	0	11	...	66	1
1992—Cleveland NFL	16	9	54	236	4.4	0	26	310	11.9	1	2	34	17.0	0	1	...	6	3
1993—Cleveland NFL	16	7	56	227	4.1	0	35	351	10.0	0	13	286	22.0	0	0	...	0	4
1994—Cleveland NFL	16	12	209	890	4.3	5	45	445	9.9	4	2	30	15.0	0	9	0	54	8
1995—Cleveland NFL	12	12	136	547	4.0	0	13	103	7.9	0	1	13	13.0	0	0	0	0	5
1996—Baltimore NFL	2	1	15	61	4.1	0	1	4	4.0	0	0	0	...	0	0	0	0	0
—Carolina NFL	3	0	5	11	2.2	0	0	0	...	0	1	19	19.0	0	0	0	0	0
—Minnesota NFL	6	6	105	420	4.0	3	10	129	12.9	0	0	0	...	0	3	0	18	3
1997—Minnesota NFL	12	1	80	235	2.9	4	11	84	7.6	0	0	0	...	0	4	0	24	0
Pro totals (8 years)	113	62	755	2930	3.9	17	199	2066	10.4	14	21	400	19.0	0	31	0	186	30

PERSONAL: Born May 23, 1968, in Victoria, Texas ... 6-2/175. ... Full name: Daryl Ray Hobbs.
HIGH SCHOOL: University (Los Angeles).
JUNIOR COLLEGE: Santa Monica (Calif.) College.
COLLEGE: Pacific.
TRANSACTIONS/CAREER NOTES: Signed as non-drafted free agent by Los Angeles Raiders (1992). ... Released by Raiders (August 31, 1992). ... Re-signed by Raiders to practice squad (September 2, 1992). ... Granted free agency after 1992 season. ... Re-signed by Raiders for 1993 season. ... Raiders franchise moved to Oakland (July 21, 1995). ... Traded by Raiders with first-round (G Chris Naeole), second-round (DE Jared Tomich) and fourth-round (traded to Houston) picks in 1997 draft to New Orleans Saints for first-round (DT Darrell Russell) and sixth-round (traded to Miami) picks in 1997 draft (March 31, 1997). ... Traded by Saints to Seattle Seahawks for seventh-round pick (WR Andy McCullough) in 1998 draft (September 30, 1997).
PRO STATISTICS: 1995—Attempted one pass without a completion. 1996—Attempted one pass with one completion for seven yards and recovered two fumbles. W.L.: 1997—Rushed 21 times for 66 yards and one touchdown.
SINGLE GAME HIGHS (regular season): Receptions—7 (September 24, 1995, vs. Philadelphia); yards—135 (September 24, 1995, vs. Philadelphia); and touchdown receptions—1 (September 21, 1997, vs. Detroit).
STATISTICAL PLATEAUS: 100-yard receiving games: 1995 (1).

Year—Team	G	GS	RECEIVING No.	Yds.	Avg.	TD	PUNT RETURNS No.	Yds.	Avg.	TD	KICKOFF RETURNS No.	Yds.	Avg.	TD	TOTALS TD	2pt.	Pts.	Fum.
1992—LA Raiders NFL									Did not play.									
1993—LA Raiders NFL	3	0	0	0	...	0	0	0	...	0	0	0	...	0	0	...	0	0
1994—LA Raiders NFL	10	0	5	52	10.4	0	0	0	...	0	0	0	...	0	0	0	0	0
1995—Oakland NFL	16	1	38	612	16.1	3	1	10	10.0	0	1	20	20.0	0	3	0	18	0
1996—Oakland NFL	16	1	44	423	9.6	3	10	84	8.4	0	1	14	14.0	0	3	0	18	4
1997—London W.L.	...	...	2	6	3.0	0	0	0	...	0	0	0	...	0	1	...	6	...
—New Orleans NFL	4	0	2	41	20.5	1	0	0	...	0	0	0	...	0	1	0	6	0
—Seattle NFL	10	0	5	44	8.8	0	0	0	...	0	0	0	...	0	1	0	6	1
W.L. totals (1 year)	...	...	2	6	3.0	0	0	0		0	0	0		0	1	0	6	0
NFL totals (5 years)	59	2	94	1172	12.5	7	11	94	8.5	0	2	34	17.0	0	8	0	42	5
Pro totals (6 years)			96	1178	12.3	7	11	94	8.5	0	2	34	17.0	0	9	0	48	5

PERSONAL: Born January 8, 1971, in Puyallup, Wash. ... 6-3/230.
HIGH SCHOOL: Puyallup (Wash.).
COLLEGE: Washington.
TRANSACTIONS/CAREER NOTES: Selected after junior season by Los Angeles Raiders in third round (58th pick overall) of 1993 NFL draft. ... Raiders franchise moved to Oakland (July 21, 1995). ... Traded by Raiders to Buffalo Bills for undisclosed draft pick (February 17, 1997). ... Released by Bills (October 15, 1997). ... Signed by New Orleans Saints (November 19, 1997).
PRO STATISTICS: 1996—Punted nine times for 371 yards (41.2 avg./35.1 net avg.) and fumbled six times. 1997—Fumbled three times and recovered one fumble for minus five yards.
SINGLE GAME HIGHS (regular season): Attempts—42 (December 7, 1997, vs. St. Louis); completions—20 (December 10, 1995, vs. Pittsburgh); yards—259 (December 7, 1997, vs. St. Louis); and touchdown passes—3 (December 14, 1997, vs. Arizona).
MISCELLANEOUS: Regular-season record as starting quarterback: 2-7 (.222).

H

Year Team	G	GS	Att.	Cmp.	Pct.	PASSING Yds.	TD	Int.	Avg.	Rat.	RUSHING Att.	Yds.	Avg.	TD	TOTALS TD	2pt.	Pts.
1995—Oakland NFL..............	4	2	80	44	55.0	540	6	4	6.75	80.2	3	5	1.7	0	0	0	0
1996—Oakland NFL..............	8	3	104	57	54.8	667	4	5	6.41	67.3	2	13	6.5	0	0	0	0
1997—Buffalo NFL..............	2	0	30	17	56.7	133	0	2	4.43	40.0	2	7	3.5	0	0	0	0
—New Orleans NFL	5	4	131	61	46.6	891	6	8	6.80	59.0	12	36	3.0	0	0	0	0
Pro totals (3 years)	19	9	345	179	51.9	2231	16	19	6.47	64.8	19	61	3.2	0	0	0	0

RECORD AS BASEBALL PLAYER

TRANSACTIONS/CAREER NOTES: Threw right, batted left. ... Selected by Chicago White Sox organization in 16th round of free-agent base-ball draft (June 3, 1993).

Year Team (League)	Pos.	G	AB	R	H	BATTING 2B	3B	HR	RBI	Avg.	BB	SO	SB	FIELDING PO	A	E	Avg.
1988—GC White Sox (GCL) ..	OF	15	39	3	10	2	0	0	4	.256	6	5	1	13	1	0	1.000

HOGANS, RICHARD   LB   BEARS

PERSONAL: Born July 8, 1975, in Columbus, Ga. ... 6-2/249.
HIGH SCHOOL: Spencer (Columbus, Ga.).
COLLEGE: Memphis.
TRANSACTIONS/CAREER NOTES: Selected by Chicago Bears in sixth round (200th pick overall) of 1997 NFL draft. ... Signed by Bears (July 10, 1997). ... On injured reserve with knee injury (July 17, 1997-entire season).

HOLCOMB, KELLY   QB   COLTS

PERSONAL: Born July 9, 1973, in Fayetteville, Tenn. ... 6-2/212. ... Full name: Bryan Kelly Holcomb.
HIGH SCHOOL: Lincoln County (Fayetteville, Tenn.).
COLLEGE: Middle Tennessee State.
TRANSACTIONS/CAREER NOTES: Played for Barcelona Dragons of World League (1995). ... Signed as non-drafted free agent by Tampa Bay Buccaneers (May 1, 1995). ... Released by Buccaneers (August 22, 1995). ... Re-signed by Buccaneers to practice squad (August 29, 1995). ... Released by Buccaneers (September 19, 1995). ... Re-signed by Buccaneers to practice squad (October 4, 1995). ... Released by Buccaneers (October 17, 1995). ... Re-signed by Buccaneers to practice squad (December 19, 1995). ... Released by Buccaneers (August 19, 1996). ... Signed by Indianapolis Colts to practice squad (November 27, 1996). ... Activated (December 12, 1996).
PRO STATISTICS: 1997—Fumbled four times and recovered one fumble for minus eight yards.
SINGLE GAME HIGHS (regular season): Attempts—32 (November 9, 1997, vs. Cincinnati); completions—19 (November 9, 1997, vs. Cincinnati); yards—236 (November 9, 1997, vs. Cincinnati); touchdown passes—1 (November 9, 1997, vs. Cincinnati).
MISCELLANEOUS: Regular-season record as starting NFL quarterback: 0-1.

Year Team	G	GS	Att.	Cmp.	Pct.	PASSING Yds.	TD	Int.	Avg.	Rat.	RUSHING Att.	Yds.	Avg.	TD	TOTALS TD	2pt.	Pts.
1995—Barcelona W.L.............	...	...	319	191	59.9	2382	14	16	7.47	76.8	38	111	2.9	2	2	0	12
1996—Indianapolis NFL						Did not play.											
1997—Indianapolis NFL	5	1	73	45	61.6	454	1	8	6.22	44.3	5	5	1.0	0	0	0	0
W.L. totals (2 years)..............	...	...	319	191	59.9	2382	14	16	7.47	76.8	38	111	2.9	2	2	0	12
NFL totals (2 years)	5	1	73	45	61.6	454	1	8	6.22	44.3	5	5	1.0	0	0	0	0
Pro totals (4 years)	...	...	392	236	60.2	2836	15	24	7.23	72.9	43	116	2.7	2	2	0	12

HOLECEK, JOHN   LB   BILLS

PERSONAL: Born May 7, 1972, in Steger, Ill. ... 6-2/242. ... Name pronounced hol-e-SECK.
HIGH SCHOOL: Marian Catholic (Chicago Heights, Ill.).
COLLEGE: Illinois.
TRANSACTIONS/CAREER NOTES: Selected by Buffalo Bills in fifth round (144th pick overall) of 1995 NFL draft. ... Signed by Bills (June 12, 1995). ... On physically unable to perform list (August 22-November 21, 1995). ... On injured reserve with knee injury (August 16, 1996-entire season). ... Granted free agency (February 13, 1998). ... Re-signed by Bills (April 27, 1998).
PLAYING EXPERIENCE: Buffalo NFL, 1995 and 1997. ... Games: 1995 (1/0), 1997 (14/8). Total: 15/8.
PRO STATISTICS: 1997—Credited with 1 1/2 sacks.

HOLLAND, DARIUS   DT   CHIEFS

PERSONAL: Born November 10, 1973, in Petersburg, Va. ... 6-5/320. ... Full name: Darius Jerome Holland.
HIGH SCHOOL: Mayfield (Las Cruces, N.M.).
COLLEGE: Colorado.
TRANSACTIONS/CAREER NOTES: Selected by Green Bay Packers in third round (65th pick overall) of 1995 NFL draft. ... Signed by Packers (July 18, 1995). ... Granted free agency (February 13, 1998). ... Re-signed by Packers (April 16, 1998). ... Traded by Packers to Kansas City Chiefs for DE Vaughn Booker (May 13, 1998).
PLAYING EXPERIENCE: Green Bay NFL, 1995-1997. ... Games/Games started: 1995 (14/4), 1996 (16/0), 1997 (12/1). Total: 42/5.
CHAMPIONSHIP GAME EXPERIENCE: Played in NFC championship game (1995 and 1996 seasons). ... Member of Super Bowl championship team (1996 season). ... Played in Super Bowl XXXII (1997 season).
PRO STATISTICS: 1995—Credited with 1 1/2 sacks.

HOLLIDAY, COREY   WR   STEELERS

H

PERSONAL: Born January 31, 1971, in Richmond, Va. ... 6-2/208. ... Full name: Corey Lamont Holliday.
HIGH SCHOOL: Huguenot (Richmond, Va.).
COLLEGE: North Carolina (degree in business administration).

TRANSACTIONS/CAREER NOTES: Signed as non-drafted free agent by Pittsburgh Steelers (April 29, 1994). ... Released by Steelers (August 22, 1994). ... Re-signed by Steelers to practice squad (November 16, 1994). ... Released by Steelers (September 12, 1995). ... Re-signed by Steelers to practice squad (September 14, 1995). ... Released by Steelers (September 22, 1995). ... Re-signed by Steelers (September 23, 1995). ... Released by Steelers (October 3, 1995). ... Re-signed by Steelers to practice squad (October 5, 1995).
PLAYING EXPERIENCE: Pittsburgh NFL, 1995-1997. ... Games/Games started: 1995 (3/0), 1996 (11/0), 1997 (2/0). Total: 16/0.
CHAMPIONSHIP GAME EXPERIENCE: Played in AFC championship game (1995 season). ... Played in Super Bowl XXX (1995 season). ... Member of Steelers for AFC championship game (1997 season); inactive.
PRO STATISTICS: 1996—Caught one pass for seven yards.
SINGLE GAME HIGHS (regular season): Receptions—1 (December 1, 1996, vs. Baltimore); yards—7 (December 1, 1996, vs. Baltimore); and touchdown receptions—0.

HOLLIER, DWIGHT — LB — DOLPHINS

PERSONAL: Born April 21, 1969, in Hampton, Va. ... 6-2/242. ... Full name: Dwight Leon Hollier.
HIGH SCHOOL: Kecoughtan (Hampton, Va.).
COLLEGE: North Carolina (degree in speech communications and psychology).
TRANSACTIONS/CAREER NOTES: Selected by Miami Dolphins in fourth round (97th pick overall) of 1992 NFL draft. ... Signed by Dolphins (July 10, 1992). ... Granted free agency (February 17, 1995). ... Re-signed by Dolphins (May 9, 1995). ... Granted unconditional free agency (February 14, 1997). ... Re-signed by Dolphins (April 17, 1997).
PLAYING EXPERIENCE: Miami NFL, 1992-1997. ... Games/Games started: 1992 (16/5), 1993 (16/10), 1994 (11/7), 1995 (16/14), 1996 (16/15), 1997 (16/3). Total: 91/54.
CHAMPIONSHIP GAME EXPERIENCE: Played in AFC championship game (1992 season).
PRO STATISTICS: 1992—Credited with one sack and recovered three fumbles. 1993—Recovered one fumble. 1994—Intercepted one pass for 36 yards. 1995—Recovered one fumble. 1996—Intercepted one pass for 11 yards and credited with one sack. 1997—Returned one kickoff for no yards.

HOLLINQUEST, LAMONT — LB — PACKERS

PERSONAL: Born October 24, 1970, in Lynwood, Calif. ... 6-3/250. ... Full name: Lamont Bertrell Hollinquest. ... Cousin of Charlie Smith, wide receiver with Philadelphia Eagles and Boston/New Orleans Breakers of USFL (1974-1981, 1983 and 1984).
HIGH SCHOOL: Pius X (Downey, Calif.).
COLLEGE: Southern California.
TRANSACTIONS/CAREER NOTES: Selected by Washington Redskins in eighth round (212th pick overall) of 1993 NFL draft. ... Signed by Redskins (July 15, 1993). ... Claimed on waivers by Cincinnati Bengals (December 21, 1994). ... Released by Bengals (August 21, 1995). ... Signed by Green Bay Packers (January 18, 1996). ... Granted free agency (February 14, 1997). ... Re-signed by Packers (June 12, 1997).
CHAMPIONSHIP GAME EXPERIENCE: Played in NFC championship game (1996 and 1997 seasons). ... Member of Super Bowl championship team (1996 season). ... Played in Super Bowl XXXII (1997 season).
PRO STATISTICS: 1994—Credited with $1/2$ sack and recovered one fumble.

Year Team	G	GS	INTERCEPTIONS No.	Yds.	Avg.	TD
1993—Washington NFL	16	0	0	0	...	0
1994—Washington NFL	14	0	1	39	39.0	0
1995—			Did not play.			
1996—Green Bay NFL	16	0	1	2	2.0	0
1997—Green Bay NFL	16	0	0	0	...	0
Pro totals (4 years)	62	0	2	41	20.5	0

HOLLIS, MIKE — K — JAGUARS

PERSONAL: Born May 22, 1972, in Kellog, Idaho. ... 5-7/178. ... Full name: Michael Shane Hollis.
HIGH SCHOOL: Central Valley (Veradale, Wash.).
COLLEGE: Idaho.
TRANSACTIONS/CAREER NOTES: Signed as non-drafted free agent by San Diego Chargers (May 6, 1994). ... Released by Chargers (August 22, 1994). ... Signed by Jacksonville Jaguars (June 5, 1994).
CHAMPIONSHIP GAME EXPERIENCE: Played in AFC championship game (1996 season).
HONORS: Played in Pro Bowl (1997 season).

Year Team	G	GS	KICKING XPM	XPA	FGM	FGA	Lg.	50+	Pts.
1995—Jacksonville NFL	16	0	27	28	20	27	53	2-3	87
1996—Jacksonville NFL	16	0	27	27	30	36	53	2-3	117
1997—Jacksonville NFL	16	0	41	41	31	36	52	2-2	*134
Pro totals (3 years)	48	0	95	96	81	99	53	6-8	338

HOLMBERG, ROB — LB — RAIDERS

PERSONAL: Born May 6, 1971, in Mt. Pleasant, Pa. ... 6-3/230. ... Full name: Robert Anthony Holmberg.
HIGH SCHOOL: Mt. Pleasant (Pa.).
COLLEGE: Penn State.
TRANSACTIONS/CAREER NOTES: Selected by Los Angeles Raiders in seventh round (217th pick overall) of 1994 NFL draft. ... Signed by Raiders (1994). ... Raiders franchise moved to Oakland (July 21, 1995).
PLAYING EXPERIENCE: Los Angeles Raiders NFL, 1994; Oakland NFL, 1995-1997. ... Games/Games started: 1994 (16/0), 1995 (16/0), 1996 (13/1), 1997 (16/0). Total: 61/1.
PRO STATISTICS: 1995—Credited with one sack and recovered one fumble. 1996—Credited with one sack. 1997—Returned one kickoff for 15 yards and recovered one fumble.

H

HOLMES, DARICK　　　　　RB　　　　　BILLS

PERSONAL: Born July 1, 1971, in Pasadena, Calif. ... 6-0/226.
HIGH SCHOOL: John Muir (Pasadena, Calif.).
JUNIOR COLLEGE: Sacramento City College.
COLLEGE: Portland State.
TRANSACTIONS/CAREER NOTES: Selected by Buffalo Bills in seventh round (244th pick overall) of 1995 NFL draft. ... Signed by Bills (June 19, 1995). ... Granted free agency (February 13, 1998). ... Re-signed by Bills (April 24, 1998).
PRO STATISTICS: 1995—Recovered two fumbles. 1996—Recovered one fumble. 1997—Recovered one fumble.
SINGLE GAME HIGHS (regular season): Attempts—30 (December 1, 1996 vs. Indianapolis); yards—122 (November 3, 1996, vs. Washington); and rushing touchdowns—3 (November 3, 1996, vs. Washington).
STATISTICAL PLATEAUS: 100-yard rushing games: 1996 (1).

			RUSHING				RECEIVING				KICKOFF RETURNS				TOTALS		
Year　Team	G	GS	Att.	Yds.	Avg.	TD	No.	Yds.	Avg.	TD	No.	Yds.	Avg.	TD	TD	2pt.	Pts.	Fum.
1995—Buffalo NFL	16	2	172	698	4.1	4	24	214	8.9	0	39	799	20.5	0	4	0	24	4
1996—Buffalo NFL	16	1	189	571	3.0	4	16	102	6.4	1	0	0	...	0	5	1	32	2
1997—Buffalo NFL	13	0	22	106	4.8	2	13	106	8.2	0	23	430	18.7	0	2	0	12	1
Pro totals (3 years)	45	3	383	1375	3.6	10	53	422	8.0	1	62	1229	19.8	0	11	1	68	7

HOLMES, EARL　　　　　LB　　　　　STEELERS

PERSONAL: Born April 28, 1973, in Tallahassee, Fla. ... 6-2/246.
HIGH SCHOOL: Florida A&M University (Tallahassee, Fla.).
COLLEGE: Florida A&M.
TRANSACTIONS/CAREER NOTES: Selected by Pittsburgh Steelers in fourth round (126th pick overall) of 1996 NFL draft. ... Signed by Steelers (July 16, 1996).
CHAMPIONSHIP GAME EXPERIENCE: Played in AFC championship game (1997 season).
PRO STATISTICS: 1997—Recovered one fumble.

Year　Team	G	GS	SACKS
1996—Pittsburgh NFL	3	1	1.0
1997—Pittsburgh NFL	16	16	4.0
Pro totals (2 years)	19	17	5.0

HOLMES, KENNY　　　　　DE　　　　　OILERS

PERSONAL: Born October 24, 1973, in Vero Beach, Fla. ... 6-4/270. ... Full name: Kenneth Holmes.
HIGH SCHOOL: Vero Beach (Fla.).
COLLEGE: Miami (Fla.).
TRANSACTIONS/CAREER NOTES: Selected by Houston Oilers in first round (18th pick overall) of 1997 NFL draft. ... Oilers franchise moved to Tennessee for 1997 season. ... Signed by Oilers (July 18, 1997).
PRO STATISTICS: 1997—Recovered one fumble.

Year　Team	G	GS	SACKS
1997—Tennessee NFL	16	5	7.0

HOLMES, LESTER　　　　　G　　　　　CARDINALS

PERSONAL: Born September 27, 1969, in Tylertown, Miss. ... 6-4/315.
HIGH SCHOOL: Tylertown (Miss.).
COLLEGE: Jackson State.
TRANSACTIONS/CAREER NOTES: Selected by Philadelphia Eagles in first round (19th pick overall) of 1993 NFL draft. ... Signed by Eagles (August 2, 1993). ... On injured reserve with knee injury (November 28, 1995-remainder of season). ... Granted free agency (February 16, 1996). ... Re-signed by Eagles (July 17, 1996). ... Granted unconditional free agency (February 14, 1997). ... Signed by Oakland Raiders (May 17, 1997). ... Released by Raiders (February 12, 1998). ... Signed by Arizona Cardinals (February 26, 1998).
PLAYING EXPERIENCE: Philadelphia NFL, 1993-1996; Oakland NFL, 1997. ... Games/Games started: 1993 (12/6), 1994 (16/16), 1995 (2/2), 1996 (16/14), 1997 (15/15). Total: 61/53.
PRO STATISTICS: 1993—Recovered one fumble. 1994—Recovered three fumbles.

HOLMES, PRIEST　　　　　RB　　　　　RAVENS

PERSONAL: Born October 7, 1973, in Fort Smith, Ark. ... 5-9/205. ... Full name: Priest Anthony Holmes.
HIGH SCHOOL: Marshall (San Antonio).
COLLEGE: Texas.
TRANSACTIONS/CAREER NOTES: Signed as non-drafted free agent by Baltimore Ravens (April 25, 1997).
PLAYING EXPERIENCE: Baltimore NFL, 1997. ... Games/Games started: 7/0.
PRO STATISTICS: 1997—Returned one kickoff for 14 yards.
SINGLE GAME HIGHS (regular season): Attempts—0; yards—0; and rushing touchdowns—0.

HOLSEY, BERNARD　　　　　DE　　　　　GIANTS

PERSONAL: Born December 10, 1973, in Cave Spring, Ga. ... 6-2/295.
HIGH SCHOOL: Coosa (Cave Spring, Ga.).
COLLEGE: Duke.
TRANSACTIONS/CAREER NOTES: Signed as non-drafted free agent by New York Giants (April 26, 1996).
PLAYING EXPERIENCE: New York Giants NFL, 1996 and 1997. ... Games/Games started: 1996 (16/0), 1997 (16/4). Total: 32/4.
PRO STATISTICS: 1997—Credited with 3 1/2 sacks.

H

PERSONAL: Born September 5, 1970, in Columbia, S.C. ... 6-3/295. ... Full name: Bradley D. Hopkins.
HIGH SCHOOL: Moline (Ill.).
COLLEGE: Illinois (degree in speech communications, 1993).
TRANSACTIONS/CAREER NOTES: Selected by Houston Oilers in first round (13th pick overall) of 1993 NFL draft. ... Signed by Oilers (August 10, 1993). ... Granted unconditional free agency (February 14, 1997). ... Re-signed by Oilers (March 10, 1997). ... Oilers franchise moved to Tennessee for 1997 season.
PLAYING EXPERIENCE: Houston NFL, 1993-1996; Tennessee NFL, 1997. ... Games/Games started: 1993 (16/11), 1994 (16/15), 1995 (16/16), 1996 (16/16), 1997 (16/16). Total: 80/74.
PRO STATISTICS: 1994—Recovered one fumble. 1995—Recovered three fumbles. 1996—Recovered one fumble. 1997—Recovered one fumble.

PERSONAL: Born February 1, 1959, in Orange, Calif. ... 5-11/192. ... Full name: Michael William Horan. ... Name pronounced hor-RAN.
HIGH SCHOOL: Sunny Hills (Fullerton, Calif.).
JUNIOR COLLEGE: Fullerton (Calif.) College.
COLLEGE: Long Beach State (degree in mechanical engineering).
TRANSACTIONS/CAREER NOTES: Selected by Atlanta Falcons in ninth round (235th pick overall) of 1982 NFL draft. ... Released by Falcons (September 4, 1982). ... Signed by Green Bay Packers (March 15, 1983). ... Released by Packers after failing physical (May 6, 1983). ... Signed by Buffalo Bills (May 25, 1983). ... Released by Bills (August 22, 1983). ... Signed by Philadelphia Eagles (May 7, 1984). ... Released by Eagles (August 28, 1986). ... Signed by Minnesota Vikings (October 31, 1986). ... Active for one game with Vikings (1986); did not play. ... Released by Vikings (November 3, 1986). ... Signed by Denver Broncos (November 25, 1986). ... Granted unconditional free agency (February 1-April 1, 1991). ... Re-signed by Broncos for 1991 season. ... Granted unconditional free agency (February 1-April 1, 1992). ... Re-signed by Broncos for 1992 season. ... On injured reserve with knee injury (October 22, 1992-remainder of season). ... Released by Broncos (August 30, 1993). ... Signed by New York Giants (November 9, 1993). ... Granted unconditional free agency (February 16, 1996). ... Re-signed by Giants (May 6, 1996). ... Released by Giants (February 14, 1997). ... Signed by St. Louis Rams (October 12, 1997). ... Granted unconditional free agency (February 13, 1998).
CHAMPIONSHIP GAME EXPERIENCE: Played in AFC championship game (1986, 1987, 1989 and 1991 seasons). ... Played in Super Bowl XXI (1986 season), Super Bowl XXII (1987 season) and Super Bowl XXIV (1989 season).
HONORS: Named punter on THE SPORTING NEWS NFL All-Pro team (1988). ... Played in Pro Bowl (1988 season).
POST SEASON RECORDS: Shares NFL postseason career record for longest punt—76 yards (January 12, 1991, at Buffalo).
PRO STATISTICS: 1985—Rushed once for 12 yards. 1986—Rushed once for no yards, fumbled once and recovered one fumble for minus 12 yards. 1991—Rushed twice for nine yards and recovered one fumble. 1995—Rushed once for no yards, fumbled once and recovered one fumble for minus 18 yards. 1997—Rushed once for minus three yards.

				PUNTING				
Year Team	G	GS	No.	Yds.	Avg.	Net avg.	In. 20	Blk.
1984—Philadelphia NFL	16	0	‡92	‡3880	42.2	35.6	21	0
1985—Philadelphia NFL	16	0	‡91	‡3777	41.5	34.2	20	0
1986—Denver NFL	4	0	13	571	43.9	34.5	8	0
1987—Denver NFL	12	0	44	1807	41.1	33.1	11	*2
1988—Denver NFL	16	0	65	2861	44.0	*37.8	19	0
1989—Denver NFL	16	0	77	3111	40.4	34.2	24	0
1990—Denver NFL	15	0	58	2575	44.4	*38.9	14	1
1991—Denver NFL	16	0	72	3012	41.8	36.7	24	1
1992—Denver NFL	7	0	37	1681	45.4	40.2	7	1
1993—New York Giants NFL	8	0	44	1882	42.8	*39.9	13	0
1994—New York Giants NFL	16	0	85	3521	41.4	35.2	25	*2
1995—New York Giants NFL	16	0	72	3063	42.5	36.2	15	0
1996—New York Giants NFL	16	0	*102	*4289	42.0	35.8	*32	0
1997—St. Louis NFL	10	0	53	2272	42.9	36.3	10	0
Pro totals (14 years)	184	0	905	38302	42.3	36.1	243	7

PERSONAL: Born January 16, 1972, in Tupelo, Miss. ... 6-1/199. ... Full name: Joseph Horn.
HIGH SCHOOL: Douglas Bird (Fayetteville, N.C.).
JUNIOR COLLEGE: Itawamba (Miss.) Junior College.
TRANSACTIONS/CAREER NOTES: Signed by Memphis Mad Dogs of CFL (March 25, 1995). ... Selected by Kansas City Chiefs in fifth round (135th pick overall) of 1996 NFL draft. ... Signed by Chiefs (June 25, 1996).
PRO STATISTICS: 1996—Rushed once for eight yards.
SINGLE GAME HIGHS (regular season): Receptions—1 (November 16, 1997, vs. Denver); yards—47 (November 9, 1997, vs. Jacksonville); and touchdown receptions—0.

			RECEIVING				KICKOFF RETURNS				TOTALS			
Year Team	G	GS	No.	Yds.	Avg.	TD	No.	Yds.	Avg.	TD	TD	2pt.	Pts.	Fum.
1995—Memphis CFL	17	17	71	1415	19.9	5	2	17	8.5	0	5	0	30	0
1996—Kansas City NFL	9	0	2	30	15.0	0	0	0	...	0	0	0	0	0
1997—Kansas City NFL	8	0	2	65	32.5	0	0	0	...	0	0	0	0	0
CFL totals (1 year)	17	17	71	1415	19.9	5	2	17	8.5	0	5	0	30	0
NFL totals (2 years)	17	0	4	95	23.8	0	0	0		0	0	0	0	0
Pro totals (3 years)	34	17	75	1510	20.1	5	2	17	8.5	0	5	0	30	0

H

HOSTETLER, JEFF   QB   REDSKINS

PERSONAL: Born April 22, 1961, in Hollsopple, Pa. ... 6-3/215. ... Full name: Jeff W. Hostetler. ... Son-in-law of Don Nehlen, head football coach, West Virginia University.
HIGH SCHOOL: Conemaugh Valley (Johnstown, Pa.).
COLLEGE: Penn State, then West Virginia.
TRANSACTIONS/CAREER NOTES: Selected by Pittsburgh Maulers in 1984 USFL territorial draft. ... Selected by New York Giants in third round (59th pick overall) of 1984 NFL draft. ... USFL rights traded by Maulers with rights to CB Dwayne Woodruff to Arizona Wranglers for draft pick (May 2, 1984). ... Signed by Giants (June 12, 1984). ... Active for 16 games with Giants (1984); did not play. ... On injured reserve with pulled hamstring (December 14, 1985-remainder of season). ... On injured reserve with leg injury (December 6, 1986-remainder of season). ... On injured reserve with kidney injury (September 7-November 7, 1987). ... Crossed picket line during players strike (October 14, 1987). ... Active for two games with Giants (1987); did not play. ... Granted free agency (February 1, 1991). ... Re-signed by Giants (July 16, 1991). ... On injured reserve with back injury (December 11, 1991-remainder of season). ... Granted unconditional free agency (March 1, 1993). ... Signed by Los Angeles Raiders (March 24, 1993). ... Raiders franchise moved to Oakland (July 21, 1995). ... Granted free agency (February 16, 1996). ... Re-signed by Raiders (April 2, 1996). ... Released by Raiders (June 17, 1997). ... Signed by Washington Redskins (June 18, 1997).
CHAMPIONSHIP GAME EXPERIENCE: Played in NFC championship game (1990 season). ... Member of Super Bowl championship team (1990 season).
HONORS: Played in Pro Bowl (1994 season).
PRO STATISTICS: 1988—Caught one pass for 10 yards, fumbled once and recovered one fumble. 1989—Fumbled twice and recovered one fumble. 1990—Fumbled four times and recovered five fumbles for minus four yards. 1991—Fumbled seven times and recovered six fumbles for minus nine yards. 1992—Fumbled six times. 1993—Fumbled six times and recovered two fumbles for minus one yard. 1994—Fumbled 10 times. 1995—Fumbled five times and recovered one fumble for minus 15 yards. 1996—Fumbled four times and recovered five fumbles for minus three yards. 1997—Fumbled three times and recovered one fumble.
SINGLE GAME HIGHS (regular season): Attempts—44 (September 22, 1996, vs. San Diego); completions—28 (September 29, 1991, vs. Dallas); yards—424 (October 31, 1993, vs. San Diego); and touchdown passes—4 (October 13, 1996, vs. Detroit).
STATISTICAL PLATEAUS: 300-yard passing games: 1991 (1), 1993 (2), 1994 (3), 1995 (1). Total: 7.
MISCELLANEOUS: Regular-season record as starting NFL quarterback: 51-32 (.614). ... Postseason record as starting NFL quarterback: 4-1 (.800).

				PASSING							RUSHING				TOTALS		
Year Team	G	GS	Att.	Cmp.	Pct.	Yds.	TD	Int.	Avg.	Rat.	Att.	Yds.	Avg.	TD	TD	2pt.	Pts.
1984—N.Y. Giants NFL..........									Did not play.								
1985—N.Y. Giants NFL..........	5	0	0	0	...	0	0	0	...	...	0	0	...	0	0	...	0
1986—N.Y. Giants NFL..........	13	0	0	0	...	0	0	0	...	...	1	1	1.0	0	0	...	0
1987—N.Y. Giants NFL..........									Did not play.								
1988—N.Y. Giants NFL..........	16	1	29	16	55.2	244	1	2	8.41	65.9	5	-3	-0.6	0	0	...	0
1989—N.Y. Giants NFL..........	16	1	39	20	51.3	294	3	2	7.54	80.5	11	71	6.5	2	2	...	12
1990—N.Y. Giants NFL..........	16	2	87	47	54.0	614	3	1	7.06	83.2	39	190	4.9	2	2	...	12
1991—N.Y. Giants NFL..........	12	12	285	179	62.8	2032	5	4	7.13	84.1	42	273	6.5	2	2	...	12
1992—N.Y. Giants NFL..........	13	9	192	103	53.6	1225	8	3	6.38	80.8	35	172	4.9	3	3	...	18
1993—L.A. Raiders NFL........	15	15	419	236	56.3	3242	14	10	7.74	82.5	55	202	3.7	5	5	...	30
1994—L.A. Raiders NFL........	16	16	455	263	57.8	3334	20	16	§7.33	80.8	46	159	3.5	2	2	0	12
1995—Oakland NFL..............	11	11	286	172	60.1	1998	12	9	6.99	82.2	31	119	3.8	0	0	0	0
1996—Oakland NFL..............	13	13	402	242	60.2	2548	23	14	6.34	83.2	37	179	4.8	1	1	0	6
1997—Washington NFL	8	3	144	79	54.9	899	5	10	6.24	56.5	14	28	2.0	0	0	0	0
Pro totals (12 years)	154	83	2338	1357	58.0	16430	94	71	7.03	80.5	316	1391	4.4	17	17	0	102

HOUSTON, BOBBY   LB   VIKINGS

PERSONAL: Born October 26, 1967, in Washington, D.C. ... 6-2/245.
HIGH SCHOOL: DeMatha Catholic (Hyattsville, Md.).
COLLEGE: North Carolina State (degree in accounting).
TRANSACTIONS/CAREER NOTES: Selected by Green Bay Packers in third round (75th pick overall) of 1990 NFL draft. ... Signed by Packers (July 23, 1990). ... On reserve/non-football injury list with pneumonia (September 22-December 19, 1990). ... Claimed on waivers by Atlanta Falcons (December 21, 1990) ... On inactive list for two games with Falcons (1990). ... Granted unconditional free agency (February 1, 1991). ... Signed by New York Jets (March 27, 1991). ... Granted unconditional free agency (February 17, 1995). ... Re-signed by Jets (February 17, 1995). ... Released by Jets (July 21, 1997). ... Signed by Kansas City Chiefs (August 4, 1997). ... Released by Chiefs (October 9, 1997). ... Signed by San Diego Chargers (October 22, 1997). ... On injured reserve with leg injury (November 4, 1997-remainder of season). ... Granted unconditional free agency (February 13, 1998). ... Signed by Minnesota Vikings (March 27, 1998).
PRO STATISTICS: 1991—Recovered one fumble. 1993—Recovered one fumble. 1994—Recovered one fumble. 1995—Recovered three fumbles. 1996—Recovered one fumble.

			INTERCEPTIONS				SACKS
Year Team	G	GS	No.	Yds.	Avg.	TD	No.
1990—Green Bay NFL..............................	1	0	0	0	...	0	0.0
1991—New York Jets NFL.........................	15	0	0	0	...	0	1.0
1992—New York Jets NFL.........................	16	15	1	20	20.0	1	4.0
1993—New York Jets NFL.........................	16	14	1	0	0.0	0	3.0
1994—New York Jets NFL.........................	16	16	0	0	...	0	3.5
1995—New York Jets NFL.........................	16	15	0	0	...	0	3.0
1996—New York Jets NFL.........................	15	15	2	3	1.5	0	0.0
1997—Kansas City NFL............................	5	0	0	0	...	0	0.0
—San Diego NFL..............................	2	0	0	0	...	0	0.0
Pro totals (8 years)	102	75	4	23	5.8	1	14.5

HOWARD, DESMOND   KR/WR   RAIDERS   H

PERSONAL: Born May 15, 1970, in Cleveland. ... 5-10/180. ... Full name: Desmond Kevin Howard.
HIGH SCHOOL: St. Joseph (Cleveland).
COLLEGE: Michigan (degree in communication studies).

TRANSACTIONS/CAREER NOTES: Selected by Washington Redskins in first round (fourth pick overall) of 1992 NFL draft. ... Signed by Redskins (August 25, 1992). ... On injured reserve with separated shoulder (December 29, 1992-remainder of 1992 season playoffs). ... Selected by Jacksonville Jaguars from Redskins in NFL expansion draft (February 15, 1995). ... Granted unconditional free agency (February 16, 1996). ... Signed by Green Bay Packers (July 11, 1996). ... Granted unconditional free agency (February 14, 1997). ... Signed by Oakland Raiders (March 4, 1997).

CHAMPIONSHIP GAME EXPERIENCE: Played in NFC championship game (1996 season). ... Member of Super Bowl championship team (1996 season).

HONORS: Heisman Trophy winner (1991). ... Named College Football Player of the Year by THE SPORTING NEWS (1991). ... Maxwell Award winner (1991). ... Named wide receiver on THE SPORTING NEWS college All-America first team (1991). ... Named punt returner on THE SPORTING NEWS NFL All-Pro team (1996). ... Named Most Valuable Player of Super Bowl XXXI (1996 season).

RECORDS: Holds NFL single-season record for most yards by punt return—875 (1996).

POST SEASON RECORDS: Holds Super Bowl career record for highest kickoff return average (minimum four returns)—38.5. ... Holds Super Bowl and NFL postseason record for longest kickoff return—99 yards (January 26, 1997, vs. New England). ... Holds Super Bowl single-game record for most yards by punt return—90 (January 26, 1997, vs. New England). ... Shares Super Bowl career and single-game records for most punt returns—6. ... Shares Super Bowl single-game records for most combined yards—244; most combined yards by kick returns—244; most touchdowns by kickoff return—1 (January 26, 1997, vs. New England). ... Shares NFL postseason single-game record for most combined yards—244; most combined kick return yards—244; and most touchdowns by kickoff return—1 (January 26, 1997, vs. New England).

PRO STATISTICS: 1992—Fumbled once. 1996—Fumbled twice and recovered one fumble. 1997—Fumbled twice and recovered two fumbles.

SINGLE GAME HIGHS (regular season): Receptions—7 (November 20, 1994, vs. Dallas); yards—130 (December 4, 1994, vs. Tampa Bay); and touchdown receptions—1 (October 1, 1995, vs. Houston).

STATISTICAL PLATEAUS: 100-yard receiving games: 1994 (2).

			RUSHING			RECEIVING				PUNT RETURNS				KICKOFF RETURNS				TOTALS		
Year Team	G	GS	Att.	Yds.	Avg.	TD	No.	Yds.	Avg.	TD	No.	Yds.	Avg.	TD	No.	Yds.	Avg.	TD	TD	2pt.	Pts.
1992—Washington NFL .	16	1	3	14	4.7	0	3	20	6.7	0	6	84	14.0	1	22	462	21.0	0	1	...	6
1993—Washington NFL .	16	5	2	17	8.5	0	23	286	12.4	0	4	25	6.3	0	21	405	19.3	0	0	...	0
1994—Washington NFL .	16	15	1	4	4.0	0	40	727	18.2	5	0	0	...	0	0	0	...	0	5	1	32
1995—Jacksonville NFL .	13	7	1	8	8.0	0	26	276	10.6	1	24	246	10.3	0	10	178	17.8	0	1	0	6
1996—Green Bay NFL....	16	0	0	0	...	0	13	95	7.3	0	*58	*875	*15.1	*3	22	460	20.9	0	3	0	18
1997—Oakland NFL........	15	0	0	0	...	0	4	30	7.5	0	27	210	7.8	0	*61	§1318	21.6	0	0	0	0
Pro totals (6 years)	92	28	7	43	6.1	0	109	1434	13.2	6	119	1440	12.1	4	136	2823	20.8	0	10	1	62

HOWARD, TY   CB   CARDINALS

PERSONAL: Born November 30, 1973, in Columbus, Ohio. ... 5-9/185.
HIGH SCHOOL: Briggs (Columbus, Ohio).
COLLEGE: Ohio State.
TRANSACTIONS/CAREER NOTES: Selected by Arizona Cardinals in third round (84th pick overall) of 1997 NFL draft. ... Signed by Cardinals (June 10, 1997).
PLAYING EXPERIENCE: Arizona NFL, 1997. ... Games/Games started: 15/2.
PRO STATISTICS: 1997—Credited with one sack.

HOYING, BOBBY   QB   EAGLES

PERSONAL: Born September 20, 1972, in St. Henry, Ohio. ... 6-3/221.
HIGH SCHOOL: St. Henry (Ohio).
COLLEGE: Ohio State.
TRANSACTIONS/CAREER NOTES: Selected by Philadelphia Eagles in third round (85th pick overall) of 1996 NFL draft. ... Signed by Eagles (July 15, 1996).
PRO STATISTICS: 1997—Fumbled seven times and recovered one fumble.
SINGLE GAME HIGHS (regular season): Attempts—42 (November 30, 1997, vs. Cincinnati); completions—26 (November 30, 1997, vs. Cincinnati); yards—313 (November 30, 1997, vs. Cincinnati); touchdown passes—4 (November 30, 1997, vs. Cincinnati).
STATISTICAL PLATEAUS: 300-yard passing games: 1997 (1).
MISCELLANEOUS: Regular-season record as starting NFL quarterback: 2-3-1 (.417).

			PASSING							RUSHING				TOTALS		
Year Team	G	GS	Att.	Cmp.	Pct.	Yds.	TD	Int.	Avg.	Rat.	Att.	Yds.	Avg.	TD	TD	2pt.	Pts.
1996—Philadelphia NFL	1	0	0	0	...	0	0	0	...	...	0	0	...	0	0	0	0
1997—Philadelphia NFL	7	6	225	128	56.9	1573	11	6	6.99	83.8	16	78	4.9	0	0	0	0
Pro totals (2 years)	8	6	225	128	56.9	1573	11	6	6.99	83.8	16	78	4.9	0	0	0	0

HUDSON, CHRIS   S   JAGUARS

PERSONAL: Born October 6, 1971, in Houston. ... 5-10/204. ... Full name: Christopher Reshard Hudson.
HIGH SCHOOL: E.E. Worthing (Houston).
COLLEGE: Colorado.
TRANSACTIONS/CAREER NOTES: Selected by Jacksonville Jaguars in third round (71st pick overall) of 1995 NFL draft. ... Signed by Jaguars (June 1, 1995). ... On injured reserve with groin injury (September 28, 1995-remainder of season). ... Granted free agency (February 13, 1998). ... Re-signed by Jaguars (June 10, 1998).
CHAMPIONSHIP GAME EXPERIENCE: Played in AFC championship game (1996 season).
HONORS: Jim Thorpe Award winner (1994).
PRO STATISTICS: 1996—Recovered two fumbles. 1997—Returned blocked field-goal attempt 58 yards for a touchdown and recovered two fumbles for 32 yards and one touchdown.
MISCELLANEOUS: Shares Jacksonville Jaguars all-time record for most interceptions (5).

H

Year Team	G	GS	INTERCEPTIONS				PUNT RETURNS				TOTALS			
			No.	Yds.	Avg.	TD	No.	Yds.	Avg.	TD	TD	2pt.	Pts.	Fum.
1995—Jacksonville NFL	1	0	0	0	...	0	0	0	...	0	0	0	0	0
1996—Jacksonville NFL	16	16	2	25	12.5	0	32	348	10.9	0	0	0	0	3
1997—Jacksonville NFL	16	16	3	26	8.7	0	0	0	...	0	2	0	12	1
Pro totals (3 years)	33	32	5	51	10.2	0	32	348	10.9	0	2	0	12	4

HUDSON, JOHN — C/G — JETS

PERSONAL: Born January 29, 1968, in Memphis, Tenn. ... 6-2/270. ... Full name: John Lewis Hudson.
HIGH SCHOOL: Henry County (Paris, Tenn.).
COLLEGE: Auburn.
TRANSACTIONS/CAREER NOTES: Selected by Philadelphia Eagles in 11th round (294th pick overall) of 1990 NFL draft. ... Signed by Eagles (July 31, 1990). ... On physically unable to perform list with knee laceration (August 2, 1990-entire season). ... Granted unconditional free agency (February 1-April 1, 1992). ... Re-signed by Eagles (July 23, 1992). ... On injured reserve with broken hand (September 28, 1992-remainder of season). ... Granted free agency (March 1, 1993). ... Re-signed by Eagles (May 12, 1993). ... Granted unconditional free agency (February 17, 1994). ... Re-signed by Eagles (April 7, 1994). ... Granted unconditional free agency (February 16, 1996). ... Signed by New York Jets (February 26, 1996).
PLAYING EXPERIENCE: Philadelphia NFL, 1991-1995; New York Jets NFL, 1996 and 1997. ... Games/Games started: 1991 (16/0), 1992 (3/0), 1993 (16/0), 1994 (16/0), 1995 (16/0), 1996 (16/0), 1997 (16/0). Total: 99/0.
PRO STATISTICS: 1991—Fumbled once. 1993—Fumbled once.

HUGHES, DANAN — WR/KR — CHIEFS

PERSONAL: Born December 11, 1970, in Bayonne, N.J. ... 6-2/211. ... Full name: Robert Danan Hughes. ... Name pronounced DAY-nin.
HIGH SCHOOL: Bayonne (N.J.).
COLLEGE: Iowa (degree in communications).
TRANSACTIONS/CAREER NOTES: Selected by Kansas City Chiefs in seventh round (186th pick overall) of 1993 NFL draft. ... Signed by Chiefs (May 27, 1993). ... Released by Chiefs (September 6, 1993). ... Re-signed by Chiefs to practice squad (September 8, 1993). ... Activated (November 17, 1993). ... Granted free agency (February 16, 1996). ... Re-signed by Chiefs (May 6, 1996). ... Granted unconditional free agency (February 13, 1998). ... Re-signed by Chiefs (April 24, 1998).
CHAMPIONSHIP GAME EXPERIENCE: Played in AFC championship game (1993 season).
PRO STATISTICS: 1995—Rushed once for five yards. 1996—Attempted one pass with one completion for 30 yards. 1997—Recovered two fumbles for seven yards and one touchdown.
SINGLE GAME HIGHS (regular season): Receptions—5 (September 15, 1996, vs. Seattle); yards—53 (November 13, 1994, vs. San Diego); and touchdown receptions—1 (November 16, 1997, vs. Denver).

Year Team	G	GS	RECEIVING				PUNT RETURNS				KICKOFF RETURNS				TOTALS			
			No.	Yds.	Avg.	TD	No.	Yds.	Avg.	TD	No.	Yds.	Avg.	TD	TD	2pt.	Pts.	Fum.
1993—Kansas City NFL	6	0	0	0	...	0	3	49	16.3	0	14	266	19.0	0	0	...	0	0
1994—Kansas City NFL	16	0	7	80	11.4	0	27	192	7.1	0	9	190	21.1	0	0	0	0	0
1995—Kansas City NFL	16	0	14	103	7.4	1	3	9	3.0	0	1	18	18.0	0	1	0	6	0
1996—Kansas City NFL	15	2	17	167	9.8	1	0	0	...	0	2	42	21.0	0	1	0	6	0
1997—Kansas City NFL	16	1	7	65	9.3	2	0	0	...	0	1	21	21.0	0	3	0	18	0
Pro totals (5 years)	69	3	45	415	9.2	4	33	250	7.6	0	27	537	19.9	0	5	0	30	0

HUGHES, TYRONE — CB/KR

PERSONAL: Born January 14, 1970, in New Orleans. ... 5-9/175. ... Full name: Tyrone Christopher Hughes.
HIGH SCHOOL: St. Augustine (New Orleans).
COLLEGE: Nebraska.
TRANSACTIONS/CAREER NOTES: Selected by New Orleans Saints in fifth round (137th pick overall) of 1993 NFL draft. ... Signed by Saints (July 16, 1993). ... Granted unconditional free agency (February 14, 1997). ... Signed by Chicago Bears (April 11, 1997). ... Released by Bears (April 24, 1998).
HONORS: Played in Pro Bowl (1993 season).
RECORDS: Holds NFL single-season records for most kickoff returns—70 (1996); yards by kickoff return—1,791 (1996). ... Holds NFL single-game records for most yards by kickoff return—304; and most yards by combined kick return—347 (October 23, 1994, vs. Los Angeles Rams). ... Shares NFL single-game record for most touchdowns by fumble recovery—2 (1994); and most touchdowns by recovery of opponents' fumbles—2 (1994). ... Shares NFL single-game records for most touchdowns by kickoff return—2; and most touchdowns by combined kick return—2 (October 23, 1994, vs. Los Angeles Rams).
PRO STATISTICS: 1994—Rushed twice for six yards and recovered three fumbles for 128 yards and two touchdowns. 1997—Rushed once for three yards, caught eight passes for 68 yards and recovered two fumbles.

Year Team	G	GS	INTERCEPTIONS				PUNT RETURNS				KICKOFF RETURNS				TOTALS			
			No.	Yds.	Avg.	TD	No.	Yds.	Avg.	TD	No.	Yds.	Avg.	TD	TD	2pt.	Pts.	Fum.
1993—New Orleans NFL	16	0	0	0	...	0	‡37	*503	*13.6	†2	30	753	25.1	†1	3	...	18	0
1994—New Orleans NFL	15	5	2	31	15.5	0	21	143	6.8	0	*63	*1556	24.7	2	4	0	24	7
1995—New Orleans NFL	16	2	2	19	9.5	0	28	262	9.4	0	*66	*1617	24.5	0	0	0	0	2
1996—New Orleans NFL	16	1	0	0	...	0	30	152	5.1	0	*70	*1791	25.6	0	0	0	0	2
1997—Chicago NFL	14	0	0	0	...	0	36	258	7.2	0	43	1008	23.4	0	0	0	0	2
Pro totals (5 years)	77	8	4	50	12.5	0	152	1318	8.7	2	272	6725	24.7	3	7	0	42	13

HUMPHRIES, STAN — QB

PERSONAL: Born April 14, 1965, in Shreveport, La. ... 6-2/223. ... Full name: William Stanley Humphries.
HIGH SCHOOL: Southwood (Shreveport, La.).
COLLEGE: Louisiana State, then Northeast Louisiana.

H

TRANSACTIONS/CAREER NOTES: Selected by Washington Redskins in sixth round (159th pick overall) of 1988 NFL draft. ... Signed by Redskins (July 13, 1988). ... On non-football injury list with blood disorder (September 3, 1988-entire season). ... On injured reserve with sprained knee (November 17, 1990-January 11, 1991). ... Active for two games (1991); did not play. ... Traded by Redskins to San Diego Chargers for third-round pick (P Ed Bunn) in 1993 draft (August 13, 1992). ... On injured reserve with concussion (December 5, 1997-remainder of season). ... Announced retirement (February 27, 1998).

CHAMPIONSHIP GAME EXPERIENCE: Member of Redskins for NFC championship game (1991 season); inactive. ... Member of Super Bowl championship team (1991 season). ... Played in AFC championship game (1994 season). ... Played in Super Bowl XXIX (1994 season).

RECORDS: Shares NFL record for longest pass completion (to Tony Martin)—99 yards, touchdown (September 18, 1994, at Seattle).

PRO STATISTICS: 1989—Fumbled once and recovered one fumble. 1992—Fumbled nine times and recovered three fumbles. 1993—Fumbled twice and recovered one fumble. 1994—Fumbled six times and recovered two fumbles for minus nine yards. 1995—Caught one pass for minus four yards, fumbled nine times and recovered seven fumbles for minus 11 yards. 1996—Fumbled seven times and recovered four fumbles for minus six yards. 1997—Fumbled seven times and recovered one fumble for minus 10 yards.

SINGLE GAME HIGHS (regular season): Attempts—51 (December 12, 1993, vs. Green Bay); completions—28 (September 12, 1993, vs. Denver); yards—358 (September 28, 1997, vs. Baltimore); and touchdown passes—4 (September 22, 1996, vs. Oakland).

STATISTICAL PLATEAUS: 300-yard passing games: 1992 (1), 1994 (1), 1995 (2), 1996 (1), 1997 (1). Total: 6.

MISCELLANEOUS: Regular-season record as starting NFL quarterback: 50-31 (.617). ... Postseason record as starting NFL quarterback: 3-3 (.500).

Year Team	G	GS	Att.	Cmp.	Pct.	PASSING Yds.	TD	Int.	Avg.	Rat.	RUSHING Att.	Yds.	Avg.	TD	TOTALS TD	2pt.	Pts.
1988—Washington NFL						Did not play.											
1989—Washington NFL	2	0	10	5	50.0	91	1	1	9.10	75.4	5	10	2.0	0	0	...	0
1990—Washington NFL	7	5	156	91	58.3	1015	3	10	6.51	57.5	23	106	4.6	2	2	...	12
1991—Washington NFL						Did not play.											
1992—San Diego NFL	16	15	454	263	57.9	3356	16	18	7.39	76.4	28	79	2.8	4	4	...	24
1993—San Diego NFL	12	10	324	173	53.4	1981	12	10	6.11	71.5	8	37	4.6	0	0	...	0
1994—San Diego NFL	15	15	453	264	58.3	3209	17	12	7.08	81.6	19	19	1.0	0	0	0	0
1995—San Diego NFL	15	15	478	282	59.0	3381	17	14	7.07	80.4	33	53	1.6	1	1	0	6
1996—San Diego NFL	13	13	416	232	55.8	2670	18	13	6.42	76.7	21	28	1.3	0	0	0	0
1997—San Diego NFL	8	8	225	121	53.8	1488	5	6	6.61	70.8	13	24	1.8	0	0	0	0
Pro totals (8 years)	88	81	2516	1431	56.9	17191	89	84	6.83	75.8	150	356	2.4	7	7	0	42

HUNDON, JAMES   WR   BENGALS

PERSONAL: Born April 9, 1971, in Daly City, Calif. ... 6-1/173.
HIGH SCHOOL: Jefferson (Daly City, Fla.).
JUNIOR COLLEGE: San Francisco Community College.
COLLEGE: Portland State.
TRANSACTIONS/CAREER NOTES: Signed as non-drafted free agent by Cincinnati Bengals (April 23, 1996). ... Released by Bengals (August 27, 1996). ... Re-signed by Bengals to practice squad (November 19, 1996). ... Activated (November 22, 1996).
PRO STATISTICS: 1996—Returned one punt for minus seven yards.
SINGLE GAME HIGHS (regular season): Receptions—5 (November 30, 1997, vs. Philadelphia); yards—118 (November 30, 1997, vs. Philadelphia); and touchdown receptions—2 (November 30, 1997, vs. Philadelphia).
STATISTICAL PLATEAUS: 100-yard receiving games: 1997 (1).

Year Team	G	GS	RECEIVING No.	Yds.	Avg.	TD	KICKOFF RETURNS No.	Yds.	Avg.	TD	TOTALS TD	2pt.	Pts.	Fum.
1996—Cincinnati NFL	5	0	1	14	14.0	1	10	237	23.7	0	1	0	6	1
1997—Cincinnati NFL	16	0	16	285	17.8	2	10	169	16.9	0	2	0	12	1
Pro totals (2 years)	21	0	17	299	17.6	3	20	406	20.3	0	3	0	18	2

HUNTER, BRICE   WR   BUCCANEERS

PERSONAL: Born April 21, 1974, in Valdosta, Ga. ... 6-0/219.
HIGH SCHOOL: Valdosta (Ga.).
COLLEGE: Georgia.
TRANSACTIONS/CAREER NOTES: Selected by Miami Dolphins in seventh round (251st pick overall) of 1996 NFL draft. ... Signed by Dolphins for 1996 season. ... Released by Dolphins (August 24, 1996). ... Signed by San Francisco 49ers to practice squad (September 16, 1996). ... Released by 49ers (September 26, 1996). ... Signed by Tampa Bay Buccaneers to practice squad (October 16, 1996). ... Released by Buccaneers (August 24, 1997). ... Re-signed by Buccaneers to practice squad (August 26, 1997). ... Activated (August 30, 1997). ... Released by Buccaneers (September 16, 1997). ... Re-signed by Buccaneers to practice squad (September 18, 1997). ... Activated (November 28, 1997). ... Released by Buccaneers (December 8, 1997). ... Re-signed by Buccaneers to practice squad (December 9, 1997).
PLAYING EXPERIENCE: Tampa Bay NFL , 1997. ... Games/Games started: 3/0.
SINGLE GAME HIGHS (regular season): Receptions—0; yards—0; and touchdown receptions—0.

HUNTINGTON, GREG   G   BEARS

PERSONAL: Born September 22, 1970, in Mountain Brook, Ala. ... 6-3/308. ... Full name: Gregory Gerard Huntington.
HIGH SCHOOL: Moeller (Cincinnati).
COLLEGE: Penn State.
TRANSACTIONS/CAREER NOTES: Selected by Washington Redskins in fifth round (128th pick overall) of 1993 NFL draft. ... Signed by Redskins for 1993 season. ... Released by Redskins (August 28, 1994). ... Signed by Jacksonville Jaguars (December 15, 1994). ... Released by Jaguars (November 21, 1995). ... Re-signed by Jaguars (December 26, 1995). ... Released by Jaguars (August 25, 1996). ... Re-signed by Jaguars (October 1, 1996). ... Released by Jaguars (October 15, 1996). ... Re-signed by Jaguars (November 19, 1996). ... Granted free agency (February 14, 1997). ... Re-signed by Jaguars (May 9, 1997). ... Released by Jaguars (August 24, 1997). ... Signed by Chicago Bears (October 28, 1997).
PLAYING EXPERIENCE: Washington NFL, 1993; Jacksonville NFL, 1995 and 1996; Chicago NFL, 1997. ... Games/Games started: 1993 (9/0), 1995 (4/0), 1996 (2/0), 1997 (1/0). Total: 16/0.
CHAMPIONSHIP GAME EXPERIENCE: Member of Jaguars for AFC championship game (1996 season); inactive.

H

HUNTLEY, RICHARD   RB   STEELERS

PERSONAL: Born September 18, 1972, in Monroe, N.C. ... 5-11/224.
HIGH SCHOOL: Monroe (N.C.).
COLLEGE: Winston-Salem (N.C.) State.
TRANSACTIONS/CAREER NOTES: Selected by Atlanta Falcons in fourth round (117th pick overall) of 1996 NFL draft. ... Signed by Falcons for 1996 season. ... Released by Falcons (August 18, 1997). ... Signed by Pittsburgh Steelers (February 13, 1998).
PLAYING EXPERIENCE: Atlanta NFL, 1996. ... Games/Games started: 1/0.
PRO STATISTICS: 1996—Rushed twice for eight yards and caught one pass for 14 yards.
SINGLE GAME HIGHS (regular season): Attempts—2 (December 22, 1996, vs. Jacksonville); yards—8 (December 22, 1996, vs. Jacksonville); and rushing touchdowns—0.

HUSTED, MICHAEL   K   BUCCANEERS

PERSONAL: Born June 16, 1970, in El Paso, Texas. ... 6-0/190. ... Full name: Michael James Husted.
HIGH SCHOOL: Hampton (Va.).
COLLEGE: Virginia (degree in sociology).
TRANSACTIONS/CAREER NOTES: Signed as non-drafted free agent by Tampa Bay Buccaneers (May 3, 1993). ... Granted free agency (February 16, 1996). ... Tendered offer sheet by San Francisco 49ers (February 21, 1996). ... Offer matched by Buccaneers (February 28, 1996).
PRO STATISTICS: 1994—Punted twice for 53 yards.

					KICKING				
Year Team	G	GS	XPM	XPA	FGM	FGA	Lg.	50+	Pts.
1993—Tampa Bay NFL	16	0	27	27	16	22	57	3-5	75
1994—Tampa Bay NFL	16	0	20	20	23	35	53	1-5	89
1995—Tampa Bay NFL	16	0	25	25	19	26	53	3-3	82
1996—Tampa Bay NFL	16	0	18	19	25	32	50	1-3	93
1997—Tampa Bay NFL	16	0	32	35	13	17	54	1-3	71
Pro totals (5 years)	80	0	122	126	96	132	57	9-19	410

HUTSON, TONY   G/OT   COWBOYS

PERSONAL: Born March 13, 1974, in Houston. ... 6-3/313.
HIGH SCHOOL: MacArthur (Houston).
JUNIOR COLLEGE: Kilgore (Texas) Junior College.
COLLEGE: Northeastern Oklahoma State.
TRANSACTIONS/CAREER NOTES: Signed as non-drafted free agent by Dallas Cowboys (April 23, 1996). ... Released by Cowboys (August 25, 1996). ... Re-signed by Cowboys to practice squad (August 27, 1996). ... Activated (January 5, 1997). ... Released by Cowboys (August 24, 1997). ... Re-signed by Cowboys to practice squad (August 26, 1997). ... Activated (November 4, 1997).
PLAYING EXPERIENCE: Dallas NFL, 1997. ... Games/Games started: 5/1.

HUTTON, TOM   P   EAGLES

PERSONAL: Born July 8, 1972, in Memphis. ... 6-1/193. ... Full name: William Thomas Hutton.
HIGH SCHOOL: Memphis University.
COLLEGE: Tennessee.
TRANSACTIONS/CAREER NOTES: Signed as non-drafted free agent by Philadelphia Eagles (April 26, 1995).
PRO STATISTICS: 1995—Fumbled once for minus 19 yards. 1996—Recovered one fumble. 1997—Rushed once for no yards, fumbled once and recovered one fumble for minus one yard.

					PUNTING			
Year Team	G	GS	No.	Yds.	Avg.	Net avg.	In. 20	Blk.
1995—Philadelphia NFL	16	0	85	3682	43.3	3.3	20	1
1996—Philadelphia NFL	16	0	73	3107	42.6	35.1	17	1
1997—Philadelphia NFL	16	0	87	3660	42.1	34.6	19	1
Pro totals (3 years)	48	0	245	10449	42.6	23.9	56	3

INGRAM, STEPHEN   OT/G   BUCCANEERS

PERSONAL: Born May 8, 1971, in Seat Pleasant, Md. ... 6-4/320.
HIGH SCHOOL: DuVal (Seat Pleasant, Md.).
COLLEGE: Maryland.
TRANSACTIONS/CAREER NOTES: Selected by Tampa Bay Buccaneers in seventh round (215th pick overall) of 1995 NFL draft. ... Signed by Buccaneers (May 3, 1995). ... Released by Buccaneers (August 22, 1996). ... Re-signed by Buccaneers (November 13, 1996). ... On injured reserve with leg injury (August 17, 1997-entire season). ... Granted free agency (February 13, 1998).
PLAYING EXPERIENCE: Tampa Bay NFL, 1995. ... Games/Games played: 2/0.

IRVIN, KEN   CB   BILLS

PERSONAL: Born July 11, 1972, in Lindale, Ga. ... 5-10/186. ... Full name: Kenneth Irvin.
HIGH SCHOOL: Pepperell (Lindale, Ga.).
COLLEGE: Memphis.
TRANSACTIONS/CAREER NOTES: Selected by Buffalo Bills in fourth round (109th pick overall) of 1995 NFL draft. ... Signed by Bills (July 10, 1995). ... Granted free agency (February 13, 1998). ... Re-signed by Bills (April 17, 1998).
PLAYING EXPERIENCE: Buffalo NFL, 1995-1997. ... Games/Games started: 1995 (16/3), 1996 (16/1), 1997 (16/0). Total: 48/4.
PRO STATISTICS: 1995—Returned one kickoff for 12 yards. 1996—Credited with two sacks and recovered one fumble. 1997—Intercepted two passes for 28 yards.

IRVIN, MICHAEL　　　　WR　　　　COWBOYS

PERSONAL: Born March 5, 1966, in Fort Lauderdale. ... 6-2/207. ... Full name: Michael Jerome Irvin.
HIGH SCHOOL: St. Thomas Aquinas (Fort Lauderdale).
COLLEGE: Miami, Fla. (degree in business management, 1988).
TRANSACTIONS/CAREER NOTES: Selected by Dallas Cowboys in first round (11th pick overall) of 1988 NFL draft. ... Signed by Cowboys (July 9, 1988). ... On injured reserve with knee injury (October 17, 1989-remainder of season). ... On injured reserve with knee injury (September 4-October 7, 1990). ... Granted free agency (February 1, 1992). ... Re-signed by Cowboys (September 3, 1992). ... Designated by Cowboys as transition player (February 25, 1993). ... On suspended list for violating league substance abuse policy (August 26-October 1, 1996).
CHAMPIONSHIP GAME EXPERIENCE: Played in NFC championship game (1992-1995 seasons). ... Member of Super Bowl championship team (1992, 1993 and 1995 seasons).
HONORS: Named wide receiver on THE SPORTING NEWS college All-America second team (1986). ... Named wide receiver on THE SPORTING NEWS NFL All-Pro team (1991). ... Played in Pro Bowl (1991-1995 seasons). ... Named Outstanding Player of Pro Bowl (1991 season).
RECORDS: Holds NFL single-season record for most games with 100 or more yards receiving—11 (1995). ... Shares NFL record for most consecutive games with 100 or more yards receiving—7 (1995).
PRO STATISTICS: 1988—Rushed once for two yards. 1989—Rushed once for six yards and recovered one fumble. 1991—Recovered one fumble. 1992—Rushed once for minus nine yards and recovered one fumble. 1993—Rushed twice for six yards.
SINGLE GAME HIGHS (regular season): Receptions—12 (October 27, 1996, vs. Miami); yards—210 (September 20, 1992, vs. Arizona); and touchdown receptions—3 (September 20, 1992, vs. Arizona).
STATISTICAL PLATEAUS: 100-yard receiving games: 1988 (1), 1989 (1), 1991 (7), 1992 (6), 1993 (5), 1994 (5), 1995 (11), 1996 (3), 1997 (4). Total: 43.
MISCELLANEOUS: Holds Dallas Cowboys all-time records for most yards receiving (10,680) and most receptions (666).

| | | | RECEIVING | | | | TOTALS | | | |
Year Team	G	GS	No.	Yds.	Avg.	TD	TD	2pt.	Pts.	Fum.
1988—Dallas NFL	14	10	32	654	‡20.4	5	5	...	30	0
1989—Dallas NFL	6	6	26	378	14.5	2	2	...	12	0
1990—Dallas NFL	12	7	20	413	20.7	5	5	...	30	0
1991—Dallas NFL	16	16	‡93	*1523	16.4	8	8	...	48	3
1992—Dallas NFL	16	14	78	1396	17.9	7	7	...	42	1
1993—Dallas NFL	16	16	88	1330	15.1	7	7	...	42	0
1994—Dallas NFL	16	16	79	1241	15.7	6	6	0	36	0
1995—Dallas NFL	16	16	111	1603	14.4	10	10	0	60	1
1996—Dallas NFL	11	11	64	962	15.0	2	2	1	14	1
1997—Dallas NFL	16	16	75	1180	15.7	9	9	0	54	0
Pro totals (10 years)	139	128	666	10680	16.0	61	61	1	368	6

IRVING, TERRY　　　　LB　　　　CARDINALS

PERSONAL: Born July 3, 1971, in Galveston, Texas. ... 6-2/236. ... Full name: Terry Duane Irving.
HIGH SCHOOL: Ball (Galveston, Texas).
COLLEGE: McNeese State.
TRANSACTIONS/CAREER NOTES: Selected by Arizona Cardinals in fourth round (115th pick overall) of 1994 NFL draft. ... Signed by Cardinals (July 15, 1994). ... Granted unconditional free agency (February 13, 1998). ... Re-signed by Cardinals (February 25, 1998).
PLAYING EXPERIENCE: Arizona NFL, 1994-1997. ... Games/Games started: 1994 (16/0), 1995 (16/8), 1996 (16/0), 1997 (16/6). Total: 64/14.
PRO STATISTICS: 1994—Recovered one fumble. 1995—Recovered three fumbles for minus two yards. 1996—Recovered one fumble for five yards. 1997—Recovered one fumble.

IRWIN, HEATH　　　　G　　　　PATRIOTS

PERSONAL: Born June 27, 1973, in Boulder, Colo. ... 6-4/300. ... Nephew of Hale Irwin, professional golfer.
HIGH SCHOOL: Boulder (Colo.).
COLLEGE: Colorado.
TRANSACTIONS/CAREER NOTES: Selected by New England Patriots in fourth round (101st pick overall) of 1996 NFL draft. ... Signed by Patriots (July 17, 1996). ... Inactive for 16 games (1996).
PLAYING EXPERIENCE: New England NFL, 1997. ... Games/Games started: 15/1.
CHAMPIONSHIP GAME EXPERIENCE: Member of Patriots for AFC championship game (1996 season); inactive. ... Member of Patriots for Super Bowl XXXI (1996 season); inactive.

ISAIA, SALE　　　　OL　　　　RAVENS

PERSONAL: Born June 13, 1972, in Honolulu. ... 6-5/315. ... Full name: Sale Isaia Jr. ... Cousin of Junior Seau, linebacker, San Diego Chargers. ... Name pronounced SAH-lay ah-SIGH-eh.
HIGH SCHOOL: Oceanside (Calif.).
COLLEGE: UCLA.
TRANSACTIONS/CAREER NOTES: Signed as non-drafted free agent by Cleveland Browns (April 2, 1995). ... On injured reserve with ankle injury (August 27, 1995-entire season). ... Browns franchise moved to Baltimore and renamed Ravens for 1996 season (March 11, 1996). ... On injured reserve with knee injury (August 18, 1997-entire season). ... Granted free agency (February 13, 1998). ... Re-signed by Ravens (April 13, 1998).
PLAYING EXPERIENCE: Baltimore NFL, 1996. ... Games/Games started: 9/0.
PRO STATISTICS: 1996—Returned one kickoff for two yards, fumbled once and recovered one fumble.

ISMAIL, QADRY　　　　　　　WR/KR　　　　　　　SAINTS

PERSONAL: Born November 8, 1970, in Newark, N.J. ... 6-0/196. ... Full name: Qadry Rahmadan Ismail. ... Brother of Rocket Ismail, wide receiver/kick returner with Toronto Argonauts (1991-92) of CFL and Los Angeles Raiders (1993-94), Oakland Raiders (1995) and Carolina Panthers (1996-97).. ... Name pronounced KAH-dree ISS-mile.
HIGH SCHOOL: Elmer L. Meyers (Wilkes-Barre, Pa.).
COLLEGE: Syracuse.
TRANSACTIONS/CAREER NOTES: Selected by Minnesota Vikings in second round (52nd pick overall) of 1993 NFL draft. ... Signed by Vikings (July 20, 1993). ... Granted unconditional free agency (February 14, 1997). ... Signed by Green Bay Packers (June 2, 1997). ... Traded by Packers to Miami Dolphins for a conditional draft pick (August 24, 1997). ... Granted unconditional free agency (February 13, 1998). ... Signed by New Orleans Saints (March 24, 1998).
HONORS: Named kick returner on THE SPORTING NEWS college All-America second team (1991).
PRO STATISTICS: 1993—Rushed three times for 14 yards. 1994—Recovered one fumble. 1995—Rushed once for seven yards. 1996—Recovered one fumble.
SINGLE GAME HIGHS (regular season): Receptions—7 (October 30, 1995, vs. Chicago); yards—142 (November 19, 1995, vs. New Orleans); an dtouchdown receptions—1 (December 1, 1996, vs. Arizona).
STATISTICAL PLATEAUS: 100-yard receiving games: 1994 (2), 1995 (1). Total: 3.

			RECEIVING				KICKOFF RETURNS			TOTALS			
Year Team	G	GS	No.	Yds.	Avg.	TD	No.	Yds.	Avg.	TD	TD	2pt.	Pts.	Fum.
1993—Minnesota NFL	15	3	19	212	11.2	1	‡42	902	21.5	0	1	...	6	1
1994—Minnesota NFL	16	3	45	696	15.5	5	35	807	23.1	0	5	0	30	2
1995—Minnesota NFL	16	2	32	597	18.7	3	42	1037	24.7	0	3	0	18	3
1996—Minnesota NFL	16	2	22	351	16.0	3	28	527	18.8	0	3	0	18	2
1997—Miami NFL	3	0	0	0	...	0	8	166	20.8	0	0	0	0	0
Pro totals (5 years)	66	10	118	1856	15.7	12	155	3439	22.2	0	12	0	72	8

ISMAIL, ROCKET　　　　　　　WR/KR　　　　　　　PANTHERS

PERSONAL: Born November 18, 1969, in Elizabeth, N.J. ... 5-11/175. ... Full name: Raghib Ramadian Ismail. ... Brother of Qadry Ismail, wide receiver/kick returner, New Orleans Saints. ... Name pronounced rahg-HEEB ISS-mile.
HIGH SCHOOL: Elmer L. Meyers (Wilkes-Barre, Pa.).
COLLEGE: Notre Dame (degree in sociology, 1994).
TRANSACTIONS/CAREER NOTES: Signed after junior season by Toronto Argonauts of CFL (April 21, 1991). ... Selected by Los Angeles Raiders in fourth round (100th pick overall) of 1991 NFL draft. ... Granted free agency from Argonauts (February 15, 1993). ... Signed by Raiders (August 30, 1993). ... Raiders franchise moved to Oakland (July 21, 1995). ... Granted free agency (February 16, 1996). ... Traded by Raiders to Carolina Panthers for undisclosed draft pick (August 25, 1996). ... Granted unconditional free agency (February 14, 1997). ... Re-signed by Panthers (February 26, 1997). ... Granted unconditional free agency (February 13, 1998). ... Re-signed by Panthers (June 2, 1998).
CHAMPIONSHIP GAME EXPERIENCE: Played in Grey Cup, CFL championship game (1991). ... Played in NFC championship game (1996 season).
HONORS: Named kick returner on THE SPORTING NEWS college All-America first team (1989). ... Named College Football Player of the Year by THE SPORTING NEWS (1990). ... Named wide receiver on THE SPORTING NEWS college All-America first team (1990).
PRO STATISTICS: CFL: 1991—Returned two unsuccessful field-goals for 90 yards, attempted one pass without a completion, fumbled eight times and recovered two fumbles. 1992—Fumbled seven times and recovered two fumbles. NFL: 1993—Recovered one fumble. 1995—Fumbled four times and recovered one fumble.
SINGLE GAME HIGHS (regular season): Receptions—6 (November 30, 1997, vs. New Orleans); yards—125 (October 22, 1995, vs. Indianapolis); and touchdown receptions—2 (October 22, 1995, vs. Indianapolis).
STATISTICAL PLATEAUS: 100-yard receiving games: 1995 (1), 1996 (1), 1997 (1). Total: 3.

			RUSHING				RECEIVING				PUNT RETURNS				KICKOFF RETURNS				TOTALS		
Year Team	G	GS	Att.	Yds.	Avg.	TD	No.	Yds.	Avg.	TD	No.	Yds.	Avg.	TD	No.	Yds.	Avg.	TD	TD	2pt.	Pts.
1991—Toronto CFL	17	...	36	271	7.5	3	64	1300	20.3	9	48	602	12.5	1	31	786	25.4	0	13	...	80
1992—Toronto CFL	16	...	34	154	4.5	3	36	651	18.1	4	59	614	10.4	1	43 ^ 1139	26.5	0	8	...	48
1993—L.A. Raiders NFL.	13	0	4	-5	-1.3	0	26	353	13.6	1	0	0	...	0	25	605	§24.2	0	1	...	6
1994—L.A. Raiders NFL.	16	0	4	31	7.8	0	34	513	15.1	5	0	0	...	0	43	923	21.5	0	5	0	30
1995—Oakland NFL	16	16	6	29	4.8	0	28	491	17.5	3	0	0	...	0	36	706	19.6	0	3	0	18
1996—Carolina NFL	13	5	8	80	10.0	1	12	214	17.8	0	0	0	...	0	5	100	20.0	0	1	0	6
1997—Carolina NFL	13	2	4	32	8.0	0	36	419	11.6	2	0	0	...	0	0	0	...	0	2	0	12
CFL totals (2 years)	33	...	70	425	6.1	6	100	1951	19.5	13	107	1216	11.4	2	74	1925	26.0	0	21	0	128
NFL totals (5 years)	71	23	26	167	6.4	1	136	1990	14.6	11	0	0	...	0	109	2334	21.4	0	12	0	72
Pro totals (7 years)	104	...	96	592	6.2	7	236	3941	16.7	24	107	1216	11.4	2	183	4259	23.3	0	33	0	200

ISRAEL, STEVE　　　　　　　CB　　　　　　　PATRIOTS

PERSONAL: Born March 16, 1969, in Lawnside, N.J. ... 5-11/194. ... Full name: Steven Douglas Israel.
HIGH SCHOOL: Haddon Heights (N.J.).
COLLEGE: Pittsburgh (degree in economics).
TRANSACTIONS/CAREER NOTES: Selected by Los Angeles Rams in second round (30th pick overall) of 1992 NFL draft. ... Signed by Rams (August 23, 1992). ... Granted roster exemption (August 25-September 4, 1992). ... Claimed on waivers by Green Bay Packers (August 7, 1995). ... Released by Packers (August 25, 1995). ... Signed by San Francisco 49ers (October 3, 1995). ... Granted unconditional free agency (February 16, 1996). ... Re-signed by 49ers (March 1, 1996). ... Granted unconditional free agency (February 14, 1997). ... Signed by New England Patriots (March 24, 1997).
PLAYING EXPERIENCE: Los Angeles Rams NFL, 1992-1994; San Francisco, NFL, 1995 and 1996; New England NFL, 1997. ... Games/Games started: 1992 (16/1), 1993 (16/12), 1994 (10/2), 1995 (8/0), 1996 (14/2), 1997 (5/0), Total: 69/17.
PRO STATISTICS: 1992—Returned one kickoff for minus three yards and recovered one fumble. 1993—Returned five kickoffs for 92 yards. 1996—Intercepted one pass for three yards and recovered one fumble. 1997—Credited with one sack.

IZZO, LARRY LB DOLPHINS

PERSONAL: Born September 26, 1974, in Fort Belvoir, Va. ... 5-10/228. ... Full name: Lawrence Alexander Izzo.
HIGH SCHOOL: McCullough (Houston).
COLLEGE: Rice.
TRANSACTIONS/CAREER NOTES: Signed as non-drafted free agent by Miami Dolphins (April 25, 1996). ... On injured reserve with foot injury (August 18, 1997-entire season).
PLAYING EXPERIENCE: Miami NFL, 1996. ... Games/Games started: 16/0.
PRO STATISTICS: 1996—Rushed once for 26 yards.

JACKE, CHRIS K

PERSONAL: Born March 12, 1966, in Richmond, Va. ... 6-0/205. ... Full name: Christopher Lee Jacke. ... Name pronounced JACK-ee.
HIGH SCHOOL: J.J. Pearce (Richardson, Texas).
COLLEGE: Texas-El Paso (degree in business, 1989).
TRANSACTIONS/CAREER NOTES: Selected by Green Bay Packers in sixth round (142nd pick overall) of 1989 NFL draft. ... Signed by Packers (July 28, 1989). ... Granted free agency (February 1, 1991). ... Re-signed by Packers (August 26, 1991). ... Granted unconditional free agency (February 14, 1997). ... Signed by Pittsburgh Steelers (July 9, 1997). ... Released by Steelers (October 14, 1997). ... Signed by Washington Redskins (December 16, 1997). ... Released by Redskins (February 3, 1998).
CHAMPIONSHIP GAME EXPERIENCE: Played in NFC championship game (1995 of 1996 seasons). ... Member of Super Bowl championship team (1996 season).

Year Team	G	GS	KICKING						
			XPM	XPA	FGM	FGA	Lg.	50+	Pts.
1989—Green Bay NFL	16	0	42	42	22	28	52	1-3	108
1990—Green Bay NFL	16	0	28	29	23	30	53	2-4	97
1991—Green Bay NFL	16	0	31	31	18	24	53	1-1	85
1992—Green Bay NFL	16	0	30	30	22	29	53	2-3	96
1993—Green Bay NFL	16	0	35	35	31	37	54	6-7	128
1994—Green Bay NFL	16	0	41	43	19	26	50	1-3	98
1995—Green Bay NFL	14	0	43	43	17	23	51	3-4	94
1996—Green Bay NFL	16	0	*51	*53	21	27	53	1-1	114
1997—Washington NFL	1	0	5	5	0	0	0	0-0	5
Pro totals (9 years)	127	0	306	311	173	224	54	17-26	825

JACKSON, CALVIN S DOLPHINS

PERSONAL: Born October 28, 1972, in Miami. ... 5-9/185. ... Full name: Calvin Bernard Jackson.
HIGH SCHOOL: Dillard (Fort Lauderdale).
COLLEGE: Auburn.
TRANSACTIONS/CAREER NOTES: Signed as non-drafted free agent by Miami Dolphins (July 21, 1994). ... Released by Dolphins (August 22, 1994). ... Re-signed by Dolphins to practice squad (August 29, 1994). ... Activated (September 17, 1994). ... Released by Dolphins (October 26, 1994). ... Re-signed by Dolphins to practice squad (October 27, 1994). ... On practice squad injured reserve with knee injury (December 24, 1994-remainder of season). ... Released by Dolphins (August 27, 1995). ... Re-signed by Dolphins to practice squad (August 30, 1995). ... Activated (September 9, 1995).
PRO STATISTICS: 1996—Credited with one sack and fumbled once. 1997—Credited with $^{1}/_{2}$ sack and recovered one fumble.

Year Team	G	GS	INTERCEPTIONS			
			No.	Yds.	Avg.	TD
1994—Miami NFL	2	0	0	0	...	0
1995—Miami NFL	9	1	1	23	23.0	0
1996—Miami NFL	16	15	3	82	27.3	1
1997—Miami NFL	16	16	0	0	...	0
Pro totals (4 years)	43	32	4	105	26.3	1

JACKSON, GRADY DE RAIDERS

PERSONAL: Born January 21, 1973, in Greensboro, Ala. ... 6-2/320.
HIGH SCHOOL: Greensboro (Ala.).
JUNIOR COLLEGE: Hinds Community College (Miss.).
COLLEGE: Knoxville.
TRANSACTIONS/CAREER NOTES: Selected by Oakland Raiders in sixth round (193rd pick overall) of 1997 NFL draft.
PLAYING EXPERIENCE: Oakland NFL, 1997. ... Games/Games started: 5/0.

JACKSON, GREG S CHARGERS

PERSONAL: Born August 20, 1966, in Hialeah, Fla. ... 6-1/217. ... Full name: Greg Allen Jackson.
HIGH SCHOOL: American (Miami).
COLLEGE: Louisiana State.
TRANSACTIONS/CAREER NOTES: Selected by New York Giants in third round (78th pick overall) of 1989 NFL draft. ... Signed by Giants (July 24, 1989). ... Granted free agency (February 1, 1992). ... Re-signed by Giants (August 3, 1992). ... Granted unconditional free agency (February 17, 1994). ... Signed by Philadelphia Eagles (June 30, 1994). ... Granted unconditional free agency (February 16, 1996). ... Signed by New Orleans Saints (June 18, 1996). ... Granted unconditional free agency (February 14, 1997). ... Signed by San Diego Chargers (June 13, 1997). ... On injured reserve with leg injury (December 1, 1997-remainder of season). ... Granted unconditional free agency (February 13, 1998). ... Re-signed by Chargers (April 28, 1998).

CHAMPIONSHIP GAME EXPERIENCE: Played in NFC championship game (1990 season). ... Member of Super Bowl championship team (1990 season).

PRO STATISTICS: 1989—Recovered one fumble. 1990—Credited with four sacks. 1991—Fumbled once. 1992—Recovered one fumble. 1993—Recovered three fumbles for three yards. 1995—Recovered three fumbles for 45 yards and one touchdown. 1996—Fumbled once. 1997—Returned one punt for no yards and recovered one fumble for 41 yards and a touchdown.

			INTERCEPTIONS			
Year Team	G	GS	No.	Yds.	Avg.	TD
1989—New York Giants NFL	16	1	0	0	...	0
1990—New York Giants NFL	14	14	5	8	1.6	0
1991—New York Giants NFL	13	12	1	3	3.0	0
1992—New York Giants NFL	16	16	4	71	17.8	0
1993—New York Giants NFL	16	16	4	32	8.0	0
1994—Philadelphia NFL	16	16	6	86	14.3	1
1995—Philadelphia NFL	16	16	1	18	18.0	0
1996—New Orleans NFL	16	15	3	24	8.0	0
1997—San Diego NFL	13	0	2	37	18.5	1
Pro totals (9 years)	136	106	26	279	10.7	2

JACKSON, JOHN — OT — CHARGERS

PERSONAL: Born January 4, 1965, in Camp Kwe, Okinawa, Japan. ... 6-6/297.
HIGH SCHOOL: Woodward (Cincinnati).
COLLEGE: Eastern Kentucky.
TRANSACTIONS/CAREER NOTES: Selected by Pittsburgh Steelers in 10th round (252nd pick overall) of 1988 NFL draft. ... Signed by Steelers (May 17, 1988). ... Granted unconditional free agency (February 13, 1998). ... Signed by San Diego Chargers (February 18, 1998).
PLAYING EXPERIENCE: Pittsburgh NFL, 1988-1997. ... Games/Games started: 1988 (16/0), 1989 (14/12), 1990 (16/16), 1991 (16/16), 1992 (16/13), 1993 (16/16), 1994 (16/16), 1995 (11/9), 1996 (16/16), 1997 (16/16). Total: 153/130.
CHAMPIONSHIP GAME EXPERIENCE: Played in AFC championship game (1994, 1995 and 1997 seasons). ... Played in Super Bowl XXX (1995 season).
PRO STATISTICS: 1988—Returned one kickoff for 10 yards. 1991—Recovered one fumble. 1993—Recovered one fumble. 1994—Recovered two fumbles. 1996—Recovered one fumble.

JACKSON, MICHAEL — WR — RAVENS

PERSONAL: Born April 12, 1969, in Tangipahoa, La. ... 6-4/195. ... Full name: Michael Dwayne Jackson. ... Formerly known as Michael Dyson.
HIGH SCHOOL: Kentwood (La.).
COLLEGE: Southern Mississippi.
TRANSACTIONS/CAREER NOTES: Selected by Cleveland Browns in sixth round (141st pick overall) of 1991 NFL draft. ... Granted free agency (February 17, 1994). ... Re-signed by Browns (1994). ... Browns franchise moved to Baltimore and renamed Ravens for 1996 season (March 11, 1996). ... Granted unconditional free agency (February 14, 1997). ... Re-signed by Ravens (February 28, 1997).
PRO STATISTICS: 1992—Rushed once for 21 yards. 1993—Attempted one pass with one completion for 25 yards, rushed once for one yard and recovered one fumble. 1994—Attempted two passes without a completion. 1995—Attempted one pass with an interception and recovered one fumble. 1996—Recovered one fumble.
SINGLE GAME HIGHS (regular season): Receptions—9 (November 24, 1996, vs. Jacksonville); yards—157 (September 3, 1995, vs. New England); and touchdown receptions—3 (December 22, 1996, vs. Houston).
STATISTICAL PLATEAUS: 100-yard receiving games: 1993 (2), 1995 (2), 1996 (4), 1997 (1). Total: 9.
MISCELLANEOUS: Holds Baltimore Ravens all-time records for most receiving yards (2,119) and most receptions (145). ... Shares Baltimore Ravens all-time records for most touchdown receptions (18) and touchdowns (18).

			RECEIVING				TOTALS			
Year Team	G	GS	No.	Yds.	Avg.	TD	TD	2pt.	Pts.	Fum.
1991—Cleveland NFL	16	7	17	268	15.8	2	0	...	0	0
1992—Cleveland NFL	16	14	47	755	16.1	7	7	...	42	0
1993—Cleveland NFL	15	11	41	756	18.4	8	8	...	48	1
1994—Cleveland NFL	9	7	21	304	14.5	2	2	0	12	0
1995—Cleveland NFL	13	10	44	714	16.2	9	9	0	54	1
1996—Baltimore NFL	16	16	76	1201	15.8	14	14	2	88	0
1997—Baltimore NFL	16	15	69	918	13.3	4	4	1	26	2
Pro totals (7 years)	101	80	315	4916	15.6	46	44	3	270	4

JACKSON, RAYMOND — DB — BILLS

PERSONAL: Born February 17, 1973, in Denver. ... 5-10/189. ... Full name: Raymond DeWayne Jackson.
HIGH SCHOOL: Montbello (Denver).
COLLEGE: Colorado State.
TRANSACTIONS/CAREER NOTES: Selected by Buffalo Bills in fifth round (156th pick overall) of 1996 NFL draft. ... Signed by Bills (June 25, 1996).
PRO STATISTICS: 1997—Returned one punt for no yards and fumbled once.

			INTERCEPTIONS			
Year Team	G	GS	No.	Yds.	Avg.	TD
1996—Buffalo NFL	12	0	1	0	0.0	0
1997—Buffalo NFL	9	0	0	0	...	0
Pro totals (2 years)	21	0	1	0	0.0	0

JACKSON, STEVE — CB — OILERS

PERSONAL: Born April 8, 1969, in Houston. ... 5-8/188. ... Full name: Steven Wayne Jackson.
HIGH SCHOOL: Klein Forest (Houston).
COLLEGE: Purdue.
TRANSACTIONS/CAREER NOTES: Selected by Houston Oilers in third round (71st pick overall) of 1991 NFL draft. ... Signed by Oilers (July 11, 1991). ... Granted free agency (February 17, 1994). ... Re-signed by Oilers (June 10, 1994). ... Granted unconditional free agency (February 14, 1997). ... Re-signed by Oilers (March 26, 1997). ... Oilers franchise moved to Tennessee for 1997 season.
PRO STATISTICS: 1991—Returned one punt for no yards and recovered two fumbles. 1996—Credited with a safety and recovered one fumble.

Year Team	G	GS	INTERCEPTIONS				SACKS	KICKOFF RETURNS				TOTALS			
			No.	Yds.	Avg.	TD	No.	No.	Yds.	Avg.	TD	TD	2pt.	Pts.	Fum.
1991—Houston NFL	15	2	0	0		0	1.0	0	0	...	0	0		0	0
1992—Houston NFL	16	1	3	18	6.0	0	1.0	0	0	...	0	0	...	0	0
1993—Houston NFL	16	12	5	54	10.8	▲1	0.0	0	0	...	0	1	...	6	0
1994—Houston NFL	11	0	1	0	0.0	0	1.0	14	285	20.4	0	0	0	0	0
1995—Houston NFL	10	1	2	0	0.0	0	1.0	0	0	...	0	0	0	0	0
1996—Houston NFL	16	1	0	0	...	0	2.0	0	0	...	0	0	0	2	0
1997—Tennessee NFL	12	6	0	0	...	0	1.0	0	0	...	0	0	0	0	0
Pro totals (7 years)	96	23	11	72	6.5	1	7.0	14	285	20.4	0	1	0	8	0

JACKSON, TYOKA — DE/DT — BUCCANEERS

PERSONAL: Born November 22, 1971, in Forestville, Md. ... 6-2/266.
HIGH SCHOOL: Bishop McNamara (Forestville, Md.).
COLLEGE: Penn State.
TRANSACTIONS/CAREER NOTES: Signed as non-drafted free agent by Atlanta Falcons (May 2, 1994). ... Released by Falcons (August 29, 1994). ... Re-signed by Falcons to practice squad (August 30, 1994). ... Signed by Miami Dolphins off Falcons practice squad (November 16, 1994). ... Released by Dolphins (August 27, 1995). ... Signed by Tampa Bay Buccaneers (December 27, 1995). ... Granted free agency (February 13, 1998).
PLAYING EXPERIENCE: Miami NFL, 1994; Tampa Bay NFL, 1996 and 1997. ... Games/Games started: 1994 (1/0), 1996 (13/2), 1997 (12/0). Total: 26/2.
PRO STATISTICS: 1994—Recovered one fumble. 1997—Credited with $2\frac{1}{2}$ sacks.

JACKSON, WILLIE — WR/KR — JAGUARS

PERSONAL: Born August 16, 1971, in Gainesville, Fla. ... 6-1/204. ... Full name: Willie Bernard Jackson.
HIGH SCHOOL: P.K. Yonge (Gainesville, Fla.).
COLLEGE: Florida.
TRANSACTIONS/CAREER NOTES: Selected by Dallas Cowboys in fourth round (109th pick overall) of 1994 NFL draft. ... Signed by Cowboys (July 16, 1994). ... Inactive for 16 games (1994). ... Selected by Jacksonville Jaguars from Cowboys in NFL expansion draft (February 15, 1995). ... Granted free agency (February 14, 1997). ... Re-signed by Jaguars (March 26, 1997).
CHAMPIONSHIP GAME EXPERIENCE: Member of Cowboys for NFC championship game (1994 season); inactive. ... Played in AFC championship game (1996 season).
PRO STATISTICS: 1995—Returned one punt for minus two yards and recovered one fumble. 1996—Rushed once for two yards. 1997—Rushed three times for 14 yards.
SINGLE GAME HIGHS (regular season): Receptions—8 (November 17, 1996, vs. Pittsburgh); yards—113 (December 10, 1995, vs. Indianapolis); and touchdown receptions—2 (December 10, 1995, vs. Indianapolis).
STATISTICAL PLATEAUS: 100-yard receiving games: 1995 (1), 1996 (1). Total: 2.
MISCELLANEOUS: Holds Jacksonville Jaguars all-time records for most receptions (86) and most touchdown receptions (8).

Year Team	G	GS	RECEIVING				KICKOFF RETURNS				TOTALS			
			No.	Yds.	Avg.	TD	No.	Yds.	Avg.	TD	TD	2pt.	Pts.	Fum.
1994—Dallas NFL			Did not play.											
1995—Jacksonville NFL	14	10	53	589	11.1	5	19	404	21.3	0	5	1	32	2
1996—Jacksonville NFL	16	2	33	486	14.7	3	7	149	21.3	0	3	1	20	0
1997—Jacksonville NFL	16	1	17	206	12.1	2	32	653	20.4	0	2	1	14	1
Pro totals (3 years)	46	13	103	1281	12.4	10	58	1206	20.8	0	10	3	66	3

JACOBS, TIM — CB — DOLPHINS

PERSONAL: Born April 5, 1970, in Washington, D.C. ... 5-10/187. ... Full name: Timothy Jacobs Jr.
HIGH SCHOOL: Eleanor Roosevelt (Greenbelt, Md.).
COLLEGE: Delaware.
TRANSACTIONS/CAREER NOTES: Signed as non-drafted free agent by Cleveland Browns (April 27, 1993). ... Released by Browns (August 30, 1993). ... Re-signed by Browns to practice squad (August 31, 1993). ... Activated (November 27, 1993). ... Granted unconditional free agency (February 16, 1996). ... Signed by Miami Dolphins (June 18, 1996). ... Granted unconditional free agency (February 14, 1997). ... Re-signed by Dolphins (April 21, 1997). ... Granted unconditional free agency (February 13, 1998). ... Re-signed by Dolphins (April 27, 1998).

Year Team	G	GS	INTERCEPTIONS			
			No.	Yds.	Avg.	TD
1993—Cleveland NFL	2	0	0	0	...	0
1994—Cleveland NFL	9	1	2	9	4.5	0
1995—Cleveland NFL	14	0	0	0	...	0
1996—Miami NFL	12	0	0	0	...	0
1997—Miami NFL	16	1	0	0	...	0
Pro totals (5 years)	53	2	2	9	4.5	0

JACOBY, MITCH   TE   RAMS

PERSONAL: Born December 8, 1973, in Port Washington, Wis. ... 6-4/260. ... Full name: Mitchel Ray Jacoby.
HIGH SCHOOL: Ozaukee (Fredonia, Wis.).
COLLEGE: Northern Illinois.
TRANSACTIONS/CAREER NOTES: Signed as non-drafted free agent by St. Louis Rams (April 29, 1997).
PLAYING EXPERIENCE: St. Louis NFL, 1997. ... Games/Games started: 14/2.
PRO STATISTICS: 1997—Caught two passes for 10 yards.
SINGLE GAME HIGHS (regular season): Receptions—1 (November 23, 1997, vs. Carolina); yards—10 (September 28, 1997. vs. Oakland); and touchdown receptions—0.

JACQUET, NATE   WR   COLTS   J

PERSONAL: Born September 2, 1975, in Duarte, Calif. ... 6-0/173. ... Full name: Nathaniel Jacquet.
HIGH SCHOOL: Duarte (Calif.).
JUNIOR COLLEGE: Mt. San Antonio College (Calif.).
COLLEGE: San Diego State.
TRANSACTIONS/CAREER NOTES: Selected by Indianapolis Colts in fifth round (150th pick overall) of 1997 NFL draft. ... Signed by Colts (June 26, 1997). ... Released by Colts (August 24, 1997). ... Re-signed by Colts to practice squad (August 25, 1997). ... Activated (November 4, 1997).
PRO STATISTICS: 1997—Recovered one fumble.
SINGLE GAME HIGHS (regular season): Receptions—0; yards—0; and touchdown receptions—0.

			PUNT RETURNS				KICKOFF RETURNS				TOTALS		
Year Team	G	GS	No.	Yds.	Avg.	TD	No.	Yds.	Avg.	TD	TD	2pt.	Pts.	Fum.
1997—Indianapolis NFL	5	0	13	96	7.4	0	8	156	19.5	0	0	0	0	1

JAEGER, JEFF   K   BEARS

PERSONAL: Born November 26, 1964, in Tacoma, Wash. ... 5-11/190. ... Full name: Jeff Todd Jaeger. ... Name pronounced JAY-ger.
HIGH SCHOOL: Meridian (Kent, Wash.).
COLLEGE: Washington.
TRANSACTIONS/CAREER NOTES: Selected by Cleveland Browns in third round (82nd pick overall) of 1987 NFL draft. ... Signed by Browns (July 26, 1987). ... Crossed picket line during players strike (October 14, 1987). ... On injured reserve with foot injury (August 26, 1988-entire season). ... Granted unconditional free agency (February 1, 1989). ... Signed by Los Angeles Raiders (March 20, 1989). ... Granted free agency (February 1, 1991). ... Re-signed by Raiders (July 13, 1991). ... Released by Raiders (August 30, 1993). ... Re-signed by Raiders (August 31, 1993). ... Raiders franchise moved to Oakland (July 21, 1995). ... Released by Raiders (August 25, 1996). ... Signed by Chicago Bears (September 17, 1996).
CHAMPIONSHIP GAME EXPERIENCE: Played in AFC championship game (1990 season).
HONORS: Played in Pro Bowl (1991 season).
PRO STATISTICS: 1987—Attempted one pass without a completion and recovered one fumble. 1997—Punted once for 18 yards.

			KICKING						
Year Team	G	GS	XPM	XPA	FGM	FGA	Lg.	50+	Pts.
1987—Cleveland NFL	10	0	33	33	14	22	48	0-1	75
1988—Cleveland NFL					Did not play.				
1989—Los Angeles Raiders NFL	16	0	34	34	23	34	50	1-2	103
1990—Los Angeles Raiders NFL	16	0	40	42	15	20	50	1-2	85
1991—Los Angeles Raiders NFL	16	0	29	30	29	34	53	2-4	116
1992—Los Angeles Raiders NFL	16	0	28	28	15	26	54	3-6	73
1993—Los Angeles Raiders NFL	16	0	27	29	*35	*44	53	4-7	*132
1994—Los Angeles Raiders NFL	16	0	31	31	22	28	51	2-2	97
1995—Oakland NFL	11	0	22	22	13	18	46	0-1	61
1996—Chicago NFL	13	0	23	23	19	23	49	0-0	80
1997—Chicago NFL	16	0	20	20	21	26	52	1-1	83
Pro totals (10 years)	146	0	287	292	206	275	54	14-26	905

JAMES, TORAN   LB   CHARGERS

PERSONAL: Born March 8, 1974, in Ahoskie, N.C. ... 6-3/247.
HIGH SCHOOL: Ahoskie (N.C.).
COLLEGE: North Carolina A&T.
TRANSACTIONS/CAREER NOTES: Selected by San Diego Chargers in seventh round (218th pick overall) of 1997 NFL draft.
PLAYING EXPERIENCE: San Diego NFL, 1997. ... Games/Games started: 14/0.

JAMES, TORY   CB   BRONCOS

PERSONAL: Born May 18, 1973, in New Orleans. ... 6-1/193. ... Full name: Tory Steven James.
HIGH SCHOOL: Archbishop Shaw (Marrero, La.).
COLLEGE: Louisiana State.
TRANSACTIONS/CAREER NOTES: Selected by Denver Broncos in second round (44th pick overall) of 1996 NFL draft. ... Signed by Broncos (July 22, 1996). ... On injured reserve with knee injury (August 18, 1997-entire season).
PRO STATISTICS: 1996—Recovered one fumble for 15 yards.

JAMISON, GEORGE   LB

PERSONAL: Born September 30, 1962, in Bridgeton, N.J. ... 6-1/235. ... Full name: George R. Jamison Jr. ... Cousin of Anthony (Bubba) Green, defensive tackle with Baltimore Colts (1981); and cousin of Larry Milbourne, major league infielder with six teams (1975-1984).
HIGH SCHOOL: Bridgeton (N.J.).
COLLEGE: Cincinnati.
TRANSACTIONS/CAREER NOTES: Selected by Philadelphia Stars in second round (34th pick overall) of 1984 USFL draft. ... Signed by Stars (January 17, 1984). ... On developmental squad for two games (February 24-March 2 and June 21, 1984-remainder of season). ... Selected by Detroit Lions in second round (47th pick overall) of 1984 NFL supplemental draft. ... Stars franchise moved to Baltimore (November 1, 1984). ... On developmental squad for one game (May 3-10, 1985). ... Granted free agency when USFL suspended operations (August 7, 1986). ... Signed by Lions (August 17, 1986). ... On injured reserve with Achilles' tendon injury (August 30, 1986-entire season). ... On injured reserve with knee injury (December 21, 1989-remainder of season). ... Granted free agency (February 1, 1992). ... Re-signed by Lions (July 23, 1992). ... Granted unconditional free agency (February 17, 1994). ... Signed by Kansas City Chiefs (July 15, 1994). ... On reserve/non-football injury list with foot injury (August 20-November 16, 1996). ... Signed by Lions (March 5, 1997). ... Granted unconditional free agency (February 13, 1998).
CHAMPIONSHIP GAME EXPERIENCE: Played in USFL championship game (1984 and 1985 seasons). ... Played in NFC championship game (1991 season).
PRO STATISTICS: 1987—Credited with one safety. 1988—Recovered three fumbles for four yards and one touchdown. 1990—Recovered one fumble. 1991—Fumbled once and recovered one fumble. 1992—Recovered one fumble. 1993—Returned one kickoff. 1994—Recovered three fumbles for 22 yards. 1995—Recovered two fumbles. 1997—Recovered one fumble.

| | | | | INTERCEPTIONS | | | SACKS |
Year Team	G	GS	No.	Yds.	Avg.	TD	No.
1984—Philadelphia USFL	15	...	0	0	...	0	4.0
1985—Baltimore USFL	17	...	1	16	16.0	0	5.0
1986—Detroit NFL				Did not play.			
1987—Detroit NFL	12	0	0	0	...	0	1.0
1988—Detroit NFL	16	11	3	56	18.7	1	5.5
1989—Detroit NFL	10	6	0	0	...	0	2.0
1990—Detroit NFL	14	7	0	0	...	0	2.0
1991—Detroit NFL	16	16	3	52	17.3	0	4.0
1992—Detroit NFL	16	16	0	0	...	0	2.0
1993—Detroit NFL	16	16	2	48	24.0	1	2.0
1994—Kansas City NFL	13	12	0	0	...	0	1.0
1995—Kansas City NFL	14	14	0	0	...	0	0.0
1996—Kansas City NFL	5	0	0	0	...	0	0.0
1997—Detroit NFL	16	10	0	0	...	0	1.0
USFL totals (2 years)	32	...	1	16	16.0	0	9.0
NFL totals (11 years)	148	108	8	156	19.5	2	20.5
Pro totals (13 years)	180	...	9	172	19.1	2	29.5

JASPER, EDWARD   DT   EAGLES

PERSONAL: Born January 18, 1973, in Troup, Texas. ... 6-2/295. ... Full name: Edward Vidal Jasper.
HIGH SCHOOL: Troup (Texas).
COLLEGE: Texas A&M.
TRANSACTIONS/CAREER NOTES: Selected by Philadelphia Eagles in sixth round (198th pick overall) of 1997 NFL draft. ... Signed by Eagles (July 16, 1997).
PLAYING EXPERIENCE: Philadelphia NFL, 1997. ... Games/Games started: 9/1.

JEFFCOAT, JIM   DE

PERSONAL: Born April 1, 1961, in Long Branch, N.J. ... 6-5/280. ... Full name: James Wilson Jeffcoat Jr.
HIGH SCHOOL: Regional (Matawan, N.J.).
COLLEGE: Arizona State (degree in communications, 1983).
TRANSACTIONS/CAREER NOTES: Selected by Arizona Wranglers in 1983 USFL territorial draft. ... Selected by Dallas Cowboys in first round (23rd pick overall) of 1983 NFL draft. ... Signed by Cowboys (May 24, 1983). ... Granted free agency (February 1, 1992). ... Re-signed by Cowboys (August 6, 1992). ... Granted unconditional free agency (February 17, 1995). ... Signed by Buffalo Bills (February 22, 1995). ... On injured reserve with knee injury (December 12, 1997-remainder of season). ... Released by Bills (February 17, 1998).
CHAMPIONSHIP GAME EXPERIENCE: Played in NFC championship game (1992-1994 seasons). ... Member of Super Bowl championship team (1992 and 1993 seasons).
PRO STATISTICS: 1984—Recovered fumble in end zone for a touchdown. 1985—Intercepted one pass for 65 yards and a touchdown and recovered two fumbles. 1986—Recovered two fumbles for eight yards. 1987—Intercepted one pass for 26 yards and recovered two fumbles for eight yards. 1989—Recovered three fumbles for 77 yards and one touchdown. 1990—Recovered one fumble for 28 yards.

Year Team	G	GS	SACKS
1983—Dallas NFL	16	0	2.0
1984—Dallas NFL	16	16	11.5
1985—Dallas NFL	16	16	12.0
1986—Dallas NFL	16	16	14.0
1987—Dallas NFL	12	12	5.0
1988—Dallas NFL	16	15	6.5
1989—Dallas NFL	16	16	11.5
1990—Dallas NFL	16	13	3.5
1991—Dallas NFL	16	16	4.0
1992—Dallas NFL	16	3	10.5
1993—Dallas NFL	16	3	6.0
1994—Dallas NFL	16	0	8.0
1995—Buffalo NFL	16	2	2.5
1996—Buffalo NFL	16	0	5.0
1997—Buffalo NFL	7	0	0.5
Pro totals (15 years)	227	128	102.5

JEFFERS, PATRICK   WR   BRONCOS

PERSONAL: Born February 2, 1973, in Fort Campbell, Ky. ... 6-3/218. ... Full name: Patrick Christopher Jeffers.
HIGH SCHOOL: Fort Worth (Texas) Country Day.
COLLEGE: Virginia.
TRANSACTIONS/CAREER NOTES: Selected by Denver Broncos in fifth round (159th pick overall) of 1996 NFL draft. ... Signed by Broncos (July 17, 1996).
PLAYING EXPERIENCE: Denver NFL, 1996 and 1997. ... Games/Games started: 1996 (4/0), 1997 (10/0). Total: 14/0.
CHAMPIONSHIP GAME EXPERIENCE: Played in AFC championship game (1997 season). ... Member of Super Bowl championship team (1997 season).
PRO STATISTICS: 1996—Returned one kickoff for 18 yards. 1997—Caught three passes for 24 yards.
SINGLE GAME HIGHS (regular season): Receptions—2 (December 7, 1997, vs. Pittsburgh); yards—19 (December 7, 1997, vs. Pittsburgh); and touchdown receptions—0.

JEFFERSON, GREG   DE   EAGLES

PERSONAL: Born August 31, 1971, in Orlando. ... 6-3/257.
HIGH SCHOOL: Bartow (Fla.).
COLLEGE: Central Florida.
TRANSACTIONS/CAREER NOTES: Selected by Philadelphia Eagles in third round (72nd pick overall) of 1995 NFL draft. ... Signed by Eagles (June 29, 1995). ... On injured reserve with knee injury (September 21, 1995-remainder of season). ... Granted free agency (February 13, 1998).
PLAYING EXPERIENCE: Philadelphia NFL, 1995-1997. ... Games/Games started: 1995 (3/0), 1996 (11/0), 1997 (12/11). Total: 26/11.
PRO STATISTICS: 1996—Credited with 2 1/2 sacks. 1997—Credited with three sacks and recovered one fumble.

JEFFERSON, SHAWN   WR   PATRIOTS

PERSONAL: Born February 22, 1969, in Jacksonville. ... 5-11/180. ... Full name: Vanchi LaShawn Jefferson.
HIGH SCHOOL: Raines (Jacksonville).
COLLEGE: Central Florida.
TRANSACTIONS/CAREER NOTES: Selected by Houston Oilers in ninth round (240th pick overall) of 1991 NFL draft. ... Signed by Oilers (July 15, 1991). ... Traded by Oilers with first-round pick (DE Chris Mims) in 1992 draft to San Diego Chargers for DL Lee Williams (August 22, 1991). ... Granted free agency (March 1, 1993). ... Re-signed by Chargers (July 15, 1993). ... Granted free agency (February 17, 1994). ... Re-signed by Chargers (May 2, 1994). ... Released by Chargers (February 29, 1996). ... Signed by New England Patriots (March 14, 1996).
CHAMPIONSHIP GAME EXPERIENCE: Played in AFC championship game (1994 and 1996 seasons). ... Played in Super Bowl XXIX (1994 season) and Super Bowl XXXI (1996 season).
SINGLE GAME HIGHS (regular season): Receptions—7 (December 22, 1997, vs. Miami); yards—120 (September 3, 1995, vs. Oakland); and touchdown receptions—2 (October 6, 1996, vs. Baltimore).
STATISTICAL PLATEAUS: 100-yard receiving games: 1995 (1), 1997 (1). Total: 2.

				RUSHING					RECEIVING				TOTALS		
Year Team	G	GS	Att.	Yds.	Avg.	TD	No.	Yds.	Avg.	TD	TD	2pt.	Pts.	Fum.
1991—San Diego NFL	16	3	1	27	27.0	0	12	125	10.4	1	1	...	6	0
1992—San Diego NFL	16	1	0	0	...	0	29	377	13.0	2	2	...	12	0
1993—San Diego NFL	16	4	5	53	10.6	0	30	391	13.0	2	2	...	12	0
1994—San Diego NFL	16	16	3	40	13.3	0	43	627	14.6	3	3	0	18	0
1995—San Diego NFL	16	15	2	1	0.5	0	48	621	12.9	2	2	0	12	0
1996—New England NFL	15	15	1	6	6.0	0	50	771	15.4	4	4	0	24	2
1997—New England NFL	16	14	0	0	...	0	54	841	15.6	2	2	0	12	2
Pro totals (7 years)	111	68	12	127	10.6	0	266	3753	14.1	16	16	0	96	4

JEFFRIES, GREG   CB   LIONS

PERSONAL: Born October 16, 1971, in High Point, N.C. ... 5-9/184. ... Full name: Greg Lemont Jeffries.
HIGH SCHOOL: T.W. Andrews (High Point, N.C.).
COLLEGE: Virginia.
TRANSACTIONS/CAREER NOTES: Selected by Detroit Lions in sixth round (147th pick overall) of 1993 NFL draft. ... Signed by Lions (July 17, 1993). ... Granted unconditional free agency (February 14, 1997). ... Re-signed by Lions (February 19, 1997).
PLAYING EXPERIENCE: Detroit NFL, 1993-1997. ... Games/Games started: 1993 (7/0), 1994 (16/1), 1995 (14/0), 1996 (16/4), 1997 (15/2). Total: 68/7.
PRO STATISTICS: 1993—Recovered one fumble. 1995—Credited with 1/2 sack. 1996—Intercepted one pass for no yards. 1997—Intercepted one pass for no yards and credited with one sack.

JELLS, DIETRICH   WR   PATRIOTS

PERSONAL: Born April 11, 1972, in Erie, Pa. ... 5-10/186. ... Name pronounced DEE-trick.
HIGH SCHOOL: Tech Memorial (Erie, Pa.).
COLLEGE: Pittsburgh.
TRANSACTIONS/CAREER NOTES: Selected by Kansas City Chiefs in sixth round (176th pick overall) of 1996 NFL draft. ... Signed by Chiefs (July 26, 1996). ... Claimed on waivers by New England Patriots (August 21, 1996).
PLAYING EXPERIENCE: New England NFL, 1996 and 1997. ... Games/Games started: 1996 (7/1), 1997 (11/0). Total: 18/1.
CHAMPIONSHIP GAME EXPERIENCE: Member of Patriots for AFC championship game (1996 season); inactive. ... Member of Patriots for Super Bowl XXXI (1996 season); inactive.
PRO STATISTICS: 1996—Caught one pass for five yards. 1997—Caught one pass for nine yards.
SINGLE GAME HIGHS (regular season): Receptions—1 (November 16, 1997, vs. Tampa Bay); yards—9 (November 16, 1997, vs. Tampa Bay); and touchdown receptions—0.

JENKINS, BILLY　　　　　　S　　　　　　RAMS

PERSONAL: Born July 8, 1974, in Albuquerque, N.M. ... 5-10/194. ... Full name: Billy Jenkins Jr.
HIGH SCHOOL: Albuquerque (N.M.).
COLLEGE: Howard.
TRANSACTIONS/CAREER NOTES: Signed as non-drafted free agent by St. Louis Rams (April 29, 1997).
PLAYING EXPERIENCE: St. Louis NFL, 1997. ... Games/Games started: 16/2.

JENKINS, DERON　　　　　　CB　　　　　　RAVENS

PERSONAL: Born November 14, 1973, in St. Louis. ... 5-11/190. ... Full name: DeRon Charles Jenkins.
HIGH SCHOOL: Ritenour (St. Louis).
COLLEGE: Tennessee.
TRANSACTIONS/CAREER NOTES: Selected by Baltimore Ravens in second round (55th pick overall) of 1996 NFL draft. ... Signed by Ravens (July 19, 1996).
PLAYING EXPERIENCE: Baltimore NFL, 1996 and 1997. ... Games/Games started: 1996 (15/2), 1997 (16/6). Total: 31/8.
PRO STATISTICS: 1996—Recovered one fumble. 1997—Intercepted one pass for 15 yards and recovered one fumble.

JENKINS, JAMES　　　　　　TE　　　　　　REDSKINS

PERSONAL: Born August 17, 1967, in Staten Island, N.Y. ... 6-2/249.
HIGH SCHOOL: Staten Island (N.Y.) Academy.
COLLEGE: Rutgers.
TRANSACTIONS/CAREER NOTES: Signed as non-drafted free agent by Washington Redskins (April 25, 1991). ... Released by Redskins (August 26, 1991). ... Re-signed by Redskins to practice squad (August 27, 1991). ... Activated (November 30, 1991). ... Released by Redskins (August 31, 1992). ... Re-signed by Redskins (September 1, 1992). ... On injured reserve with back injury (September-November 28, 1992). ... On injured reserve with shoulder injury (December 28, 1993-remainder of season). ... Granted free agency (February 17, 1995). ... Re-signed by Redskins (July 19, 1995). ... Granted unconditional free agency (February 14, 1997). ... Re-signed by Redskins (July 16, 1997).
CHAMPIONSHIP GAME EXPERIENCE: Played in NFC championship game (1991 season). ... Member of Super Bowl championship team (1991 season).
PRO STATISTICS: 1994—Returned one kickoff for four yards. 1995—Returned one kickoff for 12 yards and recovered one fumble. 1996—Recovered one fumble.
SINGLE GAME HIGHS (regular season): Receptions—2 (October 23, 1994, vs. Indianapolis); yards—20 (November 23, 1997, vs. New York Giants); and touchdown receptions—2 (October 23, 1994, vs. Indianapolis).

Year　Team	G	GS	RECEIVING				TOTALS			
			No.	Yds.	Avg.	TD	TD	2pt.	Pts.	Fum.
1991—Washington NFL	4	0	0	0	...	0	0	...	0	0
1992—Washington NFL	5	1	0	0	...	0	0	...	0	0
1993—Washington NFL	15	5	0	0	...	0	0	...	0	0
1994—Washington NFL	16	3	8	32	4.0	4	4	0	24	0
1995—Washington NFL	16	5	1	2	2.0	0	0	0	0	0
1996—Washington NFL	16	5	1	7	7.0	0	0	0	0	0
1997—Washington NFL	16	4	4	43	10.8	3	3	0	18	0
Pro totals (7 years)	88	23	14	84	6.0	7	7	0	42	0

JENKINS, KERRY　　　　　　OT　　　　　　JETS

PERSONAL: Born September 6, 1973 ... 6-5/310.
HIGH SCHOOL: Holt (Tuscaloosa, Ala.).
COLLEGE: Louisiana State, then Troy State.
TRANSACTIONS/CAREER NOTES: Signed as non-drafted free agent by Chicago Bears (April 25, 1997). ... Released by Bears (August 24, 1997). ... Re-signed by Bears to practice squad (August 27, 1997). ... Signed by New York Jets off Bears practice squad (December 3, 1997).
PLAYING EXPERIENCE: New York Jets NFL, 1997. ... Games/Games started: 2/2.

JENKINS, MIKE　　　　　　WR　　　　　　BENGALS

PERSONAL: Born August 25, 1974, in Portsmouth, Va. ... 6-3/191.
HIGH SCHOOL: I.C. Norcom (Portsmouth, Va.).
COLLEGE: Hampton.
TRANSACTIONS/CAREER NOTES: Signed as non-drafted free agent by Cincinnati Bengals (April 25, 1997). ... Released by Bengals (August 24, 1997). ... Re-signed by Bengals to practice squad (August 26, 1997). ... Activated (November 17, 1997).
PLAYING EXPERIENCE: Cincinnati NFL, 1997. ... Games/Games started: 3/0.
SINGLE GAME HIGHS (regular season): Receptions—0; yards—0; and touchdown receptions—0.

JENKINS, TREZELLE　　　　　　OT　　　　　　SAINTS

PERSONAL: Born March 13, 1973, in Chicago. ... 6-7/317. ... Full name: Trezelle Samuel Jenkins. ... Name pronounced TRUH-zell.
HIGH SCHOOL: Morgan Park (Chicago).
COLLEGE: Michigan.
TRANSACTIONS/CAREER NOTES: Selected after junior season by Kansas City Chiefs in first round (31st pick overall) of 1995 NFL draft. ... Signed by Chiefs (April 25, 1995). ... Released by Chiefs (September 16, 1997). ... Signed by New Orleans Saints (October 29, 1997). ... Granted free agency (February 13, 1998). ... Re-signed by Saints (April 19, 1998).
PLAYING EXPERIENCE: Kansas City NFL, 1995-1997. ... Games/Games started: 1995 (1/0), 1996 (6/0), 1997 (2/1). Total: 9/1.

JENNINGS, KEITH — TE

PERSONAL: Born May 19, 1966, in Summerville, S.C. ... 6-4/275. ... Full name: Keith O'Neal Jennings. ... Brother of Stanford Jennings, running back with Cincinnati Bengals (1984-1990), New Orleans Saints (1991) and Tampa Bay Buccaneers (1992); Cousin of Antonio Anderson, defensive lineman, Dallas Cowboys.
HIGH SCHOOL: Summerville (S.C.).
COLLEGE: Clemson.
TRANSACTIONS/CAREER NOTES: Selected by Dallas Cowboys in fifth round (113th pick overall) of 1989 NFL draft. ... Signed by Cowboys (August 2, 1989). ... Released by Cowboys (September 5, 1989). ... Re-signed by Cowboys to developmental squad (September 6, 1989). ... Activated (October 18, 1989). ... Released by Cowboys (September 3, 1990). ... Signed by WLAF (January 31, 1991). ... Selected by Montreal Machine in first round (first tight end) of 1991 WLAF positional draft. ... Released by Machine (April 16, 1991). ... Signed by Denver Broncos (July 3, 1991). ... Released by Broncos (August 26, 1991). ... Signed by Chicago Bears (October 9, 1991). ... Granted free agency (February 1, 1992). ... Re-signed by Bears (March 30, 1992). ... Granted free agency (February 17, 1994). ... Re-signed by Bears (May 6, 1994). ... Released by Bears (August 28, 1994). ... Re-signed by Bears (October 24, 1994). ... Granted unconditional free agency (February 17, 1995). ... Re-signed by Bears (March 6, 1995). ... On injured reserve with broken leg (November 5, 1996-remainder of season). ... Granted unconditional free agency (February 14, 1997). ... Re-signed by Bears (April 4, 1997). ... Released by Bears (December 9, 1997).
PRO STATISTICS: 1993—Recovered one fumble.
SINGLE GAME HIGHS (regular season): Receptions—4 (October 8, 1995, vs. Carolina); yards—63 (December 8, 1991, vs. Green Bay); and touchdown receptions—2 (December 24, 1995, vs. Philadelphia).

			RECEIVING					TOTALS			
Year Team	G	GS	No.	Yds.	Avg.	TD	TD	2pt.	Pts.	Fum.
1989—Dallas NFL	10	0	6	47	7.8	0	0	...	0	0
1990—				Did not play.						
1991—Montreal W.L.	4	4	4	54	13.5	1	1	...	6	0
—Chicago NFL	10	3	8	109	13.6	0	0	...	0	0
1992—Chicago NFL	16	14	23	264	11.5	1	1	...	6	0
1993—Chicago NFL	13	10	14	150	10.7	0	0	...	0	1
1994—Chicago NFL	9	1	11	75	6.8	3	3	0	18	0
1995—Chicago NFL	16	16	25	217	8.7	6	6	0	36	0
1996—Chicago NFL	6	5	6	56	9.3	0	0	0	0	0
1997—Chicago NFL	12	12	14	164	11.7	0	0	0	0	0
W.L. totals (1 year)	4	4	4	54	13.5	1	1	0	6	0
NFL totals (8 years)	92	61	107	1082	10.1	10	10	0	60	1
Pro totals (9 years)	96	65	111	1136	10.2	11	11	0	66	1

JERVEY, TRAVIS — RB — PACKERS

PERSONAL: Born May 5, 1972, in Isle of Palm, S.C. ... 6-0/222. ... Full name: Travis Richard Jervey.
HIGH SCHOOL: Wando (Mount Pleasant, S.C.).
COLLEGE: The Citadel.
TRANSACTIONS/CAREER NOTES: Selected by Green Bay Packers in fifth round (170th pick overall) of 1995 NFL draft. ... Signed by Packers (May 23, 1995). ... Granted free agency (February 13, 1998).
CHAMPIONSHIP GAME EXPERIENCE: Played in NFC championship game (1995-97 seasons). ... Member of Super Bowl championship team (1996 season). ... Played in Super Bowl XXXII (1997 season).
HONORS: Played in Pro Bowl (1997 season).
PRO STATISTICS: 1995—Recovered one fumble. 1996—Recovered one fumble.
SINGLE GAME HIGHS (regular season): Attempts—6 (October 6, 1996, vs. Chicago); yards—35 (December 22, 1996, vs. Minnesota); and rushing touchdowns—0.

			RUSHING				KICKOFF RETURNS				TOTALS			
Year Team	G	GS	Att.	Yds.	Avg.	TD	No.	Yds.	Avg.	TD	TD	2pt.	Pts.	Fum.
1995—Green Bay NFL	16	0	0	0	...	0	8	165	20.6	0	0	0	0	0
1996—Green Bay NFL	16	0	26	106	4.1	0	1	17	17.0	0	0	0	0	4
1997—Green Bay NFL	16	0	0	0	...	0	0	0	...	0	0	0	0	0
Pro totals (3 years)	48	0	26	106	4.1	0	9	182	20.2	0	0	0	0	4

JESSIE, BRANDON — TE — GIANTS

PERSONAL: Born May 20, 1974, in Detroit. ... 6-6/260. ... Son of Ron Jessie, wide receiver with Detroit Lions (1971-74) and Los Angeles Rams (1975-79).
HIGH SCHOOL: Edison (Huntington Beach, Calif.).
JUNIOR COLLEGE: Ventura (Calif.) Junior College.
COLLEGE: Utah.
TRANSACTIONS/CAREER NOTES: Signed as non-drafted free agent by New York Giants (March 17, 1997). ... On injured reserve with shoulder injury (August 11, 1997-entire season).

JETT, JAMES — WR — RAIDERS

PERSONAL: Born December 28, 1970, in Charlestown, W.Va. ... 5-10/165.
HIGH SCHOOL: Jefferson (Shenandoah Junction, W.Va.).
COLLEGE: West Virginia.
TRANSACTIONS/CAREER NOTES: Signed as non-drafted free agent by Los Angeles Raiders (May 1993). ... Raiders franchise moved to Oakland (July 21, 1995).
PRO STATISTICS: 1993—Rushed once for no yards. 1994—Recovered two fumbles for 15 yards. 1997—Recovered one fumble.
SINGLE GAME HIGHS (regular season): Receptions—7 (October 13, 1996, vs. Detroit); yards—148 (September 21, 1997, vs. New York Jets); and touchdown receptions—2 (October 26, 1997, vs. Seattle).
STATISTICAL PLATEAUS: 100-yard receiving games: 1993 (2), 1996 (1), 1997 (1). Total: 4.

Year Team			RECEIVING				TOTALS			
	G	GS	No.	Yds.	Avg.	TD	TD	2pt.	Pts.	Fum.
1993—Los Angeles Raiders NFL	16	1	33	771	*23.4	3	3	...	18	1
1994—Los Angeles Raiders NFL	16	1	15	253	16.9	0	0	0	0	0
1995—Oakland NFL	16	0	13	179	13.8	1	1	0	6	1
1996—Oakland NFL	16	16	43	601	14.0	4	4	0	24	0
1997—Oakland NFL	16	16	46	804	17.5	12	12	0	72	2
Pro totals (5 years)	80	34	150	2608	17.4	20	20	0	120	4

JETT, JOHN — P — LIONS

PERSONAL: Born November 11, 1968, in Richmond, Va. ... 6-0/199.
HIGH SCHOOL: Northumberland (Heathsville, Va.).
COLLEGE: East Carolina.
TRANSACTIONS/CAREER NOTES: Signed as non-drafted free agent by Minnesota Vikings (June 22, 1992). ... Released by Vikings (August 25, 1992). ... Signed by Dallas Cowboys (March 10, 1993). ... Granted unconditional free agency (February 16, 1996). ... Re-signed by Cowboys (April 15, 1996). ... Granted unconditional free agency (February 14, 1997). ... Signed by Detroit Lions (March 7, 1997).
CHAMPIONSHIP GAMF EXPERIENCE: Played in NFC championship game (1993-1995 seasons). ... Member of Super Bowl championship team (1993 and 1995 seasons).
PRO STATISTICS: 1996—Rushed once for minus 23 yards.

Year Team			PUNTING					
	G	GS	No.	Yds.	Avg.	Net avg.	In. 20	Blk.
1992—				Did not play.				
1993—Dallas NFL	16	0	56	2342	41.8	37.7	22	0
1994—Dallas NFL	16	0	70	2935	41.9	35.3	26	0
1995—Dallas NFL	16	0	53	2166	40.9	34.5	17	0
1996—Dallas NFL	16	0	74	3150	42.6	36.7	22	0
1997—Detroit NFL	16	0	84	3576	42.6	35.6	24	†2
Pro totals (5 years)	80	0	337	14169	42.0	36.0	111	2

JOHNSON, ALONZO — WR/KR — JETS

PERSONAL: Born April 18, 1973, in Tuscaloosa, Ala. ... 5-11/186.
HIGH SCHOOL: Bount (Tuscaloosa, Ala.).
COLLEGE: Central State (Ohio).
TRANSACTIONS/CAREER NOTES: Signed as non-drafted free agent by New York Jets (April 25, 1997). ... Released by Jets (August 23, 1997). ... Re-signed by Jets to practice squad (August 26, 1997).

JOHNSON, ANDRE — OT — LIONS

PERSONAL: Born August 25, 1973, in Southhampton, N.Y. ... 6-5/314. ... Full name: Andre T. Johnson.
HIGH SCHOOL: Southhampton (N.Y.).
COLLEGE: Penn State.
TRANSACTIONS/CAREER NOTES: Selected by Washington Redskins in first round (30th pick overall) of 1996 NFL draft. ... Signed by Redskins (July 17, 1996). ... Inactive for 16 games (1996). ... Claimed on waivers by Miami Dolphins (August 26, 1997). ... Released by Dolphins (September 29, 1997). ... Inactive for four games with Dolphins (1997). ... Signed by Detroit Lions (October 7, 1997). ... Inactive for 10 games with Lions (1997).

JOHNSON, ANTHONY — RB — PANTHERS

PERSONAL: Born October 25, 1967, in Indianapolis. ... 6-0/225. ... Full name: Anthony Scott Johnson.
HIGH SCHOOL: John Adams (South Bend, Ind.).
COLLEGE: Notre Dame.
TRANSACTIONS/CAREER NOTES: Selected by Indianapolis Colts in second round (36th pick overall) of 1990 NFL draft. ... Signed by Colts (July 27, 1990). ... On injured reserve with eye injury (November 5, 1991-remainder of season). ... Granted unconditional free agency (February 17, 1994). ... Signed by New York Jets (June 21, 1994). ... Granted unconditional free agency (February 17, 1995). ... Signed by Chicago Bears (March 21, 1995). ... Released by Bears (November 6, 1995). ... Claimed on waivers by Carolina Panthers (November 7, 1995). ... Granted unconditional free agency (February 14, 1997). ... Re-signed by Panthers (February 24, 1997).
CHAMPIONSHIP GAME EXPERIENCE: Played in NFC championship game (1996 season).
PRO STATISTICS: 1992—Attempted one pass without a completion and recovered four fumbles. 1993—Had only pass attempt intercepted and recovered two fumbles. 1994—Returned one punt for three yards. 1997—Recovered two fumbles.
SINGLE GAME HIGHS (regular season): Attempts—29 (October 20, 1996, vs. New Orleans); yards—134 (August 31, 1997, vs. Seattle); and rushing touchdowns—1 (December 15, 1996, vs. Baltimore).
STATISTICAL PLATEAUS: 100-yard rushing games: 1996 (5), 1997 (1). Total: 6. ... 100-yard receiving games: 1991 (1), 1992 (1). Total: 2.
MISCELLANEOUS: Holds Carolina Panthers all-time record for most yards rushing (1,588). ... Shares Carolina Panthers all-time record for most rushing touchdowns (7).

Year Team			RUSHING				RECEIVING				TOTALS			
	G	GS	Att.	Yds.	Avg.	TD	No.	Yds.	Avg.	TD	TD	2pt.	Pts.	Fum.
1990—Indianapolis NFL	16	0	0	0	...	0	5	32	6.4	2	2	...	12	0
1991—Indianapolis NFL	9	6	22	94	4.3	0	42	344	8.2	0	0	...	0	2
1992—Indianapolis NFL	15	13	178	592	3.3	0	49	517	10.6	3	3	...	18	6
1993—Indianapolis NFL	13	8	95	331	3.5	1	55	443	8.1	0	1	...	6	5
1994—New York Jets NFL	15	0	5	12	2.4	0	5	31	6.2	0	0	0	0	0
1995—Chicago NFL	8	0	6	30	5.0	0	13	86	6.6	0	0	0	0	2

Year Team	G	GS	RUSHING				RECEIVING				TOTALS			
			Att.	Yds.	Avg.	TD	No.	Yds.	Avg.	TD	TD	2pt.	Pts.	Fum.
—Carolina NFL	7	0	24	110	4.6	1	16	121	7.6	0	1	0	6	0
1996—Carolina NFL	16	11	300	1120	3.7	6	26	192	7.4	0	6	0	36	2
1997—Carolina NFL	16	7	97	358	3.7	0	21	158	7.5	1	1	1	8	2
Pro totals (8 years)	115	45	727	2647	3.6	8	232	1924	8.3	6	14	1	86	19

JOHNSON, BILL — DL — EAGLES

PERSONAL: Born December 9, 1968, in Chicago. ... 6-4/305. ... Full name: William Edward Johnson.
HIGH SCHOOL: Neal F. Simeon (Chicago).
COLLEGE: Michigan State.
TRANSACTIONS/CAREER NOTES: Selected by Cleveland Browns in third round (65th pick overall) of 1992 NFL draft. ... Signed by Browns (July 19, 1992). ... Granted free agency (February 17, 1995). ... Re-signed by Browns (April 13, 1995). ... Claimed on waivers by Cincinnati Bengals (August 1, 1995); released after failing physical. ... Signed by Pittsburgh Steelers (October 25, 1995). ... Granted unconditional free agency (February 14, 1997). ... Signed by St. Louis Rams (June 10, 1997). ... Granted unconditional free agency (February 13, 1998). ... Signed by Philadelphia Eagles (February 21, 1998).
CHAMPIONSHIP GAME EXPERIENCE: Played in AFC championship game (1995 season). ... Played in Super Bowl XXX (1995 season).
PRO STATISTICS: 1994—Recovered one fumble. 1995—Recovered one fumble. 1996—Recovered one fumble. 1997—Recovered one fumble.

Year Team	G	GS	SACKS
1992—Cleveland NFL	16	2	2.0
1993—Cleveland NFL	10	0	1.0
1994—Cleveland NFL	14	13	1.0
1995—Pittsburgh NFL	9	0	0.0
1996—Pittsburgh NFL	15	8	1.0
1997—St. Louis NFL	16	16	4.0
Pro totals (6 years)	80	39	9.0

JOHNSON, BRAD — QB — VIKINGS

PERSONAL: Born September 13, 1968, in Marietta, Ga. ... 6-5/224. ... Full name: James Bradley Johnson.
HIGH SCHOOL: Charles D. Owen (Swannanoa, N.C.).
COLLEGE: Florida State (degree in physical education).
TRANSACTIONS/CAREER NOTES: Selected by Minnesota Vikings in ninth round (227th pick overall) of 1992 NFL draft. ... Signed by Vikings (July 17, 1992). ... Active for one game (1992); did not play. ... Inactive for 16 games (1993). ... Granted free agency (February 17, 1995). ... Assigned by Vikings to London Monarchs in 1995 World League enhancement allocation program (February 20, 1995). ... Re-signed by Vikings (March 27, 1995). ... On injured reserve with neck injury (December 5, 1997-remainder of season).
PRO STATISTICS: 1995—Fumbled twice. 1996—Fumbled five times and recovered three fumbles for minus eight yards. 1997—Caught one pass for three yards and a touchdown, fumbled four times and recovered three fumbles.
SINGLE GAME HIGHS (regular season): Attempts—44 (September 14, 1997, vs. Tampa Bay); completions—33 (September 7, 1997, vs. Chicago); yards—334 (September 14, 1997, vs. Tampa Bay); and touchdown passes—4 (December 1, 1996, vs. Arizona).
STATISTICAL PLATEAUS: 300-yard passing games: 1997 (2).
MISCELLANEOUS: Regular-season record as starting NFL quarterback: 13-8 (.619). ... Postseason record as starting NFL quarterback: 0-1 (.000).

Year Team	G	GS	PASSING								RUSHING				TOTALS		
			Att.	Cmp.	Pct.	Yds.	TD	Int.	Avg.	Rat.	Att.	Yds.	Avg.	TD	TD	2pt.	Pts.
1992—Minnesota NFL						Did not play.											
1993—Minnesota NFL						Did not play.											
1994—Minnesota NFL	4	0	37	22	59.5	150	0	0	4.05	68.5	2	-2	-1.0	0	0	0	0
1995—London W.L.	...	...	328	194	59.1	2227	13	14	6.79	75.1	24	99	4.1	1	1	1	8
—Minnesota NFL	5	0	36	25	69.4	272	0	2	7.56	68.3	9	-9	-1.0	0	0	0	0
1996—Minnesota NFL	12	8	311	195	62.7	2258	17	10	7.26	89.4	34	90	2.6	1	1	0	6
1997—Minnesota NFL	13	13	452	275	60.8	3036	20	12	6.72	84.5	35	139	4.0	0	1	2	10
W.L. totals (1 year)	...	...	328	194	59.1	2227	13	14	6.79	75.1	24	99	4.1	1	1	1	8
NFL totals (4 years)	34	21	836	517	61.8	5716	37	24	6.84	84.9	80	218	2.7	1	2	2	16
Pro totals (5 years)	...	...	1164	711	61.1	7943	50	38	6.82	82.1	104	317	3.0	2	3	3	24

JOHNSON, CHARLES — WR — STEELERS

PERSONAL: Born January 3, 1972, in San Bernardino, Calif. ... 6-0/195. ... Full name: Charles Everett Johnson.
HIGH SCHOOL: Cajun (San Berardino, Calif.).
COLLEGE: Colorado.
TRANSACTIONS/CAREER NOTES: Selected by Pittsburgh Steelers in first round (17th pick overall) of 1994 NFL draft. ... Signed by Steelers (July 21, 1994). ... On injured reserve with knee injury (December 23, 1995-remainder of season).
CHAMPIONSHIP GAME EXPERIENCE: Played in AFC championship game (1994 and 1997 seasons).
HONORS: Named wide receiver on THE SPORTING NEWS college All-America second team (1993).
PRO STATISTICS: 1994—Fumbled twice. 1995—Recovered one fumble. 1996—Fumbled once.
SINGLE GAME HIGHS (regular season): Receptions—8 (December 1, 1996, vs. Baltimore); yards—165 (December 24, 1994, vs. San Diego); and touchdown receptions—2 (October 5, 1997, vs. Baltimore).
STATISTICAL PLATEAUS: 100-yard receiving games: 1994 (1), 1996 (4), 1997 (1). Total: 6.

Year Team	G	GS	RUSHING				RECEIVING				PUNT RETURNS				KICKOFF RETURNS				TOTALS		
			Att.	Yds.	Avg.	TD	No.	Yds.	Avg.	TD	No.	Yds.	Avg.	TD	No.	Yds.	Avg.	TD	TD	2pt.	Pts.
1994—Pittsburgh NFL	16	9	4	-1	-0.3	0	38	577	15.2	3	15	90	6.0	0	16	345	21.6	0	3	0	18
1995—Pittsburgh NFL	14	12	1	-10	-10.0	0	38	432	11.4	0	0	0	...	0	2	47	23.5	0	0	0	0
1996—Pittsburgh NFL	16	12	0	0	...	0	60	1008	16.8	3	0	0	...	0	6	111	18.5	0	3	1	20
1997—Pittsburgh NFL	13	11	0	0	...	0	46	568	12.3	2	0	0	...	0	0	0	...	0	2	0	12
Pro totals (4 years)	59	44	5	-11	-2.2	0	182	2585	14.2	8	15	90	6.0	0	24	503	21.0	0	8	1	50

JOHNSON, CLYDE   S   BEARS

PERSONAL: Born May 22, 1970, in Austin, Texas. ... 5-10/190. ... Full name: Clyde A. Johnson.
HIGH SCHOOL: Lyndon Baines Johnson (Austin, Texas).
COLLEGE: Kansas State.
TRANSACTIONS/CAREER NOTES: Signed as non-drafted free agent by Kansas City Chiefs (April 29, 1997). ... Released by Chiefs (December 18, 1997). ... Signed by Chicago Bears (December 19, 1997).
PLAYING EXPERIENCE: Kansas City NFL, 1997. ... Games/Games started: 15/0.

JOHNSON, DARRIUS   CB   BRONCOS

J

PERSONAL: Born September 17, 1972, in Terrell, Texas. ... 5-9/185.
HIGH SCHOOL: Terrell (Texas).
COLLEGE: Oklahoma.
TRANSACTIONS/CAREER NOTES: Selected by Denver Broncos in fourth round (122nd pick overall) of 1996 NFL draft. ... Signed by Broncos (July 17, 1996).
PLAYING EXPERIENCE: Denver NFL, 1996 and 1997. ... Games/Games started: 1996 (13/0), 1997 (16/0). Total: 29/0.
CHAMPIONSHIP GAME EXPERIENCE: Played in AFC championship game (1997 season). ... Member of Super Bowl championship team (1997 season).
PRO STATISTICS: 1997—Recovered one fumble for six yards and a touchdown.

JOHNSON, ELLIS   DT   COLTS

PERSONAL: Born October 30, 1973, in Wildwood, Fla. ... 6-2/292. ... Full name: Ellis B. Johnson.
HIGH SCHOOL: Wildwood (Fla.).
COLLEGE: Florida.
TRANSACTIONS/CAREER NOTES: Selected by Indianapolis Colts in first round (15th pick overall) of 1995 NFL draft. ... Signed by Colts (June 7, 1995).
CHAMPIONSHIP GAME EXPERIENCE: Played in AFC championship game (1995 season).
PRO STATISTICS: 1997—Intercepted one pass for 18 yards and recovered two fumbles.

Year Team	G	GS	SACKS
1995—Indianapolis NFL	16	2	4.5
1996—Indianapolis NFL	12	6	0.0
1997—Indianapolis NFL	15	15	4.5
Pro totals (3 years)	43	23	9.0

JOHNSON, JASON   C   COLTS

PERSONAL: Born February 6, 1974, in Kansas City, Mo. ... 6-3/281. ... Full name: Jason Joseph Johnson.
HIGH SCHOOL: Oak Park (Mo.).
COLLEGE: Kansas State.
TRANSACTIONS/CAREER NOTES: Signed as non-drafted free agent by Indianapolis Colts (April 25, 1997). ... Released by Colts (September 13, 1997). ... Re-signed by Colts to practice squad (September 15, 1997).

JOHNSON, JIMMIE   TE   EAGLES

PERSONAL: Born October 6, 1966, in Augusta, Ga. ... 6-2/257. ... Full name: Jimmie O. Johnson Jr.
HIGH SCHOOL: T.W. Josey (Augusta, Ga.).
COLLEGE: Howard (degree in consumer studies, 1989).
TRANSACTIONS/CAREER NOTES: Selected by Washington Redskins in 12th round (316th pick overall) of 1989 NFL draft. ... Signed by Redskins (July 23, 1989). ... On injured reserve with pinched nerve in neck (October 12, 1991-remainder of season). ... Granted unconditional free agency (February 1, 1992). ... Signed by Detroit Lions (April 1, 1992). ... On active/non-football injury list (July 16-August 23, 1993). ... On reserve/non-football injury list (August 23-October 15, 1993). ... Released by Lions (November 29, 1993). ... Signed by Kansas City Chiefs (1994). ... Released by Chiefs (August 29, 1994). ... Re-signed by Chiefs (October 12, 1994). ... Released by Chiefs (March 30, 1995). ... Signed by Philadelphia Eagles (August 2, 1995). ... Granted unconditional free agency (February 16, 1996). ... Re-signed by Eagles (April 18, 1996). ... Granted unconditional free agency (February 14, 1997). ... Re-signed by Eagles (June 2, 1997).
PRO STATISTICS: 1992—Returned one kickoff for no yards. 1997—Returned three kickoffs for 22 yards.
SINGLE GAME HIGHS (regular season): Receptions—4 (November 23, 1997, vs. Pittsburgh); yards—55 (November 18, 1990, vs. New Orleans); and touchdown receptions—1 (November 30, 1997, vs. Cincinnati).

Year Team	G	GS	No.	Yds.	Avg.	TD	TD	2pt.	Pts.	Fum.
1989—Washington NFL	16	0	4	84	21.0	0	0	...	0	0
1990—Washington NFL	16	5	15	218	14.5	2	2	...	12	1
1991—Washington NFL	6	0	3	7	2.3	2	2	...	12	0
1992—Detroit NFL	16	5	6	34	5.7	0	0	...	0	0
1993—Detroit NFL	6	4	2	18	9.0	0	0	...	0	0
1994—Kansas City NFL	7	1	2	7	3.5	0	0	0	0	0
1995—Philadelphia NFL	16	1	6	37	6.2	0	0	0	0	0
1996—Philadelphia NFL	16	3	7	127	18.1	0	0	0	0	0
1997—Philadelphia NFL	16	11	14	177	12.6	1	1	0	6	1
Pro totals (9 years)	115	30	59	709	12.0	5	5	0	30	2

JOHNSON, JOE — DE — SAINTS

PERSONAL: Born July 11, 1972, in St. Louis. ... 6-4/270. ... Full name: Joe T. Johnson.
HIGH SCHOOL: Jennings (Mo.).
COLLEGE: Louisville.
TRANSACTIONS/CAREER NOTES: Selected after junior season by New Orleans Saints in first round (13th pick overall) of 1994 NFL draft. ... Signed by Saints (June 7, 1994). ... Designated by Saints as franchise player (February 13, 1998).
PRO STATISTICS: 1994—Recovered one fumble. 1997—Recovered one fumble.

Year Team	G	GS	SACKS
1994—New Orleans NFL	15	14	1.0
1995—New Orleans NFL	14	14	5.5
1996—New Orleans NFL	13	13	7.5
1997—New Orleans NFL	16	16	8.5
Pro totals (4 years)	58	57	22.5

JOHNSON, KEVIN — NT

PERSONAL: Born October 30, 1970, in Los Angeles. ... 6-1/310.
HIGH SCHOOL: Westchester (Los Angeles).
JUNIOR COLLEGE: Harbor Junior College (Calif.).
COLLEGE: Texas Southern.
TRANSACTIONS/CAREER NOTES: Selected by New England Patriots in fourth round (86th pick overall) of 1993 NFL draft. ... Signed by Patriots (June 30, 1993). ... Released by Patriots (August 23, 1993). ... Signed by Minnesota Vikings to practice squad (September 1, 1993). ... Released by Vikings (September 27, 1993). ... Signed by Oakland Raiders (June 1995). ... Claimed on waivers by Philadelphia Eagles (August 29, 1995). ... Released by Eagles (December 17, 1996). ... Signed by Raiders (April 1997). ... Released by Raiders (March 12, 1998).
PRO STATISTICS: 1995—Recovered one fumble for 37 yards and a touchdown.

Year Team	G	GS	SACKS
1993—	Did not play.		
1994—	Did not play.		
1995—Philadelphia NFL	11	1	6.0
1996—Philadelphia NFL	12	5	1.0
1997—Oakland NFL	15	0	0.0
Pro totals (3 years)	38	6	7.0

JOHNSON, KEYSHAWN — WR — JETS

PERSONAL: Born July 22, 1972, in Los Angeles. ... 6-3/210. ... Cousin of Chris Miller, wide receiver, Chicago Bears.
HIGH SCHOOL: Dorsey (Los Angeles).
JUNIOR COLLEGE: West Los Angeles College.
COLLEGE: Southern California.
TRANSACTIONS/CAREER NOTES: Selected by New York Jets in first round (first pick overall) of 1996 NFL draft. ... Signed by Jets (August 6, 1996).
HONORS: Named wide receiver on THE SPORTING NEWS college All-America first team (1995).
SINGLE GAME HIGHS (regular season): Receptions—9 (November 23, 1997, vs. Minnesota); yards—104 (November 23, 1997, vs. Minnesota); and touchdown receptions—2 (October 20, 1996, vs. Buffalo).
STATISTICAL PLATEAUS: 100-yard receiving games: 1997 (1).

Year Team	G	GS	RECEIVING No.	Yds.	Avg.	TD	TOTALS TD	2pt.	Pts.	Fum.
1996—New York Jets NFL	14	11	63	844	13.4	8	8	1	50	0
1997—New York Jets NFL	16	16	70	963	13.8	5	5	0	30	0
Pro totals (2 years)	30	27	133	1807	13.6	13	13	1	80	0

JOHNSON, LEE — P — BENGALS

PERSONAL: Born November 27, 1961, in Dallas. ... 6-2/200.
HIGH SCHOOL: McCullough (The Woodlands, Texas).
COLLEGE: Brigham Young.
TRANSACTIONS/CAREER NOTES: Selected by Houston Gamblers in ninth round (125th pick overall) of 1985 USFL draft. ... Selected by Houston Oilers in fifth round (138th pick overall) of 1985 NFL draft. ... Signed by Oilers (June 25, 1985). ... Crossed picket line during players' strike (October 14, 1987). ... Claimed on waivers by Buffalo Bills (December 2, 1987). ... Claimed on waivers by Cleveland Browns (December 10, 1987). ... Claimed on waivers by Cincinnati Bengals (September 23, 1988). ... Granted free agency (February 1, 1991). ... Re-signed by Bengals (1991). ... Granted unconditional free agency (March 1, 1993). ... Re-signed by Bengals (May 10, 1993).
CHAMPIONSHIP GAME EXPERIENCE: Played in AFC championship game (1987 and 1988 seasons). ... Played in Super Bowl XXIII (1988 season).
POST SEASON RECORDS: Holds Super Bowl career record for longest punt—63 yards (January 22, 1989, vs. San Francisco).
PRO STATISTICS: 1985—Rushed once for no yards, fumbled twice and recovered one fumble for seven yards. 1987—Had 32.8-yard net punting average. 1988—Had 33.4-yard net punting average. 1989—Rushed once for minus seven yards. 1990—Attempted one pass with one completion for four yards and a touchdown. 1991—Attempted one pass with one completion for three yards, rushed once for minus two yards and fumbled once. 1993—Attempted one pass without a completion. 1994—Attempted one pass with one completion for seven yards and one touchdown. 1995—Attempted one pass with one completion for five yards, rushed once for minus 16 yards and fumbled once. 1997—Rushed once for no yards and recovered two fumbles.

Year Team	G	GS	No.	Yds.	Avg.	Net avg.	In. 20	Blk.	XPM	XPA	FGM	FGA	Lg.	50+	Pts.
				PUNTING							KICKING				
1985—Houston NFL	16	0	83	3464	41.7	35.7	22	0	0	0	0	0	0	0-0	0
1986—Houston NFL	16	0	88	3623	41.2	35.7	26	0	0	0	0	0	0	0-0	0
1987—Houston NFL	9	0	25	1008	40.3	...	5	1	0	0	0	0	0	0-0	0
—Cleveland NFL	3	0	9	317	35.2	32.2	3	0	0	0	0	0	0	0-0	0
1988—Cleveland NFL	3	0	31	1237	39.9	...	6	0	0	0	1	2	50	1-2	3
—Cincinnati NFL	12	0	14	594	42.4	...	4	0	0	0	0	0	0	0-0	0
1989—Cincinnati NFL	16	0	61	2446	40.1	30.1	14	2	0	1	0	0	0	0-0	0
1990—Cincinnati NFL	16	0	64	2705	42.3	34.2	12	0	0	0	0	1	0	0-0	0
1991—Cincinnati NFL	16	0	64	2795	43.7	34.7	15	0	0	0	1	3	53	1-3	3
1992—Cincinnati NFL	16	0	76	3196	42.1	35.8	15	0	0	0	0	1	0	0-1	0
1993—Cincinnati NFL	16	0	▲90	3954	43.9	36.6	24	0	0	0	0	0	0	0-0	0
1994—Cincinnati NFL	16	0	79	3461	43.8	35.2	19	1	0	0	0	0	0	0-0	0
1995—Cincinnati NFL	16	0	68	2861	42.1	38.6	26	0	0	0	0	0	0	0-0	0
1996—Cincinnati NFL	16	0	80	3630	45.4	34.3	16	1	0	0	0	0	0	0-0	0
1997—Cincinnati NFL	16	0	81	3471	42.9	35.9	27	0	0	0	0	0	0	0-0	0
Pro totals (13 years)	203	0	913	38762	42.5	32.5	234	5	0	1	2	7	53	2-6	6

JOHNSON, LEON RB JETS

PERSONAL: Born July 13, 1974, in Morganton (N.C.). ... 6-0/215. ... Full name: William Leon Johnson.
HIGH SCHOOL: Freedom (Morganton, N.C.).
COLLEGE: North Carolina.
TRANSACTIONS/CAREER NOTES: Selected by New York Jets in fourth round (104th pick overall) of 1997 NFL draft. ... Signed by Jets (July 17, 1997).
PRO STATISTICS: 1997—Attempted two passes without a completion and one interception, fumbled five times and recovered five fumbles.
SINGLE GAME HIGHS (regular season): Attempts—11 (August 31, 1997, vs. Seattle); yards—36 (August 31, 1997, vs. Seattle); and rushing touchdowns—1 (October 19, 1997, vs. New England).

			RUSHING				RECEIVING				PUNT RETURNS				KICKOFF RETURNS				TOTALS		
Year Team	G	GS	Att.	Yds.	Avg.	TD	No.	Yds.	Avg.	TD	No.	Yds.	Avg.	TD	No.	Yds.	Avg.	TD	TD	2pt.	Pts.
1997—N.Y. Jets NFL	16	1	48	158	3.3	2	16	142	8.9	0	§51	*619	12.1	1	12	319	26.6	▲1	4	0	24

JOHNSON, LeSHON RB GIANTS

PERSONAL: Born January 15, 1971, in Tulsa, Okla. ... 6-0/207. ... Full name: LeShon Eugene Johnson.
HIGH SCHOOL: Haskell (Okla.).
COLLEGE: Northeastern Oklahoma A&M, then Northern Illinois.
TRANSACTIONS/CAREER NOTES: Selected by Green Bay Packers in third round (84th pick overall) of 1994 NFL draft. ... Signed by Packers (July 19, 1994). ... On injured reserve with knee injury (January 3, 1995-remainder of 1994 playoffs). ... On physically unable to perform list with knee injury (August 27-October 21, 1995). ... Claimed on waivers by Arizona Cardinals (November 29, 1995). ... Granted free agency (February 14, 1997). ... Granted unconditional free agency (February 13, 1998). ... Signed by New York Giants (March 7, 1998).
HONORS: Named running back on THE SPORTING NEWS college All-America first team (1993).
PRO STATISTICS: 1995—Recovered one fumble. 1996—Recovered two fumbles.
SINGLE GAME HIGHS (regular season): Attempts—21 (September 22, 1996, vs. New Orleans); yards—214 (September 22, 1996, vs. New Orleans); and rushing touchdowns—2 (September 22, 1996, vs. New Orleans).
STATISTICAL PLATEAUS: 100-yard rushing games: 1996 (1).

			RUSHING				RECEIVING				KICKOFF RETURNS				TOTALS			
Year Team	G	GS	Att.	Yds.	Avg.	TD	No.	Yds.	Avg.	TD	No.	Yds.	Avg.	TD	TD	2pt.	Pts.	Fum.
1994—Green Bay NFL	12	0	26	99	3.8	0	13	168	12.9	0	0	0	...	0	0	0	0	0
1995—Green Bay NFL	2	0	2	-2	-1.0	0	0	0	...	0	0	0	...	0	0	0	0	0
—Arizona NFL	3	0	0	0	...	0	0	0	...	0	11	259	23.5	0	0	0	0	1
1996—Arizona NFL	15	8	141	634	4.5	3	15	176	11.7	1	10	198	19.8	0	4	0	24	5
1997—Arizona NFL	14	0	23	81	3.5	0	3	4	1.3	0	0	26	...	0	0	0	0	0
Pro totals (4 years)	46	8	192	812	4.2	3	31	348	11.2	1	21	483	23.0	0	4	0	24	6

JOHNSON, LONNIE TE BILLS

PERSONAL: Born February 14, 1971, in Miami. ... 6-3/240. ... Full name: Lonnie D. Johnson.
HIGH SCHOOL: Senior (Miami).
COLLEGE: Florida State.
TRANSACTIONS/CAREER NOTES: Selected by Buffalo Bills in second round (61st pick overall) of 1994 NFL draft. ... Signed by Bills (July 15, 1994). ... Granted free agency (February 14, 1997). ... Re-signed by Bills (June 12, 1997). ... Granted unconditional free agency (February 13, 1998). ... Re-signed by Bills (March 30, 1998).
PRO STATISTICS: 1995—Recovered one fumble. 1996—Recovered four fumbles. 1997—Rushed once for six yards and recovered one fumble.
SINGLE GAME HIGHS (regular season): Receptions—7 (October 15, 1995, vs. Seattle); yards—90 (October 20, 1996, vs. New York Jets); and touchdown receptions—1 (November 30, 1997, vs. New York Jets).

			RECEIVING				TOTALS			
Year Team	G	GS	No.	Yds.	Avg.	TD	TD	2pt.	Pts.	Fum.
1994—Buffalo NFL	10	1	3	42	14.0	0	0	0	0	0
1995—Buffalo NFL	16	16	49	504	10.3	1	1	0	6	0
1996—Buffalo NFL	16	15	46	457	9.9	0	0	0	0	1
1997—Buffalo NFL	16	16	41	340	8.3	2	2	0	12	2
Pro totals (4 years)	58	48	139	1343	9.7	3	3	0	18	3

PERSONAL: Born April 15, 1972, in Cincinnati. ... 6-0/198. ... Full name: Melvin Carlton Johnson III.
HIGH SCHOOL: St. Xavier (Cincinnati).
COLLEGE: Kentucky.
TRANSACTIONS/CAREER NOTES: Selected by Tampa Bay Buccaneers in second round (43rd pick overall) of 1995 NFL draft. ... Signed by Buccaneers (May 10, 1995). ... Traded by Buccaneers to Kansas City Chiefs for conditional pick in 1999 draft (April 19, 1998).
PRO STATISTICS: 1996—Recovered one fumble.

| | | | INTERCEPTIONS | | | |
Year Team	G	GS	No.	Yds.	Avg.	TD
1995—Tampa Bay NFL	11	3	1	0	0.0	0
1996—Tampa Bay NFL	16	16	2	24	12.0	0
1997—Tampa Bay NFL	16	7	1	19	19.0	0
Pro totals (3 years)	43	26	4	43	10.8	0

J

PERSONAL: Born May 31, 1960, in Inglewood, Calif. ... 6-2/202.
HIGH SCHOOL: Pacifica (Garden Grove, Calif.).
COLLEGE: UCLA.
TRANSACTIONS/CAREER NOTES: Signed as non-drafted free agent by Seattle Seahawks (May 4, 1982). ... Crossed picket line during players strike (October 14, 1987). ... Granted free agency (February 1, 1991). ... Re-signed by Seahawks (July 19, 1991). ... Released by Seahawks (August 26, 1991). ... Signed by Atlanta Falcons (September 9, 1991). ... Granted free agency (February 1, 1992). ... Re-signed by Falcons for 1992 season. ... Released by Falcons (July 20, 1995). ... Signed by Pittsburgh Steelers (August 22, 1995). ... Released by Steelers (July 9, 1997). ... Re-signed by Steelers (August 25, 1997).
CHAMPIONSHIP GAME EXPERIENCE: Played in AFC championship game (1983, 1995 and 1997 seasons). ... Played in Super Bowl XXX (1995 season).
HONORS: Named kicker on THE SPORTING NEWS NFL All-Pro team (1984). ... Played in Pro Bowl (1984 and 1993 seasons).
PRO STATISTICS: 1982—Attempted one pass with one completion for 27 yards. 1991—Punted once for 21 yards. 1992—Punted once for 37 yards.

| | | | KICKING | | | | | | |
Year Team	G	GS	XPM	XPA	FGM	FGA	Lg.	50+	Pts.
1982—Seattle NFL	9	0	13	14	10	14	48	0-1	43
1983—Seattle NFL	16	0	49	50	18	25	54	1-3	103
1984—Seattle NFL	16	0	50	51	20	24	50	1-3	110
1985—Seattle NFL	16	0	40	41	14	25	51	1-3	82
1986—Seattle NFL	16	0	42	42	22	35	54	5-7	108
1987—Seattle NFL	13	0	40	§40	15	20	49	0-1	85
1988—Seattle NFL	16	0	39	39	22	28	47	0-0	105
1989—Seattle NFL	16	0	27	27	15	25	50	1-5	72
1990—Seattle NFL	16	0	33	34	23	32	51	1-3	102
1991—Atlanta NFL	14	0	38	39	19	23	50	1-2	95
1992—Atlanta NFL	16	0	39	39	18	22	54	4-4	93
1993—Atlanta NFL	15	0	34	34	26	27	54	2-2	112
1994—Atlanta NFL	16	0	32	32	21	25	50	1-5	95
1995—Pittsburgh NFL	16	0	39	39	*34	*41	50	1-1	§141
1996—Pittsburgh NFL	16	0	37	37	23	30	49	0-1	106
1997—Pittsburgh NFL	16	0	40	40	22	25	52	1-2	106
Pro totals (16 years)	243	0	592	598	322	421	54	20-43	1558

PERSONAL: Born July 29, 1964, in Detroit. ... 6-3/259. ... Full name: Thomas Johnson.
HIGH SCHOOL: MacKenzie (Detroit).
COLLEGE: Ohio State.
TRANSACTIONS/CAREER NOTES: Selected by New Jersey Generals in 1986 USFL territorial draft. ... Selected by New York Giants in second round (51st pick overall) of 1986 NFL draft. ... Signed by Giants (July 30, 1986). ... Granted free agency (February 1, 1989). ... Re-signed by Giants (September 14, 1989). ... Granted roster exemption (September 14-23, 1989). ... Granted free agency (February 1, 1991). ... Re-signed by Giants (August 14, 1991). ... Designated by Giants as transition player (February 25, 1993). ... Claimed on waivers by Cleveland Browns (September 1, 1993). ... Granted unconditional free agency (February 17, 1994). ... Re-signed by Browns (June 3, 1994). ... Browns franchise moved to Baltimore and renamed Ravens for 1996 season (March 11, 1996). ... Released by Ravens (July 9, 1996). ... Signed by Detroit Lions (August 21, 1996). ... Granted unconditional free agency (February 14, 1997). ... Signed by New York Jets (February 25, 1997). ... On injured reserve with leg injury (October 20, 1997-remainder of season).
CHAMPIONSHIP GAME EXPERIENCE: Played in NFC championship game (1986 and 1990 seasons). ... Member of Super Bowl championship team (1986 and 1990 seasons).
HONORS: Named inside linebacker on THE SPORTING NEWS NFL All-Pro team (1990). ... Played in Pro Bowl (1990 and 1994 seasons).
PRO STATISTICS: 1987—Recovered one fumble. 1988—Recovered one fumble. 1989—Recovered one fumble. 1990—Recovered one fumble. 1992—Fumbled once and recovered two fumbles. 1994—Recovered one fumble for 10 yards.

| | | | INTERCEPTIONS | | | | SACKS |
Year Team	G	GS	No.	Yds.	Avg.	TD	No.
1986—New York Giants NFL	16	0	1	13	13.0	0	2.0
1987—New York Giants NFL	12	12	0	0	...	0	1.0
1988—New York Giants NFL	16	15	1	33	33.0	0	4.0
1989—New York Giants NFL	14	4	3	60	20.0	∞1	1.0
1000 New York Giants NFL	16	14	1	0	0.0	0	3.5
1991—New York Giants NFL	16	16	2	5	2.5	0	6.5

Year Team	G	GS	INTERCEPTIONS No.	Yds.	Avg.	TD	SACKS No.
1992—New York Giants NFL	16	16	2	42	21.0	0	1.0
1993—Cleveland NFL	16	11	0	0	...	0	1.0
1994—Cleveland NFL	16	16	0	0	...	0	2.5
1995—Cleveland NFL	16	16	2	22	11.0	0	2.0
1996—Detroit NFL	15	12	0	0	...	0	0.0
1997—New York Jets NFL	8	8	1	13	13.0	0	0.0
Pro totals (12 years)	177	140	13	188	14.5	2	24.5

JOHNSON, RAYLEE   DE   CHARGERS

PERSONAL: Born June 1, 1970, in Fordyce, Ark. ... 6-3/265. ... Full name: Raylee Terrell Johnson.
HIGH SCHOOL: Fordyce (Ark.).
COLLEGE: Arkansas.
TRANSACTIONS/CAREER NOTES: Selected by San Diego Chargers in fourth round (95th pick overall) of 1993 NFL draft. ... Signed by Chargers (July 15, 1993). ... Granted unconditional free agency (February 14, 1997). ... Re-signed by Chargers (March 11, 1997).
CHAMPIONSHIP GAME EXPERIENCE: Played in AFC championship game (1994 season). ... Played in Super Bowl XXIX (1994 season).

Year Team	G	GS	SACKS
1993—San Diego NFL	9	0	0.0
1994—San Diego NFL	15	0	1.5
1995—San Diego NFL	16	1	3.0
1996—San Diego NFL	16	1	3.0
1997—San Diego NFL	16	0	2.5
Pro totals (5 years)	72	2	10.0

JOHNSON, REGGIE   TE

PERSONAL: Born January 27, 1968, in Pensacola, Fla. ... 6-2/256. ... Full name: Reginald R. Johnson.
HIGH SCHOOL: Escambia (Pensacola, Fla.).
COLLEGE: Florida State (degree in criminology, 1991).
TRANSACTIONS/CAREER NOTES: Selected by Denver Broncos in second round (30th pick overall) of 1991 NFL draft. ... Signed by Broncos (July 19, 1991). ... Granted free agency (February 17, 1994). ... Re-signed by Broncos (June 16, 1994). ... Claimed on waivers by Cincinnati Bengals (August 25, 1994). ... Released by Bengals (August 26, 1994). ... Signed by Green Bay Packers (September 27, 1994). ... Granted unconditional free agency (February 17, 1995). ... Signed by Philadelphia Eagles (March 20, 1995). ... Released by Eagles (August 29, 1995). ... Re-signed by Eagles (October 25, 1995). ... Granted unconditional free agency (February 16, 1996). ... Signed by Kansas City Chiefs (May 24, 1996). ... Released by Chiefs (March 20, 1997). ... Signed by Packers (August 5, 1997). ... Activated (September 3, 1997). ... Released by Packers (August 25, 1997). ... Re-signed by Packers (September 3, 1997). ... Released by Packers (September 29, 1997).
CHAMPIONSHIP GAME EXPERIENCE: Member of Broncos for AFC championship game (1991 season); did not play.
POST SEASON RECORDS: Shares NFL postseason career and single-game records for most two-point conversions—1 (January 7, 1996, vs. Dallas).
PRO STATISTICS: 1991—Recovered one fumble. 1992—Rushed twice for seven yards, returned two kickoffs for 47 yards and recovered one fumble.
SINGLE GAME HIGHS (regular season): Receptions—4 (September 5, 1993, vs. New York Jets); yards—70 (September 5, 1993, vs. New York Jets); and touchdown receptions—1 (September 29, 1996, vs. San Diego).

Year Team	G	GS	RECEIVING No.	Yds.	Avg.	TD	TOTALS TD	2pt.	Pts.	Fum.
1991—Denver NFL	16	3	6	73	12.2	1	0	...	0	0
1992—Denver NFL	15	7	10	139	13.9	1	1	...	6	0
1993—Denver NFL	13	12	20	243	12.2	1	1	...	6	1
1994—Green Bay NFL	9	2	7	79	11.3	0	0	0	0	0
1995—Philadelphia NFL	9	2	5	68	13.6	2	2	0	12	0
1996—Kansas City NFL	11	3	18	189	10.5	1	1	0	6	0
1997—Green Bay NFL	4	0	0	0	...	0	0	0	0	0
Pro totals (7 years)	77	29	66	791	12.0	6	5	0	30	1

JOHNSON, ROB   QB   BILLS

PERSONAL: Born March 18, 1973, in Newport Beach, Calif. ... 6-4/214. ... Full name: Rob Garland Johnson. ... Cousin of Bart Johnson, pitcher with Chicago White Sox (1969-1974, 1976 and 1977).
HIGH SCHOOL: El Toro (Calif.).
COLLEGE: Southern California.
TRANSACTIONS/CAREER NOTES: Selected by Jacksonville Jaguars in fourth round (99th pick overall) of 1995 NFL draft. ... Signed by Jaguars (June 1, 1995). ... Traded by Jaguars to Buffalo Bills for first- (RB Fred Taylor) and fourth-round (RB Tavian Banks) picks in 1998 draft (February 13, 1998).
CHAMPIONSHIP GAME EXPERIENCE: Member of Jaguars for AFC championship game (1996 season); did not play.
SINGLE GAME HIGHS (regular season): Attempts—24 (August 31, 1997, vs. Baltimore); completions—20 (August 31, 1997, vs. Baltimore); yards—294 (August 31, 1997, vs. Baltimore); and touchdown passes—2 (August 31, 1997, vs. Baltimore).
MISCELLANEOUS: Selected by Minnesota Twins organization in 16th round of free-agent draft (June 4, 1991); did not sign. ... Regular-season record as starting NFL quarterback: 1-0 (1.000).

Year Team	G	GS	PASSING Att.	Cmp.	Pct.	Yds.	TD	Int.	Avg.	Rat.	RUSHING Att.	Yds.	Avg.	TD	TOTALS TD	2pt.	Pts.
1995—Jacksonville NFL	1	0	7	3	42.9	24	0	1	3.43	12.5	3	17	5.7	0	0	0	0
1996—Jacksonville NFL	2	0	0	0	...	0	0	0	...	...	0	0	...	0	0	0	0
1997—Jacksonville NFL	5	1	28	22	78.6	344	2	2	12.29	111.9	10	34	3.4	1	1	0	6
Pro totals (3 years)	8	1	35	25	71.4	368	2	3	10.51	88.8	13	51	3.9	1	1	0	6

JOHNSON, TED — LB — PATRIOTS

PERSONAL: Born December 4, 1972, in Alameda, Calif. ... 6-3/240.
HIGH SCHOOL: Carlsbad (Calif.).
COLLEGE: Colorado.
TRANSACTIONS/CAREER NOTES: Selected by New England Patriots in second round (57th pick overall) of 1995 NFL draft. ... Signed by Patriots (July 18, 1995).
CHAMPIONSHIP GAME EXPERIENCE: Played in AFC championship game (1996 season). ... Played in Super Bowl XXXI (1996 season).
HONORS: Named linebacker on THE SPORTING NEWS college All-America second team (1994).
PRO STATISTICS: 1995—Recovered two fumbles. 1996—Intercepted one pass for no yards and recovered one fumble.

Year Team	G	GS	SACKS
1995—New England NFL	12	11	0.5
1996—New England NFL	16	16	0.0
1997—New England NFL	16	16	4.0
Pro totals (3 years)	44	43	4.5

JOHNSON, TONY — DE — SAINTS

PERSONAL: Born February 5, 1972, in Como, Miss. ... 6-5/255.
HIGH SCHOOL: North Panola (Sardis, Miss.).
COLLEGE: Alabama.
TRANSACTIONS/CAREER NOTES: Selected by Philadelphia Eagles in sixth round (197th pick overall) of 1996 NFL draft. ... Signed by Eagles (July 15, 1996). ... Released by Eagles (August 20, 1996). ... Signed by New Orleans Saints to practice squad (September 18, 1996). ... Activated (October 19, 1996). ... Released by Saints (December 2, 1997). ... Re-signed by Saints (July 14, 1997).
SINGLE GAME HIGHS (regular season): Receptions—4 (November 17, 1996, vs. Atlanta); yards—48 (November 17, 1996, vs. Atlanta); and touchdown receptions—1 (November 24, 1996, vs. Tampa Bay).
MISCELLANEOUS: Played tight end during 1996 and 1997 seasons.

Year Team	G	GS	RECEIVING No.	Yds.	Avg.	TD	TOTALS TD	2pt.	Pts.	Fum.
1996—New Orleans NFL	9	7	7	76	10.9	1	1	0	6	0
1997—New Orleans NFL	7	1	1	13	13.0	0	0	0	0	1
Pro totals (2 years)	16	8	8	89	11.1	1	1	0	6	1

JOHNSON, TRE' — OT — REDSKINS

PERSONAL: Born August 30, 1971, in Manhattan, N.Y. ... 6-2/326. ... Full name: Edward Stanton Johnson III. ... Name pronounced TRAY.
HIGH SCHOOL: Peekskill (N.Y.).
COLLEGE: Temple (degree in social administration, 1993).
TRANSACTIONS/CAREER NOTES: Selected by Washington Redskins in second round (31st pick overall) of 1994 NFL draft. ... Signed by Redskins (July 22, 1994). ... On injured reserve with shoulder injury (December 16, 1997-remainder of season). ... Granted unconditional free agency (February 13, 1998). ... Re-signed by Redskins (February 13, 1998).
PLAYING EXPERIENCE: Washington NFL, 1994-1997. ... Games/Games started: 1994 (14/1), 1995 (10/9), 1996 (15/15), 1997 (11/10). Total: 50/35.
PRO STATISTICS: 1994—Ran four yards with lateral from kickoff return. 1996—Recovered one fumble.

JOHNSTON, DARYL — FB — COWBOYS

PERSONAL: Born February 10, 1966, in Youngstown, N.Y. ... 6-2/242. ... Full name: Daryl Peter Johnston. ... Nickname: Moose.
HIGH SCHOOL: Lewiston-Porter Central (Youngstown, N.Y.).
COLLEGE: Syracuse (degree in economics, 1989).
TRANSACTIONS/CAREER NOTES: Selected by Dallas Cowboys in second round (39th pick overall) of 1989 NFL draft. ... Signed by Cowboys (July 24, 1989). ... Granted free agency (March 1, 1993). ... Re-signed by Cowboys (July 16, 1993). ... Granted unconditional free agency (February 17, 1994). ... Re-signed by Cowboys (April 7, 1994). ... Granted unconditional free agency (February 14, 1997). ... Re-signed by Cowboys (March 19, 1997).
CHAMPIONSHIP GAME EXPERIENCE: Played in NFC championship game (1992-1995 seasons). ... Member of Super Bowl championship team (1992, 1993 and 1995 seasons).
HONORS: Played in Pro Bowl (1993 and 1994 seasons).
PRO STATISTICS: 1990—Recovered one fumble. 1992—Recovered one fumble. 1993—Recovered one fumble. 1995—Recovered one fumble. 1996—Recovered one fumble.
SINGLE GAME HIGHS (regular season): Attempts—16 (December 24, 1989, vs. Green Bay); yards—60 (December 24, 1989, vs. Green Bay); and rushing touchdowns—1 (October 29, 1995, vs. Atlanta).

Year Team	G	GS	RUSHING Att.	Yds.	Avg.	TD	RECEIVING No.	Yds.	Avg.	TD	TOTALS TD	2pt.	Pts.	Fum.
1989—Dallas NFL	16	10	67	212	3.2	0	16	133	8.3	3	3	...	18	3
1990—Dallas NFL	16	0	10	35	3.5	0	14	148	10.6	1	2	...	12	1
1991—Dallas NFL	16	14	17	54	3.2	0	28	244	8.7	1	1	...	6	0
1992—Dallas NFL	16	16	17	61	3.6	0	32	249	7.8	2	2	...	12	0
1993—Dallas NFL	16	16	24	74	3.1	3	50	372	7.4	1	4	...	24	1
1994—Dallas NFL	16	16	40	138	3.5	2	44	325	7.4	2	4	0	24	2
1995—Dallas NFL	16	16	25	111	4.4	2	30	248	8.3	1	3	0	18	1
1996—Dallas NFL	16	15	22	48	2.2	0	43	278	6.5	1	1	0	6	1
1997—Dallas NFL	6	6	2	3	1.5	0	18	166	9.2	1	1	0	6	1
Pro totals (9 years)	134	109	224	736	3.3	8	275	2163	7.9	13	21	0	126	10

JOHNSTONE, LANCE DE RAIDERS

PERSONAL: Born June 11, 1973, in Philadelphia. ... 6-4/252.
HIGH SCHOOL: Germantown (Pa.).
COLLEGE: Temple.
TRANSACTIONS/CAREER NOTES: Selected by Oakland Raiders in second round (57th pick overall) of 1996 NFL draft. ... Signed by Raiders for 1996 season.
PRO STATISTICS: 1997—Recovered one fumble for two yards.

Year Team	G	GS	SACKS
1996—Oakland NFL	16	10	1.0
1997—Oakland NFL	14	6	3.5
Pro totals (2 years)	30	16	4.5

JONES, BRENT TE

PERSONAL: Born February 12, 1963, in Santa Clara, Calif. ... 6-4/230. ... Full name: Brent Michael Jones. ... Son of Mike Jones, selected by Oakland Raiders in 21st round of 1961 AFL draft and by Pittsburgh Steelers in 20th round of 1961 NFL draft.
HIGH SCHOOL: Leland (San Jose, Calif.).
COLLEGE: Santa Clara (degree in economics, 1986).
TRANSACTIONS/CAREER NOTES: Selected by Pittsburgh Steelers in fifth round (135th pick overall) of 1986 NFL draft. ... Signed by Steelers (July 30, 1986). ... On injured reserve with neck injury (August 19-September 23, 1986). ... Released by Steelers (September 24, 1986). ... Signed by San Francisco 49ers (December 24, 1986). ... On injured reserve with neck injury (September 1-December 5, 1987). ... Crossed picket line during players strike (October 14, 1987). ... On injured reserve with knee injury (August 29-October 5, 1988). ... Re-signed by 49ers (October 7, 1988). ... Granted unconditional free agency (February 1-April 1, 1989). ... Re-signed by 49ers (April 28, 1989). ... On injured reserve with knee injury (September 11-November 2, 1991). ... Granted free agency (February 1, 1992). ... Re-signed by 49ers (August 4, 1992). ... Announced retirement (January 21, 1998).
CHAMPIONSHIP GAME EXPERIENCE: Played in NFC championship game (1988-1990, 1992-1994 and 1997 seasons). ... Member of Super Bowl championship team (1988, 1989 and 1994 seasons).
HONORS: Played in Pro Bowl (1992-1995 seasons).
PRO STATISTICS: 1990—Recovered two fumbles. 1991—Recovered one fumble. 1993—Recovered two fumbles. 1994—Recovered one fumble. 1995—Recovered one fumble.
SINGLE GAME HIGHS (regular season): Receptions—8 (October 3, 1993, vs. Minnesota); yards—125 (September 23, 1990, vs. Atlanta); and touchdown receptions—2 (September 14, 1997, vs. New Orleans).
STATISTICAL PLATEAUS: 100-yard receiving games: 1990 (1).

Year Team	G	GS	RECEIVING No.	Yds.	Avg.	TD	TOTALS TD	2pt.	Pts.	Fum.
1986—						Did not play.				
1987—San Francisco NFL	4	0	2	35	17.5	0	0	...	0	0
1988—San Francisco NFL	11	0	8	57	7.1	2	2	...	12	0
1989—San Francisco NFL	16	16	40	500	12.5	4	4	...	24	0
1990—San Francisco NFL	16	16	56	747	13.3	5	5	...	30	2
1991—San Francisco NFL	10	9	27	417	15.4	0	0	...	0	2
1992—San Francisco NFL	15	15	45	628	14.0	4	4	...	24	1
1993—San Francisco NFL	16	16	68	735	10.8	3	3	...	18	2
1994—San Francisco NFL	15	15	49	670	13.7	9	9	1	56	1
1995—San Francisco NFL	16	16	60	595	9.9	3	3	0	18	3
1996—San Francisco NFL	11	10	33	428	13.0	1	1	0	6	0
1997—San Francisco NFL	13	12	29	383	13.2	2	2	0	12	1
Pro totals (11 years)	143	125	417	5195	12.5	33	33	1	200	12

JONES, BRIAN LB SAINTS

PERSONAL: Born January 22, 1968, in Iowa City, Iowa. ... 6-1/250. ... Full name: Brian Keith Jones.
HIGH SCHOOL: Dunbar (Lubbock, Texas).
COLLEGE: UCLA, then Texas.
TRANSACTIONS/CAREER NOTES: Selected by Los Angeles Raiders in eighth round (213th pick overall) of 1991 NFL draft. ... Released by Raiders (August 26, 1991). ... Signed by Indianapolis Colts to practice squad (September 9, 1991). ... Activated (October 4, 1991). ... Granted unconditional free agency (February 1, 1992). ... Signed by Miami Dolphins (April 1, 1992). ... Released by Dolphins (July 20, 1992). ... Signed by Raiders for 1994 season. ... Released by Raiders (August 30, 1994). ... Selected by Scottish Claymores in 33rd round (197th pick overall) of 1995 World League Draft. ... Signed by New Orleans Saints (July 31, 1995). ... Granted free agency (February 14, 1997). ... Re-signed by Saints (June 1, 1997). ... On injured reserve with knee injury (August 18, 1997-entire season).
PLAYING EXPERIENCE: Indianapolis NFL, 1991; Scottish Claymores W.L., 1995; New Orleans NFL, 1995 and 1996 ... Games/Games started: 1991 (11/1), 1995 (W.L.-games played unavailable; NFL-16/7), 1996 (16/1). Total: 43/9.
PRO STATISTICS: W.L.: 1995—Credited with 1 1/2 sacks. NFL: 1995—Credited with one sack and recovered one fumble. 1996—Recovered one fumble for 11 yards and a touchdown.

JONES, CEDRIC DE GIANTS

PERSONAL: Born April 30, 1974, in Houston ... 6-4/285.
HIGH SCHOOL: Lamar (Houston).
COLLEGE: Oklahoma.
TRANSACTIONS/CAREER NOTES: Selected by New York Giants in first round (fifth pick overall) of 1996 NFL draft. ... Signed by Giants (July 27, 1996). ... On injured reserve with leg injury (December 11, 1997-remainder of season).
PLAYING EXPERIENCE: New York Giants NFL, 1996 and 1997. ... Games/Games started: 1996 (16/0), 1997 (9/2). Total: 25/2.
HONORS: Named defensive lineman on THE SPORTING NEWS college All-America first team (1995).

JONES, CHARLIE WR CHARGERS

PERSONAL: Born December 1, 1972, in Hanford, Calif. ... 5-8/175. ... Full name: Charlie Edward Jones.
HIGH SCHOOL: Lemoore (Calif.).
COLLEGE: Fresno State.
TRANSACTIONS/CAREER NOTES: Selected by San Diego Chargers in fourth round (114th pick overall) of 1996 NFL draft. ... Signed by Chargers for 1996 season.
PRO STATISTICS: 1996—Returned one punt for 21 yards. 1997—Rushed four times for 42 yards.
SINGLE GAME HIGHS (regular season): Receptions—7 (October 27, 1996, vs. Seattle); yards—86 (November 16, 1997, vs. Oakland); and touchdown receptions—1 (November 2, 1997, vs. Cincinnati).

			RECEIVING				TOTALS		
Year Team	G	GS	No.	Yds.	Avg.	TD	TD	2pt.	Pts.	Fum.
1996—San Diego NFL	14	4	41	524	12.8	4	4	0	24	0
1997—San Diego NFL	16	11	32	423	13.2	1	1	0	6	0
Pro totals (2 years)	30	15	73	947	13.0	5	5	0	30	0

JONES, CHRIS T. WR EAGLES

PERSONAL: Born August 7, 1971, in West Palm Beach, Fla. ... 6-3/209. ... Full name: Chris Todd Jones.
HIGH SCHOOL: Cardinal Newman (West Palm Beach, Fla.).
COLLEGE: Miami (Fla.).
TRANSACTIONS/CAREER NOTES: Selected by Philadelphia Eagles in third round (78th pick overall) of 1995 NFL draft. ... Signed by Eagles (July 12, 1995). ... Granted free agency (February 13, 1998). ... Re-signed by Eagles (June 15, 1998).
PRO STATISTICS: 1995—Returned two kickoffs for 46 yards.
SINGLE GAME HIGHS (regular season): Receptions—9 (September 15, 1996, vs. Detroit); yards—121 (September 15, 1996, vs. Detroit); and touchdown receptions—1 (December 14, 1996, vs. New York Jets).
STATISTICAL PLATEAUS: 100-yard receiving games: 1996 (2).

			RECEIVING				TOTALS		
Year Team	G	GS	No.	Yds.	Avg.	TD	TD	2pt.	Pts.	Fum.
1995—Philadelphia NFL	12	0	5	61	12.2	0	0	0	0	0
1996—Philadelphia NFL	16	16	70	859	12.3	5	5	0	30	1
1997—Philadelphia NFL	4	1	5	73	14.6	0	0	0	0	0
Pro totals (3 years)	32	17	80	993	12.4	5	5	0	30	1

JONES, CLARENCE OT SAINTS

PERSONAL: Born May 6, 1968, in Brooklyn, N.Y. ... 6-6/280. ... Full name: Clarence Thomas Jones.
HIGH SCHOOL: Central Islip (N.Y.).
COLLEGE: Maryland.
TRANSACTIONS/CAREER NOTES: Selected by New York Giants in fourth round (111th pick overall) of 1991 NFL draft. ... Placed on injured reserve with ankle injury (October 1991). ... Activated (November 1991). ... Granted free agency (February 17, 1994). ... Released by Giants (May 6, 1994). ... Signed by Los Angeles Rams (June 1, 1994). ... Rams franchise moved to St. Louis (April 12, 1995). ... Granted unconditional free agency (February 16, 1996). ... Signed by New Orleans Saints (February 20, 1996).
PLAYING EXPERIENCE: New York Giants NFL, 1991-1993; Los Angeles Rams NFL, 1994; St. Louis NFL, 1995; New Orleans NFL, 1996 and 1997. ... Games/Games started: 1991 (3/0), 1992 (3/0), 1993 (4/0), 1994 (16/16), 1995 (13/0), 1996 (16/16), 1997 (15/15). Total: 70/47.
PRO STATISTICS: 1997—Recovered two fumbles.

JONES, DAMON TE JAGUARS

PERSONAL: Born September 18, 1974, in Evanston, Ill. ... 6-5/272.
HIGH SCHOOL: Evanston (Ill.).
COLLEGE: Michigan, then Southern Illinois.
TRANSACTIONS/CAREER NOTES: Selected by Jacksonville Jaguars in fifth round (147th pick overall) of 1997 NFL draft. ... Signed by Jaguars (May 30, 1997).
SINGLE GAME HIGHS (regular season): Receptions—2 (December 14, 1997, vs. Buffalo); yards—34 (November 30, 1997, vs. Baltimore); and touchdown receptions—1 (December 21, 1997, vs. Oakland).

			RECEIVING				TOTALS		
Year Team	G	GS	No.	Yds.	Avg.	TD	TD	2pt.	Pts.	Fum.
1997—Jacksonville NFL	11	3	5	87	17.4	2	2	0	12	0

JONES, DONTA LB STEELERS

PERSONAL: Born August 27, 1972, in Washington, D.C. ... 6-2/234. ... Full name: Markeysia Donta Jones. ... Name pronounced DON-tay.
HIGH SCHOOL: McDonough (Pomfret, Md.).
COLLEGE: Nebraska (degree in accounting and business administration, 1994).
TRANSACTIONS/CAREER NOTES: Selected by Pittsburgh Steelers in fourth round (125th pick overall) of 1995 NFL draft. ... Signed by Steelers (July 19, 1995). ... Granted free agency (February 13, 1998). ... Re-signed by Steelers (June 9, 1998).
PLAYING EXPERIENCE: Pittsburgh NFL, 1995-1997. ... Games/Games started: 1995 (16/0), 1996 (15/2), 1997 (16/4). Total: 47/6.
CHAMPIONSHIP GAME EXPERIENCE: Played in AFC championship game (1995 and 1997 seasons). ... Played in Super Bowl XXX (1995 season).
PRO STATISTICS: 1996—Credited with one sack and returned one punt for three yards. 1997—Recovered one fumble for six yards.

JONES, ERNEST　　　　　DE　　　　　BRONCOS

PERSONAL: Born April 1, 1971, in Utica, N.Y. ... 6-2/255. ... Full name: Ernest Lee Jones.
HIGH SCHOOL: Utica (N.Y.) Senior Academy.
COLLEGE: Oregon.
TRANSACTIONS/CAREER NOTES: Selected by Los Angeles Rams in third round (100th pick overall) of 1994 NFL draft. ... Signed by Rams (June 20, 1994). ... On injured reserve with knee injury (August 28, 1994-entire season). ... Released by Rams (August 21, 1995). ... Signed by New Orleans Saints to practice squad (August 28, 1995). ... Activated (October 21, 1995). ... Released by Saints (October 30, 1995). ... Re-signed by Saints to practice squad (November 1, 1995). ... Granted free agency (February 16, 1996) ... Signed by Denver Broncos (March 25, 1996). ... Granted free agency (February 13, 1998). ... Re-signed by Broncos (April 7, 1998).
PLAYING EXPERIENCE: New Orleans NFL, 1995; Denver NFL, 1996 and 1997. ... Games/Games started: 1995 (1/0), 1996 (6/0), 1997 (1/0). Total: 8/0.
CHAMPIONSHIP GAME EXPERIENCE: Member of Broncos for AFC championship game (1997 season); inactive. ... Member of Super Bowl championship team (1997 season); inactive.

JONES, FREDDIE　　　　　TE　　　　　CHARGERS

PERSONAL: Born September 16, 1974, in Cheverly, Md. ... 6-4/260. ... Full name: Freddie Ray Jones.
HIGH SCHOOL: McKinley (Landover, Md.).
COLLEGE: North Carolina.
TRANSACTIONS/CAREER NOTES: Selected by San Diego Chargers in second round (45th pick overall) of 1997 NFL draft. ... Signed by Chargers (May 21, 1997). ... On injured reserve with leg injury (December 12, 1997-remainder of season).
SINGLE GAME HIGHS (regular season): Receptions—5 (November 2, 1997, vs. Cincinnati); yards—81 (October 16, 1997, vs. Kansas City); and touchdown receptions—1 (September 7, 1997, vs. New Orleans).

			RECEIVING				TOTALS			
Year　Team	G	GS	No.	Yds.	Avg.	TD	TD	2pt.	Pts.	Fum.
1997—San Diego NFL	13	8	41	505	12.3	2	2	0	12	0

JONES, GEORGE　　　　　RB　　　　　STEELERS

PERSONAL: Born December 31, 1973, in Greenville, S.C. ... 5-9/204. ... Full name: George Dee Jones.
HIGH SCHOOL: Eastside (Greenville, S.C.).
JUNIOR COLLEGE: Bakersfield (Calif.) College.
COLLEGE: San Diego State.
TRANSACTIONS/CAREER NOTES: Selected by Pittsburgh Steelers in fifth round (154th pick overall) of 1997 NFL draft. ... Signed by Steelers (July 15, 1997).
CHAMPIONSHIP GAME EXPERIENCE: Member of Steelers for AFC championship game (1997 season); inactive.
PRO STATISTICS: 1997—Recovered one fumble.
SINGLE GAME HIGHS (regular season): Attempts—16 (December 21, 1997, vs. Tennessee); yards—64 (November 16, 1997, vs. Cincinnati); and rushing touchdowns—1 (November 9, 1997, vs. Baltimore).

			RUSHING				RECEIVING				TOTALS			
Year　Team	G	GS	Att.	Yds.	Avg.	TD	No.	Yds.	Avg.	TD	TD	2pt.	Pts.	Fum.
1997—Pittsburgh NFL	16	1	72	235	3.3	1	16	96	6.0	1	2	0	12	3

JONES, GREG　　　　　LB　　　　　REDSKINS

PERSONAL: Born May 22, 1974, in Denver. ... 6-4/238. ... Full name: Greg Phillip Jones.
HIGH SCHOOL: John F. Kennedy (Denver).
COLLEGE: Colorado.
TRANSACTIONS/CAREER NOTES: Selected by Washington Redskins in second round (51st pick overall) of 1997 NFL draft. ... Signed by Redskins (July 11, 1997).
PRO STATISTICS: 1997—Returned one kickoff for six yards.

Year　Team	G	GS	SACKS
1997—Washington NFL	16	3	3.5

JONES, HENRY　　　　　S　　　　　BILLS

PERSONAL: Born December 29, 1967, in St. Louis. ... 5-11/197.
HIGH SCHOOL: St. Louis University.
COLLEGE: Illinois (degree in psychology, 1990).
TRANSACTIONS/CAREER NOTES: Selected by Buffalo Bills in first round (26th pick overall) of 1991 NFL draft. ... Signed by Bills (August 30, 1991). ... Activated (September 7, 1991). ... Designated by Bills as transition player (February 15, 1994). ... On injured reserve with broken leg (October 9, 1996-remainder of season).
CHAMPIONSHIP GAME EXPERIENCE: Played in AFC championship game (1991-1993 seasons). ... Played in Super Bowl XXVI (1991 season), Super Bowl XXVII (1992 season) and Super Bowl XXVIII (1993 season).
HONORS: Named strong safety on THE SPORTING NEWS NFL All-Pro team (1992). ... Played in Pro Bowl (1992 season).
RECORDS: Shares NFL single-game record for most touchdowns scored by interception—2 (September 20, 1992, vs. Indianapolis).
PRO STATISTICS: 1991—Recovered one fumble. 1992—Recovered two fumbles. 1993—Credited with one safety and recovered two fumbles. 1994—Recovered one fumble. 1995—Recovered one fumble. 1997—Returned one punt for no yards, fumbled once and recovered one fumble.

				INTERCEPTIONS				SACKS
Year Team	G	GS	No.	Yds.	Avg.	TD		No.
1991—Buffalo NFL	15	0	0	0	...	0		0.0
1992—Buffalo NFL	16	16	†8	*263	32.9	▲2		0.0
1993—Buffalo NFL	16	16	2	92	46.0	▲1		2.0
1994—Buffalo NFL	16	16	2	45	22.5	0		1.0
1995—Buffalo NFL	13	13	1	10	10.0	0		0.0
1996—Buffalo NFL	5	5	0	0	...	0		0.0
1997—Buffalo NFL	15	15	0	0	...	0		2.0
Pro totals (7 years)	96	81	13	410	31.5	3		5.0

JONES, JAMES — DT — RAVENS

PERSONAL: Born February 6, 1969, in Davenport, Iowa. ... 6-2/290. ... Full name: James Alfie Jones.

HIGH SCHOOL: Davenport (Iowa) Central.

COLLEGE: Northern Iowa (degree in science, 1992).

TRANSACTIONS/CAREER NOTES: Selected by Cleveland Browns in third round (57th pick overall) of 1991 NFL draft. ... Signed by Browns (1991). ... Granted unconditional free agency (February 17, 1995). ... Signed by Denver Broncos (February 24, 1995). ... Released by Broncos (July 17, 1996). ... Signed by Baltimore Ravens (August 21, 1996).

PRO STATISTICS: 1991—Credited with one safety, intercepted one pass for 20 yards and a touchdown and recovered three fumbles for 15 yards. 1992—Recovered one fumble. 1993—Rushed twice for two yards and one touchdown. 1994—Rushed once for no yards, caught one pass for one yard and recovered two fumbles. 1995—Recovered two fumbles. 1996—Caught one pass for two yards and a touchdown. 1997—Recovered one fumble.

Year Team	G	GS	SACKS
1991—Cleveland NFL	16	16	1.0
1992—Cleveland NFL	16	16	4.0
1993—Cleveland NFL	16	12	5.5
1994—Cleveland NFL	16	5	3.0
1995—Denver NFL	16	16	1.0
1996—Baltimore NFL	16	11	1.0
1997—Baltimore NFL	16	16	6.0
Pro totals (7 years)	112	92	21.5

JONES, JIMMIE — DT

PERSONAL: Born January 9, 1966, in Lakeland, Fla. ... 6-4/285. ... Full name: Jimmie Sims Jones.

HIGH SCHOOL: Okeechobee (Fla.).

COLLEGE: Miami (Fla.).

TRANSACTIONS/CAREER NOTES: Selected by Dallas Cowboys in third round (63rd pick overall) of 1990 NFL draft. ... Signed by Cowboys (August 3, 1990). ... Granted unconditional free agency (February 17, 1994). ... Signed by Los Angeles Rams (March 4, 1994). ... Rams franchise moved to St. Louis (April 12, 1995). ... Released by Rams (April 22, 1997). ... Signed by Philadelphia Eagles (July 22, 1997). ... Granted unconditional free agency (February 13, 1998).

CHAMPIONSHIP GAME EXPERIENCE: Played in NFC championship game (1992 and 1993 seasons). ... Member of Super Bowl championship team (1992 and 1993 seasons).

POST SEASON RECORDS: Shares Super Bowl career and single-game records for most fumbles recovered—2; and most touchdowns by fumble recovery—1 (January 31, 1993, vs. Buffalo).

PRO STATISTICS: 1991—Recovered two fumbles for 15 yards. 1994—Recovered one fumble. 1996—Recovered two fumbles.

Year Team	G	GS	SACKS
1990—Dallas NFL	16	6	7.5
1991—Dallas NFL	16	6	2.0
1992—Dallas NFL	16	2	4.0
1993—Dallas NFL	15	2	5.5
1994—Los Angeles Rams NFL	14	14	5.0
1995—St. Louis NFL	16	16	0.0
1996—St. Louis NFL	14	14	5.5
1997—Philadelphia NFL	14	0	2.5
Pro totals (8 years)	121	60	32.0

JONES, LENOY — LB — OILERS

PERSONAL: Born September 25, 1974, in Groesbeck, Texas. ... 6-1/232.

HIGH SCHOOL: Groesbeck (Texas).

COLLEGE: Texas Christian.

TRANSACTIONS/CAREER NOTES: Signed as non-drafted free agent by Houston Oilers (April 23, 1996). ... Released by Oilers (August 20, 1996). ... Re-signed by Oilers to practice squad (August 26, 1996). ... Activated (October 9, 1996). ... Oilers franchise moved to Tennessee for 1997 season.

PLAYING EXPERIENCE: Houston NFL, 1996; Tennessee NFL, 1997. ... Games/Games started: 1996 (11/0), 1997 (16/0). Total: 27/0.

PRO STATISTICS: 1996—Recovered one fumble. 1997—Credited with one sack.

JONES, MARCUS — DT — BUCCANEERS

PERSONAL: Born August 15, 1973, in Jacksonville, N.C. ... 6-6/286. ... Full name: Marcus Edward Jones.

HIGH SCHOOL: Southwest Onslow (Jacksonville, N.C.).

COLLEGE: North Carolina.

TRANSACTIONS/CAREER NOTES: Selected by Tampa Bay Buccaneers in first round (22nd pick overall) of 1996 NFL draft. ... Signed by Buccaneers (July 21, 1996). ... On injured reserve with ankle injury (December 23, 1997-remainder of playoffs).

HONORS: Named defensive lineman on THE SPORTING NEWS college All-America second team (1995).

PRO STATISTICS: 1997—Recovered one fumble.

Year Team	G	GS	SACKS
1996—Tampa Bay NFL	16	3	1.0
1997—Tampa Bay NFL	7	1	0.0
Pro totals (2 years)	23	4	1.0

JONES, MARVIN — LB — JETS

PERSONAL: Born June 28, 1972, in Miami. ... 6-2/244. ... Full name: Marvin Maurice Jones.
HIGH SCHOOL: Miami Northwestern.
COLLEGE: Florida State.
TRANSACTIONS/CAREER NOTES: Selected after junior season by New York Jets in first round (fourth pick overall) of 1993 NFL draft. ... Signed by Jets (August 5, 1993). ... On injured reserve with hip injury (November 16, 1993-remainder of season).
HONORS: Butkus Award winner (1992). ... Named College Football Player of the Year by THE SPORTING NEWS (1992). ... Named linebacker on THE SPORTING NEWS college All-America first team (1992).
PRO STATISTICS: 1993—Recovered one fumble. 1997—Recovered one fumble.

Year Team	G	GS	SACKS
1993—New York Jets NFL	9	0	0.0
1994—New York Jets NFL	15	11	0.5
1995—New York Jets NFL	10	10	1.5
1996—New York Jets NFL	12	12	1.0
1997—New York Jets NFL	16	16	3.0
Pro totals (5 years)	62	49	6.0

JONES, MIKE — LB — RAMS

PERSONAL: Born April 15, 1969, in Kansas City, Mo. ... 6-1/240. ... Full name: Michael Anthony Jones.
HIGH SCHOOL: Southwest (Kansas City, Mo.).
COLLEGE: Missouri.
TRANSACTIONS/CAREER NOTES: Signed as non-drafted free agent by Los Angeles Raiders (April 1991). ... Assigned by Raiders to Sacramento Surge in 1992 World League enhancement allocation program (February 20, 1992). ... Raiders franchise moved to Oakland (July 21, 1995). ... Granted unconditional free agency (February 14, 1997). ... Signed by St. Louis Rams (March 18, 1997).
PLAYING EXPERIENCE: Los Angeles Raiders NFL, 1991-1994; Sacramento W.L., 1992; Oakland NFL, 1995 and 1996; St. Louis NFL, 1997. ... Games/Games started: 1991 (16/0), 1992 (W.L.-7/7; NFL-16/0), 1993 (16/2), 1994 (16/1), 1995 (16/16), 1996 (15/15), 1997 (16/16). Total W.L.: 7/7. Total NFL: 111/50. Total Pro: 118/57.
PRO STATISTICS: W.L.: 1992—Credited with two sacks. NFL: 1995—Intercepted one pass for 23 yards, recovered two fumbles for 52 yards and a touchdown. 1996—Credited with one sack. 1997—Intercepted one pass for no yards and credited with two sacks.

JONES, MIKE — DE — PATRIOTS

PERSONAL: Born August 25, 1969, in Columbia, S.C. ... 6-4/280. ... Full name: Michael David Jones.
HIGH SCHOOL: C.A. Johnson (Columbia, S.C.).
COLLEGE: North Carolina State.
TRANSACTIONS/CAREER NOTES: Selected by Phoenix Cardinals in second round (32nd pick overall) of 1991 NFL draft. ... Signed by Cardinals (July 15, 1991). ... Granted free agency (February 17, 1994). ... Signed by New England Patriots (June 7, 1994). ... Granted unconditional free agency (February 14, 1997). ... Re-signed by Patriots (March 10, 1997).
CHAMPIONSHIP GAME EXPERIENCE: Played in Super Bowl XXXI (1996 season).
PRO STATISTICS: 1994—Recovered one fumble. 1996—Recovered one fumble for 31 yards. 1997—Recovered one fumble.

Year Team	G	GS	SACKS
1991—Phoenix NFL	16	1	0.0
1992—Phoenix NFL	15	15	6.0
1993—Phoenix NFL	16	2	3.0
1994—New England NFL	16	16	6.0
1995—New England NFL	13	3	3.0
1996—New England NFL	16	12	2.0
1997—New England NFL	16	7	4.0
Pro totals (7 years)	108	56	24.0

JONES, REGGIE — WR — CHIEFS

PERSONAL: Born May 5, 1971, in Kansas City, Kan. ... 6-0/191.
HIGH SCHOOL: Wyandotte (Kansas City, Kan.).
JUNIOR COLLEGE: Butler County (Kan.) Community College.
COLLEGE: Louisiana State (did not play football).
TRANSACTIONS/CAREER NOTES: Signed as non-drafted free agent by Washington Redskins (April 27, 1995). ... Released by Redskins (August 22, 1995). ... Signed by Carolina Panthers to practice squad (September 4, 1995). ... Activated (October 21, 1995); did not play. ... Released by Panthers (August 22, 1996). ... Signed by Kansas City Chiefs (April 7, 1997). ... On injured reserve with thigh injury (August 15, 1997-entire season). ... Assigned by Chiefs to England Monarchs in 1998 NFL Europe enhancement allocation program (February 18, 1998).

JONES, ROBERT — LB — DOLPHINS

PERSONAL: Born September 27, 1969, in Blackstone, Va. ... 6-3/249. ... Full name: Robert Lee Jones.
HIGH SCHOOL: Nottoway (Va.), then Fork Union (Va.) Military Academy.
COLLEGE: East Carolina.
TRANSACTIONS/CAREER NOTES: Selected by Dallas Cowboys in first round (24th pick overall) of 1992 NFL draft. ... Signed by Cowboys (April 26, 1992). ... Granted unconditional free agency (February 16, 1996). ... Signed by St. Louis Rams (March 5, 1996). ... Released by Rams (June 2, 1998). ... Signed by Miami Dolphins (June 10, 1998).

PLAYING EXPERIENCE: Dallas NFL, 1992-1995; St. Louis NFL, 1996 and 1997. ... Games/Games started: 1992 (15/13), 1993 (13/3), 1994 (16/16), 1995 (12/12), 1996 (16/13), 1997 (16/15). Total: 88/72.
CHAMPIONSHIP GAME EXPERIENCE: Played in NFC championship game (1992-1995 seasons). ... Member of Super Bowl championship team (1992, 1993 and 1995 seasons).
HONORS: Named linebacker on THE SPORTING NEWS college All-America second team (1990). ... Named linebacker on THE SPORTING NEWS college All-America first team (1991).
PRO STATISTICS: 1992—Credited with one sack and recovered one fumble. 1993—Returned one kickoff for 12 yards. 1994—Returned one kickoff for eight yards and recovered one fumble. 1995—Credited with one sack. 1996—Intercepted one pass for no yards. 1997—Credited with one sack.

JONES, ROD — OT/G — BENGALS

PERSONAL: Born January 11, 1974, in Detroit. ... 6-4/320. ... Full name: Rodrek E. Jones.
HIGH SCHOOL: Henry Ford (Detroit).
COLLEGE: Kansas.
TRANSACTIONS/CAREER NOTES: Selected by Cincinnati Bengals in seventh round (219th pick overall) of 1996 NFL draft. ... Signed by Bengals (July 15, 1996).
PLAYING EXPERIENCE: Cincinnati NFL, 1996 and 1997. ... Games/Games started: 1996 (6/1), 1997 (13/8). Total: 19/9.

JONES, ROGER — CB

PERSONAL: Born April 22, 1969, in Cleveland. ... 5-9/175. ... Full name: Roger Carver Jones.
HIGH SCHOOL: Pearl-Cohn (Nashville).
COLLEGE: Tennessee State.
TRANSACTIONS/CAREER NOTES: Signed as non-drafted free agent by Indianapolis Colts (April 23, 1991). ... Released by Colts (August 19, 1991). ... Signed by Tampa Bay Buccaneers to practice squad (October 1, 1991). ... Activated (November 8, 1991). ... Granted unconditional free agency (February 1-April 1, 1992). ... Re-signed by Buccaneers for 1992 season. ... On injured reserve with leg injury (September 4-October 30, 1992). ... Claimed on waivers by Cincinnati Bengals (August 29, 1994). ... Granted unconditional free agency (February 16, 1996). ... Re-signed by Bengals (March 14, 1996). ... Released by Bengals (September 9, 1997). ... Signed by Tennessee Oilers (November 5, 1997). ... On injured reserve with back injury (December 5, 1997-remainder of season). ... Granted unconditional free agency (February 13, 1998).
PRO STATISTICS: 1991—Recovered one fumble. 1992—Recovered two fumbles for 26 yards and a touchdown. 1993—Recovered three fumbles for 12 yards. 1994—Returned one punt for no yards and fumbled once.

| | | | INTERCEPTIONS | | | | SACKS |
Year Team	G	GS	No.	Yds.	Avg.	TD	No.
1991—Tampa Bay NFL	6	0	0	0	...	0	0.0
1992—Tampa Bay NFL	9	1	0	0	...	0	0.0
1993—Tampa Bay NFL	16	5	0	0	...	0	1.0
1994—Cincinnati NFL	16	0	0	0	...	0	1.5
1995—Cincinnati NFL	16	15	1	17	17.0	▲1	2.0
1996—Cincinnati NFL	14	1	1	30	30.0	0	0.0
1997—Tennessee NFL	2	0	1	24	24.0	0	0.0
Pro totals (7 years)	79	22	3	71	23.7	1	4.5

JONES, RONDELL — S — RAVENS

PERSONAL: Born May 7, 1971, in Sunderland, Mass. ... 6-2/210. ... Full name: Rondell Tony Jones.
HIGH SCHOOL: Northern (Owings, Md.).
COLLEGE: North Carolina.
TRANSACTIONS/CAREER NOTES: Selected by Denver Broncos in third round (69th pick overall) of 1993 NFL draft. ... Signed by Broncos (July 15, 1993). ... Granted free agency (February 16, 1996). ... Re-signed by Broncos (August 27, 1996). ... Granted unconditional free agency (February 14, 1997). ... Signed by Baltimore Ravens (April 8, 1997).
PRO STATISTICS: 1994—Recovered one fumble.

| | | | INTERCEPTIONS | | | |
Year Team	G	GS	No.	Yds.	Avg.	TD
1993—Denver NFL	16	0	0	0	...	0
1994—Denver NFL	16	3	2	9	4.5	0
1995—Denver NFL	14	0	0	0	...	0
1996—Denver NFL	16	0	0	0	...	0
1997—Baltimore NFL	14	12	1	15	15.0	0
Pro totals (5 years)	76	15	3	24	8.0	0

JONES, TONY — OT — BRONCOS

PERSONAL: Born May 24, 1966, in Royston, Ga. ... 6-5/291. ... Full name: Tony Edward Jones.
HIGH SCHOOL: Franklin County (Carnesville, Ga.).
COLLEGE: Western Carolina (degree in management, 1989).
TRANSACTIONS/CAREER NOTES: Signed as non-drafted free agent by Cleveland Browns (May 2, 1988). ... On injured reserve with toe injury (August 29-October 22, 1988). ... On injured reserve with toe injury (September 20-November 7, 1989). ... Granted free agency (February 1, 1992). ... Re-signed by Browns (July 29, 1992). ... Browns franchise moved to Baltimore and renamed Ravens for 1996 season (March 11, 1996). ... Traded by Ravens to Denver Broncos for second-round pick (S Kim Herring) in 1997 draft (February 14, 1997).
PLAYING EXPERIENCE: Cleveland NFL, 1988-1995; Baltimore NFL, 1996; Denver NFL, 1997. ... Games/Games started: 1988 (4/0), 1989 (9/3), 1990 (16/16), 1991 (16/16), 1992 (16/16), 1993 (16/16), 1994 (16/16), 1995 (16/16), 1996 (15/15), 1997 (16/16). Total: 140/130.
CHAMPIONSHIP GAME EXPERIENCE: Played in AFC championship game (1989 and 1997 seasons). ... Member of Super Bowl championship team (1997 season).
PRO STATISTICS: 1989—Recovered one fumble. 1991—Recovered one fumble. 1994—Recovered one fumble. 1995—Recovered one fumble.

JONES, WALTER   OT   SEAHAWKS

PERSONAL: Born January 19, 1974, in Aliceville, Ala. ... 6-5/300.
HIGH SCHOOL: Aliceville (Ala.).
JUNIOR COLLEGE: Holmes (Miss.) Junior College.
COLLEGE: Florida State.
TRANSACTIONS/CAREER NOTES: Selected by Seattle Seahawks in first round (sixth pick overall) of 1997 NFL draft. ... Signed by Seahawks (August 6, 1997).
PLAYING EXPERIENCE: Seattle NFL, 1997. ... Games/Games started: 12/12.

JORDAN, ANDREW   TE   BUCCANEERS

PERSONAL: Born June 21, 1972, in Charlotte. ... 6-4/254. ... Full name: Andrew Jordan Jr.
HIGH SCHOOL: West Charlotte.
COLLEGE: Western Carolina.
TRANSACTIONS/CAREER NOTES: Selected by Minnesota Vikings in sixth round (179th pick overall) of 1994 NFL draft. ... Signed by Vikings (June 17, 1994). ... Released by Vikings (September 23, 1997). ... Signed by Tampa Bay Buccaneers (December 9, 1997).
PRO STATISTICS: 1994—Returned one kickoff for eight yards and recovered a fumble.
SINGLE GAME HIGHS (regular season): Receptions—5 (November 13, 1994, vs. New England); yards—57 (November 13, 1994, vs. New England); and touchdown receptions—1 (November 5, 1995, vs. Green Bay).

				RECEIVING				TOTALS		
Year Team	G	GS	No.	Yds.	Avg.	TD	TD	2pt.	Pts.	Fum.
1994—Minnesota NFL	16	12	35	336	9.6	0	0	1	2	1
1995—Minnesota NFL	13	7	27	185	6.9	2	2	0	12	1
1996—Minnesota NFL	13	9	19	128	6.7	0	0	1	2	0
1997—Minnesota NFL	2	0	0	0	...	0	0	0	0	0
—Tampa Bay NFL	2	0	1	0	0.0	0	0	0	0	0
Pro totals (4 years)	46	28	82	649	7.9	2	2	2	16	2

JORDAN, CHARLES   WR   DOLPHINS

PERSONAL: Born October 9, 1969, in Los Angeles. ... 5-11/185. ... Full name: Charles Alexander Jordan.
HIGH SCHOOL: Morningside (Inglewood, Calif.).
COLLEGE: Long Beach (Calif.) City College.
TRANSACTIONS/CAREER NOTES: Signed as non-drafted free agent by Los Angeles Raiders (May 4, 1993). ... On inactive list for six games (1993). ... On injured reserve with abdominal injury (October 27, 1993-remainder of season. ... Traded by Raiders to Green Bay Packers for fifth-round pick (traded to Washington) in 1995 draft (August 28, 1994). ... Granted free agency (February 16, 1996). ... Tendered offer sheet by Miami Dolphins (March 7, 1996). ... Packers declined to match offer (March 13, 1996).
CHAMPIONSHIP GAME EXPERIENCE: Member of Packers for NFC championship game (1995 season); inactive.
PRO STATISTICS: 1994—Rushed once for five yards. 1995—Recovered one fumble. 1997—Rushed three times for 12 yards and recovered one fumble.
SINGLE GAME HIGHS (regular season): Receptions—5 (December 7, 1997, vs. Detroit); yards—103 (November 30, 1997, vs. Oakland); and touchdown receptions—2 (November 30, 1997, vs. Oakland).
STATISTICAL PLATEAUS: 100-yard receiving games: 1997 (2).

			RECEIVING				PUNT RETURNS				KICKOFF RETURNS				TOTALS			
Year Team	G	GS	No.	Yds.	Avg.	TD	No.	Yds.	Avg.	TD	No.	Yds.	Avg.	TD	TD	2pt.	Pts.	Fum.
1993—L.A. Raiders NFL									Did not play.									
1994—Green Bay NFL	10	0	0	0	...	0	1	0	0.0	0	5	115	23.0	0	0	0	0	1
1995—Green Bay NFL	6	1	7	117	16.7	0	21	213	10.1	0	21	444	21.1	0	2	0	12	1
1996—Miami NFL	6	0	7	152	21.7	0	0	0	...	0	4	81	20.3	0	0	0	0	0
1997—Miami NFL	14	1	27	471	17.4	3	26	273	10.5	0	1	6	6.0	0	3	0	18	2
Pro totals (4 years)	36	2	41	740	18.0	5	48	486	10.1	0	31	646	20.8	0	5	0	30	4

JORDAN, RANDY   RB   RAIDERS

PERSONAL: Born June 6, 1970, in Henderson, N.C. ... 5-10/213. ... Full name: Randy Loment Jordan.
HIGH SCHOOL: Warren County (Warrenton, N.C.).
COLLEGE: North Carolina.
TRANSACTIONS/CAREER NOTES: Signed as non-drafted free agent by Los Angeles Raiders (May 1993). ... Released by Raiders (August 25, 1993). ... Re-signed by Raiders to practice squad (August 31, 1993). ... Activated (October 30, 1993). ... Released by Raiders (August 28, 1994). ... Signed by Jacksonville Jaguars (December 15, 1994). ... Granted free agency (February 14, 1997). ... Re-signed by Jaguars (May 5, 1997). ... Released by Jaguars (August 19, 1997). ... Re-signed by Jaguars (September 24, 1997). ... Granted unconditional free agency (February 13, 1998). ... Signed by Oakland Raiders (June 2, 1998).
CHAMPIONSHIP GAME EXPERIENCE: Played in AFC championship game (1996 season).
PRO STATISTICS: 1993—Caught four passes for 42 yards. 1995—Caught five passes for 89 yards and a touchdown. 1996—Recovered one fumble.
SINGLE GAME HIGHS (regular season): Attempts—20 (September 10, 1995, vs. Cincinnati); yards—64 (September 10, 1995, vs. Cincinnati); and rushing touchdowns—0.

			RUSHING				KICKOFF RETURNS				TOTALS			
Year Team	G	GS	Att.	Yds.	Avg.	TD	No.	Yds.	Avg.	TD	TD	2pt.	Pts.	Fum.
1993—Los Angeles Raiders NFL	10	2	12	33	2.8	0	0	0	...	0	0	0	...	2
1994—								Did not play.						
1995—Jacksonville NFL	12	2	21	62	3.0	0	2	41	20.5	0	1	0	6	0
1996—Jacksonville NFL	15	0	0	0	...	0	26	553	21.3	0	0	0	0	1
1997—Jacksonville NFL	7	0	1	2	2.0	0	0	0	...	0	0	0	0	0
Pro totals (4 years)	44	4	34	97	2.9	0	28	594	21.2	0	1	0	6	3

JORDAN, RICHARD   LB   LIONS

PERSONAL: Born December 1, 1974, in Holdenville, Okla. ... 6-1/245. ... Full name: Richard Lamont Jordan.
HIGH SCHOOL: Vian (Okla.).
COLLEGE: Missouri Southern.
TRANSACTIONS/CAREER NOTES: Selected by Detroit Lions in seventh round (239th pick overall) of 1997 NFL draft. ... Signed by Lions (May 22, 1997). ... Released by Lions (August 25, 1997). ... Re-signed by Lions to practice squad (August 27, 1997). ... Activated (September 27, 1997).
PLAYING EXPERIENCE: Detroit NFL, 1997. ... Games/Games started: 10/0.

JOYCE, MATT   G   CARDINALS

PERSONAL: Born March 30, 1972, in St. Petersburg, Fla. ... 6-7/313.
HIGH SCHOOL: New York Military Academy (Cornwall Hudson, N.Y.).
COLLEGE: Richmond.
TRANSACTIONS/CAREER NOTES: Signed as non-drafted free agent by Dallas Cowboys (May 2, 1994). ... Claimed on waivers by Cincinnati Bengals (August 28, 1994); released after failing physical. ... Signed by Cowboys to practice squad (September 5, 1994). ... Granted free agency after 1994 season. ... Signed by Seattle Seahawks (March 1, 1995). ... Released by Seahawks (August 25, 1996). ... Signed by Arizona Cardinals (December 3, 1996). ... Assigned by Cardinals to Scottish Claymores in 1997 World League enhancement allocation program (February 19, 1997).
PLAYING EXPERIENCE: Seattle NFL, 1995; Arizona NFL, 1996 and 1997. ... Games/Games started: 1995 (16/13), 1996 (2/0), 1997 (9/6). Total: 27/19.
PRO STATISTICS: 1995—Recovered one fumble.

JOYNER, SETH   LB   PACKERS

PERSONAL: Born November 18, 1964, in Spring Valley, N.Y. ... 6-2/245.
HIGH SCHOOL: Spring Valley (N.Y.).
COLLEGE: Texas-El Paso.
TRANSACTIONS/CAREER NOTES: Selected by Philadelphia Eagles in eighth round (208th pick overall) of 1986 NFL draft. ... Signed by Eagles (July 17, 1986). ... Released by Eagles (September 1, 1986). ... Re-signed by Eagles (September 17, 1986). ... Granted free agency (February 1, 1991). ... Re-signed by Eagles (August 28, 1991). ... Activated (August 30, 1991). ... Designated by Eagles as transition player (February 25, 1993). ... Free agency status changed by Eagles from transitional to unconditional (February 17, 1994). ... Signed by Arizona Cardinals (April 17, 1994). ... Released by Cardinals (June 16, 1997). ... Signed by Green Bay Packers (July 16, 1997).
CHAMPIONSHIP GAME EXPERIENCE: Played in NFC championship game (1997 season). ... Played in Super Bowl XXXII (1997 season).
HONORS: Played in Pro Bowl (1991, 1993 and 1994 seasons).
RECORDS: Shares NFL single-season records for most touchdowns by fumble recovery—2 (1991); and most touchdowns by recovery of opponents' fumbles—2 (1991).
PRO STATISTICS: 1987—Recovered two fumbles for 18 yards and one touchdown. 1988—Fumbled once and recovered one fumble. 1990—Fumbled once. 1991—Recovered four fumbles for 47 yards and two touchdowns. 1992—Recovered one fumble. 1995—Fumbled once and recovered three fumbles. 1996—Recovered one fumble.

| | | | INTERCEPTIONS | | | | SACKS |
Year Team	G	GS	No.	Yds.	Avg.	TD	No.
1986—Philadelphia NFL	14	7	1	4	4.0	0	2.0
1987—Philadelphia NFL	12	12	2	42	21.0	0	4.0
1988—Philadelphia NFL	16	16	4	96	24.0	0	3.5
1989—Philadelphia NFL	14	14	1	0	0.0	0	4.5
1990—Philadelphia NFL	16	16	1	9	9.0	0	7.5
1991—Philadelphia NFL	16	16	3	41	13.7	0	6.5
1992—Philadelphia NFL	16	16	4	88	22.0	2	6.5
1993—Philadelphia NFL	16	16	1	6	6.0	0	2.0
1994—Arizona NFL	16	16	3	2	0.7	0	6.0
1995—Arizona NFL	16	16	3	9	3.0	0	1.0
1996—Arizona NFL	16	16	1	10	10.0	0	5.0
1997—Green Bay NFL	11	10	0	0	...	0	3.0
Pro totals (12 years)	179	171	24	307	12.8	2	51.5

JUNKIN, TREY   TE   CARDINALS

PERSONAL: Born January 23, 1961, in Conway, Ark. ... 6-2/258. ... Full name: Abner Kirk Junkin. ... Brother of Mike Junkin, linebacker with Cleveland Browns (1987 and 1988) and Kansas City Chiefs (1989).
HIGH SCHOOL: Northeast (North Little Rock, Ark.).
COLLEGE: Louisiana Tech.
TRANSACTIONS/CAREER NOTES: Selected by Buffalo Bills in fourth round (93rd pick overall) of 1983 NFL draft. ... Released by Bills (September 12, 1984). ... Signed by Washington Redskins (September 25, 1984). ... Rights relinquished by Redskins (February 1, 1985). ... Signed by Los Angeles Raiders (March 10, 1985). ... On injured reserve with knee injury (September 24, 1986-remainder of season). ... Released by Raiders (September 3, 1990). ... Signed by Seattle Seahawks (October 3, 1990). ... Granted unconditional free agency (February 1-April 1, 1991). ... Re-signed by Seahawks (July 9, 1991). ... Granted unconditional free agency (February 1-April 1, 1992). ... Re-signed by Seahawks for 1992 season. ... Granted unconditional free agency (March 1, 1993). ... Re-signed by Seahawks (March 11, 1993). ... Released by Seahawks (August 30, 1993). ... Re-signed by Seahawks (August 31, 1993). ... Granted unconditional free agency (February 17, 1994). ... Re-signed by Seahawks (May 31, 1994). ... Granted unconditional free agency (February 17, 1995). ... Re-signed by Seahawks (March 20, 1995). ... Granted unconditional free agency (February 16, 1996). ... Signed by Oakland Raiders (June 10, 1996). ... Claimed on waivers by Arizona Cardinals (October 14, 1996).
PRO STATISTICS: 1983—Recovered one fumble. 1984—Recovered one fumble. 1989—Returned one kickoff for no yards.
SINGLE GAME HIGHS (regular season): Receptions—2 (November 22, 1992, vs. Kansas City); yards—38 (September 21, 1986, vs. New York Giants); and touchdown receptions—1 (September 25, 1994, vs. Pittsburgh).

Year Team	G	GS	No.	RECEIVING Yds.	Avg.	TD	TOTALS TD	2pt.	Pts.	Fum.
1983—Buffalo NFL	16	0	0	0	...	0	0	...	0	0
1984—Buffalo NFL	2	0	0	0	...	0	0	...	0	0
—Washington NFL	12	0	0	0	...	0	0	...	0	0
1985—Los Angeles Raiders NFL	16	0	2	8	4.0	1	1	...	6	0
1986—Los Angeles Raiders NFL	3	0	2	38	19.0	0	0	...	0	0
1987—Los Angeles Raiders NFL	12	1	2	15	7.5	0	0	...	0	0
1988—Los Angeles Raiders NFL	16	1	4	25	6.3	2	2	...	12	0
1989—Los Angeles Raiders NFL	16	0	3	32	10.7	2	2	...	12	0
1990—Seattle NFL	12	0	0	0	...	0	0	...	0	0
1991—Seattle NFL	16	0	0	0	...	0	0	...	0	0
1992—Seattle NFL	16	1	3	25	8.3	1	1	...	6	0
1993—Seattle NFL	16	1	0	0	...	0	0	...	0	0
1994—Seattle NFL	16	0	1	1	1.0	1	1	0	6	0
1995—Seattle NFL	16	0	0	0	...	0	0	0	0	0
1996—Oakland NFL	6	0	0	0	...	0	0	0	0	0
—Arizona NFL	10	0	0	0	...	0	0	0	0	0
1997—Arizona NFL	16	0	0	0	...	0	0	0	0	0
Pro totals (15 years)	217	4	17	144	8.5	7	7	0	42	0

JURKOVIC, JOHN　　　DT　　　JAGUARS

PERSONAL: Born August 18, 1967, in Friedrischafen, West Germany. ... 6-2/306. ... Full name: John Ivan Jurkovic.
HIGH SCHOOL: Thornton Fractional North (Calumet City, Ill.).
COLLEGE: Eastern Illinois (degree in business).
TRANSACTIONS/CAREER NOTES: Signed as non-drafted free agent by Miami Dolphins (April 27, 1990). ... Released by Dolphins (August 28, 1990). ... Re-signed by Dolphins to practice squad (October 3, 1990). ... Granted free agency after 1990 season. ... Signed by Green Bay Packers (March 8, 1991). ... Released by Packers (August 26, 1991). ... Re-signed by Packers to practice squad (August 28, 1991). ... Activated (November 22, 1991). ... Granted unconditional free agency (February 1-April 1, 1992). ... Re-signed by Packers (April 2, 1992). ... Granted unconditional free agency (February 16, 1996). ... Signed by Jacksonville Jaguars (April 13, 1996). ... On injured reserve with leg injury (September 23, 1997-remainder of season).
CHAMPIONSHIP GAME EXPERIENCE: Played in NFC championship game (1995 season). ... Played in AFC championship game (1996 season).
PRO STATISTICS: 1992—Returned three kickoffs for 39 yards. 1993—Returned two kickoffs for 22 yards. 1994—Returned four kickoffs for 57 yards. 1995—Returned one kickoff for 17 yards. 1996—Recovered two fumbles.

Year Team	G	GS	SACKS
1991—Green Bay NFL	5	0	0.0
1992—Green Bay NFL	16	12	2.0
1993—Green Bay NFL	16	12	5.5
1994—Green Bay NFL	16	15	0.0
1995—Green Bay NFL	16	14	0.0
1996—Jacksonville NFL	16	14	1.0
1997—Jacksonville NFL	3	3	0.0
Pro totals (7 years)	88	70	8.5

JUSTIN, PAUL　　　QB　　　BENGALS

PERSONAL: Born May 19, 1968, in Schaumburg, Ill. ... 6-4/211. ... Full name: Paul Donald Justin.
HIGH SCHOOL: Schaumburg (Ill.).
COLLEGE: Arizona State.
TRANSACTIONS/CAREER NOTES: Selected by Chicago Bears in seventh round (190th pick overall) of 1991 NFL draft. ... Signed by Bears for 1991 season. ... Released by Bears (August 27, 1991). ... Re-signed by Bears to practice squad (August 28, 1991). ... Released by Bears (August 31, 1992). ... Signed by Indianapolis Colts (April 11, 1994). ... Released by Colts (August 25, 1994). ... Re-signed by Colts to practice squad (August 29, 1994). ... Assigned by Colts to Frankfurt Galaxy in 1995 World League enhancement allocation program (February 20, 1995). ... Released by Colts after 1996 season. ... Re-signed by Colts (July 5, 1997). ... On injured reserve with knee injury (December 5, 1997-remainder of season). ... Granted free agency (February 13, 1998). ... Re-signed by Colts (March 26, 1998). ... Traded by Colts to Cincinnati Bengals for fifth-round pick (LB Anthony Jordon) in 1998 draft (March 26, 1998).
CHAMPIONSHIP GAME EXPERIENCE: Member of Colts for AFC championship game (1995 season); inactive.
PRO STATISTICS: 1995—Fumbled once and recovered one fumble for minus one yard. 1996—Fumbled once and recovered one fumble. 1997—Fumbled once.
SINGLE GAME HIGHS (regular season): Attempts—40 (December 1, 1996, vs. Buffalo); completions—24 (November 16, 1997, vs. Green Bay); yards—340 (November 16, 1997, vs. Green Bay); and touchdown passes—2 (October 26, 1997, vs. San Diego).
STATISTICAL PLATEAUS: 300-yard passing games: 1997 (1).
MISCELLANEOUS: Regular-season record as starting NFL quarterback: 3-4 (.429).

Year Team	G	GS	Att.	Cmp.	Pct.	PASSING Yds.	TD	Int.	Avg.	Rat.	Att.	RUSHING Yds.	Avg.	TD	TOTALS TD	2pt.	Pts.
1991—Chicago NFL						Did not play.											
1992—Chicago NFL						Did not play.											
1993—						Did not play.											
1994—Indianapolis NFL						Did not play.											
1995—Frankfurt W.L.	...	...	279	172	61.6	2394	17	12	8.58	91.6	14	50	3.6	0	0	0	0
—Indianapolis NFL	3	1	36	20	55.6	212	0	2	5.89	49.8	3	1	0.3	0	0	0	0
1996—Indianapolis NFL	8	2	127	74	58.3	839	2	0	6.61	83.4	2	7	3.5	0	0	0	0
1997—Indianapolis NFL	8	4	140	83	59.3	1046	5	5	7.47	79.6	6	2	0.3	0	0	0	0
W.L. totals (1 year)	...	...	279	172	61.6	2394	17	12	8.58	91.6	14	50	3.6	0	0	0	0
NFL totals (2 years)	19	7	303	177	58.4	2097	7	7	6.92	77.7	11	10	0.9	0	0	0	0
Pro totals (3 years)	...	...	582	349	60.0	4491	24	19	7.72	84.3	25	60	2.4	0	0	0	0

KALU, NDUKWE   DE/LB   EAGLES

PERSONAL: Born August 3, 1975, in Baltimore. ... 6-3/246. ... Full name: Ndukwe Dike Kalu. ... Name pronounced EN-doo-kway ka-LOO.
HIGH SCHOOL: John Marshall (San Antonio).
COLLEGE: Rice.
TRANSACTIONS/CAREER NOTES: Selected by Philadelphia Eagles in fifth round (152nd pick overall) of 1997 NFL draft. ... Signed by Eagles (July 15, 1997).
PLAYING EXPERIENCE: Philadelphia NFL, 1997. ... Games/Games started: 3/0.

KANELL, DANNY   QB   GIANTS

PERSONAL: Born November 21, 1973, in Ft. Lauderdale. ... 6-3/215. ... Son of Dan Kanell, team physician, Miami Dolphins and spring training physician, New York Yankees.
HIGH SCHOOL: Westminster (Fort Lauderdale) Academy.
COLLEGE: Florida State.
TRANSACTIONS/CAREER NOTES: Selected by New York Giants in fourth round (130th pick overall) of 1996 NFL draft. ... Signed by Giants (July 18, 1996).
PRO STATISTICS: 1996—Fumbled twice for minus one yard. 1997—Fumbled six times for minus 10 yards.
SINGLE GAME HIGHS (regular season): Attempts—37 (November 23, 1997, vs. Washington); completions—20 (November 23, 1997, vs. Washington); yards—220 (October 19, 1997, vs. Detroit); and touchdown passes—3 (December 7, 1997, vs. Philadelphia).
MISCELLANEOUS: Selected by Milwaukee Brewers organization in 19th round of free-agent baseball draft (June 1, 1992); did not sign. ... Selected by New York Yankees organization in 25th round of free-agent baseball draft (June 1, 1995); did not sign. ... Regular-season record as starting NFL quarterback: 7-2-1 (.750). ... Postseason record as starting NFL quarterback: 0-1.

			PASSING								RUSHING				TOTALS		
Year Team	G	GS	Att.	Cmp.	Pct.	Yds.	TD	Int.	Avg.	Rat.	Att.	Yds.	Avg.	TD	TD	2pt.	Pts.
1996—N.Y. Giants NFL..........	4	0	60	23	38.3	227	1	1	3.78	48.4	7	6	0.9	0	0	0	0
1997—N.Y. Giants NFL..........	16	10	294	156	53.1	1740	11	9	5.92	70.7	15	2	0.1	0	0	0	0
Pro totals (2 years)	20	10	354	179	50.6	1967	12	10	5.56	66.9	22	8	0.4	0	0	0	0

KASAY, JOHN   K   PANTHERS

PERSONAL: Born October 27, 1969, in Athens, Ga. ... 5-10/198. ... Full name: John David Kasay. ... Name pronounced KAY-see.
HIGH SCHOOL: Clarke Central (Athens, Ga.).
COLLEGE: Georgia (degree in journalism).
TRANSACTIONS/CAREER NOTES: Selected by Seattle Seahawks in fourth round (98th pick overall) of 1991 NFL draft. ... Signed by Seahawks (July 19, 1991). ... Granted free agency (February 17, 1994). ... Re-signed by Seahawks (July 19, 1994). ... Granted unconditional free agency (February 17, 1995). ... Signed by Carolina Panthers (February 20, 1995).
CHAMPIONSHIP GAME EXPERIENCE: Played in NFC championship game (1996 season).
HONORS: Played in Pro Bowl (1996 season).
RECORDS: Holds NFL single-season record for most field goals made—37 (1996).
PRO STATISTICS: 1993—Recovered one fumble. 1995—Punted once for 32 yards. 1996—Punted once for 30 yards.

			KICKING						
Year Team	G	GS	XPM	XPA	FGM	FGA	Lg.	50+	Pts.
1991—Seattle NFL...	16	0	27	28	25	31	54	2-3	102
1992—Seattle NFL...	16	0	14	14	14	22	43	0-0	56
1993—Seattle NFL...	16	0	29	29	23	28	55	3-5	98
1994—Seattle NFL...	16	0	25	26	20	24	50	1-2	85
1995—Carolina NFL	16	0	27	20	28	33	52	1-1	105
1996—Carolina NFL	16	0	34	35	*37	*45	53	3-7	*145
1997—Carolina NFL	16	0	25	25	22	26	54	3-6	91
Pro totals (7 years)	112	0	181	185	167	209	55	13-24	682

KAUFMAN, NAPOLEON   RB   RAIDERS

PERSONAL: Born June 7, 1973, in Kansas City, Mo. ... 5-9/185.
HIGH SCHOOL: Lompoc (Calif.).
COLLEGE: Washington.
TRANSACTIONS/CAREER NOTES: Selected by Los Angeles Raiders in first round (18th pick overall) of 1995 NFL draft. ... Signed by Raiders (May 24, 1995). ... Raiders franchise moved to Oakland (July 21, 1995).
HONORS: Named running back on THE SPORTING NEWS college All-America second team (1994).
PRO STATISTICS: 1997—Attempted one pass without a completion and recovered one fumble.
SINGLE GAME HIGHS (regular season): Attempts—28 (October 19, 1997, vs. Denver); yards—227 (October 19, 1997, vs. Denver); and rushing touchdowns—2 (September 14, 1997, vs. Atlanta).
STATISTICAL PLATEAUS: 100-yard rushing games: 1996 (3), 1997 (6). Total: 9. ... 100-yard receiving games: 1997 (1).

			RUSHING				RECEIVING				KICKOFF RETURNS				TOTALS			
Year Team	G	GS	Att.	Yds.	Avg.	TD	No.	Yds.	Avg.	TD	No.	Yds.	Avg.	TD	TD	2pt.	Pts.	Fum.
1995—Oakland NFL................	16	1	108	490	4.5	1	9	62	6.9	0	22	572	26.0	1	2	0	12	0
1996—Oakland NFL................	16	9	150	874	*5.8	1	22	143	6.5	1	25	548	21.9	0	2	0	12	3
1997 Oakland NFL................	16	16	272	1294	4.8	6	40	403	10.1	2	0	0	...	0	8	0	48	7
Pro totals (3 years)	48	26	530	2658	5.0	8	71	608	8.6	3	47	1120	23.8	1	12	0	72	10

KAZADI, MUADIANVITA   LB   RAMS

PERSONAL: Born December 20, 1973, in Zaire. ... 6-2/240. ... Full name: Muadianvita Matt Kazadi. ... Name pronounced Mar-jon-VEE-tah ka-ZA-dee.
HIGH SCHOOL: Newton (Kan.).
COLLEGE: Tulsa.
TRANSACTIONS/CAREER NOTES: Selected by St. Louis Rams in sixth round (179th pick overall) of 1997 NFL draft. ... Signed by Rams (July 3, 1997).
PLAYING EXPERIENCE: St. Louis NFL, 1997. ... Games/Games started: 12/0.

KELLY, ROB   S   SAINTS

PERSONAL: Born June 21, 1974, in Newark, Ohio. ... 6-0/199. ... Full name: Robert James Kelly.
HIGH SCHOOL: Newark Catholic (Ohio).
COLLEGE: Ohio State.
TRANSACTIONS/CAREER NOTES: Selected by New Orleans Saints in second round (33rd pick overall) of 1997 NFL draft. ... Signed by Saints (July 17, 1997).

			INTERCEPTIONS				SACKS
Year Team	G	GS	No.	Yds.	Avg.	TD	No.
1997—New Orleans NFL	16	2	1	15	15.0	0	0.0

KENDALL, PETE   G   SEAHAWKS

PERSONAL: Born July 9, 1973, in Weymouth, Mass. ... 6-5/292. ... Full name: Peter Marcus Kendall.
HIGH SCHOOL: Archbishop Williams (Weymouth, Mass.).
COLLEGE: Boston College.
TRANSACTIONS/CAREER NOTES: Selected by Seattle Seahawks in first round (21st pick overall) of 1996 NFL draft. ... Signed by Seahawks (July 21, 1996).
PLAYING EXPERIENCE: Seattle NFL, 1996 and 1997. ... Games/Games started: 1996 (12/11), 1997 (16/16). Total: 28/27.

KENNEDY, CORTEZ   DT   SEAHAWKS

PERSONAL: Born August 23, 1968, in Osceola, Ark. ... 6-3/306.
HIGH SCHOOL: Rivercrest (Wilson, Ark.).
JUNIOR COLLEGE: Northwest Mississippi Community College.
COLLEGE: Miami, Fla. (degree in criminal justice).
TRANSACTIONS/CAREER NOTES: Selected by Seattle Seahawks in first round (third pick overall) of 1990 NFL draft. ... Signed by Seahawks (September 3, 1990). ... Granted roster exemption (September 3-9, 1990). ... On injured reserve with ankle injury (December 10, 1997-remainder of season).
HONORS: Named defensive tackle on THE SPORTING NEWS college All-America first team (1989). ... Played in Pro Bowl (1991-1996 seasons). ... Named defensive tackle on THE SPORTING NEWS NFL All-Pro team (1992 and 1993).
PRO STATISTICS: 1990—Recovered one fumble. 1991—Recovered one fumble. 1992—Fumbled once and recovered one fumble for 19 yards. 1993—Recovered one fumble. 1994—Recovered one fumble.

Year Team	G	GS	SACKS
1990—Seattle NFL	16	2	1.0
1991—Seattle NFL	16	16	6.5
1992—Seattle NFL	16	16	14.0
1993—Seattle NFL	16	16	6.5
1994—Seattle NFL	16	16	4.0
1995—Seattle NFL	16	16	6.5
1996—Seattle NFL	16	16	8.0
1997—Seattle NFL	8	8	2.0
Pro totals (8 years)	120	106	48.5

KENNEDY, LINCOLN   G/OT   RAIDERS

PERSONAL: Born February 12, 1971, in York, Pa. ... 6-6/325. ... Full name: Tamerlane Lincoln Kennedy.
HIGH SCHOOL: Samuel F. B. Morse (San Diego).
COLLEGE: Washington (degree in speech and drama, 1993).
TRANSACTIONS/CAREER NOTES: Selected by Atlanta Falcons in first round (ninth pick overall) of 1993 NFL draft (traded to Oakland). ... Signed by Falcons (August 2, 1993). ... Granted free agency (February 16, 1996). ... Traded by Falcons to Oakland Raiders for fifth-round pick (traded to Washington) in 1997 draft (May 13, 1996).
PLAYING EXPERIENCE: Atlanta NFL, 1993-1995; Oakland NFL, 1996 and 1997. ... Games/Games started: 1993 (16/16), 1994 (16/2), 1995 (16/4), 1996 (16/16), 1997 (16/16). Total: 80/54.
HONORS: Named offensive tackle on THE SPORTING NEWS college All-America first team (1992).
PRO STATISTICS: 1993—Recovered one fumble. 1994—Recovered one fumble. 1996—Recovered one fumble.

KENNISON, EDDIE   WR   RAMS

PERSONAL: Born January 20, 1973, in Lake Charles, La. ... 6-0/195. ... Full name: Eddie Joseph Kennison III.
HIGH SCHOOL: Washington-Marion (Lake Charles, La.).
COLLEGE: Louisiana State.

TRANSACTIONS/CAREER NOTES: Selected after junior season by St. Louis Rams in first round (18th pick overall) of 1996 NFL draft. ... Signed by Rams (July 27, 1996).

PRO STATISTICS: 1997—Rushed three times for 13 yards.

SINGLE GAME HIGHS (regular season): Receptions—8 (December 8, 1996, vs. Chicago); yards—226 (December 15, 1996, vs. Atlanta); and touchdown receptions—3 (December 15, 1996, vs. Atlanta).

STATISTICAL PLATEAUS: 100-yard receiving games: 1996 (2).

				RECEIVING				PUNT RETURNS				KICKOFF RETURNS				TOTALS		
Year Team	G	GS	No.	Yds.	Avg.	TD	No.	Yds.	Avg.	TD	No.	Yds.	Avg.	TD	TD	2pt.	Pts. Fum.
1996—St. Louis NFL	15	14	54	924	17.1	9	29	423	14.6	2	23	454	19.7	0	11	0	66 5
1997—St. Louis NFL	14	9	25	404	16.2	0	34	247	7.3	0	1	14	14.0	0	0	0	0 2
Pro totals (2 years)	29	23	79	1328	16.8	9	63	670	10.6	2	24	468	19.5	0	11	0	66 7

KENT, JOEY   WR   OILERS

PERSONAL: Born April 23, 1974, in Huntsville, Ala. ... 6-1/186. ... Full name: Joseph Edward Kent III.

HIGH SCHOOL: Johnson (Huntsville, Ala.).

COLLEGE: Tennessee.

TRANSACTIONS/CAREER NOTES: Selected by Houston Oilers in second round (46th pick overall) of 1997 NFL draft. ... Oilers franchise moved to Tennessee for 1997 season. ... Signed by Oilers (July 17, 1997).

HONORS: Named wide receiver on THE SPORTING NEWS college All-America second team (1996).

SINGLE GAME HIGHS (regular season): Receptions—2 (December 21, 1997, vs. Pittsburgh); yards—24 (December 21, 1997, vs. Pittsburgh); and touchdown receptions—1 (December 4, 1997, vs. Cincinnati).

			RECEIVING				TOTALS			
Year Team	G	GS	No.	Yds.	Avg.	TD	TD	2pt.	Pts.	Fum.
1997—Tennessee NFL	12	0	6	55	9.2	1	1	0	6	0

KERNER, MARLON   CB   BILLS

PERSONAL: Born March 18, 1973, in Columbus, Ohio. ... 5-10/187.

HIGH SCHOOL: Brookhaven (Columbus, Ohio).

COLLEGE: Ohio State.

TRANSACTIONS/CAREER NOTES: Selected by Buffalo Bills in third round (76th pick overall) of 1995 NFL draft. ... Signed by Bills (July 10, 1995). ... On injured reserve with knee injury (December 1, 1997-remainder of season). ... Granted free agency (February 13, 1998).

PLAYING EXPERIENCE: Buffalo NFL, 1995-1997. ... Games/Games started: 1995 (14/5), 1996 (15/0), 1997 (13/2). Total: 42/7.

PRO STATISTICS: 1996—Intercepted one pass for six yards and credited with one sack. 1997—Intercepted two passes for 20 yards and recovered one fumble.

KIDD, JOHN   P

PERSONAL: Born August 22, 1961, in Springfield, Ill. ... 6-3/214. ... Full name: Max John Kidd.

HIGH SCHOOL: Findlay (Ohio).

COLLEGE: Northwestern (degree in industrial engineering and management science, 1984).

TRANSACTIONS/CAREER NOTES: Selected by Chicago Blitz in 1984 USFL territorial draft. ... Selected by Buffalo Bills in fifth round (128th pick overall) of 1984 NFL draft. ... Signed by Bills (June 1, 1984). ... Granted unconditional free agency (February 1, 1990). ... Signed by San Diego Chargers (March 15, 1990). ... Granted free agency (February 1, 1992). ... Re-signed by Chargers (July 23, 1992). ... Granted unconditional free agency (March 1, 1993). ... Re-signed by Chargers (July 23, 1993). ... Granted unconditional free agency (February 17, 1994). ... Re-signed by Chargers (August 20, 1994). ... On injured reserve with hamstring injury (September 12-22, 1994). ... Released by Chargers (September 22, 1994). ... Signed by Miami Dolphins (November 30, 1994). ... Granted unconditional free agency (February 17, 1995). ... Re-signed by Dolphins (April 18, 1995). ... Released by Dolphins (October 3, 1997). ... Re-signed by Dolphins (October 7, 1997). ... Granted unconditional free agency (February 13, 1998).

CHAMPIONSHIP GAME EXPERIENCE: Played in AFC championship game (1988 season).

PRO STATISTICS: 1986—Rushed once for no yards and recovered one fumble. 1987—Attempted one pass without a completion. 1990—Fumbled once and recovered one fumble. 1992—Rushed twice for minus 13 yards, fumbled once and recovered one fumble for minus nine yards. 1993—Rushed three times for minus 13 yards and a touchdown. 1996—Rushed once for three yards. 1997—Rushed once for four yards.

			PUNTING					
Year Team	G	GS	No.	Yds.	Avg.	Net avg.	In. 20	Blk.
1984—Buffalo NFL	16	0	88	3696	42.0	32.7	16	2
1985—Buffalo NFL	16	0	92	3818	41.5	35.8	*33	0
1986—Buffalo NFL	16	0	75	3031	40.4	34.5	14	0
1987—Buffalo NFL	12	0	64	2495	39.0	34.5	†20	0
1988—Buffalo NFL	16	0	62	2451	39.5	35.2	13	0
1989—Buffalo NFL	16	0	65	2564	39.4	32.2	15	2
1990—San Diego NFL	16	0	61	2442	40.0	36.6	14	1
1991—San Diego NFL	16	0	76	3064	40.3	34.7	22	1
1992—San Diego NFL	16	0	68	2899	42.6	36.3	22	0
1993—San Diego NFL	14	0	57	2431	42.6	35.8	16	0
1994—San Diego NFL	2	0	7	246	35.1	32.2	1	0
—Miami NFL	4	0	14	602	43.0	29.1	2	0
1995—Miami NFL	16	0	57	2433	42.7	36.2	15	0
1996—Miami NFL	16	0	78	3611	46.3	38.7	26	0
1997—Miami NFL	13	0	52	2247	43.2	37.0	13	0
Pro totals (14 years)	205	0	916	38030	41.5	35.2	242	6

KILLENS, TERRY   LB   OILERS

PERSONAL: Born March 24, 1974, in Cincinnati. ... 6-1/227. ... Full name: Terry Deleon Killens.
HIGH SCHOOL: Purcell (Cincinnati).
COLLEGE: Penn State.
TRANSACTIONS/CAREER NOTES: Selected by Houston Oilers in third round (74th pick overall) of 1996 NFL draft. ... Signed by Oilers (July 20, 1996). ... Oilers franchise moved to Tennessee for 1997 season.
PLAYING EXPERIENCE: Houston NFL, 1996; Tennessee NFL, 1997. ... Games/Games started: 1996 (14/0), 1997 (16/0). Total: 30/0.

KINCHEN, BRIAN   TE   RAVENS

PERSONAL: Born August 6, 1965, in Baton Rouge, La. ... 6-2/240. ... Full name: Brian Douglas Kinchen. ... Brother of Todd Kinchen, wide receiver/kick returner, Atlanta Falcons.
HIGH SCHOOL: University (Baton Rouge, La.).
COLLEGE: Louisiana State.
TRANSACTIONS/CAREER NOTES: Selected by Miami Dolphins in 12th round (320th pick overall) of 1988 NFL draft. ... Signed by Dolphins (June 6, 1988). ... On injured reserve with hamstring injury (October 4, 1990-remainder of season). ... Granted unconditional free agency (February 1, 1991). ... Signed by Green Bay Packers (April 1, 1991). ... Released by Packers (August 26, 1991). ... Signed by Cleveland Browns (September 13, 1991). ... Granted unconditional free agency (February 1-April 1, 1992). ... Re-signed by Browns for 1992 season. ... Granted unconditional free agency (February 17, 1994). ... Re-signed by Browns (March 4, 1994). ... Granted unconditional free agency (February 16, 1996). ... Browns franchise moved to Baltimore and renamed Ravens for 1996 season (March 11, 1996). ... Re-signed by Ravens (April 3, 1996).
PRO STATISTICS: 1995—Recovered one fumble.
SINGLE GAME HIGHS (regular season): Receptions—9 (November 24, 1996, vs. Jacksonville); yards—87 (December 15, 1996, vs. Carolina); and touchdown receptions—1 (October 5, 1997, vs. Pittsburgh).

Year Team	G	GS	RECEIVING				KICKOFF RETURNS				TOTALS			
			No.	Yds.	Avg.	TD	No.	Yds.	Avg.	TD	TD	2pt.	Pts.	Fum.
1988—Miami NFL	16	0	1	3	3.0	0	0	0	...	0	0	...	0	0
1989—Miami NFL	16	0	1	12	12.0	0	2	26	13.0	0	0	...	0	2
1990—Miami NFL	4	0	0	0	...	0	1	16	16.0	0	0	...	0	0
1991—Cleveland NFL	14	0	0	0	...	0	0	0	...	0	0	...	0	1
1992—Cleveland NFL	16	0	0	0	...	0	0	0	...	0	0	...	0	0
1993—Cleveland NFL	16	15	29	347	12.0	2	1	0	0.0	0	2		12	1
1994—Cleveland NFL	16	11	24	232	9.7	1	3	38	12.7	0	1	0	6	1
1995—Cleveland NFL	13	12	20	216	10.8	0	0	0	...	0	0	0	0	1
1996—Baltimore NFL	16	16	55	581	10.6	1	1	19	19.0	0	1	0	6	1
1997—Baltimore NFL	16	6	11	95	8.6	1	0	0	...	0	1	0	6	0
Pro totals (10 years)	143	60	141	1486	10.5	5	8	99	12.4	0	5	0	30	7

KINCHEN, TODD   KR/WR   FALCONS

PERSONAL: Born January 7, 1969, in Baton Rouge, La. ... 5-11/187. ... Full name: Todd Whittington Kinchen. ... Brother of Brian Kinchen, tight end, Baltimore Ravens.
HIGH SCHOOL: Trafton Academy (Baton Rouge, La.).
COLLEGE: Louisiana State.
TRANSACTIONS/CAREER NOTES: Selected by Los Angeles Rams in third round (60th pick overall) of 1992 NFL draft. ... Signed by Rams (July 13, 1992). ... On injured reserve with knee injury (November 23, 1993-remainder of season). ... On physically unable to perform list (July 22-28, 1994). ... Released by Rams (September 6, 1994). ... Re-signed by Rams (September 21, 1994). ... Granted free agency (February 17, 1995). ... Rams franchise moved to St. Louis (April 12, 1995). ... Re-signed by Rams (June 16, 1995). ... Traded by Rams to Denver Broncos for undisclosed draft choice (August 27, 1996). ... Released by Broncos (February 25, 1997). ... Signed by Atlanta Falcons (April 11, 1997).
RECORDS: Shares NFL single-game records for most touchdowns by punt return—2; and most touchdowns by combined kick return—2 (December 27, 1992, vs. Atlanta).
PRO STATISTICS: 1993—Fumbled once. 1994—Fumbled five times. 1995—Attempted one pass without a completion, fumbled eight times and recovered one fumble. 1996—Fumbled five times and recovered one fumble. 1997—Fumbled five times and recovered two fumbles.
SINGLE GAME HIGHS (regular season): Receptions—5 (December 4, 1994, vs. New Orleans); yards—85 (October 19, 1997, vs. San Francisco); and touchdown receptions—1 (October 19, 1997, vs. San Francisco).

Year Team	G	GS	RUSHING				RECEIVING				PUNT RETURNS				KICKOFF RETURNS				TOTALS		
			Att.	Yds.	Avg.	TD	No.	Yds.	Avg.	TD	No.	Yds.	Avg.	TD	No.	Yds.	Avg.	TD	TD	2pt.	Pts.
1992—L.A. Rams NFL	14	0	0	0	...	0	0	0	...	0	4	103	25.8	†2	4	63	15.8	0	2	...	12
1993—L.A. Rams NFL	6	1	2	10	5.0	0	8	137	17.1	1	7	32	4.6	0	6	96	16.0	0	1	...	6
1994—L.A. Rams NFL	13	0	1	44	44.0	1	23	352	15.3	3	16	158	9.9	0	21	510	24.3	0	4	0	24
1995—St. Louis NFL	16	1	4	16	4.0	0	36	419	11.6	4	*53	416	7.8	0	35	743	21.2	0	4	0	24
1996—Denver NFL	7	0	0	0	...	0	1	27	27.0	0	26	300	11.5	0	0	0	...	0	0	0	0
1997—Atlanta NFL	16	0	0	0	...	0	16	266	16.6	1	*52	446	8.6	0	1	18	18.0	0	0	0	0
Pro totals (6 years)	72	2	7	70	10.0	1	84	1201	14.3	9	158	1455	9.2	2	67	1430	21.3	0	11	0	66

KINDER, RANDY   S   EAGLES

PERSONAL: Born April 4, 1975, in Washington, D.C. ... 6-1/210. ... Full name: Randolph Samuel Kinder III.
HIGH SCHOOL: East Lansing (Mich.).
COLLEGE: Notre Dame (degree in American studies (1997)).
TRANSACTIONS/CAREER NOTES: Signed as non-drafted free agent by Green Bay Packers (April 25, 1997). ... Released by Packers (August 24, 1997). ... Re-signed by Packers to practice squad (August 26, 1997). ... Activated (September 3, 1997). ... Claimed on waivers by Philadelphia Eagles (November 13, 1997).
PLAYING EXPERIENCE: Green Bay (6)-Philadelphia (6) NFL, 1997. ... Games/Games started: 1997 (G.B.-6/0; Phi.-6/0; Total: 12/0).

KING, ED   G

PERSONAL: Born December 3, 1969, in Fort Benning, Ga. ... 6-4/300. ... Full name: Ed E'Dainia King.
HIGH SCHOOL: Central (Phenix City, Ala.).
COLLEGE: Auburn.
TRANSACTIONS/CAREER NOTES: Selected after junior season by Cleveland Browns in second round (29th pick overall) of 1991 NFL draft. ... Signed by Browns (July 16, 1991). ... Granted free agency (February 17, 1994). ... Signed by Green Bay Packers (June 2, 1994). ... Released by Packers (August 28, 1994). ... Selected by Barcelona Dragons in ninth round (54th pick overall) of 1995 World League Draft. ... Signed by New Orleans Saints (July 19, 1995). ... Granted unconditional free agency (February 14, 1997). ... Re-signed by Saints (May 6, 1997). ... Released by Saints (October 29, 1997).
PLAYING EXPERIENCE: Cleveland NFL, 1991-1993; Barcelona W.L., 1995; New Orleans NFL, 1995-1997. ... Games/Games started: 1991 (16/15), 1992 (16/14), 1993 (6/2), 1995 (W.L.-games played unavailable; NFL-1/0), 1996 (16/16), 1997 (2/0). Total: 57/47.
HONORS: Named guard on THE SPORTING NEWS college All-America second team (1990).
PRO STATISTICS: 1991—Recovered one fumble. 1996—Recovered one fumble.

KING, SHAWN   DE   PANTHERS

PERSONAL: Born June 24, 1972, in West Monroe, La. ... 6-3/278.
HIGH SCHOOL: West Monroe (La.).
COLLEGE: Louisiana State, then Northeast Louisiana.
TRANSACTIONS/CAREER NOTES: Selected by Carolina Panthers in second round (36th pick overall) of 1995 NFL draft. ... Signed by Panthers (July 15, 1995). ... On reserve/suspended list for violating league substance abuse policy (August 24-October 17, 1997). ... On injured reserve with knee injury (December 15, 1997-remainder of season).
PRO STATISTICS: 1996—Intercepted one pass for one yard and recovered one fumble for 12 yards and a touchdown.

Year Team	G	GS	SACKS
1995—Carolina NFL	13	0	2.0
1996—Carolina NFL	16	0	3.0
1997—Carolina NFL	9	2	2.0
Pro totals (3 years)	38	2	7.0

KINNEY, KELVIN   DE   REDSKINS

PERSONAL: Born December 31, 1972, in Montgomery, W.Va. ... 6-6/264.
HIGH SCHOOL: Dupont (W.Va.), then Louisa (Va.).
COLLEGE: Virginia State.
TRANSACTIONS/CAREER NOTES: Selected by Washington Redskins in sixth round (174th pick overall) of 1996 NFL draft. ... Signed by Redskins (June 4, 1996). ... On injured reserve with foot injury (August 20, 1996-entire season).
PLAYING EXPERIENCE: Washington NFL, 1997. ... Games/Games started: 4/1.

KIRBY, TERRY   RB

PERSONAL: Born January 20, 1970, in Hampton, Va. ... 6-1/223. ... Full name: Terry Gayle Kirby. ... Brother of Wayne Kirby, outfielder, New York Mets organization; and cousin of Chris Slade, linebacker, New England Patriots.
HIGH SCHOOL: Tabb (Va.).
COLLEGE: Virginia (degree in psychology).
TRANSACTIONS/CAREER NOTES: Selected by Miami Dolphins in third round (78th pick overall) of 1993 NFL draft. ... Signed by Dolphins (July 19, 1993). ... On injured reserve with knee injury (September 26, 1994-remainder of season). ... Granted free agency (February 16, 1996). ... Traded by Dolphins to San Francisco 49ers for fourth round pick in 1997 draft (August 19, 1996). ... Released by 49ers (March 3, 1998).
CHAMPIONSHIP GAME EXPERIENCE: Played in NFC championship game (1997 season).
PRO STATISTICS: 1993—Recovered four fumbles. 1995—Attempted one pass with one completion for 31 yards and a touchdown. 1996—Attempted two passes with one completion for 24 yards and a touchdown and returned one punt for three yards. 1997—Recovered two fumbles.
SINGLE GAME HIGHS (regular season): Attempts—19 (October 8, 1995, vs. Indianapolis); yards—105 (December 2, 1996, vs. Atlanta); and rushing touchdowns—2 (October 19, 1997, vs. Atlanta).
STATISTICAL PLATEAUS: 100-yard rushing games: 1994 (1), 1996 (1). Total: 2. ... 100-yard receiving games: 1993 (2).

			RUSHING				RECEIVING				KICKOFF RETURNS				TOTALS			
Year Team	G	GS	Att.	Yds.	Avg.	TD	No.	Yds.	Avg.	TD	No.	Yds.	Avg.	TD	TD	2pt.	Pts.	Fum.
1993—Miami NFL	16	8	119	390	3.3	3	75	874	11.7	3	4	85	21.3	0	6	...	36	5
1994—Miami NFL	4	4	60	233	3.9	2	14	154	11.0	0	0	0	...	0	2	1	14	2
1995—Miami NFL	16	4	108	414	3.8	4	66	618	9.4	3	0	0	...	0	7	0	42	2
1996—San Francisco NFL	14	10	134	559	4.2	3	52	439	8.4	1	1	22	22.0	0	4	0	24	1
1997—San Francisco NFL	16	3	125	418	3.3	6	23	279	12.1	1	3	124	41.3	1	9	2	58	3
Pro totals (5 years)	66	29	546	2014	3.7	18	230	2364	10.3	8	8	231	28.9	1	28	3	174	13

KIRK, RANDY   LB   49ERS

PERSONAL: Born December 27, 1964, in San Jose, Calif. ... 6-2/242. ... Full name: Randall Scott Kirk.
HIGH SCHOOL: Bellarmine College Prep (San Jose, Calif.).
JUNIOR COLLEGE: De Anza College (Calif.).
COLLEGE: San Diego State.
TRANSACTIONS/CAREER NOTES: Signed as non-drafted free agent by New York Giants (May 10, 1987). ... Released by Giants (August 31, 1987). ... Signed as replacement player by San Diego Chargers (September 24, 1987). ... Granted unconditional free agency (February 1, 1989). ... Signed by Phoenix Cardinals (March 31, 1989). ... On injured reserve with broken ankle (October 16, 1989-remainder of season). ... On injured reserve with foot injury (August 27-September 18, 1990). Released by Cardinals (September 18, 1990). ... Signed by Washington Redskins (November 7, 1990). ... Released by Redskins (November 13, 1990). ... Signed by Cleveland Browns (July 27, 1991). ... On injured reserve with back injury (September 13-November 19, 1991). ... Claimed on waivers by Chargers (November 19, 1991). ...

Granted unconditional free agency (February 1, 1992). ... Signed by Cincinnati Bengals (March 3, 1992). ... Granted unconditional free agency (February 17, 1994). ... Signed by Cardinals (March 7, 1994). ... Cardinals franchise renamed Arizona Cardinals for 1994 season. ... Granted unconditional free agency (February 16, 1996). ... Signed by San Francisco 49ers (March 26, 1996).

PLAYING EXPERIENCE: San Diego NFL, 1987 and 1988; Phoenix NFL, 1989; Washington NFL, 1990; Cleveland (2)-San Diego (5) NFL, 1991; Cleveland NFL, 1992; Cincinnati NFL, 1993; Arizona NFL, 1994 and 1995; San Francisco NFL, 1996 and 1997. ... Games/Games started: 1987 (13/1), 1988 (16/0), 1989 (6/0), 1990 (1/0), 1991 (Cle.-2/0; S.D.-5/0; Total: 7/0), 1992 (15/0), 1993 (16/0), 1994 (16/0), 1995 (16/0), 1996 (16/0), 1997 (16/0). Total: 138/1.

CHAMPIONSHIP GAME EXPERIENCE: Played in NFC championship game (1997 season).

PRO STATISTICS: 1987—Credited with one sack. 1988—Recovered one fumble. 1992—Recovered two fumbles for seven yards.

KIRKLAND, LEVON　　　　LB　　　　STEELERS

PERSONAL: Born February 17, 1969, in Lamar, S.C. ... 6-1/274. ... Full name: Lorenzo Levon Kirkland. ... Name pronounced luh-VON.
HIGH SCHOOL: Lamar (S.C.).
COLLEGE: Clemson.
TRANSACTIONS/CAREER NOTES: Selected by Pittsburgh Steelers in second round (38th pick overall) of 1992 NFL draft. ... Signed by Steelers (July 25, 1992).
CHAMPIONSHIP GAME EXPERIENCE: Played in AFC championship game (1994, 1995 and 1997 seasons). ... Played in Super Bowl XXX (1995 season).
HONORS: Named linebacker on THE SPORTING NEWS college All-America first team (1991). ... Played in Pro Bowl (1996 and 1997 seasons). ... Named inside linebacker on THE SPORTING NEWS NFL All-Pro team (1997).
PRO STATISTICS: 1993—Recovered two fumbles for 24 yards and one touchdown. 1995—Recovered two fumbles. 1997—Recovered one fumble.

| | | | INTERCEPTIONS | | | | SACKS |
Year Team	G	GS	No.	Yds.	Avg.	TD	No.
1992—Pittsburgh NFL	16	0	0	0	...	0	0.0
1993—Pittsburgh NFL	16	13	0	0	...	0	1.0
1994—Pittsburgh NFL	16	15	2	0	0.0	0	3.0
1995—Pittsburgh NFL	16	16	0	0	...	0	1.0
1996—Pittsburgh NFL	16	16	4	12	3.0	0	4.0
1997—Pittsburgh NFL	16	16	2	14	7.0	0	5.0
Pro totals (6 years)	96	76	8	26	3.3	0	14.0

KIRSCHKE, TRAVIS　　　　DT　　　　LIONS

PERSONAL: Born September 6, 1974 ... 6-3/286.
HIGH SCHOOL: Esperanza (Anaheim).
COLLEGE: UCLA.
TRANSACTIONS/CAREER NOTES: Signed as non-drafted free agent by Detroit Lions (April 24, 1997).
PLAYING EXPERIENCE: Detroit NFL, 1997. ... Games/Games started: 3/0.

KITNA, JON　　　　QB　　　　SEAHAWKS

PERSONAL: Born September 21, 1972, in Tacoma, Wash. ... 6-2/217.
HIGH SCHOOL: Lincoln (Tacoma,Wash.).
COLLEGE: Central Washington (degree in math education, 1995).
TRANSACTIONS/CAREER NOTES: Signed as non-drafted free agent by Seattle Seahawks (April 1996). ... Released by Seahawks prior to 1996 season. ... Re-signed by Seahawks to practice squad for 1996 season. ... Assigned by Seahawks to Barcelona Dragons in 1997 World League enhancement allocation program (February 19, 1997).
PRO STATISTICS: 1997—Fumbled once and recovered one fumble for minus two yards.
SINGLE GAME HIGHS (regular season): Attempts—37 (December 14, 1997, vs. Oakland); completions—23 (December 14, 1997, vs. Oakland); yards—283 (December 14, 1997, vs. Oakland); and touchdown passes—1 (December 14, 1997, vs. Oakland).
MISCELLANEOUS: Regular-season record as starting NFL quarterback: 1-0.

| | | | PASSING | | | | | | | RUSHING | | | | TOTALS | | |
Year Team	G	GS	Att.	Cmp.	Pct.	Yds.	TD	Int.	Avg.	Rat.	Att.	Yds.	Avg.	TD	TD	2pt.	Pts.
1997—Barcelona W.L.	...	...	317	171	53.9	2448	22	15	7.72	82.6	50	334	6.7	3	3	...	18
—Seattle NFL	3	1	45	31	68.9	371	1	2	8.24	82.7	10	9	0.9	1	1	0	6
W.L. totals (1 year)	...	...	317	171	53.9	2448	22	15	7.72	82.6	50	334	6.7	3	3	0	18
NFL totals (1 year)	3	1	45	31	68.9	371	1	2	8.24	82.7	10	9	0.9	1	1	0	6
Pro totals (2 years)	...	...	362	202	55.8	2819	23	17	7.79	82.6	60	343	5.7	4	4	0	24

KITTS, JIM　　　　FB　　　　DOLPHINS

PERSONAL: Born December 28, 1972 ... 6-2/243.
HIGH SCHOOL: Great Bridge (Chesapeake, Va.).
COLLEGE: Ferrum (Va.).
TRANSACTIONS/CAREER NOTES: Played with Albany Firebirds of Arena League (1995 and 1996). ... Signed by Washington Redskins (February 19, 1997). ... Assigned by Redskins to Frankfurt Galaxy in 1997 World League enhancement allocation program (February 19, 1997). ... Released by Redskins (August 18, 1997). ... Re-signed by Redskins to practice squad (August 26, 1997). ... Released by Redskins (September 22, 1997). ... Signed by Green Bay Packers to practice squad (September 23, 1997). ... Signed by Miami Dolphins off Packers practice squad (October 1, 1997).
PLAYING EXPERIENCE: Frankfurt W.L., 1997; Miami NFL, 1997. ... Games/Games started: 1997 (W.L.: games played unavailable; NFL: 10/0). Total NFL: 10/0.
PRO STATISTICS: W.L.: 1997—Rushed three times for 10 yards and caught 10 passes for 53 yards.
SINGLE GAME HIGHS (regular season): Attempts—0; yards—0; and rushing touchdowns—0.

KLINGLER, DAVID · QB

PERSONAL: Born February 17, 1969, in Stratford, Texas. ... 6-2/205.
HIGH SCHOOL: Stratford (Houston).
COLLEGE: Houston (degree in marketing, 1991).
TRANSACTIONS/CAREER NOTES: Selected by Cincinnati Bengals in first round (sixth pick overall) of 1992 NFL draft. ... Signed by Bengals (August 30, 1992). ... Granted unconditional free agency (February 16, 1996). ... Signed by Oakland Raiders (June 8, 1996). ... Released by Raiders after 1997 season.
PRO STATISTICS: 1992—Fumbled three times. 1993—Fumbled seven times and recovered two fumbles for minus 10 yards. 1994—Caught one pass for minus six yards, fumbled seven times and recovered one fumble. 1996—Fumbled once and recovered one fumble. 1997—Fumbled once and recovered one fumble for minus five yards.
SINGLE GAME HIGHS (regular season): Attempts—43 (September 4, 1994, vs. Cleveland); completions—27 (September 4, 1994, vs. Cleveland); yards—266 (September 18, 1994, vs. New England); and touchdown passes—3 (December 26, 1993, vs. Atlanta).
MISCELLANEOUS: Regular-season record as starting NFL quarterback: 4-20 (.167).

			PASSING								RUSHING				TOTALS		
Year Team	G	GS	Att.	Cmp.	Pct.	Yds.	TD	Int.	Avg.	Rat.	Att.	Yds.	Avg.	TD	TD	2pt.	Pts.
1992—Cincinnati NFL	4	4	98	47	48.0	530	3	2	5.41	66.3	11	53	4.8	0	0	...	0
1993—Cincinnati NFL	14	13	343	190	55.4	1935	6	9	5.64	66.6	41	282	6.9	0	0	...	0
1994—Cincinnati NFL	10	7	231	131	56.7	1327	6	9	5.74	65.7	17	85	5.0	0	0	0	0
1995—Cincinnati NFL	3	0	15	7	46.7	88	1	1	5.87	59.9	0	0	...	0	0	0	0
1996—Oakland NFL	1	0	24	10	41.7	87	0	0	3.63	51.9	4	36	9.0	0	0	0	0
1997—Oakland NFL	1	0	7	4	57.1	27	0	1	3.86	26.2	1	0	0.0	0	0	0	0
Pro totals (6 years)	33	24	718	389	54.2	3994	16	22	5.56	65.1	74	456	6.2	0	0	0	0

KNIGHT, SAMMY · S · SAINTS

PERSONAL: Born September 10, 1975, in Fontana, Calif. ... 6-0/205.
HIGH SCHOOL: Rubidoux (Riverside, Calif.).
COLLEGE: Southern California.
TRANSACTIONS/CAREER NOTES: Signed as non-drafted free agent by New Orleans Saints (April 25, 1997).
PRO STATISTICS: 1997—Recovered one fumble.

			INTERCEPTIONS			
Year Team	G	GS	No.	Yds.	Avg.	TD
1997—New Orleans NFL	16	12	5	75	15.0	0

KNIGHT, TOM · CB · CARDINALS

PERSONAL: Born December 29, 1974, in Summit, N.J. ... 5-11/196. ... Full name: Thomas Lorenzo Knight.
HIGH SCHOOL: Cherokee (Marlton, N.J.).
COLLEGE: Iowa.
TRANSACTIONS/CAREER NOTES: Selected by Arizona Cardinals in first round (ninth pick overall) of 1997 NFL draft. ... Signed by Cardinals (July 16, 1997).
PLAYING EXPERIENCE: Arizona NFL, 1997. ... Games/Games started: 15/14.

KOONCE, GEORGE · LB · PACKERS

PERSONAL: Born October 15, 1968, in New Bern, N.C. ... 6-1/243. ... Full name: George Earl Koonce Jr.
HIGH SCHOOL: West Craven (Vanceboro, N.C.)
COLLEGE: Chowan College (N.C.), then East Carolina.
TRANSACTIONS/CAREER NOTES: Signed as non-drafted free agent by Atlanta Falcons (April 30, 1991). ... Released by Falcons (August 26, 1991). ... Selected by Ohio Glory in 13th round (143rd pick overall) of 1992 World League draft. ... Signed by Green Bay Packers (June 2, 1992). ... On injured reserve with shoulder injury (January 3, 1994-entire 1993 playoffs). ... Granted free agency (February 17, 1995). ... Re-signed by Packers (June 2, 1995). ... On injured reserve with knee injury (January 10, 1997-remainder of 1996 playoffs). ... On physically unable to perform list with knee injury (August 19-November 18, 1997).
CHAMPIONSHIP GAME EXPERIENCE: Played in NFC championship game (1995 and 1997 seasons). ... Member of Packers for NFC championship game (1996); inactive. ... Member of Super Bowl championship team (1996 season); inactive. ... Played in Super Bowl XXXII (1997 season).
PRO STATISTICS: W.L.: 1992—Recovered two fumbles for 35 yards. NFL: 1992—Recovered one fumble. 1993—Recovered one fumble. 1994—Recovered two fumbles. 1996—Recovered one fumble.

			INTERCEPTIONS				SACKS
Year Team	G	GS	No.	Yds.	Avg.	TD	No.
1992—Ohio W.L.	10	9	0	0	...	0	2.5
—Green Bay NFL	16	10	0	0	...	0	1.5
1993—Green Bay NFL	15	15	0	0	...	0	3.0
1994—Green Bay NFL	16	16	0	0	...	0	1.0
1995—Green Bay NFL	16	16	1	12	12.0	0	1.0
1996—Green Bay NFL	16	16	3	84	28.0	1	0.0
1997—Green Bay NFL	4	0	0	0	...	0	0.0
W.L. totals (1 year)	10	9	0	0		0	2.5
NFL totals (6 years)	83	73	4	96	24.0	1	6.5
Pro totals (7 years)	93	82	4	96	24.0	1	9.0

K

KOPP, JEFF — LB — JAGUARS

PERSONAL: Born July 8, 1971, in Danville, Calif. ... 6-3/245.
HIGH SCHOOL: San Ramon (Danville, Calif.).
COLLEGE: Southern California.
TRANSACTIONS/CAREER NOTES: Selected by Miami Dolphins in sixth round (194th pick overall) of 1995 NFL draft. ... Signed by Dolphins for 1995 season. ... Released by Dolphins (August 25, 1996). ... Signed by Jacksonville Jaguars (September 24, 1996).
PLAYING EXPERIENCE: Miami NFL, 1995; Jacksonville NFL, 1996 and 1997. ... Games/Games started: 1995 (16/0), 1996 (12/0), 1997 (16/3). Total: 44/3.
CHAMPIONSHIP GAME EXPERIENCE: Played in AFC championship game (1996 season).
PRO STATISTICS: 1997—Intercepted one pass for nine yards and credited with one sack.

KOWALKOWSKI, SCOTT — LB — LIONS

PERSONAL: Born August 23, 1968, in Royal Oak, Mich. ... 6-2/228. ... Full name: Scott Thomas Kowalkowski. ... Son of David Kowalkowski, guard with Detroit Lions (1966-1976). ... Name pronounced KO-wal-KOW-skee.
HIGH SCHOOL: St. Mary's Prep (Orchard Lake, Mich.).
COLLEGE: Notre Dame (degree in American studies).
TRANSACTIONS/CAREER NOTES: Selected by Philadelphia Eagles in eighth round (217th pick overall) of 1991 NFL draft. ... Signed by Eagles (July 10, 1991). ... On injured reserve with ankle injury (August 30-November 23, 1993). ... Released by Eagles (November 23, 1993). ... Signed by Detroit Lions (1994). ... Granted unconditional free agency (February 17, 1995). ... Re-signed by Lions (March 24, 1995). ... Granted unconditional free agency (February 16, 1996). ... Re-signed by Lions prior to 1996 season. ... Granted unconditional free agency (February 14, 1997). ... Re-signed by Lions (March 18, 1997).
PLAYING EXPERIENCE: Philadelphia NFL, 1991 and 1992; Detroit NFL, 1994-1997. ... Games/Games started: 1991 (16/0), 1992 (16/0), 1994 (16/0), 1995 (16/0), 1996 (16/1), 1997 (16/0). Total: 96/1.
PRO STATISTICS: 1991—Recovered one fumble. 1996—Recovered one fumble.

KOZLOWSKI, BRIAN — TE — FALCONS

PERSONAL: Born October 4, 1970, in Rochester, N.Y. ... 6-3/255. ... Full name: Brian Scott Kozlowski.
HIGH SCHOOL: Webster (N.Y.).
COLLEGE: Connecticut.
TRANSACTIONS/CAREER NOTES: Signed as non-drafted free agent by New York Giants (May 1, 1993). ... Released by Giants (August 16, 1993). ... Re-signed by Giants to practice squad (December 8, 1993). ... Granted unconditional free agency (February 14, 1997). ... Signed by Atlanta Falcons (March 21, 1997). ... Granted unconditional free agency (February 13, 1998). ... Re-signed by Falcons (March 4, 1998).
PRO STATISTICS: 1995—Recovered one fumble.
SINGLE GAME HIGHS (regular season): Receptions—2 (December 14, 1997, vs. Philadelphia); yards—41 (December 14, 1995, vs. Philadelphia); and touchdown receptions—1 (November 16, 1997, vs. St. Louis).

			RECEIVING				KICKOFF RETURNS				TOTALS		
Year Team	G	GS	No.	Yds.	Avg.	TD	No.	Yds.	Avg.	TD	TD	2pt.	Pts.	Fum.
1993—New York Giants NFL							Did not play.						
1994—New York Giants NFL	16	2	1	5	5.0	0	2	21	10.5	0	0	0	0	0
1995—New York Giants NFL	16	0	2	17	8.5	0	5	75	15.0	0	0	0	0	1
1996—New York Giants NFL	5	0	1	4	4.0	1	1	16	16.0	0	1	0	6	0
1997—Atlanta NFL	16	5	7	99	14.1	1	2	49	24.5	0	1	0	6	0
Pro totals (4 years)	53	7	11	125	11.4	2	10	161	16.1	0	2	0	12	1

KRAGEN, GREG — NT

PERSONAL: Born March 4, 1962, in Chicago. ... 6-3/267. ... Full name: Greg John Kragen.
HIGH SCHOOL: Amador (Pleasanton, Calif.).
COLLEGE: Utah State.
TRANSACTIONS/CAREER NOTES: Selected by Oklahoma Outlaws in 15th round (296th pick overall) of 1984 USFL draft. ... Signed as non-drafted free agent by Denver Broncos (May 2, 1984). ... Released by Broncos (August 27, 1984). ... Re-signed by Broncos (January 20, 1985). ... Released by Broncos (April 22, 1994). ... Signed by Kansas City Chiefs (August 18, 1994). ... Selected by Carolina Panthers from Chiefs in NFL expansion draft (February 15, 1995). ... Granted unconditional free agency (February 14, 1997). ... Re-signed by Panthers (February 24, 1997). ... Granted unconditional free agency (February 13, 1998).
CHAMPIONSHIP GAME EXPERIENCE: Played in AFC championship game (1986, 1987, 1989 and 1991 seasons). ... Played in Super Bowl XXI (1986 season), Super Bowl XXII (1987 season) and Super Bowl XXIV (1989 season). ... Played in NFC championship game (1996 season).
HONORS: Played in Pro Bowl (1989 season).
PRO STATISTICS: 1986—Recovered three fumbles. 1987—Recovered one fumble. 1988—Recovered four fumbles for 17 yards and a touchdown. 1990—Recovered two fumbles. 1993—Recovered one fumble. 1995—Intercepted one pass for 29 yards and recovered two fumbles for three yards and a touchdown. 1996—Recovered two fumbles.

Year Team	G	GS	SACKS
1985—Denver NFL	16	1	2.0
1986—Denver NFL	16	14	0.0
1987—Denver NFL	12	9	2.0
1988—Denver NFL	16	16	2.5
1989—Denver NFL	14	14	2.0
1990—Denver NFL	16	16	2.0
1991—Denver NFL	16	16	3.5
1992—Denver NFL	16	16	5.5
1993—Denver NFL	14	14	3.0
1994—Kansas City NFL	16	2	0.0
1995—Carolina NFL	16	14	1.0
1996—Carolina NFL	16	16	3.0
1997—Carolina NFL	16	16	2.0
Pro totals (13 years)	200	164	28.5

K

PERSONAL: Born November 6, 1964, in Encino, Calif. ... 6-1/204. ... Full name: William Erik Kramer.
HIGH SCHOOL: Conoga Park (Calif.).
JUNIOR COLLEGE: Los Angeles Pierce Junior College.
COLLEGE: North Carolina State.
TRANSACTIONS/CAREER NOTES: Signed as non-drafted free agent by New Orleans Saints (May 6, 1987). ... Released by Saints (August 31, 1987). ... Signed as replacement player by Atlanta Falcons (September 24, 1987). ... Released by Falcons (September 1, 1988). ... Signed by Calgary Stampeders of CFL (September 28, 1988). ... Released by Stampeders (July 4, 1989). ... Signed by Detroit Lions (March 21, 1990). ... On injured reserve with shoulder injury (September 4-December 28, 1990). ... Released by Lions (December 28, 1990). ... Re-signed by Lions (March 6, 1991). ... Granted free agency (March 1, 1993). ... Tendered offer sheet by Dallas Cowboys (April 1993). ... Offer matched by Lions (April 23, 1993). ... Granted unconditional free agency (February 17, 1994). ... Signed by Chicago Bears (February 21, 1994). ... On injured reserve with neck injury (October 14, 1996-remainder of season). ... Granted unconditional free agency (February 14, 1997). ... Re-signed by Bears (March 11, 1997). ... Granted unconditional free agency (February 13, 1998). ... Re-signed by Bears (February 20, 1998).
CHAMPIONSHIP GAME EXPERIENCE: Played in NFC championship game (1991 season).
PRO STATISTICS: CFL: 1988—Fumbled seven times. NFL: 1991—Fumbled eight times and recovered four fumbles for minus five yards. 1992—Fumbled four times and recovered one fumble for minus one yard. 1993—Fumbled once. 1994—Fumbled three times and recovered two fumbles for minus five yards. 1995—Fumbled six times and recovered two fumbles for minus 13 yards. 1996—Fumbled once and recovered one fumble for minus one yard. 1997—Fumbled 11 times and recovered three fumbles for minus 14 yards.
SINGLE GAME HIGHS (regular season): Attempts—60 (November 16, 1997, vs. New York Jets); completions—32 (November 16, 1997, vs. New York Jets); yards—354 (November 16, 1997, vs. New York Jets); and touchdown passes—4 (September 24, 1995, vs. St. Louis).
STATISTICAL PLATEAUS: 300-yard passing games: 1987 (1), 1992 (1), 1994 (1), 1995 (3), 1997 (2). Total: 8.
MISCELLANEOUS: Regular-season record as starting NFL quarterback: 26-29 (.473). ... Postseason record as starting NFL quarterback: 1-2 (.333).

			PASSING								RUSHING				TOTALS		
Year Team	G	GS	Att.	Cmp.	Pct.	Yds.	TD	Int.	Avg.	Rat.	Att.	Yds.	Avg.	TD	TD	2pt.	Pts.
1987—Atlanta NFL	3	2	92	45	48.9	559	4	5	6.08	60.0	2	10	5.0	0	0	...	0
1988—Calgary CFL	6	...	153	62	40.5	964	5	13	6.30	37.6	12	17	1.4	1	1	...	6
1989—							Did not play.										
1990—Detroit NFL							Did not play.										
1991—Detroit NFL	13	8	265	136	51.3	1635	11	8	6.17	71.8	35	26	0.7	1	1	...	6
1992—Detroit NFL	7	3	106	58	54.7	771	4	8	7.27	59.1	12	34	2.8	0	0	...	0
1993—Detroit NFL	5	4	138	87	63.0	1002	8	8	7.26	95.1	10	5	0.5	0	0	...	0
1994—Chicago NFL	6	5	158	99	62.7	1129	8	8	7.15	79.9	6	-2	-0.3	0	0	0	0
1995—Chicago NFL	16	16	522	315	60.3	3838	29	10	7.35	93.5	35	39	1.1	1	1	0	6
1996—Chicago NFL	4	4	150	73	48.7	781	3	6	5.21	54.3	8	4	0.5	0	0	0	0
1997—Chicago NFL	15	13	477	275	57.7	3011	14	14	6.31	74.0	27	83	3.1	2	2	0	12
CFL totals (1 year)	6	...	153	62	40.5	964	5	13	6.30	37.6	12	17	1.4	1	1	...	6
NFL totals (8 years)	69	55	1908	1088	57.0	12726	81	62	6.67	78.0	135	199	1.5	4	4	0	24
Pro totals (9 years)	75	...	2061	1150	55.8	13690	86	75	6.64	75.0	147	216	1.5	5	5	0	30

PERSONAL: Born February 8, 1973, in Cincinnati. ... 6-2/223. ... Full name: Eric Joel Kresser.
HIGH SCHOOL: Palm Beach Gardens (Fla.).
COLLEGE: Florida, then Marshall (W.Va.).
TRANSACTIONS/CAREER NOTES: Signed as non-drafted free agent by Cincinnati Bengals (April 25, 1997). ... Released by Bengals (August 24, 1997). ... Re-signed by Bengals to practice squad (October 21, 1997). ... Activated (November 17, 1997). ... Inactive for five games (1997).

PERSONAL: Born October 20, 1958, in Iola, Wis. ... 6-1/202. ... Full name: David M. Krieg. ... Name pronounced CRAIG.
HIGH SCHOOL: D.C. Everest (Schofield, Wis.).
COLLEGE: Milton College, Wis. (degree in marketing management, 1980).
TRANSACTIONS/CAREER NOTES: Signed as non-drafted free agent by Seattle Seahawks (May 6, 1980). ... On injured reserve with separated shoulder (September 19-November 12, 1988). ... On injured reserve with thumb injury (September 3-October 18, 1991). ... Granted unconditional free agency (February 1, 1992). ... Signed by Kansas City Chiefs (March 19, 1992). ... Granted unconditional free agency (February 17, 1994). ... Signed by Detroit Lions (April 22, 1994). ... Granted unconditional free agency (February 17, 1995). ... Signed by Arizona Cardinals (March 11, 1995). ... Released by Cardinals (April 8, 1996). ... Signed by Chicago Bears (May 21, 1996). ... Granted unconditional free agency (February 14, 1997). ... Signed by Houston Oilers (May 5, 1997). ... Oilers franchise moved to Tennessee for 1997 season.
CHAMPIONSHIP GAME EXPERIENCE: Played in AFC championship game (1983 and 1993 seasons).
HONORS: Played in Pro Bowl (1984, 1988 and 1989 seasons).
RECORDS: Holds NFL single-season record for most own fumbles recovered—9 (1989). ... Shares NFL single-season record for most fumbles recovered, own and opponents—9 (1989).
PRO STATISTICS: 1981—Fumbled four times. 1982—Fumbled five times and recovered two fumbles for minus 14 yards. 1983—Caught one pass for 11 yards, fumbled 10 times and recovered two fumbles. 1984—Fumbled 11 times and recovered three fumbles for minus 24 yards. 1985—Fumbled 11 times and recovered three fumbles for minus two yards. 1986—Fumbled 10 times and recovered one fumble for minus five yards. 1987—Fumbled 11 times and recovered five fumbles for minus two yards. 1988—Fumbled six times. 1989—Led league with 18 fumbles and recovered nine fumbles for minus 20 yards. 1990—Caught one pass for minus six yards, fumbled 16 times and recovered two fumbles. 1991—Fumbled six times. 1992—Fumbled 10 times and recovered six fumbles for minus 15 yards. 1993—Fumbled six times and recovered one fumble. 1994—Fumbled four times and recovered two fumbles for minus one yard. 1995—Led league with 16 fumbles and recovered seven fumbles for minus 13 yards. 1996—Caught one pass for five yards, fumbled six times and recovered three fumbles for minus nine yards.
SINGLE GAME HIGHS (regular season): Attempts—51 (October 13, 1985, vs. Atlanta); completions—33 (October 13, 1985, vs. Atlanta); yards—420 (November 20, 1983, vs. Denver); and touchdown passes—5 (November 28, 1988, vs. Los Angeles Raiders).
STATISTICAL PLATEAUS: 300-yard passing games: 1983 (1), 1984 (3), 1985 (2), 1986 (1), 1980 (1), 1989 (1), 1990 (1), 1991 (1), 1992 (2), 1994 (1), 1995 (4). Total: 18.
MISCELLANEOUS: Regular-season record as starting NFL quarterback: 98-77 (.560). ... Postseason record as starting NFL quarterback: 3-6 (.333). ... Holds Seattle Seahawks all-time records for most passing yards (26,132) and most touchdown passes (195).

Year Team	G	GS	Att.	Cmp.	Pct.	Yds.	TD	Int.	Avg.	Rat.	Att.	Yds.	Avg.	TD	TD	2pt.	Pts.
1980—Seattle NFL.................	1	0	2	0	0.0	0	0	0	...	39.6	0	0	...	0	0	...	0
1981—Seattle NFL.................	7	3	112	64	57.1	843	7	5	7.53	83.3	11	56	5.1	1	1	...	6
1982—Seattle NFL.................	3	2	78	49	62.8	501	2	2	6.42	79.1	6	-3	-0.5	0	0	...	0
1983—Seattle NFL.................	9	8	243	147	60.5	2139	18	11	§8.80	95.0	16	55	3.4	2	2	...	12
1984—Seattle NFL.................	16	16	480	276	57.5	3671	32	*24	7.65	83.3	46	186	4.0	3	3	...	18
1985—Seattle NFL.................	16	16	532	285	53.6	3602	27	20	6.77	76.2	35	121	3.5	1	1	...	6
1986—Seattle NFL.................	15	14	375	225	60.0	2921	21	11	7.79	91.0	35	122	3.5	1	1	...	6
1987—Seattle NFL.................	12	12	294	178	60.5	2131	23	15	7.25	87.6	36	155	4.3	2	2	...	12
1988—Seattle NFL.................	9	9	228	134	58.8	1741	18	8	7.64	94.6	24	64	2.7	0	0	...	0
1989—Seattle NFL.................	15	14	499	286	57.3	3309	21	20	6.63	74.8	40	160	4.0	0	0	...	0
1990—Seattle NFL.................	16	16	448	265	59.2	3194	15	20	7.13	73.6	32	115	3.6	0	0	...	0
1991—Seattle NFL.................	10	9	285	187	*65.6	2080	11	12	7.30	82.5	13	59	4.5	0	0	...	0
1992—Kansas City NFL.........	16	16	413	230	55.7	3115	15	12	§7.54	79.9	37	74	2.0	2	2	...	12
1993—Kansas City NFL.........	12	5	189	105	55.6	1238	7	3	6.55	81.4	21	24	1.1	0	0	...	0
1994—Detroit NFL.................	14	7	212	131	61.8	1629	14	3	7.68	101.7	23	35	1.5	0	0	0	0
1995—Arizona NFL................	16	16	521	304	58.3	3554	16	‡21	6.82	72.6	19	29	1.5	0	0	0	0
1996—Chicago NFL................	13	12	377	226	59.9	2278	14	12	6.04	76.3	16	12	0.8	1	1	0	6
1997—Tennessee NFL............	8	0	2	1	50.0	2	0	0	1.00	56.3	4	-2	-0.5	0	0	0	0
Pro totals (18 years)............	208	175	5290	3093	58.5	37948	261	199	7.17	81.5	414	1262	3.0	13	13	0	78

KUBERSKI, BOB — DT — PACKERS

PERSONAL: Born April 5, 1971, in Chester, Pa. ... 6-4/295. ... Full name: Robert Kenneth Kuberski Jr.
HIGH SCHOOL: Ridley (Folsom, Pa.).
COLLEGE: Navy.
TRANSACTIONS/CAREER NOTES: Selected by Green Bay Packers in seventh round (183rd pick overall) of 1993 NFL draft. ... Signed by Packers (June 7, 1993). ... On reserve/military list (August 23, 1993-April 19, 1995).
PLAYING EXPERIENCE: Green Bay NFL, 1995-1997. ... Games/Games started: 1995 (9/0), 1996 (1/0), 1997 (11/3). Total: 21/3.
CHAMPIONSHIP GAME EXPERIENCE: Played in NFC championship game (1995 and 1997 seasons). ... Member of Packers for NFC championship game (1996 season); inactive. ... Member of Super Bowl championship team (1996 season); inactive. ... Played in Super Bowl XXXII (1997 season).
PRO STATISTICS: 1995—Credited with two sacks.

KUEHL, RYAN — DT — REDSKINS

PERSONAL: Born January 18, 1972, in Washington, D.C. ... 6-4/289. ... Full name: Ryan Philip Kuehl.
HIGH SCHOOL: Walt Whitman (Bethesda, Md.).
COLLEGE: Virginia (degree in marketing, 1994).
TRANSACTIONS/CAREER NOTES: Signed as non-drafted free agent by San Francisco 49ers (April 26, 1995). ... Released by 49ers (August 19, 1995). ... Re-signed by Redskins to practice squad (August 26, 1996). ... Signed by Washington Redskins (February 16, 1996). ... Released by Redskins (August 25, 1996). ... Re-signed by Redskins to practice squad (August 26, 1996). ... Activated (October 19, 1996). ... Released by Redskins (November 6, 1996). ... Re-signed by Redskins to practice squad (November 7, 1996). ... Activated (November 11, 1996). ... Released by Redskins (August 23, 1997). ... Re-signed by Redskins (September 9, 1997).
PLAYING EXPERIENCE: Washington NFL, 1996 and 1997. ... Games/Games started: 1996 (2/0), 1997 (12/5). Total: 14/5.

KYLE, JASON — LB — SEAHAWKS

PERSONAL: Born May 12, 1972, in Mesa, Ariz. ... 6-3/242. ... Full name: Jason C. Kyle.
HIGH SCHOOL: McClintock (Tempe, Ariz.).
COLLEGE: Arizona State.
TRANSACTIONS/CAREER NOTES: Selected by Seattle Seahawks in fourth round (126th pick overall) of 1995 NFL draft. ... Signed by Seahawks (July 16, 1995). ... On injured reserve with shoulder injury (August 18, 1997-entire season). ... Granted free agency (February 13, 1998). ... Re-signed by Seahawks (April 16, 1998).
PLAYING EXPERIENCE: Seattle NFL, 1995 and 1996. ... Games/Games started: 1995 (16/0), 1996 (16/0). Total: 32/0.

LaBOUNTY, MATT — DE — SEAHAWKS

PERSONAL: Born January 3, 1969, in San Francisco. ... 6-4/275. ... Full name: Matthew James LaBounty.
HIGH SCHOOL: San Marin (Novato, Calif.).
COLLEGE: Oregon.
TRANSACTIONS/CAREER NOTES: Selected by San Francisco 49ers in 12th round (327th pick overall) of 1992 NFL draft. ... Signed by 49ers (July 13, 1992). ... Released by 49ers (August 31, 1992). ... Re-signed by 49ers to practice squad (September 1, 1992). ... Granted free agency after 1992 season. ... Re-signed by 49ers for 1993 season. ... Released by 49ers (October 17, 1993). ... Re-signed by 49ers to practice squad (October 20, 1993). ... Activated (December 2, 1993). ... Claimed on waivers by Green Bay Packers (December 8, 1993). ... On injured reserve with back injury (August 23, 1994-entire season). ... Traded by Packers to Seattle Seahawks for S Eugene Robinson (June 27, 1996). ... Granted unconditional free agency (February 13, 1998). ... Re-signed by Seahawks (February 11, 1998).
PLAYING EXPERIENCE: San Francisco NFL, 1993; Green Bay NFL, 1995; Seattle NFL, 1996 and 1997. ... Games/Games started: 1993 (6/0), 1995 (14/2), 1996 (3/0), 1997 (15/6). Total: 38/8.
CHAMPIONSHIP GAME EXPERIENCE: Played in NFC championship game (1995 season).
PRO STATISTICS: 1995—Credited with three sacks. 1997—Credited with three sacks.

LACINA, CORBIN G PANTHERS

PERSONAL: Born November 2, 1970, in Woodbury, Minn. ... 6-4/297.
HIGH SCHOOL: Cretin-Derham Hall (St. Paul, Minn.).
COLLEGE: Augustana (S.D.).
TRANSACTIONS/CAREER NOTES: Selected by Buffalo Bills in sixth round (167th pick overall) of 1993 NFL draft. ... Signed by Bills (July 12, 1993). ... Released by Bills (August 30, 1993). ... Re-signed by Bills to practice squad (September 1, 1993). ... Activated (December 30, 1993); did not play. ... On injured reserve with foot injury (December 22, 1994-remainder of season). ... On injured reserve with groin injury (November 30, 1996-remainder of season). ... Granted free agency (February 14, 1997). ... Re-signed by Bills (June 12, 1997). ... Granted unconditional free agency (February 13, 1998). ... Signed by Carolina Panthers (February 26, 1998).
PLAYING EXPERIENCE: Buffalo NFL, 1994-1997. ... Games/Games started: 1994 (11/10), 1995 (16/3), 1996 (12/2), 1997 (16/13). Total: 55/28.
CHAMPIONSHIP GAME EXPERIENCE: Member of Bills for AFC championship game (1993 season); inactive. ... Member of Bills for Super Bowl XXVIII (1993 season); inactive.
PRO STATISTICS: 1997—Recovered one fumble.

LaFLEUR, DAVID TE COWBOYS

PERSONAL: Born January 29, 1974, in Lake Charles, La. ... 6-7/280. ... Full name: David Alan LaFleur.
HIGH SCHOOL: Westlake (La.).
COLLEGE: Louisiana State.
TRANSACTIONS/CAREER NOTES: Selected by Dallas Cowboys in first round (22nd pick overall) of 1997 NFL draft. ... Signed by Cowboys (July 17, 1997).
SINGLE GAME HIGHS (regular season): Receptions—4 (December 8, 1997, vs. Carolina); yards—29 (December 14, 1997, Cincinnati); and touchdown receptions—2 (December 14, 1997, vs. Cincinnati).

			RECEIVING				TOTALS		
Year Team	G	GS	No.	Yds.	Avg.	TD	TD	2pt.	Pts.	Fum.
1997—Dallas NFL	16	5	18	122	6.8	2	2	0	12	1

LAGEMAN, JEFF DE JAGUARS

L

PERSONAL: Born July 18, 1967, in Fairfax, Va. ... 6-6/265. ... Full name: Jeffrey David Lageman. ... Name pronounced LOG-a-man.
HIGH SCHOOL: Park View (Sterling, Va.).
COLLEGE: Virginia (degree in economics, 1989).
TRANSACTIONS/CAREER NOTES: Selected by New York Jets in first round (14th pick overall) of 1989 NFL draft. ... Signed by Jets (August 24, 1989). ... On injured reserve with knee injury (September 15, 1992-remainder of season). ... Granted unconditional free agency (February 17, 1995). ... Signed by Jacksonville Jaguars (March 14, 1995). ... On injured reserve with foot injury (December 19, 1995-remainder of season). ... Granted unconditional free agency (February 13, 1998). ... Re-signed by Jaguars (February 18, 1998).
CHAMPIONSHIP GAME EXPERIENCE: Played in AFC championship game (1996 season).
PRO STATISTICS: 1989—Rushed once for minus five yards. 1993—Intercepted one pass for 15 yards. 1994—Recovered three fumbles. 1995—Recovered one fumble. 1997—Recovered one fumble.

Year Team	G	GS	SACKS
1989—New York Jets NFL	16	15	4.5
1990—New York Jets NFL	16	16	4.0
1991—New York Jets NFL	16	16	10.0
1992—New York Jets NFL	2	2	1.0
1993—New York Jets NFL	16	16	8.5
1994—New York Jets NFL	16	16	6.5
1995—Jacksonville NFL	11	11	3.0
1996—Jacksonville NFL	12	9	4.5
1997—Jacksonville NFL	16	16	5.0
Pro totals (9 years)	121	117	47.0

LAING, AARON TE RAMS

PERSONAL: Born July 19, 1971, in Houston. ... 6-3/260. ... Full name: Aaron Matthew Laing.
HIGH SCHOOL: Sharpstown (Houston).
COLLEGE: New Mexico State.
TRANSACTIONS/CAREER NOTES: Selected by San Diego Chargers in fifth round (137th pick overall) of 1994 NFL draft. ... Signed by Chargers (June 15, 1994). ... Claimed on waivers by St. Louis Rams (August 27, 1995). ... Released by Rams (August 31, 1995). ... Re-signed by Rams (January 4, 1996). ... Granted free agency (February 13, 1998). ... Re-signed by Rams (April 21, 1998).
CHAMPIONSHIP GAME EXPERIENCE: Member of Chargers for AFC championship game and Super Bowl XXIX (1994 season); inactive.
PRO STATISTICS: 1996—Returned one kickoff for 15 yards and recovered one fumble.
SINGLE GAME HIGHS (regular season): Receptions—4 (December 8, 1996, vs. Chicago); yards—35 (December 15, 1996, vs. Atlanta); and touchdown receptions—1 (September 28, 1997, vs. Oakland).

			RECEIVING				TOTALS		
Year Team	G	GS	No.	Yds.	Avg.	TD	TD	2pt.	Pts.	Fum.
1994—San Diego NFL	5	1	0	0	...	0	0	0	0	0
1995—					Did not play.					
1996—St. Louis NFL	12	0	13	116	8.9	0	0	0	0	0
1997—St. Louis NFL	15	3	5	31	6.2	1	1	0	6	0
Pro totals (3 years)	32	12	18	147	8.2	1	1	0	6	0

LAKE, CARNELL   S   STEELERS

PERSONAL: Born July 15, 1967, in Salt Lake City. ... 6-1/210. ... Full name: Carnell Augustino Lake.
HIGH SCHOOL: Culver City (Calif.).
COLLEGE: UCLA.
TRANSACTIONS/CAREER NOTES: Selected by Pittsburgh Steelers in second round (34th pick overall) of 1989 NFL draft. ... Signed by Steelers (July 23, 1989). ... Granted free agency (February 1, 1992). ... Re-signed by Steelers (August 21, 1992). ... Granted roster exemption (August 21-28, 1992). ... Designated by Steelers as franchise player (February 15, 1995).
CHAMPIONSHIP GAME EXPERIENCE: Played in AFC championship game (1994, 1995 and 1997 seasons). ... Played in Super Bowl XXX (1995 season).
HONORS: Named linebacker on The Sporting News college All-America second team (1987). ... Played in Pro Bowl (1994-1997 seasons). ... Named strong safety on The Sporting News NFL All-Pro team (1997).
POST SEASON RECORDS: Shares NFL postseason single-game record for most safeties—1 (January 7, 1995, vs. Cleveland).
PRO STATISTICS: 1989—Recovered six fumbles for two yards. 1990—Recovered one fumble. 1992—Recovered one fumble for 12 yards. 1993—Recovered two fumbles. 1994—Recovered one fumble. 1995—Recovered one fumble. 1996—Recovered two fumbles for 85 yards and one touchdown. 1997—Recovered one fumble for 38 yards and a touchdown.

				INTERCEPTIONS				SACKS
Year	Team	G	GS	No.	Yds.	Avg.	TD	No.
1989—Pittsburgh NFL		15	15	1	0	0.0	0	1.0
1990—Pittsburgh NFL		16	16	1	0	0.0	0	1.0
1991—Pittsburgh NFL		16	16	0	0	...	0	1.0
1992—Pittsburgh NFL		16	16	0	0	...	0	2.0
1993—Pittsburgh NFL		14	14	4	31	7.8	0	5.0
1994—Pittsburgh NFL		16	16	1	2	2.0	0	1.0
1995—Pittsburgh NFL		16	16	1	32	32.0	▲1	1.5
1996—Pittsburgh NFL		13	13	1	47	47.0	1	2.0
1997—Pittsburgh NFL		16	16	3	16	5.3	0	6.0
Pro totals (9 years)		138	138	12	128	10.7	2	20.5

LAND, DAN   CB   RAIDERS

PERSONAL: Born July 3, 1965, in Donalsonville, Ga. ... 6-0/195.
HIGH SCHOOL: Seminole County (Donalsonville, Ga.).
COLLEGE: Albany (Ga.) State.
TRANSACTIONS/CAREER NOTES: Signed as non-drafted free agent by Tampa Bay Buccaneers (May 4, 1987). ... Released by Buccaneers (September 7, 1987). ... Re-signed as replacement player by Buccaneers (September 24, 1987). ... Released by Buccaneers (October 19, 1987). ... Signed by Atlanta Falcons for 1988 season (December 5, 1987). ... Released by Falcons (August 30, 1988). ... Signed by Los Angeles Raiders (January 10, 1989). ... Released by Raiders (September 5, 1989). ... Re-signed by Raiders (October 4, 1989). ... Granted free agency (February 1, 1991). ... Re-signed by Raiders (1991). ... Assigned by Raiders to New York/New Jersey Knights in 1992 World League enhancement allocation program (February 20, 1992). ... Released by Raiders (August 30, 1993). ... Re-signed by Raiders (August 31, 1993). ... Released by Raiders (August 27, 1995). ... Re-signed by Raiders (August 30, 1995). ... Raiders franchise moved to Oakland (July 21, 1995). ... Granted unconditional free agency (February 16, 1996). ... Re-signed by Raiders for 1996 season.
PLAYING EXPERIENCE: Tampa Bay NFL, 1987; Los Angeles Raiders NFL, 1989-1994; New York//New Jersey W.L., 1992; Oakland NFL, 1995 -1997. ... Games/Games started: 1987 (3/2), 1989 (10/0), 1990 (16/0), 1991 (16/0), 1992 WL (10/9), 1992 NFL (16/16), 1993 (15/0), 1994 (16/0), 1995 (15/3), 1996 (16/2), 1997 (16/0). Total W.L.: 10/9. Total NFL: 139/23. Total Pro: 149/32.
CHAMPIONSHIP GAME EXPERIENCE: Played in AFC championship game (1990 season).
PRO STATISTICS: NFL: 1987—Rushed nine times for 20 yards. 1992—Returned two kickoffsfor 27 yards, intercepted one pass for no yards and fumbled once. W.L.: 1992—Rushed once for 16 yards, credited with one sack and intercepted one pass for 11 yards. 1996—Credited with a safety. and recovered two fumbles. 1997—Intercepted one pass for 13 yards.

LANDETA, SEAN   P   PACKERS

PERSONAL: Born January 6, 1962, in Baltimore. ... 6-0/215. ... Full name: Sean Edward Landeta.
HIGH SCHOOL: Loch Raven (Baltimore).
COLLEGE: Towson State.
TRANSACTIONS/CAREER NOTES: Selected by Philadelphia Stars in 14th round (161st pick overall) of 1983 USFL draft. ... Signed by Stars (January 24, 1983). ... Stars franchise moved to Baltimore (November 1, 1984). ... Granted free agency (August 1, 1985). ... Signed by New York Giants (August 5, 1985). ... On injured reserve with back injury (September 7, 1988-remainder of season). ... Granted free agency (February 1, 1990). ... Re-signed by Giants (July 23, 1990). ... On injured reserve with knee injury (November 25, 1992-remainder of season). ... Granted unconditional free agency (March 1, 1993). ... Re-signed by Giants (March 18, 1993). ... Released by Giants (November 9, 1993). ... Signed by Los Angeles Rams (November 12, 1993). ... Granted unconditional free agency (February 17, 1994). ... Re-signed by Rams (May 10, 1994). ... Granted unconditional free agency (February 17, 1995). ... Rams franchise moved to St. Louis (April 12, 1995). ... Re-signed by Rams (May 8, 1995). ... Released by Rams (March 18, 1997). ... Signed by Tampa Bay Buccaneers (October 9, 1997). ... Granted unconditional free agency (February 13, 1998). ... Signed by Green Packers (February 25, 1998).
CHAMPIONSHIP GAME EXPERIENCE: Played in USFL championship game (1983-1985 seasons). ... Played in NFC championship game (1986 and 1990 seasons). ... Member of Super Bowl championship team (1986 and 1990 seasons).
HONORS: Named punter on The Sporting News USFL All-Star team (1983 and 1984). ... Named punter on The Sporting News NFL All-Pro team (1986, 1989 and 1990). ... Played in Pro Bowl (1986 and 1990 seasons).
PRO STATISTICS: USFL: 1983—Rushed once for minus five yards, fumbled once and recovered one fumble. 1984—Recovered one fumble. NFL: 1985—Attempted one pass without a completion. 1996—Rushed twice for no yards, fumbled once and recovered one fumble for minus 11 yards.

Year Team	G	GS	No.	Yds.	Avg.	Net avg.	In. 20	Blk.
					PUNTING			
1983—Philadelphia USFL	18	0	86	3601	41.9	36.5	31	0
1984—Philadelphia USFL	18	0	53	2171	41.0	*38.1	18	0
1985—Baltimore USFL	18	0	65	2718	41.8	33.2	18	0
—New York Giants NFL	16	0	81	3472	42.9	36.3	20	0
1986—New York Giants NFL	16	0	79	3539	‡44.8	‡37.1	24	0
1987—New York Giants NFL	12	0	65	2773	42.7	31.0	13	1
1988—New York Giants NFL	1	0	6	222	37.0	35.7	1	0
1989—New York Giants NFL	16	0	70	3019	43.1	*37.7	19	0
1990—New York Giants NFL	16	0	75	3306	‡44.1	37.2	†24	0
1991—New York Giants NFL	15	0	64	2768	43.3	35.2	16	0
1992—New York Giants NFL	11	0	53	2317	43.7	31.5	13	*2
1993—New York Giants NFL	8	0	33	1390	42.1	35.0	11	1
—Los Angeles Rams NFL	8	0	42	1825	43.5	32.8	7	0
1994—Los Angeles Rams NFL	16	0	78	3494	*44.8	34.2	23	0
1995—St. Louis NFL	16	0	83	3679	‡44.3	36.7	23	0
1996—St. Louis NFL	16	0	78	3491	44.8	36.1	23	0
1997—Tampa Bay NFL	10	0	54	2274	42.1	34.1	15	1
USFL totals (3 years)	54	0	204	8490	41.6	35.9	67	0
NFL totals (13 years)	177	0	861	37569	43.6	35.3	232	5
Pro totals (16 years)	231	0	1065	46059	43.2	35.4	299	5

LANE, ERIC   FB   GIANTS

PERSONAL: Born March 17, 1974, in East Orange, N.J. ... 6-2/240.
HIGH SCHOOL: Bergen Catholic (Paramus, N.J.).
COLLEGE: Tennessee.
TRANSACTIONS/CAREER NOTES: Signed as non-drafted free agent by New York Giants (April 28, 1997).
SINGLE GAME HIGHS (regular season): Attempts—5 (December 21, 1997, vs. Dallas); yards—13 (December 21, 1997, vs. Dallas); and rushing touchdowns—0.

Year Team	G	GS	RUSHING				RECEIVING				TOTALS			
			Att.	Yds.	Avg.	TD	No.	Yds.	Avg.	TD	TD	2pt.	Pts.	Fum.
1997—New York Giants NFL	15	0	5	13	2.6	0	0	0	...	0	0	0	0	0

LANE, FRED   RB   PANTHERS

PERSONAL: Born September 6, 1975, in Nashville. ... 5-10/205. ... Full name: Freddie Brown Lane Jr.
HIGH SCHOOL: Franklin (Tenn.).
COLLEGE: Lane (Tenn.).
TRANSACTIONS/CAREER NOTES: Signed as non-drafted free agent by Carolina Panthers (April 19, 1997).
PRO STATISTICS: 1997—Recovered two fumbles.
SINGLE GAME HIGHS (regular season): Attempts—34 (December 8, 1997, vs. Dallas); yards—147 (November 2, 1997, vs. Oakland); and rushing touchdowns—3 (November 2, 1997, vs. Oakland).
STATISTICAL PLATEAUS: 100-yard rushing games: 1997 (4).
MISCELLANEOUS: Shares Carolina Panthers all-time record for most rushing touchdowns (7).

Year Team	G	GS	RUSHING				RECEIVING				TOTALS			
			Att.	Yds.	Avg.	TD	No.	Yds.	Avg.	TD	TD	2pt.	Pts.	Fum.
1997—Carolina NFL	13	7	182	809	4.4	7	8	27	3.4	0	7	0	42	4

LANE, MAX   OT   PATRIOTS

PERSONAL: Born February 22, 1971, in Norborne, Mo. ... 6-6/305. ... Full name: Max Aaron Lane.
HIGH SCHOOL: Norborne (Mo.), then Naval Academy Preparatory (Newport, R.I.).
COLLEGE: Navy.
TRANSACTIONS/CAREER NOTES: Selected by New England Patriots in sixth round (168th pick overall) of 1994 NFL draft. ... Signed by Patriots (June 1, 1994). ... Granted free agency (February 14, 1997). ... Re-signed by Patriots (June 20, 1997).
PLAYING EXPERIENCE: New England NFL, 1994-1997. ... Games/Games started: 1994 (14/0), 1995 (16/16), 1996 (16/16), 1997 (16/16). Total: 62/48.
CHAMPIONSHIP GAME EXPERIENCE: Played in AFC championship game (1996 season). ... Played in Super Bowl XXXI (1996 season).
PRO STATISTICS: 1995—Recovered one fumble. 1996—Recovered three fumbles. 1997—Recovered one fumble.

LANG, KENARD   DE   REDSKINS

PERSONAL: Born January 31, 1975, in Orlando. ... 6-4/277. ... Full name: Kenard Dushun Lang.
HIGH SCHOOL: Maynard Evans (Orlando).
COLLEGE: Miami (Fla.).
TRANSACTIONS/CAREER NOTES: Selected by Washington Redskins in first round (17th pick overall) of 1997 NFL draft. ... Signed by Redskins (July 28, 1997).
PRO STATISTICS: 1994—Intercepted one pass for one yard. 1997—Recovered two fumbles.

Year Team	G	GS	SACKS
1997—Washington NFL	12	11	1.5

LANGFORD, JEVON   DE   BENGALS

PERSONAL: Born February 16, 1974, in Washington, D.C. ... 6-3/276.
HIGH SCHOOL: Bishop Carroll (Washington, D.C.).
COLLEGE: Oklahoma State.
TRANSACTIONS/CAREER NOTES: Selected after junior season by Cincinnati Bengals in fourth round (108th pick overall) of 1996 NFL draft. ... Signed by Bengals (August 5, 1996).
PRO STATISTICS: 1996—Recovered one fumble.

Year Team	G	GS	INTERCEPTIONS No.	Yds.	Avg.	TD	SACKS No.
1996—Cincinnati NFL	12	3	1	0	0.0	0	2.0
1997—Cincinnati NFL	15	0	0	0	...	0	1.0
Pro totals (2 years)	27	3	1	0	0.0	0	3.0

LANGHAM, ANTONIO   CB   49ERS

PERSONAL: Born July 31, 1972, in Town Creek, Ala. ... 6-0/184. ... Full name: Collie Antonio Langham.
HIGH SCHOOL: Hazelwood (Town Creek, Ala.).
COLLEGE: Alabama.
TRANSACTIONS/CAREER NOTES: Selected by Cleveland Browns in first round (ninth pick overall) of 1994 NFL draft. ... Signed by Browns (August 4, 1994). ... Browns franchise moved to Baltimore and renamed Ravens for 1996 season (March 11, 1996). ... Granted unconditional free agency (February 13, 1998). ... Signed by San Francisco 49ers (March 4, 1998).
HONORS: Jim Thorpe Award winner (1993). ... Named defensive back on THE SPORTING NEWS college All-America first team (1993).
PRO STATISTICS: 1994—Fumbled once. 1997—Credited with one sack.
MISCELLANEOUS: Holds Baltimore Ravens all-time record for most interceptions (8).

Year Team	G	GS	INTERCEPTIONS No.	Yds.	Avg.	TD
1994—Cleveland NFL	16	16	2	2	1.0	0
1995—Cleveland NFL	16	16	2	29	14.5	0
1996—Baltimore NFL	15	14	5	59	11.8	0
1997—Baltimore NFL	16	15	3	40	13.3	1
Pro totals (4 years)	63	61	12	130	10.8	1

LASSITER, KWAMIE   S   CARDINALS

PERSONAL: Born December 3, 1969, in Newport News, Va. ... 6-0/202.
HIGH SCHOOL: Menchville (Newport News, Va.).
JUNIOR COLLEGE: Butler County (Kan.) Community College.
COLLEGE: Kansas.
TRANSACTIONS/CAREER NOTES: Signed as non-drafted free agent by Arizona Cardinals (April 28, 1995). ... On injured reserve with ankle injury (October 5, 1995-remainder of season). ... Granted free agency (February 13, 1998). ... Re-signed by Cardinals (May 21, 1998).
PLAYING EXPERIENCE: Arizona NFL, 1995-1997. ... Games/Games started: 1995 (5/0), 1996 (14/0), 1997 (16/1). Total: 35/1.
PRO STATISTICS: 1995—Rushed once for one yard. 1996—Intercepted one pass for 20 yards. 1997—Intercepted one pass for 10 yards and credited with three sacks.

LATHON, LAMAR   LB   PANTHERS

PERSONAL: Born December 23, 1967, in Wharton, Texas. ... 6-3/260. ... Full name: Lamar Lavantha Lathon. ... Name pronounced LAY-thin.
HIGH SCHOOL: Wharton (Texas).
COLLEGE: Houston.
TRANSACTIONS/CAREER NOTES: Selected by Houston Oilers in first round (15th pick overall) of 1990 NFL draft. ... Signed by Oilers (July 18, 1990). ... On injured reserve with shoulder injury (September 19-October 19, 1990). ... On injured reserve with knee injury (November 24, 1992-January 2, 1993). ... Granted unconditional free agency (February 17, 1995). ... Signed by Carolina Panthers (March 1, 1995).
CHAMPIONSHIP GAME EXPERIENCE: Played in NFC championship game (1996 season).
HONORS: Named linebacker on THE SPORTING NEWS NFL All-Pro team (1996). ... Played in Pro Bowl (1996 season).
PRO STATISTICS: 1990—Recovered one fumble. 1993—Recovered one fumble. 1994—Credited with one safety and recovered one fumble. 1995—Recovered one fumble. 1996—Recovered two fumbles for four yards.
MISCELLANEOUS: Holds Carolina Panthers all-time record for most sacks (23.5).

Year Team	G	GS	INTERCEPTIONS No.	Yds.	Avg.	TD	SACKS No.
1990—Houston NFL	11	1	0	0	...	0	0.0
1991—Houston NFL	16	16	3	77	25.7	1	2.0
1992—Houston NFL	11	11	0	0	...	0	1.5
1993—Houston NFL	13	1	0	0	...	0	2.0
1994—Houston NFL	16	15	0	0	...	0	8.5
1995—Carolina NFL	15	15	0	0	...	0	8.0
1996—Carolina NFL	16	16	0	0	...	0	13.5
1997—Carolina NFL	15	15	1	1	1.0	0	2.0
Pro totals (8 years)	113	90	4	78	19.5	1	37.5

LAW, TY — CB — PATRIOTS

PERSONAL: Born February 10, 1974, in Aliquippa, Pa. ... 5-11/200.
HIGH SCHOOL: Aliquippa (Pa.).
COLLEGE: Michigan.
TRANSACTIONS/CAREER NOTES: Selected after junior season by New England Patriots in first round (23rd pick overall) of 1995 NFL draft. ... Signed by Patriots (July 20, 1995).
CHAMPIONSHIP GAME EXPERIENCE: Played in AFC championship game (1996 season). ... Played in Super Bowl XXXI (1996 season).
PRO STATISTICS: 1995—Credited with one sack. 1997—Credited with 1/2 sack, fumbled once and recovered one fumble.

				INTERCEPTIONS		
Year Team	G	GS	No.	Yds.	Avg.	TD
1995—New England NFL	14	7	3	47	15.7	0
1996—New England NFL	13	12	3	45	15.0	1
1997—New England NFL	16	16	3	70	23.3	0
Pro totals (3 years)	43	35	9	162	18.0	1

LAYMAN, JASON — OT/G — OILERS

PERSONAL: Born July 29, 1973, in Sevierville, Tenn. ... 6-5/306. ... Full name: Jason Todd Layman.
HIGH SCHOOL: Sevier County (Sevierville, Tenn.).
COLLEGE: Tennessee.
TRANSACTIONS/CAREER NOTES: Selected by Houston Oilers in second round (48th pick overall) of 1996 NFL draft. ... Signed by Oilers (July 20, 1996). ... Oilers franchise moved to Tennessee for 1997 season.
PLAYING EXPERIENCE: Houston NFL, 1996; Tennessee NFL, 1997. ... Games/Games started: 1996 (16/0), 1997 (13/0). Total: 29/0.
PRO STATISTICS: 1997—Returned one kickoff for five yards.

LE BEL, HARPER — TE

PERSONAL: Born July 14, 1963, in Granada Hills, Calif. ... 6-4/250. ... Full name: Brian Harper Le Bel.
HIGH SCHOOL: Notre Dame (Sherman Oaks, Calif.).
COLLEGE: Colorado State.
TRANSACTIONS/CAREER NOTES: Selected by Kansas City Chiefs in 12th round (321st pick overall) of 1985 NFL draft. ... Signed by Chiefs (July 18, 1985). ... Released by Chiefs (August 12, 1985). ... Signed by San Francisco 49ers for 1986 season (December 20, 1985). ... Released by 49ers after failing physical (April 7, 1986). ... Signed as replacement player by San Diego Chargers (September 29, 1987). ... Released by Chargers (October 20, 1987). ... Signed by Dallas Cowboys (April 27, 1988). ... Released by Cowboys (August 2, 1988). ... Signed by Tampa Bay Buccaneers (August 15, 1988). ... Released by Buccaneers (August 23, 1988). ... Signed by Seattle Seahawks (August 8, 1989). ... Granted unconditional free agency (February 1, 1990). ... Signed by Philadelphia Eagles (March 30, 1990). ... Granted unconditional free agency (February 1, 1991). ... Signed by Atlanta Falcons (April 1, 1991). ... On injured reserve with wrist injury (September 18, 1991-remainder of season). ... Granted unconditional free agency (February 1-April 1, 1992). ... Re-signed by Falcons for 1992 season. ... Granted free agency (March 1, 1993). ... Re-signed by Falcons (June 11, 1993). ... Granted unconditional free agency (February 17, 1994). ... Re-signed by Falcons (March 30, 1994). ... Granted unconditional free agency (February 17, 1995). ... Re-signed by Falcons (March 22, 1995). ... Granted unconditional free agency (February 14, 1997). ... Signed by Green Bay Packers (March 31, 1997). ... Released by Packers (August 24, 1997). ... Signed by Chicago Bears (August 27, 1997). ... Granted unconditional free agency (February 13, 1998).
PLAYING EXPERIENCE: Seattle NFL, 1989; Philadelphia NFL, 1990; Atlanta NFL, 1991-1996; Chicago NFL, 1997. ... Games/Games started: 1989 (16/0), 1990 (16/0), 1991 (3/0), 1992 (16/2), 1993 (16/0), 1994 (16/0), 1995 (16/0), 1996 (16/0), 1997 (16/0). Total: 131/2.
PRO STATISTICS: 1989—Fumbled once for minus 25 yards. 1990—Caught one pass for nineyards and fumbled once. 1992—Fumbled once for minus 37 yards. 1993—Fumbled once. 1995—Fumbled once for minus eight yards. 1996—Recovered one fumble. 1997—Rushed once for no yards, fumbled once and recovered one fumble.
SINGLE GAME HIGHS (regular season): Receptions—1 (September 16, 1990, vs. Arizona); yards—9 (September 16, 1990, vs. Arizona); and touchdown receptions—0.

LEE, AMP — RB — RAMS

PERSONAL: Born October 1, 1971, in Chipley, Fla. ... 5-11/200. ... Full name: Anthonia Wayne Lee.
HIGH SCHOOL: Chipley (Fla.).
COLLEGE: Florida State.
TRANSACTIONS/CAREER NOTES: Selected after junior season by San Francisco 49ers in second round (45th pick overall) of 1992 NFL draft. ... Signed by 49ers (July 18, 1992). ... Released by 49ers (May 4, 1994). ... Signed by Minnesota Vikings (May 24, 1994). ... On physically unable to perform list (July 13-20, 1994). ... Granted unconditional free agency (February 14, 1997). ... Signed by St. Louis Rams (August 4, 1997). ... Granted unconditional free agency (February 13, 1998). ... Re-signed by Rams (February 20, 1998).
CHAMPIONSHIP GAME EXPERIENCE: Played in NFC championship game (1992 and 1993 seasons).
PRO STATISTICS: 1992—Fumbled once and recovered three fumbles. 1993—Fumbled once. 1994—Fumbled once and recovered one fumble. 1995—Fumbled three times and recovered two fumbles. 1996—Fumbled twice and recovered one fumble.
SINGLE GAME HIGHS (regular season): Attempts—23 (December 13, 1992, vs. Minnesota); yards—134 (December 13, 1992, vs. Minnesota); and rushing touchdowns—1 (December 3, 1995, vs. Tampa Bay).
STATISTICAL PLATEAUS: 100-yard rushing games: 1992 (1). ... 100-yard receiving games: 1997 (3).

			RUSHING				RECEIVING				PUNT RETURNS				KICKOFF RETURNS				TOTALS		
Year Team	G	GS	Att.	Yds.	Avg.	TD	No.	Yds.	Avg.	TD	No.	Yds.	Avg.	TD	No.	Yds.	Avg.	TD	TD	2pt.	Pts.
1992—San Fran. NFL	16	3	91	362	4.0	2	20	102	5.1	2	0	0	...	0	14	276	19.7	0	4	...	24
1993—San Fran. NFL	15	3	72	230	3.2	1	16	115	7.2	2	0	0	...	0	10	160	16.0	0	3	...	18
1994—Minnesota NFL	13	0	29	104	3.6	0	45	368	8.2	2	0	0	...	0	3	42	14.0	0	2	0	12
1995—Minnesota NFL	16	3	69	371	5.4	2	71	558	7.9	1	5	50	10.0	0	5	100	20.0	0	3	0	18
1996—Minnesota NFL	16	3	51	161	3.2	0	54	422	7.8	2	10	84	8.4	0	5	86	17.0	0	2	0	12
1997—St. Louis NFL	16	1	28	104	3.7	0	61	825	13.5	3	0	0	...	0	4	71	17.8	0	3	0	18
Pro totals (6 years)	92	13	340	1332	3.9	5	267	2390	9.0	12	15	134	8.9	0	41	734	17.9	0	17	0	102

LEE, SHAWN   DT   BEARS

PERSONAL: Born October 24, 1966, in Brooklyn, N.Y. ... 6-2/300. ... Full name: Shawn Swaboda Lee.
HIGH SCHOOL: Erasmus Hall (Brooklyn, N.Y.).
COLLEGE: North Alabama.
TRANSACTIONS/CAREER NOTES: Selected by Tampa Bay Buccaneers in sixth round (163rd pick overall) of 1988 NFL draft. ... Signed by Buccaneers (July 10, 1988). ... Granted unconditional free agency (February 1-April 1, 1990). ... Re-signed by Buccaneers (July 20, 1990). ... Claimed on waivers by Atlanta Falcons (August 29, 1990). ... Traded by Falcons to Miami Dolphins for conditional pick in 1991 draft (September 3, 1990). ... On injured reserve with ankle injury (September 29-October 27, 1990). ... Granted free agency (February 1, 1991). ... Re-signed by Dolphins (August 21, 1991). ... Activated (August 23, 1991). ... On injured reserve with knee injury (September 17, 1991-remainder of season). ... Granted free agency (February 1, 1992). ... Re-signed by Dolphins (July 22, 1992). ... Released by Dolphins (August 31, 1992). ... Signed by San Diego Chargers (October 28, 1992). ... Granted unconditional free agency (March 1, 1993). ... Re-signed by Chargers (April 23, 1993). ... Traded by Chargers to Chicago Bears for fifth-round pick in 1999 draft (June 8, 1998).
CHAMPIONSHIP GAME EXPERIENCE: Member of Chargers for AFC championship game (1994 season); inactive. ... Played in Super Bowl XXIX (1994 season).
PRO STATISTICS: 1991—Intercepted one pass for 14 yards. 1992—Recovered one fumble. 1993—Recovered one fumble. 1994—Recovered one fumble. 1995—Recovered one fumble. 1996—Intercepted one pass for minus one yard.

Year Team	G	GS	SACKS
1988—Tampa Bay NFL	15	0	2.0
1989—Tampa Bay NFL	15	3	1.0
1990—Miami NFL	13	10	1.5
1991—Miami NFL	3	2	0.0
1992—San Diego NFL	9	1	0.5
1993—San Diego NFL	16	15	3.0
1994—San Diego NFL	15	15	6.5
1995—San Diego NFL	16	15	8.0
1996—San Diego NFL	15	7	1.0
1997—San Diego NFL	16	15	3.0
Pro totals (10 years)	133	83	26.5

LEEUWENBURG, JAY   G/C   COLTS

PERSONAL: Born June 18, 1969, in St. Louis. ... 6-3/290. ... Full name: Jay Robert Leeuwenburg. ... Son of Richard Leeuwenburg, tackle with Chicago Bears (1965).
HIGH SCHOOL: Kirkwood (Mo.).
COLLEGE: Colorado (degree in English).
TRANSACTIONS/CAREER NOTES: Selected by Kansas City Chiefs in ninth round (244th pick overall) of 1992 NFL draft. ... Signed by Chiefs (July 20, 1992). ... Claimed on waivers by Chicago Bears (September 2, 1992). ... Granted free agency (February 17, 1995). ... Re-signed by Bears (April 12, 1995). ... Granted unconditional free agency (February 16, 1996). ... Signed by Indianapolis Colts (February 21, 1996).
PLAYING EXPERIENCE: Chicago NFL, 1992-1995; Indianapolis NFL, 1996 and 1997. ... Games/Games started: 1992 (12/0), 1993 (16/16), 1994 (16/16), 1995 (16/16), 1996 (15/7), 1997 (16/16). Total: 91/71.
HONORS: Named center on THE SPORTING NEWS college All-America first team (1991).
PRO STATISTICS: 1992—Returned one kickoff for 12 yards. 1995—Recovered one fumble. 1997—Fumbled once for minus 20 yards.

LEGETTE, TYRONE   CB   BUCCANEERS

PERSONAL: Born February 15, 1970, in Columbia, S.C. ... 5-9/179. ... Full name: Tyrone C. Legette. ... Name pronounced luh-GET.
HIGH SCHOOL: Spring Valley (Columbia, S.C.).
COLLEGE: Nebraska.
TRANSACTIONS/CAREER NOTES: Selected by New Orleans Saints in third round (72nd pick overall) of 1992 NFL draft. ... Signed by Saints (July 26, 1992). ... On injured reserve with hamstring injury (November 3, 1992-remainder of season). ... Granted free agency (February 17, 1995). ... Re-signed by Saints (July 23, 1995). ... Granted unconditional free agency (February 16, 1996). ... Signed by Tampa Bay Buccaneers (June 28, 1996). ... Granted unconditional free agency (February 14, 1997). ... Re-signed by Buccaneers (February 26, 1997).
PLAYING EXPERIENCE: New Orleans NFL, 1992-1995; Tampa Bay NFL, 1996 and 1997. ... Games/Games started: 1992 (8/0), 1993 (14/1), 1994 (15/2), 1995 (16/1), 1996 (15/0), 1997 (16/1). Total: 84/5.
PRO STATISTICS: 1994—Credited with one sack, returned one punt for no yards and fumbled once. 1995—Credited with one sack, intercepted one pass for 43 yards and returned one punt for six yards. 1997—Intercepted one pass for no yards.

LESTER, FRED   FB   FALCONS

PERSONAL: Born August 1, 1971, in Miami. ... 6-1/244. ... Full name: Fredrick Lester. ... Brother of Tim Lester, fullback, Pittsburgh Steelers.
HIGH SCHOOL: Miami Southridge.
COLLEGE: Alabama A&M.
TRANSACTIONS/CAREER NOTES: Selected by New York Jets in sixth round (173rd pick overall) of 1994 NFL draft. ... Signed by Jets (June 24, 1994). ... Released by Jets (August 27, 1994). ... Re-signed by Jets to practice squad (October 25, 1994). ... Activated (November 5, 1994). ... Released by Jets (November 8, 1994). ... Activated (June 24, 1994). ... Re-signed by Jets (December 16, 1994). ... Released by Jets (August 21, 1995). ... Signed by Tampa Bay Buccaneers to practice squad (September 27, 1995). ... Activated (December 12, 1995). Released by Buccaneers (August 25, 1996). ... Signed by Atlanta Falcons (January 30, 1997). ... On injured reserve with arm injury (August 18, 1997-entire season). ... Granted free agency (February 13, 1998).

LESTER, TIM   FB   STEELERS

PERSONAL: Born June 15, 1968, in Miami. ... 5-10/238. ... Full name: Timothy Lee Lester. ... Brother of Fred Lester, fullback, Atlanta Falcons.
HIGH SCHOOL: Miami Southridge.
COLLEGE: Eastern Kentucky.

TRANSACTIONS/CAREER NOTES: Selected by Los Angeles Rams in 10th round (255th pick overall) of 1992 NFL draft. ... Signed by Rams (July 13, 1992). ... Released by Rams (September 4, 1992). ... Re-signed by Rams to practice squad (September 7, 1992). ... Activated (October 7, 1992). ... Released by Rams (August 29, 1995). ... Signed by Pittsburgh Steelers (October 3, 1995).
CHAMPIONSHIP GAME EXPERIENCE: Played in AFC championship game (1995 and 1997 seasons). ... Played in Super Bowl XXX (1995 season).
PRO STATISTICS: 1994—Returned one kickoff for eight yards and recovered one fumble.
SINGLE GAME HIGHS (regular season): Attempts—5 (December 11, 1994, vs. Tampa Bay); yards—28 (October 14, 1993, vs. Atlanta); and rushing touchdowns—1 (November 25, 1996, vs. Miami).

| | | | RUSHING | | | | RECEIVING | | | | TOTALS | | | |
Year Team	G	GS	Att.	Yds.	Avg.	TD	No.	Yds.	Avg.	TD	TD	2pt.	Pts.	Fum.
1992—Los Angeles Rams NFL	11	0	0	0	...	0	0	0	...	0	0	...	0	0
1993—Los Angeles Rams NFL	16	14	11	74	6.7	0	18	154	8.6	0	0	...	0	0
1994—Los Angeles Rams NFL	14	4	7	14	2.0	0	1	1	1.0	0	0	0	0	1
1995—Pittsburgh NFL	6	1	5	9	1.8	1	0	0	...	0	1	0	6	0
1996—Pittsburgh NFL	16	13	8	20	2.5	1	7	70	10.0	0	1	0	6	1
1997—Pittsburgh NFL	16	13	2	9	4.5	0	10	51	5.1	0	0	0	0	0
Pro totals (6 years)	79	45	33	126	3.8	2	36	276	7.7	0	2	0	12	2

LETT, LEON — DL — COWBOYS

PERSONAL: Born October 12, 1968, in Mobile, Ala. ... 6-6/295. ... Full name: Leon Lett Jr. ... Nickname: The Big Cat.
HIGH SCHOOL: Fairhope (Ala.).
JUNIOR COLLEGE: Hinds Junior College (Miss.).
COLLEGE: Emporia (Kan.) State.
TRANSACTIONS/CAREER NOTES: Selected by Dallas Cowboys in seventh round (173rd pick overall) of 1991 NFL draft. ... Signed by Cowboys (July 14, 1991). ... On injured reserve with back injury (August 27-November 21, 1991). ... On suspended list for violating league substance abuse policy (November 3-24, 1995). ... On suspended list for violating league substance abuse policy (December 3, 1996-December 1, 1997).
CHAMPIONSHIP GAME EXPERIENCE: Played in NFC championship game (1992-1995 seasons). ... Member of Super Bowl championship team (1992, 1993 and 1995 seasons).
HONORS: Played in Pro Bowl (1994 season).
POST SEASON RECORDS: Holds Super Bowl career record for most yards by fumble recovery—64. ... Holds Super Bowl single-game record for most yards by fumble recovery—64 (January 31, 1993).
PRO STATISTICS: 1992—Recovered one fumble. 1993—Fumbled once. 1995—Recovered two fumbles. 1996—Recovered two fumbles.

Year Team	G	GS	SACKS
1991—Dallas NFL	5	0	0.0
1992—Dallas NFL	16	0	3.5
1993—Dallas NFL	11	6	0.0
1994—Dallas NFL	16	16	4.0
1995—Dallas NFL	12	12	3.0
1996—Dallas NFL	13	13	3.5
1997—Dallas NFL	3	3	0.5
Pro totals (7 years)	76	50	14.5

LEVENS, DORSEY — RB — PACKERS

PERSONAL: Born May 21, 1970, in Syracuse, N.Y. ... 6-1/230. ... Full name: Hebert Dorsey Levens.
HIGH SCHOOL: Nottingham (Syracuse, N.Y.).
COLLEGE: Notre Dame, then Georgia Tech.
TRANSACTIONS/CAREER NOTES: Selected by Green Bay Packers in fifth round (149th pick overall) of 1994 NFL draft. ... Signed by Packers (June 9, 1994). ... Granted free agency (February 14, 1997). ... Re-signed by Packers (June 20, 1997). ... Designated by Packers as franchise player (February 13, 1998).
CHAMPIONSHIP GAME EXPERIENCE: Played in NFC championship game (1995-97 seasons). ... Member of Super Bowl championship team (1996 season). ... Played in Super Bowl XXXII (1997 season).
HONORS: Played in Pro Bowl (1997 season).
PRO STATISTICS: 1996—Recovered one fumble. 1997—Recovered one fumble for minus seven yards.
SINGLE GAME HIGHS (regular season): Attempts—33 (November 23, 1997, vs. Dallas); yards—190 (November 23, 1997, vs. Dallas); and rushing touchdowns—2 (December 1, 1997, vs. Minnesota).
STATISTICAL PLATEAUS: 100-yard rushing games: 1997 (6).

| | | | RUSHING | | | | RECEIVING | | | | KICKOFF RETURNS | | | | TOTALS | | | |
Year Team	G	GS	Att.	Yds.	Avg.	TD	No.	Yds.	Avg.	TD	No.	Yds.	Avg.	TD	TD	2pt.	Pts.	Fum.
1994—Green Bay NFL	14	0	5	15	3.0	0	1	9	9.0	0	2	31	15.5	0	0	0	0	0
1995—Green Bay NFL	15	12	36	120	3.3	3	48	434	9.0	4	0	0	...	0	7	0	42	0
1996—Green Bay NFL	16	1	121	566	4.7	5	31	226	7.3	5	5	84	16.8	0	10	0	60	2
1997—Green Bay NFL	16	16	329	1435	4.4	7	53	370	7.0	5	0	0	...	0	12	1	74	5
Pro totals (4 years)	61	29	491	2136	4.4	15	133	1039	7.8	14	7	115	16.4	0	29	1	176	7

LEVITT, CHAD — RB — RAIDERS

PERSONAL: Born November 21, 1975, in Melrose Park, Pa. ... 6-1/233. ... Full name: Chad Aaron Levitt.
HIGH SCHOOL: Cheltenham (Pa.).
COLLEGE: Cornell.
TRANSACTIONS/CAREER NOTES: Selected by Oakland Raiders in fourth round (123rd pick overall) of 1997 NFL draft. ... Signed by Raiders for 1997 season.
PRO STATISTICS: 1997—Returned one kickoff for 12 yards.
SINGLE GAME HIGHS (regular season): Attempts—2 (December 21, 1997, Jacksonville); yards—3 (December 3, 1997, vs. Jacksonville); and rushing touchdowns—0

Year Team	G	GS	RUSHING Att.	Yds.	Avg.	TD	RECEIVING No.	Yds.	Avg.	TD	TOTALS TD	2pt.	Pts.	Fum.
1997—Oakland NFL	10	2	2	3	1.5	0	2	24	12.0	0	0	0	0	0

LEVY, CHUCK RB/KR 49ERS

PERSONAL: Born January 7, 1972, in Torrance, Calif. ... 6-0/206. ... Full name: Charles Levy.
HIGH SCHOOL: Lynwood (Calif.).
COLLEGE: Arizona.
TRANSACTIONS/CAREER NOTES: Selected after junior season by Arizona Cardinals in second round (38th pick overall) of 1994 NFL draft. ... Signed by Cardinals (August 10, 1994). ... On suspended list for violating league substance abuse policy (August 25, 1995-July 18, 1996). ... Released by Cardinals (August 25, 1996). ... Signed by San Francisco 49ers (December 25, 1996).
CHAMPIONSHIP GAME EXPERIENCE: Played in NFC championship game (1997 season).
POST SEASON RECORDS: Shares NFL postseason single-game record for most touchdowns by kickoff return—1 (January 11, 1998, vs. Green Bay).
PRO STATISTICS: 1994—Recovered one fumble. 1997—Returned six punts for 109 yards and one touchdown.
SINGLE GAME HIGHS (regular season): Attempts—8 (December 21, 1997, Seattle); yards—61 (December 21, 1997, vs. Seattle); and rushing touchdowns—0.

Year Team	G	GS	RUSHING Att.	Yds.	Avg.	TD	RECEIVING No.	Yds.	Avg.	TD	KICKOFF RETURNS No.	Yds.	Avg.	TD	TOTALS TD	2pt.	Pts.	Fum.
1994—Arizona NFL	11	0	3	15	5.0	0	4	35	8.8	0	26	513	19.7	0	0	0	0	0
1995—Arizona NFL								Did not play.										
1997—San Francisco NFL	14	0	16	90	5.6	0	5	68	13.6	0	36	793	22.0	0	1	0	6	1
Pro totals (2 years)	25	0	19	105	5.5	0	9	103	11.4	0	62	1306	21.1	0	1	0	6	1

LEWIS, ALBERT CB RAIDERS

PERSONAL: Born October 6, 1960, in Mansfield, La. ... 6-2/195. ... Full name: Albert Ray Lewis.
HIGH SCHOOL: DeSoto (Mansfield, La.).
COLLEGE: Grambling State (degree in political science, 1983).
TRANSACTIONS/CAREER NOTES: Selected by Philadelphia Stars in 15th round (175th pick overall) of 1983 USFL draft. ... Selected by Kansas City Chiefs in third round (61st pick overall) of 1983 NFL draft. ... Signed by Chiefs (May 19, 1983). ... On injured reserve with knee injury (December 10, 1984-remainder of season). ... On reserve/did not report list (July 24-September 17, 1990). ... On injured reserve with knee injury (December 14, 1991-remainder of season). ... On injured reserve with forearm injury (November 11, 1992-remainder of season). ... On practice squad (December 16-23, 1992). ... Granted unconditional free agency (February 17, 1994). ... Signed by Los Angeles Raiders (March 15, 1994). ... Raiders franchise moved to Oakland (July 21, 1995).
CHAMPIONSHIP GAME EXPERIENCE: Played in AFC championship game (1993 season).
HONORS: Played in Pro Bowl (1987, 1989 and 1990 seasons). ... Named to play in Pro Bowl (1988 season); replaced by Eric Thomas due to injury. ... Named cornerback on THE SPORTING NEWS NFL All-Pro team (1989 and 1990).
PRO STATISTICS: 1983—Recovered two fumbles. 1985—Recovered one fumble in end zone for a touchdown. 1986—Recovered two fumbles. 1987—Recovered one fumble. 1988—Credited with one safety and recovered one fumble. 1990—Recovered three fumbles for one yard. 1993—Recovered blocked punt in end zone for a touchdown and recovered two fumbles. 1995—Recovered one fumble for 29 yards.

Year Team	G	GS	INTERCEPTIONS No.	Yds.	Avg.	TD	SACKS No.
1983—Kansas City NFL	16	1	4	42	10.5	0	0.0
1984—Kansas City NFL	15	15	4	57	14.3	0	1.0
1985—Kansas City NFL	16	16	▲8	59	7.4	0	1.5
1986—Kansas City NFL	15	15	4	18	4.5	0	1.0
1987—Kansas City NFL	12	12	1	0	0.0	0	0.0
1988—Kansas City NFL	14	12	1	19	19.0	0	0.0
1989—Kansas City NFL	16	16	4	37	9.3	0	1.0
1990—Kansas City NFL	15	14	2	15	7.5	0	0.0
1991—Kansas City NFL	8	6	3	21	7.0	0	0.0
1992—Kansas City NFL	9	8	1	0	0.0	0	0.0
1993—Kansas City NFL	14	13	6	61	10.2	0	0.0
1994—Los Angeles Raiders NFL	14	9	0	0	...	0	1.0
1995—Oakland NFL	16	15	0	0	...	0	1.0
1996—Oakland NFL	16	13	2	0	0.0	0	3.0
1997—Oakland NFL	14	11	0	0	...	0	2.0
Pro totals (15 years)	210	176	40	329	8.2	0	11.5

LEWIS, CHAD TE EAGLES

PERSONAL: Born October 5, 1971 ... 6-6/252.
HIGH SCHOOL: Orem (Utah).
COLLEGE: Brigham Young.
TRANSACTIONS/CAREER NOTES: Signed as non-drafted free agent by Philadelphia Eagles (April 23, 1997).
PRO STATISTICS: 1997—Returned one kickoff for 11 yards.
SINGLE GAME HIGHS (regular season): Receptions—3 (August 31, 1997, vs. New York Giants); yards—34 (August 31, 1997, vs. New York Giants); and touchdown receptions—1 (November 30, 1997, vs. Cincinnati).

Year Team	G	GS	RECEIVING No.	Yds.	Avg.	TD	TOTALS TD	2pt.	Pts.	Fum.
1997—Philadelphia NFL	16	3	12	94	7.8	4	4	0	24	0

LEWIS, DARRYLL — CB — OILERS

PERSONAL: Born December 16, 1968, in Bellflower, Calif. ... 5-9/186. ... Full name: Darryll Lamont Lewis.
HIGH SCHOOL: Nogales (West Covina, Calif.).
COLLEGE: Arizona.
TRANSACTIONS/CAREER NOTES: Selected by Houston Oilers in second round (38th pick overall) of 1991 NFL draft. ... Signed by Oilers (July 19, 1991). ... On injured reserve with knee injury (October 25, 1993). ... Granted free agency (February 17, 1994). ... Re-signed by Oilers (July 17, 1994). ... Granted unconditional free agency (February 17, 1995). ... Re-signed by Oilers (March 9, 1995). ... Oilers franchise moved to Tennessee for 1997 season.
HONORS: Jim Thorpe Award winner (1990). ... Named defensive back on THE SPORTING NEWS college All-America first team (1990). ... Played in Pro Bowl (1995 season).
PRO STATISTICS: 1991—Recovered one fumble. 1992—Recovered one fumble. 1997—Recovered three fumbles for 68 yards.

			INTERCEPTIONS				SACKS	KICKOFF RETURNS				TOTALS			
Year Team	G	GS	No.	Yds.	Avg.	TD	No.	No.	Yds.	Avg.	TD	TD	2pt.	Pts.	Fum.
1991—Houston NFL	16	1	1	33	33.0	1	1.0	0	0	...	0	1	...	6	0
1992—Houston NFL	13	0	0	0	...	0	1.0	8	171	21.4	0	0	...	0	0
1993—Houston NFL	4	4	1	47	47.0	▲1	0.0	0	0	...	0	1	...	6	0
1994—Houston NFL	16	15	5	57	11.4	0	0.0	0	0	...	0	0	0	0	0
1995—Houston NFL	16	15	6	§145	24.2	1	1.0	0	0	...	0	1	0	6	0
1996—Houston NFL	16	16	5	103	20.6	▲1	0.0	0	0	...	0	1	0	6	0
1997—Tennessee NFL	16	14	5	115	23.0	1	0.0	0	0	...	0	1	0	6	1
Pro totals (7 years)	97	65	23	500	21.7	5	3.0	8	171	21.4	0	5	0	30	1

LEWIS, JEFF — QB — BRONCOS

PERSONAL: Born April 17, 1973, in Columbus, Ohio. ... 6-2/211. ... Full name: Jeff Scott Lewis.
HIGH SCHOOL: Horizon (Scottsdale, Ariz.).
COLLEGE: Northern Arizona.
TRANSACTIONS/CAREER NOTES: Selected by Denver Broncos in fourth round (100th pick overall) of 1996 NFL draft. ... Signed by Broncos (July 19, 1996).
CHAMPIONSHIP GAME EXPERIENCE: Member of Broncos for AFC championship game (1997 season); inactive. ... Member of Super Bowl championship team (1997 season); inactive.
SINGLE GAME HIGHS (regular season): Attempts—14 (December 22, 1996, vs. San Diego); completions—8 (December 22, 1996, vs. San Diego); yards—53 (December 22, 1996, vs. San Diego); and touchdown passes—0.

			PASSING								RUSHING				TOTALS		
Year Team	G	GS	Att.	Cmp.	Pct.	Yds.	TD	Int.	Avg.	Rat.	Att.	Yds.	Avg.	TD	TD	2pt.	Pts.
1996—Denver NFL	2	0	17	9	52.9	58	0	1	3.41	35.9	4	39	9.8	0	0	0	0
1997—Denver NFL	3	0	2	1	50.0	21	0	0	10.50	87.5	5	2	0.4	0	0	0	0
Pro totals (2 years)	5	0	19	10	52.6	79	0	1	4.16	41.3	9	41	4.6	0	0	0	0

LEWIS, JERMAINE — WR/KR — RAVENS

PERSONAL: Born October 16, 1974, in Lanham, Md. ... 5-7/172. ... Full name: Jermaine Edward Lewis.
HIGH SCHOOL: Eleanor Roosevelt (Lanham, Md.).
COLLEGE: Maryland.
TRANSACTIONS/CAREER NOTES: Selected by Baltimore Ravens in fifth round (153rd pick overall) of 1996 NFL draft. ... Signed by Ravens (July 18, 1996).
RECORDS: Shares NFL single-game records for most touchdowns by punt returns—2; and most touchdowns by combined kick return—2 (December 7, 1997, vs. Seattle).
PRO STATISTICS: 1996—Rushed once for minus three yards and recovered one fumble. 1997—Rushed three times for 35 yards and recovered two fumbles.
SINGLE GAME HIGHS (regular season): Receptions—8 (September 21, 1997, vs. Tennessee); yards—124 (September 21, 1997, vs. Tennessee); and touchdown receptions—2 (August 31, 1997, vs. Jacksonville).
STATISTICAL PLATEAUS: 100-yard receiving games: 1997 (2).

			RECEIVING				PUNT RETURNS				KICKOFF RETURNS				TOTALS			
Year Team	G	GS	No.	Yds.	Avg.	TD	No.	Yds.	Avg.	TD	No.	Yds.	Avg.	TD	TD	2pt.	Pts.	Fum.
1996—Baltimore NFL	16	1	5	78	15.6	1	36	339	9.4	0	41	883	21.5	0	1	0	6	4
1997—Baltimore NFL	14	7	42	648	15.4	6	28	437	*15.6	2	41	905	22.1	0	8	0	48	3
Pro totals (2 years)	30	8	47	726	15.4	7	64	776	12.1	2	82	1788	21.8	0	9	0	54	7

LEWIS, MO — LB — JETS

PERSONAL: Born October 21, 1969, in Atlanta. ... 6-3/258. ... Full name: Morris C. Lewis.
HIGH SCHOOL: J.C. Murphy (Atlanta).
COLLEGE: Georgia.
TRANSACTIONS/CAREER NOTES: Selected by New York Jets in third round (62nd pick overall) of 1991 NFL draft. ... Signed by Jets (July 18, 1991).
PRO STATISTICS: 1991—Recovered one fumble. 1992—Recovered four fumbles for 22 yards. 1994—Recovered one fumble for 11 yards. 1997—Recovered one fumble for 26 yards.

			INTERCEPTIONS				SACKS
Year Team	G	GS	No.	Yds.	Avg.	TD	No.
1991—New York Jets NFL	16	16	0	0	...	0	2.0
1992—New York Jets NFL	16	16	1	1	1.0	0	2.0
1993—New York Jets NFL	16	16	2	4	2.0	0	4.0
1994—New York Jets NFL	16	16	4	106	26.5	2	6.0
1995—New York Jets NFL	16	16	2	22	11.0	▲1	5.0
1996—New York Jets NFL	0	9	0	0	...	0	0.5
1997—New York Jets NFL	16	16	1	43	43.0	1	8.0
Pro totals (7 years)	105	105	10	176	17.6	4	27.5

LEWIS, RAY   LB   RAVENS

PERSONAL: Born May 15, 1975, in Lakeland, Fla. ... 6-1/240. ... Full name: Ray Anthony Lewis.
HIGH SCHOOL: Kathleen (Lakeland, Fla.).
COLLEGE: Miami (Fla.).
TRANSACTIONS/CAREER NOTES: Selected after junior season by Baltimore Ravens in first round (26th pick overall) of 1996 NFL draft. ... Signed by Ravens (July 15, 1996).
HONORS: Named linebacker on THE SPORTING NEWS college All-America second team (1995). ... Played in Pro Bowl (1997 season).
PRO STATISTICS: 1997—Recovered one fumble.

				INTERCEPTIONS			SACKS
Year Team	G	GS	No.	Yds.	Avg.	TD	No.
1996—Baltimore NFL	14	13	1	0	0.0	0	2.5
1997—Baltimore NFL	16	16	1	18	18.0	0	4.0
Pro totals (2 years)	30	29	2	18	9.0	0	6.5

LEWIS, ROD   TE   CHARGERS

PERSONAL: Born June 9, 1971, in Washington, D.C. ... 6-5/254. ... Full name: Roderick Albert Lewis.
HIGH SCHOOL: Bishop Dunne (Dallas).
COLLEGE: Arizona.
TRANSACTIONS/CAREER NOTES: Selected by Houston Oilers in fifth round (157th pick overall) of 1994 NFL draft. ... Signed by Oilers (July 16, 1994). ... Granted free agency (February 14, 1997). ... Oilers franchise moved to Tennessee for 1997 season. ... Re-signed by Oilers (July 10, 1997). ... Granted unconditional free agency (February 13, 1998). ... Signed by San Diego Chargers (June 10, 1998).
PRO STATISTICS: 1995—Returned one kickoff for five yards.
SINGLE GAME HIGHS (regular season): Receptions—3 (December 24, 1994, vs. New York Jets); yards—42 (December 24, 1994, vs. New York Jets); and touchdown receptions—0.

			RECEIVING				TOTALS			
Year Team	G	GS	No.	Yds.	Avg.	TD	TD	2pt.	Pts.	Fum.
1994—Houston NFL	3	1	4	48	12.0	0	0	0	0	0
1995—Houston NFL	15	8	16	116	7.3	0	0	0	0	0
1996—Houston NFL	16	7	7	50	7.1	0	0	0	0	0
1997—Tennessee NFL	10	1	1	7	7.0	0	0	0	0	0
Pro totals (4 years)	44	17	28	221	7.9	0	0	0	0	0

LEWIS, THOMAS   WR   BEARS

PERSONAL: Born January 10, 1972, in Akron, Ohio. ... 6-1/195. ... Full name: Thomas A. Lewis.
HIGH SCHOOL: Garfield Senior (Akron, Ohio).
COLLEGE: Indiana.
TRANSACTIONS/CAREER NOTES: Selected after junior season by New York Giants in first round (24th pick overall) of 1994 NFL draft. ... Signed by Giants (July 22, 1994). ... On non-football injury list (July 22-August 2, 1994). ... On injured reserve with knee injury (December 16, 1994-remainder of season). ... On injured reserve with toe injury (November 12, 1997-remainder of season). ... Granted unconditional free agency (February 13, 1998). ... Signed by Chicago Bears (April 21, 1998).
PRO STATISTICS: 1994—Recovered two fumbles.
SINGLE GAME HIGHS (regular season): Receptions—9 (October 20, 1996, vs. Washington); yards—126 (November 19, 1995, vs. Philadelpia); and touchdown receptions—1 (November 10, 1996, vs. Carolina).
STATISTICAL PLATEAUS: 100-yard receiving games: 1994 (1), 1996 (1). Total: 2.

			RECEIVING				PUNT RETURNS				KICKOFF RETURNS				TOTALS			
Year Team	G	GS	No.	Yds.	Avg.	TD	No.	Yds.	Avg.	TD	No.	Yds.	Avg.	TD	TD	2pt.	Pts.	Fum.
1994—New York Giants NFL..	9	0	4	46	11.5	0	5	64	12.8	0	26	509	19.6	0	0	0	0	2
1995—New York Giants NFL..	8	2	12	208	17.3	1	6	46	7.7	0	9	257	28.6	1	2	0	12	1
1996—New York Giants NFL..	13	11	53	694	13.1	4	10	36	3.6	0	4	107	26.8	0	4	0	24	0
1997—New York Giants NFL..	4	2	5	84	16.8	0	0	0	...	0	14	364	26.0	0	0	0	0	0
Pro totals (4 years)	34	15	74	1032	13.9	5	21	146	7.0	0	53	1237	23.3	1	6	0	36	3

LINCOLN, JEREMY   CB   GIANTS

PERSONAL: Born April 7, 1969, in Toledo, Ohio. ... 5-10/180. ... Full name: Jeremy Arlo Lincoln.
HIGH SCHOOL: DeVilbiss (Toledo, Ohio).
COLLEGE: Tennessee.
TRANSACTIONS/CAREER NOTES: Selected by Chicago Bears in third round (80th pick overall) of 1992 NFL draft. ... Signed by Bears (July 23, 1992). ... On injured reserve with knee injury (September 1, 1992-entire season). ... Granted free agency (February 17, 1995). ... Re-signed by Bears (July 15, 1995). ... Released by Bears (August 20, 1996). ... Signed by St. Louis Rams (September 5, 1996). ... Released by Rams (February 24, 1997). ... Signed by Seattle Seahawks (June 4, 1997). ... Granted unconditional free agency (February 13, 1998). ... Signed by New York Giants (June 15, 1998).
PRO STATISTICS: 1995—Credited with one sack. 1996—Recovered one fumble. 1997—Recovered one fumble.

			INTERCEPTIONS			
Year Team	G	GS	No.	Yds.	Avg.	TD
1992—Chicago NFL				Did not play.		
1993—Chicago NFL	16	7	3	109	36.3	1
1994—Chicago NFL	15	14	1	5	5.0	0
1995—Chicago NFL	16	14	1	32	32.0	0
1996—St. Louis NFL	13	1	1	3	3.0	0
1997—Seattle NFL	13	3	0	0	...	0
Pro totals (5 years)	73	39	6	149	24.8	1

LINDSAY, EVERETT   G/C   VIKINGS

PERSONAL: Born September 18, 1970, in Burlington, Iowa. ... 6-4/290. ... Full name: Everett Eric Lindsay.
HIGH SCHOOL: Millbrook (Raleigh, N.C.).
COLLEGE: Mississippi (degree in general business).
TRANSACTIONS/CAREER NOTES: Selected by Minnesota Vikings in fifth round (133rd pick overall) of 1993 NFL draft. ... Signed by Vikings (July 14, 1993). ... On injured reserve with shoulder injury (December 22, 1993-remainder of season). ... On injured reserve with shoulder injury (August 23, 1994-entire season). ... On physically unable to perform list with knee injury (July 22, 1996-August 20, 1996). ... On reserve/non-football injury list with knee injury (August 20, 1996-entire season). ... Assigned by Vikings to Barcelona Dragons in 1997 World League enhancement allocation program (February 19, 1997). ... Granted unconditional free agency (February 13, 1998). ... Re-signed by Vikings (February 17, 1998).
PLAYING EXPERIENCE: Minnesota NFL, 1993, 1995 and 1997. ... Games: 1993 (12/12), 1995 (16/0), 1997 (16/3). Total: 44/15.
HONORS: Named offensive tackle on THE SPORTING NEWS college All-America second team (1992).

LLOYD, GREG   LB   STEELERS

PERSONAL: Born May 26, 1965, in Miami. ... 6-2/235. ... Full name: Gregory Lenard Lloyd.
HIGH SCHOOL: Peach County (Ga.).
COLLEGE: Fort Valley (Ga.) State College.
TRANSACTIONS/CAREER NOTES: Selected by Pittsburgh Steelers in sixth round (150th pick overall) of 1987 NFL draft. ... Signed by Steelers (May 19, 1987). ... On injured reserve with knee injury (August 31, 1987-entire season). ... On injured reserve with knee injury (August 30-October 22, 1988). ... On injured reserve with knee injury (September 10, 1996-remainder of season).
CHAMPIONSHIP GAME EXPERIENCE: Played in AFC championship game (1994 and 1995 seasons). ... Played in Super Bowl XXX (1995 season). ... Member of Steelers for AFC championship game (1997 season); inactive.
HONORS: Played in Pro Bowl (1991-1995 seasons). ... Named outside linebacker on THE SPORTING NEWS NFL All-Pro team (1994 and 1995).
PRO STATISTICS: 1988—Recovered one fumble. 1989—Fumbled once and recovered three fumbles. 1991—Fumbled once and recovered two fumbles. 1992—Fumbled once and recovered four fumbles. 1993—Recovered one fumble. 1994—Recovered one fumble. 1997—Fumbled once and recovered three fumbles for 61 yards.

| | | | INTERCEPTIONS | | | | SACKS |
Year Team	G	GS	No.	Yds.	Avg.	TD	No.
1987—Pittsburgh NFL			Did not play.				
1988—Pittsburgh NFL	9	4	0	0	...	0	0.5
1989—Pittsburgh NFL	16	16	3	49	16.3	0	7.0
1990—Pittsburgh NFL	15	14	1	9	9.0	0	4.5
1991—Pittsburgh NFL	16	16	1	0	0.0	0	8.0
1992—Pittsburgh NFL	16	16	1	35	35.0	0	6.5
1993—Pittsburgh NFL	15	15	0	0	...	0	6.0
1994—Pittsburgh NFL	15	15	1	8	8.0	0	10.0
1995—Pittsburgh NFL	16	16	3	85	28.3	0	6.5
1996—Pittsburgh NFL	1	1	0	0	...	0	1.0
1997—Pittsburgh NFL	12	12	0	0	...	0	3.5
Pro totals (10 years)	131	125	10	186	18.6	0	53.5

LOCKETT, KEVIN   WR   CHIEFS

PERSONAL: Born September 8, 1974, in Tulsa, Okla. ... 6-0/177.
HIGH SCHOOL: Washington (Tulsa, Okla.).
COLLEGE: Kansas State.
TRANSACTIONS/CAREER NOTES: Selected by Kansas City Chiefs in second round (47th pick overall) of 1997 NFL draft. ... Signed by Chiefs (July 25, 1997).
PRO STATISTICS: 1997—Caught one pass for 35 yards.
SINGLE GAME HIGHS (regular season): Receptions—1 (November 23, 1997, vs. Seattle); yards—35 (November 23, 1997, vs. Seattle); and touchdown receptions—0.

LODISH, MIKE   DT   BRONCOS

PERSONAL: Born August 11, 1967, in Detroit. ... 6-3/280. ... Full name: Michael Timothy Lodish. ... Name pronounced LO-dish.
HIGH SCHOOL: Brother Rice (Birmingham, Mich.).
COLLEGE: UCLA (degree in history and business administration, 1990).
TRANSACTIONS/CAREER NOTES: Selected by Buffalo Bills in 10th round (265th pick overall) of 1990 NFL draft. ... Signed by Bills (July 26, 1990). ... Granted free agency (February 1, 1992). ... Re-signed by Bills (July 23, 1992). ... Granted unconditional free agency (February 17, 1995). ... Signed by Denver Broncos (April 4, 1995). ... Granted unconditional free agency (February 14, 1997). ... Re-signed by Broncos (August 6, 1997).
CHAMPIONSHIP GAME EXPERIENCE: Played in AFC championship game (1990-1993 and 1997 seasons). ... Played in Super Bowl XXV (1990 season), Super Bowl XXVI (1991 season), Super Bowl XXVII (1992 season) and Super Bowl XXVIII (1993 season). ... Member of Super Bowl championship team (1997 season).
POST SEASON RECORDS: Shares Super Bowl career record for most games—5.
PRO STATISTICS: 1992—Recovered one fumble for 18 yards and a touchdown. 1993—Recovered one fumble. 1994—Recovered one fumble in end zone for a touchdown. 1997—Recovered one fumble.

Year Team	G	GS	SACKS
1990—Buffalo NFL	12	0	2.0
1991—Buffalo NFL	16	6	1.5
1992—Buffalo NFL	16	0	0.0
1993—Buffalo NFL	15	1	0.5
1994—Buffalo NFL	15	5	0.0
1995—Denver NFL	16	0	0.0
1996—Denver NFL	16	16	1.5
1997—Denver NFL	16	0	1.0
Pro totals (8 years)	122	28	6.5

LOFTON, STEVE   CB   PATRIOTS

PERSONAL: Born November 26, 1968, in Jacksonville, Texas. ... 5-9/177. ... Full name: Steven Lynn Lofton.
HIGH SCHOOL: Alto (Texas).
COLLEGE: Texas A&M.
TRANSACTIONS/CAREER NOTES: Signed as non-drafted free agent by WLAF (January 31, 1991). ... Selected by Montreal Machine in third round (34th defensive back) of 1991 WLAF positional draft. ... Signed by Phoenix Cardinals (July 9, 1991). ... On injured reserve with hamstring injury (October 12-December 2, 1992). ... On practice squad (December 2, 1992-remainder of season). ... Cardinals franchise renamed Arizona Cardinals for 1994 season. ... Claimed on waivers by Cincinnati Bengals (August 4, 1994). ... Released by Bengals (August 7, 1994). ... Signed by Carolina Panthers (April 11, 1995). ... Granted unconditional free agency (February 14, 1997). ... Signed by New England Patriots (September 30, 1997). ... On injured reserve with hamstring injury (December 9, 1997-remainder of season).
CHAMPIONSHIP GAME EXPERIENCE: Member of Panthers for NFC championship game (1996 season); did not play.
PRO STATISTICS: W.L.: 1991—Recovered one fumble. NFL: 1993—Returned one kickoff for 18 yards.

Year Team	G	GS	INTERCEPTIONS No.	Yds.	Avg.	TD
1991—Montreal W.L.	10	8	2	16	8.0	0
—Phoenix NFL	11	1	0	0	...	0
1992—Phoenix NFL	4	0	0	0	...	0
1993—Phoenix NFL	13	0	0	0	...	0
1994—			Did not play.			
1995—Carolina NFL	9	2	0	0	...	0
1996—Carolina NFL	11	3	1	42	42.0	0
1997—New England NFL	4	0	0	0	...	0
W.L. totals (1 year)	10	8	2	16	8.0	0
NFL totals (6 years)	52	6	1	42	42.0	0
Pro totals (7 years)	62	14	3	58	19.3	0

LOGAN, ERNIE   DE   JETS

PERSONAL: Born May 18, 1968, in Fort Bragg, N.C. ... 6-3/290. ... Full name: Ernest Edward Logan.
HIGH SCHOOL: Pine Forest (Fayetteville, N.C.).
COLLEGE: East Carolina.
TRANSACTIONS/CAREER NOTES: Selected by Atlanta Falcons in ninth round (226th pick overall) of 1991 NFL draft. ... Released by Falcons (August 19, 1991). ... Signed by Cleveland Browns (August 21, 1991). ... Released by Browns (September 8, 1993). ... Signed by Falcons (October 7, 1993). ... Granted free agency (February 17, 1994). ... Re-signed by Falcons (April 28, 1994). ... Released by Falcons (August 22, 1994). ... Signed by Jacksonville Jaguars (December 15, 1994). ... Granted unconditional free agency (February 14, 1997). ... Signed by New York Jets (March 20, 1997). ... On injured reserve with leg injury (December 15, 1997-remainder of season).
CHAMPIONSHIP GAME EXPERIENCE: Member of Jaguars for AFC championship game (1996 season); inactive.
PRO STATISTICS: 1991—Recovered one fumble.

Year Team	G	GS	SACKS
1991—Cleveland NFL	15	5	0.5
1992—Cleveland NFL	16	0	1.0
1993—Atlanta NFL	8	1	1.0
1994—		Did not play.	
1995—Jacksonville NFL	15	1	3.0
1996—Jacksonville NFL	4	0	0.0
1997—New York Jets NFL	15	14	0.0
Pro totals (6 years)	73	21	5.5

LOGAN, JAMES   LB   SEAHAWKS

PERSONAL: Born December 6, 1972, in Opp, Ala. ... 6-2/225.
HIGH SCHOOL: Opp (Ala.).
JUNIOR COLLEGE: Jones County Junior College (Miss.).
COLLEGE: Memphis.
TRANSACTIONS/CAREER NOTES: Signed as non-drafted free agent by Houston Oilers (May 3, 1995). ... Released by Oilers (August 27, 1995). ... Re-signed by Oilers (August 30, 1995). ... Activated (September 7, 1995). ... Released as replacement player by Bengals (September 25, 1995). ... Claimed on waivers by Cincinnati Bengals (October 18, 1995). ... Claimed on waivers by Seattle Seahawks (October 31, 1995). ... Assigned by Seahawks to Scottish Claymores in 1997 World League enhancement allocation program (February 19, 1997).
PLAYING EXPERIENCE: Houston (3)-Cincinnati (1)-Seattle (6) NFL, 1995; Seattle NFL, 1996; Scotland W.L., 1997; Seattle NFL, 1997. ... Games/Games started: 1995 (Hou.-3/0; Cin.-1/0; Sea.-6/0; Total: 10/0), 1996 (6/0), 1997 (W.L.-games played unavailable; NFL-14/1). Total NFL: 30/1.
PRO STATISTICS: W.L.: 1997—Intercepted one pass for no yards. NFL: 1997—Recovered one fumble.

LOGAN, MARC   FB

PERSONAL: Born May 9, 1965, in Lexington, Ky. ... 6-0/228. ... Full name: Marc Anthony Logan. ... Cousin of Dermontti Dawson, center, Pittsburgh Steelers.
HIGH SCHOOL: Bryan Station (Lexington, Ky.).
COLLEGE: Kentucky (degree in political science, 1987).
TRANSACTIONS/CAREER NOTES: Selected by Cincinnati Bengals in fifth round (130th pick overall) of 1987 NFL draft. ... Signed by Bengals (July 7, 1987). ... Released by Bengals (September 7, 1987). ... Re-signed as replacement player by Bengals (September 25, 1987). ... Claimed on waivers by Cleveland Browns (October 20, 1987). ... Released by Browns (November 5, 1987). ... Re-signed by Browns for 1988 (November 7, 1987). ... Released by Browns (August 24, 1988). ... Signed by Bengals (October 4, 1988). ... Granted unconditional free agency (February 1, 1989). ... Signed by Miami Dolphins (February 16, 1989). ... On injured reserve with knee injury (October 25-December 6, 1989). ... Granted free agency (February 1, 1991). ... Re-signed by Dolphins (August 20, 1991). ... Activated (August 23, 1991). ... Granted uncon-

ditional free agency (February 1, 1992). ... Signed by San Francisco 49ers (April 1, 1992). ... Granted unconditional free agency (March 1, 1993). ... Re-signed by 49ers (July 20, 1993). ... Released by 49ers (August 30, 1993). ... Re-signed by 49ers (August 31, 1993). ... Released by 49ers (July 28, 1994). ... Re-signed by 49ers (July 29, 1994). ... Released by 49ers (March 10, 1995). ... Signed by Washington Redskins (April 25, 1995). ... Released by Redskins (June 4, 1997). ... Re-signed by Redskins (July 19, 1997). ... Granted unconditional free agency (February 13, 1998).

CHAMPIONSHIP GAME EXPERIENCE: Member of Bengals for AFC championship game (1988 season); inactive. ... Played in Super Bowl XXIII (1988 season). ... Played in NFC championship game (1992-1994 seasons). ... Member of Super Bowl championship team (1994 season).

POST SEASON RECORDS: Shares NFL postseason single-game record for most kickoff returns—8 (January 12, 1991, at Buffalo).

PRO STATISTICS: 1989—Returned blocked punt two yards for a touchdown and recovered two fumbles for minus one yard. 1990—Recovered one fumble. 1993—Recovered one fumble. 1997—Recovered one fumble.

SINGLE GAME HIGHS (regular season): Attempts—16 (December 10, 1989, vs. New England); yards—103 (October 11, 1987, vs. Seattle); and rushing touchdowns—2 (October 31, 1993, vs. Los Angeles Rams).

STATISTICAL PLATEAUS: 100-yard rushing games: 1987 (1).

			RUSHING				RECEIVING				KICKOFF RETURNS				TOTALS			
Year Team	G	GS	Att.	Yds.	Avg.	TD	No.	Yds.	Avg.	TD	No.	Yds.	Avg.	TD	TD	2pt.	Pts.	Fum.
1987—Cincinnati NFL............	3	3	37	203	5.5	1	3	14	4.7	0	3	31	10.3	0	1	...	6	0
1988—Cincinnati NFL............	9	0	2	10	5.0	0	2	20	10.0	0	4	80	20.0	0	0	...	0	1
1989—Miami NFL	10	4	57	201	3.5	0	5	34	6.8	0	24	613	25.5	†1	2	...	12	1
1990—Miami NFL	16	0	79	317	4.0	2	7	54	7.7	0	20	367	18.4	0	2	...	12	4
1991—Miami NFL	16	0	4	5	1.3	0	0	0	...	0	12	191	15.9	0	0	...	0	1
1992—San Francisco NFL	16	1	8	44	5.5	1	2	17	8.5	0	22	478	21.7	0	1	...	6	0
1993—San Francisco NFL	14	12	58	280	4.8	7	37	348	9.4	0	0	0	...	0	7	...	42	2
1994—San Francisco NFL	10	5	33	143	4.3	1	16	97	6.1	1	0	0	...	0	2	0	12	0
1995—Washington NFL	16	8	23	72	3.1	1	25	276	11.0	2	0	0	...	0	3	0	18	1
1996—Washington NFL	14	9	20	111	5.6	2	23	269	11.7	0	0	0	...	0	2	0	12	1
1997—Washington NFL	15	1	4	5	1.3	0	3	6	2.0	0	4	70	17.5	0	0	0	0	1
Pro totals (11 years)	139	43	325	1391	4.3	15	123	1135	9.2	3	89	1830	20.6	1	20	0	120	12

LOGAN, MIKE — DB — JAGUARS

PERSONAL: Born September 15, 1974, in Pittsburgh. ... 6-0/206. ... Full name: Michael V. Logan.
HIGH SCHOOL: McKeesport (Pa.).
COLLEGE: West Virginia.
TRANSACTIONS/CAREER NOTES: Selected by Jacksonville Jaguars in second round (50th pick overall) of 1997 NFL draft. ... Signed by Jaguars (May 23, 1997).

			KICKOFF RETURNS				TOTALS			
Year Team	G	GS	No.	Yds.	Avg.	TD	TD	2pt.	Pts.	Fum.
1997—Jacksonville NFL	11	0	10	236	23.6	0	0	0	0	0

LONDON, ANTONIO — LB — PACKERS

PERSONAL: Born April 14, 1971, in Tullahoma, Tenn. ... 6-2/240. ... Full name: Antonio Monte London.
HIGH SCHOOL: Tullahoma (Tenn.).
COLLEGE: Alabama.
TRANSACTIONS/CAREER NOTES: Selected by Detroit Lions in third round (62nd pick overall) of 1993 NFL draft. ... Signed by Lions (July 17, 1993). ... Released by Lions (February 3, 1998). ... Signed by Green Bay Packers (February 24, 1998).

Year Team	G	GS	SACKS
1993—Detroit NFL	14	0	1.0
1994—Detroit NFL	16	0	0.0
1995—Detroit NFL	15	0	7.0
1996—Detroit NFL	14	12	3.0
1997—Detroit NFL	16	6	2.0
Pro totals (5 years)	75	18	13.0

LONGWELL, RYAN — K — PACKERS

PERSONAL: Born August 16, 1974, in Seattle. ... 5-11/185.
HIGH SCHOOL: Bend (Ore.).
COLLEGE: California.
TRANSACTIONS/CAREER NOTES: Signed as non-drafted free agent by San Francisco 49ers (April 28, 1997). ... Claimed on waivers by Green Bay Packers (July 10, 1997).
CHAMPIONSHIP GAME EXPERIENCE: Played in NFC championship game (1997 season). ... Played in Super Bowl XXXII (1997 season).

			KICKING						
Year Team	G	GS	XPM	XPA	FGM	FGA	Lg.	50+	Pts.
1997—Green Bay NFL	16	0	*48	*48	24	30	50	1-1	120

LOTT, ANTHONE — CB

PERSONAL: Born July 22, 1974, in Jacksonville. ... 5-9/194. ... Full name: Anthone Vouchan Lott.
HIGH SCHOOL: Raines (Jacksonville).
COLLEGE: Florida.
TRANSACTIONS/CAREER NOTES: Signed as non-drafted free agent by Cincinnati Bengals (April 25, 1997). ... Released by Bengals (October 21, 1997).
PLAYING EXPERIENCE: Cincinnati NFL, 1997. ... Games/Games started: 5/0.
PRO STATISTICS: 1997—Recovered one fumble.

LOUCHIEY, COREY   OT   FALCONS

PERSONAL: Born October 10, 1971, in Greenville, S.C. ... 6-8/305. ... Name pronounced LOU-chee.
HIGH SCHOOL: Carolina (Greenville, S.C.).
COLLEGE: Tennessee (did not play football), then South Carolina.
TRANSACTIONS/CAREER NOTES: Selected by Buffalo Bills in third round (98th pick overall) of 1994 NFL draft. ... Signed by Bills (July 15, 1994). ... Inactive for 12 games (1994). ... Granted free agency (February 14, 1997). ... Re-signed by Bills (June 12, 1997). ... Granted unconditional free agency (February 13, 1998). ... Signed by Atlanta Falcons (March 2, 1998).
PLAYING EXPERIENCE: Buffalo NFL, 1995-1997. ... Games/Games started: 1995 (13/3), 1996 (16/4), 1997 (16/6). Total: 45/13.
PRO STATISTICS: 1996—Caught one pass for no yards.

LOVILLE, DEREK   RB/KR   BRONCOS

PERSONAL: Born July 4, 1968, in San Francisco. ... 5-10/205. ... Full name: Derek Kevin Loville. ... Name pronounced luh-VILL.
HIGH SCHOOL: Riordan (San Francisco).
COLLEGE: Oregon (degree in American studies).
TRANSACTIONS/CAREER NOTES: Signed as non-drafted free agent by Seattle Seahawks (May 9, 1990). ... Granted unconditional free agency (February 1-April 1, 1991). ... Re-signed by Seahawks for 1991 season. ... Granted unconditional free agency (February 1, 1992). ... Signed by Los Angeles Rams (March 27, 1992). ... Released by Rams (August 31, 1992). ... Signed by San Francisco 49ers (March 22, 1993). ... On injured reserve with knee injury (August 30-November 10, 1993). ... Released by 49ers (November 10, 1993). ... Re-signed by 49ers (June 1, 1994). ... Granted unconditional free agency (February 17, 1995). ... Re-signed by 49ers (March 1, 1995). ... Released by 49ers (February 3, 1997). ... Signed by Denver Broncos (May 2, 1997). ... Granted unconditional free agency (February 13, 1998). ... Re-signed by Broncos (June 1, 1998).
CHAMPIONSHIP GAME EXPERIENCE: Played in NFC championship game (1994 season). ... Member of Super Bowl championship team (1994 and 1997 seasons). ... Played in AFC championship game (1997 season).
PRO STATISTICS: 1991—Returned three punts for 16 yards and recovered one fumble.
SINGLE GAME HIGHS (regular season): Attempts—24 (December 3, 1995, vs. Buffalo); yards—88 (December 3, 1995, vs. Buffalo); and rushing touchdowns—1 (December 21, 1997, vs. San Diego).

			RUSHING				RECEIVING				KICKOFF RETURNS				TOTALS			
Year Team	G	GS	Att.	Yds.	Avg.	TD	No.	Yds.	Avg.	TD	No.	Yds.	Avg.	TD	TD	2pt.	Pts.	Fum.
1990—Seattle NFL	11	1	7	12	1.7	0	0	0	...	0	18	359	19.9	0	0	...	0	1
1991—Seattle NFL	16	0	22	69	3.1	0	0	0	...	0	18	412	22.9	0	0	...	0	0
1992—									Did not play.									
1993—									Did not play.									
1994—San Francisco NFL	14	0	31	99	3.2	0	2	26	13.0	0	2	34	17.0	0	0	0	0	0
1995—San Francisco NFL	16	16	218	723	3.3	10	87	662	7.6	3	0	0	...	0	13	1	80	1
1996—San Francisco NFL	12	6	70	229	3.3	2	16	138	8.6	2	10	229	22.9	0	4	0	24	0
1997—Denver NFL	16	0	25	124	5.0	1	2	10	5.0	0	5	136	27.2	0	1	0	6	1
Pro totals (6 years)	85	23	373	1256	3.4	13	107	836	7.8	5	53	1170	22.1	0	18	1	110	3

LOWERY, MICHAEL   LB   BEARS

PERSONAL: Born February 14, 1974, in McComb, Miss. ... 6-0/232.
HIGH SCHOOL: South Pike (McComb, Miss.).
COLLEGE: Mississippi.
TRANSACTIONS/CAREER NOTES: Signed as non-drafted free agent by Chicago Bears (April 22, 1996).
PLAYING EXPERIENCE: Chicago NFL, 1996 and 1997. ... Games/Games started: 1996 (16/0), 1997 (16/0). Total: 32/0.
PRO STATISTICS: 1996—Recovered one fumble in end zone for a touchdown.

LUCAS, RAY   QB   JETS

PERSONAL: Born August 6, 1972, in Harrison, N.J. ... 6-3/201.
HIGH SCHOOL: Harrison (N.J.).
COLLEGE: Rutgers.
TRANSACTIONS/CAREER NOTES: Signed as non-drafted free agent by New England Patriots (May 1, 1996). ... Released by Patriots (August 25, 1996). ... Re-signed by Patriots to practice squad (August 27, 1996). ... Activated (December 12, 1996). ... Claimed on waivers by New York Jets (August 19, 1997). ... Released by Jets (August 24, 1997). ... Re-signed by Jets to practice squad (August 26, 1997). ... Activated (November 22, 1997).
CHAMPIONSHIP GAME EXPERIENCE: Played in AFC championship game (1996 season). ... Played in Super Bowl XXXI (1996 season).
SINGLE GAME HIGHS (regular season): Attempts—4 (December 21, 1997, vs. Detroit); completions—3 (December 21, 1997, vs. Detroit); yards—28 (December 21, 1997, vs. Detroit); and touchdown passes—0.

			PASSING								RUSHING				TOTALS		
Year Team	G	GS	Att.	Cmp.	Pct.	Yds.	TD	Int.	Avg.	Rat.	Att.	Yds.	Avg.	TD	TD	2pt.	Pts.
1996—New England NFL	2	0	0	0	...	0	0	0	...	...	0	0	...	0	0	0	0
1997—New York Jets NFL	5	0	4	3	75.0	28	0	1	7.00	54.2	6	55	9.2	0	0	0	0
Pro totals (2 years)	7	0	4	3	75.0	28	0	1	7.00	54.2	6	55	9.2	0	0	0	0

LUSK, HENRY   TE   REDSKINS

PERSONAL: Born May 8, 1972, in Seaside, Calif. ... 6-2/250. ... Full name: Hendrick H. Lusk.
HIGH SCHOOL: Monterey (Calif.).
COLLEGE: Utah (degree in sociology, 1995).
TRANSACTIONS/CAREER NOTES: Selected by New Orleans Saints in seventh round (246th pick overall) of 1996 NFL draft. ... Signed by Saints (July 12, 1996). ... Released by Saints (June 4, 1997). ... Signed by Green Bay Packers (June 19, 1997). ... Released by Packers (August 13, 1997). ... Signed by Washington Redskins (December 31, 1997).

PRO STATISTICS: 1996—Returned one kickoff for 16 yards.

SINGLE GAME HIGHS (regular season): Receptions—4 (November 24, 1996, vs. Tampa Bay); yards—32 (October 6, 1996, vs. Jacksonville); and touchdown receptions—0.

			RECEIVING				TOTALS			
Year Team	G	GS	No.	Yds.	Avg.	TD	TD	2pt.	Pts.	Fum.
1996—New Orleans NFL...	16	3	27	210	7.8	0	0	0	0	1
1997—						Did not play.				

LYGHT, TODD   CB   RAMS

PERSONAL: Born February 9, 1969, in Kwajalein, Marshall Islands. ... 6-0/190. ... Full name: Todd William Lyght.

HIGH SCHOOL: Powers (Flint, Mich.).

COLLEGE: Notre Dame.

TRANSACTIONS/CAREER NOTES: Selected by Los Angeles Rams in first round (fifth pick overall) of 1991 NFL draft. ... Signed by Rams (August 16, 1991). ... On injured reserve with shoulder injury (September 22-October 22, 1992). ... On injured reserve with knee injury (November 23, 1993-remainder of season). ... Designated by Rams as transition player (February 15, 1994). ... Rams franchise moved to St. Louis (April 12, 1995). ... Tendered offer sheet by Jacksonville Jaguars (April 12, 1996). ... Offer matched by Rams (April 15, 1996).

HONORS: Named defensive back on THE SPORTING NEWS college All-America first team (1989). ... Named defensive back on THE SPORTING NEWS college All-America second team (1990).

PRO STATISTICS: 1991—Fumbled once and recovered one fumble. 1993—Recovered one fumble for 13 yards. 1994—Returned one punt for 29 yards and recovered one fumble for 74 yards and a touchdown. 1995—Ran 16 yards with lateral from punt return. 1996—Fumbled once. 1997—Credited with one sack and recovered two fumbles.

			INTERCEPTIONS			
Year Team	G	GS	No.	Yds.	Avg.	TD
1991—Los Angeles Rams NFL..	12	8	1	0	0.0	0
1992—Los Angeles Rams NFL..	12	12	3	80	26.7	0
1993—Los Angeles Rams NFL..	9	9	2	0	0.0	0
1994—Los Angeles Rams NFL..	16	16	1	14	14.0	0
1995—St. Louis NFL	16	16	4	34	8.5	1
1996—St. Louis NFL	16	16	5	43	8.6	1
1997—St. Louis NFL	16	16	4	25	6.3	0
Pro totals (7 years)	97	93	20	196	9.8	2

LYLE, KEITH   S   RAMS

L

PERSONAL: Born April 17, 1972, in Washington, D.C. ... 6-2/210. ... Full name: Keith Allen Lyle. ... Son of Garry Lyle, free safety with Chicago Bears (1968-1974).

HIGH SCHOOL: George C. Marshall (Falls Church, Va.).

COLLEGE: Virginia.

TRANSACTIONS/CAREER NOTES: Selected by Los Angeles Rams in third round (71st pick overall) of 1994 NFL draft. ... Signed by Rams (July 8, 1994). ... Rams franchise moved to St. Louis (April 12, 1995). ... Granted free agency (February 14, 1997). ... Re-signed by Rams (April 15, 1997).

PRO STATISTICS: 1995—Rushed once for four yards. 1996—Rushed three times for 39 yards and fumbled once. 1997—Credited with two sacks.

			INTERCEPTIONS			
Year Team	G	GS	No.	Yds.	Avg.	TD
1994—Los Angeles Rams NFL..	16	0	2	1	0.5	0
1995—St. Louis NFL	16	16	3	42	14.0	0
1996—St. Louis NFL	16	16	†9	‡152	16.9	0
1997—St. Louis NFL	16	16	8	102	12.8	0
Pro totals (4 years)	64	48	22	297	13.5	0

LYLE, RICK   DL   JETS

PERSONAL: Born February 26, 1971, in Monroe, La. ... 6-5/285. ... Full name: Rick James Earl Lyle.

HIGH SCHOOL: Hickman Mills (Kansas City, Mo.).

COLLEGE: Missouri.

TRANSACTIONS/CAREER NOTES: Signed as non-drafted free agent by Cleveland Browns (May 2, 1994). ... On injured reserve with back injury (September 2, 1995-entire season). ... Browns franchise moved to Baltimore and renamed Ravens for 1996 season (March 11, 1996). ... Granted unconditional free agency (February 14, 1997). ... Signed by New York Jets (March 24, 1997).

PLAYING EXPERIENCE: Cleveland NFL, 1994; Baltimore NFL, 1996; New York Jets NFL, 1997. ... Games/Games started: 1994 (3/0), 1996 (11/3), 1997 (16/16). Total: 30/19.

PRO STATISTICS: 1997—Credited with three sacks and recovered one fumble for two yards.

LYNCH, JOHN   S   BUCCANEERS

PERSONAL: Born September 25, 1971, in Hinsdale, Ill. ... 6-2/214. ... Full name: John Terrence Lynch. ... Son of John Lynch, linebacker with Pittsburgh Steelers (1969).

HIGH SCHOOL: Torrey Pines (Encinitas, Calif.).

COLLEGE: Stanford.

TRANSACTIONS/CAREER NOTES: Selected by Tampa Bay Buccaneers in third round (82nd pick overall) of 1993 NFL draft. ... Signed by Buccaneers (June 1, 1993). ... On injured reserve with knee injury (December 12, 1995-remainder of season). ... Granted free agency (February 16, 1996). ... Re-signed by Buccaneers (July 13, 1996).

HONORS: Played in Pro Bowl (1997 season).

PRO STATISTICS: 1996—Rushed once for 40 yards, credited with one sack, fumbled once and recovered one fumble. 1997—Recovered two fumbles.

Year—Team	G	GS	INTERCEPTIONS No.	Yds.	Avg.	TD
1993—Tampa Bay NFL	15	4	0	0	...	0
1994—Tampa Bay NFL	16	0	0	0	...	0
1995—Tampa Bay NFL	9	6	3	3	1.0	0
1996—Tampa Bay NFL	16	14	3	26	8.7	0
1997—Tampa Bay NFL	16	16	2	28	14.0	0
Pro totals (5 years)	72	40	8	57	7.1	0

LYNCH, LORENZO   S

PERSONAL: Born April 6, 1963, in Oakland. ... 5-11/200.
HIGH SCHOOL: Oakland.
COLLEGE: Sacramento State.
TRANSACTIONS/CAREER NOTES: Signed as non-drafted free agent by Dallas Cowboys (April 30, 1987). ... Released by Cowboys (July 27, 1987). ... Signed by Chicago Bears (July 31, 1987). ... Released by Bears (September 1, 1987). ... Re-signed as replacement player by Bears (September 24, 1987) On injured reserve with dislocated shoulder (October 16, 1987-remainder of season). ... On injured reserve with hamstring injury (August 29-October 14, 1988). ... Granted unconditional free agency (February 1, 1990). ... Signed by Phoenix Cardinals (March 30, 1990). ... Granted free agency (February 1, 1992). ... Re-signed by Cardinals (July 19, 1992). ... Granted unconditional free agency (February 17, 1994). ... Cardinals franchise renamed Arizona Cardinals for 1994 season. ... Re-signed by Cardinals (June 2, 1994). ... Granted unconditional free agency (February 17, 1995). ... Re-signed by Cardinals (February 27, 1995). ... Released by Cardinals (March 6, 1996). ... Signed by Oakland Raiders (March 8, 1996). ... Released by Raiders (February 14, 1997). ... Re-signed by Raiders (May 8, 1997). ... Granted unconditional free agency (February 13, 1998).
CHAMPIONSHIP GAME EXPERIENCE: Played in NFC championship game (1988 season).
PRO STATISTICS: 1991—Recovered one fumble for 17 yards. 1992—Recovered one fumble. 1993—Credited with one sack and recovered three fumbles for 55 yards and a touchdown. 1994—Credited with $1/2$ sack. 1995—Credited with one sack and recovered one fumble. 1997—Credited with one sack.

Year—Team	G	GS	INTERCEPTIONS No.	Yds.	Avg.	TD
1987—Chicago NFL	2	2	0	0	...	0
1988—Chicago NFL	9	0	0	0	...	0
1989—Chicago NFL	16	2	3	55	18.3	0
1990—Phoenix NFL	16	0	0	0	...	0
1991—Phoenix NFL	16	14	3	59	19.7	∞1
1992—Phoenix NFL	16	9	0	0	...	0
1993—Phoenix NFL	16	15	3	13	4.3	0
1994—Arizona NFL	15	15	2	35	17.5	0
1995—Arizona NFL	12	11	1	72	72.0	1
1996—Oakland NFL	16	16	3	75	25.0	0
1997—Oakland NFL	15	0	2	6	3.0	0
Pro totals (11 years)	199	84	17	315	18.5	2

LYNN, ANTHONY   TE   BRONCOS

PERSONAL: Born December 21, 1968, in McKinney, Texas. ... 6-3/230. ... Full name: Anthony Ray Lynn.
HIGH SCHOOL: Celina (Texas).
COLLEGE: Texas Tech.
TRANSACTIONS/CAREER NOTES: Signed as non-drafted free agent by New York Giants (May 5, 1992). ... Released by Giants (August 31, 1992). ... Signed by Denver Broncos (April 21, 1993). ... Released by Broncos (August 23, 1994). ... Signed by San Francisco 49ers (March 28, 1995). ... Granted unconditional free agency (February 14, 1997). ... Signed by Broncos (March 4, 1997).
CHAMPIONSHIP GAME EXPERIENCE: Played in AFC championship game (1997 season). ... Member of Super Bowl championship team (1997 season).
PRO STATISTICS: 1996—Caught two passes for 14 yards. 1997—Caught one pass for 21 yards.
SINGLE GAME HIGHS (regular season): Attempts—7 (October 6, 1996, vs. St. Louis); yards—67 (September 29, 1996, vs. Atlanta); and rushing touchdowns—0.
MISCELLANEOUS: Played running back (1993-1996 seasons).

Year—Team	G	GS	RUSHING Att.	Yds.	Avg.	TD	TOTALS TD	2pt.	Pts.	Fum.
1993—Denver NFL	13	0	0	0	...	0	0	...	0	0
1994—					Did not play.					
1995—San Francisco NFL	6	0	2	11	5.5	0	0	0	0	0
1996—San Francisco NFL	16	1	24	164	6.8	0	0	0	0	0
1997—Denver NFL	16	0	0	0	...	0	0	0	0	0
Pro totals (4 years)	51	1	26	175	6.7	0	0	0	0	0

LYONS, LAMAR   S   RAVENS

PERSONAL: Born March 25, 1973, in Los Angeles. ... 6-3/210.
HIGH SCHOOL: University (Los Angeles), then St. Monica Catholic (Santa Monica, Calif.).
COLLEGE: Washington.
TRANSACTIONS/CAREER NOTES: Signed as non-drafted free agent by Oakland (May 20, 1996). ... Released by Raiders (August 19, 1996). ... Re-signed by Raiders for 1997 season. ... Released by Raiders (August 19, 1997). ... Signed by Baltimore Ravens (December 10, 1997).
PLAYING EXPERIENCE: Oakland NFL, 1996; Baltimore NFL, 1997. ... Games/Games started: 1996 (6/0), 1997 (1/0). Total: 7/0.

LYONS, MITCH   TE   STEELERS

PERSONAL: Born May 13, 1970, in Grand Rapids, Mich. ... 6-5/265. ... Full name: Mitchell Warren Lyons.
HIGH SCHOOL: Forest Hills Northern (Grand Rapids, Mich.).
COLLEGE: Michigan State.
TRANSACTIONS/CAREER NOTES: Selected by Atlanta Falcons in sixth round (151st pick overall) of 1993 NFL draft. ... Signed by Falcons (May 26, 1993). ... Granted free agency (February 16, 1996). ... Re-signed by Falcons (June 12, 1996). ... Granted unconditional free agency (February 14, 1997). ... Signed by Pittsburgh Steelers (April 21, 1997). ... On injured reserve with knee injury (November 11, 1997-remainder of season).
SINGLE GAME HIGHS (regular season): Receptions—4 (October 23, 1994, vs. Los Angeles Raiders); yards—34 (November 26, 1995, vs. Arizona); and touchdown receptions—1 (December 8, 1996, vs. New Orleans).

			RECEIVING			TOTALS			
Year Team	G	GS	No.	Yds.	Avg.	TD	TD	2pt.	Pts.	Fum.
1993—Atlanta NFL	16	8	8	63	7.9	0	0	...	0	0
1994—Atlanta NFL	7	2	7	54	7.7	0	0	0	0	0
1995—Atlanta NFL	13	5	5	83	16.6	0	0	0	0	0
1996—Atlanta NFL	14	4	4	16	4.0	1	1	0	6	0
1997—Pittsburgh NFL	10	3	4	29	7.3	0	0	0	0	0
Pro totals (5 years)	60	22	28	245	8.8	1	1	0	6	0

LYONS, PRATT   DE   OILERS

PERSONAL: Born September 17, 1974, in Ft. Worth, Texas. ... 6-5/281.
HIGH SCHOOL: Trimble (Ft. Worth, Texas).
COLLEGE: Utah State, then Troy (Ala.) State.
TRANSACTIONS/CAREER NOTES: Selected by Houston Oilers in fourth round (107th pick overall) of 1997 NFL draft. ... Oilers franchise moved to Tennessee for 1997 season. ... Signed by Oilers (July 15, 1997).

Year Team	G	GS	SACKS
1997—Tennessee NFL	16	0	2.5

MACK, TREMAIN   S   BENGALS

PERSONAL: Born November 21, 1974, in Tyler, Texas. ... 6-0/193. ... Nephew of Phillip Epps, wide receiver with Green Bay Packers (1982-88).
HIGH SCHOOL: Chapel Hill (Tyler, Texas).
COLLEGE: Miami (Fla.).
TRANSACTIONS/CAREER NOTES: Selected by Cincinnati Bengals in fourth round (111th pick overall) of 1997 NFL draft. ... Signed by Bengals (June 5, 1997). ... On non-football injury reserve list with illness (November 5-December 1, 1997).

			INTERCEPTIONS			
Year Team	G	GS	No.	Yds.	Avg.	TD
1997—Cincinnati NFL	4	4	1	29	29.0	0

MADDOX, MARK   LB   CARDINALS

PERSONAL: Born March 23, 1968, in Milwaukee. ... 6-1/233. ... Full name: Mark Anthony Maddox.
HIGH SCHOOL: James Madison (Milwaukee).
COLLEGE: Northern Michigan.
TRANSACTIONS/CAREER NOTES: Selected by Buffalo Bills in ninth round (249th pick overall) of 1991 NFL draft. ... Signed by Bills (June 18, 1991). ... On injured reserve with knee injury (August 27, 1991-entire season). ... On injured reserve (October 10, 1995-remainder of season). ... Granted unconditional free agency (February 16, 1996). ... Re-signed by Bills (March 4, 1996). ... Released by Bills (June 2, 1997). ... Re-signed by Bills (July 2, 1997). ... Released by Bills (August 12, 1997). ... Re-signed by Bills (October 28, 1997). ... Granted unconditional free agency (February 13, 1998). ... Signed by Arizona Cardinals (March 19, 1998).
PLAYING EXPERIENCE: Buffalo NFL, 1992-1997. ... Games/Games started: 1992 (15/1), 1993 (11/8), 1994 (15/14), 1995 (4/4), 1996 (14/14), 1997 (8/1). Total: 67/42.
CHAMPIONSHIP GAME EXPERIENCE: Played in AFC championship game (1992 and 1993 season). ... Played in Super Bowl XXVII (1992 season) and Super Bowl XXVIII (1993 season).
PRO STATISTICS: 1993—Recovered two fumbles. 1994—Intercepted one pass for 11 yards and recovered one fumble. 1997—Intercepted one pass for 25 yards.

MADISON, SAM   CB   DOLPHINS

PERSONAL: Born April 23, 1974, in Thomasville, Ga. ... 5-11/185. ... Full name: Samuel A. Madison.
HIGH SCHOOL: Florida A&M (Monticello, Fla.).
COLLEGE: Louisville.
TRANSACTIONS/CAREER NOTES: Selected by Miami Dolphins in second round (44th pick overall) of 1997 NFL draft. ... Signed by Dolphins (June 16, 1997).

			INTERCEPTIONS			
Year Team	G	GS	No.	Yds.	Avg.	TD
1997—Miami NFL	14	3	1	21	21.0	0

MAHLUM, ERIC   G   COLTS

PERSONAL: Born December 6, 1970, in San Diego. ... 6-4/302. ... Full name: Eric Arnold Mahlum.
HIGH SCHOOL: Pacific Grove (Calif.).

L
M

COLLEGE: California.

TRANSACTIONS/CAREER NOTES: Selected by Indianapolis Colts in second round (32nd pick overall) of 1994 NFL draft. ... Signed by Colts (July 22, 1994). ... On physically unable to perform list with knee injury (July 6, 1997-entire season).

PLAYING EXPERIENCE: Indianapolis NFL, 1994-1996. ... Games/Games started: 1994 (16/2), 1995 (7/7), 1996 (13/9). Total: 36/18.

CHAMPIONSHIP GAME EXPERIENCE: Played in AFC championship game (1995 season).

PRO STATISTICS: 1995—Recovered two fumbles. 1996—Recovered one fumble.

MALAMALA, SIUPELI   G/OT   JETS

PERSONAL: Born January 15, 1969, in Tofoa, Tonga. ... 6-5/305. ... Cousin of Viliami Maumau, defensive tackle, Carolina Panthers. ... Name pronounced SEE-uh-pell-ee ma-la-ma-la.

HIGH SCHOOL: Kalahoe (Kailua, Hawaii).

COLLEGE: Washington.

TRANSACTIONS/CAREER NOTES: Selected by New York Jets in third round (68th pick overall) of 1992 NFL draft. ... Signed by Jets (July 14, 1992). ... On injured reserve with shoulder injury (August 31-September 29, 1992). ... On practice squad (September 29-October 9, 1992). ... Granted free agency (February 17, 1995). ... Re-signed by Jets (March 29, 1995). ... On injured reserve with knee injury (October 31, 1995-remainder of season). ... On physically unable to perform list with knee injury (July 21, 1996-October 18, 1996). ... Released by Jets (September 20, 1997). ... Re-signed by Jets (September 21, 1997).

PLAYING EXPERIENCE: New York Jets NFL, 1992-1997. ... Games/Games started: 1992 (9/5), 1993 (15/15), 1994 (12/10), 1995 (6/4), 1996 (4/1), 1997 (10/5). Total: 56/40.

PRO STATISTICS: 1993—Recovered one fumble.

MALONE, VAN   S   CARDINALS

PERSONAL: Born July 1, 1970, in Houston. ... 5-11/186. ... Full name: Van Buren Malone.

HIGH SCHOOL: Waltrip (Houston).

COLLEGE: Texas.

TRANSACTIONS/CAREER NOTES: Selected by Detroit Lions in second round (57th pick overall) of 1994 NFL draft. ... Signed by Lions (July 19, 1994). ... On injured reserve with groin injury (November 19, 1997-remainder of season). ... Granted unconditional free agency (February 13, 1998). ... Signed by Arizona Cardinals (April 9, 1998).

PRO STATISTICS: 1994—Returned three kickoffs for 38 yards and fumbled once. 1997—Fumbled once.

			INTERCEPTIONS			
Year Team	G	GS	No.	Yds.	Avg.	TD
1994—Detroit NFL	16	0	0	0	...	0
1995—Detroit NFL	16	0	1	0	0.0	0
1996—Detroit NFL	15	15	1	5	5.0	0
1997—Detroit NFL	8	4	1	-5	-5.0	0
Pro totals (4 years)	55	19	3	0	0.0	0

MAMULA, MIKE   LB/DE   EAGLES

PERSONAL: Born August 14, 1973, in Lackawanna, N.Y. ... 6-4/252. ... Full name: Michael Brian Mamula. ... Name pronounced ma-MOO-lah.

HIGH SCHOOL: Lackawanna (N.Y.) Secondary.

COLLEGE: Boston College.

TRANSACTIONS/CAREER NOTES: Selected after junior season by Philadelphia Eagles in first round (seventh pick overall) of 1995 NFL draft. ... Signed by Eagles (July 19, 1995).

PRO STATISTICS: 1995—Recovered one fumble for 25 yards. 1996—Recovered three fumbles for four yards and a touchdown.

Year Team	G	GS	SACKS
1995—Philadelphia NFL	14	13	5.5
1996—Philadelphia NFL	16	16	8.0
1997—Philadelphia NFL	16	16	4.0
Pro totals (3 years)	46	45	17.5

MANDARICH, TONY   OT   COLTS

PERSONAL: Born September 23, 1966, in Oakville, Ont. ... 6-5/324. ... Full name: Tony Joseph Mandarich. ... Brother of John Mandarich, defensive tackle with Edmonton Eskimos (1984-1989) and Ottawa Rough Riders of CFL (1990).

HIGH SCHOOL: White Oaks (Ont.), then Roosevelt (Kent, Ohio).

COLLEGE: Michigan State (degree in telecommunications, 1990).

TRANSACTIONS/CAREER NOTES: Selected by Green Bay Packers in first round (second pick overall) of 1989 NFL draft. ... Signed by Packers (September 5, 1989). ... Granted roster exemption (September 5-18, 1989). ... On reserve/non-football injury list with thyroid injury (September 1, 1992-entire season). ... Granted unconditional free agency (March 1, 1993). ... Signed by Indianapolis Colts (February 22, 1996). ... Granted unconditional free agency (February 13, 1998). ... Tendered offer sheet by Chicago Bears (March 14, 1998). ... Offer matched by Colts (March 18, 1998).

PLAYING EXPERIENCE: Green Bay NFL, 1989-1991; Indianapolis NFL, 1996 and 1997. ... Games/Games started: 1989 (14/0), 1990 (16/16), 1991 (15/15), 1996 (15/6), 1997 (16/16). Total: 76/53.

HONORS: Named offensive tackle on THE SPORTING NEWS college All-America second team (1987). ... Named offensive tackle on THE SPORTING NEWS college All-America first team (1988).

PRO STATISTICS: 1989—Returned one kickoff for no yards. 1990—Recovered one fumble. 1997—Recovered one fumble.

MISCELLANEOUS: Out of pro football (1993-1995).

MANGUM, JOHN   S   BEARS

PERSONAL: Born March 16, 1967, in Magee, Miss. ... 5-10/190. ... Full name: John Wayne Mangum Jr. ... Son of John Mangum, defensive tackle with Boston Patriots of AFL (1966 and 1967); brother of Kris Mangum, tight end, Carolina Panthers.
HIGH SCHOOL: Magee (Miss.).
COLLEGE: Alabama (degree in finance).
TRANSACTIONS/CAREER NOTES: Selected by Chicago Bears in sixth round (144th pick overall) of 1990 NFL draft. ... Signed by Bears (July 24, 1990). ... Released by Bears (September 3, 1990). ... Signed by Tampa Bay Buccaneers to practice squad (October 1, 1990). ... Signed by Bears off Buccaneers practice squad (October 23, 1990). ... On injured reserve with knee injury (October 8, 1992-remainder of season). ... Granted free agency (March 1, 1993). ... Re-signed by Bears (May 17, 1993). ... Granted unconditional free agency (February 17, 1995). ... Re-signed by Bears (March 2, 1995). ... Granted unconditional free agency (February 13, 1998). ... Re-signed by Bears (February 18, 1998).
PRO STATISTICS: 1990—Recovered one fumble. 1991—Recovered two fumbles. 1993—Returned one kickoff for no yards. 1997—Recovered three fumbles.

| | | | INTERCEPTIONS | | | | SACKS |
Year Team	G	GS	No.	Yds.	Avg.	TD	No.
1990—Chicago NFL	10	0	0	0	...	0	1.0
1991—Chicago NFL	16	1	1	5	5.0	0	1.0
1992—Chicago NFL	5	1	0	0	...	0	0.0
1993—Chicago NFL	12	1	1	0	0.0	0	0.0
1994—Chicago NFL	16	3	0	0	...	0	0.5
1995—Chicago NFL	11	1	1	2	2.0	0	1.0
1996—Chicago NFL	16	2	0	0	...	0	1.0
1997—Chicago NFL	16	16	2	4	2.0	0	1.0
Pro totals (8 years)	102	25	5	11	2.2	0	5.5

MANGUM, KRIS   TE   PANTHERS

PERSONAL: Born August 15, 1973, in Magee, Miss. ... 6-4/249. ... Full name: Kris Thomas Mangum. ... Son of John Mangum, defensive tackle with Boston Patriots (1966 and 1967) of AFL; and brother of John Mangum, cornerback with Chicago Bears (1990-1997).
HIGH SCHOOL: Magee (Miss.).
COLLEGE: Mississippi.
TRANSACTIONS/CAREER NOTES: Selected by Carolina Panthers in seventh round (228th pick overall) of 1997 NFL draft. ... Signed by Panthers (May 20, 1997). ... Released by Panthers (September 2, 1997). ... Re-signed by Panthers to practice squad (September 4, 1997). ... Activated (December 5, 1997).
PRO STATISTICS: 1997—Caught four passes for 56 yards.
SINGLE GAME HIGHS (regular season): Receptions—4 (December 20, 1997, vs. St. Louis); yards—56 (December 20, 1997, vs. St. Louis); and touchdown receptions—0.

MANIECKI, JASON   DT   BUCCANEERS

PERSONAL: Born August 15, 1972, in Wisconsin Dells, Wis. ... 6-4/291. ... Full name: Jason Zbiyniew Maniecki. ... Name pronounced muh-NECK-ee.
HIGH SCHOOL: Wisconsin Dells (Wis.).
COLLEGE: Wisconsin.
TRANSACTIONS/CAREER NOTES: Selected by Tampa Bay Buccaneers in fifth round (140th pick overall) of 1996 NFL draft. ... Signed by Buccaneers (July 16, 1996).
PLAYING EXPERIENCE: Tampa Bay NFL, 1996 and 1997. ... Games/Games started: 1996 (5/0), 1997 (10/0). Total: 15/0.
PRO STATISTICS: 1997—Credited with one sack and recovered one fumble.

MANLEY, JAMES   DT   RAMS

PERSONAL: Born July 11, 1974, in Birmingham, Ala. ... 6-3/320.
HIGH SCHOOL: Huffman (Birmingham, Ala.).
COLLEGE: Vanderbilt.
TRANSACTIONS/CAREER NOTES: Selected by Minnesota Vikings in second round (45th pick overall) of 1996 NFL draft. ... Signed by Vikings (July 23, 1996). ... Active for two games (1996); did not play. ... Released by Vikings (September 23, 1997). ... Signed by St. Louis Rams (January 5, 1998).

MANNING, BRIAN   WR   DOLPHINS

PERSONAL: Born April 22, 1975, in Kansas City, Kan. ... 5-11/188. ... Full name: Brian Keith Manning.
HIGH SCHOOL: Ruskin (Kansas City, Mo.).
COLLEGE: Stanford.
TRANSACTIONS/CAREER NOTES: Selected by Miami Dolphins in sixth round (170th pick overall) of 1997 NFL draft. ... Signed by Dolphins (June 17, 1997).
PRO STATISTICS: 1997—Recovered one fumble for minus one yard.
SINGLE GAME HIGHS (regular season): Receptions—5 (November 23, 1997, vs. New England); yards—60 (November 23, 1997, vs. New England); and touchdown receptions—0.

| | | | RECEIVING | | | | TOTALS | | | |
Year Team	G	GS	No	Yds.	Avg.	TD	TD	2pt.	Pts.	Fum.
1997—Miami NFL	/	0	7	85	12.1	0	0	0	0	0

M

MANUEL, ROD   DE   STEELERS

PERSONAL: Born October 8, 1974, in Fort Worth, Texas. ... 6-5/290. ... Full name: Roderick Manuel.
HIGH SCHOOL: Western Hills (Fort Worth, Texas).
COLLEGE: Oklahoma.
TRANSACTIONS/CAREER NOTES: Selected by Pittsburgh Steelers in sixth round (199th pick overall) of 1997 NFL draft. ... Signed by Steelers (June 17, 1997).
PLAYING EXPERIENCE: Pittsburgh NFL, 1997. ... Games/Games started: 1/0.
CHAMPIONSHIP GAME EXPERIENCE: Member of Steelers for AFC championship game (1997 season); inactive.

MANUEL, SEAN   TE   CHIEFS

PERSONAL: Born December 1, 1973, in Los Gatos, Calif. ... 6-2/245. ... Full name: Sandor Manuel.
HIGH SCHOOL: Pinole Valley (El Sobrante, Calif.).
JUNIOR COLLEGE: Laney (Oakland) Community College.
COLLEGE: New Mexico State.
TRANSACTIONS/CAREER NOTES: Selected by San Francisco 49ers in seventh round (239th pick overall) of 1996 NFL draft. ... Signed by 49ers (July 12, 1996). ... On injured reserve with shoulder injury (December 13, 1996-remainder of season). ... Released by 49ers (August 24, 1997). ... Signed by Kansas City Chiefs (April 7, 1998).
PLAYING EXPERIENCE: San Francisco NFL, 1996. ... Games/Games started: 1996 (11/0).
PRO STATISTICS: 1996—Caught three passes for 18 yards.
SINGLE GAME HIGHS (regular season): Receptions—1 (October 27, 1996, vs. Houston); yards—7 (October 6, 1996, vs. St. Louis); and touchdown receptions—0.

MANUSKY, GREG   LB   CHIEFS

PERSONAL: Born August 12, 1966, in Wilkes-Barre, Pa. ... 6-1/234. ... Full name: Gregory Manusky.
HIGH SCHOOL: Dallas (Pa.).
COLLEGE: Colgate (degree in education, 1988).
TRANSACTIONS/CAREER NOTES: Signed as non-drafted free agent by Washington Redskins (May 3, 1988). ... On injured reserve with thigh injury (August 29-November 4, 1988). ... Granted unconditional free agency (February 1, 1991). ... Signed by Minnesota Vikings (March 27, 1991). ... On injured reserve with kidney injury (November 24-December 23, 1992). ... Granted unconditional free agency (March 1, 1993). ... Re-signed by Vikings for 1993 season. ... Released by Vikings (August 30, 1993). ... Re-signed by Vikings (August 31, 1993). ... Released by Vikings (August 22, 1994). ... Signed by Kansas City Chiefs (August 31, 1994). ... Granted unconditional free agency (February 16, 1996). ... Re-signed by Chiefs (April 9, 1996). ... Granted unconditional free agency (February 13, 1998). ... Re-signed by Chiefs (April 24, 1998).
PLAYING EXPERIENCE: Washington NFL, 1988-1990; Minnesota NFL, 1991-1993; Kansas City NFL, 1994-1997. ... Games/Games started: 1988 (7/0), 1989 (16/7), 1990 (16/8), 1991 (16/0), 1992 (11/0), 1993 (16/0), 1994 (16/2), 1995 (16/1), 1996 (16/1), 1997 (16/1). Total: 146/20.
PRO STATISTICS: 1989—Recovered one fumble. 1994—Recovered two fumbles. 1996—Returned two kickoffs for 32 yards, fumbled once and recovered three fumbles. 1997—Returned one kickoff for 16 yards and recovered one fumble.

MARE, OLINDO   K   DOLPHINS

PERSONAL: Born June 6, 1973, in Hollywood, Fla. ... 5-10/190. ... Name pronounced oh-LYNN-doe muh-RAY.
HIGH SCHOOL: Cooper City (Fla.).
JUNIOR COLLEGE: Valencia (Orlando) Community College.
COLLEGE: Syracuse.
TRANSACTIONS/CAREER NOTES: Signed as non-drafted free agent by New York Giants (May 2, 1996). ... Released by Giants (August 25, 1996). ... Re-signed by Giants to practice squad (August 27, 1996). ... Signed by Miami Dolphins (February 27, 1997).

			PUNTING					KICKING						
Year Team	G	GS	No.	Yds.	Avg.	Net avg.	In. 20	Blk.	XPM	XPA	FGM	FGA	Lg.	50+	Pts.
1997—Miami NFL	16	0	5	235	47.0	46.2	2	0	33	33	28	36	50	1-3	117

MARINO, DAN   QB   DOLPHINS

PERSONAL: Born September 15, 1961, in Pittsburgh. ... 6-4/228. ... Full name: Daniel Constantine Marino Jr. ... Brother-in-law of Bill Maas, nose tackle with Kansas City Chiefs (1984-1993) and Green Bay Packers (1993); and current NFL broadcaster, Fox Sports.
HIGH SCHOOL: Central Catholic (Pittsburgh).
COLLEGE: Pittsburgh (degree in communications).
TRANSACTIONS/CAREER NOTES: Selected by Los Angeles Express in first round (first pick overall) of 1983 USFL draft. ... Selected by Miami Dolphins in first round (27th pick overall) of 1983 NFL draft. ... Signed by Dolphins (July 9, 1983). ... Left Dolphins camp voluntarily (July 25-August 31, 1985). ... Granted roster exemption (September 1-5, 1985). ... On injured reserve with Achilles' tendon injury (October 13, 1993-remainder of season).
CHAMPIONSHIP GAME EXPERIENCE: Played in AFC championship game (1984, 1985 and 1992 seasons). ... Played in Super Bowl XIX (1984 season).
HONORS: Named quarterback on THE SPORTING NEWS college All-America first team (1981). ... Named NFL Rookie of the Year by THE SPORTING NEWS (1983). ... Named to play in Pro Bowl (1983 season); replaced by Bill Kenney due to injury. ... Named NFL Player of the Year by THE SPORTING NEWS (1984). ... Named quarterback on THE SPORTING NEWS NFL All-Pro team (1984-1986). ... Played in Pro Bowl (1984 and 1992 seasons). ... Named to play in Pro Bowl (1985 season); replaced by Ken O'Brien due to injury. ... Named to play in Pro Bowl (1986 season); replaced by Boomer Esiason due to injury. ... Named to play in Pro Bowl (1987 season); replaced by Jim Kelly due to injury. ... Named to play in Pro Bowl (1991 season); replaced by John Elway due to injury. Elway replaced by Ken O'Brien due to injury. ... Named to play in Pro Bowl (1994 season); replaced by Jeff Hostetler due to injury. ... Named to play in Pro Bowl (1995 season); replaced by Steve Bono due to injury.
RECORDS: Holds NFL career records for most touchdown passes—385; most yards passing—55,416; most passes attempted—7,452; most

passes completed—4,453; most games with 400 or more yards passing—12; and most games with four or more touchdown passes—18. ... Holds NFL records for most seasons with 4,000 or more yards passing—6; most consecutive seasons with 3,000 or more yards passing—9 (1984-1992); most games with 300 or more yards passing—56; most consecutive games with four or more touchdown passes—4 (November 26-December 17, 1984); most seasons leading league in pass attempts—5; and most seasons leading league in pass completions—6. ... Holds NFL single-season records for most yards passing—5,084 (1984); most touchdown passes—48 (1984); most games with 400 or more yards passing—4 (1984); most games with four or more touchdown passes—6 (1984); and most consecutive games with four or more touchdown passes—4 (1984). ... Holds NFL rookie-season records for highest pass completion percentage—58.45 (1983); highest passer rating—96.0 (1983); and lowest percentage of passes intercepted—2.03 (1983). ... Shares NFL records for most seasons leading league in yards passing—5; most consecutive seasons leading league in pass completions—3 (1984-1986); most consecutive games with 400 or more yards passing—2 (December 2 and 9, 1984); and most seasons with 3,000 or more yards passing—12. ... Shares NFL single-season record for most games with 300 or more yards passing—9 (1984).

POST SEASON RECORDS: Holds NFL postseason career record for most consecutive games with one or more touchdown passes—13. ... Shares NFL postseason single-game record for pass attempts—64 (December 30, 1995, vs. Buffalo).

PRO STATISTICS: 1983—Fumbled five times and recovered two fumbles. 1984—Fumbled six times and recovered two fumbles for minus three yards. 1985—Fumbled nine times and recovered two fumbles for minus four yards. 1986—Fumbled eight times and recovered four fumbles for minus 12 yards. 1987—Fumbled five times and recovered four fumbles for minus 25 yards. 1988—Fumbled 10 times and recovered eight fumbles for minus 31 yards. 1989—Fumbled seven times. 1990—Fumbled three times and recovered two fumbles. 1991—Fumbled six times and recovered three fumbles for minus eight yards. 1992—Fumbled five times and recovered two fumbles for minus 12 yards. 1993—Fumbled four times and recovered two fumbles for minus 13 yards. 1994—Fumbled nine times and recovered three fumbles for minus four yards. 1995—Caught one pass for minus six yards, fumbled seven times and recovered three fumbles for minus 14 yards. 1996—Fumbled four times and recovered one fumble for minus three yards. 1997—Fumbled eight times and recovered three fumbles for minus 17 yards.

SINGLE GAME HIGHS (regular season): Attempts—60 (December 21, 1997, vs. New England); completions—39 (November 16, 1986, vs. Buffalo); yards—521 (October 23, 1988, vs. New York Jets); and touchdown passes—6 (September 21, 1986, vs. New York Jets).

STATISTICAL PLATEAUS: 300-yard passing games: 1983 (1), 1984 (9), 1985 (6), 1986 (6), 1987 (4), 1988 (6), 1989 (5), 1990 (1), 1991 (3), 1992 (3), 1994 (5), 1995 (3), 1997 (4). Total: 56.

MISCELLANEOUS: Selected by Kansas City Royals organization in fourth round of free-agent baseball draft (June 5, 1979); did not sign. ... Regular-season record as starting NFL quarterback: 132-81 (.620). ... Postseason record as starting NFL quarterback: 6-8 (.429). ... Active NFL leader for career passing yards (55,416) and touchdown passes (385). ... Holds Miami Dolphins all-time records for most yards passing (55,416) and most touchdown passes (385).

Year Team	G	GS	Att.	Cmp.	Pct.	Yds.	TD	Int.	Avg.	Rat.	Att.	Yds.	Avg.	TD	TD	2pt.	Pts.
						PASSING						RUSHING				TOTALS	
1983—Miami NFL	11	9	296	173	58.4	2210	20	6	7.47	§96.0	28	45	1.6	2	2	...	12
1984—Miami NFL	16	16	*564	*362	§64.2	*5084	*48	17	*9.01	*108.9	28	-7	-0.3	0	0	...	0
1985—Miami NFL	16	16	567	*336	59.3	*4137	*30	21	7.30	84.1	26	-24	-0.9	0	0	...	0
1986—Miami NFL	16	16	*623	*378	60.7	*4746	*44	23	7.62	§92.5	12	-3	-0.3	0	0	...	0
1987—Miami NFL	12	12	§444	*263	59.2	3245	§26	13	7.31	89.2	12	-5	-0.4	1	1	...	6
1988—Miami NFL	16	16	*606	*354	58.4	*4434	▲28	§23	7.32	80.8	20	-17	-0.9	0	0	...	0
1989—Miami NFL	16	16	§550	§308	56.0	§3997	24	†22	7.27	76.9	14	-7	-0.5	2	2	...	12
1990—Miami NFL	16	16	531	306	57.6	3563	21	11	6.71	82.6	16	29	1.8	0	0	...	0
1991—Miami NFL	16	16	549	318	57.9	3970	25	13	7.23	85.8	27	32	1.2	1	1	...	6
1992—Miami NFL	16	16	*554	*330	59.6	*4116	§24	16	7.43	85.1	20	66	3.3	0	0	...	0
1993—Miami NFL	5	5	150	91	60.7	1218	8	3	8.12	95.9	9	-4	-0.4	1	1	...	6
1994—Miami NFL	16	16	615	385	62.6	4453	§30	17	7.24	§89.2	22	-6	-0.3	1	1	0	6
1995—Miami NFL	14	14	482	309	§64.1	3668	24	15	7.61	90.8	11	14	1.3	0	0	0	0
1996—Miami NFL	13	13	373	221	59.2	2795	17	9	7.49	87.8	11	-3	-0.3	0	0	0	0
1997—Miami NFL	16	16	*548	*319	58.2	3780	16	11	6.90	80.7	18	-14	-0.8	0	0	0	0
Pro totals (15 years)	215	213	7452	4453	59.8	55416	385	220	7.44	87.8	274	96	0.4	8	8	0	48

MARION, BROCK   S   DOLPHINS

PERSONAL: Born June 11, 1970, in Bakersfield, Calif. ... 5-11/200. ... Full name: Brock Elliot Marion. ... Son of Jerry Marion, wide receiver with Pittsburgh Steelers (1967); and nephew of Brent McClanahan, running back with Minnesota Vikings (1973-79).
HIGH SCHOOL: West (Bakersfield, Calif.).
COLLEGE: Nevada.
TRANSACTIONS/CAREER NOTES: Selected by Dallas Cowboys in seventh round (196th overall) of 1993 NFL draft. ... Signed by Cowboys (July 14, 1993). ... Granted free agency (February 16, 1996). ... Re-signed by Cowboys (May 2, 1996). ... Granted unconditional free agency (February 14, 1997). ... Re-signed by Cowboys (April 7, 1997). ... Granted unconditional free agency (February 13, 1998). ... Signed by Miami Dolphins (March 3, 1998).
CHAMPIONSHIP GAME EXPERIENCE: Played in NFC championship game (1993-1995 seasons). ... Member of Super Bowl championship team (1993 and 1995 seasons).
PRO STATISTICS: 1993—Recovered one fumble. 1994—Credited with one sack and returned two kickoffs for 39 yards. 1995—Returned one kickoff for 16 yards. 1996—Returned three kickoffs for 68 yards, fumbled once and recovered one fumble for 45 yards. 1997—Returned 10 kickoffs for 311 yards and recovered one fumble for 13 yards.

Year Team	G	GS	No.	Yds.	Avg.	TD
			INTERCEPTIONS			
1993—Dallas NFL	15	0	1	2	2.0	0
1994—Dallas NFL	14	1	1	11	11.0	0
1995—Dallas NFL	16	16	6	40	6.7	1
1996—Dallas NFL	10	10	0	0		0
1997—Dallas NFL	16	16	0	0	...	0
Pro totals (5 years)	71	43	8	53	6.6	1

MARSH, CURTIS   WR   STEELERS

PERSONAL: Born November 24, 1970, in Simi Valley, Calif. ... 6-2/206. ... Full name: Curtis Joseph Marsh.
HIGH SCHOOL: Simi Valley (Calif.).
JUNIOR COLLEGE: Moorpark (Calif.) Community College.

COLLEGE: Utah.

TRANSACTIONS/CAREER NOTES: Selected by Jacksonville Jaguars in seventh round (219th pick overall) of 1995 NFL draft. ... Signed by Jaguars (June 1, 1995). ... Released by Jaguars (August 27, 1995). ... Re-signed by Jaguars to practice squad (August 28, 1995). ... Activated (October 17, 1995). ... Released by Jaguars (August 24, 1997). ... Signed by Pittsburgh Steelers (October 22, 1997).

CHAMPIONSHIP GAME EXPERIENCE: Member of Jaguars for AFC championship game (1996 season); inactive. ... Member of Steelers for AFC championship game (1997 season); inactive.

PRO STATISTICS: 1995—Recovered one fumble. 1997—Rushed once for two yards.

SINGLE GAME HIGHS (regular season): Receptions—3 (December 24, 1995, vs. Cleveland); yards—73 (December 24, 1995, vs. Cleveland); and touchdown receptions—0.

			RECEIVING				KICKOFF RETURNS				TOTALS		
Year Team	G	GS	No.	Yds.	Avg.	TD	No.	Yds.	Avg.	TD	TD	2pt.	Pts.	Fum.
1995—Jacksonville NFL	9	0	7	127	18.1	0	15	323	21.5	0	0	0	0	2
1996—Jacksonville NFL	1	0	0	0	...	0	0	0	...	0	0	0	0	0
1997—Pittsburgh NFL	5	0	2	14	7.0	0	0	0	...	0	0	0	0	0
Pro totals (3 years)	15	0	9	141	15.7	0	15	323	21.5	0	0	0	0	2

MARSHALL, ANTHONY   S   JETS

PERSONAL: Born September 16, 1970, in Mobile, Ala. ... 6-1/212. ... Full name: Anthony Dewayne Marshall.

HIGH SCHOOL: LeFlore (Mobile, Ala.).

COLLEGE: Louisiana State.

TRANSACTIONS/CAREER NOTES: Signed as non-drafted free agent by Chicago Bears (April 28, 1994). ... Released by Bears (August 28, 1994). ... Re-signed by Bears to practice squad (August 30, 1994). ... Activated (December 9, 1994). ... Claimed on waivers by New York Jets (December 17, 1997). ... Granted free agency (February 13, 1998). ... Re-signed by Jets (March 23, 1998).

PRO STATISTICS: 1995—Returned one blocked punt 11 yards for a touchdown. 1996—Ran 75 yards with lateral from kickoff return. 1997—Ran three yards from lateral on a kickoff, credited with three sacks, fumbled once and recovered two fumbles for 10 yards.

			INTERCEPTIONS			
Year Team	G	GS	No.	Yds.	Avg.	TD
1994—Chicago NFL	3	0	0	0	...	0
1995—Chicago NFL	16	2	1	0	0.0	0
1996—Chicago NFL	13	3	2	20	10.0	0
1997—Chicago NFL	14	1	2	0	0.0	0
Pro totals (4 years)	46	6	5	20	4.0	0

MARTIN, CURTIS   RB   JETS

PERSONAL: Born May 1, 1973, in Pittsburgh. ... 5-11/203.

HIGH SCHOOL: Allderdice (Pittsburgh).

COLLEGE: Pittsburgh.

TRANSACTIONS/CAREER NOTES: Selected after junior season by New England Patriots in third round (74th pick overall) of 1995 NFL draft. ... Signed by Patriots (July 18, 1995). ... Granted free agency (February 13, 1998). ... Tendered offer sheet by New York Jets (March 20, 1998). ... Patriots declined to match offer (March 25, 1998).

CHAMPIONSHIP GAME EXPERIENCE: Played in AFC championship game (1996 season). ... Played in Super Bowl XXXI (1996 season).

HONORS: Named NFL Rookie of the Year by THE SPORTING NEWS (1995). ... Played in Pro Bowl (1995 and 1996 seasons).

PRO STATISTICS: 1995—Recovered three fumbles. 1996—Recovered one fumble.

SINGLE GAME HIGHS (regular season): Attempts—40 (September 14, 1997, vs. New York Jets); yards—199 (September 14, 1997, vs. New York Jets); and rushing touchdowns—3 (November 3, 1996, vs. Miami).

STATISTICAL PLATEAUS: 100-yard rushing games: 1995 (9), 1996 (2), 1997 (3). Total: 14.

			RUSHING				RECEIVING				TOTALS		
Year Team	G	GS	Att.	Yds.	Avg.	TD	No.	Yds.	Avg.	TD	TD	2pt.	Pts.	Fum.
1995—New England NFL	16	15	§368	§1487	4.0	14	30	261	8.7	1	15	1	92	5
1996—New England NFL	16	15	316	1152	3.6	§14	46	333	7.2	3	§17	1	104	4
1997—New England NFL	13	13	274	1160	4.2	4	41	296	7.2	1	5	0	30	3
Pro totals (3 years)	45	43	958	3799	4.0	32	117	890	7.6	5	37	2	226	12

MARTIN, EMANUEL   S   BILLS

PERSONAL: Born July 31, 1969, in Miami. ... 5-11/184. ... Full name: Emanuel C. Martin.

HIGH SCHOOL: Central (Miami).

COLLEGE: Alabama State.

TRANSACTIONS/CAREER NOTES: Signed as non-drafted free agent by Houston Oilers (May 17, 1993). ... Released by Oilers (August 19, 1993). ... Re-signed by Oilers to practice squad (September 29, 1993). ... Activated (October 6, 1993). ... Released by Oilers (October 25, 1993). ... Re-signed by Oilers to practice squad (October 27, 1993). ... Released by Oilers (August 28, 1994). ... Signed by Ottawa Rough Riders of CFL for 1994 season. ... Granted free agency (February 16, 1996). ... Signed by Buffalo Bills (April 4, 1996).

PRO STATISTICS: CFL: 1995—Returned one punt for 33 yards and a touchdown and recovered one fumble.

			INTERCEPTIONS				SACKS
Year Team	G	GS	No.	Yds.	Avg.	TD	No.
1993—Houston NFL	1	0	0	0	...	0	0.0
1994—Ottawa CFL	3	3	0	0	...	0	0.0
1995—Ottawa CFL	17	...	2	12	6.0	0	1.0
1996—Buffalo NFL	16	1	2	35	17.5	0	0.0
1997—Buffalo NFL	16	2	1	12	12.0	0	0.0
CFL totals (2 years)	20	...	2	12	6.0	0	1.0
NFL totals (3 years)	33	3	3	47	15.7	0	0.0
Pro totals (5 years)	53	...	5	59	11.8	0	1.0

M

MARTIN, STEVE   DT   COLTS

PERSONAL: Born May 31, 1974, in St. Paul, Minn. ... 6-4/303. ... Full name: Steve Albert Martin.
HIGH SCHOOL: Jefferson City (Mo.).
COLLEGE: Missouri.
TRANSACTIONS/CAREER NOTES: Selected by Indianapolis Colts in fifth round (151st pick overall) of 1996 NFL draft. ... Signed by Colts (July 5, 1996).
PRO STATISTICS: 1996—Recovered one fumble.

Year Team	G	GS	SACKS
1996—Indianapolis NFL	14	5	1.0
1997—Indianapolis NFL	12	0	0.0
Pro totals (2 years)	26	5	1.0

MARTIN, TONY   WR   FALCONS

PERSONAL: Born September 5, 1965, in Miami. ... 6-0/181. ... Full name: Tony Derrick Martin.
HIGH SCHOOL: Miami Northwestern.
COLLEGE: Bishop (Texas), then Mesa State (Colo.).
TRANSACTIONS/CAREER NOTES: Selected by New York Jets in fifth round (126th pick overall) of 1989 NFL draft. ... Signed by New York Jets for 1989 season. ... Released by Jets (September 4, 1989). ... Signed by Miami Dolphins to developmental squad (September 5, 1989). ... Activated (December 23, 1989). ... On inactive list for one game (1989). ... Granted free agency (February 1, 1992). ... Re-signed by Dolphins (March 10, 1992). ... Traded by Dolphins to San Diego Chargers for fourth-round pick (traded to Arizona) in 1994 draft (March 24, 1994). ... Designated by Chargers as franchise player (February 13, 1997). ... Re-signed by Chargers (May 1, 1997). ... Traded by Chargers to Atlanta Falcons for second-round pick in 1999 draft (June 3, 1998).
CHAMPIONSHIP GAME EXPERIENCE: Played in AFC championship game (1992 and 1994 seasons). ... Played in Super Bowl XXIX (1994 season).
HONORS: Played in Pro Bowl (1996 season).
RECORDS: Shares NFL record for longest pass reception (from Stan Humphries)—99 yards, touchdown (September 18, 1994, at Seattle).
PRO STATISTICS: 1990—Recovered two fumbles. 1992—Attempted one pass without a completion and recovered one fumble. 1994—Attempted one pass without a completion and returned eight kickoffs for 167 yards. 1995—Attempted one pass without a completion.
SINGLE GAME HIGHS (regular season): Receptions—13 (September 10, 1995, vs. Seattle); yards—172 (December 11, 1994, vs. San Francisco); and touchdown receptions—3 (September 28, 1997, vs. Baltimore).
STATISTICAL PLATEAUS: 100-yard receiving games: 1991 (2), 1993 (1), 1994 (2), 1995 (4), 1996 (4), 1997 (2). Total: 15.

			RUSHING				RECEIVING				PUNT RETURNS				TOTALS		
Year Team	G	GS	Att.	Yds.	Avg.	TD	No.	Yds.	Avg.	TD	No.	Yds.	Avg.	TD	TD	2pt.	Pts. Fum.
1990—Miami NFL	16	5	1	8	8.0	0	29	388	13.4	2	26	140	5.4	0	2	...	12	4
1991—Miami NFL	16	0	0	0	...	0	27	434	16.1	2	1	10	10.0	0	2	...	12	2
1992—Miami NFL	16	3	1	-2	-2.0	0	33	553	16.8	2	1	0	0.0	0	2	...	12	2
1993—Miami NFL	12	0	1	6	6.0	0	20	347	17.4	3	0	0	...	0	3	...	18	1
1994—San Diego NFL	16	1	2	-9	-4.5	0	50	885	17.7	7	0	0	...	0	7	0	42	2
1995—San Diego NFL	16	16	0	0	...	0	90	1224	13.6	6	0	0	...	0	6	0	36	3
1996—San Diego NFL	16	16	0	0	...	0	85	1171	13.8	†14	0	0	...	0	14	0	84	0
1997—San Diego NFL	16	16	0	0	...	0	63	904	14.3	6	0	0	...	0	6	0	36	0
Pro totals (8 years)	124	57	5	3	0.6	0	397	5906	14.9	42	28	150	5.4	0	42	0	252	14

MARTIN, WAYNE   DT   SAINTS

PERSONAL: Born October 26, 1965, in Forrest City, Ark. ... 6-5/275. ... Full name: Gerald Wayne Martin.
HIGH SCHOOL: Cross Country (Cherry Valley, Ark.).
COLLEGE: Arkansas (degree in criminal justice, 1990).
TRANSACTIONS/CAREER NOTES: Selected by New Orleans Saints in first round (19th pick overall) of 1989 NFL draft. ... Signed by Saints (August 10, 1989). ... On injured reserve with knee injury (December 19, 1990-remainder of season). ... Granted free agency (March 1, 1993). ... Tendered offer sheet by Washington Redskins (April 8, 1993). ... Offer matched by Saints (April 14, 1993).
HONORS: Named defensive lineman on THE SPORTING NEWS college All-America first team (1988). ... Played in Pro Bowl (1994 season).
PRO STATISTICS: 1989—Recovered two fumbles. 1991—Recovered one fumble. 1992—Recovered two fumbles. 1993—Recovered two fumbles for seven yards. 1995—Intercepted one pass for 12 yards and recovered one fumble. 1996—Recovered one fumble. 1997—Recovered one fumble.

Year Team	G	GS	SACKS
1989—New Orleans NFL	16	0	2.5
1990—New Orleans NFL	11	11	4.0
1991—New Orleans NFL	16	16	3.5
1992—New Orleans NFL	16	16	15.5
1993—New Orleans NFL	16	16	5.0
1994—New Orleans NFL	16	16	10.0
1995—New Orleans NFL	16	16	∞13.0
1996—New Orleans NFL	16	16	11.0
1997—New Orleans NFL	16	16	10.5
Pro totals (9 years)	139	123	75.0

MARTS, LONNIE   LB   OILERS

PERSONAL: Born November 10, 1968, in New Orleans. ... 6-2/241. ... Full name: Lonnie Marts Jr.
HIGH SCHOOL: St. Augustine (New Orleans).
COLLEGE: Tulane (degree in sociology).
TRANSACTIONS/CAREER NOTES: Signed as non-drafted free agent by Kansas City Chiefs (May 1, 1990). ... On injured reserve with ankle injury (September 8, 1990-entire season). ... Granted unconditional free agency (February 17, 1994). ... Signed by Tampa Bay Buccaneers (March 21, 1994). ... Granted unconditional free agency (February 14, 1997). ... Signed by Houston Oilers (April 3, 1997). ... Oilers franchise moved to Tennessee for 1997 season.

M

CHAMPIONSHIP GAME EXPERIENCE: Played in AFC championship game (1993 season).

PRO STATISTICS: 1991—Recovered one fumble. 1992—Recovered one fumble for two yards. 1993—Returned one kickoff for no yards and recovered one fumble. 1994—Recovered two fumbles. 1995—Recovered one fumble. 1996—Recovered two fumbles. 1997—Recovered one fumble.

			INTERCEPTIONS				SACKS
Year Team	G	GS	No.	Yds.	Avg.	TD	No.
1990—Kansas City NFL				Did not play.			
1991—Kansas City NFL	16	2	0	0	...	0	1.0
1992—Kansas City NFL	15	3	1	36	36.0	0	0.0
1993—Kansas City NFL	16	15	1	20	20.0	0	2.0
1994—Tampa Bay NFL	16	14	0	0	...	0	0.0
1995—Tampa Bay NFL	15	13	1	8	8.0	0	0.0
1996—Tampa Bay NFL	16	13	0	0	...	0	7.0
1997—Tennessee NFL	14	14	0	0	...	0	1.0
Pro totals (7 years)	108	74	3	64	21.3	1	11.0

MARYLAND, RUSSELL　　　　　DT　　　　　RAIDERS

PERSONAL: Born March 22, 1969, in Chicago. ... 6-1/279.
HIGH SCHOOL: Whitney-Young (Chicago).
COLLEGE: Miami, Fla. (degree in psychology, 1990).
TRANSACTIONS/CAREER NOTES: Selected by Dallas Cowboys in first round (first pick overall) of 1991 NFL draft. ... Signed by Cowboys (April 22, 1991). ... Granted unconditional free agency (February 16, 1996). ... Signed by Oakland Raiders (February 22, 1996).
CHAMPIONSHIP GAME EXPERIENCE: Played in NFC championship game (1992-1995 seasons). ... Member of Super Bowl championship team (1992, 1993 and 1995 seasons).
HONORS: Named defensive tackle on The Sporting News college All-America second team (1989). ... Outland Trophy winner (1990). ... Named defensive lineman on The Sporting News college All-America first team (1990). ... Played in Pro Bowl (1993 season).
PRO STATISTICS: 1992—Recovered two fumbles for 26 yards and a touchdown. 1993—Recovered two fumbles. 1994—Recovered one fumble.

Year Team	G	GS	SACKS
1991—Dallas NFL	16	7	4.5
1992—Dallas NFL	14	13	2.5
1993—Dallas NFL	16	12	2.5
1994—Dallas NFL	16	16	3.0
1995—Dallas NFL	13	13	2.0
1996—Oakland NFL	16	16	2.0
1997—Oakland NFL	16	16	4.5
Pro totals (7 years)	107	93	21.0

MASON, DERRICK　　　　　WR　　　　　OILERS

M

PERSONAL: Born January 17, 1974, in Detroit. ... 5-10/190. ... Full name: Derrick James Mason.
HIGH SCHOOL: Mumford (Detroit).
COLLEGE: Michigan State.
TRANSACTIONS/CAREER NOTES: Selected by Houston Oilers in fourth round (98th pick overall) of 1997 NFL draft. ... Oilers franchise moved to Tennessee for 1997 season. ... Signed by Oilers (July 19, 1997).
PRO STATISTICS: 1997—Rushed once for minus seven yards.
SINGLE GAME HIGHS (regular season): Receptions—4 (December 14, 1997, vs. Baltimore); yards—47 (December 21, 1997, vs. Pittsburgh); and touchdown receptions—0

			RECEIVING				PUNT RETURNS				KICKOFF RETURNS				TOTALS			
Year Team	G	GS	No.	Yds.	Avg.	TD	No.	Yds.	Avg.	TD	No.	Yds.	Avg.	TD	TD	2pt.	Pts.	Fum.
1997—Tennessee NFL	16	2	14	186	13.3	0	13	95	7.3	0	26	551	21.2	0	0	0	0	5

MASSEY, ROBERT　　　　　CB　　　　　GIANTS

PERSONAL: Born February 17, 1967, in Rock Hill, S.C. ... 5-11/200. ... Full name: Robert Lee Massey.
HIGH SCHOOL: Garinger (Charlotte).
COLLEGE: North Carolina Central (degree in history, 1990).
TRANSACTIONS/CAREER NOTES: Selected by New Orleans Saints in second round (46th pick overall) of 1989 NFL draft. ... Signed by Saints (July 30, 1989). ... Granted free agency (February 1, 1991). ... Rights traded by Saints to Phoenix Cardinals for G Derek Kennard and fifth-round pick (traded to Tampa Bay) in 1992 draft (August 19, 1991). ... On injured reserve with viral hepatitis (October 2-30, 1991). ... Granted free agency (March 1, 1993). ... Re-signed by Cardinals (September 24, 1993). ... Granted roster exemption (September 25-October 19, 1993). ... Granted unconditional free agency (February 17, 1994). ... Signed by Detroit Lions (March 12, 1994). ... Released by Lions (March 29, 1996). ... Signed by Jacksonville Jaguars (April 24, 1996). ... Released by Jaguars (August 24, 1997). ... Signed by New York Giants (August 27, 1997). ... Granted unconditional free agency (February 13, 1998). ... Re-signed by Giants (May 5, 1998).
CHAMPIONSHIP GAME EXPERIENCE: Played in AFC championship game (1996 season).
HONORS: Played in Pro Bowl (1992 season).
RECORDS: Shares NFL single-game record for most touchdowns scored by interception—2 (October 4, 1992, vs. Washington).
PRO STATISTICS: 1989—Ran 54 yards with lateral from punt return. 1990—Recovered two fumbles. 1991—Recovered one fumble for two yards. 1993—Recovered two fumbles. 1994—Returned one punt for three yards and fumbled once.

			INTERCEPTIONS			
Year Team	G	GS	No.	Yds.	Avg.	TD
1989—New Orleans NFL	16	16	5	26	5.2	0
1990—New Orleans NFL	16	16	0	0	...	0
1991—Phoenix NFL	12	5	0	0	...	0

				INTERCEPTIONS			
Year Team	G	GS	No.	Yds.	Avg.	TD	
1992—Phoenix NFL	15	12	5	147	29.4	*3	
1993—Phoenix NFL	10	10	0	0	...	0	
1994—Detroit NFL	16	15	4	25	6.3	0	
1995—Detroit NFL	16	3	0	0	0	0	
1996—Jacksonville NFL	16	2	0	0	...	0	
1997—New York Giants NFL	16	0	0	0	...	0	
Pro totals (9 years)	133	79	14	198	14.1	3	

MATHEWS, JASON　　　　OT　　　　BUCCANEERS

PERSONAL: Born February 9, 1971, in Orange, Texas. ... 6-5/304. ... Full name: Samuel Jason Mathews.
HIGH SCHOOL: Bridge City (Texas).
COLLEGE: Texas A&M.
TRANSACTIONS/CAREER NOTES: Selected by Indianapolis Colts in third round (67th pick overall) of 1994 NFL draft. ... Signed by Colts (July 23, 1994). ... Granted free agency (February 14, 1997). ... Re-signed by Colts (April 30, 1997). ... Granted unconditional free agency (February 13, 1998). ... Signed by Tampa Bay Buccaneers (May 7, 1998).
PLAYING EXPERIENCE: Indianapolis NFL, 1994-1997. ... Games/Games started: 1994 (10/0), 1995 (16/16), 1996 (16/15), 1997 (16/0). Total: 58/31.
CHAMPIONSHIP GAME EXPERIENCE: Played in AFC championship game (1995 season).
PRO STATISTICS: 1996—Recovered one fumble.

MATHIS, DEDRIC　　　　CB　　　　BEARS

PERSONAL: Born September 26, 1973, in Cuero, Texas. ... 5-10/188. ... Brother of Wayne Mathis, outfielder/shortstop in New York Mets organization (1989 and 1990).
HIGH SCHOOL: Cuero (Texas).
COLLEGE: Houston.
TRANSACTIONS/CAREER NOTES: Selected by Indianapolis Colts in second round (51st pick overall) of 1996 NFL draft. ... Signed by Colts (July 10, 1996). ... On injured reserve with knee injury (December 5, 1997-remainder of season). ... Released by Colts (March 18, 1998). ... Signed by Chicago Bears (March 30, 1998).
PLAYING EXPERIENCE: Indianapolis NFL, 1996 and 1997. ... Games/Games started: 1996 (16/6), 1997 (13/4). Total: 29/10.
PRO STATISTICS: 1997—Intercepted one pass for 31 yards.

MATHIS, KEVIN　　　　CB　　　　COWBOYS

PERSONAL: Born April 9, 1974, in Gainesville, Texas. ... 5-9/172.
HIGH SCHOOL: Gainesville (Texas).
COLLEGE: East Texas State.
TRANSACTIONS/CAREER NOTES: Signed as non-drafted free agent by Dallas Cowboys (April 24, 1997).
PRO STATISTICS: 1997—Recovered two fumbles.

			PUNT RETURNS				TOTALS			
Year Team	G	GS	No.	Yds.	Avg.	TD	TD	2pt.	Pts.	Fum.
1997—Dallas NFL	16	3	11	91	8.3	0	0	0	0	2

MATHIS, TERANCE　　　　WR　　　　FALCONS

PERSONAL: Born June 7, 1967, in Detroit, ... 5-10/185.
HIGH SCHOOL: Redan (Stone Mountain, Ga.).
COLLEGE: New Mexico.
TRANSACTIONS/CAREER NOTES: Selected by New York Jets in sixth round (140th pick overall) of 1990 NFL draft. ... Signed by Jets (July 12, 1990). ... Granted unconditional free agency (February 17, 1994). ... Signed by Atlanta Falcons (May 3, 1994). ... Granted unconditional free agency (February 16, 1996). ... Re-signed by Falcons (April 30, 1996).
HONORS: Named wide receiver on THE SPORTING NEWS college All-America first team (1989). ... Played in Pro Bowl (1994 season).
PRO STATISTICS: 1990—Fumbled once. 1991—Fumbled four times and recovered one fumble. 1992—Fumbled twice and recovered one fumble. 1993—Fumbled five times and recovered one fumble. 1994—Recovered one fumble. 1995—Fumbled once. 1996—Recovered one fumble.
SINGLE GAME HIGHS (regular season): Receptions—13 (September 18, 1994, vs. Kansas City); yards—184 (November 19, 1995, vs. St. Louis); and touchdown receptions—3 (November 19, 1995, vs. St. Louis).
STATISTICAL PLATEAUS: 100-yard receiving games: 1992 (1), 1994 (5), 1995 (2), 1996 (2), 1997 (1). Total: 11.

			RUSHING				RECEIVING				PUNT RETURNS				KICKOFF RETURNS				TOTALS		
Year Team	G	GS	Att.	Yds.	Avg.	TD	No.	Yds.	Avg.	TD	No.	Yds.	Avg.	TD	No.	Yds.	Avg.	TD	TD	2pt.	Pts.
1990—N.Y. Jets NFL	16	1	2	9	4.5	0	19	245	12.9	0	11	165	15.0	†1	43	787	18.3	0	1	...	6
1991—N.Y. Jets NFL	16	0	1	19	19.0	0	28	329	11.8	1	23	157	6.8	0	29	599	20.7	0	1	...	6
1992—N.Y. Jets NFL	16	1	3	25	8.3	1	22	316	14.4	3	2	24	12.0	0	28	492	17.6	0	4	...	24
1993—N.Y. Jets NFL	16	3	2	20	10.0	1	24	352	14.7	0	14	99	7.1	0	7	102	14.6	0	1	...	6
1994—Atlanta NFL	16	16	0	0	...	0	111	1342	12.1	11	0	0	...	0	0	0	...	0	11	2	70
1995—Atlanta NFL	14	12	0	0	...	0	78	1039	13.3	9	0	0	...	0	0	0	...	0	9	3	60
1996—Atlanta NFL	16	16	0	0	...	0	69	771	11.2	7	3	19	6.3	0	0	0	...	0	7	1	44
1997—Atlanta NFL	16	16	3	35	11.7	0	62	802	12.9	6	0	0	...	0	0	0	...	0	6	0	36
Pro totals (8 years)	126	65	11	108	9.8	2	413	5196	12.6	37	53	464	8.8	1	107	1980	18.5	0	40	6	252

M

MATTHEWS, BRUCE　　　　　G/C　　　　　OILERS

PERSONAL: Born August 8, 1961, in Arcadia, Calif. ... 6-5/309. ... Full name: Bruce Rankin Matthews. ... Son of Clay Matthews Sr., end with San Francisco 49ers (1950 and 1953-1955); and brother of Clay Matthews Jr., linebacker with Cleveland Browns (1978-1993) and Atlanta Falcons (1994-1996).
HIGH SCHOOL: Arcadia (Calif.).
COLLEGE: Southern California (degree in industrial engineering, 1983).
TRANSACTIONS/CAREER NOTES: Selected by Los Angeles Express in 1983 USFL territorial draft. ... Selected by Houston Oilers in first round (ninth pick overall) of 1983 NFL draft. ... Signed by Oilers (July 24, 1983). ... Granted free agency (February 1, 1987). ... On reserve/unsigned list (August 31-November 3, 1987). ... Re-signed by Oilers (November 4, 1987). ... Granted roster exemption (November 4-7, 1987). ... Granted unconditional free agency (February 17, 1995). ... Re-signed by Oilers (August 8, 1995). ... Oilers franchise moved to Tennessee for 1997 season.
PLAYING EXPERIENCE: Houston NFL, 1983-1996; Tennessee NFL, 1997. ... Games/Games started: 1983 (16/15), 1984 (16/16), 1985 (16/16), 1986 (16/16), 1987 (8/5), 1988 (16/16), 1989 (16/16), 1990 (16/16), 1991 (16/16), 1992 (16/16), 1993 (16/16), 1994 (16/16), 1995 (16/16), 1996 (16/16), 1997 (16/16). Total: 232/228.
HONORS: Named guard on THE SPORTING NEWS college All-America first team (1982). ... Named guard on THE SPORTING NEWS NFL All-Pro team (1988-1990 and 1992). ... Played in Pro Bowl (1988-1994, 1996 and 1997 seasons). ... Named center on THE SPORTING NEWS NFL All-Pro team (1993). ... Named to play in Pro Bowl (1995 season); replaced by Will Shields due to injury.
PRO STATISTICS: 1985—Recovered three fumbles. 1986—Recovered one fumble for seven yards. 1989—Fumbled twice and recovered one fumble for minus 29 yards. 1990—Recovered one fumble. 1991—Fumbled once and recovered one fumble for minus three yards. 1994—Fumbled twice. 1997—Recovered two fumbles.

MATTHEWS, STEVE　　　　　QB　　　　　JAGUARS

PERSONAL: Born October 13, 1970, in Tullahoma, Tenn. ... 6-3/227.
HIGH SCHOOL: Tullahoma (Tenn.).
COLLEGE: Memphis State.
TRANSACTIONS/CAREER NOTES: Selected by Kansas City Chiefs in seventh round (199th pick overall) of 1994 NFL draft. ... On reserve/non-football injury list with knee injury (July 18, 1994-entire season. ... On reserve/non-football injury list with knee injury (July 21, 1995-entire season). ... Assigned by Chiefs to Scottish Claymores in 1996 World League enhancement allocation program (February 19, 1996). ... Claimed on waivers by Jacksonville Jaguars (August 20, 1997).
PRO STATISTICS: 1997—Fumbled once.
SINGLE GAME HIGHS (regular season): Attempts—35 (September 7, 1997, vs. New York Giants); completions—23 (September 7, 1997, vs. New York Giants); yards—252 (September 7, 1997, vs. New York Giants); and touchdown passes—0.
MISCELLANEOUS: Regular-season record as starting NFL quarterback: 1-0.

				PASSING							RUSHING				TOTALS		
Year　Team	G	GS	Att.	Cmp.	Pct.	Yds.	TD	Int.	Avg.	Rat.	Att.	Yds.	Avg.	TD	TD	2pt.	Pts.
1994—Kansas City NFL.........	...	...				Did not play.											
1995—Kansas City NFL.........	...	...				Did not play.											
1996—Scottish W.L.	...	...	205	115	56.1	1560	9	10	7.61	74.8	26	105	4.0	1	1	0	6
1996—Kansas City NFL.........						Did not play.											
1997—Jacksonville NFL........	2	1	40	26	65.0	275	0	0	6.88	84.9	1	10	10.0	0	0	0	0
W.L. totals (1 year)...............	...	...	205	115	56.1	1560	9	10	7.61	74.8	26	105	4.0	1	1	0	6
NFL totals (1 year)...............	2	1	40	26	65.0	275	0	0	6.88	84.9	1	10	10.0	0	0	0	0
Pro totals (2 years)...............	...	...	245	141	57.6	1835	9	10	7.49	76.5	27	115	4.3	1	1	0	6

MAUMALANGA, CHRIS　　　　　DT　　　　　RAMS

PERSONAL: Born December 15, 1971, in Redwood City, Calif. ... 6-3/300. ... Full name: Christian Maumalanga. ... Cousin of Viliami Maumau, defensive tackle, Carolina Panthers. ... Name pronounced MAL-ma-longa.
HIGH SCHOOL: Bishop Montgomery (Torrance, Calif.).
COLLEGE: Kansas.
TRANSACTIONS/CAREER NOTES: Selected by New York Giants in fourth round (128th pick overall) of 1994 NFL draft. ... Signed by Giants (July 18, 1994). ... Released by Giants (August 27, 1995). ... Signed by Arizona Cardinals (September 15, 1995). ... Released by Cardinals (September 25, 1995). ... Re-signed by Cardinals (October 2, 1995). ... Released by Cardinals (October 1, 1996). ... Signed by Kansas City Chiefs (April 7, 1997). ... Released by Chiefs (August 15, 1997). ... Signed by Chicago Bears (November 5, 1997). ... Active for one game with Bears (1997); did not play. ... Released by Bears (December 1, 1997). ... Signed by St. Louis Rams (December 17, 1997). ... Inactive for one game with Rams (1997).
PLAYING EXPERIENCE: New York Giants NFL, 1994; Arizona NFL, 1995 and 1996. ... Games/Games started: 1994 (7/0), 1995 (9/0), 1996 (1/0). Total: 17/0.

MAWAE, KEVIN　　　　　C　　　　　JETS

PERSONAL: Born January 23, 1971, in Leesville, La. ... 6-4/305. ... Full name: Kevin James Mawae. ... Name pronounced ma-WHY.
HIGH SCHOOL: Leesville (La.).
COLLEGE: Louisiana State.
TRANSACTIONS/CAREER NOTES: Selected by Seattle Seahawks in second round (36th pick overall) of 1994 NFL draft. ... Signed by Seahawks (July 21, 1994). ... Granted free agency (February 14, 1997). ... Re-signed by Seahawks (May 5, 1997). ... Granted unconditional free agency (February 13, 1998). ... Signed by New York Jets (February 19, 1998).
PLAYING EXPERIENCE: Seattle NFL, 1994-1997. ... Games/Games started: 1994 (14/11), 1995 (16/16), 1996 (16/16), 1997 (16/16). Total: 62/59.
PRO STATISTICS: 1994—Recovered one fumble. 1996—Recovered two fumbles. 1997—Recovered two fumbles.

MAXIE, BRETT　　　　　S　　　　　PANTHERS

PERSONAL: Born January 13, 1962, in Dallas. ... 6-2/210. ... Full name: Brett Derrell Maxie.
HIGH SCHOOL: James Madison (Dallas).
COLLEGE: Texas Southern.

M

TRANSACTIONS/CAREER NOTES: Signed as non-drafted free agent by New Orleans Saints (June 21, 1985). ... Released by Saints (September 2, 1985). ... Re-signed by Saints (September 3, 1985). ... Granted free agency (February 1, 1990). ... Re-signed by Saints (August 13, 1990). ... Granted free agency (February 1, 1992). ... Re-signed by Saints (August 22, 1992). ... On injured reserve with knee injury (November 19, 1992-remainder of season). ... On injured reserve with knee injury (September 14, 1993-remainder of season). ... Granted unconditional free agency (February 17, 1994). ... Signed by Atlanta Falcons (September 27, 1994). ... Granted unconditional free agency (February 17, 1995). ... Signed by Carolina Panthers (March 9, 1995). ... Released by Panthers (February 20, 1997). ... Signed by San Francisco 49ers (November 19, 1997). ... Granted unconditional free agency (February 13, 1998). ... Signed by Panthers (February 13, 1998).

CHAMPIONSHIP GAME EXPERIENCE: Played in NFC championship game (1996 season). ... Member of 49ers for NFC championship game (1997 season); inactive.

PRO STATISTICS: 1985—Recovered one fumble. 1986—Recovered one fumble. 1987—Credited with two sacks, credited with a safety and returned one punt for 12 yards. 1989—Recovered one fumble. 1991—Recovered one fumble. 1992—Credited with one sack and recovered one fumble. 1995—Recovered one fumble. 1997—Credited with one sack.

			INTERCEPTIONS			
Year Team	G	GS	No.	Yds.	Avg.	TD
1985—New Orleans NFL	16	1	0	0	...	0
1986—New Orleans NFL	15	0	2	15	7.5	0
1987—New Orleans NFL	12	10	3	17	5.7	0
1988—New Orleans NFL	16	16	0	0	...	0
1989—New Orleans NFL	16	2	3	41	13.7	∞1
1990—New Orleans NFL	16	16	2	88	44.0	1
1991—New Orleans NFL	16	16	3	33	11.0	∞1
1992—New Orleans NFL	10	10	2	12	6.0	0
1993—New Orleans NFL	1	1	0	0	...	0
1994—Atlanta NFL	4	2	0	0	...	0
1995—Carolina NFL	16	16	6	59	9.8	0
1996—Carolina NFL	13	13	1	35	35.0	0
1997—San Francisco NFL	2	1	1	0	0.0	0
Pro totals (13 years)	153	104	23	300	13.0	3

MAY, CHAD — QB — BENGALS

PERSONAL: Born September 28, 1971, in West Covina, Calif. ... 6-1/219.
HIGH SCHOOL: Damien (La Verne, Calif.).
COLLEGE: Cal State Fullerton, then Kansas State.
TRANSACTIONS/CAREER NOTES: Selected by Minnesota Vikings in fourth round (111th pick overall) of 1995 NFL draft. ... Signed by Vikings (July 24, 1995). ... Inactive for 16 games (1995 season). ... Released by Vikings (August 25, 1996). ... Signed by Arizona Cardinals (November 5, 1996). ... Inactive for seven games (1996 season). ... Assigned by Cardinals to Frankfurt Galaxy in 1997 World League enhancement allocation program (February 19, 1997). ... Released by Cardinals (August 19, 1997). ... Signed by Cincinnati Bengals (April 9, 1998).

			PASSING							RUSHING				TOTALS		
Year Team	G	GS	Att.	Cmp.	Pct.	Yds.	TD	Int.	Avg.	Rat.	Att.	Yds.	Avg.	TD	TD	2pt.	Pts.
1995—Minnesota NFL								Did not play.									
1996—Arizona NFL								Did not play.									
1997—Frankfurt W.L.	...	...	184	86	46.7	1016	4	3	5.52	64.5	9	24	2.7	0	0	0	0

MAY, DEEMS — TE — SEAHAWKS

M

PERSONAL: Born March 6, 1969, in Lexington, N.C. ... 6-4/263. ... Full name: Bert Deems May Jr.
HIGH SCHOOL: Lexington (N.C.) Senior.
COLLEGE: North Carolina (degree in political science).
TRANSACTIONS/CAREER NOTES: Selected by San Diego Chargers in seventh round (174th pick overall) of 1992 NFL draft. ... Signed by Chargers (July 16, 1992). ... On injured reserve with foot injury (November 2, 1994-remainder of season). ... Granted free agency (February 17, 1995). ... Re-signed by Chargers (May 19, 1995). ... On physically unable to perform list with foot injury (July 18-October 10, 1995). ... Granted unconditional free agency (February 14, 1997). ... Signed by Seattle Seahawks (May 7, 1997).

CHAMPIONSHIP GAME EXPERIENCE: Member of Chargers for Super Bowl XXIX (1994 season); inactive.

PRO STATISTICS: 1996—Recovered one fumble. 1997—Returned one kickoff for eight yards.

SINGLE GAME HIGHS (regular season): Receptions—4 (November 24, 1996, vs. Kansas City); yards—44 (November 17, 1996, vs. Tampa Bay); and touchdown receptions—0.

			RECEIVING				TOTALS			
Year Team	G	GS	No.	Yds.	Avg.	TD	TD	2pt.	Pts.	Fum.
1992—San Diego NFL	16	6	0	0	...	0	0	...	0	0
1993—San Diego NFL	15	1	0	0	...	0	0	...	0	0
1994—San Diego NFL	5	2	2	22	11.0	0	0	0	0	0
1995—San Diego NFL	5	0	0	0	...	0	0	0	0	0
1996—San Diego NFL	16	12	19	188	9.9	0	0	0	0	0
1997—Seattle NFL	16	0	2	21	10.5	0	0	0	0	0
Pro totals (6 years)	73	21	23	231	10.0	0	0	0	0	0

MAYBERRY, JERMANE — OT — EAGLES

PERSONAL: Born August 29, 1973, in Floresville, Texas. ... 6-4/325.
HIGH SCHOOL: Floresville (Texas).
JUNIOR COLLEGE: Navarro (Texas) Junior College.
COLLEGE: Texas A&M-Kingsville.
TRANSACTIONS/CAREER NOTES: Selected by Philadelphia Eagles in first round (25th pick overall) of 1996 NFL draft. ... Signed by Eagles (June 13, 1996).
PLAYING EXPERIENCE: Philadelphia NFL, 1996 and 1997. ... Games/Games started: 1996 (3/1), 1997 (16/16). Total: 19/17.
PRO STATISTICS: 1997—Recovered one fumble.

MAYBERRY, TONY   C   BUCCANEERS

PERSONAL: Born December 8, 1967, in Wurzburg, West Germany. ... 6-4/302. ... Full name: Eino Anthony Mayberry.
HIGH SCHOOL: Hayfield (Alexandria, Va.).
COLLEGE: Wake Forest (degree in sociology).
TRANSACTIONS/CAREER NOTES: Selected by Tampa Bay Buccaneers in fourth round (108th pick overall) of 1990 NFL draft. ... Signed by Buccaneers (July 19, 1990). ... Granted free agency (March 1, 1993). ... Tendered offer sheet by New England Patriots (March 11, 1993). ... Offer matched by Buccaneers (March 18, 1993). ... Granted unconditional free agency (February 16, 1996). ... Re-signed by Buccaneers (February 27, 1996).
PLAYING EXPERIENCE: Tampa Bay NFL, 1990-1997. ... Games/Games started: 1990 (16/1), 1991 (16/16), 1992 (16/16), 1993 (16/16), 1994 (16/16), 1995 (16/16), 1996 (16/16), 1997 (16/16). Total: 128/113.
HONORS: Played in Pro Bowl (1997 season).
PRO STATISTICS: 1991—Fumbled three times for minus 17 yards. 1993—Fumbled once and recovered one fumble for minus six yards. 1994—Recovered one fumble. 1996—Recovered one fumble.

MAYES, DERRICK   WR   PACKERS

PERSONAL: Born January 28, 1974, in Indianapolis. ... 6-0/205. ... Full name: Derrick B. Mayes.
HIGH SCHOOL: North Central (Indianapolis).
COLLEGE: Notre Dame.
TRANSACTIONS/CAREER NOTES: Selected by Green Bay Packers in second round (56th pick overall) of 1996 NFL draft. ... Signed by Packers (July 17, 1996).
CHAMPIONSHIP GAME EXPERIENCE: Member of Packers for NFC championship game (1996 season); inactive. ... Member of Super Bowl championship team (1996 season); inactive. ... Played in NFC championship game (1997 season). ... Played in Super Bowl XXXII (1997 season).
PRO STATISTICS: 1997—Returned 14 punts for 141 yards.
SINGLE GAME HIGHS (regular season): Receptions—4 (November 23, 1997, vs. Dallas); yards—119 (November 16, 1997, vs. Indianapolis); and touchdown receptions—1 (November 18, 1996, vs. Dallas).
STATISTICAL PLATEAUS: 100-yard receiving games: 1997 (1).

| | | | RECEIVING | | | | TOTALS | | | |
Year Team	G	GS	No.	Yds.	Avg.	TD	TD	2pt.	Pts.	Fum.
1996—Green Bay NFL	7	0	6	46	7.7	2	2	0	12	0
1997—Green Bay NFL	12	3	18	290	16.1	0	0	0	0	0
Pro totals (2 years)	19	3	24	336	14.0	2	2	0	12	0

MAYNARD, BRAD   P   GIANTS

PERSONAL: Born February 9, 1974, in Tipton, Ind. ... 6-1/185. ... Full name: Bradley Alan Maynard.
HIGH SCHOOL: Sheridan (Atlanta, Ind.).
COLLEGE: Ball State.
TRANSACTIONS/CAREER NOTES: Selected by New York Giants in third round (95th pick overall) of 1997 NFL draft. ... Signed by Giants for 1997 season.
HONORS: Named punter on THE SPORTING NEWS college All-America second team (1996).

| | | | PUNTING | | | | | |
Year Team	G	GS	No.	Yds.	Avg.	Net avg.	In. 20	Blk.
1997—New York Giants NFL	16	0	*111	*4531	40.8	34.6	*33	1

McADA, RONNIE   QB   PACKERS

PERSONAL: Born March 6, 1974, in Mesquite, Texas. ... 6-3/205. ... Full name: Ronnie Eugene McAda.
HIGH SCHOOL: Mesquite (Texas).
COLLEGE: Army.
TRANSACTIONS/CAREER NOTES: Selected by Green Bay Packers in seventh round (240th pick overall) of 1997 NFL draft. ... Signed by Packers (April 28, 1997). ... On reserve/military list (August 2, 1997-entire season).

McAFEE, FRED   RB   STEELERS

PERSONAL: Born June 20, 1968, in Philadelphia, Miss. ... 5-10/198. ... Full name: Fred Lee McAfee.
HIGH SCHOOL: Philadelphia (Miss.).
COLLEGE: Mississippi College (degree in business).
TRANSACTIONS/CAREER NOTES: Selected by New Orleans Saints in sixth round (154th pick overall) of 1991 NFL draft. ... Signed by Saints (July 14, 1991). ... Released by Saints (August 26, 1991). ... Signed by Saints to practice squad (August 28, 1991). ... Activated (October 18, 1991). ... On injured reserve with shoulder injury (December 15, 1992-remainder of season). ... Granted free agency (February 17, 1994). ... Signed by Arizona Cardinals (August 2, 1994). ... Released by Cardinals (October 31, 1994). ... Signed by Pittsburgh Steelers (November 9, 1994). ... Granted unconditional free agency (February 16, 1996). ... Re-signed by Steelers (April 12, 1996).
CHAMPIONSHIP GAME EXPERIENCE: Played in AFC championship game (1994, 1995 and 1997 seasons). ... Played in Super Bowl XXX (1995 season).
PRO STATISTICS: 1995—Recovered one fumble.
SINGLE GAME HIGHS (regular season): Attempts—28 (November 24, 1991, vs. Atlanta); yards—138 (November 24, 1991, vs. Atlanta); and rushing touchdowns—1 (September 10, 1995, vs. Houston).
STATISTICAL PLATEAUS: 100-yard rushing games: 1991 (1).

M

Year	Team	G	GS	RUSHING Att.	Yds.	Avg.	TD	RECEIVING No.	Yds.	Avg.	TD	KICKOFF RETURNS No.	Yds.	Avg.	TD	TOTALS TD	2pt.	Pts.	Fum.
1991—New Orleans NFL		9	0	109	494	4.5	2	1	8	8.0	0	1	14	14.0	0	2	...	12	2
1992—New Orleans NFL		14	1	39	114	2.9	1	1	16	16.0	0	19	393	20.7	0	1	...	6	0
1993—New Orleans NFL		15	4	51	160	3.1	1	1	3	3.0	0	28	580	20.7	0	1	...	6	3
1994—Arizona NFL		7	0	2	-5	-2.5	1	1	4	4.0	0	7	113	16.1	0	1	0	6	1
—Pittsburgh NFL		6	0	16	56	3.5	1	0	0	...	0	0	0	...	0	1	0	6	0
1995—Pittsburgh NFL		16	1	39	156	4.0	1	15	88	5.9	0	5	56	11.2	0	1	0	6	0
1996—Pittsburgh NFL		14	0	7	17	2.4	0	5	21	4.2	0	0	0	...	0	0	0	0	0
1997—Pittsburgh NFL		14	0	13	41	3.2	0	2	44	22.0	0	0	0	...	0	0	0	0	1
Pro totals (7 years)		95	6	276	1033	3.7	7	26	184	7.1	0	60	1156	19.3	0	7	0	42	7

McBURROWS, GERALD   S   RAMS

PERSONAL: Born October 7, 1973, in Detroit. ... 5-11/205. ... Full name: Gerald Lance McBurrows.
HIGH SCHOOL: Martin Luther King (Detroit).
COLLEGE: Kansas.
TRANSACTIONS/CAREER NOTES: Selected by St. Louis Rams in seventh round (214th pick overall) of 1995 NFL draft. ... Signed by Rams (June 16, 1995). ... On injured reserve with knee injury (October 29, 1997-remainder of season). ... Granted free agency (February 13, 1998). ... Re-signed by Rams (April 24, 1998).
PLAYING EXPERIENCE: St. Louis NFL, 1995-1997. ... Games/Games started: 1995 (14/3), 1996 (16/7), 1997 (8/3). Total: 38/13.
PRO STATISTICS: 1995—Credited with one sack. 1996—Intercepted one pass for three yards.

McCAFFREY, ED   WR   BRONCOS

PERSONAL: Born August 17, 1968, in Allentown, Pa. ... 6-5/215.
HIGH SCHOOL: Allentown (Pa.) Central Catholic.
COLLEGE: Stanford.
TRANSACTIONS/CAREER NOTES: Selected by New York Giants in third round (83rd pick overall) of 1991 NFL draft. ... Signed by Giants (July 23, 1991). ... Granted free agency (February 17, 1994). ... Signed by San Francisco 49ers (July 24, 1994). ... Granted unconditional free agency (February 17, 1995). ... Signed by Denver Broncos (March 7, 1995).
CHAMPIONSHIP GAME EXPERIENCE: Played in NFC championship game (1994 season). ... Member of Super Bowl championship team (1994 and 1997 seasons). ... Played in AFC championship game (1997 season).
HONORS: Named wide receiver on THE SPORTING NEWS college All-America second team (1990).
PRO STATISTICS: 1995—Rushed once for minus one yard. 1997—Recovered two fumbles.
SINGLE GAME HIGHS (regular season): Receptions—9 (December 24, 1995, vs. Oakland); yards—111 (November 30, 1997, vs. San Diego); and touchdown receptions—3 (October 20, 1996, vs. Baltimore).
STATISTICAL PLATEAUS: 100-yard receiving games: 1992 (1), 1997 (1). Total: 2.

Year	Team	G	GS	RECEIVING No.	Yds.	Avg.	TD	TOTALS TD	2pt.	Pts.	Fum.
1991—New York Giants NFL		16	0	16	146	9.1	0	0	...	0	0
1992—New York Giants NFL		16	3	49	610	12.4	5	5	...	30	2
1993—New York Giants NFL		16	1	27	335	12.4	2	2	...	12	0
1994—San Francisco NFL		16	0	11	131	11.9	2	2	0	12	0
1995—Denver NFL		16	5	39	477	12.2	2	2	1	14	1
1996—Denver NFL		15	15	48	553	11.5	7	7	0	42	0
1997—Denver NFL		15	15	45	590	13.1	8	8	0	48	0
Pro totals (7 years)		110	39	235	2842	12.1	26	26	1	158	3

M

McCARDELL, KEENAN   WR   JAGUARS

PERSONAL: Born January 6, 1970, in Houston. ... 6-1/184. ... Full name: Keenan Wayne McCardell.
HIGH SCHOOL: Waltrip (Houston).
COLLEGE: UNLV.
TRANSACTIONS/CAREER NOTES: Selected by Washington Redskins in 12th round (326th pick overall) of 1991 NFL draft. ... On injured reserve with knee injury (August 20, 1991-entire season). ... Granted unconditional free agency (February 1, 1992). ... Signed by Cleveland Browns (March 24, 1992). ... Released by Browns (September 1, 1992). ... Re-signed by Browns to practice squad (September 3, 1992). ... Activated (October 6, 1992). ... Released by Browns (October 13, 1992). ... Re-signed by Browns to practice squad (October 14, 1992). ... Activated (November 14, 1992). ... Released by Browns (November 19, 1992). ... Re-signed by Browns to practice squad (November 20, 1992). ... Activated (December 26, 1992). ... Released by Browns (September 22, 1993). ... Signed by Chicago Bears to practice squad (November 2, 1993). ... Signed by Browns off Bears practice squad (November 24, 1993). ... Granted free agency (February 17, 1994). ... Re-signed by Browns (March 4, 1994). ... Granted unconditional free agency (February 16, 1996). ... Signed by Jacksonville Jaguars (March 2, 1996).
CHAMPIONSHIP GAME EXPERIENCE: Played in AFC championship game (1996 season).
HONORS: Played in Pro Bowl (1996 season).
PRO STATISTICS: 1995—Returned 13 punts for 93 yards and returned nine kickoffs for 161 yards. 1996—Returned one punt for two yards and recovered three fumbles.
SINGLE GAME HIGHS (regular season): Receptions—16 (October 20, 1996, vs. St. Louis); yards—232 (October 20, 1996, vs. St. Louis); and touchdown receptions—2 (December 7, 1997, vs. New England).
STATISTICAL PLATEAUS: 100-yard receiving games: 1995 (1), 1996 (3), 1997 (4). Total: 8.

Year	Team	G	GS	RECEIVING No.	Yds.	Avg.	TD	TOTALS TD	2pt.	Pts.	Fum.
1991—Washington NFL				Did not play.							
1992—Cleveland NFL		2	0	1	8	8.0	0	0	...	0	0
1993—Cleveland NFL		6	3	13	234	18.0	4	4	...	24	0
1994—Cleveland NFL		13	3	10	182	18.2	0	0	0	0	0
1995—Cleveland NFL		16	5	56	709	12.7	4	4	0	24	0
1996—Jacksonville NFL		16	15	85	1129	13.3	3	3	2	22	1
1997—Jacksonville NFL		16	16	85	1164	13.7	5	5	0	30	0
Pro totals (6 years)		69	42	250	3426	13.7	16	16	2	100	1

McCLEON, DEXTER　　　　CB　　　　RAMS

PERSONAL: Born October 9, 1973, in Meridian, Miss. ... 5-10/200. ... Full name: Dexter Keith McCleon.
HIGH SCHOOL: Meridian (Miss.).
COLLEGE: Clemson.
TRANSACTIONS/CAREER NOTES: Selected by St. Louis Rams in second round (40th pick overall) of 1997 NFL draft. ... Signed by Rams (July 3, 1997).
PRO STATISTICS: 1997—Credited with one sack.
MISCELLANEOUS: Selected by Minnesota Twins organization in 13th round of free-agent baseball draft (June 3, 1993); did not sign.

| | | | INTERCEPTIONS | | | |
Year Team	G	GS	No.	Yds.	Avg.	TD
1997—St. Louis NFL	16	1	1	0	0.0	0

McCLESKEY, J.J.　　　　CB　　　　CARDINALS

PERSONAL: Born April 10, 1970, in Knoxville, Tenn. ... 5-8/184. ... Full name: Tommy Joe McCleskey.
HIGH SCHOOL: Karns Comprehensive (Knoxville, Tenn.).
COLLEGE: Tennessee.
TRANSACTIONS/CAREER NOTES: Signed as non-drafted free agent by New Orleans Saints (May 7, 1993). ... Released by Saints (August 24, 1993). ... Re-signed by Saints to practice squad (August 31, 1993). ... Activated (December 23, 1993). ... Released by Saints (August 23, 1994). ... Re-signed by Saints (September 20, 1994). ... On injured reserve with hamstring injury (October 16-18, 1996). ... Claimed on waivers by Arizona Cardinals (October 18, 1996). ... Granted free agency (February 14, 1997). ... Re-signed by Cardinals for 1997 season. ... Granted unconditional free agency (February 13, 1998). ... Re-signed by Cardinals (February 16, 1998).
PLAYING EXPERIENCE: New Orleans NFL, 1994 and 1995; New Orleans (5)-Arizona (5) NFL, 1996; Arizona NFL, 1997. ... Games/Games started: 1994 (13/0), 1995 (14/1), 1996 (N.O.-5/0; Ariz.-5/0; Total: 10/0), 1997 (13/0). Total: 50/1.
PRO STATISTICS: 1994—Recovered one fumble. 1995—Intercepted one pass for no yards, returned one kickoff for no yards and recovered one fumble. 1997—Intercepted one pass for 15 yards and credited with one sack.

McCLOUD, TYRUS　　　　LB　　　　RAVENS

PERSONAL: Born November 23, 1974, in Fort Lauderdale. ... 6-1/250. ... Full name: Tyrus Kamall McCloud.
HIGH SCHOOL: Nova (Fort Lauderdale).
COLLEGE: Louisville.
TRANSACTIONS/CAREER NOTES: Selected by Baltimore Ravens in fourth round (118th pick overall) of 1997 NFL draft. ... Signed by Ravens (July 10, 1997).
PLAYING EXPERIENCE: Baltimore NFL, 1997. ... Games/Games started: 16/0.
HONORS: Named inside linebacker on THE SPORTING NEWS college All-America second team (1996).
PRO STATISTICS: 1997—Fumbled once and recovered one fumble.

McCOLLUM, ANDY　　　　C　　　　SAINTS

PERSONAL: Born June 2, 1970, in Akron, Ohio. ... 6-4/295. ... Full name: Andrew Jon McCollum.
HIGH SCHOOL: Revere (Richfield, Ohio).
COLLEGE: Toledo.
TRANSACTIONS/CAREER NOTES: Played in Arena League with Milwaukee Mustangs (1994). ... Signed by Cleveland Browns (June 1994). ... Released by Browns (August 28, 1994). ... Re-signed by Browns to practice squad (August 30, 1994). ... Signed by New Orleans Saints off Browns practice squad (November 15, 1994). ... Assigned by Saints to Barcelona Dragons in 1995 World League enhancement allocation program (February 20, 1995).
PLAYING EXPERIENCE: Barcelona W.L., 1995; New Orleans NFL, 1995-1997. ... Games/Games started: W.L.: 1995 (games played unavailable); NFL: 1995 (11/9), 1996 (16/16), 1997 (16/16). Total: 43/41.
PRO STATISTICS: 1996—Recovered one fumble.

McCOMBS, TONY　　　　OL　　　　CARDINALS

PERSONAL: Born August 24, 1974, in Hopkinsville, Ky. ... 6-2/246. ... Full name: Antonias Orlando McCombs.
HIGH SCHOOL: Christian County (Hopkinsville, Ky.).
COLLEGE: Eastern Kentucky.
TRANSACTIONS/CAREER NOTES: Selected by Arizona Cardinals in sixth round (188th pick overall) of 1997 NFL draft. ... Signed by Cardinals (June 2, 1997).
PLAYING EXPERIENCE: Arizona NFL, 1997. ... Games/Games started: 12/0.

McCORMACK, HURVIN　　　　DL　　　　COWBOYS

PERSONAL: Born April 6, 1972, in Brooklyn, N.Y. ... 6-5/284.
HIGH SCHOOL: New Dorp (Staten Island, N.Y.).
COLLEGE: Indiana.
TRANSACTIONS/CAREER NOTES: Signed as non-drafted free agent by Dallas Cowboys (April 28, 1994). ... Granted unconditional free agency (February 14, 1997). ... Re-signed by Cowboys (July 1997). ... Granted unconditional free agency (February 13, 1998). ... Re-signed by Cowboys (March 9, 1998).

M

PLAYING EXPERIENCE: Dallas NFL, 1994-1997. ... Games/Games started: 1994 (4/0), 1995 (14/2), 1996 (16/4), 1997 (13/0). Total: 47/6.
CHAMPIONSHIP GAME EXPERIENCE: Member of Cowboys for NFC championship game (1994 season); did not play. ... Played in NFC championship game (1995 season). ... Member of Super Bowl championship team (1995 season).
PRO STATISTICS: 1995—Credited with two sacks. 1996—Credited with 2 1/2 sacks. 1997—Credited with 1/2 sack.

McCORVEY, KEZ　　　　WR　　　　LIONS

PERSONAL: Born January 23, 1972, in Gautier, Miss. ... 6-0/190.
HIGH SCHOOL: Pascagoula (Miss.).
COLLEGE: Florida State.
TRANSACTIONS/CAREER NOTES: Selected by Detroit Lions in fifth round (156th pick overall) of 1995 NFL draft. ... Signed by Lions (July 19, 1995). ... Released by Lions (October 17, 1997). ... Re-signed by Lions (October 21, 1997). ... Granted free agency (February 13, 1998). ... Re-signed by Lions (April 17, 1998).
PLAYING EXPERIENCE: Detroit NFL, 1995-1997. ... Games/Games started: 1995 (1/0), 1996 (1/0), 1997 (7/0). Total: 9/0.
PRO STATISTICS: 1997—Caught two passes for nine yards.
SINGLE GAME HIGHS (regular season): Receptions—1 (December 21, 1997, vs. New York Jets); yards—6 (December 21, 1997, vs. New York Jets); and touchdown receptions—0.

McCOY, TONY　　　　NT　　　　COLTS

PERSONAL: Born June 10, 1969, in Orlando. ... 6-0/282. ... Full name: Anthony Bernard McCoy.
HIGH SCHOOL: Maynard Evans (Orlando).
COLLEGE: Florida.
TRANSACTIONS/CAREER NOTES: Selected by Indianapolis Colts in fourth round (105th pick overall) of 1992 NFL draft. ... Signed by Colts (July 17, 1992). ... Granted free agency (February 17, 1995). ... Re-signed by Colts (June 7, 1995).
CHAMPIONSHIP GAME EXPERIENCE: Played in AFC championship game (1995 season).
PRO STATISTICS: 1992—Recovered one fumble. 1994—Recovered one fumble. 1996—Recovered one fumble.

Year　Team	G	GS	SACKS
1992—Indianapolis NFL	16	3	1.0
1993—Indianapolis NFL	6	0	0.0
1994—Indianapolis NFL	15	15	6.0
1995—Indianapolis NFL	16	16	2.5
1996—Indianapolis NFL	15	15	5.0
1997—Indianapolis NFL	16	11	2.5
Pro totals (6 years)	84	60	17.0

McCRARY, FRED　　　　FB　　　　SAINTS

PERSONAL: Born September 19, 1972, in Naples, Fla. ... 6-0/232. ... Full name: Freddy Demetrius McCrary.
HIGH SCHOOL: Naples (Fla.).
COLLEGE: Mississippi State.
TRANSACTIONS/CAREER NOTES: Selected by Philadelphia Eagles in sixth round (208th pick overall) of 1995 NFL draft. ... Signed by Eagles (June 27, 1995). ... Released by Eagles (August 25, 1996). ... Signed by New Orleans Saints (March 5, 1997).
PRO STATISTICS: 1995—Returned one kickoff for one yard. 1997—Returned two kickoffs for 26 yards.
SINGLE GAME HIGHS (regular season): Attempts—5 (November 23, 1997, vs. Atlanta); yards—13 (November 23, 1997, vs. Atlanta); and rushing touchdowns—1 (September 10, 1995, vs. Arizona).

			RUSHING				RECEIVING				TOTALS			
Year　Team	G	GS	Att.	Yds.	Avg.	TD	No.	Yds.	Avg.	TD	TD	2pt.	Pts.	Fum.
1995—Philadelphia NFL	13	5	3	1	0.3	1	9	60	6.7	0	1	0	6	0
1996—					Did not play.									
1997—New Orleans NFL	7	0	8	15	1.9	0	4	17	4.3	0	0	0	0	0
Pro totals (2 years)	20	5	11	16	1.5	1	13	77	5.9	0	1	0	6	0

McCRARY, MICHAEL　　　　DE　　　　RAVENS

PERSONAL: Born July 7, 1970, in Vienna, Va. ... 6-4/270.
HIGH SCHOOL: George C. Marshall (Falls Church, Va.).
COLLEGE: Wake Forest.
TRANSACTIONS/CAREER NOTES: Selected by Seattle Seahawks in seventh round (170th pick overall) of 1993 NFL draft. ... Signed by Seahawks (July 13, 1993). ... Granted free agency (February 16, 1996). ... Re-signed by Seahawks (June 6, 1996). ... Granted unconditional free agency (February 14, 1997). ... Signed by Baltimore Ravens (April 7, 1997).
PRO STATISTICS: 1996—Recovered one fumble. 1997—Recovered two fumbles.

Year　Team	G	GS	SACKS
1993—Seattle NFL	15	0	4.0
1994—Seattle NFL	16	0	1.5
1995—Seattle NFL	11	0	1.0
1996—Seattle NFL	16	13	▲13.5
1997—Baltimore NFL	15	15	9.0
Pro totals (5 years)	73	28	29.0

McCULLOUGH, GEORGE　　　　DB　　　　OILERS

PERSONAL: Born February 18, 1975, in Galveston, Texas. ... 5-10/187. ... Full name: George Wayne McCullough Jr.
HIGH SCHOOL: Ball (Galveston, Texas).
COLLEGE: Baylor.

TRANSACTIONS/CAREER NOTES: Selected by Houston Oilers in fifth round (143rd pick overall) of 1997 NFL draft. ... Oilers franchise moved to Tennessee for 1997 season. ... Signed by Oilers (July 19, 1997). ... Released by Oilers (August 25, 1997). ... Re-signed by Oilers to practice squad (August 26, 1997). ... Activated (December 5, 1997). ... Assigned by Oilers to Barcelona Dragons in 1998 NFL Europe enhancement allocation program (February 18, 1998).
PLAYING EXPERIENCE: Tennessee NFL, 1997. ... Games/Games started: 2/0.

McDANIEL, ED — LB — VIKINGS

PERSONAL: Born February 23, 1969, in Battesburg, S.C. ... 5-11/230.
HIGH SCHOOL: Battesburg (S.C.)-Leesville.
COLLEGE: Clemson.
TRANSACTIONS/CAREER NOTES: Selected by Minnesota Vikings in fifth round (125th pick overall) of 1992 NFL draft. ... Signed by Vikings (July 20, 1992). ... Released by Vikings (August 31, 1992). ... Re-signed by Vikings to practice squad (September 1, 1992). ... Activated (November 5, 1992). ... On injured reserve with knee injury (August 25, 1996-entire season).
PLAYING EXPERIENCE: Minnesota NFL, 1992-1995. ... Games: 1992 (8), 1993 (7), 1994 (16), 1995 (16). Total: 47.
PRO STATISTICS: 1995—Recovered one fumble.

Year Team	G	GS	INTERCEPTIONS No.	Yds.	Avg.	TD	SACKS No.
1992—Minnesota NFL	8	0	0	0	...	0	0.0
1993—Minnesota NFL	7	1	0	0	...	0	0.0
1994—Minnesota NFL	16	16	1	0	0.0	0	1.5
1995—Minnesota NFL	16	16	1	3	3.0	0	4.5
1996—Minnesota NFL			Did not play.				
1997—Minnesota NFL	16	16	1	18	18.0	0	1.5
Pro totals (5 years)	63	49	3	21	7.0	0	7.5

McDANIEL, EMMANUEL — DB — COLTS

PERSONAL: Born July 27, 1972, in Griffin, Ga. ... 5-9/180.
HIGH SCHOOL: Jonesboro (Ga.).
COLLEGE: East Carolina.
TRANSACTIONS/CAREER NOTES: Selected by Carolina Panthers in fourth round (111th pick overall) of 1996 NFL draft. ... Signed by Panthers (July 20, 1996). ... Released by Panthers (August 26, 1997). ... Signed by Indianapolis Colts (November 27, 1997).
PLAYING EXPERIENCE: Carolina NFL, 1996; Indianapolis NFL, 1997. ... Games/Games started: 1996 (2/0), 1997 (3/0). Total: 5/0.
CHAMPIONSHIP GAME EXPERIENCE: Member of Panthers for NFC championship game (1996 season); inactive.

McDANIEL, RANDALL — G — VIKINGS

PERSONAL: Born December 19, 1964, in Phoenix. ... 6-3/279. ... Full name: Randall Cornell McDaniel.
HIGH SCHOOL: Agua Fria Union (Avondale, Ariz.).
COLLEGE: Arizona State (degree in physical education, 1988).
TRANSACTIONS/CAREER NOTES: Selected by Minnesota Vikings in first round (19th pick overall) of 1988 NFL draft. ... Signed by Vikings (July 22, 1988). ... Granted free agency (February 1, 1991). ... Re-signed by Vikings (July 22, 1991). ... Designated by Vikings as transition player (February 25, 1993). ... Free agency status changed by Vikings from transitional to unconditional (February 17, 1994). ... Re-signed by Vikings (April 21, 1994). ... Designated by Vikings as franchise player (February 13, 1997). ... Re-signed by Vikings (February 21, 1997).
PLAYING EXPERIENCE: Minnesota NFL, 1988-1997. ... Games/Games started: 1988 (16/15), 1989 (14/13), 1990 (16/16), 1991 (16/16), 1992 (16/16), 1993 (16/16), 1994 (16/16), 1995 (16/16), 1996 (16/16), 1997 (16/16). Total: 158/156.
HONORS: Named guard on THE SPORTING NEWS college All-America second team (1987). ... Played in Pro Bowl (1989-1997 seasons). ... Named guard on THE SPORTING NEWS NFL All-Pro team (1991-1994, 1996 and 1997).
PRO STATISTICS: 1991—Recovered one fumble. 1994—Recovered one fumble. 1996—Rushed twice for one yard.

McDANIEL, TERRY — CB

PERSONAL: Born February 8, 1965, in Saginaw, Mich. ... 5-10/180. ... Full name: Terence Lee McDaniel.
HIGH SCHOOL: Saginaw (Mich.).
COLLEGE: Tennessee.
TRANSACTIONS/CAREER NOTES: Selected by Los Angeles Raiders in first round (ninth pick overall) of 1988 NFL draft. ... Signed by Raiders (July 13, 1988). ... On injured reserve with broken leg (September 14, 1988-remainder of season). ... Granted free agency (February 1, 1992). ... Re-signed by Raiders (August 12, 1992). ... Designated by Raiders as transition player (February 25, 1993). ... Raiders franchise moved to Oakland (July 21, 1995). ... Granted unconditional free agency (February 14, 1997). ... Re-signed by Raiders (February 14, 1997). ... Released by Raiders (June 5, 1998).
CHAMPIONSHIP GAME EXPERIENCE: Played in AFC championship game (1990 season).
HONORS: Named defensive back on THE SPORTING NEWS college All-America second team (1987). ... Played in Pro Bowl (1992-1996 seasons).
PRO STATISTICS: 1989—Credited with one sack. 1990—Credited with two sacks, recovered two fumbles for 44 yards and one touchdown. 1991—Recovered one fumble. 1992—Recovered one fumble for 40 yards. 1994—Recovered three fumbles for 48 yards and one touchdown. 1997—Fumbled once.

Year Team	G	GS	INTERCEPTIONS No.	Yds.	Avg.	TD
1988—Los Angeles Raiders NFL	2	2	0	0	...	0
1989—Los Angeles Raiders NFL	16	15	3	21	7.0	0
1990—Los Angeles Raiders NFL	16	13	3	20	6.7	0
1991—Los Angeles Raiders NFL	16	16	0	0	...	0

Year Team	G	GS	No.	Yds.	Avg.	TD
1992—Los Angeles Raiders NFL	16	16	4	180	45.0	0
1993—Los Angeles Raiders NFL	16	16	5	87	17.4	▲1
1994—Los Angeles Raiders NFL	16	16	7	103	14.7	2
1995—Oakland NFL	16	16	6	46	7.7	▲1
1996—Oakland NFL	16	15	5	150	30.0	1
1997—Oakland NFL	13	12	1	17	17.0	0
Pro totals (10 years)	143	137	34	624	18.4	5

McDANIELS, PELLOM — DE — CHIEFS

PERSONAL: Born February 21, 1968, in San Jose, Calif. ... 6-3/285. ... Full name: Pellom McDaniels III.
HIGH SCHOOL: Silver Creek (San Jose, Calif.).
COLLEGE: Oregon State (degree in communications and political science).
TRANSACTIONS/CAREER NOTES: Selected by Birmingham Fire in fifth round of 1991 World League draft. ... Signed as free agent by Philadelphia Eagles (June 19, 1991). ... Released by Eagles (August 12, 1991). ... Signed by Kansas City Chiefs (June 5, 1992). ... Released by Chiefs (August 31, 1992). ... Re-signed by Chiefs to practice squad (September 2, 1992). ... Released by Chiefs (September 16, 1992). ... Re-signed by Chiefs for 1993 season. ... On injured reserve with shoulder injury (December 20, 1994-remainder of season).
CHAMPIONSHIP GAME EXPERIENCE: Played in AFC championship game (1993 season).
PRO STATISTICS: 1994—Recovered one fumble. 1995—Returned one kickoff for no yards. 1997—Recovered one fumble.

Year Team	G	GS	SACKS
1991—Birmingham W.L.	10	...	3.0
1992—Birmingham W.L.	10	...	3.5
1993—Kansas City NFL	10	0	0.0
1994—Kansas City NFL	12	3	2.0
1995—Kansas City NFL	16	2	2.0
1996—Kansas City NFL	9	1	0.0
1997—Kansas City NFL	16	6	3.5
W.L. totals (2 years)	20	...	6.5
NFL totals (5 years)	63	12	7.5
Pro totals (7 years)	83	...	14.0

McDONALD, RICARDO — LB — BEARS

PERSONAL: Born November 8, 1969, in Kingston, Jamaica. ... 6-2/240. ... Full name: Ricardo Milton McDonald. ... Twin brother of Devon McDonald, linebacker with Indianapolis Colts (1993-1995) and Arizona Cardinals (1996).
HIGH SCHOOL: Eastside (Paterson, N.J.).
COLLEGE: Pittsburgh.
TRANSACTIONS/CAREER NOTES: Selected by Cincinnati Bengals in fourth round (88th pick overall) of 1992 NFL draft. ... Signed by Bengals (July 24, 1992). ... On injured reserve with knee injury (December 24, 1993-remainder of season). ... Granted free agency (February 17, 1995). ... Re-signed by Bengals (March 6, 1995). ... Granted unconditional free agency (February 16, 1996). ... Re-signed by Bengals (March 8, 1996). ... Granted unconditional free agency (February 13, 1998). ... Signed by Chicago Bears (May 12, 1998).
PRO STATISTICS: 1992—Intercepted one pass for no yards and recovered one fumble for four yards. 1995—Recovered one fumble.

Year Team	G	GS	SACKS
1992—Cincinnati NFL	16	13	0.0
1993—Cincinnati NFL	14	12	1.0
1994—Cincinnati NFL	13	13	1.0
1995—Cincinnati NFL	16	15	5.0
1996—Cincinnati NFL	16	15	5.0
1997—Cincinnati NFL	13	12	1.0
Pro totals (6 years)	88	80	13.0

M

McDONALD, TIM — S — 49ERS

PERSONAL: Born January 6, 1965, in Fresno, Calif. ... 6-2/219. ... Full name: Timothy McDonald.
HIGH SCHOOL: Edison (Fresno, Calif.).
COLLEGE: Southern California.
TRANSACTIONS/CAREER NOTES: Selected by St. Louis Cardinals in second round (34th pick overall) of 1987 NFL draft. ... Signed by Cardinals (August 2, 1987). ... On injured reserve with broken ankle (September 1-December 12, 1987). ... Cardinals franchise moved to Phoenix (March 15, 1988). ... Granted free agency (February 1, 1990). ... Re-signed by Cardinals (August 21, 1990). ... On injured reserve with broken leg and ankle (December 3, 1991-remainder of season). ... Designated by Cardinals as franchise player (February 25, 1993). ... Signed by San Francisco 49ers (April 7, 1993); Cardinals received first-round pick (OT Ernest Dye) in 1993 draft as compensation.
CHAMPIONSHIP GAME EXPERIENCE: Played in NFC championship game (1993, 1994 and 1997 seasons). ... Member of Super Bowl championship team (1994 season).
HONORS: Named defensive back on THE SPORTING NEWS college All-America second team (1984). ... Named defensive back on THE SPORTING NEWS college All-America first team (1985). ... Played in Pro Bowl (1989 and 1992-1995 seasons). ... Named to play in Pro Bowl (1991 season); replaced by Shaun Gayle due to injury.
PRO STATISTICS: 1988—Recovered one fumble for nine yards. 1989—Recovered one fumble for one yard. 1990—Recovered one fumble. 1991—Recovered one fumble. 1992—Recovered three fumbles for two yards. 1993—Recovered one fumble for 15 yards. 1994—Recovered one fumble for 49 yards and a touchdown. 1996—Recovered one fumble. 1997—Recovered three fumbles.

Year Team	G	GS	INTERCEPTIONS No.	Yds.	Avg.	TD	SACKS No.
1987—St. Louis NFL	3	0	0	0	...	0	0.0
1988—Phoenix NFL	16	15	2	11	5.5	0	2.0
1989—Phoenix NFL	16	16	7	‡140	20.0	∞1	0.0
1990—Phoenix NFL	16	16	4	63	15.8	0	0.0

Year Team	G	GS	INTERCEPTIONS				SACKS
			No.	Yds.	Avg.	TD	No.
1991—Phoenix NFL	13	13	5	36	7.2	0	0.0
1992—Phoenix NFL	16	16	2	35	17.5	0	0.5
1993—San Francisco NFL	16	16	3	23	7.7	0	0.0
1994—San Francisco NFL	16	16	2	79	39.5	1	0.0
1995—San Francisco NFL	16	16	4	135	33.8	†2	0.0
1996—San Francisco NFL	16	16	2	14	7.0	0	1.0
1997—San Francisco NFL	15	15	3	34	11.3	0	0.0
Pro totals (11 years)	159	155	34	570	16.8	4	3.5

McDUFFIE, O.J.   WR   DOLPHINS

PERSONAL: Born December 2, 1969, in Marion, Ohio. ... 5-10/194. ... Full name: Otis James McDuffie.
HIGH SCHOOL: Hawken (Gates Mills, Ohio).
COLLEGE: Penn State (degree in labor and industrial relations).
TRANSACTIONS/CAREER NOTES: Selected by Miami Dolphins in first round (25th pick overall) of 1993 NFL draft. ... Signed by Dolphins (July 18, 1993).
HONORS: Named wide receiver on THE SPORTING NEWS college All-America second team (1992).
POST SEASON RECORDS: Shares NFL postseason career and single-game records for most two-point conversions—1 ... (December 30, 1995, vs. Buffalo).
PRO STATISTICS: 1993—Fumbled four times and recovered one fumble. 1994—Fumbled three times. 1995—Fumbled four times and recovered two fumbles. 1996—Fumbled six times and recovered three fumbles. 1997—Recovered two fumbles for three yards.
SINGLE GAME HIGHS (regular season): Receptions—9 (November 23, 1997, vs. New England); yards—137 (October 27, 1997, vs. Chicago); and touchdown receptions—2 (October 20, 1996, vs. Philadelphia).
STATISTICAL PLATEAUS: 100-yard receiving games: 1994 (1), 1996 (2), 1997 (3). Total: 6.

Year Team	G	GS	RUSHING				RECEIVING				PUNT RETURNS				KICKOFF RETURNS				TOTALS		
			Att.	Yds.	Avg.	TD	No.	Yds.	Avg.	TD	No.	Yds.	Avg.	TD	No.	Yds.	Avg.	TD	TD	2pt.	Pts.
1993—Miami NFL	16	0	1	-4	-4.0	0	19	197	10.4	0	28	317	11.3	†2	32	755	23.6	0	2	...	12
1994—Miami NFL	15	3	5	32	6.4	0	37	488	13.2	3	32	228	7.1	0	36	767	21.3	0	3	0	18
1995—Miami NFL	16	16	3	6	2.0	0	62	819	13.2	8	24	163	6.8	0	23	564	24.5	0	8	1	50
1996—Miami NFL	16	16	2	7	3.5	0	74	918	12.4	8	22	212	9.6	0	0	0	...	0	8	0	48
1997—Miami NFL	16	16	0	0	...	0	76	943	12.4	1	2	4	2.0	0	0	0	...	0	1	0	6
Pro totals (5 years)	79	51	11	41	3.7	0	268	3365	12.6	20	108	924	8.6	2	91	2086	22.9	0	22	1	128

McELROY, LEELAND   RB   CARDINALS

PERSONAL: Born June 25, 1974, in Beaumont, Texas. ... 5-9/212. ... Brother of Reggie McElroy, offensive tackle with four NFL teams (1992-1996).
HIGH SCHOOL: Central (Beaumont, Texas).
COLLEGE: Texas A&M.
TRANSACTIONS/CAREER NOTES: Selected after junior season by Arizona Cardinals in second round (32nd pick overall) of 1996 NFL draft. ... Signed by Cardinals (August 7, 1996).
HONORS: Named kick returner on THE SPORTING NEWS college All-America first team (1994). ... Named kick returner on THE SPORTING NEWS college All-America second team (1995).
PRO STATISTICS: 1996—Recovered one fumble.
SINGLE GAME HIGHS (regular season): Attempts—18 (September 14, 1997, vs. Washington); yards—90 (December 8, 1996, vs. Dallas); and rushing touchdowns—1 (September 7, 1997, vs. Dallas).

Year Team	G	GS	RUSHING				RECEIVING				KICKOFF RETURNS				TOTALS			
			Att.	Yds.	Avg.	TD	No.	Yds.	Avg.	TD	No.	Yds.	Avg.	TD	TD	2pt.	Pts.	Fum.
1996—Arizona NFL	16	6	89	305	3.4	1	5	41	8.2	1	54	1148	21.3	0	2	0	12	3
1997—Arizona NFL	14	8	135	424	3.1	2	7	32	4.6	0	0	0	...	0	2	0	12	3
Pro totals (2 years)	30	14	224	729	3.3	3	12	73	6.1	1	54	1148	21.3	0	4	0	24	6

McELROY, RAY   CB   COLTS

PERSONAL: Born July 31, 1972, in Bellwood, Ill. ... 5-11/207. ... Full name: Raymond Edward McElroy.
HIGH SCHOOL: Proviso West (Hillside, Ill.).
COLLEGE: Eastern Illinois.
TRANSACTIONS/CAREER NOTES: Selected by Indianapolis Colts in fourth round (114th pick overall) of 1995 NFL draft. ... Signed by Colts (July 12, 1995). ... Granted free agency (February 13, 1998). ... Re-signed by Colts (February 24, 1998).
PLAYING EXPERIENCE: Indianapolis NFL, 1995-1997. ... Games/Games started: 1995 (16/0), 1996 (16/5), 1997 (16/4). Total: 48/9.
CHAMPIONSHIP GAME EXPERIENCE: Played in AFC championship game (1995 season).
PRO STATISTICS: 1997—Returned blocked field goal 42 yards for a touchdown.

McGEE, DELL   CB   CARDINALS

PERSONAL: Born September 7, 1973, in Columbus, Ga. ... 5-8/185.
HIGH SCHOOL: Kendrick (Columbus, Ga.).
COLLEGE: Auburn.
TRANSACTIONS/CAREER NOTES: Selected by Arizona Cardinals in fifth round (162nd pick overall) of 1996 NFL draft. ... Signed by Cardinals (July 21, 1996). ... Released by Cardinals (August 25, 1996). ... Re-signed by Cardinals to practice squad (August 27, 1996). ... On injured reserve with shoulder injury (August 19, 1997-entire season).

McGEE, TONY   TE   BENGALS

PERSONAL: Born April 21, 1971, in Terre Haute, Ind. ... 6-3/246.
HIGH SCHOOL: Terre Haute (Ind.) South.
COLLEGE: Michigan.
TRANSACTIONS/CAREER NOTES: Selected by Cincinnati Bengals in second round (37th pick overall) of 1993 NFL draft. ... Signed by Bengals (July 20, 1993). ... Granted free agency (February 16, 1996). ... Re-signed by Bengals for 1996 season.
PRO STATISTICS: 1994—Returned one kickoff for four yards.
SINGLE GAME HIGHS (regular season): Receptions—8 (December 22, 1996, vs. Indianapolis); yards—118 (September 3, 1995, vs. Indianapolis); and touchdown receptions—2 (November 9, 1997, vs. Indianapolis).
STATISTICAL PLATEAUS: 100-yard receiving games: 1993 (1), 1995 (1). Total: 2.

| | | | RECEIVING | | | | TOTALS | | |
Year Team	G	GS	No.	Yds.	Avg.	TD	TD	2pt.	Pts.	Fum.
1993—Cincinnati NFL	15	15	44	525	11.9	0	0	...	0	1
1994—Cincinnati NFL	16	16	40	492	12.3	1	1	0	6	0
1995—Cincinnati NFL	16	16	55	754	13.7	4	4	0	24	2
1996—Cincinnati NFL	16	16	38	446	11.7	4	4	0	24	0
1997—Cincinnati NFL	16	16	34	414	12.2	6	6	1	38	0
Pro totals (5 years)	79	79	211	2631	12.5	15	15	1	92	3

McGILL, LENNY   CB   FALCONS

PERSONAL: Born May 31, 1971, in Long Beach, Calif. ... 6-1/202. ... Full name: Charles Leonard McGill.
HIGH SCHOOL: Orange Glen (Escondido, Calif.).
COLLEGE: Arizona State.
TRANSACTIONS/CAREER NOTES: Signed as non-drafted free agent by Green Bay Packers (May 2, 1994). ... On injured reserve with torn knee ligament (November 1, 1994-remainder of season). ... Traded by Packers to Atlanta Falcons for RB Robert Baldwin (June 6, 1996). ... Granted unconditional free agency (February 14, 1997). ... Re-signed by Falcons (April 1, 1997). ... Released by Falcons (August 24, 1997). ... Re-signed by Falcons (September 3, 1997). ... Granted unconditional free agency (February 13, 1998). ... Re-signed by Falcons (April 1, 1998).
CHAMPIONSHIP GAME EXPERIENCE: Played in NFC championship game (1995 season).
PRO STATISTICS: 1995—Recovered one fumble. 1996—Recovered one fumble.

| | | | INTERCEPTIONS | | | |
Year Team	G	GS	No.	Yds.	Avg.	TD
1994—Green Bay NFL	6	0	2	16	8.0	0
1995—Green Bay NFL	15	1	0	0	...	0
1996—Atlanta NFL	16	8	0	0	...	0
1997—Atlanta NFL	15	0	1	7	7.0	0
Pro totals (4 years)	52	9	3	23	7.7	0

McGINEST, WILLIE   LB

PERSONAL: Born December 11, 1971, in Long Beach, Calif. ... 6-5/255. ... Full name: William McGinest.
HIGH SCHOOL: Polytechnic (Long Beach, Calif.).
COLLEGE: Southern California.
TRANSACTIONS/CAREER NOTES: Selected by New England Patriots in first round (fourth pick overall) of 1994 NFL draft. ... Signed by Patriots (May 17, 1994). ... Granted unconditional free agency (February 13, 1998).
CHAMPIONSHIP GAME EXPERIENCE: Played in AFC championship game (1996 season). ... Played in Super Bowl XXXI (1996 season).
PRO STATISTICS: 1994—Recovered two fumbles. 1996—Intercepted one pass for 46 yards and a touchdown and recovered two fumbles (including one in end zone for a touchdown). 1997—Recovered three fumbles.

Year Team	G	GS	SACKS
1994—New England NFL	16	7	4.5
1995—New England NFL	16	16	11.0
1996—New England NFL	16	16	9.5
1997—New England NFL	11	11	2.0
Pro totals (4 years)	59	50	27.0

M

McGLOCKTON, CHESTER   DT   CHIEFS

PERSONAL: Born September 16, 1969, in Whiteville, N.C. ... 6-4/315.
HIGH SCHOOL: Whiteville (N.C.).
COLLEGE: Clemson.
TRANSACTIONS/CAREER NOTES: Selected after junior season by Los Angeles Raiders in first round (16th pick overall) of 1992 NFL draft. ... Signed by Raiders for 1992 season. ... On injured reserve (January 11, 1994-remainder of 1993 playoffs). ... Raiders franchise moved to Oakland (July 21, 1995). ... Designated by Raiders as franchise player (February 13, 1998). ... Tendered offer sheet by Kansas City Chiefs (April 10, 1998). ... Raiders declined to match offer (April 17, 1998).
HONORS: Named defensive tackle on THE SPORTING NEWS NFL All-Pro team (1994). ... Played in Pro Bowl (1994-1997 seasons).
PRO STATISTICS: 1993—Intercepted one pass for 19 yards. 1994—Recovered one fumble. 1995—Recovered two fumbles. 1997—Recovered one fumble.

Year Team	G	GS	SACKS
1992—Los Angeles Raiders NFL	10	0	3.0
1993—Los Angeles Raiders NFL	16	16	7.0
1994—Los Angeles Raiders NFL	16	16	9.5
1995—Oakland NFL	16	16	7.5
1996—Oakland NFL	16	16	8.0
1997—Oakland NFL	16	16	4.5
Pro totals (6 years)	90	80	39.5

McGRUDER, MIKE   CB

PERSONAL: Born May 6, 1964, in Cleveland Heights, Ohio. ... 5-11/184. ... Full name: Michael J.P. McGruder. ... Nickname: Scooter.
HIGH SCHOOL: Cleveland Heights (Ohio).
COLLEGE: Kent (degree in business management).
TRANSACTIONS/CAREER NOTES: Signed as non-drafted free agent by Ottawa Rough Riders of CFL (May 1985). ... Released by Rough Riders (July 1985). ... Signed by Saskatchewan Roughriders of CFL (April 1986). ... Granted free agency (March 1, 1989). ... Signed by Green Bay Packers (April 26, 1989). ... Released by Packers (September 19, 1989). ... Re-signed by Packers to developmental squad (September 22, 1989). ... Released by Packers (January 29, 1990). ... Signed by Miami Dolphins (April 3, 1990). ... On injured reserve with shoulder injury (September 14, 1990-remainder of season). ... Granted unconditional free agency (February 1-April 1, 1991). ... Re-signed by Dolphins for 1991 season. ... Granted free agency (February 1, 1992). ... Re-signed by Dolphins (July 20, 1992). ... Released by Dolphins (August 31, 1992). ... Signed by San Francisco 49ers (October 6, 1992). ... Granted unconditional free agency (February 17, 1994). ... Signed by Tampa Bay Buccaneers (June 2, 1994). ... Granted unconditional free agency (February 16, 1996). ... Signed by New England Patriots (April 5, 1996). ... Released by Patriots (August 30, 1996). ... Re-signed by Patriots (September 4, 1996). ... Released by Patriots (September 5, 1996). ... Re-signed by Patriots (September 10, 1996). ... Released by Patriots (September 30, 1997).
CHAMPIONSHIP GAME EXPERIENCE: Played in NFC championship game (1992 and 1993 seasons). ... Played in AFC championship game (1996 season). ... Played in Super Bowl XXXI (1996 season).
PRO STATISTICS: CFL: 1986—Recovered one fumble and ran minus four yards with lateral from punt return. 1987—Recovered four fumbles for 26 yards. 1988—Recovered two fumbles for 20 yards and one touchdown. NFL: 1989—Recovered one fumble. 1991—Recovered one fumble. 1992—Recovered one fumble for seven yards. 1995—Recovered one fumble. 1996—Credited with a 1/2 sack. 1997—Credited with one sack.

| | | | INTERCEPTIONS | | | |
Year Team	G	GS	No.	Yds.	Avg.	TD
1986—Saskatchewan CFL	14	...	5	35	7.0	0
1987—Saskatchewan CFL	14	...	5	26	5.2	0
1988—Saskatchewan CFL	18	...	7	89	12.7	0
1989—Green Bay NFL	2	0	0	0	...	0
1990—Miami NFL	1	0	0	0	...	0
1991—Miami NFL	16	5	0	0	...	0
1992—San Francisco NFL	9	3	0	0	...	0
1993—San Francisco NFL	16	5	5	89	17.8	1
1994—Tampa Bay NFL	15	3	1	0	0.0	0
1995—Tampa Bay NFL	16	2	0	0	...	0
1996—New England NFL	14	0	0	0	...	0
1997—New England NFL	3	0	0	0	...	0
CFL totals (3 years)	46	...	17	150	8.8	0
NFL totals (9 years)	92	18	6	89	14.8	1
Pro totals (12 years)	138	...	23	239	10.4	1

McGUIRE, KAIPO   WR

PERSONAL: Born January 16, 1974, in Honolulu. ... 5-10/175. ... Full name: Kaiponohea McGuire.
HIGH SCHOOL: St. Louis (Pearl City, Hawaii).
COLLEGE: Brigham Young (degree in psychology, 1996).
TRANSACTIONS/CAREER NOTES: Signed as non-drafted free agent by Indianapolis Colts (May 5, 1997). ... Released by Colts (August 24, 1997). ... Re-signed by Colts to practice squad (August 25, 1997). ... Activated (September 13, 1997). ... Released by Colts (October 7, 1997).
PLAYING EXPERIENCE: Indianapolis NFL, 1997. ... Games/Games started: 3/0.
SINGLE GAME HIGHS (regular season): Receptions—0; yards—0; and touchdown receptions—0.

McIVER, EVERETT   G   COWBOYS

PERSONAL: Born August 5, 1970, in Fayetteville, N.C. ... 6-5/318.
HIGH SCHOOL: 71st Senior (Fayetteville, N.C.).
COLLEGE: Elizabeth (N.C.) City State.
TRANSACTIONS/CAREER NOTES: Signed as non-drafted free agent by San Diego Chargers (April 27, 1993). ... Claimed on waivers by Dallas Cowboys (July 27, 1993). ... Released by Cowboys (August 30, 1993). ... Re-signed by Cowboys to practice squad (August 31, 1993). ... Released by Cowboys (December 7, 1993). ... Signed by New York Jets to practice squad (December 10, 1993). ... Activated (January 2, 1994). ... Assigned by Jets to London Monarchs in 1996 World League enhancement allocation program (February 19, 1996). ... Released by Jets (August 7, 1996). ... Signed by Miami Dolphins (August 13, 1996). ... Released by Dolphins (September 2, 1996). ... Re-signed by Dolphins (October 7, 1996). ... Granted unconditional free agency (February 13, 1998). ... Signed by Dallas Cowboys (February 23, 1998).
PLAYING EXPERIENCE: New York Jets NFL, 1994 and 1995; London W.L., 1996; Miami NFL, 1996 and 1997. ... Games/Games started: 1994 (4/0), 1995 (14/4), 1996 (W.L.-games played unavailable; NFL-7/5), 1997 (14/14). Total NFL: 39/23.

McKEEHAN, JAMES   TE   OILERS

PERSONAL: Born August 9, 1973, in Houston. ... 6-3/251. ... Full name: James Bell McKeehan.
HIGH SCHOOL: Willis (Texas).
COLLEGE: Texas A&M.
TRANSACTIONS/CAREER NOTES: Signed as non-drafted free agent by Seattle Seahawks (April 25, 1995). ... Released by Seahawks (August 21, 1995). ... Re-signed by Seahawks to practice squad (August 28, 1995). ... Signed by Houston Oilers off Seahawks practice squad (November 30, 1995). ... Oilers franchise moved to Tennessee for 1997 season. ... Released by Oilers (August 25, 1997). ... Re-signed by Oilers (October 1, 1997). ... Released by Oilers (November 5, 1997). ... Re-signed by Oilers (November 21, 1997).
PLAYING EXPERIENCE: Houston NFL, 1996; Tennessee NFL, 1997. ... Games/Games started: 1996 (14/0), 1997 (10/0). Total: 24/0.
PRO STATISTICS: 1996—Returned two kickoffs for six yards.
SINGLE GAME HIGHS (regular season): Receptions—0; yards—0; and touchdown receptions—0.

McKENZIE, KEITH   LB   PACKERS

PERSONAL: Born October 17, 1973, in Detroit. ... 6-3/255. ... Full name: Keith Derrick McKenzie.
HIGH SCHOOL: Highland Park (Mich.).
COLLEGE: Ball State.
TRANSACTIONS/CAREER NOTES: Selected by Green Bay Packers in seventh round (252nd pick overall) of 1996 NFL draft. ... Signed by Packers (July 15, 1996).
CHAMPIONSHIP GAME EXPERIENCE: Member of Super Bowl championship team (1996 season). ... Played in NFC championship game (1996 and 1997 seasons). ... Played in Super Bowl XXXII (1997 season).

Year Team	G	GS	SACKS
1996—Green Bay NFL	10	0	1.0
1997—Green Bay NFL	16	0	1.5
Pro totals (2 years)	26	0	2.5

McKENZIE, RALEIGH   C/G   CHARGERS

PERSONAL: Born February 8, 1963, in Knoxville, Tenn. ... 6-2/283. ... Twin brother of Reggie McKenzie, linebacker with Los Angeles Raiders (1985-1988), Phoenix Cardinals (1989), Montreal Machine of World League (1990) and San Francisco 49ers (1992).
HIGH SCHOOL: Austin-East (Knoxville, Tenn.).
COLLEGE: Tennessee.
TRANSACTIONS/CAREER NOTES: Selected by Washington Redskins in 11th round (290th pick overall) of 1985 NFL draft. ... Signed by Redskins (June 20, 1985). ... Granted free agency (February 1, 1992). ... Re-signed by Redskins for 1992 season. ... Granted unconditional free agency (February 17, 1995). ... Signed by Philadelphia Eagles (March 28, 1995). ... Granted unconditional free agency (February 14, 1997). ... Signed by San Diego Chargers (February 20, 1997).
PLAYING EXPERIENCE: Washington NFL, 1985-1994; Philadelphia NFL, 1995 and 1996; San Diego NFL, 1997. ... Games/Games started: 1985 (6/0), 1986 (15/5), 1987 (12/12), 1988 (16/14), 1989 (15/8), 1990 (16/12), 1991 (16/14), 1992 (16/16), 1993 (16/16), 1994 (16/16), 1995 (16/16), 1996 (16/16), 1997 (16/16). Total: 192/161.
CHAMPIONSHIP GAME EXPERIENCE: Played in NFC championship game (1986, 1987 and 1991 seasons). ... Member of Super Bowl championship team (1987 and 1991 seasons).
PRO STATISTICS: 1994—Recovered one fumble. 1995—Recovered one fumble. 1997—Recovered one fumble.

McKINNON, RONALD   LB   CARDINALS

PERSONAL: Born September 20, 1973, in Fort Rucker Army Base, Ala. ... 6-0/240.
HIGH SCHOOL: Elba (Ala.).
COLLEGE: North Alabama.
TRANSACTIONS/CAREER NOTES: Signed as non-drafted free agent by Arizona Cardinals (April 23, 1996).
PLAYING EXPERIENCE: Arizona NFL, 1996 and 1997. ... Games/Games started: 1996 (16/0), 1997 (16/16). Total: 32/16.
PRO STATISTICS: 1996—Rushed once for minus four yards. 1997—Rushed once for three yards, intercepted three passes for 40 yards and credited with one sack.

McKNIGHT, JAMES   WR   SEAHAWKS

PERSONAL: Born June 17, 1972, in Orlando. ... 6-1/198.
HIGH SCHOOL: Apopka (Fla.).
COLLEGE: Liberty (Va.).
TRANSACTIONS/CAREER NOTES: Signed as non-drafted free agent by Seattle Seahawks (April 29, 1994). ... Released by Seahawks (August 28, 1994). ... Re-signed by Seahawks to practice squad (August 29, 1994). ... Activated (November 19, 1994). ... Granted unconditional free agency (February 13, 1998). ... Re-signed by Seahawks (February 17, 1998).
PRO STATISTICS: 1995—Returned one kickoff for four yards and recovered one fumble. 1996—Returned three kickoffs for 86 yards and recovered one fumble. 1997—Returned one kickoff for 14 yards.
SINGLE GAME HIGHS (regular season): Receptions—5 (November 30, 1997, vs. Atlanta); yards—100 (October 26, 1997, vs. Oakland); and touchdown receptions—1 (December 21, 1997, vs. San Francisco).
STATISTICAL PLATEAUS: 100-yard receiving games: 1997 (1).

Year Team	G	GS	RECEIVING				TOTALS			
			No.	Yds.	Avg.	TD	TD	2pt.	Pts.	Fum.
1994—Seattle NFL	2	0	1	25	25.0	1	1	0	6	0
1995—Seattle NFL	16	0	6	91	15.2	0	0	0	0	1
1996—Seattle NFL	16	0	1	73	73.0	0	0	0	0	0
1997—Seattle NFL	12	5	34	637	*18.7	6	6	0	36	1
Pro totals (4 years)	46	5	42	826	19.7	7	7	0	42	2

McKYER, TIM   CB

PERSONAL: Born September 5, 1963, in Orlando. ... 6-0/178. ... Full name: Timothy Bernard McKyer.
HIGH SCHOOL: Lincoln (Port Arthur, Texas).
COLLEGE: Texas-Arlington.
TRANSACTIONS/CAREER NOTES: Selected by San Francisco 49ers in third round (64th pick overall) of 1986 NFL draft. ... Signed by 49ers (July 20, 1986). ... On suspended list (October 7-24, 1989). ... Traded by 49ers to Miami Dolphins for 11th-round pick (S Anthony Shelton) in 1990 draft and second-round pick (traded to Cincinnati) in 1991 draft (April 22, 1990). ... Granted free agency (February 1, 1991). ... Traded by Dolphins to Atlanta Falcons for third-round pick (RB Aaron Craver) in 1991 draft (April 22, 1991). ... Granted unconditional free agency (March 1, 1993). ... Signed by Detroit Lions (August 20, 1993). ... Granted unconditional free agency (February 17, 1994). ... Signed by Pittsburgh Steelers (August 24, 1994). ... Selected by Carolina Panthers from Steelers in NFL expansion draft (February 15, 1995). ... Granted

unconditional free agency (February 16, 1996). ... Signed by Falcons (July 22, 1996). ... On injured reserve with broken arm (December 11, 1996-remainder of season). ... Released by Falcons (February 26, 1997). ... Signed by Denver Broncos (August 20, 1997). ... Granted unconditional free agency (February 13, 1998).

CHAMPIONSHIP GAME EXPERIENCE: Played in NFC championship game (1988 and 1989 seasons). ... Member of Super Bowl championship team (1988, 1989 and 1997 seasons). ... Played in AFC championship game (1994 and 1997 seasons).

PRO STATISTICS: 1986—Returned one kickoff for 15 yards and returned one punt for five yards. 1991—Ran six yards with lateral from fumble recovery. 1992—Credited with one sack. 1993—Recovered one fumble for 23 yards. 1995—Recovered two fumbles. 1996—Credited with one sack and recovered two fumbles. 1997—Credited with one sack.

				INTERCEPTIONS		
Year Team	G	GS	No.	Yds.	Avg.	TD
1986—San Francisco NFL	16	16	6	33	5.5	1
1987—San Francisco NFL	12	12	2	0	0.0	0
1988—San Francisco NFL	16	16	7	11	1.6	0
1989—San Francisco NFL	7	1	1	18	18.0	0
1990—Miami NFL	16	16	4	40	10.0	0
1991—Atlanta NFL	16	16	∞6	24	4.0	0
1992—Atlanta NFL	16	15	1	0	0.0	0
1993—Detroit NFL	15	4	2	10	5.0	0
1994—Pittsburgh NFL	16	2	0	0	...	0
1995—Carolina NFL	16	16	3	99	33.0	1
1996—Atlanta NFL	8	7	0	0	...	0
1997—Denver NFL	16	1	1	0	0.0	0
Pro totals (12 years)	170	122	33	235	7.1	2

McMANUS, TOM   LB   JAGUARS

PERSONAL: Born July 30, 1970, in Buffalo Grove, Ill. ... 6-2/255. ... Full name: Thomas Edward McManus.
HIGH SCHOOL: Wheeling (Ill.).
COLLEGE: Boston College.
TRANSACTIONS/CAREER NOTES: Signed as non-drafted free agent by New Orleans Saints (May 7, 1993). ... Released by Saints (August 24, 1993). ... Signed by Jacksonville Jaguars (February 1, 1995). ... On injured reserve with knee injury (July 30, 1997-entire season). ... Granted free agency (February 13, 1998). ... Re-signed by Jaguars (June 3, 1998).
PLAYING EXPERIENCE: Jacksonville NFL, 1995 and 1996. ... Games/Games started: 1995 (14/2), 1996 (16/11). Total: 30/13.
CHAMPIONSHIP GAME EXPERIENCE: Played in AFC championship game (1996 season).

McMILLIAN, MARK   CB   CHIEFS

PERSONAL: Born April 29, 1970, in Los Angeles. ... 5-7/148. ... Nephew of Gary Davis, running back with Miami Dolphins (1976-1979) and Tampa Bay Buccaneers (1980 and 1981). ... Name pronounced mik-MILL-en.
HIGH SCHOOL: John F. Kennedy (Granada Hills, Calif.).
JUNIOR COLLEGE: Glendale (Calif.) College.
COLLEGE: Alabama.
TRANSACTIONS/CAREER NOTES: Selected by Philadelphia Eagles in 10th round (272nd pick overall) of 1992 NFL draft. ... Signed by Eagles (July 20, 1992). ... Granted unconditional free agency (February 16, 1996). ... Signed by New Orleans Saints (February 29, 1996). ... Released by Saints (May 15, 1997). ... Signed by Kansas City Chiefs (June 16, 1997).
PRO STATISTICS: 1993—Fumbled once and recovered one fumble. 1994—Recovered one fumble. 1995—Recovered two fumbles for minus one yard. 1996—Recovered one fumble for minus six yards.

				INTERCEPTIONS		
Year Team	G	GS	No.	Yds.	Avg.	TD
1992—Philadelphia NFL	16	3	1	0	0.0	0
1993—Philadelphia NFL	16	12	2	25	12.5	0
1994—Philadelphia NFL	16	16	2	2	1.0	0
1995—Philadelphia NFL	16	16	3	27	9.0	0
1996—New Orleans NFL	16	16	2	4	2.0	0
1997—Kansas City NFL	16	2	▲8	*274	*34.3	†3
Pro totals (6 years)	96	65	18	332	18.4	3

McMULLEN, TYPAIL   DB   GIANTS

PERSONAL: Born September 3, 1973, in Brenham, Texas. ... 6-2/190. ... Full name: Typail Wahkuts McMullen.
HIGH SCHOOL: Dunbar-Struggs (Lubbock, Texas).
COLLEGE: Texas A&M, then Middle Tennessee State.
TRANSACTIONS/CAREER NOTES: Signed as non-drafted free agent by New York Giants (April 28, 1997). ... On injured reserve with knee injury (August 19, 1997-entire season). ... Granted free agency (February 13, 1998).

McNAIR, STEVE   QB   OILERS

PERSONAL: Born February 14, 1973, in Mount Olive, Miss. ... 6-2/229. ... Full name: Steve LaTreal McNair. ... Brother of Fred McNair, quarterback with Toronto Argonauts of the CFL (1991) and London Monarchs of the World League (1992).
HIGH SCHOOL: Mount Olive (Miss.).
COLLEGE: Alcorn State.
TRANSACTIONS/CAREER NOTES: Selected by Houston Oilers in first round (third pick overall) of 1995 NFL draft. ... Signed by Oilers (July 25, 1995). ... Oilers franchise moved to Tennessee for 1997 season.
HONORS: Walter Payton Award winner (1994).

M

PRO STATISTICS: 1995—Fumbled three times and recovered two fumbles for minus two yards. 1996—Fumbled seven times and recovered four fumbles. 1997—Led league with 16 fumbles and recovered seven fumbles for minus two yards.
SINGLE GAME HIGHS (regular season): Attempts—45 (December 14, 1997, vs. Baltimore); completions—24 (December 8, 1996, vs. Jacksonville); yards—308 (December 8, 1996, vs. Jacksonville); and touchdown passes—3 (October 12, 1997, vs. Cincinnati).
STATISTICAL PLATEAUS: 300-yard passing games: 1996 (1).
MISCELLANEOUS: Regular-season record as starting NFL quarterback: 12-10 (.545).

Year Team	G	GS	PASSING								RUSHING				TOTALS		
			Att.	Cmp.	Pct.	Yds.	TD	Int.	Avg.	Rat.	Att.	Yds.	Avg.	TD	TD	2pt.	Pts.
1995—Houston NFL..............	6	2	80	41	51.3	569	3	1	7.11	81.7	11	38	3.5	0	0	0	0
1996—Houston NFL..............	9	4	143	88	61.5	1197	6	4	8.37	90.6	31	169	5.5	2	2	0	12
1997—Tennessee NFL...........	16	16	415	216	52.0	2665	14	13	6.42	70.4	101	674	*6.7	8	8	0	48
Pro totals (3 years).............	31	22	638	345	54.1	4431	23	18	6.95	76.3	143	881	6.2	10	10	0	60

McNEIL, RYAN · CB · RAMS

PERSONAL: Born October 4, 1970, in Fort Pierce, Fla. ... 6-2/192. ... Full name: Ryan Darrell McNeil.
HIGH SCHOOL: Fort Pierce (Fla.) Westwood.
COLLEGE: Miami (Fla.).
TRANSACTIONS/CAREER NOTES: Selected by Detroit Lions in second round (33rd pick overall) of 1993 NFL draft. ... Signed by Lions (August 25, 1993). ... Granted unconditional free agency (February 14, 1997). ... Signed by St. Louis Rams (July 7, 1997). ... Designated by Rams as franchise player (February 13, 1998).
HONORS: Named defensive back on THE SPORTING NEWS college All-America second team (1992).
PRO STATISTICS: 1995—Recovered two fumbles. 1996—Recovered two fumbles. 1997—Fumbled once and recovered one fumble.

Year Team	G	GS	INTERCEPTIONS			
			No.	Yds.	Avg.	TD
1993—Detroit NFL...	16	2	2	19	9.5	0
1994—Detroit NFL...	14	13	1	14	14.0	0
1995—Detroit NFL...	16	16	2	26	13.0	0
1996—Detroit NFL...	16	16	5	14	2.8	0
1997—St. Louis NFL..	16	16	*9	127	14.1	1
Pro totals (5 years)...	78	63	19	200	10.5	1

McPHAIL, JERRIS · WR · DOLPHINS

PERSONAL: Born June 26, 1972, in Clinton, N.C. ... 5-11/210. ... Full name: Jerris Cornelius McPhail.
HIGH SCHOOL: Clinton (N.C.).
COLLEGE: Mount Olive (N.C.) College, then East Carolina.
TRANSACTIONS/CAREER NOTES: Selected by Miami Dolphins in fifth round (134th pick overall) of 1996 NFL draft. ... Signed by Dolphins (July 15, 1996). ... On injured reserve with fractured left wrist (December 17, 1996-remainder of season).
PRO STATISTICS: 1996—Recovered one fumble.
SINGLE GAME HIGHS (regular season): Attempts—3 (December 14, 1997, vs. Indianapolis); yards—77 (October 27, 1997, vs. Chicago); and rushing touchdowns—1 (October 27, 1997, vs. Chicago).

M

Year Team	G	GS	RUSHING				RECEIVING				KICKOFF RETURNS				TOTALS			
			Att.	Yds.	Avg.	TD	No.	Yds.	Avg.	TD	No.	Yds.	Avg.	TD	TD	2pt.	Pts.	Fum.
1996—Miami NFL	9	1	6	28	4.7	0	20	282	14.1	0	15	335	22.3	0	0	0	0	2
1997—Miami NFL	14	1	17	146	8.6	1	34	262	7.7	1	15	314	20.9	0	2	0	12	1
Pro totals (2 years)...............	23	2	23	174	7.6	1	54	544	10.1	1	30	649	21.6	0	2	0	12	3

McTYER, TIM · CB · EAGLES

PERSONAL: Born December 14, 1975, in Los Angeles ... 5-11/181.
HIGH SCHOOL: Washington (Los Angeles).
JUNIOR COLLEGE: Los Angeles Southwest.
COLLEGE: Brigham Young.
TRANSACTIONS/CAREER NOTES: Signed as non-drafted free agent by Indianapolis Colts (April 25, 1997). ... Released by Colts (August 18, 1997). ... Signed by Philadelphia Eagles to practice squad (August 27, 1997). ... Released by Eagles (September 2, 1997). ... Re-signed by Eagles to practice squad (September 18, 1997). ... Activated (October 17, 1997).
PLAYING EXPERIENCE: Philadelphia NFL, 1997. ... Games/Games started: 10/0.

McWILLIAMS, JOHNNY · TE · CARDINALS

PERSONAL: Born December 14, 1972, in Ontario, Calif. ... 6-4/271.
HIGH SCHOOL: Pomona (Calif.).
COLLEGE: Southern California.
TRANSACTIONS/CAREER NOTES: Selected by Arizona Cardinals in third round (64th pick overall) of 1996 NFL draft. ... Signed by Cardinals (August 28, 1996). ... On reserve/did not report list (August 25-September 9, 1996).
SINGLE GAME HIGHS (regular season): Receptions—5 (November 10, 1996, vs. Washington); yards—54 (November 10, 1996, vs. Washington); and touchdown receptions—1 (November 10, 1996, vs. Washington).

Year Team	G	GS	RECEIVING				TOTALS			
			No.	Yds.	Avg.	TD	TD	2pt.	Pts.	Fum.
1996—Arizona NFL................	12	0	7	80	11 4	1	1	0	6	0
1997—Arizona NFL................	16	7	7	75	10.7	0	0	0	0	0
Pro totals (2 years)	28	7	14	155	11.1	1	1	0	6	0

MEADOWS, ADAM OT COLTS

PERSONAL: Born January 25, 1974, in Powder Springs, Ga. ... 6-5/299.
HIGH SCHOOL: McEachern (Powder Springs, Ga.).
COLLEGE: Georgia.
TRANSACTIONS/CAREER NOTES: Selected by Indianapolis Colts in second round (48th pick overall) of 1997 NFL draft. ... Signed by Colts (July 8, 1997).
PLAYING EXPERIENCE: Indianapolis NFL, 1997. ... Games/Games started: 16/16.

MEANS, NATRONE RB CHARGERS

PERSONAL: Born April 26, 1972, in Harrisburg, N.C. ... 5-10/245. ... Full name: Natrone Jermaine Means. ... Name pronounced NAY-trone.
HIGH SCHOOL: Central Cabarrus (Concord, N.C.).
COLLEGE: North Carolina.
TRANSACTIONS/CAREER NOTES: Selected after junior season by San Diego Chargers in second round (41st pick overall) of 1993 NFL draft. ... Signed by Chargers (July 18, 1993). ... Claimed on waivers by Jacksonville Jaguars (March 11, 1996). ... Granted unconditional free agency (February 13, 1998). ... Signed by Chargers (March 4, 1998).
CHAMPIONSHIP GAME EXPERIENCE: Played in AFC championship game (1994 and 1996 seasons). ... Played in Super Bowl XXIX (1994 season).
HONORS: Played in Pro Bowl (1994 season).
PRO STATISTICS: 1993—Attempted one pass without a completion, returned two kickoffs for 22 yards and recovered one fumble. 1994—Attempted one pass without a completion. 1996—Recovered one fumble.
SINGLE GAME HIGHS (regular season): Attempts—27 (December 22, 1996, vs. Atlanta); yards—125 (October 9, 1994, vs. Kansas City); and rushing touchdowns—3 (October 16, 1994, vs. New Orleans).
STATISTICAL PLATEAUS: 100-yard rushing games: 1993 (2), 1994 (6), 1995 (3), 1996 (1). Total: 12.

			RUSHING				RECEIVING				TOTALS			
Year Team	G	GS	Att.	Yds.	Avg.	TD	No.	Yds.	Avg.	TD	TD	2pt.	Pts.	Fum.
1993—San Diego NFL	16	0	160	645	4.0	8	10	59	5.9	0	8	...	48	1
1994—San Diego NFL	16	16	§343	1350	3.9	§12	39	235	6.0	0	▲12	0	72	5
1995—San Diego NFL	10	9	186	730	3.9	5	7	46	6.6	0	5	0	30	2
1996—Jacksonville NFL	14	4	152	507	3.3	2	7	45	6.4	1	3	0	18	3
1997—Jacksonville NFL	14	11	244	823	3.4	9	15	104	6.9	0	9	0	54	5
Pro totals (5 years)	70	40	1085	4055	3.7	36	78	489	6.3	1	37	0	222	16

MEGGETT, DAVE RB/KR

PERSONAL: Born April 30, 1966, in Charleston, S.C. ... 5-7/190. ... Full name: David Lee Meggett.
HIGH SCHOOL: Bonds-Wilson (North Charleston, S.C.).
COLLEGE: Morgan State, then Towson State.
TRANSACTIONS/CAREER NOTES: Selected by New York Giants in fifth round (132nd pick overall) of 1989 NFL draft. ... Signed by Giants (July 24, 1989). ... Granted free agency (February 1, 1991). ... Re-signed by Giants (August 29, 1991). ... Granted free agency (March 1, 1993). ... Re-signed by Giants (July 28, 1993). ... Granted unconditional free agency (February 17, 1995). ... Signed by New England Patriots (March 3, 1995). ... Released by Patriots (May 29, 1998).
CHAMPIONSHIP GAME EXPERIENCE: Played in NFC championship game (1990 season). ... Member of Super Bowl championship team (1990 season). ... Played in AFC championship game (1996 season). ... Played in Super Bowl XXXI (1996 season).
HONORS: Walter Payton Award winner (1988). ... Played in Pro Bowl (1989 and 1996 seasons). ... Named punt returner on THE SPORTING NEWS NFL All-Pro team (1990).
RECORDS: Holds NFL career records for most punt returns—344; most yards gained by punt return—3.668; and most fair catches—114.
POST SEASON RECORDS: Shares Super Bowl single-game record for most fair catches—3 (January 27, 1991, vs. Buffalo). ... Holds NFL postseason career records for most punt returns—30; and most yards by punt return—265.
PRO STATISTICS: 1989—Fumbled eight times and recovered three fumbles. 1990—Fumbled three times and recovered two fumbles. 1991—Attempted one pass without a completion, fumbled eight times and recovered three fumbles. 1992—Fumbled five times and recovered three fumbles. 1993—Attempted two passes with two completions for 63 yards and two touchdowns, fumbled once and recovered one fumble. 1994—Attempted two passes with one completion for 16 yards and a touchdown, fumbled six times and recovered five fumbles. 1995—Attempted one pass without a completion and fumbled five times. 1996—Attempted one pass without a completion, fumbled seven times and recovered four fumbles. 1997—Attempted one pass with one completion for 35 yards and a touchdown, fumbled twice and recovered one fumble.
SINGLE GAME HIGHS (regular season): Attempts—26 (September 18, 1994, vs. Washington); yards—82 (September 18, 1994, vs. Washington); and rushing touchdowns—2 (September 18, 1994, vs. Washington).

			RUSHING				RECEIVING				PUNT RETURNS				KICKOFF RETURNS				TOTALS	
Year Team	G	GS	Att.	Yds.	Avg.	TD	No.	Yds.	Avg.	TD	No.	Yds.	Avg.	TD	No.	Yds.	Avg.	TD	TD	2pt.	Pts.
1989—N.Y. Giants NFL	16	2	28	117	4.2	0	34	531	15.6	4	‡46	*582	12.7	†1	27	577	21.4	0	5	...	30
1990—N.Y. Giants NFL	16	1	22	164	7.5	0	39	410	10.5	1	*43	*467	10.9	†1	21	492	‡23.4	0	2	...	12
1991—N.Y. Giants NFL	16	2	29	153	5.3	1	50	412	8.2	3	28	287	10.3	1	25	514	20.6	0	5	...	30
1992—N.Y. Giants NFL	16	0	32	167	5.2	0	38	229	6.0	2	27	240	8.9	0	20	455	22.8	1	3	...	18
1993—N.Y. Giants NFL	16	1	69	329	4.8	0	38	319	8.4	0	32	331	10.3	1	24	403	16.8	0	1	...	6
1994—N.Y. Giants NFL	16	3	91	298	3.3	4	32	293	9.2	0	26	323	12.4	†2	29	548	18.9	0	6	0	36
1995—New England NFL	16	0	60	250	4.2	2	52	334	6.4	0	45	383	8.5	0	38	964	25.4	0	2	2	16
1996—New England NFL	16	0	40	122	3.1	0	33	292	8.8	0	§52	§588	11.3	§1	34	781	23.0	0	1	0	6
1997—New England NFL	16	2	20	60	3.0	1	19	203	10.7	1	45	467	10.4	0	33	816	24.7	0	2	0	12
Pro totals (9 years)	144	12	391	1660	4.2	8	335	3023	9.0	11	344	3668	10.7	7	251	5550	22.1	1	27	2	166

METCALF, ERIC WR CARDINALS

PERSONAL: Born January 23, 1968, in Seattle. ... 5-10/188. ... Full name: Eric Quinn Metcalf. ... Son of Terry Metcalf, running back with St. Louis Cardinals (1973-1977), Toronto Argonauts of CFL (1978-1980) and Washington Redskins (1981); and cousin of Ray Hall, defensive tackle with Jacksonville Jaguars (1995).

M

HIGH SCHOOL: Bishop Dennis J. O'Connell (Arlington, Va.).

COLLEGE: Texas (degree in liberal arts, 1990).

TRANSACTIONS/CAREER NOTES: Selected by Cleveland Browns in first round (13th pick overall) of 1989 NFL draft. ... Signed by Browns (August 20, 1989). ... Granted free agency (February 1, 1991). ... Re-signed by Browns (1991). ... On injured reserve with shoulder injury (November 2, 1991-remainder of season). ... Granted free agency (February 1, 1992). ... Re-signed by Browns (August 30, 1992). ... Granted roster exemption (August 30-September 5, 1992). ... Traded by Browns with first-round pick (DB Devin Bush) in 1995 draft to Atlanta Falcons for first-round pick (traded to San Francisco) in 1995 draft (March 25, 1995). ... Granted unconditional free agency (February 14, 1997). ... Signed by San Diego Chargers (May 8, 1997). ... Traded by Chargers with first- (DE Andre Wadsworth) and second-round (CB Corey Chavous) picks in 1998 draft, first-round pick in 1999 draft and LB Patrick Sapp to Arizona Cardinals for first-round pick (QB Ryan Leaf) in 1998 draft (March 12, 1998).

CHAMPIONSHIP GAME EXPERIENCE: Played in AFC championship game (1989 season).

HONORS: Named all-purpose player on The Sporting News college All-America second team (1987). ... Named punt returner on The Sporting News NFL All-Pro team (1993 and 1994). ... Played in Pro Bowl (1993, 1994 and 1997 seasons).

RECORDS: Holds NFL career record for most touchdowns by punt return—9. ... Shares NFL single-game records for most touchdowns by punt return—2; and most touchdowns by combined kick return—2 (October 24, 1993, vs. Pittsburgh and November 2, 1997, vs. Cincinnati).

POST SEASON RECORDS: Shares NFL postseason career record for most touchdowns by kickoff return—1 (January 6, 1990, vs. Buffalo).

PRO STATISTICS: 1989—Attempted two passes with one completion for 32 yards and a touchdown and fumbled five times. 1990—Fumbled eight times and recovered one fumble. 1991—Fumbled once. 1992—Attempted one pass without a completion, fumbled six times and recovered two fumbles. 1993—Fumbled five times. 1994—Attempted one pass without a completion and fumbled six times. 1995—Attempted one pass without a completion, fumbled four times and recovered two fumbles. 1996—Fumbled three times. 1997—Fumbled four times and recovered two fumbles.

SINGLE GAME HIGHS (regular season): Receptions—11 (September 17, 1995, vs. New Orleans); yards—177 (September 20, 1992, vs. Los Angeles Raiders); and touchdown receptions—3 (September 20, 1992, vs. Los Angeles Raiders).

STATISTICAL PLATEAUS: 100-yard receiving games: 1992 (1), 1993 (1), 1995 (2), 1996 (1), 1997 (1). Total: 6.

				RUSHING				RECEIVING				PUNT RETURNS				KICKOFF RETURNS				TOTALS		
Year Team	G	GS	Att.	Yds.	Avg.	TD	No.	Yds.	Avg.	TD	No.	Yds.	Avg.	TD	No.	Yds.	Avg.	TD	TD	2pt.	Pts.
1989—Cleveland NFL	16	11	187	633	3.4	6	54	397	7.4	4	0	0	...	0	31	718	23.2	0	10	...	60
1990—Cleveland NFL	16	9	80	248	3.1	1	57	452	7.9	1	0	0	...	0	*52	*1052	20.2	*2	4	...	24
1991—Cleveland NFL	8	3	30	107	3.6	0	29	294	10.1	0	12	100	8.3	0	23	351	15.3	0	0	...	0
1992—Cleveland NFL	16	5	73	301	4.1	1	47	614	13.1	5	*44	§429	9.8	0	9	157	17.4	0	7	...	42
1993—Cleveland NFL	16	9	129	611	4.7	1	63	539	8.6	2	36	464	§12.9	†2	15	318	21.2	0	5	...	30
1994—Cleveland NFL	16	8	93	329	3.5	2	47	436	9.3	3	35	348	9.9	†2	9	210	23.3	0	7	0	42
1995—Atlanta NFL	16	14	28	133	4.8	1	104	1189	11.4	8	39	383	9.8	†1	12	278	23.2	0	10	0	60
1996—Atlanta NFL	16	11	3	8	2.7	0	54	599	11.1	6	27	296	11.0	0	49	1034	21.1	0	6	0	36
1997—San Diego NFL	16	1	3	-5	-1.7	0	40	576	14.4	2	45	489	10.9	†3	16	355	22.2	0	5	0	30
Pro totals (9 years)	136	71	626	2365	3.8	12	495	5096	10.3	31	238	2509	10.5	9	216	4473	20.7	2	54	0	324

METZELAARS, PETE   TE

PERSONAL: Born May 24, 1960, in Three Rivers, Mich. ... 6-7/254. ... Full name: Peter Henry Metzelaars. ... Name pronounced METZ-eh-lars.

HIGH SCHOOL: Central (Portage, Mich.).

COLLEGE: Wabash, Ind. (degree in economics, 1982).

TRANSACTIONS/CAREER NOTES: Selected by Seattle Seahawks in third round (75th pick overall) of 1982 NFL draft. ... On injured reserve with knee injury (October 17-December 1, 1984). ... Traded by Seahawks to Buffalo Bills for WR Byron Franklin (August 20, 1985). ... Granted unconditional free agency (February 1-April 1, 1992). ... Re-signed by Bills (1992). ... Granted unconditional free agency (March 1, 1993). ... Re-signed by Bills (May 21, 1993). ... Granted unconditional free agency (February 17, 1995). ... Signed by Carolina Panthers (March 8, 1995). ... Released by Panthers (February 14, 1996). ... Signed by Detroit Lions (May 7, 1996). ... Granted unconditional free agency (February 14, 1997). ... Re-signed by Lions (April 14, 1997). ... Granted unconditional free agency (February 13, 1998).

CHAMPIONSHIP GAME EXPERIENCE: Played in AFC championship game (1983, 1988 and 1990-1993 seasons). ... Played in Super Bowl XXV (1990 season), Super Bowl XXVI (1991 season), Super Bowl XXVII (1992 season) and Super Bowl XXVIII (1993 season).

PRO STATISTICS: 1982—Recovered one fumble. 1983—Returned one kickoff for no yards. 1985—Recovered one fumble for two yards. 1986—Recovered one fumble in end zone for a touchdown. 1987—Recovered one fumble. 1988—Recovered one fumble. 1996—Returned one kickoff for one yard.

SINGLE GAME HIGHS (regular season): Receptions—10 (November 28, 1993, vs. Kansas City); yards—113 (September 13, 1992, vs. San Francisco); and touchdown receptions—2 (October 30, 1994, vs. Kansas City).

STATISTICAL PLATEAUS: 100-yard receiving games: 1986 (1), 1992 (1). Total: 2.

			RECEIVING				TOTALS			
Year Team	G	GS	No.	Yds.	Avg.	TD	TD	2pt.	Pts.	Fum.
1982—Seattle NFL	9	2	15	152	10.1	0	0	...	0	2
1983—Seattle NFL	16	7	7	72	10.3	1	1	...	6	0
1984—Seattle NFL	9	4	5	80	16.0	0	0	...	0	1
1985—Buffalo NFL	16	8	12	80	6.7	1	1	...	6	0
1986—Buffalo NFL	16	16	49	485	9.9	3	4	...	24	2
1987—Buffalo NFL	12	12	28	290	10.4	0	0	...	0	3
1988—Buffalo NFL	16	16	33	438	13.3	1	1	...	6	0
1989—Buffalo NFL	16	16	18	179	9.9	2	2	...	12	0
1990—Buffalo NFL	16	4	10	60	6.0	1	1	...	6	1
1991—Buffalo NFL	16	1	5	54	10.8	2	2	...	12	0
1992—Buffalo NFL	16	7	30	298	9.9	6	6	...	36	0
1993—Buffalo NFL	16	16	68	609	9.0	4	4	...	24	1
1994—Buffalo NFL	16	16	49	428	8.7	5	5	0	30	0
1995—Carolina NFL	14	14	20	171	8.6	3	3	0	18	0
1996—Detroit NFL	15	11	17	146	8.6	0	0	0	0	0
1997—Detroit NFL	16	6	17	144	8.5	0	0	0	0	0
Pro totals (10 years)	235	156	383	3686	9.6	29	30	0	180	10

M

MICHELS, JOHN   OT   PACKERS

PERSONAL: Born March 19, 1973, in La Jolla, Calif. ... 6-7/304. ... Full name: John Spiegel Michels.
HIGH SCHOOL: La Jolla (Calif.).
COLLEGE: Southern California.
TRANSACTIONS/CAREER NOTES: Selected by Green Bay Packers in first round (27th pick overall) of 1996 NFL draft. ... Signed by Packers (July 20, 1996).
PLAYING EXPERIENCE: Green Bay NFL, 1996 and 1997. ... Games/Games started: 1996 (15/9), 1997 (9/5). Total: 24/14.
CHAMPIONSHIP GAME EXPERIENCE: Played in NFC championship game (1996 season). ... Member of Super Bowl championship team (1996 season). ... Member of Packers for NFC championship game (1997 season); inactive. ... Member of Packers for Super Bowl XXXII (1997 season); inactive.

MICKELL, DARREN   DE

PERSONAL: Born August 3, 1970, in Miami. ... 6-4/291.
HIGH SCHOOL: Senior (Miami).
COLLEGE: Florida.
TRANSACTIONS/CAREER NOTES: Selected by Kansas City Chiefs in second round of 1992 NFL supplemental draft (second of two supplemental drafts in 1992). ... Signed by Chiefs (September 16, 1992). ... Granted roster exemption (September 16-29, 1992). ... On injured reserve with knee injury (September 30-November 11, 1992). ... On practice squad (November 11-December 26, 1992). ... Granted unconditional free agency (February 16, 1996). ... Signed by New Orleans Saints (March 12, 1996). ... On reserve/did not report list (July 14-August 12, 1996). ... On physically unable to perform list (August 12-19, 1996). ... On suspended list for violating league substance abuse policy (October 4-November 10, 1996). ... Announced retirement (February 23, 1998).
CHAMPIONSHIP GAME EXPERIENCE: Played in AFC championship game (1993 season).
PRO STATISTICS: 1993—Recovered one fumble. 1994—Recovered one fumble. 1995—Recovered one fumble. 1997—Recovered one fumble for 11 yards.

Year Team	G	GS	SACKS
1992—Kansas City NFL	1	0	0.0
1993—Kansas City NFL	16	1	1.0
1994—Kansas City NFL	16	13	7.0
1995—Kansas City NFL	12	6	5.5
1996—New Orleans NFL	12	12	3.0
1997—New Orleans NFL	14	13	3.5
Pro totals (6 years)	71	45	20.0

MICKENS, RAY   CB   JETS

PERSONAL: Born January 4, 1973, in Frankfurt, West Germany. ... 5-8/180.
HIGH SCHOOL: Andress (El Paso, Texas).
COLLEGE: Texas A&M.
TRANSACTIONS/CAREER NOTES: Selected by New York Jets in third round (62nd pick overall) of 1996 NFL draft. ... Signed by Jets (July 13, 1996).
PLAYING EXPERIENCE: New York Jets NFL, 1996 and 1997. ... Games/Games started: 1996 (15/10), 1997 (16/0). Total: 31/10.
HONORS: Named defensive back on The Sporting News college All-America second team (1995).
PRO STATISTICS: 1997—Intercepted four passes for two yards, credited with one sack and returned blocked field-goal attempt 72 yards for a touchdown.

MICKENS, TERRY   WR   RAIDERS

PERSONAL: Born February 21, 1971, in Tallahassee, Fla. ... 6-0/198. ... Full name: Terry KaJuan Mickens.
HIGH SCHOOL: Leon (Tallahassee, Fla.).
COLLEGE: Florida A&M.
TRANSACTIONS/CAREER NOTES: Selected by Green Bay Packers in fifth round (146th pick overall) of 1994 NFL draft. ... Signed by Packers (July 7, 1994). ... Granted unconditional free agency (February 13, 1998). ... Signed by Oakland Raiders (April 24, 1998).
CHAMPIONSHIP GAME EXPERIENCE: Played in NFC championship game (1995-97 seasons). ... Member of Super Bowl championship team (1996 season). ... Played in Super Bowl XXXII (1997 season).
PRO STATISTICS: 1995—Returned one kickoff for no yards. 1997—Returned one kickoff for no yards.
SINGLE GAME HIGHS (regular season): Receptions—7 (November 3, 1996, vs. Detroit); yards—52 (November 3, 1996, vs. Detroit); and touchdown receptions—2 (November 3, 1996, vs. Detroit).

Year Team	G	GS	No.	Yds.	Avg.	TD	TD	2pt.	Pts.	Fum.
1994—Green Bay NFL	12	0	4	31	7.8	0	0	0	0	0
1995—Green Bay NFL	16	0	3	50	16.7	0	0	0	0	0
1996—Green Bay NFL	8	5	18	161	8.9	2	2	0	12	1
1997—Green Bay NFL	11	0	1	2	2.0	1	1	0	6	0
Pro totals (4 years)	47	5	26	244	9.4	3	3	0	18	1

(Header spanning: "RECEIVING" over No./Yds./Avg./TD; "TOTALS" over TD/2pt./Pts./Fum.)

MIDDLETON, FRANK   G   BUCCANEERS

PERSONAL: Born October 25, 1974, in Beaumont, Texas. ... 6-3/340. ... Full name: Frank Middleton Jr.
HIGH SCHOOL: West Brook (Beaumont, Texas).
JUNIOR COLLEGE: Fort Scott (Kan.) Community College.
COLLEGE: Arizona.
TRANSACTIONS/CAREER NOTES: Selected by Tampa Bay Buccaneers in third round (63rd pick overall) of 1997 NFL draft. ... Signed by Buccaneers (July 20, 1997).
PLAYING EXPERIENCE: Tampa Bay NFL, 1997. ... Games/Games started: 15/2.

M

MILANOVICH, SCOTT — QB — BUCCANEERS

PERSONAL: Born January 25, 1973, in Butler, Pa. ... 6-3/220.
HIGH SCHOOL: Butler (Pa.).
COLLEGE: Maryland.
TRANSACTIONS/CAREER NOTES: Signed as non-drafted free agent by Tampa Bay Buccaneers (April 23, 1996).
PLAYING EXPERIENCE: Tampa Bay NFL, 1996. ... Games/Games started: 1/0.
PRO STATISTICS: 1996—Attempted three passes with two completions for nine yards.
SINGLE GAME HIGHS (regular season): Attempts—3 (September 8, 1996, vs. Detroit); completions—2 (September 8, 1996, vs. Detroit); yards—9 (September 8, 1996, vs. Detroit); and touchdown passes—0.

MILBURN, GLYN — WR/KR — PACKERS

PERSONAL: Born February 19, 1971, in Santa Monica, Calif. ... 5-8/177. ... Full name: Glyn Curt Milburn. ... Cousin of Rod Milburn, gold medalist in 110-meter high hurdles in 1972 Summer Olympics.
HIGH SCHOOL: Santa Monica (Calif.).
COLLEGE: Oklahoma, then Stanford (degree in public policy).
TRANSACTIONS/CAREER NOTES: Selected by Denver Broncos in second round (43rd pick overall) of 1993 NFL draft. ... Signed by Broncos (July 15, 1993). ... Traded by Broncos to Detroit Lions for second- (traded to Baltimore) and seventh-round (P Brian Gragert) picks in 1996 NFL draft (April 12, 1996). ... Traded by Lions to Green Bay Packers for conditional pick in 1999 draft (April 21, 1998).
HONORS: Named kick returner on THE SPORTING NEWS NFL All-Pro team (1995). ... Played in Pro Bowl (1995 season).
RECORDS: Holds NFL single-season record for most combined kick returns—102. ... Holds NFL single-game record for most combined net yards gained—404 (December 10, 1995).
PRO STATISTICS: 1993—Fumbled nine times and recovered one fumble. 1994—Fumbled four times and recovered one fumble. 1995—Fumbled twice. 1997—Fumbled three times and recovered two fumbles.
SINGLE GAME HIGHS (regular season): Receptions—9 (September 18, 1994 vs. Los Angeles Raiders); yards—85 (September 18, 1994 vs. Los Angeles Raiders); touchdowns—1 (November 6, 1994 vs. Los Angeles Rams).
STATISTICAL PLATEAUS: 100-yard rushing games: 1995 (1).

			RUSHING				RECEIVING				PUNT RETURNS				KICKOFF RETURNS				TOTALS		
Year Team	G	GS	Att.	Yds.	Avg.	TD	No.	Yds.	Avg.	TD	No.	Yds.	Avg.	TD	No.	Yds.	Avg.	TD	TD	2pt.	Pts.
1993—Denver NFL	16	2	52	231	4.4	0	38	300	7.9	3	40	425	10.6	0	12	188	15.7	0	3	...	18
1994—Denver NFL	16	3	58	201	3.5	1	77	549	7.1	3	41	379	9.2	0	37	793	21.4	0	4	0	24
1995—Denver NFL	16	1	49	266	5.4	0	22	191	8.7	0	31	354	11.4	0	47	1269	27.0	0	0	0	0
1996—Detroit NFL	16	0	0	0	...	0	0	0	...	0	34	284	8.4	0	64	1627	25.4	0	0	0	0
1997—Detroit NFL	16	1	0	0	...	0	5	77	15.4	0	47	433	9.2	0	55	1315	23.9	0	0	0	0
Pro totals (5 years)	80	7	159	698	4.4	1	142	1117	7.9	6	193	1875	9.7	0	215	5192	24.1	0	7	0	42

MILI, ITULA — TE — SEAHAWKS

PERSONAL: Born April 20, 1973, in Kahuku, Hawaii. ... 6-4/265. ... Name pronounced ee-TWO-la MEE-lee.
HIGH SCHOOL: Kahuku (Hawaii).
COLLEGE: Brigham Young.
TRANSACTIONS/CAREER NOTES: Selected by Seattle Seahawks in sixth round (174th pick overall) of 1997 NFL draft. ... Signed by Seahawks (June 11, 1997). ... On physically unable to perform list with knee injury (August 18, 1997-remainder of season).

M

MILLER, ANTHONY — WR

PERSONAL: Born April 15, 1965, in Los Angeles. ... 5-11/190. ... Full name: Lawrence Anthony Miller.
HIGH SCHOOL: John Muir (Pasadena, Calif.).
JUNIOR COLLEGE: Pasadena (Calif.) City College.
COLLEGE: San Diego State, then Tennessee.
TRANSACTIONS/CAREER NOTES: Selected by San Diego Chargers in first round (15th pick overall) of 1988 NFL draft. ... Signed by Chargers (July 12, 1988). ... On injured reserve with leg injury (December 7, 1991-remainder of season). ... Designated by Chargers as transition player (February 15, 1994). ... Tendered offer sheet by Denver Broncos (March 18, 1994). ... Chargers declined to match offer (March 24, 1994). ... Released by Broncos (June 2, 1997). ... Signed by Dallas Cowboys (June 2, 1997). ... Granted unconditional free agency (February 13, 1998).
HONORS: Played in Pro Bowl (1989, 1990, 1992, 1993 and 1995 seasons).
PRO STATISTICS: 1990—Recovered one fumble. 1991—Recovered one fumble. 1992—Recovered one fumble in end zone for a touchdown. 1995—Recovered one fumble for nine yards. 1997—Recovered one fumble.
SINGLE GAME HIGHS (regular season): Receptions—10 (October 3, 1993, vs. Seattle); yards—162 (September 17, 1989, vs. Houston); and touchdown receptions—3 (September 10, 1995, vs. Dallas).
STATISTICAL PLATEAUS: 100-yard receiving games: 1989 (5), 1990 (2), 1991 (2), 1992 (4), 1993 (6), 1994 (4), 1995 (3), 1996 (1). Total: 27.

			RUSHING				RECEIVING				KICKOFF RETURNS				TOTALS		
Year Team	G	GS	Att.	Yds.	Avg.	TD	No.	Yds.	Avg.	TD	No.	Yds.	Avg.	TD	TD	2pt.	Pts.	Fum.
1988—San Diego NFL	16	15	7	45	6.4	0	36	526	14.6	3	25	648	25.9	†1	4	...	24	1
1989—San Diego NFL	16	16	4	21	5.3	0	75	1252	16.7	10	21	533	25.4	†1	11	...	66	1
1990—San Diego NFL	16	16	3	13	4.3	0	63	933	14.8	7	1	13	13.0	0	7	...	42	2
1991—San Diego NFL	13	12	0	0	...	0	44	649	14.8	3	0	0	...	0	3	...	18	1
1992—San Diego NFL	16	16	1	-1	-1.0	0	72	§1060	14.7	7	1	33	33.0	0	8	...	48	0
1993—San Diego NFL	16	16	1	0	0.0	0	84	1162	13.8	7	2	42	21.0	0	7	...	42	0
1994—Denver NFL	16	15	1	3	3.0	0	60	1107	18.5	5	0	0	...	0	5	1	32	0
1995—Denver NFL	14	14	1	5	5.0	0	59	1079	18.3	14	0	0	...	0	14	0	84	1
1996—Denver NFL	16	16	3	39	13.0	1	56	735	13.1	3	0	0	...	0	4	0	24	0
1997—Dallas NFL	16	16	1	6	6.0	0	46	645	14.0	4	0	0	...	0	4	0	24	1
Pro totals (10 years)	155	152	22	131	6.0	1	595	9148	15.4	63	50	1269	25.4	2	67	1	404	7

MILLER, BUBBA   C/G   EAGLES

PERSONAL: Born January 24, 1973, in Nashville. ... 6-1/300. ... Full name: Stephen DeJuan Miller.
HIGH SCHOOL: Brentwood Academy (Franklin, Tenn.).
COLLEGE: Tennessee.
TRANSACTIONS/CAREER NOTES: Signed as non-drafted free agent by Philadelphia Eagles (April 26, 1996). ... Inactive for 16 games (1996).
PLAYING EXPERIENCE: Philadelphia NFL, 1997. ... Games/Games started: 13/3.

MILLER, CHRIS   WR   BEARS

PERSONAL: Born July 10, 1973, in Los Angeles. ... 5-10/192. ... Full name: Christopher Kyle Miller. ... Cousin of Keyshawn Johnson, wide receiver, New York Jets.
HIGH SCHOOL: Dorsey (Los Angeles).
JUNIOR COLLEGE: West Los Angeles Community College.
COLLEGE: Southern California.
TRANSACTIONS/CAREER NOTES: Selected by Green Bay Packers in seventh round (213th pick overall) of 1997 NFL draft. ... Signed by Packers (June 3, 1997). ... Released by Packers (August 18, 1997). ... Signed by Detroit Lions to practice squad (August 26, 1997). ... Released by Lions (August 28, 1997). ... Signed by Chicago Bears to practice squad (December 4, 1997). ... Assigned by Bears to Scotland Claymores in 1998 NFL Europe enhancement allocation program (February 18, 1998).

MILLER, COREY   LB   GIANTS

PERSONAL: Born October 25, 1968, in Pageland, S.C. ... 6-2/248.
HIGH SCHOOL: Central (Pageland, S.C.).
COLLEGE: South Carolina.
TRANSACTIONS/CAREER NOTES: Selected by New York Giants in sixth round (167th pick overall) of 1991 NFL draft. ... Signed by Giants (July 15, 1991). ... Granted free agency (February 17, 1994). ... Re-signed by Giants (July 22, 1994). ... Granted unconditional free agency (February 17, 1995). ... Re-signed by Giants (March 9, 1995).
PRO STATISTICS: 1991—Recovered one fumble. 1993—Recovered two fumbles and fumbled once. 1994—Recovered one fumble.

| | | | INTERCEPTIONS | | | | SACKS |
Year Team	G	GS	No.	Yds.	Avg.	TD	No.
1991—New York Giants NFL	16	1	0	0	...	0	2.5
1992—New York Giants NFL	16	7	2	10	5.0	0	2.0
1993—New York Giants NFL	16	14	2	18	9.0	0	6.5
1994—New York Giants NFL	15	13	2	6	3.0	0	0.0
1995—New York Giants NFL	14	9	0	0	...	0	0.0
1996—New York Giants NFL	14	13	0	0	...	0	2.0
1997—New York Giants NFL	14	13	0	0	...	0	1.0
Pro totals (7 years)	105	70	6	34	5.7	0	14.0

M

MILLER, FRED   OT   RAMS

PERSONAL: Born February 6, 1973, in Aldine, Texas. ... 6-7/315. ... Full name: Fred Miller Jr.
HIGH SCHOOL: Aldine Eisenhower (Houston).
COLLEGE: Baylor.
TRANSACTIONS/CAREER NOTES: Selected by St. Louis Rams in fifth round (141st pick overall) of 1996 NFL draft. ... Signed by Rams (July 15, 1996).
PLAYING EXPERIENCE: St. Louis NFL, 1996 and 1997. ... Games/Games started: 1996 (14/0), 1997 (15/7). Total: 29/7.

MILLER, JAMIR   LB   CARDINALS

PERSONAL: Born November 19, 1973, in Philadelphia. ... 6-5/266. ... Full name: Jamir Malik Miller.
HIGH SCHOOL: El Cerrito (Calif.).
COLLEGE: UCLA.
TRANSACTIONS/CAREER NOTES: Selected after junior season by Arizona Cardinals in first round (10th pick overall) of 1994 NFL draft. ... Signed by Cardinals (August 12, 1994). ... On suspended list for violating league substance abuse policy (September 4-October 3, 1995).
HONORS: Named linebacker on THE SPORTING NEWS college All-America first team (1993).
PRO STATISTICS: 1995—Fumbled once and recovered two fumbles for 26 yards. 1996—Recovered one fumble for 26 yards and a touchdown.

Year Team	G	GS	SACKS
1994—Arizona NFL	16	0	3.0
1995—Arizona NFL	11	8	1.0
1996—Arizona NFL	16	16	1.0
1997—Arizona NFL	16	16	5.5
Pro totals (4 years)	59	40	10.5

MILLER, JEFF   OT   REDSKINS

PERSONAL: Born November 23, 1972, in Vero Beach, Fla. ... 6-4/303.
HIGH SCHOOL: Vero Beach (Fla.).
JUNIOR COLLEGE: Northwest Mississippi Community College.
COLLEGE: Mississippi.
TRANSACTIONS/CAREER NOTES: Selected by Green Bay Packers in fourth round (117th pick overall) of 1995 NFL draft. ... Signed by Packers (July 17, 1995). ... On injured reserve with knee injury (August 21, 1995-entire season). ... On injured reserve with knee injury (August 19, 1996-entire season). ... Signed by Tampa Bay Buccaneers (April 18, 1997). ... Released by Buccaneers (August 24, 1997). ... Signed by Washington Redskins to practice squad (September 2, 1997).

MILLER, JIM QB LIONS

PERSONAL: Born February 9, 1971, in Grosse Pointe, Mich. ... 6-2/210. ... Full name: James Donald Miller.
HIGH SCHOOL: Kettering (Detroit).
COLLEGE: Michigan State.
TRANSACTIONS/CAREER NOTES: Selected by Pittsburgh Steelers in sixth round (178th pick overall) of 1994 NFL draft. ... Signed by Steelers (May 12, 1994). ... Inactive for 16 games (1994). ... Assigned by Steelers to Frankfurt Galaxy in 1995 World League enhancement allocation program (February 20, 1995). ... Released by Steelers (August 23, 1997). ... Signed by Jacksonville Jaguars (September 2, 1997). ... Released by Jaguars (September 23, 1997). ... Signed by Atlanta Falcons (October 27, 1997). ... Granted unconditional free agency (February 13, 1998). ... Signed by Detroit Lions (March 2, 1998).
CHAMPIONSHIP GAME EXPERIENCE: Member of Steelers for AFC championship game (1994 and 1995 seasons); inactive. ... Member of Steelers for Super Bowl XXX (1995 season); inactive.
PRO STATISTICS: 1995—Fumbled once. 1996—Fumbled once for minus four yards.
SINGLE GAME HIGHS (regular season): Attempts—28 (September 18, 1995, vs. Miami); completions—17 (September 18, 1995, vs. Miami); yards—202 (September 18, 1995, vs. Miami); and touchdown passes—1 (September 24, 1995, vs. Minnesota).
MISCELLANEOUS: Regular-season record as starting NFL quarterback: 0-1 (.000).

Year Team	G	GS	Att.	Cmp.	Pct.	Yds.	TD	Int.	Avg.	Rat.	Att.	Yds.	Avg.	TD	TD	2pt.	Pts.
						PASSING						RUSHING				TOTALS	
1994—Pittsburgh NFL						Did not play.											
1995—Frankfurt W.L.	...	...	43	23	53.5	236	1	1	5.49	67.6	3	-2	-0.7	0	0	0	0
—Pittsburgh NFL	4	0	56	32	57.1	397	2	5	7.09	53.9	1	2	2.0	0	0	0	0
1996—Pittsburgh NFL	2	1	25	13	52.0	123	0	0	4.92	65.9	2	-4	-2.0	0	0	0	0
1997—Jacksonville NFL						Did not play.											
—Atlanta NFL						Did not play.											
W.L. totals (1 year)	...	...	43	23	53.5	236	1	1	5.49	67.6	3	-2	-0.7	0	0	0	0
NFL totals (2 years)	6	1	81	45	55.6	520	2	5	6.42	57.6	3	-2	-0.7	0	0	0	0
Pro totals (3 years)	...	...	124	68	54.8	756	3	6	6.10	61.1	6	-4	-0.7	0	0	0	0

MILLER, JOSH P STEELERS

PERSONAL: Born July 14, 1970, in East Brunswick, N.J. ... 6-3/215.
HIGH SCHOOL: East Brunswick (N.J.).
COLLEGE: Arizona.
TRANSACTIONS/CAREER NOTES: Signed as non-drafted free agent by Seattle Seahawks (May 29, 1996). ... Released by Seahawks (August 13, 1996). ... Signed by Pittsburgh Steelers (August 15, 1996).
CHAMPIONSHIP GAME EXPERIENCE: Played in AFC championship game (1997 season).
PRO STATISTICS: 1997—Rushed once for minus seven yards.

Year Team	G	GS	No.	Yds.	Avg.	Net avg.	In. 20	Blk.
				PUNTING				
1996—Pittsburgh NFL	12	0	55	2256	41.0	33.6	18	0
1997—Pittsburgh NFL	16	0	64	2729	42.6	35.0	17	0
Pro totals (2 years)	28	0	119	4985	41.9	34.4	35	0

M

MILLER, LES DE PANTHERS

PERSONAL: Born March 1, 1965, in Arkansas City, Kan. ... 6-7/305. ... Full name: Les P. Miller.
HIGH SCHOOL: Arkansas City (Kan.).
COLLEGE: Kansas State, then Fort Hays State (Kan.).
TRANSACTIONS/CAREER NOTES: Signed as non-drafted free agent by New Orleans Saints (May 11, 1987). ... Released by Saints (September 7, 1987). ... Signed as replacement player by San Diego Chargers (September 24, 1987). ... On injured reserve with back injury (December 22, 1990-remainder of season). ... Granted unconditional free agency (February 1, 1991). ... Signed by Saints (April 1, 1991). ... Granted unconditional free agency (March 1, 1993). ... Re-signed by Saints (March 9, 1993). ... Released by Saints (October 25, 1994). ... Signed by Chargers (November 2, 1994). ... Granted unconditional free agency (February 17, 1995). ... Signed by Saints (August 16, 1995). ... Released by Saints (August 27, 1995). ... Signed by Carolina Panthers (February 7, 1996). ... Granted unconditional free agency (February 14, 1997). ... Re-signed by Panthers (June 13, 1997).
CHAMPIONSHIP GAME EXPERIENCE: Member of Chargers for AFC championship game (1994 season); did not play. ... Played in Super Bowl XXIX (1994 season).
RECORDS: Shares NFL single-season records for most touchdowns by fumble recovery—2 (1990); and most touchdowns by recovery of opponents' fumbles—2 (1990).
PRO STATISTICS: 1987—Recovered two fumbles (including one in end zone for a touchdown). 1989—Recovered one fumble. 1990—Recovered three fumbles for one yard (including two in end zone for touchdowns). 1992—Recovered one fumble. 1996—Recovered one fumble for 14 yards. 1997—Recovered one fumble for three yards.

Year Team	G	GS	SACKS
1987—San Diego NFL	9	4	3.0
1988—San Diego NFL	13	0	0.0
1989—San Diego NFL	14	0	2.5
1990—San Diego NFL	14	9	1.0
1991—New Orleans NFL	16	0	1.0
1992—New Orleans NFL	16	2	1.0
1993—New Orleans NFL	13	11	2.5
1994—New Orleans NFL	8	5	0.0
—San Diego NFL	4	0	0.5
1995—		Did not play.	
1996—Carolina NFL	15	5	3.0
1997—Carolina NFL	16	11	5.5
Pro totals (10 years)	138	47	20.0

MILLER, NATE   OT/G   FALCONS

PERSONAL: Born October 8, 1971, in Tuscaloosa, Ala. ... 6-3/310. ... Full name: Nathan Udell Miller.
HIGH SCHOOL: Central East (Tuscaloosa, Ala.).
COLLEGE: Lousiana State.
TRANSACTIONS/CAREER NOTES: Signed as non-drafted free agent by Atlanta Falcons (April 24, 1995). ... Released by Falcons (August 22, 1995). ... Re-signed by Falcons to practice squad (August 29, 1995). ... Activated (December 1, 1995). ... On inactive list (December 1, 1995-remainder of season). ... Released by Falcons (September 4, 1996). ... Re-signed by Falcons to practice squad (September 5, 1996). ... Activated (December 9, 1996); did not play. ... Assigned by Falcons to Frankfurt Galaxy in 1997 World League enhancement allocation program (February 19, 1997).
PLAYING EXPERIENCE: Atlanta NFL, 1997. ... Games/Games started: 13/0.

MILLOY, LAWYER   S   PATRIOTS

PERSONAL: Born November 14, 1973, in St. Louis. ... 6-0/208.
HIGH SCHOOL: Lincoln (Tacoma, Wash.).
COLLEGE: Washington.
TRANSACTIONS/CAREER NOTES: Selected after junior season by New England Patriots in second round (36th pick overall) of 1996 NFL draft. ... Signed by Patriots (June 5, 1996).
CHAMPIONSHIP GAME EXPERIENCE: Played in AFC championship game (1996 season). ... Played in Super Bowl XXXI (1996 season).
HONORS: Named defensive back on THE SPORTING NEWS college All-America first team (1995).
PRO STATISTICS: 1996—Recovered one fumble. 1997—Recovered two fumbles.

			INTERCEPTIONS				SACKS
Year Team	G	GS	No.	Yds.	Avg.	TD	No.
1996—New England NFL	16	10	2	14	7.0	0	1.0
1997—New England NFL	16	16	3	15	5.0	0	0.0
Pro totals (2 years)	32	26	5	29	5.8	0	1.0

MILLS, ERNIE   WR   COWBOYS

PERSONAL: Born October 28, 1968, in Dunnellon, Fla. ... 5-11/192. ... Full name: Ernest Lee Mills III.
HIGH SCHOOL: Dunnellon (Fla.) Senior.
COLLEGE: Florida.
TRANSACTIONS/CAREER NOTES: Selected by Pittsburgh Steelers in third round (73rd pick overall) of 1991 NFL draft. ... Signed by Steelers (August 13, 1991). ... Granted free agency (February 17, 1994). ... Re-signed by Steelers (June 1, 1994). ... On physically unable to perform list with knee injury (August 24-October 25, 1996). ... Granted unconditional free agency (February 14, 1997). ... Signed by Carolina Panthers (March 5, 1997). ... Released by Panthers (February 13,"1998). ... Signed by Dallas Cowboys (February 27, 1998).
CHAMPIONSHIP GAME EXPERIENCE: Played in AFC championship game (1994 and 1995 seasons). ... Played in Super Bowl XXX (1995 season).
PRO STATISTICS: 1991—Recovered punt return in end zone for a touchdown, returned one punt for no yards and recovered one fumble. 1995—Recovered one fumble. 1996—Recovered one fumble for five yards.
SINGLE GAME HIGHS (regular season): Receptions—6 (December 24, 1995, vs. Green Bay); yards—99 (December 16, 1995, vs. New England); and touchdown receptions—2 (December 10, 1995, vs. Oakland).

			RUSHING				RECEIVING				KICKOFF RETURNS				TOTALS			
Year Team	G	GS	Att.	Yds.	Avg.	TD	No.	Yds.	Avg.	TD	No.	Yds.	Avg.	TD	TD	2pt.	Pts.	Fum.
1991—Pittsburgh NFL	16	2	0	0	...	0	3	79	26.3	1	11	284	25.8	0	2	...	12	0
1992—Pittsburgh NFL	16	5	1	20	20.0	0	30	383	12.8	3	1	11	11.0	0	3	...	18	2
1993—Pittsburgh NFL	14	5	3	12	4.0	0	29	386	13.3	1	0	0	...	0	1	...	6	0
1994—Pittsburgh NFL	15	6	3	18	6.0	0	19	384	20.2	1	2	6	3.0	0	1	0	6	1
1995—Pittsburgh NFL	16	4	5	39	7.8	0	39	679	17.4	8	54	1306	24.2	0	8	0	48	2
1996—Pittsburgh NFL	9	3	2	24	12.0	0	7	92	13.1	1	8	146	18.3	0	1	0	6	0
1997—Carolina NFL	10	5	0	0	...	0	11	127	11.5	1	4	65	16.3	0	1	0	6	0
Pro totals (7 years)	96	30	14	113	8.1	0	138	2130	15.4	16	80	1818	22.7	0	17	0	102	5

MILLS, JIM   OT/G   CHARGERS

PERSONAL: Born March 30, 1973, in Marysville, Wash. ... 6-4/290. ... Full name: James Gary Mills.
HIGH SCHOOL: Marysville (Wash.).
COLLEGE: Idaho.
TRANSACTIONS/CAREER NOTES: Selected by San Diego Chargers in sixth round (190th pick overall) of 1996 NFL draft. ... Signed by Chargers (June 20, 1996).
PLAYING EXPERIENCE: San Diego NFL, 1996 and 1997. ... Games/Games started: 1996 (1/0), 1997 (1/0). Total: 2/0.

MILLS, JOHN HENRY   TE   RAIDERS

PERSONAL: Born October 31, 1969, in Jacksonville. ... 6-0/222. ... Full name: John Henry Mills.
HIGH SCHOOL: Godby (Tallahassee, Fla.).
COLLEGE: Wake Forest (degree in speech communications, 1993).
TRANSACTIONS/CAREER NOTES: Selected by Houston Oilers in fifth round (131st pick overall) of 1993 NFL draft. ... Signed by Oilers (July 16, 1993). ... Released by Oilers (August 30, 1993). ... Re-signed by Oilers (August 31, 1993). ... Granted free agency (February 16, 1996). ... Re-signed by Oilers (July 20, 1996). ... Granted unconditional free agency (February 14, 1997). ... Signed by Oakland Raiders (June 6, 1997). ... Granted unconditional free agency (February 13, 1998). ... Re-signed by Raiders (February 17, 1998).
HONORS: Played in Pro Bowl (1996 season).
PRO STATISTICS: 1994—Caught one pass for four yards. 1996—Recovered two fumbles.

M

Year Team	G	GS	KICKOFF RETURNS No.	Yds.	Avg.	TD	TOTALS TD	2pt.	Pts.	Fum.
1993—Houston NFL	16	0	11	230	20.9	0	0	...	0	0
1994—Houston NFL	16	1	15	282	18.8	0	0	0	0	1
1995—Houston NFL	16	0	0	0	...	0	0	0	0	0
1996—Houston NFL	16	0	0	0	...	0	0	0	0	0
1997—Oakland NFL	16	0	0	0	...	0	0	0	0	0
Pro totals (5 years)	80	1	26	512	19.7	0	0	0	0	1

MILLS, SAM — LB

PERSONAL: Born June 3, 1959, in Neptune, N.J. ... 5-9/232. ... Full name: Samuel Davis Mills Jr.
HIGH SCHOOL: Long Branch (N.J.).
COLLEGE: Montclair (N.J.) State.
TRANSACTIONS/CAREER NOTES: Signed as non-drafted free agent by Cleveland Browns (May 3, 1981). ... Released by Browns (August 24, 1981). ... Signed by Toronto Argonauts of CFL (March 1982). ... Released by Argonauts (June 30, 1982). ... Signed by Philadelphia Stars of USFL (October 21, 1982). ... Stars franchise moved to Baltimore (November 1, 1984). ... Granted free agency (August 1, 1985). ... Re-signed by Stars (August 7, 1985). ... Granted free agency when USFL suspended operations (August 7, 1986). ... Signed by New Orleans Saints (August 12, 1986). ... Granted roster exemption (August 12-22, 1986). ... Granted unconditional free agency (February 17, 1995). ... Signed by Carolina Panthers (March 9, 1995). ... Granted unconditional free agency (February 14, 1997). ... Re-signed by Panthers (March 6, 1997). ... Announced retirement (December 20, 1997).
CHAMPIONSHIP GAME EXPERIENCE: Played in USFL championship game (1983-1985 seasons). ... Played in NFC championship game (1996 season).
HONORS: Named inside linebacker on THE SPORTING NEWS USFL All-Star team (1983 and 1985). ... Played in Pro Bowl (1987, 1988, 1991, 1992 and 1996 seasons). ... Named inside linebacker on THE SPORTING NEWS NFL All-Pro team (1991 and 1992).
PRO STATISTICS: USFL: 1983—Credited with 3$\frac{1}{2}$ sacks for 37 yards and recovered five fumbles for eight yards. 1984—Credited with five sacks for 39 yards and recovered three fumbles for two yards. 1985—Credited with 5$\frac{1}{2}$ sacks for 41 yards and recovered two fumbles. NFL: 1986—Recovered one fumble. 1987—Recovered three fumbles. 1988—Recovered four fumbles. 1989—Recovered one fumble. 1990—Recovered one fumble. 1991—Recovered two fumbles. 1992—Recovered three fumbles for 76 yards and a touchdown. 1993—Recovered one fumble for 30 yards and a touchdown. 1994—Recovered one fumble. 1995—Recovered four fumbles for seven yards. 1996—Recovered two fumbles for 41 yards and a touchdown. 1997—Returned two kickoffs for 12 yards and fumbled once.

Year Team	G	GS	INTERCEPTIONS No.	Yds.	Avg.	TD	SACKS No.
1981—				Did not play.			
1982—				Did not play.			
1983—Philadelphia USFL	18	18	3	13	4.3	0	3.5
1984—Philadelphia USFL	18	...	3	24	8.0	0	5.0
1985—Baltimore USFL	18	...	3	32	10.7	1	5.5
1986—New Orleans NFL	16	13	0	0	...	0	0.0
1987—New Orleans NFL	12	12	0	0	...	0	0.0
1988—New Orleans NFL	16	16	0	0	...	0	0.0
1989—New Orleans NFL	16	15	0	0	...	0	3.0
1990—New Orleans NFL	16	14	0	0	...	0	0.5
1991—New Orleans NFL	16	16	2	13	6.5	0	1.0
1992—New Orleans NFL	16	16	1	10	10.0	0	3.0
1993—New Orleans NFL	9	7	0	0	...	0	2.0
1994—New Orleans NFL	16	16	1	10	10.0	0	1.0
1995—Carolina NFL	16	16	5	58	11.6	1	4.5
1996—Carolina NFL	16	16	1	10	10.0	0	5.5
1997—Carolina NFL	16	16	1	18	18.0	0	0.0
USFL totals (3 years)	54	...	9	69	7.7	1	14.0
NFL totals (12 years)	181	173	11	119	10.8	1	20.5
Pro totals (15 years)	235	...	20	188	9.4	2	34.5

MILNE, BRIAN — FB — BENGALS

PERSONAL: Born January 7, 1973, in Waterford, Pa. ... 6-3/254. ... Full name: Brian Fitzsimons Milne.
HIGH SCHOOL: LeBoeuf (Pa.).
COLLEGE: Penn State.
TRANSACTIONS/CAREER NOTES: Selected by Indianapolis Colts in fourth round (115th pick overall) of 1996 NFL draft. ... Signed by Colts (July 5, 1996). ... Released by Colts (August 20, 1996). ... Claimed on waivers by Cincinnati Bengals (August 21, 1996).
SINGLE GAME HIGHS (regular season): Attempts—3 (November 9, 1997, vs. Indianapolis); yards—9 (November 9, 1997, vs. Indianapolis); and rushing touchdowns—1 (November 30, 1997, vs. Philadelphia).
MISCELLANEOUS: Won NCAA discus championship (1993).

Year Team	G	GS	RUSHING Att.	Yds.	Avg.	TD	RECEIVING No.	Yds.	Avg.	TD	TOTALS TD	2pt.	Pts.	Fum.
1996—Cincinnati NFL	6	5	8	22	2.8	1	3	29	9.7	0	1	0	6	0
1997—Cincinnati NFL	16	16	13	32	2.5	2	23	138	6.0	0	2	0	12	0
Pro totals (2 years)	22	21	21	54	2.6	3	26	167	6.4	0	3	0	18	0

MILSTEAD, ROD — G — REDSKINS

PERSONAL: Born November 10, 1969, in Washington, D.C. ... 6-2/290. ... Full name: Roderick Leon Milstead Jr.
HIGH SCHOOL: Lackey (Indian Head, Md.).
COLLEGE: Delaware State (degree in sociology and criminal justice).
TRANSACTIONS/CAREER NOTES: Selected by Dallas Cowboys in fifth round (121st pick overall) of 1992 NFL draft. ... Traded by Cowboys to Cleveland Browns for eighth-round pick (traded) in 1993 draft (August 24, 1992). ... On injured reserve with back injury (September 3,

1992-entire season). ... Released by Browns (August 30, 1993). ... Re-signed by Browns (October 6, 1993). ... Released by Browns (November 27, 1993). ... Re-signed by Browns (November 30, 1993). ... Released by Browns (August 28, 1994). ... Signed by San Francisco 49ers (September 14, 1994). ... Granted unconditional free agency (February 14, 1997). ... Re-signed by 49ers (May 1, 1997). ... Released by 49ers (August 24, 1997). ... Re-signed by 49ers (October 22, 1997). ... Granted unconditional free agency (February 13, 1998). ... Signed by Washington Redskins (March 3, 1998).

PLAYING EXPERIENCE: San Francisco NFL, 1994-1997. ... Games/Games started: 1994 (5/0), 1995 (16/12), 1996 (11/0), 1997 (4/0). Total: 36/12.

CHAMPIONSHIP GAME EXPERIENCE: Member of 49ers for NFC championship game (1994 and 1997 seasons); inactive. ... Member of Super Bowl championship team (1994 season).

MIMS, CHRIS — DE — CHARGERS

PERSONAL: Born September 29, 1970, in Los Angeles. ... 6-5/290. ... Full name: Christopher Eddie Mims.
HIGH SCHOOL: Dorsey (Los Angeles).
JUNIOR COLLEGE: Los Angeles Pierce Junior College, then Los Angeles Southwest Community College.
COLLEGE: Tennessee.
TRANSACTIONS/CAREER NOTES: Selected by San Diego Chargers in first round (23rd pick overall) of 1992 NFL draft. ... Signed by Chargers (June 5, 1992). ... Released by Chargers (April 14, 1997). ... Signed by Washington Redskins (June 10, 1997). ... Granted unconditional free agency (February 13, 1998). ... Signed by Oakland Raiders (April 23, 1998). ... Released by Raiders (May 1998). ... Signed by Chargers (June 10, 1998).
CHAMPIONSHIP GAME EXPERIENCE: Played in AFC championship game (1994 season). ... Played in Super Bowl XXIX (1994 season).
PRO STATISTICS: 1992—Credited with one safety and recovered one fumble. 1993—Recovered two fumbles. 1994—Recovered two fumbles. 1995—Recovered one fumble. 1996—Recovered two fumbles.

Year Team	G	GS	SACKS
1992—San Diego NFL	16	4	10.0
1993—San Diego NFL	16	7	7.0
1994—San Diego NFL	16	16	11.0
1995—San Diego NFL	15	15	2.0
1996—San Diego NFL	15	15	6.0
1997—Washington NFL	11	7	4.0
Pro totals (6 years)	89	64	40.0

MINCY, CHARLES — S — BUCCANEERS

PERSONAL: Born December 16, 1969, in Los Angeles. ... 5-11/195. ... Full name: Charles Anthony Mincy.
HIGH SCHOOL: Dorsey (Los Angeles).
JUNIOR COLLEGE: Pasadena (Calif.) City College.
COLLEGE: Washington.
TRANSACTIONS/CAREER NOTES: Selected by Kansas City Chiefs in fifth round (133rd pick overall) of 1991 NFL draft. ... Signed by Chiefs (July 17, 1991). ... On injured reserve with ankle/toe injury (August 30-December 25, 1991). ... Did not play during regular season (1991); played in two playoff games. ... Granted free agency (February 17, 1994). ... Re-signed by Chiefs (June 17, 1994). ... Granted unconditional free agency (February 17, 1995). ... Signed by Minnesota Vikings (March 6, 1995). ... Released by Vikings (February 9, 1996). ... Signed by Tampa Bay Buccaneers (October 2, 1996). ... Granted unconditional free agency (February 13, 1998). ... Re-signed by Buccaneers (March 30, 1998).
CHAMPIONSHIP GAME EXPERIENCE: Played in AFC championship game (1993 season).
PRO STATISTICS: 1992—Recovered one fumble for 30 yards and a touchdown. 1993—Recovered two fumbles. 1995—Recovered two fumbles for 10 yards. 1997—Recovered one fumble.

Year Team	G	GS	INTERCEPTIONS				PUNT RETURNS				TOTALS			
			No.	Yds.	Avg.	TD	No.	Yds.	Avg.	TD	TD	2pt.	Pts.	Fum.
1991—Kansas City NFL						Did not play.								
1992—Kansas City NFL	16	16	4	128	32.0	▲2	1	4	4.0	0	3	...	18	0
1993—Kansas City NFL	16	4	5	44	8.8	0	2	9	4.5	0	0	...	0	0
1994—Kansas City NFL	16	7	3	49	16.3	0	0	0	...	0	0	0	0	0
1995—Minnesota NFL	16	9	3	37	12.3	0	4	22	5.5	0	0	0	0	0
1996—Tampa Bay NFL	2	0	1	26	26.0	0	0	0	...	0	0	0	0	0
1997—Tampa Bay NFL	16	9	1	14	14.0	0	0	0	...	0	0	0	0	0
Pro totals (6 years)	82	45	17	298	17.5	2	7	35	5.0	0	3	0	18	0

MINIEFIELD, KEVIN — DB

PERSONAL: Born March 2, 1970, in Phoenix. ... 5-9/180. ... Full name: Kevin Lamar Miniefield.
HIGH SCHOOL: Camelback (Phoenix).
COLLEGE: Arizona State.
TRANSACTIONS/CAREER NOTES: Selected by Detroit Lions in eighth round (201st pick overall) of 1993 NFL draft. ... Signed by Lions (July 17, 1993). ... Released by Lions (August 30, 1993). ... Re-signed by Lions to practice squad (August 31, 1993). ... Signed by Chicago Bears off Lions practice squad (October 13, 1993). ... Granted unconditional free agency (February 14, 1997). ... Re-signed by Bears (March 2, 1997). ... Released by Bears (August 15, 1997). ... Signed by Arizona Cardinals (October 15, 1997). ... Released by Cardinals (November 8, 1997).
PRO STATISTICS: 1994—Recovered one fumble for minus five yards. 1996—Credited with 1 1/2 sacks.

Year Team	G	GS	INTERCEPTIONS			
			No.	Yds.	Avg.	TD
1993—Chicago NFL	8	0	0	0	...	0
1994—Chicago NFL	12	0	0	0	...	0
1995—Chicago NFL	15	7	3	37	12.3	0
1996—Chicago NFL	13	3	0	0	...	0
1997—Arizona NFL	3	0	0	0	...	0
Pro totals (5 years)	51	10	3	37	12.3	0

MINTER, BARRY   LB   BEARS

PERSONAL: Born January 28, 1970, in Mt. Pleasant, Texas. ... 6-2/242. ... Full name: Barry Antoine Minter.
HIGH SCHOOL: Mt. Pleasant (Texas).
COLLEGE: Tulsa.
TRANSACTIONS/CAREER NOTES: Selected by Dallas Cowboys in sixth round (168th pick overall) of 1993 NFL draft. ... Signed by Cowboys (July 14, 1993). ... Traded by Cowboys with LB Vinson Smith and sixth-round pick (DE Carl Reeves) in 1995 draft to Chicago Bears for TE Kelly Blackwell, S Markus Paul and LB John Roper (August 17, 1993). ... Granted free agency (February 16, 1996). ... Re-signed by Bears (February 26, 1996). ... Granted unconditional free agency (February 13, 1998). ... Re-signed by Bears (February 20, 1998).
PLAYING EXPERIENCE: Chicago NFL, 1993-1997. ... Games/Games started: 1993 (2/0), 1994 (13/1), 1995 (16/3), 1996 (16/7), 1997 (16/16). Total: 63/27.
PRO STATISTICS: 1994—Recovered one fumble. 1995—Intercepted one pass for two yards and a touchdown. 1996—Intercepted one pass for five yards and credited with one sack. 1997—Credited with six sacks and recovered three fumbles.

MINTER, MIKE   S   PANTHERS

PERSONAL: Born January 15, 1974, in Cleveland. ... 5-10/188. ... Full name: Michael Christopher Minter.
HIGH SCHOOL: Lawton (Okla.).
COLLEGE: Nebraska.
TRANSACTIONS/CAREER NOTES: Selected by Carolina Panthers in second round (56th pick overall) of 1997 NFL draft. ... Signed by Panthers (June 12, 1997).
PRO STATISTICS: 1997—Recovered two fumbles.

Year Team	G	GS	SACKS
1997—Carolina NFL	16	11	3.5

MIRER, RICK   QB   BEARS

PERSONAL: Born March 19, 1970, in Goshen, Ind. ... 6-2/215. ... Full name: Rick F. Mirer.
HIGH SCHOOL: Goshen (Ind.).
COLLEGE: Notre Dame.
TRANSACTIONS/CAREER NOTES: Selected by Seattle Seahawks in first round (second pick overall) of 1993 NFL draft. ... Signed by Seahawks (August 2, 1993). ... On injured reserve with thumb injury (December 20, 1994-remainder of season). ... Traded by Seahawks with fourth-round pick (RB Darnell Autry) in 1997 draft to Chicago Bears for first-round pick (traded to Atlanta) in 1997 draft (February 18, 1997).
RECORDS: Holds NFL rookie-season records for most yards passing—2,833; most passes attempted—486; and most passes completed—274 (1993).
PRO STATISTICS: 1993—Fumbled 13 times and recovered five fumbles for minus 14 yards. 1994—Fumbled twice and recovered one fumble for minus seven yards. 1995—Fumbled five times and recovered one fumble for minus one yard. 1996—Fumbled four times. 1997—Fumbled four times and recovered one fumble for minus four yards.
SINGLE GAME HIGHS (regular season): Attempts—43 (October 24, 1993, vs. New England); completions—25 (October 3, 1993, vs. San Diego); yards—287 (December 5, 1993, vs. Kansas City); and touchdown passes—3 (September 11, 1994, vs. Los Angeles Raiders).
MISCELLANEOUS: Regular-season record as starting NFL quarterback: 20-34 (.370).

Year Team	G	GS	PASSING								RUSHING				TOTALS		
			Att.	Cmp.	Pct.	Yds.	TD	Int.	Avg.	Rat.	Att.	Yds.	Avg.	TD	TD	2pt.	Pts.
1993—Seattle NFL	16	16	486	274	56.4	2833	12	17	5.83	67.0	68	343	5.0	3	3	0	18
1994—Seattle NFL	13	13	381	195	51.2	2151	11	7	5.65	70.2	34	153	4.5	0	0	0	0
1995—Seattle NFL	15	13	391	209	53.5	2564	13	§20	6.56	63.7	43	193	4.5	1	1	0	6
1996—Seattle NFL	11	9	265	136	51.3	1546	5	12	5.83	56.6	33	191	5.8	2	2	0	12
1997—Chicago NFL	7	3	103	53	51.5	420	0	6	4.08	37.7	20	78	3.9	1	1	0	8
Pro totals (5 years)	62	54	1626	867	53.3	9514	41	62	5.85	63.4	198	958	4.8	7	7	0	44

MITCHELL, BRANDON   DT   PATRIOTS

PERSONAL: Born June 19, 1975, in Abbeville, La. ... 6-3/289. ... Full name: Brandon Paul Mitchell.
HIGH SCHOOL: Abbeville (La.).
COLLEGE: Texas A&M.
TRANSACTIONS/CAREER NOTES: Selected by New England Patriots in second round (59th pick overall) of 1997 NFL draft. ... Signed by Patriots (June 6, 1997).
PLAYING EXPERIENCE: New England NFL, 1997. ... Games/Games started: 11/0.

MITCHELL, BRIAN   FB/KR   REDSKINS

PERSONAL: Born August 18, 1968, in Fort Polk, La. ... 5-10/221. ... Full name: Brian Keith Mitchell.
HIGH SCHOOL: Plaquemine (La.).
COLLEGE: Southwestern Louisiana.
TRANSACTIONS/CAREER NOTES: Selected by Washington Redskins in fifth round (130th pick overall) of 1990 NFL draft. ... Signed by Redskins (July 22, 1990). ... Granted free agency (February 1, 1992). ... Re-signed by Redskins for 1992 season. ... Granted unconditional free agency (February 17, 1994). ... Re-signed by Redskins (May 24, 1994). ... Granted free agency (February 17, 1995). ... Re-signed by Redskins (March 27, 1995). ... Granted unconditional free agency (February 13, 1998). ... Re-signed by Redskins (February 13, 1998).
CHAMPIONSHIP GAME EXPERIENCE: Played in NFC championship game (1991 season). ... Member of Super Bowl championship team (1991 season).
HONORS: Named punt returner on THE SPORTING NEWS NFL All-Pro team (1995). ... Played in Pro Bowl (1995 season).
RECORDS: Holds NFL single-season record for most yards by combined kick return—1,930 (1994).

PRO STATISTICS: 1990—Attempted six passes with three completions for 40 yards and fumbled twice. 1991—Fumbled eight times and recovered one fumble. 1992—Attempted one pass without a completion, fumbled four times and recovered two fumbles. 1993—Attempted two passes with one completion for 50 yards and an interception, fumbled three times and recovered one fumble. 1994—Had only pass attempt intercepted and fumbled four times. 1995—Fumbled twice and recovered one fumble. 1996—Attempted one pass without a completion, fumbled once and recovered two fumbles. 1997—Fumbled three times.

SINGLE GAME HIGHS (regular season): Attempts—21 (September 6, 1993, vs. Dallas); yards—116 (September 6, 1993, vs. Dallas); and rushing touchdowns—2 (September 6, 1996, vs. Dallas).

STATISTICAL PLATEAUS: 100-yard rushing games: 1993 (1).

Year Team	G	GS	RUSHING Att.	Yds.	Avg.	TD	RECEIVING No.	Yds.	Avg.	TD	PUNT RETURNS No.	Yds.	Avg.	TD	KICKOFF RETURNS No.	Yds.	Avg.	TD	TOTALS TD	2pt.	Pts.
1990—Washington NFL .	15	0	15	81	5.4	1	2	5	2.5	0	12	107	8.9	0	18	365	20.3	0	1	...	6
1991—Washington NFL .	16	0	3	14	4.7	0	0	0	...	0	45	*600	13.3	*2	29	583	20.1	0	2	...	12
1992—Washington NFL .	16	0	6	70	11.7	0	3	30	10.0	0	29	271	9.3	1	23	492	21.4	0	1	...	6
1993—Washington NFL .	16	4	63	246	3.9	3	20	157	7.9	0	29	193	6.7	0	33	678	20.5	0	3	...	18
1994—Washington NFL .	16	7	78	311	4.0	0	26	236	9.1	1	32	‡452	*14.1	†2	58	1478	25.5	0	3	1	20
1995—Washington NFL .	16	1	46	301	6.5	1	38	324	8.5	1	25	315	12.6	†1	55	1408	‡25.6	0	3	0	18
1996—Washington NFL .	16	2	39	193	4.9	0	32	286	8.9	0	23	258	11.2	0	56	1258	22.5	0	0	0	0
1997—Washington NFL .	16	1	23	107	4.7	1	36	438	12.2	1	38	442	11.6	∞1	47	1094	23.3	1	4	0	24
Pro totals (8 years)	127	15	273	1323	4.8	6	157	1476	9.4	3	233	2638	11.3	7	319	7356	23.1	1	17	1	104

MITCHELL, KEITH   LB   SAINTS

PERSONAL: Born July 24, 1974, in Garland, Texas. ... 6-2/240. ... Full name: Carlence Marquis Mitchell.
HIGH SCHOOL: Garland (Texas).
COLLEGE: Texas A&M.
TRANSACTIONS/CAREER NOTES: Signed as non-drafted free agent by New Orleans Saints (April 25, 1997).
HONORS: Named outside linebacker on THE SPORTING NEWS college All-America second team (1996).

Year Team	G	GS	SACKS
1997—New Orleans NFL...	16	2	4.0

MITCHELL, KEVIN   LB   SAINTS

PERSONAL: Born January 1, 1971, in Harrisburg, Pa. ... 6-1/250. ... Full name: Kevin Danyelle Mitchell. ... Cousin of Troy Drayton, tight end, Miami Dolphins.
HIGH SCHOOL: Harrisburg (Pa.).
COLLEGE: Syracuse.
TRANSACTIONS/CAREER NOTES: Selected by San Francisco 49ers in second round (53rd pick overall) of 1994 NFL draft. ... Signed by 49ers (July 20, 1994). ... Granted free agency (February 14, 1997). ... Re-signed by 49ers (April 24, 1997). ... Granted free agency (February 13, 1998). ... Signed by New Orleans Saints (February 19, 1998).
PLAYING EXPERIENCE: San Francisco NFL, 1994-1997. ... Games/Games started: 1994 (16/0), 1995 (15/0), 1996 (12/3), 1997 (16/0). Total: 59/3.
CHAMPIONSHIP GAME EXPERIENCE: Played in NFC championship game (1994 and 1997 seasons). ... Member of Super Bowl championship team (1994 season).
HONORS: Named defensive lineman on THE SPORTING NEWS college All-America second team (1992 and 1993).
PRO STATISTICS: 1996—Credited with one sack and recovered one fumble.

M

MITCHELL, PETE   TE   JAGUARS

PERSONAL: Born October 9, 1971, in Bloomfield Hills, Mich. ... 6-2/238. ... Full name: Peter Clark Mitchell.
HIGH SCHOOL: Brother Rice (Bloomfield Hills, Mich.).
COLLEGE: Boston College (degree in communications).
TRANSACTIONS/CAREER NOTES: Selected by Miami Dolphins in fourth round (122nd pick overall) of 1995 NFL draft. ... Signed by Dolphins (July 14, 1995). ... Traded by Dolphins to Jacksonville Jaguars for WR Mike Williams (August 27, 1995). ... Granted free agency (February 13, 1998). ... Re-signed by Jaguars (April 13, 1998).
CHAMPIONSHIP GAME EXPERIENCE: Played in AFC championship game (1996 season).
HONORS: Named tight end on THE SPORTING NEWS college All-America first team (1993 and 1994).
PRO STATISTICS: 1997—Returned two kickoffs for 17 yards and recovered one fumble.
SINGLE GAME HIGHS (regular season): Receptions—10 (November 19, 1995, vs. Tampa Bay); yards—161 (November 19, 1995, vs. Tampa Bay); and touchdown receptions—1 (November 23, 1997, vs. Cincinnati).
STATISTICAL PLATEAUS: 100-yard receiving games: 1995 (1).

Year Team	G	GS	RECEIVING No.	Yds.	Avg.	TD	TOTALS TD	2pt.	Pts.	Fum.
1995—Jacksonville NFL	16	4	41	527	12.9	2	2	0	12	0
1996—Jacksonville NFL	16	7	52	575	11.1	1	1	0	6	1
1997—Jacksonville NFL	16	12	35	380	10.9	4	4	0	24	0
Pro totals (3 years)	48	23	128	1482	11.6	7	7	0	42	1

MITCHELL, SCOTT   QB   LIONS

PERSONAL: Born January 2, 1968, in Salt Lake City. ... 6-6/230. ... Full name: William Scott Mitchell.
HIGH SCHOOL: Springville (Utah).
COLLEGE: Utah.
TRANSACTIONS/CAREER NOTES: Selected after junior season by Miami Dolphins in fourth round (93rd pick overall) of 1990 NFL draft. ... Signed by Dolphins (July 20, 1990). ... Inactive for 16 games (1990). ... Granted free agency (February 1, 1992). ... Assigned by Dolphins to Orlando Thunder in 1992 World League enhancement allocation program (February 20, 1992). ... Re-signed by Dolphins (February 21, 1992).

... Granted unconditional free agency (February 17, 1994). ... Signed by Detroit Lions (March 6, 1994). ... On injured reserve with wrist injury (November 8, 1994-remainder of season).

CHAMPIONSHIP GAME EXPERIENCE: Played in AFC championship game (1992 season).

PRO STATISTICS: W.L.: 1992—Fumbled six times and recovered two fumbles for minus 19 yards. NFL: 1993—Fumbled once and recovered one fumble for minus four yards. 1994—Fumbled eight times and recovered two fumbles for minus five yards. 1995—Fumbled eight times and recovered one fumble. 1996—Fumbled nine times and recovered five fumbles for minus three yards. 1997—Tied for NFC lead with 15 fumbles and recovered four fumbles for minus 15 yards.

SINGLE GAME HIGHS (regular season): Attempts—50 (September 7, 1997, vs. Tampa Bay); completions—31 (October 13, 1996, vs. Oakland); yards—410 (November 23, 1995, vs. Minnesota); and touchdown passes—4 (September 22, 1996, vs. Chicago).

STATISTICAL PLATEAUS: 300-yard passing games: 1993 (1), 1995 (5), 1996 (2), 1997 (1). Total: 9.

MISCELLANEOUS: Regular-season record as starting NFL quarterback: 30-32 (.484). Postseason record as starting NFL quarterback: 0-2.

				PASSING							RUSHING				TOTALS		
Year Team	G	GS	Att.	Cmp.	Pct.	Yds.	TD	Int.	Avg.	Rat.	Att.	Yds.	Avg.	TD	TD	2pt.	Pts.
1990—Miami NFL								Did not play.									
1991—Miami NFL	2	0	0	0	...	0	0	0	...	...	0	0	...	0	0	...	0
1992—Orlando W.L.	10	10	*361	*201	55.7	2213	12	7	6.13	77.0	21	45	2.1	1	1	...	6
—Miami NFL	16	0	8	2	25.0	32	0	1	4.00	-4.2	8	10	1.3	0	0	...	0
1993—Miami NFL	13	7	233	133	57.1	1773	12	8	7.61	84.2	21	89	4.2	0	0	...	0
1994—Detroit NFL...............	9	9	246	119	48.4	1456	10	11	5.92	62.0	15	24	1.6	1	1	0	6
1995—Detroit NFL...............	16	16	583	346	59.3	4338	32	12	7.44	92.3	36	104	2.9	4	4	0	24
1996—Detroit NFL...............	14	14	437	253	57.9	2917	17	17	6.68	74.9	37	83	2.2	4	4	0	24
1997—Detroit NFL...............	16	16	509	293	57.6	3484	19	14	6.84	79.6	37	83	2.2	1	1	0	6
W.L. totals (1 year)	10	10	361	201	55.7	2213	12	7	6.13	77.0	21	45	2.1	1	1	0	6
NFL totals (7 years)	86	62	2016	1146	56.8	14000	90	63	6.94	80.2	154	393	2.6	10	10	0	60
Pro totals (8 years)...............	96	72	2377	1347	56.7	16213	102	70	6.82	79.8	175	438	2.5	11	11	0	66

MITCHELL, SHANNON — TE

PERSONAL: Born March 28, 1972, in Alcoa, Tenn. ... 6-2/245. ... Full name: Shannon Lamont Mitchell.

HIGH SCHOOL: Alcoa (Tenn.).

COLLEGE: Georgia.

TRANSACTIONS/CAREER NOTES: Signed as non-drafted free agent by San Diego Chargers (April 28, 1994). ... Granted free agency (February 14, 1997). ... Released by Chargers (June 2, 1997). ... Re-signed by Chargers (November 26, 1997). ... Released by Chargers following 1997 season.

CHAMPIONSHIP GAME EXPERIENCE: Played in AFC championship game (1994 season). ... Played in Super Bowl XXIX (1994 season).

PRO STATISTICS: 1994—Returned one kickoff for 18 yards.

SINGLE GAME HIGHS (regular season): Receptions—3 (December 11, 1994, vs. San Francisco); yards—44 (December 11, 1994, vs. San Francisco); and touchdown receptions—1 (October 9, 1995, vs. Kansas City).

			RECEIVING				TOTALS			
Year Team	G	GS	No.	Yds.	Avg.	TD	TD	2pt.	Pts.	Fum.
1994—San Diego NFL	16	6	11	105	9.5	0	0	0	0	0
1995—San Diego NFL	16	2	3	31	10.3	1	1	0	6	0
1996—San Diego NFL	16	11	10	57	5.7	0	0	0	0	1
1997—San Diego NFL	4	1	1	14	14.0	0	0	...	0	0
Pro totals (4 years)	52	20	25	207	8.3	1	1	0	6	1

M

MIX, BRYANT — DE — OILERS

PERSONAL: Born July 28, 1972, in Water Valley, Miss. ... 6-3/293. ... Full name: Bryant Lee Mix.

HIGH SCHOOL: Water Valley (Miss.).

JUNIOR COLLEGE: Northwest Mississippi Community College.

COLLEGE: Alcorn State.

TRANSACTIONS/CAREER NOTES: Selected by Houston Oilers in second round (38th pick overall) of 1996 NFL draft. ... Signed by Oilers (July 20, 1996). ... Oilers franchise moved to Tennessee for 1997 season.

Year Team	G	GS	SACKS
1996—Houston NFL	6	2	1.0
1997—Tennessee NFL	1	0	0.0
Pro totals (2 years)................................	7	2	1.0

MOBLEY, JOHN — LB — BRONCOS

PERSONAL: Born October 10, 1973, in Chester, Pa. ... 6-1/236. ... Full name: John Ulysses Mobley.

HIGH SCHOOL: Chichester (Chester, Pa.).

COLLEGE: Kutztown (Pa.) University.

TRANSACTIONS/CAREER NOTES: Selected by Denver Broncos in first round (15th pick overall) of 1996 NFL draft. ... Signed by Broncos (July 23, 1996).

CHAMPIONSHIP GAME EXPERIENCE: Played in AFC championship game (1997 season). ... Member of Super Bowl championship team (1997 season).

HONORS: Named outside linebacker on THE SPORTING NEWS NFL All-Pro team (1997).

PRO STATISTICS: 1997—Recovered one fumble.

			INTERCEPTIONS				SACKS
Year Team	G	GS	No.	Yds.	Avg.	TD	No.
1996—Denver NFL................................	16	16	1	8	8.0	0	1.5
1997—Denver NFL................................	16	16	1	13	13.0	1	4.0
Pro totals (2 years)................................	32	32	2	21	10.5	1	5.5

MOBLEY, SINGOR — S — COWBOYS

PERSONAL: Born October 12, 1972, in Tacoma, Wash. ... 5-11/195.
HIGH SCHOOL: Curtis (Tacoma, Wash.).
COLLEGE: Washington State.
TRANSACTIONS/CAREER NOTES: Signed as non-drafted free agent by Edmonton Eskimos of CFL (April 1995). ... Signed by Dallas Cowboys (February 12, 1997).
PLAYING EXPERIENCE: Edmonton CFL, 1995 and 1996; Dallas NFL, 1997. ... Games/Games started: CFL: 1995 (17/games started unavailable), 1996 (16/games started unavailable); NFL: 1997 (12/0). Total CFL: 33/games started unavailable. Total NFL: 12/0. Total Pro: 45/games started unavailable.
PRO STATISTICS: CFL: 1995—Intercepted one pass for four yards, credited with one sack and recovered three fumbles for 129 yards and one touchdown. 1996—Credited with five sacks and recovered one fumble.

MOHR, CHRIS — P — BILLS

PERSONAL: Born May 11, 1966, in Atlanta. ... 6-5/215. ... Full name: Christopher Garrett Mohr. ... Name pronounced MORE.
HIGH SCHOOL: Briarwood Academy (Thomson, Ga.).
COLLEGE: Alabama (degree in criminal justice).
TRANSACTIONS/CAREER NOTES: Selected by Tampa Bay Buccaneers in sixth round (146th pick overall) of 1989 NFL draft. ... Signed by Buccaneers (July 15, 1989). ... Released by Buccaneers (September 2, 1990). ... Signed by WLAF (January 31, 1991). ... Selected by Montreal Machine in first round (eighth punter) of 1991 WLAF positional draft. ... Signed by Buffalo Bills (June 6, 1991). ... Granted unconditional free agency (February 17, 1994). ... Re-signed by Bills (March 3, 1994). ... Granted unconditional free agency (February 14, 1997). ... Re-signed by Bills (March 4, 1997).
CHAMPIONSHIP GAME EXPERIENCE: Played in AFC championship game (1991-1993 seasons). ... Played in Super Bowl XXVI (1991 season), Super Bowl XXVII (1992 season) and Super Bowl XXVIII (1993 season).
HONORS: Named punter on All-World League team (1991).
PRO STATISTICS: NFL: 1989—Converted one extra point. 1991—Attempted one pass with one completion for minus nine yards. 1992—Rushed once for 11 yards and recovered one fumble. 1993—Fumbled once and recovered one fumble. 1994—Rushed once for minus nine yards. 1997—Rushed once for no yards, attempted one pass with one completion for 29 yards, fumbled once and recovered one fumble for minus 10 yards. W.L.: 1991—Had only pass attempt intercepted and rushed three times for minus four yards.

				PUNTING				
Year Team	G	GS	No.	Yds.	Avg.	Net avg.	In. 20	Blk.
1989—Tampa Bay NFL	16	0	∞84	3311	39.4	32.1	10	2
1990—				Did not play.				
1991—Montreal W.L.	10	...	57	2436	42.7	34.0	13	2
—Buffalo NFL	16	0	54	2085	38.6	36.1	12	0
1992—Buffalo NFL	15	0	60	2531	42.2	36.7	12	0
1993—Buffalo NFL	16	0	74	2991	40.4	36.0	19	0
1994—Buffalo NFL	16	0	67	2799	41.8	36.0	13	0
1995—Buffalo NFL	16	0	86	3473	40.4	36.2	23	0
1996—Buffalo NFL	16	0	§101	§4194	41.5	36.5	§27	0
1997—Buffalo NFL	16	0	90	3764	41.8	36.0	24	1
W.L. totals (1 year)	10	...	57	2436	42.7	34.0	13	2
NFL totals (8 years)	127	0	616	25148	40.8	35.7	140	3
Pro totals (9 years)	137	...	673	27584	41.0	35.5	153	5

MOHRING, MIKE — DT — CHARGERS

PERSONAL: Born March 22, 1974, in Glen Cove, N.Y. ... 6-5/295. ... Full name: Michael Joseph Mohring. ... Cousin of John Mohring, linebacker with Cleveland Browns (1980).
HIGH SCHOOL: West Chester (Pa.) East.
COLLEGE: Pittsburgh.
TRANSACTIONS/CAREER NOTES: Signed as non-drafted free agent by Miami Dolphins (April 24, 1997). ... Released by Dolphins (August 18, 1997). ... Signed by San Diego Chargers to practice squad (August 25, 1997). ... Activated (December 12, 1997).
PLAYING EXPERIENCE: San Diego NFL, 1997. ... Games/Games started: 2/0.

MOLDEN, ALEX — CB — SAINTS

PERSONAL: Born August 4, 1973, in Detroit. ... 5-10/190. ... Full name: Alex M. Molden.
HIGH SCHOOL: Sierra (Colorado Springs, Colo.).
COLLEGE: Oregon.
TRANSACTIONS/CAREER NOTES: Selected by New Orleans Saints in first round (11th pick overall) of 1996 NFL draft. ... Signed by Saints (July 21, 1996).
HONORS: Named defensive back on THE SPORTING NEWS college All-America second team (1995).
PRO STATISTICS: 1997—Recovered two fumbles.

			INTERCEPTIONS				SACKS
Year Team	G	GS	No.	Yds.	Avg.	TD	No.
1996—New Orleans NFL	14	2	2	2	1.0	0	2.0
1997—New Orleans NFL	16	15	0	0	...	0	4.0
Pro totals (2 years)	30	17	2	2	1.0	0	6.0

M

MONTGOMERY, GREG   P   RAVENS

PERSONAL: Born October 29, 1964, in Morristown, N.J. ... 6-4/215. ... Full name: Gregory Hugh Montgomery Jr.
HIGH SCHOOL: Red Bank Regional (Little Silver, N.J.).
COLLEGE: Penn State, then Michigan State (degree in communications/sales, 1988).
TRANSACTIONS/CAREER NOTES: Selected by Houston Oilers in third round (72nd pick overall) of 1988 NFL draft. ... Signed by Oilers (August 3, 1988). ... Granted free agency (February 1, 1991). ... Re-signed by Oilers (September 6, 1991). ... Granted unconditional free agency (February 17, 1994). ... Signed by Detroit Lions (May 6, 1994). ... Granted unconditional free agency (February 17, 1995). ... Signed by Baltimore Ravens (April 3, 1996).
HONORS: Named punter on THE SPORTING NEWS NFL All-Pro team (1993). ... Played in Pro Bowl (1993 season).
PRO STATISTICS: 1989—Rushed three times for 17 yards and fumbled once. 1992—Rushed twice for minus 14 yards, fumbled once and recovered one fumble. 1996—Rushed once for no yards, fumbled once and recovered one fumble. 1997—Rushed once for 11 yards.

			PUNTING					
Year Team	G	GS	No.	Yds.	Avg.	Net avg.	In. 20	Blk.
1988—Houston NFL	16	0	65	2523	38.8	34.1	12	0
1989—Houston NFL	16	0	56	2422	§43.3	§36.1	15	2
1990—Houston NFL	16	0	34	1530	45.0	36.6	7	0
1991—Houston NFL	15	0	48	2105	43.9	36.7	13	2
1992—Houston NFL	16	0	53	2487	*46.9	37.2	14	*2
1993—Houston NFL	15	0	54	2462	*45.6	§39.1	13	0
1994—Detroit NFL	16	0	63	2782	44.2	34.2	19	1
1995—				Did not play.				
1996—Baltimore NFL	16	0	68	2980	43.8	37.7	23	1
1997—Baltimore NFL	16	0	83	3540	42.7	36.6	24	0
Pro totals (9 years)	142	0	524	22831	43.6	36.4	140	8

MONTGOMERY, MONTY   DB   COLTS

PERSONAL: Born December 8, 1973, in Dallas. ... 5-11/197. ... Full name: Delmonico Montgomery.
HIGH SCHOOL: Gladewater (Texas).
COLLEGE: Houston.
TRANSACTIONS/CAREER NOTES: Selected by Indianapolis Colts in fourth round (117th pick overall) of 1997 NFL draft. ... Signed by Colts (July 7, 1997).
PLAYING EXPERIENCE: Indianapolis NFL, 1997. ... Games/Games started: 16/3.
PRO STATISTICS: 1997—Credited with one sack.

MONTREUIL, MARK   CB   CHARGERS

PERSONAL: Born December 29, 1971, in Montreal. ... 6-2/200. ... Full name: Mark Allen Montreuil. ... Name pronounced mon-TROY.
HIGH SCHOOL: Beaconsfield (Montreal).
COLLEGE: Concordia (Canada).
TRANSACTIONS/CAREER NOTES: Selected by Toronto Argonauts in first round (third pick overall) of 1995 CFL draft. ... Selected by San Diego Chargers in seventh round (237th pick overall) of 1995 NFL draft. ... Signed by Chargers (July 12, 1995). ... Assigned by Chargers to London Monarchs in 1996 World League enhancement allocation program (February 19, 1996). ... On injured reserve with knee injury (October 29, 1997-remainder of season). ... Granted free agency (February 13, 1998). ... Re-signed by Chargers (February 25, 1998).
PLAYING EXPERIENCE: San Diego NFL, 1995-1997; London W.L., 1996. ... Games/Games started: 1995 (16/0), 1996: (W.L.-games played unavailable; NFL-13/0), 1997 (6/1). Total: 35/1.
PRO STATISTICS: 1995—Recovered one fumble.

M

MONTY, PETE   LB   GIANTS

PERSONAL: Born July 13, 1974, in Fort Collins, Colo. ... 6-2/250.
HIGH SCHOOL: Fort Collins (Colo.).
COLLEGE: Wisconsin.
TRANSACTIONS/CAREER NOTES: Selected by New York Giants in fourth round (103rd pick overall) of 1997 NFL draft. ... Signed by Giants (July 19, 1997). ... On injured reserve with knee injury (September 30, 1997-remainder of season).
PLAYING EXPERIENCE: New York Giants, NFL. ... Games/Games started: 3/0.

MOON, WARREN   QB   SEAHAWKS

PERSONAL: Born November 18, 1956, in Los Angeles. ... 6-3/213. ... Full name: Harold Warren Moon.
HIGH SCHOOL: Hamilton (Los Angeles).
COLLEGE: Washington.
TRANSACTIONS/CAREER NOTES: Signed as free agent by Edmonton Eskimos of CFL (March 1978). ... USFL rights traded by Memphis Showboats to Los Angeles Express for future draft pick (August 30, 1983). ... Granted free agency (March 1, 1984). ... Signed by Houston Oilers (March 1, 1984). ... On injured reserve with fractured scapula (September 5-October 15, 1988). ... Traded by Oilers to Minnesota Vikings for third-round pick (WR Malcolm Seabron) in 1994 draft and third-round pick (RB Rodney Thomas) in 1995 draft (April 14, 1994). ... Released by Vikings (February 21, 1997). ... Signed by Seattle Seahawks (March 7, 1997).
CHAMPIONSHIP GAME EXPERIENCE: Played in Grey Cup, CFL championship game (1978-1982 seasons).
HONORS: Played in Pro Bowl (1988-1995 and 1997 seasons). ... Named quarterback on THE SPORTING NEWS NFL All-Pro team (1990). ... Named Outstanding Player of Pro Bowl (1997 season).

RECORDS: Holds NFL career records for most fumbles—152; most own and opponents' fumbles recovered—54; and most own fumbles recovered—54. ... Holds NFL single-season record for most passes completed—404 (1991). ... Shares NFL single-season record for most games with 300 or more yards passing—9 (1990). ... Shares NFL single-game record for most times sacked—12 (September 29, 1985, vs. Dallas).

POST SEASON RECORDS: Holds NFL postseason career records for most fumbles—16; and most own fumbles recovered—8. ... Holds NFL postseason single-game records for most passes completed—36 (January 3, 1993, OT, at Buffalo); and most fumbles—5 (January 16, 1994, vs. Kansas City).

PRO STATISTICS: CFL: 1978—Fumbled once. 1979—Fumbled once. 1981—Fumbled once. 1982—Fumbled once and recovered one fumble. 1983—Fumbled seven times. NFL: 1984—Led league with 17 fumbles and recovered seven fumbles for minus one yard. 1985—Fumbled 12 times and recovered five fumbles for minus eight yards. 1986—Fumbled 11 times and recovered three fumbles for minus four yards. 1987—Fumbled eight times and recovered six fumbles for minus seven yards. 1988—Fumbled eight times and recovered four fumbles for minus 12 yards. 1989—Fumbled 11 times and recovered six fumbles for minus 13 yards. 1990—Led league with 18 fumbles and recovered four fumbles. 1991—Fumbled 11 times and recovered four fumbles for minus four yards. 1992—Fumbled seven times. 1993—Fumbled 13 times and recovered five fumbles for minus seven yards. 1994—Fumbled nine times and recovered two fumbles for minus five yards. 1995—Fumbled 13 times and recovered five fumbles for minus 12 yards. 1996—Fumbled seven times and recovered two fumbles. 1997—Fumbled seven times and recovered one fumble for minus two yards.

SINGLE GAME HIGHS (regular season): Attempts—57 (November 6, 1994, vs. New Orleans); completions—41 (November 10, 1991, vs. Dallas); yards—527 (December 16, 1990, vs. Kansas City); and touchdown passes—5 (October 26, 1997, vs. Oakland).

STATISTICAL PLATEAUS: 300-yard passing games: 1984 (4), 1985 (3), 1986 (3), 1987 (2), 1989 (4), 1990 (9), 1991 (6), 1992 (4), 1993 (3), 1994 (6), 1995 (4), 1997 (1). Total: 49.

MISCELLANEOUS: Regular-season record as starting NFL quarterback: 98-94 (.510). ... Postseason record as starting NFL quarterback: 3-7 (.300). ... Holds Oilers franchise all-time records for most yards passing (33,685) and most touchdown passes (196).

					PASSING							RUSHING				TOTALS	
Year Team	G	GS	Att.	Cmp.	Pct.	Yds.	TD	Int.	Avg.	Rat.	Att.	Yds.	Avg.	TD	TD	2pt.	Pts.
1978—Edmonton CFL	16	...	173	89	51.4	1112	5	7	6.43	64.5	30	114	3.8	1	1	...	6
1979—Edmonton CFL	16	...	274	149	54.4	2382	20	12	8.69	89.7	56	150	2.7	2	2	...	12
1980—Edmonton CFL	16	...	331	181	54.7	3127	25	11	9.45	98.3	55	352	6.4	3	3	...	18
1981—Edmonton CFL	15	9	378	237	62.7	3959	27	12	10.47	108.6	50	298	6.0	3	3	...	18
1982—Edmonton CFL	16	16	562	333	59.3	5000	36	16	8.90	98.0	54	259	4.8	4	4	...	24
1983—Edmonton CFL	16	16	664	380	57.2	5648	31	19	8.51	88.9	85	527	6.2	3	3	...	18
1984—Houston NFL	16	16	450	259	57.6	3338	12	14	7.42	76.9	58	211	3.6	1	1	...	6
1985—Houston NFL	14	14	377	200	53.1	2709	15	19	7.19	68.5	39	130	3.3	0	0	...	0
1986—Houston NFL	15	15	488	256	52.5	3489	13	*26	7.15	62.3	42	157	3.7	2	2	...	12
1987—Houston NFL	12	12	368	184	50.0	2806	21	18	7.63	74.2	34	112	3.3	3	3	...	18
1988—Houston NFL	11	11	294	160	54.4	2327	17	8	7.91	88.4	33	88	2.7	5	5	...	30
1989—Houston NFL	16	16	464	280	60.3	3631	23	14	7.83	88.9	70	268	3.8	4	4	...	24
1990—Houston NFL	15	15	*584	*362	62.0	*4689	*33	13	8.03	96.8	55	215	3.9	2	2	...	12
1991—Houston NFL	16	16	*655	*404	61.7	*4690	23	*21	7.16	81.7	33	68	2.1	2	2	...	12
1992—Houston NFL	11	10	346	224	64.7	2521	18	12	7.29	§89.3	27	147	5.4	1	1	...	6
1993—Houston NFL	15	14	520	303	58.3	3485	21	21	6.70	75.2	48	145	3.0	1	1	...	6
1994—Minnesota NFL	15	15	§601	‡371	61.7	‡4264	18	‡19	7.09	79.9	27	55	2.0	0	0	0	0
1995—Minnesota NFL	16	16	‡606	*377	62.2	4228	33	14	6.98	91.5	33	82	2.5	0	0	0	0
1996—Minnesota NFL	8	8	247	134	54.3	1610	7	9	6.52	68.7	9	6	0.7	0	0	0	0
1997—Seattle NFL	15	14	528	313	59.3	3678	25	16	6.97	83.7	17	40	2.4	1	1	0	6
CFL totals (6 years)	95	...	2382	1369	57.5	21228	144	77	8.91	93.8	330	1700	5.2	16	16	0	96
NFL totals (14 years)	195	192	6528	3827	58.6	47465	279	224	7.27	81.2	525	1724	3.3	22	22	0	132
Pro totals (20 years)	290	...	8910	5196	58.3	68693	423	301	7.71	84.6	855	3424	4.0	38	38	0	228

MOORE, DAVE   TE   BUCCANEERS

PERSONAL: Born November 11, 1969, in Morristown, N.J. ... 6-2/242. ... Full name: David Edward Moore.

HIGH SCHOOL: Roxbury (Succasunna, N.J.).

COLLEGE: Pittsburgh (degree in justice administration).

TRANSACTIONS/CAREER NOTES: Selected by Miami Dolphins in seventh round (191st pick overall) of 1992 NFL draft. ... Signed by Dolphins (July 15, 1992). ... Released by Dolphins (August 31, 1992). ... Signed by Dolphins to practice squad (September 1, 1992). ... Released by Dolphins (September 16, 1992). ... Re-signed by Dolphins to practice squad (October 21, 1992). ... Activated (October 24, 1992). ... Released by Dolphins (October 28, 1992). ... Re-signed by Dolphins to practice squad (October 28, 1992). ... Released by Dolphins (November 18, 1992). ... Signed by Tampa Bay Buccaneers to practice squad (November 24, 1992). ... Activated (December 4, 1992). ... Granted free agency (February 16, 1996). ... Re-signed by Buccaneers (May 31, 1996). ... Granted unconditional free agency (February 14, 1997). ... Re-signed by Buccaneers (February 18, 1997).

PRO STATISTICS: 1993—Attempted one pass without a completion and recovered one fumble. 1995—Rushed once for four yards.

SINGLE GAME HIGHS (regular season): Receptions—6 (November 2, 1997, vs. Indianapolis); yards—62 (November 3, 1996, vs. Chicago); and touchdown receptions—1 (November 16, 1997, vs. New England).

			RECEIVING				TOTALS			
Year Team	G	GS	No.	Yds.	Avg.	TD	TD	2pt.	Pts.	Fum.
1992—Miami NFL	1	0	0	0	...	0	0	...	0	0
—Tampa Bay NFL	4	2	1	10	10.0	0	0	...	0	0
1993—Tampa Bay NFL	15	1	4	47	11.8	1	1	...	6	0
1994—Tampa Bay NFL	15	5	4	57	14.3	0	0	0	0	0
1995—Tampa Bay NFL	16	9	13	102	7.8	0	0	0	0	0
1996—Tampa Bay NFL	16	8	27	237	8.8	3	3	0	18	0
1997—Tampa Bay NFL	16	7	19	217	11.4	4	4	0	24	0
Pro totals (6 years)	83	32	68	670	9.9	8	8	0	48	0

MOORE, HERMAN   WR   LIONS

PERSONAL: Born October 20, 1969, in Danville, Va. ... 6-4/210. ... Full name: Herman Joseph Moore.

HIGH SCHOOL: George Washington (Danville, Va.).

COLLEGE: Virginia (degree in rhetoric and communication studies, 1991).

TRANSACTIONS/CAREER NOTES: Selected after junior season by Detroit Lions in first round (10th pick overall) of 1991 NFL draft. ... Signed by Lions (July 19, 1991). ... On injured reserve with quadricep injury (September 11-October 9, 1992). ... On practice squad (October 9-14, 1992). ... Designated by Lions as transition player (February 25, 1993).

CHAMPIONSHIP GAME EXPERIENCE: Played in NFC championship game (1991 season).

HONORS: Named wide receiver on THE SPORTING NEWS college All-America first team (1990). ... Played in Pro Bowl (1994-1997 seasons). ... Named wide receiver on THE SPORTING NEWS NFL All-Pro team (1995-1997).

RECORDS: Holds NFL single-season record for most pass receptions—123 (1995).

POST SEASON RECORDS: Shares NFL postseason career and single-game records for most two-point conversions—1 (December 30, 1995, vs. Philadelphia).

SINGLE GAME HIGHS (regular season): Receptions—14 (December 4, 1995, vs. Chicago); yards—183 (December 4, 1995, vs. Chicago); and touchdown receptions—3 (October 29, 1995, vs. Green Bay).

STATISTICAL PLATEAUS: 100-yard receiving games: 1992 (3), 1993 (3), 1994 (3), 1995 (10), 1996 (5), 1997 (6). Total: 30.

MISCELLANEOUS: Holds Detroit Lions all-time records for most yards receiving (7,484), most receptions (528), and most touchdown receptions (52).

			RECEIVING				TOTALS			
Year Team	G	GS	No.	Yds.	Avg.	TD	TD	2pt.	Pts.	Fum.
1991—Detroit NFL	13	1	11	135	12.3	0	0	...	0	0
1992—Detroit NFL	12	11	51	966	‡18.9	4	4	...	24	0
1993—Detroit NFL	15	15	61	935	15.3	6	6	...	36	2
1994—Detroit NFL	16	16	72	1173	16.3	11	11	0	66	1
1995—Detroit NFL	16	16	*123	1686	13.7	14	14	0	84	2
1996—Detroit NFL	16	16	106	1296	12.2	9	9	1	56	0
1997—Detroit NFL	16	16	†104	1293	12.4	8	8	1	50	0
Pro totals (7 years)	104	91	528	7484	14.2	52	52	2	316	5

MOORE, JERALD　　FB　　RAMS

PERSONAL: Born November 20, 1974, in Houston. ... 5-9/225. ... Full name: Jerald Christopher Moore.

HIGH SCHOOL: Yates (Houston).

COLLEGE: Oklahoma.

TRANSACTIONS/CAREER NOTES: Selected after junior season by St. Louis Rams in third round (83rd pick overall) of 1996 NFL draft. ... Signed by Rams (July 15, 1996).

PRO STATISTICS: 1997—Recovered two fumbles.

SINGLE GAME HIGHS (regular season): Attempts—27 (December 20, 1997, vs. Carolina); yards—113 (December 20, 1997, vs. Carolina); and rushing touchdowns—1 (December 14, 1997, vs. Chicago).

STATISTICAL PLATEAUS: 100-yard rushing games: 1997 (1).

			RUSHING				RECEIVING				TOTALS			
Year Team	G	GS	Att.	Yds.	Avg.	TD	No.	Yds.	Avg.	TD	TD	2pt.	Pts.	Fum.
1996—St. Louis NFL	11	4	11	32	2.9	0	3	13	4.3	0	0	0	0	0
1997—St. Louis NFL	9	5	104	380	3.7	3	8	69	8.6	0	3	0	18	4
NFL totals (2 years)	20	9	115	412	3.6	3	11	82	7.5	0	3	0	18	4

M

MOORE, MARTY　　LB　　PATRIOTS

PERSONAL: Born March 19, 1971, in Phoenix. ... 6-1/244. ... Full name: Martin Neff Moore.

HIGH SCHOOL: Highlands (Fort Thomas, Ky.).

COLLEGE: Kentucky.

TRANSACTIONS/CAREER NOTES: Selected by New England Patriots in seventh round (222nd pick overall) of 1994 NFL draft. ... Signed by Patriots (June 1, 1994). ... Granted free agency (February 14, 1997). ... Re-signed by Patriots (June 6, 1997). ... Granted unconditional free agency (February 13, 1908). ... Re-signed by Patriots (April 3, 1998).

PLAYING EXPERIENCE: New England NFL, 1994-1997. ... Games/Games started: 1994 (16/4), 1995 (16/3), 1996 (16/0), 1997 (16/0). Total: 64/7.

CHAMPIONSHIP GAME EXPERIENCE: Played in AFC championship game (1996 season). ... Played in Super Bowl XXXI (1996 season).

PRO STATISTICS: 1997—Intercepted two passes for seven yards.

MOORE, ROB　　WR　　CARDINALS

PERSONAL: Born September 27, 1968, in New York. ... 6-3/203. ... Full name: Robert S. Moore.

HIGH SCHOOL: Hempstead (N.Y.).

COLLEGE: Syracuse (degree in psychology, 1990).

TRANSACTIONS/CAREER NOTES: Selected by New York Jets in first round of 1990 NFL supplemental draft. ... Signed by Jets (July 22, 1990). ... Designated by Jets as transition player (February 25, 1993). ... Free agency status changed by Jets from transitional to restricted (February 17, 1994). ... Re-signed by Jets (July 12, 1994). ... Designated by Jets as franchise player (February 15, 1995). ... Traded by Jets to Arizona Cardinals for RB Ronald Moore and first- (DE Hugh Douglas) and fourth-round (OT Melvin Hayes) picks in 1995 draft (April 21, 1995).

HONORS: Named wide receiver on THE SPORTING NEWS college All-America first team (1989). ... Played in Pro Bowl (1994 and 1997 seasons).

PRO STATISTICS: 1990—Rushed twice for minus four yards. 1992—Rushed once for 21 yards. 1993—Rushed once for minus six yards. 1994—Rushed once for minus three yards and recovered one fumble. 1995—Attempted two passes with one completion for 33 yards and an interception.

SINGLE GAME HIGHS (regular season): Receptions—9 (November 24, 1996, vs. Philadelphia); yards—175 (September 30, 1990, vs. New England); and touchdown receptions—2 (December 16, 1990, vs. Indianapolis).

STATISTICAL PLATEAUS: 100-yard receiving games: 1990 (1), 1993 (2), 1994 (2), 1995 (3), 1996 (3), 1997 (8). Total: 19.

Year Team	G	GS	RECEIVING				TOTALS			
			No.	Yds.	Avg.	TD	TD	2pt.	Pts.	Fum.
1990—New York Jets NFL	15	14	44	692	15.7	6	6	...	36	1
1991—New York Jets NFL	16	16	70	987	14.1	5	5	...	30	2
1992—New York Jets NFL	16	15	50	726	14.5	4	4	...	24	0
1993—New York Jets NFL	13	13	64	843	13.2	1	1	...	6	2
1994—New York Jets NFL	16	16	78	1010	12.9	6	6	2	40	0
1995—Arizona NFL	15	15	63	907	14.4	5	5	1	32	0
1996—Arizona NFL	16	16	58	1016	17.5	4	4	1	26	0
1997—Arizona NFL	16	16	97	*1584	16.3	8	8	1	50	0
Pro totals (8 years)	123	121	524	7765	14.8	39	39	5	244	5

MOORE, RON — RB — CARDINALS

PERSONAL: Born January 26, 1970, in Spencer, Okla. ... 5-10/220. ... Full name: Ronald L. Moore.

HIGH SCHOOL: Star Spencer (Okla.).

COLLEGE: Pittsburg (Kan.) State.

TRANSACTIONS/CAREER NOTES: Selected by Phoenix Cardinals in fourth round (87th pick overall) of 1993 NFL draft. ... Signed by Cardinals (July 22, 1993). ... Cardinals franchise renamed Arizona Cardinals for 1994 season. ... Traded by Cardinals with first-round (DE Hugh Douglas) and fourth-round (OT Melvin Hayes) picks in 1995 draft to New York Jets for WR Rob Moore (April 21, 1995). ... Granted unconditional free agency (February 14, 1997). ... Signed by St. Louis Rams (March 5, 1997). ... Released by Rams (October 29, 1997). ... Signed by Cardinals (November 3, 1997).

HONORS: Harlon Hill Trophy winner (1992).

PRO STATISTICS: 1993—Returned one kickoff for nine yards and recovered one fumble. 1994—Attempted one pass without a completion and recovered one fumble. 1995—Recovered one fumble.

SINGLE GAME HIGHS (regular season): Attempts—36 (November 7, 1993, vs. Philadelphia); yards—160 (November 7, 1993, vs. Philadelphia); and rushing touchdowns—4 (December 5, 1993, vs. Los Angeles Rams).

STATISTICAL PLATEAUS: 100-yard rushing games: 1993 (3), 1994 (1). Total: 4.

Year Team	G	GS	RUSHING				RECEIVING				KICKOFF RETURNS				TOTALS			
			Att.	Yds.	Avg.	TD	No.	Yds.	Avg.	TD	No.	Yds.	Avg.	TD	TD	2pt.	Pts.	Fum.
1993—Phoenix NFL	16	11	263	1018	3.9	9	3	16	5.3	0	1	9	9.0	0	9	...	54	3
1994—Arizona NFL	16	16	232	780	3.4	4	8	52	6.5	1	0	0	...	0	5	1	32	2
1995—New York Jets NFL	15	3	43	121	2.8	0	8	50	6.3	0	8	166	20.8	0	0	0	0	3
1996—New York Jets NFL	16	0	1	1	1.0	0	0	0	...	0	8	118	14.8	0	0	0	0	0
1997—St. Louis NFL	7	2	24	103	4.3	1	4	34	8.5	0	1	17	17.0	0	1	0	6	0
—Arizona NFL	6	2	57	175	3.1	0	0	0	...	0	0	0	...	0	0	0	0	0
Pro totals (5 years)	76	34	620	2198	3.5	14	23	152	6.6	1	18	310	17.2	0	15	1	92	8

MOORE, STEVON — S — RAVENS

PERSONAL: Born February 9, 1967, in Wiggins, Miss. ... 5-11/210. ... Full name: Stevon Nathaniel Moore. ... Name pronounced Stee-von.

HIGH SCHOOL: Stone County (Wiggins, Miss.).

COLLEGE: Mississippi.

TRANSACTIONS/CAREER NOTES: Selected by New York Jets in seventh round (181st pick overall) of 1989 NFL draft. ... Signed by Jets (July 22, 1989). ... On injured reserve with knee injury (August 28, 1989-entire season). ... Granted unconditional free agency (February 1, 1990). ... Signed by Miami Dolphins (March 30, 1990). ... On physically unable to perform list with knee injury (July 21-August 27, 1990). ... On physically unable to perform list with knee injury (August 28-October 18, 1990). ... On injured reserve with hamstring injury (November 8-December 8, 1990). ... On injured reserve with knee injury (August 27, 1991-entire season). ... Granted unconditional free agency (February 1, 1992). ... Signed by Cleveland Browns (March 25, 1992). ... On injured reserve with separated shoulder (December 15, 1992-remainder of season). ... Browns franchise moved to Baltimore and renamed Ravens for 1996 season (March 11, 1996). ... Granted unconditional free agency (February 14, 1997). ... Re-signed by Ravens (April 2, 1997).

PRO STATISTICS: 1990—Recovered one fumble. 1992—Recovered three fumbles for 115 yards and one touchdown. 1993—Recovered one fumble for 22 yards and a touchdown. 1994—Recovered five fumbles for three yards. 1996—Recovered one fumble.

Year Team	G	GS	INTERCEPTIONS				SACKS
			No.	Yds.	Avg.	TD	No.
1989—New York Jets NFL			Did not play.				
1990—Miami NFL	7	0	0	0	...	0	0.0
1991—Miami NFL			Did not play.				
1992—Cleveland NFL	14	4	0	0	...	0	2.0
1993—Cleveland NFL	16	16	0	0	...	0	0.0
1994—Cleveland NFL	16	16	0	0	...	0	0.0
1995—Cleveland NFL	16	16	5	55	11.0	0	1.0
1996—Baltimore NFL	16	16	1	10	10.0	0	0.0
1997—Baltimore NFL	13	12	4	56	14.0	0	0.0
Pro totals (8 years)	98	80	10	121	12.1	0	3.0

MOORE, WILL — WR — JAGUARS

PERSONAL: Born February 21, 1970, in Dallas. ... 6-1/185.

HIGH SCHOOL: David D. Carter (Dallas).

COLLEGE: Texas Southern.

TRANSACTIONS/CAREER NOTES: Signed by Calgary Stampeders of CFL (April 1992). ... Granted free agency (February 1995). ... Signed by New England Patriots (April 3, 1995). ... Released by Patriots (September 10, 1996). ... Signed by Jacksonville Jaguars (January 9, 1997).

PRO STATISTICS: CFL: 1994—Attempted two passes with two completions for 52 yards and returned two kickoffs for two yards. NFL: 1997—Returned one kickoff for 36 yards.

SINGLE GAME HIGHS (regular season): Receptions—8 (September 10, 1995, vs. Miami); yards—112 (September 10, 1995, vs. Miami); and touchdown receptions—1 (October 15, 1995, vs. Kansas City).

M

Year Team	G	GS	RECEIVING				TOTALS			
			No.	Yds.	Avg.	TD	TD	2pt.	Pts.	Fum.
1992—Calgary CFL	1	...	3	38	12.7	0	0	...	0	0
1993—Calgary CFL	18	...	73	1083	14.8	12	12	...	72	2
1994—Calgary CFL	18	...	44	792	18.0	11	11	0	66	0
1995—New England NFL	14	13	43	502	11.7	1	1	0	6	0
1996—New England NFL	2	1	3	37	12.3	0	0	0	0	0
1997—Jacksonville NFL	11	0	1	10	10.0	0	0	0	0	0
CFL totals (3 years)	37	...	120	1913	15.9	23	23	0	138	2
NFL totals (3 years)	27	14	47	549	11.7	1	1	0	6	0
Pro totals (6 years)	64	...	167	2462	14.7	24	24	0	144	2

MORABITO, TIM DT PANTHERS

PERSONAL: Born October 12, 1973 ... 6-3/296. ... Full name: Timothy Robert Morabito.
HIGH SCHOOL: St. Joseph's Regional.
COLLEGE: Boston College (degree in sociology).
TRANSACTIONS/CAREER NOTES: Signed as non-drafted free agent by Cincinnati Bengals (April 23, 1996). ... Released by Bengals (September 11, 1996). ... Re-signed by Bengals to practice squad (September 12, 1996). ... Activated (November 5, 1996). ... Claimed on waivers by Carolina Panthers (August 26, 1997).
PLAYING EXPERIENCE: Cincinnati NFL, 1996; Carolina NFL, 1997. ... Games/Games started: 1996 (7/1), 1997 (8/0). Total: 15/1.
PRO STATISTICS: 1997—Recovered one fumble.

MORAN, SEAN DE BILLS

PERSONAL: Born June 5, 1973, in Denver. ... 6-3/275. ... Full name: Sean Farrell Moran.
HIGH SCHOOL: Overland (Aurora, Colo.).
COLLEGE: Colorado State.
TRANSACTIONS/CAREER NOTES: Selected by Buffalo Bills in fourth round (120th pick overall) of 1996 NFL draft. ... Signed by Bills (July 9, 1996).
PLAYING EXPERIENCE: Buffalo NFL, 1996 and 1997. ... Games/Games started: 1996 (16/0), 1997 (16/7). Total: 32/7.
PRO STATISTICS: 1997—Intercepted two passes for 12 yards, credited with 4 1/2 sacks and recovered one fumble.

MORRIS, BAM RB

PERSONAL: Born January 13, 1972, in Cooper, Texas. ... 6-0/245. ... Full name: Byron Morris. ... Brother of Ron Morris, wide receiver with Chicago Bears (1987-1992); and cousin of Terry Norris, former World Boxing Council junior middleweight champion.
HIGH SCHOOL: Cooper (Texas).
COLLEGE: Texas Tech.
TRANSACTIONS/CAREER NOTES: Selected after junior season by Pittsburgh Steelers in third round (91st pick overall) of 1994 NFL draft. ... Signed by Steelers (July 15, 1994). ... Released by Steelers (July 10, 1996). ... On suspended list for violating league substance abuse policy (September 1-22, 1996). ... Signed by Baltimore Ravens (September 24, 1996). ... On suspended list for violating league substance abuse policy (August 31-September 22, 1997). ... Granted unconditional free agency (February 13, 1998).
CHAMPIONSHIP GAME EXPERIENCE: Played in AFC championship game (1994 and 1995 seasons). ... Played in Super Bowl XXX (1995 season).
HONORS: Doak Walker Award winner (1993). ... Named running back on THE SPORTING NEWS college All-America second team (1993).
PRO STATISTICS: 1994—Recovered one fumble. 1997—Recovered four fumbles.
SINGLE GAME HIGHS (regular season): Attempts—36 (October 26, 1997, vs. Washington); yards—176 (October 26, 1997, vs. Washington); and rushing touchdowns—3 (November 19, 1995, vs. Cincinnati).
STATISTICAL PLATEAUS: 100-yard rushing games: 1994 (2), 1995 (2), 1996 (3), 1997 (2). Total: 9.
MISCELLANEOUS: Holds Baltimore Ravens all-time record for most yards rushing (1,511) and most rushing touchdowns (8).

M

Year Team	G	GS	RUSHING				RECEIVING				KICKOFF RETURNS				TOTALS			
			Att.	Yds.	Avg.	TD	No.	Yds.	Avg.	TD	No.	Yds.	Avg.	TD	TD	2pt.	Pts.	Fum.
1994—Pittsburgh NFL	15	6	198	836	4.2	7	22	204	9.3	0	4	114	28.5	0	7	0	42	3
1995—Pittsburgh NFL	13	4	148	559	3.8	9	8	36	4.5	0	0	0	0	0	9	0	54	3
1996—Baltimore NFL	11	7	172	737	4.3	4	25	242	9.7	1	1	3	3.0	0	5	0	30	0
1997—Baltimore NFL	11	8	204	774	3.8	4	29	176	6.1	0	1	23	23.0	0	4	0	24	4
Pro totals (4 years)	50	25	722	2906	4.0	24	84	658	7.8	1	6	140	23.3	0	25	0	150	10

MORRIS, MIKE C VIKINGS

PERSONAL: Born February 22, 1961, in Centerville, Iowa. ... 6-5/283. ... Full name: Michael Stephen Morris.
HIGH SCHOOL: Centerville (Iowa).
COLLEGE: Northeast Missouri State (degree in psychology and physical education).
TRANSACTIONS/CAREER NOTES: Signed as non-drafted free agent by Arizona Outlaws of USFL (November 1, 1984). ... Released by Outlaws (February 11, 1985). ... Signed by Denver Broncos (May 8, 1986). ... Released by Broncos (July 21, 1986). ... Signed by St. Louis Cardinals (May 20, 1987). ... Crossed picket line during players strike (October 7, 1987). ... Cardinals franchise moved to Phoenix (March 15, 1988). ... On injured reserve with knee injury (August 23, 1988-entire season). ... Granted unconditional free agency (February 1, 1989). ... Signed by Washington Redskins (March 20, 1989). ... Claimed on waivers by Kansas City Chiefs (August 30, 1989). ... Released by Chiefs (October 11, 1989). ... Signed by New England Patriots (October 13, 1989). ... Granted unconditional free agency (February 1, 1990). ... Signed by Chiefs (April 1, 1990). ... Released by Chiefs (July 28, 1990). ... Signed by Seattle Seahawks (preseason, 1990). ... Released by Seahawks (October 4, 1990). ... Signed by Cleveland Browns (October 16, 1990). ... Granted unconditional free agency (February 1-April 1, 1991). ... Re-signed by Browns (1991). ... Released by Browns (July 22, 1991). ... Signed by Minnesota Vikings (August 10, 1991). ... Released by Vikings (August 26, 1991). ... Re-signed by Vikings (August 29, 1991). ... Granted unconditional free agency (February 1-April 1, 1992). ... Re-signed by Vikings for 1992 season. ... Granted unconditional free agency (February 17, 1994). ... Re-signed by Vikings (May 17, 1994). ... Granted unconditional free agency (February 17, 1995). ... Re-signed by Vikings (March 27, 1995).
PLAYING EXPERIENCE: St. Louis NFL, 1987; Kansas City (5)-New England (11) NFL, 1989; Seattle (4)-Cleveland (10) NFL, 1990; Minnesota NFL, 1991-1996. ... Games/Games started: 1987 (14/0), 1989 (K.C.-5/0; N.E.-11/0; Total: 16,0), 1990 (Sea.-4/0; Clev.-10/0; Total: 14/0), 1991 (16/0), 1992 (16/0), 1993 (16/0), 1994 (16/0), 1995 (16/0), 1996 (16/0), 1997 (16/0). Total: 150/0.
PRO STATISTICS: 1990—Fumbled once for minus 23 yards.

MORRISON, STEVE   LB ·   COLTS

PERSONAL: Born December 28, 1971, in Birmingham, Mich. ... 6-3/246. ... Full name: Steve Craig Morrison.
HIGH SCHOOL: Brother Rice (Bloomfield Hills, Mich.).
COLLEGE: Michigan.
TRANSACTIONS/CAREER NOTES: Signed as non-drafted free agent by Indianapolis Colts (April 27, 1995). ... Granted free agency (February 13, 1998). ... Re-signed by Colts (March 12, 1998).
PLAYING EXPERIENCE: Indianapolis NFL, 1995-1997. ... Games/Games started: 1995 (10/0), 1996 (16/8), 1997 (16/9). Total: 42/17.
CHAMPIONSHIP GAME EXPERIENCE: Member of Colts for AFC championship game (1995 season); inactive.
PRO STATISTICS: 1995—Returned two kickoffs for six yards. 1996—Intercepted one pass for 20 yards and recovered two fumbles. 1997—Intercepted one pass for two yards, credited with one sack and recovered two fumbles for 27 yards.

MORROW, HAROLD   RB   VIKINGS

PERSONAL: Born February 24, 1973, in Maplesville, Ala. ... 5-11/215. ... Full name: Harold Morrow Jr. ... Cousin of Tommie Agee, fullback with Seattle Seahawks (1987 and 1988), Kansas City Chiefs (1989) and Dallas Cowboys (1990-1994).
HIGH SCHOOL: Maplesville (Ala.).
COLLEGE: Auburn.
TRANSACTIONS/CAREER NOTES: Signed as non-drafted free agent by Dallas Cowboys (April 25, 1996). ... Claimed on waivers by Minnesota Vikings (August 26, 1996).
PLAYING EXPERIENCE: Minnesota NFL, 1996 and 1997. ... Games/Games started: 1996 (8/0), 1997 (16/0). Total: 24/0.
PRO STATISTICS: 1996—Returned six kickoffs for 117 yards. 1997—Returned five kickoffs for 99 yards.
SINGLE GAME HIGHS (regular season): Attempts—0; yards—0; and rushing touchdowns—0.

MORTON, JOHNNIE   WR   LIONS

PERSONAL: Born October 7, 1971, in Inglewood, Calif. ... 6-0/190. ... Full name: Johnnie James Morton.
HIGH SCHOOL: South Torrance (Calif.).
COLLEGE: Southern California.
TRANSACTIONS/CAREER NOTES: Selected by Detroit Lions in first round (21st pick overall) of 1994 NFL draft. ... Signed by Lions (July 18, 1994).
HONORS: Named wide receiver on THE SPORTING NEWS college All-America first team (1993).
PRO STATISTICS: 1994—Recovered one fumble. 1995—Returned seven punts for 48 yards.
SINGLE GAME HIGHS (regular season): Receptions—9 (December 7, 1997, vs. Miami); yards—174 (September 22, 1996, vs. Chicago); and touchdown receptions—2 (September 22, 1996, vs. Chicago).
STATISTICAL PLATEAUS: 100-yard receiving games: 1995 (1), 1996 (2), 1997 (3). Total: 6.

			RUSHING				RECEIVING				KICKOFF RETURNS				TOTALS			
Year Team	G	GS	Att.	Yds.	Avg.	TD	No.	Yds.	Avg.	TD	No.	Yds.	Avg.	TD	TD	2pt.	Pts.	Fum.
1994—Detroit NFL	14	0	0	0	...	0	3	39	13.0	1	4	143	35.8	1	2	0	12	1
1995—Detroit NFL	16	14	3	33	11.0	0	44	590	13.4	8	18	390	21.7	0	8	0	48	1
1996—Detroit NFL	16	15	9	35	3.9	0	55	714	13.0	6	0	0	...	0	6	0	36	1
1997—Detroit NFL	16	16	3	33	11.0	0	80	1057	13.2	6	0	0	...	0	6	0	36	2
Pro totals (4 years)	62	45	15	101	6.7	0	182	2400	13.2	21	22	533	24.2	1	22	0	132	5

MORTON, MIKE   LB   RAIDERS

PERSONAL: Born March 28, 1972, in Kannapolis, N.C. ... 6-4/235. ... Full name: Michael Anthony Morton Jr.
HIGH SCHOOL: A.L. Brown (Kannapolis, N.C.).
COLLEGE: North Carolina.
TRANSACTIONS/CAREER NOTES: Selected by Los Angeles Raiders in fourth round (118th pick overall) of 1995 NFL draft. ... Signed by Raiders (July 21, 1995). ... Raiders franchise moved to Oakland (July 21, 1995).
PLAYING EXPERIENCE: Oakland NFL, 1995-1997. ... Games/Games started: 1995 (12/0), 1996 (16/6), 1997 (11/11). Total: 39/17.
PRO STATISTICS: 1995—Recovered one fumble. 1996—Intercepted two passes for 13 yards and credited with one sack. 1997—Returned one kickoff for 14 yards and recovered one fumble.

MOSS, WINSTON   LB

PERSONAL: Born December 24, 1965, in Miami. ... 6-3/245. ... Full name: Winston N. Moss. ... Brother of Anthony Moss, linebacker with New York Giants (1991).
HIGH SCHOOL: Southridge (Miami).
COLLEGE: Miami (Fla.).
TRANSACTIONS/CAREER NOTES: Selected by Tampa Bay Buccaneers in second round (50th pick overall) of 1987 NFL draft. ... Signed by Buccaneers (July 18, 1987). ... Granted free agency (February 1, 1990). ... Re-signed by Buccaneers (July 27, 1990). ... Traded by Buccaneers to Los Angeles Raiders for third- (RB Robert Wilson) and fifth-round (G Tim Ryan) picks in 1991 draft (April 22, 1991). ... Granted free agency (February 1, 1992). ... Re-signed by Raiders (August 26, 1992). ... Granted roster exemption (August 26-28, 1992). ... Granted unconditional free agency (February 17, 1995). ... Signed by Seattle Seahawks (March 15, 1995). ... On injured reserve with neck injury (December 10, 1997-remainder of season). ... Announced retirement (March 26, 1998).
PRO STATISTICS: 1987—Recovered one fumble in end zone for a touchdown. 1990—Intercepted one pass for 31 yards and recovered one fumble. 1991—Recovered two fumbles. 1995—Intercepted one pass for no yards and recovered two fumbles. 1996—Intercepted one pass for one yard. 1997—Recovered one fumble.

Year Team	G	GS	SACKS
1987—Tampa Bay NFL	12	6	1.5
1988—Tampa Bay NFL	16	15	0.0
1989—Tampa Bay NFL	16	16	5.5

Year	Team	G	GS	SACKS
1990—Tampa Bay NFL		16	15	3.5
1991—Los Angeles Raiders NFL		16	16	3.0
1992—Los Angeles Raiders NFL		15	15	2.0
1993—Los Angeles Raiders NFL		16	16	0.0
1994—Los Angeles Raiders NFL		16	15	2.0
1995—Seattle NFL		16	16	2.0
1996—Seattle NFL		16	16	1.0
1997—Seattle NFL		14	14	0.0
Pro totals (11 years)		**169**	**160**	**20.5**

MOSS, ZEFROSS — OT — PATRIOTS

PERSONAL: Born August 17, 1966, in Holt, Ala. ... 6-6/325.
HIGH SCHOOL: Holt (Ala.).
COLLEGE: Alabama State.
TRANSACTIONS/CAREER NOTES: Signed as non-drafted free agent by Dallas Cowboys (April 29, 1988). ... Released by Cowboys (August 24, 1988). ... Re-signed by Cowboys (December 8, 1988). ... Traded by Cowboys to Indianapolis Colts for 10th-round pick (traded to Minnesota) in 1990 draft (August 22, 1989). ... On injured reserve with ankle injury (December 20, 1991-remainder of season). ... Granted unconditional free agency (February 17, 1995). ... Signed by Detroit Lions (April 28, 1995). ... Granted unconditional free agency (February 14, 1997). ... Signed by New England Patriots (March 31, 1997).
PLAYING EXPERIENCE: Indianapolis NFL, 1989-1994; Detroit NFL, 1995 and 1996; New England NFL, 1997. ... Games/Games started: 1989 (16/0), 1990 (16/16), 1991 (11/10), 1992 (13/13), 1993 (16/16), 1994 (11/11), 1995 (14/14), 1996 (15/15), 1997 (15/15). Total: 127/110.

MOULDS, ERIC — WR/KR — BILLS

PERSONAL: Born July 17, 1973, in Lucedale, Miss. ... 6-0/204. ... Full name: Eric Shannon Moulds.
HIGH SCHOOL: George County (Miss.).
COLLEGE: Mississippi State.
TRANSACTIONS/CAREER NOTES: Selected by Buffalo Bills in first round (24th pick overall) of 1996 NFL draft. ... Signed by Bills (July 16, 1996).
PRO STATISTICS: 1997—Returned two punts for 20 yards and recovered one fumble.
SINGLE GAME HIGHS (regular season): Receptions—6 (December 14, 1997, vs. Jacksonville); yards—89 (December 8, 1996, vs. Seattle); and touchdown receptions—1 (December 16, 1996, vs. Miami).

				RUSHING			RECEIVING				KICKOFF RETURNS				TOTALS			
Year	Team	G	GS	Att.	Yds.	Avg.	TD	No.	Yds.	Avg.	TD	No.	Yds.	Avg.	TD	TD	2pt.	Pts. Fum.
1996—Buffalo NFL		16	5	12	44	3.7	0	20	279	14.0	2	52	1205	23.2	▲1	3	0	18 1
1997—Buffalo NFL		16	8	4	59	14.8	0	29	294	10.1	0	43	921	21.4	0	0	1	2 3
Pro totals (2 years)		**32**	**13**	**16**	**103**	**6.4**	**0**	**49**	**573**	**11.7**	**2**	**95**	**2126**	**22.4**	**1**	**3**	**1**	**20 4**

MUHAMMAD, MUHSIN — WR — PANTHERS

M

PERSONAL: Born May 5, 1973, in Lansing, Mich. ... 6-2/217. ... Name pronounced moo-SEEN moo-HAH-med.
HIGH SCHOOL: Waverly (Lansing, Mich.).
COLLEGE: Michigan State.
TRANSACTIONS/CAREER NOTES: Selected by Carolina Panthers in second round (43rd pick overall) of 1996 NFL draft. ... Signed by Panthers (July 23, 1996).
CHAMPIONSHIP GAME EXPERIENCE: Played in NFC championship game (1996 season).
PRO STATISTICS: 1996—Rushed once for minus one yard.
SINGLE GAME HIGHS (regular season): Receptions—8 (September 7, 1997, vs. Atlanta); yards—96 (September 29, 1996, vs. Jacksonville); and touchdown receptions—1 (October 13, 1996, vs. St. Louis).

				RECEIVING				TOTALS			
Year	Team	G	GS	No	Yds.	Avg.	TD	TD	2pt.	Pts.	Fum.
1996—Carolina NFl		9	5	25	407	16.3	1	1	0	6	0
1997—Carolina NFL		13	5	27	317	11.7	0	0	1	2	0
Pro totals (2 years)		**22**	**10**	**52**	**724**	**13.9**	**1**	**1**	**1**	**8**	**0**

MULLEN, RODERICK — DB — PACKERS

PERSONAL: Born December 5, 1972, in Baton Rouge, La. ... 6-1/204. ... Full name: Roderick Louis Mullen.
HIGH SCHOOL: West Feleciana (St. Francisville, La.).
COLLEGE: Grambling State.
TRANSACTIONS/CAREER NOTES: Selected by New York Giants in fifth round (153rd pick overall) of 1995 NFL draft. ... Signed by Giants (July 23, 1995). ... Released by Giants (August 29, 1995). ... Signed by Green Bay Packers (October 18, 1995).
PLAYING EXPERIENCE: Green Bay NFL, 1995-1997. ... Games/Games started: 1995 (8/0), 1996 (14/0), 1997 (16/1). Total: 38/1.
CHAMPIONSHIP GAME EXPERIENCE: Played in NFC championship game (1995-97 seasons). ... Member of Super Bowl championship team (1996 season). ... Played in Super Bowl XXXII (1997 season).
PRO STATISTICS: 1997—Intercepted one pass for 17 yards and recovered one fumble for one yard.

MURRAY, EDDIE — K

PERSONAL: Born August 29, 1956, in Halifax, Nova Scotia. ... 5-11/195. ... Full name: Edward Peter Murray. ... Cousin of Mike Rogers, center with Edmonton Oilers, New England/Hartford Whalers and New York Rangers of World Hockey Association and NHL (1974-75 through 1985-86).
HIGH SCHOOL: Spectrum (Victoria, B.C.).

COLLEGE: Tulane (degree in education, 1980).
TRANSACTIONS/CAREER NOTES: Selected by Detroit Lions in seventh round (166th pick overall) of 1980 NFL draft. ... On suspended list (September 10-November 20, 1982). ... On injured reserve with hip injury (October 12-November 20, 1990). ... Granted unconditional free agency (February 1-April 1, 1991). ... Re-signed by Lions for 1991 season. ... Granted unconditional free agency (February 1-April 1, 1992). ... Rights relinquished by Lions (April 29, 1992). ... Signed by Kansas City Chiefs (October 24, 1992). ... Released by Chiefs (October 28, 1992). ... Signed by Tampa Bay Buccaneers (November 10, 1992). ... Granted unconditional free agency (March 1, 1993). ... Re-signed by Buccaneers (1993). ... Released by Buccaneers (August 23, 1993). ... Signed by Dallas Cowboys (September 14, 1993). ... Granted unconditional free agency (February 17, 1994). ... Signed by Philadelphia Eagles (March 22, 1994). ... Released by Eagles (July 23, 1995). ... Signed by Washington Redskins (August 8, 1995). ... Granted unconditional free agency (February 16, 1996). ... Re-signed by Redskins (May 15, 1996). ... Released by Redskins (August 25, 1996). ... Signed by Minnesota Vikings (September 24, 1997). ... Granted unconditional free agency (February 13, 1998).
CHAMPIONSHIP GAME EXPERIENCE: Played in NFC championship game (1991 and 1993 seasons). ... Member of Super Bowl championship team (1993 season).
HONORS: Played in Pro Bowl (1980 and 1989 seasons). ... Named Outstanding Player of Pro Bowl (1980 season).
PRO STATISTICS: 1986—Punted once for 37 yards. 1987—Punted four times for 155 yards (38.8-yard average).

							KICKING			
Year Team	G	GS	XPM	XPA	FGM	FGA	Lg.	50+	Pts.
1980—Detroit NFL	16	0	35	36	*27	*42	52	1-4	116
1981—Detroit NFL	16	0	46	46	25	35	53	3-4	†121
1982—Detroit NFL	7	0	16	16	11	12	49	0-0	49
1983—Detroit NFL	16	0	38	38	25	32	54	3-4	113
1984—Detroit NFL	16	0	31	31	20	27	52	1-4	91
1985—Detroit NFL	16	0	31	33	26	31	51	2-3	109
1986—Detroit NFL	16	0	31	32	18	25	52	2-5	85
1987—Detroit NFL	12	0	21	21	20	32	53	1-2	81
1988—Detroit NFL	16	0	22	23	20	21	48	0-1	82
1989—Detroit NFL	16	0	36	36	20	21	50	1-1	96
1990—Detroit NFL	11	0	34	34	13	19	47	0-2	73
1991—Detroit NFL	16	0	40	40	19	28	50	2-4	97
1992—Kansas City NFL	1	0	0	0	1	1	52	1-1	3
—Tampa Bay NFL	7	0	13	13	4	8	47	0-0	25
1993—Dallas NFL	14	0	38	38	28	33	52	3-5	122
1994—Philadelphia NFL	16	0	33	33	21	25	42	0-0	96
1995—Washington NFL	16	0	33	33	27	36	52	1-2	114
1996—					Did not play.				
1997—Minnesota NFL	12	0	23	24	12	17	49	0-1	59
Pro totals (17 years)	240	0	521	527	337	445	54	21-43	1532

MURRELL, ADRIAN   RB   CARDINALS

PERSONAL: Born October 16, 1970, in Lafayette, La. ... 5-11/214. ... Full name: Adrian Bryan Murrell.
HIGH SCHOOL: Leilehua (Wahiawa, Hawaii).
COLLEGE: West Virginia.
TRANSACTIONS/CAREER NOTES: Selected by New York Jets in fifth round (120th pick overall) of 1993 NFL draft. ... Signed by Jets (July 22, 1993). ... Granted free agency (February 16, 1996). ... Re-signed by Jets (April 21, 1996). ... Traded by Jets with seventh-round pick (DE Jomo Cousins) in 1998 draft to Arizona Cardinals for third-round pick (traded to St. Louis) in 1998 draft (April 7, 1998).
PRO STATISTICS: 1993—Recovered two fumbles. 1995—Recovered two fumbles. 1996—Recovered two fumbles for minus 16 yards. 1997—Recovered two fumbles.
SINGLE GAME HIGHS (regular season): Attempts—40 (September 28, 1997, vs. Cincinnati); yards—199 (October 27, 1996, vs. Arizona); and rushing touchdowns—2 (November 10, 1996, vs. New England).
STATISTICAL PLATEAUS: 100-yard rushing games: 1995 (1), 1996 (5), 1997 (3). Total: 9.

			RUSHING				RECEIVING				KICKOFF RETURNS				TOTALS		
Year Team	G	GS	Att.	Yds.	Avg.	TD	No.	Yds.	Avg.	TD	No.	Yds.	Avg.	TD	TD	2pt.	Pts. Fum.
1993—New York Jets NFL	16	0	34	157	4.6	1	5	12	2.4	0	23	342	14.9	0	1	...	6 4
1994—New York Jets NFL	10	1	33	160	4.8	0	7	76	10.9	0	14	268	19.1	0	0	0	0 1
1995—New York Jets NFL	15	9	192	795	4.1	1	71	465	6.5	2	1	5	5.0	0	3	0	18 2
1996—New York Jets NFL	16	16	301	1249	4.1	6	17	81	4.8	1	0	0	...	0	7	0	42 6
1997—New York Jets NFL	16	15	300	1086	3.6	7	27	106	3.9	0	0	0	...	0	7	0	42 4
Pro totals (5 years)	73	41	860	3447	4.0	15	127	740	5.8	3	38	615	16.2	0	18	0	108 17

MUSGRAVE, BILL   QB   COLTS

PERSONAL: Born November 11, 1967, in Grand Junction, Colo. ... 6-3/220. ... Full name: William Scott Musgrave.
HIGH SCHOOL: Grand Junction (Colo.).
COLLEGE: Oregon (degree in finance).
TRANSACTIONS/CAREER NOTES: Selected by Dallas Cowboys in fourth round (106th pick overall) of 1991 NFL draft. ... Signed by Cowboys (July 14, 1991). ... Released by Cowboys (August 26, 1991). ... Signed by San Francisco 49ers to practice squad (August 28, 1991). ... Activated (November 9, 1991). ... Granted unconditional free agency (February 1-April 1, 1992). ... Re-signed by 49ers for 1992 season. ... Active for one game (1992); did not play. ... On injured reserve with knee injury (December 15, 1992-remainder of season). ... Released by 49ers (June 10, 1994). ... Re-signed by 49ers (July 21, 1994). ... Granted unconditional free agency (February 17, 1995). ... Signed by Denver Broncos (March 7, 1995). ... On injured reserve with shoulder injury (December 26, 1996-remainder of playoffs). ... Granted unconditional free agency (February 14, 1997). ... Re-signed by Denver Broncos (July 16, 1997). ... Released by Broncos (August 18, 1997). ... Signed by Indianapolis Colts (April 8, 1998).
CHAMPIONSHIP GAME EXPERIENCE: Member of 49ers for NFC championship game (1993 season); inactive. ... Member of 49ers for NFC championship game (1994 season); inactive. ... Member of Super Bowl championship team (1994 season).
PRO STATISTICS: 1995—Fumbled once. 1996—Fumbled three times for minus four yards.
SINGLE GAME HIGHS (regular season): Attempts—21 (December 8, 1996, vs. Green Bay); completions—12 (December 8, 1996, vs. Green Bay); yards—101 (December 8, 1996, vs. Green Bay); and touchdown passes—1 (December 23, 1991, vs. Chicago).
MISCELLANEOUS: Regular-season record as starting NFL quarterback: 0-1.

Year Team	G	GS	Att.	Cmp.	Pct.	Yds.	TD	Int.	Avg.	Rat.	Att.	Yds.	Avg.	TD	TD	2pt.	Pts.
						PASSING						RUSHING				TOTALS	
1991—San Francisco NFL......	1	0	5	4	80.0	33	1	0	6.60	133.8	0	0	...	0	0	...	0
1992—San Francisco NFL......								Did not play.									
1993—San Francisco NFL......	1	0	0	0	...	0	0	0	...	...	3	-3	-1.0	0	0	...	0
1994—San Francisco NFL......								Did not play.									
1995—Denver NFL................	4	0	12	8	66.7	93	0	0	7.75	89.9	4	-4	-1.0	0	0	0	0
1996—Denver NFL................	6	1	52	31	59.6	276	0	2	5.31	57.9	12	-4	-0.3	0	0	0	0
1997—								Did not play.									
Pro totals (4 years)................	12	1	69	43	62.3	402	1	2	5.83	71.0	19	-11	-0.6	0	0	0	0

MYERS, GREG   S/PR   BENGALS

PERSONAL: Born September 30, 1972, in Tampa. ... 6-1/202. ... Full name: Gregory Jay Myers.
HIGH SCHOOL: Windsor (Colo.).
COLLEGE: Colorado State.
TRANSACTIONS/CAREER NOTES: Selected by Cincinnati Bengals in fifth round (144th pick overall) of 1996 NFL draft. ... Signed by Bengals (July 2, 1996).
HONORS: Named defensive back on THE SPORTING NEWS college All-America first team (1994 and 1995). ... Jim Thorpe Award winner (1995).
PRO STATISTICS: 1996—Fumbled once. 1997—Recovered two fumbles.

Year Team	G	GS	No.	Yds.	Avg.	TD	No.	Yds.	Avg.	TD	TD	2pt.	Pts.	Fum.
			INTERCEPTIONS				PUNT RETURNS				TOTALS			
1996—Cincinnati NFL	14	0	2	10	5.0	0	9	51	5.7	0	0	0	0	1
1997—Cincinnati NFL	16	14	1	25	25.0	0	26	201	7.7	0	0	0	0	3
Pro totals (2 years)..	30	14	3	35	11.7	0	35	252	7.2	0	0	0	0	4

MYSLINSKI, TOM   OL   COLTS

PERSONAL: Born December 7, 1968, in Rome, N.Y. ... 6-3/293. ... Full name: Thomas Joseph Myslinski.
HIGH SCHOOL: Free Academy (Rome, N.Y.).
COLLEGE: Tennessee.
TRANSACTIONS/CAREER NOTES: Selected by Dallas Cowboys in fourth round (109th pick overall) of 1992 NFL draft. ... Signed by Cowboys (July 15, 1992). ... Released by Cowboys (August 31, 1992). ... Re-signed by Cowboys to practice squad (September 1, 1992). ... Signed by Cleveland Browns off Cowboys practice squad (September 8, 1992). ... Inactive for three games with Browns (1992). ... Released by Browns (October 9, 1992). ... Re-signed by Browns to practice squad (October 14, 1992). ... Released by Browns (October 17, 1992). ... Signed by Washington Redskins to practice squad (October 21, 1992). ... Activated (November 11, 1992). ... Released by Redskins (November 28, 1992). ... Signed by Buffalo Bills (April 6, 1993). ... Released by Bills (August 30, 1993). ... Re-signed by Bills (August 31, 1993). ... Released by Bills (November 15, 1993). ... Signed by Chicago Bears (November 30, 1993). ... Selected by Jacksonville Jaguars from Bears in NFL expansion draft (February 15, 1995). ... Granted free agency (February 17, 1995). ... Re-signed by Jaguars (April 19, 1995). ... Granted free agency (February 16, 1996). ... Signed by Pittsburgh Steelers (April 24, 1996). ... Released by Steelers (August 24, 1996). ... Re-signed by Steelers (August 27, 1996). ... Granted unconditional free agency (February 13, 1998). ... Signed by Indianapolis Colts (February 19, 1998).
PLAYING EXPERIENCE: Washington NFL, 1992; Buffalo (1)-Chicago (1) NFL, 1993; Chicago NFL, 1994; Jacksonville NFL, 1995; Pittsburgh NFL, 1996 and 1997. ... Games/Games started: 1992 (1/0), 1993 (Buf.-1/0; Chi.-1/0; Total: 2/0), 1994 (4/0), 1995 (9/9), 1996 (8/6), 1997 (16/7). Total: 40/22.
CHAMPIONSHIP GAME EXPERIENCE: Played in AFC championship game (1997 season).

NAEOLE, CHRIS   G   SAINTS

PERSONAL: Born December 25, 1974, in Kailua, Hawaii. ... 6-3/313. ... Name pronounced nay-OH-lee. ... Full name: Chris Kealoha Naeole.
HIGH SCHOOL: Kahuka (Kaaava, Hawaii).
COLLEGE: Colorado.
TRANSACTIONS/CAREER NOTES: Selected by New Orleans Saints in first round (10th pick overall) of 1997 NFL draft. ... Signed by Saints (July 17, 1997). ... On injured reserve with ankle injury (October 17, 1997-remainder of season).
PLAYING EXPERIENCE: New Orleans NFL, 1997. ... Games/Games started: 4/0.
HONORS: Named guard on THE SPORTING NEWS college All-America second team (1996).

M
N

NAILS, JAMIE   OT   BILLS

PERSONAL: Born June 3, 1975, in Baxley, Ga. ... 6-6/354.
HIGH SCHOOL: Appling County (Baxley, Ga.).
COLLEGE: Florida A&M.
TRANSACTIONS/CAREER NOTES: Selected by Buffalo Bills in fourth round (120th pick overall) of 1997 NFL draft. ... Signed by Bills (July 2, 1997).
PLAYING EXPERIENCE: Buffalo NFL, 1997. ... Games/Games started: 2/0.

NALEN, TOM   C   BRONCOS

PERSONAL: Born May 13, 1971, in Foxboro, Mass. ... 6-2/286. ... Full name: Thomas Andrew Nalen.
HIGH SCHOOL: Foxboro (Mass.).
COLLEGE: Boston College.
TRANSACTIONS/CAREER NOTES: Selected by Denver Broncos in seventh round (218th pick overall) of 1994 NFL draft. ... Signed by Broncos (July 16, 1994). ... Released by Broncos (September 2, 1994). ... Re-signed by Broncos to practice squad (September 6, 1994). ... Activated (October 7, 1994).

PLAYING EXPERIENCE: Denver NFL, 1994-1997. ... Games/Games started: 1994 (7/1), 1995 (15/15), 1996 (16/16), 1997 (16/16). Total: 54/48.
CHAMPIONSHIP GAME EXPERIENCE: Played in AFC championship game (1997 season).
HONORS: Played in Pro Bowl (1997 season).
PRO STATISTICS: 1997—Caught one pass for minus one yard.

NEAL, LEON   RB

PERSONAL: Born September 11, 1972, in St. Paul, Minn. ... 5-9/185.
HIGH SCHOOL: Paramount (Calif.).
COLLEGE: Washington.
TRANSACTIONS/CAREER NOTES: Selected by Buffalo Bills in sixth round (196th pick overall) of 1996 NFL draft. ... Signed by Bills (June 28, 1996). ... Released by Bills (August 25, 1996). ... Signed by Indianapolis Colts to practice squad (October 15, 1996). ... Activated (December 12, 1996). ... Active for two games (1996); did not play. ... Released by Colts (August 27, 1997). ... Re-signed by Colts to practice squad (September 16, 1997). ... Activated (December 5, 1997). ... Released by Colts (February 27, 1998).

			RUSHING				KICKOFF RETURNS		
Year Team	G	GS	Att.	Yds.	Avg.	TD	No.	Yds.	Avg.	TD
1997—Indianapolis NFL	1	0	0	0	...	0	1	23	23.0	0

NEAL, LORENZO   FB   BUCCANEERS

PERSONAL: Born December 27, 1970, in Hanford, Calif. ... 5-11/240. ... Full name: Lorenzo LaVon Neal.
HIGH SCHOOL: Lemoore (Calif.).
COLLEGE: Fresno State.
TRANSACTIONS/CAREER NOTES: Selected by New Orleans Saints in fourth round (89th pick overall) of 1993 NFL draft. ... Signed by Saints (July 15, 1993). ... On injured reserve with ankle injury (September 15, 1993-remainder of season). ... Granted free agency (February 16, 1996). ... Re-signed by Saints (July 1, 1996). ... Granted unconditional free agency (February 14, 1997). ... Signed by New York Jets (March 31, 1997). ... Traded by Jets to Tampa Bay Buccaneers for fifth-round pick (TE Blake Spence) in 1998 draft (March 12, 1998).
PRO STATISTICS: 1994—Returned one kickoff for 17 yards. 1995—Returned two kickoffs for 28 yards. 1996—Recovered two fumbles. 1997—Returned two kickoffs for 22 yards.
SINGLE GAME HIGHS (regular season): Attempts—14 (October 9, 1994, vs. Chicago); yards—89 (September 5, 1993, vs. Houston); and rushing touchdowns—1 (December 15, 1996, vs. New York Giants).

			RUSHING				RECEIVING				TOTALS			
Year Team	G	GS	Att.	Yds.	Avg.	TD	No.	Yds.	Avg.	TD	TD	2pt.	Pts.	Fum.
1993—New Orleans NFL	2	2	21	175	8.3	1	0	0	...	0	1	...	6	1
1994—New Orleans NFL	16	7	30	90	3.0	1	2	9	4.5	0	1	0	6	1
1995—New Orleans NFL	16	7	5	3	0.6	0	12	123	10.3	1	1	0	6	2
1996—New Orleans NFL	16	11	21	58	2.8	1	31	194	6.3	1	2	0	12	1
1997—New York Jets NFL	16	3	10	28	2.8	0	8	40	5.0	1	1	0	6	0
Pro totals (5 years)	66	30	87	354	4.1	3	53	366	6.9	3	6	0	36	5

NEALY, RAY   RB   DOLPHINS

PERSONAL: Born April 30, 1975, in Little Rock, Ark. ... 5-11/235. ... Full name: Ray T. Nealy.
HIGH SCHOOL: Central (Little Rock, Ark.).
COLLEGE: Arkansas-Pine Bluff.
TRANSACTIONS/CAREER NOTES: Signed as non-drafted free agent by Miami Dolphins (April 24, 1997). ... Released by Dolphins (August 18, 1997). ... Re-signed by Dolphins to practice squad (August 26, 1997). ... Activated (November 19, 1997).
PLAYING EXPERIENCE: Miami NFL, 1997. ... Games/Games started: 1/0.
PRO STATISTICS: 1997—Rushed once for two yards.
SINGLE GAME HIGHS (regular season): Attempts—1 (November 23, 1997, New England); yards—2 (November 23, 1997, vs. New England); and rushing touchdowns—0.

NEDNEY, JOE   K   CARDINALS

PERSONAL: Born March 22, 1973, in San Jose, Calif. ... 6-4/215. ... Full name: Joseph Thomas Nedney.
HIGH SCHOOL: Santa Teresa (San Jose, Calif.).
COLLEGE: San Jose State.
TRANSACTIONS/CAREER NOTES: Signed as non-drafted free agent by Oakland Raiders (August 19, 1995). ... Released by Raiders from practice squad (September 6, 1995). ... Signed by Miami Dolphins to practice squad (September 21, 1995). ... Activated by Miami Dolphins (March 29, 1996). ... Claimed on waivers by New York Jets (August 12, 1997). ... Released by Jets (August 25, 1997). ... Signed by Dolphins (October 3, 1997). ... Released by Dolphins (October 6, 1997). ... Signed by Arizona Cardinals (October 15, 1997).

			KICKING						
Year Team	G	GS	XPM	XPA	FGM	FGA	Lg.	50+	Pts.
1996—Miami NFL	16	0	35	36	18	29	44	0-2	89
1997—Arizona NFL	10	0	19	19	11	17	45	0-2	52
Pro totals (2 years)	26	0	54	55	29	46	45	0-4	141

NEIL, DAN   G/C   BRONCOS

PERSONAL: Born October 21, 1973, in Houston. ... 6-2/281.
HIGH SCHOOL: Cypress Creek (Texas).
COLLEGE: Texas.

TRANSACTIONS/CAREER NOTES: Selected by Denver Broncos in third round (67th pick overall) of 1997 NFL draft. ... Signed by Broncos (July 17, 1997).

PLAYING EXPERIENCE: Denver NFL, 1997. ... Games/Games started: 3/0.

CHAMPIONSHIP GAME EXPERIENCE: Member of Broncos for AFC championship game (1997 season); inactive. ... Member of Super Bowl championship team (1997 season); inactive.

HONORS: Named guard on THE SPORTING NEWS college All-America first team (1996).

NEUJAHR, QUENTIN   C   JAGUARS

PERSONAL: Born January 30, 1971, in Seward, Neb. ... 6-4/305. ... Full name: Quentin T. Neujahr. ... Name pronounced NEW-year.

HIGH SCHOOL: Centennial (Ulysses, Neb.).

COLLEGE: Kansas State.

TRANSACTIONS/CAREER NOTES: Signed as non-drafted free agent by Los Angeles Raiders (April 3, 1994). ... Released by Raiders (August 23, 1994). ... Signed by Cleveland Browns to practice squad (December 27, 1994). ... Active for one game (1995); did not play. ... Browns franchise moved to Baltimore and renamed Ravens for 1996 season (March 11, 1996). ... Granted free agency (February 13, 1998). ... Tendered offer sheet by Jacksonville Jaguars (February 24, 1998). ... Ravens declined to match offer (March 4, 1998).

PLAYING EXPERIENCE: Baltimore NFL, 1996 and 1997. ... Games/Games started: 1996 (5/0), 1997 (9/7). Total: 14/7.

PRO STATISTICS: 1996—Recovered one fumble.

NEWMAN, ANTHONY   S   RAIDERS

PERSONAL: Born November 21, 1965, in Bellingham, Wash. ... 6-0/200. ... Full name: Anthony Q. Newman.

HIGH SCHOOL: Beaverton (Ore.).

COLLEGE: Oregon.

TRANSACTIONS/CAREER NOTES: Selected by Los Angeles Rams in second round (35th pick overall) of 1988 NFL draft. ... Signed by Rams (July 11, 1988). ... On injured reserve with fractured elbow (December 21, 1989-remainder of season). ... Granted free agency (February 1, 1992). ... Re-signed by Rams (July 21, 1992). ... Released by Rams (August 27, 1995). ... Signed by New Orleans Saints (August 28, 1995). ... Granted unconditional free agency (February 16, 1996). ... Re-signed by Saints (March 6, 1996). ... Granted unconditional free agency (February 13, 1998). ... Signed by Oakland Raiders (March 26, 1998).

PRO STATISTICS: 1988—Recovered one fumble. 1990—Recovered one fumble. 1991—Credited with a sack and recovered one fumble for 17 yards and a touchdown. 1992—Recovered three fumbles. 1994—Recovered one fumble. 1995—Caught one pass for 18 yards. 1996—Recovered two fumbles. 1997—Recovered one fumble.

MISCELLANEOUS: Selected by Toronto Blue Jays organization in 26th round of free-agent baseball draft (June 4, 1984); did not sign. ... Selected by Cleveland Indians organization in secondary phase of free-agent baseball draft (January 9, 1985); did not sign. ... Selected by Texas Rangers organization in secondary phase of free-agent baseball draft (June 3, 1985); did not sign.

				INTERCEPTIONS		
Year Team	G	GS	No.	Yds.	Avg.	TD
1988—Los Angeles Rams NFL	16	0	2	27	13.5	0
1989—Los Angeles Rams NFL	15	1	0	0	...	0
1990—Los Angeles Rams NFL	16	6	2	0	0.0	0
1991—Los Angeles Rams NFL	16	1	1	58	58.0	0
1992—Los Angeles Rams NFL	16	16	4	33	8.3	0
1993—Los Angeles Rams NFL	16	16	0	0	...	0
1994—Los Angeles Rams NFL	16	14	2	46	23.0	1
1995—New Orleans NFL	13	1	0	0	...	0
1996—New Orleans NFL	16	16	3	40	13.3	0
1997—New Orleans NFL	12	12	3	19	6.3	0
Pro totals (10 years)	152	83	17	223	13.1	1

NEWNAM, BRIAN   G

PERSONAL: Born February 11, 1974, in Stroud, Okla. ... 6-3/296.

HIGH SCHOOL: Stroud (Okla.).

COLLEGE: Tulsa.

TRANSACTIONS/CAREER NOTES: Signed as non-drafted free agent by Tampa Bay Buccaneers (April 21, 1997). ... On injured reserve with knee injury (August 17, 1997-entire season). ... Released by Buccaneers (June 16, 1998).

N

NEWSOME, CRAIG   CB   PACKERS

PERSONAL: Born August 10, 1971, in San Bernardino, Calif. ... 6-0/190.

HIGH SCHOOL: Eisenhower (Rialto, Calif.).

JUNIOR COLLEGE: San Bernardino (Calif.) Valley.

COLLEGE: Arizona State.

TRANSACTIONS/CAREER NOTES: Selected by Green Bay Packers in first round (32nd pick overall) of 1995 NFL draft. ... Signed by Packers (May 23, 1995). ... On injured reserve with knee injury (September 3, 1997-remainder of season).

CHAMPIONSHIP GAME EXPERIENCE: Played in NFC championship game (1995 and 1996 seasons). ... Member of Super Bowl championship team (1996 season).

PRO STATISTICS: 1996—Recovered one fumble.

				INTERCEPTIONS		
Year Team	G	GS	No.	Yds.	Avg.	TD
1995—Green Bay NFL	16	16	1	3	3.0	0
1996—Green Bay NFL	16	16	2	22	11.0	0
1997—Green Bay NFL	1	1	0	0	...	0
Pro totals (3 years)	33	33	3	25	8.3	0

NEWTON, NATE — G — COWBOYS

PERSONAL: Born December 20, 1961, in Orlando. ... 6-3/295. ... Full name: Nathaniel Newton Jr. ... Brother of Tim Newton, defensive tackle with Minnesota Vikings, Tampa Bay Buccaneers and Kansas City Chiefs (1985-1991 and 1993).
HIGH SCHOOL: Jones (Orlando).
COLLEGE: Florida A&M.
TRANSACTIONS/CAREER NOTES: Selected by Tampa Bay Bandits in 1983 USFL territorial draft. ... Signed as non-drafted free agent by Washington Redskins (May 5, 1983). ... Released by Redskins (August 29, 1983). ... Signed by Bandits (November 6, 1983). ... Granted free agency when USFL suspended operations (August 7, 1986). ... Signed by Dallas Cowboys (August 14, 1986). ... Granted roster exemption (August 14-21, 1986). ... Crossed picket line during players strike (October 24, 1987). ... Granted unconditional free agency (February 17, 1994). ... Re-signed by Cowboys (April 7, 1994).
PLAYING EXPERIENCE: Tampa Bay USFL, 1984 and 1985; Dallas NFL, 1986-1997. ... Games/Games started: 1984 (18/18), 1985 (18/18), 1986 (11/0), 1987 (11/11), 1988 (15/15), 1989 (16/16), 1990 (16/16), 1991 (14/14), 1992 (15/15), 1993 (16/16), 1994 (16/16), 1995 (16/16), 1996 (16/16), 1997 (13/13). Total USFL: 36/36. Total NFL: 175/164. Total Pro: 211/200.
CHAMPIONSHIP GAME EXPERIENCE: Played in NFC championship game (1992-1995 seasons). ... Member of Super Bowl championship team (1992, 1993 and 1995 seasons).
HONORS: Played in Pro Bowl (1992-1996 seasons). ... Named guard on THE SPORTING NEWS NFL All-Pro team (1995).
PRO STATISTICS: 1900—Caught one pass for two yards. 1990—Recovered two fumbles. 1991—Recovered one fumble. 1992—Recovered one fumble. 1997—Recovered one fumble.

NICKERSON, HARDY — LB — BUCCANEERS

PERSONAL: Born September 1, 1965, in Los Angeles. ... 6-2/230. ... Full name: Hardy Otto Nickerson.
HIGH SCHOOL: Verbum Dei (Los Angeles).
COLLEGE: California.
TRANSACTIONS/CAREER NOTES: Selected by Pittsburgh Steelers in fifth round (122nd pick overall) of 1987 NFL draft. ... Signed by Steelers (July 26, 1987). ... On injured reserve with ankle and knee injuries (November 3-December 16, 1989). ... Granted free agency (February 1, 1992). ... Re-signed by Steelers (June 15, 1992). ... Granted unconditional free agency (March 1, 1993). ... Signed by Tampa Bay Buccaneers (March 18, 1993). ... Granted unconditional free agency (February 16, 1996). ... Re-signed by Buccaneers (February 22, 1996).
HONORS: Named linebacker on THE SPORTING NEWS college All-America second team (1985). ... Named inside linebacker on THE SPORTING NEWS NFL All-Pro team (1993). ... Played in Pro Bowl (1993, 1996 and 1997 seasons).
PRO STATISTICS: 1987—Recovered one fumble. 1988—Intercepted one pass for no yards and recovered one fumble. 1992—Recovered two fumbles for 44 yards. 1993—Intercepted one pass for six yards and recovered one fumble. 1994—Intercepted two passes for nine yards. 1995—Recovered three fumbles. 1996—Intercepted two passes for 24 yards and recovered two fumbles. 1997—Recovered two fumbles.

Year Team	G	GS	SACKS
1987—Pittsburgh NFL	12	0	0.0
1988—Pittsburgh NFL	15	10	3.5
1989—Pittsburgh NFL	10	8	1.0
1990—Pittsburgh NFL	16	14	2.0
1991—Pittsburgh NFL	16	14	1.0
1992—Pittsburgh NFL	15	15	2.0
1993—Tampa Bay NFL	16	16	1.0
1994—Tampa Bay NFL	14	14	1.0
1995—Tampa Bay NFL	16	16	1.5
1996—Tampa Bay NFL	16	16	3.0
1997—Tampa Bay NFL	16	16	1.0
Pro totals (11 years)	162	139	17.0

NORGARD, ERIK — G/C — OILERS

N

PERSONAL: Born November 4, 1965, in Bellevue, Wash. ... 6-1/289. ... Full name: Erik Christian Norgard.
HIGH SCHOOL: Arlington (Wash.).
COLLEGE: Colorado (degree in communications, 1989).
TRANSACTIONS/CAREER NOTES: Signed as non-drafted free agent by Houston Oilers (May 12, 1989). ... Released by Oilers (August 30, 1989). ... Re-signed by Oilers to developmental squad (September 6, 1989). ... Released by Oilers (January 2, 1990). ... Re-signed by Oilers (March 8, 1990). ... Released by Oilers (August 26, 1991). ... Re-signed by Oilers (August 27, 1991). ... On injured reserve with shoulder injury (August 29, 1991-entire season). ... Granted unconditional free agency (February 1-April 1, 1992). ... Assigned by Oilers to San Antonio Riders in 1992 World League enhancement allocation program. ... Re-signed by Oilers for 1992 season. ... Released by Oilers (August 31, 1992). ... Re-signed by Oilers (September 11, 1992). ... Granted unconditional free agency (February 17, 1994). ... Re-signed by Oilers (March 9, 1994). ... Released by Oilers (July 14, 1995). ... Signed by Atlanta Falcons (August 2, 1995); released after failing physical. ... Signed by Oilers (August 8, 1995). ... Oilers franchise moved to Tennessee for 1997 season.
PLAYING EXPERIENCE: Houston NFL, 1990 and 1992-1996; San Antonio W.L., 1992; Tennessee NFL, 1997. ... Games/Games started: 1990 (16/0), 1992 (W.L.-10/10; NFL-15/0; Total: 25/10), 1993 (16/4), 1994 (16/7), 1995 (15/0), 1996 (13/0), 1997 (15/0). W.L.:10/10. Total NFL: 106/11. Total Pro: 116/21.
PRO STATISTICS: NFL: 1990—Returned two kickoffs for no yards. 1993—Caught one pass for 13 yards and recovered one fumble. 1996—Caught one pass for one yard and a touchdown. 1997—Recovered one fumble. W.L.: 1992—Caught two passes for 22 yards.

NORTHERN, GABE — LB/DE — BILLS

PERSONAL: Born June 8, 1974, in Baton Rouge, La. ... 6-2/240. ... Full name: Gabriel O'Kara Northern.
HIGH SCHOOL: Glen Oaks (Baton Rouge, La.).
COLLEGE: Louisiana State.
TRANSACTIONS/CAREER NOTES: Selected by Buffalo Bills in second round (53rd pick overall) of 1996 NFL draft. ... Signed by Bills (July 17, 1996).
PRO STATISTICS: 1996—Returned blocked punt 18 yards for a touchdown.

Year Team	G	GS	SACKS
1996—Buffalo NFL	16	2	5.0
1997—Buffalo NFL	16	1	0.0
Pro totals (2 years)	32	3	5.0

NORTON, KEN ·   LB   49ERS

PERSONAL: Born September 29, 1966, in Jacksonville, Ill. ... 6-2/254. ... Full name: Kenneth Howard Norton Jr. ... Son of Ken Norton Sr., former world heavyweight boxing champion.

HIGH SCHOOL: Westchester (Los Angeles).

COLLEGE: UCLA.

TRANSACTIONS/CAREER NOTES: Selected by Dallas Cowboys in second round (41st pick overall) of 1988 NFL draft. ... Signed by Cowboys (July 13, 1988). ... On injured reserve with broken arm (August 23-December 3, 1988). ... On injured reserve with knee injury (December 24, 1990-remainder of season). ... Granted free agency (February 1, 1992). ... Re-signed by Cowboys (August 12, 1992). ... Granted unconditional free agency (February 17, 1994). ... Signed by San Francisco 49ers (April 20, 1994).

CHAMPIONSHIP GAME EXPERIENCE: Played in NFC championship game (1992-1994 and 1997 seasons). ... Member of Super Bowl championship team (1992-1994 seasons).

HONORS: Named linebacker on THE SPORTING NEWS college All-America first team (1987). ... Played in Pro Bowl (1993, 1995 and 1997 seasons).

POST SEASON RECORDS: Shares Super Bowl career record for most touchdowns by fumble recovery—1 (January 31, 1993, vs. Buffalo).

PRO STATISTICS: 1988—Recovered one fumble. 1990—Recovered two fumbles. 1992—Recovered two fumbles. 1993—Recovered one fumble for three yards. 1996—Recovered one fumble for 21 yards. 1997—Recovered two fumbles.

Year Team	G	GS	No.	Yds.	Avg.	TD	No.
			INTERCEPTIONS				SACKS
1988—Dallas NFL	3	0	0	0	...	0	0.0
1989—Dallas NFL	13	13	0	0	...	0	2.5
1990—Dallas NFL	15	15	0	0	...	0	2.5
1991—Dallas NFL	16	16	0	0	...	0	0.0
1992—Dallas NFL	16	16	0	0	...	0	0.0
1993—Dallas NFL	16	16	1	25	25.0	0	2.0
1994—San Francisco NFL	16	16	1	0	0.0	0	0.0
1995—San Francisco NFL	16	16	3	102	34.0	†2	1.0
1996—San Francisco NFL	16	16	0	0	...	0	0.0
1997—San Francisco NFL	16	16	0	0	...	0	1.5
Pro totals (10 years)	143	140	5	127	25.4	2	9.5

NOTTAGE, DEXTER   DE ·   PACKERS

PERSONAL: Born November 14, 1970, in Miami. ... 6-4/280.

HIGH SCHOOL: Hollywood (Fla.) Hills.

COLLEGE: Florida A&M.

TRANSACTIONS/CAREER NOTES: Selected by Washington Redskins in sixth round (163rd pick overall) of 1994 NFL draft. ... Signed by Redskins (June 2, 1994). ... Released by Redskins (August 24, 1997). ... Signed by Kansas City Chiefs (September 23, 1997). ... Released by Chiefs (November 7, 1997). ... Signed by Green Bay Packers (March 19, 1998).

PRO STATISTICS: 1995—Recovered three fumbles.

Year Team	G	GS	SACKS
1994—Washington NFL	15	1	1.0
1995—Washington NFL	16	0	0.0
1996—Washington NFL	16	4	5.0
1997—Kansas City NFL	1	0	0.0
Pro totals (4 years)	48	5	6.0

NOVAK, JEFF   G/OT   JAGUARS

PERSONAL: Born July 27, 1967, in Cook County, Ill. ... 6-6/292. ... Full name: Jeff Ladd Novak.

HIGH SCHOOL: Clear Lake (Houston).

COLLEGE: Southwest Texas State (degree in hospital administration).

TRANSACTIONS/CAREER NOTES: Selected by San Diego Chargers in seventh round (172nd pick overall) of 1990 NFL draft. ... Signed by Chargers for 1990 season. ... Released by Chargers (August 30, 1990). ... Selected by Montreal Machine in first round of 1991 World League draft. ... Signed by New York Giants (June 1, 1992). ... Released by Giants (August 31, 1992). ... Re-signed by Giants to practice squad (September 2, 1992). ... On injured reserve with hand injury (October 12, 1992-remainder of season). ... Granted free agency after 1992 season. ... Re-signed by Giants (March 5, 1993). ... Released by Giants (August 30, 1993). ... Re-signed by Giants to practice squad (August 31, 1993). ... Signed by Miami Dolphins off Giants practice squad (December 15, 1993). ... Selected by Jacksonville Jaguars from Dolphins in NFL expansion draft (February 15, 1995).

PLAYING EXPERIENCE: Montreal W.L., 1991 and 1992; Miami NFL, 1994; Jacksonville NFL, 1995-1997. ... Games/Games started: W.L.: 1991 (9/games started unavailable), 1992 (10/games started unavailable), 1994 (6/0), 1995 (16/13), 1996 (5/0), 1997 (7/2). Total W.L.: 19/games started unavailable. Total NFL: 34/15. Total Pro: 53/games started unavailable.

CHAMPIONSHIP GAME EXPERIENCE: Member of Jaguars for AFC championship game (1996 season); did not play.

NUSSMEIER, DOUG   QB   BRONCOS

PERSONAL: Born December 11, 1970, in Portland, Ore. ... 6-3/211. ... Full name: Douglas Keith Nussmeier.

HIGH SCHOOL: Lakeridge (Lake Oswego, Ore.).

COLLEGE: Idaho.

TRANSACTIONS/CAREER NOTES: Selected by New Orleans Saints in fourth round (116th pick overall) of 1994 NFL draft. ... Signed by Saints (May 31, 1994). ... Active for 16 games (1994); did not play. ... Assigned by Saints to Rhein Fire in 1995 World League enhancement allocation program (February 20, 1995). ... Granted free agency (February 14, 1997). ... Re-signed by Saints (June 7, 1997). ... Granted unconditional free agency (February 13, 1998). ... Signed by Denver Broncos (March 4, 1998).
HONORS: Walter Payton Award winner (1993).
PRO STATISTICS: 1996—Fumbled twice. 1997—Fumbled once for minus four yards.
SINGLE GAME HIGHS (regular season): Attempts—35 (December 8, 1996, vs. Atlanta); completions—21 (December 8, 1996, vs. Atlanta); yards—171 (December 8, 1996, vs. Atlanta); and touchdown passes—1 (December 8, 1996, vs. Atlanta).
MISCELLANEOUS: Regular-season record as starting NFL quarterback: 0-2.

Year Team	G	GS	Att.	Cmp.	Pct.	Yds.	TD	Int.	Avg.	Rat.	Att.	Yds.	Avg.	TD	TD	2pt.	Pts.
						PASSING							RUSHING			TOTALS	
1994—New Orleans NFL						Did not play.											
1995—Rhein W.L.	...	...	9	4	44.4	27	0	1	3.00	12.0	2	3	1.5	0	0	0	0
1996—New Orleans NFL	2	1	50	28	56.0	272	1	1	5.44	69.8	3	6	2.0	0	0	0	0
1997—New Orleans NFL	4	1	32	18	56.3	183	0	3	5.72	33.7	8	30	3.8	0	0	0	0
W.L. totals (1 year)	...	...	9	4	44.4	27	0	1	3.00	12.0	2	3	1.5	0	0	0	0
NFL totals (2 years)	6	2	82	46	56.1	455	1	4	5.55	55.7	11	36	3.3	0	0	0	0
Pro totals (3 years)	...	...	91	50	54.9	482	1	5	5.30	50.7	13	39	3.0	0	0	0	0

OBEN, ROMAN   OT   GIANTS

PERSONAL: Born October 9, 1972, in Cameroon, West Africa. ... 6-4/310.
HIGH SCHOOL: Gonzaga (Washington, D.C.), then Fork Union (Va.) Military Academy.
COLLEGE: Louisville.
TRANSACTIONS/CAREER NOTES: Selected by New York Giants in third round (66th pick overall) of 1996 NFL draft. ... Signed by Giants (July 20, 1996).
PLAYING EXPERIENCE: New York Giants NFL, 1996 and 1997. ... Games/Games started: 1996 (2/0), 1997 (16/16). Total: 18/16.

ODOM, JASON   OT   BUCCANEERS

PERSONAL: Born March 31, 1974, in Bartow, Fla. ... 6-5/307. ... Full name: Jason Brian Odom.
HIGH SCHOOL: Bartow (Fla.).
COLLEGE: Florida.
TRANSACTIONS/CAREER NOTES: Selected by Tampa Bay Buccaneers in fourth round (96th pick overall) of 1996 NFL draft. ... Signed by Buccaneers (July 16, 1996).
PLAYING EXPERIENCE: Tampa Bay NFL, 1996 and 1997. ... Games/Games started: 1996 (12/7), 1997 (16/16). Total: 28/23.
HONORS: Named offensive lineman on THE SPORTING NEWS college All-America first team (1995).
PRO STATISTICS: 1996—Recovered one fumble.

O'DONNELL, NEIL   QB   JETS

PERSONAL: Born July 3, 1966, in Morristown, N.J. ... 6-3/228. ... Full name: Neil Kennedy O'Donnell.
HIGH SCHOOL: Madison (N.J.)-Boro.
COLLEGE: Maryland (degree in economics, 1990).
TRANSACTIONS/CAREER NOTES: Selected by Pittsburgh Steelers in third round (70th pick overall) of 1990 NFL draft. ... Signed by Steelers (August 8, 1990). ... Active for three games (1990); did not play. ... Granted free agency (March 1, 1993). ... Tendered offer sheet by Tampa Bay Buccaneers (April 2, 1993). ... Offer matched by Steelers (April 12, 1993). ... Granted unconditional free agency (February 16, 1996). ... Signed by New York Jets (February 29, 1996).
CHAMPIONSHIP GAME EXPERIENCE: Played in AFC championship game (1994 and 1995 seasons). ... Played in Super Bowl XXX (1995 season).
HONORS: Played in Pro Bowl (1992 season).
RECORDS: Holds NFL career record for lowest interception percentage—2.10.
POST SEASON RECORDS: Holds NFL postseason single-game record for most passes attempted without an interception—54 (January 15, 1995, vs. San Diego).
PRO STATISTICS: 1991—Fumbled 11 times and recovered two fumbles for minus three yards. 1992—Fumbled six times and recovered four fumbles for minus 20 yards. 1993—Fumbled five times. 1994—Fumbled four times and recovered one fumble. 1995—Fumbled twice and recovered one fumble. 1996—Fumbled twice. 1997—Fumbled nine times and recovered two fumbles for minus one yard.
SINGLE GAME HIGHS (regular season): Attempts—55 (December 24, 1995, vs. Green Bay); completions—34 (November 5, 1995, vs. Chicago); yards—377 (November 19, 1995, vs. Cincinnati); and touchdown passes—5 (August 31, 1997, vs. Seattle).
STATISTICAL PLATEAUS: 300-yard passing games: 1991 (1), 1993 (1), 1995 (4), 1996 (2), 1997 (1). Total: 9.
MISCELLANEOUS: Regular-season record as starting NFL quarterback: 47-34 (.580). ... Postseason record as starting NFL quarterback: 3-4 (.429).

Year Team	G	GS	Att.	Cmp.	Pct.	Yds.	TD	Int.	Avg.	Rat.	Att.	Yds.	Avg.	TD	TD	2pt.	Pts.
						PASSING							RUSHING			TOTALS	
1990—Pittsburgh NFL...........						Did not play.											
1991—Pittsburgh NFL...........	12	8	286	156	54.5	1963	11	7	6.86	78.8	18	82	4.6	1	1	...	6
1992—Pittsburgh NFL.........	12	12	313	185	59.1	2283	13	9	7.29	83.6	27	5	0.2	1	1	...	6
1993—Pittsburgh NFL.........	16	15	486	270	55.6	3208	14	7	6.60	79.5	26	111	4.3	0	0	...	0
1994—Pittsburgh NFL.........	14	14	370	212	57.3	2443	13	9	6.60	78.9	31	80	2.6	1	1	0	6
1995—Pittsburgh NFL.........	12	12	416	246	59.1	2970	17	7	7.14	87.7	24	45	1.9	0	0	0	0
1996—New York Jets NFL.....	6	6	188	110	58.5	1147	4	7	6.10	67.8	6	30	5.0	0	0	0	0
1997—New York Jets NFL......	15	14	460	259	56.3	2796	17	7	6.08	80.3	32	36	1.1	1	1	0	6
Pro totals (7 years)	87	81	2519	1438	57.1	16810	89	53	6.67	80.5	164	389	2.4	4	4	0	24

O'DWYER, MATT — G — JETS

PERSONAL: Born September 1, 1972, in Lincolnshire, Ill. ... 6-5/300. ... Full name: Matthew Phillip O'Dwyer.
HIGH SCHOOL: Adlai E. Stevenson (Prairie View, Ill.).
COLLEGE: Northwestern.
TRANSACTIONS/CAREER NOTES: Selected by New York Jets in second round (33rd pick overall) of 1995 NFL draft. ... Signed by Jets (July 20, 1995).
PLAYING EXPERIENCE: New York Jets NFL, 1995-1997. ... Games/Games started: 1995 (12/2), 1996 (16/16), 1997 (16/16). Total: 44/34.

OFODILE, A.J. — TE — RAVENS

PERSONAL: Born October 10, 1973, in Detroit. ... 6-6/260. ... Full name: Anselm Junior Ofodile. ... Name pronounced oh-FAH-duh-lay.
HIGH SCHOOL: Cass Technical (Detroit).
COLLEGE: Missouri.
TRANSACTIONS/CAREER NOTES: Selected after junior season by Buffalo Bills in fifth round (158th pick overall) of 1994 NFL draft. ... Signed by Bills (July 15, 1994). ... On physically unable to perform list with knee injury (August 23, 1994-entire season). ... Released by Bills (August 22, 1995). ... Signed by Pittsburgh Steelers to practice squad (August 29, 1995). ... Released by Steelers (August 19, 1996). ... Signed by Baltimore Ravens (February 12, 1997). ... Assigned by Ravens to Rhein Fire in 1997 World League enhancement allocation program (February 19, 1997).
PLAYING EXPERIENCE: Rhein W.L., 1997; Baltimore NFL, 1997. ... Games/Games started: W.L. 1997 (games played unavailable), NFL 1997 (12/0).
PRO STATISTICS: W.L.: 1997—Caught 10 passes for 146 yards and one touchdown.
SINGLE GAME HIGHS (regular season): Receptions—0; yards—0; and touchdown receptions—0.

OGDEN, JONATHAN — OT — RAVENS

PERSONAL: Born July 31, 1974, in Washington, D.C. ... 6-8/318. ... Full name: Jonathan Phillip Ogden.
HIGH SCHOOL: St. Alban's (Washington, D.C.).
COLLEGE: UCLA.
TRANSACTIONS/CAREER NOTES: Selected by Baltimore Ravens in first round (fourth pick overall) of 1996 NFL draft. ... Signed by Ravens (July 15, 1996).
PLAYING EXPERIENCE: Baltimore NFL, 1996 and 1997. ... Games/Games started: 1996 (16/16), 1997 (16/16). Total: 32/32.
HONORS: Outland Trophy winner (1995). ... Named offensive lineman on THE SPORTING NEWS college All-America first team (1995). ... Named offensive tackle on the THE SPORTING NEWS NFL All-Pro team (1997). ... Played in Pro Bowl (1997 season).
PRO STATISTICS: 1996—Caught one pass for one yard and a touchdown.

OLDHAM, CHRIS — CB — STEELERS

PERSONAL: Born October 26, 1968, in Sacramento. ... 5-9/200. ... Full name: Christopher Martin Oldham.
HIGH SCHOOL: O. Perry Walker (New Orleans).
COLLEGE: Oregon (degree in communications).
TRANSACTIONS/CAREER NOTES: Selected by Detroit Lions in fourth round (105th pick overall) of 1990 NFL draft. ... Signed by Lions (July 19, 1990). ... Released by Lions (August 26, 1991). ... Signed by Buffalo Bills (September 25, 1991). ... Released by Bills (October 8, 1991). ... Signed by Phoenix Cardinals (October 15, 1991). ... Released by Cardinals (November 13, 1991). ... Signed by San Diego Chargers (February 15, 1992). ... Assigned by Chargers to San Antonio Riders in 1992 World League enhancement allocation program (February 20, 1992). ... Released by Chargers (August 25, 1992). ... Signed by Cardinals (December 22, 1992). ... Granted unconditional free agency (February 17, 1994). ... Cardinals franchise renamed Arizona Cardinals for 1994 season. ... Re-signed by Cardinals (June 7, 1994). ... Granted unconditional free agency (February 17, 1995). ... Signed by Pittsburgh Steelers (April 12, 1995).
CHAMPIONSHIP GAME EXPERIENCE: Played in AFC championship game (1995 and 1997 seasons). ... Played in Super Bowl XXX (1995 season).
PRO STATISTICS: W.L.: 1992—Credited with one sack and recovered one fumble. NFL: 1993—Credited with one sack. 1995—Recovered one fumble for 23 yards and a touchdown. 1996—Credited with two sacks. 1997—Credited with four sacks.

Year Team	G	GS	INTERCEPTIONS				KICKOFF RETURNS				TOTALS			
			No.	Yds.	Avg.	TD	No.	Yds.	Avg.	TD	TD	2pt.	Pts.	Fum.
1990—Detroit NFL	16	0	1	28	28.0	0	13	234	18.0	0	0	...	0	2
1991—Buffalo NFL	2	0	0	0	...	0	0	0	...	0	0	...	0	0
—Phoenix NFL	2	0	0	0	...	0	0	0	...	0	0	...	0	0
1992—San Antonio W.L.	9	9	3	52	17.3	*1	1	11	11.0	0	1	...	6	0
—Phoenix NFL	1	0	0	0	...	0	0	0	...	0	0	...	0	0
1993—Phoenix NFL	16	6	1	0	0.0	0	0	0	...	0	0	...	0	0
1994—Arizona NFL	11	1	0	0	...	0	0	0	...	0	0	0	0	0
1995—Pittsburgh NFL	15	0	1	12	12.0	0	0	0	...	0	1	0	6	0
1996—Pittsburgh NFL	16	0	0	0	...	0	0	0	...	0	0	0	0	0
1997—Pittsburgh NFL	16	0	2	16	8.0	0	0	0	...	0	0	0	0	0
W.L. totals (1 year)	9	9	3	52	17.3	1	1	11	11.0	0	1	0	6	0
NFL totals (8 years)	95	7	5	56	11.2	0	13	234	18.0	0	1	0	6	2
Pro totals (9 years)	104	16	8	108	13.5	1	14	245	17.5	0	2	0	12	2

OLIVER, JIMMY — WR — COWBOYS

PERSONAL: Born January 30, 1973, in Dallas. ... 5-10/186.
HIGH SCHOOL: W.H. Adamson (Dallas).
COLLEGE: Texas Christian.
TRANSACTIONS/CAREER NOTES: Selected by San Diego Chargers in second round (61st pick overall) of 1995 NFL draft. ... Signed by Chargers (June 15, 1995). ... Inactive for nine games (1995). ... On injured reserve with shoulder injury (November 10, 1995-remainder of season). ... Inactive for six games (1996). ... On injured reserve with knee injury (October 9, 1996-remainder of season). ... Released by Chargers (July 21, 1997). ... Signed by Dallas Cowboys (March 11, 1998).

OLIVER, WINSLOW   RB   PANTHERS

PERSONAL: Born March 3, 1973, in Houston. ... 5-7/180. ... Full name: Winslow Paul Oliver.
HIGH SCHOOL: Clements (Sugar Land, Texas), then Kempner (Sugar Land, Texas).
COLLEGE: New Mexico.
TRANSACTIONS/CAREER NOTES: Selected by Carolina Panthers in third round (73rd pick overall) of 1996 NFL draft. ... Signed by Panthers (July 20, 1996).
CHAMPIONSHIP GAME EXPERIENCE: Played in NFC championship game (1996 season).
PRO STATISTICS: 1996—Fumbled four times. 1997—Fumbled twice.
SINGLE GAME HIGHS (regular season): Attempts—8 (November 10, 1996, vs. New York Giants); yards—37 (September 1, 1996, vs. Atlanta); and rushing touchdowns—0.

			RUSHING				RECEIVING				PUNT RETURNS				KICKOFF RETURNS				TOTALS		
Year Team	G	GS	Att.	Yds.	Avg.	TD	No.	Yds.	Avg.	TD	No.	Yds.	Avg.	TD	No.	Yds.	Avg.	TD	TD	2pt.	Pts.
1996—Carolina NFL	16	0	47	183	3.9	0	15	144	9.6	0	52	598	11.5	1	7	160	22.9	0	1	0	6
1997—Carolina NFL	6	0	1	0	0.0	0	6	47	7.8	0	14	111	7.9	0	0	0	...	0	0	0	0
Pro totals (2 years)	22	0	48	183	3.8	0	21	191	9.1	0	66	709	10.7	1	7	160	22.9	0	1	0	6

OLSAVSKY, JERRY   LB   BENGALS

PERSONAL: Born March 29, 1967, in Youngstown, Ohio. ... 6-1/224. ... Full name: Jerome Donald Olsavsky. ... Name pronounced ol-SAV-skee.
HIGH SCHOOL: Chaney (Youngstown, Ohio).
COLLEGE: Pittsburgh (degree in information science).
TRANSACTIONS/CAREER NOTES: Selected by Pittsburgh Steelers in 10th round (258th pick overall) of 1989 NFL draft. ... Signed by Steelers (July 18, 1989). ... On injured reserve with foot injury (November 6-December 27, 1992; on practice squad (December 2-27, 1992). ... On injured reserve with knee injury (October 26, 1993-remainder of season). ... Released by Steelers (February 17, 1994). ... Re-signed by Steelers (November 16, 1994). ... Granted unconditional free agency (February 16, 1996). ... Re-signed by Steelers (April 21, 1996). ... Released by Steelers (February 2, 1998). ... Signed by Cincinnati Bengals (March 3, 1998).
PLAYING EXPERIENCE: Pittsburgh NFL, 1989-1997. ... Games/Games started: 1989 (16/8), 1990 (15/0), 1991 (16/4), 1992 (7/0), 1993 (7/7), 1994 (1/0), 1995 (15/5), 1996 (15/13), 1997 (16/0). Total: 108/37.
CHAMPIONSHIP GAME EXPERIENCE: Member of Steelers for AFC championship game (1994 season); inactive. ... Played in AFC championship game (1995 and 1997 seasons). ... Played in Super Bowl XXX (1995 season).
PRO STATISTICS: 1989—Credited with one sack. 1995—Credited with one sack. 1996—Intercepted one pass for five yards and recovered one fumble for six yards.

O'NEAL, LESLIE   DE   CHIEFS

PERSONAL: Born May 7, 1964, in Pulaski County, Ark. ... 6-4/270. ... Full name: Leslie Cornelius O'Neal.
HIGH SCHOOL: Hall (Little Rock, Ark.).
COLLEGE: Oklahoma State.
TRANSACTIONS/CAREER NOTES: Selected by New Jersey Generals in 1986 USFL territorial draft. ... Selected by San Diego Chargers in first round (eighth pick overall) of 1986 NFL draft. ... Signed by Chargers (August 5, 1986). ... On injured reserve with knee injury (December 4, 1986-remainder of season). ... On physically unable to perform list with knee injury (August 30, 1987-entire season). ... On physically unable to perform list with knee injury (July 23-August 21, 1988). ... On physically unable to perform list with knee injury (August 22-October 15, 1988). ... Granted free agency (February 1, 1990). ... Re-signed by Chargers (August 21, 1990). ... Granted free agency (February 1, 1992). ... Re-signed by Chargers (July 23, 1992). ... Designated by Chargers as franchise player (February 25, 1993). ... Free agency status changed by Chargers from franchise player to restricted free agent (June 15, 1993). ... Re-signed by Chargers (August 19, 1993). ... Granted unconditional free agency (February 16, 1996). ... Signed by St. Louis Rams (March 1, 1996). ... Released by Rams (February 18, 1998). ... Signed by Kansas City Chiefs (April 17, 1998).
CHAMPIONSHIP GAME EXPERIENCE: Played in AFC championship game (1994 season). ... Played in Super Bowl XXIX (1994 season).
HONORS: Named defensive lineman on THE SPORTING NEWS college All-America first team (1984 and 1985). ... Played in Pro Bowl (1989, 1990 and 1992-1995 seasons).
RECORDS: Shares NFL rookie-season record for most sacks—12.5 (1986).
PRO STATISTICS: 1986—Intercepted two passes for 22 yards and one touchdown and recovered two fumbles. 1989—Recovered two fumbles for 10 yards. 1990—Fumbled once and recovered two fumbles for 10 yards. 1992—Recovered one fumble. 1993—Recovered one fumble for 13 yards. 1994—Recovered one fumble. 1996—Recovered three fumbles. 1997—Intercepted one pass for five yards and recovered two fumbles for 66 yards and one touchdown.
MISCELLANEOUS: Holds San Diego Chargers all-time record for most sacks (105.5).

Year Team	G	GS	SACKS
1986—San Diego NFL	13	13	12.5
1987—San Diego NFL	Did not play.		
1988—San Diego NFL	9	1	4.0
1989—San Diego NFL	16	16	12.5
1990—San Diego NFL	16	16	13.5
1991—San Diego NFL	16	16	9.0
1992—San Diego NFL	15	15	§17.0
1993—San Diego NFL	16	16	12.0
1994—San Diego NFL	16	16	12.5
1995—San Diego NFL	16	16	12.5
1996—St. Louis NFL	16	16	7.0
1997—St. Louis NFL	15	14	10.0
Pro totals (11 years)	164	155	122.5

ORLANDO, BO   S   STEELERS

PERSONAL: Born April 3, 1966, in Berwick, Pa. ... 5-10/180. ... Full name: Joseph John Orlando.
HIGH SCHOOL: Berwick (Pa.) Area Senior.
COLLEGE: West Virginia.
TRANSACTIONS/CAREER NOTES: Selected by Houston Oilers in sixth round (157th pick overall) of 1989 NFL draft. ... Signed by Oilers (July 26, 1989). ... Released by Oilers (September 5, 1989). ... Re-signed by Oilers to developmental squad (September 8, 1989). ... Released by Oilers (January 2, 1990). ... Re-signed by Oilers (April 17, 1990). ... Granted free agency (February 1, 1992). ... Re-signed by Oilers (August 11, 1992). ... On injured reserve with knee injury (September 11-November 24, 1992). ... Granted unconditional free agency (February 17, 1995). ... Signed by San Diego Chargers (April 18, 1995). ... Granted unconditional free agency (February 16, 1996). ... Signed by Cincinnati Bengals (March 5, 1996). ... Released by Bengals (April 20, 1998). ... Signed by Pittsburgh Steelers (June 12, 1998).
PRO STATISTICS: 1991—Recovered two fumbles. 1995—Ran 37 yards with lateral from interception return. 1996—Credited with one sack and recovered one fumble. 1997—Credited with one sack and recovered one fumble.

| | | | INTERCEPTIONS | | | |
Year Team	G	GS	No.	Yds.	Avg.	TD
1989—Houston NFL			Did not play.			
1990—Houston NFL	16	0	0	0	...	0
1991—Houston NFL	16	16	4	18	4.5	0
1992—Houston NFL	6	1	0	0	...	0
1993—Houston NFL	16	3	3	68	22.7	▲1
1994—Houston NFL	16	0	0	0	...	0
1995—San Diego NFL	16	16	0	37	...	0
1996—Cincinnati NFL	16	16	2	0	0.0	0
1997—Cincinnati NFL	16	2	1	3	3.0	0
Pro totals (8 years)	118	54	10	126	12.6	1

OSTROSKI, JERRY   G   BILLS

PERSONAL: Born July 12, 1970, in Collegeville, Pa. ... 6-4/310. ... Full name: Gerald Ostroski Jr.
HIGH SCHOOL: Owen J. Roberts (Pottstown, Pa.).
COLLEGE: Tulsa.
TRANSACTIONS/CAREER NOTES: Selected by Kansas City Chiefs in 10th round (271st pick overall) of 1992 NFL draft. ... Signed by Chiefs (July 21, 1992). ... Released by Chiefs (August 25, 1992). ... Signed by Atlanta Falcons (May 7, 1993). ... Released by Falcons (August 24, 1993). ... Signed by Buffalo Bills to practice squad (November 18, 1993). ... Released by Bills (August 28, 1994). ... Re-signed by Bills to practice squad (August 29, 1994). ... Activated (November 30, 1994). ... Granted free agency (February 13, 1998). ... Re-signed by Bills (April 8, 1998).
PLAYING EXPERIENCE: Buffalo NFL, 1994-1997. ... Games/Games started: 1994 (4/3), 1995 (16/13), 1996 (16/16), 1997 (16/16). Total: 52/48.
PRO STATISTICS: 1997—Recovered three fumbles.

OTTIS, BRAD   DT   CARDINALS

PERSONAL: Born August 2, 1972, in Wahoo, Neb. ... 6-5/281. ... Full name: Brad Allen Ottis. ... Name pronounced Ah-tis.
HIGH SCHOOL: Fremont (Neb.) Bergan.
COLLEGE: Wayne State (Neb.).
TRANSACTIONS/CAREER NOTES: Selected by Los Angeles Rams in second round (56th pick overall) of 1994 NFL draft. ... Signed by Rams (June 23, 1994). ... Rams franchise moved to St. Louis (April 12, 1995). ... Released by Rams (August 20, 1996). ... Signed by Arizona Cardinals (October 1, 1996). ... Granted free agency (February 14, 1997). ... Re-signed by Cardinals for 1997 season. ... Granted unconditional free agency (February 13, 1998).
PLAYING EXPERIENCE: Los Angeles Rams NFL, 1994; St. Louis NFL, 1995; Arizona NFL, 1996 and 1997. ... Games/Games started: 1994 (13/0), 1995 (12/0), 1996 (11/1), 1997 (16/4). Total: 52/5.
PRO STATISTICS: 1994—Credited with one sack. 1996—Credited with one sack.

OWENS, DAN   DE   LIONS

PERSONAL: Born March 16, 1967, in Whittier, Calif. ... 6-3/290. ... Full name: Daniel William Owens.
HIGH SCHOOL: La Habra (Calif.).
COLLEGE: Southern California (bachelor of arts degree).
TRANSACTIONS/CAREER NOTES: Selected by Detroit Lions in second round (35th pick overall) of 1990 NFL draft. ... Signed by Lions (July 26, 1990). ... Granted free agency (March 1, 1993). ... Re-signed by Lions (August 14, 1993). ... Granted unconditional free agency (February 17, 1995). ... Re-signed by Lions (March 13, 1995). ... Granted unconditional free agency (February 16, 1996). ... Signed by Atlanta Falcons (March 26, 1996). ... Granted unconditional free agency (February 13, 1998). ... Signed by Lions (February 19, 1998).
CHAMPIONSHIP GAME EXPERIENCE: Played in NFC championship game (1991 season).
PRO STATISTICS: 1991—Recovered two fumbles. 1992—Recovered one fumble. 1993—Intercepted one pass for one yard and recovered two fumbles for 17 yards. 1995—Returned one kickoff for nine yards. 1996—Recovered one fumble. 1997—Intercepted one pass for 14 yards, returned one kickoff for nine yards, fumbled once and recovered one fumble for two yards.

Year Team	G	GS	SACKS
1990—Detroit NFL	16	12	3.0
1991—Detroit NFL	16	16	5.5
1992—Detroit NFL	16	4	2.0
1993—Detroit NFL	15	11	3.0
1994—Detroit NFL	16	8	3.0
1995—Detroit NFL	16	0	0.0
1996—Atlanta NFL	16	9	6.5
1997 Atlanta NFL	15	15	8.0
Pro totals (8 years)	126	75	30.0

O

OWENS, RICH   DE   REDSKINS

PERSONAL: Born May 22, 1972, in Philadelphia. ... 6-6/281.
HIGH SCHOOL: Lincoln (Philadelphia).
COLLEGE: Lehigh.
TRANSACTIONS/CAREER NOTES: Selected by Washington Redskins in fifth round (152nd pick overall) of 1995 NFL draft. ... Signed by Redskins (May 23, 1995). ... Granted free agency (February 13, 1998). ... Re-signed by Redskins (May 7, 1998).
PRO STATISTICS: 1997—Recovered one fumble.

Year Team	G	GS	SACKS
1995—Washington NFL	10	3	3.0
1996—Washington NFL	16	16	11.0
1997—Washington NFL	16	15	2.5
Pro totals (3 years)	42	34	16.5

OWENS, TERRELL   WR   49ERS

PERSONAL: Born December 7, 1973, in Alexander City, Ala. ... 6-3/217.
HIGH SCHOOL: Benjamin Russell (Alexander City, Ala.).
COLLEGE: Tennessee-Chattanooga.
TRANSACTIONS/CAREER NOTES: Selected by San Francisco 49ers in third round (89th pick overall) of 1996 NFL draft. ... Signed by 49ers (July 18, 1996). ... On physically unable to perform list with foot injury (July 17-August 11, 1997).
CHAMPIONSHIP GAME EXPERIENCE: Played in NFC championship game (1997 season).
PRO STATISTICS: 1996—Returned three kickoffs for 47 yards. 1997—Returned two kickoffs for 31 yards and recovered one fumble.
SINGLE GAME HIGHS (regular season): Receptions—7 (October 26, 1997, vs. New Orleans); yards—110 (December 8, 1996, vs. Carolina); and touchdown receptions—2 (October 19, 1997, vs. Atlanta).
STATISTICAL PLATEAUS: 100-yard receiving games: 1996 (1).

Year Team	G	GS	RECEIVING No.	Yds.	Avg.	TD	TOTALS TD	2pt.	Pts.	Fum.
1996—San Francisco NFL	16	10	35	520	14.9	4	4	0	24	1
1997—San Francisco NFL	16	15	60	936	15.6	8	8	0	48	1
Pro totals (2 years)	32	25	95	1456	15.3	12	12	0	72	2

PACE, ORLANDO   OT   RAMS

PERSONAL: Born November 4, 1975, in Sandusky, Ohio. ... 6-7/320. ... Full name: Orlando Lamar Pace.
HIGH SCHOOL: Sandusky (Ohio).
COLLEGE: Ohio State.
TRANSACTIONS/CAREER NOTES: Selected after junior season by St. Louis Rams in first round (first pick overall) of 1997 NFL draft. ... Signed by Rams (August 16, 1997).
PLAYING EXPERIENCE: St. Louis NFL, 1997. ... Games/Games started: 13/9.
HONORS: Lombardi Award winner (1995 and 1996). ... Named offensive tackle on THE SPORTING NEWS college All-America first team (1995 and 1996). ... Outland Trophy winner (1996).
PRO STATISTICS: 1997—Recovered one fumble.

PALELEI, LONNIE   G   JETS

PERSONAL: Born October 15, 1970, in Nu'uuli, American Samoa. ... 6-3/315. ... Full name: Siulagi Jack Palelei. ... Name pronounced SEE-oo-lon-nee pah-le-LAY.
HIGH SCHOOL: Blue Springs (Mo.).
COLLEGE: Purdue, then UNLV.
TRANSACTIONS/CAREER NOTES: Selected by Pittsburgh Steelers in fifth round (135th pick overall) of 1993 NFL draft. ... Signed by Steelers (July 9, 1993). ... Inactive for 16 games (1994). ... On reserve/non-football injury list with knee injury (August 21-November 3, 1995). ... Claimed on waivers by Cleveland Browns (November 28, 1995). ... Browns franchise moved to Baltimore and renamed Ravens for 1996 season (March 11, 1996). ... Released by Ravens (August 25, 1996). ... Signed by New York Jets (March 3, 1997).
PLAYING EXPERIENCE: Pittsburgh NFL, 1993 and 1995; New York Jets NFL, 1997. ... Games/Games started: 1993 (3/0), 1995 (1/0), 1997 (15/14). Total: 19/14.
CHAMPIONSHIP GAME EXPERIENCE: Member of Steelers for AFC championship game (1994 season); inactive.
PRO STATISTICS: 1997—Recovered one fumble.

PALMER, DAN   C   CHARGERS

PERSONAL: Born August 24, 1973, in Anderson, S.C. ... 6-4/290. ... Full name: Daniel Palmer.
HIGH SCHOOL: T.L. Hanna (Anderson, S.C.).
COLLEGE: Air Force.
TRANSACTIONS/CAREER NOTES: Selected by San Diego Chargers in sixth round (178th pick overall) of 1997 NFL draft. ... Signed by Chargers (July 14, 1997). ... On military reserve list (August 8, 1997-entire season).

PALMER, DAVID   RB   VIKINGS

PERSONAL: Born November 19, 1972, in Birmingham, Ala. ... 5-8/176. ... Full name: David L. Palmer.
HIGH SCHOOL: Jackson-Olin (Birmingham, Ala.).
COLLEGE: Alabama.

O
P

TRANSACTIONS/CAREER NOTES: Selected after junior season by Minnesota Vikings in second round (40th pick overall) of 1994 NFL draft. ... Signed by Vikings (July 19, 1994). ... Granted free agency (February 14, 1997). ... Re-signed by Vikings (May 7, 1997).
HONORS: Named kick returner on THE SPORTING NEWS college All-America first team (1993).
PRO STATISTICS: 1994—Fumbled twice. 1995—Fumbled once. 1996—Fumbled three times and recovered one fumble. 1997—Fumbled twice.
SINGLE GAME HIGHS (regular season): Attempts—4 (November 16, 1997, vs. Detroit); yards—15 (November 9, 1997, vs. Chicago); and rushing touchdowns—1 (November 9, 1997, vs. Chicago).

			RUSHING				RECEIVING				PUNT RETURNS				KICKOFF RETURNS				TOTALS		
Year Team	G	GS	Att.	Yds.	Avg.	TD	No.	Yds.	Avg.	TD	No.	Yds.	Avg.	TD	No.	Yds.	Avg.	TD	TD	2pt.	Pts.
1994—Minnesota NFL....	13	1	1	1	1.0	0	6	90	15.0	0	30	193	6.4	0	0	0	...	0	0	0	0
1995—Minnesota NFL....	14	0	7	15	2.1	0	12	100	8.3	0	26	342*13.2		†1	17	354	20.8	0	1	0	6
1996—Minnesota NFL....	11	1	2	9	4.5	0	6	40	6.7	0	22	216	9.8	1	13	292	22.5	0	1	0	6
1997—Minnesota NFL....	16	0	11	36	3.3	1	26	193	7.4	1	34	444‡13.1		0	32	711	22.2	0	2	0	12
Pro totals (4 years)........	54	2	21	61	2.9	1	50	423	8.5	1	112	1195	10.7	2	62	1357	21.9	0	4	0	24

PANOS, JOE — G/C — BILLS

PERSONAL: Born January 24, 1971, in Brookfield, Wis. ... 6-2/293.
HIGH SCHOOL: East (Brookfield, Wis.).
COLLEGE: Wisconsin.
TRANSACTIONS/CAREER NOTES: Selected by Philadelphia Eagles in third round (77th pick overall) of 1994 NFL draft. ... Signed by Eagles (July 11, 1994). ... On injured reserve with shoulder injury (November 12, 1995-remainder of season). ... Granted free agency (February 14, 1997). ... Re-signed by Eagles (July 19, 1997). ... Granted unconditional free agency (February 13, 1998). ... Signed by Buffalo Bills (February 20, 1998).
PLAYING EXPERIENCE: Philadelphia NFL, 1994-1997. ... Games/Games started: 1994 (16/2), 1995 (9/9), 1996 (16/16), 1997 (13/13). Total: 54/30.
PRO STATISTICS: 1997—Recovered one fumble.

PARKER, ANTHONY — CB — BUCCANEERS

PERSONAL: Born February 11, 1966, in Sylacauga, Ala. ... 5-10/181. ... Full name: Will Anthony Parker. ... Son of Billy Parker, second base-man/third baseman with California Angels (1971-73).
HIGH SCHOOL: McClintock (Tempe, Ariz.).
COLLEGE: Arizona State (degree in physical education, 1989).
TRANSACTIONS/CAREER NOTES: Signed as non-drafted free agent by Indianapolis Colts (April 21, 1989). ... On injured reserve with hamstring injury (September 5-November 17, 1989). ... Granted unconditional free agency (February 1, 1990). ... Signed by New York Jets (March 31, 1990). ... Released by Jets (September 4, 1990). ... Signed by WLAF (January 31, 1991). ... Selected by New York/New Jersey Knights in first round (second defensive back) of 1991 WLAF positional draft. ... Signed by Phoenix Cardinals (July 9, 1991). ... Released by Cardinals (August 13, 1991). ... Signed by Kansas City Chiefs to practice squad (September 11, 1991). ... Activated (September 15, 1991). ... Released by Chiefs (September 25, 1991). ... Re-signed by Chiefs to practice squad (October 1, 1991). ... Activated (December 14, 1991). ... Granted unconditional free agency (February 1, 1992). ... Signed by Minnesota Vikings (March 26, 1992). ... Granted free agency (February 17, 1994). ... Re-signed by Vikings (May 7, 1994). ... Granted unconditional free agency (February 17, 1995). ... Signed by Los Angeles Rams (April 4, 1995). ... Rams franchise moved to St. Louis (April 12, 1995). ... Released by Rams (July 15, 1997). ... Signed by Tampa Bay Buccaneers (July 20, 1997).
HONORS: Named cornerback on All-World League team (1991).
PRO STATISTICS: 1992—Returned two kickoffs for 30 yards and recovered two fumbles for 58 yards and a touchdown. 1994—Recovered one fumble for 23 yards and a touchdown. 1995—Recovered four fumbles for 35 yards and a touchdown. 1996—Recovered one fumble. 1997—Credited with one sack.
MISCELLANEOUS: Only player in NFL history to score a defensive touchdown in three consecutive games (1994).

			INTERCEPTIONS				PUNT RETURNS				TOTALS			
Year Team	G	GS	No.	Yds.	Avg.	TD	No.	Yds.	Avg	TD	TD	2pt.	Pts.	Fum.
1989—Indianapolis NFL............	1	0	0	0	...	0	0	0	...	0	0	...	0	0
1990—							Did not play.							
1991—New York/New Jersey W.L.	10	10	*11	*270	24.5	*2	0	0	...	0	2	...	12	0
—Kansas City NFL	2	0	0	0	...	0	0	0	...	0	0	...	0	0
1992—Minnesota NFL	16	3	3	23	7.7	0	33	336	10.2	0	1	...	6	2
1993—Minnesota NFL	14	0	1	1	1.0	0	9	64	7.1	0	0	...	0	0
1994—Minnesota NFL	15	15	4	99	24.8	2	4	31	7.8	0	3	0	18	1
1995—St. Louis NFL	16	16	2	-5	-2.5	0	0	0	...	0	1	0	6	0
1996—St. Louis NFL	14	14	4	128	32.0	†2	0	0	...	0	2	0	12	0
1997—Tampa Bay NFL	15	14	1	5	5.0	0	0	0	...	0	0	0	0	1
W.L. totals (1 year)	10	10	11	270	24.5	2	0	0		0	2	0	12	0
NFL totals (8 years)	93	62	15	251	16.7	4	46	431	9.4	0	7	0	42	4
Pro totals (9 years)	103	72	26	521	20.0	6	46	431	9.4	0	9	0	54	4

PARKER, CHRIS — RB — JAGUARS

PERSONAL: Born December 31, 1972, in Lynchburg, Va. ... 5-11/213. ... Full name: Christopher Lee Parker.
HIGH SCHOOL: Heritage (Lynchburg, Va.).
COLLEGE: Marshall (degree in business, 1996).
TRANSACTIONS/CAREER NOTES: Signed as non-drafted free agent by Jacksonville Jaguars (April 25, 1996). ... Released by Jaguars (August 19, 1996). ... Re-signed by Jaguars to practice squad (September 24, 1996). ... On injured reserve with knee injury (September 2, 1997-remainder of season).
PLAYING EXPERIENCE: Jacksonville NFL, 1997. ... Games/Games started: 1/0.
PRO STATISTICS: 1997—Returned one kickoff for nine yards.
SINGLE GAME HIGHS (regular season): Attempts—0; yards—0; and rushing touchdowns—0.

P

PARKER, GLENN   G/OT   CHIEFS

PERSONAL: Born April 22, 1966, in Westminster, Calif. ... 6-5/305. ... Full name: Glenn Andrew Parker.
HIGH SCHOOL: Edison (Huntington Beach, Calif.).
COLLEGE: Arizona.
TRANSACTIONS/CAREER NOTES: Selected by Buffalo Bills in third round (69th pick overall) of 1990 NFL draft. ... Signed by Bills (July 26, 1990). ... Granted free agency (March 1, 1993). ... Re-signed by Bills (March 11, 1993). ... Released by Bills (August 24, 1997). ... Signed by Kansas City Chiefs (August 28, 1997).
PLAYING EXPERIENCE: Buffalo NFL, 1990-1996; Kansas City NFL, 1997. ... Games/Games started: 1990 (16/3), 1991 (16/5), 1992 (13/13), 1993 (16/9), 1994 (16/16), 1995 (13/13), 1996 (14/13), 1997 (15/15). Total: 119/87.
CHAMPIONSHIP GAME EXPERIENCE: Played in AFC championship game (1990, 1992 and 1993 seasons). ... Member of Bills for AFC championship game (1991 season); inactive. ... Played in Super Bowl XXV (1990 season), Super Bowl XXVI (1991 season), Super Bowl XXVII (1992 season) and Super Bowl XXVIII (1993 season).
PRO STATISTICS: 1992—Recovered one fumble. 1995—Recovered one fumble. 1996—Recovered two fumbles.

PARKER, RICKY   DB   JAGUARS

PERSONAL: Born December 4, 1974, in Burlington, Vt. ... 6-1/209. ... Full name: Ricky Duwayne Parker.
HIGH SCHOOL: Hiram Johnson (Sacramento).
COLLEGE: San Diego State.
TRANSACTIONS/CAREER NOTES: Selected by Chicago Bears in sixth round (201st pick overall) of 1997 NFL draft. ... Signed by Bears (July 10, 1997). ... Released by Bears (August 18, 1997). ... Signed by Jacksonville Jaguars to practice squad (September 8, 1997). ... Activated (September 23, 1997). ... Assigned by Jaguars to Amsterdam Admirals in 1998 NFL Europe enhancement allocation program (February 18, 1998).
PLAYING EXPERIENCE: Jacksonville NFL, 1997. ... Games/Games started: 12/0.

PARKER, RIDDICK   DT   SEAHAWKS

PERSONAL: Born November 20, 1972, in Emporia, Va. ... 6-3/274.
HIGH SCHOOL: Southampton (Courtland, Va.).
COLLEGE: North Carolina.
TRANSACTIONS/CAREER NOTES: Signed as non-drafted free agent by San Diego Chargers (April 28, 1995). ... Released by Chargers (August 22, 1995). ... Signed by Seattle Seahawks (July 8, 1996). ... Released by Seahawks (August 24, 1996). ... Re-signed by Seahawks to practice squad (August 26, 1996).
PLAYING EXPERIENCE: Seattle NFL, 1997. ... Games/Games started: 11/0.

PARKER, VAUGHN   OT   CHARGERS

PERSONAL: Born June 5, 1971, in Buffalo. ... 6-3/296. ... Full name: Vaughn Antoine Parker.
HIGH SCHOOL: Saint Joseph's Collegiate Institute (Buffalo).
COLLEGE: UCLA.
TRANSACTIONS/CAREER NOTES: Selected by San Diego Chargers in second round (63rd pick overall) of 1994 NFL draft. ... Signed by Chargers (July 12, 1994). ... Granted free agency (February 14, 1997). ... Re-signed by Chargers (June 6, 1997).
PLAYING EXPERIENCE: San Diego NFL, 1994-1997. ... Games/Games started: 1994 (6/0), 1995 (14/7), 1996 (16/16), 1997 (16/16). Total: 52/39.
CHAMPIONSHIP GAME EXPERIENCE: Played in AFC championship game (1994 season). ... Played in Super Bowl XXIX (1994 season).
PRO STATISTICS: 1994—Returned one kickoff for one yard. 1996—Recovered one fumble. 1997—Recovered two fumbles.

PARKS, NATHAN   OT   CHIEFS

PERSONAL: Born October 25, 1974, in Chico, Calif. ... 6-5/303. ... Full name: Nathan Jacob Parks.
HIGH SCHOOL: Durham (Calif.).
JUNIOR COLLEGE: Butte Junior College (Calif.).
COLLEGE: Stanford.
TRANSACTIONS/CAREER NOTES: Selected by Kansas City Chiefs in seventh round (214th pick overall) of 1997 NFL draft. ... Signed by Chiefs (May 1, 1997).
PLAYING EXPERIENCE: Kansas City NFL, 1997. ... Games/Games started: 1/0.

PARMALEE, BERNIE   RB   DOLPHINS

PERSONAL: Born September 16, 1967, in Jersey City, N.J. ... 5-11/210. ... Full name: Bernard Parmalee.
HIGH SCHOOL: Lincoln (Jersey City, N.J.).
COLLEGE: Ball State.
TRANSACTIONS/CAREER NOTES: Signed as non-drafted free agent by Miami Dolphins (May 1, 1992). ... Released by Dolphins (August 31, 1992). ... Re-signed by Dolphins to practice squad (September 1, 1992). ... Activated (October 21, 1992). ... Deactivated for remainder of 1992 playoffs (January 16, 1993). ... Granted free agency (February 17, 1995). ... Re-signed by Dolphins (March 31, 1995). ... Granted unconditional free agency (February 14, 1997). ... Re-signed by Dolphins (April 17, 1997). ... Granted unconditional free agency (February 13, 1998). ... Re-signed by Dolphins (March 2, 1998).
PRO STATISTICS: 1994—Recovered three fumbles for 20 yards.
SINGLE GAME HIGHS (regular season): Attempts—30 (October 16, 1994, vs. Los Angeles Raiders); yards—150 (October 16, 1994, vs. Los Angeles Raiders); and rushing touchdowns—3 (December 25, 1994, vs. Detroit).
STATISTICAL PLATEAUS: 100-yard rushing games: 1994 (3), 1995 (3). Total: 6.

P

			RUSHING				RECEIVING				KICKOFF RETURNS				TOTALS			
Year Team	G	GS	Att.	Yds.	Avg.	TD	No.	Yds.	Avg.	TD	No.	Yds.	Avg.	TD	TD	2pt.	Pts.	Fum.
1992—Miami NFL	10	0	6	38	6.3	0	0	0	...	0	14	289	20.6	0	0	...	0	3
1993—Miami NFL	16	0	4	16	4.0	0	1	1	1.0	0	0	0	...	0	0	...	0	0
1994—Miami NFL	15	10	216	868	4.0	6	34	249	7.3	1	2	0	0.0	0	7	1	44	5
1995—Miami NFL	16	12	236	878	3.7	9	39	345	8.8	5	0	0	...	0	10	0	60	5
1996—Miami NFL	16	0	25	80	3.2	0	21	189	9.0	0	0	0	...	0	0	0	0	1
1997—Miami NFL	16	4	18	59	3.3	0	28	301	10.8	1	0	0	...	0	1	0	6	1
Pro totals (6 years)	89	26	505	1939	3.8	15	123	1085	8.8	3	16	289	18.1	0	18	1	110	15

PARRELLA, JOHN — DT — CHARGERS

PERSONAL: Born November 22, 1969, in Topeka, Kan. ... 6-3/290. ... Full name: John Lorin Parrella.
HIGH SCHOOL: Central Catholic (Grand Island, Neb.).
COLLEGE: Nebraska.
TRANSACTIONS/CAREER NOTES: Selected by Buffalo Bills in second round (55th pick overall) of 1993 NFL draft. ... Signed by Bills (July 12, 1993). ... Released by Bills (August 28, 1994). ... Signed by San Diego Chargers (September 12, 1994). ... Granted free agency (February 16, 1996). ... Re-signed by Chargers (June 14, 1996).
CHAMPIONSHIP GAME EXPERIENCE: Member of Bills for AFC championship game (1993 season); inactive. ... Member of Bills for Super Bowl XXVIII (1993 season); inactive. ... Played in AFC championship game (1994 season). ... Played in Super Bowl XXIX (1994 season).
PRO STATISTICS: 1997—Recovered one fumble.

Year Team	G	GS	SACKS
1993—Buffalo NFL..	10	0	1.0
1994—San Diego NFL...	13	1	1.0
1995—San Diego NFL...	16	1	2.0
1996—San Diego NFL...	16	9	2.0
1997—San Diego NFL...	16	16	3.5
Pro totals (5 years)...	71	27	9.5

PARTEN, TY — DE — CHIEFS

PERSONAL: Born October 13, 1969, in Washington, D.C. ... 6-5/295. ... Full name: Ty Daniel Parten.
HIGH SCHOOL: Horizon (Scottsdale, Ariz.).
COLLEGE: Arizona.
TRANSACTIONS/CAREER NOTES: Selected by Cincinnati Bengals in third round (63rd pick overall) of 1993 draft. ... Signed by Bengals (July 19, 1993). ... On injured reserve with left thumb injury (November 29, 1993-remainder of season). ... Released by Bengals (September 20, 1995). ... Selected by Scottish Claymores in 1996 World League draft (February 22, 1996). ... Signed by St. Louis Rams (April 2, 1997). ... Released by Rams (August 24, 1997). ... Signed by Kansas City Chiefs (December 10, 1997).
PLAYING EXPERIENCE: Cincinnati NFL, 1993-1995; Kansas City NFL, 1997. ... Games/Games started: 1993 (11/1), 1994 (14/4), 1995 (1/1), 1997 (2/0). Total: 28/6.

PATTEN, DAVID — WR — GIANTS

PERSONAL: Born August 19, 1974, in Hopkins, S.C. ... 5-9/180.
HIGH SCHOOL: Lower Richland (Columbia, S.C.).
COLLEGE: Western Carolina.
TRANSACTIONS/CAREER NOTES: Played in Arena League with Albany Firebirds (1996). ... Signed by New York Giants (March 24, 1997). ... Released by Giants (August 24, 1997). ... Re-signed by Giants to practice squad (August 27, 1997). ... Activated (August 29, 1997).
PRO STATISTICS: 1997—Rushed once for two yards, returned eight kickoffs for 123 yards and recovered one fumble.
SINGLE GAME HIGHS (regular season): Receptions—3 (December 7, 1997, vs Philadelphia); yards—66 (October 12, 1997, vs. Arizona); and touchdown receptions—1 (December 7, 1997, vs. Philadelphia).

			RECEIVING				TOTALS			
Year Team	G	GS	No.	Yds.	Avg.	TD	TD	2pt.	Pts.	Fum.
1997—New York Giants NFL	16	3	13	226	17.4	2	2	0	12	2

PATTON, JOE — G — REDSKINS

PERSONAL: Born January 5, 1972, in Birmingham, Ala. ... 6-5/306. ... Full name: Joseph Patton.
HIGH SCHOOL: Jones Valley (Birmingham, Ala.).
COLLEGE: Alabama A&M.
TRANSACTIONS/CAREER NOTES: Selected by Washington Redskins in third round (97th pick overall) of 1994 NFL draft. ... Signed by Redskins (July 19, 1994). ... Granted free agency (February 14, 1997). ... Re-signed by Redskins (June 2, 1997). ... Granted unconditional free agency (February 13, 1998). ... Re-signed by Redskins (February 19, 1998).
PLAYING EXPERIENCE: Washington NFL, 1994-1997. ... Games/Games started: 1994 (2/0), 1995 (16/13), 1996 (16/15), 1997 (16/16). Total: 50/44.
PRO STATISTICS: 1995—Recovered one fumble. 1996—Recovered one fumble. 1997—Recovered one fumble.

PATTON, MARVCUS — LB — REDSKINS

PERSONAL: Born May 1, 1967, in Los Angeles. ... 6-2/236. ... Full name: Marvcus Raymond Patton.
HIGH SCHOOL: Leuzinger (Lawndale, Calif.).
COLLEGE: UCLA (degree in political science, 1990).

TRANSACTIONS/CAREER NOTES: Selected by Buffalo Bills in eighth round (208th pick overall) of 1990 NFL draft. ... Signed by Bills (July 27, 1990). ... On injured reserve with broken leg (January 26, 1991-remainder of 1990 playoffs). ... Granted free agency (February 1, 1992). ... Re-signed by Bills (July 23, 1992). ... Granted unconditional free agency (February 17, 1995). ... Signed by Washington Redskins (February 22, 1995).

CHAMPIONSHIP GAME EXPERIENCE: Played in AFC championship game (1991-1993 seasons). ... Played in Super Bowl XXVI (1991 season), Super Bowl XXVII (1992 season) and Super Bowl XXVIII (1993 season).

PRO STATISTICS: 1993—Recovered three fumbles for five yards. 1994—Recovered one fumble and fumbled once. 1995—Recovered one fumble. 1997—Returned one kickoff for 10 yards and recovered one fumble.

			INTERCEPTIONS				SACKS
Year Team	G	GS	No.	Yds.	Avg.	TD	No.
1990—Buffalo NFL	16	0	0	0	...	0	0.5
1991—Buffalo NFL	16	2	0	0	...	0	0.0
1992—Buffalo NFL	16	4	0	0	...	0	2.0
1993—Buffalo NFL	16	16	2	0	0.0	0	1.0
1994—Buffalo NFL	16	16	2	8	4.0	0	0.0
1995—Washington NFL	16	16	2	7	3.5	0	2.0
1996—Washington NFL	16	16	2	26	13.0	0	2.0
1997—Washington NFL	16	16	2	5	2.5	0	4.5
Pro totals (8 years)	128	86	10	46	4.6	0	12.0

PAUL, TITO   DB   BRONCOS

PERSONAL: Born May 24, 1972, in Kissimmee, Fla. ... 6-0/200. ... Cousin of Markus Paul, safety with Chicago Bears (1989-1992) and Tampa Bay Buccaneers (1993).
HIGH SCHOOL: Osceola (Fla.).
COLLEGE: Ohio State.
TRANSACTIONS/CAREER NOTES: Selected by Arizona Cardinals in fifth round (167th pick overall) of 1995 NFL draft. ... Signed by Cardinals (July 20, 1995). ... Released by Cardinals (September 1, 1997). ... Signed by Cincinnati Bengals (September 9, 1997). ... Released by Bengals (April 20, 1998). ... Signed by Denver Broncos (May 7, 1998).
PLAYING EXPERIENCE: Arizona NFL, 1995 and 1996; Arizona (1)-Cincinnati (14) NFL, 1997. ... Games/Games started: 1995 (14/4), 1996 (16/3), 1997 (Ari.-1/0; Cin.-14/5; Total: 15/5). Total: 45/12.
PRO STATISTICS: 1994—Intercepted one pass for four yards. 1996—Recovered one fumble. 1997—Recovered one fumble.

PAUP, BRYCE   LB   JAGUARS

PERSONAL: Born February 29, 1968, in Scranton, Iowa. ... 6-5/247. ... Full name: Bryce Eric Paup.
HIGH SCHOOL: Scranton (Iowa).
COLLEGE: Northern Iowa (degree in business).
TRANSACTIONS/CAREER NOTES: Selected by Green Bay Packers in sixth round (159th pick overall) of 1990 NFL draft. ... Signed by Packers (July 22, 1990). ... On injured reserve with hand injury (September 4-November 17, 1990). ... On injured reserve with calf injury (December 12, 1991-remainder of season). ... Granted free agency (February 1, 1992). ... Re-signed by Packers (August 13, 1992). ... Granted unconditional free agency (February 17, 1995). ... Signed by Buffalo Bills (March 9, 1995). ... Granted unconditional free agency (February 13, 1998). ... Signed by Jacksonville Jaguars (February 16, 1998).
HONORS: Played in Pro Bowl (1994-1997 seasons). ... Named linebacker on THE SPORTING NEWS NFL All-Pro team (1995).
PRO STATISTICS: 1991—Credited with a safety. 1992—Recovered two fumbles. 1994—Recovered two fumbles. 1995—Recovered one fumble. 1997—Recovered one fumble.

			INTERCEPTIONS				SACKS
Year Team	G	GS	No.	Yds.	Avg.	TD	No.
1990—Green Bay NFL	5	0	0	0	...	0	0.0
1991—Green Bay NFL	12	1	0	0	...	0	7.5
1992—Green Bay NFL	16	10	0	0	...	0	6.5
1993—Green Bay NFL	15	14	1	8	8.0	0	11.0
1994—Green Bay NFL	16	16	3	47	15.7	1	7.5
1995—Buffalo NFL	15	15	2	0	0.0	0	*17.5
1996—Buffalo NFL	12	11	0	0	...	0	6.0
1997—Buffalo NFL	16	16	0	0	...	0	9.5
Pro totals (8 years)	107	83	6	55	9.2	1	65.5

PAYNE, ROD   C   BENGALS

PERSONAL: Born June 14, 1974, in Miami. ... 6-4/295. ... Full name: Reginald Gerald Payne.
HIGH SCHOOL: Killian (Miami).
COLLEGE: Michigan.
TRANSACTIONS/CAREER NOTES: Selected by Cincinnati Bengals in third round (76th pick overall) of 1997 NFL draft. ... Signed by Bengals (July 17, 1997). ... Inactive for 16 games (1997).

PAYNE, SETH   DT   JAGUARS

PERSONAL: Born February 12, 1975, in Victor, N.Y. ... 6-4/292. ... Full name: Seth C. Payne.
HIGH SCHOOL: Victor (N.Y.) Central.
COLLEGE: Cornell.
TRANSACTIONS/CAREER NOTES: Selected by Jacksonville Jaguars in fourth round (114th pick overall) of 1997 NFL draft. ... Signed by Jaguars (May 23, 1997).
PLAYING EXPERIENCE: Jacksonville NFL, 1997. ... Games/Games started: 12/5.

P

PERSONAL: Born January 31, 1968, in Bellingham, Wash. ... 6-3/216. ... Full name: Doug I. Pederson.
HIGH SCHOOL: Ferndale (Wash.).
COLLEGE: Northeast Louisiana (degree in business management).
TRANSACTIONS/CAREER NOTES: Signed as non-drafted free agent by Miami Dolphins (April 30, 1991). ... Released by Dolphins (August 16, 1991). ... Selected by New York/New Jersey Knights in fifth round (49th pick overall) of 1992 World League draft. ... Re-signed by Dolphins (June 1, 1992). ... Released by Dolphins (August 31, 1992). ... Re-signed by Dolphins to practice squad (September 1, 1992). ... Released by Dolphins (October 7, 1992). ... Re-signed by Dolphins (March 3, 1993). ... Released by Dolphins (August 30, 1993). ... Re-signed by Dolphins to practice squad (August 31, 1993). ... Activated (October 22, 1993). ... Released by Dolphins (December 15, 1993). ... Re-signed by Dolphins (April 15, 1994). ... Inactive for 16 games (1994). ... Selected by Carolina Panthers from Dolphins in NFL expansion draft (February 15, 1995). ... Released by Panthers (May 22, 1995). ... Re-signed by Dolphins (July 11, 1995). ... Released by Dolphins (August 21, 1995). ... Re-signed by Dolphins (October 10, 1995). ... Released by Dolphins (October 25, 1995). ... Inactive for two games with Dolphins (1995). ... Signed by Green Bay Packers (November 22, 1995). ... Inactive for five games with Packers (1995). ... Granted unconditional free agency (February 14, 1997). ... Re-signed by Packers (February 20, 1997).
CHAMPIONSHIP GAME EXPERIENCE: Member of Packers for NFC championship game (1995-97 seasons); inactive. ... Member of Super Bowl championship team (1996 season); inactive. ... Member of Packers for Super Bowl XXXII (1997 season); inactive.
PRO STATISTICS: 1993—Recovered one fumble for minus one yard.
SINGLE GAME HIGHS (regular season): Attempts—6 (November 14, 1993, vs. Philadelphia); completions—3 (November 14, 1993, vs. Philadelphia); yards—34 (November 14, 1993, vs. Philadelphia); and touchdown passes—0.

			PASSING							RUSHING				TOTALS		
Year Team	G	GS	Att.	Cmp.	Pct.	Yds.	TD	Int.	Avg.	Rat.	Att.	Yds.	Avg.	TD	TD	2pt.	Pts.
1992—N.Y./N.J. W.L.	7	1	128	70	54.7	1077	8	3	8.41	93.8	15	46	3.1	0	0	...	0
1993—Miami NFL	7	0	8	4	50.0	41	0	0	5.13	65.1	2	-1	-0.5	0	0	...	0
1994—Miami NFL						Did not play.											
1995—Miami NFL						Did not play.											
—Green Bay NFL						Did not play.											
1996—Green Bay NFL	1	0	0	0	...	0	0	0	...	...	0	0	...	0	0	0	0
1997—Green Bay NFL	1	0	0	0	...	0	0	0	...	...	3	-4	-1.3	0	0	0	0
W.L. totals (1 year)	7	1	128	70	54.7	1077	8	3	8.41	93.8	15	46	3.1	0	0	0	0
NFL totals (3 years)	9	0	8	4	50.0	41	0	0	5.13	65.1	5	-5	-1.0	0	0	0	0
Pro totals (4 years)	16	1	136	74	54.4	1118	8	3	8.22	92.1	20	41	2.1	0	0	0	0

PERSONAL: Born March 16, 1966, in Mesa, Ariz. ... 6-0/225. ... Son of Willie Peete, running backs coach, Chicago Bears; and cousin of Calvin Peete, professional golfer.
HIGH SCHOOL: Sahuaro (Tucson, Ariz.), then Shawnee Mission South (Overland Park, Kan.).
COLLEGE: Southern California (degree in communications, 1989).
TRANSACTIONS/CAREER NOTES: Selected by Detroit Lions in sixth round (141st pick overall) of 1989 NFL draft. ... Signed by Lions (July 13, 1989). ... On injured reserve with Achilles' tendon injury (October 30, 1991-remainder of season). ... Granted free agency (February 1, 1992). ... Re-signed by Lions (July 30, 1992). ... Granted unconditional free agency (February 17, 1994). ... Signed by Dallas Cowboys (May 4, 1994). ... Granted unconditional free agency (February 17, 1995). ... Signed by Philadelphia Eagles (April 22, 1995). ... Granted unconditional free agency (February 14, 1996). ... Re-signed by Eagles (March 14, 1996). ... On injured reserve with knee injury (October 3, 1996-remainder of season). ... Granted unconditional free agency (February 14, 1997). ... Re-signed by Eagles (April 1, 1997).
CHAMPIONSHIP GAME EXPERIENCE: Member of Cowboys for NFC championship game (1994 season); did not play.
HONORS: Named quarterback on The Sporting News college All-America second team (1988).
PRO STATISTICS: 1989—Fumbled nine times and recovered three fumbles. 1990—Fumbled nine times and recovered one fumble. 1991—Fumbled twice and recovered one fumble for minus one yard. 1992—Fumbled six times and recovered two fumbles for minus seven yards. 1993—Fumbled 11 times and recovered four fumbles for minus eight yards. 1994—Fumbled three times and recovered two fumbles for minus one yard. 1995—Fumbled 13 times and recovered five fumbles. 1996—Fumbled twice and recovered one fumble. 1997—Fumbled five times and recovered two fumbles for minus two yards.
SINGLE GAME HIGHS (regular season): Attempts—45 (October 8, 1995, vs. Washington); completions—30 (October 8, 1995, vs. Washington); yards—323 (September 27, 1992, vs. Tampa Bay); and touchdown passes—4 (December 16, 1990, vs. Chicago).
STATISTICAL PLATEAUS: 300-yard passing games: 1990 (1), 1992 (1). Total: 2.
MISCELLANEOUS: Selected by Toronto Blue Jays organization in 30th round of free-agent baseball draft (June 4, 1984); did not sign. ... Selected by Oakland Athletics organization in 14th round of free-agent baseball draft (June 1, 1988); did not sign. ... Selected by Athletics organization in 13th round of free-agent baseball draft (June 5, 1989); did not sign. ... Regular-season record as starting NFL quarterback: 36-32 (.529). ... Postseason record as starting NFL quarterback: 1-1 (.500).

			PASSING							RUSHING				TOTALS		
Year Team	G	GS	Att.	Cmp.	Pct.	Yds.	TD	Int.	Avg.	Rat.	Att.	Yds.	Avg.	TD	TD	2pt.	Pts.
1989—Detroit NFL	8	8	195	103	52.8	1479	5	9	7.58	67.0	33	148	4.5	4	4	...	24
1990—Detroit NFL	11	11	271	142	52.4	1974	13	8	7.28	79.8	47	363	7.7	6	6	...	36
1991—Detroit NFL	8	8	194	116	59.8	1339	5	9	6.90	69.9	25	125	5.0	2	2	...	12
1992—Detroit NFL	10	10	213	123	57.7	1702	9	9	7.99	80.0	21	83	4.0	0	0	...	0
1993—Detroit NFL	10	10	252	157	62.3	1670	6	14	6.63	66.4	45	165	3.7	1	1	...	6
1994—Dallas NFL	7	1	56	33	58.9	470	4	1	8.39	102.5	9	-2	-0.2	0	0	0	0
1995—Philadelphia NFL	15	12	375	215	57.3	2326	8	14	6.20	67.3	32	147	4.6	1	1	0	6
1996—Philadelphia NFL	5	5	134	80	59.7	992	3	5	7.40	74.6	20	31	1.6	1	1	0	6
1997—Philadelphia NFL	5	3	118	68	57.6	869	4	4	7.36	78.0	8	37	4.6	0	0	0	0
Pro totals (9 years)	79	68	1808	1037	57.4	12821	57	73	7.09	73.1	240	1097	4.6	15	15	0	90

PERSONAL: Born January 7, 1969, in Dallas. ... 5-10/195. ... Full name: Erric Demont Pegram. ... Name pronounced PEE-grum.
HIGH SCHOOL: Hillcrest (Dallas).

COLLEGE: North Texas.

TRANSACTIONS/CAREER NOTES: Selected by Atlanta Falcons in sixth round (145th pick overall) of 1991 NFL draft. ... Signed by Falcons (July 20, 1991). ... Granted free agency (February 17, 1994). ... Re-signed by Falcons (June 3, 1994). ... Granted unconditional free agency (February 17, 1995). ... Signed by Pittsburgh Steelers (April 27, 1995). ... On injured reserve with calf injury (December 20, 1996-remainder of season). ... Traded by Steelers to San Diego Chargers for seventh-round pick in 1999 draft (July 2, 1997). ... Released by Chargers (September 23, 1997). ... Signed by New York Giants (September 30, 1997). ... Granted unconditional free agency (February 13, 1998).

CHAMPIONSHIP GAME EXPERIENCE: Played in AFC championship game (1995 season). ... Played in Super Bowl XXX (1995 season).

PRO STATISTICS: 1992—Recovered three fumbles for one yard. 1993—Recovered four fumbles. 1995—Recovered one fumble. 1996—Recovered one fumble. 1997—Recovered one fumble.

SINGLE GAME HIGHS (regular season): Attempts—37 (December 26, 1993, vs. Cincinnati); yards—192 (September 19, 1993, vs. San Francisco); and rushing touchdowns—2 (November 5, 1995, vs. Chicago).

STATISTICAL PLATEAUS: 100-yard rushing games: 1993 (4), 1995 (2). Total: 6.

			RUSHING				RECEIVING				KICKOFF RETURNS				TOTALS			
Year Team	G	GS	Att.	Yds.	Avg.	TD	No.	Yds.	Avg.	TD	No.	Yds.	Avg.	TD	TD	2pt.	Pts.	Fum.
1991—Atlanta NFL	16	7	101	349	3.5	1	1	-1	-1.0	0	16	260	16.3	0	1	...	6	1
1992—Atlanta NFL	16	1	21	89	4.2	0	2	25	12.5	0	9	161	17.9	0	0	...	0	0
1993—Atlanta NFL	16	14	292	1185	4.1	3	33	302	9.2	0	4	63	15.8	0	3	...	18	6
1994—Atlanta NFL	13	5	103	358	3.5	1	16	99	6.2	0	9	145	16.1	0	1	0	6	2
1995—Pittsburgh NFL	15	11	213	813	3.8	5	28	200	7.0	1	4	85	21.3	0	6	1	38	9
1996—Pittsburgh NFL	12	4	97	509	5.2	1	17	112	6.6	0	17	419	24.6	▲1	2	0	12	1
1997—San Diego NFL	4	0	9	23	2.6	1	2	7	3.5	0	0	0	...	0	1	0	6	0
—New York Giants NFL..	11	0	19	72	3.8	1	19	83	4.4	0	22	382	17.4	0	1	0	6	1
Pro totals (7 years)	103	42	855	3398	4.0	13	116	833	7.2	1	81	1515	18.7	1	15	1	92	20

PELFREY, DOUG   K   BENGALS

PERSONAL: Born September 25, 1970, in Fort Thomas, Ky. ... 5-11/185. ... Full name: Thomas Douglas Pelfrey.

HIGH SCHOOL: Scott (Covington, Ky.).

COLLEGE: Kentucky (degree in biology, 1993).

TRANSACTIONS/CAREER NOTES: Selected by Cincinnati Bengals in eighth round (202nd pick overall) of 1993 NFL draft. ... Signed by Bengals (July 19, 1993). ... Granted free agency (February 16, 1996). ... Re-signed by Bengals (June 8, 1996).

PRO STATISTICS: 1995—Punted twice for 52 yards. 1996—Punted once for four yards.

			KICKING							
Year Team	G	GS	XPM	XPA	FGM	FGA	Lg.	50+	Pts.
1993—Cincinnati NFL	15	0	13	16	24	31	53	2-3	85
1994—Cincinnati NFL	16	0	24	25	28	33	54	2-4	108
1995—Cincinnati NFL	16	0	34	34	29	36	51	1-2	121
1996—Cincinnati NFL	16	0	41	41	23	28	49	0-0	110
1997—Cincinnati NFL	16	0	41	43	12	16	46	0-2	77
Pro totals (5 years)	79	0	153	159	116	144	54	5-11	501

PENN, CHRIS   WR   BEARS

PERSONAL: Born April 20, 1971, in Lenapah, Okla. ... 6-0/200. ... Full name: Christopher Anthony Penn.

HIGH SCHOOL: Oklahoma Union (Lenapah Okla.).

COLLEGE: Northeastern Oklahoma A&M, then Tulsa.

TRANSACTIONS/CAREER NOTES: Selected by Kansas City Chiefs in third round (96th pick overall) of 1994 NFL draft. ... Signed by Chiefs (June 2, 1994). ... Granted free agency (February 14, 1997). ... Re-signed by Chiefs (July 18, 1997). ... Traded by Chiefs to Chicago Bears for fifth-round pick (DB Robert Williams) in 1998 draft (August 24, 1997).

PRO STATISTICS: 1997—Rushed once for minus one yard.

SINGLE GAME HIGHS (regular season): Receptions—7 (November 16, 1997, vs. New York Jets); yards—90 (November 24, 1996, vs. San Diego); and touchdown receptions—2 (September 15, 1996, vs. Seattle).

			RECEIVING				PUNT RETURNS				KICKOFF RETURNS				TOTALS			
Year Team	G	GS	No.	Yds.	Avg.	TD	No.	Yds.	Avg.	TD	No.	Yds.	Avg.	TD	TD	2pt.	Pts.	Fum.
1994—Kansas City NFL	8	0	3	24	8.0	0	0	0	...	0	9	194	21.6	0	0	0	0	0
1995—Kansas City NFL	2	0	1	12	12.0	0	4	12	3.0	0	2	26	13.0	0	0	0	0	0
1996—Kansas City NFL	16	16	49	628	12.8	5	14	148	10.6	0	0	0	...	0	5	0	30	3
1997—Chicago NFL	14	4	47	576	12.3	3	0	0	...	0	0	0	...	0	3	0	18	1
Pro totals (4 years)	40	20	100	1240	12.4	8	18	160	8.9	0	11	220	20.0	0	8	0	48	4

PEOPLES, SHONT'E   LB   BEARS

PERSONAL: Born August 30, 1972, in Saginaw, Mich. ... 6-2/249.

HIGH SCHOOL: Arthur Hill (Saginaw, Mich.).

COLLEGE: Michigan.

TRANSACTIONS/CAREER NOTES: Signed by Las Vegas Posse of CFL (June 1994). ... Selected by Birmingham Barracudas in first round (second pick overall) of 1995 Las Vegas dispersal draft. ... Selected by Saskatchewan Roughriders in third round (21st pick overall) of 1996 U.S. team dispersal draft. ... Signed by Winnipeg Blue Bombers of CFL (May 9, 1997). ... Signed by Chicago Bears (February 18, 1998).

Year Team	G	GS	SACKS
1994—Las Vegas CFL	16	...	14.0
1995—Birmingham CFL	18	...	15.0
1996—	Did not play.		
1997—Winnipeg CFL	15	...	13.0
Pro totals (3 years)	49	...	42.0

PERRIMAN, BRETT　　　　　　　WR

PERSONAL: Born October 10, 1965, in Miami. ... 5-9/180.
HIGH SCHOOL: Northwestern (Miami).
COLLEGE: Miami (Fla.).
TRANSACTIONS/CAREER NOTES: Selected by New Orleans Saints in second round (52nd pick overall) of 1988 NFL draft. ... Signed by Saints (May 19, 1988). ... Granted free agency (February 1, 1991). ... Traded by Saints to Detroit Lions for fifth-round pick (WR Torrance Small) in 1992 draft (August 21, 1991). ... Activated (September 2, 1991). ... Granted free agency (February 1, 1992). ... Re-signed by Lions (1992). ... Granted unconditional free agency (February 17, 1994). ... Re-signed by Lions (March 11, 1994). ... Granted free agency (February 14, 1997). ... Signed by Kansas City Chiefs (June 9, 1997). ... Released by Chiefs (October 7, 1997). ... Signed by Miami Dolphins (October 8, 1997). ... Granted unconditional free agency (February 13, 1998). ... Re-signed by Dolphins (February 23, 1998). ... Released by Dolphins (April 22, 1998).
CHAMPIONSHIP GAME EXPERIENCE: Played in NFC championship game (1991 season).
PRO STATISTICS: 1989—Returned one punt for 10 yards. 1990—Recovered one fumble. 1992—Returned four kickoffs for 59 yards. 1994—Attempted one pass without a completion. 1995—Returned five punts for 50 yards, returned five kickoffs for 65 yards and recovered one fumble.
SINGLE GAME HIGHS (regular season): Receptions—12 (November 23, 1995, vs. Minnesota); yards—153 (November 23, 1995, vs. Minnesota); and touchdown receptions—2 (September 22, 1996, vs. Chicago).
STATISTICAL PLATEAUS: 100-yard receiving games: 1991 (1), 1992 (2), 1994 (1), 1995 (8), 1996 (1). Total: 13.

			RUSHING				RECEIVING				TOTALS			
Year　Team	G	GS	Att.	Yds.	Avg.	TD	No.	Yds.	Avg.	TD	TD	2pt.	Pts.	Fum.
1988—New Orleans NFL	16	0	3	17	5.7	0	16	215	13.4	2	2	...	12	1
1989—New Orleans NFL	14	1	1	-10	-10.0	0	20	356	17.8	0	0	...	0	0
1990—New Orleans NFL	16	15	0	0	...	0	36	382	10.6	2	2	...	12	2
1991—Detroit NFL	15	14	4	10	2.5	0	52	668	12.8	1	1	...	6	0
1992—Detroit NFL	16	16	0	0	...	0	69	810	11.7	4	4	...	24	1
1993—Detroit NFL	15	15	4	16	4.0	0	49	496	10.1	2	2	...	12	1
1994—Detroit NFL	16	14	9	86	9.6	0	56	761	13.6	4	4	2	28	1
1995—Detroit NFL	16	16	5	48	9.6	0	108	1488	13.8	9	9	1	56	1
1996—Detroit NFL	16	16	1	13	13.0	0	94	1021	10.9	5	5	0	30	0
1997—Kansas City NFL	5	4	0	0	...	0	6	83	13.8	0	0	0	0	0
—Miami NFL	8	5	0	0	...	0	19	309	16.3	1	1	0	6	0
Pro totals (10 years)	153	116	27	180	6.7	0	525	6589	12.6	30	30	3	186	7

PERRY, DARREN　　　　　　　S　　　　　　　STEELERS

PERSONAL: Born December 29, 1968, in Chesapeake, Va. ... 5-11/196.
HIGH SCHOOL: Deep Creek (Chesapeake, Va.).
COLLEGE: Penn State.
TRANSACTIONS/CAREER NOTES: Selected by Pittsburgh Steelers in eighth round (203rd pick overall) of 1992 NFL draft. ... Signed by Steelers (July 16, 1992). ... Granted free agency (February 17, 1995). ... Re-signed by Steelers (June 15, 1995).
CHAMPIONSHIP GAME EXPERIENCE: Played in AFC championship game (1994, 1995 and 1997 seasons). ... Played in Super Bowl XXX (1995 season).
HONORS: Named defensive back on THE SPORTING NEWS college All-America second team (1991).
PRO STATISTICS: 1992—Recovered one fumble. 1994—Recovered two fumbles. 1995—Fumbled once and recovered two fumbles. 1996—Returned one kickoff for eight yards, fumbled once and recovered two fumbles. 1997—Credited with one sack.

			INTERCEPTIONS			
Year　Team	G	GS	No.	Yds.	Avg.	TD
1992—Pittsburgh NFL	16	16	6	69	11.5	0
1993—Pittsburgh NFL	16	16	4	61	15.3	0
1994—Pittsburgh NFL	16	16	7	112	16.0	0
1995—Pittsburgh NFL	16	16	4	71	17.8	0
1996—Pittsburgh NFL	16	16	5	115	23.0	1
1997—Pittsburgh NFL	16	16	4	77	19.3	0
Pro totals (6 years)	96	96	30	505	16.8	1

PERRY, ED　　　　　　　TE　　　　　　　DOLPHINS

PERSONAL: Born September 1, 1974, in Richmond. ... 6-4/250. ... Full name: Edwin Lewis Perry.
HIGH SCHOOL: Highlands Springs (Richmond).
COLLEGE: James Madison.
TRANSACTIONS/CAREER NOTES: Selected by Miami Dolphins in sixth round (177th pick overall) of 1997 NFL draft. ... Signed by Dolphins (June 13, 1997).
PRO STATISTICS: 1997—Returned one kickoff for seven yards and recovered one fumble.
SINGLE GAME HIGHS (regular season): Receptions—3 (November 23, 1997, vs. New England); yards—19 (November 9, 1997, vs. New York Jets); and touchdown receptions—1 (November 17, 1997, vs. Buffalo).

			RECEIVING				TOTALS			
Year　Team	G	GS	No.	Yds.	Avg.	TD	TD	2pt.	Pts.	Fum.
1997—Miami NFL	16	4	11	45	4.1	1	1	0	6	0

PERRY, MARLO　　　　　　　LB

PERSONAL: Born August 25, 1972, in Forest, Miss. ... 6-4/250. ... Full name: Malcolm Marlo Perry.
HIGH SCHOOL: Scott Central (Forest, Miss.).
COLLEGE: Jackson State.

P

TRANSACTIONS/CAREER NOTES: Selected by Buffalo Bills in third round (81st pick overall) of 1994 NFL draft. ... Signed by Bills (July 18, 1994). ... Granted free agency (February 14, 1997). ... Re-signed by Bills (June 12, 1997). ... Granted unconditional free agency (February 13, 1998).
PLAYING EXPERIENCE: Buffalo NFL, 1994-1997. ... Games/Games started: 1994 (2/0), 1995 (16/11), 1996 (13/0), 1997 (13/0). Total: 44/11.
PRO STATISTICS: 1996—Intercepted one pass for six yards. 1997—Intercepted one pass for four yards and recovered one fumble.

PERRY, MICHAEL DEAN   DT

PERSONAL: Born August 27, 1965, in Aiken, S.C. ... 6-1/285. ... Full name: Michael Dean Perry. ... Brother of William Perry, defensive tackle with Chicago Bears (1985-1993), Philadelphia Eagles (1993 and 1994) and London Monarchs of World League (1996).
HIGH SCHOOL: South Aiken (S.C.).
COLLEGE: Clemson.
TRANSACTIONS/CAREER NOTES: Selected by Cleveland Browns in second round (50th pick overall) of 1988 NFL draft. ... Signed by Browns (July 23, 1988). ... Granted free agency (February 1, 1991). ... Re-signed by Browns (August 27, 1991). ... Released by Browns (February 16, 1995). ... Signed by Denver Broncos (February 28, 1995). ... Claimed on waivers by Kansas City Chiefs (December 18, 1997). ... Granted unconditional free agency (February 13, 1998).
CHAMPIONSHIP GAME EXPERIENCE: Played in AFC championship game (1989 season).
HONORS: Named defensive lineman on THE SPORTING NEWS college All-America second team (1987). ... Played in Pro Bowl (1989-1991, 1993, 1994 and 1996 seasons). ... Named defensive tackle on THE SPORTING NEWS NFL All-Pro team (1989-1993).
PRO STATISTICS: 1988—Returned one kickoff for 13 yards and recovered two fumbles for 10 yards and one touchdown. 1989—Recovered two fumbles. 1990—Recovered one fumble. 1993—Recovered two fumbles for four yards. 1996—Recovered two fumbles.

Year—Team	G	GS	SACKS
1988—Cleveland NFL	16	2	6.0
1989—Cleveland NFL	16	16	7.0
1990—Cleveland NFL	16	16	11.5
1991—Cleveland NFL	16	15	8.5
1992—Cleveland NFL	14	14	8.5
1993—Cleveland NFL	16	13	6.0
1994—Cleveland NFL	15	14	4.0
1995—Denver NFL	14	14	6.0
1996—Denver NFL	15	15	3.5
1997—Denver NFL	8	8	0.0
—Kansas City NFL	1	0	0.0
Pro totals (10 years)	147	127	61.0

PERRY, TODD   G   BEARS

PERSONAL: Born November 28, 1970, in Elizabethtown, Ky. ... 6-5/308. ... Full name: Todd Joseph Perry.
HIGH SCHOOL: Elizabethtown (Ky.).
COLLEGE: Kentucky.
TRANSACTIONS/CAREER NOTES: Selected by Chicago Bears in fourth round (97th pick overall) of 1993 NFL draft. ... Signed by Bears (June 16, 1993). ... On injured reserve with back injury (December 19, 1997-remainder of season).
PLAYING EXPERIENCE: Chicago NFL, 1993-1997. ... Games/Games started: 1993 (13/3), 1994 (15/4), 1995 (15/15), 1996 (16/16), 1997 (11/11). Total: 70/49.
PRO STATISTICS: 1996—Recovered one fumble.

PETER, CHRISTIAN   DT   GIANTS

PERSONAL: Born October 5, 1972, in Locust, N.J. ... 6-3/300. ... Brother of Jason Peter, defensive tackle, Carolina Panthers.
HIGH SCHOOL: Middletown South (Middleton, N.J.), then Milford (Conn.) Academy.
COLLEGE: Nebraska.
TRANSACTIONS/CAREER NOTES: Selected by New England Patriots in fifth round (149th pick overall) of 1996 NFL draft. ... Patriots released rights (April 24, 1996). ... Signed by New York Giants (January 22, 1997).

Year—Team	G	GS	SACKS
1997—New York Giants NFL	7	0	0.5

PETERS, TYRELL   LB   RAVENS

PERSONAL: Born August 4, 1974 ... 6-0/230.
HIGH SCHOOL: Norman (Okla.).
COLLEGE: Oklahoma.
TRANSACTIONS/CAREER NOTES: Signed as non-drafted free agent by Seattle Seahawks (April 25, 1997). ... Released by Seahawks (August 18, 1997). ... Signed by Baltimore Ravens (August 25, 1997). ... Released by Ravens (October 14, 1997). ... Re-signed by Ravens to practice squad (October 16, 1997). ... Activated (December 19, 1997).
PLAYING EXPERIENCE: Baltimore NFL, 1997. ... Games/Games started: 4/0.

PETERSON, TODD   K   SEAHAWKS

PERSONAL: Born February 4, 1970, in Valdosta, Ga. ... 5-10/171. ... Full name: Joseph Todd Peterson.
HIGH SCHOOL: Valdosta (Ga.).
COLLEGE: Navy, then Georgia (degree in finance).
TRANSACTIONS/CAREER NOTES: Selected by New York Giants in seventh round (177th pick overall) of 1993 NFL draft. ... Signed by Giants (July 19, 1993). ... Released by Giants (August 24, 1993). ... Signed by New England Patriots to practice squad (November 30, 1993). ... Released by Patriots (December 6, 1993). ... Signed by Atlanta Falcons (May 3, 1994). ... Released by Falcons (August 29, 1994). ... Signed by Arizona Cardinals (October 12, 1994). ... Released by Cardinals (October 24, 1994). ... Signed by Seattle Seahawks (January 17, 1995). ... Granted free agency (February 13, 1998).

P

Year	Team	G	GS	XPM	XPA	FGM	FGA	Lg.	50+	Pts.
						KICKING				
1993—						Did not play.				
1994—Arizona NFL		2	0	4	4	2	4	35	0-0	10
1995—Seattle NFL		16	0	§40	40	23	28	49	0-2	109
1996—Seattle NFL		16	0	27	27	28	34	54	2-3	111
1997—Seattle NFL		16	0	37	37	22	28	52	1-2	103
Pro totals (4 years)		50	0	108	108	75	94	54	3-7	333

PETERSON, TONY   LB   49ERS

PERSONAL: Born January 23, 1972, in Cleveland. ... 6-1/232. ... Full name: Anthony Wayne Peterson.
HIGH SCHOOL: Ringgold (Monongahela, Pa.).
COLLEGE: Notre Dame.
TRANSACTIONS/CAREER NOTES: Selected by San Francisco 49ers in fifth round (153rd pick overall) of 1994 NFL draft. ... Signed by 49ers (July 20, 1994). ... On injured reserve with hamstring injury (January 18, 1995-remainder of 1994 playoffs). ... Granted unconditional free agency (February 14, 1997). ... Signed by Chicago Bears (March 7, 1997). ... Traded by Bears to 49ers for seventh-round pick (OT Chad Overhauser) in 1998 draft (April 15, 1998).
PLAYING EXPERIENCE: San Francisco NFL, 1994-1996; Chicago NFL, 1997. ... Games/Games started: 1994 (15/0), 1995 (15/0), 1996 (13/0), 1997 (16/0). Total: 59/0.
CHAMPIONSHIP GAME EXPERIENCE: Member of 49ers for NFC championship game (1994 season); inactive.
PRO STATISTICS: 1997—Recovered one fumble.

PHIFER, ROMAN   LB   RAMS

PERSONAL: Born March 5, 1968, in Plattsburgh, N.Y. ... 6-2/240. ... Full name: Roman Zubinsky Phifer.
HIGH SCHOOL: South Mecklenburg (Charlotte).
COLLEGE: UCLA.
TRANSACTIONS/CAREER NOTES: Selected by Los Angeles Rams in second round (31st pick overall) of 1991 NFL draft. ... Signed by Rams (July 19, 1991). ... On injured reserve with broken leg (November 26, 1991-remainder of season). ... Granted unconditional free agency (February 17, 1995). ... Re-signed by Rams (March 22, 1995). ... Rams franchise moved to St. Louis (April 12, 1995).
PRO STATISTICS: 1992—Recovered two fumbles. 1993—Recovered two fumbles for 10 yards. 1995—Fumbled once.

Year	Team	G	GS	No.	Yds.	Avg.	TD	No.
				INTERCEPTIONS				SACKS
1991—Los Angeles Rams NFL		12	5	0	0	...	0	2.0
1992—Los Angeles Rams NFL		16	14	1	3	3.0	0	0.0
1993—Los Angeles Rams NFL		16	16	0	0	...	0	0.0
1994—Los Angeles Rams NFL		16	15	2	7	3.5	0	1.5
1995—St. Louis NFL		16	16	3	52	17.3	0	3.0
1996—St. Louis NFL		15	15	0	0	...	0	1.5
1997—St. Louis NFL		16	15	0	0	...	0	2.0
Pro totals (7 years)		107	96	6	62	10.3	0	10.0

PHILCOX, TODD   QB

PERSONAL: Born September 25, 1966, in Norwalk, Conn. ... 6-4/225. ... Full name: Todd Stuart Philcox.
HIGH SCHOOL: Norwalk (Conn.).
COLLEGE: Syracuse (degree in finance, 1988).
TRANSACTIONS/CAREER NOTES: Signed as non-drafted free agent by Cincinnati Bengals (May 1989). ... Released by Bengals (September 5, 1989). ... Re-signed by Bengals to developmental squad (September 6, 1989). ... Released by Bengals (January 29, 1990). ... Re-signed by Bengals (May 1990). ... Granted unconditional free agency (February 1, 1991). ... Signed by Cleveland Browns (April 1, 1991). ... Granted unconditional free agency (February 1-April 1, 1992). ... Re-signed by Browns for 1992 season. ... On injured reserve with broken thumb (September 22-November 14, 1992). ... Granted free agency (March 1, 1993). ... Re-signed by Browns (July 24, 1993). ... Released by Browns (August 30, 1993). ... Re-signed by Browns (September 1, 1993). ... Granted unconditional free agency (February 17, 1994). ... Signed by Bengals (October 5, 1994). ... Released by Bengals (November 8, 1994). ... Signed by Miami Dolphins (February 21, 1995). ... Released by Dolphins (April 24, 1995). ... Signed by Tampa Bay Buccaneers (April 27, 1995). ... Released by Buccaneers (August 27, 1995). ... Re-signed by Buccaneers (August 29, 1995). ... Inactive for 16 games (1995). ... Granted unconditional free agency (February 16, 1996). ... Signed by Jacksonville Jaguars (April 11, 1996). ... Released by Jaguars (August 24, 1997). ... Signed by San Diego Chargers (November 4, 1997). ... Granted unconditional free agency (February 13, 1998).
CHAMPIONSHIP GAME EXPERIENCE: Member of Jaguars for AFC championship game (1996 season); inactive.
PRO STATISTICS: 1997—Fumbled twice.
STATISTICAL PLATEAUS: 300-yard passing games: 1993 (1).
MISCELLANEOUS: Regular-season record as starting NFL quarterback: 2-3 (.400).

Year	Team	G	GS	Att.	Cmp.	Pct.	Yds.	TD	Int.	Avg.	Rat.	Att.	Yds.	Avg.	TD	TD	2pt.	Pts.
				PASSING								RUSHING				TOTALS		
1989—Cincinnati NFL										Did not play.								
1990—Cincinnati NFL		2	0	2	0	0.0	0	0	1	...	0.0	0	0	...	0	0	...	0
1991—Cleveland NFL		4	0	8	4	50.0	49	0	1	6.13	29.7	1	-1	-1.0	0	0	...	0
1992—Cleveland NFL		2	1	27	13	48.1	217	3	1	8.04	97.3	0	0	...	0	0	...	0
1993—Cleveland NFL		5	4	108	52	48.1	699	4	7	6.47	54.5	2	3	1.5	1	1	...	6
1994—Cincinnati NFL										Did not play.								
1995—Tampa Bay NFL										Did not play.								
1996—Jacksonville NFL										Did not play.								
1997—San Diego NFL		2	0	28	16	57.1	173	0	1	6.18	60.6	1	3	3.0	0	0	0	0
Pro totals (5 years)		15	5	173	85	49.1	1138	7	11	6.58	57.4	4	5	1.3	1	1	0	6

P

PHILLIPS, JOE   DT   RAMS

PERSONAL: Born July 15, 1963, in Portland, Ore. ... 6-5/305. ... Full name: Joseph Gordon Phillips.
HIGH SCHOOL: Columbia River (Vancouver, Wash.).
JUNIOR COLLEGE: Chemeketa Community College (Ore.).
COLLEGE: Oregon State, then Southern Methodist (degree in economics, 1986).
TRANSACTIONS/CAREER NOTES: Selected by Minnesota Vikings in fourth round (93rd pick overall) of 1986 NFL draft. ... Signed by Vikings (July 28, 1986). ... Released by Vikings (September 7, 1987). ... Signed as replacement player by San Diego Chargers (September 24, 1987). ... Granted free agency (February 1, 1988). ... Re-signed by Chargers (August 29, 1988). ... On reserve/non-football injury list with head injuries (September 26, 1990-remainder of season). ... Granted free agency (February 1, 1992). ... Rights relinquished by Chargers (September 21, 1992). ... Signed by Kansas City Chiefs (September 30, 1992). ... Granted unconditional free agency (February 17, 1994). ... Re-signed by Chiefs (March 29, 1994). ... Released by Chiefs (February 13, 1998). ... Signed by St. Louis Rams (April 24, 1998).
CHAMPIONSHIP GAME EXPERIENCE: Played in AFC championship game (1993 season).
PRO STATISTICS: 1986—Recovered one fumble. 1991—Recovered one fumble. 1992—Recovered one fumble. 1994—Recovered one fumble. 1995—Intercepted one pass for two yards and recovered one fumble. 1997—Recovered one fumble and credited with a safety.

Year Team	G	GS	SACKS
1986—Minnesota NFL	16	1	0.0
1987—San Diego NFL	13	7	5.0
1988—San Diego NFL	16	16	2.0
1989—San Diego NFL	16	15	1.0
1990—San Diego NFL	3	3	0.5
1991—San Diego NFL	16	15	1.0
1992—Kansas City NFL	12	10	2.5
1993—Kansas City NFL	16	16	1.5
1994—Kansas City NFL	16	16	3.0
1995—Kansas City NFL	16	16	4.5
1996—Kansas City NFL	16	16	2.0
1997—Kansas City NFL	15	15	0.5
Pro totals (12 years)	171	146	23.5

PHILLIPS, LAWRENCE   RB   DOLPHINS

PERSONAL: Born May 12, 1975, in Little Rock, Ark. ... 6-0/223. ... Full name: Lawrence Lamond Phillips.
HIGH SCHOOL: Baldwin Park (Calif.).
COLLEGE: Nebraska.
TRANSACTIONS/CAREER NOTES: Selected after junior season by St. Louis Rams in first round (sixth pick overall) of 1996 NFL draft. ... Signed by Rams (July 30, 1996). ... Released by Rams (November 20, 1997). ... Signed by Miami Dolphins (December 2, 1997).
PRO STATISTICS: 1996—Returned four kickoffs for 74 yards and recovered one fumble.
SINGLE GAME HIGHS (regular season): Attempts—31 (October 27, 1996, vs. Baltimore Ravens); yards—125 (August 31, 1997, vs. New Orleans); and rushing touchdowns—3 (August 31, 1997, vs. New Orleans).
STATISTICAL PLATEAUS: 100-yard rushing games: 1996 (2), 1997 (1). Total: 3.

Year Team	G	GS	RUSHING Att.	Yds.	Avg.	TD	RECEIVING No.	Yds.	Avg.	TD	TOTALS TD	2pt.	Pts.	Fum.
1996—St. Louis NFL	15	11	193	632	3.3	4	8	28	3.5	1	5	0	30	2
1997—St. Louis NFL	10	9	183	633	3.5	8	10	33	3.3	0	8	0	48	3
—Miami NFL	2	0	18	44	2.4	0	1	6	6.0	0	0	0	0	0
Pro totals (2 years)	27	20	394	1309	3.3	12	19	67	3.5	1	13	0	78	5

PHILLIPS, RYAN   LB   GIANTS

PERSONAL: Born February 7, 1974, in Renton, Wash. ... 6-4/252.
HIGH SCHOOL: Auburn (Wash.).
COLLEGE: Idaho.
TRANSACTIONS/CAREER NOTES: Selected by New York Giants in third round (68th pick overall) of 1997 NFL draft. ... Signed by Giants (July 19, 1997).

Year Team	G	GS	SACKS
1997—New York Giants NFL	10	0	1.0

PHILYAW, DINO   RB

PERSONAL: Born October 30, 1970, in Kenansville, N.C. ... 5-10/203. ... Full name: Delvic Dyvon Philyaw.
HIGH SCHOOL: Southern Wayne (Dudley, N.C.).
JUNIOR COLLEGE: Taft (Calif.) College.
COLLEGE: Oregon.
TRANSACTIONS/CAREER NOTES: Selected by New England Patriots in sixth round (195th pick overall) of 1995 NFL draft. ... Signed by Patriots (July 10, 1995). ... Released by Patriots (August 30, 1995). ... Re-signed by Patriots to practice squad (September 1, 1995). ... Signed by Carolina Panthers off Patriots practice squad (November 8, 1995). ... Granted unconditional free agency (February 14, 1997). ... Signed by St. Louis Rams (February 24, 1997). ... Released by Rams (August 17, 1997). ... Signed by Green Bay Packers (February 5, 1998). ... Assigned by Packers to Scottish Claymores in 1998 NFL Europe enhancement allocation program (February 18, 1998). ... Released by Packers (June 1, 1998).
PLAYING EXPERIENCE: Carolina NFL, 1995 and 1996. ... Games/Games started: 1995 (1/0), 1996 (9/0). Total: 10/0.
CHAMPIONSHIP GAME EXPERIENCE: Member of Panthers for NFC championship game (1996 season); inactive.
PRO STATISTICS: 1995—Returned one kickoff for 23 yards. 1996—Rushed 12 times for 38 yards and one touchdown.
SINGLE GAME HIGHS (regular season): Attempts—9 (October 13, 1996, vs. St. Louis Rams); yards—22 (October 13, 1996, vs. St. Louis Rams); and rushing touchdowns—1 (October 13, 1996, vs. St. Louis Rams).

P

PICKENS, CARL　　　　　　WR　　　　　　BENGALS

PERSONAL: Born March 23, 1970, in Murphy, N.C. ... 6-2/206. ... Full name: Carl McNally Pickens.
HIGH SCHOOL: Murphy (N.C.).
COLLEGE: Tennessee.
TRANSACTIONS/CAREER NOTES: Selected after junior season by Cincinnati Bengals in second round (31st pick overall) of 1992 NFL draft. ... Signed by Bengals (August 4, 1992). ... Granted free agency (February 17, 1995). ... Tendered offer sheet by Arizona Cardinals (March 17, 1995). ... Offer matched by Bengals (March 24, 1995). ... On injured reserve with groin injury (December 15, 1997-remainder of season).
HONORS: Named wide receiver on THE SPORTING NEWS college All-America first team (1991). ... Played in Pro Bowl (1995 and 1996 seasons).
PRO STATISTICS: 1992—Recovered two fumbles. 1993—Attempted one pass without a completion. 1994—Recovered one fumble. 1995—Rushed once for six yards. 1996—Rushed twice for two yards and attempted one pass with one completion for 12 yards.
SINGLE GAME HIGHS (regular season): Receptions—12 (November 10, 1996, vs. Pittsburgh); yards—188 (November 13, 1994, vs. Houston); and touchdown receptions—3 (December 1, 1996, vs. Jacksonville).
STATISTICAL PLATEAUS: 100-yard receiving games: 1993 (1), 1994 (5), 1995 (5), 1996 (2), 1997 (1). Total: 14.

| | | | | RECEIVING | | | PUNT RETURNS | | | | TOTALS | | | |
Year　Team	G	GS	No.	Yds.	Avg.	TD	No.	Yds.	Avg.	TD	TD	2pt.	Pts.	Fum.
1992—Cincinnati NFL	16	10	26	326	12.5	1	18	229	12.7	1	2	...	12	3
1993—Cincinnati NFL	13	12	43	565	13.1	6	4	16	4.0	0	6	...	36	1
1994—Cincinnati NFL	15	15	71	1127	15.9	11	9	62	6.9	0	11	0	66	1
1995—Cincinnati NFL	16	15	§99	1234	12.5	17	5	-2	-0.4	0	17	0	102	1
1996—Cincinnati NFL	16	16	§100	1180	11.8	12	1	2	2.0	0	12	1	74	0
1997—Cincinnati NFL	12	12	52	695	13.4	5	0	0	...	0	5	0	30	1
Pro totals (6 years)	88	80	391	5127	13.1	52	37	307	8.3	1	53	1	320	7

PIERCE, AARON　　　　　　TE

PERSONAL: Born September 6, 1969, in Seattle. ... 6-5/250.
HIGH SCHOOL: Franklin (Seattle).
COLLEGE: Washington.
TRANSACTIONS/CAREER NOTES: Selected by New York Giants in third round (69th pick overall) of 1992 NFL draft. ... Signed by Giants (July 21, 1992). ... On injured reserve with wrist injury (September 1-December 26, 1992); on practice squad (October 7-November 4, 1992). ... Granted free agency (February 17, 1995). ... Re-signed by Giants (April 5, 1995). ... Released by Giants (February 13, 1998).
PRO STATISTICS: 1995—Rushed once for six yards and recovered one fumble. 1996—Rushed once for one yard and a touchdown and recovered one fumble. 1997—Returned one kickoff for 10 yards.
SINGLE GAME HIGHS (regular season): Receptions—5 (October 30, 1994, vs. Detroit); yards—98 (December 5, 1993, vs. Miami); and touchdown receptions—1 (September 15, 1996, vs. Washington).

| | | | | RECEIVING | | | TOTALS | | | |
Year　Team	G	GS	No.	Yds.	Avg.	TD	TD	2pt.	Pts.	Fum.
1992—New York Giants NFL	1	0	0	0	...	0	0	...	0	0
1993—New York Giants NFL	13	6	12	212	17.7	0	0	...	0	2
1994—New York Giants NFL	16	11	20	214	10.7	4	4	0	24	0
1995—New York Giants NFL	16	11	33	310	9.4	0	0	0	0	0
1996—New York Giants NFL	10	3	11	144	13.1	1	2	0	12	0
1997—New York Giants NFL	16	4	10	47	4.7	0	0	0	0	0
Pro totals (6 years)	72	35	86	927	10.8	5	6	0	36	2

PIERI, DAMON　　　　　　S　　　　　　PANTHERS

PERSONAL: Born September 25, 1970, in Phoenix. ... 6-0/186. ... Full name: Mark Damon Pieri.
HIGH SCHOOL: St. Mary's (Phoenix).
JUNIOR COLLEGE: Phoenix College.
COLLEGE: San Diego State.
TRANSACTIONS/CAREER NOTES: Signed as non-drafted free agent by New York Jets (April 27, 1993). ... Released by Jets (August 30, 1993). ... Re-signed by Jets (August 31, 1993). ... Released by Jets (October 13, 1993). ... Re-signed by Jets to practice squad (October 22, 1993). ... Granted free agency after 1993 season. ... Signed by San Francisco 49ers (April 14, 1995). ... Released by 49ers (August 19, 1995). ... Signed by Carolina Panthers (August 30, 1995). ... Inactive for 10 games (1995). ... Released by Panthers (November 15, 1995). ... Re-signed by Panthers (March 19, 1996). ... Granted free agency (February 13, 1998).
PLAYING EXPERIENCE: New York Jets NFL, 1993; Carolina NFL, 1996 and 1997. ... Games/Games started: 1993 (5/0), 1996 (16/1), 1997 (16/0). Total: 37/1.
CHAMPIONSHIP GAME EXPERIENCE: Played in NFC championship game (1996 season).
PRO STATISTICS: 1996—Intercepted one pass for no yards.

PIERSON, PETE　　　　　　OT　　　　　　BUCCANEERS

PERSONAL: Born February 4, 1971, in Portland, Ore. ... 6-5/295. ... Full name: Peter Samuel Pierson.
HIGH SCHOOL: David Douglas (Portland, Ore.).
COLLEGE: Washington (degree in political science, 1994).
TRANSACTIONS/CAREER NOTES: Selected by Tampa Bay Buccaneers in fifth round (136th pick overall) of 1994 NFL draft. ... Signed by Buccaneers (July 6, 1994). ... Released by Buccaneers (August 28, 1994). ... Re-signed by Buccaneers to practice squad (September 2, 1994). ... Activated (November 22, 1994). ... Released by Buccaneers (August 18, 1996). ... Re-signed by Buccaneers (September 10, 1996). ... Granted free agency (February 13, 1998).
PLAYING EXPERIENCE: Tampa Bay NFL, 1995-1997. ... Games/Games started: 1995 (12/4), 1996 (11/2), 1997 (15/0). Total: 38/6.
PRO STATISTICS: 1995—Recovered one fumble.

P

PIKE, MARK   DE   BILLS

PERSONAL: Born December 27, 1963, in Elizabethtown, Ky. ... 6-4/272. ... Full name: Mark Harold Pike.
HIGH SCHOOL: Dixie Heights (Edgewood, Ky.).
COLLEGE: Georgia Tech.
TRANSACTIONS/CAREER NOTES: Selected by Jacksonville Bulls in 1986 USFL territorial draft. ... Selected by Buffalo Bills in seventh round (178th pick overall) of 1986 NFL draft. ... Signed by Bills (July 20, 1986). ... On injured reserve with shoulder injury (August 26, 1986-entire season). ... On injured reserve with leg injury (September 16-November 14, 1987). ... On injured reserve with foot injury (December 8, 1987-remainder of season). ... Granted free agency (February 1, 1991). ... Re-signed by Bills (1991). ... Granted unconditional free agency (February 1-April 1, 1992). ... Re-signed by Bills for 1992 season. ... Granted unconditional free agency (March 1, 1993). ... Re-signed by Bills (May 26, 1993). ... Granted unconditional free agency (February 17, 1995). ... Re-signed by Bills (March 14, 1995). ... Granted unconditional free agency (February 13, 1998). ... Re-signed by Bills (June 1, 1998).
PLAYING EXPERIENCE: Buffalo NFL, 1987-1997. ... Games/Games started: 1987 (3/0), 1988 (16/0), 1989 (16/0), 1990 (16/0), 1991 (16/0), 1992 (16/0), 1993 (14/0), 1994 (16/0), 1995 (16/0), 1996 (16/0), 1997 (15/0). Total: 160/0.
CHAMPIONSHIP GAME EXPERIENCE: Played in AFC championship game (1988 and 1990-1993 seasons). ... Played in Super Bowl XXV (1990 season), Super Bowl XXVI (1991 season), Super Bowl XXVII (1992 season) and Super Bowl XXVIII (1993 season).
PRO STATISTICS: 1988—Returned one kickoff for five yards. 1989—Recovered one fumble. 1992—Credited with one sack. 1994—Returned two kickoffs for nine yards. 1995—Returned one kickoff for 20 yards. 1997—Returned one kickoff for 11 yards.

PILGRIM, EVAN   G   OILERS

PERSONAL: Born August 14, 1972, in Pittsburg, Calif. ... 6-4/304.
HIGH SCHOOL: Antioch (Calif.).
COLLEGE: Brigham Young.
TRANSACTIONS/CAREER NOTES: Selected by Chicago Bears in third round (87th pick overall) of 1995 NFL draft. ... Signed by Bears (July 19, 1995). ... Released by Bears (December 9, 1997). ... Signed by Tennessee Oilers (May 15, 1998).
PLAYING EXPERIENCE: Chicago NFL, 1996 and 1997. ... Games/Games started: 1996 (6/0), 1997 (13/6). Total: 19/6.
PRO STATISTICS: 1997—Recovered one fumble.

PITTMAN, KAVIKA   DE   COWBOYS

PERSONAL: Born October 9, 1974, in Leesville, La. ... 6-6/267. ... Name pronounced kah-VEEK-ah.
HIGH SCHOOL: Leesville (La.).
COLLEGE: McNeese State.
TRANSACTIONS/CAREER NOTES: Selected by Dallas Cowboys in second round (37th pick overall) of 1996 NFL draft. ... Signed by Cowboys (July 16, 1996).
PLAYING EXPERIENCE: Dallas NFL, 1996 and 1997. ... Games/Games started: 1996 (15/0), 1997 (15/0). Total: 30/0.
PRO STATISTICS: 1997—Returned one kickoff for no yards and credited with one sack.

PLEASANT, ANTHONY   DE   JETS

PERSONAL: Born January 27, 1968, in Century, Fla. ... 6-5/280. ... Full name: Anthony Devon Pleasant.
HIGH SCHOOL: Century (Fla.).
COLLEGE: Tennessee State.
TRANSACTIONS/CAREER NOTES: Selected by Cleveland Browns in third round (73rd pick overall) of 1990 NFL draft. ... Signed by Browns (July 22, 1990). ... Browns franchise moved to Baltimore and renamed Ravens for 1996 season (March 11, 1996). ... Granted unconditional free agency (February 14, 1997). ... Signed by Atlanta Falcons (June 21, 1997). ... Released by Falcons (February 13, 1998). ... Signed by New York Jets (March 12, 1998).
PRO STATISTICS: 1991—Recovered one fumble for four yards. 1993—Credited with one safety. 1996—Recovered one fumble for 36 yards.

Year Team	G	GS	SACKS
1990—Cleveland NFL	16	7	3.5
1991—Cleveland NFL	16	7	2.5
1992—Cleveland NFL	16	14	4.0
1993—Cleveland NFL	16	13	11.0
1994—Cleveland NFL	14	14	4.5
1995—Cleveland NFL	16	16	8.0
1996—Baltimore NFL	12	12	4.0
1997—Atlanta NFL	11	0	0.5
Pro totals (8 years)	117	83	38.0

PLUMMER, GARY   LB

PERSONAL: Born January 26, 1960, in Fremont, Calif. ... 6-2/247. ... Full name: Gary Lee Plummer.
HIGH SCHOOL: Mission San Jose (Fremont, Calif.).
JUNIOR COLLEGE: Ohlone (Calif.) College.
COLLEGE: California.
TRANSACTIONS/CAREER NOTES: Selected by Oakland Invaders in 1983 USFL territorial draft. ... Signed by Invaders (January 26, 1983). ... On developmental squad for one game (March 30-April 6, 1984). ... Protected in merger of Invaders and Michigan Panthers (December 6, 1984). ... Claimed on waivers by Tampa Bay Bandits (August 3, 1985). ... Granted free agency when USFL suspended operations (August 7, 1986). ... Signed by San Diego Chargers (August 18, 1986). ... Granted roster exemption (August 18-22, 1986). ... On injured reserve with broken wrist (October 27-November 28, 1987). ... Granted free agency (February 1, 1992). ... Re-signed by Chargers (July 27, 1992). ... Granted unconditional free agency (March 1, 1993). ... Re-signed by Chargers (July 23, 1993). ... Granted unconditional free agency (February 17, 1994). ... Signed by San Francisco 49ers (March 24, 1994). ... On physically unable to perform list with knee injury (July 20-26, 1997). ... Announced retirement (March 12, 1998).

P

CHAMPIONSHIP GAME EXPERIENCE: Played in USFL championship game (1985 season). ... Played in NFC championship game (1994 season). ... Member of Super Bowl championship team (1994 season).

PRO STATISTICS: USFL: 1983—Recovered one fumble. 1984—Recovered one fumble. 1985— Returned three kickoffs for 31 yards and recovered one fumble. NFL: 1986—Returned one kickoff for no yards and recovered two fumbles. 1989—Rushed once for six yards and recovered one fumble. 1990—Caught one pass for two yards and a touchdown and rushed twice for three yards and one touchdown. 1991— Recovered one fumble. 1992—Recovered two fumbles. 1994—Recovered one fumble.

				INTERCEPTIONS				SACKS
Year Team	G	GS	No.	Yds.	Avg.	TD		No.
1983—Oakland USFL	18	18	3	20	6.7	0		0.0
1984—Oakland USFL	17	17	2	11	5.5	0		1.0
1985—Oakland USFL	18	18	1	46	46.0	0		1.0
1986—San Diego NFL	15	13	0	0	...	0		2.5
1987—San Diego NFL	8	7	1	2	2.0	0		0.0
1988—San Diego NFL	16	12	0	0	...	0		0.0
1989—San Diego NFL	16	16	0	0	...	0		0.0
1990—San Diego NFL	16	15	0	0	...	0		0.0
1991—San Diego NFL	16	15	0	0	...	0		1.0
1992—San Diego NFL	16	13	2	40	20.0	0		0.0
1993—San Diego NFL	16	15	2	7	3.5	0		0.0
1994—San Francisco NFL	16	16	1	1	1.0	0		0.0
1995—San Francisco NFL	16	15	0	0	...	0		1.0
1996—San Francisco NFL	13	11	0	0	...	0		0.0
1997—San Francisco NFL	16	16	0	0	...	0		0.0
USFL totals (3 years)	53	53	6	77	12.8	0		2.0
NFL totals (12 years)	180	164	6	50	8.3	0		4.5
Pro totals (15 years)	233	217	12	127	10.6	0		6.5

PLUMMER, JAKE   QB   CARDINALS

PERSONAL: Born December 19, 1974, in Boise, Idaho. ... 6-2/197. ... Full name: Jason Steven Plummer.

HIGH SCHOOL: Capital (Boise, Idaho).

COLLEGE: Arizona State.

TRANSACTIONS/CAREER NOTES: Selected by Arizona Cardinals in second round (42nd pick overall) of 1997 NFL draft. ... Signed by Cardinals (July 14, 1997).

HONORS: Named quarterback on THE SPORTING NEWS college All-America second team (1996).

PRO STATISTICS: 1997—Caught one pass for two yards, fumbled six times and recovered one fumble for minus one yard.

SINGLE GAME HIGHS (regular season): Attempts—40 (October 26, 1997, vs. Tennessee); completions—22 (November 16, 1997, vs. New York Giants); yards—388 (November 16, 1997, vs. New York Giants); and touchdown passes—4 (December 7, 1997, vs. Washington).

STATISTICAL PLATEAUS: 300-yard passing games: 1997 (2).

MISCELLANEOUS: Regular-season record as starting NFL quarterback: 3-6 (.333).

			PASSING							RUSHING				TOTALS		
Year Team	G	GS	Att.	Cmp.	Pct.	Yds.	TD	Int.	Avg.	Rat.	Att.	Yds.	Avg.	TD	TD	2pt.	Pts.
1997—Arizona NFL	10	9	296	157	53.0	2203	15	15	7.44	73.1	39	216	5.5	2	2	1	14

POLLACK, FRANK   G/OT   49ERS

PERSONAL: Born November 5, 1967, in Camp Springs, Md. ... 6-5/295. ... Full name: Frank Steven Pollack.

HIGH SCHOOL: Greenway (Phoenix).

COLLEGE: Northern Arizona (degree in advertising, 1990).

TRANSACTIONS/CAREER NOTES: Selected by San Francisco 49ers in sixth round (165th pick overall) of 1990 NFL draft. ... Signed by 49ers (July 18, 1990). ... Granted unconditional free agency (February 1-April 1, 1991). ... Re-signed by 49ers for 1991 season. ... Granted unconditional free agency (February 1, 1992). ... Signed by Denver Broncos (March 20, 1992). ... On injured reserve with back injury (August 24, 1992-entire season). ... Released by Broncos (August 18, 1993). ... Signed by 49ers (May 18, 1994). ... Granted unconditional free agency (February 17, 1995). ... Re-signed by 49ers (May 15, 1995). ... Granted unconditional free agency (February 16, 1996). ... Selected by Scottish Claymores in 1996 World League draft (February 22, 1996). ... Re-signed by 49ers (June 3, 1996). ... Released by 49ers after 1996 season. ... Re-signed by 49ers (March 25, 1997).

PLAYING EXPERIENCE: San Francisco NFL, 1990, 1991, 1994-1997. ... Games/Games started: 1990 (15/0), 1991 (15/0), 1994 (12/4), 1995 (15/0), 1996 (16/2), 1997 (16/0). Total: 89/6.

CHAMPIONSHIP GAME EXPERIENCE: Played in NFC championship game (1990 and 1997 seasons). ... Member of 49ers for NFC championship game (1994 season); inactive. ... Member of Super Bowl championship team (1994 season).

POLLARD, MARCUS   TE   COLTS

PERSONAL: Born February 8, 1972, in Lanett, Ala. ... 6-4/257. ... Full name: Marcus LaJuan Pollard.

HIGH SCHOOL: Valley (Ala.).

JUNIOR COLLEGE: Seward County (Kan.) Community College (did not play football).

COLLEGE: Bradley (did not play football).

TRANSACTIONS/CAREER NOTES: Signed as non-drafted free agent by Indianapolis Colts (January 24, 1995). ... Released by Colts (August 22, 1995). ... Re-signed by Colts to practice squad (August 28, 1995). ... Activated (October 10, 1995). ... Granted free agency (February 13, 1998). ... Tendered offer sheet by Philadelphia Eagles (March 4, 1998). ... Offer matched by Colts (March 9, 1998).

CHAMPIONSHIP GAME EXPERIENCE: Played in AFC championship game (1995 season).

PRO STATISTICS: 1996—Recovered one fumble.

SINGLE GAME HIGHS (regular season): Receptions—3 (October 12, 1997, vs. Pittsburgh); yards—55 (October 12, 1997, vs. Pittsburgh); and touchdown receptions—1 (September 15, 1996, vs. Dallas).

MISCELLANEOUS: Played basketball during college.

P

Year Team	G	GS	No.	RECEIVING Yds.	Avg.	TD	TD	TOTALS 2pt.	Pts.	Fum.
1995—Indianapolis NFL	8	0	0	0	...	0	0	0	0	0
1996—Indianapolis NFL	16	4	6	86	14.3	1	1	0	6	0
1997—Indianapolis NFL	16	5	10	116	11.6	0	0	1	2	0
Pro totals (3 years)	40	9	16	202	12.6	1	1	1	8	0

POOLE, KEITH — WR — SAINTS

PERSONAL: Born June 18, 1974, in San Jose, Calif. ... 6-0/188. ... Full name: Keith Robert Poole.
HIGH SCHOOL: Clovis (Calif.).
COLLEGE: Arizona State.
TRANSACTIONS/CAREER NOTES: Selected by New Orleans Saints in fourth round (116th pick overall) of 1997 NFL draft. ... Signed by Saints (June 10, 1997).
PLAYING EXPERIENCE: New Orleans NFL, 1997. ... Games/Games started: 3/0.
PRO STATISTICS: 1997—Caught four passes for 98 yards and two touchdowns.
SINGLE GAME HIGHS (regular season): Receptions—3 (December 21, 1997, vs. Kansas City); yards—49 (December 21, 1997, vs. Kansas City); and touchdown receptions—2 (December 21, 1997, vs. Kansas City).

POOLE, TYRONE — CB/KR — PANTHERS

PERSONAL: Born February 3, 1972, in LaGrange, Ga. ... 5-8/188.
HIGH SCHOOL: LaGrange (Ga.).
COLLEGE: Fort Valley (Ga.) State.
TRANSACTIONS/CAREER NOTES: Selected by Carolina Panthers in first round (22nd pick overall) of 1995 NFL draft. ... Signed by Panthers (July 15, 1995).
CHAMPIONSHIP GAME EXPERIENCE: Played in NFC championship game (1996 season).
PRO STATISTICS: 1996—Recovered one fumble. 1997—Returned one kickoff for five yards and recovered three fumbles for 11 yards.

Year Team	G	GS	No.	INTERCEPTIONS Yds.	Avg.	TD	SACKS No.	No.	PUNT RETURNS Yds.	Avg.	TD	TD	TOTALS 2pt.	Pts.	Fum.
1995—Carolina NFL	16	13	2	8	4.0	0	2.0	0	0	...	0	0	0	0	0
1996—Carolina NFL	15	15	1	35	35.0	0	0.0	3	26	8.7	0	0	0	0	0
1997—Carolina NFL	16	16	2	0	0.0	0	1.0	26	191	7.3	0	0	0	0	3
Pro totals (3 years)	47	44	5	43	8.6	0	3.0	29	217	7.5	0	0	0	0	3

POPE, MARQUEZ — CB — 49ERS

PERSONAL: Born October 29, 1970, in Nashville. ... 5-11/193. ... Full name: Marquez Phillips Pope. ... Name pronounced MARK-ez.
HIGH SCHOOL: Polytechnic (Long Beach, Calif.).
COLLEGE: Fresno State.
TRANSACTIONS/CAREER NOTES: Selected by San Diego Chargers in second round (33rd pick overall) of 1992 NFL draft. ... Signed by Chargers (July 16, 1992). ... On reserve/non-football illness list with virus (September 1-28, 1992). ... On practice squad (September 28-November 7, 1992). ... Traded by Chargers to Los Angeles Rams for sixth-round pick in 1995 draft (April 11, 1994). ... Granted free agency (February 17, 1995). ... Tendered offer sheet by San Francisco 49ers (April 9, 1995). ... Rams declined to match offer (April 12, 1995); received second-round pick (OL Jesse James) in 1995 draft as compensation.
CHAMPIONSHIP GAME EXPERIENCE: Played in NFC championship game (1997 season).
PRO STATISTICS: 1993—Credited with $1/2$ sack. 1996—Recovered one fumble for four yards.

Year Team	G	GS	No.	INTERCEPTIONS Yds.	Avg.	TD
1992—San Diego NFL	7	0	0	0	...	0
1993—San Diego NFL	16	1	2	14	7.0	0
1994—Los Angeles Rams NFL	16	16	3	66	22.0	0
1995—San Francisco NFL	16	16	1	-7	-7.0	0
1996—San Francisco NFL	16	16	6	98	16.3	1
1997—San Francisco NFL	5	5	1	7	7.0	0
Pro totals (6 years)	76	54	13	178	13.7	1

POPSON, TED — TE — CHIEFS

PERSONAL: Born September 10, 1966, in Granada Hills, Calif. ... 6-4/250. ... Full name: Theodore Paul Popson.
HIGH SCHOOL: Tahoe Truckee (Truckee, Calif.).
JUNIOR COLLEGE: Marin Community College (Calif.).
COLLEGE: Portland State.
TRANSACTIONS/CAREER NOTES: Selected by New York Giants in 11th round (306th pick overall) of 1991 NFL draft. ... Signed by Giants for 1991 season. ... Selected by London Monarchs in 1992 World League draft. ... Released by Giants (August 31, 1992). ... Re-signed by Giants to practice squad (September 2, 1992). ... Released by Giants (October 7, 1992). ... Signed by San Francisco 49ers (April 30, 1993). ... Released by 49ers (August 27, 1993). ... Re-signed by 49ers to practice squad (August 31, 1993). ... Granted free agency after 1993 season. ... Re-signed by 49ers (February 15, 1994). ... Released by 49ers (February 15, 1996). ... Re-signed by 49ers (June 13, 1996). ... Granted unconditional free agency (February 14, 1997). ... Signed by Kansas City Chiefs (June 17, 1997).
CHAMPIONSHIP GAME EXPERIENCE: Played in NFC championship game (1994 season). ... Member of Super Bowl championship team (1994 season).
PRO STATISTICS: W.L.: 1992—Returned three kickoffs for 31 yards. NFL: 1995—Fumbled once. 1996—Recovered one fumble.
SINGLE GAME HIGHS (regular season): Receptions—8 (October 20, 1996, vs. Cincinnati); yards—116 (October 20, 1996, vs. Cincinnati); and touchdown receptions—2 (October 20, 1996, vs. Cincinnati).
STATISTICAL PLATEAUS: 100-yard receiving games: 1996 (1).

P

Year Team	G	GS	RECEIVING			TD	TOTALS			Fum.
			No.	Yds.	Avg.	TD	TD	2pt.	Pts.	Fum.
1991—New York Giants NFL			Did not play.							
1992—London W.L.	10	5	4	24	6.0	0	0	...	0	0
1993—San Francisco NFL			Did not play.							
1994—San Francisco NFL	16	1	13	141	10.8	0	0	0	0	0
1995—San Francisco NFL	12	0	16	128	8.0	0	0	0	0	1
1996—San Francisco NFL	15	6	26	301	11.6	6	6	0	36	0
1997—Kansas City NFL	13	12	35	320	9.1	2	2	0	12	0
W.L. totals (1 year)	10	5	4	24	6.0	0	0	...	0	0
NFL totals (4 years)	56	19	90	890	9.9	8	8	0	48	1
Pro totals (5 years)	66	24	94	914	9.7	8	8	0	48	1

PORCHER, ROBERT · DE · LIONS

PERSONAL: Born July 30, 1969, in Wando, S.C. ... 6-3/270. ... Full name: Robert Porcher III. ... Name pronounced por-SHAY.
HIGH SCHOOL: Cainhoy (Huger, S.C.).
COLLEGE: Tennessee State, then South Carolina State.
TRANSACTIONS/CAREER NOTES: Selected by Detroit Lions in first round (26th pick overall) of 1992 NFL draft. ... Signed by Lions (July 25, 1992). ... Granted unconditional free agency (February 16, 1996). ... Re-signed by Lions (March 29, 1996). ... Granted unconditional free agency (February 14, 1997). ... Re-signed by Lions (March 4, 1997).
PRO STATISTICS: 1994—Recovered one fumble. 1996—Recovered two fumbles.

Year Team	G	GS	SACKS
1992—Detroit NFL	16	1	1.0
1993—Detroit NFL	16	4	8.5
1994—Detroit NFL	15	15	3.0
1995—Detroit NFL	16	16	5.0
1996—Detroit NFL	16	16	10.0
1997—Detroit NFL	16	15	12.5
Pro totals (6 years)	95	67	40.0

PORTER, DARYL · CB · LIONS

PERSONAL: Born January 16, 1974, in Ft. Lauderdale, Fla. ... 5-9/190. ... Full name: Daryl Maurice Porter. ... Cousin of Bennie Blades, cornerback with Detroit Lions (1988-96) and Seattle Seahawks (1997); and cousin of Brian Blades, wide receiver, Seattle Seahawks.
HIGH SCHOOL: St. Thomas Aquinas (Ft. Lauderdale, Fla.).
COLLEGE: Boston College.
TRANSACTIONS/CAREER NOTES: Selected by Pittsburgh Steelers in sixth round (186th pick overall) of 1997 NFL draft. ... Signed by Steelers (June 6, 1997). ... Released by Steelers (August 19, 1997). ... Re-signed by Steelers to practice squad (August 26, 1997). ... Released by Steelers (October 20, 1997). ... Signed by Detroit Lions (October 21, 1997). ... Released by Lions after 1997 season. ... Re-signed by Lions (April 22, 1998).
PLAYING EXPERIENCE: Detroit NFL, 1997. ... Games/Games started: 7/0.

PORTER, JUAN · C · PATRIOTS

PERSONAL: Born November 26, 1973, in Cleveland. ... 6-3/295.
HIGH SCHOOL: St. Ignatius (Cleveland).
COLLEGE: Ohio State.
TRANSACTIONS/CAREER NOTES: Signed as non-drafted free agent by New England Patriots (April 20, 1997). ... Released by Patriots (August 19, 1997). ... Re-signed by Patriots to practice squad (August 26, 1997).

PORTER, RUFUS · LB

PERSONAL: Born May 18, 1965, in Amite, La. ... 6-1/230.
HIGH SCHOOL: Capitol (Baton Rouge, La.).
COLLEGE: Southern (La.).
TRANSACTIONS/CAREER NOTES: Signed as non-drafted free agent by Seattle Seahawks (May 11, 1988). ... On injured reserve with groin injury (December 5, 1990-remainder of season). ... On injured reserve with Achilles' tendon injury (November 10, 1993-remainder of season). ... Granted unconditional free agency (February 17, 1995). ... Signed by New Orleans Saints (March 10, 1995). ... Released by Saints (February 13, 1997). ... Signed by Tampa Bay Buccaneers (March 11, 1997). ... Released by Buccaneers (February 12, 1998).
HONORS: Played in Pro Bowl (1988 and 1989 seasons).
PRO STATISTICS: 1988—Recovered one fumble. 1990—Recovered four fumbles for 11 yards. 1991—Intercepted one pass for no yards. 1994—Intercepted one pass for 33 yards. 1995—Recovered one fumble.

Year Team	G	GS	SACKS
1988—Seattle NFL	16	0	0.0
1989—Seattle NFL	16	3	10.5
1990—Seattle NFL	12	12	5.0
1991—Seattle NFL	15	15	10.0
1992—Seattle NFL	16	16	9.5
1993—Seattle NFL	7	6	1.0
1994—Seattle NFL	16	15	1.5
1995—New Orleans NFL	14	12	3.0
1996—New Orleans NFL	13	0	0.0
1997—Tampa Bay NFL	11	10	0.5
Pro totals (10 years)	136	98	41.0

P

POTTS, ROOSEVELT　　　　　　RB　　　　　　RAVENS

PERSONAL: Born January 8, 1971, in Rayville, La. ... 6-0/250. ... Full name: Roosevelt Bernard Potts. ... Cousin of Reggie Burnette, linebacker with Green Bay Packers (1991) and Tampa Bay Buccaneers (1992 and 1993).
HIGH SCHOOL: Rayville (La.).
COLLEGE: Northeast Louisiana.
TRANSACTIONS/CAREER NOTES: Selected by Indianapolis Colts in second round (49th pick overall) of 1993 NFL draft. ... Signed by Colts (July 20, 1993). ... On injured reserve with knee injury (December 19, 1995-remainder of season). ... Granted free agency (February 16, 1996). ... Suspended by NFL for violating league substance abuse policy (August 19, 1996-July 15, 1997). ... Re-signed by Colts (August 11, 1997). ... Released by Colts (November 4, 1997). ... Signed by Miami Dolphins (November 10, 1997). ... Granted unconditional free agency (February 13, 1998). ... Signed by Baltimore Ravens (March 4, 1998).
PRO STATISTICS: 1993—Recovered two fumbles. 1994—Recovered one fumble. 1997—Returned one kickoff for 16 yards.
SINGLE GAME HIGHS (regular season): Attempts—23 (October 31, 1991, vs. New England); yards—113 (October 10, 1993, vs. Dallas); and rushing touchdowns—1 (September 11, 1994, vs. Tampa Bay).
STATISTICAL PLATEAUS: 100-yard rushing games: 1993 (2).

			RUSHING				RECEIVING				TOTALS			
Year　Team	G	GS	Att.	Yds.	Avg.	TD	No.	Yds.	Avg.	TD	TD	2pt.	Pts.	Fum.
1993—Indianapolis NFL	16	15	179	711	4.0	0	26	189	7.3	0	0	...	0	8
1994—Indianapolis NFL	16	16	77	336	4.4	1	26	251	9.7	1	2	0	12	5
1995—Indianapolis NFL	15	15	65	309	4.8	0	21	228	10.9	1	1	0	0	0
1996—Indianapolis NFL							Did not play.							
1997—Indianapolis NFL	1	0	1	1	1.0	0	0	0	...	0	0	0	0	0
—Miami NFL	6	1	1	3	3.0	0	3	27	9.0	0	0	0	0	0
Pro totals (4 years)	54	46	323	1360	4.2	1	76	695	9.1	2	3	0	18	13

POUNDS, DARRYL　　　　　　CB　　　　　　REDSKINS

PERSONAL: Born July 21, 1972, in Fort Worth, Texas. ... 5-10/189.
HIGH SCHOOL: South Pike (Magnolia, Miss.).
COLLEGE: Nicholls State.
TRANSACTIONS/CAREER NOTES: Selected by Washington Redskins in third round (68th pick overall) of 1995 NFL draft. ... Signed by Redskins (May 26, 1995). ... On physically unable to perform list with back injury (August 22-October 17, 1995). ... Granted free agency (February 13, 1998). ... Re-signed by Redskins (April 9, 1998).
PRO STATISTICS: 1995—Fumbled once. 1996—Recovered one fumble. 1997—Credited with two sacks and recovered three fumbles for 18 yards and one touchdown.

			INTERCEPTIONS			
Year　Team	G	GS	No.	Yds.	Avg.	TD
1995—Washington NFL	9	0	1	26	26.0	0
1996—Washington NFL	12	1	2	11	5.5	0
1997—Washington NFL	16	0	3	42	14.0	1
Pro totals (3 years)	37	1	6	79	13.2	1

POURDANESH, SHAR　　　　　　OT　　　　　　REDSKINS

PERSONAL: Born July 19, 1970, in Iran. ... 6-6/312. ... Full name: Shahriar Pourdanesh. ... Name pronounced Shar-E-are PORE-donish.
HIGH SCHOOL: University (Irvine, Calif.).
COLLEGE: Nevada.
TRANSACTIONS/CAREER NOTES: Signed as non-drafted free agent by Cleveland Browns (1993). ... Released by Browns before 1993 season. ... Signed by Baltimore of CFL (1994). ... Signed by Washington Redskins (March 20, 1995).
PLAYING EXPERIENCE: Baltimore CFL, 1994 and 1995; Washington NFL, 1996 and 1997. ... Games/Games started: 1994 (18/18), 1995 (14/14), 1996 (16/8), 1997 (16/14). Total CFL: 32/32. Total NFL: 32/22. Total Pro: 64/54.
HONORS: Named tackle on CFL All-Star team (1994). ... Named CFL Most Outstanding Offensive Lineman (1994).

POWELL, CARL　　　　　　DE　　　　　　COLTS

PERSONAL: Born January 4, 1974, in Detroit. ... 6-3/265. ... Full name: Carl Demetris Powell.
HIGH SCHOOL: Northern (Detroit).
JUNIOR COLLEGE: Grand Rapids (Mich.) Community College.
COLLEGE: Louisville.
TRANSACTIONS/CAREER NOTES: Selected by Indianapolis Colts in fifth round (156th pick overall) of 1997 NFL draft. ... Signed by Colts (July 3, 1997).
PLAYING EXPERIENCE: Indianapolis NFL, 1997. ... Games/Games started: 11/0.

PRESTON, ROELL　　　　　　WR/KR　　　　　　PACKERS

PERSONAL: Born June 23, 1972, in Miami. ... 5-10/185. ... Name pronounced ROW-ell.
HIGH SCHOOL: Hialeah (Fla.).
JUNIOR COLLEGE: Northwest Mississippi Community College.
COLLEGE: Mississippi.
TRANSACTIONS/CAREER NOTES: Selected by Atlanta Falcons in fifth round (145th pick overall) of 1995 NFL draft. ... Signed by Falcons (July 13, 1995). ... Released by Falcons (August 24, 1997). ... Signed by Green Bay Packers (November 12, 1997). ... Released by Packers (November 18, 1997). ... Signed by Washington Redskins (December 3, 1997). ... Released by Redskins (December 9, 1997). ... Signed by Packers (March 4, 1998).

P

PRO STATISTICS: 1995—Fumbled once. 1997—Returned one punt for no yards.
SINGLE GAME HIGHS (regular season): Receptions—9 (October 13, 1996, vs. Houston); yards—79 (November 26, 1995, vs. Arizona); and touchdown receptions—1 (September 29, 1996, vs. San Francisco).

| | | | RECEIVING | | | | KICKOFF RETURNS | | | | TOTALS | | |
Year Team	G	GS	No.	Yds.	Avg.	TD	No.	Yds.	Avg.	TD	TD	2pt.	Pts.	Fum.
1995—Atlanta NFL	14	0	7	129	18.4	1	30	627	20.9	0	1	0	6	1
1996—Atlanta NFL	15	2	21	208	9.9	1	32	681	21.3	0	1	0	6	0
1997—Green Bay NFL	1	0	0	0	...	0	7	211	30.1	0	0	0	0	0
Pro totals (3 years)	30	2	28	337	12.0	2	69	1519	22.0	0	2	0	12	1

PRICE, DARYL   DE   49ERS

PERSONAL: Born October 23, 1972, in Galveston, Texas. ... 6-3/287.
HIGH SCHOOL: Central (Beaumont, Texas).
COLLEGE: Colorado.
TRANSACTIONS/CAREER NOTES: Selected by San Francisco 49ers in fourth round (128th pick overall) of 1996 NFL draft. ... Signed by 49ers (July 18, 1996).
PLAYING EXPERIENCE: San Francisco NFL, 1996 and 1997. ... Games/Games started: 1996 (14/0), 1997 (4/0). Total: 18/0.
CHAMPIONSHIP GAME EXPERIENCE: Member of 49ers for NFC championship game (1997 season); inactive.
PRO STATISTICS: 1996—Recovered one fumble.

PRICE, MARCUS   OT/G   CHARGERS

PERSONAL: Born March 3, 1972, in Port Arthur, Texas. ... 6-6/321. ... Full name: Marcus Raymond Price.
HIGH SCHOOL: Lincoln (Port Arthur, Texas).
COLLEGE: Louisiana State.
TRANSACTIONS/CAREER NOTES: Selected by Jacksonville Jaguars in sixth round (172nd pick overall) of 1995 NFL draft. ... Signed by Jaguars (June 1, 1995). ... On injured reserve with ankle injury (August 19, 1995-entire season). ... Released by Jaguars (August 25, 1996). ... Signed by Denver Broncos to practice squad (December 3, 1996). ... Released by Broncos (December 30, 1996). ... Signed by Jaguars (January 31, 1997). ... Released by Jaguars (August 19, 1997). ... Re-signed by Jaguars to practice squad (October 28, 1997). ... Signed by San Diego Chargers off Jaguars practice squad (November 26, 1997).
PLAYING EXPERIENCE: San Diego NFL, 1997. ... Games/Games started: 2/0.

PRICE, SHAWN   DE   BILLS

PERSONAL: Born March 28, 1970, in Jacksonville. ... 6-5/260. ... Full name: Shawn Sterling Price.
HIGH SCHOOL: North Tahoe (Nev.).
JUNIOR COLLEGE: Sierra College (Calif.).
COLLEGE: Pacific.
TRANSACTIONS/CAREER NOTES: Signed as non-drafted free agent by Tampa Bay Buccaneers (April 29, 1993). ... Released by Buccaneers (August 30, 1993). ... Re-signed by Buccaneers to practice squad (August 31, 1993). ... Activated (November 5, 1993). ... Selected by Carolina Panthers from Buccaneers in NFL expansion draft (February 15, 1995). ... Granted unconditional free agency (February 16, 1996). ... Signed by Buffalo Bills (April 12, 1996). ... Granted unconditional free agency (February 13, 1998). ... Re-signed by Bills (March 9, 1998).
PLAYING EXPERIENCE: Tampa Bay NFL, 1993 and 1994; Carolina NFL, 1995; Buffalo NFL, 1996 and 1997. ... Games/Games started: 1993 (9/6), 1994 (6/0), 1995 (16/0), 1996 (15/0), 1997 (10/0). Total: 56/6.
PRO STATISTICS: 1993 Credited with three sacks. 1995—Credited with one sack.

PRIOR, ANTHONY   CB   CHIEFS

PERSONAL: Born March 27, 1970, in Mira Loma, Calif. ... 5-11/186.
HIGH SCHOOL: Rubidoux (Riverside, Calif.).
COLLEGE: Washington State.
TRANSACTIONS/CAREER NOTES: Selected by New York Giants in ninth round (238th pick overall) of 1992 NFL draft. ... Signed by Giants (July 21, 1992). ... Released by Giants (August 25, 1992). ... Signed by New York Jets to practice squad (September 9, 1992). ... Released by Jets (September 29, 1992). ... Re-signed by Jets for 1993 season. ... Re-signed by Jets (March 29, 1995). ... Released by Jets (March 1, 1996). ... Signed by Cincinnati Bengals (March 12, 1996). ... Released by Bengals (July 15, 1996). ... Signed by San Francisco 49ers (July 19, 1996). ... Released by 49ers (August 20, 1996). ... Signed by Minnesota Vikings (December 4, 1996). ... Granted unconditional free agency (February 14, 1997). ... Re-signed by Vikings (April 9, 1997). ... On injured reserve with groin injury (November 29, 1997-remainder of season). ... Released by Vikings (February 2, 1998). ... Signed by Kansas City Chiefs (April 6, 1998).
PRO STATISTICS: 1993—Recovered one fumble.

| | | | KICKOFF RETURNS | | | | TOTALS | | | |
Year Team	G	GS	No.	Yds.	Avg.	TD	TD	2pt.	Pts.	Fum.
1992—New York Jets NFL						Did not play.				
1993—New York Jets NFL	16	0	9	126	14.0	0	0	...	0	0
1994—New York Jets NFL	13	0	16	316	19.8	0	0	0	0	0
1995—New York Jets NFL	11	0	0	0	...	0	0	0	0	0
1996—Minnesota NFL	3	0	0	0	...	0	0	0	0	0
1997—Minnesota NFL	12	0	0	0	...	0	0	0	0	0
Pro totals (5 years)	55	0	25	440	17.6	0	0	0	0	0

PRIOR, MIKE   S   PACKERS P

PERSONAL: Born November 14, 1963, in Chicago Heights, Ill. ... 6-0/208. ... Full name: Michael Robert Prior.
HIGH SCHOOL: Marian Catholic (Chicago Heights, Ill.).
COLLEGE: Illinois State (degree in business administration, 1985).

TRANSACTIONS/CAREER NOTES: Selected by Memphis Showboats in fourth round (60th pick overall) of 1985 USFL draft. ... Selected by Tampa Bay Buccaneers in seventh round (176th pick overall) of 1985 NFL draft. ... Signed by Buccaneers (June 10, 1985). ... On injured reserve with fractured wrist (August 25-September 28, 1986). ... Released by Buccaneers (September 29, 1986). ... Signed by Indianapolis Colts (May 11, 1987). ... Released by Colts (August 31, 1987). ... Re-signed as replacement player by Colts (September 23, 1987). ... On injured reserve with abdomen injury (October 11-December 6, 1991). ... Granted unconditional free agency (March 1, 1993). ... Signed by Green Bay Packers (April 16, 1993). ... Released by Packers (July 27, 1994). ... Re-signed by Packers (July 27, 1994). ... Granted unconditional free agency (February 17, 1995). ... Re-signed by Packers (April 28, 1995). ... Granted unconditional free agency (February 14, 1997). ... Re-signed by Packers (April 2, 1997). ... Released by Packers (March 4, 1998). ... Re-signed by Packers (April 24, 1998).

CHAMPIONSHIP GAME EXPERIENCE: Played in NFC championship game (1995-97 seasons). ... Member of Super Bowl championship team (1996 season). ... Played in Super Bowl XXXII (1997 season).

PRO STATISTICS: 1985—Recovered three fumbles. 1987—Credited with one sack and recovered three fumbles. 1988—Credited with one sack and recovered one fumble for 12 yards. 1989—Recovered one fumble for 10 yards. 1990—Caught one pass for 40 yards and recovered two fumbles for six yards. 1991—Recovered one fumble. 1992—Caught one pass for 17 yards and recovered one fumble. 1993—Recovered two fumbles. 1994—Recovered two fumbles. 1995—Credited with 1 1/2 sacks and recovered one fumble.

MISCELLANEOUS: Selected by Baltimore Orioles organization in 18th round of free-agent baseball draft (June 4, 1984); did not sign. ... Selected by Los Angeles Dodgers organization in fourth round of free-agent baseball draft (June 3, 1985); did not sign.

Year Team	G	GS	INTERCEPTIONS No.	Yds.	Avg.	TD	PUNT RETURNS No.	Yds.	Avg.	TD	KICKOFF RETURNS No.	Yds.	Avg.	TD	TOTALS TD	2pt.	Pts.	Fum.
1985—Tampa Bay NFL	16	0	0	0	...	0	13	105	8.1	0	10	131	13.1	0	0	...	0	4
1986—									Did not play.									
1987—Indianapolis NFL	13	7	6	57	9.5	0	0	0	...	0	3	47	15.7	0	0	...	0	0
1988—Indianapolis NFL	16	16	3	46	15.3	0	1	0	0.0	0	0	0	...	0	0	...	0	1
1989—Indianapolis NFL	16	16	6	88	14.7	1	0	0	...	0	0	0	...	0	1	...	6	0
1990—Indianapolis NFL	16	16	3	66	22.0	0	2	0	0.0	0	0	0	...	0	0	...	0	1
1991—Indianapolis NFL	9	7	3	50	16.7	0	0	0	...	0	0	0	...	0	0	...	0	0
1992—Indianapolis NFL	16	16	6	44	7.3	0	1	7	7.0	0	0	0	...	0	0	...	0	0
1993—Green Bay NFL	16	4	1	1	1.0	0	17	194	11.4	0	0	0	...	0	0	...	0	3
1994—Green Bay NFL	16	0	0	0	...	0	8	62	7.8	0	0	0	...	0	0	0	0	3
1995—Green Bay NFL	16	2	1	9	9.0	0	1	10	10.0	0	0	0	...	0	0	0	0	0
1996—Green Bay NFL	16	0	1	7	7.0	0	0	0	...	0	0	0	...	0	0	0	0	0
1997—Green Bay NFL	16	0	4	72	18.0	0	1	0	0.0	0	0	0	...	0	0	0	0	1
Pro totals (12 years)	182	84	34	440	12.9	1	44	378	8.6	0	13	178	13.7	0	1	0	6	13

PRITCHARD, MIKE — WR — SEAHAWKS

PERSONAL: Born October 26, 1969, in Shaw AFB, S.C. ... 5-10/193. ... Full name: Michael Robert Pritchard.
HIGH SCHOOL: Rancho (North Las Vegas, Nev.).
COLLEGE: Colorado.
TRANSACTIONS/CAREER NOTES: Selected by Atlanta Falcons in first round (13th pick overall) of 1991 NFL draft. ... Signed by Falcons (July 24, 1991). ... Traded by Falcons with seventh-round pick (WR Byron Chamberlain) in 1995 draft to Denver Broncos for first-round pick (traded to Minnesota) in 1995 draft (April 24, 1994). ... On injured reserve with kidney injury (November 2, 1994-remainder of season). ... Released by Broncos (June 3, 1996). ... Signed by Seattle Seahawks (June 19, 1996).
PRO STATISTICS: 1991—Returned one kickoff for 18 yards.
SINGLE GAME HIGHS (regular season): Receptions—10 (September 5, 1993, vs. Detroit); yards—119 (September 4, 1994, vs. San Diego); and touchdown receptions—2 (November 21, 1993, vs. Dallas).
STATISTICAL PLATEAUS: 100-yard receiving games: 1992 (1), 1994 (2). Total: 3.

Year Team	G	GS	RUSHING Att.	Yds.	Avg.	TD	RECEIVING No.	Yds.	Avg.	TD	TOTALS TD	2pt.	Pts.	Fum.
1991—Atlanta NFL	16	11	0	0	...	0	50	624	12.5	2	2	...	12	2
1992—Atlanta NFL	16	15	5	37	7.4	0	77	827	10.7	5	5	...	30	3
1993—Atlanta NFL	15	14	2	4	2.0	0	74	736	9.9	7	7	...	42	1
1994—Denver NFL	3	0	0	0	...	0	19	271	14.3	1	1	0	6	1
1995—Denver NFL	15	13	6	17	2.8	0	33	441	13.4	3	3	0	18	1
1996—Seattle NFL	16	5	2	13	6.5	0	21	328	15.6	1	1	0	6	0
1997—Seattle NFL	16	15	1	14	14.0	0	64	843	13.2	2	2	0	12	2
Pro totals (7 years)	97	73	16	85	5.3	0	338	4070	12.0	21	21	0	126	10

PRITCHETT, KELVIN — DT — JAGUARS

PERSONAL: Born October 24, 1969, in Atlanta. ... 6-3/300. ... Full name: Kelvin Bratodd Pritchett.
HIGH SCHOOL: Therrell (Atlanta).
COLLEGE: Mississippi.
TRANSACTIONS/CAREER NOTES: Selected by Dallas Cowboys in first round (20th pick overall) of 1991 NFL draft. ... Rights traded by Cowboys to Detroit Lions for second- (LB Dixon Edwards), third- (G James Richards) and fourth-round (DE Tony Hill) picks in 1991 draft (April 21, 1991). ... Granted free agency (February 17, 1994). ... Re-signed by Lions (August 12, 1994). ... Granted unconditional free agency (February 17, 1995). ... Signed by Jacksonville Jaguars (March 11, 1995). ... On injured reserve with knee injury (November 4, 1997-remainder of season).
CHAMPIONSHIP GAME EXPERIENCE: Played in NFC championship game (1991 season). ... Played in AFC championship game (1996 season).
PRO STATISTICS: 1994—Recovered one fumble. 1996—Recovered two fumbles. 1997—Recovered one fumble.

Year Team	G	GS	SACKS
1991—Detroit NFL	16	0	1.5
1992—Detroit NFL	16	15	6.5
1993—Detroit NFL	16	5	4.0
1994—Detroit NFL	16	15	5.5
1995—Jacksonville NFL	16	16	1.5
1996—Jacksonville NFL	13	4	2.0
1997—Jacksonville NFL	8	5	3.0
Pro totals (7 years)	101	60	24.0

P

PRITCHETT, STANLEY FB DOLPHINS

PERSONAL: Born December 12, 1973, in Atlanta. ... 6-1/245. ... Full name: Stanley Jerome Pritchett.
HIGH SCHOOL: Frederick Douglass (College Park, Ga.).
COLLEGE: South Carolina.
TRANSACTIONS/CAREER NOTES: Selected by Miami Dolphins in fourth round (118th pick overall) of 1996 NFL draft. ... Signed by Dolphins (July 10, 1996).
PRO STATISTICS: 1996—Recovered one fumble.
SINGLE GAME HIGHS (regular season): Attempts—2 (November 25, 1996, vs. Pittsburgh); yards—16 (October 13, 1996, vs. Buffalo); and rushing touchdowns—0.

				RUSHING				RECEIVING				TOTALS		
Year Team	G	GS	Att.	Yds.	Avg.	TD	No.	Yds.	Avg.	TD	TD	2pt.	Pts.	Fum.
1996—Miami NFL	16	16	7	27	3.9	0	33	354	10.7	2	2	0	12	3
1997—Miami NFL	6	5	3	7	2.3	0	5	35	7.0	0	0	0	0	0
Pro totals (2 years)	22	21	10	34	3.4	0	38	389	10.2	2	2	0	12	3

PROEHL, RICKY WR RAMS

PERSONAL: Born March 7, 1968, in Belle Mead, N.J. ... 6-0/190. ... Full name: Richard Scott Proehl.
HIGH SCHOOL: Hillsborough (N.J.).
COLLEGE: Wake Forest.
TRANSACTIONS/CAREER NOTES: Selected by Phoenix Cardinals in third round (58th pick overall) of 1990 NFL draft. ... Signed by Cardinals (July 23, 1990). ... Granted free agency (March 1, 1993). ... Tendered offer sheet by New England Patriots (April 13, 1993). ... Offer matched by Cardinals (April 19, 1993). ... Cardinals franchise renamed Arizona Cardinals for 1994 season. ... Traded by Cardinals to Seattle Seahawks for fourth-round pick (traded to New York Jets) in 1995 draft (April 3, 1995). ... Released by Seahawks (March 7, 1997). ... Signed by Chicago Bears (April 10, 1997). ... Granted unconditional free agency (February 13, 1998). ... Signed by St. Louis Rams (February 24, 1998).
PRO STATISTICS: 1990—Returned one punt for two yards and returned four kickoffs for 53 yards. 1991—Returned four punts for 26 yards and recovered one fumble. 1992—Had only pass attempt intercepted and fumbled five times. 1993—Fumbled once. 1994—Fumbled twice and recovered two fumbles. 1997—Returned eight punts for 59 yards.
SINGLE GAME HIGHS (regular season): Receptions—11 (November 16, 1997, vs. New York Jets); yards—164 (November 27, 1997, vs. Detroit); and touchdown receptions—2 (October 10, 1993, vs. New England).
STATISTICAL PLATEAUS: 100-yard receiving games: 1990 (2), 1991 (1), 1992 (3), 1993 (1), 1997 (3). Total: 10.

				RUSHING				RECEIVING				TOTALS		
Year Team	G	GS	Att.	Yds.	Avg.	TD	No.	Yds.	Avg.	TD	TD	2pt.	Pts.	Fum.
1990—Phoenix NFL	16	2	1	4	4.0	0	56	802	14.3	4	4	...	24	0
1991—Phoenix NFL	16	16	3	21	7.0	0	55	766	13.9	2	2	...	12	0
1992—Phoenix NFL	16	15	3	23	7.7	0	60	744	12.4	3	3	...	18	5
1993—Phoenix NFL	16	16	8	47	5.9	0	65	877	13.5	7	7	...	42	1
1994—Arizona NFL	16	16	0	0	...	0	51	651	12.8	5	5	0	30	2
1995—Seattle NFL	8	0	0	0	...	0	5	29	5.8	0	0	0	0	0
1996—Seattle NFL	16	7	0	0	...	0	23	309	13.4	2	2	0	12	0
1997—Chicago NFL	15	10	0	0	...	0	58	753	13.0	7	7	1	44	2
Pro totals (8 years)	119	82	15	95	6.3	0	373	4931	13.2	30	30	1	182	10

PRYCE, TREVOR DT BRONCOS

PERSONAL: Born August 3, 1975, in Winter Park, Fla. ... 6-5/284.
HIGH SCHOOL: Lake Howell (Casselberry, Fla.).
COLLEGE: Clemson.
TRANSACTIONS/CAREER NOTES: Selected by Denver Broncos in first round (28th pick overall) of 1997 NFL draft. ... Signed by Broncos (July 24, 1997).
CHAMPIONSHIP GAME EXPERIENCE: Played in AFC championship game (1997 season). ... Member of Super Bowl championship team (1997 season).

Year Team	G	GS	SACKS
1997—Denver NFL	8	3	2.0

PUPUNU, ALFRED TE GIANTS

PERSONAL: Born October 17, 1969, in Tonga. ... 6-2/260. ... Full name: Alfred Sione Pupunu. ... Name pronounced puh-POO-noo.
HIGH SCHOOL: Salt Lake City South.
JUNIOR COLLEGE: Dixie College (Utah).
COLLEGE: Weber State.
TRANSACTIONS/CAREER NOTES: Signed as non-drafted free agent by Kansas City Chiefs (May 2, 1992). ... Claimed on waivers by San Diego Chargers (September 1, 1992). ... Granted unconditional free agency (February 16, 1996). ... Re-signed by Chargers (March 5, 1996). ... Released by Chargers (November 4, 1997). ... Signed by Chiefs (November 11, 1997). ... Released by Chiefs (November 25, 1997). ... Signed by New York Giants (December 22, 1997).
CHAMPIONSHIP GAME EXPERIENCE: Played in AFC championship game (1994 season). ... Played in Super Bowl XXIX (1994 season).
POST SEASON RECORDS: Shares Super Bowl and NFL postseason career and single-game records for most two-point conversions—1 (January 29, 1995, vs. San Francisco).
PRO STATISTICS: 1993—Recovered one fumble. 1995—Fumbled once. 1996—Returned one kickoff for 15 yards and recovered two fumbles. 1997—Recovered one fumble.
SINGLE GAME HIGHS (regular season): Receptions—6 (December 19, 1993, vs. Kansas City); yards—83 (September 29, 1996, vs. Kansas City); and touchdown receptions—1 (November 11, 1996, vs. Detroit).

P

Year Team	G	GS	RECEIVING				TOTALS			
			No.	Yds.	Avg.	TD	TD	2pt.	Pts.	Fum.
1992—San Diego NFL	15	2	0	0	...	0	0	...	0	0
1993—San Diego NFL	16	7	13	142	10.9	0	0	...	0	0
1994—San Diego NFL	13	10	21	214	10.2	2	2	0	12	0
1995—San Diego NFL	15	14	35	315	9.0	0	0	0	0	1
1996—San Diego NFL	9	8	24	271	11.3	1	1	0	6	1
1997—San Diego NFL	8	1	1	7	7.0	0	0	0	0	0
—Kansas City NFL	1	0	0	0	...	0	0	0	0	0
Pro totals (6 years)	77	42	94	949	10.1	3	3	0	18	2

PURNELL, LOVETT   TE   PATRIOTS

PERSONAL: Born April 7, 1972, in Seaford, Del. ... 6-3/245.
HIGH SCHOOL: Seaford (Del.).
COLLEGE: West Virginia.
TRANSACTIONS/CAREER NOTES: Selected by New England Patriots in seventh round (216th pick overall) of 1996 NFL draft. ... Signed by Patriots (July 11, 1996). ... Released by Patriots (October 9, 1996). ... Re-signed by Patriots to practice squad (October 11, 1996). ... Activated (December 10, 1996).
PLAYING EXPERIENCE: New England NFL, 1996 and 1997. ... Games/Games started: 1996 (2/0), 1997 (16/2). Total: 18/2.
CHAMPIONSHIP GAME EXPERIENCE: Member of Patriots for AFC championship game (1996 season); inactive. ... Member of Patriots for Super Bowl XXXI (1996 season); inactive.
PRO STATISTICS: 1997—Caught five passes for 57 yards and three touchdowns and recovered one fumble.
SINGLE GAME HIGHS (regular season): Receptions—2 (September 14, 1997, vs. New York Jets); yards—25 (September 14, 1997, vs. New York Jets); and touchdown receptions—1 (November 16, 1997, vs. Tampa Bay).

PURVIS, ANDRE   NT   BENGALS

PERSONAL: Born July 14, 1973, in Jacksonville. ... 6-4/304. ... Full name: Andre Lamont Purvis.
HIGH SCHOOL: White Oak (Jacksonville), then Swansboro (N.C.).
COLLEGE: North Carolina.
TRANSACTIONS/CAREER NOTES: Selected by Cincinnati Bengals in fifth round (144th overall) of 1997 NFL draft. ... Signed by Bengals (June 5, 1997).
PLAYING EXPERIENCE: Cincinnati NFL, 1997. ... Games/Games started: 7/1.

PYNE, JIM   C   LIONS

PERSONAL: Born November 23, 1971, in Milford, Mass. ... 6-2/297. ... Full name: James M. Pyne. ... Son of George Pyne III, tackle with Boston Patriots of AFL (1965); and grandson of George Pyne Jr., tackle with Providence Steamrollers of NFL (1931).
HIGH SCHOOL: Milford (Mass.).
COLLEGE: Virginia Tech.
TRANSACTIONS/CAREER NOTES: Selected by Tampa Bay Buccaneers in seventh round (200th pick overall) of 1994 NFL draft. ... Signed by Buccaneers (July 14, 1994). ... On injured reserve with broken leg (December 17, 1996-remainder of season). ... Granted free agency (February 14, 1997). ... Re-signed by Buccaneers (April 18, 1997). ... Granted unconditional free agency (February 13, 1998). ... Signed by Detroit Lions (February 21, 1998).
PLAYING EXPERIENCE: Tampa Bay NFL, 1995-1997. ... Games/Games started: 1995 (15/13), 1996 (12/11), 1997 (15/14). Total: 42/38.
HONORS: Named offensive lineman on THE SPORTING NEWS college All-America first team (1993).
PRO STATISTICS: 1995—Recovered one fumble. 1997—Fumbled one for minus five yards.

QUARLES, SHELTON   LB   BUCCANEERS

PERSONAL: Born September 11, 1971, in Nashville. ... 6-1/236.
HIGH SCHOOL: Whites Creek (Nashville).
COLLEGE: Vanderbilt.
TRANSACTIONS/CAREER NOTES: Signed as free agent by B.C. Lions of CFL (December 1, 1994). ... Granted free agency (February 16, 1997). ... Signed by Tampa Bay Buccaneers (March 21, 1997).
PLAYING EXPERIENCE: B.C. CFL, 1995 and 1996; Tampa Bay NFL, 1997. ... Games/Games started: 1995 (16/games started unavailable), 1996 (16/games started unavailable), 1997 (16/0). Total CFL: 32/games started unavailable. Total NFL: 16/0. Total Pro: 48/games started unavailable.
PRO STATISTICS: CFL: 1995—Intercepted one pass for no yards and recovered one fumble for 14 yards. 1996—Credited with 10 sacks and intercepted one pass for 22 yards. NFL: 1997—Recovered two fumbles.

QUINN, MIKE   QB   STEELERS

PERSONAL: Born April 15, 1974, in Houston. ... 6-3/220. ... Full name: Michael Patrick Quinn.
HIGH SCHOOL: Robert E. Lee (Houston).
COLLEGE: Stephen F. Austin.
TRANSACTIONS/CAREER NOTES: Signed as non-drafted free agent by Pittsburgh Steelers (April 21, 1997). ... Assigned by Steelers to Rhein Fire in 1998 NFL Europe enhancement allocation program (February 18, 1998).
PLAYING EXPERIENCE: Pittsburgh NFL, 1997. ... Games/Games started: 1/0.
CHAMPIONSHIP GAME EXPERIENCE: Member of Steelers for AFC championship game (1997 season); inactive.
PRO STATISTICS: 1997—Attempted two passes with one completion for 10 yards.
SINGLE GAME HIGHS (regular season): Attempts—2 (November 9, 1997, vs. Baltimore); completions—1 (November 9, 1997, vs. Baltimore); yards—10 (November 9, 1997, vs. Baltimore); and touchdown passes—0.

RACHAL, LATARIO — WR/KR — CHARGERS

PERSONAL: Born January 31, 1973, in Lynwood, Calif. ... 5-11/183. ... Full name: Latario Deshawn Rachal.
HIGH SCHOOL: Carson (Calif.).
JUNIOR COLLEGE: El Camino (Torrance, Calif.).
COLLEGE: Fresno State.
TRANSACTIONS/CAREER NOTES: Signed as non-drafted free agent by San Diego Chargers (February 27, 1997). ... Assigned by Chargers to Amsterdam Admirals in 1997 World League enhancement allocation program (February 27, 1997).
PLAYING EXPERIENCE: Amsterdam W.L., 1997; San Diego NFL, 1997. ... Games/Games started: W.L. 1997 (games played unavailable); NFL 1997 (14/0).
PRO STATISTICS: W.L.: 1997—Caught 14 passes for 141 yards and one touchdown and returned one kickoff for 37 yards. NFL: 1997— Returned 15 kickoffs for 336 yards, fumbled once and recovered one fumble.
SINGLE GAME HIGHS (regular season): Receptions—0; yards—0; and touchdown receptions—0.

RAMIREZ, TONY — OT — LIONS

PERSONAL: Born January 26, 1973, in Lincoln, Neb. ... 6-6/296.
HIGH SCHOOL: Northglenn (Colo.), then Lincoln (Neb.).
COLLEGE: Northern Colorado.
TRANSACTIONS/CAREER NOTES: Selected by Detroit Lions in sixth round (168th pick overall) of 1997 NFL draft. ... Signed by Lions (July 11, 1997).
PLAYING EXPERIENCE: Detroit NFL, 1997. ... Games/Games started: 2/0.

RANDLE, JOHN — DT — VIKINGS

PERSONAL: Born December 12, 1967, in Hearne, Texas. ... 6-1/285. ... Brother of Ervin Randle, linebacker with Tampa Bay Buccaneers (1985-1990) and Kansas City Chiefs (1991 and 1992).
HIGH SCHOOL: Hearne (Texas).
JUNIOR COLLEGE: Trinity Valley Community College (Texas).
COLLEGE: Texas A&I.
TRANSACTIONS/CAREER NOTES: Signed as non-drafted free agent by Minnesota Vikings (May 4, 1990). ... Designated by Vikings as transition player (January 15, 1994). ... Designated by Vikings as transition player (February 13, 1998). ... Tendered offer sheet by Miami Dolphins (February 16, 1998). ... Offer matched by Vikings (February 17, 1998).
HONORS: Played in Pro Bowl (1993-1997 seasons). ... Named defensive tackle on THE SPORTING NEWS NFL All-Pro team (1994-1997).
PRO STATISTICS: 1992—Recovered one fumble. 1994—Recovered two fumbles. 1997—Recovered two fumbles for five yards.

Year Team	G	GS	SACKS
1990—Minnesota NFL	16	0	1.0
1991—Minnesota NFL	16	8	9.5
1992—Minnesota NFL	16	14	11.5
1993—Minnesota NFL	16	16	12.5
1994—Minnesota NFL	16	16	∞13.5
1995—Minnesota NFL	16	16	10.5
1996—Minnesota NFL	16	16	11.5
1997—Minnesota NFL	16	16	*15.5
Pro totals (8 years)	128	102	85.5

RANDOLPH, THOMAS — CB — BENGALS

PERSONAL: Born October 5, 1970, in Norfolk, Va. ... 5-9/185. ... Full name: Thomas C. Randolph.
HIGH SCHOOL: Manhattan (Kan.).
COLLEGE: Kansas State.
TRANSACTIONS/CAREER NOTES: Selected by New York Giants in second round (47th pick overall) of 1994 NFL draft. ... Signed by Giants (July 17, 1994). ... Granted unconditional free agency (February 13, 1998). ... Signed by Cincinnati Bengals (March 4, 1998).
PRO STATISTICS: 1995—Recovered one fumble. 1996—Recovered one fumble for 17 yards.

Year Team	G	GS	INTERCEPTIONS No.	Yds.	Avg.	TD
1994—New York Giants NFL	16	10	1	0	0.0	0
1995—New York Giants NFL	16	16	2	15	7.5	0
1996—New York Giants NFL	16	2	0	0	...	0
1997—New York Giants NFL	16	4	1	1	1.0	0
Pro totals (4 years)	64	32	4	16	4.0	0

RASBY, WALTER — TE — LIONS

PERSONAL: Born September 7, 1972, in Washington, D.C. ... 6-3/247. ... Full name: Walter Herbert Rasby.
HIGH SCHOOL: Washington (N.C.).
COLLEGE: Wake Forest.
TRANSACTIONS/CAREER NOTES: Signed as non-drafted free agent by Pittsburgh Steelers (April 29, 1994). ... Released by Steelers (August 27, 1995). ... Signed by Carolina Panthers (October 17, 1995). ... Granted free agency (February 14, 1997). ... Re-signed by Panthers (June 3, 1997). ... On injured reserve with knee injury (December 10, 1997-remainder of season). ... Granted unconditional free agency (February 13, 1998). ... Signed by Detroit Lions (April 23, 1998).
PLAYING EXPERIENCE: Pittsburgh NFL, 1994; Carolina NFL, 1995-1997. ... Games/Games started: 1994 (2/0), 1995 (9/2), 1996 (16/1), 1997 (14/2). Total: 41/5.

CHAMPIONSHIP GAME EXPERIENCE: Played in AFC championship game (1994 season). ... Played in NFC championship game (1996 season).
PRO STATISTICS: 1995—Credited with one two-point conversion and caught five passes for 47 yards. 1996—Recovered one fumble. 1997—Caught one pass for one yard and returned three kickoffs for 32 yards.
SINGLE GAME HIGHS (regular season): Receptions—1 (December 8, 1997, vs. Dallas); yards—15 (November 12, 1995, vs. St. Louis); and touchdown receptions—0.

RAVOTTI, ERIC — LB — STEELERS

PERSONAL: Born March 16, 1971, in Freeport, Pa. ... 6-2/250. ... Full name: Eric Allen Ravotti.
HIGH SCHOOL: Freeport (Pa.) Area.
COLLEGE: Penn State.
TRANSACTIONS/CAREER NOTES: Selected by Pittsburgh Steelers in sixth round (180th pick overall) of 1994 NFL draft. ... Signed by Steelers (May 6, 1994). ... Granted unconditional free agency (February 14, 1997). ... Re-signed by Steelers (April 17, 1997). ... Released by Steelers (August 24, 1997). ... Re-signed by Steelers (April 23, 1998).
PLAYING EXPERIENCE: Pittsburgh NFL, 1994-1996. ... Games/Games started: 1994 (2/0), 1995 (6/1), 1996 (15/2). Total: 23/3.
CHAMPIONSHIP GAME EXPERIENCE: Member of Steelers for AFC championship game (1994 and 1995 seasons); inactive.
PRO STATISTICS: 1996—Credited with two sacks and recovered one fumble for nine yards.

RAYBON, ISRAEL — DE

PERSONAL: Born February 5, 1973, in Lee, Ala. ... 6-6/293. ... Full name: Israel Deshon Raybon.
HIGH SCHOOL: Lee (Huntsville, Ala.).
COLLEGE: North Alabama.
TRANSACTIONS/CAREER NOTES: Selected by Pittsburgh Steelers in fifth round (163rd pick overall) of 1996 NFL draft. ... Signed by Steelers (July 16, 1996). ... Traded by Steelers to Carolina Panthers for seventh-round pick (traded to Atlanta) in 1998 draft (August 24, 1997). ... Released by Panthers (December 15, 1997).

Year Team	G	GS	SACKS
1996—Pittsburgh NFL	3	0	1.0
1997—Carolina NFL	9	0	0.5
Pro totals (2 years)	12	0	1.5

RAYMER, CORY — C — REDSKINS

PERSONAL: Born March 3, 1973, in Fond du Lac, Wis. ... 6-2/289.
HIGH SCHOOL: Goodrich (Fond du Lac, Wis.).
COLLEGE: Wisconsin.
TRANSACTIONS/CAREER NOTES: Selected by Washington Redskins in second round (37th pick overall) of 1995 NFL draft. ... Signed by Redskins (July 24, 1995). ... On injured reserve with back injury (November 25, 1996-remainder of season).
PLAYING EXPERIENCE: Washington NFL, 1995-1997. ... Games/Games started: 1995 (3/2), 1996 (6/5), 1997 (6/3). Total: 15/10.
HONORS: Named offensive lineman on THE SPORTING NEWS college All-America first team (1994).
PRO STATISTICS: 1996—Recovered one fumble.

RAYMOND, COREY — CB

PERSONAL: Born July 28, 1969, in New Iberia, La. ... 5-11/185.
HIGH SCHOOL: New Iberia (La.).
COLLEGE: Louisiana State.
TRANSACTIONS/CAREER NOTES: Signed as non-drafted free agent by New York Giants (May 5, 1992). ... Selected by Jacksonville Jaguars from Giants in NFL expansion draft (February 15, 1995). ... Granted free agency (February 17, 1995). ... Traded by Jaguars to Detroit Lions for TE Ty Hallock (May 30, 1995). ... Granted unconditional free agency (February 16, 1996). ... Released by Lions (February 3, 1998).
PRO STATISTICS: 1992—Credited with one sack. 1995—Credited with two sacks and recovered one fumble for nine yards.

Year Team	G	GS	INTERCEPTIONS No.	Yds.	Avg.	TD
1992—New York Giants NFL	16	0	0	0	...	0
1993—New York Giants NFL	16	8	2	11	5.5	0
1994—New York Giants NFL	16	12	1	0	0.0	0
1995—Detroit NFL	16	15	6	44	7.3	0
1996—Detroit NFL	13	13	1	24	24.0	1
1997—Detroit NFL	13	12	1	17	17.0	0
Pro totals (6 years)	90	60	11	96	8.7	1

REDMON, ANTHONY — G

PERSONAL: Born April 9, 1971, in Brewton, Ala. ... 6-5/308. ... Full name: Kendrick Anthony Redmon.
HIGH SCHOOL: T. R. Miller (Brewton, Ala.).
COLLEGE: Auburn.
TRANSACTIONS/CAREER NOTES: Selected by Arizona Cardinals in fifth round (139th pick overall) of 1994 NFL draft. ... Signed by Cardinals (June 13, 1994). ... Granted free agency (February 14, 1997). ... Re-signed by Cardinals (June 13, 1997). ... Granted unconditional free agency (February 13, 1998).
PLAYING EXPERIENCE: Arizona NFL, 1994-1997. ... Games/Games started: 1994 (6/5), 1995 (12/9), 1996 (16/16), 1997 (16/16). Total: 50/46.
PRO STATISTICS: 1996—Recovered one fumble.

REED, ANDRE WR BILLS

PERSONAL: Born January 29, 1964, in Allentown, Pa. ... 6-2/190. ... Full name: Andre Darnell Reed.

HIGH SCHOOL: Louis E. Dieruff (Allentown, Pa.).

COLLEGE: Kutztown (Pa.) State.

TRANSACTIONS/CAREER NOTES: Selected by Orlando Renegades in third round (39th pick overall) of 1985 USFL draft. ... Selected by Buffalo Bills in fourth round (86th pick overall) of 1985 NFL draft. ... Signed by Bills (July 19, 1985). ... Granted unconditional free agency (February 16, 1996). ... Re-signed by Bills (May 7, 1996). ... On injured reserve with shoulder injury (December 18, 1997-remainder of season).

CHAMPIONSHIP GAME EXPERIENCE: Played in AFC championship game (1988 and 1990-1993 seasons). ... Played in Super Bowl XXV (1990 season), Super Bowl XXVI (1991 season), Super Bowl XXVII (1992 season) and Super Bowl XXVIII (1993 season).

HONORS: Played in Pro Bowl (1988-1990, 1992 and 1994 seasons). ... Member of Pro Bowl squad (1991 season); did not play. ... Named to play in Pro Bowl (1993 season); replaced by Haywood Jeffires due to injury.

POST SEASON RECORDS: Shares NFL postseason single-game record for most touchdown receptions—3 (January 3, 1993, OT, vs. Houston).

PRO STATISTICS: 1985—Returned five punts for 12 yards and recovered two fumbles. 1986—Recovered two fumbles for two yards. 1990—Recovered one fumble. 1994—Attempted one pass with one completion for 32 yards and recovered two fumbles.

SINGLE GAME HIGHS (regular season): Receptions—15 (November 20, 1994, vs. Green Bay); yards—191 (November 20, 1994, vs. Green Bay); and touchdown receptions—3 (September 5, 1993, vs. New England).

STATISTICAL PLATEAUS: 100-yard receiving games: 1985 (1), 1987 (2), 1988 (3), 1989 (6), 1990 (2), 1991 (4), 1992 (2), 1993 (2), 1994 (5), 1996 (5), 1997 (2). Total: 34.

MISCELLANEOUS: Active AFC leader for career receiving yards (11,764). ... Holds Buffalo Bills all-time record for most receptions (826), most yards receiving (11,764) and most touchdown receptions (80).

| | | | RUSHING | | | | RECEIVING | | | | TOTALS | | | |
Year Team	G	GS	Att.	Yds.	Avg.	TD	No.	Yds.	Avg.	TD	TD	2pt.	Pts.	Fum.
1985—Buffalo NFL	16	15	3	-1	-0.3	1	48	637	13.3	4	5	...	30	1
1986—Buffalo NFL	15	15	3	-8	-2.7	0	53	739	13.9	7	7	...	42	2
1987—Buffalo NFL	12	12	1	1	1.0	0	57	752	13.2	5	5	...	30	0
1988—Buffalo NFL	15	14	6	64	10.7	0	71	968	13.6	6	6	...	36	1
1989—Buffalo NFL	16	16	2	31	15.5	0	§88	§1312	14.9	9	9	...	54	4
1990—Buffalo NFL	16	16	3	23	7.7	0	71	945	13.3	8	8	...	48	1
1991—Buffalo NFL	16	16	12	136	11.3	0	81	1113	13.7	10	10	...	60	1
1992—Buffalo NFL	16	16	8	65	8.1	0	65	913	14.0	3	3	...	18	4
1993—Buffalo NFL	15	15	9	21	2.3	0	52	854	16.4	6	6	...	36	3
1994—Buffalo NFL	16	16	10	87	8.7	0	90	1303	14.5	8	8	0	48	3
1995—Buffalo NFL	6	6	7	48	6.9	0	24	312	13.0	3	3	0	18	2
1996—Buffalo NFL	16	16	8	22	2.8	0	66	1036	15.7	6	6	0	36	1
1997—Buffalo NFL	15	15	3	11	3.7	0	60	880	14.7	5	5	0	30	1
Pro totals (13 years)	190	188	75	500	6.7	1	826	11764	14.2	80	81	0	486	24

REED, JAKE WR VIKINGS

PERSONAL: Born September 28, 1967, in Covington, Ga. ... 6-3/219. ... Full name: Willis Reed. ... Brother of Dale Carter, cornerback, Kansas City Chiefs.

HIGH SCHOOL: Newton County (Covington, Ga.).

COLLEGE: Grambling State (degree in criminal justice).

TRANSACTIONS/CAREER NOTES: Selected by Minnesota Vikings in third round (68th pick overall) of 1991 NFL draft. ... Signed by Vikings (July 22, 1991). ... On injured reserve with ankle injury (November 2, 1991-remainder of season). ... Granted free agency (February 17, 1994). ... Re-signed by Vikings (May 6, 1994). ... Granted unconditional free agency (February 17, 1995). ... Re-signed by Vikings (February 28, 1995).

PRO STATISTICS: 1992—Returned one kickoff for one yard. 1995—Recovered one fumble.

SINGLE GAME HIGHS (regular season): Receptions—12 (September 7, 1997, vs. Chicago); yards—157 (November 6, 1994, vs. New Orleans); and touchdown receptions—2 (November 23, 1997, vs. New York Jets).

STATISTICAL PLATEAUS: 100-yard receiving games: 1994 (3), 1995 (3), 1996 (3), 1997 (5). Total: 14.

| | | | RECEIVING | | | | TOTALS | | | |
Year Team	G	GS	No.	Yds.	Avg.	TD	TD	2pt.	Pts.	Fum.
1991—Minnesota NFL	1	0	0	0	...	0	0	...	0	0
1992—Minnesota NFL	16	0	6	142	23.7	0	0	...	0	0
1993—Minnesota NFL	10	1	5	65	13.0	0	0	...	0	0
1994—Minnesota NFL	16	16	85	1175	13.8	4	4	0	24	3
1995—Minnesota NFL	16	16	72	1167	16.2	9	9	0	54	1
1996—Minnesota NFL	16	15	72	1320	18.3	7	7	0	42	0
1997—Minnesota NFL	16	16	68	1138	16.7	6	6	0	36	0
Pro totals (7 years)	91	64	308	5007	16.3	26	26	0	156	4

REESE, ALBERT DT 49ERS

PERSONAL: Born April 29, 1973, in Mobile, Ala. ... 6-6/294.

HIGH SCHOOL: Vigor (Mobile, Ala.).

COLLEGE: Grambling State.

TRANSACTIONS/CAREER NOTES: Signed as non-drafted free agent by San Francisco 49ers (April 23, 1996). ... Released by 49ers (August 20, 1996). ... Re-signed by 49ers to practice squad (August 26, 1996). ... Released by 49ers (August 24, 1997). ... Re-signed by 49ers to practice squad (August 25, 1997). ... Released by 49ers (October 21, 1997). ... Re-signed by 49ers (November 5, 1997).

PLAYING EXPERIENCE: San Francisco NFL, 1997. ... Games/Games started: 5/0.

CHAMPIONSHIP GAME EXPERIENCE: Member of 49ers for NFC championship game (1997 season); inactive.

REESE, JERRY   WR/KR   BILLS

PERSONAL: Born March 18, 1973, in Berkeley, Calif. ... 5-11/190. ... Full name: Jerry Maurice Reese.
HIGH SCHOOL: Mount Diablo (Concord, Calif.).
COLLEGE: San Jose State.
TRANSACTIONS/CAREER NOTES: Played with San Jose SaberCats of Arena League (1995 and 1996). ... Signed by Buffalo Bills (March 26, 1997). ... Released by Bills (September 5, 1997). ... Re-signed by Bills to practice squad (September 6, 1997). ... Activated (October 5, 1997). ... Released by Bills (November 5, 1997). ... Re-signed by Bills to practice squad (November 6, 1997). ... Activated (December 1, 1997). ... Released by Bills (December 12, 1997). ... Re-signed by Bills to practice squad (December 15, 1997). ... Activated (December 18, 1997). ... Assigned by Bills to Scotland Claymores in 1998 NFL Europe enhancement allocation program (February 18, 1998).
PLAYING EXPERIENCE: Buffalo NFL, 1997. ... Games/Games started: 5/0.
PRO STATISTICS: 1997—Caught one pass for 13 yards.
SINGLE GAME HIGHS (regular season): Receptions—1 (December 20, 1997, vs. Green Bay); yards—13 (December 20, 1997, vs. Green Bay); and touchdown receptions—0.

REEVES, CARL   DE   BEARS

PERSONAL: Born December 17, 1971, in Durham, N.C. ... 6-4/270.
HIGH SCHOOL: Northern Durham (N.C.).
COLLEGE: North Carolina State.
TRANSACTIONS/CAREER NOTES: Selected by Chicago Bears in sixth round (198th pick overall) of 1995 NFL draft. ... Signed by Bears (June 27, 1995). ... On injured reserve with back injury (August 22, 1995-entire season). ... Assigned by Bears to Barcelona Dragons in 1997 World League enhancement allocation program (February 19, 1997).
PLAYING EXPERIENCE: Chicago NFL, 1996 and 1997. ... Games/Games started: 1996 (5/0), 1997 (15/11). Total: 20/11.
PRO STATISTICS: 1997—Credited with 1/2 sack and recovered one fumble.

REHBERG, SCOTT   OT   PATRIOTS

PERSONAL: Born November 17, 1973, in Kalamazoo, Mich. ... 6-8/336. ... Full name: Scott Joseph Rehberg. ... Name pronounced RAY-berg.
HIGH SCHOOL: Central (Kalamazoo, Mich.).
COLLEGE: Central Michigan.
TRANSACTIONS/CAREER NOTES: Selected by New England Patriots in seventh round (230th pick overall) of 1997 NFL draft. ... Signed by Patriots (June 19, 1997).
PLAYING EXPERIENCE: New England NFL, 1997. ... Games/Games started: 6/0.

REICH, FRANK   QB   LIONS

PERSONAL: Born December 4, 1961, in Freeport, N.Y. ... 6-4/210. ... Full name: Frank Michael Reich. ... Name pronounced RIKE.
HIGH SCHOOL: Cedar Crest (Lebanon, Pa.).
COLLEGE: Maryland (degree in finance, 1984).
TRANSACTIONS/CAREER NOTES: Selected by Tampa Bay Bandits in 1985 USFL territorial draft. ... Selected by Buffalo Bills in third round (57th pick overall) of 1985 NFL draft. ... Signed by Bills (August 1, 1985). ... On injured reserve with Achilles' tendon injury (September 3-December 6, 1985). ... Active for 12 games with Bills (1987); did not play. ... Granted unconditional free agency (February 17, 1995). ... Signed by Carolina Panthers (March 27, 1995). ... Granted unconditional free agency (February 16, 1996). ... Signed by New York Jets (April 11, 1996). ... Released by Jets (March 3, 1997). ... Signed by Detroit Lions (March 6, 1997).
CHAMPIONSHIP GAME EXPERIENCE: Member of Bills for AFC championship game (1988 season); did not play. ... Played in AFC championship game (1990-1993 seasons). ... Played in Super Bowl XXV (1990 season), Super Bowl XXVI (1991 season), Super Bowl XXVII (1992 season) and Super Bowl XXVIII (1993 season).
POST SEASON RECORDS: Shares Super Bowl single-game record for most fumbles—3 (January 31, 1993, vs. Dallas).
PRO STATISTICS: 1986—Fumbled once. 1989—Fumbled twice. 1990—Fumbled once. 1992—Fumbled three times and recovered two fumbles for minus four yards. 1994—Fumbled once and recovered one fumble. 1995—Fumbled three times and recovered one fumble. 1996—Fumbled nine times and recovered one fumble for minus 70 yards.
SINGLE GAME HIGHS (regular season): Attempts—50 (November 24, 1996, vs. Buffalo); completions—26 (December 24, 1994, vs. Indianapolis); yards—352 (November 17, 1996, vs. Indianapolis); and touchdown passes—3 (November 17, 1996, vs. Indianapolis).
STATISTICAL PLATEAUS: 300-yard passing games: 1995 (1), 1996 (1). Total: 2.
MISCELLANEOUS: Regular-season record as starting NFL quarterback: 5-13 (.278). Postseason record as starting NFL quarterback: 2-0.

				PASSING							RUSHING				TOTALS		
Year	Team	G	GS	Att.	Cmp.	Pct.	Yds.	TD	Int.	Avg.	Rat.	Att.	Yds.	Avg.	TD	TD	2pt.	Pts.
1985—Buffalo NFL		1	0	1	1	100.0	19	0	0	19.00	118.8	0	0	...	0	0	...	0
1986—Buffalo NFL		3	0	19	9	47.4	104	0	2	5.47	24.8	1	0	0.0	0	0	...	0
1987—Buffalo NFL										Did not play.								
1988—Buffalo NFL		3	0	0	0		0	0	0	...	...	3	-3	-1.0	0	0	...	0
1989—Buffalo NFL		7	3	87	53	60.9	701	7	2	8.06	103.7	9	30	3.3	0	0	...	0
1990—Buffalo NFL		16	2	63	36	57.1	469	2	0	7.44	91.3	15	24	1.6	0	0	...	0
1991—Buffalo NFL		16	1	41	27	65.9	305	6	2	7.44	107.2	13	6	0.5	0	0	...	0
1992—Buffalo NFL		16	0	47	24	51.1	221	0	2	4.70	46.5	9	-9	-1.0	0	0	...	0
1993—Buffalo NFL		15	0	26	16	61.5	153	2	0	5.88	103.5	6	-6	-1.0	0	0	...	0
1994—Buffalo NFL		16	2	93	56	60.2	568	1	4	6.11	63.4	6	3	0.5	0	0	0	0
1995—Carolina NFL		3	3	84	37	44.0	441	2	2	5.25	58.7	1	3	3.0	0	0	0	0
1996—New York Jets NFL		10	7	331	175	52.9	2205	15	16	6.66	68.9	18	31	1.7	0	0	0	0
1997—Detroit NFL		6	0	30	11	36.7	121	0	0	4.03	21.7	4	-4	-1.0	0	0	0	0
Pro totals (12 years)		112	18	822	445	54.1	5307	35	32	6.46	72.1	85	75	0.9	0	0	0	0

REYNOLDS, JERRY   OT   GIANTS

PERSONAL: Born April 2, 1970, in Fort Thomas, Ky. ... 6-6/325. ... Full name: Jerry Bradford Reynolds.
HIGH SCHOOL: Highlands (Fort Thomas, Ky.).
COLLEGE: UNLV.
TRANSACTIONS/CAREER NOTES: Selected by Cincinnati Bengals in sixth round (184th pick overall) of 1994 NFL draft. ... Signed by Bengals for 1994 season. ... Released by Bengals (August 25, 1994). ... Re-signed by Bengals to practice squad (August 30, 1994). ... Signed by Dallas Cowboys off Bengals practice squad (November 2, 1994). ... Active for one game (1994); did not play. ... Granted free agency after 1994 season and re-signed by Cowboys (April 25, 1995). ... Released by Cowboys (August 27, 1995). ... Signed by New York Giants (August 31, 1995). ... Granted free agency (February 14, 1997). ... Re-signed by Giants (August, 1997). ... Granted unconditional free agency (February 13, 1998). ... Re-signed by Giants (March 10, 1998).
PLAYING EXPERIENCE: New York Giants NFL, 1996 and 1997. ... Games/Games started: 1996 (8/0), 1997 (5/0). Total: 13/0.
CHAMPIONSHIP GAME EXPERIENCE: Member of Cowboys for NFC championship game (1994 season); inactive.

R

RHETT, ERRICT   RB   RAVENS

PERSONAL: Born December 11, 1970, in Pembroke Pines, Fla. ... 5-11/210. ... Full name: Errict Undra Rhett.
HIGH SCHOOL: McArthur (Hollywood, Fla.).
COLLEGE: Florida (degree in commercial management).
TRANSACTIONS/CAREER NOTES: Selected by Tampa Bay Buccaneers in second round (34th pick overall) of 1994 NFL draft. ... Signed by Buccaneers (August 9, 1994). ... Granted free agency (February 13, 1998). ... Traded by Buccaneers to Baltimore Ravens for third-round pick in 1999 draft (February 17, 1998).
HONORS: Named running back on THE SPORTING NEWS college All-America second team (1993).
PRO STATISTICS: 1994—Recovered one fumble. 1995—Recovered one fumble. 1996—Recovered one fumble. 1997—Returned one kickoff for 16 yards.
SINGLE GAME HIGHS (regular season): Attempts—40 (December 4, 1994, vs. Washington); yards—192 (December 4, 1994, vs. Washington); and rushing touchdowns—2 (November 19, 1995, vs. Jacksonville).
STATISTICAL PLATEAUS: 100-yard rushing games: 1994 (4), 1995 (4). Total: 8.

			RUSHING				RECEIVING				TOTALS		
Year Team	G	GS	Att.	Yds.	Avg.	TD	No.	Yds.	Avg.	TD	TD	2pt.	Pts.	Fum.
1994—Tampa Bay NFL	16	8	284	1011	3.6	7	22	119	5.4	0	7	1	44	2
1995—Tampa Bay NFL	16	16	332	1207	3.6	11	14	110	7.9	0	11	0	66	2
1996—Tampa Bay NFL	9	7	176	539	3.1	3	4	11	2.8	1	4	0	24	3
1997—Tampa Bay NFL	11	0	31	96	3.1	3	0	0	...	0	3	0	18	0
Pro totals (4 years)	52	31	823	2853	3.5	24	40	240	6.0	1	25	1	152	7

RICE, JERRY   WR   49ERS

PERSONAL: Born October 13, 1962, in Starkville, Miss. ... 6-2/196. ... Full name: Jerry Lee Rice.
HIGH SCHOOL: B.L. Moor (Crawford, Miss.).
COLLEGE: Mississippi Valley State.
TRANSACTIONS/CAREER NOTES: Selected by Birmingham Stallions in first round (first pick overall) of 1985 USFL draft. ... Selected by San Francisco 49ers in first round (16th pick overall) of 1985 NFL draft. ... Signed by 49ers (July 23, 1985). ... Granted free agency (February 1, 1992). ... Re-signed by 49ers (August 25, 1992). ... On injured reserve with knee injury (December 23, 1997-remainder of season).
CHAMPIONSHIP GAME EXPERIENCE: Played in NFC championship game (1988-1990 and 1992-1994 seasons). ... Member of Super Bowl championship team (1988, 1989 and 1994 seasons).
HONORS: Named wide receiver on THE SPORTING NEWS college All-America first team (1984). ... Named wide receiver on THE SPORTING NEWS NFL All-Pro team (1986-1996). ... Played in Pro Bowl (1986, 1987, 1989-1993 and 1995 seasons). ... Named NFL Player of the Year by THE SPORTING NEWS (1987 and 1990). ... Named Most Valuable Player of Super Bowl XXIII (1988 season). ... Named to play in Pro Bowl (1988 season); replaced by J.T. Smith due to injury. ... Named to play in Pro Bowl (1994 season); replaced by Herman Moore due to injury. ... Named Outstanding Player of Pro Bowl (1995 season). ... Named to play in Pro Bowl (1996 season); replaced by Irving Fryar due to injury.
RECORDS: Holds NFL career records for most touchdowns—166; most touchdown receptions—155; most receiving yards—16,455; most pass receptions—1,057; most seasons with 1,000 or more yards receiving—11; most games with 100 or more yards receiving—61; and most consecutive games with one or more touchdown reception—13 (December 19, 1986-December 27, 1987). ... Holds NFL single-season record for most yards receiving—1,848 (1995); and most touchdown receptions—22 (1987). ... Shares NFL single-game record for most touchdown receptions—5 (October 14, 1990, at Atlanta).
POST SEASON RECORDS: Holds Super Bowl career records for most points—42; most touchdowns—7; most touchdown receptions—7; most receptions—28; most combined yards—527; and most yards receiving—512. ... Holds Super Bowl single-game records for most touchdowns receptions—3 (January 28, 1990, vs. Denver and January 29, 1995, vs. San Diego); and most yards receiving—215 (January 22, 1989, vs. Cincinnati). ... Shares Super Bowl single-game records for most points—18; most touchdowns—3 (January 28, 1990, vs. Denver and January 29, 1995, vs. San Diego); and most receptions—11 (January 22, 1989, vs. Cincinnati). ... Holds NFL postseason career records for most touchdowns—18; most touchdown receptions—18; most receptions—120; most yards receiving—1,742; and most games with 100 or more yards receiving—7. ... Shares NFL postseason career record for most consecutive games with 100 or more yards receiving—3. ... Shares NFL postseason single-game record for most touchdown receptions—3 (January 28, 1990, vs. Denver; January 1, 1989, vs. Minnesota; and January 29, 1995, vs. San Diego).
PRO STATISTICS: 1985—Returned one kickoff for six yards. 1986—Attempted two passes with one completion for 16 yards and recovered three fumbles. 1987—Recovered one fumble. 1988—Attempted three passes with one completion for 14 yards and one interception and recovered one fumble. 1993—Recovered one fumble. 1995—Attempted one pass with one completion for 41 yards and a touchdown and recovered one fumble in end zone for a touchdown. 1996—Attempted one pass without a completion.
SINGLE GAME HIGHS (regular season): Receptions—16 (November 20, 1994, vs. Los Angeles Rams); yards—289 (December 18, 1995, vs. Minnesota); and touchdown receptions—5 (October 14, 1990, vs. Atlanta).
STATISTICAL PLATEAUS: 100-yard receiving games: 1985 (2), 1986 (6), 1987 (4), 1988 (5), 1989 (8), 1990 (7), 1991 (4), 1992 (3), 1993 (5), 1994 (5), 1995 (9), 1996 (3). Total: 61.
MISCELLANEOUS: Active NFL leader for career receiving yards (16,455) and touchdowns (166). ... Holds San Francisco 49ers all-time records for most yards receiving (16,455), most touchdowns (166), most receptions (1,057) and most touchdown receptions (155).

Year Team	G	GS	RUSHING				RECEIVING				TOTALS			
			Att.	Yds.	Avg.	TD	No.	Yds.	Avg.	TD	TD	2pt.	Pts.	Fum.
1985—San Francisco NFL	16	4	6	26	4.3	1	49	927	18.9	3	4	...	24	1
1986—San Francisco NFL	16	15	10	72	7.2	1	‡86	*1570	18.3	15	16	...	96	2
1987—San Francisco NFL	12	12	8	51	6.4	1	65	1078	16.6	22	*23	...	*138	2
1988—San Francisco NFL	16	16	13	107	8.2	1	64	1306	20.4	9	10	...	60	2
1989—San Francisco NFL	16	16	5	33	6.6	0	82	*1483	18.1	17	17	...	102	0
1990—San Francisco NFL	16	16	2	0	0.0	0	*100	*1502	15.0	13	13	...	78	1
1991—San Francisco NFL	16	16	1	2	2.0	1	80	1206	15.1	14	14	...	84	1
1992—San Francisco NFL	16	16	9	58	6.4	1	84	1201	14.3	10	11	...	66	2
1993—San Francisco NFL	16	16	3	69	23.0	1	98	*1503	15.3	15	*16	...	96	3
1994—San Francisco NFL	16	16	7	93	13.3	2	112	*1499	13.4	13	15	1	92	1
1995—San Francisco NFL	16	16	5	36	7.2	1	122	*1848	15.1	15	17	1	104	3
1996—San Francisco NFL	16	16	11	77	7.0	1	*108	1254	11.6	8	9	0	54	0
1997—San Francisco NFL	2	1	1	-10	-10.0	0	7	78	11.1	1	1	0	6	0
Pro totals (13 years)	190	176	81	614	7.6	10	1057	16455	15.6	155	166	2	1000	18

RICE, RON   S   LIONS

PERSONAL: Born November 9, 1972, in Detroit. ... 6-1/206. ... Full name: Ronald Wilson Rice.
HIGH SCHOOL: University of Detroit Jesuit.
COLLEGE: Eastern Michigan.
TRANSACTIONS/CAREER NOTES: Signed as non-drafted free agent by Detroit Lions (April 24, 1995). ... Released by Lions (August 18, 1995). ... Re-signed by Lions to practice squad (August 29, 1995). ... Activated (November 1, 1995); did not play. ... Granted free agency (February 13, 1998).
PLAYING EXPERIENCE: Detroit NFL, 1996 and 1997. ... Games/Games started: 1996 (13/2), 1997 (12/8). Total: 25/10.
PRO STATISTICS: 1997—Intercepted one pass for 18 yards and credited with one sack.

RICE, SIMEON   DE   CARDINALS

PERSONAL: Born February 24, 1974, in Chicago. ... 6-5/260.
HIGH SCHOOL: Mt. Carmel (Chicago).
COLLEGE: Illinois.
TRANSACTIONS/CAREER NOTES: Selected by Arizona Cardinals in first round (third pick overall) of 1996 NFL draft. ... Signed by Cardinals (August 19, 1996).
HONORS: Named linebacker on The Sporting News college All-America second team (1995).
RECORDS: Shares NFL rookie-season record for most sacks—12.5 (1996).
PRO STATISTICS: 1996—Recovered one fumble. 1997—Intercepted one pass for no yards.

Year Team	G	GS	SACKS
1996—Arizona NFL	16	15	12.5
1997—Arizona NFL	16	15	5.0
Pro totals (2 years)	32	30	17.5

RICHARD, STANLEY   S   REDSKINS

PERSONAL: Born October 21, 1967, in Miniola, Texas. ... 6-2/198. ... Full name: Stanley Palmer Richard.
HIGH SCHOOL: Hawkins (Texas).
COLLEGE: Texas.
TRANSACTIONS/CAREER NOTES: Selected by San Diego Chargers in first round (ninth pick overall) of 1991 NFL draft. ... Signed by Chargers (August 5, 1991). ... Granted free agency (February 17, 1994). ... Re-signed by Chargers (May 2, 1994). ... Granted unconditional free agency (February 17, 1995). ... Signed by Washington Redskins (March 10, 1995).
CHAMPIONSHIP GAME EXPERIENCE: Played in AFC championship game (1994 season). ... Played in Super Bowl XXIX (1994 season).
PRO STATISTICS: 1992—Recovered one fumble. 1993—Credited with two sacks and recovered one fumble. 1995—Recovered one fumble. 1997—Recovered one fumble.

Year Team	G	GS	INTERCEPTIONS			
			No.	Yds.	Avg.	TD
1991—San Diego NFL	15	14	2	5	2.5	0
1992—San Diego NFL	14	14	3	26	8.7	0
1993—San Diego NFL	16	16	1	-2	-2.0	0
1994—San Diego NFL	16	16	4	§224	56.0	2
1995—Washington NFL	16	16	3	24	8.0	0
1996—Washington NFL	16	15	3	47	15.7	0
1997—Washington NFL	16	16	4	28	7.0	0
Pro totals (7 years)	109	107	20	352	17.6	2

RICHARDSON, C.J.   S

PERSONAL: Born June 10, 1972, in Dallas. ... 5-10/209. ... Full name: Carl Ray Richardson Jr.
HIGH SCHOOL: H. Grady Spruce (Dallas).
COLLEGE: Miami, Fla. (degree in criminal justice).
TRANSACTIONS/CAREER NOTES: Selected by Houston Oilers in seventh round (211th pick overall) of 1995 NFL draft. ... Signed by Oilers (July 10, 1995). ... Released by Oilers (August 27, 1995). ... Re-signed by Oilers to practice squad (August 30, 1995). ... Signed by Arizona Cardinals off Oilers practice squad (November 8, 1995). ... Claimed on waivers by Seattle Seahawks (June 19, 1996). ... Released by Seahawks (August 18, 1996). ... Re-signed by Seahawks (March 5, 1997). ... Granted free agency (February 13, 1998).
PLAYING EXPERIENCE: Arizona NFL, 1995; Seattle NFL, 1997. ... Games/Games started: 1995 (1/0), 1997 (14/0). Total: 15/0.
HONORS: Named defensive back on The Sporting News college All-America second team (1994).

RICHARDSON, KYLE   P   RAVENS

PERSONAL: Born March 2, 1973, in Farmington, Mo. ... 6-2/210.
HIGH SCHOOL: Farmington (Mo.).
COLLEGE: Arkansas State.
TRANSACTIONS/CAREER NOTES: Signed as non-drafted free agent by Miami Dolphins (September 3, 1997). ... Released by Dolphins (September 8, 1997). ... Re-signed by Dolphins (September 18, 1997). ... Released by Dolphins (October 7, 1997). ... Signed by Seattle Seahawks to practice squad (November 12, 1997). ... Released by Seahawks (November 25, 1997). ... Signed by Baltimore Ravens (March 25, 1998).
PRO STATISTICS: 1997—Rushed once for no yards and fumbled once for minus 13 yards.

					PUNTING			
Year Team	G	GS	No.	Yds.	Avg.	Net avg.	In. 20	Blk.
1997—Miami NFL	3	0	11	480	43.6	33.1	0	0
—Seattle NFL	2	0	8	324	40.5	23.8	2	†2
Pro totals (1 years)	5	0	19	804	42.3	29.2	2	2

RICHARDSON, TONY   RB   CHIEFS

PERSONAL: Born December 17, 1971, in Frankfurt, West Germany. ... 6-1/237. ... Full name: Antonio Richardson.
HIGH SCHOOL: Daleville (Ala.).
COLLEGE: Auburn.
TRANSACTIONS/CAREER NOTES: Signed as non-drafted free agent by Dallas Cowboys (April 28, 1994). ... Released by Cowboys (August 28, 1994). ... Re-signed by Cowboys to practice squad (August 30, 1994). ... Granted free agency after 1994 season. ... Signed by Kansas City Chiefs (February 28, 1995). ... On injured reserve with wrist injury (December 11, 1996-remainder of season).
PRO STATISTICS: 1996—Recovered one fumble.
SINGLE GAME HIGHS (regular season): Attempts—2 (December 21, 1997, vs. New Orleans); yards—11 (December 21, 1997, vs. New Orleans); and rushing touchdowns—0.

			RUSHING				RECEIVING				TOTALS			
Year Team	G	GS	Att.	Yds.	Avg.	TD	No.	Yds.	Avg.	TD	TD	2pt.	Pts.	Fum.
1995—Kansas City NFL	14	1	8	18	2.3	0	0	0		0	0	0	0	0
1996—Kansas City NFL	13	0	4	10	2.5	0	2	18	9.0	1	1	0	6	0
1997—Kansas City NFL	14	0	2	11	5.5	0	3	6	2.0	3	3	0	18	0
Pro totals (3 years)	41	1	14	39	2.8	0	5	24	4.8	4	4	0	24	0

RICHARDSON, WALLY   QB   RAVENS

PERSONAL: Born February 11, 1974, in Sumter, S.C. ... 6-4/225. ... Full name: Wallace Herman Richardson.
HIGH SCHOOL: Sumter (S.C.).
COLLEGE: Penn State.
TRANSACTIONS/CAREER NOTES: Selected by Baltimore Ravens in seventh round (234th pick overall) of 1997 NFL draft. ... Signed by Ravens (July 10, 1997). ... Assigned by Ravens to England Monarchs in the 1998 NFL Europe enhancement allocation program (February 18, 1998).
PLAYING EXPERIENCE: Baltimore NFL, 1997. ... Games/Games started: 1/0.

RICHIE, DAVID   DT   BRONCOS

PERSONAL: Born September 26, 1973, in Orange, Calif. ... 6-4/280.
HIGH SCHOOL: Kelso (Wash.).
COLLEGE: Washington.
TRANSACTIONS/CAREER NOTES: Signed as non-drafted free agent by Denver Broncos (April 28, 1997).
PLAYING EXPERIENCE: Denver NFL, 1997. ... Games/Games started: 2/0.
CHAMPIONSHIP GAME EXPERIENCE: Member of Broncos for AFC championship game (1997 season); inactive. Member of Super Bowl championship team (1997 season); inactive.
PRO STATISTICS: 1997—Credited with 1/2 sack.

RIEMERSMA, JAY   TE   BILLS

PERSONAL: Born May 17, 1973, in Zeeland, Mich. ... 6-5/254. ... Full name: Allen Jay Riemersma. ... Name pronounced REE-mers-muh.
HIGH SCHOOL: Zeeland (Mich.).
COLLEGE: Michigan.
TRANSACTIONS/CAREER NOTES: Selected by Buffalo Bills in seventh round (244th pick overall) of 1996 NFL draft. ... Signed by Bills (July 9, 1996). ... Released by Bills (August 25, 1996). ... Re-signed by Bills to practice squad (August 26, 1996). ... Activated (October 15, 1996); did not play.
SINGLE GAME HIGHS (regular season): Receptions—5 (November 23, 1997, vs. Tennessee); yards—54 (August 31, 1997, vs. Minnesota); and touchdown receptions—1 (September 7, 1997, vs. New York Jets).

			RECEIVING				TOTALS			
Year Team	G	GS	No.	Yds.	Avg.	TD	TD	2pt.	Pts.	Fum.
1996—Buffalo NFL						Did not play.				
1997—Buffalo NFL	16	8	26	208	8.0	2	2	1	14	1

RISON, ANDRE   WR   CHIEFS

PERSONAL: Born March 18, 1967, in Flint, Mich. ... 6-1/188. ... Full name: Andre Previn Rison. ... Name pronounced RYE-zun.
HIGH SCHOOL: Northwestern (Flint, Mich.).
COLLEGE: Michigan State.

TRANSACTIONS/CAREER NOTES: Selected by Indianapolis Colts in first round (22nd pick overall) of 1989 NFL draft. ... Signed by Colts (May 2, 1989). ... Traded by Colts with OT Chris Hinton, fifth-round pick (OT Reggie Redding) in 1990 draft and first-round pick (WR Mike Pritchard) in 1991 draft to Atlanta Falcons for first-round (QB Jeff George) and fourth-round (WR Stacey Simmons) picks in 1990 draft (April 20, 1990). ... Granted roster exemption for one game (September 1992). ... Designated by Falcons as transition player (February 25, 1993). ... On reserve/did not report list (July 23-August 20, 1993). ... Granted roster exemption (August 20-26, 1993). ... On suspended list (November 21-22, 1994). ... Free agency status changed by Falcons from transitional to unconditional (February 17, 1995). ... Signed by Cleveland Browns (March 24, 1995). ... Browns franchise moved to Baltimore and renamed Ravens for 1996 season (March 11, 1996). ... Released by Ravens (July 9, 1996). ... Signed by Jacksonville Jaguars (July 17, 1996). ... Released by Jaguars (November 18, 1996). ... Claimed on waivers by Green Bay Packers (November 19, 1996). ... Released by Packers (March 25, 1997). ... Signed by Kansas City Chiefs (June 18, 1997).
CHAMPIONSHIP GAME EXPERIENCE: Played in NFC championship game (1996 season). ... Member of Super Bowl championship team (1996 season).
HONORS: Named wide receiver on THE SPORTING NEWS NFL All-Pro team (1990). ... Played in Pro Bowl (1990-1993 and 1997 seasons). ... Named Outstanding Player of Pro Bowl (1993 season).
PRO STATISTICS: 1989—Rushed three times for 18 yards and returned two punts for 20 yards. 1990—Returned two punts for 10 yards. 1991—Rushed once for minus nine yards. 1995—Rushed twice for no yards and recovered one fumble. 1997—Rushed once for two yards.
SINGLE GAME HIGHS (regular season): Receptions—14 (September 4, 1994, vs. Detroit); yards—193 (September 4, 1994, vs. Detroit); and touchdown receptions—3 (September 19, 1993, vs. San Francisco).
STATISTICAL PLATEAUS: 100-yard receiving games: 1989 (3), 1990 (5), 1991 (1), 1992 (2), 1993 (4), 1994 (3), 1995 (2), 1996 (1), 1997 (2). Total: 23.
MISCELLANEOUS: Holds Atlanta Falcons all-time records for most touchdowns (56), most receptions (423) and most touchdown receptions (56).

Year Team	G	GS	RECEIVING No.	Yds.	Avg.	TD	KICKOFF RETURNS No.	Yds.	Avg.	TD	TOTALS TD	2pt.	Pts.	Fum.
1989—Indianapolis NFL	16	13	52	820	15.8	4	8	150	18.8	0	4	...	24	1
1990—Atlanta NFL	16	15	82	1208	14.7	10	0	0	...	0	10	...	60	2
1991—Atlanta NFL	16	15	81	976	12.0	12	0	0	...	0	12	...	72	1
1992—Atlanta NFL	15	13	93	1119	12.0	11	0	0	...	0	11	...	66	2
1993—Atlanta NFL	16	16	86	1242	14.4	15	0	0	...	0	15	...	90	2
1994—Atlanta NFL	15	14	81	1088	13.4	8	0	0	...	0	8	1	50	1
1995—Cleveland NFL	16	14	47	701	14.9	3	0	0	...	0	3	1	18	1
1996—Jacksonville NFL	10	9	34	458	13.5	2	0	0	...	0	2	0	12	1
—Green Bay NFL	5	4	13	135	10.4	1	0	0	...	0	1	0	6	1
1997—Kansas City NFL	16	16	72	1092	15.2	7	0	0	...	0	7	0	42	0
Pro totals (9 years)	141	129	641	8839	13.8	73	8	150	18.8	0	73	1	440	11

RITCHEY, JAMES — QB — OILERS

PERSONAL: Born July 10, 1973, in Copperas Cove, Texas. ... 6-2/210. ... Full name: James Alan Ritchey.
HIGH SCHOOL: Copperas Cove (Texas).
COLLEGE: Stephen F. Austin.
TRANSACTIONS/CAREER NOTES: Signed as non-drafted free agent by Houston Oilers (May 21, 1996). ... Oilers franchise moved to Tennessee for 1997 season. ... Assigned by Oilers to Barcelona Dragons in 1998 NFL Europe enhancement allocation program (February 18, 1998).
PLAYING EXPERIENCE: Tennessee NFL, 1997. ... Games/Games started: 1/0.
PRO STATISTICS: 1997—Attempted two passes with two completions for 15 yards and rushed once for six yards.
SINGLE GAME HIGHS (regular season): Attempts—2 (September 21, 1997, vs. Baltimore); completions—2 (September 21, 1997, vs. Baltimore); yards—15 (September 21, 1997, vs. Baltimore); touchdown passes—0.

RIVERA, MARCO — G — PACKERS

PERSONAL: Born April 26, 1972, in Elmont, N.Y. ... 6-4/295. ... Full name: Marco Anthony Rivera.
HIGH SCHOOL: Elmont (N.Y.) Memorial.
COLLEGE: Penn State.
TRANSACTIONS/CAREER NOTES: Selected by Green Bay Packers in sixth round (208th pick overall) of 1996 NFL draft. ... Signed by Packers (July 15, 1996). ... Inactive for 16 games (1996). ... Assigned by Packers to Scottish Claymores in 1997 World League enhancement allocation program (February 19, 1997).
PLAYING EXPERIENCE: Green Bay NFL, 1997. ... Games/Games started: 14/0.
CHAMPIONSHIP GAME EXPERIENCE: Member of Packers for NFC championship game (1996 season); inactive. ... Member of Super Bowl championship team (1996 season); inactive. ... Played in NFC championship game (1997 season). ... Played in Super Bowl XXXII (1997 season).

RIVERS, RON — RB — LIONS

PERSONAL: Born November 13, 1971, in Elizabeth, N.J. ... 5-8/205. ... Full name: Ronald Leroy Rivers.
HIGH SCHOOL: San Gorgonio (San Bernardino, Calif.).
COLLEGE: Fresno State.
TRANSACTIONS/CAREER NOTES: Signed as non-drafted free agent by San Diego Chargers (May 2, 1994). ... Released by Chargers (August 29, 1994). ... Signed by Detroit Lions to practice squad (September 21, 1994). ... Activated (December 22, 1994); did not play. ... Granted free agency (February 13, 1998). ... Re-signed by Lions (April 28, 1998).
POST SEASON RECORDS: Shares NFL postseason career and single-game records for most two-point conversions—1 (December 30, 1995, vs. Philadelphia).
PRO STATISTICS: 1995—Caught one pass for five yards and recovered one fumble. 1997—Recovered one fumble.
SINGLE GAME HIGHS (regular season): Attempts—11 (December 17, 1995, vs. Jacksonville); yards—59 (December 17, 1995, vs. Jacksonville); and rushing touchdowns—1 (November 27, 1997, vs. Chicago).

Year Team	G	GS	RUSHING Att.	Yds.	Avg.	TD	RECEIVING No.	Yds.	Avg.	TD	KICKOFF RETURNS No.	Yds.	Avg.	TD	TOTALS TD	2pt.	Pts.	Fum.
1994—Detroit NFL							Did not play.											
1995—Detroit NFL	16	0	18	73	4.1	1	1	5	5.0	0	19	420	22.1	0	1	0	6	2
1996—Detroit NFL	15	0	19	86	4.5	0	2	28	14.0	0	1	8	8.0	0	0	0	0	0
1997—Detroit NFL	16	0	29	166	5.7	1	0	0	...	0	2	34	17.0	0	1	0	6	0
Pro totals (3 years)	47	0	66	325	4.9	2	3	33	11.0	0	22	462	21.0	0	2	0	12	2

ROAF, WILLIE　　　　　OT　　　　　SAINTS

PERSONAL: Born April 18, 1970, in Pine Bluff, Ark. ... 6-5/300. ... Full name: William Layton Roaf.
HIGH SCHOOL: Pine Bluff (Ark.).
COLLEGE: Louisiana Tech.
TRANSACTIONS/CAREER NOTES: Selected by New Orleans Saints in first round (eighth pick overall) of 1993 NFL draft. ... Signed by Saints (July 15, 1993). ... Designated by Saints as transition player (February 15, 1994).
PLAYING EXPERIENCE: New Orleans NFL, 1993-1997. ... Games/Games started: 1993 (16/16), 1994 (16/16), 1995 (16/16), 1996 (13/13), 1997 (16/16). Total: 77/77.
HONORS: Named offensive tackle on THE SPORTING NEWS college All-America second team (1992). ... Named offensive tackle on THE SPORTING NEWS NFL All-Pro team (1994-1996). ... Played in Pro Bowl (1994-1997 seasons).
PRO STATISTICS: 1994—Recovered one fumble. 1996—Recovered one fumble.

ROAN, MICHAEL　　　　　TE　　　　　OILERS

PERSONAL: Born August 29, 1972, in Iowa City, Iowa. ... 6-3/242. ... Full name: Michael Phillip Roan.
HIGH SCHOOL: Iowa City (Iowa).
COLLEGE: Wisconsin.
TRANSACTIONS/CAREER NOTES: Selected by Houston Oilers in fourth round (101st pick overall) of 1995 NFL draft. ... Signed by Oilers (July 10, 1995). ... Oilers franchise moved to Tennessee for 1997 season.
PLAYING EXPERIENCE: Houston NFL, 1995 and 1996; Tennessee NFL, 1997. ... Games/Games started: 1995 (5/2), 1996 (15/1), 1997 (14/13). Total: 34/16.
PRO STATISTICS: 1995—Caught eight passes for 46 yards, fumbled once and recovered one fumble. 1996—Returned one kickoff for 13 yards. 1997—Caught 12 passes for 159 yards and returned two kickoffs for 20 yards.
SINGLE GAME HIGHS (regular season): Receptions—3 (November 2, 1997, vs. Jacksonville); yards—51 (November 2, 1997, vs. Jacksonville); and touchdown receptions—0.

ROBBINS, AUSTIN　　　　　DT　　　　　SAINTS

PERSONAL: Born March 1, 1971, in Washington, D.C. ... 6-6/290. ... Full name: Austin Dion Robbins.
HIGH SCHOOL: Howard D. Woodson (Washington D.C.).
COLLEGE: North Carolina.
TRANSACTIONS/CAREER NOTES: Selected by Los Angeles Raiders in fourth round (120th pick overall) of 1994 NFL draft. ... Signed by Raiders (July 14, 1994). ... Raiders franchise moved to Oakland (July 21, 1995). ... Traded by Raiders to New Orleans Saints for undisclosed pick in 1997 draft (August 25, 1996). ... Granted free agency (February 14, 1997). ... Re-signed by Saints (June 7, 1997). ... Granted unconditional free agency (February 13, 1998). ... Re-signed by Saints (March 6, 1998).
PRO STATISTICS: 1995—Recovered two fumbles for six yards and one touchdown.

Year　Team	G	GS	SACKS
1994—Los Angeles Raiders NFL	2	0	0.0
1995—Oakland NFL	16	0	2.0
1996—New Orleans NFL	15	7	1.0
1997—New Orleans NFL	12	0	0.0
Pro totals (4 years)	45	7	3.0

ROBBINS, BARRET　　　　　C　　　　　RAIDERS

PERSONAL: Born August 26, 1973, in Houston. ... 6-3/305.
HIGH SCHOOL: Sharpstown (Houston).
COLLEGE: Texas Christian.
TRANSACTIONS/CAREER NOTES: Selected by Los Angeles Raiders in second round (49th pick overall) of 1995 NFL draft. ... Signed by Raiders (June 20, 1995). ... Raiders franchise moved to Oakland (July 21, 1995).
PLAYING EXPERIENCE: Oakland NFL, 1995-1997. ... Games/Games started: 1995 (16/0), 1996 (14/14), 1997 (16/16). Total: 46/30.
PRO STATISTICS: 1996—Recovered one fumble.

ROBERSON, JAMES　　　　　DE　　　　　OILERS

PERSONAL: Born May 3, 1971, in Lake Wales, Fla. ... 6-3/275.
HIGH SCHOOL: Lake Wales (Fla.).
COLLEGE: Florida State.
TRANSACTIONS/CAREER NOTES: Signed as non-drafted free agent by New Orleans Saints (April 27, 1995). ... Released by Saints (July 25, 1995). ... Claimed on waivers by Green Bay Packers (July 27, 1995). ... Released by Packers (August 21, 1995). ... Signed by Rhein Fire for 1996 season. ... Signed by Houston Oilers (July 20, 1996). ... Released by Oilers (August 25, 1996). ... Re-signed by Oilers to practice squad (August 26, 1996). ... Activated (September 6, 1996). ... Oilers franchise moved to Tennessee for 1997 season.
PRO STATISTICS: 1996—Recovered one fumble for four yards. 1997—Recovered one fumble.

Year　Team	G	GS	SACKS
1996—Rhein W.L.	...	...	3.0
—Houston NFL	15	5	3.0
1997—Tennessee NFL	15	11	2.0
W.L. totals (1 year)		...	3.0
NFL totals (2 years)	30	16	5.0
Pro totals (3 years)	...	...	8.0

ROBERTS, RAY   OT   LIONS

PERSONAL: Born June 3, 1969, in Asheville, N.C. ... 6-6/308. ... Full name: Richard Ray Roberts Jr.
HIGH SCHOOL: Asheville (N.C.).
COLLEGE: Virginia (degree in communication studies, 1991).
TRANSACTIONS/CAREER NOTES: Selected by Seattle Seahawks in first round (10th pick overall) of 1992 NFL draft. ... Signed by Seahawks (August 1, 1992). ... Designated by Seahawks as transition player (February 15, 1994). ... On injured reserve with ankle/leg injury (December 11, 1994-remainder of season). ... Free agency status changed by Seahawks from transitional to unconditional (February 16, 1996). ... Signed by Detroit Lions (March 11, 1996). ... Granted unconditional free agency (February 13, 1998). ... Re-signed by Lions (February 19, 1998).
PLAYING EXPERIENCE: Seattle NFL, 1992-1995; Detroit NFL, 1996 and 1997. ... Games/Games started: 1992 (16/16), 1993 (16/16), 1994 (14/14), 1995 (11/0), 1996 (16/16), 1997 (14/14). Total: 87/76.
HONORS: Named offensive tackle on The Sporting News college All-America second team (1991).
PRO STATISTICS: 1993—Caught one pass for four yards. 1996—Ran five yards with lateral from reception and recovered two fumbles. 1997—Recovered two fumbles for four yards.

ROBERTS, WILLIAM   G

PERSONAL: Born August 5, 1962, in Miami. ... 6-5/298. ... Full name: William Harold Roberts. ... Cousin of Reggie Sandilands, wide receiver with Memphis Showboats of USFL (1984).
HIGH SCHOOL: Carol City (Miami).
COLLEGE: Ohio State.
TRANSACTIONS/CAREER NOTES: Selected by New Jersey Generals in 1984 USFL territorial draft. ... Selected by New York Giants in first round (27th pick overall) of 1984 NFL draft. ... Signed by Giants (June 4, 1984). ... On injured reserve with knee injury (July 20, 1985-entire season). ... Granted free agency (February 1, 1991). ... Re-signed by Giants (August 29, 1991). ... Activated (September 2, 1991). ... Granted unconditional free agency (February 17, 1994). ... Re-signed by Giants (July 17, 1994). ... Released by Giants (May 17, 1995). ... Signed by New England Patriots (July 23, 1995). ... Granted unconditional free agency (February 16, 1996). ... Re-signed by Patriots (February 27, 1996). ... Released by Patriots (September 4, 1996). ... Re-signed by Patriots (September 5, 1996). ... Granted unconditional free agency (February 14, 1997). ... Signed by New York Jets (July 27, 1997). ... On injured reserve with knee injury (November 27, 1997-remainder of season). ... Granted unconditional free agency (February 13, 1998).
PLAYING EXPERIENCE: New York Giants NFL, 1984 and 1986-1994; New England NFL, 1995 and 1996; New York Jets NFL, 1997. ... Games/Games started: 1984 (11/8), 1986 (16/0), 1987 (12/12), 1988 (16/13), 1989 (16/16), 1990 (16/16), 1991 (16/16), 1992 (16/15), 1993 (16/16), 1994 (16/15), 1995 (16/11), 1996 (16/16), 1997 (12/0). Total: 195/154.
CHAMPIONSHIP GAME EXPERIENCE: Played in NFC championship game (1986 and 1990 seasons). ... Member of Super Bowl championship team (1986 and 1990 seasons). ... Played in AFC championship game (1996 season). ... Played in Super Bowl XXXI (1996 season).
HONORS: Played in Pro Bowl (1990 season).
PRO STATISTICS: 1984—Recovered one fumble. 1988—Recovered two fumbles. 1993—Recovered one fumble.

ROBERTSON, MARCUS   S   OILERS

PERSONAL: Born October 2, 1969, in Pasadena, Calif. ... 5-11/202. ... Full name: Marcus Aaron Robertson.
HIGH SCHOOL: John Muir (Pasadena, Calif.).
COLLEGE: Iowa State.
TRANSACTIONS/CAREER NOTES: Selected by Houston Oilers in fourth round (102nd pick overall) of 1991 NFL draft. ... Signed by Oilers (July 16, 1991). ... On injured reserve with knee injury (December 30, 1993-remainder of season). ... Granted free agency (February 17, 1994). ... Re-signed by Oilers (July 11, 1994). ... On injured reserve with knee injury (November 30, 1995-remainder of season). ... Oilers franchise moved to Tennessee for 1997 season.
HONORS: Named free safety on The Sporting News NFL All-Pro team (1993).
PRO STATISTICS: 1991—Credited with one sack, returned one punt for no yards and fumbled once. 1993—Recovered three fumbles for 107 yards and one touchdown. 1994—Returned one punt for no yards, fumbled once and recovered one fumble. 1996—Recovered one fumble for five yards. 1997—Returned one punt for no yards and recovered three fumbles for 67 yards and two touchdowns.

				INTERCEPTIONS		
Year Team	G	GS	No.	Yds.	Avg.	TD
1991—Houston NFL	16	0	0	0	...	0
1992—Houston NFL	16	14	1	27	27.0	0
1993—Houston NFL	13	13	7	137	19.6	0
1994—Houston NFL	16	16	3	90	30.0	0
1995—Houston NFL	2	2	0	0	...	0
1996—Houston NFL	16	16	4	44	11.0	0
1997—Tennessee NFL	14	14	5	127	25.4	0
Pro totals (7 years)	93	75	20	425	21.3	0

ROBINSON, BRYAN   DL   RAMS

PERSONAL: Born June 22, 1974 ... 6-4/295.
HIGH SCHOOL: Woodward (Toledo, Ohio).
JUNIOR COLLEGE: College of the Desert (Palm Desert, Calif.).
COLLEGE: Fresno State.
TRANSACTIONS/CAREER NOTES: Signed as non-drafted free agent by St. Louis Rams (April 29, 1997).
PLAYING EXPERIENCE: St. Louis NFL, 1997. ... Games/Games started: 11/0.
PRO STATISTICS: 1997—Credited with one sack.

ROBINSON, DAMIEN   S   BUCCANEERS

PERSONAL: Born December 22, 1973, in Dallas. ... 6-2/210.
HIGH SCHOOL: Hillcrest (Dallas).
COLLEGE: Iowa.
TRANSACTIONS/CAREER NOTES: Selected by Philadelphia Eagles in fourth round (119th pick overall) of 1997 NFL draft. ... Signed by Eagles (June 4, 1997). ... Released by Eagles (August 25, 1997). ... Re-signed by Eagles to practice squad (August 27, 1997). ... Signed by Tampa Bay Buccaneers off Eagles practice squad (September 17, 1997). ... Inactive for 13 games (1997).

ROBINSON, EDDIE   LB   JAGUARS

PERSONAL: Born April 13, 1970, in New Orleans. ... 6-1/233. ... Full name: Eddie Joseph Robinson.
HIGH SCHOOL: Brother Martin (New Orleans).
COLLEGE: Alabama State.
TRANSACTIONS/CAREER NOTES: Selected by Houston Oilers in second round (50th pick overall) of 1992 NFL draft. ... Signed by Oilers (July 16, 1992). ... Granted free agency (February 17, 1995). ... Re-signed by Oilers (July 1995). ... Granted unconditional free agency (February 16, 1996). ... Signed by Jacksonville Jaguars (March 1, 1996).
CHAMPIONSHIP GAME EXPERIENCE: Played in AFC championship game (1996 season).
PRO STATISTICS: 1995—Intercepted one pass for 49 yards and a touchdown and recovered one fumble. 1996—Recovered one fumble. 1997—Intercepted one pass for no yards and recovered two fumbles.

Year Team	G	GS	SACKS
1992—Houston NFL	16	11	1.0
1993—Houston NFL	16	15	1.0
1994—Houston NFL	15	15	0.0
1995—Houston NFL	16	16	3.5
1996—Jacksonville NFL	16	15	1.0
1997—Jacksonville NFL	16	14	2.0
Pro totals (6 years)	95	86	8.5

ROBINSON, EUGENE   S   FALCONS

PERSONAL: Born May 28, 1963, in Hartford, Conn. ... 6-1/197. ... Full name: Eugene Keefe Robinson.
HIGH SCHOOL: Weaver (Hartford, Conn.).
COLLEGE: Colgate.
TRANSACTIONS/CAREER NOTES: Selected by New Jersey Generals in 1985 USFL territorial draft. ... Signed as non-drafted free agent by Seattle Seahawks (May 15, 1985). ... On injured reserve with Achilles' tendon injury (December 11, 1994-remainder of season). ... Traded by Seahawks to Green Bay Packers for LB Matt LaBounty (June 27, 1996). ... Granted unconditional free agency (February 13, 1998). ... Signed by Atlanta Falcons (March 6, 1998).
CHAMPIONSHIP GAME EXPERIENCE: Played in NFC championship game (1996 and 1997 seasons). ... Member of Super Bowl championship team (1996 season). ... Played in Super Bowl XXXII (1997 season).
HONORS: Played in Pro Bowl (1992 and 1993 seasons).
PRO STATISTICS: 1985—Returned one kickoff for 10 yards. 1986—Recovered three fumbles for six yards. 1987—Returned blocked punt eight yards for a touchdown and recovered one fumble. 1989—Fumbled once and recovered one fumble. 1990—Recovered four fumbles for 16 yards and a touchdown. 1991—Recovered one fumble. 1992—Recovered one fumble. 1993—Recovered two fumbles for seven yards. 1994—Recovered one fumble. 1995—Returned one punt for one yard and recovered one fumble. 1997—Fumbled once and recovered two fumbles.
MISCELLANEOUS: Active NFL leader for career interceptions (49).

Year Team	G	GS	INTERCEPTIONS No.	Yds.	Avg.	TD	SACKS No.
1985—Seattle NFL	16	0	2	47	23.5	0	0.0
1986—Seattle NFL	16	16	3	39	13.0	0	0.0
1987—Seattle NFL	12	12	3	75	25.0	0	0.0
1988—Seattle NFL	16	16	1	0	0.0	0	1.0
1989—Seattle NFL	16	14	5	24	4.8	0	0.0
1990—Seattle NFL	16	16	3	89	29.7	0	0.0
1991—Seattle NFL	16	16	5	56	11.2	0	1.0
1992—Seattle NFL	16	16	7	126	18.0	0	0.0
1993—Seattle NFL	16	16	*9	80	8.9	0	2.0
1994—Seattle NFL	14	14	3	18	6.0	0	1.0
1995—Seattle NFL	16	16	1	32	32.0	0	0.0
1996—Green Bay NFL	16	16	6	107	17.8	0	0.0
1997—Green Bay NFL	16	16	1	26	26.0	0	2.5
Pro totals (13 years)	202	184	49	719	14.7	0	7.5

ROBINSON, GREG   RB   CHIEFS

PERSONAL: Born August 7, 1969, in Grenada, Miss. ... 5-10/205.
HIGH SCHOOL: Grenada (Miss.).
JUNIOR COLLEGE: Holmes (Miss.) Community College.
COLLEGE: Northeast Louisiana.
TRANSACTIONS/CAREER NOTES: Selected by Los Angeles Raiders in eighth round (208th pick overall) of 1993 NFL draft. ... Signed by Raiders (July 13, 1993). ... On injured reserve with knee injury (August 22, 1994-entire season). ... Traded by Raiders to Green Bay Packers for undisclosed draft pick (August 21, 1995); trade voided when Robinson failed physical. ... Released by Raiders (August 22, 1995). ... Signed by St. Louis Rams (November 1, 1995). ... Granted free agency (February 16, 1996). ... Re-signed by Rams (June 20, 1996). ... Granted unconditional free agency (February 14, 1997). ... Signed by Kansas City Chiefs (April 7, 1998).

PRO STATISTICS: 1993—Returned four kickoffs for 57 yards and recovered one fumble.
SINGLE GAME HIGHS (regular season): Attempts—21 (November 21, 1993, vs. San Diego); yards—90 (November 14, 1993, vs. Kansas City); and rushing touchdowns—1 (November 10, 1996, vs. Atlanta).

			RUSHING				RECEIVING				TOTALS		
Year Team	G	GS	Att.	Yds.	Avg.	TD	No.	Yds.	Avg.	TD	TD	2pt.	Pts.	Fum.
1993—Los Angeles Raiders NFL	12	12	156	591	3.8	1	15	142	9.5	0	1	...	6	3
1994—Los Angeles Raiders NFL							Did not play.							
1995—St. Louis NFL	6	1	40	165	4.1	0	2	12	6.0	0	0	0	0	0
1996—St. Louis NFL	11	0	32	134	4.2	1	1	6	6.0	0	1	0	6	1
1997—							Did not play.							
Pro totals (3 years)	29	13	228	890	3.9	2	18	160	8.9	0	2	0	12	4

R

ROBINSON, JEFF   DE   RAMS

PERSONAL: Born February 20, 1970, in Kennewick, Wash. ... 6-4/275. ... Full name: Jeffrey William Robinson.
HIGH SCHOOL: Joel E. Ferris (Spokane, Wash.).
COLLEGE: Idaho.
TRANSACTIONS/CAREER NOTES: Selected by Denver Broncos in fourth round (98th pick overall) of 1993 NFL draft. ... Signed by Broncos (July 13, 1993). ... Granted free agency (February 16, 1996). ... Re-signed by Broncos (March 28, 1996). ... Granted unconditional free agency (February 14, 1997). ... Signed by St. Louis Rams (March 14, 1997).
PRO STATISTICS: 1993—Recovered one fumble for minus 10 yards. 1995—Returned one kickoff for 14 yards and recovered one fumble. 1996—Recovered one fumble.

Year Team	G	GS	SACKS
1993—Denver NFL	16	0	3.5
1994—Denver NFL	16	0	1.0
1995—Denver NFL	16	0	1.0
1996—Denver NFL	16	0	0.5
1997—St. Louis NFL	16	0	0.5
Pro totals (5 years)	80	0	6.5

ROBINSON, MARCUS   WR   BEARS

PERSONAL: Born February 27, 1975, in Ft. Valley, Ga. ... 6-3/215.
HIGH SCHOOL: Peach County (Ft. Valley, Ga.).
COLLEGE: South Carolina.
TRANSACTIONS/CAREER NOTES: Selected by Chicago Bears in fourth round (108th pick overall) of 1997 NFL draft. ... Signed by Bears (July 11, 1997). ... On injured reserve with thumb injury (September 24, 1997-remainder of season). ... Inactive for four games (1997). ... Assigned by Bears to Rhein Fire in 1998 NFL Europe enhancement allocation program (February 18, 1998).

ROBINSON, RAFAEL   S

PERSONAL: Born June 19, 1969, in Marshall, Texas. ... 5-11/200. ... Full name: Eugene Rafael Robinson.
HIGH SCHOOL: Jefferson (Texas).
COLLEGE: Wisconsin.
TRANSACTIONS/CAREER NOTES: Signed as non-drafted free agent by Seattle Seahawks (May 1, 1992). ... Released by Seahawks (August 31, 1992). ... Signed by Seahawks to practice squad (September 2, 1992). ... Activated (September 26, 1992). ... Released by Seahawks (October 5, 1992). ... Re-signed by Seahawks to practice squad (October 6, 1992). ... Activated (October 14, 1992). ... Released by Seahawks (October 24, 1992). ... Re-signed by Seahawks to practice squad (October 26, 1992). ... Activated (December 9, 1992). ... Granted free agency (February 17, 1995). ... Re-signed by Seahawks (April 24, 1995). ... Granted unconditional free agency (February 16, 1996). ... Signed by Houston Oilers (April 22, 1996). ... Oilers franchise moved to Tennessee for 1997 season. ... Released by Oilers (August 27, 1997). ... Re-signed by Oilers (September 5, 1997). ... Released by Oilers (September 29, 1997).
PLAYING EXPERIENCE: Seattle NFL, 1992-1995; Houston NFL, 1996; Tennessee NFL, 1997. ... Games/Games started: 1992 (6/0), 1993 (16/1), 1994 (16/1), 1995 (13/3), 1996 (16/2), 1997 (3/0). Total: 70/7.
PRO STATISTICS: 1993—Credited with 1 ¹/₂ sacks and recovered one fumble. 1994—Intercepted one pass for no yards and recovered one fumble. 1996—Intercepted one pass for two yards and recovered one fumble.

ROBY, REGGIE   P

PERSONAL: Born July 30, 1961, in Waterloo, Iowa. ... 6-2/258. ... Full name: Reginald Henry Roby. ... Brother of Mike Roby, first baseman/outfielder with San Francisco Giants organization (1967 and 1968).
HIGH SCHOOL: East (Waterloo, Iowa).
COLLEGE: Iowa.
TRANSACTIONS/CAREER NOTES: Selected by Chicago Blitz in 16th round (187th pick overall) of 1983 USFL draft. ... Selected by Miami Dolphins in sixth round (167th pick overall) of 1983 NFL draft. ... Signed by Dolphins (July 9, 1983). ... On injured reserve with knee, ankle and groin injuries (September 16-October 31, 1987). ... Crossed picket line during players strike (October 14, 1987). ... On injured reserve with knee injury (September 18-November 4, 1992). ... Released by Dolphins (August 30, 1993). ... Signed by Washington Redskins (September 7, 1993). ... Granted unconditional free agency (February 17, 1995). ... Signed by Tampa Bay Buccaneers (February 20, 1995). ... Released by Buccaneers (May 13, 1996). ... Signed by Houston Oilers (June 13, 1996). ... Oilers franchise moved to Tennessee for 1997 season. ... Released by Oilers (February 14, 1998).
CHAMPIONSHIP GAME EXPERIENCE: Played in AFC championship game (1984, 1985 and 1992 seasons). ... Played in Super Bowl XIX (1984 season).
HONORS: Named punter on THE SPORTING NEWS NFL All-Pro team (1984 and 1994). ... Played in Pro Bowl (1984, 1989 and 1994 seasons).
PRO STATISTICS: 1986—Rushed twice for minus eight yards, fumbled twice and recovered two fumbles for minus 11 yards. 1987—Rushed once for no yards and recovered one fumble. 1993—Rushed twice for no yards and recovered two fumbles. 1993—Rushed once for no yards and recovered one fumble. 1994—Fumbled once and recovered one fumble. 1995—Rushed once for no yards, attempted one pass with one completion for 48 yards. 1997—Rushed once for 12 yards.

					PUNTING				
Year Team	G	GS	No.	Yds.	Avg.	Net avg.	In. 20	Blk.
1983—Miami NFL	16	0	74	3189	43.1	36.5	§26	1
1984—Miami NFL	16	0	51	2281	44.7	*38.1	15	0
1985—Miami NFL	16	0	59	2576	43.7	34.7	19	0
1986—Miami NFL	15	0	56	2476	44.2	*37.3	13	0
1987—Miami NFL	10	0	32	1371	42.8	38.2	8	0
1988—Miami NFL	15	0	64	2754	43.0	35.2	18	0
1989—Miami NFL	16	0	58	2458	42.4	35.2	18	1
1990—Miami NFL	16	0	72	3022	42.0	35.6	20	0
1991—Miami NFL	16	0	54	2466	*45.7	36.3	17	1
1992—Miami NFL	9	0	35	1443	41.2	34.2	11	0
1993—Washington NFL	15	0	78	3447	44.2	37.2	25	0
1994—Washington NFL	16	0	82	3639	44.4	36.1	21	0
1995—Tampa Bay NFL	16	0	77	3296	42.8	36.2	23	1
1996—Houston NFL	16	0	67	2973	44.4	38.0	25	1
1997—Tennessee NFL	16	0	73	3049	41.8	35.6	25	0
Pro totals (15 years)	224	0	932	40440	43.4	36.3	284	5

ROCHE, BRIAN   TE   CHARGERS

PERSONAL: Born May 5, 1973, in Downey, Calif. ... 6-4/255. ... Full name: Brian Matthew Roche.
HIGH SCHOOL: Damien (LaVerne, Calif.).
COLLEGE: Cal Poly-SLO, then San Jose State.
TRANSACTIONS/CAREER NOTES: Selected by San Diego Chargers in third round (81st pick overall) of 1996 NFL draft. ... Signed by Chargers (July 14, 1996). ... On injured reserve with knee injury (November 26, 1997-remainder of season).
SINGLE GAME HIGHS (regular season): Receptions—3 (December 22, 1996, vs. Denver); yards—23 (December 22, 1996, vs. Denver); and touchdown receptions—0.

			RECEIVING				TOTALS			
Year Team	G	GS	No.	Yds.	Avg.	TD	TD	2pt.	Pts.	Fum.
1996—San Diego NFL	13	0	13	111	8.5	0	0	0	0	0
1997—San Diego NFL	5	0	0	0	...	0	0	0	0	0
Pro totals (2 years)	18	0	13	111	8.5	0	0	0	0	0

ROCKWOOD, MIKE   OT   BILLS

PERSONAL: Born June 8, 1973, in Mira Loma, Calif. ... 6-10/345. ... Full name: Michael Lural Rockwood.
HIGH SCHOOL: Rubidoux (Riverside, Calif.).
JUNIOR COLLEGE: Riverside (Calif.) Junior College.
COLLEGE: Nevada-Reno.
TRANSACTIONS/CAREER NOTES: Signed as non-drafted free agent by Buffalo Bills (May 3, 1996). ... Released by Bills (August 25, 1996). ... Re-signed by Bills to practice squad (August 26, 1996). ... Released by Bills (August 18, 1997). ... Re-signed by Bills to practice squad (August 26, 1997). ... Activated (December 1, 1997). ... Assigned by Bills to Scottish Claymores in 1998 NFL Europe enhancement allocation program (February 18, 1998).
PLAYING EXPERIENCE: Buffalo NFL, 1997. ... Games/Games started: 1/0.

RODENHAUSER, MARK   C   PANTHERS

PERSONAL: Born June 1, 1961, in Elmhurst, Ill. ... 6-5/280. ... Full name: Mark Todd Rodenhauser. ... Name pronounced RO-den-how-ser.
HIGH SCHOOL: Addison (Ill.) Trail.
COLLEGE: Illinois State (degree in industrial technology).
TRANSACTIONS/CAREER NOTES. Signed as non-drafted free agent by Michigan Panthers of USFL (January 15, 1984). ... Released by Panthers (February 13, 1984). ... Signed by Memphis Showboats of USFL (December 3, 1984). ... Released by Showboats (January 22, 1985). ... Signed by Chicago Bruisers of Arena Football League (June 29, 1987). ... Granted free agency (August 15, 1987). ... Signed as replacement player by Chicago Bears (September 24, 1987). ... Left camp voluntarily (August 16, 1988). ... Released by Bears (August 17, 1988). ... Signed by Minnesota Vikings (March 16, 1989). ... Granted unconditional free agency (February 1, 1990). ... Signed by San Diego Chargers (March 1, 1990). ... Granted unconditional free agency (February 1-April 1, 1991). ... Re-signed by Chargers (April 5, 1991). ... On injured reserve with foot injury (November 13, 1991-remainder of season). ... Granted unconditional free agency (February 1, 1992). ... Signed by Bears (March 6, 1992). ... Released by Bears (December 18, 1992). ... Signed by Detroit Lions (April 30, 1993). ... Granted unconditional free agency (February 17, 1994). ... Re-signed by Lions (August 15, 1994). ... Selected by Carolina Panthers from Lions in NFL expansion draft (February 15, 1995). ... Granted unconditional free agency (February 16, 1996). ... Re-signed by Panthers (March 15, 1996). ... Granted unconditional free agency (February 14, 1997). ... Re-signed by Panthers (February 25, 1997). ... Granted unconditional free agency (February 1, 1998). ... Re-signed by Panthers (April 1, 1998).
PLAYING EXPERIENCE: Chicago Bruisers Arena Football, 1987; Chicago NFL, 1987 and 1992; Minnesota NFL, 1989; San Diego NFL, 1990 and 1991; Detroit NFL, 1993 and 1994; Carolina NFL, 1995-1997. ... Games/Games started: 1987 Arena Football (4/4), 1987 NFL (9/3), 1989 (16/0), 1990 (16/0), 1991 (10/0), 1992 (13/0), 1993 (16/0), 1994 (16/0), 1995 (16/0), 1996 (16/0), 1997 (16/0). Total Arena League: 4/4. Total NFL: 144/3. Total Pro: 148/7.
CHAMPIONSHIP GAME EXPERIENCE: Played in NFC championship game (1996 season).

RODGERS, ANTHONY   WR   CHARGERS

PERSONAL: Born December 11, 1973, in Los Angeles. ... 6-3/190. ... Full name: Anthony Tyrone Rodgers.
HIGH SCHOOL: Verbum Dei (Los Angeles).
JUNIOR COLLEGE: El Camino College (Calif.).
COLLEGE: Cal State Northridge (did not play football).

TRANSACTIONS/CAREER NOTES: Signed by Anaheim Piranhas of Arena League (April 9, 1996). ... Released by Piranhas (April 23, 1996). ... Signed by San Diego Chargers (March 12, 1997). ... Released by Chargers (August 18, 1997). ... Signed by Kansas City Chiefs to practice squad (November 12, 1997). ... Released by Chiefs (December 10, 1997). ... Signed by Chargers to practice squad (December 10, 1997).

RODGERS, DERRICK — LB — DOLPHINS

PERSONAL: Born October 14, 1971, in Cordova, Tenn. ... 6-1/225. ... Full name: Derrick Andre Rodgers.
HIGH SCHOOL: St. Augustine (New Orleans).
JUNIOR COLLEGE: Riverside (Calif.) Community College.
COLLEGE: Arizona State.
TRANSACTIONS/CAREER NOTES: Selected by Miami Dolphins in third round (92nd pick overall) of 1997 NFL draft. ... Signed by Dolphins (July 8, 1997).
PRO STATISTICS: 1997—Recovered one fumble.

Year Team	G	GS	SACKS
1997—Miami NFL	15	14	5.0

ROE, JAMES — WR — RAVENS

PERSONAL: Born August 23, 1973, in Richmond, Va. ... 6-1/187. ... Full name: James Edward Roe II.
HIGH SCHOOL: Henrico (Richmond, Va.).
COLLEGE: Norfolk State.
TRANSACTIONS/CAREER NOTES: Selected by Baltimore Ravens in sixth round (186th pick overall) of 1996 NFL draft. ... Signed by Ravens for 1996 season.
PRO STATISTICS: 1997—Recovered one fumble.
SINGLE GAME HIGHS (regular season): Receptions—4 (November 30, 1997, vs. Jacksonville); yards—80 (November 30, 1997, vs. Jacksonville); and touchdown receptions—0.

Year Team	G	GS	RECEIVING No.	Yds.	Avg.	TD	PUNT RETURNS No.	Yds.	Avg.	TD	KICKOFF RETURNS No.	Yds.	Avg.	TD	TOTALS TD	2pt.	Pts.	Fum.
1996—Baltimore NFL	1	0	0	0	...	0	0	0	...	0	0	0	...	0	0	0	0	0
1997—Baltimore NFL	12	4	7	124	17.7	0	8	72	9.0	0	9	189	21.0	0	0	0	0	1
Pro totals (2 years)	13	4	7	124	17.7	0	8	72	9.0	0	9	189	21.0	0	0	0	0	1

ROGERS, SAM — LB — BILLS

PERSONAL: Born May 30, 1970, in Pontiac, Mich. ... 6-3/245. ... Full name: Sammy Lee Rogers.
HIGH SCHOOL: Saint Mary's Preparatory (Orchard Lake, Mich.).
JUNIOR COLLEGE: West Hills College (Calif.), then West Los Angeles College.
COLLEGE: Colorado.
TRANSACTIONS/CAREER NOTES: Selected by Buffalo Bills in second round (64th pick overall) of 1994 NFL draft. ... Signed by Bills (July 12, 1994). ... Granted free agency (February 14, 1997). ... Re-signed by Bills (June 12, 1997). ... Granted unconditional free agency (February 13, 1998). ... Re-signed by Bills (February 23, 1998).
PRO STATISTICS: 1995—Recovered one fumble. 1996—Recovered two fumbles.

Year Team	G	GS	SACKS
1994—Buffalo NFL	14	0	0.0
1995—Buffalo NFL	16	8	2.0
1996—Buffalo NFL	14	14	3.5
1997—Buffalo NFL	15	15	3.5
Pro totals (4 years)	59	37	9.0

ROMANOWSKI, BILL — LB — BRONCOS

PERSONAL: Born April 2, 1966, in Vernon, Conn. ... 6-4/245. ... Full name: William Thomas Romanowski.
HIGH SCHOOL: Rockville (Vernon, Conn.).
COLLEGE: Boston College (degree in general management, 1988).
TRANSACTIONS/CAREER NOTES: Selected by San Francisco 49ers in third round (80th pick overall) of 1988 NFL draft. ... Signed by 49ers (July 15, 1988). ... Granted free agency (February 1, 1991). ... Re-signed by 49ers (July 17, 1991). ... Granted unconditional free agency (March 1, 1993). ... Re-signed by 49ers (March 23, 1993). ... Traded by 49ers to Philadelphia Eagles for third-round (traded to Los Angeles Rams) and sixth-round (traded to Green Bay) picks in 1994 draft (April 24, 1994). ... Granted unconditional free agency (February 16, 1996). ... Signed by Denver Broncos (February 23, 1996).
CHAMPIONSHIP GAME EXPERIENCE: Played in NFC championship game (1988-1990, 1992 and 1993 seasons). ... Member of Super Bowl championship team (1988, 1989 and 1997 seasons). ... Played in AFC championship game (1997 season).
HONORS: Played in Pro Bowl (1996 season).
PRO STATISTICS: 1988—Recovered one fumble. 1989—Returned one punt for no yards, fumbled once and recovered two fumbles. 1991—Recovered two fumbles. 1992—Recovered one fumble. 1993—Recovered one fumble. 1994—Recovered one fumble. 1995—Recovered one fumble. 1996—Recovered three fumbles.

Year Team	G	GS	INTERCEPTIONS No.	Yds.	Avg.	TD	SACKS No.
1988—San Francisco NFL	16	8	0	0	...	0	0.0
1989—San Francisco NFL	16	4	1	13	13.0	0	1.0
1990—San Francisco NFL	16	16	0	0	...	0	1.0
1991—San Francisco NFL	16	16	1	7	7.0	0	1.0
1992—San Francisco NFL	16	16	0	0	...	0	1.0
1993—San Francisco NFL	16	16	0	0	...	0	3.0

| Year | Team | G | GS | INTERCEPTIONS | | | | SACKS |
				No.	Yds.	Avg.	TD	No.
1994—Philadelphia NFL		16	15	2	8	4.0	0	2.5
1995—Philadelphia NFL		16	16	2	5	2.5	0	1.0
1996—Denver NFL		16	16	3	1	0.3	0	3.0
1997—Denver NFL		16	16	1	7	7.0	0	2.0
Pro totals (10 years)		160	139	10	41	4.1	0	15.5

ROQUE, JUAN — OT — LIONS

PERSONAL: Born January 6, 1974, in San Diego. ... 6-8/333. ... Full name: Juan Armando Roque. ... Name pronounced row-KAY.
HIGH SCHOOL: Ontario (Calif.).
COLLEGE: Arizona State.
TRANSACTIONS/CAREER NOTES: Selected by Detroit Lions in second round (35th pick overall) of 1997 NFL draft. ... Signed by Lions (July 13, 1997). ... On injured reserve with knee injury (December 2, 1997-remainder of season).
PLAYING EXPERIENCE: Detroit NFL, 1997. ... Games/Games started: 13/1.
HONORS: Named offensive tackle on THE SPORTING NEWS college All-America second team (1996).

ROSENSTIEL, ROBERT — TE — RAIDERS

PERSONAL: Born February 7, 1974, in Prineville, Ore. ... 6-3/240.
HIGH SCHOOL: Junction City (Ore.).
JUNIOR COLLEGE: Shasta College (Calif.), then College of Sequoias (Calif.).
COLLEGE: Eastern Illinois.
TRANSACTIONS/CAREER NOTES: Signed as non-drafted free agent by Oakland Raiders (April 28, 1997). ... Released by Raiders (August 19, 1997). ... Re-signed by Raiders to practice squad (August 1997). ... Activated (November 1997).
PLAYING EXPERIENCE: Oakland NFL, 1997. ... Games/Games started: 4/0.
SINGLE GAME HIGHS (regular season): Receptions—0; yards—0; and touchdown receptions—0.

ROSS, JERMAINE — WR — JAGUARS

PERSONAL: Born April 27, 1971, in Jeffersonville, Ind. ... 6-0/191. ... Full name: Jermaine Lewis Ross.
HIGH SCHOOL: Jeffersonville (Ind.).
COLLEGE: Purdue.
TRANSACTIONS/CAREER NOTES: Signed as non-drafted free agent by Los Angeles Rams (April 29, 1994). ... Released by Rams (August 22, 1994). ... Re-signed by Rams to practice squad (August 29, 1994). ... Activated (November 30, 1994). ... Rams franchise moved to St. Louis (April 12, 1995). ... On injured reserve with right knee injury (August 21, 1995-entire season). ... Released by Rams (September 30, 1997). ... Signed by Jacksonville Jaguars (January 6, 1998).
PRO STATISTICS: 1996—Rushed once for three yards and a touchdown and recovered one fumble. 1997—Returned two punts for 12 yards and six kickoffs for 130 yards.
SINGLE GAME HIGHS (regular season): Receptions—2 (December 15, 1996, vs. Atlanta); yards—36 (December 24, 1994 vs. Washington); and touchdown receptions—1 (December 24, 1994, vs. Washington).

| Year | Team | G | GS | RECEIVING | | | | TOTALS | | | |
				No.	Yds.	Avg.	TD	TD	2pt.	Pts.	Fum.
1994—Los Angeles Rams NFL		4	0	1	36	36.0	1	1	0	6	0
1995—St. Louis NFL						Did not play.					
1996—St. Louis NFL		15	0	15	160	10.7	0	1	0	6	0
1997—St. Louis NFL		4	0	3	37	12.3	0	0	0	0	0
Pro totals (3 years)		23	0	19	233	12.3	1	2	0	12	0

ROSS, KEVIN — S — CHIEFS

PERSONAL: Born January 16, 1962, in Camden, N.J. ... 5-9/185. ... Full name: Kevin Lesley Ross.
HIGH SCHOOL: Paulsboro (N.J.).
COLLEGE: Temple.
TRANSACTIONS/CAREER NOTES: Selected by Philadelphia Stars in 1984 USFL territorial draft. ... Selected by Kansas City Chiefs in seventh round (173rd pick overall) of 1984 NFL draft. ... Signed by Chiefs (June 21, 1984). ... Crossed picket line during players strike (October 14, 1987). ... Granted roster exemption (September 3-8, 1990). ... Granted unconditional free agency (February 17, 1994). ... Signed by Atlanta Falcons (March 17, 1994). ... Released by Falcons (February 16, 1996). ... Signed by San Diego Chargers (March 5, 1996). ... Released by Chargers (February 20, 1997). ... Signed by Chiefs (June 9, 1997). ... On injured reserve with knee injury (October 9, 1997-remainder of season).
CHAMPIONSHIP GAME EXPERIENCE: Played in AFC championship game (1993 season).
HONORS: Played in Pro Bowl (1989 and 1990 seasons).
PRO STATISTICS: 1984—Recovered one fumble. 1985—Recovered one fumble. 1986—Recovered three fumbles for 33 yards and one touchdown. 1987—Returned blocked field-goal attempt 65 yards for a touchdown. 1989—Returned two punts for no yards and fumbled once. 1990—Returned blocked punt four yards for a touchdown and recovered three fumbles. 1991—Recovered one fumble for 13 yards. 1992—Recovered two fumbles. 1993—Recovered one fumble for 22 yards. 1995—Returned blocked field-goal attempt 83 yards for a touchdown and recovered two fumbles. 1996—Recovered one fumble.

| Year | Team | G | GS | INTERCEPTIONS | | | | SACKS |
				No.	Yds.	Avg.	TD	No.
1984—Kansas City NFL		16	16	6	124	20.7	1	0.0
1985—Kansas City NFL		16	15	3	47	15.7	0	0.0
1986—Kansas City NFL		16	16	4	66	16.5	0	2.0
1987—Kansas City NFL		12	11	3	40	13.3	0	1.0

Year Team	G	GS	INTERCEPTIONS No.	Yds.	Avg.	TD	SACKS No.
1988—Kansas City NFL	15	14	1	0	0.0	0	0.0
1989—Kansas City NFL	15	13	4	29	7.3	0	0.0
1990—Kansas City NFL	16	15	5	97	19.4	0	0.0
1991—Kansas City NFL	14	13	1	0	0.0	0	0.0
1992—Kansas City NFL	16	16	1	99	99.0	1	0.5
1993—Kansas City NFL	15	15	2	49	24.5	0	0.5
1994—Atlanta NFL	16	16	3	26	8.7	0	1.0
1995—Atlanta NFL	16	15	3	70	23.3	0	0.0
1996—San Diego NFL	16	16	2	7	3.5	0	0.0
1997—Kansas City NFL	5	0	0	0	...	0	0.0
Pro totals (14 years)	204	191	38	654	17.2	2	5.0

R

ROUEN, TOM   P   BRONCOS

PERSONAL: Born June 9, 1968, in Hinsdale, Ill. ... 6-3/225. ... Full name: Thomas Francis Rouen Jr. ... Name pronounced RUIN.
HIGH SCHOOL: Heritage (Littleton, Colo.).
COLLEGE: Colorado State, then Colorado.
TRANSACTIONS/CAREER NOTES: Signed as non-drafted free agent by New York Giants (April 29, 1991). ... Released by Giants (August 19, 1991). ... Selected by Ohio Glory in fourth round (44th pick overall) of 1992 World League draft. ... Signed by Los Angeles Rams (July 1992). ... Released by Rams (August 24, 1992). ... Signed by Denver Broncos (April 29, 1993). ... Granted unconditional free agency (February 14, 1997). ... Re-signed by Broncos (March 6, 1997).
CHAMPIONSHIP GAME EXPERIENCE: Played in AFC championship game (1997 season). ... Member of Super Bowl championship team (1997 season).
HONORS: Named punter on THE SPORTING NEWS college All-America second team (1989).
PRO STATISTICS: 1993—Rushed once for no yards.

Year Team	G	GS	PUNTING No.	Yds.	Avg.	Net avg.	In. 20	Blk.
1992—Ohio W.L.	10	0	48	1992	41.5	36.1	14	1
1993—Denver NFL	16	0	67	3017	45.0	37.1	17	1
1994—Denver NFL	16	0	76	3258	42.9	*37.1	23	0
1995—Denver NFL	16	0	52	2192	42.2	37.6	22	1
1996—Denver NFL	16	0	65	2714	41.8	36.2	16	0
1997—Denver NFL	16	0	60	2598	43.3	38.1	22	0
W.L. totals (1 year)	10	0	48	1992	41.5	36.1	14	1
NFL totals (5 years)	80	0	320	13779	43.1	37.2	100	2
Pro totals (6 years)	90	0	368	15771	42.9	37.0	114	3

ROUNDTREE, RALEIGH   OT   CHARGERS

PERSONAL: Born August 31, 1975, in Augusta, Ga. ... 6-4/295. ... Full name: Raleigh Cito Roundtree.
HIGH SCHOOL: Josey (Augusta, Ga.).
COLLEGE: South Carolina State.
TRANSACTIONS/CAREER NOTES: Selected by San Diego Chargers in fourth round (109th pick overall) of 1997 NFL draft. ... Signed by Chargers (July 14, 1997). ... Inactive for 16 games (1997).

ROWE, JOE   CB   RAMS

PERSONAL: Born December 8, 1973, in East Elmhurst, N.Y. ... 6-0/195. ... Full name: Joseph Rowe III.
HIGH SCHOOL: Greensville County (N.Y.).
COLLEGE: Virginia.
TRANSACTIONS/CAREER NOTES: Signed as non-drafted free agent by St. Louis Rams (April 29, 1997). ... Claimed on waivers by Green Bay Packers (August 19, 1997). ... Released by Packers (August 24, 1997). ... Re-signed by Packers to practice squad (August 26, 1997). ... Signed by Rams off Packers practice squad (November 18, 1997).
PLAYING EXPERIENCE: St. Louis NFL, 1997. ... Games/Games started: 2/0.

ROYAL, ANDRE   LB   SAINTS

PERSONAL: Born December 1, 1972, in Northport, Ala. ... 6-2/238. ... Full name: Andre Tierre Royal.
HIGH SCHOOL: Tuscaloosa County (Northport, Ala.).
COLLEGE: Alabama.
TRANSACTIONS/CAREER NOTES: Signed as non-drafted free agent by Cleveland Browns (May 2, 1995). ... Released by Browns (August 21, 1995). ... Signed by Carolina Panthers to practice squad (August 30, 1995). ... Activated (September 26, 1995). ... Granted free agency (February 13, 1998). ... Tendered offer sheet by New Orleans Saints (March 19, 1998). ... Panthers declined to match offer (March 25, 1998).
PLAYING EXPERIENCE: Carolina NFL, 1995-1997. ... Games/Games started: 1995 (12/0), 1996 (16/0), 1997 (16/13). Total: 44/13.
CHAMPIONSHIP GAME EXPERIENCE: Played in NFC championship game (1996 season).
PRO STATISTICS: 1996—Recovered one fumble. 1997—Credited with five sacks and recovered one fumble.

ROYALS, MARK   P   SAINTS

PERSONAL: Born June 22, 1964, in Hampton, Va. ... 6-5/215. ... Full name: Mark Alan Royals.
HIGH SCHOOL: Mathews (Va.).

COLLEGE: Chowan College (N.C.), then Appalachian State (degree in political science).

TRANSACTIONS/CAREER NOTES: Signed as non-drafted free agent by Dallas Cowboys (June 6, 1986). ... Released by Cowboys (August 8, 1986). ... Signed as replacement player by St. Louis Cardinals (September 30, 1987). ... Released by Cardinals (October 7, 1987). ... Signed as replacement player by Philadelphia Eagles (October 14, 1987). ... Released by Eagles (November 1987). ... Signed by Cardinals (December 12, 1987). ... Released by Cardinals (July 27, 1988). ... Signed by Miami Dolphins (May 2, 1989). ... Released by Dolphins (August 28, 1989). ... Signed by Tampa Bay Buccaneers (April 24, 1990). ... Granted unconditional free agency (February 1, 1992). ... Signed by Pittsburgh Steelers (March 15, 1992). ... Granted unconditional free agency (February 17, 1995). ... Signed by Detroit Lions (April 26, 1995). ... Granted free agency (February 16, 1996). ... Re-signed by Lions (June 19, 1996). ... Granted unconditional free agency (February 14, 1997). ... Signed by New Orleans Saints (April 25, 1997).

CHAMPIONSHIP GAME EXPERIENCE: Played in AFC championship game (1994 season).

PRO STATISTICS: 1987—Had 23.3-yard net punting average. 1992—Attempted one pass with one completion for 44 yards. 1994—Rushed once for minus 13 yards. 1995—Rushed once for minus seven yards. 1996—Attempted one pass with one completion for minus eight yards and recovered one fumble.

Year Team	G	GS	No.	Yds.	Avg.	Net avg.	In. 20	Blk.
1986—				Did not play.				
1987—St. Louis NFL	1	0	6	222	37.0	...	2	0
—Philadelphia NFL	1	0	5	209	41.8	...	1	0
1988—				Did not play.				
1989—				Did not play.				
1990—Tampa Bay NFL	16	0	72	2902	40.3	34.0	8	0
1991—Tampa Bay NFL	16	0	84	3389	40.3	32.2	22	0
1992—Pittsburgh NFL	16	0	73	3119	42.7	35.6	22	1
1993—Pittsburgh NFL	16	0	89	3781	42.5	34.2	§28	0
1994—Pittsburgh NFL	16	0	§97	3849	39.7	35.7	*35	0
1995—Detroit NFL	16	0	57	2393	42.0	31.0	15	2
1996—Detroit NFL	16	0	69	3020	43.8	33.3	11	1
1997—New Orleans NFL	16	0	88	4038	45.9	34.9	21	0
Pro totals (9 years)	130	0	640	26922	42.1	33.8	165	4

ROYE, ORPHEUS — DE/DT — STEELERS

PERSONAL: Born January 21, 1974, in Miami. ... 6-4/290. ... Name pronounced OR-fee-us ROY.

HIGH SCHOOL: Miami Springs.

JUNIOR COLLEGE: Jones County Junior College (Miss.).

COLLEGE: Florida State.

TRANSACTIONS/CAREER NOTES: Selected by Pittsburgh Steelers in sixth round (200th pick overall) of 1996 NFL draft. ... Signed by Steelers (July 16, 1996).

PLAYING EXPERIENCE: Pittsburgh NFL, 1996 and 1997. ... Games/Games started: 1996 (13/1), 1997 (16/0). Total: 29/1.

CHAMPIONSHIP GAME EXPERIENCE: Played in AFC championship game (1997 season).

PRO STATISTICS: 1996—Recovered one fumble. 1997—Credited with one sack.

RUCCI, TODD — G — PATRIOTS

PERSONAL: Born July 14, 1970, in Upper Darby, Pa. ... 6-5/296. ... Full name: Todd L. Rucci.

HIGH SCHOOL: Upper Darby (Pa.).

COLLEGE: Penn State.

TRANSACTIONS/CAREER NOTES: Selected by New England Patriots in second round (51st pick overall) of 1993 NFL draft. ... Signed by Patriots (July 22, 1993). ... On injured reserve with pectoral muscle injury (September 19, 1993-remainder of season). ... Granted unconditional free agency (February 13, 1998). ... Re-signed by Patriots (February 24, 1998).

PLAYING EXPERIENCE: New England NFL, 1993-1997. ... Games/Games started: 1993 (?/1), 1994 (13/10), 1995 (6/5), 1996 (16/12), 1997 (16/16). Total: 53/44.

CHAMPIONSHIP GAME EXPERIENCE: Played in AFC championship game (1996 season). ... Played in Super Bowl XXXI (1996 season).

RUCKER, KEITH — DT

PERSONAL: Born November 20, 1968, in University Park, Ill. ... 6-3/331.

HIGH SCHOOL: Shaker Heights (Cleveland).

COLLEGE: Eastern Michigan, then Ohio Wesleyan.

TRANSACTIONS/CAREER NOTES: Signed as non-drafted free agent by Phoenix Cardinals (May 8, 1992). ... Released by Cardinals (September 11, 1992). ... Re-signed by Cardinals to practice squad (September 14, 1992). ... Activated (September 16, 1992). ... Released by Cardinals (July 7, 1994). ... Signed by Cincinnati Bengals (July 11, 1994). ... Released by Bengals (August 19, 1996). ... Signed by Philadelphia Eagles (December 17, 1996). ... Released by Eagles (December 24, 1996). ... Signed by Washington Redskins (January 27, 1997). ... Released by Redskins (September 9, 1997). ... Signed by Kansas City Chiefs (October 9, 1997). ... Released by Chiefs (October 27, 1997).

PRO STATISTICS: 1993—Recovered one fumble.

Year Team	G	GS	SACKS
1992—Phoenix NFL	14	5	2.0
1993—Phoenix NFL	16	15	0.0
1994—Cincinnati NFL	16	14	2.0
1995—Cincinnati NFL	15	15	2.0
1996—		Did not play.	
1997—Washington NFL	2	0	0.0
Pro totals (5 years)	63	49	6.0

RUDD, DWAYNE   LB   VIKINGS

PERSONAL: Born February 3, 1976, in Batesville, Miss. ... 6-2/245. ... Full name: Dwayne Dupree Rudd.
HIGH SCHOOL: South Panola (Miss.).
COLLEGE: Alabama.
TRANSACTIONS/CAREER NOTES: Selected by Minnesota Vikings in first round (20th pick overall) of 1997 NFL draft. ... Signed by Vikings (July 18, 1997).

Year Team	G	GS	SACKS
1997—Minnesota NFL	16	2	5.0

RUDDY, TIM   C   DOLPHINS

PERSONAL: Born April 27, 1972, in Scranton, Pa. ... 6-3/300. ... Full name: Timothy Daniel Ruddy.
HIGH SCHOOL: Dunmore (Pa.).
COLLEGE: Notre Dame.
TRANSACTIONS/CAREER NOTES: Selected by Miami Dolphins in second round (65th pick overall) of 1994 NFL draft. ... Signed by Dolphins (July 18, 1994).
PLAYING EXPERIENCE: Miami NFL, 1994-1997. ... Games/Games started: 1994 (16/0), 1995 (16/16), 1996 (16/16), 1997 (15/15). Total: 63/47.
PRO STATISTICS: 1995—Fumbled once. 1996—Fumbled once for minus 14 yards.

RUDOLPH, JOE   G   49ERS

PERSONAL: Born July 21, 1972, in Belle Vernon, Pa. ... 6-2/284.
HIGH SCHOOL: Belle Vernon (Pa.).
COLLEGE: Wisconsin.
TRANSACTIONS/CAREER NOTES: Signed as non-drafted free agent by Philadelphia Eagles (April 26, 1995). ... Released by Eagles (August 27, 1995). ... Re-signed by Eagles (October 4, 1995). ... Released by Eagles (December 22, 1995). ... Re-signed by Eagles to practice squad (December 22, 1995). ... Activated (January 5, 1996). ... Released by Eagles (August 20, 1996). ... Signed by San Francisco 49ers (January 23, 1997).
PLAYING EXPERIENCE: Philadelphia NFL, 1995; San Francisco NFL, 1997. ... Games/Games started: 1995 (4/0), 1997 (6/1). Total: 10/1.
CHAMPIONSHIP GAME EXPERIENCE: Member of 49ers for NFC championship game (1997 season); inactive.

RUNYAN, JON   OT   OILERS

PERSONAL: Born November 27, 1973, in Flint, Mich. ... 6-7/316. ... Full name: Jon Daniel Runyan.
HIGH SCHOOL: Carman-Ainsworth (Flint, Mich.).
COLLEGE: Michigan.
TRANSACTIONS/CAREER NOTES: Selected after junior season by Houston Oilers in fourth round (109th pick overall) of 1996 NFL draft. ... Signed by Oilers (July 20, 1996). ... Oilers franchise moved to Tennessee for 1997 season.
PLAYING EXPERIENCE: Houston NFL, 1996; Tennessee NFL, 1997. ... Games/Games started: 1996 (10/0), 1997 (16/16). Total: 26/16.
HONORS: Named offensive lineman on THE SPORTING NEWS college All-America second team (1995).

RUSK, REGGIE   CB   SEAHAWKS

PERSONAL: Born October 19, 1972, in Galveston, Texas. ... 5-10/190. ... Full name: Reggie Leon Rusk.
HIGH SCHOOL: Texas City (Texas).
COLLEGE: Kentucky.
TRANSACTIONS/CAREER NOTES: Selected by Tampa Bay Buccaneers in seventh round (221st pick overall) of 1996 NFL draft. ... Signed by Buccaneers (July 12, 1996). ... Released by Buccaneers (August 18, 1996). ... Re-signed by Buccaneers to practice squad (August 27, 1996). ... Activated (September 28, 1996). ... Released by Buccaneers (October 2, 1996). ... Re-signed by Buccaneers to practice squad (October 3, 1996). ... Assigned by Buccaneers to Scottish Claymores in 1997 World League enhancement allocation program (February 19, 1997). ... Released by Buccaneers (September 27, 1997). ... Re-signed by Buccaneers to practice squad (September 29, 1997). ... Signed by Seattle Seahawks off Buccaneers practice squad (December 5, 1997).
PLAYING EXPERIENCE: Tampa Bay NFL, 1996; Tampa Bay (4)-Seattle (2) NFL, 1997. ... Games/Games started: 1996 (1/0), 1997 (T.B.-4/0; Sea.-2/0; Total: 6/0). Total: 7/0.

RUSS, BERNARD   LB   PATRIOTS

PERSONAL: Born November 4, 1973 ... 6-0/225. ... Full name: Bernard Dion Russ.
HIGH SCHOOL: Collinwood (Utica, N.Y.).
JUNIOR COLLEGE: Arizona Western.
COLLEGE: West Virginia.
TRANSACTIONS/CAREER NOTES: Signed as non-drafted free agent by Baltimore Ravens (April 25, 1997). ... Released by Ravens (August 24, 1997). ... Signed by New England Patriots to practice squad (August 27, 1997). ... Activated (December 9, 1997).
PLAYING EXPERIENCE: New England NFL, 1997. ... Games/Games started: 2/0.

RUSS, STEVE   LB   BRONCOS

PERSONAL: Born September 16, 1972, in Stetsonville, Wis. ... 6-4/245.
HIGH SCHOOL: Stetsonville, Wis.
COLLEGE: Air Force.

TRANSACTIONS/CAREER NOTES: Selected by Denver Broncos in seventh round (218th pick overall) of 1995 NFL draft. ... Signed by Broncos (July 12, 1995). ... On reserved/military list entire 1995 season. ... On reserved/military list (August 13, 1996-entire season).
PLAYING EXPERIENCE: Denver NFL, 1997. ... Games/Games started: 14/0.
CHAMPIONSHIP GAME EXPERIENCE: Member of Broncos for AFC championship game (1997 season); inactive. ... Member of Super Bowl championship team (1997 season); inactive.

RUSSELL, DARRELL   DT   RAIDERS

PERSONAL: Born May 27, 1976, in Pensacola, Fla. ... 6-4/321.
HIGH SCHOOL: St. Augustine (San Diego).
COLLEGE: Southern California.
TRANSACTIONS/CAREER NOTES: Selected by Oakland Raiders in first round (second pick overall) of 1997 NFL draft. ... Signed by Raiders (July 23, 1997).

Year Team	G	GS	SACKS
1997—Oakland NFL	16	10	3.5

RUSSELL, DEREK   WR

PERSONAL: Born June 22, 1969, in Little Rock, Ark. ... 6-0/195. ... Full name: Derek Dwayne Russell. ... Cousin of Sidney Moncrief, guard with Milwaukee Bucks (1979-80 through 1988-89) and Atlanta Hawks (1990-91).
HIGH SCHOOL: Little Rock (Ark.) Central.
COLLEGE: Arkansas.
TRANSACTIONS/CAREER NOTES: Selected by Denver Broncos in fourth round (89th pick overall) of 1991 NFL draft. ... Signed by Broncos (July 12, 1991). ... On injured reserve with thumb injury (December 1, 1992-remainder of season). ... Granted unconditional free agency (February 17, 1995). ... Signed by Houston Oilers (June 2, 1995). ... Oilers franchise moved to Tennessee for 1997 season. ... Released by Oilers (July 18, 1997). ... Re-signed by Oilers (July 24, 1997). ... Released by Oilers (April 15, 1998).
CHAMPIONSHIP GAME EXPERIENCE: Played in AFC championship game (1991 season).
PRO STATISTICS: 1993—Recovered one fumble in end zone for a touchdown.
SINGLE GAME HIGHS (regular season): Receptions—6 (November 28, 1993, vs. Seattle); yards—111 (October 18, 1993, vs. Los Angeles Raiders); and touchdown receptions—1 (November 23, 1997, vs. Buffalo).
STATISTICAL PLATEAUS: 100-yard receiving games: 1993 (2).

Year Team	G	GS	RECEIVING				KICKOFF RETURNS				TOTALS			
			No.	Yds.	Avg.	TD	No.	Yds.	Avg.	TD	TD	2pt.	Pts.	Fum.
1991—Denver NFL	13	5	21	317	15.1	1	7	120	17.1	0	1	...	6	0
1992—Denver NFL	12	6	12	140	11.7	0	7	154	22.0	0	0	...	0	0
1993—Denver NFL	13	12	44	719	16.3	3	18	374	20.8	0	4	...	24	1
1994—Denver NFL	12	12	25	342	13.7	1	5	105	21.0	0	1	0	6	0
1995—Houston NFL	11	5	24	321	13.4	0	0	0	...	0	0	0	0	0
1996—Houston NFL	16	5	34	421	12.4	2	0	0	...	0	2	0	12	0
1997—Tennessee NFL	11	2	12	141	11.8	1	0	0	...	0	1	0	6	0
Pro totals (7 years)	88	47	172	2401	14.0	8	37	753	20.4	0	9	0	54	1

RUSSELL, MATT   LB   LIONS

PERSONAL: Born July 5, 1973, in Tokyo. ... 6-2/245.
HIGH SCHOOL: Belleville East (Ill.).
COLLEGE: Colorado.
TRANSACTIONS/CAREER NOTES: Selected by Detroit Lions in fourth round (130th pick overall) of 1997 NFL draft. ... Signed by Lions (July 13, 1997).
PLAYING EXPERIENCE: Detroit NFL, 1997. ... Games/Games started: 14/0.
HONORS: Butkus Award winner (1996). ... Named inside linebacker on THE SPORTING NEWS college All-America first team (1996).
PRO STATISTICS: 1997—Returned one kickoff for no yards and recovered one fumble.

RUSSELL, TWAN   LB   REDSKINS

PERSONAL: Born April 25, 1974, in Fort Lauderdale, Fla. ... 6-1/219. ... Full name: Twan Sanchez Russell.
HIGH SCHOOL: St. Thomas Aquinas (Fort Lauderdale, Fla.).
COLLEGE: Miami, Fla. (degree in broadcasting, 1996).
TRANSACTIONS/CAREER NOTES: Selected by Washington Redskins in fifth round (148th pick overall) of 1997 NFL draft. ... Signed by Redskins (May 9, 1997).
PLAYING EXPERIENCE: Washington NFL, 1997. ... Games/Games started: 14/0.

RUTHERFORD, REYNARD   RB   49ERS

PERSONAL: Born May 15, 1973, in San Francisco. ... 6-0/210. ... Name pronounced ruh-NARD.
HIGH SCHOOL: McAteer (San Francisco), then Benica (Calif.).
COLLEGE: California.
TRANSACTIONS/CAREER NOTES: Signed as non-drafted free agent by Kansas City Chiefs (April 30, 1996). ... Released by Chiefs (August 1, 1996). ... Signed by San Francisco 49ers (August 7, 1996). ... Released by 49ers (August 20, 1996). ... Signed by 49ers to practice squad (September 4, 1996). ... Released by 49ers (September 17, 1996). ... Re-signed by 49ers (July 22, 1997). ... Released by 49ers (August 19, 1997). ... Re-signed by 49ers to practice squad (August 25, 1997). ... Assigned by 49ers to Frankfurt Galaxy in 1998 NFL Europe enhancement allocation program (February 18, 1998).

RYPIEN, MARK   QB   FALCONS

PERSONAL: Born October 2, 1962, in Calgary, Alberta. ... 6-4/225. ... Full name: Mark Robert Rypien. ... Brother of Tim Rypien, catcher in Toronto Blue Jays organization (1984-1986); and cousin of Shane Churla, forward, New York Rangers of NHL. ... Name pronounced RIP-in.
HIGH SCHOOL: Shadle Park (Spokane, Wash.).
COLLEGE: Washington State.
TRANSACTIONS/CAREER NOTES: Selected by Washington Redskins in sixth round (146th pick overall) of 1986 NFL draft. ... Signed by Redskins (July 18, 1986). ... On injured reserve with knee injury (September 5, 1986-entire season). ... On injured reserve with back injury (September 7-November 28, 1987). ... Active for one game with Redskins (1987); did not play. ... On injured reserve with knee injury (September 26-November 17, 1990). ... Granted free agency (February 1, 1991). ... Re-signed by Redskins (July 24, 1991). ... Granted free agency (February 1, 1992). ... Re-signed by Redskins (August 11, 1992). ... Released by Redskins (April 13, 1994). ... Signed by Cleveland Browns (May 10, 1994). ... Granted unconditional free agency (February 17, 1995). ... Signed by St. Louis Rams (May 8, 1995). ... Granted free agency (February 16, 1996). ... Signed by Philadelphia Eagles (October 3, 1996). ... Granted unconditional free agency (February 14, 1997). ... Signed by Rams (March 5, 1997). ... Granted unconditional free agency (February 13, 1998). ... Signed by Atlanta Falcons (April 1, 1998).
CHAMPIONSHIP GAME EXPERIENCE: Played in NFC championship game (1991 season). ... Member of Super Bowl championship team (1987 and 1991 seasons).
HONORS: Played in Pro Bowl (1989 and 1991 seasons). ... Named Most Valuable Player of Super Bowl XXVI (1991 season).
PRO STATISTICS: 1988—Fumbled six times. 1989—Fumbled 14 times and recovered two fumbles. 1990—Fumbled twice. 1991—Fumbled nine times and recovered three fumbles for minus five yards. 1992—Fumbled four times and recovered two fumbles. 1993—Fumbled seven times. 1994—Fumbled twice. 1995—Fumbled once.
SINGLE GAME HIGHS (regular season): Attempts—55 (December 10, 1995, vs. Buffalo; completions—34 (December 17, 1995, vs. Washington); yards—442 (November 10, 1991, vs. Atlanta); and touchdown passes—6 (November 10, 1991, vs. Atlanta).
STATISTICAL PLATEAUS: 300-yard passing games: 1988 (2), 1989 (5), 1990 (1), 1991 (2), 1995 (3). Total: 13.
MISCELLANEOUS: Regular-season record as starting NFL quarterback: 47-31 (.603). ... Postseason record as starting NFL quarterback: 5-2 (.714).

Year Team	G	GS	Att.	Cmp.	Pct.	Yds.	TD	Int.	Avg.	Rat.	Att.	Yds.	Avg.	TD	TD	2pt.	Pts.
						PASSING						RUSHING				TOTALS	
1986—Washington NFL						Did not play.											
1987—Washington NFL						Did not play.											
1988—Washington NFL	9	6	208	114	54.8	1730	18	13	8.32	85.2	9	31	3.4	1	1	...	6
1989—Washington NFL	14	14	476	280	58.8	3768	22	13	7.92	88.1	26	56	2.2	1	1	...	6
1990—Washington NFL	10	10	304	166	54.6	2070	16	11	6.81	78.4	15	4	0.3	0	0	...	0
1991—Washington NFL	16	16	421	249	59.1	‡3564	‡28	11	8.47	97.9	15	6	0.4	1	1	...	6
1992—Washington NFL	16	16	‡479	269	56.2	3282	13	17	6.85	71.7	36	50	1.4	2	2	...	12
1993—Washington NFL	12	10	319	166	52.0	1514	4	10	4.75	56.3	9	4	0.4	3	3	...	18
1994—Cleveland NFL	6	3	128	59	46.1	694	4	3	5.42	63.7	7	4	0.6	0	0	0	0
1995—St. Louis NFL	11	3	217	129	59.4	1448	9	8	6.67	77.9	9	10	1.1	0	0	0	0
1996—Philadelphia NFL	1	0	13	10	76.9	76	1	0	5.85	116.2	0	0	...	0	0	0	0
1997—St. Louis NFL	5	0	39	19	48.7	270	2	2	6.92	50.2	1	1	1.0	0	0	0	0
Pro totals (10 years)	100	78	2604	1461	56.1	18416	115	88	7.07	78.9	127	166	1.3	8	8	...	48

SABB, DWAYNE   LB   BILLS

PERSONAL: Born October 9, 1969, in Union City, N.J. ... 6-4/248. ... Full name: Dwayne Irving Sabb.
HIGH SCHOOL: Hudson Catholic (Jersey City, N.J.).
COLLEGE: New Hampshire.
TRANSACTIONS/CAREER NOTES: Selected by New England Patriots in fifth round (116th pick overall) of 1992 NFL draft. ... Signed by Patriots (July 15, 1992). ... Granted free agency (February 17, 1995). ... Re-signed by Patriots (May 24, 1995). ... Granted unconditional free agency (February 14, 1997). ... Signed by St. Louis Rams (June 14, 1997). ... Released by Rams (August 24, 1997). ... Signed by Buffalo Bills for 1998 season.
CHAMPIONSHIP GAME EXPERIENCE: Played in Super Bowl XXXI (1996 season).
PRO STATISTICS: 1993—Returned two kickoffs for no yards.

Year Team	G	GS	No.	Yds.	Avg.	TD	No.
			INTERCEPTIONS				SACKS
1992—New England NFL	16	2	0	0	...	0	1.0
1993—New England NFL	14	7	0	0	...	0	2.0
1994—New England NFL	16	8	2	6	3.0	0	3.5
1995—New England NFL	12	0	0	0	...	0	0.0
1996—New England NFL	16	7	1	0	0.0	0	0.5
1997—			Did not play.				
Pro totals (5 years)	74	24	3	6	2.0	0	7.0

SADOWSKI, TROY   TE   STEELERS

PERSONAL: Born December 8, 1965, in Atlanta. ... 6-5/252. ... Full name: Troy Robert Sadowski.
HIGH SCHOOL: Chamblee (Ga.).
COLLEGE: Georgia.
TRANSACTIONS/CAREER NOTES: Selected by Atlanta Falcons in sixth round (145th pick overall) of 1989 NFL draft. ... Signed by Falcons for 1989 season. ... Released by Falcons (August 30, 1989). ... Re-signed by Falcons to developmental squad (December 6, 1989). ... Released by Falcons (January 9, 1990). ... Re-signed by Falcons (February 20, 1990). ... Released by Falcons (September 3, 1990). ... Re-signed by Falcons (September 4, 1990). ... Granted unconditional free agency (February 1, 1991). ... Signed by Kansas City Chiefs (April 2, 1991). ... Released by Chiefs (December 17, 1991). ... Signed by New York Jets (March 23, 1992). ... Released by Jets (April 20, 1993). ... Released by Jets (August 24, 1993). ... Re-signed by Jets (September 28, 1993). ... Granted unconditional free agency (February 17, 1994). ... Signed by Cincinnati Bengals (April 26, 1994). ... Released by Bengals (August 18, 1997). ... Signed by Pittsburgh Steelers (November 11, 1997).
CHAMPIONSHIP GAME EXPERIENCE: Played in AFC championship game (1997 season).
PRO STATISTICS: 1993—Returned one kickoff for no yards. 1994—Recovered one fumble. 1995—Recovered one fumble. 1996—Returned two kickoffs for seven yards.
SINGLE GAME HIGHS (regular season): Receptions—3 (November 6, 1994, vs. Seattle); yards—20 (September 6, 1992, vs. Atlanta); and touchdown receptions—0.

Year Team	G	GS	No.	Yds.	Avg.	TD	TD	2pt.	Pts.	Fum.
			RECEIVING				TOTALS			
1990—Atlanta NFL	13	1	0	0	...	0	0	...	0	0
1991—Kansas City NFL	14	1	0	0	...	0	0	...	0	0
1992—New York Jets NFL	6	2	1	20	20.0	0	0	...	0	0
1993—New York Jets NFL	13	1	2	14	7.0	0	0	...	0	0
1994—Cincinnati NFL	15	1	11	54	4.9	0	0	0	0	0
1995—Cincinnati NFL	12	1	5	37	7.4	0	0	0	0	0
1996—Cincinnati NFL	16	0	3	15	5.0	0	0	0	0	0
1997—Pittsburgh NFL	5	0	1	12	12.0	0	0	0	0	0
Pro totals (8 years)	94	7	23	152	6.6	0	0	0	0	0

SAGAPOLUTELE, PIO — DL — SAINTS

PERSONAL: Born November 28, 1969, in American Samoa. ... 6-6/297. ... Full name: Pio Alika Sagapolutele. ... Name pronounced PEE-o Saang-a-POO-la-tel-lee.

HIGH SCHOOL: Maryknoll (Honolulu).

COLLEGE: San Diego State (degree in criminal justice, 1991).

TRANSACTIONS/CAREER NOTES: Selected by Cleveland Browns in fourth round (85th pick overall) of 1991 NFL draft. ... Signed by Browns for 1991 season. ... Granted free agency (February 17, 1994). ... Re-signed by Browns (May 11, 1994). ... Granted unconditional free agency (February 17, 1995). ... Re-signed by Browns (April 17, 1995). ... Granted unconditional free agency (February 16, 1996). ... Signed by New England Patriots (March 20, 1996). ... Released by Patriots (June 12, 1997). ... Signed by New Orleans Saints (July 21, 1997).

CHAMPIONSHIP GAME EXPERIENCE: Played in AFC championship game (1996 season). ... Played in Super Bowl XXXI (1996 season).

Year Team	G	GS	SACKS
1991—Cleveland NFL	15	8	1.5
1992—Cleveland NFL	14	0	0.0
1993—Cleveland NFL	8	0	0.0
1994—Cleveland NFL	11	0	0.0
1995—Cleveland NFL	15	3	0.5
1996—New England NFL	15	10	3.0
1997—New Orleans NFL	15	13	2.0
Pro totals (7 years)	93	34	7.0

S

SALAAM, RASHAAN — RB — BEARS

PERSONAL: Born October 8, 1974, in San Diego. ... 6-1/224. ... Full name: Rashaan Iman Salaam. ... Son of Sulton Salaam (formerly known as Teddy Washington), running back with Cincinnati Bengals of AFL (1968). ... Name pronounced rah-SHAHN sah-LAHM.

HIGH SCHOOL: La Jolla (Calif.) Country Day.

COLLEGE: Colorado.

TRANSACTIONS/CAREER NOTES: Selected after junior season by Chicago Bears in first round (21st pick overall) of 1995 NFL draft. ... Signed by Bears (August 3, 1995). ... On injured reserve with leg injury (September 23, 1997-remainder of season). ... Traded by Bears to Miami Dolphins for conditional pick in 1999 draft (April 22, 1998); trade later voided because Salaam failed physical (April 24, 1998).

HONORS: Heisman Trophy winner (1994). ... Named College Football Player of the Year by THE SPORTING NEWS (1994). ... Doak Walker Award winner (1994). ... Named running back on THE SPORTING NEWS college All-America first team (1994).

PRO STATISTICS: 1995—Recovered one fumble. 1996—Recovered one fumble.

SINGLE GAME HIGHS (regular season): Attempts—30 (December 24, 1995, vs. Philadelphia); yards—134 (December 17, 1995, vs. Tampa Bay); and rushing touchdowns—3 (December 17, 1995, vs. Tampa Bay).

STATISTICAL PLATEAUS: 100-yard rushing games: 1995 (5), 1996 (1). Total: 6.

Year Team	G	GS	Att.	Yds.	Avg.	TD	No.	Yds.	Avg.	TD	TD	2pt.	Pts.	Fum.
			RUSHING				RECEIVING				TOTALS			
1995—Chicago NFL	16	12	296	1074	3.6	10	7	56	8.0	0	10	0	60	9
1996—Chicago NFL	12	6	143	496	3.5	3	7	44	6.3	1	4	0	24	3
1997—Chicago NFL	3	3	31	112	3.6	0	2	20	10.0	0	0	0	0	2
Pro totals (3 years)	31	21	470	1682	3.6	13	16	120	7.5	1	14	0	84	14

SALEAUMUA, DAN — DT — SEAHAWKS

PERSONAL: Born November 25, 1964, in San Diego. ... 6-0/315. ... Full name: Raymond Daniel Saleaumua. ... Name pronounced SOL-ee-uh-MOO-uh.

HIGH SCHOOL: Sweetwater (National City, Calif.).

COLLEGE: Arizona State.

TRANSACTIONS/CAREER NOTES: Selected by Detroit Lions in seventh round (175th pick overall) of 1987 NFL draft. ... Signed by Lions (July 25, 1987). ... On injured reserve with hamstring injury (September 7-October 31, 1987). ... Granted unconditional free agency (February 1, 1989). ... Signed by Kansas City Chiefs (March 20, 1989). ... Designated by Chiefs as transition player (February 25, 1993). ... Free agency status changed by Chiefs from transitional to unconditional (February 17, 1994). ... Re-signed by Chiefs (August 23, 1994). ... Released by Chiefs (July 28, 1997). ... Signed by Seattle Seahawks (August 6, 1997).

CHAMPIONSHIP GAME EXPERIENCE: Played in AFC championship game (1993 season).

HONORS: Played in Pro Bowl (1995 season).

PRO STATISTICS: 1987—Returned three kickoffs for 57 yards. 1988—Returned one kickoff for no yards and fumbled once. 1989—Intercepted one pass for 21 yards, returned one kickoff for eight yards and recovered five fumbles for two yards. 1990—Recovered six fumbles (including one in end zone for a touchdown). 1991—Credited with one safety and recovered two fumbles. 1992—Recovered one fumble. 1993—Intercepted one pass for 13 yards and recovered one fumble for 16 yards and a touchdown. 1994—Recovered one fumble. 1995—Intercepted one pass for no yards and recovered one fumble. 1997—Recovered one fumble and credited with a safety.

Year Team	G	GS	SACKS
1987—Detroit NFL	9	0	2.0
1988—Detroit NFL	16	0	2.0
1989—Kansas City NFL	16	8	2.0
1990—Kansas City NFL	16	16	7.0
1991—Kansas City NFL	16	16	1.5
1992—Kansas City NFL	16	16	6.0
1993—Kansas City NFL	16	16	3.5
1994—Kansas City NFL	14	14	1.0
1995—Kansas City NFL	16	16	7.0
1996—Kansas City NFL	15	14	0.0
1997—Seattle NFL	16	8	3.5
Pro totals (11 years)	**166**	**124**	**35.5**

SALEH, TAREK — LB — PANTHERS

PERSONAL: Born November 7, 1974, in Woodbridge, Conn. ... 6-1/240. ... Name pronounced TAR-ick SAH-luh.
HIGH SCHOOL: Notre Dame (Woodbridge, Conn.).
COLLEGE: Wisconsin.
TRANSACTIONS/CAREER NOTES: Selected by Carolina Panthers in fourth round (122nd pick overall) of 1997 NFL draft. ... Signed by Panthers for 1997 season.

Year Team	G	GS	SACKS
1997—Carolina NFL	3	0	1.0

SALMON, MIKE — S

PERSONAL: Born December 27, 1970, in Long Beach, Calif. ... 6-1/208. ... Brother of Tim Salmon, outfielder, Anaheim Angels.
HIGH SCHOOL: Greenway (Phoenix).
COLLEGE: Southern California.
TRANSACTIONS/CAREER NOTES: Signed as non-drafted free agent by San Francisco 49ers (July 21, 1994). ... Released by 49ers (August 21, 1994). ... Signed by Houston Oilers prior to 1995 season. ... Released by Oilers (August 22, 1995). ... Signed by 49ers (August 8, 1996). ... Released by 49ers (August 20, 1996). ... Re-signed to 49ers practice squad (August 26, 1996). ... Signed by Buffalo Bills off 49ers practice squad (October 9, 1996). ... Released by Bills (November 22, 1996). ... Re-signed by Bills to practice squad (November 24, 1996). ... Granted free agency after 1996 season. ... Signed by 49ers (April 29, 1997). ... Released by 49ers (August 26, 1997). ... Signed by 49ers (September 17, 1997). ... Released by 49ers (October 21, 1997).
PLAYING EXPERIENCE: San Francisco NFL, 1997. ... Games/Games started: 1/0.

SANDERS, BARRY — RB — LIONS

PERSONAL: Born July 16, 1968, in Wichita, Kan. ... 5-8/200.
HIGH SCHOOL: North (Wichita, Kan.).
COLLEGE: Oklahoma State.
TRANSACTIONS/CAREER NOTES: Selected after junior season by Detroit Lions in first round (third pick overall) of 1989 NFL draft. ... Signed by Lions (September 7, 1989).
CHAMPIONSHIP GAME EXPERIENCE: Played in NFC championship game (1991 season).
HONORS: Named kick returner on THE SPORTING NEWS college All-America first team (1987). ... Heisman Trophy winner (1988). ... Named College Football Player of the Year by THE SPORTING NEWS (1988). ... Maxwell Award winner (1988). ... Named running back on THE SPORTING NEWS college All-America first team (1988). ... Named NFL Rookie of the Year by THE SPORTING NEWS (1989). ... Named running back on THE SPORTING NEWS NFL All-Pro team (1989-1991 and 1993-1997). ... Played in Pro Bowl (1989-1992 and 1994-1997 seasons). ... Named to play in Pro Bowl (1993 season); replaced by Ricky Watters due to injury. ... Named NFL Player of the Year by THE SPORTING NEWS (1997).
RECORDS: Holds NFL record for most consecutive seasons with 1,000 or more yards rushing—9 (1989-1997); and most consecutive games with 100 or more yards rushing—14 (September 14-December 21, 1997). ... Holds NFL single-season record for most games with 100 or more yards rushing—14 (1997); and most consecutive games with 100 or more yards rushing—14 (September 14-December 21, 1997).
PRO STATISTICS: 1989—Returned five kickoffs for 118 yards. 1990—Recovered two fumbles. 1991—Recovered one fumble. 1992—Attempted one pass without a completion and recovered two fumbles. 1993—Recovered three fumbles. 1995—Attempted two passes with one completion for 11 yards and recovered one fumble. 1996—Attempted one pass without a completion and an interception and recovered two fumbles. 1997—Recovered one fumble.
SINGLE GAME HIGHS (regular season): Attempts—40 (September 19, 1994, vs. Dallas); yards—237 (November 13, 1994, vs. Tampa Bay); and rushing touchdowns—4 (November 24, 1991, vs. Minnesota).
STATISTICAL PLATEAUS: 100-yard rushing games: 1989 (7), 1990 (4), 1991 (8), 1992 (7), 1993 (4), 1994 (10), 1995 (7), 1996 (6), 1997 (14). Total: 67. ... 100-yard receiving games: 1990 (1), 1997 (1). Total: 2.
MISCELLANEOUS: Active NFL leader for career rushing yards (13,778). ... Holds Detroit Lions all-time records for most yards rushing (13,778), most touchdowns (105) and most rushing touchdowns (95).

			RUSHING				RECEIVING				TOTALS			
Year Team	G	GS	Att.	Yds.	Avg.	TD	No.	Yds.	Avg.	TD	TD	2pt.	Pts.	Fum.
1989—Detroit NFL	15	13	280	‡1470	5.3	14	24	282	11.8	0	14	...	84	10
1990—Detroit NFL	16	16	255	*1304	5.1	13	36	480	13.3	3	*16	...	96	4
1991—Detroit NFL	15	15	342	1548	4.5	*16	41	307	7.5	1	*17	...	102	5
1992—Detroit NFL	16	16	312	1352	4.3	9	29	225	7.8	1	10	...	60	6
1993—Detroit NFL	11	11	243	1115	4.6	3	36	205	5.7	0	3	...	18	3
1994—Detroit NFL	16	16	331	*1883	*5.7	7	44	283	6.4	1	8	0	48	0
1995—Detroit NFL	16	16	314	1500	4.8	11	48	398	8.3	1	12	0	72	3
1996—Detroit NFL	16	16	307	*1553	‡5.1	11	24	147	6.1	0	11	0	66	4
1997—Detroit NFL	16	16	‡335	*2053	‡6.1	‡11	33	305	9.2	3	‡14	0	84	3
Pro totals (9 years)	**137**	**135**	**2719**	**13778**	**5.1**	**95**	**315**	**2632**	**8.4**	**10**	**105**	**0**	**630**	**38**

SANDERS, BRANDON — S

PERSONAL: Born June 10, 1973, in San Diego. ... 5-9/185. ... Full name: Brandon Christopher Sanders.
HIGH SCHOOL: Helix (La Mesa, Calif.).
COLLEGE: Arizona.
TRANSACTIONS/CAREER NOTES: Signed as non-drafted free agent by Kansas City Chiefs (April 27, 1996). ... Released by Chiefs (August 20, 1996). ... Signed by New York Giants (March 10, 1997).
PLAYING EXPERIENCE: New York Giants NFL, 1997. ... Games/Games started: 12/0.

SANDERS, CHRIS — TE — REDSKINS

PERSONAL: Born April 22, 1973 ... 6-3/241. ... Full name: Christopher Sanders.
HIGH SCHOOL: LBJ (Austin).
COLLEGE: Texas A&M.
TRANSACTIONS/CAREER NOTES: Signed as non-drafted free agent by Houston Oilers (April 23, 1996). ... Released by Oilers (August 25, 1996). ... Re-signed by Oilers to practice squad (August 26, 1996). ... Granted free agency after 1996 season. ... Signed by Washington Redskins (February 27, 1997). ... Released by Redskins (September 18, 1997). ... Re-signed by Redskins to practice squad (September 22, 1997).
PLAYING EXPERIENCE: Washington NFL, 1997. ... Games/Games started: 1/0.
SINGLE GAME HIGHS (regular season): Attempts—0; yards—0; and rushing touchdowns—0.

SANDERS, CHRIS — WR — OILERS

PERSONAL: Born May 8, 1972, in Denver. ... 6-1/180. ... Full name: Christopher Dwayne Sanders.
HIGH SCHOOL: Montbello (Denver).
COLLEGE: Ohio State.
TRANSACTIONS/CAREER NOTES: Selected by Houston Oilers in third round (67th pick overall) of 1995 NFL draft. ... Signed by Oilers (July 20, 1995). ... Oilers franchise moved to Tennessee for 1997 season.
PRO STATISTICS: 1995—Rushed twice for minus 19 yards. 1997—Rushed once for minus eight yards.
SINGLE GAME HIGHS (regular season): Receptions—7 (December 14, 1997, vs. Baltimore); yards—147 (November 26, 1995, vs. Denver); and touchdown receptions—2 (October 26, 1997, vs. Arizona).
STATISTICAL PLATEAUS: 100-yard receiving games: 1995 (1), 1996 (3), 1997 (1). Total: 5.

| | | | RECEIVING | | | | TOTALS | | |
Year Team	G	GS	No.	Yds.	Avg.	TD	TD	2pt.	Pts.	Fum.
1995—Houston NFL	16	10	35	823	*23.5	9	9	0	54	0
1996—Houston NFL	16	15	48	882	§18.4	4	4	0	24	0
1997—Tennessee NFL	15	14	31	498	16.1	3	3	0	18	1
Pro totals (3 years)	47	39	114	2203	19.3	16	16	0	96	1

SANDERS, DEION — CB — COWBOYS

PERSONAL: Born August 9, 1967, in Fort Myers, Fla. ... 6-1/195. ... Full name: Deion Luwynn Sanders. ... Nickname: Prime Time.
HIGH SCHOOL: North Fort Myers (Fla.).
COLLEGE: Florida State.
TRANSACTIONS/CAREER NOTES: Selected by Atlanta Falcons in first round (fifth pick overall) of 1989 NFL draft. ... Signed by Falcons (September 7, 1989). ... On reserve/did not report list (July 27-August 13, 1990). ... Granted roster exemption for one game (September 1992). ... On reserve/did not report list (July 23-October 14, 1993). ... Designated by Falcons as transition player (February 15, 1994). ... Free agency status changed by Falcons from transitional to unconditional (April 28, 1994). ... Signed by San Francisco 49ers (September 15, 1994). ... Granted unconditional free agency (February 17, 1995). ... Signed by Dallas Cowboys (September 9, 1995). ... On reserve/did not report list (July 16-August 29, 1997).
CHAMPIONSHIP GAME EXPERIENCE: Played in NFC championship game (1994 and 1995 seasons). ... Member of Super Bowl championship team (1994 and 1995 seasons).
HONORS: Named defensive back on THE SPORTING NEWS college All-America first team (1986-1988). ... Jim Thorpe Award winner (1988). ... Named cornerback on THE SPORTING NEWS NFL All-Pro team (1991-1997). ... Played in Pro Bowl (1991-1994 seasons). ... Named kick returner on THE SPORTING NEWS NFL All-Pro team (1992). ... Named to play in Pro Bowl (1996 season); replaced by Darrell Green due to injury. ... Named to play in Pro Bowl (1997 season); replaced by Cris Dishman due to injury.
PRO STATISTICS: 1989—Fumbled twice and recovered one fumble. 1990—Fumbled four times and recovered two fumbles. 1991—Credited with a sack, fumbled once and recovered one fumble. 1992—Rushed once for minus four yards, fumbled three times and recovered two fumbles. 1993—Attempted one pass without a completion. 1994—Recovered one fumble. 1995—Rushed twice for nine yards. 1996—Rushed three times for two yards, fumbled twice and recovered three fumbles for 15 yards and a touchdown. 1997—Rushed once for minus 11 yards and fumbled once.
MISCELLANEOUS: Only person in history to play in both the World Series (1992) and Super Bowl (1994 and 1995 seasons).

| | | | INTERCEPTIONS | | | | RECEIVING | | | | PUNT RETURNS | | | | KICKOFF RETURNS | | | | TOTALS | | |
Year Team	G	GS	No.	Yds.	Avg.	TD	No.	Yds.	Avg.	TD	No.	Yds.	Avg.	TD	No.	Yds.	Avg.	TD	TD	2pt.	Pts.
1989—Atlanta NFL	15	10	5	52	10.4	0	1	-8	-8.0	0	28	307	11.0	†1	35	725	20.7	0	1	...	6
1990—Atlanta NFL	16	16	∞3	153	51.0	2	0	0	...	0	29	250	8.6	†1	39	851	21.8	0	3	...	18
1991—Atlanta NFL	15	15	6	119	19.8	∞1	1	17	17.0	0	21	170	8.1	0	26	576	22.2	†1	2	...	12
1992—Atlanta NFL	13	12	3	105	35.0	0	3	45	15.0	1	13	41	3.2	0	40	*1067	‡26.7	*2	3	...	18
1993—Atlanta NFL	11	10	‡7	91	13.0	0	6	106	17.7	1	2	21	10.5	0	7	169	24.1	0	1	...	6
1994—S.F. NFL	14	12	6	*303	50.5	†3	0	0	...	0	0	0	...	0	0	0	...	0	3	0	18
1995—Dallas NFL	9	9	2	34	17.0	0	2	25	12.5	0	1	54	54.0	0	1	15	15.0	0	0	0	0
1996—Dallas NFL	16	15	2	3	1.5	0	36	475	13.2	1	0	0	...	0	0	0	...	0	2	0	12
1997—Dallas NFL	13	12	2	81	40.5	1	0	0	...	0	33	407	12.3	∞1	1	10	18.0	0	2	0	12
Pro totals (9 years)	122	111	36	941	26.1	7	49	660	13.5	3	128	1254	9.8	3	149	3421	23.0	3	17	0	102

RECORD AS BASEBALL PLAYER

TRANSACTIONS/CAREER NOTES: Selected by Kansas City Royals organization in sixth round of free-agent draft (June 3, 1985); did not sign. ... Selected by New York Yankees organization in 30th round of free-agent draft (June 1, 1988). ... On disqualified list (August 1-September 24, 1990). ... Released by Yankees organization (September 24, 1990). ... Signed by Atlanta Braves (January 29, 1991). ... Placed on Richmond temporarily inactive list (August 1, 1991). ... On disqualified list (April 29-May 21, 1993). ... On disabled list (August 22-September 6, 1993). ... Traded by Braves to Cincinnati Reds for OF Roberto Kelly and P Roger Etheridge (May 29, 1994). ... On Cincinnati disabled list (June 1-July 16, 1995); included rehabilitation assignment to Chattanooga (July 12-14). ... Traded by Reds with P John Roper, P Ricky Pickett, P Scott Service and IF Dave McCarty to San Francisco Giants for OF Darren Lewis, P Mark Portugal and P Dave Burba (July 21, 1995). ... Granted free agency (December 21, 1995). ... Did not play baseball during 1996 season. ... Granted free agency (November 5, 1997). ... Re-signed by Reds (February 17, 1997). ... Granted free agency after 1997 season. ... Re-signed by Reds organization (January 8, 1998).

STATISTICAL NOTES: Led N.L. in caught stealing with 16 in 1994.

MISCELLANEOUS: Only person in history to play in both the World Series (1992) and Super Bowl (1994 and 1995 seasons).

Year	Team (League)	Pos.	G	AB	R	H	2B	3B	HR	RBI	Avg.	BB	SO	SB	PO	A	E	Avg.
1988—GC Yankees (GCL)		OF	17	75	7	21	4	2	0	6	.280	2	10	11	33	1	2	.944
—Fort Lauderdale (FSL)		OF	6	21	5	9	2	0	0	2	.429	1	3	2	22	2	0	1.000
—Columbus (Int'l)		OF	5	20	3	3	1	0	0	0	.150	1	4	1	13	0	0	1.000
1989—Alb./Colon. (Eastern)		OF	33	119	28	34	2	2	1	6	.286	11	20	17	79	3	0	1.000
—New York (A.L.)		OF	14	47	7	11	2	0	2	7	.234	3	8	1	30	1	1	.969
—Columbus (Int'l)		OF	70	259	38	72	12	5	5	30	.278	22	46	16	165	0	4	.976
1990—New York (A.L.)		OF-DH	57	133	24	21	2	2	3	9	.158	13	27	8	69	2	2	.973
—Columbus (Int'l)		OF	22	84	21	27	7	1	2	10	.321	17	15	9	49	1	0	1.000
1991—Atlanta (N.L.)■		OF	54	110	16	21	1	2	4	13	.191	12	23	11	57	3	3	.952
—Richmond (Int'l)		OF	29	130	20	34	6	3	5	16	.262	10	28	12	73	1	1	.987
1992—Atlanta (N.L.)		OF	97	303	54	92	6	*14	8	28	.304	18	52	26	174	4	3	.983
1993—Atlanta (N.L.)		OF	95	272	42	75	18	6	6	28	.276	16	42	19	137	1	2	.986
1994—Atlanta (N.L.)		OF	46	191	32	55	10	0	4	21	.288	16	28	19	99	0	2	.980
—Cincinnati (N.L.)■		OF	46	184	26	51	7	4	0	7	.277	16	35	19	110	2	0	1.000
1995—Cincinnati (N.L.)		OF	33	129	19	31	2	3	1	10	.240	9	18	16	88	2	3	.968
—Chattanooga (Sou.)		OF	2	7	1	4	0	0	1	2	.571	0	1	1	3	1	0	1.000
—San Fran. (N.L.)■		OF	52	214	29	61	9	5	5	18	.285	18	42	8	127	0	2	.984
1996—									Did not play.									
1997—Cincinnati (N.L.)■		OF	115	465	53	127	13	7	5	23	.273	34	67	56	236	3	4	.984
American League totals (2 years)			71	180	31	32	4	2	5	16	.178	16	35	9	99	3	3	.971
National League totals (6 years)			538	1868	271	513	66	41	33	148	.275	139	307	174	1028	15	19	.982
Major league totals (8 years)			609	2048	302	545	70	43	38	164	.266	155	342	183	1127	18	22	.981

CHAMPIONSHIP SERIES RECORD

Year	Team (League)	Pos.	G	AB	R	H	2B	3B	HR	RBI	Avg.	BB	SO	SB	PO	A	E	Avg.
1992—Atlanta (N.L.)		OF-PH	4	5	0	0	0	0	0	0	.000	0	3	0	1	0	0	1.000
1993—Atlanta (N.L.)		PH-OF-PR	5	3	0	0	0	0	0	0	.000	0	1	0	0	0	0	...
Championship series totals (2 years)			9	8	0	0	0	0	0	0	.000	0	4	0	1	0	0	1.000

WORLD SERIES RECORD

Year	Team (League)	Pos.	G	AB	R	H	2B	3B	HR	RBI	Avg.	BB	SO	SB	PO	A	E	Avg.
1992—Atlanta (N.L.)		OF	4	15	4	8	2	0	0	1	.533	2	1	5	5	1	0	1.000

SANDERS, FRANK   WR   CARDINALS

PERSONAL: Born February 17, 1973, in Fort Lauderdale. ... 6-2/197. ... Full name: Frank Vondel Sanders.

HIGH SCHOOL: Dillard (Fort Lauderdale).

COLLEGE: Auburn.

TRANSACTIONS/CAREER NOTES: Selected by Arizona Cardinals in second round (47th pick overall) of 1995 NFL draft. ... Signed by Cardinals (July 17, 1995). ... Granted free agency (February 13, 1998). ... Re-signed by Cardinals (March 13, 1998).

HONORS: Named wide receiver on THE SPORTING NEWS college All-America second team (1994).

PRO STATISTICS: 1995—Rushed once for one yard. 1996—Rushed twice for minus four yards and recovered one fumble. 1997—Attempted one pass with one completion for 26 yards and rushed once for five yards.

SINGLE GAME HIGHS (regular season): Receptions—10 (October 26, 1997, vs. Tennessee); yards—188 (November 16, 1997, vs. New York Giants); and touchdown receptions—2 (October 8, 1995, vs. New York Giants).

STATISTICAL PLATEAUS: 100-yard receiving games: 1995 (2), 1997 (2). Total: 4.

			RECEIVING				TOTALS			
Year Team	G	GS	No.	Yds.	Avg.	TD	TD	2pt.	Pts.	Fum.
1995—Arizona NFL	16	15	52	883	17.0	2	2	2	16	0
1996—Arizona NFL	16	16	69	813	11.8	4	4	0	24	1
1997—Arizona NFL	16	16	75	1017	13.6	4	4	1	26	3
Pro totals (3 years)	48	47	196	2713	13.8	10	10	3	66	4

SANDERSON, SCOTT   OT   OILERS

PERSONAL: Born July 25, 1974, in Walnut Creek, Calif. ... 6-6/278. ... Full name: Scott Michael Sanderson.

HIGH SCHOOL: Clayton Valley (Calif.).

COLLEGE: Washington State.

TRANSACTIONS/CAREER NOTES: Selected by Houston Oilers in third round (81st pick overall) of 1997 NFL draft. ... Oilers franchise moved to Tennessee for 1997 season. ... Signed by Oilers (July 17, 1997).

PLAYING EXPERIENCE: Tennessee NFL, 1997. ... Games/Games started: 10/0.

HONORS: Named offensive tackle on THE SPORTING NEWS college All-America first team (1996).

SANTIAGO, O.J.　　　　　TE　　　　　FALCONS

PERSONAL: Born April 4, 1974, in Toronto. ... 6-7/267. ... Full name: Otis Jason Santiago.
HIGH SCHOOL: St. Michael's (Toronto).
COLLEGE: Kent State.
TRANSACTIONS/CAREER NOTES: Selected by Atlanta Falcons in third round (70th pick overall) of 1997 NFL draft. ... Signed by Falcons (July 11, 1997). ... On injured reserve with leg injury (November 20, 1997-remainder of season).
SINGLE GAME HIGHS (regular season): Reception—5 (September 14, 1997, vs. Oakland); yards—47 (August 31, 1997, vs. Detroit); and touchdown receptions—1 (October 19, 1997, vs. San Francisco).

| | | | RECEIVING | | | | TOTALS | | |
Year Team	G	GS	No.	Yds.	Avg.	TD	TD	2pt.	Pts.	Fum.
1997—Atlanta NFL	11	11	17	217	12.8	2	2	0	12	1

SAPOLU, JESSE　　　　　G

PERSONAL: Born March 10, 1961, in Laie, Western Samoa. ... 6-4/278. ... Full name: Manase Jesse Sapolu.
HIGH SCHOOL: Farrington (Honolulu).
COLLEGE: Hawaii.
TRANSACTIONS/CAREER NOTES: Selected by Oakland Invaders in 17th round (199th pick overall) of 1983 USFL draft. ... Selected by San Francisco 49ers in 11th round (289th pick overall) of 1983 NFL draft. ... Signed by 49ers (July 10, 1983). ... On physically unable to perform list with fractured foot (July 19-August 12, 1984). ... On physically unable to perform list with fractured foot (August 13-November 8, 1984). ... On injured reserve with fractured foot (November 16, 1984-remainder of season). ... On injured reserve with broken foot (August 12, 1985-entire season). ... On injured reserve with broken leg (July 30, 1986-entire season). ... On reserve/did not report list (July 30-August 27, 1990). ... Released by 49ers (February 13, 1997). ... Re-signed by 49ers (August 22, 1997). ... Granted unconditional free agency (February 13, 1998).
PLAYING EXPERIENCE: San Francisco NFL, 1983, 1984 and 1987-1997. ... Games/Games started: 1983 (16/1), 1984 (1/0), 1987 (12/9), 1988 (16/16), 1989 (16/16), 1990 (16/16), 1991 (16/16), 1992 (16/16), 1993 (16/16), 1994 (13/13), 1995 (16/16), 1996 (16/16), 1997 (12/3). Total: 182/154.
CHAMPIONSHIP GAME EXPERIENCE: Played in NFC championship game (1983, 1988-1990, 1992-1994 and 1997 seasons). ... Member of Super Bowl championship team (1988, 1989 and 1994 seasons).
HONORS: Played in Pro Bowl (1993 and 1994 seasons).
PRO STATISTICS: 1994—Recovered one fumble.

SAPP, BOB　　　　　G　　　　　VIKINGS

PERSONAL: Born September 22, 1973, in Colorado Springs, Colo. ... 6-4/303. Full name: Robert Malcom Sapp.
HIGH SCHOOL: General Mitchell (Colorado Springs, Colo.).
COLLEGE: Washington.
TRANSACTIONS/CAREER NOTES: Selected by Chicago Bears in third round (69th pick overall) of 1997 NFL draft. ... Signed by Bears (July 10, 1997). ... Released by Bears (August 26, 1997). ... Signed by Minnesota Vikings (August 27, 1997).
PLAYING EXPERIENCE: Minnesota NFL, 1997. ... Games/Games started: 1/0.

SAPP, PATRICK　　　　　LB　　　　　CARDINALS

PERSONAL: Born May 11, 1973, in Jacksonville. ... 6-4/258. ... Full name: Patrick Zolley Sapp.
HIGH SCHOOL: Raines (Jacksonville).
COLLEGE: Clemson.
TRANSACTIONS/CAREER NOTES: Selected by San Diego Chargers in second round (50th pick overall) of 1996 NFL draft. ... Traded by Chargers with first- (DE Andre Wadsworth) and second-round (CB Corey Chavous) picks in 1998 draft, first-round pick in 1999 draft and KR Eric Metcalf to Arizona Cardinals for first-round pick (QB Ryan Leaf) in 1998 draft (March 12, 1998).
PLAYING EXPERIENCE: San Diego NFL, 1996 and 1997. ... Games/Games started: 1996 (16/0), 1997 (16/9). Total: 32/9.

SAPP, WARREN　　　　　DT　　　　　BUCCANEERS

PERSONAL: Born December 19, 1972, in Plymouth, Fla. ... 6-2/276. ... Full name: Warren Carlos Sapp.
HIGH SCHOOL: Apopka (Fla.).
COLLEGE: Miami (Fla.).
TRANSACTIONS/CAREER NOTES: Selected after junior season by Tampa Bay Buccaneers in first round (12th pick overall) of 1995 NFL draft. ... Signed by Buccaneers (April 27, 1995).
HONORS: Lombardi Award winner (1994). ... Named defensive lineman on THE SPORTING NEWS college All-America first team (1994). ... Played in Pro Bowl (1997 season).
PRO STATISTICS: 1995—Intercepted one pass for five yards and a touchdown. 1996—Recovered one fumble. 1997—Recovered one fumble for 23 yards.

Year Team	G	GS	SACKS
1995—Tampa Bay NFL	16	8	3.0
1996—Tampa Bay NFL	15	14	9.0
1997—Tampa Bay NFL	15	15	10.5
Pro totals (3 years)	46	37	22.5

SARGENT, KEVIN　　　　　OT　　　　　BENGALS

PERSONAL: Born March 31, 1969, in Bremerton, Wash. ... 6-6/295.
HIGH SCHOOL: Bremerton (Wash.).

COLLEGE: Eastern Washington.
TRANSACTIONS/CAREER NOTES: Signed as non-drafted free agent by Cincinnati Bengals (April 1992). ... On injured reserve with fractured right forearm (December 3, 1993-remainder of season). ... On injured reserve with neck injury (August 14, 1996-entire season). ... Granted unconditional free agency (February 14, 1997). ... Re-signed by Bengals (March 13, 1997). ... On physically unable to perform list with neck injury (August 24-October 18, 1997).
PLAYING EXPERIENCE: Cincinnati NFL, 1992-1995 and 1997. ... Games/Games started: 1992 (16/8), 1993 (1/1), 1994 (16/15), 1995 (15/15), 1997 (10/8). Total: 58/52.
PRO STATISTICS: 1992—Recovered two fumbles. 1995—Recovered one fumble.

SASA, DON DT PANTHERS

PERSONAL: Born September 16, 1972, in American Samoa. ... 6-3/303. ... Name pronounced SAW-sa.
HIGH SCHOOL: Polytechnic (Long Beach, Calif.).
JUNIOR COLLEGE: Long Beach (Calif.) City College.
COLLEGE: Washington State.
TRANSACTIONS/CAREER NOTES: Selected by San Diego Chargers in third round (93rd pick overall) of 1995 NFL draft. ... Signed by Chargers (July 17, 1995). ,,, On injured reserve with knee injury (October 17, 1995-remainder of season). ... Released by Chargers (August 24, 1997). ... Signed by Washington Redskins (October 9, 1997). ... Released by Redskins (October 31, 1997). ... Signed by Carolina Panthers (December 16, 1997).
PLAYING EXPERIENCE: San Diego NFL, 1995 and 1996; Washington NFL, 1997. ... Games/Games started: 1995 (5/0), 1996 (4/1), 1997 (1/0). Total: 10/1.

SAUER, CRAIG LB FALCONS

PERSONAL: Born December 13, 1972, in Sartell, Minn. ... 6-1/240.
HIGH SCHOOL: Sartell (Minn.).
COLLEGE: Minnesota.
TRANSACTIONS/CAREER NOTES: Selected by Atlanta Falcons in sixth round (188th pick overall) of 1996 NFL draft. ... Signed by Falcons (June 6, 1996).
PLAYING EXPERIENCE: Atlanta NFL, 1996 and 1997. ... Games/Games started: 1996 (16/1), 1997 (16/1). Total: 32/2.
PRO STATISTICS: 1997—Recovered one fumble.

SAUERBRUN, TODD P BEARS

PERSONAL: Born January 4, 1973, in Setauket, N.Y. ... 5-10/209. ... Name pronounced SOW-er-bruhn.
HIGH SCHOOL: Ward Melville (Setauket, N.Y.).
COLLEGE: West Virginia.
TRANSACTIONS/CAREER NOTES: Selected by Chicago Bears in second round (56th pick overall) of 1995 NFL draft. ... Signed by Bears (July 20, 1995). ... Granted free agency (February 13, 1998).
HONORS: Named punter on THE SPORTING NEWS college All-America first team (1994).
PRO STATISTICS: 1996—Rushed once for three yards, attempted two passes with two completions for 63 yards. 1997—Rushed twice for eight yards and fumbled once for minus nine yards.

| | | | PUNTING | | | | | |
Year Team	G	GS	No.	Yds.	Avg.	Net avg.	In. 20	Blk.
1995—Chicago NFL	15	0	55	2080	37.8	31.1	16	0
1996—Chicago NFL	16	0	78	3491	44.8	34.8	15	0
1997—Chicago NFL	16	0	95	4059	42.7	32.8	26	0
Pro totals (3 years)	47	0	228	9630	42.2	33.1	57	0

SAVOIE, NICKY TE SAINTS

PERSONAL: Born September 21, 1973, in Cut Off, La. ... 6-5/253. ... Name pronounced sav-WAH. ... Full name: Nicky John Savoie.
HIGH SCHOOL: South LaFourche (La.).
JUNIOR COLLEGE: Gulf Coast Community College (Fla.).
COLLEGE: Louisiana State.
TRANSACTIONS/CAREER NOTES: Selected by New Orleans Saints in sixth round (165th pick overall) of 1997 NFL draft. ... Signed by Saints (June 5, 1997).
PLAYING EXPERIENCE: New Orleans NFL, 1997. ... Games/Games started: 1/0.
PRO STATISTICS: 1997—Caught one pass for 14 yards.

SAWYER, COREY CB BENGALS

PERSONAL: Born October 4, 1971, in Key West, Fla. ... 5-11/177. ... Full name: Corey F. Sawyer.
HIGH SCHOOL: Key West (Fla.).
COLLEGE: Florida State.
TRANSACTIONS/CAREER NOTES: Selected after junior season by Cincinnati Bengals in fourth round (104th pick overall) of 1994 NFL draft. ... Signed by Bengals (July 22, 1994).
HONORS: Named defensive back on THE SPORTING NEWS college All-America first team (1993).
PRO STATISTICS: 1994—Recovered one fumble. 1996—Recovered one fumble.

Year Team	G	GS	INTERCEPTIONS				SACKS	PUNT RETURNS				KICKOFF RETURNS				TOTALS			
			No.	Yds.	Avg.	TD	No.	No.	Yds.	Avg.	TD	No.	Yds.	Avg.	TD	TD	2pt.	Pts.	Fum.
1994—Cincinnati NFL..........	15	0	2	0	0.0	0	0.0	26	307	11.8	1	1	14	14.0	0	1	0	6	2
1995—Cincinnati NFL..........	12	8	2	61	30.5	0	2.0	9	58	6.4	0	2	50	25.0	0	0	0	0	1
1996—Cincinnati NFL..........	15	2	2	0	0.0	0	1.5	15	117	7.8	0	12	241	20.1	0	0	0	0	2
1997—Cincinnati NFL..........	15	2	4	44	11.0	0	0.0	0	0	...	0	0	0	...	0	0	0	0	0
Pro totals (4 years)	57	12	10	105	10.5	0	3.5	50	482	9.6	1	15	305	20.3	0	1	0	6	5

SAXTON, BRIAN   TE   FALCONS

PERSONAL: Born March 13, 1972, in Whippany Park, N.J. ... 6-6/265. ... Full name: Paul Brian Saxton.
HIGH SCHOOL: Whippany Park (N.J.).
COLLEGE: Boston College (bachelor's degree in marketing and master's degree in human development).
TRANSACTIONS/CAREER NOTES: Signed as non-drafted free agent by New York Giants (May 8, 1995). ... Released by Giants (August 27, 1995). ... Re-signed by Giants to practice squad (August 29, 1995). ... Activated (August 31, 1996). ... Released by Giants (August 24, 1997). ... Signed by Atlanta Falcons (December 2, 1997).
PLAYING EXPERIENCE: New York Giants NFL, 1996; Atlanta NFL, 1997. ... Games/Games started: 1996 (16/2), 1997 (3/0). Total: 19/2.
PRO STATISTICS: 1996—Caught four passes for 31 yards, returned three kickoffs for 31 yards and recovered one fumble.
SINGLE GAME HIGHS (regular season): Receptions—2 (November 17, 1996, vs. Arizona); yards—14 (December 8, 1996, vs. Miami); and touchdown receptions—0.

SCHLERETH, MARK   G   BRONCOS

PERSONAL: Born January 25, 1966, in Anchorage, Alaska. ... 6-3/287. ... Name pronounced SHLARE-eth.
HIGH SCHOOL: Robert Service (Anchorage, Alaska).
COLLEGE: Idaho.
TRANSACTIONS/CAREER NOTES: Selected by Washington Redskins in 10th round (263rd pick overall) of 1989 NFL draft. ... Signed by Redskins (July 23, 1989). ... On injured reserve with knee injury (September 5-November 11, 1989). ... On injured reserve with a nerve condition known as Guillain-Barre Syndrome (November 16, 1993-remainder of season). ... Released by Redskins (September 2, 1994). ... Re-signed by Redskins (September 3, 1994). ... Granted unconditional free agency (February 17, 1995). ... Signed by Denver Broncos (March 27, 1995). ... Released by Broncos (February 14, 1997). ... Re-signed by Broncos (April 11, 1997). ... Granted unconditional free agency (February 13, 1998). ... Re-signed by Broncos (February 23, 1998).
PLAYING EXPERIENCE: Washington NFL, 1989-1994; Denver NFL, 1995-1997. ... Games/Games started: 1989 (6/6), 1990 (12/7), 1991 (16/16), 1992 (16/16), 1993 (9/8), 1994 (16/6), 1995 (16/16), 1996 (14/14), 1997 (11/11). Total: 116/100.
CHAMPIONSHIP GAME EXPERIENCE: Played in NFC championship game (1991 season). ... Member of Super Bowl championship team (1991 and 1997 seasons). ... Played in AFC championship game (1997 season).
HONORS: Played in Pro Bowl (1991 season).
PRO STATISTICS: 1989—Recovered one fumble. 1993—Recovered one fumble. 1997—Recovered one fumble.

SCHLESINGER, CORY   FB   LIONS

PERSONAL: Born June 23, 1972, in Columbus, Neb. ... 6-0/230.
HIGH SCHOOL: Columbus (Neb.).
COLLEGE: Nebraska.
TRANSACTIONS/CAREER NOTES: Selected by Detroit Lions in sixth round (192nd pick overall) of 1995 NFL draft. ... Signed by Lions (July 19, 1995).
PRO STATISTICS: 1995—Recovered one fumble for 11 yards.
SINGLE GAME HIGHS (regular season): Attempts—4 (November 27, 1997, vs. Chicago); yards—9 (November 27, 1997, vs. Chicago); and rushing touchdowns—0.

Year Team	G	GS	RUSHING				RECEIVING				TOTALS			
			Att.	Yds.	Avg.	TD	No.	Yds.	Avg.	TD	TD	2pt.	Pts.	Fum.
1995—Detroit NFL	16	1	1	1	1.0	0	1	2	2.0	0	0	0	0	0
1996— Detroit NFL	16	1	0	0	...	0	0	0	...	0	0	0	0	0
1997—Detroit NFL	16	2	7	11	1.6	0	5	69	13.8	1	1	0	6	0
Pro totals (3 years)	48	4	8	12	1.5	0	6	71	11.8	1	1	0	6	0

SCHREIBER, ADAM   C   FALCONS

PERSONAL: Born February 20, 1962, in Galveston, Texas. ... 6-4/298. ... Full name: Adam Blayne Schreiber.
HIGH SCHOOL: Butler (Huntsville, Ala.).
COLLEGE: Texas.
TRANSACTIONS/CAREER NOTES: Selected by Seattle Seahawks in ninth round (243rd pick overall) of 1984 NFL draft. ... Signed by Seahawks (June 20, 1984). ... Released by Seahawks (August 27, 1984). ... Re-signed by Seahawks (October 10, 1984). ... Released by Seahawks (August 29, 1985). ... Signed by New Orleans Saints (November 20, 1985). ... Released by Saints (September 1, 1986). ... Signed by Philadelphia Eagles (October 16, 1986). ... Claimed on waivers by New York Jets (October 19, 1988). ... Granted unconditional free agency (February 1, 1990). ... Signed by Minnesota Vikings (March 21, 1990). ... Granted unconditional free agency (February 1-April 1, 1992). ... Re-signed by Vikings for 1992 season. ... Granted unconditional free agency (March 1, 1993). ... Re-signed by Vikings (May 7, 1993). ... Released by Vikings (July 12, 1994). ... Signed by New York Giants (August 16, 1994). ... Granted unconditional free agency (February 17, 1995). ... Re-signed by Giants (May 8, 1995). ... Granted unconditional free agency (February 14, 1997). ... Signed by Atlanta Falcons (August 5, 1997).
PLAYING EXPERIENCE: Seattle NFL, 1984; New Orleans NFL, 1985; Philadelphia NFL, 1986 and 1987; Philadelphia (6)-New York Jets (7) NFL, 1988; New York Jets NFL, 1989; Minnesota NFL, 1990-1993; New York Giants NFL, 1994-1996; Atlanta NFL, 1997. ... Games/Games started: 1984 (6/0), 1985 (1/0), 1986 (9/0), 1987 (12/12), 1988 (Phi.-6/0; N.Y. Jets-7/0; Total: 13/0), 1989 (16/0), 1990 (10/0), 1991 (15/0), 1992 (16/1), 1993 (16/16), 1994 (16/2), 1995 (16/0), 1996 (15/2), 1997 (16/0). Total: 183/33.
PRO STATISTICS: 1990—Returned one kickoff for five yards. 1992—Recovered one fumble.

SCHROEDER, BILL   WR   PACKERS

PERSONAL: Born January 9, 1971, in Eau Claire, Wis. ... 6-2/200.
HIGH SCHOOL: Sheboygan (Wis.) South.
COLLEGE: Wisconsin-La Crosse.
TRANSACTIONS/CAREER NOTES: Selected by Green Bay Packers in sixth round (181st pick overall) of 1994 NFL draft. ... Signed by Packers (May 10, 1994). ... Released by Packers (August 28, 1994). ... Re-signed by Packers to practice squad (August 30, 1994). ... Activated (December 29, 1994). ... Traded by Packers with TE Jeff Wilner to New England Patriots for C Mike Arthur (August 11, 1995). ... On injured reserve list with foot injury (August 27, 1995-entire season). ... Released by Patriots (August 14, 1996). ... Signed by Packers to practice squad (August 28, 1996). ... Assigned by Packers to Rhein Fire in 1997 World League enhancement allocation program (February 19, 1997).
CHAMPIONSHIP GAME EXPERIENCE: Member of Packers for NFC championship game (1997 season); inactive. ... Member of Packers for Super Bowl XXXII (1997 season); inactive.
PRO STATISTICS: W.L.: 1997—Rushed twice of 18 yards. NFL: 1997—Recovered one fumble.
SINGLE GAME HIGHS (regular season): Receptions—1 (September 28, 1997, vs. Detroit); yards—8 (September 14, 1997, vs. Miami); and touchdown receptions—1 (September 28, 1997, vs. Detroit).

			RECEIVING				PUNT RETURNS				KICKOFF RETURNS				TOTALS			
Year Team	G	GS	No.	Yds.	Avg.	TD	No.	Yds.	Avg.	TD	No.	Yds.	Avg.	TD	TD	2pt.	Pts.	Fum.
1997—Rhein W.L.	...	...	43	702	16.3	6	0	0	...	0	1	20	20.0	0	6	0	36	...
Green Bay NFL	15	1	2	15	7.5	1	33	342	10.4	0	24	562	23.4	0	1	0	6	4
W.L. totals (1 year)	...	...	43	702	16.3	6	0	0	...	0	1	20	20.0	0	6	0	36	...
NFL totals (1 year)	15	1	2	15	7.5	1	33	342	10.4	0	24	562	23.4	0	1	0	6	4
Pro totals (2 years)	...	...	45	717	15.9	7	33	342	10.4	0	25	582	23.3	0	7	0	42	4

SCHULTZ, BILL   G/OT

PERSONAL: Born May 1, 1967, in Granada Hills, Calif. ... 6-5/305. ... Full name: William Schultz.
HIGH SCHOOL: John F. Kennedy (Granada Hills, Calif.).
JUNIOR COLLEGE: Glendale (Calif.) College.
COLLEGE: Southern California.
TRANSACTIONS/CAREER NOTES: Selected by Indianapolis Colts in fourth round (94th pick overall) of 1990 NFL draft. ... Signed by Colts (July 23, 1990). ... On injured reserve with knee injury (September 11-October 11, 1991). ... On injured reserve with illness (December 13, 1991-remainder of season). ... On injured reserve with ankle injury (November 13-December 12, 1992); on practice squad (December 9-12, 1992). ... Granted free agency (March 1, 1993). ... Re-signed by Colts (July 18, 1993). ... Released by Colts (April 26, 1994). ... Signed by Los Angeles Rams (July 8, 1994). ... Released by Rams (August 28, 1994). ... Signed by Houston Oilers (September 7, 1994). ... On inactive list for 10 games (1994). ... Granted unconditional free agency (February 17, 1995). ... Signed by Denver Broncos (March 23, 1995). ... Released by Broncos (October 3, 1995). ... Re-signed by Broncos (October 30, 1995). ... Released by Broncos (August 25, 1996). ... Signed by Chicago Bears (July 16, 1997). ... Released by Bears (October 29, 1997).
PLAYING EXPERIENCE: Indianapolis NFL, 1990-1993; Denver NFL, 1995; Chicago NFL, 1997. ... Games/Games started: 1990 (12/0), 1991 (10/9); 1992 (10/2), 1993 (14/14), 1995 (2/0), 1997 (8/3). Total: 56/27.
PRO STATISTICS: 1991—Recovered two fumbles. 1992—Caught one pass for three yards and a touchdown.

SCHULZ, KURT   S   BILLS

PERSONAL: Born December 12, 1968, in Wenatchee, Wash. ... 6-1/208. ... Full name: Kurt Erich Schulz.
HIGH SCHOOL: Eisenhower (Yakima, Wash.).
COLLEGE: Eastern Washington.
TRANSACTIONS/CAREER NOTES: Selected by Buffalo Bills in seventh round (195th pick overall) of 1992 NFL draft. ... Signed by Bills (July 22, 1992). ... On injured reserve with knee injury (October 26-December 19, 1992).
CHAMPIONSHIP GAME EXPERIENCE: Played in AFC championship game (1993 season). ... Member of Bills for Super Bowl XXVII (1992 season); inactive. ... Played in Super Bowl XXVIII (1993 season).
PRO STATISTICS: 1992—Recovered two fumbles.

			INTERCEPTIONS			
Year Team	G	GS	No.	Yds.	Avg.	TD
1992—Buffalo NFL	8	1	0	0	...	0
1993—Buffalo NFL	12	0	0	0	...	0
1994—Buffalo NFL	16	0	0	0	...	0
1995—Buffalo NFL	13	13	6	48	8.0	▲1
1996—Buffalo NFL	15	15	4	24	6.0	0
1997—Buffalo NFL	15	14	2	23	11.5	0
Pro totals (6 years)	79	43	12	95	7.9	1

SCHWANTZ, JIM   LB   49ERS

PERSONAL: Born January 23, 1970, in Arlington Heights, Ill. ... 6-2/240. ... Full name: James William Schwantz.
HIGH SCHOOL: William Fremd (Palatine, Ill).
COLLEGE: Purdue.
TRANSACTIONS/CAREER NOTES: Signed as non-drafted free agent by Chicago Bears (1992). ... Released by Bears (August 31, 1992). ... Re-signed by Bears to practice squad (September 1992). ... Activated (December 26, 1992). ... Released by Bears (August 30, 1993). ... Re-signed by Bears to practice squad (August 31, 1993). ... Traded by Bears to Dallas Cowboys for sixth-round pick (traded to St. Louis) in 1996 draft (August 28, 1994). ... Granted free agency (February 14, 1997). ... Signed by San Francisco 49ers (May 2, 1997).
PLAYING EXPERIENCE: Chicago NFL, 1992; Dallas NFL, 1994-1996; San Francisco NFL,1997. ... Games/Games started: 1992 (1/0), 1994 (7/0), 1995 (16/0), 1996 (16/0), 1997 (16/0). Totals: 56/10.
CHAMPIONSHIP GAME EXPERIENCE: Member of Cowboys for NFC championship game (1994 season); inactive. ... Played in NFC championship game (1995 and 1997 seasons). ... Member of Super Bowl championship team (1995 season).
HONORS: Played in Pro Bowl (1996 season).
PRO STATISTICS: 1995—Returned one kickoff for nine yards.

SCHWARTZ, BRYAN   LB   JAGUARS

PERSONAL: Born December 5, 1971, in St. Lawrence, S.D. ... 6-4/251. ... Full name: Bryan Lee Schwartz.
HIGH SCHOOL: Miller (S.D.).
COLLEGE: Augustana (S.D.).
TRANSACTIONS/CAREER NOTES: Selected by Jacksonville Jaguars in second round (64th pick overall) of 1995 NFL draft. ... Signed by Jaguars (June 1, 1995). ... On injured reserve with knee injury (September 24, 1996-remainder of season). ... Granted free agency (February 13, 1998). ... Re-signed by Jaguars (May 7, 1998).
PLAYING EXPERIENCE: Jacksonville NFL, 1995-1997. ... Games/Games started: 1995 (14/9), 1996 (4/3), 1997 (16/16). Total: 34/28.
PRO STATISTICS: 1995—Recovered one fumble. 1997—Credited with 1/2 sack and recovered one fumble.

SCIFRES, STEVE   G/OT   COWBOYS

PERSONAL: Born January 22, 1972, in Colorado Springs, Colo. ... 6-4/300. ... Full name: Steve William Scifres. ... Name pronounced SCI-ferz.
HIGH SCHOOL: Mitchell (Colorado Springs, Colo.).
COLLEGE: Wyoming.
TRANSACTIONS/CAREER NOTES: Selected by Dallas Cowboys in third round (83rd pick overall) of 1997 NFL draft. ... Signed by Cowboys (July 14, 1997).
PLAYING EXPERIENCE: Dallas NFL, 1997. ... Games/Games started: 5/0.

SCOTT, CHAD   DB   STEELERS

PERSONAL: Born September 6, 1974, in Washington, D.C. ... 6-1/203. ... Full name: Chad Oliver Scott.
HIGH SCHOOL: Suitland (Capitol Heights, Md.).
COLLEGE: Towson State, then Maryland.
TRANSACTIONS/CAREER NOTES: Selected by Pittsburgh Steelers in first round (24th pick overall) of 1997 NFL draft. ... Signed by Steelers (July 16, 1997).
CHAMPIONSHIP GAME EXPERIENCE: Played in AFC championship game (1997 season).

			INTERCEPTIONS			
Year Team	G	GS	No.	Yds.	Avg.	TD
1997—Pittsburgh NFL	13	9	2	-4	-2.0	0

SCOTT, DARNAY   WR   BENGALS

PERSONAL: Born July 7, 1972, in St. Louis. ... 6-1/180.
HIGH SCHOOL: Kearny (San Diego).
COLLEGE: San Diego State.
TRANSACTIONS/CAREER NOTES: Selected after junior season by Cincinnati Bengals in second round (30th pick overall) of 1994 NFL draft. ... Signed by Bengals (July 18, 1994). ... Granted free agency (February 14, 1997). ... Re-signed by Bengals (June 16, 1997).
PRO STATISTICS: 1994—Attempted one pass with one completion for 53 yards.
SINGLE GAME HIGHS (regular season): Receptions—8 (December 8, 1996, vs. Baltimore); yards—157 (November 6, 1994, vs. Seattle); and touchdown receptions—2 (October 30, 1994, vs. Dallas).
STATISTICAL PLATEAUS: 100-yard receiving games: 1994 (2), 1995 (1), 1996 (1), 1997 (2). Total: 6.

			RUSHING				RECEIVING				KICKOFF RETURNS				TOTALS			
Year Team	G	GS	Att.	Yds.	Avg.	TD	No.	Yds.	Avg.	TD	No.	Yds.	Avg.	TD	TD	2pt.	Pts.	Fum.
1994—Cincinnati NFL	16	12	10	106	10.6	0	46	866	§18.8	5	15	342	22.8	0	5	0	30	0
1995—Cincinnati NFL	16	16	5	11	2.2	0	52	821	15.8	5	0	0	...	0	5	0	30	0
1996—Cincinnati NFL	16	16	3	4	1.3	0	58	833	14.4	5	0	0	...	0	5	0	30	0
1997—Cincinnati NFL	16	15	1	6	6.0	0	54	797	14.8	5	0	0	...	0	5	0	30	0
Pro totals (4 years)	64	59	19	127	6.7	0	210	3317	15.8	20	15	342	22.8	0	20	0	120	0

SCOTT, FREDDIE   WR   COLTS

PERSONAL: Born August 26, 1974, in Southfield, Mich. ... 5-10/188. ... Full name: Freddie Lee Scott. ... Son of Fred Scott, wide receiver with Baltimore Colts (1974-77), Detroit Lions (1978-1983) and Los Angeles Express of USFL (1984).
HIGH SCHOOL: Detroit Country Day.
COLLEGE: Penn State.
TRANSACTIONS/CAREER NOTES: Signed as non-drafted free agent by Atlanta Falcons (April 24, 1996). ... Released by Falcons (October 27, 1997). ... Signed by Colts (April 8, 1998).
PLAYING EXPERIENCE: Atlanta NFL, 1996 and 1997. ... Games/Games started: 1996 (10/0), 1997 (2/0). Total: 12/0.
PRO STATISTICS: 1996—Caught seven passes for 80 yards.
SINGLE GAME HIGHS (regular season): Receptions—4 (October 13, 1996, vs. Houston); yards—32 (October 13, 1996, vs. Houston); and touchdown receptions—0.

SCOTT, LANCE   C   GIANTS

PERSONAL: Born February 15, 1972, in Salt Lake City. ... 6-3/285.
HIGH SCHOOL: Taylorsville (Salt Lake City).
COLLEGE: Utah.
TRANSACTIONS/CAREER NOTES: Selected by Arizona Cardinals in fifth round (165th pick overall) of 1995 NFL draft. ... Signed by Cardinals (July 24, 1995). ... Released by Cardinals (August 27, 1995). ... Re-signed by Cardinals to practice squad (October 2, 1995). ... Released by Cardinals (August 19, 1997). ... Signed by New York Giants (August 25, 1997). ... Granted free agency (February 13, 1998). Re-signed by Giants (April 8, 1998).
PLAYING EXPERIENCE: New York Giants NFL, 1997. ... Games/Games started: 16/11.

SCOTT, TODD   S

PERSONAL: Born January 23, 1968, in Galveston, Texas. ... 5-11/205. ... Full name: Todd Carlton Scott.
HIGH SCHOOL: Ball (Galveston, Texas).
COLLEGE: Southwestern Louisiana (degree in business management).
TRANSACTIONS/CAREER NOTES: Selected by Minnesota Vikings in sixth round (163rd pick overall) of 1991 NFL draft. ... Signed by Vikings (July 24, 1991). ... Granted unconditional free agency (February 17, 1995). ... Signed by New York Jets (March 21, 1995). ... Claimed on waivers by Tampa Bay Buccaneers (November 29, 1995). ... On injured reserve with Achilles' tendon injury (September 10, 1996-remainder of season). ... Granted unconditional free agency (February 14, 1997). ... Re-signed by Buccaneers (April 14, 1997). ... Released by Buccaneers (August 17, 1997). ... Signed by Kansas City Chiefs (October 9, 1997). ... Granted unconditional free agency (February 13, 1998).
HONORS: Played in Pro Bowl (1992 season).
PRO STATISTICS: 1992—Credited with a sack. 1993—Recovered one fumble. 1996—Recovered one fumble.

Year Team	G	GS	INTERCEPTIONS No.	Yds.	Avg.	TD
1991—Minnesota NFL	16	1	0	0	...	0
1992—Minnesota NFL	16	16	5	79	15.8	1
1993—Minnesota NFL	13	12	2	26	13.0	0
1994—Minnesota NFL	15	15	0	0	...	0
1995—New York Jets NFL	10	9	0	0	...	0
—Tampa Bay NFL	1	0	0	0	...	0
1996—Tampa Bay NFL	2	2	0	0	...	0
1997—Kansas City NFL	10	0	0	0	...	0
Pro totals (7 years)	83	55	7	105	15.0	1

SCRAFFORD, KIRK   OT

PERSONAL: Born March 15, 1967, in Billings, Mont. ... 6-6/275. ... Full name: Kirk Tippet Scrafford.
HIGH SCHOOL: Billings (Mont.) West.
COLLEGE: Montana.
TRANSACTIONS/CAREER NOTES: Signed as non-drafted free agent by Cincinnati Bengals (May 1990). ... On injured reserve with knee injury (September 4-November 23, 1990). ... On practice squad (November 23-December 22, 1990). ... On injured reserve with knee injury (August 27-October 15, 1991). ... Claimed on waivers by Seattle Seahawks (November 16, 1992). ... Released by Seahawks after failing physical (November 17, 1992). ... Signed by Bengals (November 1992). ... Claimed on waivers by Denver Broncos (August 17, 1993). ... Granted unconditional free agency (February 17, 1995). ... Signed by San Francisco 49ers (March 29, 1995). ... Announced retirement (March 5, 1998).
PLAYING EXPERIENCE: Cincinnati NFL, 1990-1992; Denver NFL, 1993 and 1994; San Francisco NFL, 1995-1997. ... Games/Games started: 1990 (2/0), 1991 (9/5), 1992 (8/4), 1993 (16/0), 1994 (16/7), 1995 (16/11), 1996 (7/1), 1997 (16/16). Total: 90/44.
CHAMPIONSHIP GAME EXPERIENCE: Played in NFC championship game (1997 season).
PRO STATISTICS: 1994—Recovered one fumble.

SCROGGINS, TRACY   DE   LIONS

PERSONAL: Born September 11, 1969, in Checotah, Okla. ... 6-2/255.
HIGH SCHOOL: Checotah (Okla.).
JUNIOR COLLEGE: Coffeyville (Kan.) Community College.
COLLEGE: Tulsa.
TRANSACTIONS/CAREER NOTES: Selected by Detroit Lions in second round (53rd pick overall) of 1992 NFL draft. ... Signed by Lions (July 23, 1992). ... Granted free agency (February 17, 1995). ... Re-signed by Lions (May 17, 1995).
PRO STATISTICS: 1993—Intercepted one pass for no yards and recovered one fumble. 1994—Recovered one fumble. 1995—Recovered one fumble for 81 yards and a touchdown. 1996—Recovered one fumble. 1997—Recovered one fumble for 17 yards and a touchdown and credited with a safety.

Year Team	G	GS	SACKS
1992—Detroit NFL	16	7	7.5
1993—Detroit NFL	16	0	8.0
1994—Detroit NFL	16	9	2.5
1995—Detroit NFL	16	16	9.5
1996—Detroit NFL	6	6	2.0
1997—Detroit NFL	15	6	7.5
Pro totals (6 years)	85	44	37.0

SCURLOCK, MIKE   CB   RAMS

PERSONAL: Born February 26, 1972, in Casa Grande, Ariz. ... 5-10/199. ... Full name: Michael Lee Scurlock Jr. ... Cousin of Randy Robbins, safety with Denver Broncos (1984-1991). ... Name pronounced SKER-lock.
HIGH SCHOOL: Sunnyside (Tucson, Ariz.), then Cholla (Tucson, Ariz.).
COLLEGE: Arizona.
TRANSACTIONS/CAREER NOTES: Selected by St. Louis Rams in fifth round (140th pick overall) of 1995 NFL draft. ... Signed by Rams (June 20, 1995). ... On injured reserve with sprained left knee (December 20, 1995-remainder of season). ... Released by Rams (August 24, 1997). ... Re-signed by Rams (November 4, 1997). ... Granted free agency (February 13, 1998). ... Re-signed by Rams (April 21, 1998).
PLAYING EXPERIENCE: St. Louis NFL, 1995-1997. ... Games/Games started: 1995 (14/1), 1996 (16/0), 1997 (5/0). Total: 35/1.
PRO STATISTICS: 1995—Intercepted one pass for 13 yards and recovered one fumble.

SEALS, RAY — DE — BENGALS

PERSONAL: Born June 17, 1965, in Syracuse, N.Y. ... 6-3/306. ... Full name: Raymond Seals.
HIGH SCHOOL: Henninger (Syracuse, N.Y.).
COLLEGE: None.
TRANSACTIONS/CAREER NOTES: Played semipro football for Syracuse Express of Eastern Football League (1986 and 1987). ... Signed as non-drafted free agent by Tampa Bay Buccaneers for 1988 (November 18, 1987). ... On injured reserve with back injury (August 8, 1988-entire season). ... On injured reserve with broken bone in foot (September 20, 1989-remainder of season). ... Released by Buccaneers (November 2, 1990). ... Signed by Detroit Lions (November 8, 1990). ... On inactive list for two games with Lions (1990). ... Released by Lions (November 20, 1990). ... Signed by Indianapolis Colts (November 27, 1990). ... Active for one game with Colts (1990); did not play. ... Released by Colts (December 5, 1990). ... Signed by Buccaneers (March 6, 1991). ... On injured reserve with sprained ankle (November 14-December 13, 1991). ... Granted free agency (February 1, 1992). ... Re-signed by Buccaneers (July 28, 1992). ... On injured reserve with knee injury (November 25, 1992-remainder of season). ... Granted unconditional free agency (February 17, 1994). ... Signed by Pittsburgh Steelers (March 21, 1994). ... On injured reserve with shoulder injury (August 27, 1996-entire season). ... Granted unconditional free agency (February 14, 1997). ... Signed by Carolina Panthers (March 5, 1997). ... Released by Panthers (February 4, 1998). ... Signed by Cincinnati Bengals (April 15, 1998).
CHAMPIONSHIP GAME EXPERIENCE: Played in AFC championship game (1994 and 1995 seasons). ... Played in Super Bowl XXX (1995 season).
PRO STATISTICS: 1991—Recovered two fumbles. 1993—Intercepted deflected pass in end zone for a touchdown and recovered one fumble. 1994—Recovered two fumbles. 1995—Intercepted one pass for no yards and recovered one fumble.

Year Team	G	GS	SACKS
1988—Tampa Bay NFL	Did not play.		
1989—Tampa Bay NFL	2	0	0.0
1990—Tampa Bay NFL	8	0	0.0
1991—Tampa Bay NFL	10	9	0.0
1992—Tampa Bay NFL	11	8	5.0
1993—Tampa Bay NFL	16	11	8.5
1994—Pittsburgh NFL	13	11	7.0
1995—Pittsburgh NFL	16	16	8.5
1996—Pittsburgh NFL	Did not play.		
1997—Carolina NFL	14	7	1.0
Pro totals (8 years)	90	62	30.0

SEARCY, LEON — OT — JAGUARS

PERSONAL: Born December 21, 1969, in Washington, D.C. ... 6-3/316. ... Name pronounced SEER-see.
HIGH SCHOOL: Maynard Evans (Orlando).
COLLEGE: Miami, Fla. (degree in sociology).
TRANSACTIONS/CAREER NOTES: Selected by Pittsburgh Steelers in first round (11th pick overall) of 1992 NFL draft. ... Signed by Steelers (August 3, 1992). ... Granted unconditional free agency (February 16, 1996). ... Signed by Jacksonville Jaguars (February 18, 1996).
PLAYING EXPERIENCE: Pittsburgh NFL, 1992-1995; Jacksonville NFL, 1996 and 1997. ... Games/Games started: 1992 (15/0), 1993 (16/16), 1994 (16/16), 1995 (16/16), 1996 (16/16), 1997 (16/16). Total: 95/80.
CHAMPIONSHIP GAME EXPERIENCE: Played in AFC championship game (1994-1996 seasons). ... Played in Super Bowl XXX (1995 season).
HONORS: Named offensive tackle on THE SPORTING NEWS college All-America second team (1991).
PRO STATISTICS: 1993—Recovered one fumble. 1995—Recovered one fumble. 1996—Recovered one fumble.

SEAU, JUNIOR — LB — CHARGERS

PERSONAL: Born January 19, 1969, in San Diego. ... 6-3/250. ... Full name: Tiaina Seau Jr. ... Name pronounced SAY-ow.
HIGH SCHOOL: Oceanside (Calif.).
COLLEGE: Southern California.
TRANSACTIONS/CAREER NOTES: Selected after junior season by San Diego Chargers in first round (fifth pick overall) of 1990 NFL draft. ... Signed by Chargers (August 27, 1990).
CHAMPIONSHIP GAME EXPERIENCE: Played in AFC championship game (1994 season). ... Played in Super Bowl XXIX (1994 season).
HONORS: Named linebacker on THE SPORTING NEWS college All-America first team (1989). ... Played in Pro Bowl (1991-1997 seasons). ... Named inside linebacker on THE SPORTING NEWS NFL All-Pro team (1992-1996).
PRO STATISTICS: 1992—Recovered one fumble for 10 yards. 1993—Recovered one fumble for 21 yards. 1994—Recovered three fumbles. 1995—Recovered three fumbles for 30 yards and one touchdown. 1996—Recovered three fumbles. 1997—Fumbled once and recovered two fumbles for five yards.

Year Team	G	GS	INTERCEPTIONS No.	Yds.	Avg.	TD	SACKS No.
1990—San Diego NFL	16	15	0	0	...	0	1.0
1991—San Diego NFL	16	16	0	0	...	0	7.0
1992—San Diego NFL	15	15	2	51	25.5	0	4.5
1993—San Diego NFL	16	16	2	58	29.0	0	0.0
1994—San Diego NFL	16	16	0	0	...	0	5.5
1995—San Diego NFL	16	16	2	5	2.5	0	2.0
1996—San Diego NFL	15	15	2	18	9.0	0	7.0
1997—San Diego NFL	15	15	2	33	16.5	0	7.0
Pro totals (8 years)	125	124	10	165	16.5	0	34.0

SEAY, MARK — WR

PERSONAL: Born April 11, 1967, in Los Angeles. ... 6-0/175. ... Full name: Mark Edward Seay. ... Name pronounced SAY.
HIGH SCHOOL: San Bernardino (Calif.).
COLLEGE: Long Beach State.

S

TRANSACTIONS/CAREER NOTES: Signed as non-drafted free agent by San Francisco 49ers (May 8, 1992). ... Released by 49ers (August 31, 1992). ... Re-signed by 49ers to practice squad (September 1, 1992). ... Claimed on waivers by San Diego Chargers (August 31, 1993). ... Granted unconditional free agency (February 16, 1996). ... Signed by Philadelphia Eagles (April 9, 1996). ... Granted unconditional free agency (February 14, 1997). ... Re-signed by Eagles (July 19, 1997). ... Released by Eagles (December 10, 1997).

CHAMPIONSHIP GAME EXPERIENCE: Played in AFC championship game (1994 season). ... Played in Super Bowl XXIX (1994 season).

POST SEASON RECORDS: Shares Super Bowl and NFL postseason career and single-game records for most two-point conversions—1 (January 29, 1995, vs. San Francisco).

PRO STATISTICS: 1996—Returned four kickoffs for 51 yards. 1997—Recovered one fumble.

SINGLE GAME HIGHS (regular season): Receptions—8 (September 11, 1994, vs. Cincinnati); yards—119 (September 11, 1994, vs. Cincinnati); and touchdown receptions—2 (December 9, 1995, vs. Arizona).

STATISTICAL PLATEAUS: 100-yard receiving games: 1994 (1), 1995 (1). Total: 2.

| | | | RECEIVING | | | | PUNT RETURNS | | | | TOTALS | | |
Year Team	G	GS	No.	Yds.	Avg.	TD	No.	Yds.	Avg.	TD	TD	2pt.	Pts.	Fum.
1993—San Diego NFL	1	0	0	0	...	0	0	0	...	0	0	...	0	0
1994—San Diego NFL	16	14	58	645	11.1	6	0	0	...	0	6	0	36	0
1995—San Diego NFL	16	0	45	537	11.9	3	0	0	...	0	3	1	20	0
1996—Philadelphia NFL	16	0	19	260	13.7	0	35	305	8.7	0	0	0	0	2
1997—Philadelphia NFL	12	2	13	187	14.4	1	16	172	10.8	0	1	0	6	3
Pro totals (5 years)	61	16	135	1629	12.1	10	51	477	9.4	0	10	1	62	5

SEHORN, JASON   CB   GIANTS

PERSONAL: Born April 15, 1971, in Sacramento ... 6-2/210. ... Name pronounced SEE-horn.

HIGH SCHOOL: Mt. Shasta (Calif.).

JUNIOR COLLEGE: Shasta Community College (Calif.).

COLLEGE: Southern California.

TRANSACTIONS/CAREER NOTES: Selected by New York Giants in second round (59th pick overall) of 1994 NFL draft. ... Signed by Giants (July 17, 1994). ... Granted free agency (February 14, 1997). ... Re-signed by Giants (August 9, 1997).

PRO STATISTICS: 1996—Credited with three sacks, returned one punt for no yards, fumbled once and recovered one fumble. 1997—Credited with 1 1/2 sacks and recovered one fumble for two yards.

| | | | INTERCEPTIONS | | | |
Year Team	G	GS	No.	Yds.	Avg.	TD
1994—New York Giants NFL	8	0	0	0	...	0
1995—New York Giants NFL	14	0	0	0	...	0
1996—New York Giants NFL	16	15	5	61	12.2	1
1997—New York Giants NFL	16	16	6	74	12.3	1
Pro totals (4 years)	54	31	11	135	12.3	2

RECORD AS BASEBALL PLAYER

TRANSACTIONS/CAREER NOTES: Threw right, batted right. ... Signed as non-drafted free agent by Chicago Cubs organization (July 24, 1989). ... Released by Cubs organization (April 4, 1991).

| | | | | | BATTING | | | | | | | | FIELDING | | |
Year Team (League)	Pos.	G	AB	R	H	2B	3B	HR	RBI	Avg.	BB	SO	SB	PO	A	E	Avg.
1990—Huntington (Appal.)	OF	49	125	21	23	3	1	1	10	.184	8	52	9	82	3	5	.944

SEIGLER, DEXTER   CB   CARDINALS

PERSONAL: Born January 11, 1972, in Avon Park, Fla. ... 5-9/178.

HIGH SCHOOL: Avon Park (Fla.).

COLLEGE: Miami (Fla.).

TRANSACTIONS/CAREER NOTES: Signed as non-drafted free agent by Miami Dolphins (April 28, 1994). ... Released by Dolphins (August 19, 1994). ... Signed by Toronto Argonauts of the CFL (September 16, 1994). ... Released by Argonauts (November 10, 1994). ... Signed by Seattle Seahawks (July 27, 1995). ... Released by Seahawks (August 27, 1995). ... Re-signed by Seahawks to practice squad (August 28, 1995). ... Released by Seahawks (September 3, 1997). ... Re-signed by Seahawks (November 5, 1997). ... Released by Seahawks (November 14, 1997). ... Re-signed by Seahawks (November 19, 1997). ... Released by Seahawks (November 21, 1997). ... Re-signed by Seahawks (November 25, 1997). ... Released by Seahawks (November 28, 1997). ... Re-signed by Seahawks (December 2, 1997). ... Granted free agency (February 13, 1998). ... Signed by Arizona Cardinals (June 17, 1998).

PLAYING EXPERIENCE: Seattle NFL, 1996 and 1997. ... Games/Games started: 1996 (12/0), 1997 (2/0). Total: 14/0.

SELBY, ROB   G

PERSONAL: Born October 11, 1967, in Birmingham, Ala. ... 6-3/290. ... Full name: Robert Seth Selby Jr.

HIGH SCHOOL: Berry (Ala.).

COLLEGE: Auburn.

TRANSACTIONS/CAREER NOTES: Selected by Philadelphia Eagles in third round (76th pick overall) of 1991 NFL draft. ... Signed by Eagles (July 14, 1991). ... On injured reserve with knee injury (September 8, 1993-remainder of season). ... Granted free agency (February 17, 1994). ... Re-signed by Eagles (June 22, 1994). ... Granted unconditional free agency (February 17, 1995). ... Signed by Atlanta Falcons (May 18, 1995). ... Released by Falcons (August 27, 1995). ... Signed by Arizona Cardinals (October 17, 1995). ... Granted unconditional free agency (February 16, 1996). ... Re-signed by Cardinals (March 22, 1996). ... On injured reserve with knee injury (December 3, 1996-remainder of season). ... Granted unconditional free agency (February 14, 1997). ... Re-signed by Cardinals (July 1, 1997). ... Granted unconditional free agency (February 13, 1998).

PLAYING EXPERIENCE: Philadelphia NFL, 1991-1994; Arizona NFL, 1995-1997. ... Games/Games started: 1991 (13/0), 1992 (16/1), 1993 (1/0), 1994 (2/0), 1995 (7/4), 1996 (13/4), 1997 (10/9). Total: 62/18.

SEMPLE, TONY   G   LIONS

PERSONAL: Born December 20, 1970, in Springfield, Ill. ... 6-4/286. ... Full name: Anthony Lee Semple.
HIGH SCHOOL: Lincoln Community (Ill.).
COLLEGE: Memphis State.
TRANSACTIONS/CAREER NOTES: Selected by Detroit Lions in fifth round (154th pick overall) of 1994 NFL draft. ... Signed by Lions (July 21, 1994). ... On injured reserve with knee injury (August 19, 1994-entire season). ... Granted free agency (February 14, 1997). ... Re-signed by Lions (June 13, 1997). ... Granted unconditional free agency (February 13, 1998). ... Re-signed by Lions (February 21, 1998).
PLAYING EXPERIENCE: Detroit NFL, 1995-1997. ... Games/Games started: 1995 (16/0), 1996 (15/1), 1997 (16/1). Total: 47/2.

SHADE, SAM   S   BENGALS

PERSONAL: Born June 14, 1973, in Birmingham, Ala. ... 6-1/201.
HIGH SCHOOL: Wenonah (Birmingham, Ala.).
COLLEGE: Alabama.
TRANSACTIONS/CAREER NOTES: Selected by Cincinnati Bengals in fourth round (102nd pick overall) of 1995 NFL draft. ... Signed by Bengals (July 18, 1995). ... Granted free agency (February 13, 1998).
PLAYING EXPERIENCE: Cincinnati NFL, 1995-1997. ... Games/Games started: 1995 (16/2), 1996 (12/0), 1997 (16/12). Total: 44/14.
PRO STATISTICS: 1997—Intercepted one pass for 21 yards, credited with four sacks, fumbled once and recovered one fumble.

SHARPE, SHANNON   TE   BRONCOS

PERSONAL: Born June 26, 1968, in Chicago. ... 6-2/228. ... Brother of Sterling Sharpe, wide receiver with Green Bay Packers (1988-1994).
HIGH SCHOOL: Glennville (Ga.).
COLLEGE: Savannah (Ga.) State.
TRANSACTIONS/CAREER NOTES: Selected by Denver Broncos in seventh round (192nd pick overall) of 1990 NFL draft. ... Signed by Broncos (July 1990). ... Granted free agency (February 1, 1992). ... Re-signed by Broncos (July 31, 1992). ... Designated by Broncos as transition player (February 15, 1994).
CHAMPIONSHIP GAME EXPERIENCE: Played in AFC championship game (1991 and 1997 seasons). ... Member of Super Bowl championship team (1997 season).
HONORS: Played in Pro Bowl (1992, 1993 and 1995-1997 seasons). ... Named tight end on THE SPORTING NEWS NFL All-Pro team (1993, 1996 and 1997). ... Named to play in Pro Bowl (1994 season); replaced by Eric Green due to injury.
POST SEASON RECORDS: Shares NFL postseason single-game record for most receptions—13 (January 9, 1994, vs. Los Angeles Raiders).
PRO STATISTICS: 1991—Rushed once for 15 yards and recovered one fumble. 1992—Rushed twice for minus six yards. 1993—Returned one kickoff for no yards. 1995—Recovered one fumble.
SINGLE GAME HIGHS (regular season): Receptions—13 (October 6, 1996, vs. San Diego); yards—180 (September 3, 1995, vs. Buffalo); and touchdown receptions—3 (October 6, 1996, vs. San Diego).
STATISTICAL PLATEAUS: 100-yard receiving games: 1992 (2), 1993 (2), 1994 (1), 1995 (2), 1996 (3), 1997 (4). Total: 14.

| | | | RECEIVING | | | | TOTALS | | | |
Year Team	G	GS	No.	Yds.	Avg.	TD	TD	2pt.	Pts.	Fum.
1990—Denver NFL	16	2	7	99	14.1	1	1	...	6	1
1991—Denver NFL	16	9	22	322	14.6	1	1	...	6	0
1992—Denver NFL	16	11	53	640	12.1	2	2	...	12	1
1993—Denver NFL	16	12	81	995	12.3	9	9	...	54	1
1994—Denver NFL	15	13	87	1010	11.6	4	4	2	28	1
1995—Denver NFL	13	12	63	756	12.0	4	4	0	24	1
1996—Denver NFL	15	15	80	1062	13.3	10	10	0	60	1
1997—Denver NFL	16	16	72	1107	15.4	3	3	1	20	1
Pro totals (8 years)	123	90	465	5991	12.9	34	34	3	210	7

SHARPER, DARREN   DB   PACKERS

PERSONAL: Born November 3, 1975, in Richmond. ... 6-2/205. ... Full name: Darren Mallory Sharper. ... Brother of Jamie Sharper, linebacker with Baltimore Ravens.
HIGH SCHOOL: Hermitage (Glen Allen, Va.).
COLLEGE: William & Mary.
TRANSACTIONS/CAREER NOTES: Selected by Green Bay Packers in second round (60th pick overall) of 1997 NFL draft. ... Signed by Packers (July 11, 1997).
CHAMPIONSHIP GAME EXPERIENCE: Played in NFC championship game (1997 season). ... Played in Super Bowl XXXII (1997 season).
PRO STATISTICS: 1997—Returned one kickoff for three yards and recovered one fumble for 34 yards and a touchdown.

| | | | INTERCEPTIONS | | | | PUNT RETURNS | | | | TOTALS | | | |
Year Team	G	GS	No.	Yds.	Avg.	TD	No.	Yds.	Avg.	TD	TD	2pt.	Pts.	Fum.
1997—Green Bay NFL	14	0	2	70	35.0	∞2	7	32	4.6	0	3	0	18	1

SHARPER, JAMIE   LB   RAVENS

PERSONAL: Born November 23, 1974, in Richmond. ... 6-3/240. ... Full name: Harry Jamie Sharper Jr. ... Brother of Darren Sharper, defensive back, Green Bay Packers.
HIGH SCHOOL: Hermitage (Glen Allen, Va.).
COLLEGE: Virginia (degree in psychology, 1996).
TRANSACTIONS/CAREER NOTES: Selected by Baltimore Ravens in second round (34th pick overall) of 1997 NFL draft. ... Signed by Ravens (July 23, 1997).
PRO STATISTICS: 1997—Fumbled once.

Year Team	G	GS	INTERCEPTIONS No.	Yds.	Avg.	TD	SACKS No.
1997—Baltimore NFL	16	15	1	4	4.0	0	3.0

SHAW, SEDRICK   RB   PATRIOTS

PERSONAL: Born November 16, 1973, in Austin, Texas. ... 6-0/214.
HIGH SCHOOL: Lyndon B. Johnson (Austin, Texas).
COLLEGE: Iowa.
TRANSACTIONS/CAREER NOTES: Selected by New England Patriots in third round (61st pick overall) of 1997 NFL draft. ... Signed by Patriots (July 15, 1997).
PLAYING EXPERIENCE: New England NFL, 1997. ... Games/Games started: 1/0.
SINGLE GAME HIGHS (regular season): Attempts—0; yards—0; and rushing touchdowns—0.

SHAW, TERRANCE   CB   CHARGERS

PERSONAL: Born November 11, 1973, in Marshall, Texas. ... 5-11/190. ... Full name: Terrance Bernard Shaw.
HIGH SCHOOL: Marshall (Texas).
COLLEGE: Stephen F. Austin State.
TRANSACTIONS/CAREER NOTES: Selected by San Diego Chargers in second round (34th pick overall) of 1995 NFL draft. ... Signed by Chargers (June 15, 1995).
PRO STATISTICS: 1997—Recovered one fumble.

Year Team	G	GS	INTERCEPTIONS No.	Yds.	Avg.	TD
1995—San Diego NFL	16	14	1	31	31.0	0
1996—San Diego NFL	16	16	3	78	26.0	0
1997—San Diego NFL	16	16	1	11	11.0	0
Pro totals (3 years)	48	46	5	120	24.0	0

SHEDD, KENNY   WR   RAIDERS

PERSONAL: Born February 14, 1971, in Davenport, Iowa. ... 5-9/171.
HIGH SCHOOL: West (Davenport, Iowa).
COLLEGE: Northern Iowa.
TRANSACTIONS/CAREER NOTES: Selected by New York Jets in fifth round (129th pick overall) of 1993 NFL draft. ... Signed by Jets (July 13, 1993). ... Released by Jets (August 24, 1993). ... Re-signed by Jets to practice squad (September 1, 1993). ... Activated (December 31, 1993); did not play. ... Released by Jets (September 17, 1994). ... Re-signed by Jets to practice squad (September 21, 1994). ... Signed by Chicago Bears off Jets practice squad (October 25, 1994). ... Inactive for nine games (1994). ... Released by Bears (August 27, 1995). ... Selected by London Monarchs in 1996 World League draft (February 22, 1996). ... Signed by Barcelona Dragons of World League (May 23, 1996). ... Signed by Oakland Raiders (June 1996).
PRO STATISTICS: 1996—Credited with a safety and returned three kickoffs for 51 yards. 1997—Returned two kickoffs for 38 yards and recovered two fumbles for 25 yards and one touchdown.
SINGLE GAME HIGHS (regular season): Receptions—3 (September 21, 1997, vs. New York Jets); yards—51 (December 22, 1996, vs. Seattle); and touchdown receptions—1 (September 22, 1996, vs. San Diego).

Year Team	G	GS	RECEIVING No.	Yds.	Avg.	TD	TOTALS TD	2pt.	Pts.	Fum.
1996—Barcelona W.L.	...	...	14	328	23.4	1	1	0	6	...
—Oakland NFL	16	1	3	87	29.0	1	1	0	8	0
1997—Oakland NFL	16	0	10	115	11.5	0	1	0	6	0
W.L. totals (1 year)	...	...	14	328	23.4	1	1	0	6	0
NFL totals (2 years)	32	1	13	202	15.5	1	2	0	14	0
Pro totals (3 years)	...	...	27	530	19.6	2	3	0	20	0

SHELDON, MIKE   OT   DOLPHINS

PERSONAL: Born June 8, 1973, in Hinsdale, Ill. ... 6-4/305. ... Full name: Michael Thomas Sheldon.
HIGH SCHOOL: Willowbrook (Villa Park, Ill.).
COLLEGE: Grand Valley State.
TRANSACTIONS/CAREER NOTES: Signed as non-drafted free agent by Buffalo Bills (April 1995). ... Released by Bills (August 27, 1995). ... Re-signed by Bills to practice squad (August 29, 1995). ... Released by Bills (August 20, 1996). ... Signed by Miami Dolphins to practice squad (August 27, 1996). ... Assigned by Dolphins to Rhein Fire in 1998 World League enhancement allocation program (February 17, 1997).
PLAYING EXPERIENCE: Rhein W.L., 1997; Miami NFL, 1997. ... Games/Games started: 1997 (W.L.-10/10; NFL-11/0; Total: 21/10).

SHELLING, CHRISTOPHER   S

PERSONAL: Born November 3, 1972, in Columbus, Ga. ... 5-10/180. ... Full name: Christopher A. Shelling.
HIGH SCHOOL: Baker (Columbus, Ga.).
COLLEGE: Auburn.
TRANSACTIONS/CAREER NOTES: Signed as non-drafted free agent by Cincinnati Bengals (April 26, 1995). ... Released by Bengals (September 3, 1996). ... Selected by Rhein Fire in 1997 World League draft (February 17, 1997). ... Signed by Atlanta Falcons (July 11, 1997). ... Released by Falcons (September 24, 1997).
PLAYING EXPERIENCE: Cincinnati NFL, 1995 and 1996; Atlanta NFL, 1997. ... Games/Games started: 1995 (13/0), 1996 (1/0), 1997 (2/0). Total: 16/0.

SHELLO, KENDEL DT COLTS

PERSONAL: Born November 24, 1973, in New Iberia, La. ... 6-3/301.
HIGH SCHOOL: New Iberia (La.).
COLLEGE: Southern.
TRANSACTIONS/CAREER NOTES: Signed as non-drafted free agent by Indianapolis Colts (April 26, 1996). ... Released by Colts (August 25, 1996). ... Re-signed by Colts to practice squad (August 27, 1996). ... Activated (September 22, 1996); did not play.
PLAYING EXPERIENCE: Indianapolis NFL, 1997. ... Games/Games started: 6/0.
PRO STATISTICS: 1997—Credited with one sack.

SHELTON, DAIMON RB JAGUARS

PERSONAL: Born September 15, 1972, in Duarte, Calif. ... 6-0/251.
HIGH SCHOOL: Duarte (Calif.).
JUNIOR COLLEGE: Fresno (Calif.) City College.
COLLEGE: Cal State Sacramento.
TRANSACTIONS/CAREER NOTES: Selected by Jacksonville Jaguars in sixth round (184th pick overall) of 1997 NFL draft. ... Signed by Jaguars (May 23, 1997).
SINGLE GAME HIGHS (regular season): Attempts—4 (September 7, 1997, vs. New York Giants); yards —2 (October 12, 1997, vs. Philadelphia); and rushing touchdowns—0.

			RUSHING				TOTALS		
Year Team	G	GS	Att.	Yds.	Avg.	TD	TD	2pt.	Pts.	Fum.
1997—Jacksonville NFL	13	0	6	4	0.7	0	0	0	0	1

SHEPHERD, LESLIE WR REDSKINS

PERSONAL: Born November 3, 1969, in Washington, D.C. ... 5-11/186. ... Full name: Leslie Glenard Shepherd.
HIGH SCHOOL: Forestville (Md.).
COLLEGE: Temple.
TRANSACTIONS/CAREER NOTES: Signed as non-drafted free agent by Tampa Bay Buccaneers (May 2, 1992). ... Released by Buccaneers (August 31, 1992). ... Signed by Pittsburgh Steelers (March 17, 1993). ... Released by Steelers (August 24, 1993). ... Re-signed by Steelers to practice squad (August 31, 1993). ... Claimed on waivers by Washington Redskins (September 4, 1994). ... Released by Redskins (September 16, 1994). ... Re-signed by Redskins to practice squad (September 20, 1994). ... Activated (December 2, 1994). ... On injured reserve with elbow and wrist injuries (November 19, 1997-remainder of season).
PRO STATISTICS: 1995—Returned three kickoffs for 85 yards and recovered one fumble. 1996—Recovered one fumble.
SINGLE GAME HIGHS (regular season): Receptions—7 (October 29, 1995, vs. New York Giants); yards—135 (October 29, 1995, vs. New York Giants); and touchdown receptions—2 (September 28, 1997, vs. Jacksonville).
STATISTICAL PLATEAUS: 100-yard receiving games: 1995 (1).

			RUSHING				RECEIVING				TOTALS		
Year Team	G	GS	Att.	Yds.	Avg.	TD	No.	Yds.	Avg.	TD	TD	2pt.	Pts.	Fum.
1994—Washington NFL	3	0	0	0	...	0	1	8	8.0	0	0	0	0	0
1995—Washington NFL	14	4	7	63	9.0	1	29	486	16.8	2	3	0	18	0
1996—Washington NFL	12	6	6	96	16.0	2	23	344	15.0	3	5	0	30	0
1997—Washington NFL	11	9	4	27	6.8	0	29	562	19.4	5	5	0	30	0
Pro totals (4 years)	40	19	17	186	10.9	3	82	1400	17.1	10	13	0	78	0

SHIELDS, WILL G CHIEFS

PERSONAL: Born September 15, 1971, in Fort Riley, Kan. ... 6-3/305. ... Full name: Will Herthie Shields.
HIGH SCHOOL: Lawton (Okla.).
COLLEGE: Nebraska (degree in communications).
TRANSACTIONS/CAREER NOTES: Selected by Kansas City Chiefs in the third round (74th pick overall) of 1993 NFL draft. ... Signed by Chiefs (May 3, 1993).
PLAYING EXPERIENCE: Kansas City NFL, 1993-1997. ... Games/Games started: 1993 (16/15), 1994 (16/16), 1995 (16/16), 1996 (16/16), 1997 (16/16). Total: 80/79.
CHAMPIONSHIP GAME EXPERIENCE: Played in AFC championship game (1993 season).
HONORS: Named guard on THE SPORTING NEWS college All-America second team (1991). ... Named guard on THE SPORTING NEWS college All-America first team (1992). ... Played in Pro Bowl (1995-1997 seasons).
PRO STATISTICS: 1993—Recovered two fumbles. 1994—Recovered one fumble. 1995—Recovered one fumble.

SHIVER, CLAY C COWBOYS

PERSONAL: Born December 7, 1972, in Tifton, Ga. ... 6-2/294.
HIGH SCHOOL: Tift County (Tifton, Ga.).
COLLEGE: Florida State.
TRANSACTIONS/CAREER NOTES: Selected by Dallas Cowboys in third round (67th pick overall) of 1996 NFL draft. ... Signed by Cowboys (July 16, 1996).
PLAYING EXPERIENCE: Dallas NFL, 1996 and 1997. ... Games/Games started. 1996 (14/0), 1997 (16/16). Total: 30/16.
HONORS: Named offensive lineman on THE SPORTING NEWS college All-America first team (1995).
PRO STATISTICS: 1997—Fumbled twice and recovered one fumble.

SHULER, HEATH   QB   SAINTS

PERSONAL: Born December 31, 1971, in Bryson City, N.C. ... 6-2/216. ... Full name: Joseph Heath Shuler.
HIGH SCHOOL: Swain County (Bryson City, N.C.).
COLLEGE: Tennessee.
TRANSACTIONS/CAREER NOTES: Selected after junior season by Washington Redskins in first round (third pick overall) of 1994 NFL draft. ... Signed by Redskins (August 3, 1994). ... Granted free agency (February 14, 1997). ... Traded by Redskins to New Orleans Saints for fifth-round pick (S Jamel Williams) in 1997 draft and third-round pick (RB Skip Hicks) in 1998 draft (April 16, 1997). ... On injured reserve with foot injury (November 19, 1997-remainder of season).
HONORS: Named quarterback on THE SPORTING NEWS college All-America second team (1993).
PRO STATISTICS: 1994—Fumbled three times. 1995—Fumbled once and recovered one fumble. 1996—Fumbled once for minus 14 yards. 1997—Fumbled eight times and recovered three fumbles for minus 20 yards.
SINGLE GAME HIGHS (regular season): Attempts—38 (September 27, 1997, vs. San Diego); completions—21 (November 9, 1997, vs. Oakland); yards—286 (December 11, 1994, vs. Arizona); and touchdown passes—2 (December 18, 1994, vs. Tampa Bay).
MISCELLANEOUS: Regular-season record as starting NFL quarterback: 8-14 (.364).

| | | | | | PASSING | | | | | | RUSHING | | | | TOTALS | | |
Year Team	G	GS	Att.	Cmp.	Pct.	Yds.	TD	Int.	Avg.	Rat.	Att.	Yds.	Avg.	TD	TD	2pt.	Pts.
1994—Washington NFL	11	8	265	120	45.3	1658	10	12	6.26	59.6	26	103	4.0	0	0	0	0
1995—Washington NFL	7	5	125	66	52.8	745	3	7	5.96	55.6	18	57	3.2	0	0	0	0
1996—Washington NFL	1	0	0	0	...	0	0	0	...	...	1	0	0.0	0	0	0	0
1997—New Orleans NFL	10	9	203	106	52.2	1288	2	14	6.34	46.6	22	38	1.7	1	1	0	6
Pro totals (4 years)	29	22	593	292	49.2	3691	15	33	6.22	54.3	67	198	3.0	1	1	0	6

SIENKIEWICZ, TROY   G/OT   CHARGERS

PERSONAL: Born May 27, 1972, in Charleston, S.C. ... 6-5/310. ... Full name: Troy Allen Sienkiewicz. ... Name pronounced sen-KEV-itch.
HIGH SCHOOL: Alamogordo (N.M.).
COLLEGE: New Mexico State.
TRANSACTIONS/CAREER NOTES: Selected by San Diego Chargers in sixth round (177th pick overall) of 1995 NFL draft. ... Signed by Chargers (July 14, 1995). ... On injured reserve list with neck injury (October 25, 1996-remainder of season). ... Granted free agency (February 13, 1998).
PLAYING EXPERIENCE: San Diego NFL, 1996 and 1997. ... Games/Games started: 1996 (7/0), 1997 (14/6). Total: 21/6.
PRO STATISTICS: 1997—Recovered two fumbles for seven yards.

SIGLAR, RICKY   OT   SAINTS

PERSONAL: Born June 14, 1966, in Albuquerque, N.M. ... 6-7/308. ... Full name: Ricky Allan Siglar.
HIGH SCHOOL: Manzano (Albuquerque, N.M.).
JUNIOR COLLEGE: Arizona Western College.
COLLEGE: San Jose State.
TRANSACTIONS/CAREER NOTES: Signed as non-drafted free agent by Dallas Cowboys (March 24, 1989). ... Released by Cowboys (September 5, 1989). ... Signed by San Francisco 49ers to developmental squad (September 20, 1989). ... Released by 49ers (January 29, 1990). ... Re-signed by 49ers (February 5, 1990). ... Released by 49ers (August 20, 1991). ... Re-signed by 49ers (February 4, 1992). ... Released by 49ers (August 31, 1992). ... Signed by Kansas City Chiefs (April 1993). ... Granted free agency (February 17, 1995). ... Tendered offer sheet by Jacksonville Jaguars (March 3, 1995). ... Offer matched by Chiefs (March 10, 1995). ... Granted unconditional free agency (February 14, 1997). ... Signed by New Orleans Saints (June 13, 1997).
PLAYING EXPERIENCE: San Francisco NFL, 1990; Kansas City NFL, 1993-1996; New Orleans NFL, 1997. ... Games/Games started: 1990 (15/0), 1993 (14/14), 1994 (16/8), 1995 (16/12), 1996 (16/16), 1997 (16/1). Total: 93/51.
CHAMPIONSHIP GAME EXPERIENCE: Played in NFC championship game (1990 season). ... Played in AFC championship game (1993 season).

SIMIEN, TRACY   LB

PERSONAL: Born May 21, 1967, in Bay City, Texas. ... 6-1/255. ... Full name: Tracy Anthony Simien. ... Related to Elmo Wright, wide receiver with Kansas City Chiefs (1971-1974), Houston Oilers (1975) and New England Patriots (1975).
HIGH SCHOOL: Sweeny (Texas).
COLLEGE: Texas Christian.
TRANSACTIONS/CAREER NOTES: Signed as non-drafted free agent by Pittsburgh Steelers (May 3, 1989). ... Released by Steelers (September 5, 1989). ... Re-signed by Steelers to developmental squad (September 6, 1989). ... On developmental squad (September 6, 1989-January 5, 1990). ... Played in one playoff game with Steelers (1989 season). ... Granted unconditional free agency (February 1, 1990). ... Signed by New Orleans Saints (March 30, 1990). ... Released by Saints (September 3, 1990). ... Signed by Kansas City Chiefs to practice squad (November 30, 1990). ... Granted free agency after 1990 season. ... Re-signed by Chiefs (February 2, 1991). ... Assigned by Chiefs to Montreal Machine in 1991 WLAF enhancement allocation program (March 4, 1991). ... Granted unconditional free agency (February 13, 1998).
CHAMPIONSHIP GAME EXPERIENCE: Played in AFC championship game (1993 season).
HONORS: Named outside linebacker on All-World League team (1991).
PRO STATISTICS: W.L.: 1991—Recovered one fumble for five yards. NFL: 1991—Recovered one fumble. 1994—Recovered two fumbles. 1995—Recovered three fumbles. 1996—Recovered one fumble.

| | | | INTERCEPTIONS | | | | SACKS |
Year Team	G	GS	No.	Yds.	Avg.	TD	No.
1989—Pittsburgh NFL			Did not play.				
1990—			Did not play.				
1991—Montreal W.L.	10	10	0	0	...	0	5.0
—Kansas City NFL	15	12	0	0	...	0	2.0
1992—Kansas City NFL	15	15	3	18	6.0	0	1.0
1993—Kansas City NFL	16	14	0	0	...	0	0.0
1994—Kansas City NFL	15	15	0	0	...	0	0.0

S

Year Team	G	GS	INTERCEPTIONS No.	Yds.	Avg.	TD	SACKS No.
1995—Kansas City NFL	16	16	0	0	...	0	1.0
1996—Kansas City NFL	16	13	1	2	2.0	0	0.0
1997—Kansas City NFL	16	0	0	0	...	0	0.0
W.L. totals (1 year)	10	10	0	0	...	0	5.0
NFL totals (6 years)	109	85	4	20	5.0	0	4.0
Pro totals (7 years)	119	95	4	20	5.0	0	9.0

SIMMONS, CLYDE   DE   BENGALS

PERSONAL: Born August 4, 1964, in Lanes, S.C. ... 6-6/281.
HIGH SCHOOL: New Hanover (Wilmington, N.C.).
COLLEGE: Western Carolina.
TRANSACTIONS/CAREER NOTES: Selected by Philadelphia Eagles in ninth round (233rd pick overall) of 1986 NFL draft. ... Signed by Eagles (July 3, 1986). ... Granted free agency (February 1, 1991). ... Re-signed by Eagles (August 28, 1991). ... Activated (August 30, 1991). ... Designated by Eagles as transition player (February 15, 1994). ... Signed by Phoenix Cardinals (March 17, 1994); Eagles received second-round pick (DB Brian Dawkins) in 1996 draft as compensation. ... Cardinals franchise renamed Arizona Cardinals for 1994 season. ... Released by Cardinals (August 19, 1996). ... Signed by Jacksonville Jaguars (August 23, 1996). ... Released by Jaguars (March 6, 1998). ... Signed by Cincinnati Bengals (May 13, 1998).
CHAMPIONSHIP GAME EXPERIENCE: Played in AFC championship game (1996 season).
HONORS: Played in Pro Bowl (1991 and 1992 seasons). ... Named defensive end on THE SPORTING NEWS NFL All-Pro team (1991).
PRO STATISTICS: 1986—Returned one kickoff for no yards. 1987—Recovered one fumble. 1988—Credited with one safety, ran 15 yards with blocked field-goal attempt and recovered three fumbles. 1989—Intercepted one pass for 60 yards and a touchdown. 1990—Recovered two fumbles for 28 yards and one touchdown. 1991—Recovered three fumbles (including one in end zone for a touchdown). 1992—Recovered one fumble. 1993—Intercepted one pass for no yards. 1995—Intercepted one pass for 25 yards and a touchdown and recovered one fumble. 1996—Recovered one fumble.
MISCELLANEOUS: Holds Jacksonville Jaguars all-time record for most sacks (16).

Year Team	G	GS	SACKS
1986—Philadelphia NFL	16	0	2.0
1987—Philadelphia NFL	12	12	6.0
1988—Philadelphia NFL	16	16	8.0
1989—Philadelphia NFL	16	16	15.5
1990—Philadelphia NFL	16	16	7.5
1991—Philadelphia NFL	16	16	13.0
1992—Philadelphia NFL	16	16	*19.0
1993—Philadelphia NFL	16	16	5.0
1994—Arizona NFL	16	16	6.0
1995—Arizona NFL	16	16	11.0
1996—Jacksonville NFL	16	14	7.5
1997—Jacksonville NFL	16	13	8.5
Pro totals (12 years)	188	167	109.0

SIMMONS, ED   OT   RAMS

PERSONAL: Born December 31, 1963, in Seattle. ... 6-5/334.
HIGH SCHOOL: Nathan Hale (Seattle).
COLLEGE: Eastern Washington.
TRANSACTIONS/CAREER NOTES: Selected by Washington Redskins in sixth round (164th pick overall) of 1987 NFL draft. ... Signed by Redskins (July 24, 1987). ... On injured reserve with knee injury (November 23, 1987-remainder of season). ... On injured reserve with knee injury (December 11, 1990-remainder of season). ... On injured reserve with knee injury (September 11-November 1991). ... Released by Redskins (February 26, 1998). ... Signed by St. Louis Rams (June 4, 1998).
PLAYING EXPERIENCE: Washington NFL, 1987-1997. ... Games/Games started: 1987 (5/3), 1988 (16/0), 1989 (13/8), 1990 (13/11), 1991 (6/2), 1992 (16/11), 1993 (13/13), 1994 (16/16), 1995 (16/16), 1996 (11/11), 1997 (14/13). Total: 142/104.
CHAMPIONSHIP GAME EXPFRIENCE: Played in NFC championship game (1991 season). ... Member of Super Bowl championship team (1991 season).
PRO STATISTICS: 1993—Recovered one fumble. 1995—Recovered two fumbles.

SIMMONS, WAYNE   LB   CHIEFS

PERSONAL: Born December 15, 1969, in Beauford, S.C. ... 6-2/250. ... Full name: Wayne General Simmons.
HIGH SCHOOL: Hilton Head (S.C.).
COLLEGE: Clemson (degree in finance).
TRANSACTIONS/CAREER NOTES: Selected by Green Bay Packers in first round (15th pick overall) of 1993 NFL draft. ... Signed by Packers (July 1, 1993). ... Granted unconditional free agency (February 14, 1997). ... Re-signed by Packers (May 25, 1997). ... Traded by Packers to Kansas City Chiefs for fifth-round pick (WR Corey Bradford) in 1998 draft (October 7, 1997).
CHAMPIONSHIP GAME EXPERIENCE: Played in NFC championship game (1995 and 1996 seasons). ... Member of Super Bowl championship team (1996 season).
PRO STATISTICS: 1993—Recovered one fumble. 1995—Recovered one fumble.

Year Team	G	GS	INTERCEPTIONS No.	Yds.	Avg.	TD	SACKS No.
1993—Green Bay NFL	14	8	2	21	10.5	0	1.0
1994—Green Bay NFL	12	1	0	0	...	0	0.0
1995—Green Bay NFL	16	16	0	0	...	0	4.0
1996—Green Bay NFL	16	16	1	0	0.0	0	2.5
1997—Green Bay NFL	6	6	0	0	...	0	0.0
—Kansas City NFL	10	8	0	0	...	0	3.5
Pro totals (5 years)	74	55	3	21	7.0	0	11.0

SIMPSON, CARL　　　　　DT　　　　　BEARS

PERSONAL: Born April 18, 1970, in Baxley, Ga. ... 6-2/292. ... Full name: Carl Wilhelm Simpson.
HIGH SCHOOL: Appling County (Baxley, Ga.).
COLLEGE: Florida State (degree in criminology).
TRANSACTIONS/CAREER NOTES: Selected by Chicago Bears in second round (35th pick overall) of 1993 NFL draft. ... Signed by Bears (July 17, 1993).
PRO STATISTICS: 1995—Recovered two fumbles. 1996—Recovered two fumbles for two yards.

Year　Team	G	GS	SACKS
1993—Chicago NFL	11	0	0.5
1994—Chicago NFL	15	8	0.0
1995—Chicago NFL	16	8	1.0
1996—Chicago NFL	16	16	1.5
1997—Chicago NFL	16	16	4.5
Pro totals (5 years)	74	48	7.5

SIMS, KEITH　　　　　G　　　　　EAGLES

PERSONAL: Born June 17, 1967, in Baltimore. ... 6-3/318. ... Full name: Keith A. Sims.
HIGH SCHOOL: Watchung Hills Regional (Warren, N.J.).
COLLEGE: Iowa State (degree in industrial technology).
TRANSACTIONS/CAREER NOTES: Selected by Miami Dolphins in second round (39th pick overall) of 1990 NFL draft. ... Signed by Dolphins (July 30, 1990). ... On injured reserve with knee injury (October 12-November 18, 1991). ... Granted free agency (March 1, 1993). ... Re-signed by Dolphins (July 16, 1993). ... Granted unconditional free agency (February 16, 1996). ... Re-signed by Dolphins (March 8, 1996). ... Released by Dolphins (December 9, 1997). ... Signed by Washington Redskins (December 11, 1997). ... Granted unconditional free agency (February 13, 1998). ... Signed by Philadelphia Eagles (March 2, 1998).
PLAYING EXPERIENCE: Miami NFL, 1990-1997. ... Games/Games started: 1990 (14/13), 1991 (12/12), 1992 (16/16), 1993 (16/16), 1994 (16/16), 1995 (16/16), 1996 (15/15), 1997 (8/4). Total: 113/108.
CHAMPIONSHIP GAME EXPERIENCE: Played in AFC championship game (1992 season).
HONORS: Played in Pro Bowl (1993-1995 seasons).
PRO STATISTICS: 1990—Returned one kickoff for nine yards and recovered one fumble. 1991—Caught one pass for nine yards. 1993—Recovered one fumble. 1994—Recovered two fumbles. 1995—Recovered one fumble.

SINCLAIR, MICHAEL　　　　　DE　　　　　SEAHAWKS

PERSONAL: Born January 31, 1968, in Galveston, Texas. ... 6-4/267. ... Full name: Michael Glenn Sinclair.
HIGH SCHOOL: Charlton-Pollard (Beaumont, Texas).
COLLEGE: Eastern New Mexico (degree in physical education).
TRANSACTIONS/CAREER NOTES: Selected by Seattle Seahawks in sixth round (155th pick overall) of 1991 NFL draft. ... Signed by Seahawks (July 18, 1991). ... Released by Seahawks (August 26, 1991). ... Re-signed by Seahawks to practice squad (August 28, 1991). ... Activated (November 30, 1991). ... On injured reserve with back injury (December 14, 1991-remainder of season). ... Active for two games (1991); did not play. ... Assigned by Seahawks to Sacramento Surge in 1992 World League enhancement allocation program (February 20, 1992). ... On injured reserve with ankle injury (September 1-October 3, 1992). ... On injured reserve with thumb injury (November 10, 1993-remainder of season). ... Granted free agency (February 17, 1995). ... Re-signed by Seahawks (May 24, 1995). ... Granted unconditional free agency (February 16, 1996). ... Re-signed by Seahawks (February 17, 1996).
HONORS: Named defensive end on All-World League team (1992). ... Played in Pro Bowl (1996 and 1997 seasons).
PRO STATISTICS: W.L.: 1992—Recovered one fumble. NFL: 1995—Recovered two fumbles. 1997—Recovered one fumble in end zone for a touchdown.

Year　Team	G	GS	SACKS
1991—Seattle NFL	Did not play.		
1992—Sacramento W.L.	10	10	10.0
—Seattle NFL	12	1	1.0
1993—Seattle NFL	9	1	8.0
1994—Seattle NFL	12	2	4.5
1995—Seattle NFL	16	15	5.5
1996—Seattle NFL	16	16	13.0
1997—Seattle NFL	16	16	12.0
W.L. totals (1 year)	10	10	10.0
NFL totals (5 years)	81	51	44.0
Pro totals (6 years)	91	61	54.0

SINGLETON, ALSHERMOND　　　　　LB　　　　　BUCCANEERS

PERSONAL: Born August 7, 1975, in Newark, N.J. ... 6-2/227. ... Full name: Alshermond Glendale Singleton.
HIGH SCHOOL: Irvington (N.J.).
COLLEGE: Temple.
TRANSACTIONS/CAREER NOTES: Selected by Tampa Bay Buccaneers in fourth round (128th pick overall) of 1997 NFL draft. ... Signed by Buccaneers (July 17, 1997).
PLAYING EXPERIENCE: Tampa Bay NFL, 1997. ... Games/Games started: 12/0.
PRO STATISTICS: 1997—Returned blocked punt for 28 yards and a touchdown.

SINGLETON, NATE　　　　　WR

PERSONAL: Born July 5, 1968, in New Orleans. ... 5-11/190. ... Full name: Nathaniel Singleton III. ... Nephew of Ron Singleton, offensive tackle with San Diego Chargers (1976) and San Francisco 49ers (1977-1980).
HIGH SCHOOL: Higgins (New Orleans).

COLLEGE: Grambling State.

TRANSACTIONS/CAREER NOTES: Selected by New York Giants in 11th round (292nd pick overall) of 1992 NFL draft. ... Signed by Giants (July 21, 1992). ... Released by Giants (August 24, 1992). ... Signed by San Francisco 49ers (May 3, 1993). ... On injured reserve with broken collarbone (October 19, 1996-remainder of season). ... Granted unconditional free agency (February 14, 1997). ... Signed by Philadelphia Eagles (April 4, 1997). ... Released by Eagles (August 24, 1997). ... Signed by Tennessee Oilers (October 1, 1997). ... Released by Oilers (November 5, 1997). ... Signed by Baltimore Ravens (November 19, 1997). ... On injured reserve with hip injury (December 19, 1997-remainder of season). ... Granted unconditional free agency (February 13, 1998).

CHAMPIONSHIP GAME EXPERIENCE: Member of 49ers for NFC Championship game (1993 season); inactive. ... Played in NFC championship game (1994 season). ... Member of Super Bowl championship team (1994 season).

PRO STATISTICS: 1995—Recovered one fumble.

SINGLE GAME HIGHS (regular season): Receptions—6 (December 26, 1994, vs. Minnesota); yards—92 (January 3, 1994, vs. Philadelphia); and touchdown receptions—1 (September 25, 1995, vs. Detroit).

Year Team	G	GS	RECEIVING				PUNT RETURNS				KICKOFF RETURNS				TOTALS			
			No.	Yds.	Avg.	TD	No.	Yds.	Avg.	TD	No.	Yds.	Avg.	TD	TD	2pt.	Pts.	Fum.
1992—									Did not play.									
1993—San Francisco NFL	16	0	8	126	15.8	1	0	0	...	0	0	0	...	0	1	...	6	0
1994—San Francisco NFL	16	1	21	294	14.0	2	2	13	6.5	0	2	23	11.5	0	2	0	12	0
1995—San Francisco NFL	6	2	8	108	13.5	1	5	27	5.4	0	0	0	...	0	1	0	6	1
1996—San Francisco NFL	2	0	1	11	11.0	0	2	32	16.0	0	1	10	10.0	0	0	0	0	0
1997—Baltimore NFL	5	0	0	0	...	0	0	0	...	0	4	64	16.0	0	0	0	0	0
Pro totals (5 years)	45	3	38	539	14.2	4	9	72	8.0	0	7	97	13.9	0	4	0	24	1

SIRAGUSA, TONY — DT — RAVENS

PERSONAL: Born May 14, 1967, in Kenilworth, N.J. ... 6-3/320. ... Full name: Anthony Siragusa.

HIGH SCHOOL: David Brearley Regional (Kenilworth, N.J.).

COLLEGE: Pittsburgh.

TRANSACTIONS/CAREER NOTES: Signed as non-drafted free agent by Indianapolis Colts (April 30, 1990). ... Granted unconditional free agency (February 14, 1997). ... Signed by Baltimore Ravens (April 24, 1997).

CHAMPIONSHIP GAME EXPERIENCE: Played in AFC championship game (1995 season).

PRO STATISTICS: 1990—Recovered one fumble. 1991—Recovered one fumble for five yards. 1992—Recovered one fumble. 1994—Recovered one fumble. 1996—Recovered one fumble. 1997—Recovered one fumble for seven yards.

Year Team	G	GS	SACKS
1990—Indianapolis NFL	13	6	1.0
1991—Indianapolis NFL	13	6	2.0
1992—Indianapolis NFL	16	12	3.0
1993—Indianapolis NFL	14	14	1.5
1994—Indianapolis NFL	16	16	5.0
1995—Indianapolis NFL	14	14	2.0
1996—Indianapolis NFL	10	10	2.0
1997—Baltimore NFL	14	13	0.0
Pro totals (8 years)	110	91	16.5

SKREPENAK, GREG — OT

PERSONAL: Born January 31, 1970, in Wilkes-Barre, Pa. ... 6-7/325. ... Full name: Gregory Andrew Skrepenak.

HIGH SCHOOL: G.A.R. Memorial (Wilkes-Barre, Pa.).

COLLEGE: Michigan.

TRANSACTIONS/CAREER NOTES: Selected by Los Angeles Raiders in second round (32nd pick overall) of 1992 NFL draft. ... On injured reserve (December 1992-remainder of season). ... Inactive for 16 games (1993). ... Raiders franchise moved to Oakland (July 21, 1995). ... Granted unconditional free agency (February 16, 1996). ... Signed by Carolina Panthers (February 19, 1996). ... Released by Panthers (June 2, 1998).

PLAYING EXPERIENCE: Los Angeles Raiders NFL, 1992 and 1994; Oakland NFL, 1995; Carolina NFL, 1996 and 1997. ... Games/Games started: 1992 (10/0), 1994 (12/10), 1995 (14/14), 1996 (16/16), 1997 (16/16). Total: 68/56.

CHAMPIONSHIP GAME EXPERIENCE: Played in NFC championship game (1996 season).

HONORS: Named offensive tackle on THE SPORTING NEWS college All-America first team (1991).

SLADE, CHRIS — LB — PATRIOTS

PERSONAL: Born January 30, 1971, in Newport News, Va. ... 6-5/245. ... Full name: Christopher Carroll Slade. ... Cousin of Terry Kirby, running back with Miami Dolphins (1993-95) and San Francisco 49ers (1996-1997); and cousin of Wayne Kirby, outfielder, New York Mets organization.

HIGH SCHOOL: Tabb (Va.).

COLLEGE: Virginia.

TRANSACTIONS/CAREER NOTES: Selected by New England Patriots in second round (31st pick overall) of 1993 NFL draft. ... Signed by Patriots (July 24, 1993). ... Granted free agency (February 16, 1996). ... Re-signed by Patriots (May 28, 1996).

CHAMPIONSHIP GAME EXPERIENCE: Played in AFC championship game (1996 season). ... Played in Super Bowl XXXI (1996 season).

HONORS: Named defensive lineman on THE SPORTING NEWS college All-America first team (1992). ... Played in Pro Bowl (1997 season).

PRO STATISTICS: 1993—Recovered one fumble. 1995—Recovered two fumbles for 38 yards and one touchdown. 1996—Intercepted one pass for two yards and fumbled once. 1997—Intercepted one pass for one yard and a touchdown.

Year Team	G	GS	SACKS
1993—New England NFL	16	5	9.0
1994—New England NFL	16	16	9.5
1995—New England NFL	16	16	4.0
1996—New England NFL	16	9	7.0
1997—New England NFL	16	16	9.0
Pro totals (5 years)	80	62	38.5

PERSONAL: Born October 19, 1964, in Stockton, Calif. ... 6-1/175. ... Full name: Webster M. Slaughter.
HIGH SCHOOL: Franklin (Stockton, Calif.).
JUNIOR COLLEGE: Delta College (Calif.).
COLLEGE: San Diego State.
TRANSACTIONS/CAREER NOTES: Selected by Cleveland Browns in second round (43rd pick overall) of 1986 NFL draft. ... Signed by Browns (July 24, 1986). ... On injured reserve with broken arm (October 21-December 12, 1988). ... Granted free agency (February 1, 1992). ... Granted unconditional free agency (September 24, 1992). ... Signed by Houston Oilers (September 29, 1992). ... On injured reserve with knee injury (December 30, 1993-remainder of season). ... Released by Oilers (July 20, 1995). ... Re-signed by Oilers (June 6, 1994). ... Released by Oilers (July 20, 1995). ... Signed by Kansas City Chiefs (August 9, 1995). ... Released by Chiefs (February 15, 1996). ... Signed by New York Jets (July 23, 1996). ... Granted unconditional free agency (February 14, 1997). ... Signed by San Diego Chargers (April 21, 1998).
CHAMPIONSHIP GAME EXPERIENCE: Played in AFC championship game (1986, 1987 and 1989 seasons).
HONORS: Played in Pro Bowl (1989 season). ... Named to play in Pro Bowl (1993 season); did not play due to injury.
PRO STATISTICS: 1986—Recovered one fumble in end zone for a touchdown. 1992—Returned one kickoff for 21 yards and recovered two fumbles. 1994—Recovered one fumble.
SINGLE GAME HIGHS (regular season): Receptions—11 (December 22, 1991, vs. Pittsburgh); yards—186 (October 23, 1989, vs. Chicago); and touchdown receptions—2 (October 17, 1993, vs. New England).
STATISTICAL PLATEAUS: 100-yard receiving games: 1986 (1), 1987 (2), 1988 (1), 1989 (4), 1990 (3), 1991 (3), 1993 (2), 1994 (2). Total: 18.

			RUSHING				RECEIVING				PUNT RETURNS				TOTALS			
Year Team	G	GS	Att.	Yds.	Avg.	TD	No.	Yds.	Avg.	TD	No.	Yds.	Avg.	TD	TD	2pt.	Pts.	Fum.
1986—Cleveland NFL	16	16	1	1	1.0	0	40	577	14.4	4	1	2	2.0	0	5	...	30	1
1987—Cleveland NFL	12	12	0	0	...	0	47	806	17.1	7	0	0	...	0	7	...	42	1
1988—Cleveland NFL	8	8	0	0	...	0	30	462	15.4	3	0	0	...	0	3	...	18	1
1989—Cleveland NFL	16	16	0	0	...	0	65	1236	§19.0	6	0	0	...	0	6	...	36	2
1990—Cleveland NFL	16	16	5	29	5.8	0	59	847	14.4	4	0	0	...	0	4	...	24	2
1991—Cleveland NFL	16	16	0	0	...	0	64	906	14.2	3	17	112	6.6	0	3	...	18	1
1992—Houston NFL	12	9	3	20	6.7	0	39	486	12.5	4	20	142	7.1	0	4	...	24	3
1993—Houston NFL	14	14	0	0	...	0	77	904	11.7	5	0	0	...	0	5	...	30	4
1994—Houston NFL	16	12	0	0	...	0	68	846	12.4	2	0	0	...	0	2	0	12	2
1995—Kansas City NFL	16	7	0	0	...	0	34	514	15.1	4	0	0	...	0	4	0	24	0
1996—New York Jets NFL	10	1	0	0	...	0	32	434	13.6	2	0	0	...	0	2	0	12	0
1997—							Did not play.											
Pro totals (11 years)	152	127	9	50	5.6	0	555	8018	14.4	44	38	256	6.7	0	45	0	270	17

PERSONAL: Born June 8, 1972, in Fresno, Calif. ... 6-6/254. ... Full name: David Lyle Sloan.
HIGH SCHOOL: Sierra Joint Union (Tollhouse, Calif.).
JUNIOR COLLEGE: Fresno (Calif.) City College.
COLLEGE: New Mexico.
TRANSACTIONS/CAREER NOTES: Selected by Detroit Lions in third round (70th pick overall) of 1995 NFL draft. ... Signed by Lions (July 20, 1995). ... Granted free agency (February 13, 1998). ... Re-signed by Lions (June 10, 1998).
PRO STATISTICS: 1995—Returned one kickoff for 14 yards. 1996—Recovered one fumble.
SINGLE GAME HIGHS (regular season): Receptions—7 (September 7, 1997, vs. Tampa Bay); yards—49 (September 7, 1997, vs. Chicago); and touchdown receptions—1 (November 12, 1995, vs. Tampa Bay).

			RECEIVING				TOTALS			
Year Team	G	GS	No.	Yds.	Avg.	TD	TD	2pt.	Pts.	Fum.
1995—Detroit NFL	16	8	17	184	10.8	1	1	0	6	0
1996—Detroit NFL	4	4	7	51	7.3	0	0	0	0	0
1997—Detroit NFL	14	12	29	264	9.1	0	0	0	0	0
Pro totals (3 years)	34	24	53	499	9.4	1	1	0	6	0

PERSONAL: Born December 20, 1972, in Hasbrouck Heights, N.J. ... 6-4/250.
HIGH SCHOOL: Hasbrouck Heights (N.J.).
COLLEGE: Iowa.
TRANSACTIONS/CAREER NOTES: Selected by Indianapolis Colts in third round (82nd pick overall) of 1996 NFL draft. ... Signed by Colts (July 11, 1996). ... On injured reserve with ankle injury (November 27, 1997-remainder of season).
PLAYING EXPERIENCE: Indianapolis NFL, 1996 and 1997. ... Games/Games started: 1996 (15/0), 1997 (12/2). Total: 27/2.
PRO STATISTICS: 1997—Caught three passes for 22 yards and recovered two fumbles.
SINGLE GAME HIGHS (regular season): Receptions—2 (October 5, 1997, vs. New York Jets); yards—16 (October 5, 1997, vs. New York Jets); and touchdown receptions—0.

PERSONAL: Born September 4, 1970, in Tampa. ... 6-3/209. ... Full name: Torrance Ramon Small.
HIGH SCHOOL: Thomas Jefferson (Tampa).
COLLEGE: Alcorn State.
TRANSACTIONS/CAREER NOTES: Selected by New Orleans Saints in fifth round (138th pick overall) of 1992 NFL draft. ... Signed by Saints (July 15, 1992). ... Released by Saints (September 3, 1992). ... Re-signed by Saints to practice squad (September 4, 1992). ... Activated (September 19, 1992). ... Granted free agency (February 17, 1995). ... Tendered offer sheet by Seattle Seahawks (March 8, 1995). ... Offer matched by Saints (March 15, 1995). ... Released by Saints (May 28, 1997). ... Signed by St. Louis Rams (June 7, 1997). ... Granted unconditional free agency (February 13, 1998). ... Signed by Indianapolis Colts (April 15, 1998).

S

PRO STATISTICS: 1994—Recovered one fumble. 1995—Rushed six times for 75 yards and one touchdown and recovered one fumble. 1996—Rushed four times for 51 yards and a touchdown.
SINGLE GAME HIGHS (regular season): Receptions—8 (November 20, 1994, vs. Los Angeles Raiders); yards—200 (December 24, 1994, vs. Denver); and touchdown receptions—2 (December 16, 1995, vs. Green Bay).
STATISTICAL PLATEAUS: 100-yard receiving games: 1994 (1).

| Year Team | G | GS | RECEIVING | | | | TOTALS | | | |
			No.	Yds.	Avg.	TD	TD	2pt.	Pts.	Fum.
1992—New Orleans NFL	13	2	23	278	12.1	3	3	...	18	0
1993—New Orleans NFL	11	0	16	164	10.3	1	1	...	6	0
1994—New Orleans NFL	16	0	49	719	14.7	5	5	1	32	0
1995—New Orleans NFL	16	1	38	461	12.1	5	6	0	36	0
1996—New Orleans NFL	16	13	50	558	11.2	2	3	0	18	1
1997—St. Louis NFL	13	7	32	488	15.3	1	1	0	6	0
Pro totals (6 years)	85	23	208	2668	12.8	17	19	1	116	1

SMEDLEY, ERIC　　　　DB　　　　BILLS

PERSONAL: Born July 23, 1973, in Charleston, W.Va. ... 5-11/199. ... Full name: Eric Alan Smedley.
HIGH SCHOOL: Capital (Chesterton, W.Va.).
COLLEGE: Indiana.
TRANSACTIONS/CAREER NOTES: Selected by Buffalo Bills in seventh round (249th pick overall) of 1996 NFL draft. ... Signed by Bills (July 2, 1996).
PLAYING EXPERIENCE: Buffalo NFL, 1996 and 1997. ... Games/Games started: 1996 (6/0), 1997 (13/1). Total: 19/1.

SMEENGE, JOEL　　　　DE　　　　JAGUARS

PERSONAL: Born April 1, 1968, in Holland, Mich. ... 6-6/270. ... Full name: Joel Andrew Smeenge. ... Name pronounced SMEN-ghee.
HIGH SCHOOL: Hudsonville (Mich.).
COLLEGE: Western Michigan.
TRANSACTIONS/CAREER NOTES: Selected by New Orleans Saints in third round (70th pick overall) of 1990 NFL draft. ... Signed by Saints (July 17, 1990). ... Granted free agency (March 1, 1993). ... Re-signed by Saints (July 9, 1993). ... Granted unconditional free agency (February 17, 1995). ... Signed by Jacksonville Jaguars (February 28, 1995). ... On injured reserve with broken jaw (November 12, 1996-remainder of season).
PRO STATISTICS: 1991—Recovered one fumble. 1992—Recovered one fumble. 1995—Intercepted one pass for 12 yards and fumbled once. 1997—Recovered two fumbles for one yard.

Year Team	G	GS	SACKS
1990—New Orleans NFL	15	0	0.0
1991—New Orleans NFL	14	0	0.0
1992—New Orleans NFL	11	0	0.5
1993—New Orleans NFL	16	2	1.0
1994—New Orleans NFL	16	2	0.0
1995—Jacksonville NFL	15	15	4.0
1996—Jacksonville NFL	10	10	5.0
1997—Jacksonville NFL	16	0	6.5
Pro totals (8 years)	113	29	17.0

SMITH, ANTHONY　　　　DE　　　　RAIDERS

PERSONAL: Born June 28, 1967, in Elizabeth City, N.C. ... 6-3/265. ... Full name: Anthony Wayne Smith.
HIGH SCHOOL: Northeastern (Elizabeth City, N.C.).
COLLEGE: Alabama, then Arizona.
TRANSACTIONS/CAREER NOTES: Selected by Los Angeles Raiders in first round (11th pick overall) of 1990 NFL draft. ... On injured reserve (September 3, 1990-entire season). ... Raiders franchise moved to Oakland (July 21, 1995). ... Granted unconditional free agency (February 13, 1998).
PRO STATISTICS: 1991—Recovered one fumble. 1994—Recovered one fumble for 25 yards and a touchdown. 1995—Recovered three fumbles. 1996—Recovered one fumble for three yards. 1997—Recovered one fumble and credited with a safety.

Year Team	G	GS	SACKS
1990—Los Angeles Raiders NFL	Did not play.		
1991—Los Angeles Raiders NFL	16	2	10.5
1992—Los Angeles Raiders NFL	15	1	13.0
1993—Los Angeles Raiders NFL	16	2	12.5
1994—Los Angeles Raiders NFL	16	16	6.0
1995—Oakland NFL	16	11	7.0
1996—Oakland NFL	6	4	2.0
1997—Oakland NFL	13	13	6.5
Pro totals (7 years)	98	49	57.5

SMITH, ANTOWAIN　　　　RB　　　　BILLS

PERSONAL: Born March 14, 1972, in Montgomery, Ala. ... 6-2/224. ... Name pronounced an-TWAN.
HIGH SCHOOL: Elmore (Ala.).
JUNIOR COLLEGE: East Mississippi College.
COLLEGE: Houston.
TRANSACTIONS/CAREER NOTES: Selected by Buffalo Bills in first round (23rd pick overall) of 1997 NFL draft. ... Signed by Bills (July 11, 1997).

SINGLE GAME HIGHS (regular season): Attempts—22 (November 2, 1997, vs. Miami); yards—129 (September 21, 1997, vs. Indianapolis); and rushing touchdowns—3 (September 21, 1997, vs. Indianapolis).
STATISTICAL PLATEAUS: 100-yard rushing games: 1997 (1).

Year Team				RUSHING				RECEIVING				TOTALS		
	G	GS	Att.	Yds.	Avg.	TD	No.	Yds.	Avg.	TD	TD	2pt.	Pts.	Fum.
1997—Buffalo NFL	16	0	194	840	4.3	8	28	177	6.3	0	8	0	48	4

SMITH, ARTIE — DE — PATRIOTS

PERSONAL: Born May 15, 1970, in Stillwater, Okla. ... 6-5/305. ... Full name: Artie Enlow Smith.
HIGH SCHOOL: Stillwater (Okla.).
COLLEGE: Louisiana Tech.
TRANSACTIONS/CAREER NOTES: Selected by San Francisco 49ers in fifth round (116th pick overall) of 1993 NFL draft. ... Signed by 49ers (July 14, 1993). ... Claimed on waivers by Cincinnati Bengals (September 16, 1994). ... Granted free agency (February 16, 1996). ... Re-signed by Bengals (May 4, 1996). ... Released by Bengals (August 5, 1997). ... Signed by New England Patriots (March 12, 1998).
CHAMPIONSHIP GAME EXPERIENCE: Played in NFC championship game (1993 season).
PRO STATISTICS: 1996—Recovered one fumble.

Year Team	G	GS	SACKS
1993—San Francisco NFL	16	6	1.5
1994—San Francisco NFL	2	0	0.0
—Cincinnati NFL	7	0	0.0
1995—Cincinnati NFL	16	16	2.0
1996—Cincinnati NFL	16	12	1.0
1997—	Did not play.		
Pro totals (4 years)	57	34	4.5

SMITH, BRADY — DE — SAINTS

PERSONAL: Born June 5, 1973, in Royal Oak, Mich. ... 6-5/260. ... Full name: Brady McKay Smith. ... Son of Steve Smith, offensive tackle for three NFL teams (1966 and 1968-1974).
HIGH SCHOOL: Barrington (Ill.).
COLLEGE: Colorado State.
TRANSACTIONS/CAREER NOTES: Selected by New Orleans Saints in third round (70th pick overall) of 1996 NFL draft. ... Signed by Saints (July 12, 1996).
PRO STATISTICS: 1996—Returned two kickoffs for 14 yards.

Year Team	G	GS	SACKS
1996—New Orleans NFL	16	4	2.0
1997—New Orleans NFL	16	2	5.0
Pro totals (2 years)	32	6	7.0

SMITH, BRENT — G — DOLPHINS

PERSONAL: Born November 21, 1973, in Dallas. ... 6-5/305. ... Full name: Gary Brent Smith.
HIGH SCHOOL: Pontotoc (Miss.).
COLLEGE: Mississippi State.
TRANSACTIONS/CAREER NOTES: Selected by Miami Dolphins in third round (96th pick overall) of 1997 NFL draft. ... Signed by Dolphins (July 8, 1997). ... Active for two games (1997); did not play.

SMITH, BRUCE — DE — BILLS

PERSONAL: Born June 18, 1963, in Norfolk, Va. ... 6-4/273. ... Full name: Bruce Bernard Smith.
HIGH SCHOOL: Booker T. Washington (Norfolk, Va.).
COLLEGE: Virginia Tech.
TRANSACTIONS/CAREER NOTES: Selected by Baltimore Stars in 1985 USFL territorial draft. ... Signed by Buffalo Bills (February 28, 1985). ... Selected officially by Bills in first round (first pick overall) of 1985 NFL draft. ... On non-football injury list with substance abuse problem (September 2-28, 1988). ... Granted free agency (February 1, 1989). ... Tendered offer sheet by Denver Broncos (March 23, 1989). ... Offer matched by Bills (March 29, 1989). ... On injured reserve with knee injury (October 12-November 30, 1991).
CHAMPIONSHIP GAME EXPERIENCE: Played in AFC championship game (1988 and 1990-1993 seasons). ... Played in Super Bowl XXV (1990 season), Super Bowl XXVI (1991 season), Super Bowl XXVII (1992 season) and Super Bowl XXVIII (1993 season).
HONORS: Named defensive lineman on THE SPORTING NEWS college All-America second team (1983 and 1984). ... Outland Trophy winner (1984). ... Named defensive end on THE SPORTING NEWS NFL All-Pro team (1987, 1988, 1990 and 1992-1997). ... Played in Pro Bowl (1987-1990, 1994, 1995 and 1997 seasons). ... Named Outstanding Player of Pro Bowl (1987 season). ... Named to play in Pro Bowl (1992 season); replaced by Howie Long due to injury. ... Named to play in Pro Bowl (1993 season); replaced by Sean Jones due to injury. ... Named to play in Pro Bowl (1996 season); replaced by Willie McGinest due to injury.
POST SEASON RECORDS: Shares Super Bowl single-game record for most safeties—1 (January 27, 1991, vs. New York Giants). ... Shares NFL postseason career record for most sacks—12. ... Shares NFL postseason single-game record for most safeties—1 (January 27, 1991, vs. New York Giants).
PRO STATISTICS: 1985—Rushed once for no yards and recovered four fumbles. 1987—Recovered two fumbles for 15 yards and one touchdown. 1988—Credited with one safety. 1993—Intercepted one pass for no yards and recovered one fumble. 1994—Intercepted one pass for no yards and recovered two fumbles. 1995—Recovered one fumble. 1996—Recovered one fumble.
MISCELLANEOUS: Active AFC leader for career sacks (154). ... Holds Buffalo Bills all-time record for most sacks (154).

Year Team	G	GS	SACKS
1985—Buffalo NFL	16	13	6.5
1986—Buffalo NFL	16	15	15.0
1987—Buffalo NFL	12	12	12.0
1988—Buffalo NFL	12	12	11.0
1989—Buffalo NFL	16	16	13.0
1990—Buffalo NFL	16	16	19.0
1991—Buffalo NFL	5	5	1.5
1992—Buffalo NFL	15	15	14.0
1993—Buffalo NFL	16	16	14.0
1994—Buffalo NFL	15	15	10.0
1995—Buffalo NFL	15	15	10.5
1996—Buffalo NFL	16	16	▲13.5
1997—Buffalo NFL	16	16	§14.0
Pro totals (13 years)	186	182	154.0

SMITH, CEDRIC FB CARDINALS

PERSONAL: Born May 27, 1968, in Enterprise, Ala. ... 5-11/250. ... Full name: Cedric Delon Smith.
HIGH SCHOOL: Enterprise (Ala.).
COLLEGE: Florida (degree in rehabilitative counseling).
TRANSACTIONS/CAREER NOTES: Selected by Minnesota Vikings in fifth round (131st pick overall) of 1990 NFL draft. ... Signed by Vikings (July 27, 1990). ... Released by Vikings (August 26, 1991). ... Signed by New Orleans Saints (November 6, 1991). ... Released by Saints (November 9, 1991). ... Re-signed by Saints (November 11, 1991). ... Granted unconditional free agency (February 1-April 1, 1992). ... Re-signed by Saints for 1992 season. ... Released by Saints (August 26, 1992). ... Signed by Miami Dolphins (March 3, 1993). ... Released by Dolphins (August 24, 1993). ... Signed by Washington Redskins (April 11, 1994). ... Released by Redskins (August 28, 1994). ... Re-signed by Redskins (August 31, 1994). ... Released by Redskins (September 20, 1994). ... Re-signed by Redskins (October 4, 1994). ... Granted free agency (February 17, 1995). ... Re-signed by Redskins (March 24, 1995). ... Released by Redskins (October 17, 1995). ... Signed by Arizona Cardinals (April 23, 1996). ... Granted unconditional free agency (February 13, 1998). ... Re-signed by Cardinals (February 18, 1998).
PRO STATISTICS: 1990—Returned one kickoff for 16 yards. 1996—Returned one kickoff for 14 yards. 1997—Returned three kickoffs for 50 yards and recovered one fumble.
SINGLE GAME HIGHS (regular season): Attempts—5 (September 16, 1990, vs. New Orleans); yards—24 (December 24, 1994, vs. Los Angeles Rams); and rushing touchdowns—1 (August 31, 1997, vs. Cincinnati).

			RUSHING				RECEIVING				TOTALS			
Year Team	G	GS	Att.	Yds.	Avg.	TD	No.	Yds.	Avg.	TD	TD	2pt.	Pts.	Fum.
1990—Minnesota NFL	15	1	9	19	2.1	0	0	0	...	0	0	...	0	0
1991—New Orleans NFL	6	0	0	0	...	0	0	0	...	0	0	...	0	0
1992—							Did not play.							
1993—							Did not play.							
1994—Washington NFL	14	8	10	48	4.8	0	15	118	7.9	1	1	0	6	1
1995—Washington NFL	6	0	3	13	4.3	0	0	0	...	0	0	0	0	0
1996—Arizona NFL	15	2	14	15	1.1	1	3	3	1.0	1	2	0	12	0
1997—Arizona NFL	16	3	4	5	1.3	1	2	20	10.0	0	1	0	6	0
Pro totals (6 years)	72	14	40	100	2.5	2	20	141	7.1	2	4	0	24	1

SMITH, CHUCK DE FALCONS

PERSONAL: Born December 21, 1969, in Athens, Ga. ... 6-2/265. ... Full name: Charles Henry Smith III.
HIGH SCHOOL: Clarke Central (Athens, Ga.).
COLLEGE: Northeastern Oklahoma A&M, then Tennessee.
TRANSACTIONS/CAREER NOTES: Selected by Atlanta Falcons in second round (51st pick overall) of 1992 NFL draft. ... Signed by Falcons (July 27, 1992). ... On suspended list (July 25-August 15, 1994). ... On injured reserve with knee injury (December 21, 1994-remainder of season). ... Granted free agency (February 17, 1995). ... Re-signed by Falcons (July 14, 1995). ... Granted unconditional free agency (February 16, 1996). ... Re-signed by Falcons (February 27, 1996).
PRO STATISTICS: 1993—Recovered two fumbles. 1994—Intercepted one pass for 36 yards and a touchdown and recovered two fumbles. 1995—Recovered two fumbles. 1996—Intercepted one pass for 21 yards and recovered one fumble. 1997—Intercepted one pass for four yards.

Year Team	G	GS	SACKS
1992—Atlanta NFL	16	0	2.0
1993—Atlanta NFL	15	1	3.5
1994—Atlanta NFL	15	10	11.0
1995—Atlanta NFL	14	13	5.5
1996—Atlanta NFL	15	15	6.0
1997—Atlanta NFL	16	15	12.0
Pro totals (6 years)	91	54	40.0

SMITH, DARRIN LB SEAHAWKS

PERSONAL: Born April 15, 1970, in Miami. ... 6-1/230. ... Full name: Darrin Andrew Smith.
HIGH SCHOOL: Norland (Miami).
COLLEGE: Miami, Fla. (degree in business management, 1991; master's degree in business administration, 1993).
TRANSACTIONS/CAREER NOTES: Selected by Dallas Cowboys in second round (54th pick overall) of 1993 NFL draft. ... Signed by Cowboys (July 21, 1993). ... On reserve/did not report list (July 20-October 14, 1995). ... Granted free agency (February 16, 1996). ... Re-signed by Cowboys (June 17, 1996). ... Granted unconditional free agency (February 14, 1997). ... Signed by Philadelphia Eagles (April 19, 1997). ... On injured reserve with ankle injury (November 19, 1997-remainder of season). ... Granted unconditional free agency (February 13, 1998). ... Signed by Seattle Seahawks (February 19, 1998).

CHAMPIONSHIP GAME EXPERIENCE: Played in NFC championship game (1993 and 1995 seasons). ... Member of Super Bowl championship team (1993 and 1995 seasons).

PRO STATISTICS: 1993—Recovered one fumble. 1994—Recovered two fumbles for 11 yards. 1995—Recovered one fumble for 63 yards. 1997—Recovered one fumble.

Year Team	G	GS	INTERCEPTIONS No.	Yds.	Avg.	TD	SACKS No.
1993—Dallas NFL	16	13	0	0	...	0	1.0
1994—Dallas NFL	16	16	2	13	6.5	1	4.0
1995—Dallas NFL	9	9	0	0	...	0	3.0
1996—Dallas NFL	16	16	0	0	...	0	1.0
1997—Philadelphia NFL	7	7	0	0	...	0	1.0
Pro totals (5 years)	64	61	2	13	6.5	1	10.0

SMITH, DEREK   LB   REDSKINS

PERSONAL: Born January 18, 1975, in American Fork, Utah. ... 6-2/239. ... Full name: Derek Mecham Smith.

HIGH SCHOOL: American Fork (Utah).

JUNIOR COLLEGE: Snow (Utah) College.

COLLEGE: Arizona State.

TRANSACTIONS/CAREER NOTES: Selected by Washington Redskins in third round (80th pick overall) of 1997 NFL draft. ... Signed by Redskins (July 11, 1997).

PRO STATISTICS: 1997—Recovered two fumbles for five yards.

Year Team	G	GS	SACKS
1997—Washington NFL	16	16	2.0

SMITH, DETRON   FB   BRONCOS

PERSONAL: Born February 25, 1974, in Dallas. ... 5-9/230. ... Full name: Detron Negil Smith.

HIGH SCHOOL: Lake Highlands (Dallas).

COLLEGE: Texas A&M.

TRANSACTIONS/CAREER NOTES: Selected by Denver Broncos in third round (65th pick overall) of 1996 NFL draft. ... Signed by Broncos (July 20, 1996).

PLAYING EXPERIENCE: Denver NFL, 1996 and 1997. ... Games/Games started: 1996 (13/0), 1997 (16/0). Total: 29/0.

CHAMPIONSHIP GAME EXPERIENCE: Played in AFC championship game (1997 season). ... Member of Super Bowl championship team (1997 season).

PRO STATISTICS: 1997—Rushed four times for 10 yards, caught four passes for 41 yards and one touchdown and returned one kickoff for no yards.

SINGLE GAME HIGHS (regular season): Attempts—2 (December 21, 1997, vs. San Diego); yards—11 (December 21, 1997, vs. San Diego); and rushing touchdowns—0.

SMITH, ED   TE   FALCONS

PERSONAL: Born June 5, 1969, in Trenton, N.J. ... 6-4/253. ... Full name: Edward Martin Smith. ... Brother of Irv Smith, tight end, San Francisco 49ers.

HIGH SCHOOL: Pemberton (N.J.).

COLLEGE: None.

TRANSACTIONS/CAREER NOTES: Played for Frankfurt Galaxy of World League (1996). ... Signed by St. Louis Rams (July 6, 1996). ... Released by Rams (August 20, 1996). ... Signed by Washington Redskins to practice squad (August 26, 1996). ... Granted free agency after 1996 season. ... Signed by Atlanta Falcons (March 3, 1997). ... Released by Falcons (August 24, 1997). ... Re-signed by Falcons to practice squad (August 26, 1997). ... Activated (November 20, 1997).

PLAYING EXPERIENCE: Atlanta NFL, 1997. ... Games/Games started: 5/1.

PRO STATISTICS: 1997—Caught one pass for two yards.

SINGLE GAME HIGHS (regular season): Receptions—1 (November 30, 1997, vs. Seattle); yards—2 (November 30, 1997, vs. Seattle); and touchdown receptions—0.

RECORD AS BASEBALL PLAYER

TRANSACTIONS/CAREER NOTES: Threw right, batted right. ... Selected by Chicago White Sox organization in seventh round of free-agent draft (June 2, 1987). ... Traded by White Sox organization to Milwaukee Brewers organization for P Mike Hooper (June 13, 1991). ... Granted free agency after 1993 season. ... Signed by Chicago Cubs organization (November 5, 1993). ... Granted free agency after 1994 season. ... Signed by Cleveland Indians organization (December 9, 1994).

STATISTICAL NOTES: Led Gulf Coast League third basemen with nine double player 1987. ... Led Midwest League third basemen with 37 double plays 1988. ... Led Midwest League third basemen with 40 errors in 1989.

Year Team (League)	Pos.	G	AB	R	H	2B	3B	HR	RBI	Avg.	BB	SO	SB	PO	A	E	Avg.
1987—GC Whi. Sox (GCL)	3B	32	114	10	27	3	0	2	18	.237	6	28	3	31	73	12	.897
1988—South Bend (Mid.)	3B	130	462	51	107	14	1	3	46	.232	51	87	5	110	272	37	.912
1989—South Bend (Mid.)	3B-1B	115	382	52	94	20	2	8	49	.246	43	84	1	180	140	43	.882
1990—Sarasota (Fla. St.)	3B-1B	63	239	22	46	10	3	4	23	.192	11	61	0	91	97	17	.917
—Birmingham (Sou.)	3B-1B	72	247	22	61	14	3	1	23	.247	22	49	2	103	138	15	.941
1991—Sarasota (FSL)	1B-3B	54	198	27	43	7	0	3	27	.217	15	52	4	248	45	2	.993
—Beloit (Midwest)	3B-1B	61	218	31	57	13	2	4	37	.261	21	41	5	64	112	10	.946
1992—Stockton (California)	3B-1B	99	355	57	93	21	4	11	57	.262	49	72	6	108	90	20	.908
—El Paso (Texas)	3B-1B	22	86	11	25	5	0	2	15	.291	8	20	0	104	43	7	.955
1993—El Paso (Texas)	1B-OF-3B	118	419	64	123	23	6	8	69	.294	38	97	13	505	63	14	.976
1994—Orlando (South.)	3B-1B	115	401	51	104	17	5	16	60	.259	37	75	4	167	199	21	.946
1995—Buffalo (A.A.)	3B-1B	13	31	4	10	0	1	3	9	.323	3	5	0	108	164	14	.951
—Cant./Akr. (Eastern)	OF-3B-1B	103	365	41	88	18	2	11	52	.241	36	93	0	13	1	3	.824

SMITH, EMMITT   RB   COWBOYS

PERSONAL: Born May 15, 1969, in Pensacola, Fla. ... 5-9/209. ... Full name: Emmitt J. Smith III.
HIGH SCHOOL: Escambia (Pensacola, Fla.).
COLLEGE: Florida (degree in public recreation, 1996).
TRANSACTIONS/CAREER NOTES: Selected after junior season by Dallas Cowboys in first round (17th pick overall) of 1990 NFL draft. ... Signed by Cowboys (September 4, 1990). ... Granted roster exemption (September 4-8, 1990). ... Granted free agency (March 1, 1993). ... Re-signed by Cowboys (September 16, 1993).
CHAMPIONSHIP GAME EXPERIENCE: Played in NFC championship game (1992-1995 seasons). ... Member of Super Bowl championship team (1992, 1993 and 1995 seasons).
HONORS: Named running back on THE SPORTING NEWS college All-America first team (1989). ... Played in Pro Bowl (1990-1992 and 1995 seasons). ... Named running back on THE SPORTING NEWS NFL All-Pro team (1992-1995). ... Named NFL Player of the Year by THE SPORTING NEWS (1993). ... Named Most Valuable Player of Super Bowl XXVIII (1993 season). ... Named to play in Pro Bowl (1993 season); replaced by Rodney Hampton due to injury. ... Named Sportsman of the Year by THE SPORTING NEWS (1994). ... Named to play in Pro Bowl (1994 season); replaced by Ricky Watters due to injury.
RECORDS: Holds NFL single-season records for most touchdowns—25 (1995); and most rushing touchdowns—25 (1995).
POST SEASON RECORDS: Holds Super Bowl career record for most rushing touchdowns—5. ... Holds NFL postseason career records for most games with 100 or more yards rushing—7; most rushing touchdowns—18; and most consecutive games with one or more rushing touchdowns—8. ... Shares NFL postseason record for most touchdowns—20.
PRO STATISTICS: 1991—Recovered one fumble. 1992—Recovered one fumble. 1993—Recovered three fumbles. 1996—Recovered one fumble. 1997—Recovered one fumble.
SINGLE GAME HIGHS (regular season): Attempts—35 (November 7, 1994, vs. New York Giants); yards—237 (October 31, 1993, vs. Philadelphia); and rushing touchdowns—4 (September 4, 1995, vs. New York Giants).
STATISTICAL PLATEAUS: 100-yard rushing games: 1990 (3), 1991 (8), 1992 (7), 1993 (7), 1994 (6), 1995 (11), 1996 (4), 1997 (2). Total: 48. ... 100-yard receiving games: 1990 (1), 1993 (1). Total: 2.
MISCELLANEOUS: Holds Dallas Cowboys all-time records for most touchdowns (119) and most rushing touchdowns (112).

			RUSHING				RECEIVING				TOTALS			
Year Team	G	GS	Att.	Yds.	Avg.	TD	No.	Yds.	Avg.	TD	TD	2pt.	Pts.	Fum.
1990—Dallas NFL	16	15	241	937	3.9	11	24	228	9.5	0	11	...	66	7
1991—Dallas NFL	16	16	*365	*1563	4.3	12	49	258	5.3	1	13	...	78	8
1992—Dallas NFL	16	16	‡373	*1713	4.6	*18	59	335	5.7	1	*19	...	114	4
1993—Dallas NFL	14	13	283	*1486	*5.3	9	57	414	7.3	1	10	...	60	4
1994—Dallas NFL	15	15	*368	1484	4.0	*21	50	341	6.8	1	*22	0	132	1
1995—Dallas NFL	16	16	*377	*1773	4.7	*25	62	375	6.0	1	*25	0	*150	7
1996—Dallas NFL	15	15	327	1204	3.7	12	47	249	5.3	3	15	0	90	5
1997—Dallas NFL	16	16	261	1074	4.1	4	40	234	5.9	0	4	1	26	1
Pro totals (8 years)	124	122	2595	11234	4.3	112	388	2434	6.3	7	119	1	716	37

SMITH, ERIC   WR   BEARS

PERSONAL: Born January 5, 1971, in Vero Beach, Fla. ... 5-11/183. ... Full name: Eric Lamonte Smith.
HIGH SCHOOL: Vero Beach (Fla.).
JUNIOR COLLEGE: Northwest Mississippi Junior College.
COLLEGE: Louisiana State.
TRANSACTIONS/CAREER NOTES: Signed as non-drafted free agent by Kansas City Chiefs (April 19, 1996). ... Released by Chiefs (August 25, 1996). ... Re-signed by Chiefs to practice squad (August 27, 1996). ... Assigned by Chiefs to Scottish Claymore in 1997 World League enhancement allocation program (February 17, 1997). ... Released by Chiefs (August 19, 1997). ... Signed by Chicago Bears to practice squad (August 27, 1997). ... Activated (September 23, 1997).
PRO STATISTICS: W.L.: 1997—Attempted one pass with a completion for 43 yards and a touchdown and returned seven punts for 94 yards. NFL: 1997—Rushed once for 12 yards.
SINGLE GAME HIGHS (regular season): Receptions—1 (November 9, 1997, vs. Minnesota); yards—12 (September 28, 1997, vs. Dallas); and touchdown receptions—0.

			RECEIVING				KICKOFF RETURNS				TOTALS			
Year Team	G	GS	No.	Yds.	Avg.	TD	No.	Yds.	Avg.	TD	TD	2pt.	Pts.	Fum.
1997—Scottish W.L.	...	...	19	202	10.6	0	21	552	26.3	1	1	0	6	...
—Chicago NFL	7	0	2	22	11.0	0	10	196	19.6	0	0	0	0	0
W.L. totals (1 year)	...	...	19	202	10.6	0	21	552	26.3	1	1	0	6	0
NFL totals (1 year)	7	0	2	22	11.0	0	10	196	19.6	0	0	0	0	0
Pro totals (2 years)	...	...	21	224	10.7	0	31	748	24.1	1	1	0	6	0

SMITH, FERNANDO   DE   VIKINGS

PERSONAL: Born August 2, 1971, in Flint, Mich. ... 6-6/283. ... Full name: Fernando Dewitt Smith.
HIGH SCHOOL: Northwestern Community (Flint, Mich.).
COLLEGE: Jackson State.
TRANSACTIONS/CAREER NOTES: Selected by Minnesota Vikings in second round (55th pick overall) of 1994 NFL draft. ... Signed by Vikings (July 15, 1994). ... Granted free agency (February 14, 1997). ... Re-signed by Vikings (February 20, 1997).
PRO STATISTICS: 1996—Recovered two fumbles for four yards. 1997—Recovered one fumble for six yards.

Year Team	G	GS	SACKS
1994—Minnesota NFL	7	0	0.0
1995—Minnesota NFL	12	1	2.5
1996—Minnesota NFL	16	16	9.5
1997—Minnesota NFL	12	11	4.0
Pro totals (4 years)	47	28	16.0

S

SMITH, FRANKIE · CB

PERSONAL: Born October 8, 1968, in Groesbeck, Texas. ... 5-9/182. ... Full name: Frankie L. Smith.
HIGH SCHOOL: Groesbeck (Texas).
COLLEGE: Baylor.
TRANSACTIONS/CAREER NOTES: Selected by Atlanta Falcons in fourth round (104th pick overall) of 1992 NFL draft. ... Signed by Falcons (July 7, 1992). ... Released by Falcons (August 25, 1992). ... Signed by Miami Dolphins (March 17, 1993). ... Released by Dolphins (October 22, 1993). ... Re-signed by Dolphins to practice squad (October 23, 1993). ... Activated (November 29, 1993). ... Claimed on waivers by New England Patriots (February 27, 1996). ... Released by Patriots (August 17, 1996). ... Signed by San Francisco 49ers (September 12, 1996). ... Granted unconditional free agency (February 14, 1997). ... Re-signed by 49ers (March 26, 1997). ... Granted unconditional free agency (February 13, 1998).
PLAYING EXPERIENCE: Miami NFL, 1993-1995; San Francisco NFL, 1996 and 1997. ... Games/Games started: 1993 (5/1), 1994 (13/2), 1995 (11/1), 1996 (14/0), 1997 (16/0). Total: 49/4.
CHAMPIONSHIP GAME EXPERIENCE: Played in NFC championship game (1997 season).
PRO STATISTICS: 1994—Credited with one sack. 1997—Recovered one fumble.

SMITH, IRV · TE · 49ERS

PERSONAL: Born October 13, 1971, in Trenton, N.J. ... 6-3/262. ... Full name: Irvin Martin Smith. ... Brother of Ed Smith, tight end, Atlanta Falcons.
HIGH SCHOOL: Township (Pemberton, N.J.).
COLLEGE: Notre Dame (degree in marketing).
TRANSACTIONS/CAREER NOTES: Selected by New Orleans Saints in first round (20th pick overall) of 1993 NFL draft. ... Signed by Saints (July 25, 1993). ... On physically unable to perform list (July 14-29, 1996). ... On inactive list for six games (1996). ... On injured reserve with knee injury (December 14, 1996-remainder of season). ... Granted unconditional free agency (February 13, 1998). ... Signed by San Francisco 49ers (February 19, 1998).
PRO STATISTICS: 1993—Recovered one fumble. 1994—Returned two kickoffs for 10 yards. 1995—Returned one kickoff for six yards.
SINGLE GAME HIGHS (regular season): Receptions—9 (November 12, 1995, vs. Indianapolis); yards—83 (November 12, 1995, vs. Indianapolis); and touchdown receptions—2 (December 10, 1995, vs. Atlanta).

| | | | RECEIVING | | | | | TOTALS | | |
Year Team	G	GS	No.	Yds.	Avg.	TD	TD	2pt.	Pts.	Fum.
1993—New Orleans NFL	16	8	16	180	11.3	2	2	...	12	1
1994—New Orleans NFL	16	16	41	330	8.0	3	3	0	18	0
1995—New Orleans NFL	16	16	45	466	10.4	3	3	1	20	1
1996—New Orleans NFL	7	7	15	144	9.6	0	0	0	0	0
1997—New Orleans NFL	11	8	17	180	10.6	1	1	0	6	1
Pro totals (5 years)	66	55	134	1300	9.7	9	9	1	56	3

SMITH, JEFF · C · CHIEFS

PERSONAL: Born May 25, 1973, in Decatur, Tenn. ... 6-3/322. ... Full name: Jeffery Lee Smith.
HIGH SCHOOL: Meigs County (Decatur, Tenn.).
COLLEGE: Tennessee.
TRANSACTIONS/CAREER NOTES: Selected by Kansas City Chiefs in seventh round (241st pick overall) of 1996 NFL draft. ... Signed by Chiefs (July 24, 1996). ... Active for one game (1996); did not play. ... Assigned by Chiefs to Scottish Claymores in 1997 World League enhancement allocation program (February 19, 1997).
PLAYING EXPERIENCE: Scottish W.L., 1997; Kansas City NFL, 1997. ... Games/Games started: W.L. 1997 (10/games started unavailable), NFL 1997 (3/0).

SMITH, JERMAINE · DT · PACKERS

PERSONAL: Born February 3, 1972, in Augusta, Ga. ... 6-3/289. ... Full name: Matt Jermaine Smith.
HIGH SCHOOL: Laney (Augusta, Ga.).
JUNIOR COLLEGE: Georgia Military College.
COLLEGE: Georgia.
TRANSACTIONS/CAREER NOTES: Selected by Green Bay Packers in fourth round (126th pick overall) of 1997 NFL draft. ... Signed by Packers (July 9, 1997).
CHAMPIONSHIP GAME EXPERIENCE: Member of Packers for NFC championship game (1997 season); inactive. ... Member of Packers for Super Bowl XXXII (1997 season); inactive.

Year Team	G	GS	SACKS
1997—Green Bay NFL	9	0	1.0

SMITH, JIMMY · WR · JAGUARS

PERSONAL: Born February 9, 1969, in Detroit. ... 6-1/205. ... Full name: Jimmy Lee Smith Jr.
HIGH SCHOOL: Callaway (Jackson, Miss.).
COLLEGE: Jackson State.
TRANSACTIONS/CAREER NOTES: Selected by Dallas Cowboys in second round (36th pick overall) of 1992 NFL draft. ... Signed by Cowboys (April 26, 1992). ... On injured reserve with fibula injury (September 2-October 7, 1992); on practice squad (September 28-October 7, 1992). ... On non-football injury list with appendicitis (September 2, 1993-remainder of season). ... Released by Cowboys (July 11, 1994). ... Signed by Philadelphia Eagles (July 19, 1994). ... Released by Eagles (August 29, 1994). ... Signed by Jacksonville Jaguars (February 28, 1995). ... Granted free agency (February 16, 1996). ... Re-signed by Jaguars (May 28, 1996).
CHAMPIONSHIP GAME EXPERIENCE: Played in NFC championship game (1992 season). ... Member of Super Bowl championship team (1992 season). ... Played in AFC championship game (1996 season).

S

HONORS: Played in Pro Bowl (1997 season).
PRO STATISTICS: 1995—Recovered blocked punt in end zone for a touchdown and recovered one fumble. 1997—Recovered one fumble.
SINGLE GAME HIGHS (regular season): Receptions—10 (September 22, 1997, vs. Pittsburgh); yards—164 (September 22, 1997, vs. Pittsburgh); and touchdown receptions—2 (August 31, 1997, vs. Baltimore).
STATISTICAL PLATEAUS: 100-yard receiving games: 1996 (4), 1997 (6). Total: 10.
MISCELLANEOUS: Holds Jacksonville Jaguars all-time record for most yards receiving (2,856), most receptions (187) and most touchdown receptions (14).

| | | | RECEIVING | | | KICKOFF RETURNS | | | | TOTALS | | | |
Year Team	G	GS	No.	Yds.	Avg.	TD	No.	Yds.	Avg.	TD	TD	2pt.	Pts.	Fum.
1992—Dallas NFL	7	0	0	0	...	0	0	0	...	0	0	...	0	0
1993—Dallas NFL							Did not play.							
1994—							Did not play.							
1995—Jacksonville NFL	16	4	22	288	13.1	3	24	540	22.5	1	5	0	30	2
1996—Jacksonville NFL	16	9	83	§1244	15.0	7	2	49	24.5	0	7	0	42	1
1997—Jacksonville NFL	16	16	82	1324	16.1	4	0	0	...	0	4	0	24	1
Pro totals (4 years)	55	29	187	2856	15.3	14	26	589	22.7	1	16	0	96	4

SMITH, KEVIN — CB — COWBOYS

PERSONAL: Born April 7, 1970, in Orange, Texas. ... 5-11/190. ... Full name: Kevin Rey Smith.
HIGH SCHOOL: West Orange-Stark (Orange, Texas).
COLLEGE: Texas A&M.
TRANSACTIONS/CAREER NOTES: Selected by Dallas Cowboys in first round (17th pick overall) of 1992 NFL draft. ... Signed by Cowboys (April 26, 1992). ... On injured reserve with Achilles' tendon injury (September 22, 1995-remainder of season).
CHAMPIONSHIP GAME EXPERIENCE: Played in NFC championship game (1992-1994 seasons). ... Member of Super Bowl championship team (1992, 1993 and 1995 seasons).
HONORS: Named defensive back on THE SPORTING NEWS college All-America first team (1991).
PRO STATISTICS: 1992—Returned one punt for 17 yards and returned one kickoff for nine yards. 1993—Returned one kickoff for 33 yards and recovered one fumble for 14 yards.

| | | | INTERCEPTIONS | | | |
Year Team	G	GS	No.	Yds.	Avg.	TD
1992—Dallas NFL	16	6	2	10	5.0	0
1993—Dallas NFL	16	16	6	56	9.3	1
1994—Dallas NFL	16	16	2	11	5.5	0
1995—Dallas NFL	1	1	0	0	...	0
1996—Dallas NFL	16	16	5	45	9.0	0
1997—Dallas NFL	16	16	1	21	21.0	0
Pro totals (6 years)	81	71	16	143	8.9	1

SMITH, LAMAR — RB — SAINTS

PERSONAL: Born November 29, 1970, in Fort Wayne, Ind. ... 5-11/218.
HIGH SCHOOL: South Side (Fort Wayne, Ind.).
COLLEGE: Houston.
TRANSACTIONS/CAREER NOTES: Selected by Seattle Seahawks in third round (73rd pick overall) of 1994 NFL draft. ... Signed by Seahawks (July 19, 1994). ... On non-football injury list with back injury (December 13, 1994-remainder of season). ... Granted free agency (February 14, 1997). ... Re-signed by Seahawks (February 1997). ... Granted unconditional free agency (February 13, 1998). ... Signed by New Orleans Saints (February 28, 1998).
PRO STATISTICS: 1995—Returned one kickoff for 20 yards. 1996—Recovered one fumble. 1997—Returned one kickoff for 14 yards.
SINGLE GAME HIGHS (regular season): Attempts—33 (November 17, 1996, vs. Detroit); yards—148 (November 17, 1996, vs. Detroit); and rushing touchdowns—2 (December 22, 1996, vs. Oakland).
STATISTICAL PLATEAUS: 100-yard rushing games: 1996 (1).

| | | | RUSHING | | | | RECEIVING | | | | TOTALS | | | |
Year Team	G	GS	Att.	Yds.	Avg.	TD	No.	Yds.	Avg.	TD	TD	2pt.	Pts.	Fum.
1994—Seattle NFL	2	0	2	-1	-0.5	0	0	0	...	0	0	0	0	0
1995—Seattle NFL	13	0	36	215	6.0	0	1	10	10.0	0	0	0	0	1
1996—Seattle NFL	16	2	153	680	4.4	8	9	58	6.4	0	8	3	54	4
1997—Seattle NFL	12	2	91	392	4.3	2	23	183	8.0	0	2	1	14	0
Pro totals (4 years)	43	4	282	1286	4.6	10	33	251	7.6	0	10	4	68	5

SMITH, MARK — DE — CARDINALS

PERSONAL: Born August 28, 1974, in Vicksburg, Miss. ... 6-4/290. ... Full name: Mark Anthony Smith.
HIGH SCHOOL: Vicksburg (Miss.).
JUNIOR COLLEGE: Navarro (Texas) Junior College, then Hinds Community College (Miss.).
COLLEGE: Auburn.
TRANSACTIONS/CAREER NOTES: Selected by Arizona Cardinals in seventh round (212th pick overall) of 1997 NFL draft. ... Signed by Cardinals (May 5, 1997).

Year Team	G	GS	SACKS
1997—Arizona NFL	16	4	6.0

SMITH, NEIL — DE — BRONCOS

PERSONAL: Born April 10, 1966, in New Orleans. ... 6-4/269.
HIGH SCHOOL: McDonogh 35 (New Orleans).

COLLEGE: Nebraska.

TRANSACTIONS/CAREER NOTES: Selected by Kansas City Chiefs in first round (second pick overall) of 1988 NFL draft. ... Signed by Chiefs (July 19, 1988). ... Designated by Chiefs as franchise player (February 25, 1993). ... Granted unconditional free agency (February 14, 1997). ... Signed by Denver Broncos (April 14, 1997). ... Granted unconditional free agency (February 13, 1998). ... Re-signed by Broncos (March 11, 1998).

CHAMPIONSHIP GAME EXPERIENCE: Played in AFC championship game (1993 and 1997 seasons). ... Member of Super Bowl championship team (1997 season).

HONORS: Named defensive lineman on THE SPORTING NEWS college All-America first team (1987). ... Played in Pro Bowl (1991-1993, 1995 and 1997 seasons). ... Named to play in Pro Bowl (1994 season); replaced by Rob Burnett due to injury.

PRO STATISTICS: 1989—Recovered two fumbles for three yards and one touchdown. 1990—Recovered one fumble. 1991—Recovered two fumbles for 10 yards. 1992—Intercepted one pass for 22 yards and a touchdown and recovered two fumbles. 1993—Intercepted one pass for three yards and recovered three fumbles. 1994—Intercepted one pass for 41 yards and recovered one fumble for six yards. 1995—Recovered one fumble.

Year Team	G	GS	SACKS
1988—Kansas City NFL	13	7	2.5
1989—Kansas City NFL	15	15	6.5
1990—Kansas City NFL	16	15	9.5
1991—Kansas City NFL	16	16	8.0
1992—Kansas City NFL	16	16	14.5
1993—Kansas City NFL	16	15	*15.0
1994—Kansas City NFL	14	13	11.5
1995—Kansas City NFL	16	14	12.0
1996—Kansas City NFL	16	16	6.0
1997—Denver NFL	14	13	8.5
Pro totals (10 years)	152	140	94.0

SMITH, OTIS CB JETS

PERSONAL: Born October 22, 1965, in New Orleans. ... 5-11/190. ... Full name: Otis Smith III.

HIGH SCHOOL: East Jefferson (Metairie, La.).

JUNIOR COLLEGE: Taft (Calif.) College.

COLLEGE: Missouri.

TRANSACTIONS/CAREER NOTES: Signed as non-drafted free agent by Philadelphia Eagles (April 25, 1990). ... On physically unable to perform list with appendectomy (August 2, 1990-entire season). ... Granted free agency (February 1, 1992). ... Re-signed by Eagles (August 11, 1992). ... Granted unconditional free agency (February 17, 1994). ... Re-signed by Eagles (April 25, 1994). ... Released by Eagles (March 22, 1995). ... Signed by New York Jets (April 13, 1995). ... Released by Jets (September 24, 1996). ... Signed by New England Patriots (October 9, 1996). ... Granted unconditional free agency (February 14, 1997). ... Re-signed by Jets (May 20, 1997). ... Granted unconditional free agency (February 13, 1998). ... Re-signed by Jets (April 9, 1998).

CHAMPIONSHIP GAME EXPERIENCE: Played in AFC championship game (1996 season). ... Played in Super Bowl XXXI (1996 season).

PRO STATISTICS: 1991—Recovered one fumble. 1994—Credited with one sack and returned one kickoff for 14 yards. 1995—Returned one kickoff for six yards. 1996—Credited with one sack. 1997—Recovered two fumbles for 40 yards.

Year Team	G	GS	INTERCEPTIONS No.	Yds.	Avg.	TD
1990—Philadelphia NFL			Did not play.			
1991—Philadelphia NFL	15	1	2	74	37.0	∞1
1992—Philadelphia NFL	16	1	1	0	0.0	0
1993—Philadelphia NFL	15	0	1	0	0.0	0
1994—Philadelphia NFL	16	2	0	0	...	0
1995—New York Jets NFL	11	10	6	101	16.8	▲1
1996—New York Jets NFL	2	0	0	0	...	0
—New England NFL	11	6	2	20	10.0	0
1997—New York Jets NFL	16	16	6	158	26.3	†3
Pro totals (7 years)	102	36	18	353	19.6	5

SMITH, ROBERT RB VIKINGS

PERSONAL: Born March 4, 1972, in Euclid, Ohio. ... 6-2/209. ... Full name: Robert Scott Smith.

HIGH SCHOOL: Senior (Euclid, Ohio).

COLLEGE: Ohio State.

TRANSACTIONS/CAREER NOTES: Selected after sophomore season by Minnesota Vikings in first round (21st pick overall) of 1993 NFL draft. ... Signed by Vikings (July 16, 1993). ... On injured reserve with knee injury (December 7, 1993-remainder of season). ... On physically unable to perform list (July 13-19, 1994). ... Granted free agency (February 16, 1996). ... Re-signed by Vikings (August 10, 1996). ... On injured reserve with knee injury (November 15, 1996-remainder of season). ... Granted unconditional free agency (February 14, 1997). ... Re-signed by Vikings (April 18, 1997). ... Designated by Vikings as franchise player (February 13, 1998). ... Free agency status changed from franchise to transitional (February 25, 1998). ... Re-signed by Vikings (March 3, 1998).

PRO STATISTICS: 1993—Returned one punt for four yards. 1996—Recovered one fumble. 1997—Recovered one fumble.

SINGLE GAME HIGHS (regular season): Attempts—30 (September 8, 1996, vs. Atlanta); yards—169 (August 31, 1997, vs. Buffalo); and rushing touchdowns—1 (December 14, 1997, vs. Detroit).

STATISTICAL PLATEAUS: 100-yard rushing games: 1993 (1), 1995 (2), 1996 (3), 1997 (6). Total: 12.

Year Team	G	GS	RUSHING Att.	Yds.	Avg.	TD	RECEIVING No.	Yds.	Avg.	TD	KICKOFF RETURNS No.	Yds.	Avg.	TD	TOTALS TD	2pt.	Pts.	Fum.
1993—Minnesota NFL	10	2	82	399	4.9	2	24	111	4.6	0	3	41	13.7	0	2		12	0
1994—Minnesota NFL	14	0	31	106	3.4	1	15	105	7.0	0	16	419	26.2	0	1	0	6	0
1995—Minnesota NFL	9	7	139	632	4.5	5	7	35	5.0	0	0	0	...	0	5	1	32	0
1996—Minnesota NFL	8	7	162	692	4.3	3	7	39	5.6	0	0	0	...	0	3	0	18	2
1997—Minnesota NFL	14	14	232	1266	5.5	6	37	197	5.3	1	0	0	...	0	7	0	42	0
Pro totals (5 years)	55	30	646	3095	4.8	17	90	487	5.4	1	19	460	24.2	0	18	1	110	3

SMITH, ROD   WR   BRONCOS

PERSONAL: Born May 15, 1970, in Texarkana, Ark. ... 6-0/196.
HIGH SCHOOL: Arkansas (Texarkana, Ark.).
COLLEGE: Missouri Southern.
TRANSACTIONS/CAREER NOTES: Signed as non-drafted free agent by Denver Broncos (March 23, 1995).
CHAMPIONSHIP GAME EXPERIENCE: Played in AFC championship game (1997 season). ... Member of Super Bowl championship team (1997 season).
PRO STATISTICS: 1996—Rushed once for one yard. 1997—Rushed five times for 16 yards and recovered one fumble.
SINGLE GAME HIGHS (regular season): Receptions—7 (November 16, 1997, vs. Kansas City); yards—130 (October 30, 1997, vs. New England); and touchdown receptions—2 (December 21, 1997, vs. San Diego).
STATISTICAL PLATEAUS: 100-yard receiving games: 1997 (6).

			RECEIVING			PUNT RETURNS				KICKOFF RETURNS				TOTALS			
Year Team	G	GS	No.	Yds.	Avg.	TD	No.	Yds.	Avg.	TD	No.	Yds.	Avg.	TD	TD	2pt.	Pts. Fum.
1995—Denver NFL	16	1	6	152	25.3	1	0	0	...	0	4	54	13.5	0	1	0	6 0
1996—Denver NFL	10	1	16	237	14.8	2	23	283	12.3	0	1	29	29.0	0	2	0	12 1
1997—Denver NFL	16	16	70	1180	16.9	12	1	12	12.0	0	0	0	...	0	12	0	72 3
Pro totals (3 years)	42	18	92	1569	17.1	15	24	295	12.3	0	5	83	16.6	0	15	0	90 4

SMITH, ROD   CB   PANTHERS

PERSONAL: Born March 12, 1970, in St. Paul, Minn. ... 5-11/187. ... Full name: Rodney Marc Smith.
HIGH SCHOOL: Roseville (Minn.).
COLLEGE: Notre Dame (degree in economics).
TRANSACTIONS/CAREER NOTES: Selected by New England Patriots in second round (35th pick overall) of 1992 NFL draft. ... Signed by Patriots (August 3, 1992). ... Selected by Carolina Panthers from Patriots in NFL expansion draft (February 15, 1995). ... Granted free agency (February 17, 1995). ... Signed by Panthers (May 5, 1995). ... Granted unconditional free agency (February 16, 1996). ... Signed by Minnesota Vikings (May 3, 1996). ... Released by Vikings (October 9, 1996). ... Signed by Panthers (October 22, 1996). ... Granted unconditional free agency (February 14, 1997). ... Re-signed by Panthers (February 26, 1997).
CHAMPIONSHIP GAME EXPERIENCE: Played in NFC championship game (1996 season).
PRO STATISTICS: 1993—Returned one punt for no yards. 1994—Credited with ½ sack. 1996—Credited with one sack.

			INTERCEPTIONS			
Year Team	G	GS	No.	Yds.	Avg.	TD
1992—New England NFL	16	1	1	0	0.0	0
1993—New England NFL	16	9	0	0	...	0
1994—New England NFL	16	7	2	10	5.0	0
1995—Carolina NFL	16	5	0	0	...	0
1996—Carolina NFL	8	1	0	0	...	0
1997—Carolina NFL	16	2	0	0	...	0
Pro totals (6 years)	88	25	3	10	3.3	0

SMITH, THOMAS   CB   BILLS

PERSONAL: Born December 5, 1970, in Gates, N.C. ... 5-11/188. ... Full name: Thomas Lee Smith Jr. ... Cousin of Sam Perkins, forward/center, Seattle SuperSonics.
HIGH SCHOOL: Gates County (Gatesville, N.C.).
COLLEGE: North Carolina.
TRANSACTIONS/CAREER NOTES: Selected by Buffalo Bills in first round (28th pick overall) of 1993 NFL draft. ... Signed by Bills (July 16, 1993). ... Granted free agency (February 16, 1996). ... Re-signed by Bills (February 27, 1996).
PRO STATISTICS: 1993—Recovered one fumble. 1997—Fumbled once and recovered one fumble for one yard.

			INTERCEPTIONS			
Year Team	G	GS	No.	Yds.	Avg.	TD
1993—Buffalo NFL	16	1	0	0	...	0
1994—Buffalo NFL	16	16	1	4	4.0	0
1995—Buffalo NFl	16	16	2	23	11.5	0
1996—Buffalo NFL	16	16	1	0	0.0	0
1997—Buffalo NFL	16	16	0	0	...	0
Pro totals (5 years)	80	65	4	27	6.8	0

SMITH, VERNICE   G

PERSONAL: Born October 24, 1965, in Orlando. ... 6-3/300. ... Full name: Vernice Carlton Smith.
HIGH SCHOOL: Oak Ridge (Orlando).
COLLEGE: Florida A&M.
TRANSACTIONS/CAREER NOTES: Signed as non-drafted free agent by Miami Dolphins (May 22, 1987). ... Released by Dolphins (September 7, 1987). ... Signed by Dallas Cowboys (March 8, 1988). ... Released by Cowboys (August 30, 1988). ... Signed by Cleveland Browns (March 24, 1989). ... Released by Browns (August 30, 1989). ... Signed by Phoenix Cardinals to developmental squad (September 14, 1989). ... Released by Cardinals (November 1, 1989). ... Re-signed by Cardinals to developmental squad (November 8, 1989). ... Released by Cardinals (January 3, 1990). ... Re-signed by Cardinals (off-season, 1990). ... Granted unconditional free agency (February 1-April 1, 1992). ... Re-signed by Cardinals for 1992 season. ... Granted free agency (March 1, 1993). ... Tendered offer sheet by Chicago Bears (April 24, 1993). ... Cardinals declined to match offer (April 25, 1993). ... Released by Bears (October 29, 1993). ... Signed by Washington Redskins (November 9, 1993). ... Released by Redskins (August 24, 1994). ... Re-signed by Redskins (August 25, 1994). ... Granted unconditional free agency (February 17, 1995). ... Re-signed by Redskins (June 6, 1995). ... Granted unconditional free agency (February 16, 1996). ... Signed by New York Jets (June 26, 1996). ... Released by Jets (August 19, 1996). ... Re-signed by Redskins (August 20, 1996). ... Released by Redskins (August 25, 1996). ... Signed by St. Louis Rams (May 30, 1997). ... Granted unconditional free agency (February 13, 1998).
PLAYING EXPERIENCE: Phoenix NFL, 1990-1992; Chicago (6)-Washington (8) NFL, 1993; Washington NFL, 1994 and 1995; St. Louis NFL, 1997. ... Games/Games started: 1990 (11/1), 1991 (14/7), 1992 (12/2), 1993 (Chi.-5/5; Wash.-8/3; Total: 13/8), 1994 (3/0), 1995 (9/0), 1997 (11/2). Total: 73/20.
PRO STATISTICS: 1995—Recovered one fumble.

SMITH, VINSON   LB

PERSONAL: Born July 3, 1965, in Statesville, N.C. ... 6-2/247. ... Full name: Vinson Robert Smith.
HIGH SCHOOL: Statesville (N.C.).
COLLEGE: East Carolina (degree in communications, 1989).
TRANSACTIONS/CAREER NOTES: Signed as non-drafted free agent by Atlanta Falcons (May 2, 1988). ... On injured reserve with elbow injury (August 29-November 4, 1988). ... On injured reserve with knee injury (December 10, 1988-remainder of season). ... Granted unconditional free agency (February 1, 1989). ... Signed by Pittsburgh Steelers (February 28, 1989). ... On injured reserve with broken foot (August 29, 1989-entire season). ... Granted unconditional free agency (February 1, 1990). ... Signed by Dallas Cowboys (March 3, 1990). ... Granted free agency (February 1, 1992). ... Re-signed by Cowboys (August 4, 1992). ... Traded by Cowboys with LB Barry Minter and sixth-round pick (DE Carl Reeves) in 1995 draft to Chicago Bears for TE Kelly Blackwell, S Markus Paul and LB John Roper (August 17, 1993). ... Granted unconditional free agency (February 17, 1995). ... Re-signed by Bears (March 2, 1995). ... Granted unconditional free agency (February 14, 1997). ... Signed by Cowboys (July 19, 1997). ... Granted unconditional free agency (February 13, 1998).
CHAMPIONSHIP GAME EXPERIENCE: Played in NFC championship game (1992 season). ... Member of Super Bowl championship team (1992 season).
PRO STATISTICS: 1990—Recovered two fumbles. 1992—Recovered two fumbles. 1995—Fumbled once for two yards and recovered one fumble. 1996—Recovered two fumbles for 34 yards.

Year Team	G	GS	SACKS
1988—Atlanta NFL	3	0	0.0
1989—Pittsburgh NFL	Did not play.		
1990—Dallas NFL	16	1	0.0
1991—Dallas NFL	13	12	0.0
1992—Dallas NFL	16	13	1.0
1993—Chicago NFL	16	13	0.0
1994—Chicago NFL	12	10	1.0
1995—Chicago NFL	16	13	4.0
1996—Chicago NFL	15	12	1.0
1997—Dallas NFL	14	3	1.0
Pro totals (9 years)	121	77	8.0

SOLOMON, FREDDIE   WR   EAGLES

PERSONAL: Born August 15, 1972, in Gainesville, Fla. ... 5-10/180.
HIGH SCHOOL: Santa Fe (Alachua, Fla.).
COLLEGE: South Carolina State.
TRANSACTIONS/CAREER NOTES: Signed as non-drafted free agent by Philadelphia Eagles (April 26, 1995). ... Released by Eagles (August 27, 1995). ... Re-signed by Eagles to practice squad (September 6, 1995). ... Activated (December 22, 1995); did not play. ... Released by Eagles (August 19, 1997). ... Re-signed by Eagles (September 1, 1997).
PRO STATISTICS: 1997—Recovered one fumble.
SINGLE GAME HIGHS (regular season): Receptions—4 (November 2, 1997, vs. Arizona); yards—77 (November 2, 1997, vs. Arizona); and touchdown receptions—1 (December 21, 1997, vs. Washington).

Year Team	G	GS	RECEIVING No.	Yds.	Avg.	TD	PUNT RETURNS No.	Yds.	Avg.	TD	TOTALS TD	2pt.	Pts.	Fum.
1996—Philadelphia NFL	12	0	8	125	15.6	0	5	27	5.4	0	0	0	0	0
1997—Philadelphia NFL	15	5	29	455	15.7	3	10	55	5.5	0	3	1	20	3
Pro totals (2 years)	27	5	37	580	15.7	3	15	82	5.5	0	3	1	20	3

SOWELL, JERALD   RB   JETS

PERSONAL: Born January 21, 1974, in Baton Rouge, La. ... 6-0/248. ... Full name: Jerald Monye Sowell.
HIGH SCHOOL: Baker (La.).
COLLEGE: Tulane.
TRANSACTIONS/CAREER NOTES: Selected by Green Bay Packers in seventh round (231st pick overall) of 1997 NFL draft. ... Signed by Packers (July 10, 1997). ... Claimed on waivers by New York Jets (August 25, 1997).
SINGLE GAME HIGHS (regular season): Attempts—7 (December 14, 1997, Tampa Bay); yards—35 (December 14, 1997, vs. Tampa Bay); and rushing touchdowns—0.

Year Team	G	GS	RUSHING Att.	Yds.	Avg.	TD	RECEIVING No.	Yds.	Avg.	TD	TOTALS TD	2pt.	Pts.	Fum.
1997—New York Jets NFL	9	0	7	35	5.0	0	1	8	8.0	0	0	0	0	0

SPARKS, PHILLIPPI   CB   GIANTS

PERSONAL: Born April 15, 1969, in Phoenix. ... 5-11/195. ... Full name: Phillippi Dwaine Sparks.
HIGH SCHOOL: Maryvale (Phoenix).
JUNIOR COLLEGE: Glendale (Ariz.) Community College.
COLLEGE: Arizona State.
TRANSACTIONS/CAREER NOTES: Selected by New York Giants in second round (41st pick overall) of 1992 NFL draft. ... Signed by Giants (July 21, 1992). ... Granted free agency (February 17, 1995). ... Re-signed by Giants (May 8, 1995).
PRO STATISTICS: 1992—Returned two kickoffs for 23 yards. 1997—Returned one kickoff for eight yards and credited with one sack.

Year Team	G	GS	INTERCEPTIONS No.	Yds.	Avg.	TD
1992—New York Giants NFL	16	2	1	0	0.0	0
1993—New York Giants NFL	5	3	0	0	...	0
1994—New York Giants NFL	11	11	3	4	1.3	0
1995—New York Giants NFL	16	16	5	11	2.2	0
1996—New York Giants NFL	14	14	3	23	7.7	0
1997—New York Giants NFL	13	13	5	72	14.4	0
Pro totals (6 years)	75	59	17	110	6.5	0

SPEARS, MARCUS   G/OT   CHIEFS

PERSONAL: Born September 28, 1971, in Baton Rouge, La. ... 6-4/305. ... Full name: Marcus Dewayne Spears.
HIGH SCHOOL: Belaire (Baton Rouge, La.).
COLLEGE: Northwestern (La.) State.
TRANSACTIONS/CAREER NOTES: Selected by Chicago Bears in second round (39th pick overall) of 1994 NFL draft. ... Signed by Bears (July 16, 1994). ... Assigned by Bears to Amsterdam Admirals in 1996 World League enhancement allocation program (February 19, 1996). ... Granted unconditional free agency (February 14, 1997). ... Signed by Green Bay Packers (March 12, 1997). ... Released by Packers (August 19, 1997). ... Signed by Kansas City Chiefs (September 16, 1997).
PLAYING EXPERIENCE: Chicago NFL, 1996; Kansas City NFL, 1997. ... Games/Games started: 1996 (9/0), 1997 (3/0). Total: 12/0.
HONORS: Named offensive lineman on THE SPORTING NEWS college All-America second team (1993).
PRO STATISTICS: 1996—Caught one pass for one yard and a touchdown.

SPELLMAN, ALONZO   DE

PERSONAL: Born September 27, 1971, in Mount Holly, N.J. ... 6-4/292. ... Full name: Alonzo Robert Spellman.
HIGH SCHOOL: Rancocas Valley Regional (Mount Holly, N.J.).
COLLEGE: Ohio State.
TRANSACTIONS/CAREER NOTES: Selected after junior season by Chicago Bears in first round (22nd pick overall) of 1992 NFL draft. ... Signed by Bears (July 13, 1992). ... Designated by Bears as transition player (February 16, 1996). ... Tendered offer sheet by Jacksonville Jaguars (February 17, 1996). ... Offer matched by Bears (February 23, 1996). ... Released by Bears (June 12, 1998).
PRO STATISTICS: 1994—Intercepted one pass for 31 yards. 1995—Recovered one fumble.

Year Team	G	GS	SACKS
1992—Chicago NFL	15	0	4.0
1993—Chicago NFL	16	0	2.5
1994—Chicago NFL	16	16	7.0
1995—Chicago NFL	16	16	8.5
1996—Chicago NFL	16	15	8.0
1997—Chicago NFL	7	5	2.0
Pro totals (6 years)	86	52	32.0

SPENCER, JIMMY   CB   BENGALS

PERSONAL: Born March 29, 1969, in Manning, S.C. ... 5-10/185. ... Full name: James Arthur Spencer Jr.
HIGH SCHOOL: Glades Central (Belle Glade, Fla.).
COLLEGE: Florida.
TRANSACTIONS/CAREER NOTES: Selected by Washington Redskins in eighth round (215th pick overall) of 1991 NFL draft. ... Signed by Redskins for 1991 season. ... Released by Redskins (August 26, 1991). ... Signed by New Orleans Saints (April 2, 1992). ... Granted unconditional free agency (February 16, 1996). ... Signed by Cincinnati Bengals (March 21, 1996).
PRO STATISTICS: 1992—Recovered one fumble. 1993—Recovered three fumbles for 53 yards. 1994—Recovered one fumble. 1996—Recovered one fumble for 59 yards.

Year Team	G	GS	INTERCEPTIONS No.	Yds.	Avg.	TD
1992—New Orleans NFL	16	4	0	0	...	0
1993—New Orleans NFL	16	3	0	0	...	0
1994—New Orleans NFL	16	16	5	24	4.8	0
1995—New Orleans NFL	16	15	4	11	2.8	0
1996—Cincinnati NFL	15	14	5	48	9.6	0
1997—Cincinnati NFL	16	9	1	-2	-2.0	0
Pro totals (6 years)	95	61	15	81	5.4	0

SPIELMAN, CHRIS   LB   BILLS

PERSONAL: Born October 11, 1965, in Canton, Ohio. ... 6-0/247. ... Full name: Charles Christopher Spielman.
HIGH SCHOOL: Washington (Massillon, Ohio).
COLLEGE: Ohio State.
TRANSACTIONS/CAREER NOTES: Selected by Detroit Lions in second round (29th pick overall) of 1988 NFL draft. ... Signed by Lions (July 15, 1988). ... On injured reserve with separated shoulder (September 19-October 26, 1990). ... Granted unconditional free agency (February 16, 1996). ... Signed by Buffalo Bills (March 19, 1996). ... On injured reserve with neck injury (October 28, 1997-remainder of season).
CHAMPIONSHIP GAME EXPERIENCE: Played in NFC championship game (1991 season).
HONORS: Named linebacker on THE SPORTING NEWS college All-America first team (1986 and 1987). ... Lombardi Award winner (1987). ... Played in Pro Bowl (1989-1991 and 1994 seasons). ... Named inside linebacker on THE SPORTING NEWS NFL All-Pro team (1994).
PRO STATISTICS: 1988—Recovered one fumble. 1989—Recovered two fumbles for 31 yards. 1990—Recovered two fumbles. 1991—Recovered three fumbles. 1992—Recovered one fumble. 1993—Recovered two fumbles. 1994—Recovered three fumbles for 25 yards and a touchdown. 1995—Recovered three fumbles for eight yards. 1996—Recovered two fumbles.

Year Team	G	GS	INTERCEPTIONS No.	Yds.	Avg.	TD	SACKS No.
1988—Detroit NFL	16	16	0	0	...	0	0.0
1989—Detroit NFL	16	16	0	0	...	0	5.0
1990—Detroit NFL	12	12	1	12	12.0	0	2.0
1991—Detroit NFL	16	16	0	0	...	0	1.0
1992—Detroit NFL	16	16	0	0	...	0	1.0
1993—Detroit NFL	16	16	2	-2	-1.0	0	0.5
1994—Detroit NFL	16	16	0	0	...	0	0.0
1995—Detroit NFL	16	16	1	4	4.0	0	1.0
1996—Buffalo NFL	16	16	1	14	14.0	0	0.0
1997—Buffalo NFL	8	8	1	8	8.0	0	0.0
Pro totals (10 years)	148	148	6	36	6.0	0	10.5

SPIKES, IRVING RB

PERSONAL: Born December 21, 1970, in Ocean Springs, Miss. ... 5-8/206. ... Full name: Irving E. Spikes.
HIGH SCHOOL: Ocean Springs (Miss.).
COLLEGE: Alabama, then Northeast Louisiana.
TRANSACTIONS/CAREER NOTES: Signed as non-drafted free agent by Miami Dolphins (April 28, 1994). ... Granted free agency (February 14, 1997). ... Re-signed by Dolphins (February 27, 1997). ... Released by Dolphins (April 22, 1998).
PRO STATISTICS: 1997—Recovered two fumbles.
SINGLE GAME HIGHS (regular season): Attempts—19 (October 16, 1996, vs. Seattle); yards—79 (September 8, 1996, vs. Arizona); and rushing touchdowns—1 (October 12, 1997, vs. New York Jets).

			RUSHING				RECEIVING				KICKOFF RETURNS				TOTALS		
Year Team	G	GS	Att.	Yds.	Avg.	TD	No.	Yds.	Avg.	TD	No.	Yds.	Avg.	TD	TD	2pt.	Pts. Fum.
1994—Miami NFL	12	1	70	312	4.5	2	4	16	4.0	0	19	434	22.8	0	2	0	12 1
1995—Miami NFL	9	0	32	126	3.9	1	5	18	3.6	1	18	378	21.0	0	2	0	12 0
1996—Miami NFL	15	1	87	316	3.6	3	8	81	10.1	1	28	681	24.3	0	4	0	24 1
1997—Miami NFL	12	1	63	180	2.9	2	7	70	10.0	0	24	565	23.5	0	2	0	12 3
Pro totals (4 years)	48	3	252	934	3.7	8	24	185	7.7	2	89	2058	23.1	0	10	0	60 5

SPINDLER, MARC DE/DT LIONS

PERSONAL: Born November 28, 1969, in West Scranton, Pa. ... 6-5/290. ... Full name: Marc Rudolph Spindler.
HIGH SCHOOL: West Scranton (Pa.).
COLLEGE: Pittsburgh.
TRANSACTIONS/CAREER NOTES: Selected after junior season by Detroit Lions in third round (62nd pick overall) of 1990 NFL draft. ... Signed by Lions (July 24, 1990). ... On injured reserve with knee injury (September 27, 1990-remainder of season). ... On injured reserve with hamstring injury (September 18-October 14, 1992). ... Granted free agency (March 1, 1993). ... Re-signed by Lions (August 2, 1993). ... Granted unconditional free agency (February 17, 1995). ... Signed by Tampa Bay Buccaneers (April 25, 1995). ... Traded by Buccaneers with WR Charles Wilson to New York Jets for fourth-round pick (OT Jason Odom) in 1996 draft (August 27, 1995). ... Released by Jets (February 13, 1997). ... Signed by Seattle Seahawks (June 2, 1997). ... Released by Seahawks (August 6, 1997). ... Signed by Chicago Bears (August 12, 1997). ... Released by Bears (August 24, 1997). ... Signed by Lions (August 26, 1997). ... Released by Lions (September 27, 1997). ... Re-signed by Lions (September 30, 1997). ... Granted unconditional free agency (February 13, 1998). ... Re-signed by Lions (March 4, 1998).
CHAMPIONSHIP GAME EXPERIENCE: Played in NFC championship game (1991 season).
HONORS: Named defensive tackle on THE SPORTING NEWS college All-America first team (1989).
PRO STATISTICS: 1991—Recovered one fumble. 1993—Recovered two fumbles. 1996—Recovered one fumble.

Year Team	G	GS	SACKS
1990—Detroit NFL	3	2	1.0
1991—Detroit NFL	16	16	3.5
1992—Detroit NFL	13	13	2.5
1993—Detroit NFL	16	16	2.0
1994—Detroit NFL	9	8	0.0
1995—New York Jets NFL	10	4	0.0
1996—New York Jets NFL	15	5	0.5
1997—Detroit NFL	10	0	0.0
Pro totals (8 years)	92	64	9.5

SPRIGGS, MARCUS OT BILLS

PERSONAL: Born May 17, 1974, in Hattiesburg, Miss. ... 6-3/295. ... Full name: Thomas Marcus Spriggs.
HIGH SCHOOL: Byram (Jackson, Miss.).
JUNIOR COLLEGE: Hinds Community College (Miss.).
COLLEGE: Houston.
TRANSACTIONS/CAREER NOTES: Selected by Buffalo Bills in sixth round (185th pick overall) of 1997 NFL draft. ... Signed by Bills (June 13, 1997).
PLAYING EXPERIENCE: Buffalo NFL, 1997. ... Games/Games started: 2/0.

SPRINGS, SHAWN CB SEAHAWKS

PERSONAL: Born March 11, 1975, in Silver Spring, Md. ... 6-0/195. ... Son of Ron Springs, running back with Dallas Cowboys (1979-84).
HIGH SCHOOL: Springbrook (Silver Spring, Md.).
COLLEGE: Ohio State.
TRANSACTIONS/CAREER NOTES: Selected by Seattle Seahawks in first round (third pick overall) of 1997 NFL draft. ... Signed by Seahawks (August 4, 1997).
HONORS: Named cornerback on THE SPORTING NEWS college All-America second team (1996).
MISCELLANEOUS: Returned blocked field-goal attempt 12 yards and ran one yard with lateral from interception return (1994).

			INTERCEPTIONS			
Year Team	G	GS	No.	Yds.	Avg.	TD
1997—Seattle NFL	10	10	1	0	0.0	0

STABLEIN, BRIAN WR PATRIOTS

PERSONAL: Born April 14, 1970, in Erie, Pa. ... 6-1/193. ... Full name: Brian Patrick Stablein.
HIGH SCHOOL: McDowell (Erie, Pa.).
COLLEGE: Ohio State.

TRANSACTIONS/CAREER NOTES: Selected by Denver Broncos in eighth round (210nd pick overall) of 1993 NFL draft. ... Signed by Broncos (June 7, 1993). ... Released by Broncos (August 24, 1993). ... Signed by Indianapolis Colts to practice squad (September 7, 1993). ... Granted free agency after 1993 season. ... Re-signed by Colts (March 4, 1994). ... Active for two games (1994); did not play. ... Granted free agency (February 14, 1997). ... Re-signed by Colts (June 10, 1997). ... Granted unconditional free agency (February 13, 1998). ... Signed by New England Patriots (March 19, 1998).

CHAMPIONSHIP GAME EXPERIENCE: Played in AFC championship game (1995 season).

PRO STATISTICS: 1996—Returned six punts for 56 yards. 1997—Returned 17 punts for 133 yards.

SINGLE GAME HIGHS (regular season): Receptions—5 (November 24, 1996, vs. New England); yards—47 (October 5, 1997, vs. New York Jets); and touchdown receptions—1 (October 12, 1997, vs. Pittsburgh).

				RECEIVING			TOTALS			
Year Team	G	GS	No.	Yds.	Avg.	TD	TD	2pt.	Pts.	Fum.
1995—Indianapolis NFL	15	0	8	95	11.9	0	0	0	0	0
1996—Indianapolis NFL	16	0	18	192	10.7	1	1	0	6	0
1997—Indianapolis NFL	16	0	25	253	10.1	1	1	1	8	0
Pro totals (3 years)	47	0	51	540	10.6	2	2	1	14	0

STAI, BRENDEN   G   STEELERS

PERSONAL: Born March 30, 1972, in Phoenix. ... 6-4/305. ... Name pronounced STY.

HIGH SCHOOL: Anaheim (Calif.) Esperanza.

COLLEGE: Nebraska.

TRANSACTIONS/CAREER NOTES: Selected by Pittsburgh Steelers in third round (91st pick overall) of 1995 NFL draft. ... Signed by Steelers (July 18, 1995). ... Granted free agency (February 13, 1998). ... Re-signed by Steelers (June 9, 1998).

PLAYING EXPERIENCE: Pittsburgh NFL, 1995-1997. ... Games/Games started: 1995 (16/9), 1996 (9/9), 1997 (10/9). Total: 35/27.

CHAMPIONSHIP GAME EXPERIENCE: Played in AFC championship game (1995 and 1997 seasons). ... Played in Super Bowl XXX (1995 season).

HONORS: Named offensive lineman on THE SPORTING NEWS college All-America second team (1994).

STALEY, DUCE   RB   EAGLES

PERSONAL: Born February 27, 1975, in Columbia, S.C. ... 5-11/220.

HIGH SCHOOL: Airport (Columbia, S.C.).

JUNIOR COLLEGE: Itawamba (Miss.) Junior College.

COLLEGE: South Carolina.

TRANSACTIONS/CAREER NOTES: Selected by Philadelphia Eagles in third round (71st pick overall) of 1997 NFL draft. ... Signed by Eagles (June 12, 1997).

PRO STATISTICS: 1997—Recovered one fumble.

SINGLE GAME HIGHS (regular season): Attempts—6 (December 21, 1997, vs. Washington); yards—30 (December 21, 1997, vs. Washington); and rushing touchdowns—0.

			RUSHING				RECEIVING				KICKOFF RETURNS				TOTALS			
Year Team	G	GS	Att.	Yds.	Avg.	TD	No.	Yds.	Avg.	TD	No.	Yds.	Avg.	TD	TD	2pt.	Pts.	Fum.
1997—Philadelphia NFL	16	0	7	29	4.1	0	2	22	11.0	0	47	1139	24.2	0	0	0	0	0

STALLINGS, DENNIS   LB   OILERS

PERSONAL: Born May 25, 1974, in East St. Louis, Ill. ... 6-0/234. ... Full name: Dennis Dawon Stallings.

HIGH SCHOOL: East St. Louis (Ill.).

COLLEGE: Illinois.

TRANSACTIONS/CAREER NOTES: Selected by Houston Oilers in sixth round (181st pick overall) of 1997 NFL draft. ... Oilers franchise moved to Tennessee for 1997 season. ... Signed by Oilers (July 19, 1997).

PLAYING EXPERIENCE: Tennessee NFL, 1997. ... Games/Games started: 13/0.

STALLINGS, RAMONDO   DE   BENGALS

PERSONAL: Born November 21, 1971, in Winston-Salem, N.C. ... 6-7/290. ... Full name: Ramondo Antonio Stallings.

HIGH SCHOOL: Ansonia (Conn.).

COLLEGE: San Diego State.

TRANSACTIONS/CAREER NOTES: Selected by Cincinnati Bengals in seventh round (195th pick overall) of 1994 NFL draft. ... Signed by Bengals (June 2, 1994). ... Released by Bengals (August 23, 1994). ... Re-signed by Bengals to practice squad (August 30, 1994). ... Activated (November 8, 1994). ... Granted free agency (February 14, 1997). ... Re-signed by Bengals (April 2, 1997). ... On injured reserve with groin injury (December 1, 1997-remainder of season).

PRO STATISTICS: 1995—Fumbled once and recovered one fumble.

Year Team	G	GS	SACKS
1994—Cincinnati NFL	6	0	0.0
1995—Cincinnati NFL	13	2	1.0
1996—Cincinnati NFL	13	3	2.0
1997—Cincinnati NFL	6	0	0.0
Pro totals (4 years)	38	5	3.0

STARGELL, TONY   CB

PERSONAL: Born August 7, 1966, in LaGrange, Ga. ... 5-11/192. ... Full name: Tony L. Stargell.

HIGH SCHOOL: LaGrange (Ga.).

COLLEGE: Tennessee State (degree in health and physical education, 1990).

S

TRANSACTIONS/CAREER NOTES: Selected by New York Jets in third round (56th pick overall) of 1990 NFL draft. ... Signed by Jets (July 22, 1990). ... Claimed on waivers by Indianapolis Colts (August 31, 1992). ... Granted unconditional free agency (February 17, 1994). ... Signed by Tampa Bay Buccaneers (April 20, 1994). ... On injured reserve with knee injury (November 22, 1994-remainder of season). ... Released by Buccaneers (August 29, 1995). ... Re-signed by Buccaneers (August 31, 1995). ... Granted unconditional free agency (February 16, 1996). ... Signed by Kansas City Chiefs (October 14, 1996). ... On injured reserve with ankle injury (August 24-September 8, 1997). ... Released by Chiefs (September 8, 1997). ... Signed by Chicago Bears (November 12, 1997). ... Released by Bears (November 15, 1997). ... Re-signed by Bears (November 18, 1997). ... Granted unconditional free agency (February 13, 1998).

PRO STATISTICS: 1990—Recovered one fumble. 1991—Recovered one fumble. 1993—Credited with one sack. 1994—Recovered one fumble for two yards.

				INTERCEPTIONS		
Year Team	G	GS	No.	Yds.	Avg.	TD
1990—New York Jets NFL	16	16	2	-3	-1.5	0
1991—New York Jets NFL	16	7	0	0	...	0
1992—Indianapolis NFL	13	3	2	26	13.0	0
1993—Indianapolis NFL	16	1	0	0	...	0
1994—Tampa Bay NFL	10	2	1	0	0.0	0
1995—Tampa Bay NFL	14	6	0	0	...	0
1996—Kansas City NFL	8	4	1	9	9.0	0
1997—Chicago NFL	1	0	0	0	...	0
Pro totals (8 years)	94	39	6	32	5.3	0

STARK, ROHN   P

PERSONAL: Born May 4, 1959, in Minneapolis. ... 6-3/203. ... Full name: Rohn Taylor Stark. ... Name pronounced RON.

HIGH SCHOOL: Pine River (Minn.).

COLLEGE: U.S. Air Force Academy Prep School, then Florida State (degree in finance, 1982).

TRANSACTIONS/CAREER NOTES: Selected by Baltimore Colts in second round (34th pick overall) of 1982 NFL draft. ... Colts franchise moved to Indianapolis (March 31, 1984). ... Granted unconditional free agency (February 17, 1995). ... Signed by Pittsburgh Steelers (March 28, 1995). ... Released by Steelers (August 20, 1996). ... Signed by Carolina Panthers (August 27, 1996). ... Granted unconditional free agency (February 14, 1997). ... Signed by Seattle Seahawks (November 25, 1997). ... Released by Seahawks after 1997 season.

CHAMPIONSHIP GAME EXPERIENCE: Played in AFC championship game (1995 season). ... Played in Super Bowl XXX (1995 season). ... Played in NFC championship game (1996 season).

HONORS: Named punter on THE SPORTING NEWS college All-America first team (1980 and 1981). ... Played in Pro Bowl (1985, 1986, 1990 and 1992 seasons). ... Named punter on THE SPORTING NEWS NFL All-Pro team (1992).

PRO STATISTICS: 1982—Attempted one pass without a completion, rushed once for eight yards and fumbled once. 1983—Attempted one pass without a completion and rushed once for eight yards. 1984—Had only pass attempt intercepted, rushed twice for no yards and recovered one fumble. 1985—Attempted one pass without a completion and recovered one fumble. 1986—Fumbled once and recovered one fumble. 1989—Rushed once for minus 11 yards. 1990—Attempted one pass with one completion for 40 yards. 1991—Rushed once for minus 13 yards, fumbled once and recovered two fumbles. 1992—Attempted one pass with one completion for 17 yards. 1993—Rushed once for 11 yards.

				PUNTING				
Year Team	G	GS	No.	Yds.	Avg.	Net avg.	In. 20	Blk.
1982—Baltimore NFL	9	0	46	2044	44.4	34.2	8	0
1983—Baltimore NFL	16	0	91	*4124	*45.3	36.2	20	0
1984—Indianapolis NFL	16	0	*98	4383	44.7	37.2	21	0
1985—Indianapolis NFL	16	0	78	3584	*45.9	34.2	12	*2
1986—Indianapolis NFL	16	0	76	3432	*45.2	37.2	22	0
1987—Indianapolis NFL	12	0	61	2440	40.0	30.8	12	*2
1988—Indianapolis NFL	16	0	64	2784	43.5	34.5	15	0
1989—Indianapolis NFL	16	0	79	3392	42.9	32.8	14	1
1990—Indianapolis NFL	16	0	71	3084	43.4	37.3	†24	1
1991—Indianapolis NFL	16	0	§82	§3492	42.6	34.7	14	0
1992—Indianapolis NFL	16	0	83	3716	44.8	§39.2	22	0
1993—Indianapolis NFL	16	0	83	3595	43.3	35.8	18	0
1994—Indianapolis NFL	16	0	73	3092	42.4	34.1	22	1
1995—Pittsburgh NFL	16	0	59	2368	40.1	33.2	20	0
1996—Carolina NFL	16	0	77	3128	40.6	36.0	21	0
1997—Seattle NFL	4	0	20	813	40.7	26.9	7	0
Pro totals (16 years)	233	0	1141	49471	43.4	35.2	272	7

STATEN, RALPH   S   RAVENS

PERSONAL: Born December 3, 1974, in Semmes, Ala. ... 6-3/205. ... Full name: Ralph Lahquan Staten.

HIGH SCHOOL: Montgomery (Semmes, Ala.).

COLLEGE: Alabama.

TRANSACTIONS/CAREER NOTES: Selected by Baltimore Ravens in seventh round (236th pick overall) of 1997 NFL draft. ... Signed by Ravens (July 14, 1997).

				INTERCEPTIONS				SACKS
Year Team	G	GS	No.	Yds.	Avg.	TD		No.
1997—Baltimore NFL	10	3	2	12	6.0	0		0.0

STEED, JOEL   NT   STEELERS

PERSONAL: Born February 17, 1969, in Frankfurt, West Germany. ... 6-2/310. ... Full name: Joel Edward Steed.

HIGH SCHOOL: W.C. Hinkley (Aurora, Colo.).

COLLEGE: Colorado.

TRANSACTIONS/CAREER NOTES: Selected by Pittsburgh Steelers in third round (67th pick overall) of 1992 NFL draft. ... Signed by Steelers (July 27, 1992). ... On suspended list for anabolic steroid use (October 23-November 20, 1995). ... Granted unconditional free agency (February 13, 1998). ... Re-signed by Steelers (February 18, 1998).

CHAMPIONSHIP GAME EXPERIENCE: Played in AFC championship game (1994, 1995 and 1997 seasons). ... Played in Super Bowl XXX (1995 season).

HONORS: Named defensive lineman on THE SPORTING NEWS college All-America second team (1991). ... Played in Pro Bowl (1997 season).

PRO STATISTICS: 1993—Recovered one fumble. 1996—Recovered one fumble. 1997—Recovered one fumble.

Year Team	G	GS	SACKS
1992—Pittsburgh NFL	11	4	0.0
1993—Pittsburgh NFL	14	12	1.5
1994—Pittsburgh NFL	16	16	2.0
1995—Pittsburgh NFL	12	11	1.0
1996—Pittsburgh NFL	16	14	0.0
1997—Pittsburgh NFL	16	16	1.0
Pro totals (6 years)	85	73	5.5

STENSTROM, STEVE — QB — BEARS

PERSONAL: Born December 23, 1971, in El Toro (Calif.). ... 6-2/202.
HIGH SCHOOL: El Toro (Calif.).
COLLEGE: Stanford (degree in public policy, 1994).
TRANSACTIONS/CAREER NOTES: Selected by Kansas City Chiefs in fourth round (134th pick overall) of 1995 NFL draft. ... Signed by Chiefs (September 11, 1995). ... Claimed on waivers by Chicago Bears (September 13, 1995). ... Activated (September 25, 1995). ... Active for 12 games during the 1995 season; did not play. ... Granted free agency (February 13, 1998).
PRO STATISTICS: 1997—Fumbled once.
SINGLE GAME HIGHS (regular season): Attempts—5 (November 16, 1997, vs. New York Jets); completions—4 (November 2, 1997, vs. Washington); yards—50 (November 2, 1997, vs. Washington); and touchdown passes—0.

					PASSING						RUSHING				TOTALS	
Year Team	G	GS	Att.	Cmp.	Pct.	Yds.	TD	Int.	Avg.	Rat.	Att.	Yds.	Avg.	TD	TD	2pt.	Pts.
1995—Chicago NFL	2	0	0	0	...	0	0	0	...	...	0	0	...	0	0	0	0
1996—Chicago NFL	1	0	4	3	75.0	37	0	0	9.25	103.1	0	0	...	0	0	0	0
1997—Chicago NFL	3	0	14	8	57.1	70	0	2	5.00	31.0	1	6	6.0	0	0	0	0
Pro totals (3 years)	6	0	18	11	61.1	107	0	2	5.94	38.2	1	6	6.0	0	0	0	0

STEPHENS, JAMAIN — OT — STEELERS

PERSONAL: Born January 9, 1974, in Lumberton , N.C. ... 6-6/336.
HIGH SCHOOL: Lumberton (N.C.).
COLLEGE: North Carolina A&T.
TRANSACTIONS/CAREER NOTES: Selected by Pittsburgh Steelers in first round (29th pick overall) of 1996 NFL draft. ... Signed by Steelers (July 17, 1996). ... Inactive for 16 games (1996).
PLAYING EXPERIENCE: Pittsburgh NFL, 1997. ... Games/Games started: 7/1.
CHAMPIONSHIP GAME EXPERIENCE: Member of Steelers for AFC championship game (1997 season); inactive.

STEPNOSKI, MARK — C — OILERS

PERSONAL: Born January 20, 1967, in Erie, Pa. ... 6-2/263. ... Full name: Mark Matthew Stepnoski.
HIGH SCHOOL: Cathedral Prep (Erie, Pa.).
COLLEGE: Pittsburgh (degree in communications).
TRANSACTIONS/CAREER NOTES: Selected by Dallas Cowboys in third round (57th pick overall) of 1989 NFL draft. ... Signed by Cowboys (July 23, 1989). ... Granted free agency (February 1, 1992). ... Re-signed by Cowboys (September 5, 1992). ... Granted roster exemption (September 5-14, 1992). ... On injured reserve with knee injury (December 22, 1993-remainder of season). ... Granted unconditional free agency (February 17, 1994). ... Re-signed by Cowboys (June 29, 1994). ... Granted unconditional free agency (February 17, 1995). ... Signed by Houston Oilers (March 11, 1995). ... Oilers franchise moved to Tennessee for 1997 season (May 1997).
PLAYING EXPERIENCE: Dallas NFL, 1989-1994; Houston NFL, 1995 and 1996; Tennessee NFL, 1997. ... Games/Games started: 1989 (16/4), 1990 (16/16), 1991 (16/16), 1992 (14/14), 1993 (13/13), 1994 (16/16), 1995 (16/16), 1996 (16/16), 1997 (16/16). Total: 139/127.
CHAMPIONSHIP GAME EXPERIENCE: Played in NFC championship game (1992 and 1994 seasons). ... Member of Super Bowl championship team (1992 season).
HONORS: Named guard on THE SPORTING NEWS college All-America first team (1988). ... Played in Pro Bowl (1992 and 1994-1996 seasons).
PRO STATISTICS: 1989—Recovered three fumbles. 1990—Returned one kickoff for 15 yards. 1992—Recovered one fumble. 1993—Fumbled once. 1994—Fumbled four times for minus three yards. 1997—Fumbled twice and recovered one fumble for minus seven yards.

STEUSSIE, TODD — OT — VIKINGS

PERSONAL: Born December 1, 1970, in Canoga Park, Calif. ... 6-6/321. ... Full name: Todd Edward Steussie.
HIGH SCHOOL: Agoura (Calif.).
COLLEGE: California.
TRANSACTIONS/CAREER NOTES: Selected by Minnesota Vikings in first round (19th pick overall) of 1994 NFL draft. ... Signed by Vikings (July 13, 1994).
PLAYING EXPERIENCE: Minnesota NFL, 1994-1997. ... Games/Games started: 1994 (16/16), 1995 (16/16), 1996 (16/16), 1997 (16/16). Total: 64/64.
HONORS: Named offensive lineman on THE SPORTING NEWS college All-America second team (1993). ... Played in Pro Bowl (1997 season).
PRO STATISTICS: 1994—Recovered one fumble. 1996—Recovered one fumble.

S

STEVENS, MATT   S   EAGLES

PERSONAL: Born June 15, 1973, in Chapel Hill, N.C. ... 6-0/206. ... Full name: Matt Brian Stevens.
HIGH SCHOOL: Chapel Hill (N.C.).
COLLEGE: Appalachian State.
TRANSACTIONS/CAREER NOTES: Selected by Buffalo Bills in third round (87th pick overall) of 1996 NFL draft. ... Signed by Bills (July 15, 1996). ... Claimed on waivers by Philadelphia Eagles (August 25, 1997). ... On suspended list for anabolic steroid use (August 27-September 29, 1997).
PRO STATISTICS: 1996—Recovered one fumble. 1997—Recovered one fumble.

			INTERCEPTIONS		
Year Team	G	GS	No.	Yds.	Avg.	TD
1996—Buffalo NFL	13	11	2	0	0.0	0
1997—Philadelphia NFL	11	0	1	0	0.0	0
Pro totals (2 years)	24	11	3	0	0.0	0

STEWART, JAMES   RB   JAGUARS

PERSONAL: Born December 27, 1971, in Morristown, Tenn. ... 6-1/224. ... Full name: James Ottis Stewart.
HIGH SCHOOL: Morristown (Tenn.)-Hamblen West.
COLLEGE: Tennessee.
TRANSACTIONS/CAREER NOTES: Selected by Jacksonville Jaguars in first round (19th pick overall) of 1995 NFL draft. ... Signed by Jaguars (June 1, 1995).
CHAMPIONSHIP GAME EXPERIENCE: Played in AFC championship game (1996 season).
PRO STATISTICS: 1996—Recovered one fumble.
SINGLE GAME HIGHS (regular season): Attempts—29 (October 20, 1996, vs. St. Louis Rams); yards—112 (October 20, 1996, vs. St. Louis Rams); and rushing touchdowns—5 (October 12, 1997, vs. Philadelphia).
STATISTICAL PLATEAUS: 100-yard rushing games: 1996 (1), 1997 (1). Total: 2.
MISCELLANEOUS: Holds Jacksonville Jaguars all-time records for most rushing yards (1,803), most rushing touchdowns (18) and most touchdowns (22).

			RUSHING				RECEIVING				TOTALS			
Year Team	G	GS	Att.	Yds.	Avg.	TD	No.	Yds.	Avg.	TD	TD	2pt.	Pts.	Fum.
1995—Jacksonville NFL	14	7	137	525	3.8	2	21	190	9.0	1	3	0	18	1
1996—Jacksonville NFL	13	11	190	723	3.8	8	30	177	5.9	2	10	0	60	2
1997—Jacksonville NFL	16	5	136	555	4.1	8	41	336	8.2	1	9	0	54	0
Pro totals (3 years)	43	23	463	1803	3.9	18	92	703	7.6	4	22	0	132	3

STEWART, KORDELL   QB   STEELERS

PERSONAL: Born October 16, 1972, in New Orleans. ... 6-1/212.
HIGH SCHOOL: John Ehret (Marrero, La.).
COLLEGE: Colorado.
TRANSACTIONS/CAREER NOTES: Selected by Pittsburgh Steelers in second round (60th pick overall) of 1995 NFL draft. ... Signed by Steelers (July 17, 1995).
CHAMPIONSHIP GAME EXPERIENCE: Played in AFC championship game (1995 and 1997 seasons). ... Played in Super Bowl XXX (1995 season).
PRO STATISTICS: 1995—Compiled a quarterback rating of 136.9. 1996—Compiled a quarterback rating of 18.8 and fumbled once. 1997—Compiled a quarterback rating of 75.2, fumbled six times and recovered one fumble for minus one yard.
SINGLE GAME HIGHS (regular season): Attempts—48 (December 13, 1997, vs. New England); completions—26 (December 13, 1997, vs. New England); yards—317 (October 26, 1997, vs. Jacksonville); and touchdown passes—3 (December 7, 1997, vs. Denver).
STATISTICAL PLATEAUS: 300-yard passing games: 1997 (2). ... 100-yard rushing games: 1996 (1).
MISCELLANEOUS: Regular-season record as starting NFL quarterback: 11-5 (.688). ... Postseason record as starting NFL quarterback: 1-1 (.500).

			PASSING							RUSHING				RECEIVING				TOTALS		
Year Team	G	GS	Att.	Cmp.	Pct.	Yds.	TD	Int.	Avg.	Att.	Yds.	Avg.	TD	No.	Yds.	Avg.	TD	TD	2pt.	Pts.
1995—Pittsburgh NFL	10	2	7	5	71.4	60	1	0	8.57	15	86	5.7	1	14	235	16.8	1	2	0	12
1996—Pittsburgh NFL	16	2	30	11	36.7	100	0	2	3.33	39	171	4.4	5	17	293	17.2	3	8	0	48
1997—Pittsburgh NFL	16	16	440	236	53.6	3020	21	§17	6.86	88	476	5.4	11	0	0	...	0	11	0	66
Pro totals (3 years)	42	20	477	252	52.8	3180	22	19	6.67	142	733	5.2	17	31	528	17.0	4	21	0	126

STEWART, RAYNA   CB   OILERS

PERSONAL: Born June 18, 1973, in Oklahoma City. ... 5-10/198. ... Full name: Rayna C. Stewart II. ... Name pronounced ruh-NAY.
HIGH SCHOOL: Chatsworth (Calif.).
COLLEGE: Northern Arizona (advertising, 1995).
TRANSACTIONS/CAREER NOTES: Selected by Houston Oilers in fifth round (143rd pick overall) of 1996 NFL draft. ... Signed by Oilers (June 27, 1996). ... Oilers franchise moved to Tennessee for 1997 season.
PLAYING EXPERIENCE: Houston NFL, 1996; Tennessee NFL, 1997. ... Games/Games started: 1996 (15/0), 1997 (16/5). Total: 31/5.
PRO STATISTICS: 1997—Credited with $^1/_2$ sack and recovered one fumble.

STEWART, RYAN   S   LIONS

PERSONAL: Born September 30, 1973, in Moncks Corner, S.C. ... 6-1/207.
HIGH SCHOOL: Berkeley (Moncks Corner, S.C.).
COLLEGE: Georgia Tech.

TRANSACTIONS/CAREER NOTES: Selected by Detroit Lions in third round (76th pick overall) of 1996 NFL draft. ... Signed by Lions (July 21, 1996). ... Released by Lions (August 24, 1997). ... Re-signed by Lions (October 30, 1997). ... Released by Lions after 1997 season. ... Re-signed by Lions (March 26, 1998).

				INTERCEPTIONS		
Year Team	G	GS	No.	Yds.	Avg.	TD
1996—Detroit NFL	14	2	1	14	14.0	0
1997—Detroit NFL	8	0	0	0	...	0
Pro totals (2 years)	22	2	1	14	14.0	0

STILL, BRYAN   WR   CHARGERS

PERSONAL: Born June 3, 1974, in Newport News, Va. ... 5-11/174. ... Full name: Bryan Andrei Still.
HIGH SCHOOL: Huguenot (Richmond, Va.).
COLLEGE: Virginia Tech.
TRANSACTIONS/CAREER NOTES: Selected by San Diego Chargers in second round (41st pick overall) of 1996 NFL draft. ... Signed by Chargers (June 25, 1996).
PRO STATISTICS: 1996—Returned one punt for one yard.
SINGLE GAME HIGHS (regular season): Receptions—4 (November 30, 1997, vs. Denver); yards—64 (October 27, 1996, vs. Seattle); and touchdown receptions—0.

			RECEIVING				KICKOFF RETURNS				TOTALS			
Year Team	G	GS	No.	Yds.	Avg.	TD	No.	Yds.	Avg.	TD	TD	2pt.	Pts.	Fum.
1996—San Diego NFL	16	0	6	142	23.7	0	4	113	28.3	0	0	0	0	2
1997—San Diego NFL	15	4	24	324	13.5	0	0	0	...	0	0	0	0	0
Pro totals (2 years)	31	4	30	466	15.5	0	4	113	28.3	0	0	0	0	2

STOCZ, ERIC   TE   LIONS

PERSONAL: Born May 25, 1974, in Cortland, Ohio. ... 6-4/265. ... Name pronounced STOKES.
HIGH SCHOOL: Lakeview (Cortland, Ohio).
COLLEGE: Westminster (Pa.).
TRANSACTIONS/CAREER NOTES: Signed as non-drafted free agent by Houston Oilers (April 23, 1996). ... Released by Oilers (August 20, 1996). ... Signed by Detroit Lions to practice squad (August 27, 1996). ... Released by Lions (October 15, 1996). ... Re-signed by Lions to practice squad (October 23, 1996). ... Activated (December 13, 1996). ... Released by Lions (September 19, 1997). ... Re-signed by Lions to practice squad (September 29, 1997). ... Activated (October 17, 1997). ... Released by Lions (October 21, 1997). ... Re-signed by Lions to practice squad (October 27, 1997). ... Activated (November 26, 1997).
PLAYING EXPERIENCE: Detroit NFL, 1996 and 1997. ... Games/Games started: 1996 (1/0), 1997 (6/0). Total: 7/0.
SINGLE GAME HIGHS (regular season): Receptions—0; yards—0; and touchdown receptions—0.

STOKES, ERIC   S   SEAHAWKS

PERSONAL: Born December 18, 1973, in Hebron, Neb. ... 5-11/201.
HIGH SCHOOL: Lincoln (Neb.) East.
COLLEGE: Nebraska.
TRANSACTIONS/CAREER NOTES: Selected by Seattle Seahawks in fifth round (142nd pick overall) of 1997 NFL draft. ... Signed by Seahawks (July 11, 1997). ... Released by Seahawks (August 24, 1997). ... Re-signed by Seahawks to practice squad (August 27, 1997). ... Activated (October 27, 1997).
PLAYING EXPERIENCE: Seattle NFL, 1997. ... Games/Games started: 7/0.

STOKES, J.J.   WR   49ERS

PERSONAL: Born October 6, 1972, in San Diego. ... 6-4/223. ... Full name: Jerel Jamal Stokes.
HIGH SCHOOL: Point Loma (San Diego).
COLLEGE: UCLA.
TRANSACTIONS/CAREER NOTES: Selected by San Francisco 49ers in first round (10th pick overall) of 1995 NFL draft. ... Signed by 49ers (July 27, 1995). ... On injured reserve with wrist injury (October 26, 1996-remainder of season).
CHAMPIONSHIP GAME EXPERIENCE: Played in NFC championship game (1997 season).
HONORS: Named wide receiver on THE SPORTING NEWS college All-America first team (1993).
PRO STATISTICS: 1997—Recovered two fumbles.
SINGLE GAME HIGHS (regular season): Receptions—8 (December 18, 1995, vs. Minnesota); yards—106 (December 24, 1995, vs. Atlanta); and touchdown receptions—2 (November 26, 1995, vs. St. Louis Rams).
STATISTICAL PLATEAUS: 100-yard receiving games: 1995 (1).

			RECEIVING				TOTALS			
Year Team	G	GS	No.	Yds.	Avg.	TD	TD	2pt.	Pts.	Fum.
1995—San Francisco NFL	12	2	38	517	13.6	4	4	0	24	0
1996—San Francisco NFL	6	6	18	249	13.8	0	0	0	0	0
1997—San Francisco NFL	16	16	58	733	12.6	4	4	0	24	1
Pro totals (3 years)	34	24	114	1499	13.1	8	8	0	48	1

STOLTENBERG, BRYAN   C   GIANTS

PERSONAL: Born August 25, 1972, in Kearney, Neb. ... 6-1/293. ... Full name: Bryan Douglas Stoltenberg.
HIGH SCHOOL: Clements (Sugar Land, Texas).
COLLEGE: Colorado.

TRANSACTIONS/CAREER NOTES: Selected by San Diego Chargers in sixth round (192nd pick overall) of 1996 NFL draft. ... Signed by Chargers (July 2, 1996). ... Released by Chargers (August 25, 1996). ... Re-signed by Chargers to practice squad (August 26, 1996). ... Activated (October 9, 1996). ... Released by Chargers (August 18, 1997). ... Signed by New York Giants (September 30, 1997). ... Granted free agency (February 13, 1998). ... Re-signed by Giants (May 5, 1998).
PLAYING EXPERIENCE: San Diego NFL, 1996; New York Giants NFL, 1997. ... Games/Games started: 1996 (9/0), 1997 (3/0). Total: 12/0.
HONORS: Named offensive lineman on THE SPORTING NEWS college All-America second team (1995).
PRO STATISTICS: 1997—Fumbled once.

STONE, DWIGHT — WR/KR — PANTHERS

PERSONAL: Born January 28, 1964, in Florala, Ala. ... 6-0/195.
HIGH SCHOOL: Florala (Ala.), then Marion (Ala.) Military Institute.
COLLEGE: Middle Tennessee State.
TRANSACTIONS/CAREER NOTES: Signed as non-drafted free agent by Pittsburgh Steelers (May 19, 1987). ... Crossed picket line during players strike (October 7, 1987). ... Granted free agency (February 1, 1992). ... Re-signed by Steelers (May 15, 1992). ... Released by Steelers (August 30, 1993). ... Re-signed by Steelers (August 31, 1993). ... Granted unconditional free agency (February 17, 1995). ... Signed by Carolina Panthers (May 16, 1995). ... Granted unconditional free agency (February 16, 1996). ... Re-signed by Panthers (March 19, 1996). ... Granted unconditional free agency (February 14, 1997). ... Re-signed by Panthers (July 17, 1997). ... Granted unconditional free agency (February 13, 1998). ... Re-signed by Panthers (March 17, 1998).
CHAMPIONSHIP GAME EXPERIENCE: Played in AFC championship game (1994 season). ... Played in NFC championship game (1996 season).
PRO STATISTICS: 1987—Recovered one fumble. 1989—Recovered one fumble. 1990—Recovered two fumbles. 1993—Recovered one fumble. 1997—Recovered one fumble and credited with a safety.
SINGLE GAME HIGHS (regular season): Receptions—6 (October 19, 1992, vs. Cincinnati); yards—124 (September 1, 1991, vs. San Diego); and touchdown receptions—2 (October 19, 1992, vs. Cincinnati).
STATISTICAL PLATEAUS: 100-yard receiving games: 1991 (1), 1992 (1), 1993 (1). Total: 3.

			RUSHING				RECEIVING				KICKOFF RETURNS				TOTALS			
Year Team	G	GS	Att.	Yds.	Avg.	TD	No.	Yds.	Avg.	TD	No.	Yds.	Avg.	TD	TD	2pt	Pts.	Fum.
1987—Pittsburgh NFL	14	0	17	135	7.9	0	1	22	22.0	0	28	568	20.3	0	0	...	0	0
1988—Pittsburgh NFL	16	6	40	127	3.2	0	11	196	17.8	1	29	610	21.0	†1	2	...	12	5
1989—Pittsburgh NFL	16	8	10	53	5.3	0	7	92	13.1	0	7	173	24.7	0	0	...	0	2
1990—Pittsburgh NFL	16	2	2	-6	-3.0	0	19	332	17.5	1	5	91	18.2	0	1	...	6	1
1991—Pittsburgh NFL	16	8	1	2	2.0	0	32	649	§20.3	5	6	75	12.5	0	5	...	30	0
1992—Pittsburgh NFL	15	12	12	118	9.8	0	34	501	14.7	3	12	219	18.3	0	3	...	18	0
1993—Pittsburgh NFL	16	15	12	121	10.1	1	41	587	14.3	2	11	168	15.3	0	3	...	18	2
1994—Pittsburgh NFL	15	1	2	7	3.5	0	7	81	11.6	0	11	182	16.5	0	0	1	2	0
1995—Carolina NFL	16	0	1	3	3.0	0	0	0	...	0	12	269	22.4	0	0	0	0	0
1996—Carolina NFL	16	0	1	6	6.0	0	1	11	11.0	0	0	0	...	0	0	0	0	0
1997—Carolina NFL	16	0	0	0	...	0	0	0	...	0	3	76	25.3	0	0	0	2	0
Pro totals (11 years)	172	52	98	566	5.8	1	153	2471	16.2	12	124	2431	19.6	1	14	1	88	10

STONE, RON — G — GIANTS

PERSONAL: Born July 20, 1971, in West Roxbury, Mass. ... 6-5/325.
HIGH SCHOOL: West Roxbury (Mass.).
COLLEGE: Boston College.
TRANSACTIONS/CAREER NOTES: Selected by Dallas Cowboys in fourth round (96th pick overall) of 1993 NFL draft. ... Signed by Cowboys (July 16, 1993). ... Active for four games with Cowboys (1993); did not play. ... Granted free agency (February 16, 1996). ... Tendered offer sheet by New York Giants (March 1, 1996). ... Cowboys declined to match offer (March 7, 1996).
PLAYING EXPERIENCE: Dallas NFL, 1994 and 1995; New York Giants NFL, 1996 and 1997. ... Games/Games started: 1994 (16/0), 1995 (16/1), 1996 (16/16), 1997 (16/16). Total: 64/33.
CHAMPIONSHIP GAME EXPERIENCE: Member of Cowboys for NFC championship game (1993 season); inactive. ... Member of Super Bowl championship team (1993 and 1995 seasons). ... Played in NFC championship game (1994 and 1995 seasons).
PRO STATISTICS: 1994—Recovered one fumble. 1997—Recovered one fumble.

STOUTMIRE, OMAR — S — COWBOYS

PERSONAL: Born July 9, 1974, in Pensacola, Fla. ... 5-11/198.
HIGH SCHOOL: Polytechnic (Long Beach, Calif.).
COLLEGE: Fresno State.
TRANSACTIONS/CAREER NOTES: Selected by Dallas Cowboys in seventh round (224th pick overall) of 1997 NFL draft. ... Signed by Cowboys (July 14, 1997).
PRO STATISTICS: 1997—Recovered one fumble.

			INTERCEPTIONS				SACKS
Year Team	G	GS	No.	Yds.	Avg.	TD	No.
1997—Dallas NFL	16	2	2	8	4.0	0	2.0

STOVER, MATT — K — RAVENS

PERSONAL: Born January 27, 1968, in Dallas. ... 5-11/178. ... Full name: John Matthew Stover.
HIGH SCHOOL: Lake Highlands (Dallas).
COLLEGE: Louisiana Tech (degree in marketing, 1991).
TRANSACTIONS/CAREER NOTES: Selected by New York Giants in 12th round (329th pick overall) of 1990 NFL draft. ... Signed by Giants (July 23, 1990). ... On injured reserve with leg injury (September 4, 1990-entire season). ... Granted unconditional free agency (February 1, 1991).

... Signed by Cleveland Browns (March 15, 1991). ... Granted free agency (March 1, 1993). ... Re-signed by Browns (July 24, 1993). ... Released by Browns (August 30, 1993). ... Re-signed by Browns (August 31, 1993). ... Granted unconditional free agency (February 17, 1994). ... Re-signed by Browns (March 4, 1994). ... Browns franchise moved to Baltimore and renamed Ravens for 1996 season (March 11, 1996).

PRO STATISTICS: 1992—Had only pass attempt intercepted.

					KICKING				
Year Team	G	GS	XPM	XPA	FGM	FGA	Lg.	50+	Pts.
1990—New York Giants NFL					Did not play.				
1991—Cleveland NFL	16	0	33	34	16	22	55	2-2	81
1992—Cleveland NFL	16	0	29	30	21	29	51	1-3	92
1993—Cleveland NFL	16	0	36	36	16	22	53	1-4	84
1994—Cleveland NFL	16	0	32	32	26	28	45	0-1	110
1995—Cleveland NFL	16	0	26	26	29	33	47	0-1	113
1996—Baltimore NFL	16	0	34	35	19	25	50	1-1	91
1997—Baltimore NFL	16	0	32	32	26	34	49	0-2	110
Pro totals (7 years)	112	0	222	225	153	193	55	5-14	681

STOYANOVICH, PETE   K   CHIEFS

PERSONAL: Born April 28, 1967, in Dearborn, Mich. ... 5-11/195. ... Full name: Peter Stoyanovich. ... Name pronounced sto-YAWN-o-vich.

HIGH SCHOOL: Crestwood (Dearborn Heights, Mich.).

COLLEGE: Indiana (degree in public affairs, 1989).

TRANSACTIONS/CAREER NOTES: Selected by Miami Dolphins in eighth round (203rd pick overall) of 1989 NFL draft. ... Signed by Dolphins (July 27, 1989). ... Granted free agency (February 1, 1991). ... Re-signed by Dolphins (September 6, 1991). ... Granted unconditional free agency (February 17, 1994). ... Re-signed by Dolphins (February 21, 1994). ... Traded by Dolphins to Kansas City Chiefs for an undisclosed draft pick (August 21, 1996).

CHAMPIONSHIP GAME EXPERIENCE: Played in AFC championship game (1992 season).

HONORS: Named kicker on THE SPORTING NEWS college All-America second team (1988). ... Named kicker on THE SPORTING NEWS NFL All-Pro team (1992).

POST SEASON RECORDS: Holds NFL postseason record for longest field goal—58 yards (January 5, 1991, vs. Kansas City).

			PUNTING							KICKING					
Year Team	G	GS	No.	Yds.	Avg.	Net avg.	In. 20	Blk.	XPM	XPA	FGM	FGA	Lg.	50+	Pts.
1989—Miami NFL	16	0	0	0	...	...	0	0	38	39	19	26	59	1-3	95
1990—Miami NFL	16	0	0	0	...	...	0	0	37	37	21	25	53	2-3	100
1991—Miami NFL	14	0	2	85	42.5	38.5	1	0	28	29	*31	37	53	3-5	§121
1992—Miami NFL	16	0	2	90	45.0	45.0	0	0	34	36	†30	§37	53	3-8	*124
1993—Miami NFL	16	0	0	0	...	...	0	0	37	37	24	32	52	2-2	109
1994—Miami NFL	16	0	0	0	...	...	0	0	35	35	24	31	50	1-2	107
1995—Miami NFL	16	0	0	0	...	...	0	0	37	37	27	34	51	2-5	118
1996—Kansas City NFL	16	0	0	0	...	...	0	0	34	34	17	24	45	0-1	85
1997—Kansas City NFL	16	0	1	24	24.0	24.0	1	0	35	36	26	27	54	2-2	113
Pro totals (9 years)	142	0	5	199	39.8	38.2	2	0	315	320	219	273	59	16-31	972

STRAHAN, MICHAEL   DE   GIANTS

PERSONAL: Born November 21, 1971, in Houston. ... 6-4/285. ... Full name: Michael Anthony Strahan. ... Nephew of Art Strahan, defensive tackle with Atlanta Falcons (1968).

HIGH SCHOOL: Westbury (Houston), then Mannheim (Germany) American.

COLLEGE: Texas Southern.

TRANSACTIONS/CAREER NOTES: Selected by New York Giants in second round (40th pick overall) of 1993 NFL draft. ... Signed by Giants (July 25, 1993). ... On injured reserve with foot injury (January 13, 1994-remainder of 1993 playoffs). ... Granted free agency (February 16, 1996). ... Re-signed by Giants (July 8, 1996).

HONORS: Named defensive end on THE SPORTING NEWS NFL All-Pro team (1997). ... Played in Pro Bowl (1997 season).

PRO STATISTICS: 1995—Intercepted two passes for 56 yards. 1997—Recovered one fumble.

Year Team	G	GS	SACKS
1993—New York Giants NFL	9	0	1.0
1994—New York Giants NFL	15	15	4.5
1995—New York Giants NFL	15	15	7.5
1996—New York Giants NFL	16	16	5.0
1997—New York Giants NFL	16	16	14.0
Pro totals (5 years)	71	62	32.0

STRICKLAND, FRED   LB   COWBOYS

PERSONAL: Born August 15, 1966, in Ringwood, N.J. ... 6-2/251. ... Full name: Fredrick William Strickland Jr.

HIGH SCHOOL: Lakeland Regional (Wanaque, N.J.).

COLLEGE: Purdue.

TRANSACTIONS/CAREER NOTES: Selected by Los Angeles Rams in second round (47th pick overall) of 1988 NFL draft. ... Signed by Rams (July 10, 1988). ... On injured reserve with foot injury (October 16, 1990-remainder of season). ... Granted free agency (February 1, 1991). ... Re-signed by Rams (August 13, 1991). ... Granted unconditional free agency (March 1, 1993). ... Signed by Minnesota Vikings (May 7, 1993). ... Granted unconditional free agency (February 17, 1994). ... Signed by Green Bay Packers (June 24, 1994). ... Granted unconditional free agency (February 16, 1996). ... Signed by Dallas Cowboys (March 11, 1996).

CHAMPIONSHIP GAME EXPERIENCE: Played in NFC championship game (1989 and 1995 seasons).

PRO STATISTICS: 1988—Recovered two fumbles. 1989—Recovered one fumble for minus three yards. 1993—Recovered four fumbles for four yards. 1994—Recovered one fumble. 1996—Recovered one fumble. 1997—Recovered two fumbles.

Year Team	G	GS	INTERCEPTIONS No.	Yds.	Avg.	TD	SACKS No.
1988—Los Angeles Rams NFL	16	0	0	0	...	0	4.0
1989—Los Angeles Rams NFL	12	12	2	56	28.0	0	2.0
1990—Los Angeles Rams NFL	5	5	0	0	...	0	0.0
1991—Los Angeles Rams NFL	14	10	0	0	...	0	1.0
1992—Los Angeles Rams NFL	16	0	0	0	...	0	0.0
1993—Minnesota NFL	16	15	0	0	...	0	0.0
1994—Green Bay NFL	16	14	1	7	7.0	0	0.0
1995—Green Bay NFL	14	10	0	0	...	0	0.0
1996—Dallas NFL	16	16	1	0	0.0	0	1.0
1997—Dallas NFL	15	14	0	0	...	0	0.5
Pro totals (10 years)	140	96	4	63	15.8	0	8.5

STRINGER, KOREY   OT   VIKINGS

PERSONAL: Born May 8, 1974, in Warren, Ohio. ... 6-4/353.
HIGH SCHOOL: Harding (Warren, Ohio).
COLLEGE: Ohio State.
TRANSACTIONS/CAREER NOTES: Selected after junior season by Minnesota Vikings in first round (24th pick overall) of 1995 NFL draft. ... Signed by Vikings (July 22, 1995).
PLAYING EXPERIENCE: Minnesota NFL, 1995-1997. ... Games/Games started: 1995 (16/15), 1996 (16/15), 1997 (15/15). Total: 47/45.
HONORS: Named offensive lineman on THE SPORTING NEWS college All-America second team (1993). ... Named offensive lineman on THE SPORTING NEWS college All-America first team (1994).
PRO STATISTICS: 1995—Caught one pass for minus one yard and recovered two fumbles.

STRONG, MACK   FB   SEAHAWKS

PERSONAL: Born September 11, 1971, in Fort Benning, Ga. ... 6-0/235.
HIGH SCHOOL: Brookstone (Columbus, Ga.).
COLLEGE: Georgia.
TRANSACTIONS/CAREER NOTES: Signed as non-drafted free agent by Seattle Seahawks (April 28, 1993). ... Released by Seahawks (September 4, 1993). ... Re-signed by Seahawks to practice squad (September 6, 1993).
PRO STATISTICS: 1995—Returned four kickoffs for 65 yards and recovered one fumble. 1996—Recovered one fumble. 1997—Returned one kickoff for 16 yards and recovered one fumble.
SINGLE GAME HIGHS (regular season): Attempts—10 (December 11, 1994, vs. Houston); yards—44 (December 11, 1994, vs. Houston); rushing touchdowns—1 (November 12, 1995, vs. Jacksonville).

Year Team	G	GS	RUSHING Att.	Yds.	Avg.	TD	RECEIVING No.	Yds.	Avg.	TD	TOTALS TD	2pt.	Pts.	Fum.
1994—Seattle NFL	8	1	27	114	4.2	2	3	3	1.0	0	2	0	12	1
1995—Seattle NFL	16	1	8	23	2.9	1	12	117	9.8	3	4	0	24	2
1996—Seattle NFL	14	8	5	8	1.6	0	9	78	8.7	0	0	0	0	0
1997—Seattle NFL	16	10	4	8	2.0	0	13	91	7.0	2	2	0	12	0
Pro totals (4 years)	54	20	44	153	3.5	3	37	289	7.8	5	8	0	48	3

STRYZINSKI, DAN   P   FALCONS

PERSONAL: Born May 15, 1965, in Indianapolis. ... 6-2/200. ... Full name: Daniel Thomas Stryzinski. ... Name pronounced stri-ZIN-skee.
HIGH SCHOOL: Lincoln (Vincennes, Ind.).
COLLEGE: Indiana (bachelor of science degree in public finance and management, 1988).
TRANSACTIONS/CAREER NOTES: Signed as non-drafted free agent by Indianapolis Colts (July 1988). ... Released by Colts (August 23, 1988). ... Signed by Cleveland Browns (August 25, 1988). ... Released by Browns (August 30, 1988). ... Re-signed by Browns for 1989 season). ... Released by Browns (August 30, 1989). ... Signed by New Orleans Saints to developmental squad (October 11, 1989). ... Granted free agency after 1989 season. ... Signed by Pittsburgh Steelers (March 14, 1990). ... Granted unconditional free agency (February 1, 1992). ... Signed by Tampa Bay Buccaneers (February 21, 1992). ... Granted unconditional free agency (February 17, 1995). ... Signed by Atlanta Falcons (February 20, 1995).
PRO STATISTICS: 1990—Rushed three times for 17 yards and recovered one fumble. 1991—Rushed four times for minus 11 yards, fumbled once and recovered two fumbles. 1992—Attempted two passes with two completions for 14 yards and rushed once for seven yards. 1994—Attempted once pass with one completion for 21 yards. 1995—Rushed once for no yards.

Year Team	G	GS	PUNTING No.	Yds.	Avg.	Net avg.	In. 20	Blk.
1990—Pittsburgh NFL	16	0	65	2454	37.8	34.1	18	1
1991—Pittsburgh NFL	16	0	74	2996	40.5	36.2	10	1
1992—Tampa Bay NFL	16	0	74	3015	40.7	36.2	15	0
1993—Tampa Bay NFL	16	0	*93	3772	40.6	35.2	24	1
1994—Tampa Bay NFL	16	0	72	2800	38.9	35.8	20	0
1995—Atlanta NFL	16	0	67	2759	41.2	36.2	21	0
1996—Atlanta NFL	16	0	75	3152	42.0	35.5	22	0
1997—Atlanta NFL	16	0	89	3498	39.3	36.7	20	0
Pro totals (8 years)	128	0	609	24446	40.1	35.8	150	3

STRZELCZYK, JUSTIN   G/OT   STEELERS

PERSONAL: Born August 18, 1968, in Seneca, N.Y. ... 6-6/305. ... Full name: Justin Conrad Strzelczyk. ... Name pronounced STREL-zik.
HIGH SCHOOL: West Seneca (N.Y.) West.

COLLEGE: Maine.

TRANSACTIONS/CAREER NOTES: Selected by Pittsburgh Steelers in 11th round (293rd pick overall) of 1990 NFL draft. ... Signed by Steelers (July 18, 1990).

PLAYING EXPERIENCE: Pittsburgh NFL, 1990-1997. ... Games/Games started: 1990 (16/0), 1991 (16/0), 1992 (16/7), 1993 (16/12), 1994 (16/5), 1995 (16/14), 1996 (16/16), 1997 (14/14). Total: 126/68.

CHAMPIONSHIP GAME EXPERIENCE: Played in AFC championship game (1994, 1995 and 1997 seasons). ... Played in Super Bowl XXX (1995 season).

PRO STATISTICS: 1993—Recovered one fumble.

STUBBLEFIELD, DANA DT REDSKINS

PERSONAL: Born November 14, 1970, in Cleves, Ohio. ... 6-2/315. ... Full name: Dana William Stubblefield.

HIGH SCHOOL: Taylor (North Bend, Ohio).

COLLEGE: Kansas.

TRANSACTIONS/CAREER NOTES: Selected by San Francisco 49ers in first round (26th pick overall) of 1993 NFL draft. ... Signed by 49ers (July 14, 1993). ... Granted unconditional free agency (February 13, 1998). ... Signed by Washington Redskins (February 23, 1998).

CHAMPIONSHIP GAME EXPERIENCE: Played in NFC championship game (1993, 1994 and 1997 seasons). ... Member of Super Bowl championship team (1994 season).

HONORS: Played in Pro Bowl (1994, 1995 and 1997 seasons). ... Named defensive tackle on THE SPORTING NEWS NFL All-Pro team (1997).

PRO STATISTICS: 1995—Intercepted one pass for 12 yards. 1996—Intercepted one pass for 15 yards and recovered one fumble.

Year Team	G	GS	SACKS
1993—San Francisco NFL	16	14	10.5
1994—San Francisco NFL	14	14	8.5
1995—San Francisco NFL	16	16	4.5
1996—San Francisco NFL	15	15	1.0
1997—San Francisco NFL	16	16	15.0
Pro totals (5 years)	77	75	39.5

STUBBS, DANIEL DE DOLPHINS

PERSONAL: Born January 3, 1965, in Long Branch, N.J. ... 6-4/270. ... Full name: Daniel Stubbs II.

HIGH SCHOOL: Red Bank Regional (Little Silver, N.J.).

COLLEGE: Miami, Fla. (degree in criminal justice, 1988).

TRANSACTIONS/CAREER NOTES: Selected by San Francisco 49ers in second round (33rd pick overall) of 1988 NFL draft. ... Signed by 49ers (July 19, 1988). ... Traded by 49ers with RB Terrence Flagler and third- (traded to Pittsburgh) and 11th-round (traded to Los Angeles Raiders) picks in 1990 draft to Dallas Cowboys for second- (DL Dennis Brown) and third-round (WR Ronald Lewis) picks in 1990 draft (April 19, 1990). ... Granted free agency (February 1, 1991). ... Re-signed by Cowboys (August 10, 1991). ... Claimed on waivers by Cincinnati Bengals (November 6, 1991). ... Granted unconditional free agency (February 17, 1994). ... Re-signed by Bengals (June 14, 1994). ... Released by Bengals (August 16, 1994). ... Signed by Philadelphia Eagles (April 7, 1995). ... Granted unconditional free agency (February 16, 1996). ... Signed by Miami Dolphins (April 4, 1996). ... Granted unconditional free agency (February 14, 1997). ... Re-signed by Dolphins (March 18, 1997). ... On injured reserve with knee injury (September 3, 1997-remainder of season).

CHAMPIONSHIP GAME EXPERIENCE: Played in NFC championship game (1988 season). ... Member of Super Bowl championship team (1988 season).

HONORS: Named defensive lineman on THE SPORTING NEWS college All-America second team (1986). ... Named defensive lineman on THE SPORTING NEWS college All-America first team (1987).

PRO STATISTICS: 1988—Recovered one fumble. 1990—Recovered two fumbles. 1991—Recovered one fumble. 1992—Recovered one fumble. 1993—Recovered one fumble. 1995—Recovered one fumble.

Year Team	G	GS	SACKS
1988—San Francisco NFL	16	1	6.0
1989—San Francisco NFL	16	0	4.5
1990—Dallas NFL	16	15	7.5
1991—Dallas NFl	9	0	1.0
—Cincinnati NFL	7	0	3.0
1992—Cincinnati NFL	16	12	9.0
1993—Cincinnati NFL	16	0	5.0
1994—	Did not play.		
1995—Philadelphia NFL	16	5	5.5
1996—Miami NFL	16	15	9.0
1997—Miami NFL	1	0	1.0
Pro totals (9 years)	129	48	51.5

STYLES, LORENZO LB RAMS

PERSONAL: Born January 31, 1974, in Columbus, Ohio. ... 6-1/245.

HIGH SCHOOL: Columbus (Ohio), then Farrell (Pa.).

COLLEGE: Ohio State.

TRANSACTIONS/CAREER NOTES: Selected after junior season by Atlanta Falcons in third round (77th pick overall) of 1995 NFL draft. ... Signed by Falcons (July 21, 1995). ... Released by Falcons (August 26, 1997). ... Signed by St. Louis Rams (November 4, 1997). ... On injured reserve with shoulder injury (December 9, 1997-remainder of season). ... Granted free agency (February 13, 1998). ... Re-signed by Rams (March 25, 1998).

PLAYING EXPERIENCE: Atlanta NFL, 1995 and 1996; St. Louis NFL, 1997.. ... Games/Games started: 1995 (12/0), 1996 (16/0), 1997 (3/0). Total: 31/0.

PRO STATISTICS: 1996—Returned one kickoff for 12 yards.

SUALUA, NICKY   FB   COWBOYS

PERSONAL: Born April 15, 1975, in Santa Ana, Calif. ... 5-11/257.
HIGH SCHOOL: Mater Dei (Santa Ana, Calif.).
COLLEGE: Ohio State.
TRANSACTIONS/CAREER NOTES: Selected by Dallas Cowboys in fourth round (129th pick overall) of 1997 NFL draft. ... Signed by Cowboys (July 14, 1997).
PLAYING EXPERIENCE: Dallas NFL, 1997. ... Games/Games started: 10/1.
SINGLE GAME HIGHS (regular season): Attempts—0; yards—0; and rushing touchdowns—0.

SULLIVAN, CHRIS   DE   PATRIOTS

PERSONAL: Born March 14, 1973, in North Attleboro, Mass. ... 6-4/279. ... Full name: Christopher Patrick Sullivan.
HIGH SCHOOL: North Attleboro (Mass.).
COLLEGE: Boston College (degree in sociology, 1995).
TRANSACTIONS/CAREER NOTES: Selected by New England Patriots in fourth round (119th pick overall) of 1996 NFL draft. ... Signd by Patriots (July 12, 1996).
PLAYING EXPERIENCE: New England NFL, 1996 and 1997. ... Games/Games started: 1996 (16/0), 1997 (16/10). Total: 32/10.
CHAMPIONSHIP GAME EXPERIENCE: Played in AFC championship game (1996 season). ... Played in Super Bowl XXXI (1996 season).
PRO STATISTICS: 1996—Recovered one fumble.

SUTTER, EDDIE   LB   FALCONS

PERSONAL: Born October 3, 1969, in Peoria, Ill. ... 6-3/239. ... Full name: Edward Lee Sutter.
HIGH SCHOOL: Richwoods (Peoria, Ill.).
COLLEGE: Northwestern (degree in organizational studies).
TRANSACTIONS/CAREER NOTES: Signed as non-drafted free agent by Minnesota Vikings (May 1, 1992). ... Released by Vikings (August 25, 1992). ... Signed by Cleveland Browns to practice squad (September 9, 1992). ... Released by Browns (October 21, 1992). ... Re-signed by Browns to practice squad (October 23, 1992). ... Activated (November 20, 1992). ... On inactive list for one game (1992). ... Released by Browns (November 28, 1992). ... Re-signed by Browns to practice squad (December 1, 1992). ... Granted free agency after 1992 season. ... Signed by New England Patriots (February 22, 1993). ... Claimed on waivers by Browns (August 30, 1993). ... Granted unconditional free agency (February 16, 1996). ... Browns franchise moved Baltimore and renamed Ravens for 1996 season (March 11, 1996). ... Re-signed by Ravens (April 26, 1996). ... Granted unconditional free agency (February 14, 1997). ... Signed by Cincinnati Bengals (March 12, 1997). ... Released by Bengals (August 18, 1997). ... Signed by Miami Dolphins (August 20, 1997). ... Released by Dolphins (August 24, 1997). ... Signed by Atlanta Falcons (August 26, 1997). ... Granted unconditional free agency (February 13, 1998). ... Re-signed by Falcons (April 1, 1998).
PLAYING EXPERIENCE: Cleveland NFL, 1993-1995; Baltimore NFL, 1996; Atlanta NFL, 1997. ... Games/Games started: 1993 (15/0), 1994 (16/0), 1995 (16/0), 1996 (16/4), 1997 (16/0). Total: 79/4.
PRO STATISTICS: 1996—Recovered one fumble.

SWANN, ERIC   DT   CARDINALS

PERSONAL: Born August 16, 1970, in Pinehurst, N.C. ... 6-5/313. ... Full name: Eric Jerrod Swann.
HIGH SCHOOL: Western Harnett (Lillington, N.C.).
COLLEGE: Wake Technical College, N.C. (did not play football).
TRANSACTIONS/CAREER NOTES: Played on Bay State Titans of Minor League Football System (1990). ... Selected by Phoenix Cardinals in first round (sixth pick overall) of 1991 NFL draft. ... Signed by Cardinals (April 24, 1991). ... On injured reserve with knee injury (August 27-September 27, 1991). ... On injured reserve with knee injury (November 17, 1993-remainder of season). ... Cardinals franchise renamed Arizona Cardinals for 1994 season. ... Designated by Cardinals as franchise player (February 16, 1996). ... On injured reserve with dislocated finger (December 17, 1997-remainder of season)
HONORS: Named defensive tackle on THE SPORTING NEWS NFL All-Pro team (1995). ... Played in Pro Bowl (1995 and 1996 seasons).
PRO STATISTICS: 1992—Credited with one safety. 1993—Credited with one safety and recovered one fumble. 1994—Credited with one safety and recovered one fumble for 10 yards. 1995—Recovered two fumbles. 1996—Recovered three fumbles for 11 yards. 1997—Rushed once for no yards, fumbled once and recovered one fumble.

Year Team	G	GS	SACKS
1991—Phoenix NFL	12	3	4.0
1992—Phoenix NFL	16	11	2.0
1993—Phoenix NFL	9	9	3.5
1994—Arizona NFL	16	16	7.0
1995—Arizona NFL	13	12	8.5
1996—Arizona NFL	16	15	5.0
1997—Arizona NFL	13	13	7.5
Pro totals (7 years)	95	79	37.5

SWAYNE, HARRY   OT   BRONCOS

PERSONAL: Born February 2, 1965, in Philadelphia. ... 6-5/293. ... Full name: Harry Vonray Swayne.
HIGH SCHOOL: Cardinal Dougherty (Philadelphia).
COLLEGE: Rutgers.
TRANSACTIONS/CAREER NOTES: Selected by Tampa Bay Buccaneers in seventh round (190th pick overall) of 1987 NFL draft. ... Signed by Buccaneers (July 18, 1987). ... On injured reserve with fractured hand (September 8-October 31, 1987). ... On injured reserve with neck injury (November 18, 1988-remainder of season). ... Granted free agency (February 1, 1990). ... Re-signed by Buccaneers (July 19, 1990). ... Granted unconditional free agency (February 1, 1991). ... Signed by San Diego Chargers (April 1, 1991). ... On injured reserve with fractured leg (November 26, 1991-remainder of season). ... Designated by Chargers as transition player (February 25, 1993). ... Tendered offer sheet by Phoenix Cardinals (April 9, 1993). ... Offer matched by Chargers (April 15, 1993). ... On physically unable to perform list (July 24-August 21, 1995). ... Free agency status changed by Chargers from transitional to unconditional (February 16, 1996). ... Re-signed by Chargers (July 24, 1996). ... Granted unconditional free agency (February 14, 1997). ... Signed by Denver Broncos (April 17, 1997).

PLAYING EXPERIENCE: Tampa Bay NFL, 1987-1990; San Diego NFL, 1991-1996; Denver NFL, 1997. ... Games/Games started: 1987 (8/2), 1988 (10/1), 1989 (16/0), 1990 (10/0), 1991 (12/12), 1992 (16/16), 1993 (11/11), 1994 (16/16), 1995 (16/16), 1996 (16/3), 1997 (7/0). Total: 138/77.
CHAMPIONSHIP GAME EXPERIENCE: Played in AFC championship game (1994 and 1997 seasons). ... Played in Super Bowl XXIX (1994 season). ... Member of Super Bowl championship team (1997 season).

SWEENEY, JIM　　　　　C　　　　　STEELERS

PERSONAL: Born August 8, 1962, in Pittsburgh. ... 6-4/298. ... Full name: James Joseph Sweeney.
HIGH SCHOOL: Seton LaSalle (Pittsburgh).
COLLEGE: Pittsburgh.
TRANSACTIONS/CAREER NOTES: Selected by Pittsburgh Maulers in 1984 USFL territorial draft. ... Selected by New York Jets in second round (37th pick overall) of 1984 NFL draft. ... Signed by Jets (July 12, 1984). ... Granted free agency (February 1, 1990). ... Re-signed by Jets (August 27, 1990). ... Released by Jets (August 30, 1993). ... Re-signed by Jets (August 31, 1993). ... Granted unconditional free agency (February 17, 1994). ... Re-signed by Jets (May 2, 1994). ... Granted unconditional free agency (February 17, 1995). ... Signed by Seattle Seahawks (March 23, 1995). ... Released by Seahawks (July 19, 1996). ... Signed by Pittsburgh Steelers (August 19, 1996).
PLAYING EXPERIENCE: New York Jets NFL, 1984-1994; Seattle NFL, 1995; Pittsburgh NFL, 1996 and 1997. ... Games/Games started: 1984 (10/2), 1985 (16/16), 1986 (16/16), 1987 (12/12), 1988 (16/16), 1989 (16/16), 1990 (16/16), 1991 (16/16), 1992 (16/16), 1993 (16/16), 1994 (16/16), 1995 (16/16), 1996 (16/0), 1997 (16/1). Total: 214/175.
CHAMPIONSHIP GAME EXPERIENCE: Played in AFC championship game (1997 season).
PRO STATISTICS: 1990—Recovered one fumble. 1994—Recovered one fumble.

SWIFT, MICHAEL　　　　　DB　　　　　PANTHERS

PERSONAL: Born February 28, 1974, in Dyersburg, Tenn. ... 5-10/165. ... Full name: Michael Aaron Swift.
HIGH SCHOOL: Lake County (Tiptonville, Tenn.).
COLLEGE: Austin Peay.
TRANSACTIONS/CAREER NOTES: Signed as non-drafted free agent by San Diego Chargers (April 26, 1996). ... Released by Chargers (August 25, 1996). ... Re-signed by Chargers to practice squad (October 14, 1996). ... Released by Chargers (November 24, 1996). ... Re-signed by Chargers to practice squad (November 27, 1996). ... Assigned by Chargers to Rhein Fire in 1997 World League enhancement allocation program (February 19, 1997). ... Released by Chargers (August 18, 1997). ... Re-signed by Chargers to practice squad (August 25, 1997). ... Activated (September 26, 1997). ... Granted free agency (February 13, 1998). ... Signed by Carolina Panthers (June 2, 1998).
PLAYING EXPERIENCE: Rhein W.L., 1997; San Diego NFL, 1997. ... Games/Games started: 1997: (W.L.-games played unavailable; NFL-12/1).
PRO STATISTICS: W.L.: 1997—Intercepted one pass for eight yards. NFL: 1997—Recovered one fumble for six yards.

SWILLING, PAT　　　　　DE/LB　　　　　RAIDERS

PERSONAL: Born October 25, 1964, in Toccoa, Ga. ... 6-3/245. ... Full name: Patrick Travis Swilling.
HIGH SCHOOL: Stephens County (Toccoa, Ga.).
COLLEGE: Georgia Tech.
TRANSACTIONS/CAREER NOTES: Selected by Jacksonville Bulls in 1986 USFL territorial draft. ... Selected by New Orleans Saints in third round (60th pick overall) of 1986 NFL draft. ... Signed by Saints (July 21, 1986). ... Granted free agency (February 1, 1990). ... Re-signed by Saints (September 1, 1990). ... Granted free agency (February 1, 1992). ... Tendered offer sheet by Detroit Lions (March 23, 1992). ... Offer matched by Saints (March 30, 1992). ... Traded by Saints to Lions for first- (OT Willie Roaf) and fourth-round (RB Lorenzo Neal) picks in 1993 draft (April 25, 1993). ... Granted unconditional free agency (February 17, 1995). ... Signed by Los Angeles Raiders (April 11, 1995). ... Raiders franchise moved to Oakland (July 21, 1995). ... Released by Raiders following 1996 season. ... Re-signed by Raiders (May 29, 1998).
HONORS: Named defensive lineman on The Sporting News college All-America second team (1985). ... Played in Pro Bowl (1990-1993 seasons). ... Named outside linebacker on The Sporting News NFL All-Pro team (1991 and 1992).
PRO STATISTICS: 1987—Recovered three fumbles for one yard. 1988—Recovered one fumble. 1989—Recovered one fumble. 1991—Recovered one fumble for five yards. 1992—Recovered one fumble. 1993—Recovered one fumble. 1994—Recovered one fumble for five yards. 1996—Recovered one fumble for 49 yards.

| | | | INTERCEPTIONS | | | | SACKS |
Year　Team	G	GS	No.	Yds.	Avg.	TD	No.
1986—New Orleans NFL	16	0	0	0	...	0	4.0
1987—New Orleans NFL	12	12	1	10	10.0	0	10.5
1988—New Orleans NFL	15	14	0	0	...	0	7.0
1989—New Orleans NFL	16	15	1	14	14.0	0	16.5
1990—New Orleans NFL	16	16	0	0	...	0	11.0
1991—New Orleans NFL	16	16	1	39	39.0	∞1	17.0
1992—New Orleans NFL	16	16	0	0	...	0	10.5
1993—Detroit NFL	14	14	3	16	5.3	0	6.5
1994—Detroit NFL	16	7	0	0	...	0	3.5
1995—Oakland NFL	16	16	0	0	...	0	13.0
1996—Oakland NFL	16	16	0	0	...	0	6.0
1997—			Did not play.				
Pro totals (11 years)	169	142	6	79	13.2	1	105.5

SWINGER, RASHOD　　　　　DT　　　　　CARDINALS

PERSONAL: Born November 27, 1974, in Paterson, N.J. ... 6-2/286. ... Full name: Rashod Alexander Swinger.
HIGH SCHOOL: Manalapan (N.J.).
COLLEGE: Rutgers.
TRANSACTIONS/CAREER NOTES: Signed as non-drafted free agent by San Diego Chargers (April 21, 1997). ... Released by Chargers (August 25, 1997). ... Re-signed by Chargers to practice squad (August 26, 1997). ... Released by Chargers (September 2, 1997). ... Signed by Arizona Cardinals to practice squad (September 8, 1997). ... Activated (December 17, 1997).
PLAYING EXPERIENCE: Arizona NFL, 1997. ... Games/Games started: 1/0.

SZOTT, DAVID   G   CHIEFS

PERSONAL: Born December 12, 1967, in Passaic, N.J. ... 6-4/293. ... Full name: David Andrew Szott. ... Name pronounced ZOT.
HIGH SCHOOL: Clifton (N.J.).
COLLEGE: Penn State (degree in political science).
TRANSACTIONS/CAREER NOTES: Selected by Kansas City Chiefs in seventh round (180th pick overall) of 1990 NFL draft. ... Signed by Chiefs (July 25, 1990). ... Granted free agency (March 1, 1993). ... Re-signed by Chiefs for 1993 season.
PLAYING EXPERIENCE: Kansas City NFL, 1990-1997. ... Games/Games started: 1990 (16/11), 1991 (16/16), 1992 (16/16), 1993 (14/13), 1994 (16/16), 1995 (16/16), 1996 (16/16), 1997 (16/16). Total: 126/120.
CHAMPIONSHIP GAME EXPERIENCE: Played in AFC championship game (1993 season).
PRO STATISTICS: 1990—Recovered one fumble. 1991—Recovered one fumble. 1997—Recovered one fumble.

TALLEY, BEN   LB   FALCONS

PERSONAL: Born July 14, 1972, in Griffin, Ga. ... 6-3/248. ... Full name: Benjamin Jermaine Talley.
HIGH SCHOOL: Griffin (Ga.).
COLLEGE: Tennessee.
TRANSACTIONS/CAREER NOTES: Selected by New York Giants in fourth round (133rd pick overall) of 1995 NFL draft. ... Signed by Giants (July 23, 1995). ... On injured reserve with knee injury (August 12, 1996-entire season). ... Released by Giants (July 18, 1997). ... Signed by Atlanta Falcons for 1998 season.
PLAYING EXPERIENCE: New York Giants NFL, 1995. ... Games/Games started: 4/0.

TAMM, RALPH   G/C   CHIEFS

PERSONAL: Born March 11, 1966, in Philadelphia. ... 6-4/280. ... Full name: Ralph Earl Tamm.
HIGH SCHOOL: Bensalem (Pa.).
COLLEGE: West Chester (Pa.).
TRANSACTIONS/CAREER NOTES: Selected by New York Jets in ninth round (230th pick overall) of 1988 NFL draft. ... On injured reserve (August 29, 1988-entire season). ... Granted unconditional free agency (February 1, 1989). ... Signed by Washington Redskins (1989). ... On injured reserve with shoulder injury (September 1989-entire season). ... Granted unconditional free agency (February 1, 1990). ... Signed by Cleveland Browns (March 21, 1990). ... Released by Browns (September 5, 1991). ... Signed by Redskins (September 11, 1991). ... Released by Redskins (November 1991). ... Signed by Cincinnati Bengals (December 9, 1991). ... Granted unconditional free agency (February 1, 1992). ... Signed by San Francisco 49ers (March 29, 1992). ... On injured reserve with knee injury (December 15, 1992-January 16, 1993). ... Released by 49ers (May 5, 1995). ... Signed by Denver Broncos (June 7, 1995). ... Granted unconditional free agency (February 14, 1997). ... Signed by Kansas City Chiefs (June 9, 1997).
PLAYING EXPERIENCE: Cleveland NFL, 1990; Cleveland (1)-Washington (2)-Cincinnati (1) NFL, 1991; San Francisco NFL, 1992-1994; Denver NFL, 1995 and 1996; Kansas City NFL, 1997. ... Games/Games started: 1990 (16/12), 1991 (Clev.-1/0; Wash.-2/0; Cin.-1/0; Total: 4/0), 1992 (14/1), 1993 (16/16), 1994 (1/1), 1995 (13/1), 1996 (9/0), 1997 (16/0). Total: 89/31.
CHAMPIONSHIP GAME EXPERIENCE: Played in NFC championship game (1992-1994 seasons). ... Member of Super Bowl championship team (1994 season).
PRO STATISTICS: 1993—Recovered one fumble in end zone for a touchdown. 1995—Recovered one fumble.

TANNER, BARRON   DT   DOLPHINS

PERSONAL: Born September 14, 1973, in Athens, Texas. ... 6-3/310. ... Full name: Barron Keith Tanner.
HIGH SCHOOL: Athens (Texas).
COLLEGE: Oklahoma.
TRANSACTIONS/CAREER NOTES: Selected by Miami Dolphins in fifth round (149th pick overall) of 1997 NFL draft. ... Signed by Dolphins (July 8, 1997).
PLAYING EXPERIENCE: Miami NFL, 1997. ... Games/Games started: 16/0.

TANUVASA, MAA   DT   BRONCOS

PERSONAL: Born November 6, 1970, in America Samoa. ... 6-2/267. ... Full name: Maa Junior Tanuvasa. ... Name pronounced MAW-aw TAW-new-VA-suh.
HIGH SCHOOL: Mililani (Hawaii).
COLLEGE: Hawaii.
TRANSACTIONS/CAREER NOTES: Selected by Los Angeles Rams in eighth round (209th pick overall) of 1993 NFL draft. ... Signed by Rams for 1993 season. ... On injured reserve with knee injury (August 21, 1993-entire season). ... Released by Rams (August 23, 1994). ... Signed by Steelers to practice squad (December 1, 1994). ... Granted free agency after 1994 season. ... Signed by Denver Broncos (February 22, 1995). ... Released by Broncos (August 27, 1995). ... Re-signed by Broncos to practice squad (August 28, 1995). ... Activated (October 24, 1995). ... Granted free agency (February 14, 1997). ... Re-signed by Broncos (February 14, 1997).
CHAMPIONSHIP GAME EXPERIENCE: Played in AFC championship game (1997 season). ... Member of Super Bowl championship team (1997 season).
PRO STATISTICS: 1996—Recovered one fumble.

Year Team	G	GS	SACKS
1995—Denver NFL	1	0	0.0
1996—Denver NFL	16	1	5.0
1997—Denver NFL	15	5	8.5
Pro totals (3 years)	32	6	13.5

TASKER, STEVE   WR

PERSONAL: Born April 10, 1962, in Leoti, Kan. ... 5-9/183. ... Full name: Steven Jay Tasker.
HIGH SCHOOL: Wichita County (Leoti, Kan.).
JUNIOR COLLEGE: Dodge City (Kan.) Community College.
COLLEGE: Northwestern (degree in communication studies).
TRANSACTIONS/CAREER NOTES: Selected by Houston Oilers in ninth round (226th pick overall) of 1985 NFL draft. ... Signed by Oilers (June 14, 1985). ... On injured reserve with knee injury (October 23, 1985-remainder of season). ... On injured reserve with knee injury (September 15-November 5, 1986). ... Claimed on waivers by Buffalo Bills (November 7, 1986). ... Granted unconditional free agency (February 1-April 1, 1992). ... Re-signed by Bills for 1992 season. ... Granted unconditional free agency (February 17, 1994). ... Re-signed by Bills (April 7, 1994). ... On injured reserve with arm injury (December 22, 1994-remainder of season). ... Granted unconditional free agency (February 14, 1997). ... Re-signed by Bills (May 23, 1997). ... Released by Bills (September 20, 1997). ... Re-signed by Bills (September 22, 1997). ... Announced retirement (December 14, 1997).
CHAMPIONSHIP GAME EXPERIENCE: Played in AFC championship game (1988 and 1990-1993 seasons). ... Played in Super Bowl XXV (1990 season), Super Bowl XXVI (1991 season), Super Bowl XXVII (1992 season) and Super Bowl XXVIII (1993 season).
HONORS: Played in Pro Bowl (1987 and 1990-1995 seasons). ... Named Outstanding Player of Pro Bowl (1992 season).
PRO STATISTICS: 1985—Rushed twice for 16 yards. 1987—Credited with one safety. 1990—Recovered two fumbles for five yards. 1992—Rushed once for nine yards and recovered one fumble. 1993—Recovered one fumble. 1995—Rushed eight times for 74 yards. 1996—Rushed nine times for 31 yards and returned two punts for 18 yards. 1997—Returned 12 punts for 113 yards and recovered two fumbles.
SINGLE GAME HIGHS (regular season): Receptions—6 (November 24, 1996, vs. New York Jets); yards—160 (November 24, 1996, vs. New York Jets); and touchdown receptions—2 (November 24, 1996, vs. New York Jets).
STATISTICAL PLATEAUS: 100-yard receiving games: 1996 (1).

			RECEIVING				KICKOFF RETURNS				TOTALS			
Year Team	G	GS	No.	Yds.	Avg.	TD	No.	Yds.	Avg.	TD	TD	2pt.	Pts.	Fum.
1985—Houston NFL	7	0	2	19	9.5	0	17	447	26.3	0	0	...	0	0
1986—Houston NFL	2	0	0	0	...	0	3	65	21.7	0	0	...	0	0
—Buffalo NFL	7	0	0	0	...	0	9	148	16.4	0	0	...	0	0
1987—Buffalo NFL	12	0	0	0	...	0	11	197	17.9	0	0	...	2	2
1988—Buffalo NFL	14	0	0	0	...	0	0	0	...	0	0	...	0	0
1989—Buffalo NFL	16	0	0	0	...	0	2	39	19.5	0	0	...	0	0
1990—Buffalo NFL	16	0	2	44	22.0	2	0	0	...	0	2	...	12	0
1991—Buffalo NFL	16	0	2	39	19.5	1	0	0	...	0	1	...	6	0
1992—Buffalo NFL	15	2	2	24	12.0	0	0	0	...	0	0	...	0	0
1993—Buffalo NFL	15	0	2	26	13.0	0	0	0	...	0	0	...	0	1
1994—Buffalo NFL	14	0	0	0	...	0	1	2	2.0	0	0	0	0	0
1995—Buffalo NFL	13	3	20	255	12.8	3	0	0	...	0	3	0	18	0
1996—Buffalo NFL	8	5	21	372	17.7	3	0	0	...	0	3	0	18	3
1997—Buffalo NFL	14	0	0	0	...	0	1	12	12.0	0	0	0	0	1
Pro totals (13 years)	169	10	51	779	15.3	9	44	910	20.7	0	9	0	56	7

TATE, DAVID   DB

PERSONAL: Born November 22, 1964, in Denver. ... 6-1/209.
HIGH SCHOOL: Mullen (Denver).
COLLEGE: Colorado.
TRANSACTIONS/CAREER NOTES: Selected by Chicago Bears in eighth round (208th pick overall) of 1988 NFL draft. ... Signed by Bears (July 6, 1988). ... On injured reserve with knee injury (December 31, 1990-remainder of season playoffs). ... Granted unconditional free agency (March 1, 1993). ... Signed by New York Jets (May 4, 1993). ... Released by Jets (August 30, 1993). ... Signed by New York Giants (September 1, 1993). ... Granted unconditional free agency (February 17, 1994). ... Signed by Indianapolis Colts (July 20, 1994). ... Granted unconditional free agency (February 17, 1995). ... Re-signed by Colts (July 26, 1995). ... On injured reserve with neck injury (December 4, 1996-remainder of season). ... Released by Colts (June 3, 1997). ... Re-signed by Colts (October 7, 1997). ... Released by Colts (February 4, 1998).
CHAMPIONSHIP GAME EXPERIENCE: Played in NFC championship game (1988 season). ... Played in AFC championship game (1995 season).
PRO STATISTICS: 1989—Returned one kickoff for 12 yards. 1992—Recovered one fumble. 1993—Fumbled once. 1995—Recovered one fumble. 1996—Credited with one sack.

			INTERCEPTIONS			
Year Team	G	GS	No.	Yds.	Avg.	TD
1988—Chicago NFL	16	4	4	35	8.8	0
1989—Chicago NFL	14	4	1	0	0.0	0
1990—Chicago NFL	16	1	0	0	...	0
1991—Chicago NFL	16	0	2	35	17.5	0
1992—Chicago NFL	16	3	0	0	...	0
1993—New York Giants NFL	14	1	1	12	12.0	0
1994—Indianapolis NFL	16	8	3	51	17.0	0
1995—Indianapolis NFL	16	16	0	0	...	0
1996—Indianapolis NFL	10	10	0	0	...	0
1997—Indianapolis NFL	8	2	0	0	...	0
Pro totals (10 years)	142	49	11	133	12.1	0

TATE, MARK   CB   PATRIOTS

PERSONAL: Born March 20, 1974, in Erie, Pa. ... 6-0/185. ... Full name: Mark Anthony Tate.
HIGH SCHOOL: Cathedral (Erie, Pa.).
COLLEGE: Penn State.
TRANSACTIONS/CAREER NOTES: Signed as non-drafted free agent by New England Patriots (April 20, 1997). ... Released by Patriots (August 24, 1997). ... Re-signed by Patriots to practice squad (August 26, 1997).

TATE, ROBERT   WR   VIKINGS

PERSONAL: Born October 19, 1973, in Harrisburg, Pa. ... 5-10/187.
HIGH SCHOOL: John Harris (Harrisburg, Pa.), then Milford (Conn.) Academy.
COLLEGE: Cincinnati.
TRANSACTIONS/CAREER NOTES: Selected by Minnesota Vikings in sixth round (183rd pick overall) of 1997 NFL draft. ... Signed by Vikings (June 17, 1997). ... On injured reserve with ankle injury (October 8, 1997-remainder of season).
SINGLE GAME HIGHS (regular season): Receptions—0; yards—0; and touchdown receptions—0.

| | | | KICKOFF RETURNS | | |
Year Team	G	GS	No.	Yds.	Avg.	TD
1997—Minnesota NFL	4	0	10	196	19.6	0

TATUM, KINNON   LB   PANTHERS

PERSONAL: Born July 19, 1975, in Fayetteville, N.C. ... 6-0/222. ... Full name: Kinnon R. Tatum III.
HIGH SCHOOL: Fayetteville (N.C.).
COLLEGE: Notre Dame.
TRANSACTIONS/CAREER NOTES: Selected by Carolina Panthers in third round (87th pick overall) of 1997 NFL draft. ... Signed by Panthers for 1997 season.
PLAYING EXPERIENCE: Carolina NFL, 1997. ... Games/Games started: 16/0.

TAYLOR, AARON   G   CHARGERS

PERSONAL: Born November 14, 1972, in San Francisco. ... 6-4/305. ... Full name: Aaron Matthew Taylor.
HIGH SCHOOL: De La Salle Catholic (Concord, Calif.).
COLLEGE: Notre Dame.
TRANSACTIONS/CAREER NOTES: Selected by Green Bay Packers in first round (16th pick overall) of 1994 NFL draft. ... Signed by Packers (July 26, 1994). ... On physically unable to perform list with knee injury (August 25, 1994-entire season). ... On injured reserve with knee injury (January 11, 1996-remainder of 1995 playoffs). ... Granted unconditional free agency (February 13, 1998). ... Signed by San Diego Chargers (March 6, 1998).
PLAYING EXPERIENCE: Green Bay NFL, 1995-1997. ... Games/Games started: 1995 (16/16), 1996 (16/16), 1997 (14/14). Total: 46/46.
CHAMPIONSHIP GAME EXPERIENCE: Played in NFC championship game (1996 and 1997 seasons). ... Member of Super Bowl championship team (1996 season). ... Played in Super Bowl XXXII (1997 season).
HONORS: Named offensive lineman on THE SPORTING NEWS college All-America first team (1992 and 1993). ... Lombardi Award winner (1993).
PRO STATISTICS: 1995—Recovered two fumbles. 1996—Recovered one fumble.

TAYLOR, BOBBY   CB   EAGLES

PERSONAL: Born December 28, 1973, in Houston. ... 6-3/216. ... Full name: Robert Taylor. ... Son of Robert Taylor, silver medalist in 100-meter dash and member of gold-medal winning 400-meter relay team at 1972 Summer Olympics.
HIGH SCHOOL: Longview (Texas).
COLLEGE: Notre Dame.
TRANSACTIONS/CAREER NOTES: Selected after junior season by Philadelphia Eagles in second round (49th pick overall) of 1995 NFL draft. ... Signed by Eagles (July 19, 1995). ... On injured reserve with knee injury (October 17, 1997-remainder of season). ... Granted free agency (February 13, 1998). ... Re-signed by Eagles (June 11, 1998).
HONORS: Named defensive back on THE SPORTING NEWS college All-America first team (1993 and 1994).
PRO STATISTICS: 1996—Credited with one sack, fumbled once and recovered two fumbles for nine yards. 1997—Credited with two sacks.

| | | | INTERCEPTIONS | | |
Year Team	G	GS	No.	Yds.	Avg.	TD
1995—Philadelphia NFL	16	12	2	52	26.0	0
1996—Philadelphia NFL	16	16	3	-1	-0.3	0
1997—Philadelphia NFL	6	5	0	0	...	0
Pro totals (3 years)	38	33	5	51	10.2	0

TAYLOR, JASON   DE   DOLPHINS

PERSONAL: Born September 1, 1974, in Pittsburgh. ... 6-6/255. ... Full name: Jason Paul Taylor.
HIGH SCHOOL: Woodland Hills (Pa.).
COLLEGE: Akron.
TRANSACTIONS/CAREER NOTES: Selected by Miami Dolphins in third round (73rd pick overall) of 1997 NFL draft. ... Signed by Dolphins (July 9, 1997).
PRO STATISTICS: 1997—Recovered two fumbles.

Year Team	G	GS	SACKS
1997—Miami NFL	13	11	5.0

TAYLOR, LELAND   DT

PERSONAL: Born October 25, 1972, in Louisville. ... 6-3/305. ... Full name: Leland Morrisclay Taylor.
HIGH SCHOOL: Fairdale (Louisville).

COLLEGE: Louisville.
TRANSACTIONS/CAREER NOTES: Selected by Baltimore Ravens in seventh round (238th pick overall) of 1997 NFL draft. ... Signed by Ravens (July 14, 1997). ... On non-football injury list with leg injury (November 26, 1997-remainder of season). ... Released by Ravens (March 13, 1998).
PLAYING EXPERIENCE: Baltimore NFL, 1997. ... Games/Games played: 1/0.

TEAGUE, GEORGE — S — COWBOYS

PERSONAL: Born February 18, 1971, in Lansing, Mich. ... 6-1/196. ... Full name: George Theo Teague. ... Name pronounced TEEG.
HIGH SCHOOL: Jeff Davis (Montgomery, Ala.).
COLLEGE: Alabama.
TRANSACTIONS/CAREER NOTES: Selected by Green Bay Packers in first round (29th pick overall) of 1993 NFL draft. ... Signed by Packers (July 9, 1993). ... Granted free agency (February 16, 1996). ... Re-signed by Packers (April 12, 1996). ... Traded by Packers to Atlanta Falcons for conditional draft pick (July 16, 1996). ... Released by Falcons (August 17, 1996). ... Signed by Dallas Cowboys (August 23, 1996). ... Granted unconditional free agency (February 14, 1997). ... Signed by Miami Dolphins (March 20, 1997). ... Traded by Dolphins to Cowboys (May 6, 1998), as compensation for Dolphins signing free agent S Brock Marion (March 3, 1998).
CHAMPIONSHIP GAME EXPERIENCE: Played in NFC championship game (1995 season).
POST SEASON RECORDS: Holds NFL postseason single-game record for longest interception return—101 yards, touchdown (January 8, 1994, at Detroit).
PRO STATISTICS: 1993—Returned one punt for minus one yard and recovered two fumbles. 1995—Recovered one fumble for four yards.

| | | | INTERCEPTIONS | | | |
Year Team	G	GS	No.	Yds.	Avg.	TD
1993—Green Bay NFL	16	12	1	22	22.0	0
1994—Green Bay NFL	16	16	3	33	11.0	0
1995—Green Bay NFL	15	15	2	100	50.0	0
1996—Dallas NFL	16	8	4	47	11.8	0
1997—Miami NFL	15	6	2	25	12.5	0
Pro totals (5 years)	78	57	12	227	18.9	0

TERRELL, PAT — S — PACKERS

PERSONAL: Born March 18, 1968, in Memphis, Tenn. ... 6-1/210. ... Full name: Patrick Christopher Terrell. ... Name pronounced TAIR-el.
HIGH SCHOOL: Lakewood Senior (St. Petersburg, Fla.).
COLLEGE: Notre Dame (degree in business administration with emphasis in marketing).
TRANSACTIONS/CAREER NOTES: Selected by Los Angeles Rams in second round (49th pick overall) of 1990 NFL draft. ... Signed by Rams (August 1, 1990). ... Granted unconditional free agency (February 17, 1994). ... Signed by New York Jets (May 19, 1994). ... Released by Jets (August 21, 1995). ... Signed by Carolina Panthers (August 23, 1995). ... Granted unconditional free agency (February 16, 1996). ... Re-signed by Panthers (February 26, 1996). ... Granted unconditional free agency (February 13, 1998). ... Signed by Green Bay Packers (April 6, 1998).
CHAMPIONSHIP GAME EXPERIENCE: Played in NFC championship game (1996 season).
PRO STATISTICS: 1990—Recovered one fumble. 1991—Recovered one fumble. 1995—Recovered one fumble. 1997—Recovered one fumble.

| | | | INTERCEPTIONS | | | |
Year Team	G	GS	No.	Yds.	Avg.	TD
1990—Los Angeles Rams NFL	15	1	1	6	6.0	0
1991—Los Angeles Rams NFL	16	16	1	4	4.0	0
1992—Los Angeles Rams NFL	15	11	0	0	...	0
1993—Los Angeles Rams NFL	13	3	2	1	0.5	0
1994—New York Jets NFL	16	2	0	0	...	0
1995—Carolina NFL	16	13	3	33	11.0	0
1996—Carolina NFL	16	16	3	6	2.0	0
1997—Carolina NFL	16	5	0	0	...	0
Pro totals (8 years)	123	67	10	50	5.0	0

TERRY, RICK — DT — JETS

PERSONAL: Born April 5, 1974, in Lexington, N.C. ... 6-4/302. ... Full name: Richard Ross Terry Jr.
HIGH SCHOOL: Lexington (N.C.).
COLLEGE: North Carolina.
TRANSACTIONS/CAREER NOTES: Selected by New York Jets in second round (31st pick overall) of 1997 NFL draft. ... Signed by Jets (July 14, 1997).

Year Team	G	GS	SACKS
1997—New York Jets NFL	14	0	2.0

TERRY, TIM — LB — BENGALS

PERSONAL: Born July 26, 1974, in Hempstead, N.Y. ... 6-3/248.
HIGH SCHOOL: Hempstead (N.Y.).
COLLEGE: Temple.
TRANSACTIONS/CAREER NOTES: Signed as non-drafted free agent by Cincinnati Bengals (April 25, 1997). ... Released by Bengals (August 24, 1997). ... Re-signed by Bengals to practice squad (August 26, 1997). ... Activated (September 27, 1997). ... On injured reserve with knee injury (December 8, 1997-remainder of season).
PLAYING EXPERIENCE: Cincinnati NFL, 1997. ... Games/Games started: 5/0.

TESTAVERDE, VINNY — QB

PERSONAL: Born November 13, 1963, in Brooklyn, N.Y. ... 6-5/238. ... Full name: Vincent Frank Testaverde. ... Name pronounced TESS-tuh-VER-dee.

HIGH SCHOOL: Sewanhaka (Floral Park, N.Y.), then Fork Union (Va.) Military Academy.

COLLEGE: Miami (Fla.).

TRANSACTIONS/CAREER NOTES: Signed by Tampa Bay Buccaneers (April 3, 1987). ... Selected officially by Buccaneers in first round (first pick overall) of 1987 NFL draft. ... On injured reserve with ankle injury (December 20, 1989-remainder of season). ... Granted unconditional free agency (March 1, 1993). ... Signed by Cleveland Browns (March 31, 1993). ... Browns franchise moved to Baltimore and renamed Ravens for 1996 season (March 11, 1996). ... Released by Ravens (June 2, 1998).

HONORS: Named quarterback on THE SPORTING NEWS college All-America second team (1985). ... Heisman Trophy winner (1986). ... Named College Football Player of the Year by THE SPORTING NEWS (1986). ... Maxwell Award winner (1986). ... Davey O'Brien Award winner (1986). ... Named quarterback on THE SPORTING NEWS college All-America first team (1986). ... Played in Pro Bowl (1996 season).

PRO STATISTICS: 1987—Fumbled seven times and recovered four fumbles for minus three yards. 1988—Fumbled eight times and recovered two fumbles. 1989—Fumbled four times and recovered two fumbles. 1990—Caught one pass for three yards, fumbled 10 times and recovered three fumbles. 1991—Fumbled five times and recovered three fumbles. 1992—Fumbled four times and recovered four fumbles for minus eight yards. 1993—Fumbled four times. 1994—Fumbled three times and recovered two fumbles for two yards. 1995—Caught one pass for seven yards and fumbled four times for minus four yards. 1996—Fumbled nine times for minus 11 yards. 1997—Caught one pass for minus four yards, fumbled 11 times and recovered five fumbles for minus nine yards.

SINGLE GAME HIGHS (regular season): Attempts—52 (November 6, 1988, vs. Chicago); completions—32 (October 19, 1997, vs. Miami); yards—469 (October 16, 1988, vs. Indianapolis); and touchdown passes—4 (October 20, 1996, vs. Denver).

STATISTICAL PLATEAUS: 300-yard passing games: 1987 (1), 1988 (4), 1989 (4), 1991 (1), 1992 (1), 1993 (1), 1995 (2), 1996 (5), 1997 (3). Total: 22. ... 100-yard rushing games: 1990 (1).

MISCELLANEOUS: Regular-season record as starting NFL quarterback: 48-83-1 (.367). ... Postseason record as starting NFL quarterback: 1-1 (.500). ... Holds Tampa Bay Buccaneers all-time records for most yards passing (14,820) and most touchdown passes (77). ... Holds Baltimore Ravens all-time records for most yards passing (7,148) and most touchdown passes (51).

Year	Team	G	GS	Att.	Cmp.	Pct.	Yds.	TD	Int.	Avg.	Rat.	Att.	Yds.	Avg.	TD	TD	2pt.	Pts.
1987—Tampa Bay NFL		6	4	165	71	43.0	1081	5	6	6.55	60.2	13	50	3.8	1	1	...	6
1988—Tampa Bay NFL		15	15	466	222	47.6	3240	13	*35	6.95	48.8	28	138	4.9	1	1	...	6
1989—Tampa Bay NFL		14	14	480	258	53.8	3133	20	22	6.53	68.9	25	139	5.6	0	0	...	0
1990—Tampa Bay NFL		14	13	365	203	55.6	2818	17	∞18	‡7.72	75.6	38	280	7.4	1	1	...	6
1991—Tampa Bay NFL		13	12	326	166	50.9	1994	8	15	6.12	59.0	32	101	3.2	0	0	...	0
1992—Tampa Bay NFL		14	14	358	206	57.5	2554	14	16	7.13	74.2	36	197	5.5	2	2	...	12
1993—Cleveland NFL		10	6	230	130	56.5	1797	14	9	‡7.81	85.7	18	74	4.1	0	0	...	0
1994—Cleveland NFL		14	13	376	207	55.1	2575	16	18	6.85	70.7	21	37	1.8	2	2	0	12
1995—Cleveland NFL		13	12	392	241	61.5	2883	17	10	7.35	87.8	18	62	3.4	2	2	0	12
1996—Baltimore NFL		16	16	549	325	59.2	4177	§33	19	7.61	88.7	34	188	5.5	2	2	1	14
1997—Baltimore NFL		13	13	470	271	57.7	2971	18	15	6.32	75.9	34	138	4.1	0	0	...	0
Pro totals (11 years)		142	132	4177	2300	55.1	29223	175	183	7.00	72.8	297	1404	4.7	11	11	1	68

THARPE, LARRY — OT — LIONS

PERSONAL: Born November 19, 1970, in Macon, Ga. ... 6-4/300.

HIGH SCHOOL: Southwest (Macon, Ga.).

COLLEGE: Tennessee State.

TRANSACTIONS/CAREER NOTES: Selected by Detroit Lions in sixth round (145th pick overall) of 1992 NFL draft. ... Signed by Lions (July 23, 1992). ... On injured reserve with back and knee injuries (September 4-October 14, 1992). ... On inactive list for 15 games with Lions (1994). ... Granted free agency (February 17, 1995). ... Signed by Arizona Cardinals (March 25, 1995). ... Lions received sixth-round pick (TE Kevin Hickman) in 1995 draft as compensation. ... Granted unconditional free agency (February 16, 1996). ... Signed by New England Patriots (April 29, 1996). ... Released by Patriots (October 23, 1996). ... Signed by Lions (February 21, 1997). ... Granted unconditional free agency (February 13, 1998). ... Re-signed by Lions (June 10, 1998).

PLAYING EXPERIENCE: Detroit NFL, 1992, 1993 and 1997; Arizona NFL, 1995. ... Games/Games started: 1992 (11/0), 1993 (5/3), 1995 (16/16), 1997 (16/15). Total: 48/34.

THIBODEAUX, KEITH — DB — REDSKINS

PERSONAL: Born May 16, 1974, in Opelousan, La. ... 5-11/189. ... Full name: Keith Trevis Thibodeaux. ... Name pronounced TIB-o-dough.

HIGH SCHOOL: Beau Chene (Arnandville, La.).

COLLEGE: Northwestern (La.) State.

TRANSACTIONS/CAREER NOTES: Selected by Washington Redskins in fifth round (140th pick overall) of 1997 NFL draft. ... Signed by Redskins (May 28, 1997).

PLAYING EXPERIENCE: Washington NFL, 1997. ... Games/Games started: 15/0.

THIERRY, JOHN — DE — BEARS

PERSONAL: Born September 4, 1971, in Opelousas, La. ... 6-4/265. ... Full name: John Fitzgerald Thierry.

HIGH SCHOOL: Plaisance (Opelousas, La.).

COLLEGE: Alcorn State.

TRANSACTIONS/CAREER NOTES: Selected by Chicago Bears in first round (11th pick overall) of 1994 NFL draft. ... Signed by Bears (June 21, 1994). ... On injured reserve with knee injury (November 5, 1997-remainder of season).

PRO STATISTICS: 1994—Returned one kickoff for no yards. 1995—Recovered four fumbles.

Year	Team	G	GS	SACKS
1994—Chicago NFL		16	1	0.0
1995—Chicago NFL		16	7	4.0
1996—Chicago NFL		16	2	2.0
1997—Chicago NFL		9	9	3.0
Pro totals (4 years)		57	19	9.0

THIGPEN, YANCEY WR OILERS

PERSONAL: Born August 15, 1969, in Tarboro, N.C. ... 6-1/202. ... Full name: Yancey Dirk Thigpen.
HIGH SCHOOL: Southwest Edgecombe (Tarboro, N.C.).
COLLEGE: Winston-Salem (N.C.) State.
TRANSACTIONS/CAREER NOTES: Selected by San Diego Chargers in fourth round (90th pick overall) of 1991 NFL draft. ... Signed by Chargers (July 15, 1991). ... Released by Chargers (August 26, 1991). ... Re-signed by Chargers to practice squad (August 28, 1991). ... Activated (September 20, 1991). ... Released by Chargers (September 26, 1991). ... Re-signed by Chargers to practice squad (September 28, 1991). ... Activated (December 7, 1991). ... Released by Chargers (August 31, 1992). ... Signed by Pittsburgh Steelers (October 5, 1992). ... On injured reserve with foot injury (January 14, 1997-remainder of playoffs). ... Granted unconditional free agency (February 13, 1998). ... Signed by Tennessee Oilers (February 14, 1998).
CHAMPIONSHIP GAME EXPERIENCE: Played in AFC championship game (1994, 1995 and 1997 seasons). ... Played in Super Bowl XXX (1995 season).
HONORS: Played in Pro Bowl (1995 and 1997 seasons).
PRO STATISTICS: 1995—Rushed once for one yard. 1997—Rushed once for three yards and recovered one fumble.
SINGLE GAME HIGHS (regular season): Receptions—11 (October 26, 1997, vs. Jacksonville); yards—196 (October 26, 1997, vs. Jacksonville); and touchdown receptions—3 (December 7, 1997, vs. Denver).
STATISTICAL PLATEAUS: 100-yard receiving games: 1995 (4), 1997 (6). Total: 10.

			RECEIVING				KICKOFF RETURNS				TOTALS		
Year Team	G	GS	No.	Yds.	Avg.	TD	No.	Yds.	Avg.	TD	TD	2pt.	Pts.	Fum.
1991—San Diego NFL	4	1	0	0	...	0	0	0	...	0	0	...	0	0
1992—Pittsburgh NFL	12	0	1	2	2.0	0	2	44	22.0	0	0	...	0	0
1993—Pittsburgh NFL	12	0	9	154	17.1	3	1	23	23.0	0	3	...	18	0
1994—Pittsburgh NFL	15	6	36	546	15.2	4	5	121	24.2	0	4	0	24	0
1995—Pittsburgh NFL	16	15	85	1307	15.4	5	0	0	...	0	5	0	30	1
1996—Pittsburgh NFL	6	2	12	244	20.3	2	0	0	...	0	2	0	12	0
1997—Pittsburgh NFL	16	15	79	1398	17.7	7	0	0	...	0	7	1	44	1
Pro totals (7 years)	81	39	222	3651	16.4	21	8	188	23.5	0	21	1	128	2

THOMAS, BRODERICK DE/LB COWBOYS

PERSONAL: Born February 20, 1967, in Houston. ... 6-4/254. ... Nephew of Mike Singletary, Hall of Fame linebacker with Chicago Bears (1981-1992).
HIGH SCHOOL: James Madison (Houston).
COLLEGE: Nebraska.
TRANSACTIONS/CAREER NOTES: Selected by Tampa Bay Buccaneers in first round (sixth pick overall) of 1989 NFL draft. ... Signed by Buccaneers (August 29, 1989). ... Released by Buccaneers (June 30, 1994). ... Signed by Detroit Lions (July 15, 1994). ... Granted unconditional free agency (February 17, 1995). ... Signed by Minnesota Vikings (March 9, 1995). ... Released by Vikings (February 9, 1996). ... Signed by Dallas Cowboys (March 22, 1996). ... Granted unconditional free agency (February 14, 1997). ... Re-signed by Cowboys (March 24, 1997). ... Granted free agency (February 13, 1998). ... Re-signed by Cowboys (March 16, 1998).
HONORS: Named defensive lineman on The Sporting News college All-America second team (1987). ... Named linebacker on The Sporting News college All-America first team (1988).
PRO STATISTICS: 1990—Recovered two fumbles. 1991—Recovered two fumbles for 12 yards. 1992—Intercepted two passes for 81 yards and one touchdown and recovered three fumbles for minus one yard. 1993—Recovered one fumble. 1994—Recovered two fumbles for 11 yards. 1995—Recovered one fumble. 1996—Recovered three fumbles for 23 yards. 1997—Recovered one fumble.

Year Team	G	GS	SACKS
1989—Tampa Bay NFL	16	0	2.0
1990—Tampa Bay NFL	16	15	7.5
1991—Tampa Bay NFL	16	16	11.0
1992—Tampa Bay NFL	16	16	5.0
1993—Tampa Bay NFL	16	8	1.0
1994—Detroit NFL	16	16	7.0
1995—Minnesota NFL	16	16	6.0
1996—Dallas NFL	16	9	4.5
1997—Dallas NFL	16	0	3.5
Pro totals (9 years)	144	96	47.5

THOMAS, CHRIS WR REDSKINS

PERSONAL: Born July 16, 1971, in Ventura, Calif. ... 6-2/190. ... Full name: Chris Eric Thomas.
HIGH SCHOOL: Ventura (Calif.).
COLLEGE: Cal Poly-SLO.
TRANSACTIONS/CAREER NOTES: Signed as non-drafted free agent by San Diego Chargers (May 6, 1993). ... Released by Chargers (August 30, 1993). ... Re-signed by Chargers to practice squad (September 1, 1993). ... Granted free agency after 1993 season. ... Signed by San Francisco 49ers (May 16, 1995). ... Released by 49ers (February 15, 1996). ... Re-signed by 49ers (May 15, 1996). ... Released by 49ers (August 20, 1996). ... Selected by Rhein Fire in 1997 World League draft (February 17, 1997). ... Signed by Washington Redskins (February 25, 1997). ... Released by Redskins (August 19, 1997). ... Re-signed by Redskins (August 21, 1997). ... Released by Redskins (August 23, 1997). ... Re-signed by Redskins (September 22, 1997).
PRO STATISTICS: 1995—Returned one punt for 25 yards.
SINGLE GAME HIGHS (regular season): Receptions—3 (December 13, 1997, vs. New York Giants); yards—30 (November 12, 1995, vs. Dallas); and touchdown receptions—0.

			RECEIVING				KICKOFF RETURNS				TOTALS		
Year Team	G	GS	No.	Yds.	Avg.	TD	No.	Yds.	Avg.	TD	TD	2pt.	Pts.	Fum.
1995—San Francisco NFL	14	0	6	73	12.2	0	3	49	16.3	0	0	0	0	0
1996—							Did not play.							
1997—Washington NFL	13	0	11	93	8.5	0	0	0	...	0	0	0	0	0
Pro totals (2 years)	27	0	17	166	9.8	0	3	49	16.3	0	0	0	0	0

THOMAS, DAVE   CB   JAGUARS

PERSONAL: Born August 25, 1968, in Miami. ... 6-3/214. ... Full name: David Thomas.
HIGH SCHOOL: Miami Beach (Fla.).
COLLEGE: Tennessee.
TRANSACTIONS/CAREER NOTES: Selected by Dallas Cowboys in eighth round (203rd pick overall) of 1993 NFL draft. ... Signed by Cowboys (July 15, 1993). ... Selected by Jacksonville Jaguars from Cowboys in NFL expansion draft (February 15, 1995). ... Granted free agency (February 16, 1996). ... Re-signed by Jaguars (June 3, 1996). ... On injured reserve with broken leg (October 29, 1996-remainder of season). ... Granted unconditional free agency (February 14, 1997). ... Re-signed by Jaguars (March 3, 1997).
PLAYING EXPERIENCE: Dallas NFL, 1993 and 1994; Jacksonville NFL, 1995-1997. ... Games/Games started: 1993 (12/0), 1994 (16/0), 1995 (16/2), 1996 (9/5), 1997 (16/15). Total: 69/22.
CHAMPIONSHIP GAME EXPERIENCE: Played in NFC championship game (1993 and 1994 seasons). ... Member of Super Bowl championship team (1993 season).
PRO STATISTICS: 1995—Recovered one fumble. 1996—Intercepted two passes for seven yards, returned one punt for one yard and fumbled once. 1997—Intercepted two passes for 34 yards and recovered one fumble.

THOMAS, DERRICK   LB   CHIEFS

PERSONAL: Born January 1, 1967, in Miami. ... 6-3/247. ... Full name: Derrick Vincent Thomas.
HIGH SCHOOL: South (Miami).
COLLEGE: Alabama.
TRANSACTIONS/CAREER NOTES: Selected by Kansas City Chiefs in first round (fourth pick overall) of 1989 NFL draft. ... Signed by Chiefs (August 24, 1989). ... Granted free agency (March 1, 1993). ... Re-signed by Chiefs (May 21, 1993). ... Granted unconditional free agency (February 14, 1997). ... Re-signed by Chiefs (March 26, 1997).
CHAMPIONSHIP GAME EXPERIENCE: Played in AFC championship game (1993 season).
HONORS: Named linebacker on THE SPORTING NEWS college All-America second team (1987). ... Butkus Award winner (1988). ... Named linebacker on THE SPORTING NEWS college All-America first team (1988). ... Played in Pro Bowl (1989-1997 seasons). ... Named outside linebacker on THE SPORTING NEWS NFL All-Pro team (1990-1992).
RECORDS: Holds NFL single-game record for most sacks—7 (November 11, 1990, vs. Seattle).
PRO STATISTICS: 1989—Recovered one fumble. 1990—Recovered two fumbles for 14 yards. 1991—Recovered four fumbles for 23 yards and one touchdown. 1992—Recovered three fumbles (including one in end zone for a touchdown). 1993—Recovered one fumble for 86 yards and a touchdown. 1994—Credited with one safety and recovered three fumbles for 11 yards. 1995—Recovered one fumble. 1996—Recovered one fumble. 1997—Credited with a safety.
MISCELLANEOUS: Holds Kansas City Chiefs all-time record for most sacks (107.5).

Year Team	G	GS	SACKS
1989—Kansas City NFL	16	16	10.0
1990—Kansas City NFL	15	15	*20.0
1991—Kansas City NFL	16	15	13.5
1992—Kansas City NFL	16	16	14.5
1993—Kansas City NFL	16	15	8.0
1994—Kansas City NFL	16	15	11.0
1995—Kansas City NFL	15	15	8.0
1996—Kansas City NFL	16	13	13.0
1997—Kansas City NFL	12	10	9.5
Pro totals (9 years)	138	130	107.5

THOMAS, FRED   CB   SEAHAWKS

PERSONAL: Born September 11, 1973, in Grand Rapids, Mich. ... 5-9/172.
HIGH SCHOOL: Bruce (Miss.).
JUNIOR COLLEGE: Northwest Mississippi College.
COLLEGE: Mississippi Valley State (did not play football), then Mississippi, then Tennessee-Martin.
TRANSACTIONS/CAREER NOTES: Selected by Seattle Seahawks in second round (47th pick overall) of 1996 NFL draft. ... Signed by Seahawks (July 19, 1996).
PLAYING EXPERIENCE: Seattle NFL, 1996 and 1997. ... Games/Games started: 1996 (15/0), 1997 (16/3). Total: 31/3.

THOMAS, HENRY   DL   PATRIOTS

PERSONAL: Born January 12, 1965, in Houston. ... 6-2/277. ... Full name: Henry Lee Thomas Jr.
HIGH SCHOOL: Dwight D. Eisenhower (Houston).
COLLEGE: Louisiana State.
TRANSACTIONS/CAREER NOTES: Selected by Minnesota Vikings in third round (72nd pick overall) of 1987 NFL draft. ... Signed by Vikings (July 14, 1987). ... Designated by Vikings as transition player (February 25, 1993). ... Designated by Vikings as franchise player (February 15, 1994). ... Free agency status changed by Vikings from franchise to unconditional (February 15, 1995). ... Signed by Detroit Lions (February 27, 1995). ... Released by Lions (April 23, 1997). ... Signed by New England Patriots (June 12, 1997).
CHAMPIONSHIP GAME EXPERIENCE: Played in NFC championship game (1987 season).
HONORS: Named defensive lineman on THE SPORTING NEWS college All-America second team (1986). ... Played in Pro Bowl (1991 and 1992 seasons).
PRO STATISTICS: 1987—Intercepted one pass for no yards and recovered one fumble. 1988—Intercepted one pass for seven yards and recovered one fumble for two yards and a touchdown. 1989—Recovered three fumbles for 37 yards and one touchdown. 1990—Recovered one fumble. 1991—Recovered one fumble. 1993—Credited with one safety. 1994—Recovered one fumble. 1995—Recovered two fumbles. 1996—Recovered one fumble. 1997—Recovered one fumble.

Year Team	G	GS	SACKS
1987—Minnesota NFL	12	12	2.5
1988—Minnesota NFL	15	15	6.0
1989—Minnesota NFL	14	14	9.0

Year Team	G	GS	SACKS
1990—Minnesota NFL	16	16	8.5
1991—Minnesota NFL	16	15	8.0
1992—Minnesota NFL	16	16	6.0
1993—Minnesota NFL	13	13	9.0
1994—Minnesota NFL	16	16	7.0
1995—Detroit NFL	16	16	10.5
1996—Detroit NFL	15	15	6.0
1997—New England NFL	16	16	7.0
Pro totals (11 years)	165	164	79.5

THOMAS, HOLLIS — DT — EAGLES

PERSONAL: Born January 10, 1974, in St. Louis. ... 6-0/306.
HIGH SCHOOL: Sumner (St. Louis).
COLLEGE: Northern Illinois.
TRANSACTIONS/CAREER NOTES: Signed as non-drafted free agent by Philadelphia Eagles (April 26, 1996).
PLAYING EXPERIENCE: Philadelphia NFL, 1996 and 1997. ... Games/Games started: 1996 (16/5), 1997 (16/16). Total: 32/21.
PRO STATISTICS: 1996—Credited with one sack. 1997—Credited with 2 1/2 sacks and recovered one fumble.

THOMAS, J.T. — WR — RAMS

PERSONAL: Born July 11, 1971, in San Bernardino, Calif. ... 5-10/180. ... Full name: Johnny le'Mon Thomas.
HIGH SCHOOL: San Bernardino (Calif.).
JUNIOR COLLEGE: San Bernardino (Calif.) Valley.
COLLEGE: Arizona State.
TRANSACTIONS/CAREER NOTES: Selected after junior season by St. Louis Rams in seventh round (240th pick overall) of 1995 NFL draft. ... Signed by Rams (June 16, 1995). ... Granted free agency (February 13, 1998). ... Re-signed by Rams (May 6, 1998).
PRO STATISTICS: 1995—Ran 61 yards with lateral from punt return, fumbled once and recovered one fumble for five yards.
SINGLE GAME HIGHS (regular season): Receptions—3 (December 8, 1996, vs. Chicago); yards—25 (September 28, 1997, vs. Oakland); and touchdown receptions—0.

			RUSHING				RECEIVING				KICKOFF RETURNS				TOTALS			
Year Team	G	GS	Att.	Yds.	Avg.	TD	No.	Yds.	Avg.	TD	No.	Yds.	Avg.	TD	TD	2pt.	Pts.	Fum.
1995—St. Louis NFL	15	1	0	0	...	0	5	42	8.4	0	32	752	23.5	0	0	0	0	1
1996—St. Louis NFL	16	1	1	-1	-1.0	0	7	46	6.6	0	30	643	21.4	0	0	0	0	1
1997—St. Louis NFL	5	0	0	0	...	0	2	25	12.5	0	5	97	19.4	0	0	0	0	0
Pro totals (3 years)	36	2	1	-1	-1.0	0	14	113	8.1	0	67	1492	22.3	0	0	0	0	2

THOMAS, JOHNNY — CB — CHARGERS

PERSONAL: Born August 3, 1964, in Houston. ... 5-9/191. ... Full name: Johnny Thomas Jr.
HIGH SCHOOL: Sterling (Houston).
COLLEGE: Baylor.
TRANSACTIONS/CAREER NOTES: Selected by Washington Redskins in seventh round (192nd pick overall) of 1987 NFL draft. ... Signed by Redskins (July 24, 1987). ... On injured reserve with ankle injury (August 31, 1987-entire season). ... On injured reserve with knee injury (September 30, 1988-remainder of season). ... Granted unconditional free agency (February 1, 1989). ... Signed by San Diego Chargers (March 30, 1989). ... Released by Chargers (September 5, 1989). ... Re-signed by Chargers (September 13, 1989). ... Released by Chargers (December 16, 1989). ... Signed by Kansas City Chiefs (March 12, 1990). ... Released by Chiefs (August 28, 1990). ... Signed by Redskins (September 26, 1990). ... On injured reserve (October 17-November 16, 1990). ... Released by Redskins (November 27, 1990). ... Signed by Frankfurt Galaxy of World League (March 3, 1992). ... Signed by Redskins for 1992. ... Released by Redskins (August 31, 1992). ... Re-signed by Redskins (September 2, 1992). ... Released by Redskins (August 30, 1993). ... Re-signed by Redskins (August 31, 1993). ... Granted unconditional free agency (February 17, 1995). ... Signed by Cleveland Browns (April 17, 1995). ... Browns franchise moved to Baltimore and renamed Ravens for 1996 season (March 11, 1996). ... Released by Ravens (July 20, 1996). ... Signed by Philadelphia Eagles (October 22, 1996). ... Granted unconditional free agency (February 14, 1997). ... Signed by Chargers (March 20, 1997). ... On injured reserve with knee injury (August 19, 1997-entire season).
PLAYING EXPERIENCE: Washington NFL, 1988, 1990 and 1992-1994; San Diego NFL, 1989; Frankfurt W.L., 1992; Cleveland NFL, 1995; Philadelphia NFL, 1996. ... Games/Games started: 1988 (4/0), 1989 (13/0), 1990 (4/0), 1992 W.L. (9/9), 1992 NFL (16/0), 1993 (16/0), 1994 (16/0), 1995 (16/0), 1996 (9/0). Total NFL: 94/0. Total W.L.: 9/9. Total Pro: 103/9.
PRO STATISTICS: NFL: 1990—Returned one punt for no yards and fumbled once. 1992—Returned one punt for no yards, fumbled once and recovered one fumble. 1993—Recovered two fumbles. 1995—Recovered one fumble.

THOMAS, LAMAR — WR — DOLPHINS

PERSONAL: Born February 12, 1970, in Ocala, Fla. ... 6-1/175. ... Full name: Lamar Nathaniel Thomas.
HIGH SCHOOL: Buchholz (Gainesville, Fla.).
COLLEGE: Miami, Fla. (degree in sociology).
TRANSACTIONS/CAREER NOTES: Selected by Tampa Bay Buccaneers in third round (60th pick overall) of 1993 NFL draft. ... Signed by Buccaneers (July 14, 1993). ... Granted free agency (February 16, 1996). ... Re-signed by Buccaneers (May 16, 1996). ... Released by Buccaneers (July 17, 1996). ... Signed by Miami Dolphins (July 27, 1996). ... Granted unconditional free agency (February 14, 1997). ... Re-signed by Dolphins (March 11, 1997).
HONORS: Named wide receiver on THE SPORTING NEWS college All-America second team (1992).
PRO STATISTICS: 1995—Rushed once for five yards.
SINGLE GAME HIGHS (regular season): Receptions—4 (October 9, 1994, vs. Atlanta); yards—78 (September 26, 1993, vs. Chicago); and touchdown receptions—1 (September 8, 1990, vs. Arizona).

Year Team	G	GS	RECEIVING No.	Yds.	Avg.	TD	TOTALS TD	2pt.	Pts.	Fum.
1993—Tampa Bay NFL	14	2	8	186	23.3	2	2	...	12	0
1994—Tampa Bay NFL	11	0	7	94	13.4	0	0	0	0	0
1995—Tampa Bay NFL	11	0	10	107	10.7	0	0	0	0	0
1996—Miami NFL	9	3	10	166	16.6	1	1	0	6	0
1997—Miami NFL	12	6	28	402	14.4	2	2	0	12	1
Pro totals (5 years)	57	11	63	955	15.2	5	5	0	30	1

THOMAS, MARK — DE — BEARS

PERSONAL: Born May 6, 1969, in Lilburn, Ga. ... 6-5/272. ... Full name: Mark Andrew Thomas.
HIGH SCHOOL: Parkview (Lilburn, Ga.).
COLLEGE: North Carolina State.
TRANSACTIONS/CAREER NOTES: Selected by San Francisco 49ers in fourth round (89th pick overall) of 1992 NFL draft. ... Signed by 49ers (July 16, 1992). ... On injured reserve with ankle injury (September 1-October 7, 1992). ... On practice squad (October 7-November 11, 1992). ... On injured reserve (November 11, 1992-remainder of season). ... Selected by Carolina Panthers from 49ers in NFL expansion draft (February 15, 1995). ... Granted free agency (February 17, 1995). ... On injured reserve with thumb injury (November 27, 1995-remainder of season). ... Granted unconditional free agency (February 16, 1996). ... Re-signed by Panthers (February 20, 1996). ... Granted unconditional free agency (February 14, 1997). ... Signed by Chicago Bears (March 30, 1997).
CHAMPIONSHIP GAME EXPERIENCE: Member of 49ers for NFC championship game (1993 and 1994 seasons); inactive. ... Member of Super Bowl championship team (1994 season). ... Played in NFC championship game (1996 season).
PRO STATISTICS: 1993—Recovered one fumble. 1996—Recovered one fumble for 18 yards. 1997—Recovered one fumble.

Year Team	G	GS	SACKS
1992—San Francisco NFL	Did not play.		
1993—San Francisco NFL	11	1	0.5
1994—San Francisco NFL	9	0	1.0
1995—Carolina NFL	10	0	2.0
1996—Carolina NFL	12	0	4.0
1997—Chicago NFL	16	7	4.5
Pro totals (5 years)	58	8	12.0

T

THOMAS, MARVIN — DE — LIONS

PERSONAL: Born October 19, 1973, in Bay Minette, Ala. ... 6-5/264.
HIGH SCHOOL: Baldwin (Ala.).
COLLEGE: Memphis.
TRANSACTIONS/CAREER NOTES: Selected by Chicago Bears in seventh round (233rd pick overall) of 1997 NFL draft. ... Signed by Bears (July 10, 1997). ... Inactive for four games (1997). ... Released by Bears (August 18, 1997). ... Signed by Detroit Lions to practice squad (August 26, 1997). ... Activated (November 24, 1997); did not play.

THOMAS, ORLANDO — S — VIKINGS

PERSONAL: Born October 21, 1972, in Crowley, La. ... 6-1/216.
HIGH SCHOOL: Crowley (La.).
COLLEGE: Southwestern Louisiana.
TRANSACTIONS/CAREER NOTES: Selected by Minnesota Vikings in second round (42nd pick overall) of 1995 NFL draft. ... Signed by Vikings (July 25, 1995).
PRO STATISTICS: 1995—Fumbled once and recovered four fumbles for 19 yards and one touchdown. 1996—Recovered one fumble. 1997—Fumbled once and recovered two fumbles for 26 yards and one touchdown.

Year Team	G	GS	INTERCEPTIONS No.	Yds.	Avg.	TD
1995—Minnesota NFL	16	11	*9	108	12.0	1
1996—Minnesota NFL	16	16	5	57	11.4	0
1997—Minnesota NFL	15	13	2	1	0.5	0
Pro totals (3 years)	47	40	16	166	10.4	1

THOMAS, ROBB — WR — BUCCANEERS

PERSONAL: Born March 29, 1966, in Portland, Ore. ... 5-11/178. ... Full name: Robb Douglas Thomas. ... Son of Aaron Thomas, wide receiver with San Francisco 49ers (1961) and New York Giants (1962-1970).
HIGH SCHOOL: Corvallis (Ore.).
COLLEGE: Oregon State.
TRANSACTIONS/CAREER NOTES: Selected by Kansas City Chiefs in sixth round (143rd pick overall) of 1989 NFL draft. ... Signed by Chiefs (May 30, 1989). ... On injured reserve with dislocated shoulder (October 24-December 4, 1989). ... On developmental squad (December 5-23, 1989). ... Released by Chiefs (August 31, 1992). ... Signed by Seattle Seahawks (September 8, 1992). ... Granted free agency (March 1, 1993). ... Re-signed by Seahawks (July 2, 1993). ... Released by Seahawks (August 30, 1993). ... Re-signed by Seahawks (August 31, 1993). ... Granted unconditional free agency (February 17, 1994). ... Re-signed by Seahawks (July 13, 1994). ... Granted unconditional free agency (February 17, 1996). ... Signed by Tampa Bay Buccaneers (August 27, 1996). ... Re-signed by Buccaneers (December 9, 1996).
PRO STATISTICS: 1992—Rushed once for minus one yard.
SINGLE GAME HIGHS (regular season): Receptions—7 (November 17, 1991, vs. Denver); yards—89 (November 17, 1991, vs. Denver); and touchdown receptions—2 (October 13, 1996, vs. Minnesota).

Year Team	G	GS	RECEIVING No.	Yds.	Avg.	TD	TOTALS TD	2pt.	Pts.	Fum.
1989—Kansas City NFL	8	1	8	58	7.3	2	2	...	12	1
1990—Kansas City NFL	16	12	41	545	13.3	4	4	...	24	0

Year Team	G	GS	RECEIVING				TOTALS			
			No.	Yds.	Avg.	TD	TD	2pt.	Pts.	Fum.
1991—Kansas City NFL	15	12	43	495	11.5	1	1	...	6	0
1992—Seattle NFL	15	0	11	136	12.4	0	0	...	0	1
1993—Seattle NFL	16	0	7	67	9.6	0	0	...	0	0
1994—Seattle NFL	16	1	4	70	17.5	0	0	0	0	0
1995—Seattle NFL	15	2	12	239	19.9	1	1	0	6	0
1996—Tampa Bay NFL	12	8	33	427	12.9	2	2	0	12	0
1997—Tampa Bay NFL	16	1	13	129	9.9	0	0	0	0	0
Pro totals (9 years)	129	37	172	2166	12.6	10	10	0	60	2

THOMAS, RODNEY   RB   OILERS

PERSONAL: Born March 30, 1973, in Groveton, Texas. ... 5-10/213. ... Full name: Rodney Dejuane Thomas.
HIGH SCHOOL: Groveton (Texas).
COLLEGE: Texas A&M.
TRANSACTIONS/CAREER NOTES: Selected by Houston Oilers in third round (89th pick overall) of 1995 NFL draft. ... Signed by Oilers (August 1, 1995). ... Oilers franchise moved to Tennessee for 1997 season. ... Granted free agency (February 13, 1998).
SINGLE GAME HIGHS (regular season): Attempts—25 (November 19, 1995 vs. Kansas City); yards—108 (November 5, 1995, vs. Cleveland); and rushing touchdowns—2 (December 24, 1995, vs. Buffalo).
STATISTICAL PLATEAUS: 100-yard rushing games: 1995 (2).

Year Team	G	GS	RUSHING				RECEIVING				KICKOFF RETURNS				TOTALS			
			Att.	Yds.	Avg.	TD	No.	Yds.	Avg.	TD	No.	Yds.	Avg.	TD	TD	2pt.	Pts.	Fum.
1995—Houston NFL	16	10	251	947	3.8	5	39	204	5.2	2	3	48	16.0	0	7	1	44	8
1996—Houston NFL	16	0	49	151	3.1	1	13	128	9.8	0	5	80	16.0	0	1	0	6	0
1997—Tennessee NFL	16	1	67	310	4.6	3	14	111	7.9	0	17	346	20.4	0	3	0	18	1
Pro totals (3 years)	48	11	367	1408	3.8	9	66	443	6.7	2	25	474	19.0	0	11	1	68	9

THOMAS, THURMAN   RB   BILLS

PERSONAL: Born May 16, 1966, in Houston. ... 5-10/198. ... Full name: Thurman Lee Thomas.
HIGH SCHOOL: Willow Ridge (Missouri City, Texas).
COLLEGE: Oklahoma State.
TRANSACTIONS/CAREER NOTES: Selected by Buffalo Bills in second round (40th pick overall) of 1988 NFL draft. ... Signed by Bills (July 14, 1988).
CHAMPIONSHIP GAME EXPERIENCE: Played in AFC championship game (1988 and 1990-1993 seasons). ... Played in Super Bowl XXV (1990 season), Super Bowl XXVI (1991 season), Super Bowl XXVII (1992 season) and Super Bowl XXVIII (1993 season).
HONORS: Named running back on THE SPORTING NEWS college All-America second team (1985). ... Played in Pro Bowl (1989-1991 and 1993 seasons). ... Named to play in Pro Bowl (1992 season); replaced by Ronnie Harmon due to injury. ... Named running back on THE SPORTING News NFL All-Pro team (1990 and 1991). ... Named NFL Player of the Year by THE SPORTING NEWS (1991).
POST SEASON RECORDS: Shares NFL postseason career record for most games with 100 or more rushing yards—7. ... Shares NFL post-season single-game record for most receptions—13 (January 6, 1990, at Cleveland).
PRO STATISTICS: 1988—Recovered one fumble. 1989—Recovered two fumbles. 1990—Recovered two fumbles. 1992—Recovered one fumble. 1993—Attempted one pass without a completion and recovered one fumble. 1994—Recovered two fumbles. 1996—Recovered one fumble.
SINGLE GAME HIGHS (regular season): Attempts—37 (November 8, 1992, vs. Pittsburgh); yards—214 (September 24, 1990, vs. New York Jets); and rushing touchdowns—3 (September 6, 1992, vs. Los Angeles).
STATISTICAL PLATEAUS: 100-yard rushing games: 1988 (2), 1989 (5), 1990 (5), 1991 (8), 1992 (9), 1993 (7), 1994 (4), 1995 (3), 1996 (2), 1997 (1). Total: 46. ... 100-yard receiving games: 1991 (2), 1996 (1). Total: 3.
MISCELLANEOUS: Holds Buffalo Bills all-time record for most yards rushing (11,405), most touchdowns (83) and most rushing touchdowns (63). ... Active AFC leader for career rushing yards (11,405) and touchdowns (83).

Year Team	G	GS	RUSHING				RECEIVING				TOTALS			
			Att.	Yds.	Avg.	TD	No.	Yds.	Avg.	TD	TD	2pt.	Pts.	Fum.
1988—Buffalo NFL	15	15	207	881	4.3	2	18	208	11.6	0	2	...	12	9
1989—Buffalo NFL	16	16	298	1244	4.2	6	60	669	11.2	6	▲12	...	72	7
1990—Buffalo NFL	16	16	271	§1297	4.8	11	49	532	10.9	2	13	...	78	6
1991—Buffalo NFL	15	15	§288	§1407	*4.9	7	62	631	10.2	5	12	...	72	5
1992—Buffalo NFL	16	16	312	1487	§4.8	9	58	626	10.8	3	12	...	72	6
1993—Buffalo NFL	16	16	*355	§1315	3.7	6	48	387	8.1	0	6	...	36	6
1994—Buffalo NFL	15	15	287	1093	3.8	7	50	349	7.0	2	9	0	54	1
1995—Buffalo NFL	14	14	267	1005	3.8	6	26	220	8.5	2	8	0	48	6
1996—Buffalo NFL	15	15	281	1033	3.7	8	26	254	9.8	0	8	0	48	1
1997—Buffalo NFL	16	16	154	643	4.2	1	30	208	6.9	0	1	0	6	2
Pro totals (10 years)	154	154	2720	11405	4.2	63	427	4084	9.6	20	83	0	498	49

THOMAS, WILLIAM   LB   EAGLES

PERSONAL: Born August 13, 1968, in Amarillo, Texas. ... 6-2/223. ... Full name: William Harrison Thomas Jr.
HIGH SCHOOL: Palo Duro (Amarillo, Texas).
COLLEGE: Texas A&M.
TRANSACTIONS/CAREER NOTES: Selected by Philadelphia Eagles in fourth round (105th pick overall) of 1991 NFL draft. ... Signed by Eagles (July 17, 1991). ... Granted free agency (February 17, 1994). ... Re-signed by Eagles (July 1994).
HONORS: Played in Pro Bowl (1995 and 1996 seasons).
POST SEASON RECORDS: Shares NFL postseason record for most touchdowns by interception return—1 (December 30, 1995, vs. Detroit).
PRO STATISTICS: 1991—Recovered one fumble. 1992—Recovered two fumbles for two yards. 1993—Recovered three fumbles. 1995—Recovered one fumble. 1996—Recovered one fumble for 23 yards and a touchdown. 1997—Recovered one fumble for 37 yards and a touchdown.

Year Team	G	GS	INTERCEPTIONS No.	Yds.	Avg.	TD	SACKS No.
1991—Philadelphia NFL	16	7	0	0	...	0	2.0
1992—Philadelphia NFL	16	15	2	4	2.0	0	1.5
1993—Philadelphia NFL	16	16	2	39	19.5	0	6.5
1994—Philadelphia NFL	16	16	1	7	7.0	0	6.0
1995—Philadelphia NFL	16	16	7	104	14.9	1	2.0
1996—Philadelphia NFL	16	16	3	47	15.7	0	5.5
1997—Philadelphia NFL	14	14	2	11	5.5	0	5.0
Pro totals (7 years)	110	100	17	212	12.5	1	28.5

THOMAS, ZACH — LB — DOLPHINS

PERSONAL: Born September 1, 1973, in Lubbock, Texas. ... 5-11/235. ... Full name: Zach Michael Thomas.
HIGH SCHOOL: White Deer (Texas), then Pampa (Texas).
COLLEGE: Texas Tech.
TRANSACTIONS/CAREER NOTES: Selected by Miami Dolphins in fifth round (154th pick overall) of 1996 NFL draft. ... Signed by Dolphins (July 10, 1996).
HONORS: Named linebacker on The Sporting News college All-America second team (1994). ... Named linebacker on The Sporting News college All-America first team (1995).
PRO STATISTICS: 1996—Returned one kickoff for 17 yards and recovered two fumbles for seven yards.

Year Team	G	GS	INTERCEPTIONS No.	Yds.	Avg.	TD	SACKS No.
1996—Miami NFL	16	16	3	64	21.3	1	2.0
1997—Miami NFL	15	15	1	10	10.0	0	0.5
Pro totals (2 years)	31	31	4	74	18.5	1	2.5

THOMASON, JEFF — TE — PACKERS

PERSONAL: Born December 30, 1969, in San Diego. ... 6-5/250. ... Full name: Jeffrey David Thomason.
HIGH SCHOOL: Corona Del Mar (Newport Beach, Calif.).
COLLEGE: Oregon.
TRANSACTIONS/CAREER NOTES: Signed as non-drafted free agent by Cincinnati Bengals (April 29, 1992). ... Placed on injured reserve with sprained knee (September 1-December 5, 1992). ... Released by Bengals (August 30, 1993). ... Re-signed by Bengals (September 15, 1993). ... Claimed on waivers by Green Bay Packers (August 2, 1994). ... Released by Packers (August 21, 1994). ... Re-signed by Packers (January 20, 1995). ... Granted unconditional free agency (February 13, 1998). ... Re-signed by Packers (March 17, 1998).
CHAMPIONSHIP GAME EXPERIENCE: Played in NFC championship game (1995-97 seasons). ... Member of Super Bowl championship team (1996 season). ... Played in Super Bowl XXXII (1997 season).
PRO STATISTICS: 1995—Returned one kickoff for 16 yards and recovered one fumble. 1996—Returned one kickoff for 20 yards.
SINGLE GAME HIGHS (regular season): Receptions—5 (September 1, 1997, vs. Chicago); yards—58 (September 1, 1997, vs. Chicago); and touchdown receptions—1 (September 1, 1997, vs. Chicago).

Year Team	G	GS	RECEIVING No.	Yds.	Avg.	TD	TOTALS TD	2pt.	Pts.	Fum.
1992—Cincinnati NFL	4	0	2	14	7.0	0	0	...	0	0
1993—Cincinnati NFL	3	0	2	8	4.0	0	0	...	0	0
1994—						Did not play.				
1995—Green Bay NFL	16	1	3	32	10.7	0	0	0	0	0
1996—Green Bay NFL	16	1	3	45	15.0	0	0	0	0	0
1997—Green Bay NFL	13	1	9	115	12.8	1	1	0	6	1
Pro totals (5 years)	52	3	19	214	11.3	1	1	0	6	1

THOMPSON, BENNIE — S — RAVENS

PERSONAL: Born February 10, 1963, in New Orleans. ... 6-0/214.
HIGH SCHOOL: John McDonogh (New Orleans).
COLLEGE: Grambling State.
TRANSACTIONS/CAREER NOTES: Signed as non-drafted free agent by Kansas City Chiefs (May 9, 1985). ... Released by Chiefs (August 5, 1985). ... Signed by Winnipeg Blue Bombers of CFL (April 21, 1987). ... Granted free agency (March 1, 1989). ... Signed by New Orleans Saints (April 12, 1989). ... Released by Saints (September 5, 1989). ... Re-signed by Saints to practice squad (September 6, 1989). ... Activated (December 15, 1989). ... Granted unconditional free agency (February 1-April 1, 1991). ... Re-signed by Saints for 1991 season. ... Granted unconditional free agency (February 1, 1992). ... Signed by Chiefs (March 28, 1992). ... Granted unconditional free agency (February 17, 1994). ... Rights relinquished by Chiefs (April 29, 1994). ... Signed by Cleveland Browns (July 14, 1994). ... Browns franchise moved to Baltimore and renamed Ravens for 1996 season (March 11, 1996). ... Granted unconditional free agency (February 13, 1998). ... Re-signed by Ravens (March 10, 1998).
CHAMPIONSHIP GAME EXPERIENCE: Played in AFC championship game (1993 season).
HONORS: Played in Pro Bowl (1991 season).
PRO STATISTICS: CFL: 1987—Recovered one fumble. 1988—Fumbled once and recovered two fumbles for two yards. NFL: 1991—Recovered two fumbles. 1994—Recovered one fumble. 1997—Recovered two fumbles.

Year Team	G	GS	INTERCEPTIONS No.	Yds.	Avg.	TD	SACKS No.
1986—Winnipeg CFL	9	...	2	49	24.5	0	0.0
1987—Winnipeg CFL	8	...	1	0	0.0	0	0.0
1988—Winnipeg CFL	18	...	4	58	14.5	0	0.0
1989—New Orleans NFL	2	0	0	0	...	0	0.0
1990—New Orleans NFL	16	2	2	0	0.0	0	0.0
1991—New Orleans NFL	16	0	1	14	14.0	0	0.0
1992—Kansas City NFL	16	0	4	26	6.5	0	1.5

Year Team	G	GS	No.	Yds.	Avg.	TD	No.
1993—Kansas City NFL	16	0	0	0	...	0	0.5
1994—Cleveland NFL	16	0	0	0	...	0	1.0
1995—Cleveland NFL	13	0	0	0	...	0	0.0
1996—Baltimore NFL	16	0	0	0	...	0	3.0
1997—Baltimore NFL	16	1	0	0	...	0	0.0
CFL totals (3 years)	35	...	7	107	15.3	0	0.0
NFL totals (9 years)	127	3	7	40	5.7	0	6.0
Pro totals (12 years)	162	...	14	147	10.5	0	6.0

(Column headers above: Year Team, G, GS, INTERCEPTIONS — No., Yds., Avg., TD; SACKS — No.)

THOMPSON, DAVID   RB   RAMS

PERSONAL: Born January 13, 1975, in Okmulgee, Okla. ... 5-8/200. ... Full name: David Farrod Thompson.
HIGH SCHOOL: Okmulgee (Okla.).
COLLEGE: Oklahoma State (degree in speech communications, 1997).
TRANSACTIONS/CAREER NOTES: Signed as non-drafted free agent by Jacksonville Jaguars (April 20, 1997). ... Released by Jaguars (August 19, 1997). ... Signed by St. Louis Rams to practice squad (August 25, 1997). ... Activated (October 9, 1997).
PRO STATISTICS: 1997—Recovered one fumble.
SINGLE GAME HIGHS (regular season): Attempts—9 (December 7, 1997, vs. New Orleans); yards—18 (December 7, 1997, vs. New Orleans); and rushing touchdowns—1 (December 20, 1997, vs. Carolina).

			RUSHING				KICKOFF RETURNS				TOTALS			
Year Team	G	GS	Att.	Yds.	Avg.	TD	No.	Yds.	Avg.	TD	TD	2pt.	Pts.	Fum.
1997—St. Louis NFL	11	0	16	30	1.9	1	49	1110	22.7	0	1	0	6	2

THOMPSON, TOMMY   P   49ERS

PERSONAL: Born April 27, 1972, in Ventura, Calif. ... 5-10/179. ... Full name: Tommy Ralph Thompson.
HIGH SCHOOL: Lompoc (Calif.).
COLLEGE: Oregon.
TRANSACTIONS/CAREER NOTES: Signed as non-drafted free agent by San Francisco 49ers (May 4, 1994). ... Released by 49ers (August 20, 1994). ... Re-signed by 49ers (March 10, 1995). ... Granted free agency (February 13, 1998). ... Re-signed by 49ers (February 25, 1998).
CHAMPIONSHIP GAME EXPERIENCE: Played in NFC championship game (1997 season).

			PUNTING					
Year Team	G	GS	No.	Yds.	Avg.	Net avg.	In. 20	Blk.
1995—San Francisco NFL	16	0	57	2312	40.6	33.7	13	0
1996—San Francisco NFL	16	0	73	3217	44.1	38.2	20	2
1997—San Francisco NFL	16	0	78	3182	40.8	34.6	22	1
Pro totals (3 years)	48	0	208	8711	41.9	35.6	55	3

THRASH, JAMES   WR   REDSKINS

PERSONAL: Born April 28, 1975, in Denver. ... 6-0/200.
HIGH SCHOOL: Wewoka (Okla.).
COLLEGE: Missouri Southern.
TRANSACTIONS/CAREER NOTES: Signed as non-drafted free agent by Philadelphia Eagles (April 22, 1997). ... Released by Eagles (July 8, 1997). ... Signed by Washington Redskins (July 11, 1997).
PLAYING EXPERIENCE: Washington NFL, 1997. ... Games/Games started: 4/0.
PRO STATISTICS: 1997—Caught two passes for 24 yards.
SINGLE GAME HIGHS (regular season): Receptions—2 (December 13, 1997, vs. New York Giants); yards—24 (December 13, 1997, vs. New York Giants); and touchdown receptions—0.

THREATS, JABBAR   DE   JAGUARS

PERSONAL: Born April 26, 1975, in Springfield, Ohio. ... 6-5/264. ... Full name: Anthayus Jabbar Threats.
HIGH SCHOOL: Sprinfield (Ohio) North.
JUNIOR COLLEGE: Garden City (Kan.) Community College.
COLLEGE: Michigan State.
TRANSACTIONS/CAREER NOTES: Signed as non-drafted free agent by Jacksonville Jaguars (July 15, 1997).
PLAYING EXPERIENCE: Jacksonville NFL, 1997. ... Games/Games started: 1/0.

TIMMERMAN, ADAM   G   PACKERS

PERSONAL: Born August 14, 1971, in Cherokee, Iowa. ... 6-4/295. ... Full name: Adam Larry Timmerman.
HIGH SCHOOL: Washington (Cherokee, Iowa).
COLLEGE: South Dakota State (degree in agriculture business).
TRANSACTIONS/CAREER NOTES: Selected by Green Bay Packers in seventh round (230th pick overall) of 1995 NFL draft. ... Signed by Packers (June 2, 1995). ... Granted free agency (February 13, 1998). ... Re-signed by Packers (April 16, 1998).
PLAYING EXPERIENCE: Green Bay NFL, 1995-1997. ... Games/Games started: 1995 (13/0), 1996 (16/16), 1997 (16/16). Total: 45/32.
CHAMPIONSHIP GAME EXPERIENCE: Played in NFC championship game (1995-97 seasons). ... Member of Super Bowl championship team (1996 season). ... Played in Super Bowl XXXII (1997 season).

TIMPSON, MICHAEL — WR

PERSONAL: Born June 6, 1967, in Baxley, Ga. ... 5-10/180. ... Full name: Michael Dwain Timpson.
HIGH SCHOOL: Hialeah (Fla.) Miami Lakes.
COLLEGE: Penn State.
TRANSACTIONS/CAREER NOTES: Selected after junior season by New England Patriots in fourth round (100th pick overall) of 1989 NFL draft. ... Signed by Patriots (July 18, 1989). ... On injured reserve with hamstring injury (September 9-October 26, 1989). ... On developmental squad (October 27-November 3, 1989). ... On injured reserve with knee injury (November 16, 1989-remainder of season). ... On injured reserve with finger injury (September 4-December 1, 1990). ... Granted free agency (February 1, 1992). ... Re-signed by Patriots (July 27, 1992). ... Granted unconditional free agency (February 17, 1994). ... Re-signed by Patriots (May 24, 1994). ... Granted free agency (February 17, 1995). ... Tendered offer sheet by Chicago Bears (March 8, 1995). ... Patriots declined to match offer (March 15, 1995). ... Released by Bears (April 10, 1997). ... Signed by Philadelphia Eagles (June 2, 1997). ... Granted unconditional free agency (February 13, 1998).
PRO STATISTICS: 1991—Rushed once for minus four yards. 1992—Returned eight punts for 47 yards. 1994—Rushed twice for 14 yards. 1995—Rushed three times for 28 yards and a touchdown and recovered one fumble. 1996—Rushed three times for 21 yards and rcovered one fumble.
SINGLE GAME HIGHS (regular season): Receptions—10 (November 13, 1994, vs. Minnesota); yards—150 (December 22, 1991, vs. Cincinnati); and touchdown receptions 1 (December 14, 1997, vs. Atlanta).
STATISTICAL PLATEAUS: 100-yard receiving games: 1991 (1), 1994 (3), 1996 (1), 1997 (1). Total: 6.

Year Team	G	GS	RECEIVING				KICKOFF RETURNS				TOTALS			
			No.	Yds.	Avg.	TD	No.	Yds.	Avg.	TD	TD	2pt.	Pts.	Fum.
1989—New England NFL	2	0	0	0	...	0	2	13	6.5	0	0	...	0	1
1990—New England NFL	5	0	5	91	18.2	0	3	62	20.7	0	0	...	0	0
1991—New England NFL	16	2	25	471	18.8	2	2	37	18.5	0	2	...	12	2
1992—New England NFL	16	2	26	315	12.1	1	2	28	14.0	0	1	...	6	0
1993—New England NFL	16	7	42	654	15.6	2	0	0	...	0	2	...	12	1
1994—New England NFL	15	14	74	941	12.7	3	1	28	28.0	0	3	0	18	0
1995—Chicago NFL	16	0	24	289	12.0	2	18	420	23.3	0	3	0	18	1
1996—Chicago NFL	15	15	62	802	12.9	0	0	0	...	0	0	0	0	2
1997—Philadelphia NFL	15	10	42	484	11.5	2	0	0	...	0	2	0	12	1
Pro totals (9 years)	116	50	300	4047	13.5	12	28	588	21.0	0	13	0	78	8

TINDALE, TIM — FB — BEARS

PERSONAL: Born April 15, 1971, in London, Ont. ... 5-10/220. ... Full name: Tim Scott Tindale.
HIGH SCHOOL: Saunders (London, Ont.).
COLLEGE: Western Ontario.
TRANSACTIONS/CAREER NOTES: Signed as non-drafted free agent by Buffalo Bills (May 6, 1994). ... Active for one game (1994); did not play. ... On injured reserve with knee injury (December 1, 1997-remainder of season). ... Granted free agency (February 13, 1998). ... Signed by Chicago Bears (April 23, 1998).
PRO STATISTICS: 1995—Returned six kickoffs for 62 yards and recovered one fumble for two yards.
SINGLE GAME HIGHS (regular season): Attempts—4 (September 22, 1996, vs. Dallas); yards—15 (November 3, 1996, vs. Washington); and rushing touchdowns—0.
STATISTICAL PLATEAUS: 100-yard receiving games: 1997 (1).

Year Team	G	GS	RUSHING				RECEIVING				TOTALS			
			Att.	Yds.	Avg.	TD	No.	Yds.	Avg.	TD	TD	2pt.	Pts.	Fum.
1995—Buffalo NFL	16	0	5	16	3.2	0	0	0	...	0	0	0	0	0
1996—Buffalo NFL	14	3	14	49	3.5	0	1	-1	-1.0	0	0	0	0	1
1997—Buffalo NFL	7	0	0	0	...	0	4	105	26.3	0	0	0	0	0
Pro totals (3 years)	37	3	19	65	3.4	0	5	104	20.8	0	0	0	0	1

TOBECK, ROBBIE — C — FALCONS

PERSONAL: Born March 6, 1970, in Tarpon Springs, Fla. ... 6-4/300. ... Full name: Robert L. Tobeck.
HIGH SCHOOL: New Port Richey (Fla.); did not play football.
COLLEGE: Washington State.
TRANSACTIONS/CAREER NOTES: Signed as non-drafted free agent by Atlanta Falcons (May 7, 1993). ... Released by Falcons (August 30, 1993). ... Re-signed by Falcons to practice squad (August 31, 1993). ... Activated (January 1, 1994).
PLAYING EXPERIENCE: Atlanta NFL, 1994-1997. ... Games/Games started: 1994 (5/0), 1995 (16/16), 1996 (16/16), 1997 (16/15). Total: 53/47.
PRO STATISTICS: 1996—Caught two passes for 15 yards and a touchdown. 1997—Recovered one fumble.

TOLBERT, TONY — DE

PERSONAL: Born December 29, 1967, in Tuskegee, Ala. ... 6-6/263. ... Full name: Tony Lewis Tolbert.
HIGH SCHOOL: Dwight Morrow (Englewood, N.J.).
COLLEGE: Texas-El Paso (degree in criminal justice, 1991).
TRANSACTIONS/CAREER NOTES: Selected by Dallas Cowboys in fourth round (85th pick overall) of 1989 NFL draft. ... Signed by Cowboys (July 23, 1989). ... Granted free agency (February 1, 1992). ... Re-signed by Cowboys (August 23, 1992). ... Granted roster exemption (August 23-September 2, 1992). ... Granted unconditional free agency (February 17, 1995). ... Re-signed by Cowboys (February 22, 1995). ... Released by Cowboys (June 16, 1998).
CHAMPIONSHIP GAME EXPERIENCE: Played in NFC championship game (1992-1995 seasons). ... Member of Super Bowl championship team (1992, 1993 and 1995 seasons).

HONORS: Played in Pro Bowl (1996 season).
PRO STATISTICS: 1991—Recovered one fumble. 1994—Intercepted one pass for 54 yards and a touchdown and recovered one fumble. 1996—Recovered two fumbles.

Year	Team	G	GS	SACKS
1989—Dallas NFL		16	5	2.0
1990—Dallas NFL		16	4	6.0
1991—Dallas NFL		16	16	7.0
1992—Dallas NFL		16	16	8.5
1993—Dallas NFL		16	16	7.5
1994—Dallas NFL		16	16	5.5
1995—Dallas NFL		16	16	5.5
1996—Dallas NFL		16	16	12.0
1997—Dallas NFL		16	16	5.0
Pro totals (9 years)		144	121	59.0

TOLLIVER, BILLY JOE   QB   CHIEFS

PERSONAL: Born February 7, 1966, in Dallas. ... 6-1/217. ... Full name: Billy Joe Tolliver.
HIGH SCHOOL: Boyd (Texas).
COLLEGE: Texas Tech.
TRANSACTIONS/CAREER NOTES: Selected by San Diego Chargers in second round (51st pick overall) of 1989 NFL draft. ... Signed by Chargers (July 30, 1989). ... On injured reserve with broken collarbone (September 5-October 18, 1989). ... On developmental squad (October 19-20, 1989). ... Traded by Chargers to Atlanta Falcons for fifth-round pick (LB Kevin Little) in 1992 draft (August 28, 1991). ... Granted free agency (March 1, 1993). ... Re-signed by Falcons (August 9, 1993). ... Granted unconditional free agency (February 17, 1994). ... Signed by Houston Oilers (September 7, 1994). ... Granted unconditional free agency (February 17, 1995). ... Signed by Falcons (October 23, 1996). ... Inactive for nine games (1996). ... Granted unconditional free agency (February 14, 1997). ... Re-signed by Falcons (March 19, 1997). ... Released by Falcons (October 27, 1997). ... Signed by Kansas City Chiefs (November 5, 1997).
PRO STATISTICS: 1989—Fumbled four times and recovered one fumble for minus six yards. 1990—Fumbled six times and recovered two fumbles. 1991—Fumbled three times. 1992—Fumbled five times. 1994—Fumbled seven times. 1997—Fumbled seven times and recovered two fumbles for minus one yard.
SINGLE GAME HIGHS (regular season): Attempts—51 (December 16, 1990, vs. Denver); completions—26 (December 16, 1990, vs. Denver); yards—350 (December 10, 1989, vs. Washington); and touchdown passes—2 (November 13, 1994, vs. Cincinnati).
STATISTICAL PLATEAUS: 300-yard passing games: 1989 (2), 1990 (1). Total: 3.
MISCELLANEOUS: Regular-season record as starting NFL quarterback: 13-23 (.361).

						PASSING						RUSHING				TOTALS	
Year	Team	G	GS	Att.	Cmp.	Pct.	Yds.	TD	Int.	Avg.	Rat.	Att.	Yds.	Avg.	TD	TD	2pt.	Pts.
1989—San Diego NFL		5	5	185	89	48.1	1097	5	8	5.93	57.9	7	0	0.0	0	0	...	0
1990—San Diego NFL		15	14	410	216	52.7	2574	16	16	6.28	68.9	14	22	1.6	0	0	...	0
1991—Atlanta NFL		7	2	82	40	48.8	531	4	2	6.48	75.8	9	6	0.7	0	0	...	0
1992—Atlanta NFL		9	5	131	73	55.7	787	5	5	6.01	70.4	4	15	3.8	0	0	...	0
1993—Atlanta NFL		7	2	76	39	51.3	464	3	5	6.11	56.0	7	48	6.9	0	0	...	0
1994—Houston NFL		10	7	240	121	50.4	1287	6	7	5.36	62.6	12	37	3.1	2	2	0	12
1995—									Did not play.									
1996—Atlanta NFL									Did not play.									
1997—Atlanta NFL		6	1	115	63	54.8	685	5	1	5.96	83.4	7	8	1.1	0	0	0	0
—Kansas City NFL		3	0	1	1	100.0	-8	0	0	-8.00	79.2	2	-1	-0.5	0	0	0	0
Pro totals (7 years)		62	36	1240	642	51.8	7417	44	44	5.98	67.2	62	135	2.2	2	2	0	12

TOMCZAK, MIKE   QB   STEELERS

PERSONAL: Born October 23, 1962, in Calumet City, Ill. ... 6-1/207. ... Full name: Michael John Tomczak. ... Name pronounced TOM-zak.
HIGH SCHOOL: Thornton Fractional North (Calumet City, Ill.).
COLLEGE: Ohio State.
TRANSACTIONS/CAREER NOTES: Selected by New Jersey Generals in 1985 USFL territorial draft. ... Signed as non-drafted free agent by Chicago Bears (May 9, 1985). ... Granted free agency (February 1, 1990). ... Re-signed by Bears (July 25, 1990). ... Granted unconditional free agency (February 1, 1991). ... Signed by Green Bay Packers (March 30, 1991). ... Granted free agency (February 1, 1992). ... Re-signed by Packers (August 19, 1992). ... Released by Packers (August 31, 1992). ... Signed by Cleveland Browns (September 16, 1992). ... Granted unconditional free agency (March 1, 1993). ... Signed by Pittsburgh Steelers (April 6, 1993). ... Granted unconditional free agency (February 14, 1997). ... Re-signed by Steelers (March 6, 1997).
CHAMPIONSHIP GAME EXPERIENCE: Member of Bears for NFC championship game (1985 season); did not play. ... Member of Super Bowl championship team (1985 season). ... Played in NFC championship game (1988 season). ... Member of Steelers for AFC championship game (1994 and 1995 seasons); did not play. ... Member of Steelers for Super Bowl XXX (1995 season); did not play. ... Played in AFC championship game (1997 season).
PRO STATISTICS: 1985—Fumbled once and recovered one fumble for minus 13 yards. 1986—Fumbled twice. 1987—Fumbled six times and recovered one fumble. 1988—Fumbled once. 1989—Fumbled twice. 1990—Caught one pass for five yards and fumbled twice. 1991—Fumbled five times and recovered two fumbles for minus one yard. 1992—Fumbled five times. 1993—Fumbled twice and recovered one fumble. 1994—Fumbled twice. 1995—Fumbled twice and recovered one fumble. 1996—Fumbled seven times and recovered two fumbles.
SINGLE GAME HIGHS (regular season): Attempts—43 (December 15, 1996, vs. San Francisco); completions—26 (November 20, 1994, vs. Miami); yards—343 (November 20, 1994, vs. Miami); and touchdown passes—3 (December 1, 1991, vs. Atlanta).
STATISTICAL PLATEAUS: 300-yard passing games: 1989 (1), 1991 (1), 1992 (1), 1994 (1), 1996 (1). Total: 5.
MISCELLANEOUS: Regular-season record as starting NFL quarterback: 41-27 (.603). ... Postseason record as starting NFL quarterback: 3-2 (.600).

						PASSING						RUSHING				TOTALS	
Year	Team	G	GS	Att.	Cmp.	Pct.	Yds.	TD	Int.	Avg.	Rat.	Att.	Yds.	Avg.	TD	TD	2pt.	Pts.
1985—Chicago NFL		6	0	6	2	33.3	33	0	0	5.50	52.8	2	3	1.5	0	0	...	0
1986—Chicago NFL		13	7	151	74	49.0	1105	2	10	7.32	50.2	23	117	5.1	3	3	...	18
1987—Chicago NFL		12	6	178	97	54.5	1220	5	10	6.85	62.0	18	54	3.0	1	1	...	6

Year	Team	G	GS	PASSING Att.	Cmp.	Pct.	Yds.	TD	Int.	Avg.	Rat.	RUSHING Att.	Yds.	Avg.	TD	TOTALS TD	2pt.	Pts.
1988—Chicago NFL		14	5	170	86	50.6	1310	7	6	7.71	75.4	13	40	3.1	1	1	...	6
1989—Chicago NFL		16	1	306	156	51.0	2058	16	16	6.73	68.2	24	71	3.0	1	1	...	6
1990—Chicago NFL		16	2	104	39	37.5	521	3	5	5.01	43.8	12	41	3.4	2	2	...	12
1991—Green Bay NFL		12	7	238	128	53.8	1490	11	9	6.26	72.6	17	93	5.5	1	1	...	6
1992—Cleveland NFL		12	8	211	120	56.9	1693	7	7	8.02	80.1	24	39	1.6	0	0	...	0
1993—Pittsburgh NFL		7	1	54	29	53.7	398	2	5	7.37	51.3	5	-4	-0.8	0	0	...	0
1994—Pittsburgh NFL		6	2	93	54	58.1	804	4	0	8.65	100.8	4	22	5.5	0	0	0	0
1995—Pittsburgh NFL		7	4	113	65	57.5	666	1	9	5.89	44.3	11	25	2.3	0	0	0	0
1996—Pittsburgh NFL		16	15	401	222	55.4	2767	15	17	6.90	71.8	22	-7	-0.3	0	0	0	0
1997—Pittsburgh NFL		16	0	24	16	66.7	185	1	2	7.71	68.9	7	13	1.9	0	0	0	0
Pro totals (13 years)		153	58	2049	1088	53.1	14250	74	96	6.95	67.8	182	507	2.8	9	9	0	54

TOMICH, JARED   DE   SAINTS

PERSONAL: Born April 24, 1974, in St. John, Ind. ... 6-2/258. ... Full name: Jared James Tomich.
HIGH SCHOOL: Lake Central (St. John, Ind.).
COLLEGE: Nebraska.
TRANSACTIONS/CAREER NOTES: Selected by New Orleans Saints in second round (39th pick overall) of 1997 NFL draft. ... Signed by Saints (July 17, 1997).
PLAYING EXPERIENCE: New Orleans NFL, 1997. ... Games/Games started: 16/1.
PRO STATISTICS: 1997—Returned one kickoff for no yards, credited with one sack, fumbled once and recovered one fumble.

TONGUE, REGGIE   S   CHIEFS

PERSONAL: Born April 11, 1973, in Baltimore. ... 6-0/201. ... Full name: Reginald Clinton Tongue. ... Name pronounced TONG.
HIGH SCHOOL: Lathrop (Fairbanks, Alaska).
COLLEGE: Oregon State.
TRANSACTIONS/CAREER NOTES: Selected by Kansas City Chiefs in second round (58th pick overall) of 1996 NFL draft. ... Signed by Chiefs (July 26, 1996).
PLAYING EXPERIENCE: Kansas City NFL, 1996 and 1997. ... Games/Games started: 1996 (16/0), 1997 (16/16). Total: 32/16.
PRO STATISTICS: 1997—Intercepted one pass for no yards and credited with $2\frac{1}{2}$ sacks.

TOOMER, AMANI   WR   GIANTS

PERSONAL: Born September 8, 1974, in Berkely, Calif. ... 6-3/202. ... Name pronounced ah-MAH-nee.
HIGH SCHOOL: De La Salle Catholic (Concord, Calif.).
COLLEGE: Michigan.
TRANSACTIONS/CAREER NOTES: Selected by New York Giants in second round (34th pick overall) of 1996 NFL draft. ... Signed by Giants (July 21, 1996). ... On injured reserve with knee injury (October 31, 1996-remainder of season).
PRO STATISTICS: 1996—Caught one pass for 12 yards and recovered two fumbles.
SINGLE GAME HIGHS (regular season): Receptions—3 (September 14, 1997, vs. Baltimore); yards—64 (November 16, 1997, vs. Arizona); and touchdown receptions—1 (November 16, 1997, vs. Arizona).

Year	Team	G	GS	RECEIVING No.	Yds.	Avg.	TD	PUNT RETURNS No.	Yds.	Avg.	TD	KICKOFF RETURNS No.	Yds.	Avg.	TD	TOTALS TD	2pt.	Pts.	Fum.
1996—New York Giants NFL		7	1	1	12	12.0	0	18	298	16.6	2	11	191	17.4	0	2	0	12	1
1997—New York Giants NFL		16	0	16	263	16.4	1	47	455	9.7	∞1	0	0	...	0	2	0	12	0
Pro totals (2 years)		23	1	17	275	16.2	1	65	753	11.6	3	11	191	17.4	0	4	0	24	1

TOVAR, STEVE   LB   BENGALS

PERSONAL: Born April 25, 1970, in Elyria, Ohio. ... 6-3/244. ... Full name: Steven Eric Tovar.
HIGH SCHOOL: West (Elyria, Ohio).
COLLEGE: Ohio State.
TRANSACTIONS/CAREER NOTES: Selected by the Cincinnati Bengals in third round (59th pick overall) of 1993 NFL draft. ... Signed by Bengals (July 19, 1993). ... Granted free agency (February 16, 1996). ... Re-signed by Bengals (April 15, 1996). ... On injured list with knee injury (December 2, 1996-remainder of season).
PRO STATISTICS: 1993—Recovered one fumble. 1994—Returned one kickoff for eight yards and recovered two fumbles. 1996—Fumbled once.

Year	Team	G	GS	INTERCEPTIONS No.	Yds.	Avg.	TD	SACKS No.
1993—Cincinnati NFL		16	9	1	0	0.0	0	0.0
1994—Cincinnati NFL		16	16	1	14	14.0	0	3.0
1995—Cincinnati NFL		14	13	1	13	13.0	0	1.0
1996—Cincinnati NFL		13	13	4	42	10.5	0	3.0
1997—Cincinnati NFL		14	5	0	0	...	0	0.0
Pro totals (5 years)		73	56	7	69	9.9	0	7.0

TOWNSEND, GREG   DE

PERSONAL: Born November 3, 1961, in Los Angeles. ... 6-3/270.
HIGH SCHOOL: Dominguez (Compton, Calif.).

JUNIOR COLLEGE: Long Beach (Calif.) City College.

COLLEGE: Texas Christian.

TRANSACTIONS/CAREER NOTES: Selected by Oakland Invaders in seventh round (79th pick overall) of 1983 USFL draft. ... Selected by Los Angeles Raiders in fourth round (110th pick overall) of 1983 NFL draft. ... Signed by Raiders (July 7, 1983). ... On suspended list (October 9, 1986). ... Reinstated (October 10, 1986). ... On suspended list (October 13-20, 1986). ... Crossed picket line during players strike (October 14, 1987). ... On non-football injury list with substance abuse problem (August 5-31, 1988). ... On reserve//did not report list (August 25-September 1992). ... Granted roster exemption for two games (September 1992). ... Released by Raiders (July 19, 1994). ... Signed by Philadelphia Eagles (July 21, 1994). ... Granted unconditional free agency (February 17, 1995). ... Signed by Raiders (July 27, 1997). ... Released by Raiders (September 30, 1997).

CHAMPIONSHIP GAME EXPERIENCE: Played in AFC championship game (1983 and 1990 seasons). ... Played in Super Bowl XVIII (1983 season).

HONORS: Named defensive end on THE SPORTING NEWS NFL All-Pro team (1990). ... Played in Pro Bowl (1990 and 1991 seasons).

PRO STATISTICS: 1983—Recovered one fumble for 66 yards and a touchdown. 1985—Recovered one fumble. 1986—Credited with a safety. 1988—Recovered one fumble in end zone for a touchdown. 1989—Recovered one fumble. 1990—Recovered one fumble for one yard and a touchdown. 1991—Recovered one fumble. 1992—Recovered one fumble. 1994—Recovered one fumble for 24 yards.

			INTERCEPTIONS				SACKS
Year Team	G	GS	No.	Yds.	Avg.	TD	No.
1983—Los Angeles Raiders NFL	16	7	0	0	...	0	10.5
1984—Los Angeles Raiders NFL	16	6	0	0	...	0	7.0
1985—Los Angeles Raiders NFL	16	9	0	0	...	0	10.0
1986—Los Angeles Raiders NFL	15	4	0	0	...	0	11.5
1987—Los Angeles Raiders NFL	13	1	0	0	...	0	8.5
1988—Los Angeles Raiders NFL	16	11	1	86	86.0	1	§11.5
1989—Los Angeles Raiders NFL	16	11	0	0	...	0	10.5
1990—Los Angeles Raiders NFL	16	16	1	0	0.0	0	12.5
1991—Los Angeles Raiders NFL	16	16	1	31	31.0	0	13.0
1992—Los Angeles Raiders NFL	14	14	0	0	...	0	5.0
1993—Los Angeles Raiders NFL	16	16	0	0	...	0	7.5
1994—Philadelphia NFL	16	12	0	0	...	0	2.0
1995—			Did not play.				
1996—			Did not play.				
1997—Oakland NFL	4	0	0	0	...	0	0.0
Pro totals (13 years)	190	123	3	117	39.0	1	109.5

TRAPP, JAMES — CB — RAIDERS

PERSONAL: Born December 28, 1969, in Greenville, S.C. ... 6-0/185. ... Full name: James Harold Trapp.

HIGH SCHOOL: Lawton (Okla.).

COLLEGE: Clemson.

TRANSACTIONS/CAREER NOTES: Selected by Los Angeles Raiders in third round (72nd pick overall) of 1993 NFL draft. ... Signed by Raiders (July 13, 1993). ... Raiders franchise moved to Oakland (July 21, 1995). ... Granted free agency (February 16, 1996). ... Re-signed by Raiders (March 30, 1996).

PLAYING EXPERIENCE: Los Angeles Raiders NFL, 1993 and 1994; Oakland NFL, 1995-1997. ... Games/Games started: 1993 (14/2), 1994 (16/2), 1995 (14/2), 1996 (12/4), 1997 (16/16). Total: 72/26.

PRO STATISTICS: 1993—Intercepted one pass for seven yards. 1994—Credited with one sack. 1995—Recovered one fumble. 1996—Intercepted one pass for 23 yards. 1997—Intercepted two passes for 24 yards and recovered two fumbles.

TRAYLOR, KEITH — DT — BRONCOS

PERSONAL: Born September 3, 1969, in Malvern, Ark. ... 6-2/304. ... Full name: Byron Keith Traylor. ... Cousin of Isaac Davis, guard with San Diego Chargers (1994-1997).

HIGH SCHOOL: Malvern (Ark.).

JUNIOR COLLEGE: Coffeyville (Kan.) Community College.

COLLEGE: Oklahoma, then Central Oklahoma.

TRANSACTIONS/CAREER NOTES: Selected by Denver Broncos in third round (61st pick overall) of 1991 NFL draft. ... Released by Broncos (June 7, 1993). ... Signed by Los Angeles Raiders (June 1993). ... Released by Raiders (August 30, 1993). ... Signed by Green Bay Packers (September 14, 1993). ... Released by Packers (November 9, 1993). ... Signed by Kansas City Chiefs (January 7, 1994). ... Released by Chiefs (January 14, 1994). ... Re-signed by Chiefs (May 18, 1994). ... Released by Chiefs (August 28, 1994). ... Re-signed by Chiefs (February 28, 1995). ... Granted unconditional free agency (February 14, 1997). ... Signed by Broncos (March 10, 1997).

PLAYING EXPERIENCE: Denver NFL, 1991, 1992 and 1997; Green Bay NFL, 1993; Kansas City NFL, 1995 and 1996. ... Games/Games started: 1991 (16/2), 1992 (16/3), 1993 (5/0), 1995 (16/0), 1996 (15/2), 1997 (16/16). Total: 84/23.

CHAMPIONSHIP GAME EXPERIENCE: Played in AFC championship game (1991 and 1997 seasons). ... Member of Super Bowl championship team (1997 season).

PRO STATISTICS: 1992—Credited with one sack and returned one kickoff for 13 yards. 1995—Credited with 1 1/2 sacks and recovered one fumble. 1996—Credited with one sack. 1997—Intercepted one pass for 62 yards and a touchdown and credited with two sacks.

TREU, ADAM — G — RAIDERS

PERSONAL: Born June 24, 1974, in Lincoln, Neb. ... 6-5/302. ... Name pronounced TRUE.

HIGH SCHOOL: Pius X (Lincoln, Neb.).

COLLEGE: Nebraska.

TRANSACTIONS/CAREER NOTES: Selected by Oakland Raiders in third round (72nd pick overall) of 1997 NFL draft. ... Signed by Raiders for 1997 season.

PLAYING EXPERIENCE: Oakland NFL, 1997. ... Games/Games started: 16/0.

TRUITT, GREG   C   BENGALS

PERSONAL: Born December 8, 1965, in Sarasota, Fla. ... 6-0/235.
HIGH SCHOOL: Riverview (Sarasota, Fla.).
COLLEGE: Penn State.
TRANSACTIONS/CAREER NOTES: Signed as non-drafted free agent by Cincinnati Bengals (April 6, 1994).
PLAYING EXPERIENCE: Cincinnati NFL, 1994-1997. ... Games/Games started: 1994 (16/0), 1995 (16/0), 1996 (16/0), 1997 (16/0). Total: 64/0.
PRO STATISTICS: 1997—Fumbled twice for minus 11 yards.

TRUITT, OLANDA   WR   RAIDERS

PERSONAL: Born January 4, 1971, in Birmingham, Ala. ... 6-0/195.
HIGH SCHOOL: A.H. Parker (Birmingham, Ala.).
COLLEGE: Pittsburgh, then Mississippi State.
TRANSACTIONS/CAREER NOTES: Selected after junior season by Los Angeles Raiders in fifth round (125th pick overall) of 1993 NFL draft. ... Signed by Raiders (July 19, 1993). ... Claimed on waivers by Minnesota Vikings (August 31, 1993). ... Released by Vikings (August 27, 1994). ... Signed by Washington Redskins (August 29, 1994). ... Released by Redskins (August 27, 1995). ... Re-signed by Redskins (October 17, 1995). ... Granted unconditional free agency (February 16, 1996). ... Signed by Raiders (May 1996)
PRO STATISTICS: 1997—Returned two kickoffs for 51 yards.
SINGLE GAME HIGHS (regular season): Receptions—4 (November 26, 1995, vs. Philadelphia); yards—77 (December 4, 1994, vs. Tampa Bay); and touchdown receptions—1 (December 14, 1997, vs. Seattle).

				RECEIVING				TOTALS		
Year Team	G	GS	No.	Yds.	Avg.	TD	TD	2pt.	Pts.	Fum.
1993—Minnesota NFL	8	0	4	40	10.0	0	0	...	0	0
1994—Washington NFL	9	0	2	89	44.5	1	1	0	6	0
1995—Washington NFL	5	2	9	154	17.1	1	1	0	6	1
1996—Oakland NFL	10	0	0	0	...	0	0	0	0	0
1997—Oakland NFL	14	0	7	91	13.0	1	1	0	6	1
Pro totals (5 years)	46	2	22	374	17.0	3	3	0	18	2

TUAOLO, ESERA   DT   FALCONS

PERSONAL: Born July 11, 1968, in Honolulu. ... 6-3/276. ... Full name: Esera Tavai Tuaolo. ... Name pronounced ess-ER-uh TOO-ah-OH-lo.
HIGH SCHOOL: Don Antonio Lugo (Chino, Calif.).
COLLEGE: Oregon State.
TRANSACTIONS/CAREER NOTES: Selected by Green Bay Packers in second round (35th pick overall) of 1991 NFL draft. ... Signed by Packers (July 19, 1991). ... Released by Packers (October 1, 1992). ... Signed by Minnesota Vikings (November 24, 1992). ... Granted free agency (February 17, 1994). ... Re-signed by Vikings (July 18, 1994). ... Granted unconditional free agency (February 17, 1995). ... Re-signed by Vikings (March 7, 1995). ... On physically unable to perform list with Achilles' tendon injury (July 22-August 26, 1996). ... Released by Vikings (February 27, 1997). ... Signed by Buffalo Bills (June 25, 1997). ... Released by Bills (August 18, 1997). ... Signed by Jacksonville Jaguars (November 4, 1997). ... Granted unconditional free agency (February 13, 1998). ... Signed by Atlanta Falcons (May 7, 1998).
PRO STATISTICS: 1991—Intercepted one pass for 23 yards. 1995—Recovered two fumbles.

Year Team	G	GS	SACKS
1991—Green Bay NFL	16	16	3.5
1992—Green Bay NFL	4	0	1.0
—Minnesota NFL	3	0	0.0
1993—Minnesota NFL	11	3	0.0
1994—Minnesota NFL	16	0	0.0
1995—Minnesota NFL	16	16	3.0
1996—Minnesota NFL	14	9	2.5
1997—Jacksonville NFL	6	1	1.0
Pro totals (7 years)	86	45	11.0

TUBBS, WINFRED   LB   49ERS

PERSONAL: Born September 24, 1970, in Hollywood, Fla. ... 6-4/260. ... Full name: Winfred O'Neal Tubbs.
HIGH SCHOOL: Fairfield (Texas).
COLLEGE: Texas.
TRANSACTIONS/CAREER NOTES: Selected by New Orleans Saints in third round (79th pick overall) of 1994 NFL draft. ... Signed by Saints (July 20, 1994). ... On injured reserve with knee injury (December 22, 1995-remainder of season). ... Granted free agency (February 14, 1997). ... Re-signed by Saints (July 17, 1997). ... Granted unconditional free agency (February 13, 1998). ... Signed by San Francisco 49ers (February 15, 1998).
PRO STATISTICS: 1995—Recovered one fumble. 1996—Recovered one fumble. 1997—Recovered two fumbles.

			INTERCEPTIONS				SACKS
Year Team	G	GS	No.	Yds.	Avg.	TD	No.
1994—New Orleans NFL	13	7	1	0	0.0	0	1.0
1995—New Orleans NFL	7	6	1	6	6.0	0	1.0
1996—New Orleans NFL	16	13	1	11	11.0	0	1.0
1997—New Orleans NFL	16	16	2	21	10.5	0	2.5
Pro totals (4 years)	52	42	5	38	7.6	0	5.5

TUCKER, RYAN — C — RAMS

PERSONAL: Born June 12, 1975, in Midland, Texas. ... 6-5/305. ... Full name: Ryan Huey Tucker.
HIGH SCHOOL: Lee (Midland, Texas).
COLLEGE: Texas Christian.
TRANSACTIONS/CAREER NOTES: Selected by St. Louis Rams in fourth round (112th pick overall) of 1997 NFL draft. ... Signed by Rams (July 3, 1997). ... On physically unable to perform list with knee injury (August 19-October 29, 1997).
PLAYING EXPERIENCE: St. Louis NFL, 1997. ... Games/Games started: 7/0.

TUGGLE, JESSIE — LB — FALCONS

PERSONAL: Born April 4, 1965, in Spalding County, Ga. ... 5-11/230. ... Full name: Jessie Lloyd Tuggle.
HIGH SCHOOL: Griffin (Ga.).
COLLEGE: Valdosta (Ga.) State.
TRANSACTIONS/CAREER NOTES: Signed as non-drafted free agent by Atlanta Falcons (May 2, 1987). ... Granted free agency (February 1, 1991). ... Re-signed by Falcons (August 7, 1991). ... On reserve/did not report list (July 23-August 30, 1993). ... Granted roster exemption (August 30-September 3, 1993).
HONORS: Played in Pro Bowl (1992, 1994, 1995 and 1997 seasons).
RECORDS: Holds NFL career record for most touchdowns by recovery of opponents' fumbles—4. ... Shares NFL career record for most touchdowns by fumble recovery—4.
PRO STATISTICS: 1988—Recovered one fumble for two yards and one touchdown. 1989—Recovered one fumble. 1990—Recovered two fumbles for 65 yards and a touchdown. 1991—Recovered two fumbles for 18 yards and one touchdown. 1992—Recovered one fumble for 69 yards and a touchdown. 1993—Recovered one fumble. 1994—Recovered one fumble.

			INTERCEPTIONS				SACKS
Year Team	G	GS	No.	Yds.	Avg.	TD	No.
1987—Atlanta NFL	12	4	0	0	...	0	1.0
1988—Atlanta NFL	16	8	0	0	...	0	0.0
1989—Atlanta NFL	16	16	0	0	...	0	1.0
1990—Atlanta NFL	16	14	0	0	...	0	5.0
1991—Atlanta NFL	16	16	1	21	21.0	0	1.0
1992—Atlanta NFL	15	15	1	1	1.0	0	1.0
1993—Atlanta NFL	16	16	0	0	...	0	2.0
1994—Atlanta NFL	16	16	1	0	0.0	0	0.0
1995—Atlanta NFL	16	16	3	84	28.0	1	1.0
1996—Atlanta NFL	16	16	0	0	...	0	1.0
1997—Atlanta NFL	16	15	0	0	...	0	1.5
Pro totals (11 years)	171	152	6	106	17.7	1	14.5

TUINEI, MARK — OT

PERSONAL: Born March 31, 1960, in Nanakuli, Oahu, Hawaii. ... 6-5/314. ... Full name: Mark Pulemau Tuinei. ... Brother of Tom Tuinei, defensive end with Edmonton Eskimos of CFL (1982-1987). ... Name pronounced TOO-eh-nay.
HIGH SCHOOL: Punahou (Honolulu).
COLLEGE: UCLA, then Hawaii.
TRANSACTIONS/CAREER NOTES: Selected by Boston Breakers in 19th round (227th pick overall) of 1983 USFL draft. ... Signed as non-drafted free agent by Dallas Cowboys (April 28, 1983). ... On injured reserve with knee injury (December 2, 1987-remainder of season). ... On injured reserve with knee injury (October 19, 1988-remainder of season). ... Granted free agency (February 1, 1990). ... Re-signed by Cowboys (May 21, 1990). ... Released by Cowboys (April 14, 1998).
PLAYING EXPERIENCE: Dallas NFL, 1983-1997. ... Games/Games started: 1983 (10/0), 1984 (16/0), 1985 (16/0), 1986 (16/11), 1987 (8/8), 1988 (5/4), 1989 (16/16), 1990 (13/13), 1991 (12/12), 1992 (15/15), 1993 (16/16), 1994 (15/15), 1995 (16/16), 1996 (15/15), 1997 (6/6). Total: 195/147.
CHAMPIONSHIP GAME EXPERIENCE: Played in NFC championship game (1992-1995 seasons). ... Member of Super Bowl championship team (1992, 1993 and 1995 seasons).
HONORS: Played in Pro Bowl (1994 and 1995 seasons).
PRO STATISTICS: 1984—Credited with one sack. 1986—Returned one kickoff for no yards, fumbled once and recovered three fumbles. 1987—Recovered one fumble. 1993—Recovered one fumble.
MISCELLANEOUS: Switched from defensive lineman to offensive lineman (1985).

TUINEI, VAN — DE — CHARGERS

PERSONAL: Born February 16, 1971, in Garden Grove, Calif. ... 6-3/266. ... Full name: Vaega Van Tuinei.
HIGH SCHOOL: Westminster (Calif.).
JUNIOR COLLEGE: Golden West (Calif.) College.
COLLEGE: Arizona.
TRANSACTIONS/CAREER NOTES: Signed as non-drafted free agent by San Diego Chargers (April 21, 1997).
PLAYING EXPERIENCE: San Diego NFL, 1997. ... Games/Games started: 3/0.

TUMULTY, TOM — LB — BENGALS

PERSONAL: Born February 11, 1973, in Penn Hills, Pa. ... 6-3/247. ... Full name: Thomas Patrick Tumulty.
HIGH SCHOOL: Penn Hills (Pa.).
COLLEGE: Pittsburgh.

TRANSACTIONS/CAREER NOTES: Selected by Cincinnati Bengals in sixth round (178th pick overall) of 1996 NFL draft. ... Signed by Bengals (July 15, 1996). ... On injured reserve with foot injury (December 1, 1997-remainder of season).
PLAYING EXPERIENCE: Cincinnati NFL, 1996 and 1997. ... Games/Games started: 1996 (16/3), 1997 (11/11). Total: 27/14.
PRO STATISTICS: 1997—Credited with one sack.

TUPA, TOM — P — PATRIOTS

PERSONAL: Born February 6, 1966, in Cleveland. ... 6-4/220. ... Full name: Thomas Joseph Tupa.
HIGH SCHOOL: Brecksville (Broadview Heights, Ohio).
COLLEGE: Ohio State.
TRANSACTIONS/CAREER NOTES: Selected by Phoenix Cardinals in third round (68th pick overall) of 1988 NFL draft. ... Signed by Cardinals (July 12, 1988). ... Granted free agency (February 1, 1991). ... Re-signed by Cardinals (July 17, 1991). ... Granted unconditional free agency (February 1, 1992). ... Signed by Indianapolis Colts (March 31, 1992). ... Released by Colts (August 30, 1993). ... Signed by Cleveland Browns (November 9, 1993). ... Released by Browns (November 24, 1993). ... Re-signed by Browns (March 30, 1994). ... Granted unconditional free agency (February 16, 1996). ... Signed by New England Patriots (March 15, 1996).
CHAMPIONSHIP GAME EXPERIENCE: Played in AFC championship game (1996 season). ... Played in Super Bowl XXXI (1996 season).
PRO STATISTICS: 1988—Attempted six passes with four completions for 49 yards. 1989—Rushed 15 times for 75 yards, attempted 134 passes with 65 completions for 973 yards (three touchdowns and nine interceptions), fumbled twice and recovered one fumble for minus six yards. 1990—Rushed once for no yards and fumbled once for minus seven yards. 1991—Rushed 28 times for 97 yards and a touchdown, attempted 315 passes with 165 completions for 2,053 yards (six touchdowns and 13 interceptions), fumbled eight times and recovered two fumbles. 1992—Rushed three times for nine yards, attempted 33 passes with 17 completions for 156 yards (one touchdwon and two interceptions), fumbled once and recovered one fumble for minus one yard. 1995—Rushed once for nine yards, attempted one pass with one completion for 25 yards. 1996—Attempted two passes with no completions.
STATISTICAL PLATEAUS: 300-yard passing games: 1991 (1).
MISCELLANEOUS: Regular-season starting record as starting NFL quarterback: 4-9 (.308).

Year Team	G	GS	No.	Yds.	Avg.	Net avg.	In. 20	Blk.
1988—Phoenix NFL	2	0	0	0	...	...	0	0
1989—Phoenix NFL	14	0	6	280	46.7	39.7	2	0
1990—Phoenix NFL	15	0	0	0	...	...	0	0
1991—Phoenix NFL	11	0	0	0	...	...	0	0
1992—Indianapolis NFL	3	0	0	0	...	...	0	0
1993—Cleveland NFL					Did not play.			
1994—Cleveland NFL	16	0	80	3211	40.1	35.3	27	0
1995—Cleveland NFL	16	0	65	2831	43.6	36.2	18	0
1996—New England NFL	16	0	63	2739	43.5	36.0	14	0
1997—New England NFL	16	0	78	3569	45.8	36.1	24	1
Pro totals (9 years)	109	0	292	12630	43.3	36.0	85	1

TURK, DAN — C — REDSKINS

PERSONAL: Born June 25, 1962, in Milwaukee. ... 6-4/290. ... Full name: Daniel Anthony Turk. ... Brother of Matt Turk, punter, Washington Redskins.
HIGH SCHOOL: James Madison (Milwaukee).
COLLEGE: Drake, then Wisconsin.
TRANSACTIONS/CAREER NOTES: Selected by Jacksonville Bulls in USFL territorial draft. ... USFL rights traded by Bulls with rights to RB Marck Harrison and TE Ken Whisenhunt to Tampa Bay Bandits for rights to RB Cedric Jones, K Bobby Raymond and DB Eric Riley (January 3, 1985). ... Selected by Pittsburgh Steelers in fourth round (101st pick overall) of 1985 NFL draft. ... Signed by Steelers (July 19, 1985). ... On injured reserve with broken wrist (September 16, 1985-remainder of season). ... Traded by Steelers to Tampa Bay Buccaneers for sixth-round pick (DE Tim Johnson) in 1987 draft (April 13, 1987). ... Crossed picket line during players strike (October 14, 1987). ... On injured reserve with knee injury (October 18-November 18, 1988). ... Granted free agency (February 1, 1989). ... Rights relinquished by Buccaneers (June 6, 1989). ... Signed by Los Angeles Raiders (June 21, 1989). ... Granted free agency (February 1, 1991). ... Re-signed by Raiders (July 12, 1991). ... Granted unconditional free agency (February 17, 1994). ... Re-signed by Raiders (February 23, 1994). ... Raiders franchise moved to Oakland (July 21, 1995). ... Granted unconditional free agency (February 14, 1997). ... Signed by Washington Redskins (July 10, 1997).
PLAYING EXPERIENCE: Pittsburgh NFL, 1985 and 1986; Tampa Bay NFL, 1987 and 1988; Los Angeles Raiders NFL, 1989-1994; Oakland NFL, 1995 and 1996; Washington NFL, 1997. ... Games/Games started: 1985 (1/0), 1986 (16/4), 1987 (13/3), 1988 (12/10), 1989 (16/5), 1990 (16/0), 1991 (16/0), 1992 (16/0), 1993 (16/0), 1994 (16/0), 1995 (16/16), 1996 (16/2), 1997 (16/0). Total: 186/40.
CHAMPIONSHIP GAME EXPERIENCE: Played in AFC championship game (1990 season).
PRO STATISTICS: 1988—Fumbled once and recovered one fumble for minus 19 yards. 1989—Returned one kickoff for two yards and fumbled once for minus eight yards. 1990—Returned one kickoff for seven yards. 1991—Returned one kickoff for no yards. 1992—Returned one kickoff for three yards. 1993—Returned one kickoff for no yards and recovered one fumble. 1996—Fumbled once and recovered one fumble for minus 29 yards.

TURK, MATT — P — REDSKINS

PERSONAL: Born June 16, 1968, in Greenfield, Wis. ... 6-5/237. ... Brother of Dan Turk, center, Washington Redskins.
HIGH SCHOOL: Greenfield (Wis.).
COLLEGE: Wisconsin-Whitewater.
TRANSACTIONS/CAREER NOTES: Signed as non-drafted free agent by Green Bay Packers (July 13, 1993). ... Released by Packers (August 4, 1993). ... Signed by Los Angeles Rams (April 1994). ... Released by Rams (August 22, 1994). ... Signed by Washington Redskins (April 5, 1995).
HONORS: Played in Pro Bowl (1996 and 1997 seasons). ... Named punter on THE SPORTING NEWS NFL All-Pro team (1997).
PRO STATISTICS: 1996—Rushed once for no yards and fumbled once. 1997—Rushed once for no yards and fumbled once for minus 16 yards.

Year	Team	G	GS	No.	Yds.	Avg.	Net avg.	In. 20	Blk.
							PUNTING		
1993—						Did not play.			
1994—						Did not play.			
1995—Washington NFL		16	0	74	3140	42.4	37.7	†29	0
1996—Washington NFL		16	0	75	3386	45.1	*39.2	25	0
1997—Washington NFL		16	0	84	3788	45.1	*39.2	32	1
Pro totals (3 years)		48	0	233	10314	44.3	38.7	86	1

TURNBULL, RENALDO   DE

PERSONAL: Born January 5, 1966, in St. Thomas, Virgin Islands. ... 6-4/250. ... Full name: Renaldo Antonio Turnbull.
HIGH SCHOOL: Charlotte Amalie (St. Thomas, Virgin Islands).
COLLEGE: West Virginia (degree in communications).
TRANSACTIONS/CAREER NOTES: Selected by New Orleans Saints in first round (14th pick overall) of 1990 NFL draft. ... Signed by Saints (July 15, 1990). ... Released by Saints (August 22, 1997). ... Signed by Carolina Panthers (August 25, 1997). ... Released by Panthers (February 4, 1998).
HONORS: Played in Pro Bowl (1993 season).
PRO STATISTICS: 1990—Recovered one fumble. 1991—Recovered one fumble. 1993—Intercepted one pass for two yards and recovered two fumbles. 1995—Recovered two fumbles. 1996—Recovered one fumble.

Year	Team	G	GS	SACKS
1990—New Orleans NFL		16	6	9.0
1991—New Orleans NFL		16	0	1.0
1992—New Orleans NFL		14	0	1.5
1993—New Orleans NFL		15	14	∞13.0
1994—New Orleans NFL		16	16	6.5
1995—New Orleans NFL		15	15	7.0
1996—New Orleans NFL		12	7	6.5
1997—Carolina NFL		16	2	1.0
Pro totals (8 years)		120	60	45.5

TURNER, ERIC   S   RAIDERS

PERSONAL: Born September 20, 1968, in Ventura, Calif. ... 6-1/207. ... Full name: Eric Ray Turner.
HIGH SCHOOL: Ventura (Calif.).
COLLEGE: UCLA (degree in history, 1992).
TRANSACTIONS/CAREER NOTES: Selected by Cleveland Browns in first round (second pick overall) of 1991 NFL draft. ... Signed by Browns (July 14, 1991). ... On injured reserve with stress fracture in leg (August 28-November 2, 1991). ... Designated by Browns as transition player (February 25, 1993). ... Free agency status changed by Browns from transitional to franchise player (February 15, 1995). ... On injured reserve with back injury (December 15, 1995). ... Browns franchise moved to Baltimore and renamed Ravens for 1996 season (March 11, 1996). ... Released by Ravens (February 28, 1997). ... Signed by Oakland Raiders (April 24, 1997).
HONORS: Played in Pro Bowl (1994 and 1996 seasons).
PRO STATISTICS: 1991—Recovered one fumble. 1992—Credited with one sack and recovered two fumbles. 1994—Credited with one sack, returned one punt for no yards and recovered one fumble. 1997—Fumbled once and recovered three fumbles for 65 yards and one touchdown.

Year	Team	G	GS	No.	Yds.	Avg.	TD
					INTERCEPTIONS		
1991—Cleveland NFL		8	7	2	42	21.0	1
1992—Cleveland NFL		15	13	1	6	6.0	0
1993—Cleveland NFL		16	16	5	25	5.0	0
1994—Cleveland NFL		16	16	†9	199	22.1	1
1995—Cleveland NFL		8	8	0	0	...	0
1996—Baltimore NFL		14	14	5	1	0.2	0
1997—Oakland NFL		16	15	2	45	22.5	0
Pro totals (7 years)		93	89	24	318	13.3	2

TURNER, KEVIN   FB   EAGLES

PERSONAL: Born June 12, 1969, in Prattville, Ala. ... 6-1/231. ... Full name: Paul Kevin Turner.
HIGH SCHOOL: Prattville (Ala.).
COLLEGE: Alabama.
TRANSACTIONS/CAREER NOTES: Selected by New England Patriots in third round (71st pick overall) of 1992 NFL draft. ... Signed by Patriots (July 21, 1992). ... Granted free agency (February 17, 1995). ... Tendered offer sheet by Philadelphia Eagles (February 26, 1995). ... Patriots declined to match offer (March 2, 1995). ... On injured reserve with knee injury (September 15, 1995-remainder of season).
PRO STATISTICS: 1992—Returned one kickoff for 11 yards and recovered two fumbles. 1993—Attempted one pass without a completion and recovered two fumbles for six yards. 1994—Recovered two fumbles for minus three yards. 1997—Returned three kickoffs for 48 yards.
SINGLE GAME HIGHS (regular season): Attempts—12 (October 24, 1993 vs. Seattle; yards—63 (December 19, 1993, vs. Cleveland); rushing touchdowns—1 (September 4, 1994, vs. Miami).

Year	Team	G	GS	Att.	Yds.	Avg.	TD	No.	Yds.	Avg.	TD	TD	2pt.	Pts.	Fum.
				RUSHING				RECEIVING				TOTALS			
1992—New England NFL		16	1	10	40	4.0	0	7	52	7.4	2	2	...	12	2
1993—New England NFL		16	9	50	231	4.6	0	39	333	8.5	2	2	...	12	1
1994—New England NFL		16	9	36	111	3.1	1	52	471	9.1	2	3	0	18	4
1995—Philadelphia NFL		2	2	2	9	4.5	0	4	29	7.3	0	0	0	0	0
1996—Philadelphia NFL		16	12	18	39	2.2	0	43	409	9.5	1	1	0	6	1
1997—Philadelphia NFL		16	10	18	96	5.3	0	48	443	9.2	3	3	0	18	1
Pro totals (6 years)		82	43	134	526	3.9	1	193	1737	9.0	10	11	0	66	9

TURNER, SCOTT   CB   REDSKINS

PERSONAL: Born February 26, 1972, in Richardson, Texas. ... 5-10/180.
HIGH SCHOOL: J.J. Pearce (Richardson, Texas).
COLLEGE: Illinois.
TRANSACTIONS/CAREER NOTES: Selected by Washington Redskins in seventh round (226th pick overall) of 1995 NFL draft. ... Signed by Redskins (July 18, 1995). ... On injured reserve with ankle injury (December 11, 1997-remainder of season). ... Granted free agency (February 13, 1998). ... Re-signed by Redskins (April 30, 1998).
PRO STATISTICS: 1995—Returned one punt for no yards, credited with one sack, fumbled once and recovered one fumble. 1996—Recovered one fumble in end zone for a touchdown.

			INTERCEPTIONS			
Year Team	G	GS	No.	Yds.	Avg.	TD
1995—Washington NFL	16	0	1	0	0.0	0
1996—Washington NFL	16	0	2	16	8.0	0
1997—Washington NFL	9	0	0	0	...	0
Pro totals (3 years)	41	0	3	16	5.3	0

TUTEN, RICK   P   RAMS

PERSONAL: Born January 5, 1965, in Perry, Fla. ... 6-2/221. ... Full name: Richard Lamar Tuten. ... Name pronounced TOOT-en.
HIGH SCHOOL: Forest (Ocala, Fla.).
COLLEGE: Miami (Fla.), then Florida State (degree in economics, 1986).
TRANSACTIONS/CAREER NOTES: Signed as non-drafted free agent by San Diego Chargers (May 10, 1988). ... Released by Chargers (August 23, 1988). ... Signed by Washington Redskins (June 2, 1989). ... Released by Redskins (August 27, 1989). ... Signed by Philadelphia Eagles (December 13, 1989). ... Granted unconditional free agency (February 1, 1990). ... Signed by Buffalo Bills (March 28, 1990). ... Released by Bills (August 15, 1990). ... Re-signed by Bills (September 19, 1990). ... Granted unconditional free agency (February 1-April 1, 1991). ... Re-signed by Bills for 1991 season. ... Released by Bills (August 20, 1991). ... Signed by Green Bay Packers (August 27, 1991). ... Released by Packers (August 30, 1991). ... Signed by Seattle Seahawks (October 9, 1991). ... Granted unconditional free agency (February 1-April 1, 1992). ... Re-signed by Seahawks for 1992 season. ... Granted unconditional free agency (February 16, 1996). ... Re-signed by Seahawks (August 12, 1996). ... On injured reserve with pelvis injury (December 5, 1997-remainder of season). ... Granted unconditional free agency (February 13, 1998). ... Signed by St. Louis Rams (March 6, 1998).
CHAMPIONSHIP GAME EXPERIENCE: Played in AFC championship game (1990 season). ... Played in Super Bowl XXV (1990 season).
HONORS: Played in Pro Bowl (1994 season).
PRO STATISTICS: 1992—Attempted one pass without a completion, rushed once for no yards, fumbled twice and recovered two fumbles for minus nine yards. 1993—Attempted one pass without a completion. 1994—Credited with one two-point conversion and attempted one pass without a completion.

			PUNTING					
Year Team	G	GS	No.	Yds.	Avg.	Net avg.	In. 20	Blk.
1988—				Did not play.				
1989—Philadelphia NFL	2	0	7	256	36.6	33.6	1	0
1990—Buffalo NFL	14	0	53	2107	39.8	34.2	12	0
1991—Seattle NFL	10	0	49	2106	43.0	36.8	8	0
1992—Seattle NFL	16	0	*108	*4760	44.1	38.7	*29	0
1993—Seattle NFL	16	0	▲90	*4007	44.5	37.2	21	1
1994—Seattle NFL	16	0	91	3905	42.9	36.7	33	0
1995—Seattle NFL	16	0	83	3735	*45.0	36.5	21	0
1996—Seattle NFL	16	0	85	3746	44.1	34.5	20	1
1997—Seattle NFL	11	0	48	2007	41.8	36.4	15	0
Pro totals (9 years)	117	0	614	26629	43.4	36.5	160	2

TWYNER, GUNNARD   WR   SAINTS

PERSONAL: Born July 14, 1973, in Bettendorf, Iowa. ... 5-10/165.
HIGH SCHOOL: Pleasant Valley (Iowa).
COLLEGE: Western Illinois.
TRANSACTIONS/CAREER NOTES: Signed as non-drafted free agent by Cincinnati Bengals (April 23, 1996). ... Released by Bengals (August 24, 1996). ... Re-signed by Bengals to practice squad (August 26, 1996). ... Released by Bengals (September 27, 1997). ... Signed by New Orleans Saints to practice squad (October 1, 1997). ... Activated (December 12, 1997).
PLAYING EXPERIENCE: Cincinnati (2)-New Orleans (2) NFL, 1997. ... Games/Games started: 1997 (Cin.-2/0; N.O.-2/0; Total: 4/0).
PRO STATISTICS: 1997—Caught four passes for 45 yards and returned four kickoffs for 72 yards.
SINGLE GAME HIGHS (regular season): Receptions—3 (September 7, 1997, vs. Baltimore); yards—41 (September 7, 1997, vs. Baltimore); and touchdown receptions—0.

TYLSKI, RICH   G/C   JAGUARS

PERSONAL: Born February 27, 1971, in San Diego. ... 6-5/306. ... Full name: Richard Lee Tylski. ... Name pronounced TILL-skee.
HIGH SCHOOL: Madison (San Diego).
COLLEGE: Utah State.
TRANSACTIONS/CAREER NOTES: Signed as non-drafted free agent by New England Patriots (April 25, 1994). ... Released by Patriots (August 20, 1994). ... Re-signed by Patriots to practice squad (August 30, 1994). ... Claimed on waivers by Jacksonville Jaguars (July 26, 1995). ... Released by Jaguars (August 27, 1995). ... Re-signed by Jaguars to practice squad (August 28, 1995). ... Activated (September 1, 1996).
PLAYING EXPERIENCE: Jacksonville NFL, 1996 and 1997. ... Games/Games started: 1996 (16/7), 1997 (13/13). Total: 29/20.

UHLENHAKE, JEFF   C   REDSKINS

PERSONAL: Born January 28, 1966, in Indianapolis. ... 6-3/291. ... Full name: Jeffrey Alan Uhlenhake. ... Name pronounced you-lun-HAKE.
HIGH SCHOOL: Newark (Ohio) Catholic.
COLLEGE: Ohio State.
TRANSACTIONS/CAREER NOTES: Selected by Miami Dolphins in fifth round (121st pick overall) of 1989 NFL draft. ... Signed by Dolphins (July 21, 1989). ... Granted free agency (February 1, 1991). ... Re-signed by Dolphins (September 3, 1991). ... Activated (September 7, 1991). ... Granted free agency (March 1, 1993). ... Re-signed by Dolphins (August 3, 1993). ... On physically unable to perform list (August 3-August 30, 1993). ... On injured reserve with knee injury (November 10, 1993-remainder of season). ... Granted unconditional free agency (February 17, 1994). ... Signed by New Orleans Saints (April 22, 1994). ... Granted unconditional free agency (February 16, 1996). ... Signed by Washington Redskins (August 25, 1996). ... Granted unconditional free agency (February 14, 1997). ... Re-signed by Redskins (May 6, 1997).
PLAYING EXPERIENCE: Miami NFL, 1989-1993; New Orleans NFL, 1994 and 1995; Washington NFL, 1996 and 1997. ... Games/Games started: 1989 (16/15), 1990 (16/16), 1991 (13/10), 1992 (13/13), 1993 (5/5), 1994 (16/15), 1995 (14/14), 1996 (12/11), 1997 (14/13). Total: 119/112.
CHAMPIONSHIP GAME EXPERIENCE: Played in AFC championship game (1992 season).
HONORS: Named center on THE SPORTING NEWS college All-America first team (1988).
PRO STATISTICS: 1989—Fumbled once for minus 19 yards. 1992—Fumbled once and recovered two fumbles for minus four yards.

UNUTOA, MORRIS   C   EAGLES

PERSONAL: Born March 10, 1971, in Torrance, Calif. ... 6-1/284.
HIGH SCHOOL: Carson (Calif.).
COLLEGE: Brigham Young.
TRANSACTIONS/CAREER NOTES: Signed as non-drafted free agent by Philadelphia Eagles (April 26, 1996).
PLAYING EXPERIENCE: Philadelphia NFL, 1996 and 1997. ... Games/Games started: 1996 (16/0), 1997 (16/0). Total: 32/0.
PRO STATISTICS: 1996—Fumbled once.

UNVERZAGT, ERIC   LB   SEAHAWKS

PERSONAL: Born December 18, 1972, in Central Islip, N.Y. ... 6-1/241. ... Name pronounced UN-ver-zott.
HIGH SCHOOL: Central Islip (N.Y.).
COLLEGE: Wisconsin.
TRANSACTIONS/CAREER NOTES: Selected by Seattle Seahawks in fourth round (131st pick overall) of 1996 NFL draft. ... Signed by Seahawks (July 17, 1996). ... Assigned by Seahawks to Scottish Claymores in 1997 World League enhancement allocation program (February 19, 1997). ... Released by Seahawks (August 24, 1997). ... Re-signed by Seahawks (December 10, 1997). ... Granted free agency (February 13, 1998).
PLAYING EXPERIENCE: Seattle NFL, 1996 and 1997; Scotland W.L., 1997. ... Games/Games started: 1996 (8/0), 1997 (W.L.-games played unavailable; NFL-1/0). Total: 9/0.
PRO STATISTICS: W.L.: 1997—Returned one kickoff for no yards.

UPSHAW, REGAN   DE   BUCCANEERS

PERSONAL: Born August 12, 1975, in Detroit. ... 6-4/268. ... Full name: Regan Charles Upshaw.
HIGH SCHOOL: Pittsburg (Calif.).
COLLEGE: California.
TRANSACTIONS/CAREER NOTES: Selected after junior season by Tampa Bay Buccaneers in first round (12th pick overall) of 1996 NFL draft. ... Signed by Buccaneers (July 21, 1996).
PRO STATISTICS: 1996—Recovered one fumble. 1997—Recovered one fumble.

Year Team	G	GS	SACKS
1996—Tampa Bay NFL	16	16	4.0
1997—Tampa Bay NFL	15	15	7.5
Pro totals (2 years)	31	31	11.5

UWAEZUOKE, IHEANYI   WR   49ERS

PERSONAL: Born July 24, 1973, in Lagos, Nigeria ... 6-2/198. ... Name pronounced ee-HAHN-ee ooh-WAY-zoh-kay.
HIGH SCHOOL: Harvard (North Hollywood, Calif.).
COLLEGE: California.
TRANSACTIONS/CAREER NOTES: Selected by San Francisco 49ers in fifth round (160th pick overall) of 1996 NFL draft. ... Signed by 49ers (July 18, 1996).
CHAMPIONSHIP GAME EXPERIENCE: Played in NFC championship game (1997 season).
PRO STATISTICS: 1997—Recovered two fumbles.
SINGLE GAME HIGHS (regular season): Receptions—3 (November 2, 1997, vs. Dallas); yards—41 (September 21, 1997, vs. Atlanta); and touchdown receptions—1 (November 10, 1996, vs. Dallas).

Year Team	G	GS	RECEIVING No.	RECEIVING Yds.	RECEIVING Avg.	RECEIVING TD	PUNT RETURNS No.	PUNT RETURNS Yds.	PUNT RETURNS Avg.	PUNT RETURNS TD	KICKOFF RETURNS No.	KICKOFF RETURNS Yds.	KICKOFF RETURNS Avg.	KICKOFF RETURNS TD	TOTALS TD	TOTALS 2pt.	TOTALS Pts.	TOTALS Fum.
1996—San Francisco NFL	14	0	7	91	13.0	1	0	0		0	1	21	21.0	0	1	0	6	0
1997—San Francisco NFL	14	0	14	165	11.8	0	34	373	11.0	0	6	131	21.8	0	0	0	0	4
Pro totals (2 years)	28	0	21	256	12.2	1	34	373	11.0	0	7	152	21.7	0	1	0	6	4

VAN DYKE, ALEX   WR   JETS

PERSONAL: Born July 24, 1974, in Sacramento. ... 6-0/200. ... Full name: Frank Alexander Van Dyke.
HIGH SCHOOL: Luther Burbank (Sacramento).

JUNIOR COLLEGE: Sacramento City College.
COLLEGE: Nevada.
TRANSACTIONS/CAREER NOTES: Selected by New York Jets in second round (31st pick overall) of 1996 NFL draft. ... Signed by Jets (July 15, 1996).
HONORS: Named wide receiver on THE SPORTING NEWS college All-America second team (1995).
SINGLE GAME HIGHS (regular season): Receptions—4 (October 13, 1996, vs. Jacksonville); yards—35 (December 7, 1997, vs. Indianapolis); and touchdown receptions—2 (December 7, 1997, vs. Indianapolis).

			RECEIVING				KICKOFF RETURNS				TOTALS			
Year Team	G	GS	No.	Yds.	Avg.	TD	No.	Yds.	Avg.	TD	TD	2pt.	Pts.	Fum.
1996—New York Jets NFL	15	1	17	118	6.9	1	15	289	19.3	0	1	0	6	0
1997—New York Jets NFL	5	0	3	53	17.7	2	6	138	23.0	0	2	0	12	0
Pro totals (2 years)	20	1	20	171	8.6	3	21	427	20.3	0	3	0	18	0

VANOVER, TAMARICK   WR/KR   CHIEFS

PERSONAL: Born February 25, 1974, in Tallahassee, Fla. ... 5-11/218. ... Name pronounced tom-ARE-ik.
HIGH SCHOOL: Leon (Tallahassee, Fla.).
COLLEGE: Florida State
TRANSACTIONS/CAREER NOTES: Signed after sophomore season with Las Vegas Posse of CFL (February 10, 1994). ... Selected by Kansas City Chiefs in third round (81st pick overall) of 1995 NFL draft. ... Signed by Chiefs for 1995 season.
HONORS: Named kick returner on THE SPORTING NEWS college All-America first team (1992). ... Named kick returner on THE SPORTING NEWS college All-America second team (1993).
PRO STATISTICS: CFL: 1994—Returned four unsuccessful field-goals for 31 yards, fumbled three times and recovered one fumble. NFL: 1996—Fumbled once. 1997—Fumbled six times and recovered one fumble.
SINGLE GAME HIGHS (regular season): Receptions—7 (September 1, 1996, vs. Houston); yards—85 (November 23, 1995, vs. Dallas); and touchdown receptions—1 (September 1, 1996, vs. Houston).

			RUSHING				RECEIVING				PUNT RETURNS				KICKOFF RETURNS				TOTALS		
Year Team	G	GS	Att.	Yds.	Avg.	TD	No.	Yds.	Avg.	TD	No.	Yds.	Avg.	TD	No.	Yds.	Avg.	TD	TD	2pt.	Pts.
1994—Las Vegas CFL	15	...	1	6	6.0	0	23	385	16.7	3	36	341	9.5	1	31	718	23.2	1	5	1	32
1995—Kansas City NFL	15	0	6	31	5.2	0	11	231	21.0	2	51	*540	10.6	†1	43	1095	25.5	†2	5	0	30
1996—Kansas City NFL	13	6	4	6	1.5	0	21	241	11.5	1	17	116	6.8	0	33	854	§25.9	▲1	2	0	12
1997—Kansas City NFL	16	0	5	50	10.0	0	7	92	13.1	0	35	383	10.9	1	51	1308	25.6	▲1	2	1	14
CFL totals (1 year)	15	...	1	6	6.0	0	23	385	16.7	3	36	341	9.5	1	31	718	23.2	1	5	1	32
NFL totals (3 years)	44	6	15	87	5.8	0	39	564	14.5	3	103	1039	10.1	2	127	3257	25.6	4	9	1	56
Pro totals (4 years)	59	...	16	93	5.8	0	62	949	15.3	6	139	1380	9.9	3	158	3975	25.2	5	14	2	88

VAN PELT, ALEX   QB   BILLS

PERSONAL: Born May 1, 1970, in Graffton, W.Va. ... 6-0/220. ... Full name: Gregory Alexander Van Pelt.
HIGH SCHOOL: Grafton (W.Va.), then Winston Churchill (San Antonio).
COLLEGE: Pittsburgh.
TRANSACTIONS/CAREER NOTES: Selected by Pittsburgh Steelers in eighth round (216th pick overall) of 1993 NFL draft. ... Released by Steelers (August 30, 1993). ... Signed by Kansas City Chiefs to practice squad (November 3, 1993). ... Activated (November 8, 1993); did not play. ... Released by Chiefs (November 17, 1993). ... Re-signed by Chiefs (May 18, 1994). ... Released by Chiefs (August 23, 1994). ... Signed by Buffalo Bills to practice squad (December 14, 1994). ... Activated (December 17, 1994); did not play.
PRO STATISTICS: 1997—Fumbled three times and recovered three fumbles for minus seven yards.
SINGLE GAME HIGHS (regular season): Attempts—44 (December 20, 1997, vs. Green Bay); completions—23 (December 20, 1997, vs. Green Bay); yards—255 (December 20, 1997, vs. Green Bay); and touchdown passes—2 (October 26, 1997, vs. Denver).
MISCELLANEOUS: Regular-season record as starting NFL quarterback: 1-2 (.333).

			PASSING								RUSHING				TOTALS		
Year Team	G	GS	Att.	Cmp.	Pct.	Yds.	TD	Int.	Avg.	Rat.	Att.	Yds.	Avg.	TD	TD	2pt.	Pts.
1995—Buffalo NFL	1	0	18	10	55.6	106	2	0	5.89	110.0	0	0	...	0	0	0	0
1996—Buffalo NFL	1	0	5	2	40.0	9	0	0	1.80	47.9	3	-5	-1.7	0	0	0	0
1997—Buffalo NFL	6	3	124	60	48.4	684	2	10	5.52	37.2	11	33	3.0	1	1	0	6
Pro totals (3 years)	8	3	147	72	49.0	799	4	10	5.44	46.3	14	28	2.0	1	1	0	6

VARDELL, TOMMY   FB   LIONS

PERSONAL: Born February 20, 1969, in El Cajon, Calif. ... 6-2/230. ... Full name: Thomas Arthur Vardell.
HIGH SCHOOL: Granite Hills (El Cajon, Calif.).
COLLEGE: Stanford (degree in industrial engineering, 1992).
TRANSACTIONS/CAREER NOTES: Selected by Cleveland Browns in first round (ninth pick overall) of 1992 NFL draft. ... Signed by Browns (July 26, 1992). ... On injured reserve with calf injury (December 26, 1992-remainder of season). ... On injured reserve with knee injury (October 5, 1994-remainder of season). ... On physically unable to perform list with knee injury (July 17-23, 1995). ... Granted unconditional free agency (February 16, 1996). ... Signed by San Francisco 49ers (March 25, 1996). ... Released by 49ers (February 13, 1997). ... Signed by Detroit Lions (April 23, 1997).
PRO STATISTICS: 1992—Returned two kickoffs for 14 yards. 1993—Returned four kickoffs for 58 yards. 1997—Returned one kickoff for 15 yards and recovered one fumble.
SINGLE GAME HIGHS (regular season): Attempts—25 (October 17, 1993, vs. Cincinnati); yards—104 (September 19, 1993, vs. Los Angeles Raiders); and rushing touchdowns—3 (November 16, 1997, vs. Minnesota).
STATISTICAL PLATEAUS: 100-yard rushing games: 1993 (1).

V

Year Team	G	GS	RUSHING				RECEIVING				TOTALS			
			Att.	Yds.	Avg.	TD	No.	Yds.	Avg.	TD	TD	2pt.	Pts.	Fum.
1992—Cleveland NFL	14	10	99	369	3.7	0	13	128	9.8	0	0	...	0	0
1993—Cleveland NFL	16	12	171	644	3.8	3	19	151	7.9	1	4	...	24	3
1994—Cleveland NFL	5	5	15	48	3.2	0	16	137	8.6	1	1	0	6	0
1995—Cleveland NFL	5	0	4	9	2.3	0	6	18	3.0	0	0	0	0	0
1996—San Francisco NFL	11	7	58	192	3.3	2	28	179	6.4	0	2	0	12	0
1997—Detroit NFL	16	10	32	122	3.8	6	16	218	13.6	0	6	0	36	1
Pro totals (6 years)	67	44	379	1384	3.7	11	98	831	8.5	2	13	0	78	4

VAUGHN, LEE   CB   COWBOYS

PERSONAL: Born November 27, 1974, in Little Rock, Ark. ... 5-11/184.
HIGH SCHOOL: Cheyenne (Wyo.) East.
COLLEGE: Wyoming.
TRANSACTIONS/CAREER NOTES: Selected by Dallas Cowboys in sixth round (187th pick overall) of 1997 NFL draft. ... Signed by Cowboys (July 14, 1997). ... On injured reserve with knee injury (July 26, 1997-entire season).

VELAND, TONY   S   BRONCOS

PERSONAL: Born March 11, 1973, in Omaha, Neb. ... 6-1/209.
HIGH SCHOOL: Benson (Omaha, Neb.).
COLLEGE: Nebraska.
TRANSACTIONS/CAREER NOTES: Selected by Denver Broncos in sixth round (181st pick overall) of 1996 NFL draft. ... Signed by Broncos (July 16, 1996). ... Released by Broncos (August 25, 1996). ... Re-signed by Broncos to practice squad (August 27, 1996).
PLAYING EXPERIENCE: Denver NFL, 1997. ... Games/Games started: 12/0.
CHAMPIONSHIP GAME EXPERIENCE: Played in AFC championship game (1997 season). ... Member of Super Bowl championship team (1997 season).
PRO STATISTICS: 1997—Recovered one fumble.

VERBA, ROSS   OT   PACKERS

PERSONAL: Born October 31, 1973, in Des Moines, Iowa. ... 6-4/299. ... Full name: Ross Robert Verba.
HIGH SCHOOL: Dowling (West Des Moines, Iowa).
COLLEGE: Iowa.
TRANSACTIONS/CAREER NOTES: Selected by Green Bay Packers in first round (30th pick overall) of 1997 NFL draft. ... Signed by Packers (July 31, 1997).
PLAYING EXPERIENCE: Green Bay NFL, 1997. ... Games/Games started: 16/11.
CHAMPIONSHIP GAME EXPERIENCE: Played in NFC championship game (1997 season). ... Played in Super Bowl XXXII (1997 season).

VERSTEGEN, MIKE   G/OT   SAINTS

PERSONAL: Born October 24, 1971, in Appleton, Wis. ... 6-6/311. ... Full name: Mike Robert Verstegen. ... Name pronounced ver-STAY-gun.
HIGH SCHOOL: Kimberly (Wis.).
COLLEGE: Wisconsin.
TRANSACTIONS/CAREER NOTES: Selected by New Orleans Saints in third round (75th pick overall) of 1995 NFL draft. ... Signed by Saints (July 20, 1995). ... Inactive for 13 games (1995). ... Granted free agency (February 13, 1998). ... Re-signed by Saints (April 27, 1998).
PLAYING EXPERIENCE: New Orleans NFL, 1996 and 1997. ... Games/Games started: 1996 (8/4), 1997 (14/8). Total: 22/12.

V

VICKERS, KIPP   OT/G   COLTS

PERSONAL: Born August 27, 1969, in Holiday, Fla. ... 6-2/298. ... Full name: Kipp E. Vickers.
HIGH SCHOOL: Tarpon Springs (Fla.).
COLLEGE: Miami (Fla.).
TRANSACTIONS/CAREER NOTES: Signed as non-drafted free agent by Indianapolis Colts (April 30, 1993). ... Released by Colts (August 30, 1993). ... Re-signed by Colts to practice squad (September 1, 1993). ... Activated (December 21, 1993); did not play. ... Released by Colts (August 28, 1994). ... Re-signed by Colts to practice squad (August 31, 1994). ... Released by Colts (November 1, 1994). ... Re-signed by Colts to practice squad (November 16, 1994). ... Activated (December 24, 1994); did not play. ... Assigned by Colts to Frankfurt Galaxy in 1995 World League enhancement allocation program (February 20, 1995). ... Released by Colts (February 4, 1998). ... Re-signed by Colts for 1997 season. ... Granted free agency (February 13, 1998). ... Re-signed by Colts (February 24, 1998).
PLAYING EXPERIENCE: Frankfurt W.L., 1995; Indianapolis NFL, 1995-1997. ... Games/Games started: 1995 (W.L.-games played unavailable; NFL-9/0; Total: games played unavailable), 1996 (10/6), 1997 (9/0). Total W.L.: games played unavailable; Total NFL: 28/6.
CHAMPIONSHIP GAME EXPERIENCE: Played in AFC championship game (1995 season).

VILLA, DANNY   G

PERSONAL: Born September 21, 1964, in Nogales, Ariz. ... 6-5/308. ... Full name: Daniel Villa. ... Name pronounced VEE-uh.
HIGH SCHOOL: Nogales (Ariz.).
COLLEGE: Arizona State.

TRANSACTIONS/CAREER NOTES: Selected by New England Patriots in fifth round (113th pick overall) of 1987 NFL draft. ... Signed by Patriots (July 25, 1987). ... On injured reserve with ankle injury (October 4-November 8, 1991). ... On injured reserve with ankle injury (December 11, 1991-remainder of season). ... Traded by Patriots to Phoenix Cardinals for sixth-round pick (traded to Detroit) in 1992 draft (January 30, 1992). ... Granted unconditional free agency (March 1, 1993). ... Signed by Kansas City Chiefs (April 19, 1993). ... Granted unconditional free agency (February 14, 1997). ... Signed by Oakland Raiders (April 1, 1997). ... Released by Raiders (August 24, 1997). ... Signed by Patriots (November 6 ,1997). ... Granted unconditional free agency (February 13, 1998).

PLAYING EXPERIENCE: New England NFL, 1987-1991 and 1997; Phoenix NFL, 1992; Kansas City NFL, 1993-1996. ... Games/Games started: 1987 (11/7), 1988 (16/14), 1989 (15/15), 1990 (16/16), 1991 (10/10), 1992 (16/12), 1993 (13/3), 1994 (14/0), 1995 (16/0), 1996 (16/0), 1997 (7/0). Total: 150/77.

CHAMPIONSHIP GAME EXPERIENCE: Played in AFC championship game (1993 season).

PRO STATISTICS: 1987—Fumbled once for minus 13 yards. 1988—Fumbled once for minus 39 yards. 1990—Recovered one fumble. 1991—Recovered two fumbles.

VILLARRIAL, CHRIS　　　　C　　　　BEARS

PERSONAL: Born June 9, 1973, in Hummelstown, Pa. ... 6-4/310. ... Name pronounced vill-uh-ree-AL.
HIGH SCHOOL: Hershey (Pa.).
COLLEGE: Indiana (Pa.).
TRANSACTIONS/CAREER NOTES: Selected by Chicago Bears in fifth round (152nd pick overall) of 1996 NFL draft. ... Signed by Bears (July 11, 1996).
PLAYING EXPERIENCE: Chicago NFL, 1996 and 1997. ... Games/Games started: 1996 (14/8), 1997 (11/11). Total: 25/19.

VINATIERI, ADAM　　　　K　　　　PATRIOTS

PERSONAL: Born December 28, 1972, in Yunkton, S.D. ... 6-0/200.
HIGH SCHOOL: Rapid City (S.D.) Central.
COLLEGE: South Dakota State (degree in fitness and wellness).
TRANSACTIONS/CAREER NOTES: Signed by Amsterdam Admirals of World League (March 1996). ... Signed by New England Patriots (June 28, 1996).
CHAMPIONSHIP GAME EXPERIENCE: Played in AFC championship game (1996 season). ... Played in Super Bowl XXXI (1996 season).
PRO STATISTICS: 1996—Punted once for 27 yards.

Year Team	G	GS	KICKING						
			XPM	XPA	FGM	FGA	Lg.	50+	Pts.
1996—Amsterdam W.L.	10	0	4	4	9	10	43	0-0	31
—New England NFL	16	0	39	42	27	35	50	1-2	120
1997—New England NFL	16	0	40	40	25	29	52	1-1	115
W.L. totals (1 year)	10	0	4	4	9	10	43	0-0	31
NFL totals (2 years)	32	0	79	82	52	64	52	2-3	235
Pro totals (3 years)	42	0	83	86	61	74	52	2-0	266

VINCENT, TROY　　　　CB　　　　EAGLES

PERSONAL: Born June 8, 1970, in Trenton, N.J. ... 6-0/194. ... Full name: Troy D. Vincent. ... Nephew of Steve Luke, safety with Green Bay Packers (1975-1980).
HIGH SCHOOL: Pennsbury (Fairless Hills, Pa.).
COLLEGE: Wisconsin.
TRANSACTIONS/CAREER NOTES: Selected by Miami Dolphins in first round (seventh pick overall) of 1992 NFL draft. ... Signed by Dolphins (August 8, 1992). ... Designated by Dolphins as transition player (February 25, 1993). ... On injured reserve with knee injury (December 15, 1993-remainder of season). ... Tendered offer sheet by Philadelphia Eagles (February 24, 1996). ... Dolphins declined to match offer (March 3, 1996).
CHAMPIONSHIP GAME EXPERIENCE: Played in AFC championship game (1992 season).
HONORS: Named defensive back on THE SPORTING NEWS college All-America first team (1991).
RECORDS: Holds NFL record for longest interception return for a touchdown—104 yards (November 3, 1996; with lateral from LB James Willis).
PRO STATISTICS: 1992—Returned five punts for 16 yards and recovered two fumbles. 1993—Recovered one fumble. 1994—Ran 58 yards with lateral from interception for a touchdown. 1996—Ran minus two yards with lateral from punt return. 1997—Returned one punt for minus eight yards, fumbled once and recovered two fumbles for five yards.

Year Team	G	GS	INTERCEPTIONS			
			No.	Yds.	Avg.	TD
1992—Miami NFL	15	14	2	47	23.5	0
1993—Miami NFL	13	13	2	29	14.5	0
1994—Miami NFL	13	12	5	113	22.6	1
1995—Miami NFL	16	16	5	95	19.0	▲1
1996—Philadelphia NFL	16	16	3	144	48.0	1
1997—Philadelphia NFL	16	16	3	14	4.7	0
Pro totals (6 years)	89	87	20	442	22.1	3

VINSON, TONY　　　　RB　　　　RAVENS

PERSONAL: Born March 13, 1971, in Frankfurt, West Germany ... 6-1/229. ... Full name: Anthony Cho Vinson.
HIGH SCHOOL: Denbigh (Newport News, Va.).
COLLEGE: Towson State.
TRANSACTIONS/CAREER NOTES: Selected by San Diego Chargers in fifth round (160th pick overall) of 1994 NFL draft. ... Signed by Chargers (July 14, 1994). ... Released by Chargers (August 22, 1994). ... Re-signed by Chargers to practice squad (August 29, 1994). ... Granted free agency after 1994 season. ... Signed by Atlanta Falcons (April 13, 1995). ... Released by Falcons (August 21, 1995). ... Re-signed by Falcons to practice squad (August 29, 1995). ... Assigned by Falcons to London Monarchs in 1996 World League enhancement allocation program (February 19, 1996). ... Released by Falcons (August 5, 1996). ... Signed by Baltimore Ravens (July 9, 1997).

V

PLAYING EXPERIENCE: London W.L., 1996 and 1997; Baltimore NFL, 1997. ... Games/Games started: 1996 (W.L.-games played unavailable), 1997 (W.L.-games played unavailable; NFL-13/0).
PRO STATISTICS: W.L.: 1996—Rushed 105 times for 516 yards and three touchdowns and caught 25 passes for 169 yards and two touchdowns. 1997—Rushed 67 times for 163 yards and one touchdown and caught three passes for minus five yards.

VON DER AHE, SCOTT   LB   COLTS

PERSONAL: Born October 12, 1975, in Lancaster, Calif. ... 5-11/242. ... Full name: Scott Fraser Von Der Ahe. ... Name pronounced VON-der-ah-hee.
HIGH SCHOOL: Mission Viejo (Calif.).
JUNIOR COLLEGE: Saddleback Community College (Calif.).
COLLEGE: Arizona State.
TRANSACTIONS/CAREER NOTES: Selected by Indianapolis Colts in sixth round (182nd pick overall) of 1997 NFL draft. ... Signed by Colts for 1997 season.
PLAYING EXPERIENCE: Indianapolis NFL, 1997. ... Games/Games started: 9/2.

VON OELHOFFEN, KIMO   NT   BENGALS

PERSONAL: Born January 30, 1971, in Kaunakaki, Hawaii. ... 6-4/305. ... Full name: Kimo K. von Oelhoffen.
HIGH SCHOOL: Malokai (Hoolehua, Hawaii).
JUNIOR COLLEGE: Walla Walla (Wash.) Community College.
COLLEGE: Hawaii, then Boise State.
TRANSACTIONS/CAREER NOTES: Selected by Cincinnati Bengals in sixth round (162nd pick overall) of 1994 NFL draft. ... Signed by Bengals (May 9, 1994).
PLAYING EXPERIENCE: Cincinnati NFL, 1994-1997. ... Games/Games started: 1994 (7/0), 1995 (16/0), 1996 (11/1), 1997 (13/12). Total: 47/13.
PRO STATISTICS: 1995—Returned one kickoff for 10 yards. 1996—Credited with one sack.

VRABEL, MIKE   DE   STEELERS

PERSONAL: Born August 14, 1975, in Akron, Ohio. ... 6-4/275. ... Full name: Michael George Vrabel.
HIGH SCHOOL: Walsh Jesuit (Stow, Ohio).
COLLEGE: Ohio State.
TRANSACTIONS/CAREER NOTES: Selected by Pittsburgh Steelers in third round (91st pick overall) of 1997 NFL draft. ... Signed by Steelers (July 15, 1997).
CHAMPIONSHIP GAME EXPERIENCE: Played in AFC championship game (1997 season).
PRO STATISTICS: 1997—Returned one kickoff for no yards and recovered one fumble.

Year Team	G	GS	SACKS
1997—Pittsburgh NFL	15	0	1.5

WAINRIGHT, FRANK   TE   DOLPHINS

PERSONAL: Born October 10, 1967, in Peoria, Ill. ... 6-3/250. ... Full name: Frank Wesley Wainright.
HIGH SCHOOL: Pomona (Arvada, Colo.).
COLLEGE: Northern Colorado.
TRANSACTIONS/CAREER NOTES: Selected by New Orleans Saints in eighth round (210th pick overall) of 1991 NFL draft. ... Signed by Saints (July 14, 1991). ... Released by Saints (August 26, 1991). ... Re-signed by Saints to practice squad (August 28, 1991). ... Activated (September 14, 1991). ... Granted unconditional free agency (February 1-April 1, 1992). ... Re-signed by Saints for 1992 season. ... Granted unconditional free agency (February 17, 1995). ... Signed by Denver Broncos (April 17, 1995). ... Released by Broncos (August 22, 1995). ... Signed by Philadelphia Eagles (August 29, 1995). ... Released by Eagles (October 25, 1995). ... Signed by Miami Dolphins (November 15, 1995). ... Granted unconditional free agency (February 16, 1996). ... Re-signed by Dolphins (March 5, 1996). ... Granted unconditional free agency (February 14, 1997). ... Re-signed by Dolphins (February 27, 1997). ... On injured reserve with chest injury (December 9, 1997-remainder of season).
PRO STATISTICS: 1995—Recovered one fumble. 1996—Returned one kickoff for 10 yards.
SINGLE GAME HIGHS (regular season): Receptions—2 (December 3, 1992, vs. Atlanta); yards—42 (December 3, 1992, vs. Atlanta); and touchdown receptions—1 (September 15, 1996, vs. New York Jets).

Year Team	G	GS	RECEIVING No.	Yds.	Avg.	TD	TOTALS TD	2pt.	Pts.	Fum.
1991—New Orleans NFL	14	2	1	3	3.0	0	0	...	0	0
1992—New Orleans NFL	13	4	9	143	15.9	0	0	...	0	0
1993—New Orleans NFL	16	2	0	0	...	0	0	...	0	0
1994—New Orleans NFL					Did not play.					
1995—Philadelphia NFL	7	0	0	0	...	0	0	0	0	0
—Miami NFL	6	0	0	0	...	0	0	0	0	0
1996—Miami NFL	16	0	1	2	2.0	1	1	0	6	0
1997—Miami NFL	9	0	0	0	...	0	0	0	0	0
Pro totals (6 years)	81	8	11	148	13.5	1	1	0	6	0

WALDROUP, KERWIN   DT   LIONS

PERSONAL: Born August 1, 1974, in Chicago. ... 6-3/260.
HIGH SCHOOL: Rich Central (Olympia Fields, Ill.).

COLLEGE: Michigan, then Central State (Ohio).
TRANSACTIONS/CAREER NOTES: Selected by Detroit Lions in fifth round (158th pick overall) of 1996 NFL draft. ... Signed by Lions (July 15, 1996). ... On injured reserve with knee injury (November 24, 1997-remainder of season).
PRO STATISTICS: 1997—Recovered one fumble.

Year Team	G	GS	SACKS
1996—Detroit NFL	16	10	2.5
1997—Detroit NFL	11	11	1.0
Pro totals (2 years)	27	21	3.5

WALKER, BRACEY   S   DOLPHINS

PERSONAL: Born October 28, 1970, in Spring Lake, N.C. ... 6-0/200. ... Full name: Bracey Wordell Walker.
HIGH SCHOOL: Pine Forest (Fayetteville, N.C.).
COLLEGE: North Carolina.
TRANSACTIONS/CAREER NOTES: Selected by Kansas City Chiefs in fourth round (127th pick overall) of 1994 NFL draft. ... Signed by Chiefs (July 20, 1994). ... Claimed on waivers by Cincinnati Bengals (October 12, 1994). ... Granted free agency (February 14, 1997). ... Re-signed by Bengals (April 18, 1997). ... Claimed on waivers by Miami Dolphins (August 20, 1997). ... On injured reserve with leg injury (December 2, 1997-remainder of season). ... Granted unconditional free agency (February 13, 1998). ... Re-signed by Dolphins (April 27, 1998).
HONORS: Named defensive back on THE SPORTING NEWS college All-America second team (1993).
PRO STATISTICS: 1995—Recovered two fumbles. 1997—Recovered one fumble.

Year Team	G	GS	INTERCEPTIONS No.	Yds.	Avg.	TD
1994—Kansas City NFL	2	0	0	0	...	0
—Cincinnati NFL	7	0	0	0	...	0
1995—Cincinnati NFL	14	14	4	56	14.0	0
1996—Cincinnati NFL	16	16	2	35	17.5	0
1997—Miami NFL	12	0	0	0	...	0
Pro totals (4 years)	49	30	6	91	15.2	0

WALKER, BRIAN   S   DOLPHINS

PERSONAL: Born May 31, 1972, in Colorado Springs, Colo. ... 6-1/190.
HIGH SCHOOL: Widefield (Colorado Springs, Colo.).
JUNIOR COLLEGE: Snow College (Utah).
COLLEGE: Washington State.
TRANSACTIONS/CAREER NOTES: Signed as non-drafted free agent by Washington Redskins (May 1, 1996). ... Released by Redskins (October 9, 1997). ... Signed by Miami Dolphins (December 9, 1997). ... Active for two games for Dolphins (1997); did not play.
PLAYING EXPERIENCE: Washington NFL, 1996 and 1997. ... Games/Games started: 1996 (16/4), 1997 (5/0). Total: 21/4.
PRO STATISTICS: 1996—Credited with one sack.

WALKER, DARNELL   CB   49ERS

PERSONAL: Born January 17, 1970, in St. Louis. ... 5-8/167. ... Full name: Darnell Robert Walker. ... Brother of Marquis Walker, cornerback with Washington Redskins (1996) and St. Louis Rams (1996-1997).
HIGH SCHOOL: Sumner (St. Louis).
JUNIOR COLLEGE: Coffeyville (Kan.) Community College.
COLLEGE: Oklahoma.
TRANSACTIONS/CAREER NOTES: Selected by Atlanta Falcons in seventh round (178th pick overall) of 1993 NFL draft. ... Signed by Falcons (July 14, 1993). ... Granted free agency (February 16, 1996). ... Re-signed by Falcons (June 12, 1996). ... Granted unconditional free agency (February 14, 1997). ... Signed by San Francisco 49ers (March 28, 1997).
CHAMPIONSHIP GAME EXPERIENCE: Played in NFC championship game (1997 season).
PRO STATISTICS: 1994—Credited with one sack. 1996—Recovered one fumble. 1997—Credited with one sack.

Year Team	G	GS	INTERCEPTIONS No.	Yds.	Avg.	TD
1993—Atlanta NFL	15	8	3	7	2.3	0
1994—Atlanta NFL	16	5	3	105	35.0	1
1995—Atlanta NFL	16	7	0	0	...	0
1996—Atlanta NFL	15	9	1	0	0.0	0
1997—San Francisco NFL	16	11	3	49	16.3	0
Pro totals (5 years)	78	40	10	161	16.1	1

WALKER, DENARD   DB   OILERS

PERSONAL: Born August 9, 1973, in Dallas. ... 6-1/192. ... Full name: Denard Antuan Walker.
HIGH SCHOOL: South Garland (Texas), than Harlingen (Texas) Military Institute.
COLLEGE: Louisiana State.
TRANSACTIONS/CAREER NOTES: Selected by Houston Oilers in third round (75th pick overall) of 1997 NFL draft. ... Oilers franchise moved to Tennessee for 1997 season. ... Signed by Oilers (July 18, 1997).
PLAYING EXPERIENCE: Tennessee NFL, 1997. ... Games/Games started: 15/11.
PRO STATISTICS: 1997—Intercepted two passes for 53 yards and one touchdown.

W

WALKER, DERRICK   TE

PERSONAL: Born June 23, 1967, in Glenwood, Ill. ... 6-0/250. ... Full name: Derrick Norval Walker.

HIGH SCHOOL: Bloom (Chicago Heights, Ill.).

COLLEGE: Michigan (degree in communications).

TRANSACTIONS/CAREER NOTES: Selected by San Diego Chargers in sixth round (163rd pick overall) of 1990 NFL draft. ... Signed by Chargers (July 21, 1990). ... Granted free agency (March 1, 1993). ... Re-signed by Chargers for 1993 season. ... On injured reserve with knee injury (December 15, 1993-remainder of season). ... Released by Chargers (March 9, 1994). ... Signed by Kansas City Chiefs (August 29, 1994). ... Granted free agency (February 17, 1995). ... Tendered offer sheet by Washington Redskins (March 11, 1995). ... Offer matched by Chiefs (March 18, 1995). ... Released by Chiefs (February 13, 1998).

PRO STATISTICS: 1991—Recovered one fumble. 1996—Recovered one fumble.

SINGLE GAME HIGHS (regular season): Receptions—8 (October 17, 1994, vs. Denver); yards—104 (October 25, 1992, vs. Denver); and touchdown receptions—1 (November 28, 1996, vs. Detroit).

STATISTICAL PLATEAUS: 100-yard receiving games: 1992 (1).

				RECEIVING				TOTALS		
Year Team	G	GS	No.	Yds.	Avg.	TD	TD	2pt.	Pts.	Fum.
1990—San Diego NFL	16	13	23	240	10.4	1	1	...	6	1
1991—San Diego NFL	16	16	20	134	6.7	0	0	...	0	0
1992—San Diego NFL	16	16	34	393	11.6	2	2	...	12	0
1993—San Diego NFL	12	11	21	212	10.1	1	1	...	6	0
1994—Kansas City NFL	15	11	36	382	10.6	2	2	0	12	1
1995—Kansas City NFL	16	3	25	205	8.2	1	1	0	6	0
1996—Kansas City NFL	11	9	9	73	8.1	1	1	0	6	0
1997—Kansas City NFL	16	5	5	60	12.0	0	0	0	0	0
Pro totals (8 years)	118	84	173	1699	9.8	8	8	0	48	2

WALKER, GARY   DE   OILERS

PERSONAL: Born February 28, 1973, in Lavonia, Ga. ... 6-2/288. ... Full name: Gary Lamar Walker.

HIGH SCHOOL: Franklin County (Lavonia, Ga.).

COLLEGE: Auburn.

TRANSACTIONS/CAREER NOTES: Selected by Houston Oilers in fifth round (159th pick overall) of 1995 NFL draft. ... Signed by Oilers (July 10, 1995). ... Oilers franchise moved to Tennessee for 1997 season. ... Granted free agency (February 13, 1998).

PRO STATISTICS: 1996—Recovered one fumble.

Year Team	G	GS	SACKS
1995—Houston NFL	15	9	2.5
1996—Houston NFL	16	16	5.5
1997—Tennessee NFL	15	15	7.0
Pro totals (3 years)	46	40	15.0

WALKER, HERSCHEL   RB

PERSONAL: Born March 3, 1962, in Wrightsville, Ga. ... 6-1/225.

HIGH SCHOOL: Johnson County (Wrightsville, Ga.).

COLLEGE: Georgia (degree in criminal justice, 1984).

TRANSACTIONS/CAREER NOTES: Signed after junior season by New Jersey Generals of USFL (February 22, 1983); Generals forfeited first-round pick in 1984 draft. ... On developmental squad (April 8-14, 1984). ... Selected by Dallas Cowboys in fifth round (114th pick overall) of 1985 NFL draft. ... Granted free agency when USFL suspended operations (August 7, 1986). ... Signed by Cowboys (August 13, 1986). ... Granted roster exemption (August 13-23, 1986). ... Traded as part of a six-player, 12 draft-pick deal in which Cowboys sent Walker to Minnesota Vikings in exchange for DB Issiac Holt, LB David Howard, LB Jesse Solomon, DE Alex Stewart, first-round pick in 1992 draft and conditional first-round picks in 1990 and 1991 drafts, conditional second-round picks in 1990, 1991 and 1992 drafts and conditional third-round pick in 1992 draft (October 12, 1989); Nelson refused to report to Cowboys and was traded to San Diego Chargers, with Vikings giving Cowboys a sixth-round pick in 1990 as well as the original conditional second-round pick in 1991 and Chargers sending a fifth-round pick in 1990 to Vikings through Cowboys (October 17, 1989); deal completed with Cowboys retaining Howard, Solomon and Holt and all conditional picks and Cowboys sending third-round picks in 1990 and 1991 and 10th-round pick in 1990 to Vikings (February 2, 1990). ... Granted free agency (February 1, 1991). ... Re-signed by Vikings (June 24, 1991). ... Granted free agency (February 1, 1992). ... Released by Vikings (May 29, 1992). ... Signed by Philadelphia Eagles (June 22, 1992). ... Released by Eagles (March 28, 1995). ... Signed by New York Giants (April 3, 1995). ... Released by Giants (June 18, 1996). ... Signed by Cowboys (July 11, 1996). ... Granted unconditional free agency (February 14, 1997). ... Re-signed by Cowboys (June 2, 1997). ... Granted unconditional free agency (February 13, 1998).

HONORS: Named running back on THE SPORTING NEWS college All-America first team (1980-1982). ... Heisman Trophy winner (1982). ... Named College Football Player of the Year by THE SPORTING NEWS (1982). ... Maxwell Award winner (1982). ... Named running back on THE SPORTING NEWS USFL All-Star team (1983 and 1985). ... Named USFL Player of the Year by THE SPORTING NEWS (1985). ... Played in Pro Bowl (1987 and 1988 seasons).

PRO STATISTICS: USFL: 1983—Recovered four fumbles. 1984—Recovered two fumbles. 1985—Recovered three fumbles. NFL: 1986—Recovered two fumbles. 1987—Recovered one fumble. 1988—Recovered three fumbles. 1990—Attempted two passes with one completion for 12 yards. 1991—Recovered one fumble. 1992—Attempted one pass without a completion and recovered two fumbles. 1993—Recovered two fumbles. 1994—Recovered one fumble. 1996—Recovered one fumble. 1997—Recovered two fumbles.

SINGLE GAME HIGHS (regular season): Attempts—29 (September 12, 1988, vs. Phoenix); yards—173 (November 15, 1987, vs. New England); rushing touchdowns—3 (October 27, 1991, vs. Arizona).

STATISTICAL PLATEAUS: USFL: 100-yard rushing games: 1983 (7), 1984 (5), 1985 (14). Total: 26. ... 100-yard receiving games: 1983 (1), 1985 (1). Total: 2. ... NFL: 100-yard rushing games: 1986 (2), 1987 (3), 1988 (4), 1991 (3), 1992 (5). Total: 17. ... 100-yard receiving games: 1986 (3), 1993 (2). Total: 5.

MISCELLANEOUS: Only player in NFL history to have a run from scrimmage, pass reception and kickoff return of 90 yards or more in one season (1994).

Year Team	G	GS	RUSHING				RECEIVING				KICKOFF RETURNS				TOTALS			
			Att.	Yds.	Avg.	TD	No.	Yds.	Avg.	TD	No.	Yds.	Avg.	TD	TD	2pt.	Pts.	Fum.
1983—New Jersey USFL.......	18	18	*412	*1812	4.4	*17	53	489	9.2	*1	3	69	23.0	0	*18	...	*110	12
1984—New Jersey USFL.......	17	17	293	1339	4.6	16	40	528	13.2	5	0	0	...	0	*21	...	128	6
1985—New Jersey USFL.......	18	18	*438	*2411	5.5	*21	37	467	12.6	*1	0	0	...	0	*22	...	*132	9
1986—Dallas NFL.............	16	9	151	737	‡4.9	12	76	837	11.0	2	0	0	...	0	14	...	84	5
1987—Dallas NFL.............	12	11	209	891	4.3	7	60	715	11.9	1	0	0	...	0	8	...	48	4
1988—Dallas NFL.............	16	16	‡361	‡1514	4.2	5	53	505	9.5	2	0	0	...	0	7	...	42	6
1989—Dallas NFL.............	5	5	81	246	3.0	2	22	261	11.9	1	0	0	...	0	3	...	18	2
—Minnesota NFL.........	11	9	169	669	4.0	5	18	162	9.0	1	13	374	28.8	†1	7	...	42	5
1990—Minnesota NFL.........	16	16	184	770	4.2	5	35	315	9.0	4	‡44	‡966	22.0	0	9	...	54	4
1991—Minnesota NFL.........	15	15	198	825	4.2	10	33	204	6.2	0	5	83	16.6	0	10	...	60	2
1992—Philadelphia NFL........	16	16	267	1070	4.0	8	38	278	7.3	2	3	69	23.0	0	10	...	60	6
1993—Philadelphia NFL........	16	16	174	746	4.3	1	75	610	8.1	3	11	184	16.7	0	4	...	24	3
1994—Philadelphia NFL........	16	14	113	528	4.7	5	50	500	10.0	2	21	581	27.7	1	8	0	48	4
1995—New York Giants NFL..	16	3	31	126	4.1	0	31	234	7.5	1	41	881	21.5	0	1	0	6	0
1996—Dallas NFL.............	16	1	10	83	8.3	1	7	89	12.7	0	27	779	28.9	0	1	0	6	0
1997—Dallas NFL.............	16	6	6	20	3.3	0	14	149	10.6	2	50	1167	23.3	0	2	0	12	0
USFL totals (3 years)...........	53	53	1143	5562	4.9	54	130	1484	11.4	7	3	69	23.0	0	61	0	370	27
NFL totals (12 years)...........	187	137	1954	8225	4.2	61	512	4859	9.5	21	215	5084	23.6	2	84	0	504	41
Pro totals (15 years)...........	240	190	3097	13787	4.5	115	642	6343	9.9	28	218	5153	23.6	2	145	0	874	68

WALKER, JAY   QB   VIKINGS

PERSONAL: Born January 24, 1972, in Los Angeles. ... 6-3/229. ... Full name: Jewell Jay Walker.
HIGH SCHOOL: University (Los Angeles).
COLLEGE: Howard.
TRANSACTIONS/CAREER NOTES: Selected by New England Patriots in seventh round (198th pick overall) of 1994 NFL draft. ... Signed by Patriots (June 1, 1994). ... Assigned by Patriots to Barcelona Dragons in 1995 World League enhancement allocation program (February 20, 1995). ... Released by Patriots (August 27, 1995). ... Signed by Minnesota Vikings (March 15, 1996). ... Active for four games (1997); did not play. ... Granted free agency (February 13, 1998).
PLAYING EXPERIENCE: Minnesota NFL, 1996. ... Games/Games started: 1/0.
PRO STATISTICS: 1996—Attempted two passes with two completions for 31 yards.
SINGLE GAME HIGHS (regular season): Attempts—2 (December 1, 1996, vs. Arizona); completions—2 (December 1, 1996, vs. Arizona); yards—31 (December 1, 1996, vs. Arizona); and touchdown passes—0.

RECORD AS BASEBALL PLAYER

TRANSACTIONS/CAREER NOTES: Threw right, batted right. ... Selected by California Angels organization in 21st round of free-agent draft (June 5, 1989). ... Released by Angels (June 24, 1990).

Year Team (League)	W	L	Pct.	ERA	G	GS	CG	ShO	Sv.	IP	H	R	ER	BB	SO
1989—Mesa (Arizona).........	0	0	...	12.15	8	0	0	0	0	13⅓	27	30	18	23	6

WALKER, MARQUIS   CB   RAIDERS

PERSONAL: Born July 6, 1972, in St. Louis. ... 5-10/173. ... Full name: Marquis Roshe Walker. ... Brother of Darnell Walker, cornerback, San Francisco 49ers.
HIGH SCHOOL: Berkeley (St. Louis).
JUNIOR COLLEGE: Blinn College (Texas), then Cisco (Texas) Junior College.
COLLEGE: Southeast Missouri State.
TRANSACTIONS/CAREER NOTES: Signed as non-drafted free agent by St. Louis Rams (April 24, 1996). ... Released by Rams (September 4, 1996). ... Signed by Washington Redskins to practice squad (September 4, 1996). ... Signed by Rams off Redskins practice squad (November 6, 1996). ... Released by Rams (November 19, 1997).
PLAYING EXPERIENCE: St. Louis NFL, 1996 and 1997; Washington NFL, 1996. ... Games/Games started: 1996 (St.L-8/4; Wash.-1/0; Total: 9/4), 1997 (10/0). Total: 19/4.
PRO STATISTICS: 1997—Recovered one fumble.

WALLACE, AARON   LB   RAIDERS

PERSONAL: Born April 17, 1967, in Paris, Texas. ... 6-3/245.
HIGH SCHOOL: Franklin D. Roosevelt (Dallas).
COLLEGE: Texas A&M.
TRANSACTIONS/CAREER NOTES: Selected by Los Angeles Raiders in second round (37th pick overall) of 1990 NFL draft. ... Signed by Raiders (July 16, 1990). ... Granted free agency (March 1, 1993). ... Re-signed by Raiders (July 21, 1993). ... Raiders franchise moved to Oakland (July 21, 1995). ... Granted unconditional free agency (February 16, 1996). ... Signed by Denver Broncos (May 14, 1996). ... Released by Broncos (July 24, 1996). ... Signed by Raiders (June 19, 1997). ... Released by Raiders (August 19, 1997). ... Re-signed by Raiders (October 15, 1997). ... Granted unconditional free agency (February 13, 1998). ... Re-signed by Raiders (February 17, 1998).
CHAMPIONSHIP GAME EXPERIENCE: Played in AFC championship game (1990 season).
HONORS: Named linebacker on THE SPORTING NEWS college All-America second team (1988).
PRO STATISTICS: 1992—Recovered two fumbles. 1993—Recovered two fumbles. 1995—Recovered one fumble.

Year Team	G	GS	SACKS
1990—Los Angeles Raiders NFL	16	0	9.0
1991—Los Angeles Raiders NFL	16	0	2.0
1992—Los Angeles Raiders NFL	16	16	4.0
1993—Los Angeles Raiders NFL	16	14	2.0
1994—Los Angeles Raiders NFL	16	5	2.0
1995—Oakland NFL	13	0	2.0
1996—	Did not play.		
1997—Oakland NFL	5	0	0.0
Pro totals (7 years)	98	35	21.0

W

WALLACE, AL   LB/DE   EAGLES

PERSONAL: Born March 25, 1974, in Delray Beach, Fla. ... 6-5/258. ... Full name: Alonzo Dwight Wallace.
HIGH SCHOOL: Spanish River (Delray Beach, Fla.).
COLLEGE: Maryland (degree in health education, 1997).
TRANSACTIONS/CAREER NOTES: Signed as non-drafted free agent by Jacksonville Jaguars (April 21, 1997). ... Released by Jaguars (August 19, 1997). ... Re-signed by Jaguars to practice squad (August 25, 1997). ... Signed by Philadelphia Eagles off Jaguars practice squad (December 2, 1997).
PLAYING EXPERIENCE: Philadelphia NFL, 1997. ... Games/Games started: 1/0.

WALLACE, STEVE   OT

PERSONAL: Born December 27, 1964, in Atlanta. ... 6-5/280. ... Full name: Barron Steven Wallace. ... Related to Leonard Humphries, defensive back with Indianapolis Colts (1994).
HIGH SCHOOL: Chamblee (Ga.).
COLLEGE: Auburn.
TRANSACTIONS/CAREER NOTES: Selected by Birmingham Stallions in 1986 USFL territorial draft. ... Selected by San Francisco 49ers in fourth round (101st pick overall) of 1986 NFL draft. ... Signed by 49ers (July 18, 1986). ... Granted free agency (February 1, 1992). ... Re-signed by 49ers (August 1, 1992). ... Designated by 49ers as transition player (February 25, 1993). ... Released by 49ers (March 4, 1996). ... Signed by Philadelphia Eagles (April 18, 1996). ... Released by Eagles (August 20, 1996). ... Signed by 49ers (August 28, 1996). ... Granted unconditional free agency (February 14, 1997). ... Signed by Kansas City Chiefs (July 30, 1997). ... Granted unconditional free agency (February 13, 1998).
PLAYING EXPERIENCE: San Francisco NFL, 1986-1996; Kansas City NFL, 1997. ... Games/Games started: 1986 (16/0), 1987 (11/4), 1988 (16/16), 1989 (16/1), 1990 (16/16), 1991 (16/16), 1992 (16/16), 1993 (15/15), 1994 (15/15), 1995 (13/12), 1996 (16/16), 1997 (10/0). Total: 176/127.
CHAMPIONSHIP GAME EXPERIENCE: Played in NFC championship game (1988-1990 and 1992-1994 seasons). ... Member of Super Bowl championship team (1988, 1989 and 1994 seasons).
HONORS: Played in Pro Bowl (1992 season).
PRO STATISTICS: 1992—Recovered one fumble. 1993—Recovered one fumble. 1994—Recovered two fumbles.

WALLERSTEDT, BRETT   LB

PERSONAL: Born November 24, 1970, in Tacoma, Wash. ... 6-1/240. ... Full name: Brett Robert Wallerstedt.
HIGH SCHOOL: Manhattan (Kan.).
COLLEGE: Arizona State (degree in general business).
TRANSACTIONS/CAREER NOTES: Selected by Phoenix Cardinals in sixth round (143rd pick overall) of 1993 NFL draft. ... Signed by Cardinals (July 16, 1993). ... On injured reserve with knee injury (November 17, 1993-remainder of season). ... Cardinals franchise renamed Arizona Cardinals for 1994 season. ... Released by Cardinals (August 23, 1994). ... Signed by Denver Broncos (September 6, 1994). ... Claimed on waivers by Cincinnati Bengals (September 22, 1994). ... Granted free agency (February 16, 1996). ... Re-signed by Bengals (May 6, 1996). ... On injured reserve with foot injury (August 25, 1996-entire season). ... Granted unconditional free agency (February 14, 1997). ... Signed by St. Louis Rams (July 25, 1997). ... Released by Rams (August 19, 1997). ... Re-signed by Rams (December 13, 1997). ... Granted unconditional free agency (February 13, 1998).
PLAYING EXPERIENCE: Phoenix NFL, 1993; Cincinnati NFL, 1994 and 1995; St. Louis NFL, 1997. ... Games/Games started: 1993 (7/0), 1994 (10/0), 1995 (11/2), 1997 (2/0). Total: 30/2.

WALLS, WESLEY   TE   PANTHERS

PERSONAL: Born February 26, 1966, in Batesville, Miss. ... 6-5/250. ... Full name: Charles Wesley Walls.
HIGH SCHOOL: Pontotoc (Miss.).
COLLEGE: Mississippi.
TRANSACTIONS/CAREER NOTES: Selected by San Francisco 49ers in second round (56th pick overall) of 1989 NFL draft. ... Signed by 49ers (July 26, 1989). ... Granted free agency (February 1, 1992). ... Re-signed by 49ers (July 18, 1992). ... On injured reserve with shoulder injury (September 1, 1992-January 16, 1993). ... On injured reserve with shoulder injury (October 27, 1993-remainder of season). ... Granted unconditional free agency (February 17, 1994). ... Signed by New Orleans Saints (April 27, 1994). ... Granted unconditional free agency (February 16, 1996). ... Signed by Carolina Panthers (February 21, 1996).
CHAMPIONSHIP GAME EXPERIENCE: Played in NFC championship game (1989, 1990 and 1996 seasons). ... Member of Super Bowl championship team (1989 season).
HONORS: Named tight end on THE SPORTING NEWS college All-America second team (1988). ... Played in Pro Bowl (1996 and 1997 seasons).
PRO STATISTICS: 1989—Recovered one fumble. 1990—Returned one kickoff for 16 yards. 1993—Recovered one fumble. 1995—Returned one kickoff for six yards, fumbled once and recovered one fumble.
SINGLE GAME HIGHS (regular season): Receptions—8 (November 30, 1997, vs. New Orleans); yards—147 (September 7, 1997, vs. Atlanta); and touchdown receptions—2 (September 14, 1997, vs. San Diego).
STATISTICAL PLATEAUS: 100-yard receiving games: 1997 (2).
MISCELLANEOUS: Holds Carolina Panthers all-time records for most touchdown receptions (16) and most touchdowns (16).

W

| | | | RECEIVING | | | | TOTALS | | | |
Year Team	G	GS	No.	Yds.	Avg.	TD	TD	2pt.	Pts.	Fum.
1989—San Francisco NFL	16	0	4	16	4.0	1	1	...	6	1
1990—San Francisco NFL	16	0	5	27	5.4	0	0	...	0	0
1991—San Francisco NFL	15	0	2	24	12.0	0	0	...	0	0
1992—San Francisco NFL					Did not play.					
1993—San Francisco NFL	6	0	0	0	...	0	0	...	0	0
1994—New Orleans NFL	15	7	38	406	10.7	4	4	1	26	0
1995—New Orleans NFL	16	10	57	694	12.2	4	4	1	26	1
1996—Carolina NFL	16	15	61	713	11.7	10	10	0	60	0
1997—Carolina NFL	15	15	58	746	12.9	6	6	0	36	0
Pro totals (8 years)	115	47	225	2626	11.7	25	25	2	154	2

WALSH, CHRIS   WR   VIKINGS

PERSONAL: Born December 12, 1968, in Cleveland. ... 6-1/198. ... Full name: Christopher Lee Walsh.
HIGH SCHOOL: Ygnacio Valley (Concord, Calif.).
COLLEGE: Stanford (degree in quantitative economics).
TRANSACTIONS/CAREER NOTES: Selected by Buffalo Bills in ninth round (251st pick overall) of 1992 NFL draft. ... Signed by Bills (July 22, 1992). ... Released by Bills (August 31, 1992). ... Re-signed by Bills to practice squad (September 1, 1992). ... Activated (September 19, 1992). ... Released by Bills (October 2, 1992). ... Re-signed by Bills to practice squad (October 2, 1992). ... Released by Bills (March 10, 1994). ... Signed by Minnesota Vikings (May 6, 1994). ... Granted unconditional free agency (February 16, 1996). ... Re-signed by Vikings (March 4, 1996). ... Granted unconditional free agency (February 13, 1998). ... Re-signed by Vikings (March 9, 1998).
CHAMPIONSHIP GAME EXPERIENCE: Member of Bills for AFC championship game (1993 season); inactive. ... Member of Bills for Super Bowl XXVIII (1993 season); inactive.
PRO STATISTICS: 1994—Returned one kickoff for six yards. 1995—Returned three kickoffs for 42 yards. 1996—Attempted one pass without a completion and credited with one two-point conversion. 1997—Returned one kickoff for 10 yards.
SINGLE GAME HIGHS (regular season): Receptions—4 (October 22, 1995, vs. Green Bay); yards—31 (October 22, 1995, vs. Green Bay); and touchdown receptions—1 (September 7, 1997, vs. Chicago).

| | | | RECEIVING | | | | TOTALS | | | |
Year Team	G	GS	No.	Yds.	Avg.	TD	TD	2pt.	Pts.	Fum.
1992—Buffalo NFL	2	0	0	0	...	0	0	...	0	0
1993—Buffalo NFL	3	0	0	0	...	0	0	...	0	0
1994—Minnesota NFL	10	0	0	0	...	0	0	0	0	0
1995—Minnesota NFL	16	0	7	66	9.4	0	0	0	0	0
1996—Minnesota NFL	15	0	4	39	9.8	1	1	1	8	0
1997—Minnesota NFL	14	0	11	114	10.4	1	1	0	6	0
Pro totals (6 years)	60	0	22	219	10.0	2	2	1	14	0

WALSH, STEVE   QB   BUCCANEERS

PERSONAL: Born December 1, 1966, in St. Paul, Minn. ... 6-3/215. ... Full name: Stephen John Walsh.
HIGH SCHOOL: Cretin-Derham Hall (St. Paul, Minn.).
COLLEGE: Miami (Fla.).
TRANSACTIONS/CAREER NOTES: Selected by Dallas Cowboys in first round of 1989 NFL supplemental draft (July 7, 1989). ... Signed by Cowboys (July 29, 1989). ... Traded by Cowboys to New Orleans Saints for first-round and third-round (OT Erik Williams) picks in 1991 draft and second-round pick (traded to Cleveland) in 1992 draft (September 25, 1990). ... Active for two games (1992); did not play. ... Granted free agency (March 1, 1993). ... Re-signed by Saints (July 15, 1993). ... Released by Saints (April 23, 1994). ... Signed by Chicago Bears (April 26, 1994). ... Granted unconditional free agency (February 17, 1995). ... Re-signed by Bears (April 17, 1995). ... Granted unconditional free agency (February 16, 1996). ... Signed by St. Louis Rams (April 10, 1996). ... Granted unconditional free agency (February 14, 1997). ... Signed by Tampa Bay Buccaneers (April 16, 1997).
PRO STATISTICS: 1989—Fumbled three times and recovered two fumbles for minus 14 yards. 1990—Fumbled six times and recovered two fumbles. 1991—Fumbled three times and recovered one fumble for minus 20 yards. 1994—Fumbled seven times and recovered three fumbles for minus eight yards. 1996—Fumbled once and recovered one fumble. 1997—Fumbled once and recovered two fumbles.
SINGLE GAME HIGHS (regular season): Attempts—49 (October 29, 1989, vs. Phoenix); completions—26 (December 8, 1991, vs. Dallas); yards—317 (December 1, 1991, vs. San Francisco); and touchdown passes—3 (October 14, 1990, vs. Cleveland).
STATISTICAL PLATEAUS: 300-yard passing games: 1991 (1).
MISCELLANEOUS: Regular-season record as starting NFL quarterback: 20-18 (.526). Postseason record as starting NFL quarterback: 1-2 (.333).

| | | | PASSING | | | | | | | | RUSHING | | | | TOTALS | | |
Year Team	G	GS	Att.	Cmp.	Pct.	Yds.	TD	Int.	Avg.	Rat.	Att.	Yds.	Avg.	TD	TD	2pt.	Pts.
1989—Dallas NFL	8	5	219	110	50.2	1371	5	9	6.26	60.5	6	16	2.7	0	0	...	0
1990—Dallas NFL	1	0	9	4	44.4	40	0	0	4.44	57.6	1	0	0.0	0	0	...	0
—New Orleans NFL	12	11	327	175	53.5	1970	12	13	6.02	67.5	19	25	1.3	0	0	...	0
1991—New Orleans NFL	8	7	255	141	55.3	1638	11	6	6.42	79.5	8	0	0.0	0	0	...	0
1992—New Orleans NFL								Did not play.									
1993—New Orleans NFL	2	1	38	20	52.6	271	2	3	7.13	60.3	4	-4	-1.0	0	0	...	0
1994—Chicago NFL	12	11	343	208	60.6	2078	10	8	6.06	77.9	30	4	0.1	1	1	0	6
1995—Chicago NFL	1	0	0	0	...	0	0	0	...	...	0	0	...	0	0	...	0
1996—St. Louis NFL	3	3	77	33	42.9	344	0	5	4.47	29.4	6	10	1.7	0	0	...	0
1997—Tampa Bay NFL	13	0	17	6	35.3	58	0	1	3.41	21.2	6	-4	-0.7	0	0	...	0
Pro totals (8 years)	60	38	1285	697	54.2	7770	40	45	6.05	68.3	80	47	0.6	1	1	0	6

W

WALTER, JOE   OT

PERSONAL: Born June 18, 1963, in Dallas. ... 6-7/292. ... Full name: Joseph Follmann Walter Jr.
HIGH SCHOOL: North (Garland, Texas).
COLLEGE: Texas Tech.
TRANSACTIONS/CAREER NOTES: Selected by Denver Gold in 1985 USFL territorial draft. ... Selected by Cincinnati Bengals in seventh round (181st pick overall) of 1985 NFL draft. ... Signed by Bengals (July 15, 1985). ... On injured reserve with knee injury (December 30, 1988-remainder of season playoffs). ... On physically unable to perform list with knee injury (September 4-October 21, 1989). ... Granted free agency (February 1, 1992). ... Re-signed by Bengals (September 2, 1992). ... On injured reserve with knee injury (August 23, 1994-entire season). ... Released by Bengals (October 18, 1997).
PLAYING EXPERIENCE: Cincinnati NFL, 1985-1993, 1995-1997. ... Games/Games started: 1985 (14/0), 1986 (15/8), 1987 (12/12), 1988 (16/16), 1989 (10/7), 1990 (16/16), 1991 (15/14), 1992 (16/16), 1993 (16/16), 1995 (16/16), 1996 (15/15), 1997 (5/0). Total: 166/136.
PRO STATISTICS: 1987—Recovered two fumbles. 1991—Recovered one fumble. 1992—Recovered one fumble. 1996—Recovered one fumble.

WALTER, KEN — P — PANTHERS

PERSONAL: Born August 15, 1972, in Cleveland. ... 6-1/195. ... Full name: Kenneth Matthew Walter.
HIGH SCHOOL: Euclid (Ohio).
COLLEGE: Kent.
TRANSACTIONS/CAREER NOTES: Signed as non-drafted free agent by Carolina Panthers (April 14, 1997).
PRO STATISTICS: 1997—Rushed once for minus five yards.

			PUNTING					
Year Team	G	GS	No.	Yds.	Avg.	Net avg.	In. 20	Blk.
1997—Carolina NFL	16	0	85	3604	42.4	36.4	29	0

WARD, CHRIS — DE — RAVENS

PERSONAL: Born February 4, 1974, in Decatur, Ga. ... 6-3/275. ... Full name: Chris Jamal Ward.
HIGH SCHOOL: DeKalb (Decatur, Ga.).
COLLEGE: Kentucky.
TRANSACTIONS/CAREER NOTES: Selected by Baltimore Ravens in seventh round (205th pick overall) of 1997 NFL draft. ... Signed by Ravens (July 14, 1997).
PLAYING EXPERIENCE: Baltimore NFL, 1997. ... Games/Games started: 5/0.

WARD, DEDRIC — WR — JETS

PERSONAL: Born September 29, 1974, in Cedar Rapids, Iowa. ... 5-9/180. ... Full name: Dedric Lamar Ward.
HIGH SCHOOL: Washington (Cedar Rapids, Iowa).
COLLEGE: Northern Iowa.
TRANSACTIONS/CAREER NOTES: Selected by New York Jets in third round (88th pick overall) of 1997 NFL draft. ... Signed by Jets (July 17, 1997).
PRO STATISTICS: 1997—Rushed twice for 25 yards.
STATISTICAL PLATEAUS: 100-yard receiving games: 1997 (1).

			RECEIVING				PUNT RETURNS				KICKOFF RETURNS				TOTALS			
Year Team	G	GS	No.	Yds.	Avg.	TD	No.	Yds.	Avg.	TD	No.	Yds.	Avg.	TD	TD	2pt.	Pts.	Fum.
1997—New York Jets NFL	11	1	18	212	11.8	1	8	55	6.9	0	2	10	5.0	0	1	0	6	1

WARD, RONNIE — LB — DOLPHINS

PERSONAL: Born February 11, 1974, in St. Louis. ... 6-0/232. ... Full name: Ronnie V. Ward.
HIGH SCHOOL: Hazelwood East (St. Louis).
COLLEGE: Kansas.
TRANSACTIONS/CAREER NOTES: Selected by Miami Dolphins in third round (93rd pick overall) of 1997 NFL draft. ... Signed by Dolphins (July 8, 1997). ... On injured reserve with leg injury (September 29, 1997-remainder of season).
PLAYING EXPERIENCE: Miami NFL, 1997. ... Games/Games started: 4/0.

WARREN, CHRIS — RB — COWBOYS

PERSONAL: Born January 24, 1968, in Silver Spring, Md. ... 6-2/228. ... Full name: Christopher Collins Warren Jr.
HIGH SCHOOL: Robinson Secondary (Fairfax, Va.).
COLLEGE: Virginia, then Ferrum, Va. (degree in psychology).
TRANSACTIONS/CAREER NOTES: Selected by Seattle Seahawks in fourth round (89th pick overall) of 1990 NFL draft. ... Signed by Seahawks (July 24, 1990). ... Granted free agency (March 1, 1993). ... Tendered offer sheet by New York Jets (April 23, 1993). ... Offer matched by Seahawks (April 23, 1993). ... Released by Seahawks (March 13, 1998). ... Signed by Dallas Cowboys (April 13, 1998).
HONORS: Played in Pro Bowl (1993-1995 seasons).
PRO STATISTICS: 1990—Fumbled three times and recovered one fumble. 1991—Fumbled three times and recovered one fumble. 1992—Fumbled twice and recovered two fumbles. 1993—Fumbled three times. 1994—Fumbled five times and recovered two fumbles. 1995—Fumbled five times and recovered two fumbles. 1996—Fumbled three times and recovered two fumbles for four yards. 1997—Fumbled twice.
SINGLE GAME HIGHS (regular season): Attempts—36 (September 19, 1993, vs. New England); yards—185 (December 11, 1994, vs. Houston); and rushing touchdowns—3 (December 17, 1995, vs. Oakland).
STATISTICAL PLATEAUS: 100-yard rushing games: 1992 (3), 1993 (3), 1994 (7), 1995 (8), 1996 (3). Total: 24.
MISCELLANEOUS: Holds Seattle Seahawks all-time record for most yards rushing (6,706).

			RUSHING				RECEIVING				PUNT RETURNS				KICKOFF RETURNS				TOTALS		
Year Team	G	GS	Att.	Yds.	Avg.	TD	No.	Yds.	Avg.	TD	No.	Yds.	Avg.	TD	No.	Yds.	Avg.	TD	TD	2pt.	Pts.
1990—Seattle NFL	16	0	6	11	1.8	1	0	0	...	0	28	269	9.6	0	23	478	20.8	0	1	...	6
1991—Seattle NFL	16	1	11	13	1.2	0	2	9	4.5	0	32	298	9.3	▲1	35	792	22.6	0	1	...	6
1992—Seattle NFL	16	16	223	1017	4.6	3	16	134	8.4	0	34	252	7.4	0	28	524	18.7	0	3	...	18
1993—Seattle NFL	14	14	273	1072	3.9	7	15	99	6.6	0	0	0	...	0	0	0	...	0	7	...	42
1994—Seattle NFL	16	15	333	§1545	§4.6	9	41	323	7.9	2	0	0	...	0	0	0	...	0	11	1	68
1995—Seattle NFL	16	16	310	1346	4.3	§15	35	247	7.1	1	0	0	...	0	0	0	...	0	16	0	96
1996—Seattle NFL	14	14	203	855	4.2	5	40	273	6.8	0	0	0	...	0	0	0	...	0	5	1	32
1997—Seattle NFL	15	13	200	847	4.2	4	45	257	5.7	0	0	0	...	0	0	0	...	0	4	0	24
Pro totals (8 years)	123	89	1559	6706	4.3	44	194	1342	6.9	3	94	819	8.7	1	86	1794	20.9	0	48	2	292

W

WARREN, LAMONT — RB — COLTS

PERSONAL: Born January 4, 1973, in Indianapolis. ... 5-11/202.
HIGH SCHOOL: Dorsey (Los Angeles).
COLLEGE: Colorado.
TRANSACTIONS/CAREER NOTES: Selected after junior season by Indianapolis Colts in sixth round (164th pick overall) of 1994 NFL draft. ... Signed by Colts (July 13, 1994).
CHAMPIONSHIP GAME EXPERIENCE: Played in AFC championship game (1995 season).
PRO STATISTICS: 1994—Attempted one pass without a completion. 1996—Recovered one fumble. 1997—Attempted one pass without a completion and recovered one fumble.
SINGLE GAME HIGHS (regular season): Attempts—22 (December 23, 1995, vs. New England); yards—90 (December 23, 1995, vs. New England); and rushing touchdowns—1 (November 16, 1997, vs. Green Bay).

| | | | RUSHING | | | | RECEIVING | | | | KICKOFF RETURNS | | | | TOTALS | | |
Year Team	G	GS	Att.	Yds.	Avg.	TD	No.	Yds.	Avg.	TD	No.	Yds.	Avg.	TD	TD	2pt.	Pts.	Fum.
1994—Indianapolis NFL	11	0	18	80	4.4	0	3	47	15.7	0	2	56	28.0	0	0	0	0	0
1995—Indianapolis NFL	12	1	47	152	3.2	1	17	159	9.4	0	15	315	21.0	0	1	0	6	1
1996—Indianapolis NFL	13	3	67	230	3.4	1	22	174	7.9	0	3	54	18.0	0	1	0	6	3
1997—Indianapolis NFL	13	0	28	80	2.9	2	20	192	9.6	0	1	19	19.0	0	2	0	12	0
Pro totals (4 years)	49	4	160	542	3.4	4	62	572	9.2	0	21	444	21.1	0	4	0	24	4

WASHINGTON, DEWAYNE — CB — STEELERS

PERSONAL: Born December 27, 1972, in Durham, N.C. ... 6-0/190. ... Full name: Dewayne Neron Washington.
HIGH SCHOOL: Northern (Durham, N.C.).
COLLEGE: North Carolina State.
TRANSACTIONS/CAREER NOTES: Selected by Minnesota Vikings in first round (18th pick overall) of 1994 NFL draft. ... Signed by Vikings (July 14, 1994). ... Granted unconditional free agency (February 13, 1998). ... Signed by Pittsburgh Steelers (February 25, 1998).
PRO STATISTICS: 1994—Recovered two fumbles for 17 yards and one touchdown.

| | | | INTERCEPTIONS | | | |
Year Team	G	GS	No.	Yds.	Avg.	TD
1994—Minnesota NFL	16	16	3	135	45.0	2
1995—Minnesota NFL	15	15	1	25	25.0	0
1996—Minnesota NFL	16	16	2	27	13.5	1
1997—Minnesota NFL	16	16	4	71	17.8	0
Pro totals (4 years)	63	63	10	258	25.8	3

WASHINGTON, KEITH — DE — RAVENS

PERSONAL: Born December 18, 1972, in Dallas. ... 6-4/270.
HIGH SCHOOL: Wilmer-Hutchins (Dallas).
COLLEGE: UNLV.
TRANSACTIONS/CAREER NOTES: Signed as non-drafted free agent by Minnesota Vikings (April 1995). ... Released by Vikings (August 27, 1995). ... Re-signed by Vikings to practice squad (August 28, 1995). ... Activated (October 9, 1995); did not play. ... On injured reserve with ankle injury (November 15, 1995-remainder of season). ... Released by Vikings (August 25, 1996). ... Signed by Detroit Lions (August 26, 1996). ... Released by Lions (August 26, 1997). ... Signed by Baltimore Ravens (October 15, 1997). ... Granted free agency (February 13, 1998). ... Re-signed by Ravens (April 14, 1998).
PLAYING EXPERIENCE: Detroit NFL, 1996; Baltimore NFL, 1997. ... Games/Games started: 1996 (12/0), 1997 (10/1). Total: 22/1.
PRO STATISTICS: 1996—Returned one kickoff for 14 yards. 1997—Credited with two sacks.

WASHINGTON, LIONEL — CB

PERSONAL: Born October 21, 1960, in New Orleans. ... 6-0/185.
HIGH SCHOOL: Lutcher (La.).
COLLEGE: Tulane (degree in sports administration).
TRANSACTIONS/CAREER NOTES: Selected by Tampa Bay Bandits in 20th round (229th pick overall) of 1983 USFL draft. ... Selected by St. Louis Cardinals in fourth round (103rd pick overall) of 1983 NFL draft. ... Signed by Cardinals (May 6, 1983). ... On injured reserve with broken fibula (September 16-November 22, 1985). ... Granted free agency (February 1, 1987). ... Re-signed by Cardinals and traded to Los Angeles Raiders for fifth-round pick (P John Bruno) in 1987 draft (March 18, 1987). ... Granted free agency (February 1, 1992). ... Re-signed by Raiders (August 6, 1992). ... Granted unconditional free agency (February 17, 1995). ... Signed by Denver Broncos (March 6, 1995). ... Released by Broncos (February 14, 1997). ... Signed by Raiders (June 19, 1997). ... Granted unconditional free agency (February 13, 1998).
CHAMPIONSHIP GAME EXPERIENCE: Played in AFC championship game (1990 season).
PRO STATISTICS: 1983—Recovered one fumble. 1984—Recovered one fumble. 1986—Recovered one fumble. 1989—Recovered three fumbles for 44 yards and one touchdown. 1993—Credited with one sack.

| | | | INTERCEPTIONS | | | |
Year Team	G	GS	No.	Yds.	Avg.	TD
1983—St. Louis NFL	16	8	8	92	11.5	0
1984—St. Louis NFL	15	15	5	42	8.4	0
1985—St. Louis NFL	5	3	1	48	48.0	†1
1986—St. Louis NFL	16	12	2	19	9.5	0
1987—Los Angeles Raiders NFL	11	10	0	0	...	0
1988—Los Angeles Raiders NFL	12	0	1	0	0.0	0
1989—Los Angeles Raiders NFL	16	16	3	46	15.3	1
1990—Los Angeles Raiders NFL	16	15	1	2	2.0	0
1991—Los Angeles Raiders NFL	16	16	5	22	4.4	0
1992—Los Angeles Raiders NFL	16	16	2	21	10.5	0

W

Year Team	G	GS	INTERCEPTIONS			
			No.	Yds.	Avg.	TD
1993—Los Angeles Raiders NFL	16	16	2	0	0.0	0
1994—Los Angeles Raiders NFL	11	7	3	65	21.7	1
1995—Denver NFL	16	16	0	0	...	0
1996—Denver NFL	14	12	2	17	8.5	0
1997—Oakland NFL	9	3	2	44	22.0	1
Pro totals (15 years)	205	165	37	418	11.3	4

WASHINGTON, MARVIN DE BRONCOS

PERSONAL: Born October 22, 1965, in Denver. ... 6-6/285. ... Full name: Marvin Andrew Washington. ... Cousin of Andrew Lang, center, Milwaukee Bucks.

HIGH SCHOOL: Justin F. Kimball (Dallas).

JUNIOR COLLEGE: Hinds Community College (Miss.).

COLLEGE: Texas-El Paso, then Idaho.

TRANSACTIONS/CAREER NOTES: Selected by New York Jets in sixth round (151st pick overall) of 1989 NFL draft. ... Signed by Jets (July 21, 1989). ... Granted free agency (February 1, 1991). ... Re-signed by Jets (May 5, 1991). ... Granted free agency (March 1, 1993). ... Tendered offer sheet by Seattle Seahawks (March 25, 1993). ... Offer matched by Jets (March 31, 1993). ... Released by Jets (August 11, 1997). ... Signed by San Francisco 49ers (August 21, 1997). ... On injured reserve with ankle injury (November 12, 1997-remainder of season). ... Granted unconditional free agency (February 13, 1998). ... Signed by Denver Broncos (March 2, 1998).

PRO STATISTICS: 1989—Returned one kickoff for 11 yards and recovered one fumble. 1992—Credited with one safety. 1994—Intercepted one pass for seven yards, fumbled once and recovered one fumble. 1997—Recovered one fumble.

Year Team	G	GS	SACKS
1989—New York Jets NFL	16	0	1.5
1990—New York Jets NFL	16	0	4.5
1991—New York Jets NFL	15	15	6.0
1992—New York Jets NFL	16	14	8.5
1993—New York Jets NFL	16	16	5.5
1994—New York Jets NFL	15	15	3.0
1995—New York Jets NFL	16	16	6.0
1996—New York Jets NFL	14	14	2.5
1997—San Francisco NFL	10	1	1.0
Pro totals (9 years)	134	91	38.5

WASHINGTON, MICKEY CB SAINTS

PERSONAL: Born July 8, 1968, in Galveston, Texas. ... 5-9/195. ... Full name: Mickey Lynn Washington. ... Cousin of Joe Washington, running back with four NFL teams (1977-1985).

HIGH SCHOOL: West Brook Senior (Beaumont, Texas).

COLLEGE: Texas A&M (degree in sociology).

TRANSACTIONS/CAREER NOTES: Selected by Phoenix Cardinals in eighth round (199th pick overall) of 1990 NFL draft. ... Signed by Cardinals (July 23, 1990). ... Released by Cardinals (September 3, 1990). ... Signed by Indianapolis Colts to practice squad (October 1, 1990). ... Signed by New England Patriots off Colts practice squad (October 30, 1990). ... Granted unconditional free agency (February 1-April 1, 1991). ... Re-signed by Patriots for 1991 season. ... Granted free agency (February 1, 1992). ... Re-signed by Patriots (July 26, 1992). ... Claimed on waivers by Pittsburgh Steelers (August 25, 1992). ... Released by Steelers (August 31, 1992). ... Signed by Washington Redskins (November 18, 1992). ... Released by Redskins (December 16, 1992). ... Signed by Buffalo Bills (March 23, 1993). ... Granted unconditional free agency (February 17, 1995). ... Signed by Jacksonville Jaguars (March 14, 1995). ... Released by Jaguars (April 21, 1997). ... Signed by New Orleans Saints (May 28, 1997). ... Signed by Barcelona Dragons of World League for 1997 season.

CHAMPIONSHIP GAME EXPERIENCE: Played in AFC championship game (1993 season). ... Played in Super Bowl XXVIII (1993 season). ... Played in AFC championship game (1996 season).

PRO STATISTICS: 1993—Credited with 1/2 sack and recovered two fumbles for six yards. 1994—Credited with 1/2 sack and recovered one fumble. 1995—Recovered two fumbles. 1996—Returned blocked field-goal attempt 65 yards for a touchdown.

Year Team	G	GS	INTERCEPTIONS			
			No.	Yds.	Avg.	TD
1990—New England NFL	9	0	0	0	...	0
1991—New England NFL	16	4	2	0	0.0	0
1992—Washington NFL	3	0	0	0	...	0
1993—Buffalo NFL	16	6	1	27	27.0	▲1
1994—Buffalo NFL	16	16	3	63	21.0	0
1995—Jacksonville NFL	16	16	1	48	48.0	▲1
1996—Jacksonville NFL	16	16	1	1	1.0	0
1997—Barcelona W.L.	...	...	1	24	24.0	0
—New Orleans NFL	16	2	2	30	15.0	0
W.L. totals (1 year)	...	...	1	24	24.0	0
NFL totals (8 years)	108	60	10	169	16.9	2
Pro totals (9 years)	...	...	11	193	17.5	2

WASHINGTON, TED NT BILLS

PERSONAL: Born April 13, 1968, in Tampa. ... 6-4/325. ... Full name: Theodore Washington. ... Son of Ted Washington, linebacker with Houston Oilers (1973-1982).

HIGH SCHOOL: Tampa Bay Vocational Tech Senior.

COLLEGE: Louisville.

TRANSACTIONS/CAREER NOTES: Selected by San Francisco 49ers in first round (25th pick overall) of 1991 NFL draft. ... Signed by 49ers (July 10, 1991). ... Traded by 49ers to Denver Broncos for fifth-round pick (traded to Green Bay) in 1994 draft (April 19, 1994). ... Granted unconditional free agency (February 17, 1995). ... Signed by Buffalo Bills (February 25, 1995). ... Designated by Bills as franchise player (February 13, 1998). ... Free agency status changed from franchise to transitional (February 27, 1998). ... Re-signed by Bills (March 2, 1998).

CHAMPIONSHIP GAME EXPERIENCE: Played in NFC championship game (1992 and 1993 seasons).

W

HONORS: Played in Pro Bowl (1997 season).
PRO STATISTICS: 1993—Recovered one fumble. 1994—Intercepted one pass for five yards. 1997—Recovered one fumble.

Year Team	G	GS	SACKS
1991—San Francisco NFL	16	0	1.0
1992—San Francisco NFL	16	6	2.0
1993—San Francisco NFL	12	12	3.0
1994—Denver NFL	15	15	2.5
1995—Buffalo NFL	16	15	2.5
1996—Buffalo NFL	16	16	3.5
1997—Buffalo NFL	16	16	4.0
Pro totals (7 years)	107	80	18.5

WATSON, TIM   S

PERSONAL: Born August 13, 1970, in Fort Valley, Ga. ... 6-2/221. ... Full name: James Timothy Watson Jr.
HIGH SCHOOL: Peach County (Fort Valley, Ga.).
COLLEGE: Howard (degree in business marketing and fashion merchandising).
TRANSACTIONS/CAREER NOTES: Selected by Green Bay Packers in sixth round (156th overall) in 1993 NFL draft. ... Signed by Packers (July 9, 1993). ... Released by Packers (August 23, 1993). ... Signed by Cleveland Browns (August 25, 1993). ... On non-football injury list (August 30-September 2, 1993). ... Released by Browns (September 2, 1993). ... Signed by Packers (September 6, 1993). ... Released by Packers (September 20, 1993). ... Signed by Kansas City Chiefs to practice squad (September 27, 1993). ... Activated (November 15, 1993). ... On injured reserve with knee injury (September 14, 1994-remainder of season). ... Released by Chiefs (September 27, 1995). ... Signed by New York Giants (November 8, 1995). ... Released by Giants (December 21, 1995). ... Signed by Oakland Raiders for 1996 season. ... Assigned by Raiders to Barcelona Dragons in 1996 World League enhancement allocation program (February 19, 1996). ... Signed by Philadelphia Eagles (March 6, 1997). ... Released by Eagles (September 17, 1997).
PLAYING EXPERIENCE: Kansas City NFL, 1993 and 1994; Kansas City (4)-New York Giants (1) NFL, 1995; Philadelphia NFL, 1997. ... Games/Games started: 1993 (4/0), 1994 (1/0), 1995 (5/0), 1997 (3/0). Total: 13/0.
CHAMPIONSHIP GAME EXPERIENCE: Played in AFC championship game (1993 season).

WATTERS, RICKY   RB   SEAHAWKS

PERSONAL: Born April 7, 1969, in Harrisburg, Pa. ... 6-1/217. ... Full name: Richard James Watters.
HIGH SCHOOL: Bishop McDevitt (Harrisburg, Pa.).
COLLEGE: Notre Dame (degree in design).
TRANSACTIONS/CAREER NOTES: Selected by San Francisco 49ers in second round (45th pick overall) of 1991 NFL draft. ... Signed by 49ers (July 11, 1991). ... On injured reserve with foot injury (August 27, 1991-entire season). ... Designated by 49ers as transition player (February 15, 1994). ... Tendered offer sheet by Philadelphia Eagles (March 18, 1995). ... 49ers declined to match offer (March 25, 1995). ... Granted unconditional free agency (February 13, 1998). ... Signed by Seattle Seahawks (March 4, 1998).
CHAMPIONSHIP GAME EXPERIENCE: Played in NFC championship game (1992-1994 seasons). ... Member of Super Bowl championship team (1994 season).
HONORS: Played in Pro Bowl (1992-1996 seasons).
POST SEASON RECORDS: Shares Super Bowl single-game records for most points—18; and most touchdowns—3 (January 29, 1995, vs. San Diego). ... Holds NFL postseason single-game records for most points—30; most touchdowns—5; and most rushing touchdowns—5 (January 15, 1994, vs. New York Giants).
PRO STATISTICS: 1992—Attempted one pass without a completion and recovered one fumble. 1993—Recovered one fumble. 1994—Recovered two fumbles. 1997—Recovered one fumble.
SINGLE GAME HIGHS (regular season): Attempts—33 (December 10, 1995, vs. Dallas); yards—173 (October 20, 1996, vs. Miami); rushing touchdowns—3 (December 5, 1993, vs. Cincinnati).
STATISTICAL PLATEAUS: 100-yard rushing games: 1992 (4), 1993 (3), 1994 (2), 1995 (4), 1996 (6), 1997 (2). Total: 21. ... 100-yard receiving games: 1994 (1).

Year Team	G	GS	RUSHING				RECEIVING				TOTALS			
			Att.	Yds.	Avg.	TD	No.	Yds.	Avg.	TD	TD	2pt.	Pts.	Fum.
1991—San Francisco NFL							Did not play.							
1992—San Francisco NFL	14	13	206	1013	4.9	9	43	405	9.4	2	11	...	66	2
1993—San Francisco NFL	13	13	208	950	4.6	‡10	31	326	10.5	1	11	...	66	5
1994—San Francisco NFL	16	16	239	877	3.7	6	66	719	10.9	5	11	0	66	8
1995—Philadelphia NFL	16	16	337	1273	3.8	11	62	434	7.0	1	12	0	72	6
1996—Philadelphia NFL	16	16	*353	1411	4.0	13	51	444	8.7	0	13	0	78	5
1997—Philadelphia NFL	16	16	285	1110	3.9	7	48	440	9.2	0	7	0	42	3
Pro totals (6 years)	91	90	1628	6634	4.1	56	301	2768	9.2	9	65	0	390	29

W

WATTS, DAMON   DB

PERSONAL: Born April 8, 1972, in Indianapolis. ... 5-10/190. ... Full name: Damon Shanel Watts.
HIGH SCHOOL: Lawrence North (Indianapolis).
COLLEGE: Indiana.
TRANSACTIONS/CAREER NOTES: Signed as non-drafted free agent by Indianapolis Colts (July 12, 1994). ... On injured reserve with fractured forearm (December 6, 1996-remainder of season). ... Granted free agency (February 14, 1997). ... Re-signed by Colts (June 10, 1997). ... On injured reserve with neck injury (November 11, 1997-remainder of season). ... Announced retirement (February 4, 1998).
CHAMPIONSHIP GAME EXPERIENCE: Played in AFC championship game (1995 season).

Year Team	G	GS	INTERCEPTIONS			
			No.	Yds.	Avg.	TD
1994—Indianapolis NFL	16	8	1	0	0.0	0
1995—Indianapolis NFL	13	0	1	9	9.0	0
1996—Indianapolis NFL	10	0	1	21	21.0	0
1997—Indianapolis NFL	8	6	0	0	...	0
Pro totals (4 years)	47	14	3	30	10.0	0

WAY, CHARLES   FB   GIANTS

PERSONAL: Born December 27, 1972, in Philadelphia. ... 6-0/247. ... Full name: Charles Christopher Way.
HIGH SCHOOL: Northeast (Philadelphia).
COLLEGE: Virginia.
TRANSACTIONS/CAREER NOTES: Selected by New York Giants in sixth round (206th pick overall) of 1995 NFL draft. ... Signed by Giants (July 23, 1995).
PRO STATISTICS: 1995—Returned one kickoff for eight yards. 1996—Returned two kickoffs for 19 yards and recovered three fumbles. 1997—Returned two kickoffs for 46 yards and recovered five fumbles.
SINGLE GAME HIGHS (regular season): Attempts—20 (October 26, 1997, vs. Cincinnati); yards—114 (November 16, 1997, vs. Arizona); rushing touchdowns—2 (October 26, 1997, vs. Cincinnati).
STATISTICAL PLATEAUS: 100-yard rushing games: 1997 (1).

				RUSHING				RECEIVING				TOTALS		
Year Team	G	GS	Att.	Yds.	Avg.	TD	No.	Yds.	Avg.	TD	TD	2pt.	Pts.	Fum.
1995—New York Giants NFL	16	4	2	6	3.0	0	7	76	10.9	1	1	0	6	0
1996—New York Giants NFL	16	12	22	79	3.6	1	32	328	10.3	1	2	0	12	0
1997—New York Giants NFL	16	16	151	698	4.6	4	37	304	8.2	1	5	0	30	3
Pro totals (3 years)	48	32	175	783	4.5	5	76	708	9.3	3	8	0	48	3

WEBB, RICHMOND   OT   DOLPHINS

PERSONAL: Born January 11, 1967, in Dallas. ... 6-6/320. ... Full name: Richmond Jewel Webb.
HIGH SCHOOL: Franklin D. Roosevelt (Dallas).
COLLEGE: Texas A&M (degree in industrial distribution).
TRANSACTIONS/CAREER NOTES: Selected by Miami Dolphins in first round (ninth pick overall) of 1990 NFL draft. ... Signed by Dolphins (July 27, 1990).
PLAYING EXPERIENCE: Miami NFL, 1990-1997. ... Games/Games started: 1990 (16/16), 1991 (14/14), 1992 (16/16), 1993 (16/16), 1994 (16/16), 1995 (16/16), 1996 (16/16), 1997 (16/16). Total: 126/126.
CHAMPIONSHIP GAME EXPERIENCE: Played in AFC championship game (1992 season).
HONORS: Named NFL Rookie of the Year by THE SPORTING NEWS (1990). ... Played in Pro Bowl (1990-1996 seasons). ... Named offensive tackle on THE SPORTING NEWS NFL All-Pro team (1992 and 1994).
PRO STATISTICS: 1995—Recovered one fumble.

WEBSTER, LARRY   DL   RAVENS

PERSONAL: Born January 18, 1969, in Elkton, Md. ... 6-5/288. ... Full name: Larry Melvin Webster Jr.
HIGH SCHOOL: Elkton (Md.).
COLLEGE: Maryland.
TRANSACTIONS/CAREER NOTES: Selected by Miami Dolphins in third round (70th pick overall) of 1992 NFL draft. ... Signed by Dolphins (July 10, 1992). ... Granted free agency (February 17, 1995). ... Signed by Cleveland Browns (May 4, 1995). ... On suspended list for violating league substance abuse policy (September 4-26, 1995). ... Browns franchise moved to Baltimore and renamed Ravens for 1996 season (March 11, 1996). ... Suspended by NFL for violating league substance abuse policy (August 20, 1996-July 13, 1997). ... Granted unconditional free agency (February 13, 1998). ... Re-signed by Ravens (February 16, 1998).
PLAYING EXPERIENCE: Miami NFL, 1994; Cleveland NFL, 1995; Baltimore NFL, 1997. ... Games/Games started: 1992 (16/0), 1993 (13/9), 1994 (16/7), 1995 (10/0), 1997 (16/3). Total: 71/19.
CHAMPIONSHIP GAME EXPERIENCE: Played in AFC championship game (1992 season).
PRO STATISTICS: 1992—Credited with 1 1/2 sacks. 1993—Recovered one fumble.

WELDON, CASEY   QB   CHARGERS

PERSONAL: Born February 3, 1969, in Americus, Ga. ... 6-1/206. ... Full name: William Casey Weldon.
HIGH SCHOOL: North Florida Christian (Tallahassee, Fla.).
COLLEGE: Florida State.
TRANSACTIONS/CAREER NOTES: Selected by Philadelphia Eagles in fourth round (102nd pick overall) of 1992 NFL draft. ... Signed by Eagles (July 26, 1992). ... On inactive list for all 16 games (1992). ... Claimed on waivers by Tampa Bay Buccaneers (September 1, 1993). ... Assigned by Buccaneers to Barcelona Dragons in 1995 World League enhancement allocation program (February 20, 1995). ... Granted unconditional free agency (February 14, 1997). ... Signed by San Diego Chargers (November 14, 1997). ... Inactive for six games during 1997 season. ... Granted unconditional free agency (February 13, 1998). ... Re-signed by Chargers (April 13, 1998).
HONORS: Named quarterback on THE SPORTING NEWS college All-America second team (1991).
PRO STATISTICS: 1995—Fumbled four times. 1996—Fumbled once for minus one yard.
SINGLE GAME HIGHS (regular season): Attempts—28 (December 23, 1995, vs. Detroit); completions—11 (December 23, 1995, vs. Detroit); yards—156 (October 1, 1995, vs. Carolina); and touchdown passes—1 (December 3, 1995, vs. Minnesota).

					PASSING						RUSHING				TOTALS	
Year Team	G	GS	Att.	Cmp.	Pct.	Yds.	TD	Int.	Avg.	Rat.	Att.	Yds.	Avg.	TD	TD	2pt.	Pts.
1992—Philadelphia NFL						Did not play.											
1993—Tampa Bay NFL	3	0	11	6	54.5	55	0	1	5.00	30.5	0	0	...	0	0		0
1994—Tampa Bay NFL	2	0	9	7	77.8	63	0	0	7.00	95.8	0	0	...	0	0	0	0
1995—Barcelona W.L.	...	...	91	41	45.1	543	3	9	5.97	35.9	8	44	5.5	0	0	0	0
—Tampa Bay W.L.	16	0	91	42	46.2	519	1	2	5.70	58.8	5	5	1.0	1	1	0	6
1996—Tampa Bay NFL	3	0	9	5	55.6	76	0	1	8.44	44.0	2	-1	-0.5	0	0	0	0
1997—San Diego NFL						Did not play.											
W.L. totals (1 year)	...	...	91	41	45.1	543	3	9	5.97	35.9	8	44	5.5	0	0	0	0
NFL totals (4 years)	24	0	120	60	50.0	713	1	4	5.94	57.4	7	4	0.6	1	1	0	6
Pro totals (5 years)	...	...	211	101	47.9	1256	4	13	5.95	47.4	15	48	3.2	1	1	0	6

W

WELLS, DEAN   LB   SEAHAWKS

PERSONAL: Born July 20, 1970, in Louisville, Ky. ... 6-3/248. ... Full name: Donald Dean Wells.
HIGH SCHOOL: Holy Cross (Louisville, Ky.).
COLLEGE: Kentucky (degree in marketing, 1992).
TRANSACTIONS/CAREER NOTES: Selected by Seattle Seahawks in fourth round (85th pick overall) of 1993 NFL draft. ... Signed by Seahawks (July 13, 1993).
PLAYING EXPERIENCE: Seattle NFL, 1993-1997. ... Games/Games started: 1993 (14/1), 1994 (15/0), 1995 (14/10), 1996 (16/15), 1997 (16/16). Total: 75/42.
PRO STATISTICS: 1995—Recovered one fumble. 1996—Credited with one sack and recovered two fumbles. 1997—Credited with one sack and recovered one fumble.

WELLS, MIKE   DE   BEARS

PERSONAL: Born January 6, 1971, in Arnold, Mo. ... 6-3/310. ... Full name: Mike Allan Wells.
HIGH SCHOOL: Fox (Arnold, Mo.).
COLLEGE: Iowa.
TRANSACTIONS/CAREER NOTES: Selected by Minnesota Vikings in fourth round (125th pick overall) of 1994 NFL draft. ... Signed by Vikings (June 24, 1994). ... Released by Vikings (August 28, 1994). ... Signed by Detroit Lions (August 29, 1994). ... Granted free agency (February 14, 1997). ... Re-signed by Lions (June 2, 1997). ... Granted unconditional free agency (February 13, 1998). ... Signed by Chicago Bears (February 17, 1998).
PLAYING EXPERIENCE: Detroit NFL, 1994-1997. ... Games/Games started: 1994 (4/0), 1995 (15/0), 1996 (16/1), 1997 (16/16). Total: 51/17.
PRO STATISTICS: 1994—Credited with 1/2 sack. 1996—Recovered one fumble in end zone for a touchdown. 1997—Credited with one sack and recovered one fumble.

WEST, DEREK   OT

PERSONAL: Born March 28, 1972, in Denver. ... 6-8/312.
HIGH SCHOOL: Pomona (Arvada, Colo.).
COLLEGE: Colorado.
TRANSACTIONS/CAREER NOTES: Selected by Indianapolis Colts in fifth round (149th pick overall) of 1995 NFL draft. ... Signed by Colts (July 12, 1995). ... On physically unable to perform list with broken foot (August 20-October 30, 1996). ... Released by Colts (February 4, 1998).
PLAYING EXPERIENCE: Indianapolis NFL, 1995-1997. ... Games/Games started: 1995 (3/0), 1996 (1/0), 1997 (1/0). Total: 5/0.
CHAMPIONSHIP GAME EXPERIENCE: Played in AFC championship game (1995 season).

WEST, ED   TE

PERSONAL: Born August 2, 1961, in Colbert County, Ala. ... 6-1/250. ... Full name: Edward Lee West III.
HIGH SCHOOL: Colbert County (Leighton, Ala.).
COLLEGE: Auburn.
TRANSACTIONS/CAREER NOTES: Selected by Birmingham Stallions in 1984 USFL territorial draft. ... Signed as non-drafted free agent by Green Bay Packers (May 3, 1984). ... Released by Packers (August 27, 1984). ... Re-signed by Packers (August 30, 1984). ... Granted free agency (February 1, 1992). ... Re-signed by Packers (July 27, 1992). ... Released by Packers (August 30, 1993). ... Re-signed by Packers (August 31, 1993). ... Granted unconditional free agency (February 17, 1994). ... Re-signed by Packers (June 22, 1994). ... Granted unconditional free agency (February 17, 1995). ... Signed by Indianapolis Colts (March 28, 1995). ... Released by Colts (August 27, 1995). ... Signed by Philadelphia Eagles (August 28, 1995). ... Granted unconditional free agency (February 16, 1996). ... Re-signed by Eagles (April 18, 1996). ... Granted unconditional free agency (February 14, 1997). ... Signed by Atlanta Falcons (March 6, 1997). ... On injured reserve with knee injury (December 2, 1997-remainder of season). ... Announced retirement (May 3, 1998).
PRO STATISTICS: 1984—Rushed once for two yards and a touchdown and recovered one fumble. 1985—Rushed once for no yards. 1986—Recovered one fumble. 1990—Returned one kickoff for no yards. 1992—Returned one kickoff for no yards. 1995—Recovered one fumble.
SINGLE GAME HIGHS (regular season): Receptions—7 (December 22, 1990, vs. Detroit); yards—103 (December 22, 1990, vs. Detroit); and touchdown receptions—2 (September 9, 1990, vs. Los Angeles Rams).
STATISTICAL PLATEAUS: 100-yard receiving games: 1986 (1), 1990 (1). Total: 2.

| | | | RECEIVING | | | | TOTALS | | | |
Year Team	G	GS	No.	Yds.	Avg.	TD	TD	2pt.	Pts.	Fum.
1984—Green Bay NFL	16	0	6	54	9.0	4	5	...	30	0
1985—Green Bay NFL	16	0	8	95	11.9	1	1	...	6	1
1986—Green Bay NFL	16	6	15	199	13.3	1	1	...	6	0
1987—Green Bay NFL	12	11	19	261	13.7	1	1	...	6	0
1988—Green Bay NFL	16	16	30	276	9.2	3	3	...	18	1
1989—Green Bay NFL	13	12	22	269	12.2	5	5	...	30	0
1990—Green Bay NFL	16	16	27	356	13.2	5	5	...	30	3
1991—Green Bay NFL	16	16	15	151	10.1	3	3	...	18	0
1992—Green Bay NFL	16	8	4	30	7.5	0	0	...	0	0
1993—Green Bay NFL	16	7	25	253	10.1	0	0	...	0	0
1994—Green Bay NFL	14	12	31	377	12.2	2	2	1	14	1
1995—Philadelphia NFL	16	14	20	190	9.5	1	1	0	6	0
1996—Philadelphia NFL	16	4	8	91	11.4	0	0	0	0	0
1997—Atlanta NFL	12	3	7	63	9.0	1	1	0	6	0
Pro totals (14 years)	211	125	237	2665	11.2	27	28	1	170	6

W

WESTBROOK, BRYANT   CB   LIONS

PERSONAL: Born December 19, 1974, in Charlotte. ... 6-0/199. ... Full name: Bryant Antoine Westbrook.
HIGH SCHOOL: El Camino (Oceanside, Calif.).
COLLEGE: Texas.
TRANSACTIONS/CAREER NOTES: Selected by Detroit Lions in first round (fifth pick overall) of 1997 NFL draft. ... Signed by Lions (August 9, 1997).

			INTERCEPTIONS		
Year Team	G	GS	No.	Yds.	Avg.	TD
1997—Detroit NFL	15	14	2	64	32.0	1

WESTBROOK, MICHAEL   WR   REDSKINS

PERSONAL: Born July 7, 1972, in Detroit. ... 6-3/220.
HIGH SCHOOL: Chadsey (Detroit).
COLLEGE: Colorado.
TRANSACTIONS/CAREER NOTES: Selected by Washington Redskins in first round (fourth pick overall) of 1995 NFL draft. ... Signed by Redskins (August 14, 1995).
HONORS: Named wide receiver on THE SPORTING NEWS college All-America first team (1994).
SINGLE GAME HIGHS (regular season): Receptions—9 (November 23, 1997, vs. New York Giants); yards—126 (November 24, 1996, vs. San Francisco); and touchdown receptions—2 (September 14, 1997, vs. Arizona).
STATISTICAL PLATEAUS: 100-yard receiving games: 1996 (1), 1997 (1). Total: 2.

			RUSHING				RECEIVING				TOTALS			
Year Team	G	GS	Att.	Yds.	Avg.	TD	No.	Yds.	Avg.	TD	TD	2pt.	Pts.	Fum.
1995—Washington NFL	11	9	6	114	19.0	1	34	522	15.4	1	2	0	12	0
1996—Washington NFL	11	6	2	2	1.0	0	34	505	14.9	1	1	0	6	0
1997—Washington NFL	13	9	3	-11	-3.7	0	34	559	16.4	3	3	0	18	0
Pro totals (3 years)	35	24	11	105	9.5	1	102	1586	15.5	5	6	0	36	0

WETNIGHT, RYAN   TE   BEARS

PERSONAL: Born November 5, 1970, in Fresno, Calif. ... 6-2/236. ... Full name: Ryan Scott Wetnight.
HIGH SCHOOL: Hoover (Fresno, Calif.).
JUNIOR COLLEGE: Fresno (Calif.) City College.
COLLEGE: Stanford.
TRANSACTIONS/CAREER NOTES: Signed as non-drafted free agent by Chicago Bears (April 29, 1993). ... Released by Bears (October 10, 1993). ... Re-signed by Bears to practice squad (October 11, 1993). ... Activated (October 29, 1993). ... Released by Bears (October 7, 1994). ... Re-signed by Bears (October 10, 1994). ... On injured reserve with knee injury (December 7, 1995-remainder of season). ... Granted unconditional free agency (February 14, 1997). ... Re-signed by Bears (April 2, 1997). ... Granted unconditional free agency (February 13, 1998). ... Re-signed by Bears (February 23, 1998).
PRO STATISTICS: 1997—Returned one kickoff for nine yards.
SINGLE GAME HIGHS (regular season): Receptions—6 (October 27, 1997, vs. Miami); yards—70 (December 7, 1997, vs. Buffalo); and touchdown receptions—1 (December 7, 1997, vs. Buffalo).

			RECEIVING				TOTALS			
Year Team	G	GS	No.	Yds.	Avg.	TD	TD	2pt.	Pts.	Fum.
1993—Chicago NFL	10	1	9	93	10.3	1	1	...	6	0
1994—Chicago NFL	11	0	11	104	9.5	1	1	0	6	0
1995—Chicago NFL	12	2	24	193	8.0	2	2	0	12	0
1996—Chicago NFL	11	5	21	223	10.6	1	1	0	6	0
1997—Chicago NFL	16	3	46	464	10.1	1	1	0	6	1
Pro totals (5 years)	60	11	111	1077	9.7	6	6	0	36	1

WHEATLEY, TYRONE   RB   GIANTS

PERSONAL: Born January 19, 1972, in Inkster, Mich. ... 6-0/230.
HIGH SCHOOL: Robichaud (Dearborn Heights, Mich.).
COLLEGE: Michigan.
TRANSACTIONS/CAREER NOTES: Selected by New York Giants in first round (17th pick overall) of 1995 NFL draft. ... Signed by Giants (August 9, 1995).
PRO STATISTICS: 1996—Attempted one pass with one completion for 24 yards and a touchdown and recovered one fumble for minus 18 yards. 1997—Recovered three fumbles.
SINGLE GAME HIGHS (regular season): Attempts—22 (October 12, 1997, vs. Arizona); yards—103 (October 12, 1997, vs. Arizona; rushing touchdowns—2 (October 26, 1997, vs. Cincinnati).
STATISTICAL PLATEAUS: 100-yard rushing games: 1997 (1).

			RUSHING				RECEIVING				KICKOFF RETURNS				TOTALS			
Year Team	G	GS	Att.	Yds.	Avg.	TD	No.	Yds.	Avg.	TD	No.	Yds.	Avg.	TD	TD	2pt.	Pts.	Fum.
1995—New York Giants NFL	13	1	78	245	3.1	3	5	27	5.4	0	10	186	18.6	0	3	0	18	2
1996—New York Giants NFL	14	0	112	400	3.6	3	12	51	4.3	2	23	503	21.9	0	3	0	18	6
1997—New York Giants NFL	14	7	152	583	3.8	4	16	140	8.8	0	0	0	...	0	4	0	24	3
Pro totals (3 years)	41	8	342	1228	3.6	8	33	210	6.0	2	33	689	20.9	0	10	0	60	11

W

WHEATON, KENNY   CB   COWBOYS

PERSONAL: Born March 8, 1975, in Phoenix. ... 5-10/190. ... Full name: Kenneth Tyrone Wheaton.
HIGH SCHOOL: McClintock (Tempe, Ariz.).
COLLEGE: Oregon.
TRANSACTIONS/CAREER NOTES: Selected by Dallas Cowboys in third round (94th pick overall) of 1997 NFL draft. ... Signed by Cowboys (July 14, 1997).
PLAYING EXPERIENCE: Dallas NFL, 1997. ... Games/Games started: 2/0.

WHEELER, LEONARD   CB   PANTHERS

PERSONAL: Born January 15, 1969, in Taccoa, Ga. ... 5-11/189. ... Full name: Leonard Tyrone Wheeler.
HIGH SCHOOL: Stephens County (Taccoa, Ga.).
JUNIOR COLLEGE: Northwest Mississippi Community College (did not play football).
COLLEGE: Lees-McRae College (N.C.), then Mississippi (did not play football), then Troy (Ala.) State.
TRANSACTIONS/CAREER NOTES: Selected by Cincinnati Bengals in third round (84th pick overall) of 1992 NFL draft. ... Signed by Bengals (July 25, 1992). ... On injured reserve with wrist injury (August 28, 1994-entire season). ... Granted free agency (February 17, 1995). ... Re-signed by Bengals (April 13, 1995). ... Granted unconditional free agency (February 16, 1996). ... Re-signed by Bengals (April 26, 1996). ... Granted free agency (February 14, 1997). ... Signed by Minnesota Vikings (July 17, 1997). ... Granted unconditional free agency (February 13, 1998). ... Signed by Carolina Panthers (February 20, 1998).
PLAYING EXPERIENCE: Cincinnati NFL, 1992, 1993, 1995 and 1996; Minnesota NFL, 1997. ... Games/Games started: 1992 (16/2), 1993 (16/2), 1995 (16/1), 1996 (13/0), 1997 (15/0). Total: 76/5.
PRO STATISTICS: 1992—Intercepted one pass for 12 yards. 1993—Recovered one fumble. 1997—Credited with two sacks and recovered one fumble.

WHEELER, MARK   DT   PATRIOTS

PERSONAL: Born April 1, 1970, in San Marcos, Texas. ... 6-3/285. ... Full name: Mark Anthony Wheeler.
HIGH SCHOOL: San Marcos (Texas).
JUNIOR COLLEGE: Navarro College (Texas).
COLLEGE: Texas A&M.
TRANSACTIONS/CAREER NOTES: Selected by Tampa Bay Buccaneers in third round (59th pick overall) of 1992 NFL draft. ... Signed by Buccaneers (July 9, 1992). ... Granted unconditional free agency (February 16, 1996). ... Signed by New England Patriots (March 21, 1996).
CHAMPIONSHIP GAME EXPERIENCE: Played in AFC championship game (1996 season). ... Played in Super Bowl XXXI (1996 season).
PRO STATISTICS: 1996—Recovered one fumble.

Year Team	G	GS	SACKS
1992—Tampa Bay NFL	16	16	5.0
1993—Tampa Bay NFL	10	10	2.0
1994—Tampa Bay NFL	15	8	3.0
1995—Tampa Bay NFL	14	12	1.0
1996—New England NFL	16	15	1.0
1997—New England NFL	14	14	4.0
Pro totals (6 years)	85	75	16.0

WHELIHAN, CRAIG   QB   CHARGERS

PERSONAL: Born April 15, 1971, in San Jose. ... 6-5/220.
HIGH SCHOOL: Santa Teresa (San Jose).
COLLEGE: Oregon State, then Pacific.
TRANSACTIONS/CAREER NOTES: Selected by San Diego Chargers in sixth round (197th pick overall) of 1995 NFL draft. ... Signed by Chargers (July 6, 1995). ... Inactive for 16 games (1995). ... Active for three games (1996); did not play.
PRO STATISTICS: 1997—Fumbled seven times and recovered two fumbles for minus 11 yards.
SINGLE GAME HIGHS (regular season): Attempts—51 (November 30, 1997, vs. Denver); completions—23 (November 30, 1997; vs. Denver); yards—259 (December 7, 1997, vs. Atlanta); and touchdown passes—2 (November 30, 1997, vs. Denver).
MISCELLANEOUS: Regular-season record as starting NFL quarterback: 0-7.

Year Team	G	GS	Att.	Cmp.	Pct.	Yds.	TD	Int.	Avg.	Rat.	Att.	Yds.	Avg.	TD	TD	2pt.	Pts.
						PASSING							RUSHING			TOTALS	
1995—San Diego NFL						Did not play.											
1996—San Diego NFL						Did not play.											
1997—San Diego NFL	9	7	237	118	49.8	1357	6	10	5.73	58.3	13	29	2.2	0	0	0	0

WHIGHAM, LARRY   S   PATRIOTS

PERSONAL: Born June 23, 1972, in Hattiesburg, Miss. ... 6-2/205. ... Full name: Larry Jerome Whigham.
HIGH SCHOOL: Hattiesburg (Miss.).
COLLEGE: Northeast Louisiana.
TRANSACTIONS/CAREER NOTES: Selected by Seattle Seahawks in fourth round (110th pick overall) of 1994 NFL draft. ... Signed by Seahawks (June 9, 1994). ... Released by Seahawks (August 28, 1994). ... Re-signed by Seahawks to practice squad (August 29, 1994). ... Signed by New England Patriots off Seahawks practice squad (September 13, 1994). ... Granted free agency (February 14, 1997). ... Re-signed by Patriots (May 1, 1997).
CHAMPIONSHIP GAME EXPERIENCE: Played in AFC championship game (1996 season). ... Played in Super Bowl XXXI (1996 season).
HONORS: Played in Pro Bowl (1997 season).
PRO STATISTICS: 1994—Fumbled once. 1995—Recovered one fumble. 1996—Recovered one fumble. 1997—Credited with two sacks.

W

Year Team		G	GS	INTERCEPTIONS			
				No.	Yds.	Avg.	TD
1994—New England NFL		12	0	1	21	21.0	0
1995—New England NFL		16	0	0	0	...	0
1996—New England NFL		16	1	0	0	...	0
1997—New England NFL		16	0	2	60	30.0	1
Pro totals (4 years)		60	1	3	81	27.0	1

WHITE, JOSE   DT   JAGUARS

PERSONAL: Born March 2, 1973, in Washington, D.C. ... 6-3/274. ... Full name: Jose C. White.

HIGH SCHOOL: Howard D. Woodson (Washington, D.C.).

COLLEGE: Howard.

TRANSACTIONS/CAREER NOTES: Selected by Minnesota Vikings in seventh round (232nd pick overall) of 1995 NFL draft. ... Signed by Vikings (July 22, 1995). ... Inactive for three games (1995). ... Released by Vikings (September 21, 1995). ... Re-signed by Vikings to practice squad (September 22, 1995). ... Released by Vikings (August 20, 1996). ... Signed by New York Jets to practice squad (September 11, 1996). ... Released by Jets (October 1, 1996). ... Signed by New Orleans Saints to practice squad (October 31, 1996). ... Signed by Jacksonville Jaguars from Saints practice squad (December 3, 1996). ... Inactive for four games (1996). ... Released by Jaguars (August 19, 1997). ... Re-signed by Jaguars (November 11, 1997).

PLAYING EXPERIENCE: Jacksonville NFL, 1997. ... Games/Games started: 3/0.

CHAMPIONSHIP GAME EXPERIENCE: Member of Jaguars for AFC championship game (1996 season); inactive.

WHITE, REGGIE   DE   PACKERS

PERSONAL: Born December 19, 1961, in Chattanooga, Tenn. ... 6-5/304. ... Full name: Reginald Howard White.

HIGH SCHOOL: Howard (Chattanooga, Tenn.).

COLLEGE: Tennessee.

TRANSACTIONS/CAREER NOTES: Selected by Memphis Showboats in 1984 USFL territorial draft. ... Signed by Showboats (January 15, 1984). ... On developmental squad (March 9-24, 1984). ... Selected by Philadelphia Eagles in first round (fourth pick overall) of 1984 NFL supplemental draft. ... Released by Showboats (September 19, 1985). ... Signed by Eagles (September 21, 1985). ... Granted roster exemption (September 21-27, 1985). ... On reserve/did not report list (July 28-August 23, 1989). ... Designated by Eagles as franchise player (February 25, 1993). ... Signed by Green Bay Packers (April 6, 1993); Eagles received first-round pick (G Lester Holmes) in 1993 draft and first-round pick (traded to Cleveland) in 1994 draft as compensation. ... Announced retirement (April 19, 1998); decided to return for 1998 season.

CHAMPIONSHIP GAME EXPERIENCE: Played in NFC championship game (1995-97 seasons). ... Member of Super Bowl championship team (1996 season). ... Played in Super Bowl XXXII (1997 season).

HONORS: Named defensive end on THE SPORTING NEWS college All-America first team (1983). ... Named defensive end on THE SPORTING NEWS USFL All-Star team (1985). ... Played in Pro Bowl (1986-1993, 1995-1997 seasons). ... Named Outstanding Player of Pro Bowl (1986 season). ... Named defensive end on THE SPORTING NEWS NFL All-Pro team (1987, 1988, 1991, 1993 and 1995). ... Named to play in Pro Bowl (1994 season); replaced by Wayne Martin due to injury.

RECORDS: Holds NFL career record for most sacks—176.5.

POST SEASON RECORDS: Holds Super Bowl single-game record for most sacks (since 1982)—3 ... (January 26, 1997, vs. New England). ... Shares NFL postseason career record for most sacks—12. ... Shares NFL postseason single-game record for most safeties—1 (January 3, 1993, at New Orleans).

PRO STATISTICS: USFL: 1984—Recovered one fumble. 1985—Credited with one safety and recovered one fumble for 20 yards and a touchdown. NFL: 1985—Recovered two fumbles. 1987—Recovered one fumble for 70 yards and a touchdown. 1988—Recovered two fumbles. 1989—Recovered one fumble for 10 yards. 1990—Intercepted one pass for 33 yards and recovered one fumble. 1991—Intercepted one pass for no yards and recovered three fumbles for eight yards. 1992—Recovered one fumble for 37 yards and a touchdown. 1993—Recovered two fumbles for 10 yards. 1994—Recovered one fumble. 1996—Intercepted one pass for 46 yards, fumbled twice and recovered three fumbles for two yards. 1997—Recovered two fumbles.

MISCELLANEOUS: Active NFL leader for career sacks (176.5). ... Holds Philadelphia Eagles all-time record for most sacks (124).

Year Team	G	GS	SACKS
1984—Memphis USFL	16	16	12.0
1905—Memphis USFL	18	18	11.5
—Philadelphia NFL	13	12	13.0
1986—Philadelphia NFL	16	16	18.0
1987—Philadelphia NFL	12	12	*21.0
1988—Philadelphia NFL	16	16	*18.0
1989—Philadelphia NFL	16	16	11.0
1990—Philadelphia NFL	16	16	14.0
1991—Philadelphia NFL	16	16	15.0
1992—Philadelphia NFL	16	16	14.0
1993—Green Bay NFL	16	16	‡13.0
1994—Green Bay NFL	16	15	8.0
1995—Green Bay NFL	15	13	12.0
1996—Green Bay NFL	16	16	8.5
1997—Green Bay NFL	16	16	11.0
USFL totals (2 years)	34	34	23.5
NFL totals (13 years)	200	196	176.5
Pro totals (15 years)	234	230	200.0

WHITE, STAN   QB   DOLPHINS

PERSONAL: Born August 14, 1971, in Birmingham, Ala. ... 6-2/220. ... Full name: Stanley Cleve White.

HIGH SCHOOL: Berry (Birmingham, Ala.).

COLLEGE: Auburn.

W

TRANSACTIONS/CAREER NOTES: Signed as non-drafted free agent by New York Giants (July 17, 1994). ... Inactive for 16 games (1994 season). ... Inactive for 15 games (1995 season). ... Inactive for 10 games (1996 season). ... Assigned by Giants to London Monarchs in 1997 World League enhancement allocation program (February 19, 1997). ... On non-football injury list with shoulder injury (July 18, 1997-entire season). ... Released by Giants (February 12, 1998). ... Signed by Miami Dolphins (March 23, 1998).
PLAYING EXPERIENCE: London W.L., 1997. ... Games/Games started: W.L. 1997 (games played unavailable).
PRO STATISTICS: W.L.: 1997—Attempted 131 passes with 62 completions for 676 yards, three touchdowns and four interceptions and rushed 13 times for 32 yards and one touchdown.
SINGLE GAME HIGHS (regular season): Attempts—0; completions—0; yards—0; and touchdown passes—0.

WHITE, STEVE — LB — BUCCANEERS

PERSONAL: Born October 25, 1973, in Memphis. ... 6-2/265. ... Full name: Stephen Gregory White.
HIGH SCHOOL: Westwood (Memphis).
COLLEGE: Tennessee (degree in psychology, 1996).
TRANSACTIONS/CAREER NOTES: Selected by Philadelphia Eagles in sixth round (194th pick overall) of 1996 NFL draft. ... Signed by Eagles (July 17, 1996). ... Released by Eagles (August 20, 1996). ... Signed by Tampa Bay Buccaneers to practice squad (August 27, 1996). ... Activated (October 15, 1996). ... Released by Buccaneers (November 9, 1996). ... Re-signed by Buccaneers (November 12, 1996).
PLAYING EXPERIENCE: Tampa Bay NFL, 1996 and 1997. ... Games/Games started: 1996 (4/0), 1997 (15/1). Total: 19/1.
PRO STATISTICS: 1997—Returned one kickoff for no yards.

WHITE, WILLIAM — S — FALCONS

PERSONAL: Born February 19, 1966, in Lima, Ohio. ... 5-10/205. ... Full name: William Eugene White.
HIGH SCHOOL: Lima (Ohio).
COLLEGE: Ohio State.
TRANSACTIONS/CAREER NOTES: Selected by Detroit Lions in fourth round (85th pick overall) of 1988 NFL draft. ... Signed by Lions (July 11, 1988). ... Granted unconditional free agency (March 1, 1993). ... Re-signed by Lions (April 6, 1993). ... Traded by Lions to Kansas City Chiefs for conditional pick in 1995 draft (July 13, 1994). ... Granted unconditional free agency (February 14, 1997). ... Signed by Atlanta Falcons (March 13, 1997).
CHAMPIONSHIP GAME EXPERIENCE: Played in NFC championship game (1991 season).
PRO STATISTICS: 1988—Recovered one fumble. 1989—Recovered one fumble for 20 yards and a touchdown. 1991—Returned blocked field-goal attempt 55 yards for a touchdown. 1992—Fumbled once.

			INTERCEPTIONS			SACKS
Year Team	G	GS	No.	Yds.	Avg.	TD	No.
1988—Detroit NFL	16	0	0	0	...	0	0.0
1989—Detroit NFL	15	15	1	0	0.0	0	1.0
1990—Detroit NFL	16	16	5	120	24.0	1	0.0
1991—Detroit NFL	16	16	2	35	17.5	0	0.0
1992—Detroit NFL	16	16	4	54	13.5	0	0.0
1993—Detroit NFL	16	16	1	5	5.0	0	1.5
1994—Kansas City NFL	15	14	2	0	0.0	0	0.0
1995—Kansas City NFL	16	5	2	48	24.0	0	1.0
1996—Kansas City NFL	12	2	0	0	...	0	0.0
1997—Atlanta NFL	16	16	1	11	11.0	0	0.0
Pro totals (10 years)	154	116	18	273	15.2	1	3.5

WHITFIELD, BOB — OT — FALCONS

PERSONAL: Born October 18, 1971, in Carson, Calif. ... 6-5/310. ... Full name: Bob Whitfield Jr.
HIGH SCHOOL: Banning (Los Angeles).
COLLEGE: Stanford.
TRANSACTIONS/CAREER NOTES: Selected after junior season by Atlanta Falcons in first round (eighth pick overall) of 1992 NFL draft. ... Signed by Falcons (September 4, 1992). ... Granted roster exemption for one game (September 1992).
PLAYING EXPERIENCE: Atlanta NFL, 1992-1997. ... Games/Games started: 1992 (11/0), 1993 (16/16), 1994 (16/16), 1995 (16/16), 1996 (16/16), 1997 (16/16). Total: 91/80.
HONORS: Named offensive tackle on THE SPORTING NEWS college All-America first team (1991).
PRO STATISTICS: 1993—Recovered two fumbles. 1996—Recovered one fumble.

W

WHITLEY, CURTIS — C — RAIDERS

PERSONAL: Born May 10, 1969, in Lowgrounds, N.C. ... 6-1/295. ... Full name: Curtis Wayne Whitley.
HIGH SCHOOL: Smithfield (N.C.)-Selma Senior.
COLLEGE: Chowan College (N.C.), then Clemson.
TRANSACTIONS/CAREER NOTES: Selected by San Diego Chargers in fifth round (117th pick overall) of 1992 NFL draft. ... Signed by Chargers (July 16, 1992). ... Released by Chargers (July 18, 1994). ... Re-signed by Chargers (August 20, 1994). ... Selected by Carolina Panthers from Chargers in NFL expansion draft (February 15, 1995). ... Granted free agency (February 17, 1995). ... Signed by Panthers (May 5, 1995). ... Granted unconditional free agency (February 16, 1996). ... Re-signed by Panthers (February 26, 1996). ... On reserved/suspended list (October 31-November 29, 1996). ... Released by Panthers (July 14, 1997). ... Signed by Raiders for 1997 season. ... Granted unconditional free agency (February 13, 1998). ... Re-signed by Raiders (February 19, 1998).
PLAYING EXPERIENCE: San Diego NFL, 1992-1994; Carolina NFL, 1995 and 1996; Oakland NFL, 1997. ... Games/Games started: 1992 (3/0), 1993 (15/0), 1994 (12/2), 1995 (16/16), 1996 (11/8), 1997 (15/1). Total: 72/27.
CHAMPIONSHIP GAME EXPERIENCE: Played in AFC championship game (1994 season). ... Member of Chargers for Super Bowl XXIX (1994 season); did not play. ... Played in NFC championship game (1996 season).
PRO STATISTICS: 1994—Recovered one fumble. 1995—Recovered one fumble.

WHITTAKER, SCOTT — OT — RAIDERS

PERSONAL: Born May 7, 1974, in Long Beach, Calif. ... 6-7/300.
HIGH SCHOOL: Etiwanda (Alta Loma, Calif.).
COLLEGE: Kansas.
TRANSACTIONS/CAREER NOTES: Signed as non-drafted free agent by Oakland Raiders (April 1997). ... Inactive for all 16 games (1997).

WHITTINGTON, BERNARD — DE — COLTS

PERSONAL: Born August 20, 1971, in St. Louis. ... 6-6/280. ... Full name: Bernard M. Whittington.
HIGH SCHOOL: Hazelwood East (St. Louis).
COLLEGE: Indiana.
TRANSACTIONS/CAREER NOTES: Signed as non-drafted free agent by Indianapolis Colts (May 5, 1994). ... Granted free agency (February 14, 1997). ... Re-signed by Colts (June 13, 1997).
CHAMPIONSHIP GAME EXPERIENCE: Played in AFC championship game (1995 season).
PRO STATISTICS: 1995—Recovered one fumble.

Year Team	G	GS	SACKS
1994—Indianapolis NFL	13	8	0.0
1995—Indianapolis NFL	16	13	2.0
1996—Indianapolis NFL	16	14	3.0
1997—Indianapolis NFL	15	6	0.0
Pro totals (4 years)	60	41	5.0

WIDELL, DAVE — C — FALCONS

PERSONAL: Born May 14, 1965, in Hartford, Conn. ... 6-7/312. ... Full name: David Harold Widell. ... Brother of Doug Widell, guard, Green Bay Packers. ... Name pronounced WY-dell.
HIGH SCHOOL: South Catholic (Hartford, Conn.).
COLLEGE: Boston College (degree in finance, 1988).
TRANSACTIONS/CAREER NOTES: Selected by Dallas Cowboys in fourth round (94th pick overall) of 1988 NFL draft. ... Signed by Cowboys (July 12, 1988). ... Traded by Cowboys to Denver Broncos for seventh-round pick (DT Leon Lett) in 1991 draft and eighth-round pick (traded to Cleveland) in 1992 draft (August 24, 1990). ... Granted unconditional free agency (February 17, 1994). ... Re-signed by Broncos for 1994 season. ... Granted unconditional free agency (February 17, 1995). ... Signed by Jacksonville Jaguars (March 15, 1995). ... Granted unconditional free agency (February 13, 1998). ... Signed by Atlanta Falcons (May 8, 1998).
PLAYING EXPERIENCE: Dallas NFL, 1988 and 1989; Denver NFL, 1990-1994; Jacksonville NFL, 1995-1997. ... Games/Games started: 1988 (14/9), 1989 (15/2), 1990 (16/5), 1991 (16/2), 1992 (16/1), 1993 (15/15), 1994 (16/16), 1995 (16/16), 1996 (15/14), 1997 (16/12). Total: 155/92.
CHAMPIONSHIP GAME EXPERIENCE: Played in AFC championship game (1991 and 1996 seasons).
PRO STATISTICS: 1988—Recovered one fumble. 1991—Fumbled once for minus 15 yards. 1994—Fumbled once. 1997—Recovered one fumble.

WIDELL, DOUG — G — PACKERS

PERSONAL: Born September 23, 1966, in Hartford, Conn. ... 6-4/296. ... Full name: Douglas Joseph Widell. ... Brother of Dave Widell, center, Atlanta Falcons. ... Name pronounced WY-dell.
HIGH SCHOOL: South Catholic (Hartford, Conn.).
COLLEGE: Boston College (degree in marketing, 1989).
TRANSACTIONS/CAREER NOTES: Selected by Denver Broncos in second round (41st pick overall) of 1989 NFL draft. ... Signed by Broncos (July 23, 1989). ... Granted free agency (February 1, 1992). ... Re-signed by Broncos (July 22, 1992). ... Traded by Broncos to Green Bay Packers for seventh-round pick (RB Butler By'not'e) in 1994 draft (August 24, 1993). ... Granted unconditional free agency (February 17, 1994). ... Signed by Detroit Lions (June 2, 1994). ... Granted unconditional free agency (February 16, 1996). ... Signed by Indianapolis Colts (March 16, 1996). ... Released by Colts (February 20, 1998). ... Signed by Green Bay Packers (April 18, 1998).
PLAYING EXPERIENCE: Denver NFL, 1989-1992; Green Bay NFL, 1993; Detroit NFL, 1994 and 1995; Indianapolis NFL, 1996 and 1997. ... Games/Games started: 1989 (16/10), 1990 (16/16), 1991 (16/16), 1992 (16/16), 1993 (16/9), 1994 (16/16), 1995 (11/11), 1996 (16/16), 1997 (16/16). Total: 139/126.
CHAMPIONSHIP GAME EXPERIENCE: Played in AFC championship game (1989 and 1991 seasons). ... Played in Super Bowl XXIV (1989 season).
PRO STATISTICS: 1990—Recovered one fumble. 1991—Recovered one fumble. 1992—Caught one pass for minus seven yards and recovered two fumbles.

WIDMER, COREY — LB — GIANTS

PERSONAL: Born December 25, 1968, in Alexandria, Va. ... 6-3/255. ... Full name: Corey Edward Widmer.
HIGH SCHOOL: Bozeman (Mont.).
COLLEGE: Montana State.
TRANSACTIONS/CAREER NOTES: Selected by New York Giants in seventh round (180th pick overall) of 1992 NFL draft. ... Signed by Giants (July 21, 1992). ... On injured reserve with back injury (September 5-30, 1992). ... On practice squad (September 30-November 15, 1992). ... Granted free agency (February 17, 1995). ... Re-signed by Giants (April 18, 1995).
PLAYING EXPERIENCE: New York Giants NFL, 1992-1997. ... Games/Games started: 1992 (8/0), 1993 (11/0), 1994 (16/5), 1995 (16/0), 1996 (16/16), 1997 (16/15). Total: 83/36.
PRO STATISTICS: 1994—Credited with one sack. 1995—Returned one kickoff for no yards. 1996—Intercepted two passes for eight yards, credited with two sacks, fumbled once and recovered one fumble. 1997—Intercepted two passes for no yards and credited with 1 1/2 sacks.

W

WIEGERT, ZACH   OT   RAMS

PERSONAL: Born August 16, 1972, in Fremont, Neb. ... 6-4/310. ... Full name: Zach Allan Wiegert. ... Name pronounced WEE-gert.
HIGH SCHOOL: Bergan (Fremont, Neb.).
COLLEGE: Nebraska.
TRANSACTIONS/CAREER NOTES: Selected by St. Louis Rams in second round (38th pick overall) of 1995 NFL draft. ... Signed by Rams (July 18, 1995). ... Granted free agency (February 13, 1998).
PLAYING EXPERIENCE: St. Louis NFL, 1995-1997. ... Games/Games started: 1995 (5/2), 1996 (16/16), 1997 (15/15). Total: 36/33.
HONORS: Outland Trophy Award winner (1994). ... Named offensive lineman on THE SPORTING NEWS college All-America first team (1994).
PRO STATISTICS: 1996—Recovered two fumbles. 1997—Caught one pass for one yard and recovered four fumbles for no yards and one touchdown.

WIEGMANN, CASEY   C   BEARS

PERSONAL: Born July 20, 1973, in Parkersburg, Iowa. ... 6-3/295.
HIGH SCHOOL: Parkersburg (Iowa).
COLLEGE: Iowa.
TRANSACTIONS/CAREER NOTES: Signed as non-drafted free agent by Indianapolis Colts (April 26, 1996). ... Released by Colts (August 25, 1996). ... Re-signed by Colts to practice squad (August 27, 1996). ... Activated (September 10, 1996); did not play. ... Released by Colts (September 22, 1996). ... Re-signed by Colts to practice squad (September 23, 1996). ... Activated (October 15, 1996); did not play. ... Claimed on waivers by New York Jets (October 29, 1996). ... Released by Jets (September 21, 1997). ... Signed by Chicago Bears (September 24, 1997).
PLAYING EXPERIENCE: New York Jets (3)-Chicago (1) NFL, 1997. ... Games/Games started: 1997 (NYJ-3/0; Chi.-1/0; Total: 4/0).

WIGGINS, PAUL   OT   STEELERS

PERSONAL: Born August 17, 1973, in Portland. ... 6-3/307. ... Full name: Paul Anthony Wiggins.
HIGH SCHOOL: Benson (Portland).
COLLEGE: Oregon.
TRANSACTIONS/CAREER NOTES: Selected by Pittsburgh Steelers in third round (82nd pick overall) of 1997 NFL draft. ... Signed by Steelers (July 14, 1997).
CHAMPIONSHIP GAME EXPERIENCE: Member of Steelers for AFC championship game (1997 season); inactive.
PLAYING EXPERIENCE: Pittsburgh NFL, 1997. ... Games/Games started: 1/0.

WILEY, MARCELLUS   DE   BILLS

PERSONAL: Born November 30, 1974, in Los Angeles. ... 6-5/271.
HIGH SCHOOL: Saint Monica (Los Angeles).
COLLEGE: Columbia.
TRANSACTIONS/CAREER NOTES: Selected by Buffalo Bills in second round (52nd pick overall) of 1997 NFL draft. ... Signed by Bills (June 20, 1997).
PLAYING EXPERIENCE: Buffalo NFL, 1997. ... Games/Games started: 16/0.
PRO STATISTICS: 1997—Returned one kickoff for 12 yards, fumbled once and recovered two fumbles for 40 yards.

WILKERSON, BRUCE   OT/G   PACKERS

PERSONAL: Born July 28, 1964, in Loudon, Tenn. ... 6-5/310. ... Full name: Bruce Alan Wilkerson.
HIGH SCHOOL: Loudon (Tenn.).
COLLEGE: Tennessee.
TRANSACTIONS/CAREER NOTES: Selected by Los Angeles Raiders in second round (52nd pick overall) of 1987 NFL draft. ... Signed by Raiders (July 10, 1987). ... Crossed picket line during players strike (October 2, 1987). ... On injured reserve with knee injury (September 4-November 4, 1990). ... Granted free agency (February 1, 1991). ... Re-signed by Raiders (July 23, 1991). ... On injured reserve with broken foot (December 22, 1992-remainder of season). ... Granted free agency (February 17, 1995). ... Signed by Jacksonville Jaguars (June 15, 1995). ... Released by Jaguars (April 16, 1996). ... Signed by Green Bay Packers (April 19, 1996).
PLAYING EXPERIENCE: Los Angeles Raiders NFL, 1987-1994; Jacksonville NFL, 1995; Green Bay NFL, 1996 and 1997. ... Games/Games started: 1987 (11/5), 1988 (16/16), 1989 (16/16), 1990 (8/1), 1991 (16/16), 1992 (15/15), 1993 (14/14), 1994 (11/6), 1995 (10/0), 1996 (14/2), 1997 (16/3). Total: 147/94.
CHAMPIONSHIP GAME EXPERIENCE: Played in AFC championship game (1990 season). ... Played in NFC championship game (1996 and 1997 seasons). ... Member of Super Bowl championship team (1996 season). ... Played in Super Bowl XXXII (1997 season).
HONORS: Named offensive guard on THE SPORTING NEWS college All-America second team (1985).
PRO STATISTICS: 1989—Recovered two fumbles. 1992—Recovered one fumble. 1993—Recovered one fumble. 1994—Recovered one fumble.

WILKINS, GABE   DE   49ERS

PERSONAL: Born September 1, 1971, in Cowpens, S.C. ... 6-5/315. ... Full name: Gabriel Nicholas Wilkins.
HIGH SCHOOL: Gettys D. Broome (Spartanburg, S.C.).
COLLEGE: Gardner-Webb (N.C.).
TRANSACTIONS/CAREER NOTES: Selected by Green Bay Packers in fourth round (126th pick overall) of 1994 NFL draft. ... Signed by Packers (June 17, 1994). ... Granted free agency (February 14, 1997). ... Re-signed by Packers (April 28, 1997). ... Granted unconditional free agency (February 13, 1998). ... Signed by San Francisco 49ers (February 19, 1998).
CHAMPIONSHIP GAME EXPERIENCE: Played in NFC championship game (1995-97 season). ... Member of Super Bowl championship team (1996 season). ... Played in Super Bowl XXXII (1997 season).
PRO STATISTICS: 1997—Intercepted one pass for 77 yards and a touchdown and recovered three fumbles for one yard and one touchdown.

W

Year—Team	G	GS	SACKS
1994—Green Bay NFL	15	0	1.0
1995—Green Bay NFL	13	8	3.0
1996—Green Bay NFL	16	1	3.0
1997—Green Bay NFL	16	16	5.5
Pro totals (4 years)	60	25	12.5

WILKINS, JEFF   K   RAMS

PERSONAL: Born April 19, 1972, in Youngstown, Ohio. ... 6-2/205. ... Full name: Jeff Allen Wilkins.
HIGH SCHOOL: Austintown Fitch (Youngstown, Ohio).
COLLEGE: Youngstown State.
TRANSACTIONS/CAREER NOTES: Signed as non-drafted free agent by Dallas Cowboys (April 28, 1994). ... Released by Cowboys (July 18, 1994). ... Signed by Philadelphia Eagles (November 14, 1994). ... Released by Eagles (August 14, 1995). ... Signed by San Francisco 49ers (November 8, 1995). ... Granted unconditional free agency (February 14, 1997). ... Signed by St. Louis Rams (March 6, 1997).

Year—Team	G	GS	XPM	XPA	FGM	FGA	Lg.	50+	Pts.
1994—Philadelphia NFL	6	0	0	0	0	0	...	0-0	0
1995—San Francisco NFL	7	0	27	29	12	13	40	0-0	63
1996—San Francisco NFL	16	0	40	40	30	34	49	0-0	130
1997—St. Louis NFL	16	0	32	32	25	∞37	52	2-2	107
Pro totals (4 years)	45	0	99	101	67	84	52	2-2	300

WILKINSON, DAN   DT   REDSKINS

PERSONAL: Born March 13, 1973, in Dayton, Ohio. ... 6-5/313. ... Nickname: Big Daddy.
HIGH SCHOOL: Paul L. Dunbar (Dayton, Ohio).
COLLEGE: Ohio State.
TRANSACTIONS/CAREER NOTES: Selected after sophomore season by Cincinnati Bengals in first round (first pick overall) of 1994 NFL draft. ... Signed by Bengals (May 5, 1994). ... Designated by Bengals as franchise player (February 11, 1998). ... Tendered offer sheet by Washington Redskins (February 25, 1998). ... Bengals declined to match offer (February 26, 1998).
HONORS: Named defensive lineman on THE SPORTING NEWS college All-America first team (1993).
PRO STATISTICS: 1996—Intercepted one pass for seven yards, fumbled once and recovered one fumble.

Year—Team	G	GS	SACKS
1994—Cincinnati NFL	16	14	5.5
1995—Cincinnati NFL	14	14	8.0
1996—Cincinnati NFL	16	16	6.5
1997—Cincinnati NFL	15	15	5.0
Pro totals (4 years)	61	59	25.0

WILLIAMS, AENEAS   CB   CARDINALS

PERSONAL: Born January 29, 1968, in New Orleans. ... 5-11/202. ... Full name: Aeneas Demetrius Williams.
HIGH SCHOOL: Fortier (New Orleans).
COLLEGE: Southern, La. (degree in accounting, 1990).
TRANSACTIONS/CAREER NOTES: Selected by Phoenix Cardinals in third round (59th pick overall) of 1991 NFL draft. ... Signed by Cardinals (July 26, 1991). ... Granted free agency (February 17, 1994). ... Cardinals franchise renamed Arizona Cardinals for 1994 season. ... Re-signed by Cardinals (June 1, 1994). ... Granted unconditional free agency (February 16, 1996). ... Re-signed by Cardinals (February 27, 1996).
HONORS: Played in Pro Bowl (1994-1997 seasons). ... Named cornerback on THE SPORTING NEWS NFL All-Pro team (1995 and 1997).
PRO STATISTICS: 1991—Fumbled once and recovered two fumbles for 10 yards. 1992—Recovered one fumble for 39 yards. 1993—Recovered two fumbles for 20 yards and a touchdown. 1994—Recovered one fumble. 1995—Fumbled once and recovered three fumbles. 1996—Credited with one sack and recovered one fumble.

Year—Team	G	GS	No.	Yds.	Avg.	TD
1991—Phoenix NFL	16	15	∞6	60	10.0	0
1992—Phoenix NFL	16	16	3	25	8.3	0
1993—Phoenix NFL	16	16	2	87	43.5	1
1994—Arizona NFL	16	16	†9	89	9.9	0
1995—Arizona NFL	16	16	6	86	14.3	†2
1996—Arizona NFL	16	16	6	89	14.8	1
1997—Arizona NFL	16	16	6	95	15.8	∞2
Pro totals (7 years)	112	111	38	531	14.0	6

WILLIAMS, ALFRED   DE   BRONCOS

PERSONAL: Born November 6, 1968, in Houston. ... 6-6/263. ... Full name: Alfred Hamilton Williams.
HIGH SCHOOL: Jesse H. Jones Sr. (Houston).
COLLEGE: Colorado.
TRANSACTIONS/CAREER NOTES: Selected by Cincinnati Bengals in first round (18th pick overall) of 1991 NFL draft. ... Signed by Bengals (July 18, 1991). ... Granted free agency (February 17, 1994). ... Re-signed by Bengals (June 15, 1994). ... Granted unconditional free agency (February 17, 1995). ... Signed by San Francisco 49ers (July 15, 1995). ... Granted unconditional free agency (February 16, 1996). ... Signed by Denver Broncos (February 27, 1996).
CHAMPIONSHIP GAME EXPERIENCE: Played in AFC championship game (1997 season). ... Member of Super Bowl championship team (1997 season).
HONORS: Named defensive end on THE SPORTING NEWS college All-America second team (1989). ... Butkus Award winner (1990). ... Named linebacker on THE SPORTING NEWS college All-America first team (1990). ... Named defensive end on THE SPORTING NEWS NFL All-Pro team (1996). ... Played in Pro Bowl (1996 season).

W

PRO STATISTICS: 1991—Recovered two fumbles for 24 yards. 1993—Credited with one safety. 1994—Credited with one safety and recovered one fumble. 1995—Recovered one fumble. 1996—Recovered one fumble. 1997—Recovered one fumble for 51 yards and a touchdown.

Year	Team	G	GS	SACKS
1991—Cincinnati NFL		16	15	3.0
1992—Cincinnati NFL		15	6	10.0
1993—Cincinnati NFL		16	16	4.0
1994—Cincinnati NFL		16	16	9.5
1995—San Francisco NFL		16	0	4.5
1996—Denver NFL		16	16	13.0
1997—Denver NFL		16	16	8.5
Pro totals (7 years)		111	85	52.5

WILLIAMS, ARMON   DB   OILERS

PERSONAL: Born August 13, 1973, in Tempe, Ariz. ... 6-0/215. ... Full name: Armon Abdule Williams.
HIGH SCHOOL: Valley Christian (Tempe, Ariz.).
COLLEGE: Arizona.
TRANSACTIONS/CAREER NOTES: Selected by Houston Oilers in seventh round (216th pick overall) of 1997 NFL draft. ... Oilers franchise moved to Tennessee for 1997 season. ... Signed by Oilers (July 15, 1997). ... Assigned by Oilers to Barcelona Dragons in 1998 NFL Europe enhancement allocation program (February 18, 1998).
PLAYING EXPERIENCE: Tennessee NFL, 1997. ... Games/Games started: 6/0.

WILLIAMS, BRIAN   LB   PACKERS

PERSONAL: Born December 17, 1972, in Dallas. ... 6-1/240. ... Full name: Brian Marcee Williams.
HIGH SCHOOL: Bishop Dunne (Dallas).
COLLEGE: Southern California.
TRANSACTIONS/CAREER NOTES: Selected by Green Bay Packers in third round (73rd pick overall) of 1995 NFL draft. ... Signed by Packers (May 9, 1995). ... Granted free agency (February 13, 1998). ... Re-signed by Packers (February 13, 1998).
PLAYING EXPERIENCE: Green Bay NFL, 1995-1997. ... Games/Games started: 1995 (13/0), 1996 (16/16), 1997 (16/16). Total: 45/32.
CHAMPIONSHIP GAME EXPERIENCE: Played in NFC championship game (1995-97 seasons). ... Member of Super Bowl championship team (1996 season). ... Played in Super Bowl XXXII (1997 season).
PRO STATISTICS: 1996—Credited with ¹/₂ sack and recovered three fumbles. 1997—Intercepted two passes for 30 yards, credited with one sack and recovered one fumble.

WILLIAMS, CHARLIE   S   COWBOYS

PERSONAL: Born February 2, 1972, in Detroit. ... 6-0/189.
HIGH SCHOOL: Henry Ford (Detroit).
COLLEGE: Bowling Green State.
TRANSACTIONS/CAREER NOTES: Selected by Dallas Cowboys in third round (92nd pick overall) of 1995 NFL draft. ... Signed by Cowboys (July 18, 1995). ... On physically unable to perform list with knee injury (July 18-November 8, 1996). ... Granted free agency (February 13, 1998). ... Re-signed by Cowboys (April 17, 1998).
PLAYING EXPERIENCE: Dallas NFL, 1995-1997. ... Games/Games started: 1995 (16/0), 1996 (7/0), 1997 (16/0). Total: 39/0.
CHAMPIONSHIP GAME EXPERIENCE: Played in NFC championship game (1995 season). ... Member of Super Bowl championship team (1995 season).
PRO STATISTICS: 1996—Returned two kickoffs for 21 yards and fumbled once. 1997—Credited with two sacks.

WILLIAMS, DAN   DE   CHIEFS

PERSONAL: Born December 15, 1969, in Ypsilanti, Mich. ... 6-4/290. ... Full name: Daniel Williams II. ... Brother of Lamanzer Williams, defensive end, Jacksonville Jaguars.
HIGH SCHOOL: Ypsilanti (Mich.).
COLLEGE: Tennessee State, then Toledo.
TRANSACTIONS/CAREER NOTES: Selected by Denver Broncos in first round (11th pick overall) of 1993 NFL draft. ... Signed by Broncos (July 19, 1993). ... On injured reserve with knee injury (December 19, 1995-remainder of season). ... Released by Broncos (July 18, 1997). ... Signed by Kansas City Chiefs (July 24, 1997). ... Designated by Chiefs as franchise player (February 13, 1998).
PRO STATISTICS: 1993—Recovered one fumble. 1994—Intercepted one pass for minus three yards. 1996—Recovered one fumble. 1997—Recovered two fumbles for two yards.

Year	Team	G	GS	SACKS
1993—Denver NFL		13	11	1.0
1994—Denver NFL		12	7	0.0
1995—Denver NFL		6	6	2.0
1996—Denver NFL		15	15	1.0
1997—Kansas City NFL		15	6	10.5
Pro totals (5 years)		61	45	14.5

WILLIAMS, DARRYL   S   SEAHAWKS

PERSONAL: Born January 8, 1970, in Miami. ... 6-0/202. ... Full name: Darryl Edwin Williams.
HIGH SCHOOL: American (Hialeah, Fla.).
COLLEGE: Miami (Fla.).
TRANSACTIONS/CAREER NOTES: Selected after junior season by Cincinnati Bengals in first round (28th pick overall) of 1992 NFL draft. ... Signed by Bengals (July 25, 1992). ... Designated by Bengals as transition player (February 15, 1994). ... Free agency status changed by Bengals from transitional to unconditional (February 16, 1996). ... Signed by Seattle Seahawks (February 21, 1996).

W

HONORS: Named defensive back on THE SPORTING NEWS college All-America second team (1991). ... Played in Pro Bowl (1997 season).
PRO STATISTICS: 1992—Recovered one fumble. 1993—Recovered two fumbles. 1994—Returned one punt for four yards and recovered two fumbles. 1995—Recovered three fumbles. 1996—Recovered one fumble for two yards. 1997—Recovered one fumble.

				INTERCEPTIONS			SACKS
Year	Team	G	GS	No.	Yds.	Avg.	TD	No.
1992—Cincinnati NFL		16	12	4	65	16.3	0	2.0
1993—Cincinnati NFL		16	16	2	126	63.0	▲1	2.0
1994—Cincinnati NFL		16	16	2	45	22.5	0	1.0
1995—Cincinnati NFL		16	16	1	1	1.0	0	1.0
1996—Seattle NFL		16	16	5	148	29.6	1	0.0
1997—Seattle NFL		16	16	▲8	172	21.5	1	0.0
Pro totals (6 years)		96	92	22	557	25.3	3	6.0

WILLIAMS, DAVID — OT

PERSONAL: Born June 21, 1966, in Mulberry, Fla. ... 6-5/300. ... Full name: David Wayne Williams.
HIGH SCHOOL: Lakeland (Fla.).
COLLEGE: Florida.
TRANSACTIONS/CAREER NOTES: Selected by Houston Oilers in first round (23rd pick overall) of 1989 NFL draft. ... Signed by Oilers (July 29, 1989). ... Granted free agency (March 1, 1993). ... Re-signed by Oilers (August 16, 1993). ... Designated by Oilers as franchise player (February 16, 1995). ... Released by Oilers (November 21, 1995). ... Signed by New York Jets (February 14, 1996). ... Released by Jets (June 1, 1998).
PLAYING EXPERIENCE: Houston NFL 1989-1995; New York Jets NFL, 1996 and 1997. ... Games/Games started: 1989 (14/0), 1990 (15/9), 1991 (16/16), 1992 (16/16), 1993 (15/15), 1994 (16/16), 1995 (10/9), 1996 (14/14), 1997 (12/11). Total: 128/106.
PRO STATISTICS: 1989—Returned two kickoffs for eight yards. 1990—Recovered one fumble. 1991—Recovered one fumble. 1992—Recovered one fumble. 1993—Recovered one fumble for seven yards. 1994—Recovered one fumble.

WILLIAMS, ERIK — OT — COWBOYS

PERSONAL: Born September 7, 1968, in Philadelphia. ... 6-6/328. ... Full name: Erik George Williams.
HIGH SCHOOL: John Bartram (Philadelphia).
COLLEGE: Central State (Ohio).
TRANSACTIONS/CAREER NOTES: Selected by Dallas Cowboys in third round (70th pick overall) of 1991 NFL draft. ... Signed by Cowboys (July 14, 1991). ... Designated by Cowboys as transition player (February 15, 1994). ... On reserve/non-football injury list (November 21, 1994-remainder of season).
PLAYING EXPERIENCE: Dallas NFL, 1991-1997. ... Games/Games started: 1991 (11/3), 1992 (16/16), 1993 (16/16), 1994 (7/7), 1995 (15/15), 1996 (16/16), 1997 (15/15). Total: 96/88.
CHAMPIONSHIP GAME EXPERIENCE: Played in NFC championship game (1992, 1993 and 1995 seasons). ... Member of Super Bowl championship team (1992, 1993 and 1995 seasons).
HONORS: Named offensive tackle on THE SPORTING NEWS NFL All-Pro team (1993 and 1995). ... Played in Pro Bowl (1993, 1996 and 1997 seasons).
PRO STATISTICS: 1991—Recovered one fumble.

WILLIAMS, GENE — OT/G — FALCONS

PERSONAL: Born October 14, 1968, in Blair, Neb. ... 6-2/315. ... Full name: Eugene Williams.
HIGH SCHOOL: Creighton Preparatory (Omaha, Neb.).
COLLEGE: Iowa State (degree in speech communications, 1991).
TRANSACTIONS/CAREER NOTES: Selected by Miami Dolphins in fifth round (121st pick overall) of 1991 NFL draft. ... Signed by Dolphins (July 11, 1991). ... Traded by Dolphins to Cleveland Browns for fourth-round pick (LB Ronnie Woolfork) in 1994 draft (July 12, 1993). ... Granted free agency (February 17, 1994). ... Re-signed by Browns for 1994 season. ... Traded by Browns to Atlanta Falcons for fifth-round pick (WR Jermaine Lewis) in 1996 draft (August 28, 1995).
PLAYING EXPERIENCE: Miami NFL, 1991 and 1992; Cleveland NFL, 1993 and 1994; Atlanta NFL, 1995—1997. ... Games/Games started: 1991 (10/0), 1992 (5/0), 1993 (16/14), 1994 (15/9), 1995 (12/3), 1996 (10/0), 1997 (15/15). Total: 83/41.
PRO STATISTICS: 1997—Recovered two fumbles.

WILLIAMS, GERALD — DE

PERSONAL: Born September 8, 1963, in Waycross, Ga. ... 6-3/290.
HIGH SCHOOL: Valley (Ala.).
COLLEGE: Auburn.
TRANSACTIONS/CAREER NOTES: Selected by Birmingham Stallions in 1986 USFL territorial draft. ... Selected by Pittsburgh Steelers in second round (36th pick overall) of 1986 NFL draft. ... Signed by Steelers (July 25, 1986). ... Crossed picket line during players strike (October 13, 1987). ... Granted free agency (February 1, 1990). ... Re-signed by Steelers (July 18, 1990). ... Granted free agency (February 1, 1992). ... Re-signed by Steelers (July 13, 1992). ... On injured reserve with knee injury (October 13-November 10, 1992). ... On practice squad (November 10-28, 1992). ... On injured reserve with tricep injury (November 22, 1994-remainder of season). ... Granted unconditional free agency (February 17, 1995). ... Signed by Carolina Panthers (March 28, 1995). ... Granted unconditional free agency (February 14, 1997). ... Re-signed by Panthers for 1997 season. ... Released by Panthers (October 17, 1997). ... Signed by Green Bay Packers (October 22, 1997). ... Released by Packers (November 27, 1997).
CHAMPIONSHIP GAME EXPERIENCE: Played in NFC championship game (1996 season).
PRO STATISTICS: 1987—Recovered one fumble. 1988—Recovered one fumble for one yard. 1989—Recovered one fumble. 1994—Recovered one fumble in end zone for a touchdown.

W

Year Team	G	GS	SACKS
1986—Pittsburgh NFL	16	0	3.5
1987—Pittsburgh NFL	9	1	1.0
1988—Pittsburgh NFL	16	16	3.5
1989—Pittsburgh NFL	16	16	3.0
1990—Pittsburgh NFL	16	15	6.0
1991—Pittsburgh NFL	16	15	2.0
1992—Pittsburgh NFL	10	10	3.0
1993—Pittsburgh NFL	10	8	1.0
1994—Pittsburgh NFL	11	11	1.5
1995—Carolina NFL	16	16	...
1996—Carolina NFL	16	14	1.0
1997—Carolina NFL	5	5	0.0
—Green Bay NFL	4	0	0.0
Pro totals (12 years)	161	127	25.5

WILLIAMS, GEROME   S   CHARGERS

PERSONAL: Born July 9, 1973, in Houston. ... 6-2/210. ... Full name: Meltrix Gerome Williams.
HIGH SCHOOL: Kempner (Houston).
COLLEGE: Houston.
TRANSACTIONS/CAREER NOTES: Signed as non-drafted free agent by San Diego Chargers (April 24, 1997). ... Released by Chargers (August 24, 1997). ... Re-signed by Chargers to practice squad (August 25, 1997). ... Activated (November 15, 1997).
PLAYING EXPERIENCE: San Diego NFL, 1997. ... Games/Games started: 6/0.

WILLIAMS, GRANT   OT   SEAHAWKS

PERSONAL: Born May 10, 1974, in Hattiesburg, Miss. ... 6-7/323.
HIGH SCHOOL: Clinton (Miss.).
COLLEGE: Louisiana Tech (degree in biology, 1995).
TRANSACTIONS/CAREER NOTES: Signed as non-drafted free agent by Seattle Seahawks (April 22, 1996).
PLAYING EXPERIENCE: Seattle NFL, 1996 and 1997. ... Games/Games started: 1996 (8/0), 1997 (16/8). Total: 24/8.
PRO STATISTICS: 1997—Recovered two fumbles.

WILLIAMS, HARVEY   RB   RAIDERS

PERSONAL: Born April 22, 1967, in Hempstead, Texas. ... 6-2/215. ... Full name: Harvey Lavance Williams.
HIGH SCHOOL: Hempstead (Texas).
COLLEGE: Louisiana State.
TRANSACTIONS/CAREER NOTES: Selected by Kansas City Chiefs in first round (21st pick overall) of 1991 NFL draft. ... Signed by Chiefs (August 7, 1991). ... Released by Chiefs (April 6, 1994). ... Signed by Los Angeles Raiders (April 28, 1994). ... Granted unconditional free agency (February 17, 1995). ... Re-signed by Raiders (March 3, 1995). ... Raiders franchise moved to Oakland (July 21, 1995). ... On injured reserve with knee injury (December 15, 1997-remainder of season).
CHAMPIONSHIP GAME EXPERIENCE: Member of Chiefs for AFC championship game (1993 season); inactive.
PRO STATISTICS: 1991—Attempted one pass without a completion. 1994—Recovered two fumbles. 1995—Attempted one pass with one completion for 13 yards and a touchdown and recovered one fumble. 1996—Attempted two passes with one completion for 18 yards and a touchdown.
SINGLE GAME HIGHS (regular season): Attempts—29 (October 30, 1994, vs. Houston); yards—160 (October 8, 1995, vs. Seattle); rushing touchdowns—2 (November 16, 1997, vs. San Diego).
STATISTICAL PLATEAUS: 100-yard rushing games: 1991 (1), 1994 (2), 1995 (3). Total: 6.

			RUSHING				RECEIVING				KICKOFF RETURNS				TOTALS			
Year Team	G	GS	Att.	Yds.	Avg.	TD	No.	Yds.	Avg.	TD	No.	Yds.	Avg.	TD	TD	2pt.	Pts.	Fum.
1991—Kansas City NFL	14	1	97	447	4.6	1	16	147	9.2	2	24	524	21.8	0	3	...	18	1
1992—Kansas City NFL	14	0	78	262	3.4	1	5	24	4.8	0	21	405	19.3	0	1	...	6	1
1993—Kansas City NFL	7	6	42	149	3.5	0	7	42	6.0	0	3	53	17.7	0	0	...	0	3
1994—L.A. Raiders NFL	16	10	282	983	3.5	4	47	391	8.3	3	8	153	19.1	0	7	1	44	4
1995—Oakland NFL	16	16	255	1114	4.4	9	54	375	6.9	0	0	0	...	0	9	0	54	5
1996—Oakland NFL	13	5	121	431	3.6	0	22	143	6.5	0	0	0	...	0	0	0	0	3
1997—Oakland NFL	14	6	18	70	3.9	3	16	147	9.2	2	0	0	...	0	5	1	32	0
Pro totals (7 years)	94	44	893	3456	3.9	18	167	1269	7.6	7	56	1135	20.3	0	25	2	154	17

WILLIAMS, JAMEL   DB   REDSKINS

PERSONAL: Born December 22, 1973, in Gary, Ind. ... 5-11/205. ... Full name: Jamel Ishmael Williams. ... Name pronounced ja-MELL.
HIGH SCHOOL: Merrillville (Indiana).
COLLEGE: Nebraska.
TRANSACTIONS/CAREER NOTES: Selected by Washington Redskins in fifth round (132nd pick overall) of 1997 NFL draft. ... Signed by Redskins (June 2, 1997).
PLAYING EXPERIENCE: Washington NFL, 1997. ... Games/Games started: 16/0.

W

WILLIAMS, JAMES — LB — 49ERS

PERSONAL: Born October 10, 1968, in Natchez, Miss. ... 6-0/246. ... Full name: James Edward Williams.
HIGH SCHOOL: Natchez (Miss.).
COLLEGE: Mississippi State.
TRANSACTIONS/CAREER NOTES: Selected by New Orleans Saints in sixth round (158th pick overall) of 1990 NFL draft. ... Signed by Saints (May 9, 1990). ... Granted unconditional free agency (February 1-April 1, 1991). ... Re-signed by Saints for 1991 season. ... Granted unconditional free agency (February 17, 1994). ... Re-signed by Saints (March 18, 1994). ... Selected by Jacksonville Jaguars from Saints in NFL expansion draft (February 15, 1995). ... Released by Jaguars (December 5, 1995). ... Signed by Atlanta Falcons (May 9, 1996). ... On injured reserve with hamstring injury (August 20-22, 1996). ... Released by Falcons (August 22, 1996). ... Signed by New England Patriots (March 6, 1997). ... Played with Amsterdam Admirals of World League (1996). ... Released by Patriots (August 19, 1997). ... Signed by San Francisco 49ers (August 20, 1997). ... Granted unconditional free agency (February 13, 1998). ... Re-signed by 49ers (March 20, 1998).
CHAMPIONSHIP GAME EXPERIENCE: Played in NFC championship game (1997 season).
PRO STATISTICS: 1991—Recovered one fumble. 1994—Intercepted two passes for 42 yards and one touchdown. 1995—Intercepted two passes for 19 yards. 1997—Recovered one fumble.

Year Team	G	GS	SACKS
1990—New Orleans NFL	14	0	0.0
1991—New Orleans NFL	16	4	1.0
1992—New Orleans NFL	16	0	0.0
1993—New Orleans NFL	16	9	2.0
1994—New Orleans NFL	16	7	0.0
1995—Jacksonville NFL	12	6	0.0
1996—Amsterdam W.L.	...	...	1.0
—Atlanta NFL	Did not play.		
1997—San Francisco NFL	16	0	0.0
W.L. totals (1 year)	...	...	1.0
NFL totals (7 years)	106	26	3.0
Pro totals (8 years)	...	...	4.0

WILLIAMS, JAMES — OT — BEARS

PERSONAL: Born March 29, 1968, in Pittsburgh. ... 6-7/340. ... Full name: James Otis Williams.
HIGH SCHOOL: Allderdice (Pittsburgh).
COLLEGE: Cheyney (Pa.).
TRANSACTIONS/CAREER NOTES: Signed as non-drafted free agent by Chicago Bears (April 25, 1991). ... Granted free agency (February 16, 1996). ... Re-signed by Bears (March 15, 1996).
PLAYING EXPERIENCE: Chicago NFL, 1991-1997. ... Games/Games started: 1991 (14/0), 1992 (5/0), 1993 (3/0), 1994 (16/15), 1995 (16/16), 1996 (16/16), 1997 (16/16). Total: 86/63.
PRO STATISTICS: 1991—Credited with one sack. 1996—Recovered two fumbles.
MISCELLANEOUS: Switched from defensive line to offensive line during the 1992 season.

WILLIAMS, JAY — DT — RAMS

PERSONAL: Born October 13, 1971, in Washington, D.C. ... 6-3/280. ... Full name: Jay Omar Williams.
HIGH SCHOOL: St. John's (Washington, D.C.).
COLLEGE: Wake Forest.
TRANSACTIONS/CAREER NOTES: Signed as non-drafted free agent by Miami Dolphins (April 28, 1994). ... Released by Dolphins (August 28, 1994). ... Signed by Los Angeles Rams to practice squad (September 27, 1994). ... Activated (December 7, 1994); did not play. ... Rams franchise moved from Los Angeles to St. Louis (April 12, 1995). ... On physically unable to perform list with forearm injury (July 31-November 18, 1996). ... Released by Rams (November 20, 1996). ... Re-signed by Rams (Devember 11, 1996).
PLAYING EXPERIENCE: St. Louis NFL, 1996 and 1997. ... Games/Games started: 1996 (2/0), 1997 (16/2). Total: 18/2.
PRO STATISTICS: 1997—Returned one kickoff for 10 yards and credited with one sack.

WILLIAMS, JOHN — DB — RAVENS

PERSONAL: Born July 26, 1974, in Hammond, La. ... 5-7/180. ... Full name: John Wesley Williams. ... Nephew of David Williams, running back/kick returner with San Francisco 49ers (1977 and 1978) and Chicago Bears (1974-1981); and nephew of Clyde Williams, punt returner/kick returner with St. Louis Cardinals (1967-1971).
HIGH SCHOOL: Hammond (La.).
COLLEGE: Southern.
TRANSACTIONS/CAREER NOTES: Signed as non-drafted free agent by Baltimore Ravens (April 25, 1997). ... Released by Ravens (August 24, 1997). ... Re-signed by Ravens to practice squad (August 26, 1997). ... Activated (November 26, 1997).
PLAYING EXPERIENCE: Baltimore NFL, 1997. ... Games/Games started: 4/0.

WILLIAMS, KARL — WR — BUCCANEERS

PERSONAL: Born April 10, 1971 ... 5-10/174.
HIGH SCHOOL: Rowlett (Texas).
COLLEGE: Texas A&M-Kingsville.
TRANSACTIONS/CAREER NOTES: Signed as non-drafted free agent by Tampa Bay Buccaneers (April 23, 1996).
PRO STATISTICS: 1996—Rushed once for minus three yards and recovered one fumble. 1997—Rushed once for five yards and recovered one fumble.
SINGLE GAME HIGHS (regular season): Receptions—5 (December 7, 1997, vs. Green Bay); yards—87 (December 7, 1997, vs. Green Bay); and touchdown receptions—2 (November 2, 1997, vs. Indianapolis).

W

Year Team	G	GS	RECEIVING				PUNT RETURNS				KICKOFF RETURNS				TOTALS			
			No.	Yds.	Avg.	TD	No.	Yds.	Avg.	TD	No.	Yds.	Avg.	TD	TD	2pt.	Pts.	Fum.
1996—Tampa Bay NFL..........	16	0	22	246	11.2	0	13	274	21.1	1	14	383	27.4	0	2	0	12	2
1997—Tampa Bay NFL..........	16	8	33	486	14.7	4	46	‡597	13.0	∞1	15	277	18.5	0	5	0	30	5
Pro totals (2 years)	32	8	55	732	13.3	4	59	871	14.8	2	29	660	22.8	0	7	0	42	7

WILLIAMS, KEVIN — WR/KR — BILLS

PERSONAL: Born January 25, 1971, in Dallas. ... 5-9/195. ... Full name: Kevin Ray Williams.
HIGH SCHOOL: Franklin D. Roosevelt (Dallas).
COLLEGE: Miami (Fla.).
TRANSACTIONS/CAREER NOTES: Selected after junior season by Dallas Cowboys in second round (46th overall) of 1993 NFL draft. ... Signed by Cowboys (April 29, 1993). ... Granted unconditional free agency (February 14, 1997). ... Signed by Arizona Cardinals (July 15, 1997). ... Granted unconditional free agency (February 13, 1998). ... Signed by Buffalo Bills (February 17, 1998).
CHAMPIONSHIP GAME EXPERIENCE: Played in NFC championship game (1993-1995 seasons). ... Member of Super Bowl championship team (1993 and 1995 seasons).
PRO STATISTICS: 1993—Fumbled eight times and recovered four fumbles. 1994—Fumbled four times and recovered three fumbles. 1995—Fumbled three times. 1997—Fumbled three times and recovered one fumble.
SINGLE GAME HIGHS (regular season): Receptions—9 (December 25, 1995, vs. Arizona); yards—203 (December 25, 1995, vs. Arizona); and touchdown receptions—2 (December 25, 1995, vs. Arizona).
STATISTICAL PLATEAUS: 100-yard receiving games: 1995 (1).

Year Team	G	GS	RUSHING				RECEIVING				PUNT RETURNS				KICKOFF RETURNS				TOTALS		
			Att.	Yds.	Avg.	TD	No.	Yds.	Avg.	TD	No.	Yds.	Avg.	TD	No.	Yds.	Avg.	TD	TD	2pt.	Pts.
1993—Dallas NFL..........	16	1	7	26	3.7	2	20	151	7.6	2	36	381	10.6	†2	31	689	22.2	0	6	...	36
1994—Dallas NFL..........	15	2	6	20	3.3	0	13	181	13.9	0	39	349	8.9	1	43	1148	26.7	1	2	0	12
1995—Dallas NFL..........	16	16	10	53	5.3	0	38	613	16.1	2	18	166	9.2	0	49	1108	22.6	0	2	0	12
1996—Dallas NFL..........	10	9	4	11	2.8	0	27	323	12.0	1	2	17	8.5	0	21	471	22.4	0	1	0	6
1997—Arizona NFL..........	16	0	1	-2	-2.0	0	20	273	13.7	1	40	462	11.6	0	‡59	*1458	24.7	0	1	0	6
Pro totals (5 years)	73	28	28	108	3.9	2	118	1541	13.1	6	135	1375	10.2	3	203	4874	24.0	1	12	0	72

WILLIAMS, MOE — RB — VIKINGS

PERSONAL: Born July 26, 1974, in Columbus, Ga. ... 6-1/200. ... Full name: Maurice Jabari Williams.
HIGH SCHOOL: Spencer (Columbus, Ga.).
COLLEGE: Kentucky.
TRANSACTIONS/CAREER NOTES: Selected after junior season by Minnesota Vikings in third round (75th pick overall) of 1996 NFL draft. ... Signed by Vikings (July 22, 1996).
SINGLE GAME HIGHS (regular season): Attempts—19 (November 2, 1997, vs. New England); yards—43 (November 2, 1997, vs. New England); and rushing touchdowns—1 (November 2, 1997, vs. New England).

Year Team	G	GS	RUSHING				RECEIVING				KICKOFF RETURNS				TOTALS			
			Att.	Yds.	Avg.	TD	No.	Yds.	Avg.	TD	No.	Yds.	Avg.	TD	TD	2pt.	Pts.	Fum.
1996—Minnesota NFL..........	9	0	0	0	...	0	0	0	...	0	0	0	...	0	0	0	0	0
1997—Minnesota NFL..........	14	0	22	59	2.7	1	4	14	3.5	0	16	388	24.3	0	1	0	6	0
Pro totals (2 years)	23	0	22	59	2.7	1	4	14	3.5	0	16	388	24.3	0	1	0	6	0

WILLIAMS, PAT — DT — BILLS

PERSONAL: Born October 24, 1972, in Monroe, La. ... 6-3/270. ... Full name: Patrick Williams.
HIGH SCHOOL: Worsman (Monroe, La.).
JUNIOR COLLEGE: Navarro College (Texas).
COLLEGE: Northeast Oklahoma, then Texas A&M.
TRANSACTIONS/CAREER NOTES: Signed as non-drafted free agent by Buffalo Bills (April 25, 1997).
PLAYING EXPERIENCE: Buffalo NFL, 1997. ... Games/Games started: 1/0.

WILLIAMS, SHERMAN — RB — COWBOYS

W

PERSONAL: Born August 13, 1973, in Mobile, Ala. ... 5-8/202.
HIGH SCHOOL: M.T. Blount (Prichard, Ala.).
COLLEGE: Alabama.
TRANSACTIONS/CAREER NOTES: Selected by Dallas Cowboys in second round (46th pick overall) of 1995 NFL draft. ... Signed by Cowboys (July 21, 1995).
CHAMPIONSHIP GAME EXPERIENCE: Played in NFC championship game (1995 season). ... Member of Super Bowl championship team (1995 season).
HONORS: Named running back on THE SPORTING NEWS college All-America second team (1994).
PRO STATISTICS: 1996—Attempted one pass without a completion. 1997—Recovered one fumble.
SINGLE GAME HIGHS (regular season): Attempts—19 (December 8, 1997, vs. Carolina); yards—79 (September 24, 1995, vs. Arizona); rushing touchdowns—1 (December 14, 1997, vs. Cincinnati).

Year Team	G	GS	RUSHING				RECEIVING				TOTALS			
			Att.	Yds.	Avg.	TD	No.	Yds.	Avg.	TD	TD	2pt.	Pts.	Fum.
1995—Dallas NFL	11	0	48	205	4.3	1	3	28	9.3	0	1	0	6	2
1996—Dallas NFL	16	1	69	269	3.9	0	5	41	8.2	0	0	0	0	2
1997—Dallas NFL	16	0	121	468	3.9	2	21	159	7.6	0	2	0	12	5
Pro totals (3 years)...................	43	1	238	942	4.0	3	29	228	7.9	0	3	0	18	9

WILLIAMS, STEPFRET   WR   COWBOYS

PERSONAL: Born June 14, 1973, in Minden, La. ... 6-0/170.
HIGH SCHOOL: Minden (La.).
COLLEGE: Northeast Louisiana.
TRANSACTIONS/CAREER NOTES: Selected by Dallas Cowboys in third round (94th pick overall) of 1996 NFL draft. ... Signed by Cowboys (July 18, 1996).
PRO STATISTICS: 1997—Returned two punts for 14 yards.
SINGLE GAME HIGHS (regular season): Receptions—5 (November 2, 1997, vs. San Francisco); yards—53 (September 7, 1997, vs. Arizona); and touchdown receptions—1 (October 19, 1997, vs. Jacksonville).

			RECEIVING				TOTALS			
Year Team	G	GS	No.	Yds.	Avg.	TD	TD	2pt.	Pts.	Fum.
1996—Dallas NFL	5	0	1	32	32.0	0	0	0	0	0
1997—Dallas NFL	16	0	30	308	10.3	1	1	0	6	0
Pro totals (2 years)	21	0	31	340	11.0	1	1	0	6	0

WILLIAMS, TONY   DT   VIKINGS

PERSONAL: Born July 9, 1975, in Germantown, Tenn. ... 6-1/291. ... Full name: Anthony Demetric Williams
HIGH SCHOOL: Oakhaven (Memphis), then Germantown (Tenn.).
COLLEGE: Memphis.
TRANSACTIONS/CAREER NOTES: Selected by Minnesota Vikings in fifth round (151st pick overall) of 1997 NFL draft. ... Signed by Vikings (June 17, 1997).
PLAYING EXPERIENCE: Minnesota NFL, 1997. ... Games/Games started: 6/2.

WILLIAMS, TYRONE   CB   PACKERS

PERSONAL: Born May 31, 1973, in Bradenton, Fla. ... 5-11/195. ... Full name: Upton Tyrone Williams.
HIGH SCHOOL: Manatee (Bradenton, Fla.).
COLLEGE: Nebraska.
TRANSACTIONS/CAREER NOTES: Selected by Green Bay Packers in third round (93rd pick overall) of 1996 NFL draft. ... Signed by Packers (May 15, 1996).
PLAYING EXPERIENCE: Green Bay NFL, 1996 and 1997. ... Games/Games started: 1996 (16/0), 1997 (16/15). Total: 32/15.
CHAMPIONSHIP GAME EXPERIENCE: Played in NFC championship game (1996 and 1997 seasons). ... Member of Super Bowl championship team (1996 season). ... Played in Super Bowl XXXII (1997 season).
PRO STATISTICS: 1996—Recovered one fumble. 1997—Intercepted one pass for no yards.

WILLIAMS, TYRONE   DT   BEARS

PERSONAL: Born October 22, 1972, in Philadelphia. ... 6-4/292. ... Full name: Tyrone M. Williams.
HIGH SCHOOL: LaVista (Papillion, Neb.).
COLLEGE: Wyoming.
TRANSACTIONS/CAREER NOTES: Signed as non-drafted free agent by St. Louis Rams (July 25, 1996). ... Released by Rams (August 25, 1996). ... Re-signed by Rams to practice squad (August 26, 1996). ... Allocated by Rams to Rhein Fire in 1997 World League enhancement allocation program (February 19, 1997). ... Released by Rams (August 19, 1997). ... Signed by Chicago Bears to practice squad (August 27, 1997). ... Released by Bears (September 9, 1997). ... Re-signed by Rams to practice squad (September 25, 1997). ... Signed by Bears off Rams practice squad (October 29, 1997).
PLAYING EXPERIENCE: Rhein W.L., 1997; Chicago NFL, 1997. ... Games/Games started: W.L. 1997 (games played unavailable); NFL 1997 (3/0).

WILLIAMS, WALLY   G/C   RAVENS

PERSONAL: Born February 19, 1971, in Tallahassee, Fla. ... 6-2/305. ... Full name: Wally James Williams Jr.
HIGH SCHOOL: James S. Rickards (Tallahassee, Fla.).
COLLEGE: Florida A&M.
TRANSACTIONS/CAREER NOTES: Signed as non-drafted free agent by Cleveland Browns (April 27, 1993). ... Browns franchise moved to Baltimore and renamed Ravens for 1996 season (March 11, 1996). ... Designated by Ravens as franchise player (February 13, 1998).
PLAYING EXPERIENCE: Cleveland NFL, 1993-1995; Baltimore NFL, 1996 and 1997. ... Games/Games started: 1993 (2/0), 1994 (11/7), 1995 (16/16), 1996 (15/13), 1997 (10/10). Total: 54/46.
PRO STATISTICS: 1994—Recovered one fumble.

W

WILLIAMS, WILLIE   CB   SEAHAWKS

PERSONAL: Born December 26, 1970, in Columbia, S.C. ... 5-9/180. ... Full name: Willie James Williams Jr.
HIGH SCHOOL: Spring Valley (Columbia, S.C.).
COLLEGE: Western Carolina.
TRANSACTIONS/CAREER NOTES: Selected by Pittsburgh Steelers in sixth round (162nd pick overall) of 1993 NFL draft. ... Signed by Steelers (July 9, 1993). ... Granted free agency (February 16, 1996). ... Re-signed by Steelers (June 12, 1996). ... Granted unconditional free agency (February 14, 1997). ... Signed by Seattle Seahawks (February 18, 1997).
CHAMPIONSHIP GAME EXPERIENCE: Played in AFC championship game (1994 and 1995 seasons). ... Played in Super Bowl XXX (1995 season).

PRO STATISTICS: 1993—Returned one kickoff for 19 yards. 1996—Credited with one sack and recovered one fumble.

				INTERCEPTIONS		
Year Team	G	GS	No.	Yds.	Avg.	TD
1993—Pittsburgh NFL	16	0	0	0	...	0
1994—Pittsburgh NFL	16	1	0	0	...	0
1995—Pittsburgh NFL	16	15	§7	122	17.4	▲1
1996—Pittsburgh NFL	15	14	1	1	1.0	0
1997—Seattle NFL	16	16	1	0	0.0	0
Pro totals (5 years)	79	46	9	123	13.7	1

WILLIG, MATT　　　OT　　　PACKERS

PERSONAL: Born January 21, 1969, in Whittier, Calif. ... 6-8/317. ... Full name: Matthew J. Willig.
HIGH SCHOOL: St. Paul (Santa Fe Springs, Calif.).
COLLEGE: Southern California.
TRANSACTIONS/CAREER NOTES: Signed as non-drafted free agent by New York Jets (May 5, 1992). ... Released by Jets (August 24, 1992). ... Re-signed by Jets to practice squad (September 2, 1992). ... Activated (December 24, 1992). ... Active for one game (1992); did not play. ... Signed by Jets (February 14, 1995). ... Released by Jets (April 23, 1996). ... Signed by Atlanta Falcons (May 2, 1996). ... Granted unconditional free agency (February 13, 1998). ... Signed by Green Bay Packers (May 5, 1998).
PLAYING EXPERIENCE: New York Jets NFL, 1993-1995; Atlanta NFL, 1996 and 1997. ... Games/Games started: 1993 (3/0), 1994 (16/3), 1995 (15/12), 1996 (12/0), 1997 (16/13). Total: 62/28.

WILLIS, JAMES　　　LB　　　EAGLES

PERSONAL: Born September 2, 1972, in Huntsville, Ala. ... 6-2/237. ... Full name: James Edward Willis III.
HIGH SCHOOL: J.O. Johnson (Huntsville, Ala.).
COLLEGE: Auburn.
TRANSACTIONS/CAREER NOTES: Selected after junior season by Green Bay Packers in fifth round (119th pick overall) of 1993 NFL draft. ... Signed by Packers (May 21, 1993). ... On injured reserve with knee injury (December 23, 1993-remainder of season). ... Released by Packers (October 25, 1995). ... Signed by Philadelphia Eagles (October 31, 1995). ... Granted free agency (February 16, 1996). ... Re-signed by Eagles (March 1, 1996).
PRO STATISTICS: 1993—Recovered one fumble. 1994—Fumbled once and recovered one fumble. 1997—Credited with two sacks and recovered two fumbles.

				INTERCEPTIONS		
Year Team	G	GS	No.	Yds.	Avg.	TD
1993—Green Bay NFL	13	0	0	0	...	0
1994—Green Bay NFL	12	0	2	20	10.0	0
1995—Philadelphia NFL	5	0	0	0	...	0
1996—Philadelphia NFL	16	13	1	14	14.0	0
1997—Philadelphia NFL	15	15	1	0	0.0	0
Pro totals (5 years)	61	28	4	34	8.5	0

WILMSMEYER, KLAUS　　　P　　　DOLPHINS

PERSONAL: Born December 4, 1967, in Mississauga, Ont. ... 6-1/210. ... Full name: Klaus Wilmsmeyer Jr.
HIGH SCHOOL: Lorne Park Secondary (Mississauga, Ont.).
COLLEGE: Louisville.
TRANSACTIONS/CAREER NOTES: Selected by Tampa Bay Buccaneers in 12th round (311th pick overall) of 1992 NFL draft. ... Signed by Buccaneers (June 9, 1992). ... Released by Buccaneers (August 24, 1992). ... Signed by San Francisco 49ers to practice squad (September 2, 1992). ... Activated (September 4, 1992). ... Granted unconditional free agency (February 17, 1995). ... Signed by New Orleans Saints (March 7, 1995). ... Granted unconditional free agency (February 14, 1997). ... Signed by Miami Dolphins (February 23, 1998).
CHAMPIONSHIP GAME EXPERIENCE: Played in NFC championship game (1992-1994 seasons). ... Member of Super Bowl championship team (1994 season).
PRO STATISTICS: 1992—Rushed twice for no yards, fumbled once and recovered one fumble. 1993—Rushed twice for no yards, fumbled twice and recovered one fumble for minus 10 yards. 1995—Attempted one pass with one completion for 18 yards. 1996—Credited with one two-point conversion.

				PUNTING				
Year Team	G	GS	No.	Yds.	Avg.	Net avg.	In. 20	Blk.
1992—San Francisco NFL	15	0	49	1918	39.1	34.7	19	0
1993—San Francisco NFL	15	0	42	1718	40.9	34.5	11	0
1994—San Francisco NFL	16	0	54	2235	41.4	35.7	18	0
1995—New Orleans NFL	16	0	73	2965	40.6	35.6	21	1
1996—New Orleans NFL	16	0	87	3551	40.8	32.5	16	0
1997—				Did not play.				
Pro totals (5 years)	78	0	305	12387	40.6	34.4	85	1

WILSON, BERNARD　　　DT　　　CARDINALS

PERSONAL: Born August 17, 1970, in Nashville. ... 6-3/318.
HIGH SCHOOL: Maplewood (Nashville).
COLLEGE: Tennessee State.
TRANSACTIONS/CAREER NOTES: Signed as non-drafted free agent by Detroit Lions (May 1, 1992). ... Released by Lions (August 31, 1992). ... Re-signed by Lions to practice squad (September 1, 1992). ... Released by Lions (September 6, 1993). ... Re-signed by Lions to practice squad (September 8, 1993). ... Signed by Tampa Bay Buccaneers off Lions practice squad (September 16, 1993). ... Claimed

W

on waivers by Arizona Cardinals (September 7, 1994). ... Granted unconditional free agency (February 14, 1997). ... Re-signed by Cardinals (February 19, 1997).

PRO STATISTICS: 1996—Recovered one fumble. 1997—Intercepted one pass for 66 yards and a touchdown.

Year Team	G	GS	SACKS
1993—Tampa Bay NFL	13	2	0.0
1994—Tampa Bay NFL	1	0	0.0
—Arizona NFL	13	12	1.0
1995—Arizona NFL	16	14	1.0
1996—Arizona NFL	16	16	1.0
1997—Arizona NFL	16	14	0.0
Pro totals (5 years)	75	58	3.0

WILSON, JERRY   CB   DOLPHINS

PERSONAL: Born July 17, 1973, in Lake Charles, La. ... 5-10/187. ... Full name: Jerry Lee Wilson Jr.
HIGH SCHOOL: LaGrange (Lake Charles, La.).
COLLEGE: Southern (La.).
TRANSACTIONS/CAREER NOTES: Selected by Tampa Bay Buccaneers in fourth round (105th pick overall) of 1995 NFL draft. ... Signed by Buccaneers (May 9, 1995). ... On injured reserve with knee injury (August 31, 1995-entire season). ... Released by Buccaneers (August 20, 1996). ... Signed by Miami Dolphins to practice squad (October 29, 1996). ... Activated (November 5, 1996).
PLAYING EXPERIENCE: Miami NFL, 1996 and 1997. ... Games/Games started: 1996 (2/0), 1997 (16/0). Total: 18/0.
PRO STATISTICS: 1997—Credited with two sacks and recovered one fumble.

WILSON, REINARD   LB   BENGALS

PERSONAL: Born December 12, 1973, in Lake City, Fla. ... 6-2/251.
HIGH SCHOOL: Columbia (Lake City, Fla.).
COLLEGE: Florida State.
TRANSACTIONS/CAREER NOTES: Selected by Cincinnati Bengals in first round (14th pick overall) of 1997 NFL draft. ... Signed by Bengals (July 18, 1997).
HONORS: Named defensive end on THE SPORTING NEWS college All-America second team (1996).

Year Team	G	GS	SACKS
1997—Cincinnati NFL	16	4	3.0

WILSON, SHEDDRICK   WR   EAGLES

PERSONAL: Born November 23, 1973, in Thomasville, Ga. ... 6-3/210.
HIGH SCHOOL: Thomasville (Ga.).
COLLEGE: Louisiana State.
TRANSACTIONS/CAREER NOTES: Signed as non-drafted free agent by Houston Oilers (April 23, 1996). ... Assigned by Oilers to Barcelona Dragons in 1997 World League enhancement allocation program (February 19, 1997). ... Oilers franchise moved to Tennessee for 1997 season. ... Released by Oilers (August 25, 1997). ... Signed by Philadelphia Eagles (March 2, 1998).
SINGLE GAME HIGHS (regular season): Receptions—1 (December 8, 1996, vs. Jacksonville); yards—14 (November 24, 1996, vs. Carolina); and touchdown receptions—0.

			RECEIVING				TOTALS			
Year Team	G	GS	No.	Yds.	Avg.	TD	TD	2pt.	Pts.	Fum.
1996—Houston NFL	11	0	2	24	12.0	0	0	0	0	0
1997—Barcelona W.L.	...	...	41	633	15.4	9	9	1	56	...
W.L. totals (1 year)	...	...	41	633	15.4	9	9	1	56	0
NFL totals (1 year)	11	0	2	24	12.0	0	0	0	0	0
Pro totals (2 years)	...	...	43	657	15.3	9	9	1	56	0

WILSON, SIR MAWN   WR   BRONCOS

PERSONAL: Born June 4, 1973, in Killeen,Texas. ... 6-2/213. ... Full name: Sir Mawn Jeyson Wilson.
HIGH SCHOOL: Tampa Catholic.
COLLEGE: Syracuse (degree in sociology).
TRANSACTIONS/CAREER NOTES: Signed as non-drafted free agent by Miami Dolphins (April 21, 1996). ... Released by Dolphins (August 21, 1996). ... Signed as free agent by Arizona Rattlers of Arena League (February 18, 1997). ... Signed by Denver Broncos (May 28, 1997). ... Released by Broncos (August 24, 1997). ... Re-signed by Broncos to practice squad (August 25, 1997). ... Activated (December 8, 1997); did not play.
PLAYING EXPERIENCE: Denver NFL, 1997. ... Games/Games started: 1/0.
CHAMPIONSHIP GAME EXPERIENCE: Played in AFC championship game (1997 season). ... Member of Super Bowl championship team (1997 season); inactive.
SINGLE GAME HIGHS (regular season): Receptions—0; yards—0; and touchdown receptions—0.

W

WILSON, WADE   QB

PERSONAL: Born February 1, 1959, in Greenville, Texas. ... 6-3/208. ... Full name: Charles Wade Wilson.
HIGH SCHOOL: Commerce (Texas).
COLLEGE: East Texas State.
TRANSACTIONS/CAREER NOTES: Selected by Minnesota Vikings in eighth round (210th pick overall) of 1981 NFL draft. ... On inactive list (September 12, 1982). ... On commissioner's exempt list (November 20-December 8, 1982). ... Active for four games with Vikings (1982); did not play. ... On injured reserve with broken thumb (September 26-November 24, 1990). ... On injured reserve with separated shoulder

(December 26, 1990-remainder of season). ... Released by Vikings (July 9, 1992). ... Signed by Atlanta Falcons (July 15, 1992). ... Granted unconditional free agency (March 1, 1993). ... Signed by New Orleans Saints (April 12, 1993). ... Released by Saints (March 18, 1994). ... Re-signed by Saints (April 13, 1994). ... Released by Saints (March 20, 1995). ... Signed by Dallas Cowboys (May 22, 1995). ... Released by Cowboys (February 24, 1998).

CHAMPIONSHIP GAME EXPERIENCE: Played in NFC championship game (1987 season). ... Member of Cowboys for NFC championship game (1995 season); did not play. ... Member of Super Bowl championship team (1995 season).

HONORS: Played in Pro Bowl (1988 season).

PRO STATISTICS: 1981—Fumbled twice and recovered one fumble. 1983—Fumbled once. 1984—Fumbled twice. 1986—Punted twice for 76 yards (38.0-yard avg.) with one punt blocked, fumbled three times and recovered one fumble for minus two yards. 1987—Fumbled three times. 1988—Fumbled four times and recovered four fumbles for minus nine yards. 1989—Fumbled five times and recovered two fumbles for minus seven yards. 1990—Fumbled three times and recovered one fumble for minus two yards. 1991—Fumbled three times and recovered one fumble for minus three yards. 1993—Fumbled nine times and recovered four fumbles for minus three yards. 1994—Fumbled once. 1995—Fumbled once and recovered one fumble.

SINGLE GAME HIGHS (regular season): Attempts—47 (December 27, 1992, vs. Los Angeles Rams); completions—31 (December 27, 1992, vs. Los Angeles Rams); yards—391 (November 6, 1988, vs. Detroit); and touchdown passes—5 (December 13, 1992, vs. Tampa Bay).

STATISTICAL PLATEAUS: 300-yard passing games: 1986 (2), 1988 (2), 1989 (2), 1990 (1), 1992 (3), 1993 (1). Total: 11.

MISCELLANEOUS: Regular-season record as starting NFL quarterback: 35-31 (.530). ... Postseason record as starting NFL quarterback: 2-3 (.400).

					PASSING						RUSHING				TOTALS		
Year Team	G	GS	Att.	Cmp.	Pct.	Yds.	TD	Int.	Avg.	Rat.	Att.	Yds.	Avg.	TD	TD	2pt.	Pts.
1981—Minnesota NFL...........	3	0	13	6	46.2	48	0	2	3.69	16.3	0	0	...	0	0	...	0
1982—Minnesota NFL...........							Did not play.										
1983—Minnesota NFL...........	1	1	28	16	57.1	124	1	2	4.43	50.3	3	-3	-1.0	0	0	...	0
1984—Minnesota NFL...........	8	5	195	102	52.3	1019	5	11	5.23	52.5	9	30	3.3	0	0	...	0
1985—Minnesota NFL...........	4	1	60	33	55.0	404	3	3	6.73	71.8	0	0	...	0	0	...	0
1986—Minnesota NFL...........	9	3	143	80	55.9	1165	7	5	8.15	84.4	13	9	0.7	1	1	...	6
1987—Minnesota NFL...........	12	7	264	140	53.0	2106	14	13	*7.98	76.7	41	263	6.4	5	5	...	30
1988—Minnesota NFL...........	14	10	332	204	*61.4	2746	15	9	8.27	‡91.5	36	136	3.8	2	2	...	12
1989—Minnesota NFL...........	14	12	362	194	53.6	2543	9	12	7.02	70.5	32	132	4.1	1	1	...	6
1990—Minnesota NFL...........	6	4	146	82	56.2	1155	9	8	7.91	79.6	12	79	6.6	0	0	...	0
1991—Minnesota NFL...........	5	5	122	72	59.0	825	3	10	6.76	53.5	13	33	2.5	0	0	...	0
1992—Atlanta NFL................	9	3	163	111	68.1	1366	13	4	8.38	110.1	15	62	4.1	0	0	...	0
1993—New Orleans NFL........	14	14	388	221	57.0	2457	12	15	6.33	70.1	31	230	7.4	0	0	...	0
1994—New Orleans NFL........	4	0	28	20	71.4	172	0	6	6.14	87.2	7	15	2.1	0	0	0	0
1995—Dallas NFL.................	7	0	57	38	66.7	391	1	3	6.86	70.1	10	12	1.2	0	0	0	0
1996—Dallas NFL.................	3	1	18	8	44.4	79	0	1	4.39	34.3	4	5	1.3	0	0	0	0
1997—Dallas NFL.................	7	0	21	12	57.1	115	0	0	5.48	72.5	6	-2	-0.3	0	0	0	0
Pro totals (16 years)............	120	66	2340	1339	57.2	16715	92	98	7.14	75.2	232	1001	4.3	9	9	0	54

WIMBERLY, MARCUS   S   FALCONS

PERSONAL: Born July 8, 1974, in Memphis. ... 5-11/192. ... Full name: Marcus Juanald Wimberly.
HIGH SCHOOL: East (Memphis).
COLLEGE: Miami (Fla.).
TRANSACTIONS/CAREER NOTES: Selected by Atlanta Falcons in fifth round (133rd pick overall) of 1997 NFL draft. ... Signed by Falcons (June 16, 1997).
PLAYING EXPERIENCE: Atlanta NFL, 1997. ... Games/Games started: 6/0.

WING, CHRIS   LB   JETS

PERSONAL: Born May 28, 1971, in Redmond, Wash. ... 6-2/240.
HIGH SCHOOL: Redmond (Wash.).
COLLEGE: Boise State.
TRANSACTIONS/CAREER NOTES: Signed as non-drafted free agent by New England Patriots (April 20, 1997). ... Released by Patriots (August 19, 1997). ... Signed by New York Jets to practice squad (August 26, 1997). ... Activated (October 20, 1997). ... Released by Jets (December 2, 1997). ... Re-signed by Jets to practice squad (December 3, 1997).
PLAYING EXPERIENCE: New York Jets NFL, 1997. ... Games/Games started: 2/0.

WINTERS, FRANK   C   PACKERS

W

PERSONAL: Born January 23, 1964, in Hoboken, N.J. ... 6-3/300. ... Full name: Frank Mitchell Winters.
HIGH SCHOOL: Emerson (Union City, N.J.).
JUNIOR COLLEGE: College of Eastern Utah.
COLLEGE: Western Illinois (degree in political science administration, 1987).
TRANSACTIONS/CAREER NOTES: Selected by Cleveland Browns in 10th round (276th pick overall) of 1987 NFL draft. ... Signed by Browns (July 25, 1987). ... Granted unconditional free agency (February 1, 1989). ... Signed by New York Giants (March 17, 1989). ... Granted unconditional free agency (February 1, 1990). ... Signed by Kansas City Chiefs (March 26, 1990). ... Granted unconditional free agency (February 1, 1992). ... Signed by Green Bay Packers (March 17, 1992). ... Granted unconditional free agency (February 17, 1994). ... Re-signed by Packers (April 1, 1994). ... Granted unconditional free agency (February 14, 1997). ... Re-signed by Packers (March 26, 1997).
PLAYING EXPERIENCE: Cleveland NFL, 1987 and 1988; New York Giants NFL, 1989; Kansas City NFL, 1990 and 1991; Green Bay NFL, 1992-1997. ... Games/Games started: 1987 (12/0), 1988 (16/0), 1989 (15/0), 1990 (16/6), 1991 (16/0), 1992 (16/11), 1993 (16/16), 1994 (16/16), 1995 (16/16), 1996 (16/16), 1997 (13/13). Total: 168/94.
CHAMPIONSHIP GAME EXPERIENCE: Played in AFC championship game (1987 season). ... Played in NFC championship game (1995-97 seasons). ... Member of Super Bowl championship team (1996 season). ... Played in Super Bowl XXXII (1997 season).
HONORS: Played in Pro Bowl (1996 season).
PRO STATISTICS: 1987—Fumbled once. 1990—Recovered two fumbles. 1992—Fumbled once. 1994—Fumbled once and recovered one fumble for minus two yards. 1996—Recovered one fumble.

WISNIEWSKI, STEVE　　　　　G　　　　　RAIDERS

PERSONAL: Born April 7, 1967, in Rutland, Vt. ... 6-4/285. ... Full name: Stephen Adam Wisniewski. ... Brother of Leo Wisniewski, nose tackle with Baltimore/Indianapolis Colts (1982-1984). ... Name pronounced wiz-NEWS-ki.
HIGH SCHOOL: Westfield (Houston).
COLLEGE: Penn State.
TRANSACTIONS/CAREER NOTES: Selected by Dallas Cowboys in second round (29th pick overall) of 1989 NFL draft. ... Draft rights traded by Cowboys with sixth-round pick (LB Jeff Francis) in 1989 draft to Los Angeles Raiders for second-(RB Darryl Johnston), third-(DE Rhondy Weston) and fifth-round (LB Willis Crockett) picks in 1989 draft (April 23, 1989). ... Signed by Raiders (July 22, 1989). ... Granted free agency (March 1, 1993). ... Re-signed by Raiders for 1993 season. ... Raiders franchise moved to Oakland (July 21, 1995).
PLAYING EXPERIENCE: Los Angeles Raiders NFL, 1989-1994; Oakland NFL, 1995-1997. ... Games/Games started: 1989 (15/15), 1990 (16/16), 1991 (15/15), 1992 (16/16), 1993 (16/16), 1994 (16/16), 1995 (16/16), 1996 (16/16), 1997 (16/16). Total: 142/142.
CHAMPIONSHIP GAME EXPERIENCE: Played in AFC championship game (1990 season).
HONORS: Named guard on THE SPORTING NEWS college All-America first team (1987 and 1988). ... Named guard on THE SPORTING NEWS NFL All-Pro team (1990-1994). ... Played in Pro Bowl (1990, 1991, 1993 and 1995 seasons). ... Named to play in Pro Bowl (1992 season); replaced by Jim Ritcher due to injury.
PRO STATISTICS: 1989—Recovered three fumbles. 1995—Recovered one fumble.

WITHERSPOON, DERRICK　　　　　RB

PERSONAL: Born February 14, 1971, in Sumter, S.C. ... 5-10/196. ... Full name: Derrick Leon Witherspoon.
HIGH SCHOOL: Sumter (S.C.).
COLLEGE: Clemson.
TRANSACTIONS/CAREER NOTES: Signed as non-drafted free agent by New England Patriots (April 28, 1994). ... Released by Patriots (August 20, 1994). ... Signed by Philadelphia Eagles (April 20, 1995). ... Granted free agency (February 14, 1997). ... Re-signed by Eagles (July 1, 1997). ... Released by Eagles (September 23, 1997).
PRO STATISTICS: 1995—Rushed two times for seven yards.
SINGLE GAME HIGHS (regular season): Attempts—2 (November 12, 1995, vs. Denver); yards—7 (November 12, 1995, vs. Denver); rushing touchdowns—0.

			KICKOFF RETURNS				TOTALS			
Year　Team	G	GS	No.	Yds.	Avg.	TD	TD	2pt.	Pts.	Fum.
1995—Philadelphia NFL	15	0	18	459	25.5	1	1	0	6	0
1996—Philadelphia NFL	16	0	53	1271	24.0	*2	2	0	12	1
1997—Philadelphia NFL	3	0	9	171	19.0	0	0	0	0	0
Pro totals (3 years)	34	0	80	1901	23.8	3	3	0	18	1

WITMAN, JON　　　　　FB　　　　　STEELERS

PERSONAL: Born June 1, 1972, in Wrightsville, Pa. ... 6-1/240. ... Full name: Jon Doyle Witman.
HIGH SCHOOL: Eastern York (Pa.).
COLLEGE: Penn State.
TRANSACTIONS/CAREER NOTES: Selected by Pittsburgh Steelers in third round (92nd pick overall) of 1996 NFL draft. ... Signed by Steelers (July 16, 1996).
CHAMPIONSHIP GAME EXPERIENCE: Played in AFC championship game (1997 season).
PRO STATISTICS: 1996—Returned one kickoff for 20 yards.
SINGLE GAME HIGHS (regular season): Attempts—7 (November 3, 1996, vs. St. Louis); yards—33 (November 3, 1996, vs. St. Louis); rushing touchdowns—0.

			RUSHING				RECEIVING				TOTALS			
Year　Team	G	GS	Att.	Yds.	Avg.	TD	No.	Yds.	Avg.	TD	TD	2pt.	Pts.	Fum.
1996—Pittsburgh NFL	16	4	17	69	4.1	0	2	15	7.5	0	0	0	0	0
1997—Pittsburgh NFL	16	2	5	11	2.2	0	1	3	3.0	0	0	0	0	0
Pro totals (2 years)	32	6	22	80	3.6	0	3	18	6.0	0	0	0	0	0

WOHLABAUGH, DAVE　　　　　C　　　　　PATRIOTS

PERSONAL: Born April 13, 1972, in Lackawanna, N.Y. ... 6-3/292. ... Full name: David Vincent Wohlabaugh. ... Name pronounced WOOL-uh-buh.
HIGH SCHOOL: Frontier (Hamburg, N.Y.).
COLLEGE: Syracuse.
TRANSACTIONS/CAREER NOTES: Selected by New England Patriots in fourth round (112th pick overall) of 1995 NFL draft. ... Signed by Patriots (June 26, 1995). ... Granted free agency (February 13, 1998). ... Re-signed by Patriots (May 28, 1998).
PLAYING EXPERIENCE: New England NFL, 1995-1997. ... Games/Games started: 1995 (11/11), 1996 (16/16), 1997 (14/14). Total: 41/41.
CHAMPIONSHIP GAME EXPERIENCE: Played in AFC championship game (1996 season). ... Played in Super Bowl XXXI (1996 season).
PRO STATISTICS: 1995—Recovered one fumble. 1996—Recovered two fumbles for one yard.

W

WOLF, JOE　　　　　OL　　　　　CARDINALS

PERSONAL: Born December 28, 1966, in Allentown, Pa. ... 6-6/297. ... Full name: Joseph Francis Wolf Jr.
HIGH SCHOOL: William Allen (Allentown, Pa.).
COLLEGE: Boston College (degree in communications, 1988).
TRANSACTIONS/CAREER NOTES: Selected by Phoenix Cardinals in first round (17th pick overall) of 1989 NFL draft. ... Signed by Cardinals (August 15, 1989)　On injured reserve with shoulder injury (October 19-December 7, 1991). ... On injured reserve with torn pectoral muscle (September 3-December 4, 1992). ... Granted free agency (March 1, 1993). ... Re-signed by Cardinals (July 13, 1993). ... Granted uncon-

ditional free agency (February 17, 1994). ... Cardinals franchise renamed Arizona Cardinals for 1994 season. ... Re-signed by Cardinals (May 17, 1994). ... Granted unconditional free agency (February 17, 1995). ... Re-signed by Cardinals (June 16, 1995). ... Granted unconditional free agency (February 16, 1996). ... Re-signed by Cardinals (May 3, 1996). ... Granted unconditional free agency (February 14, 1997). ... Re-signed by Cardinals (May 30, 1997). ... On injured reserve with knee injury (December 17, 1997-remainder of season). ... Granted unconditional free agency (February 13, 1998).

PLAYING EXPERIENCE: Phoenix NFL, 1989-1993; Arizona NFL, 1994-1997. ... Games/Games started: 1989 (16/15), 1990 (15/0), 1991 (8/6), 1992 (3/2), 1993 (8/5), 1994 (7/6), 1995 (6/1), 1996 (16/16), 1997 (15/9). Total: 94/60.

PRO STATISTICS: 1996—Recovered two fumbles. 1997—Recovered one fumble.

WOLFORD, WILL   OT   STEELERS

PERSONAL: Born May 18, 1964, in Louisville, Ky. ... 6-5/300. ... Full name: William Charles Wolford. ... Name pronounced WOOL-ford.
HIGH SCHOOL: St. Xavier (Louisville, Ky.).
COLLEGE: Vanderbilt.
TRANSACTIONS/CAREER NOTES: Selected by Memphis Showboats in 1986 USFL territorial draft. ... Selected by Buffalo Bills in first round (20th pick overall) of 1986 NFL draft. ... Signed by Bills (August 12, 1986). ... Granted roster exemption (August 12-22, 1986). ... Granted free agency (February 1, 1990). ... Re-signed by Bills (August 28, 1990). ... Granted roster exemption (September 9, 1990). ... Designated by Bills as transition player (February 25, 1993). ... Tendered offer sheet by Indianapolis Colts (March 28, 1993). ... Bills declined to match offer (April 23, 1993). ... On injured reserve with shoulder injury (December 10, 1993-remainder of season). ... Designated by Colts as transition player (February 15, 1994). ... Free agency status changed by Colts from transitional to unconditional (February 29, 1996). ... Signed by Pittsburgh Steelers (March 1, 1996).
PLAYING EXPERIENCE: Buffalo NFL, 1986-1992; Indianapolis NFL, 1993-1995; Pittsburgh NFL, 1996 and 1997. ... Games/Games started: 1986 (16/16), 1987 (9/9), 1988 (16/16), 1989 (16/16), 1990 (14/14), 1991 (15/15), 1992 (16/16), 1993 (12/12), 1994 (16/16), 1995 (16/16), 1996 (16/16), 1997 (16/16). Total: 178/178.
CHAMPIONSHIP GAME EXPERIENCE: Played in AFC championship game (1988, 1990-1992, 1995 and 1997 seasons). ... Played in Super Bowl XXV (1990 season), Super Bowl XXVI (1991 season) and Super Bowl XXVII (1992 season).
HONORS: Played in Pro Bowl (1990 and 1995 seasons). ... Named to play in Pro Bowl (1992 season); replaced by John Alt due to injury.
PRO STATISTICS: 1988—Recovered one fumble. 1994—Recovered one fumble.

WOODALL, LEE   LB   49ERS

PERSONAL: Born October 31, 1969, in Carlisle, Pa. ... 6-1/224. ... Full name: Lee Artis Woodall.
HIGH SCHOOL: Carlisle (Pa.).
COLLEGE: West Chester (Pa.).
TRANSACTIONS/CAREER NOTES: Selected by San Francisco 49ers in sixth round (182nd pick overall) of 1994 NFL draft. ... Signed by 49ers (July 20, 1994).
CHAMPIONSHIP GAME EXPERIENCE: Played in NFC championship game (1994 and 1997 seasons). ... Member of Super Bowl championship team (1994 season).
HONORS: Played in Pro Bowl (1995 and 1997 seasons).
PRO STATISTICS: 1994—Recovered one fumble. 1995—Recovered two fumbles for 98 yards and a touchdown.

| | | | INTERCEPTIONS | | | | SACKS |
Year Team	G	GS	No.	Yds.	Avg.	TD	No.
1994—San Francisco NFL	15	13	0	0	...	0	1.0
1995—San Francisco NFL	16	16	2	0	0.0	0	3.0
1996—San Francisco NFL	16	13	0	0	...	0	2.5
1997—San Francisco NFL	16	16	2	55	27.5	0	0.0
Pro totals (4 years)	63	58	4	55	13.8	0	6.5

WOODEN, SHAWN   S   DOLPHINS

PERSONAL: Born October 23, 1973, in Willow Grove, Pa. ... 5-11/205. ... Full name: Shawn Anthony Wooden.
HIGH SCHOOL: Abington (Pa.).
COLLEGE: Notre Dame.
TRANSACTIONS/CAREER NOTES: Selected by Miami Dolphins in sixth round (189th pick overall) of 1996 NFL draft. ... Signed by Dolphins (July 10, 1996).
PRO STATISTICS: 1996—Recovered two fumbles. 1997—Fumbled once and recovered two fumbles.

| | | | INTERCEPTIONS | | | |
Year Team	G	GS	No.	Yds.	Avg.	TD
1996—Miami NFL	16	11	2	15	7.5	0
1997—Miami NFL	16	15	2	10	5.0	0
Pro totals (2 years)	32	26	4	25	6.3	0

WOODEN, TERRY   LB   CHIEFS

PERSONAL: Born January 14, 1967, in Hartford, Conn. ... 6-3/239. ... Full name: Terrence Tylon Wooden.
HIGH SCHOOL: Farmington (Conn.).
COLLEGE: Syracuse (degree in sociology).
TRANSACTIONS/CAREER NOTES: Selected by Seattle Seahawks in second round (29th pick overall) of 1990 NFL draft. ... Signed by Seahawks (July 27, 1990). ... On injured reserve with knee injury (November 10, 1990-remainder of season). ... On injured reserve with knee injury (October 28, 1992-remainder of season). ... Granted free agency (March 1, 1993). ... Re-signed by Seahawks (August 25, 1993). ... Activated (September 4, 1993). ... Granted unconditional free agency (February 14, 1997). ... Signed by Kansas City Chiefs (April 21, 1997).
PRO STATISTICS: 1991—Recovered four fumbles for five yards. 1993—Recovered one fumble. 1994—Recovered two fumbles. 1995—Recovered one fumble for 20 yards. 1996—Recovered two fumbles. 1997—Recovered one fumble.

Year Team	G	GS	INTERCEPTIONS				SACKS
			No.	Yds.	Avg.	TD	No.
1990—Seattle NFL	8	8	0	0	...	0	0.0
1991—Seattle NFL	16	15	0	0	...	0	2.0
1992—Seattle NFL	8	8	1	3	3.0	0	0.0
1993—Seattle NFL	16	16	0	0	...	0	2.5
1994—Seattle NFL	16	15	3	78	26.0	1	1.5
1995—Seattle NFL	16	16	1	9	9.0	0	0.0
1996—Seattle NFL	9	9	1	13	13.0	0	0.0
1997—Kansas City NFL	15	8	0	0	...	0	2.0
Pro totals (8 years)	104	95	6	103	17.2	1	8.0

WOODS, JEROME   CB/SS   CHIEFS

PERSONAL: Born March 17, 1973, in Memphis. ... 6-2/200.
HIGH SCHOOL: Melrose (Memphis).
JUNIOR COLLEGE: Northeast Mississippi Community College.
COLLEGE: Memphis.
TRANSACTIONS/CAREER NOTES: Selected by Kansas City Chiefs in first round (28th pick overall) of 1996 NFL draft. ... Signed by Chiefs (August 12, 1996).
PRO STATISTICS: 1996—Recovered one fumble. 1997—Credited with one sack and recovered two fumbles for 13 yards.

Year Team	G	GS	INTERCEPTIONS				TOTALS			
			No.	Yds.	Avg.	TD	TD	2pt.	Pts.	Fum.
1996—Kansas City NFL	16	0	0	0	...	0	0	0	0	1
1997—Kansas City NFL	16	16	4	57	14.3	0	0	0	0	0
Pro totals (2 years)	32	16	4	57	14.3	0	0	0	0	1

WOODSON, DARREN   S   COWBOYS

PERSONAL: Born April 25, 1969, in Phoenix. ... 6-1/219. ... Full name: Darren Ray Woodson.
HIGH SCHOOL: Maryvale (Phoenix).
COLLEGE: Arizona State.
TRANSACTIONS/CAREER NOTES: Selected by Dallas Cowboys in second round (37th pick overall) of 1992 NFL draft. ... Signed by Cowboys (April 26, 1992).
CHAMPIONSHIP GAME EXPERIENCE: Played in NFC championship game (1992-1995 seasons). ... Member of Super Bowl championship team (1992, 1993 and 1995 seasons).
HONORS: Named strong safety on THE SPORTING NEWS NFL All-Pro team (1994-1996). ... Played in Pro Bowl (1994-1996 seasons). ... Named to play in Pro Bowl (1997 season); replaced by John Lynch due to injury.
PRO STATISTICS: 1992—Credited with a sack. 1993—Recovered three fumbles for three yards. 1994—Recovered one fumble. 1996—Credited with three sacks, fumbled once and recovered one fumble. 1997—Credited with two sacks, fumbled once and recovered two fumbles.

Year Team	G	GS	INTERCEPTIONS			
			No.	Yds.	Avg.	TD
1992—Dallas NFL	16	2	0	0	...	0
1993—Dallas NFL	16	15	0	0	...	0
1994—Dallas NFL	16	16	5	140	28.0	1
1995—Dallas NFL	16	16	2	46	23.0	0
1996—Dallas NFL	16	16	5	43	8.6	0
1997—Dallas NFL	14	14	1	14	14.0	0
Pro totals (6 years)	94	79	13	243	18.7	2

WOODSON, ROD   CB   RAVENS

PERSONAL: Born March 10, 1965, in Fort Wayne, Ind. ... 6-0/200. ... Full name: Roderick Kevin Woodson.
HIGH SCHOOL: R. Nelson Snider (Fort Wayne, Ind.).
COLLEGE: Purdue.
TRANSACTIONS/CAREER NOTES: Selected by Pittsburgh Steelers in first round (10th pick overall) of 1987 NFL draft. ... On reserve/unsigned list (August 31-October 27, 1987). ... Signed by Steelers (October 28, 1987). ... Granted roster exemption (October 28-November 7, 1987). ... Granted free agency (February 1, 1991). ... Re-signed by Steelers (August 22, 1991). ... Activated (August 30, 1991). ... Granted unconditional free agency (February 14, 1997). ... Signed by San Francisco 49ers (July 17, 1997). ... Released by 49ers (February 13, 1998). ... Signed by Baltimore Ravens (February 20, 1998).
CHAMPIONSHIP GAME EXPERIENCE: Played in AFC championship game (1994 season). ... Member of Steelers for AFC championship game (1995 season); inactive. ... Played in Super Bowl XXX (1995 season). ... Played in NFC championship game (1997 season).
HONORS: Named defensive back on THE SPORTING NEWS college All-America second team (1985). ... Named kick returner on THE SPORTING NEWS college All-America first team (1986). ... Named kick returner on THE SPORTING NEWS NFL All-Pro team (1989). ... Played in Pro Bowl (1989-1994 and 1996 seasons). ... Named cornerback on THE SPORTING NEWS NFL All-Pro team (1990 and 1992-1994).
PRO STATISTICS: 1987—Recovered two fumbles. 1988— Recovered three fumbles for two yards. 1989— Recovered four fumbles for one yard. 1990— Recovered three fumbles. 1991— Recovered three fumbles for 15 yards. 1992—Recovered one fumble for nine yards. 1993—Rushed once for no yards and recovered one fumble. 1994—Recovered one fumble. 1996—Recovered three fumbles for 42 yards and a touchdown. 1997—Recovered one fumble.
MISCELLANEOUS: Active AFC leader for career interceptions (41).

Year Team	G	GS	INTERCEPTIONS				SACKS	PUNT RETURNS				KICKOFF RETURNS				TOTALS			
			No.	Yds.	Avg.	TD	No.	No.	Yds.	Avg.	TD	No.	Yds.	Avg.	TD	TD	2pt.	Pts.	Fum.
1987—Pittsburgh NFL	8	0	1	45	45.0	1	0.0	16	135	8.4	0	13	290	22.3	0	1		6	3
1988—Pittsburgh NFL	16	16	4	90	24.5	0	0.5	33	281	8.5	0	37	850	23.0	*1	1	...	6	3

W

Year Team	G	GS	INTERCEPTIONS				SACKS	PUNT RETURNS				KICKOFF RETURNS				TOTALS			
			No.	Yds.	Avg.	TD	No.	No.	Yds.	Avg.	TD	No.	Yds.	Avg.	TD	TD	2pt.	Pts.	Fum.
1989—Pittsburgh NFL	15	14	3	39	13.0	0	0.0	29	207	7.1	0	§36	§982	*27.3	†1	1	...	6	3
1990—Pittsburgh NFL	16	16	5	67	13.4	0	0.0	§38	§398	10.5	†1	35	764	21.8	0	1	...	6	3
1991—Pittsburgh NFL	15	15	3	72	24.0	0	1.0	28	320	§11.4	0	*44	880	20.0	0	0	...	0	3
1992—Pittsburgh NFL	16	16	4	90	22.5	0	6.0	32	364	§11.4	1	25	469	18.8	0	1	...	6	2
1993—Pittsburgh NFL	16	16	8	§138	17.3	▲1	2.0	42	338	8.0	0	15	294	19.6	0	1	...	6	2
1994—Pittsburgh NFL	15	15	4	109	27.3	2	3.0	39	319	8.2	0	15	365	24.3	0	2	0	12	2
1995—Pittsburgh NFL	1	1	0	0	...	0	0.0	0	0	...	0	0	0	...	0	0	0	0	0
1996—Pittsburgh NFL	16	16	6	121	20.2	1	1.0	0	0	...	0	0	0	...	0	2	0	12	1
1997—San Francisco NFL	14	14	3	81	27.0	0	0.0	1	0	0.0	0	0	0	...	0	0	0	0	0
Pro totals (11 years)	148	139	41	860	21.0	5	13.5	258	2362	9.2	2	220	4894	22.2	2	10	0	60	22

WOODSON, SEAN   S   BILLS

PERSONAL: Born August 27, 1974, in Jackson, Miss. ... 6-0/214. ... Full name: Sean Andre Woodson.
HIGH SCHOOL: Jim Hill (Jackson, Miss.).
COLLEGE: Jackson State.
TRANSACTIONS/CAREER NOTES: Selected by Buffalo Bills in fifth round (153rd pick overall) of 1997 NFL draft. ... Signed by Bills (June 6, 1997). ... Released by Bills (August 18, 1997). ... Re-signed by Bills to practice squad (August 26, 1997). ... Activated (November 5, 1997).
PLAYING EXPERIENCE: Buffalo NFL, 1997. ... Games/Games started: 1/0.

WOOLFORD, DONNELL   CB

PERSONAL: Born January 6, 1966, in Baltimore. ... 5-9/200.
HIGH SCHOOL: Douglas Byrd (Fayetteville, N.C.).
COLLEGE: Clemson.
TRANSACTIONS/CAREER NOTES: Selected by Chicago Bears in first round (11th pick overall) of 1989 NFL draft. ... Signed by Bears (August 16, 1989). ... Designated by Bears as transition player (February 25, 1993). ... Free agency status changed from transitional to unconditional (March 6, 1997). ... Signed by Pittsburgh Steelers (April 19, 1997). ... Released by Steelers (June 1, 1998).
CHAMPIONSHIP GAME EXPERIENCE: Played in AFC championship game (1997 season).
HONORS: Named kick returner on THE SPORTING NEWS college All-America second team (1987). ... Named defensive back on THE SPORTING NEWS college All-America first team (1988).
PRO STATISTICS: 1991—Recovered one fumble for 28 yards. 1992—Recovered one fumble. 1994—Returned one kickoff for 28 yards.

Year Team	G	GS	INTERCEPTIONS				SACKS	PUNT RETURNS				TOTALS			
			No.	Yds.	Avg.	TD	No.	No.	Yds.	Avg.	TD	TD	2pt.	Pts.	Fum.
1989—Chicago NFL	11	11	3	0	0.0	0	0.0	1	12	12.0	0	0	...	0	0
1990—Chicago NFL	13	13	3	18	6.0	0	2.0	0	0	...	0	0	...	0	0
1991—Chicago NFL	15	15	2	21	10.5	0	1.0	0	0	...	0	0	...	0	0
1992—Chicago NFL	16	16	7	67	9.6	0	0.0	12	127	10.6	0	0	...	0	2
1993—Chicago NFL	16	16	2	18	9.0	0	0.0	0	0	...	0	0	...	0	0
1994—Chicago NFL	16	16	5	30	6.0	0	0.0	0	0	...	0	0	0	0	1
1995—Chicago NFL	9	9	4	21	5.3	0	0.0	0	0	...	0	0	0	0	0
1996—Chicago NFL	15	15	6	37	6.2	1	0.0	0	0	...	0	1	0	6	0
1997—Pittsburgh NFL	15	12	4	91	22.8	0	0.0	0	0	...	0	0	0	0	0
Pro totals (9 years)	126	123	36	303	8.4	1	3.0	13	139	10.7	0	1	0	6	3

WOOTEN, TITO   S   GIANTS

PERSONAL: Born December 12, 1971, in Goldsboro, N.C. ... 6-0/195.
HIGH SCHOOL: Goldsboro (N.C.).
COLLEGE: North Carolina, then Northeast Louisiana.
TRANSACTIONS/CAREER NOTES: Selected by New York Giants in fourth round of 1994 NFL supplemental draft. ... Signed by Giants (July 22, 1994). ... Granted free agency (February 14, 1997). ... Re-signed by Giants (June, 1997). ... Granted unconditional free agency (February 13, 1998). ... Re-signed by Giants (February 13, 1998).
PRO STATISTICS: 1995—Recovered one fumble for one yard and a touchdown. 1996—Credited with a safety and recovered one fumble for 54 yards and a touchdown. 1997—Fumbled once and recovered one fumble.

Year Team	G	GS	INTERCEPTIONS			
			No.	Yds.	Avg.	TD
1994—New York Giants NFL	16	2	0	0	...	0
1995—New York Giants NFL	16	3	1	38	38.0	0
1996—New York Giants NFL	13	12	1	35	35.0	0
1997—New York Giants NFL	16	16	5	‡146	29.2	1
Pro totals (4 years)	61	33	7	219	31.3	1

WORTHAM, BARRON   LB   OILERS

PERSONAL: Born November 1, 1969, in Everman, Texas. ... 5-11/244. ... Full name: Barron Winfield Wortham.
HIGH SCHOOL: Everman (Texas).
COLLEGE: Texas-El Paso.
TRANSACTIONS/CAREER NOTES: Selected by Houston Oilers in sixth round (194th pick overall) of 1994 NFL draft. ... Signed by Oilers (July 12, 1994). ... Granted free agency (February 14, 1997). ... Oilers franchise moved to Tennessee for 1997 season. ... Re-signed by Oilers (July 9, 1997). ... Granted unconditional free agency (February 13, 1998). ... Re-signed by Oilers (February 23, 1998).
HONORS: Named linebacker on THE SPORTING NEWS college All-America second team (1993).
PRO STATISTICS: 1994—Recovered one fumble. 1995—Returned one kickoff for minus three yards. 1996—Recovered two fumbles.

Year Team	G	GS	SACKS
1994—Houston NFL	16	1	0.0
1995—Houston NFL	16	5	1.0
1996—Houston NFL	15	14	2.0
1997—Tennessee NFL	16	16	0.0
Pro totals (4 years)	63	36	3.0

WRIGHT, LAWRENCE   S   BENGALS

PERSONAL: Born September 6, 1973 ... 6-1/211. ... Full name: Lawrence D. Wright III.
HIGH SCHOOL: North Miami, then Valley Forge Military Academy (Fort Wayne, Pa.).
COLLEGE: Florida.
TRANSACTIONS/CAREER NOTES: Signed as non-drafted free agent by Cincinnati Bengals (April 25, 1997). ... Released by Bengals (August 24, 1997). ... Re-signed by Bengals to practice squad (August 26, 1997). ... Activated (November 5, 1997).
PLAYING EXPERIENCE: Cincinnati NFL, 1997. ... Games/Games started: 4/0.
HONORS: Jim Thorpe Award winner (1996).

WRIGHT, TOBY   S   RAMS

PERSONAL: Born November 19, 1970, in Phoenix ... 5-11/212. ... Full name: Toby Lin Wright. ... Brother of Terry Wright, defensive back with Indianapolis Colts (1987 and 1988) and Hamilton Tiger-Cats of CFL (1991-1995).
HIGH SCHOOL: Dobson (Mesa, Ariz.).
COLLEGE: Nebraska.
TRANSACTIONS/CAREER NOTES: Selected by Los Angeles Rams in second round (49th pick overall) of 1994 NFL draft. ... Signed by Rams (May 18, 1994). ... Rams franchise moved to St. Louis (April 12, 1995).
PRO STATISTICS: 1994—Recovered one fumble for 98 yards and a touchdown. 1995—Rushed once for nine yards, recovered one fumble for 73 yards and a touchdown. 1997—Recovered one fumble for 34 yards.

			INTERCEPTIONS			
Year Team	G	GS	No.	Yds.	Avg.	TD
1994—Los Angeles Rams NFL	16	2	0	0	...	0
1995—St. Louis NFL	16	16	6	79	13.2	0
1996—St. Louis NFL	12	12	1	19	19.0	1
1997—St. Louis NFL	11	11	0	0	...	0
Pro totals (4 years)	55	41	7	98	14.0	1

WUERFFEL, DANNY   QB   SAINTS

PERSONAL: Born May 27, 1974, in Ft. Walton, Fla. ... 6-1/212. ... Full name: Daniel Carl Wuerffel.
HIGH SCHOOL: Ft. Walton Beach (Fla.).
COLLEGE: Florida.
TRANSACTIONS/CAREER NOTES: Selected by New Orleans Saints in fourth round (99th pick overall) of 1997 NFL draft. ... Signed by Saints (July 17, 1997).
HONORS: Davey O'Brien Award winner (1995 and 1996). ... Heisman Trophy winner (1996). ... Named College Player of the Year by THE SPORTING NEWS (1996). ... Named quarterback on THE SPORTING NEWS college All-America first team (1996).
PRO STATISTICS: 1997—Fumbled twice and recovered two fumbles.
SINGLE GAME HIGHS (regular season): Attempts—32 (October 19, 1997, vs. Carolina); completions—13 (October 19, 1997, vs. Carolina); yards—132 (October 19, 1997, vs. Carolina); and touchdown passes—1 (December 21, 1997, vs. Kansas City).
MISCELLANEOUS: Regular-season record as starting NFL quarterback: 0-2.

			PASSING							RUSHING				TOTALS		
Year Team	G	GS	Att.	Cmp.	Pct.	Yds.	TD	Int.	Avg.	Rat.	Att.	Yds.	Avg.	TD	TD	2pt.	Pts.
1997—New Orleans NFL	7	2	91	42	46.2	518	4	8	5.69	42.3	6	26	4.3	0	0	0	0

WUNSCH, JERRY   OT   BUCCANEERS

PERSONAL: Born January 21, 1974, in Eau Claire, Wis. ... 6-6/333. ... Full name: Gerald Wunsch. ... Name pronounced WUNCH.
HIGH SCHOOL: West (Wausau, Wis.).
COLLEGE: Wisconsin.
TRANSACTIONS/CAREER NOTES: Selected by Tampa Bay Buccaneers in second round (37th pick overall) of 1997 NFL draft. ... Signed by Buccaneers (July 18, 1997).
PLAYING EXPERIENCE: Tampa Bay NFL, 1997. ... Games/Games started: 16/0.
PRO STATISTICS: 1997—Recovered one fumble.

W

WYATT, ANTWUAN   WR   EAGLES

PERSONAL: Born July 18, 1975, in Daytona Beach, Fla. ... 5-10/199. ... Son of Alvin Wyatt, defensive back for three NFL teams (1970-73) and head football coach, Bethune-Cookman College.
HIGH SCHOOL: Mainland (Daytona Beach, Fla.).
COLLEGE: Bethune-Cookman.
TRANSACTIONS/CAREER NOTES: Selected by Philadelphia Eagles in sixth round (190th pick overall) of 1997 NFL draft. ... Signed by Eagles (July 1, 1997). ... On injured reserve with knee injury (September 1, 1997-remainder of season).
SINGLE GAME HIGHS (regular season): Receptions—0; yards—0; and touchdown receptions—0.

			PUNT RETURNS				KICKOFF RETURNS				TOTALS			
Year Team	G	GS	No.	Yds.	Avg.	TD	No.	Yds.	Avg.	TD	TD	2pt.	Pts.	Fum.
1997—Philadelphia NFL	1	0	2	-2	-1.0	0	2	50	25.0	0	0	0	0	0

WYCHECK, FRANK　　　　TE　　　　OILERS

PERSONAL: Born October 14, 1971, in Philadelphia. ... 6-3/248.
HIGH SCHOOL: Archbishop Ryan (Philadelphia).
COLLEGE: Maryland.
TRANSACTIONS/CAREER NOTES: Selected after junior season by Washington Redskins in sixth round (160th pick overall) of 1993 NFL draft. ... Signed by Redskins (July 15, 1993). ... On suspended list for anabolic steroid use (November 29, 1994-remainder of season). ... Released by Redskins (August 17, 1995). ... Signed by Houston Oilers (August 18, 1995). ... Granted free agency (February 16, 1996). ... Re-signed by Oilers (June 28, 1996). ... Oilers franchise moved to Tennessee for 1997 season.
PRO STATISTICS: 1993—Recovered one fumble. 1995—Rushed once for one yard and a touchdown and recovered one fumble. 1996—Rushed twice for three yards. 1997—Recovered one fumble.
SINGLE GAME HIGHS (regular season): Receptions—9 (September 28, 1997, vs. Pittsburgh); yards—78 (October 12, 1997, vs. Cincinnati); and touchdown receptions—1 (November 16, 1997, vs. Jacksonville).

			RECEIVING				KICKOFF RETURNS				TOTALS			
Year　Team	G	GS	No.	Yds.	Avg.	TD	No.	Yds.	Avg.	TD	TD	2pt.	Pts.	Fum.
1993—Washington NFL	9	7	16	113	7.1	0	0	0	...	0	0	...	0	1
1994—Washington NFL	9	1	7	55	7.9	1	4	84	21.0	0	1	0	6	0
1995—Houston NFL	16	11	40	471	11.8	1	0	0	...	0	2	0	12	0
1996—Houston NFL	16	16	53	511	9.6	6	2	5	2.5	0	6	0	36	2
1997—Tennessee NFL	16	16	63	748	11.9	4	1	3	3.0	0	4	1	26	0
Pro totals (5 years)	66	51	179	1898	10.6	12	7	92	13.1	0	10	1	80	3

WYMAN, DEVIN　　　　DT　　　　PATRIOTS

PERSONAL: Born August 29, 1973, in East Palo Alto, Calif. ... 6-7/290.
HIGH SCHOOL: Carlmont (Belmont, Calif.).
JUNIOR COLLEGE: San Mateo (Calif.) Junior College.
COLLEGE: Kentucky State.
TRANSACTIONS/CAREER NOTES: Selected by New England Patriots in sixth round (206th pick overall) of 1996 NFL draft. ... Signed by Patriots (July 18, 1996). ... Assigned by Patriots to Barcelona Dragons in 1998 NFL Europe enhancement allocation program (February 18, 1998).
CHAMPIONSHIP GAME EXPERIENCE: Member of Patriots for AFC championship game (1996 season); inactive. ... Member of Patriots for Super Bowl XXXI (1996 season); inactive.

Year　Team	G	GS	SACKS
1996—New England NFL	9	4	1.0
1997—New England NFL	6	0	0.0
Pro totals (2 years)	15	4	1.0

WYNN, RENALDO　　　　DT　　　　JAGUARS

PERSONAL: Born September 3, 1974, in Chicago. ... 6-3/290. ... Full name: Renaldo Lavalle Wynn.
HIGH SCHOOL: De La Salle Institute (Chicago).
COLLEGE: Notre Dame.
TRANSACTIONS/CAREER NOTES: Selected by Jacksonville Jaguars in first round (21st pick overall) of 1997 NFL draft. ... Signed by Jaguars (July 21, 1997).
PRO STATISTICS: 1997—Recovered one fumble.

Year　Team	G	GS	SACKS
1997—Jacksonville NFL	16	8	2.5

YARBOROUGH, RYAN　　　　WR　　　　RAVENS

PERSONAL: Born April 26, 1971, in Baltimore. ... 6-2/195. ... Full name: Ryan K. Yarborough.
HIGH SCHOOL: Rich East (Park Forest, Ill.).
COLLEGE: Wyoming.
TRANSACTIONS/CAREER NOTES: Selected by New York Jets in second round (41st pick overall) of 1994 NFL draft. ... Signed by Jets (June 21, 1994). ... Traded by Jets to Green Bay Packers for conditional pick in 1997 draft (July 26, 1996). ... Claimed on waivers by Baltimore Ravens (July 15, 1997).
HONORS: Named wide receiver on THE SPORTING NEWS college All-America second team (1993).
STATISTICAL PLATEAUS: 100-yard receiving games: 1995 (1).

			RECEIVING				TOTALS			
Year　Team	G	GS	No.	Yds.	Avg.	TD	TD	2pt.	Pts.	Fum.
1994—New York Jets NFL	13	0	6	42	7.0	1	1	0	6	0
1995—New York Jets NFL	16	2	18	230	12.8	2	2	0	12	0
1997—Baltimore NFL	16	3	16	183	11.4	0	0	0	0	3
Pro totals (3 years)	45	5	40	455	11.4	3	3	0	18	3

YOUNG, BRYANT　　　　DT　　　　49ERS

PERSONAL: Born January 27, 1972, in Chicago Heights, Ill. ... 6-3/291. ... Full name: Bryant Colby Young.
HIGH SCHOOL: Bloom (Chicago Heights, Ill.).
COLLEGE: Notre Dame.
TRANSACTIONS/CAREER NOTES: Selected by San Francisco 49ers in first round (seventh pick overall) of 1994 NFL draft. ... Signed by 49ers (July 26, 1994).
CHAMPIONSHIP GAME EXPERIENCE: Played in NFC championship game (1994 and 1997 seasons). ... Member of Super Bowl championship team (1994 season).

W
Y

HONORS: Named defensive tackle on THE SPORTING NEWS NFL All-Pro team (1996). ... Played in Pro Bowl (1996 season).
PRO STATISTICS: 1994—Recovered one fumble. 1995—Recovered two fumbles. 1996—Recovered one fumble for 43 yards.

Year Team	G	GS	SACKS
1994—San Francisco NFL	16	16	6.0
1995—San Francisco NFL	12	12	6.0
1996—San Francisco NFL	16	16	11.5
1997—San Francisco NFL	12	12	4.0
Pro totals (4 years)	56	56	27.5

YOUNG, FLOYD   CB   BUCCANEERS

PERSONAL: Born November 23, 1975, in New Orleans. ... 6-0/170.
HIGH SCHOOL: Clark (New Orleans).
COLLEGE: Texas A&M-Kingsville.
TRANSACTIONS/CAREER NOTES: Signed as non-drafted free agent by Tampa Bay Buccaneers (May 5, 1997). ... Released by Buccaneers (July 18, 1997). ... Re-signed by Buccaneers (July 22, 1997). ... Released by Buccaneers (August 17, 1997). ... Re-signed by Buccaneers to practice squad (August 26, 1997). ... Activated (September 27, 1997).
PLAYING EXPERIENCE: Tampa Bay NFL, 1997. ... Games/Games started: 12/1.

YOUNG, RODNEY   S   GIANTS

PERSONAL: Born January 25, 1973, in Grambling, La. ... 6-1/210. ... Full name: Rodney Menard Young.
HIGH SCHOOL: Ruston (La.).
COLLEGE: Louisiana State.
TRANSACTIONS/CAREER NOTES: Selected by New York Giants in third round (85th pick overall) of 1995 NFL draft. ... Signed by Giants (July 25, 1995). ... Granted free agency (February 13, 1998).
PLAYING EXPERIENCE: New York Giants NFL, 1995-1997. ... Games/Games started: 1995 (10/0), 1996 (12/0), 1997 (9/0). Total: 31/0.
PRO STATISTICS: 1995—Returned one punt for no yards and fumbled once.

YOUNG, STEVE   QB   49ERS

PERSONAL: Born October 11, 1961, in Salt Lake City. ... 6-2/215. ... Full name: Jon Steven Young.
HIGH SCHOOL: Greenwich (Conn.).
COLLEGE: Brigham Young (law degree, 1994).
TRANSACTIONS/CAREER NOTES: Selected by Los Angeles Express in first round (10th pick overall) of 1984 USFL draft. ... Signed by Express (March 5, 1984). ... Granted roster exemption (March 5-30, 1984). ... Selected by Tampa Bay Buccaneers in first round (first pick overall) of 1984 NFL supplemental draft. ... On developmental squad (March 31-April 16, 1985). ... Released by Express (September 9, 1985). ... Signed by Buccaneers (September 10, 1985). ... Granted roster exemption (September 10-23, 1985). ... Traded by Buccaneers to San Francisco 49ers for second-round (LB Winston Moss) and fourth-round (WR Bruce Hill) picks in 1987 draft and cash (April 24, 1987). ... Granted free agency (February 1, 1991). ... Re-signed by 49ers (May 3, 1991). ... Designated by 49ers as franchise player (February 25, 1993).
CHAMPIONSHIP GAME EXPERIENCE: Played in NFC championship game (1988-1990, 1992-1994 and 1997 seasons). ... Member of 49ers for Super Bowl XXIII (1988 season); did not play. ... Member of Super Bowl championship team (1989 and 1994 seasons).
HONORS: Davey O'Brien Award winner (1983). ... Named quarterback on THE SPORTING NEWS college All-America first team (1983). ... Named NFL Player of the Year by THE SPORTING NEWS (1992 and 1994). ... Named quarterback on THE SPORTING NEWS NFL All-Pro team (1992 and 1994). ... Played in Pro Bowl (1992-1995 and 1997 seasons). ... Named Most Valuable Player of Super Bowl XXIX (1994 season). ... Named to play in Pro Bowl (1996 season); replaced by Kerry Collins due to injury.
RECORDS: Holds NFL career records for highest completion percentage—64.8; highest passer rating—97.0; and most consecutive seasons leading league in passer rating—4 (1991-1994). ... Holds NFL single-season record for highest passer rating—112.8 (1994).
POST SEASON RECORDS: Holds Super Bowl single-game record for most touchdown passes—6 (January 29, 1995, vs. San Diego). ... Shares Super Bowl single-game record for most passes attempted without an interception—36 (January 29, 1995, vs. San Diego). ... Shares NFL postseason single-game record for most touchdown passes—6 (January 29, 1995, vs. San Diego).
PRO STATISTICS: USFL: 1984 Fumbled seven times and recovered four fumbles. 1985—Fumbled seven times and recovered one fumble for minus 11 yards. NFL: 1985—Fumbled four times and recovered one fumble for minus one yard. 1986—Fumbled 11 times and recovered four fumbles for minus 24 yards. 1988—Fumbled five times and recovered two fumbles for minus 10 yards. 1989—Fumbled twice and recovered one fumble. 1990—Fumbled once. 1991—Fumbled three times and recovered one fumble for minus six yards. 1992—Fumbled nine times and recovered three fumbles for minus 13 yards. 1993—Caught two passes for two yards, fumbled eight times and recovered two fumbles for minus four yards. 1994—Fumbled four times and recovered one fumble for minus four yards. 1995—Fumbled three times. 1996—Fumbled three times and recovered one fumble. 1997—Fumbled four times and recovered two fumbles for minus 11 yards.
SINGLE GAME HIGHS (regular season): Attempts—49 (December 18, 1995, vs. Minnesota); completions—33 (November 24, 1996, vs. Washington); yards—462 (November 28, 1993, vs. Los Angeles Rams); and touchdown passes—4 (November 28, 1994, vs. New Orleans).
STATISTICAL PLATEAUS: USFL: 300-yard passing games: 1984 (2). ... 100-yard rushing games: 1984 (1), 1985 (1). Total: 2. ... NFL: 300-yard passing games: 1991 (3), 1992 (3), 1993 (3), 1994 (5), 1995 (5). Total: 19. ... 100-yard rushing games: 1990 (1).
MISCELLANEOUS: Active NFC leader for career passing yards (28,508); and career touchdown passes (193). Regular-season record as starting NFL quarterback: 81-44 (.648). ... Postseason record as starting NFL quarterback: 7-5 (.583).

			PASSING								RUSHING				TOTALS		
Year Team	G	GS	Att.	Cmp.	Pct.	Yds.	TD	Int.	Avg.	Rat.	Att.	Yds.	Avg.	TD	TD	2pt.	Pts.
1984—Los Angeles USFL	12	12	310	179	57.7	2361	10	9	7.62	80.6	79	515	6.5	7	7	3	48
1985—Los Angeles USFL	13	...	250	137	54.8	1741	6	13	6.96	63.1	56	368	6.6	2	2	0	12
—Tampa Bay NFL	5	5	138	72	52.2	935	3	8	6.78	56.9	40	233	5.8	1	1	...	6
1986—Tampa Bay NFL	14	14	363	195	53.7	2282	8	13	6.29	65.5	74	425	5.7	5	5	...	30
1987—San Francisco NFL	8	3	69	37	53.6	570	10	0	8.26	120.8	26	190	7.3	1	1	...	6
1988—San Francisco NFL	11	3	101	54	53.5	680	3	3	6.73	72.2	27	184	6.8	1	1	...	6
1989—San Francisco NFL	10	3	92	64	69.6	1001	8	3	10.88	120.8	38	126	3.3	2	2	...	12
1990—San Francisco NFL	6	1	62	38	61.3	427	2	0	6.89	92.6	15	159	10.6	0	0	...	0
1991 San Francisco NFL	11	10	279	180	64.5	2517	17	8	*9.02	*101.8	66	415	6.3	4	4	...	24
1992—San Francisco NFL	16	16	402	268	*66.7	‡3465	*25	7	*8.62	*107.0	76	537	7.1	4	4	...	24

Year Team	G	GS	PASSING								RUSHING				TOTALS		
			Att.	Cmp.	Pct.	Yds.	TD	Int.	Avg.	Rat.	Att.	Yds.	Avg.	TD	TD	2pt.	Pts.
1993—San Francisco NFL......	16	16	462	314	68.0	‡4023	*29	16	*8.71	*101.5	69	407	5.9	2	2	...	12
1994—San Francisco NFL......	16	16	461	324	*70.3	3969	*35	10	*8.61	*112.8	58	293	5.1	7	7	0	42
1995—San Francisco NFL......	11	11	447	299	*66.9	3200	20	11	7.16	92.3	50	250	5.0	3	3	0	18
1996—San Francisco NFL......	12	12	316	214	*67.7	2410	14	6	‡7.63	*97.2	52	310	6.0	4	4	1	26
1997—San Francisco NFL......	15	15	356	241	*67.7	3029	19	6	*8.51	*104.7	50	199	4.0	3	3	0	18
USFL totals (2 years)............	25	...	560	316	56.4	4102	16	22	7.33	72.8	135	883	6.5	9	9	3	60
NFL totals (13 years)............	151	125	3548	2300	64.8	28508	193	91	8.03	97.0	641	3728	5.8	37	37	1	224
Pro totals (15 years)............	176	...	4108	2616	63.7	32610	209	113	7.94	93.7	776	4611	5.9	46	46	4	284

ZANDOFSKY, MIKE — G — BEARS

PERSONAL: Born November 30, 1965, in Corvallis, Ore. ... 6-2/308. ... Full name: Michael Leslie Zandofsky. ... Name pronounced zan-DOFF-skee.
HIGH SCHOOL: Corvallis (Ore.).
COLLEGE: Washington.
TRANSACTIONS/CAREER NOTES: Selected by Phoenix Cardinals in third round (67th pick overall) of 1989 NFL draft. ... Signed by Cardinals (July 22, 1989). ... Traded by Cardinals to San Diego Chargers for eighth-round pick (TE Jerry Evans) in 1991 draft (August 29, 1990). ... On injured reserve with knee injury (August 27-October 12, 1991). ... Granted free agency (February 1, 1992). ... Re-signed by Chargers (July 23, 1992). ... Granted free agency (March 1, 1993). ... Re-signed by Chargers (July 25, 1993). ... Granted unconditional free agency (February 17, 1994). ... Signed by Atlanta Falcons (March 6, 1994). ... Granted unconditional free agency (February 14, 1997). ... Signed by Philadelphia Eagles (April 23, 1997). ... Released by Eagles (November 12, 1997). ... Signed by Chicago Bears (March 18, 1998).
PLAYING EXPERIENCE: Phoenix NFL, 1989; San Diego NFL, 1990-1993; Atlanta NFL, 1994-1996; Philadelphia NFL, 1997. ... Games/Games started: 1989 (15/7), 1990 (13/0), 1991 (10/5), 1992 (15/0), 1993 (16/16), 1994 (16/16), 1995 (12/12), 1996 (14/14), 1997 (4/2). Total: 115/72.
HONORS: Named offensive tackle on The Sporting News college All-America second team (1987).
PRO STATISTICS: 1995—Recovered one fumble.

ZATECHKA, ROB — G — GIANTS

PERSONAL: Born December 1, 1971, in Lansing, Mich. ... 6-4/320. ... Full name: Robert Zatechka. ... Name pronounced ZAT-es-ka.
HIGH SCHOOL: Lincoln (Neb.) East.
COLLEGE: Nebraska (degree in biological sciences).
TRANSACTIONS/CAREER NOTES: Selected by New York Giants in fourth round (128th pick overall) of 1995 NFL draft. ... Signed by Giants (July 6, 1995). ... Granted free agency (February 13, 1998).
PLAYING EXPERIENCE: New York Giants NFL, 1995-1997. ... Games/Games started: 1995 (16/3), 1996 (15/6), 1997 (16/0). Total: 47/9.
PRO STATISTICS: 1995—Returned one kickoff for five yards.

ZEIER, ERIC — QB — RAVENS

PERSONAL: Born September 6, 1972, in Marietta, Ga. ... 6-1/205. ... Full name: Eric Royce Zeier. ... Name pronounced ZY-er.
HIGH SCHOOL: Heidelberg (West Germany), then Marietta (Ga.).
COLLEGE: Georgia.
TRANSACTIONS/CAREER NOTES: Selected by Cleveland Browns in third round (84th pick overall) of 1995 NFL draft. ... Signed by Browns (July 14, 1995). ... Browns franchise moved to Baltimore and renamed Ravens for 1996 season (March 11, 1996). ... Granted free agency (February 13, 1998). ... Tendered offer sheet by Atlanta Falcons (March 5, 1998). ... Offer matched by Ravens (March 10, 1998).
HONORS: Named quarterback on The Sporting News college All-America second team (1994).
PRO STATISTICS: 1995—Fumbled three times. 1996—Fumbled twice and recovered one fumble. 1997—Fumbled three times for minus 14 yards.
SINGLE GAME HIGHS (regular season): Attempts—54 (November 5, 1995, vs. Houston); completions—28 (December 21, 1997, vs. Cincinnati); yards—310 (October 29, 1995, vs. Cincinnati); and touchdown passes—3 (December 14, 1997, vs. Tennessee).
STATISTICAL PLATEAUS: 300-yard passing games: 1995 (1), 1997 (2). Total: 3.
MISCELLANEOUS: Regular-season record as starting NFL quarterback: 3-4 (.429).

Year Team	G	GS	PASSING								RUSHING				TOTALS		
			Att.	Cmp.	Pct.	Yds.	TD	Int.	Avg.	Rat.	Att.	Yds.	Avg.	TD	TD	2pt.	Pts.
1995—Cleveland NFL............	7	4	161	82	50.9	864	4	9	5.37	51.9	15	80	5.3	0	0	1	2
1996—Baltimore NFL............	1	0	21	10	47.6	97	1	1	4.62	57.0	2	8	4.0	0	0	0	0
1997—Baltimore NFL............	5	3	116	67	57.8	958	7	1	8.26	101.1	10	17	1.7	0	0	0	0
Pro totals (3 years)...............	13	7	298	159	53.4	1919	12	11	6.44	71.4	27	105	3.9	0	0	1	2

ZEIGLER, DUSTY — C/G — BILLS

PERSONAL: Born September 27, 1973, in Rincon, Ga. ... 6-5/298. ... Full name: Curtis Dustin Zeigler.
HIGH SCHOOL: Effingham County (Springfield, Ga.).
COLLEGE: Notre Dame.
TRANSACTIONS/CAREER NOTES: Selected by Buffalo Bills in sixth round (202nd pick overall) of 1996 NFL draft. ... Signed by Bills (June 25, 1996).
PLAYING EXPERIENCE: Buffalo NFL, 1996 and 1997. ... Games/Games started: 1996 (2/0), 1997 (13/13). Total: 15/13.
PRO STATISTICS: 1997—Fumbled once and recovered one fumble for minus 12 yards.

ZELLARS, RAY — RB — SAINTS

PERSONAL: Born March 25, 1973, in Pittsburgh. ... 5-11/233. ... Full name: Raymond Mark Zellars.
HIGH SCHOOL: David B. Oliver (Pittsburgh).

COLLEGE: Notre Dame.
TRANSACTIONS/CAREER NOTES: Selected by New Orleans Saints in second round (44th pick overall) of 1995 NFL draft. ... Signed by Saints (July 19, 1995). ... On inactive list for five games (1996 season). ... On injured reserve with neck injury (December 19, 1996-remainder of season).
PRO STATISTICS: 1997—Recovered two fumbles.
SINGLE GAME HIGHS (regular season): Attempts—20 (November 3, 1996, vs. San Francisco); yards—174 (October 13, 1996, vs. Chicago); rushing touchdowns—2 (November 16, 1997, vs. Seattle).
STATISTICAL PLATEAUS: 100-yard rushing games: 1996 (1).

			RUSHING				RECEIVING				TOTALS		
Year Team	G	GS	Att.	Yds.	Avg.	TD	No.	Yds.	Avg.	TD	TD	2pt.	Pts.	Fum.
1995—New Orleans NFL	12	0	50	162	3.2	2	7	33	4.7	0	2	0	12	1
1996—New Orleans NFL	9	6	120	475	4.0	4	9	45	5.0	0	4	0	24	2
1997—New Orleans NFL	16	16	156	552	3.5	4	31	263	8.5	0	4	0	24	6
Pro totals (3 years)	37	22	326	1189	3.6	10	47	341	7.3	0	10	0	60	9

ZGONINA, JEFF — DT — RAMS

PERSONAL: Born May 24, 1970, in Long Grove, Ill. ... 6-2/300. ... Full name: Jeffrey Marc Zgonina. ... Name pronounced skah-NEE-nah.
HIGH SCHOOL: Carmel (Long Grove, Ill.).
COLLEGE: Purdue (degree in community health promotion, 1992).
TRANSACTIONS/CAREER NOTES: Selected by Pittsburgh Steelers in seventh round (185th pick overall) of 1993 NFL draft. ... Signed by Steelers (July 16, 1993). ... Claimed on waivers by Carolina Panthers (August 28, 1995). ... Granted free agency (February 16, 1996). ... Re-signed by Panthers (April 11, 1996). ... Released by Panthers (August 19, 1996). ... Signed by Atlanta Falcons (October 8, 1996). ... Granted unconditional free agency (February 14, 1997). ... Signed by St. Louis Rams (March 17, 1997).
PLAYING EXPERIENCE: Pittsburgh NFL, 1993 and 1994; Carolina NFL, 1995; Atlanta NFL, 1996; St. Louis NFL, 1997. ... Games/Games started: 1993 (5/0), 1994 (16/0), 1995 (2/0), 1996 (8/0), 1997 (15/0). Total: 46/0.
CHAMPIONSHIP GAME EXPERIENCE: Played in AFC championship game (1994 season).
PRO STATISTICS: 1993—Recovered one fumble. 1994—Returned two kickoffs for eight yards, fumbled once and recovered one fumble. 1996—Credited with one sack and recovered one fumble. 1997—Returned one kickoff for five yards and credited with two sacks.

ZIMMERMAN, GARY — OT — BRONCOS

PERSONAL: Born December 13, 1961, in Fullerton, Calif. ... 6-6/294. ... Full name: Gary Wayne Zimmerman.
HIGH SCHOOL: Walnut (Calif.).
COLLEGE: Oregon.
TRANSACTIONS/CAREER NOTES: Selected by Los Angeles Express in second round (36th pick overall) of 1984 USFL draft. ... Signed by Express (February 13, 1984). ... Granted roster exemption (February 13-24, 1984). ... Selected by New York Giants in first round (third pick overall) of 1984 NFL supplemental draft. ... NFL rights traded by Giants to Minnesota Vikings for two second-round picks (CB Mark Collins and S Greg Lasker) in 1986 draft (April 29, 1986). ... Released by Express (May 19, 1986). ... Signed by Vikings (May 21, 1986). ... Granted free agency (February 1, 1988). ... Re-signed by Vikings (August 29, 1988). ... Placed on reserve/did not report list (July 20, 1993). ... Traded by Vikings to Denver Broncos for first- (CB Dewayne Washington) and sixth-round (TE Andrew Jordan) picks in 1994 draft and second-round pick (DB Orlando Thomas) in 1995 draft (August 23, 1993). ... Granted unconditional free agency (February 14, 1997). ... Re-signed by Denver Broncos (September 9, 1997).
PLAYING EXPERIENCE: Los Angeles USFL, 1984 and 1985; Minnesota NFL, 1986-1992; Denver NFL, 1993-1997. ... Games/Games started: 1984 (16/16), 1985 (16/16), 1986 (16/16), 1987 (12/12), 1988 (16/16), 1989 (16/16), 1990 (16/16), 1991 (16/16), 1992 (16/16), 1993 (16/16), 1994 (16/16), 1995 (16/16), 1996 (14/14), 1997 (14/14). Total USFL: 32/32 Total NFL: 184/184. Total Pro: 216/216.
CHAMPIONSHIP GAME EXPERIENCE: Played in NFC championship game (1987 season). ... Played in AFC championship game (1997 season). ... Member of Super Bowl championship team (1997 season).
HONORS: Named offensive tackle on THE SPORTING NEWS college All-America second team (1983). ... Named offensive tackle on THE SPORTING NEWS USFL All-Star team (1984 and 1985). ... Named offensive tackle on THE SPORTING NEWS NFL All-Pro team (1987 and 1996). ... Played in Pro Bowl (1987-1989, 1992 and 1994 seasons). ... Named to play in Pro Bowl (1995 season); replaced by Will Wolford due to injury. ... Named to play in Pro Bowl (1996 season); replaced by Tony Boselli due to injury.
PRO STATISTICS: USFL: 1984—Returned one kickoff for no yards, fumbled once and recovered two fumbles. NFL: 1986—Recovered two fumbles. 1987—Recovered one fumble for four yards. 1993—Recovered one fumble for no yards.

ZOLAK, SCOTT — QB — PATRIOTS

PERSONAL: Born December 13, 1967, in Pittsburgh. ... 6-5/235. ... Full name: Scott David Zolak.
HIGH SCHOOL: Ringgold (Monongahela, Pa.).
COLLEGE: Maryland (degree in business administration).
TRANSACTIONS/CAREER NOTES: Selected by New England Patriots in fourth round (84th pick overall) of 1991 NFL draft. ... On inactive list for all 16 games (1991). ... On injured reserve with ankle injury (December 18, 1992-remainder of season). ... Granted free agency (February 17, 1994). ... Re-signed by Patriots (April 2, 1994).
CHAMPIONSHIP GAME EXPERIENCE: Member of Patriots for AFC championship game (1996 season); inactive. ... Member of Patriots for Super Bowl XXXI (1996 season); inactive.
PRO STATISTICS: 1992—Fumbled five times and recovered three fumbles for minus 21 yards. 1995—Fumbled four times and recovered one fumble for minus two yards.
SINGLE GAME HIGHS (regular season): Attempts—45 (October 1, 1995, vs. Atlanta); completions—24 (October 1, 1995, vs. Atlanta); yards—261 (November 15, 1992, vs. Indianapolis); and touchdown passes—2 (November 15, 1992, vs. Indianapolis).
MISCELLANEOUS: Regular-season record as starting NFL quarterback: 2-3 (.400).

			PASSING							RUSHING				TOTALS		
Year Team	G	GS	Att.	Cmp.	Pct.	Yds.	TD	Int.	Avg.	Rat.	Att.	Yds.	Avg.	TD	TD	2pt.	Pts.
1991—New England NFL							Did not play.										
1992—New England NFL	6	4	100	52	52.0	561	2	4	5.61	58.8	18	71	3.9	0	0	...	0
1993—New England NFL	3	0	2	0	0.0	0	0	0	...	39.6	1	0	0.0	0	0	...	0

Year Team	G	GS	Att.	Cmp.	Pct.	Yds.	TD	Int.	Avg.	Rat.	Att.	Yds.	Avg.	TD	TD	2pt.	Pts.
					PASSING							**RUSHING**				**TOTALS**	
1994—New England NFL........	16	0	8	5	62.5	28	0	0	3.50	68.8	1	-1	-1.0	0	0	0	0
1995—New England NFL........	16	1	49	28	57.1	282	1	0	5.76	80.5	4	19	4.8	0	0	0	0
1996—New England NFL........	3	0	1	1	100.0	5	0	0	5.00	87.5	4	-3	-0.8	0	0	0	0
1997—New England NFL........	4	0	9	6	66.7	67	2	0	7.44	128.2	3	-3	-1.0	0	0	0	0
Pro totals (6 years)	48	5	169	92	54.4	943	5	4	5.58	70.7	31	83	2.7	0	0	0	0

ZORDICH, MICHAEL   S   EAGLES

PERSONAL: Born October 12, 1963, in Youngstown, Ohio ... 6-1/212. ... Full name: Michael Edward Zordich.

HIGH SCHOOL: Chaney (Youngstown, Ohio).

COLLEGE: Penn State (degree in hotel, restaurant and institutional management, 1986).

TRANSACTIONS/CAREER NOTES: Selected by Baltimore Stars in 1986 USFL territorial draft. ... Selected by San Diego Chargers in ninth round (235th pick overall) of 1986 NFL draft. ... Signed by Chargers (June 24, 1986). ... Released by Chargers (August 22, 1986). ... Signed by New York Jets (April 9, 1987). ... Released by Jets (September 6, 1987). ... Re-signed by Jets (September 14, 1987). ... Granted unconditional free agency (February 1, 1989). ... Signed by Phoenix Cardinals (March 2, 1989). ... Granted free agency (February 1, 1991). ... Re-signed by Cardinals (July 22, 1991). ... Granted unconditional free agency (March 1, 1993). ... Re-signed by Cardinals (July 23, 1993). ... Granted unconditional free agency (February 17, 1994). ... Signed by Philadelphia Eagles (June 28, 1994).

PRO STATISTICS: 1990—Recovered one fumble. 1991—Recovered three fumbles for 19 yards. 1994—Returned one kickoff for no yards and recovered three fumbles for five yards. 1995—Recovered two fumbles for 58 yards and one touchdown. 1997—Recovered one fumble for minus one yard.

Year Team	G	GS	No.	Yds.	Avg.	TD	No.
				INTERCEPTIONS			**SACKS**
1987—New York Jets NFL..	10	0	0	0	...	0	1.0
1988—New York Jets NFL..	16	0	1	35	35.0	1	0.0
1989—Phoenix NFL...	16	6	1	16	16.0	∞1	1.0
1990—Phoenix NFL...	16	1	1	25	25.0	0	0.0
1991—Phoenix NFL...	16	16	1	27	27.0	0	0.0
1992—Phoenix NFL...	16	16	3	37	12.3	0	0.0
1993—Phoenix NFL...	16	9	1	0	0.0	0	0.0
1994—Philadelphia NFL...	16	16	4	39	9.8	1	1.0
1995—Philadelphia NFL...	15	15	1	10	10.0	0	1.0
1996—Philadelphia NFL...	16	16	4	54	13.5	0	0.0
1997—Philadelphia NFL...	16	16	1	21	21.0	0	2.0
Pro totals (11 years)	169	111	18	264	14.7	3	6.0

ZORICH, CHRIS   DT

PERSONAL: Born March 13, 1969, in Chicago. ... 6-1/282. ... Full name: Christopher Robert Zorich.

HIGH SCHOOL: Chicago Vocational.

COLLEGE: Notre Dame (degree in American studies).

TRANSACTIONS/CAREER NOTES: Selected by Chicago Bears in second round (49th pick overall) of 1991 NFL draft. ... Signed by Bears (June 24, 1991). ... Granted unconditional free agency (February 17, 1995). ... Re-signed by Bears (March 1, 1995). ... On injured reserve with knee injury (August 19, 1996-entire season). ... Released by Bears (October 28, 1997). ... Signed by Washington Redskins (October 31, 1997). ... Granted unconditional free agency (February 13, 1998).

HONORS: Named nose tackle on THE SPORTING NEWS college All-America first team (1989). ... Lombardi Award winner (1990). ... Named defensive lineman on THE SPORTING NEWS college All-America first team (1990).

PRO STATISTICS: 1992—Recovered one fumble for 42 yards and a touchdown. 1993—Recovered two fumbles. 1994—Recovered one fumble. 1995—Recovered two fumbles.

Year Team	G	GS	SACKS
1991—Chicago NFL	12	0	0.0
1992—Chicago NFL	16	2	2.0
1993—Chicago NFL	16	16	7.0
1994—Chicago NFL	16	16	5.5
1995—Chicago NFL	16	15	1.0
1996—Chicago NFL		Did not play.	
1997—Chicago NFL	3	0	0.0
—Washington NFL	6	0	1.0
Pro totals (6 years)..	85	49	16.5

1998 DRAFT PICKS

ADAMS, FLOZELL   OT   COWBOYS

PERSONAL: Born May 10, 1975, in Chicago. ... 6-7/335. ... Full name: Flozell Jootin Adams. ... Cousin of Hersey Hawkins, guard, Seattle SuperSonics.
HIGH SCHOOL: Proviso West (Maywood, Ill.).
COLLEGE: Michigan State.
TRANSACTIONS/CAREER NOTES: Selected by Dallas Cowboys in second round (38th pick overall) of 1998 NFL draft.
HONORS: Named offensive tackle on THE SPORTING NEWS college All-America third team (1997).
COLLEGE PLAYING EXPERIENCE: Michigan State, 1993-1997. ... Games: 1993 (redshirted), 1994 (6), 1995 (11), 1996 (11), 1997 (11). Total: 39.

AKINS, CHRIS   DT   EAGLES

PERSONAL: Born January 7, 1976, in Paris, Texas. ... 6-1/323.
HIGH SCHOOL: Paris (Texas).
COLLEGE: Texas.
TRANSACTIONS/CAREER NOTES: Selected by Philadelphia Eagles in seventh round (220th pick overall) of 1998 NFL draft. ... Signed by Eagles (June 11, 1998).

Year—Team	G	SACKS
1994—Texas	11	0.0
1995—Texas	12	4.0
1996—Texas	12	1.5
1997—Texas	3	0.0
College totals (4 years)	38	5.5

ALEXANDER, CURTIS   RB   BRONCOS

PERSONAL: Born June 11, 1974, in Memphis. ... 6-0/204.
HIGH SCHOOL: Whitehaven (Memphis).
COLLEGE: Alabama.
TRANSACTIONS/CAREER NOTES: Selected by Denver Broncos in fourth round (122nd pick overall) of 1998 NFL draft. ... Signed by Broncos (June 10, 1998).

		RUSHING				RECEIVING				TOTALS	
Year—Team	G	Att.	Yds.	Avg.	TD	No.	Yds.	Avg.	TD	TD	Pts.
1993—Alabama					Redshirted.						
1994—Alabama	3	19	75	3.9	1	0	0	...	0	1	6
1995—Alabama	6	22	75	3.4	0	0	0	...	0	0	0
1996—Alabama	7	61	240	3.9	2	7	105	15.0	1	3	18
1997—Alabama	11	155	720	4.6	6	16	133	8.3	2	8	48
College totals (4 years)	27	257	1110	4.3	9	23	238	10.3	3	12	72

ALEXANDER, JAMAAL   S   LIONS

PERSONAL: Born September 18, 1976, in New Orleans. ... 5-11/200.
HIGH SCHOOL: John F. Kennedy (New Orleans).
COLLEGE: Southern Mississippi.
TRANSACTIONS/CAREER NOTES: Selected by Detroit Lions in sixth round (185th pick overall) of 1998 NFL draft.

		INTERCEPTIONS			
Year—Team	G	No.	Yds.	Avg.	TD
1994—Southern Mississippi	11	0	0	...	0
1995—Southern Mississippi	11	1	0	0.0	0
1996—Southern Mississippi	11	4	117	29.3	1
1997—Southern Mississippi	11	2	21	10.5	1
College totals (4 years)	44	7	138	19.7	2

ALEXANDER, STEPHEN   TE   REDSKINS

PERSONAL: Born November 7, 1975, in Chickasha, Okla. ... 6-4/246.
HIGH SCHOOL: Chickasha (Okla.).
COLLEGE: Oklahoma.
TRANSACTIONS/CAREER NOTES: Selected by Washington Redskins in second round (48th pick overall) of 1998 NFL draft.

		RECEIVING			
Year—Team	G	No.	Yds.	Avg.	TD
1994—Oklahoma	6	10	123	12.3	1
1995—Oklahoma	11	43	580	13.5	2
1996—Oklahoma	7	22	438	19.9	2
1997—Oklahoma	11	29	450	15.5	1
College totals (4 years)	35	104	1591	15.3	6

ALFORD, BRIAN WR GIANTS

PERSONAL: Born June 7, 1975, in Oak Park, Mich. ... 6-1/187. ... Full name: Brian Wayne Alford.
HIGH SCHOOL: Oak Park (Mich.).
COLLEGE: Purdue.
TRANSACTIONS/CAREER NOTES: Selected by New York Giants in third round (70th pick overall) of 1998 NFL draft.
HONORS: Named wide receiver on THE SPORTING NEWS college All-America third team (1997).
COLLEGE NOTES: Returned two kickoffs for 36 yards (1995); and returned two punts for 19 yards (1997).

			RUSHING				RECEIVING				TOTALS	
Year Team	G	Att.	Yds.	Avg.	TD	No.	Yds.	Avg.	TD	TD	Pts.
1993—Purdue						Redshirted.					
1994—Purdue	5	0	0	...	0	4	58	14.5	1	1	6
1995—Purdue	11	1	-13	-13.0	0	34	686	20.2	8	8	48
1996—Purdue	11	3	22	7.3	0	63	1057	16.8	12	12	72
1997—Purdue	11	1	-8	-8.0	0	59	1167	19.8	9	9	54
College totals (4 years)	38	5	1	0.2	0	160	2968	18.6	30	30	180

ALLOTEY, VICTOR G BILLS

PERSONAL: Born April 8, 1975, in Brooklyn, N.Y. ... 6-3/325.
HIGH SCHOOL: Abraham Lincoln (Brooklyn, N.Y.).
COLLEGE: Indiana.
TRANSACTIONS/CAREER NOTES: Selected by Buffalo Bills in seventh round (198th pick overall) of 1998 NFL draft. ... Signed by Bills (June 8, 1998).
COLLEGE NOTES: Played defensive tackle during 1994, 1995 and 1996 seasons. ... Credited with two sacks (1995).
COLLEGE PLAYING EXPERIENCE: Indiana, 1993-1997. ... Games: 1993 (redshirted), 1994 (11), 1995 (9), 1996 (7), 1997 (11). Total: 38.

AMEY, VINCE DE RAIDERS

PERSONAL: Born February 9, 1975, in Hollywood, Calif. ... 6-2/290. ... Full name: Vincent Wayne Amey.
HIGH SCHOOL: James Logan (Union City, Calif.).
COLLEGE: Arizona State.
TRANSACTIONS/CAREER NOTES: Selected by Oakland Raiders in seventh round (230th pick overall) of 1998 NFL draft. ... Signed by Raiders (May 21, 1998).

Year Team	G	SACKS
1994—Arizona State	8	0.0
1995—Arizona State	10	0.0
1996—Arizona State	7	1.0
1997—Arizona State	11	2.5
College totals (4 years)	36	3.5

ANDERSEN, JASON OT PATRIOTS

PERSONAL: Born September 3, 1975, in Hayward, Calif. ... 6-6/312.
HIGH SCHOOL: Piedmont (Calif.).
COLLEGE: Brigham Young.
TRANSACTIONS/CAREER NOTES: Selected by New England Patriots in seventh round (211th pick overall) of 1998 NFL draft.
COLLEGE PLAYING EXPERIENCE: Brigham Young, 1993-1997. ... Games: 1993 (redshirted), 1994 (games played unavailable), 1995 (games played unavailable), 1996 (14), 1997 (11). Total: 25.

AVERY, JOHN RB DOLPHINS

PERSONAL: Born January 11, 1976, in Richmond, Va. ... 5-9/184. ... Full name: John Edward Avery.
HIGH SCHOOL: Asheville (N.C.).
JUNIOR COLLEGE: Northwest Mississippi Community College.
COLLEGE: Mississippi.
TRANSACTIONS/CAREER NOTES: Selected by Miami Dolphins in first round (29th pick overall) of 1998 NFL draft.
COLLEGE NOTES: Returned eight punts for 85 yards (1995).

			RUSHING				RECEIVING				KICKOFF RETURNS				TOTALS	
Year Team	G	Att.	Yds.	Avg.	TD	No.	Yds.	Avg.	TD	No.	Yds.	Avg.	TD	TD	Pts.
1994—Northwest Mississippi	10	226	1233	5.5	13	17	132	7.8	0	12	410	34.2	2	15	90
1995—Northwest Mississippi	10	178	1003	5.6	12	4	7	1.8	0	6	197	32.8	1	13	78
1996—Mississippi	11	181	788	4.4	5	16	99	6.2	0	17	473	27.8	2	7	42
1997—Mississippi	9	166	862	5.2	7	19	113	5.9	0	13	315	24.2	1	8	48
Junior college totals (2 years)	20	404	2236	5.5	25	21	139	6.6	0	18	607	33.7	3	28	168
College totals (2 years)	20	347	1650	4.8	12	35	212	6.1	0	30	788	26.3	3	15	90

BANKS, TAVIAN   RB   JAGUARS

PERSONAL: Born February 17, 1974, in Moline, Ill. ... 5-10/198. ... Full name: Tavian R. Banks.
HIGH SCHOOL: Bettendorf (Iowa).
COLLEGE: Iowa.
TRANSACTIONS/CAREER NOTES: Selected by Jacksonville Jaguars in fourth round (101st pick overall) of 1998 NFL draft. ... Signed by Jaguars (May 14, 1998).
COLLEGE NOTES: Returned one punt for five yards (1996).

		RUSHING				RECEIVING				KICKOFF RETURNS				TOTALS	
Year Team	G	Att.	Yds.	Avg.	TD	No.	Yds.	Avg.	TD	No.	Yds.	Avg.	TD	TD	Pts.
1993—Iowa							Redshirted.								
1994—Iowa	11	35	257	7.3	5	6	30	5.0	0	28	638	22.8	0	5	30
1995—Iowa	6	53	278	5.2	2	2	9	4.5	0	5	97	19.4	0	2	12
1996—Iowa	11	131	599	4.6	9	21	137	6.5	1	2	44	22.0	0	10	60
1997—Iowa	11	246	1639	6.7	17	18	200	11.1	2	0	0	...	0	19	114
College totals (4 years)	39	465	2773	6.0	33	47	376	8.0	3	35	779	22.3	0	36	216

BARBER, SHAWN   LB   REDSKINS

PERSONAL: Born January 14, 1975, in Richmond, Va. ... 6-2/224.
HIGH SCHOOL: Hermitage (Richmond, Va.).
COLLEGE: Richmond.
TRANSACTIONS/CAREER NOTES: Selected by Washington Redskins in fourth round (113th pick overall) of 1998 NFL draft. ... Signed by Redskins (May 13, 1998).
COLLEGE NOTES: Returned three kickoffs for 68 yards (1994); and caught one pass for 56 yards and a touchdown (1997).

		INTERCEPTIONS				SACKS
Year Team	G	No.	Yds.	Avg.	TD	No.
1993—Richmond				Redshirted.		
1994—Richmond	11	0	0	...	0	1.0
1995—Richmond	11	1	23	23.0	0	7.0
1996—Richmond	11	1	60	60.0	1	6.0
1997—Richmond	11	3	33	11.0	1	6.0
College totals (4 years)	44	5	116	23.2	2	20.0

BATCH, CHARLIE   QB   LIONS

PERSONAL: Born December 5, 1974, in Pittsburgh. ... 6-2/216. ... Full name: Charles D'Donte Batch.
HIGH SCHOOL: Steel Valley (Homestead, Pa.).
COLLEGE: Eastern Michigan (degree in business, 1997).
TRANSACTIONS/CAREER NOTES: Selected by Detroit Lions in second round (60th pick overall) of 1998 NFL draft.
COLLEGE NOTES: Granted medical redshirt due to ankle injury (1996).

		PASSING								RUSHING				TOTALS	
Year Team	G	Att.	Cmp.	Pct.	Yds.	TD	Int.	Avg.	Rat.	Att.	Yds.	Avg.	TD	TD	Pts.
1992—Eastern Michigan							Did not play.								
1993—Eastern Michigan							Redshirted.								
1994—Eastern Michigan	8	78	49	62.8	617	7	1	7.91	156.3	23	0	0.0	1	1	6
1995—Eastern Michigan	11	421	244	58.0	3177	21	17	7.55	129.7	61	52	0.9	3	3	18
1996—Eastern Michigan	2	65	39	60.0	518	2	2	7.97	130.9	12	-39	-3.3	0	0	0
1997—Eastern Michigan	11	434	247	56.9	3280	23	11	7.56	132.8	85	110	1.3	1	1	6
College totals (4 years)	32	998	579	58.0	7592	53	31	7.61	133.2	181	123	0.7	5	5	30

BATEMAN, ERIC   G   JETS

PERSONAL: Born December 28, 1973, in Santa Barbara, Calif. ... 6-7/319.
HIGH SCHOOL: Camarillo (Calif.).
COLLEGE: Brigham Young.
TRANSACTIONS/CAREER NOTES: Selected after junior season by New York Jets in fifth round (149th pick overall) of 1998 NFL draft.
COLLEGE NOTES: On Mormon mission (1993 and 1994).
COLLEGE PLAYING EXPERIENCE: Brigham Young, 1992 and 1995-1997. ... Games: 1992 (redshirted), 1995 (11), 1996 (13), 1997 (11). Total: 35.

BEASLEY, FRED   RB   49ERS

PERSONAL: Born September 18, 1974, in Montgomery, Ala. ... 6-0/220. ... Full name: Frederick Jerome Beasley.
HIGH SCHOOL: Robert E. Lee (Montgomery, Ala.).
COLLEGE: Auburn.
TRANSACTIONS/CAREER NOTES: Selected by San Francisco 49ers in sixth round (180th pick overall) of 1998 NFL draft.

		RUSHING				RECEIVING				TOTALS	
Year Team	G	Att.	Yds.	Avg.	TD	No.	Yds.	Avg.	TD	TD	Pts.
1994—Auburn	10	47	223	4.7	1	11	119	10.8	0	1	6
1995—Auburn	12	66	346	5.2	5	11	194	17.6	1	6	36
1996—Auburn	12	94	428	4.6	5	4	29	7.3	0	5	30
1997—Auburn	12	75	244	3.3	7	16	225	14.1	2	9	54
College totals (4 years)	46	282	1241	4.4	18	42	567	13.5	3	21	126

IN MEMORIAM — LEON BENDER

PERSONAL: Born August 8, 1975, in Santee, Calif. ... Died May 30, 1998. ... 6-4/300. ... Full name: Leon D. Bender.
HIGH SCHOOL: Santana (Santee, Calif.).
JUNIOR COLLEGE: Walla Walla (Wash.) Community College; did not play.
COLLEGE: Washington State.
TRANSACTIONS/CAREER NOTES: Selected by Oakland Raiders in second round (31st pick overall) of 1998 NFL draft. ... Signed by Raiders (May 12, 1998).

Year Team	G	SACKS
1993—Washington State		Did not play.
1994—Washington State	2	0.0
1995—Walla Walla		Did not play.
1996—Washington State	11	6.5
1997—Washington State	11	3.0
College totals (3 years)	24	9.5

BIRK, MATT   OT   VIKINGS

PERSONAL: Born July 23, 1976, in St. Paul, Minn. ... 6-4/308. ... Full name: Matthew Robert Birk.
HIGH SCHOOL: Cretin-Derham Hall (St. Paul, Minn.).
COLLEGE: Harvard.
TRANSACTIONS/CAREER NOTES: Selected by Minnesota Vikings in sixth round (173rd pick overall) of 1998 NFL draft.
COLLEGE PLAYING EXPERIENCE: Harvard, 1994-1997. ... Games: 1994 (4), 1995 (10), 1996 (10), 1997 (10). Total: 34.

BLACKMON, ROOSEVELT   CB   PACKERS

PERSONAL: Born September 10, 1974, in Belle Glade, Fla. ... 6-1/180.
HIGH SCHOOL: Belle Glade (Fla.).
COLLEGE: Morris Brown College (Ga.).
TRANSACTIONS/CAREER NOTES: Selected by Green Bay Packers in fourth round (121st pick overall) of 1998 NFL draft.
COLLEGE NOTES: Attempted four passes with two completions for 99 yards and one touchdown, rushed once for seven yards and returned 19 punts for 305 yards and two touchdowns (1996).

			INTERCEPTIONS		
Year Team	G	No.	Yds.	Avg.	TD.
1993—Morris Brown			Did not play.		
1994—Morris Brown	10	5	98	19.6	1
1995—Morris Brown	10	4	18	4.5	0
1996—Morris Brown	11	2	158	79.0	1
1997—Morris Brown	3	0	0	...	0
College totals (4 years)	34	11	274	24.9	2

BLACKWELL, ERNEST   FB   CHIEFS

PERSONAL: Born August 7, 1975, in St. Louis, Mo. ... 6-2/242. ... Full name: Ernest Jerome Blackwell.
HIGH SCHOOL: Eureka (Mo.).
COLLEGE: Missouri.
TRANSACTIONS/CAREER NOTES: Selected by Kansas City Chiefs in seventh round (224th pick overall) of 1998 NFL draft. ... Signed by Chiefs (June 4, 1998).

		RUSHING				RECEIVING				TOTALS	
Year Team	G	Att.	Yds.	Avg.	TD	No.	Yds.	Avg.	TD	TD	Pts.
1994—Missouri	4	7	32	4.6	0	0	0	...	0	0	0
1995—Missouri	9	33	220	6.7	1	1	6	6.0	0	1	6
1996—Missouri	11	79	506	6.4	5	0	0	...	0	5	30
1997—Missouri	11	73	551	7.5	6	2	8	4.0	0	6	36
College totals (4 years)	35	192	1309	6.8	12	3	14	4.7	0	12	72

BOOSE, DORIAN   DE   JETS

PERSONAL: Born January 29, 1974, in Frankfurt, West Germany. ... 6-5/283. ... Full name: Dorian Alexander Boose.
HIGH SCHOOL: Foss (Tacoma, Wash.).
JUNIOR COLLEGE: Walla Walla (Wash.) Community College.
COLLEGE: Washington State.
TRANSACTIONS/CAREER NOTES: Selected by New York Jets in second round (56th pick overall) of 1998 NFL draft.
COLLEGE NOTES: Granted medical redshirt due to foot injury (1995). ... Returned one punt for seven yards (1997).

		INTERCEPTIONS				SACKS
Year Team	G	No.	Yds.	Avg.	TD	No.
1993—Walla Walla	11	0	0	...	...	9.0
1994—Walla Walla	11	1	85	85.0	1	15.0
1995—Washington State			Redshirted.			
1996—Washington State	11	0	0	...	0	6.5
1997—Washington State	11	0	0	...	0	8.0
Junior college totals (2 years)	22	1	85	85.0	1	24.0
College totals (2 years)	22	0	0	...	0	14.5

BORDANO, CHRIS   LB   SAINTS

PERSONAL: Born December 30, 1974, in San Antonio. ... 6-1/241.
HIGH SCHOOL: Southwest (San Antonio).
COLLEGE: Southern Methodist.
TRANSACTIONS/CAREER NOTES: Selected by New Orleans Saints in sixth round (161st pick overall) of 1998 NFL draft. ... Signed by Saints (June 11, 1998).

		INTERCEPTIONS				SACKS
Year Team	G	No.	Yds.	Avg.	TD	No.
1993—SMU	9	0	0	...	0	1.0
1994—SMU	9	0	0	...	0	0.0
1995—SMU				Redshirted.		
1996—SMU	11	0	0	...	0	3.0
1997—SMU	10	1	1	1.0	0	1.5
College totals (4 years)	39	1	1	1.0	0	5.5

BRADFORD, COREY   WR   PACKERS

PERSONAL: Born December 8, 1975, in Clinton, La. ... 6-1/200.
HIGH SCHOOL: Clinton (La.).
JUNIOR COLLEGE: Hinds Community College (Miss.).
COLLEGE: Jackson State.
TRANSACTIONS/CAREER NOTES: Selected by Green Bay Packers in fifth round (150th pick overall) of 1998 NFL draft.

		RUSHING				RECEIVING				KICKOFF RETURNS				TOTALS	
Year Team	G	Att.	Yds.	Avg.	TD	No.	Yds.	Avg.	TD	No.	Yds.	Avg.	TD	TD	Pts.
1994—Hinds							Statistics unavailable.								
1995—Hinds							Statistics unavailable.								
1996—Jackson State							Did not play.								
1997—Jackson State	12	2	70	35.0	1	51	958	18.8	9	14	354	25.3	1	11	66
College totals (1 years)	12	2	70	35.0	1	51	958	18.8	9	14	354	25.3	1	11	66

BRAZZELL, CHRIS   WR   JETS

PERSONAL: Born May 22, 1976, in Fort Worth, Texas ... 6-2/182. ... Name rhymes with DAZZLE.
HIGH SCHOOL: Alice (Texas).
JUNIOR COLLEGE: Blinn College (Texas).
COLLEGE: Angelo State (Texas).
TRANSACTIONS/CAREER NOTES: Selected by New York Jets in sixth round (174th pick overall) of 1998 NFL draft. ... Signed by Jets (May 29, 1998).

		RECEIVING				PUNT RETURNS				KICKOFF RETURNS				TOTALS	
Year Team	G	No.	Yds.	Avg.	TD	No.	Yds.	Avg.	TD	No.	Yds.	Avg.	TD	TD	Pts.
1994—Blinn							Statistics unavailable.								
1995—Blinn							Statistics unavailable.								
1996—Angelo State	10	34	474	13.9	5	0	0	...	0	0	0	...	0	5	30
1997—Angelo State	10	47	1091	23.2	13	2	1	0.5	0	5	129	25.8	0	13	78
College totals (2 years)	20	81	1565	19.3	18	2	1	0.5	0	5	129	25.8	0	18	108

BRIGHAM, JEREMY   TE   RAIDERS

PERSONAL: Born March 22, 1975, in Boston. ... 6-4/250.
HIGH SCHOOL: Saguara (Scottsdale, Ariz.).
COLLEGE: Washington.
TRANSACTIONS/CAREER NOTES: Selected by Oakland Raiders in fifth round (127th pick overall) of 1998 NFL draft.

		RECEIVING		
Year Team	G	No.	Yds.	Avg.	TD
1993—Washington			Redshirted.		
1994—Washington			Did not play.		
1995—Washington	11	1	1	1.0	1
1996—Washington	11	4	22	5.5	0
1997—Washington	8	3	16	5.3	1
College totals (3 years)	30	8	39	4.9	2

BROMELL, LORENZO   DE   DOLPHINS

PERSONAL: Born September 23, 1975, in Chopee, S.C. ... 6-6/266.
HIGH SCHOOL: Chopee (S.C.).
JUNIOR COLLEGE: Georgia Military College.
COLLEGE: Clemson.
TRANSACTIONS/CAREER NOTES: Selected by Miami Dolphins in fourth round (102nd pick overall) of 1998 NFL draft.

Year Team	G	SACKS
1995—Georgia Military	10	8.0
1996—Clemson	11	2.0
1997—Clemson	11	6.0
Junior college totals (1 year)	10	8.0
College totals (2 years)	22	8.0

BROOKING, KEITH — LB — FALCONS

PERSONAL: Born October 30, 1975, in Senoia, Ga. ... 6-2/244. ... Full name: Keith Howard Brooking.
HIGH SCHOOL: East Coweta (Ga.).
COLLEGE: Georgia Tech.
TRANSACTIONS/CAREER NOTES: Selected by Atlanta Falcons in first round (12th pick overall) of 1998 NFL draft.

Year Team	G	INTERCEPTIONS No.	Yds.	Avg.	TD	SACKS No.
1994—Georgia Tech	11	0	0	...	0	0.0
1995—Georgia Tech	11	0	0	...	0	0.5
1996—Georgia Tech	11	1	0	0.0	0	3.0
1997—Georgia Tech	11	2	25	12.5	0	2.0
College totals (4 years)	44	3	25	8.3	0	5.5

BROWN, ERIC — S — BRONCOS

PERSONAL: Born March 20, 1975, in San Antonio. ... 6-0/203. ... Full name: Eric Jon Brown.
HIGH SCHOOL: Converse-Judson (San Antonio).
JUNIOR COLLEGE: Blinn College (Texas).
COLLEGE: Mississippi State.
TRANSACTIONS/CAREER NOTES: Selected by Denver Broncos in second round (61st pick overall) of 1998 NFL draft.

Year Team	G	INTERCEPTIONS No.	Yds.	Avg.	TD	SACKS No.
1994—Blinn		Statistics unavailable.				
1995—Blinn		Statistics unavailable.				
1996—Mississippi State	8	2	13	6.5	1	2.0
1997—Mississippi State	10	1	20	20.0	0	4.0
College totals (2 years)	18	3	33	11.0	1	6.0

BROWN, JONATHON — DE — PACKERS

PERSONAL: Born November 28, 1975, in Tulsa, Okla. ... 6-4/270. ... Full name: Jonathon Bernard Brown.
HIGH SCHOOL: Booker T. Washington (Tulsa, Okla.).
COLLEGE: Tennessee.
TRANSACTIONS/CAREER NOTES: Selected by Green Bay Packers in third round (90th pick overall) of 1998 NFL draft. ... Signed by Packers (June 12, 1998).

Year Team	G	SACKS
1994—Tennessee	11	2.0
1995—Tennessee	11	3.0
1996—Tennessee	11	6.5
1997—Tennessee	12	13.5
College totals (4 years)	45	25.0

BROWN, OMAR — S — FALCONS

PERSONAL: Born March 28, 1975, in York, Pa. ... 5-10/200. ... Full name: Omar L. Brown.
HIGH SCHOOL: William Penn (York, Pa.).
COLLEGE: North Carolina.
TRANSACTIONS/CAREER NOTES: Selected by Atlanta Falcons in fourth round (103rd pick overall) of 1998 NFL draft.

Year Team	G	INTERCEPTIONS No.	Yds.	Avg.	TD
1993—North Carolina		Redshirted.			
1994—North Carolina	11	0	0	...	0
1995—North Carolina	10	1	0	0.0	0
1996—North Carolina	11	0	0	...	0
1997—North Carolina	11	2	0	0.0	0
College totals (4 years)	43	3	0	0.0	0

BUNDREN, JIM — G — DOLPHINS

PERSONAL: Born October 6, 1974, in Pontiac, Mich. ... 6-3/303.
HIGH SCHOOL: Alexis I. Dupont (Greenville, Del.), then Valley Forge Military Academy (Wayne, Pa.).
COLLEGE: Clemson.
TRANSACTIONS/CAREER NOTES: Selected by Miami Dolphins in seventh round (210th pick overall) of 1998 NFL draft.
HONORS: Named offensive tackle on THE SPORTING NEWS college All-America third team (1997).
COLLEGE PLAYING EXPERIENCE: Clemson, 1993-1997. ... Games: 1993 (redshirted), 1994 (11), 1995 (12), 1996 (12), 1997 (12). Total: 47.

BURNETT, CHESTER — LB — VIKINGS

PERSONAL: Born April 15, 1975, in Denver. ... 5-10/226. ... Full name: Chester Dean Burnett.
HIGH SCHOOL: Mullen (Denver).
COLLEGE: Arizona.
TRANSACTIONS/CAREER NOTES: Selected by Minnesota Vikings in seventh round (208th pick overall) of 1998 NFL draft.

Year	Team	G	INTERCEPTIONS				SACKS
			No.	Yds.	Avg.	TD	No.
1993—Arizona		6	0	0	...	0	0.0
1994—Arizona				Redshirted.			
1995—Arizona		11	0	0	...	0	1.0
1996—Arizona		11	2	33	16.5	1	5.0
1997—Arizona		11	2	45	22.5	0	4.0
College totals (4 years)		39	4	78	19.5	1	10.0

CANNIDA, JAMES — DT — BUCCANEERS

PERSONAL: Born January 3, 1975, in Savannah, Ga. ... 6-2/275. ... Full name: James Thomas Cannida II.
HIGH SCHOOL: American (Fremont, Calif.).
COLLEGE: Nevada.
TRANSACTIONS/CAREER NOTES: Selected by Tampa Bay Buccaneers in sixth round (175th pick overall) of 1998 NFL draft. ... Signed by Buccaneers (June 4, 1998).

Year	Team	G	SACKS
1994—Nevada		11	1.0
1995—Nevada		11	1.0
1996—Nevada		11	10.0
1997—Nevada		10	5.0
College totals (4 years)		43	17.0

CHASE, MARTIN — DT — RAVENS

PERSONAL: Born December 19, 1974, in Lawton, Okla. ... 6-2/295. ... Full name: Cecil Martin Chase.
HIGH SCHOOL: Eisenhower (Lawton, Okla.).
COLLEGE: Oklahoma.
TRANSACTIONS/CAREER NOTES: Selected by Baltimore Ravens in fifth round (124th pick overall) of 1998 NFL draft.
COLLEGE NOTES: Intercepted one pass for 12 yards (1995).

Year	Team	G	SACKS
1994—Oklahoma		10	0.5
1995—Oklahoma		11	0.0
1996—Oklahoma		11	0.0
1997—Oklahoma		12	14.0
College totals (4 years)		44	14.5

CHAVOUS, COREY — S/CB — CARDINALS

PERSONAL: Born January 15, 1976, in Aiken, S.C. ... 6-0/204.
HIGH SCHOOL: Silver Bluff (Aiken, S.C.).
COLLEGE: Vanderbilt.
TRANSACTIONS/CAREER NOTES: Selected by Arizona Cardinals in second round (33rd pick overall) of 1998 NFL draft.

Year	Team	G	INTERCEPTIONS				PUNT RETURNS				KICKOFF RETURNS				TOTALS	
			No.	Yds.	Avg.	TD	No.	Yds.	Avg.	TD	No.	Yds.	Avg.	TD	TD	Pts.
1994—Vanderbilt		11	3	6	2.0	0	0	0	...	0	0	0	...	0	0	0
1995—Vanderbilt		11	2	0	0.0	0	6	13	2.2	0	3	36	12.0	0	0	0
1996—Vanderbilt		11	3	0	0.0	0	0	3	...	0	16	394	24.6	0	0	0
1997—Vanderbilt		11	4	-2	-0.5	0	0	0	...	0	0	0	...	0	0	0
College totals (4 years)		44	12	4	0.3	0	6	16	2.7	0	19	430	22.6	0	0	0

CHORAK, JASON — DE — RAMS

PERSONAL: Born September 23, 1974, in Vashon, Wash. ... 6-4/253.
HIGH SCHOOL: Vashon (Wash.).
COLLEGE: Washington.
TRANSACTIONS/CAREER NOTES: Selected by St. Louis Rams in seventh round (236th pick overall) of 1998 NFL draft.
HONORS: Named outside linebacker on THE SPORTING NEWS college All-America first team (1996).

Year	Team	G	SACKS
1993—Washington			Redshirted.
1994—Washington		11	0.5
1995—Washington		11	3.5
1996—Washington		11	14.5
1997—Washington		11	7.0
College totals (4 years)		44	25.5

CLEELAND, CAM — TE — SAINTS

PERSONAL: Born April 15, 1975, in Sedro Woolley, Wash. ... 6-4/272. ... Full name: Cameron Cleeland. ... Nephew of Phil Misley, pitcher in Milwaukee Braves organization (1956-58).
HIGH SCHOOL: Sedro Woolley (Wash.).
COLLEGE: Washington.
TRANSACTIONS/CAREER NOTES: Selected by New Orleans Saints in second round (40th pick overall) of 1998 NFL draft. ... Signed by Saints (June 9, 1998).
COLLEGE NOTES: Returned two kickoffs for 17 yards (1995).

Year Team	G	RECEIVING No.	Yds.	Avg.	TD
1993—Washington			Redshirted.		
1994—Washington	10	0	0	...	0
1995—Washington	11	8	146	18.3	1
1996—Washington	11	23	354	15.4	3
1997—Washington	11	19	276	14.5	2
College totals (4 years)	43	50	776	15.5	6

CLEMENT, ANTHONY — OT — CARDINALS

PERSONAL: Born April 10, 1976, in Lafayette, La. ... 6-7/355.
HIGH SCHOOL: Cecilia (Breaux Bridge, La.).
COLLEGE: Southwestern Louisiana.
TRANSACTIONS/CAREER NOTES: Selected by Arizona Cardinals in second round (36th pick overall) of 1998 NFL draft. ... Signed by Cardinals (June 16, 1998).
COLLEGE PLAYING EXPERIENCE: Southwestern Louisiana, 1994-1997. ... Games: 1994 (11), 1995 (11), 1996 (11), 1997 (11). Total: 44.

COLEMAN, FRED — WR — BILLS

PERSONAL: Born January 31, 1975, in Tyler, Texas. ... 6-1/190.
HIGH SCHOOL: Robert E. Lee (Tyler, Texas).
COLLEGE: Washington.
TRANSACTIONS/CAREER NOTES: Selected by Buffalo Bills in sixth round (160th pick overall) of 1998 NFL draft.
COLLEGE NOTES: Returned nine kickoffs for 186 yards (1995); and rushed three times for 24 yards (1997).

		RECEIVING				PUNT RETURNS				TOTALS	
Year Team	G	No.	Yds.	Avg.	TD	No.	Yds.	Avg.	TD	TD	Pts.
1993—Washington						Redshirted.					
1994—Washington	11	4	19	4.8	0	1	7	7.0	0	0	0
1995—Washington	11	32	498	15.6	4	3	25	8.3	0	4	24
1996—Washington	11	19	348	18.3	0	0	0	...	0	0	0
1997—Washington	11	42	723	17.2	7	2	12	6.0	0	7	42
College totals (4 years)	44	97	1588	16.4	11	6	44	7.3	0	11	66

COLLINS, MO — OT — RAIDERS

PERSONAL: Born September 22, 1976, in Charlotte, N.C. ... 6-4/337. ... Full name: Damon Jamal Collins.
HIGH SCHOOL: West Charlotte (N.C.).
COLLEGE: Florida.
TRANSACTIONS/CAREER NOTES: Selected after junior season by Oakland Raiders in first round (23rd pick overall) of 1998 NFL draft.
COLLEGE NOTES: Granted medical redshirt due to foot and ankle injury (1994).
COLLEGE PLAYING EXPERIENCE: Florida, 1994-1997. ... Games: 1994 (3), 1995 (12), 1996 (5), 1997 (11). Total: 31.

CONRAD, CHRIS — OT — STEELERS

PERSONAL: Born May 27, 1975, in Fullerton, Calif. ... 6-6/301.
HIGH SCHOOL: Olinda (Brea, Calif.).
COLLEGE: Fresno State.
TRANSACTIONS/CAREER NOTES: Selected by Pittsburgh Steelers in third round (66th pick overall) of 1998 NFL draft.
COLLEGE PLAYING EXPERIENCE: Fresno State, 1993-1997. ... Games: 1993 (redshirted), 1994 (10), 1995 (5), 1996 (11), 1997 (10). Total: 36.

COOKS, KERRY — S — VIKINGS

PERSONAL: Born March 28, 1974, in Irving, Texas. ... 5-11/198.
HIGH SCHOOL: Nimitz (Irving, Texas).
COLLEGE: Iowa.
TRANSACTIONS/CAREER NOTES: Selected by Minnesota Vikings in fifth round (144th pick overall) of 1998 NFL draft.
COLLEGE NOTES: Credited with two sacks (1996).

Year Team	G	INTERCEPTIONS No.	Yds.	Avg.	TD
1993—Iowa			Redshirted.		
1994—Iowa	11	1	27	27.0	0
1995—Iowa	11	0	0	...	0
1996—Iowa	11	1	20	20.0	0
1997—Iowa	11	2	45	22.5	1
College totals (4 years)	44	4	92	23.0	1

COUSINS, JOMO — DE — CARDINALS

PERSONAL: Born September 2, 1974, in Baltimore. ... 6-5/277. ... Full name: Jomo George Cousins.
HIGH SCHOOL: Seneca Valley (Calif.).

COLLEGE: Florida A&M.
TRANSACTIONS/CAREER NOTES: Selected by Arizona Cardinals in seventh round (209th pick overall) of 1998 NFL draft. ... Signed by Cardinals (May 21, 1998).

Year Team	G	SACKS
1994—Florida A&M	Did not play.	
1995—Florida A&M	Did not play.	
1996—Florida A&M	9	8.0
1997—Florida A&M	10	10.5
College totals (2 years)	19	18.5

COWART, SAM   LB   BILLS

PERSONAL: Born February 26, 1975, in Jacksonville. ... 6-2/239.
HIGH SCHOOL: Mandarin (Jacksonville).
COLLEGE: Florida State.
TRANSACTIONS/CAREER NOTES: Selected by Buffalo Bills in second round (39th pick overall) of 1998 NFL draft.
HONORS: Named outside linebacker on THE SPORTING NEWS college All-America first team (1997).
COLLEGE NOTES: Intercepted one pass for minus one yard (1995); advanced three fumbles for 39 yards and three touchdowns (1997). ... Granted medical redshirt due to knee injury (1996).

Year Team	G	SACKS
1993—Florida State	12	1.0
1994—Florida State	11	1.0
1995—Florida State	11	3.0
1996—Florida State	Redshirted.	
1997—Florida State	11	4.0
College totals (4 years)	45	9.0

CROWELL, GERMANE   WR   LIONS

PERSONAL: Born September 13, 1976, in Winston-Salem, N.C. ... 6-3/213. ... Full name: Germane L. Crowell.
HIGH SCHOOL: North Forsyth (Winston-Salem, N.C.).
COLLEGE: Virginia.
TRANSACTIONS/CAREER NOTES: Selected by Detroit Lions in second round (50th pick overall) of 1998 NFL draft.

Year Team	G	RUSHING				RECEIVING				TOTALS	
		Att.	Yds.	Avg.	TD	No.	Yds.	Avg.	TD	TD	Pts.
1994—Virginia	8	0	0	...	0	9	115	12.8	2	2	12
1995—Virginia	12	0	0	...	0	27	371	13.7	5	5	30
1996—Virginia	10	3	15	5.0	0	33	687	20.8	3	3	18
1997—Virginia	11	1	1	1.0	0	53	969	18.3	9	9	54
College totals (4 years)	41	4	16	4.0	0	122	2142	17.6	19	19	114

DAILEY, CASEY   LB   JETS

PERSONAL: Born June 11, 1975, in La Verne, Calif. ... 6-3/249.
HIGH SCHOOL: Damien (La Verne, Calif.).
COLLEGE: Northwestern.
TRANSACTIONS/CAREER NOTES: Selected by New York Jets in fifth round (134th pick overall) of 1998 NFL draft.
COLLEGE NOTES: Caught one pass for 23 yards (1994); and returned one fumble for 43 yards and a touchdown (1995).

Year Team	G	SACKS
1993—Northwestern	Redshirted.	
1994—Northwestern	9	2.0
1995—Northwestern	11	6.0
1996—Northwestern	11	8.0
1997—Northwestern	12	12.0
College totals (4 years)	43	28.0

DARDEN, TONY   CB   VIKINGS

PERSONAL: Born August 11, 1975, in Baton Rouge, La. ... 5-11/187.
HIGH SCHOOL: Holmes (San Antonio).
COLLEGE: Texas Tech.
TRANSACTIONS/CAREER NOTES: Selected by Minnesota Vikings in seventh round (225th pick overall) of 1998 NFL draft.
COLLEGE NOTES: Played quarterback during 1994 season and wide receiver during 1994 and 1995 seasons. ... Attempted 61 passes with 26 completions for 381 yards, two touchdowns and two interceptions and rushed 28 times for 73 yards and one touchdown (1994).

Year Team	G	INTERCEPTIONS				RECEIVING				TOTALS	
		No.	Yds.	Avg.	TD	No.	Yds.	Avg.	TD	TD	Pts.
1993—Texas Tech					Redshirted.						
1994—Texas Tech	11	0	0	...	0	11	234	21.3	1	1	6
1995—Texas Tech	11	0	0	...	0	11	183	16.6	1	1	6
1996—Texas Tech	11	3	18	6.0	0	0	0	...	0	0	0
1997—Texas Tech	10	2	0	0.0	0	0	0	...	0	0	0
College totals (4 years)	43	5	18	3.6	0	22	417	19.0	2	2	12

DARIUS, DONOVIN   S   JAGUARS

PERSONAL: Born August 12, 1975, in Camden, N.J. ... 6-1/211.
HIGH SCHOOL: Woodrow Wilson (Camden, N.J.).
COLLEGE: Syracuse.
TRANSACTIONS/CAREER NOTES: Selected by Jacksonville Jaguars in first round (25th pick overall) of 1998 NFL draft.
HONORS: Named free safety on THE SPORTING NEWS college All-America first team (1997).

Year Team	G	INTERCEPTIONS No.	Yds.	Avg.	TD	SACKS No.
1993—Syracuse		Redshirted.				
1994—Syracuse	11	1	0	0.0	0	0.0
1995—Syracuse	11	2	17	8.5	0	0.0
1996—Syracuse	11	2	0	0.0	0	0.0
1997—Syracuse	12	7	56	8.0	0	1.0
College totals (4 years)	45	12	73	6.1	0	1.0

DELIGIANIS, HARRY   DL   JAGUARS

PERSONAL: Born August 4, 1975, in Ashtabula, Ohio. ... 0-4/305. ... Full name: Harry Nicholas Deligianis.
HIGH SCHOOL: Ashtabula (Ohio).
COLLEGE: Youngstown State.
TRANSACTIONS/CAREER NOTES: Selected by Jacksonville Jaguars in fourth round (118th pick overall) of 1998 NFL draft. ... Signed by Jaguars (May 14, 1998).

Year Team	G	SACKS
1993—Youngstown State		Redshirted.
1994—Youngstown State		Did not play.
1995—Youngstown State	9	0.0
1996—Youngstown State	11	1.0
1997—Youngstown State	15	17.0
College totals (3 years)	35	18.0

DiNAPOLI, GENNARO   G   RAIDERS

PERSONAL: Born May 25, 1975, in Manhassat, N.Y. ... 6-3/301. ... Full name: Gennaro L. DiNapoli.
HIGH SCHOOL: Cazenovia (N.Y.).
COLLEGE: Virginia Tech.
TRANSACTIONS/CAREER NOTES: Selected by Oakland Raiders in fourth round (109th pick overall) of 1998 NFL draft.
COLLEGE PLAYING EXPERIENCE: Virginia Tech, 1994-1997. ... Games: 1994 (9), 1995 (11), 1996 (11), 1997 (11). Total: 42.

DRAFT, CHRIS   LB   BEARS

PERSONAL: Born February 26, 1976, in Anaheim. ... 5-11/222.
HIGH SCHOOL: Valencia (Calif.).
COLLEGE: Stanford.
TRANSACTIONS/CAREER NOTES: Selected by Chicago Bears in sixth round (157th pick overall) of 1998 NFL draft.
COLLEGE NOTES: Intercepted two passes for two yards (1997).

Year Team	G	SACKS
1994—Stanford	11	2.0
1995—Stanford	11	0.0
1996—Stanford	11	2.0
1997—Stanford	8	2.0
College totals (4 years)	41	6.0

DUNCAN, JAMIE   LB   BUCCANEERS

PERSONAL: Born July 20, 1975, in Wilmington, Del. ... 6-0/244.
HIGH SCHOOL: Christiana (Wilmington, Del.).
COLLEGE: Vanderbilt.
TRANSACTIONS/CAREER NOTES: Selected by Tampa Bay Buccaneers in third round (84th pick overall) of 1998 NFL draft.
HONORS: Named inside linebacker on THE SPORTING NEWS college All-America second team (1997).
COLLEGE NOTES: Returned one fumble for 31 yards and a touchdown (1996).

Year Team	G	INTERCEPTIONS No.	Yds.	Avg.	TD	SACKS No.
1993—Vanderbilt		Redshirted.				
1994—Vanderbilt	3	0	0	...	0	3.0
1995—Vanderbilt	11	1	4	4.0	0	1.0
1996—Vanderbilt	11	0	...	...	0	6.0
1997—Vanderbilt	11	1	12	12.0	0	2.0
College totals (4 years)	36	2	16	8.0	0	12.0

DUTTON, JOHN   QB   DOLPHINS

PERSONAL: Born September 20, 1975, in Newport Beach, Calif. ... 6-4/219.
HIGH SCHOOL: Fallbrook (Calif.).
COLLEGE: Texas, then Nevada.
TRANSACTIONS/CAREER NOTES: Selected by Miami Dolphins in sixth round (172nd pick overall) of 1998 NFL draft.

Year Team	G	PASSING Att.	Cmp.	Pct.	Yds.	TD	Int.	Avg.	Rat.	RUSHING Att.	Yds.	Avg.	TD	TOTALS TD	Pts.
1993—Texas							Redshirted.								
1994—Texas							Did not play.								
1995—Nevada							Did not play.								
1996—Nevada	11	334	222	66.5	2750	22	6	8.23	153.8	27	-56	-2.1	1	1	6
1997—Nevada	11	367	222	60.5	3526	20	6	9.61	155.9	44	-4	-0.1	1	1	6
College totals (2 years)	22	701	444	63.3	6276	42	12	8.95	154.9	71	-60	-0.8	2	2	12

DWIGHT, TIM — WR/KR — FALCONS

PERSONAL: Born July 13, 1975, in Iowa City, Iowa. ... 5-8/184.
HIGH SCHOOL: Iowa City (Iowa).
COLLEGE: Iowa.
TRANSACTIONS/CAREER NOTES: Selected by Atlanta Falcons in fourth round (114th pick overall) of 1998 NFL draft.
HONORS: Named kick returner on THE SPORTING NEWS college All-America second team (1996). ... Named kick returner on THE SPORTING NEWS college All-America first team (1997).
COLLEGE NOTES: Attempted one pass with one completion for nine yards and a touchdown (1994); had only pass attempt intercepted (1995); attempted two passes without a completion and one interception (1996); and attempted two passes with two completions for 86 yards and one touchdown (1997).

Year Team	G	RUSHING Att.	Yds.	Avg.	TD	RECEIVING No.	Yds.	Avg.	TD	PUNT RETURNS No.	Yds.	Avg.	TD	KICKOFF RETURNS No.	Yds.	Avg.	TD	TOTALS TD	Pts.
1994—Iowa	11	13	58	4.5	1	0	0	...	0	13	161	12.4	0	14	278	19.9	0	1	6
1995—Iowa	11	7	111	15.9	2	43	776	18.0	9	13	106	8.2	0	21	407	19.4	0	11	66
1996—Iowa	11	9	68	7.6	3	45	646	14.4	4	22	417	19.0	2	12	227	18.9	0	9	54
1997—Iowa	11	8	85	10.6	0	39	653	16.7	8	19	367	19.3	3	8	229	28.6	0	11	66
College totals (4 years)	44	37	322	8.7	6	127	2075	16.3	21	67	1051	15.7	5	55	1141	20.7	0	32	192

DYSON, KEVIN — WR — OILERS

PERSONAL: Born June 23, 1975, in Clinton, Utah. ... 5-11/199.
HIGH SCHOOL: Clearfield (Utah).
COLLEGE: Utah.
TRANSACTIONS/CAREER NOTES: Selected by Tennessee Oilers in first round (16th pick overall) of 1998 NFL draft.

Year Team	G	RUSHING Att.	Yds.	Avg.	TD	RECEIVING No.	Yds.	Avg.	TD	PUNT RETURNS No.	Yds.	Avg.	TD	KICKOFF RETURNS No.	Yds.	Avg.	TD	TOTALS TD	Pts.
1993—Utah								Redshirted.											
1994—Utah	11	0	0	...	0	24	339	14.1	2	0	0	...	0	0	0	...	0	2	12
1995—Utah	11	1	3	3.0	0	55	751	13.7	6	0	0	...	0	1	23	23.0	0	6	36
1996—Utah	11	0	0	...	0	53	812	15.3	8	2	15	7.5	0	12	289	24.1	0	8	48
1997—Utah	11	1	14	14.0	0	60	824	13.7	2	20	223	11.2	1	12	268	22.3	0	3	18
College totals (4 years)	44	2	17	8.5	0	192	2726	14.2	18	22	238	10.8	1	25	580	23.2	0	19	114

EDWARDS, ROBERT — RB — PATRIOTS

PERSONAL: Born October 2, 1974, in Tennille, Ga. ... 5-11/218.
HIGH SCHOOL: Washington County (Tennille, Ga.).
COLLEGE: Georgia.
TRANSACTIONS/CAREER NOTES: Selected by New England Patriots in first round (18th pick overall) of 1998 NFL draft.
COLLEGE NOTES: Played cornerback during 1993 and 1994 seasons. ... Returned one punt for 10 yards and intercepted four passes for 30 yards (1994). ... Granted medical redshirt due to foot injury (1995).

Year Team	G	RUSHING Att.	Yds.	Avg.	TD	RECEIVING No.	Yds.	Avg.	TD	KICKOFF RETURNS No.	Yds.	Avg.	TD	TOTALS TD	Pts.
1993—Georgia	6	0	0	...	0	0	0	...	0	0	0	...	0	0	0
1994—Georgia	11	0	0	...	0	0	0	...	0	1	12	12.0	0	0	0
1995—Georgia	2	45	325	7.2	6	2	42	21.0	1	0	0	...	0	7	42
1996—Georgia	11	184	800	4.3	9	23	199	8.7	1	2	27	13.5	0	10	60
1997—Georgia	9	142	830	5.8	12	17	172	10.1	1	2	12	6.0	0	13	78
College totals (5 years)	39	371	1955	5.3	27	42	413	9.8	3	5	51	10.2	0	30	180

ELLIS, GREG — DE — COWBOYS

PERSONAL: Born August 14, 1975, in Wendell. N.C. ... 6-6/283. ... Full name: Gregory Lemont Ellis.
HIGH SCHOOL: East Wake (Wendell, N.C.).
COLLEGE: North Carolina.
TRANSACTIONS/CAREER NOTES: Selected by Dallas Cowboys in first round (eighth pick overall) of 1998 NFL draft.
HONORS: Named defensive end on THE SPORTING NEWS college All-America second team (1996 and 1997).

Year Team	G	SACKS
1994—North Carolina	10	4.0
1995—North Carolina	11	7.0
1996—North Carolina	11	12.5
1997—North Carolina	11	9.0
College totals (4 years)	43	32.5

ENIS, CURTIS — RB — BEARS

PERSONAL: Born June 15, 1976, in Union City, Ohio. ... 6-1/242. ... Full name: Curtis D. Enis.
HIGH SCHOOL: Mississinawa Valley (Union City, Ohio), then Kiski Prep (Saltsburg, Pa.).
COLLEGE: Penn State.
TRANSACTIONS/CAREER NOTES: Selected after junior season by Chicago Bears in first round (fifth pick overall) of 1998 NFL draft.
HONORS: Named running back on THE SPORTING NEWS college All-America second team (1997).

		RUSHING				RECEIVING				KICKOFF RETURNS				TOTALS	
Year Team	G	Att.	Yds.	Avg.	TD	No.	Yds.	Avg.	TD	No.	Yds.	Avg.	TD	TD	Pts.
1995—Penn State	10	113	683	6.0	4	0	0	...	0	14	272	19.4	0	4	24
1996—Penn State	11	224	1210	5.4	13	32	291	9.1	1	0	0	...	0	14	84
1997—Penn State	11	228	1363	6.0	19	25	215	8.6	1	0	0	...	0	20	122
College totals (3 years)	32	565	3256	5.8	36	57	506	8.9	2	14	272	19.4	0	38	230

FABINI, JASON — OT — JETS

PERSONAL: Born August 25, 1974, in Fort Wayne, Ind. ... 6-7/318.
HIGH SCHOOL: Bishop Dwenger (Fort Wayne, Ind.).
COLLEGE: Cincinnati.
TRANSACTIONS/CAREER NOTES: Selected by New York Jets in fourth round (111th pick overall) of 1998 NFL draft.
COLLEGE PLAYING EXPERIENCE: Cincinnati, 1993-1997. ... Games: 1993 (redshirted), 1994 (11), 1995 (11), 1996 (11), 1997 (11). Total: 44.

FAIR, TERRY — CB — LIONS

PERSONAL: Born July 20, 1976, in Phoenix. ... 5-9/185. ... Full name: Terrance Delon Fair.
HIGH SCHOOL: South Mountain (Phoenix).
COLLEGE: Tennessee.
TRANSACTIONS/CAREER NOTES: Selected by Detroit Lions in first round (20th pick overall) of 1998 NFL draft.

		INTERCEPTIONS				PUNT RETURNS				KICKOFF RETURNS				TOTALS	
Year Team	G	No.	Yds.	Avg.	TD	No.	Yds.	Avg.	TD	No.	Yds.	Avg.	TD	TD	Pts.
1994—Tennessee	11	0	0	...	0	0	0	...	0	0	0	...	0	0	0
1995—Tennessee	10	2	15	7.5	0	5	73	14.6	0	6	166	27.7	0	0	0
1996—Tennessee	10	4	94	23.5	0	29	400	13.8	2	3	57	19.0	0	2	12
1997—Tennessee	11	5	1	0.2	0	19	272	14.3	0	2	30	15.0	0	0	0
College totals (4 years)	42	11	110	10.0	0	53	745	14.1	2	11	253	23.0	0	2	12

FANECA, ALAN — G — STEELERS

PERSONAL: Born December 7, 1976, in New Orleans. ... 6-5/322. ... Full name: Alan Joseph Faneca.
HIGH SCHOOL: Lamar (Houston).
COLLEGE: Louisiana State.
TRANSACTIONS/CAREER NOTES: Selected after junior season by Pittsburgh Steelers in first round (26th pick overall) of 1998 NFL draft.
HONORS: Named guard on THE SPORTING NEWS college All-America first team (1997).
COLLEGE PLAYING EXPERIENCE: Louisiana State, 1994-1997. ... Games: 1994 (redshirted), 1995 (11), 1996 (11), 1997 (11). Total: 33.

FAVORS, GREGORY — LB — CHIEFS

PERSONAL: Born September 30, 1974, in Atlanta. ... 6-1/236. ... Full name: Gregory Bernard Favors.
HIGH SCHOOL: Southside (Atlanta).
COLLEGE: Mississippi State (degree in correction, 1997).
TRANSACTIONS/CAREER NOTES: Selected by Kansas City Chiefs in fourth round (120th pick overall) of 1998 NFL draft.
COLLEGE NOTES: Intercepted one pass for one yard (1997).

Year Team	G	SACKS
1993—Mississippi State		Redshirted.
1994—Mississippi State	6	0.0
1995—Mississippi State	11	0.0
1996—Mississippi State	11	12.5
1997—Mississippi State	10	7.0
College totals (4 years)	38	19.5

FISCHER, MARK — C — REDSKINS

PERSONAL: Born July 29, 1974, in Cincinnati. ... 6-3/293. ... Full name: Mark Raymond Fischer.
HIGH SCHOOL: LaSalle (Cincinnati).
COLLEGE: Purdue.
TRANSACTIONS/CAREER NOTES: Selected by Washington Redskins in fifth round (140th pick overall) of 1998 NFL draft. ... Signed by Redskins (May 26, 1998).
COLLEGE PLAYING EXPERIENCE: Purdue, 1993-1997. ... Games: 1993 (redshirted), 1994 (8), 1995 (8), 1996 (11), 1997 (11). Total: 38.

FLEMING, ANTONIO   G   COWBOYS

PERSONAL: Born February 6, 1974, in Edison, Ga. ... 6-3/309. ... Full name: Antonio Marquise Fleming.
HIGH SCHOOL: Calhoun County (Edison, Ga.).
COLLEGE: Georgia.
TRANSACTIONS/CAREER NOTES: Selected by Dallas Cowboys in seventh round (227th pick overall) of 1998 NFL draft.
COLLEGE PLAYING EXPERIENCE: Georgia, 1993-1997. ... Games: 1993 (redshirted), 1994 (5), 1995 (9), 1996 (11), 1997 (11). Total: 36.

FLOYD, CHRIS   FB   PATRIOTS

PERSONAL: Born June 23, 1975, in Detroit. ... 6-0/231. ... Full name: Christopher Michael Floyd.
HIGH SCHOOL: Cooley (Detroit).
COLLEGE: Michigan.
TRANSACTIONS/CAREER NOTES: Selected by New England Patriots in third round (81st pick overall) of 1998 NFL draft.

		RUSHING				RECEIVING				TOTALS	
Year Team	G	Att.	Yds.	Avg.	TD	No.	Yds.	Avg.	TD	TD	Pts.
1994—Michigan	11	6	69	11.5	0	0	0	...	0	0	0
1995—Michigan	12	48	182	3.8	0	4	19	4.8	0	0	0
1996—Michigan	11	24	66	2.8	0	3	23	7.7	0	0	0
1997—Michigan	11	63	269	4.3	2	7	83	11.9	0	2	12
College totals (4 years)	45	141	586	4.2	2	14	125	8.9	0	2	12

FOLEY, STEVE   LB   BENGALS

PERSONAL: Born September 9, 1975, in Little Rock, Ark. ... 6-4/270.
HIGH SCHOOL: Hall (Little Rock, Ark.).
COLLEGE: Northeast Louisiana.
TRANSACTIONS/CAREER NOTES: Selected by Cincinnati Bengals in third round (75th pick overall) of 1998 NFL draft.

Year Team	G	SACKS
1994—Northeast Louisiana		Did not play.
1995—Northeast Louisiana	11	0.0
1996—Northeast Louisiana	10	5.0
1997—Northeast Louisiana	12	18.5
College totals (3 years)	33	23.5

FRICKE, BEN   C   GIANTS

PERSONAL: Born November 13, 1975, in Austin, Texas. ... 6-0/282. ... Name pronounced frick-EE.
HIGH SCHOOL: L.C. Anderson (Austin, Texas).
COLLEGE: Houston.
TRANSACTIONS/CAREER NOTES: Selected by New York Giants in seventh round (213th pick overall) of 1998 NFL draft.
HONORS: Named center on THE SPORTING NEWS college All-America second team (1997).
COLLEGE PLAYING EXPERIENCE: Houston, 1994-1997. ... Games: 1994 (6), 1995 (10), 1996 (11), 1997 (11). Total: 38.

FROST, SCOTT   S   JETS

PERSONAL: Born January 4, 1975, in Wood River, Neb. ... 6-3/219.
HIGH SCHOOL: Wood River (Neb.).
COLLEGE: Stanford, then Nebraska (degree in finance, 1997).
TRANSACTIONS/CAREER NOTES: Selected by New York Jets in third round (67th pick overall) of 1998 NFL draft.
COLLEGE NOTES: Played safety during 1994 season and quarterback during 1993, 1994, 1996 and 1997 seasons. ... Intercepted one pass for no yards (1994); and caught one pass for minus 11 yards (1996).

		PASSING								RUSHING				TOTALS	
Year Team	G	Att.	Cmp.	Pct.	Yds.	TD	Int.	Avg.	Rat.	Att.	Yds.	Avg.	TD	TD	Pts.
1993—Stanford	8	9	2	22.2	6	0	0	0.67	27.8	15	63	4.2	0	0	0
1994—Stanford	4	77	33	42.9	464	2	5	6.03	89.1	38	193	5.1	2	2	12
1995—Nebraska					Redshirted.										
1996—Nebraska	12	200	104	52.0	1440	13	3	7.20	130.9	126	438	3.5	9	9	54
1997—Nebraska	12	159	88	55.3	1237	5	4	7.78	126.0	176	1095	6.2	19	19	114
College totals (4 years)	36	445	227	51.0	3147	20	12	7.07	119.9	355	1789	5.0	30	30	180

FUAMATU-MA'AFALA, CHRIS   FB   STEELERS

PERSONAL: Born March 4, 1977, in Honolulu. ... 5-11/252. ... Name pronounced foo-ah-MAH-two mah-ah-FAH-la.
HIGH SCHOOL: St. Louis (Honolulu).
COLLEGE: Utah.
TRANSACTIONS/CAREER NOTES: Selected after junior season by Pittsburgh Steelers in sixth round (178th pick overall) of 1998 NFL draft.

		RUSHING				RECEIVING				TOTALS	
Year Team	G	Att.	Yds.	Avg.	TD	No.	Yds.	Avg.	TD	TD	Pts.
1995—Utah	11	141	834	5.9	9	1	6	6.0	0	9	54
1996—Utah	8	168	982	5.8	9	10	80	8.0	0	9	54
1997—Utah	11	154	814	5.3	4	4	39	9.8	1	5	30
College totals (3 years)	30	463	2630	5.7	22	15	125	8.3	1	23	138

GAINES, CORY S COLTS

PERSONAL: Born May 9, 1976, in Baton Rouge, La. ... 5-11/195. ... Full name: Cory LeRoy Gaines.
HIGH SCHOOL: Catholic (Baton Rouge, La.).
COLLEGE: Tennessee.
TRANSACTIONS/CAREER NOTES: Selected by Indianapolis Colts in seventh round (231st pick overall) of 1998 NFL draft.
COLLEGE NOTES: Credited with one sack and intercepted one pass for 57 yards and a touchdown (1997).
COLLEGE PLAYING EXPERIENCE: Tennessee, 1994-1997. ... Games: 1994 (6), 1995 (12), 1996 (12), 1997 (12). Total: 42.

GERMAN, JAMMI WR FALCONS

PERSONAL: Born July 4, 1974, in Fort Myers, Fla. ... 6-1/187. ... Name pronounced JAY-me.
HIGH SCHOOL: Fort Myers (Fla.).
COLLEGE: Miami.
TRANSACTIONS/CAREER NOTES: Selected by Atlanta Falcons in third round (74th pick overall) of 1998 NFL draft.

			RECEIVING				PUNT RETURNS				KICKOFF RETURNS				TOTALS	
Year Team	G	No.	Yds.	Avg.	TD	No.	Yds.	Avg.	TD	No.	Yds.	Avg.	TD	TD	Pts.
1993—Miami (Fla.)	8	16	213	13.3	1	13	129	9.9	0	4	69	17.3	0	1	6
1994—Miami (Fla.)	11	33	391	11.8	2	27	245	9.1	0	11	237	21.5	0	2	12
1995—Miami (Fla.)	11	41	730	17.8	3	0	0	...	0	0	0	...	0	3	18
1996—Miami (Fla.)							Did not play.								
1997—Miami (Fla.)							Did not play.								
College totals (3 years)	30	90	1334	14.8	6	40	374	9.4	0	15	306	20.4	0	6	36

GOFF, MIKE G BENGALS

PERSONAL: Born January 6, 1976, in Spring Valley, Ill. ... 6-5/311. ... Full name: Michael J. Goff.
HIGH SCHOOL: Lasalle-Peru (Peru, Ill.).
COLLEGE: Iowa.
TRANSACTIONS/CAREER NOTES: Selected by Cincinnati Bengals in third round (78th pick overall) of 1998 NFL draft.
COLLEGE PLAYING EXPERIENCE: Iowa, 1994-1997. ... Games: 1994 (11), 1995 (11), 1996 (11), 1997 (11). Total: 44.

GREEN, AHMAN RB SEAHAWKS

PERSONAL: Born February 16, 1977, in Omaha, Neb. ... 6-0/213.
HIGH SCHOOL: Central (Omaha, Neb.).
COLLEGE: Nebraska.
TRANSACTIONS/CAREER NOTES: Selected after junior season by Seattle Seahawks in third round (76th pick overall) of 1998 NFL draft.
HONORS: Named running back on THE SPORTING NEWS college All-America second team (1997).

			RUSHING				RECEIVING				KICKOFF RETURNS				TOTALS	
Year Team	G	Att.	Yds.	Avg.	TD	No.	Yds.	Avg.	TD	No.	Yds.	Avg.	TD	TD	Pts.
1995—Nebraska	11	141	1086	7.7	13	12	102	8.5	3	4	71	17.8	0	16	96
1996—Nebraska	10	155	917	5.9	7	9	93	10.3	0	1	29	29.0	0	7	42
1997—Nebraska	12	278	1877	6.8	22	14	105	7.5	0	0	0	...	0	22	132
College totals (3 years)	33	574	3880	6.8	42	35	300	8.6	3	5	100	20.0	0	45	270

GREEN, E.G. WR COLTS

PERSONAL: Born June 28, 1975, in Ft. Walton Beach, Fla. ... 5-11/187. ... Full name: Ernie G. Green.
HIGH SCHOOL: Ft. Walton Beach (Fla.).
COLLEGE: Florida State.
TRANSACTIONS/CAREER NOTES: Selected by Indianapolis Colts in third round (71st pick overall) of 1998 NFL draft.

			RUSHING				RECEIVING				TOTALS	
Year Team	G	Att.	Yds.	Avg.	TD	No.	Yds.	Avg.	TD	TD	Pts.
1993—Florida State				Redshirted.								
1994—Florida State	11	5	-18	-3.6	0	18	192	10.7	1	1	6
1995—Florida State	11	4	56	14.0	1	60	1007	16.8	10	11	66
1996—Florida State	11	0	0	...	0	34	662	19.5	7	7	42
1997—Florida State	11	1	9	9.0	0	54	1059	19.6	11	11	66
College totals (4 years)	44	10	47	4.7	1	166	2920	17.6	29	30	180

GREEN, JACQUEZ WR BUCCANEERS

PERSONAL: Born January 15, 1976, in Ft. Valley, Ga. ... 5-9/172. ... Full name: D'Tanyian Jacquez Green.
HIGH SCHOOL: Peach County (Ga.).
COLLEGE: Florida.
TRANSACTIONS/CAREER NOTES: Selected after junior season by Tampa Bay Buccaneers in second round (34th pick overall) of 1998 NFL draft.
HONORS: Named wide receiver on THE SPORTING NEWS college All-America second team (1997).

			RUSHING				RECEIVING				PUNT RETURNS				KICKOFF RETURNS				TOTALS	
Year Team	G	Att.	Yds.	Avg.	TD	No.	Yds.	Avg.	TD	No.	Yds.	Avg.	TD	No.	Yds.	Avg.	TD	TD	Pts.
1994—Florida						Redshirted.														
1995—Florida	11	7	93	13.3	1	19	531	27.9	5	9	50	5.6	0	16	312	19.5	0	6	36
1996—Florida	12	6	21	3.5	1	33	626	19.0	9	25	324	13.0	2	10	216	21.6	0	12	72
1997—Florida	11	7	51	7.3	1	61	1024	16.8	9	27	392	14.5	2	0	0	...	0	12	72
College totals (3 years)	34	20	165	8.3	3	113	2181	19.3	23	61	766	12.6	4	26	528	20.3	0	30	180

GRIESE, BRIAN | QB | BRONCOS

PERSONAL: Born March 18, 1975, in Miami. ... 6-3/215. ... Full name: Brian David Griese. ... Son of Bob Griese, Hall of Fame quarterback, Miami Dolphins (1967-80).
HIGH SCHOOL: Columbus (Miami).
COLLEGE: Michigan.
TRANSACTIONS/CAREER NOTES: Selected by Denver Broncos in third round (91st pick overall) of 1998 NFL draft.
COLLEGE NOTES: Punted 13 times for 429 yards (1996); and punted three times for 117 yards (1997).

Year Team	G	PASSING Att.	Cmp.	Pct.	Yds.	TD	Int.	Avg.	Rat.	RUSHING Att.	Yds.	Avg.	TD	TOTALS TD	Pts.
1993—Michigan					Redshirted.										
1994—Michigan	9	0	0	...	0	0	0	...	...	0	0	...	0	0	0
1995—Michigan	12	238	127	53.4	1577	13	10	6.63	118.6	34	-95	-2.8	2	2	12
1996—Michigan	12	61	35	57.4	513	3	2	8.41	137.7	16	-6	-0.4	0	0	0
1997—Michigan	12	307	193	62.9	2293	17	6	7.47	140.0	58	20	0.3	2	2	12
College totals (4 years)	45	606	355	58.6	4383	33	18	7.23	131.4	108	-81	-0.8	4	4	24

HAKIM, AZ-ZAHIR | WR | RAMS

PERSONAL: Born June 3, 1977, in Los Angeles. ... 5-10/178. ... Full name: Az-zahir Ali Hakim. ... Name pronounced ahz zah-HEER hah-KEEM.
HIGH SCHOOL: Fairfax (Los Angeles).
COLLEGE: San Diego State.
TRANSACTIONS/CAREER NOTES: Selected by St. Louis Rams in fourth round (96th pick overall) of 1998 NFL draft.
COLLEGE NOTES: Returned three punts for 68 yards (1997).

Year Team	G	RUSHING Att.	Yds.	Avg.	TD	RECEIVING No.	Yds.	Avg.	TD	KICKOFF RETURNS No.	Yds.	Avg.	TD	TOTALS TD	Pts.
1994—San Diego State	9	2	6	3.0	0	17	370	21.8	2	2	64	32.0	0	2	12
1995—San Diego State	12	7	8	1.1	0	57	1022	17.9	8	21	491	23.4	0	8	48
1996—San Diego State	7	2	1	0.5	0	36	635	17.6	5	3	77	25.7	0	5	30
1997—San Diego State	8	0	0	...	0	37	595	16.1	6	14	367	26.2	1	7	42
College totals (4 years)	36	11	15	1.4	0	147	2622	17.8	21	40	999	25.0	1	22	132

HALLEN, BOB | C | FALCONS

PERSONAL: Born March 9, 1975, in Mentor, Ohio. ... 6-4/292. ... Full name: Robert Joseph Hallen.
HIGH SCHOOL: Mentor (Ohio).
COLLEGE: Kent State.
TRANSACTIONS/CAREER NOTES: Selected by Atlanta Falcons in second round (53rd pick overall) of 1998 NFL draft. ... Signed by Falcons (June 3, 1998).
COLLEGE PLAYING EXPERIENCE: Kent, 1993-1997. ... Games: 1993 (redshirted), 1994 (11), 1995 (11), 1996 (11), 1997 (11). Total: 44.

HAMBRECK, DARREN | LB | COWBOYS

PERSONAL: Born August 30, 1975, in Lacoochee, Fla. ... 6-2/216. ... Nephew of Mudcat Grant, major league pitcher for seven teams (1958-71).
HIGH SCHOOL: Pasco (Dade City, Fla.).
COLLEGE: Florida, then South Carolina.
TRANSACTIONS/CAREER NOTES: Selected by Dallas Cowboys in fifth round (130th pick overall) of 1998 NFL draft.

Year Team	G	INTERCEPTIONS No.	Yds.	Avg.	TD	SACKS No.
1993—Florida	12	2	35	17.5	0	1.0
1994—Florida	11	2	81	40.5	1	1.0
1995—South Carolina				Redshirted.		
1996—South Carolina	11	0	0	...	0	1.5
1997—South Carolina	4	0	0	...	0	0.0
College totals (4 years)	38	4	116	29.0	1	3.5

HANSEN, CARL | DE | SEAHAWKS

PERSONAL: Born January 25, 1976, in Houston. ... 6-5/282.
HIGH SCHOOL: Stratford (Houston).
COLLEGE: Stanford.
TRANSACTIONS/CAREER NOTES: Selected by Seattle Seahawks in sixth round (162nd pick overall) of 1998 NFL draft. ... Signed by Seahawks (June 5, 1998).

Year Team	G	INTERCEPTIONS No.	Yds.	Avg.	TD	SACKS No.
1994—Stanford	11	0	0	...	0	0.0
1995—Stanford	11	1	0	0.0	0	8.0
1990—Stanford	11	1	6	6.0	0	6.5
1997—Stanford	11	0	0	...	0	6.0
College totals (4 years)	44	2	6	3.0	0	20.5

HARDEN, CEDRIC — DE — CHARGERS

PERSONAL: Born October 19, 1974, in Atlanta. ... 6-6/260.
HIGH SCHOOL: D.M. Therrell (Atlanta).
COLLEGE: Florida A&M.
TRANSACTIONS/CAREER NOTES: Selected by San Diego Chargers in fifth round (126th pick overall) of 1998 NFL draft.
COLLEGE PLAYING EXPERIENCE: Florida A&M, 1993-97. ... Games: 1993 (redshirted), 1994 (11), 1995 (11), 1996 (11), 1997 (11). Total:44.
COLLEGE NOTES: Played tight end during 1994, 1995 and 1996 seasons. ... Credited with seven sacks (1997).

HARDY, TERRY — TE — CARDINALS

PERSONAL: Born May 31, 1976, in Montgomery, Ala. ... 6-4/266.
HIGH SCHOOL: Carver (Montgomery, Ala.).
COLLEGE: Southern Mississippi (degree in coaching and sports information, 1997).
TRANSACTIONS/CAREER NOTES: Selected by Arizona Cardinals in fifth round (125th pick overall) of 1998 NFL draft. ... Signed by Cardinals (June 15, 1998).

		RECEIVING			
Year Team	G	No.	Yds.	Avg.	TD
1994—Southern Mississippi	10	5	50	10.0	0
1995—Southern Mississippi	11	7	83	11.9	1
1996—Southern Mississippi	11	4	49	12.3	0
1997—Southern Mississippi	11	12	108	9.0	2
College totals (4 years)	43	28	290	10.4	3

HART, LAWRENCE — TE — JETS

PERSONAL: Born September 19, 1976, in Shreveport, La. ... 6-4/261.
HIGH SCHOOL: Woodlawn (Shreveport, La.).
COLLEGE: Southern (La.).
TRANSACTIONS/CAREER NOTES: Selected by New York Jets in seventh round (195th pick overall) of 1998 NFL draft. ... Signed by Jets (June 15, 1998).
COLLEGE NOTES: Rushed once for no yards (1996).

		RECEIVING			
Year Team	G	No.	Yds.	Avg.	TD
1994—Southern	4	5	49	9.8	0
1995—Southern	5	5	67	13.4	1
1996—Southern	8	11	134	12.2	1
1997—Southern	7	13	175	13.5	1
College totals (4 years)	24	34	425	12.5	3

HASKINS, JON — LB — CHARGERS

PERSONAL: Born October 6, 1975, in Sarasota, Fla. ... 6-2/245.
HIGH SCHOOL: Riverview (Sarasota, Fla.).
COLLEGE: Stanford.
TRANSACTIONS/CAREER NOTES: Selected by San Diego Chargers in seventh round (194th pick overall) of 1998 NFL draft.

		INTERCEPTIONS				SACKS
Year Team	G	No.	Yds.	Avg.	TD	No.
1994—Stanford	11	0	0	...	0	2.0
1995—Stanford	11	0	0	...	0	1.0
1996—Stanford	11	0	0	...	0	7.0
1997—Stanford	11	1	22	22.0	1	1.0
College totals (4 years)	44	1	22	22.0	1	11.0

HASSELBECK, MATT — QB — PACKERS

PERSONAL: Born September 25, 1975, in Norfolk, Mass. ... 6-4/219. ... Full name: Matthew Michael Hasselbeck.
HIGH SCHOOL: Xaverian Brothers (Norfolk, Mass.).
COLLEGE: Boston College (degree in marketing, 1997).
TRANSACTIONS/CAREER NOTES: Selected by Green Bay Packers in sixth round (187th pick overall) of 1998 NFL draft.

		PASSING								RUSHING				TOTALS	
Year Team	G	Att.	Cmp.	Pct.	Yds.	TD	Int.	Avg.	Rat.	Att.	Yds.	Avg.	TD	TD	Pts.
1993—Boston College						Redshirted.									
1994—Boston College	5	6	4	66.7	39	0	0	6.50	121.3	5	8	1.6	0	0	0
1995—Boston College	11	60	27	45.0	280	2	7	4.67	71.9	10	-6	-0.6	1	1	6
1996—Boston College	11	330	171	51.8	1990	9	9	6.03	106.0	87	-214	-2.5	2	2	12
1997—Boston College	10	305	188	61.6	2239	11	10	7.34	128.6	71	24	0.3	1	1	6
College totals (4 years)	37	701	390	55.6	4548	22	26	6.49	113.1	173	-188	-1.1	4	4	24

HAWKINS, ARTRELL — CB — BENGALS

PERSONAL: Born November 24, 1975, in Johnstown, Pa. ... 5-10/190.
HIGH SCHOOL: Bishop McCort (Johnstown, Pa.).
COLLEGE: Cincinnati.

TRANSACTIONS/CAREER NOTES: Selected by Cincinnati Bengals in second round (43rd pick overall) of 1998 NFL draft. ... Signed by Bengals (May 14, 1998).

Year Team	G	INTERCEPTIONS				KICKOFF RETURNS				TOTALS	
		No.	Yds.	Avg.	TD	No.	Yds.	Avg.	TD	TD	Pts.
1993—Cincinnati						Redshirted.					
1994—Cincinnati	8	0	0	...	0	3	59	19.7	0	0	0
1995—Cincinnati	11	1	0	0.0	0	1	19	19.0	0	0	0
1996—Cincinnati	11	1	0	0.0	0	2	35	17.5	0	0	0
1997—Cincinnati	11	1	38	38.0	1	19	474	24.9	0	1	6
College totals (4 years)	41	3	38	12.7	1	25	587	23.5	0	1	6

HAYES, DONALD — WR — PANTHERS

PERSONAL: Born July 13, 1975, in Madison, Wis. ... 6-5/208.
HIGH SCHOOL: East (Madison, Wis.).
COLLEGE: Wisconsin.
TRANSACTIONS/CAREER NOTES: Selected by Carolina Panthers in fourth round (106th pick overall) of 1998 NFL draft.
COLLEGE NOTES: Returned one kickoff for 14 yards (1994).

Year Team	G	RECEIVING			
		No.	Yds.	Avg.	TD
1994—Wisconsin	9	0	0	...	0
1995—Wisconsin	11	17	328	19.3	1
1996—Wisconsin	12	43	620	14.4	1
1997—Wisconsin	12	40	574	14.4	2
College totals (4 years)	44	100	1522	15.2	4

HICKS, ROBERT — OT — BILLS

PERSONAL: Born November 17, 1974, in Atlanta ... 6-7/338. ... Full name: Robert Otis Hicks Jr.
HIGH SCHOOL: Douglass (Atlanta).
COLLEGE: Mississippi State.
TRANSACTIONS/CAREER NOTES: Selected by Buffalo Bills in third round (68th pick overall) of 1998 NFL draft.
COLLEGE PLAYING EXPERIENCE: Mississippi State, 1993-1997. ... Games: 1993 (redshirted), 1994 (2), 1995 (11), 1996 (10), 1997 (11). Total: 34.

HICKS, SKIP — RB — REDSKINS

PERSONAL: Born October 13, 1974, in Corsicana, Texas. ... 6-0/230. ... Full name: Brian LaVell Hicks.
HIGH SCHOOL: Burkburnett (Texas).
COLLEGE: UCLA.
TRANSACTIONS/CAREER NOTES: Selected by Washington Redskins in third round (69th pick overall) of 1998 NFL draft.
HONORS: Named running back on THE SPORTING NEWS college All-America first team (1997).
COLLEGE NOTES: Granted medical redshirt due to knee injury (1995).

Year Team	G	RUSHING				RECEIVING				TOTALS	
		Att.	Yds.	Avg.	TD	No.	Yds.	Avg.	TD	TD	Pts.
1993—UCLA	9	100	563	5.6	5	0	0	...	0	5	30
1994—UCLA	7	40	161	4.0	3	2	10	5.0	0	3	18
1995—UCLA	3	16	100	6.3	1	1	15	15.0	0	1	6
1996—UCLA	11	224	1034	4.6	17	21	283	13.5	3	20	120
1997—UCLA	12	258	1282	5.0	22	22	389	17.7	4	26	156
College totals (5 years)	42	638	3140	4.9	48	46	697	15.2	7	55	330

HOLCOMBE, ROBERT — RB — RAMS

PERSONAL: Born December 11, 1975, in Houston. ... 5-11/220. ... Full name: Robert Wayne Holcombe.
HIGH SCHOOL: Jeff Davis Senior (Houston), then Mesa (Ariz.).
COLLEGE: Illinois.
TRANSACTIONS/CAREER NOTES: Selected by St. Louis Rams in second round (37th pick overall) of 1998 NFL draft.

Year Team	G	RUSHING				RECEIVING				KICKOFF RETURNS				TOTALS	
		Att.	Yds.	Avg.	TD	No.	Yds.	Avg.	TD	No.	Yds.	Avg.	TD	TD	Pts.
1994—Illinois	10	125	520	4.2	4	6	44	7.3	0	1	6	6.0	0	4	24
1995—Illinois	11	264	1051	4.0	5	8	57	7.1	0	1	14	14.0	0	5	30
1996—Illinois	11	260	1281	4.9	12	23	241	10.5	1	0	0	...	0	13	78
1997—Illinois	11	294	1253	4.3	4	35	277	7.9	2	0	0	...	0	6	36
College totals (4 years)	43	943	4105	4.4	25	72	619	8.6	3	2	20	10.0	0	28	168

HOLLIDAY, VONNIE — DT — PACKERS

PERSONAL: Born May 20, 1976, in Camden (S.C.). ... 6-5/300. ... Full name: Dimetry Giovonni Holliday.
HIGH SCHOOL: Camden (S.C.).
COLLEGE: North Carolina.
TRANSACTIONS/CAREER NOTES: Selected by Green Bay Packers in first round (19th pick overall) of 1998 NFL draft. ... Signed by Packers (June 12, 1998).

Year Team	G	SACKS
1994—North Carolina	10	0.0
1995—North Carolina	10	1.0
1996—North Carolina	11	5.0
1997—North Carolina	11	5.0
College totals (4 years)	42	11.0

HOWARD, CHRIS — RB — BRONCOS

PERSONAL: Born May 5, 1975, in River Ridge, La. ... 5-10/223.
HIGH SCHOOL: John Curtis (River Ridge, La.).
COLLEGE: Michigan.
TRANSACTIONS/CAREER NOTES: Selected by Denver Broncos in fifth round (153rd pick overall) of 1998 NFL draft.
COLLEGE NOTES: Returned one kickoff for 13 yards (1994).

Year Team	G	RUSHING				RECEIVING				TOTALS	
		Att.	Yds.	Avg.	TD	No.	Yds.	Avg.	TD	TD	Pts.
1994—Michigan	12	11	38	3.5	0	0	0	...	0	0	0
1995—Michigan	13	48	175	3.6	0	14	91	6.5	2	2	12
1996—Michigan	11	160	725	4.5	10	9	62	6.9	0	10	60
1997—Michigan	12	199	938	4.7	7	37	276	7.5	1	8	48
College totals (4 years)	48	418	1876	4.5	17	60	429	7.2	3	20	120

IVORY, CLIFFORD — CB — CHARGERS

PERSONAL: Born August 1, 1975, in Quitman, Ga. ... 5-11/183.
HIGH SCHOOL: Brooks County (Quitman, Ga.).
COLLEGE: Troy (Ala.) State.
TRANSACTIONS/CAREER NOTES: Selected by San Diego Chargers in sixth round (155th pick overall) of 1998 NFL draft.
COLLEGE NOTES: Played wide receiver during 1995 season. ... Caught six passes for 32 yards (1995).

Year Team	G	INTERCEPTIONS			
		No.	Yds.	Avg.	TD
1994—Troy State		Did not play.			
1995—Troy State	11	0	0	...	0
1996—Troy State	11	2	6	3.0	0
1997—Troy State	11	7	201	28.7	2
College totals (3 years)	33	9	207	23.0	2

JACKSON, BRAD — LB — DOLPHINS

PERSONAL: Born January 11, 1975, in Canton, Ohio. ... 6-0/228.
HIGH SCHOOL: Firestone (Akron, Ohio).
COLLEGE: Cincinnati.
TRANSACTIONS/CAREER NOTES: Selected by Miami Dolphins in third round (79th pick overall) of 1998 NFL draft.
HONORS: Named outside linebacker on THE SPORTING NEWS college All-America third team (1997).

Year Team	G	INTERCEPTIONS				SACKS
		No.	Yds.	Avg.	TD	No.
1993—Cincinnati		Redshirted.				
1994—Cincinnati	10	1	9	9.0	0	0.0
1995—Cincinnati	11	4	74	18.5	1	5.0
1996—Cincinnati	11	1	13	13.0	0	5.0
1997—Cincinnati	11	0	0	...	0	3.0
College totals (4 years)	43	6	96	16.0	1	13.0

JANES, RON — FB — CARDINALS

PERSONAL: Born February 14, 1975, in Macon, Mo. ... 6-1/276.
HIGH SCHOOL: South Shelby (Clarence, Mo.).
COLLEGE: Missouri.
TRANSACTIONS/CAREER NOTES: Selected by Arizona Cardinals in seventh round (233rd pick overall) of 1998 NFL draft. ... Signed by Cardinals (May 21, 1998).

Year Team	G	RUSHING				RECEIVING				TOTALS	
		Att.	Yds.	Avg.	TD	No.	Yds.	Avg.	TD	TD	Pts.
1993—Missouri		Redshirted.									
1994—Missouri	12	10	39	3.9	0	3	16	5.3	0	0	0
1995—Missouri	11	21	81	3.9	0	2	18	9.0	0	0	0
1996—Missouri	11	51	156	3.1	0	7	102	14.6	1	1	6
1997—Missouri	11	32	123	3.8	0	2	18	9.0	0	0	0
College totals (4 years)	45	114	399	3.5	0	14	154	11.0	1	1	6

JENSEN, JERRY — LB — PANTHERS

PERSONAL: Born February 26, 1975, in Downey, Calif. ... 6-0/237.
HIGH SCHOOL: Cascade (Everett, Wash.).

COLLEGE: Washington.
TRANSACTIONS/CAREER NOTES: Selected by Carolina Panthers in fifth round (136th pick overall) of 1998 NFL draft.
COLLEGE NOTES: Intercepted two passes for two yards (1997).

Year Team	G	SACKS
1993—Washington	Redshirted.	
1994—Washington	11	0.0
1995—Washington	11	5.0
1996—Washington	11	7.0
1997—Washington	11	6.0
College totals (4 years)	44	18.0

JOHNSON, DUSTIN — FB — JETS

PERSONAL: Born August 5, 1973, in Eagar, Ariz. ... 6-2/236.
HIGH SCHOOL: Round Valley (Springerville, Ariz.).
COLLEGE: Brigham Young.
TRANSACTIONS/CAREER NOTES: Selected by New York Jets in sixth round (183rd pick overall) of 1998 NFL draft.
COLLEGE NOTES: On Mormon mission (1992 and 1993). ... Played fullback and tight end during 1997 season.

Year Team	G	RUSHING				RECEIVING				TOTALS	
		Att.	Yds.	Avg.	TD	No.	Yds.	Avg.	TD	TD	Pts.
1991—Brigham Young						Redshirted.					
1992—Brigham Young						Did not play.					
1993—Brigham Young						Did not play.					
1994—Brigham Young						Did not play.					
1995—Brigham Young	11	5	71	14.2	0	3	25	8.3	0	0	0
1996—Brigham Young	13	45	257	5.7	1	30	464	15.5	3	4	24
1997—Brigham Young	11	18	113	6.3	0	33	394	11.9	1	1	6
College totals (3 years)	35	68	441	6.5	1	66	883	13.4	4	5	30

JOHNSON, PAT — WR — RAVENS

PERSONAL: Born August 10, 1976, in Gainesville, Ga. ... 5-10/180. ... Full name: Patrick Jevon Johnson.
HIGH SCHOOL: Redlands (Calif.).
COLLEGE: Oregon.
TRANSACTIONS/CAREER NOTES: Selected by Baltimore Ravens in second round (42nd pick overall) of 1998 NFL draft.
HONORS: Named kick returner on THE SPORTING NEWS college All-America second team (1997).

Year Team	G	RUSHING				RECEIVING				PUNT RETURNS				KICKOFF RETURNS				TOTALS	
		Att.	Yds.	Avg.	TD	No.	Yds.	Avg.	TD	No.	Yds.	Avg.	TD	No.	Yds.	Avg.	TD	TD	Pts.
1994—Oregon	11	1	-3	-3.0	0	30	472	15.7	2	9	76	8.4	0	7	104	14.9	0	2	12
1995—Oregon	12	2	2	1.0	0	11	157	14.3	0	42	344	8.2	0	2	107	53.5	1	1	6
1996—Oregon	10	4	39	9.8	0	14	218	15.6	3	17	129	7.6	0	12	368	30.7	1	4	24
1997—Oregon	12	1	-6	-6.0	0	55	1072	19.5	8	21	249	11.9	1	19	516	27.2	0	9	54
College totals (4 years)	45	8	32	4.0	0	110	1919	17.4	13	89	798	9.0	1	40	1095	27.4	2	16	96

JONES, TEBUCKY — S — PATRIOTS

PERSONAL: Born October 6, 1974. ... 6-2/216. ... Full name: Tebucky S. Jones.
HIGH SCHOOL: New Britain, Conn.
COLLEGE: Syracuse.
TRANSACTIONS/CAREER NOTES: Selected by New England Patriots in first round (22nd pick overall) of 1998 NFL draft.
COLLEGE NOTES: Played running back during 1994, 1995 and 1996 seasons.

Year Team	G	RUSHING				INTERCEPTIONS				RECEIVING				KICKOFF RETURNS				TOTALS	
		Att.	Yds.	Avg.	TD	No.	Yds.	Avg.	TD	No.	Yds.	Avg.	TD	No.	Yds.	Avg.	TD	TD	Pts.
1994—Syracuse	7	7	49	7.0	0	0	0	...	0	0	0	...	0	1	13	13.0	0	0	0
1995—Syracuse	9	62	223	3.6	5	0	0	...	0	1	2	2.0	0	8	163	20.4	0	5	30
1996—Syracuse	11	54	223	4.1	3	0	0	...	0	1	7	7.0	0	0	0	...	0	3	18
1997—Syracuse	10	1	1	1.0	1	4	104	26.0	1	0	0	...	0	0	0	...	0	2	12
College totals (4 years)	37	124	496	4.0	9	4	104	26.0	1	2	9	4.5	0	9	176	19.6	0	10	60

JORDAN, ANTONY — LB — COLTS

PERSONAL: Born December 19, 1974, in Sewell, N.J. ... 6-2/234.
HIGH SCHOOL: Washington Township (Sewell, N.J.).
COLLEGE: Vanderbilt.
TRANSACTIONS/CAREER NOTES: Selected by Indianapolis Colts in fifth round (135th pick overall) of 1998 NFL draft.

Year Team	G	INTERCEPTIONS				SACKS
		No.	Yds.	Avg.	TD	No.
1993—Vanderbilt			Redshirted.			
1994—Vanderbilt	11	1	0	0.0	0	4.0
1995—Vanderbilt	11	0	0	...	0	0.0
1996—Vanderbilt	11	1	41	41.0	1	2.0
1997—Vanderbilt	10	0	0	...	0	2.5
College totals (4 years)	43	2	41	20.5	1	8.5

JUREVICIUS, JOE WR GIANTS

PERSONAL: Born December 23, 1974, in Cleveland. ... 6-5/231. ... Full name: Joe Michael Jurevicius. ... Name pronounced jur-ih-VISH-us.
HIGH SCHOOL: Lake Catholic (Mentor, Ohio).
COLLEGE: Penn State.
TRANSACTIONS/CAREER NOTES: Selected by New York Giants in second round (55th pick overall) of 1998 NFL draft.
COLLEGE NOTES: Punted 15 times for 553 yards (1994); and rushed once for six yards (1996).

			RECEIVING		
Year Team	G	No.	Yds.	Avg.	TD
1993—Penn State		Redshirted.			
1994—Penn State	1	1	9	9.0	0
1995—Penn State	11	13	199	15.3	1
1996—Penn State	11	41	869	21.2	4
1997—Penn State	11	39	817	20.9	10
College totals (4 years)	34	94	1894	20.1	15

KARCZEWSKI, DOUG G JETS

PERSONAL: Born February 6, 1975, in Washington, D.C. ... 6-5/298. ... Full name: Doug Lindsay Karczewski.
HIGH SCHOOL: DeMatha Catholic (Hyattsville, Md.).
COLLEGE: Virginia (degree in sociology).
TRANSACTIONS/CAREER NOTES: Selected by New York Jets in fifth round (141st pick overall) of 1998 NFL draft.
COLLEGE PLAYING EXPERIENCE: Virginia, 1993-1997. ... Games: 1993 (redshirted), 1994 (10), 1995 (8), 1996 (11), 1997 (11). Total: 40.

KELLY, BRIAN CB BUCCANEERS

PERSONAL: Born January 14, 1976, in Las Vegas. ... 5-11/195.
HIGH SCHOOL: Overland (Aurora, Colo.).
COLLEGE: Southern California.
TRANSACTIONS/CAREER NOTES: Selected by Tampa Bay Buccaneers in second round (45th pick overall) of 1998 NFL draft.

			INTERCEPTIONS		
Year Team	G	No.	Yds.	Avg.	TD
1994—Southern California	11	1	9	9.0	0
1995—Southern California	11	3	19	6.3	0
1996—Southern California	10	1	18	18.0	0
1997—Southern California	11	2	32	16.0	0
College totals (4 years)	43	7	78	11.1	0

KING, CARLOS FB STEELERS

PERSONAL: Born November 27, 1973, in Booneville, N.C. ... 6-0/235.
HIGH SCHOOL: Starmount (Booneville, N.C.), then Hargrave Military Academy (Chatham, Va.).
COLLEGE: North Carolina State.
TRANSACTIONS/CAREER NOTES: Selected by Pittsburgh Steelers in fourth round (123rd pick overall) of 1998 NFL draft.

		RUSHING				RECEIVING				TOTALS	
Year Team	G	Att.	Yds.	Avg.	TD	No.	Yds.	Avg.	TD	TD	Pts.
1994—North Carolina State	11	63	257	4.1	6	11	62	5.6	1	7	42
1995—North Carolina State	5	22	124	5.6	1	5	48	9.6	0	1	6
1996—North Carolina State	11	50	227	4.5	3	13	161	12.4	1	4	24
1997—North Carolina State	11	70	380	5.4	1	20	207	10.4	1	2	12
College totals (4 years)	38	205	988	4.8	11	49	478	9.8	3	14	84

KREUTZ, OLIN C BEARS

PERSONAL: Born June 9, 1977, in Honolulu. ... 6-2/300. ... Name pronounced KROOTZ.
HIGH SCHOOL: St. Louis (Honolulu).
COLLEGE: Washington.
TRANSACTIONS/CAREER NOTES: Selected after junior season by Chicago Bears in third round (64th pick overall) of 1998 NFL draft.
HONORS: Named center on THE SPORTING NEWS college All-America first team (1997).
COLLEGE PLAYING EXPERIENCE: Washington, 1995-1997. ... Games: 1995 (10), 1996 (11), 1997 (11). Total: 32.

LEAF, RYAN QB CHARGERS

PERSONAL: Born May 15, 1976, in Great Falls, Mont. ... 6-5/240. ... Full name: Ryan David Leaf.
HIGH SCHOOL: Russell (Great Falls, Mont.).
COLLEGE: Washington State.
TRANSACTIONS/CAREER NOTES: Selected after junior season by San Diego Chargers in first round (second pick overall) of 1998 NFL draft.
HONORS: Named quarterback on THE SPORTING NEWS college All-America first team (1997).

		PASSING								RUSHING				TOTALS	
Year Team	G	Att.	Cmp.	Pct.	Yds.	TD	Int.	Avg.	Rat.	Att.	Yds.	Avg.	TD	TD	Pts.
1994—Washington State					Redshirted.										
1995—Washington State	9	97	52	53.6	654	4	1	6.74	121.8	22	13	0.6	2	2	12
1996—Washington State	11	373	194	52.0	2811	21	12	7.54	127.5	69	-136	-2.0	6	6	36
1997—Washington State	11	375	210	56.0	3637	33	10	9.70	161.2	72	-54	-0.8	6	6	36
College totals (3 years)	31	845	456	54.0	7102	58	23	8.40	141.8	163	-177	-1.1	14	14	84

LINTON, JONATHAN   FB   BILLS

PERSONAL: Born October 7, 1974, in Catasauqua, Pa. ... 6-0/248. ... Full name: Jonathan C. Linton.
HIGH SCHOOL: Catasauqua (Pa.).
COLLEGE: North Carolina.
TRANSACTIONS/CAREER NOTES: Selected by Buffalo Bills in fifth round (131st pick overall) of 1998 NFL draft. ... Signed by Bills (June 8, 1998).

		RUSHING				RECEIVING				KICKOFF RETURNS				TOTALS	
Year Team	G	Att.	Yds.	Avg.	TD	No.	Yds.	Avg.	TD	No.	Yds.	Avg.	TD	TD	Pts.
1993—North Carolina								Redshirted.							
1994—North Carolina	11	0	0	...	0	0	0	...	0	0	0	...	0	0	0
1995—North Carolina	11	90	350	3.9	4	8	67	8.4	0	1	17	17.0	0	4	24
1996—North Carolina	11	55	200	3.6	0	5	56	11.2	1	1	23	23.0	0	1	6
1997—North Carolina	11	248	1004	4.0	10	29	286	9.9	1	...	...	...	...	11	66
College totals (4 years)	44	393	1554	4.0	14	42	409	9.7	2	2	40	20.0	0	16	96

LITTLE, LEONARD   LB   RAMS

PERSONAL: Born October 19, 1974, in Asheville, N.C. ... 6-3/237. ... Full name: Leonard Antonio Little.
HIGH SCHOOL: Asheville (N.C.).
JUNIOR COLLEGE: Coffeyville (Kan.) Community College.
COLLEGE: Tennessee.
TRANSACTIONS/CAREER NOTES: Selected by St. Louis Rams in third round (65th pick overall) of 1998 NFL draft.

Year Team	G	SACKS
1994—Coffeyville	7	5.0
1995—Tennessee	11	11.0
1996—Tennessee	7	8.5
1997—Tennessee	12	8.5
Junior college totals (1 year)	7	5.0
College totals (3 years)	30	28.0

LIWIENSKI, CHRIS   G   LIONS

PERSONAL: Born August 2, 1975, in Sterling Heights, Mich. ... 6-5/304.
HIGH SCHOOL: Stevenson (Sterling Heights, Mich.).
COLLEGE: Indiana.
TRANSACTIONS/CAREER NOTES: Selected by Detroit Lions in seventh round (207th pick overall) of 1998 NFL draft.
COLLEGE PLAYING EXPERIENCE: Indiana, 1993-1997. ... Games: 1993 (redshirted), 1994 (11), 1995 (10), 1996 (11), 1997 (11). Total: 43.

LONG, KEVIN   C   OILERS

PERSONAL: Born May 2, 1975, in Summerville, S.C. ... 6-5/296.
HIGH SCHOOL: Summerville (S.C.).
COLLEGE: Florida State.
TRANSACTIONS/CAREER NOTES: Selected by Tennessee Oilers in seventh round (229th pick overall) of 1998 NFL draft.
COLLEGE PLAYING EXPERIENCE: Florida State, 1993-1997. ... Games: 1993 (redshirted), 1994 (11), 1995 (10), 1996 (10), 1997 (11). Total: 42.

LOUD, KAMIL   WR   BILLS

PERSONAL: Born June 25, 1976, in Richmond, Calif. ... 6-0/190. ... Full name: Kamil Kassam Loud.
HIGH SCHOOL: El Cerrito (Calif.).
COLLEGE: Cal Poly-SLO.
TRANSACTIONS/CAREER NOTES: Selected by Buffalo Bills in seventh round (238th pick overall) of 1998 NFL draft. ... Signed by Bills (June 8, 1998).

		RECEIVING			
Year Team	G	No.	Yds.	Avg.	TD
1994—Cal Poly-San Luis Obispo	8	19	276	14.5	2
1995—Cal Poly-San Luis Obispo	11	57	1098	19.3	9
1996—Cal Poly-San Luis Obispo	11	60	1042	17.4	7
1997—Cal Poly-San Luis Obispo	10	33	708	21.5	8
College totals (4 years)	40	169	3124	18.5	26

LOVE, CLARENCE   CB   EAGLES

PERSONAL: Born June 16, 1976, in Jackson, Mich. ... 5-10/181. ... Full name: Clarence Eugene Love.
HIGH SCHOOL: Jackson (Mich.).
COLLEGE: Toledo.
TRANSACTIONS/CAREER NOTES: Selected by Philadelphia Eagles in fourth round (116th pick overall) of 1998 NFL draft.
COLLEGE NOTES: Credited with one sack and returned one fumble for 28 yards and a touchdown (1996).

Year Team		INTERCEPTIONS			
	G	No.	Yds.	Avg.	TD
1993—Toledo			Redshirted.		
1994—Toledo	8	1	11	11.0	0
1995—Toledo	11	1	31	31.0	0
1996—Toledo	11	1	0	0.0	0
1997—Toledo	12	3	36	12.0	0
College totals (4 years)	42	6	78	13.0	0

MANNELLY, PATRICK OT BEARS

PERSONAL: Born April 18, 1975, in Atlanta. ... 6-5/285. ... Full name: James Patrick Mannelly.
HIGH SCHOOL: Marist (Atlanta).
COLLEGE: Duke.
TRANSACTIONS/CAREER NOTES: Selected by Chicago Bears in sixth round (189th pick overall) of 1998 NFL draft.
COLLEGE NOTES: Duke, 1993-1997. ... Games: 1993 (11), 1994 (12), 1995 (11), 1996 (redshirted), 1997 (8). Total: 42.

MANNING, PEYTON QB COLTS

PERSONAL: Born March 24, 1976, in New Orleans. ... 6-5/230. ... Full name: Peyton Williams Manning.
HIGH SCHOOL: Isidore Newman (New Orleans).
COLLEGE: Tennessee.
TRANSACTIONS/CAREER NOTES: Selected by Indianapolis Colts in first round (first pick overall) of 1998 NFL draft.
HONORS: Davey O'Brien Award winner (1997). ... Named quarterback on THE SPORTING NEWS college All-America second team (1997).
COLLEGE NOTES: Caught one pass for 10 yards (1997).

Year Team		PASSING								RUSHING				TOTALS	
	G	Att.	Cmp.	Pct.	Yds.	TD	Int.	Avg.	Rat.	Att.	Yds.	Avg.	TD	TD	Pts.
1994—Tennessee	10	144	89	61.8	1141	11	6	7.92	145.2	21	-26	-1.2	1	1	6
1995—Tennessee	11	380	244	64.2	2954	22	4	7.77	146.5	41	6	0.1	5	5	30
1996—Tennessee	11	380	243	63.9	3287	20	12	8.65	147.7	42	-131	-3.1	3	3	18
1997—Tennessee	13	477	287	60.2	3819	36	11	8.01	147.7	49	-30	-0.6	3	3	18
College totals (4 years)	45	1381	863	62.5	11201	89	33	8.11	147.1	153	-181	-1.2	12	12	72

MARROW, MITCH DT PANTHERS

PERSONAL: Born July 16, 1975, in Mt. Vernon, N.Y. ... 6-4/280.
HIGH SCHOOL: Brunswick (Conn.).
COLLEGE: Pennsylvania.
TRANSACTIONS/CAREER NOTES: Selected by Carolina Panthers in third round (73rd pick overall) of 1998 NFL draft.

Year Team	G	SACKS
1994—Pennsylvania	1	0.0
1995—Pennsylvania	10	6.0
1996—Pennsylvania	10	16.5
1997—Pennsylvania	10	3.0
College totals (4 years)	31	25.5

MAUMAU, VILIAMI DT PANTHERS

PERSONAL: Born April 3, 1975, in Fu'ui, Tonga. ... 6-2/302. ... Cousin of Chris Maumalanga, defensive tackle, St. Louis Rams; and cousin of Siupeli Malamala, guard/tackle, New York Jets. ... Name pronounced vihl-ee-AHM-ee mow-mow (like now-now).
HIGH SCHOOL: St. Louis (Honolulu).
COLLEGE: Colorado.
TRANSACTIONS/CAREER NOTES: Selected by Carolina Panthers in seventh round (196th pick overall) of 1998 NFL draft.
COLLEGE NOTES: Returned one interception for 33 yards and a touchdown (1996).

Year Team	G	SACKS
1993—Colorado		Redshirted.
1994—Colorado	7	1.0
1995—Colorado	11	0.0
1996—Colorado	11	1.5
1997—Colorado	11	1.0
College totals (4 years)	40	3.5

MAYES, ALONZO TE BEARS

PERSONAL: Born June 4, 1975, in Oklahoma City. ... 6-4/259.
HIGH SCHOOL: Douglass (Oklahoma City).
JUNIOR COLLEGE: Rose State College (Okla.); did not play.
COLLEGE: Oklahoma State.
TRANSACTIONS/CAREER NOTES: Selected by Chicago Bears in fourth round (94th pick overall) of 1998 NFL draft.
HONORS: Named tight end on THE SPORTING NEWS college All-America first team (1997).

Year	Team	G	RECEIVING			
			No.	Yds.	Avg.	TD
1993—Rose State			Did not play.			
1994—Oklahoma State		10	1	15	15.0	1
1995—Oklahoma State		11	32	421	13.2	4
1996—Oklahoma State		10	30	512	17.1	3
1997—Oklahoma State		7	29	424	14.6	7
College totals (4 years)		38	92	1372	14.9	15

MAYS, KIVUUSAMA   LB   VIKINGS

PERSONAL: Born January 7, 1975, in Anniston, Ala. ... 6-3/244. ... Name pronounced kah-VAH-YOU-sum-uh.
HIGH SCHOOL: Anniston (Ala.).
COLLEGE: North Carolina.
TRANSACTIONS/CAREER NOTES: Selected by Minnesota Vikings in fourth round (110th pick overall) of 1998 NFL draft.
COLLEGE NOTES: Intercepted one pass for minus one yard (1997).

Year	Team	G	SACKS
1993—North Carolina		Redshirted.	
1994—North Carolina		11	0.0
1995—North Carolina		11	1.0
1996—North Carolina		11	2.0
1997—North Carolina		11	3.0
College totals (4 years)		44	6.0

McCARTY, CHANCE   DE/LB   BUCCANEERS

PERSONAL: Born August 29, 1975, in Fort Worth,Texas. ... 6-3/248.
HIGH SCHOOL: Eastern Hills (Fort Worth, Texas).
COLLEGE: Texas Christian.
TRANSACTIONS/CAREER NOTES: Selected by Tampa Bay Buccaneers in seventh round (212th pick overall) of 1998 NFL draft. ... Signed by Buccaneers (June 11, 1998).
COLLEGE NOTES: Played quarterback during 1993 season. ... Attempted one pass without a completion and rushed six times for minus 15 yards (1993).

Year	Team	G	SACKS
1993—Texas Christian		4	0.0
1994—Texas Christian		Redshirted.	
1995—Texas Christian		11	1.0
1996—Texas Christian		8	1.0
1997—Texas Christian		11	8.0
College totals (4 years)		34	10.0

McCULLOUGH, ANDY   WR   SAINTS

PERSONAL: Born November 11, 1975, in Dayton (Ohio). ... 6-3/210. ... Full name: Antwone McCullough.
HIGH SCHOOL: Meadowdale (Dayton, Ohio).
COLLEGE: Tennessee.
TRANSACTIONS/CAREER NOTES: Selected by New Orleans Saints in seventh round (204th pick overall) of 1998 NFL draft. ... Signed by Saints (May 20, 1998).

Year	Team	G	RECEIVING			
			No.	Yds.	Avg.	TD
1994—Tennessee		8	4	45	11.3	0
1995—Tennessee		11	9	81	9.0	1
1996—Tennessee		12	24	352	14.7	4
1997—Tennessee		12	22	425	19.3	3
College totals (4 years)		43	59	903	15.3	8

McDONALD, RAMOS   CB   VIKINGS

PERSONAL: Born April 30, 1976, in Dallas. ... 5-11/195.
HIGH SCHOOL: Liberty Eylau (Texarkana, Texas).
JUNIOR COLLEGE: Navarro College (Texas).
COLLEGE: New Mexico.
TRANSACTIONS/CAREER NOTES: Selected by Minnesota Vikings in third round (80th pick overall) of 1998 NFL draft.

Year	Team	G	INTERCEPTIONS			
			No.	Yds.	Avg.	TD
1994—Navarro College			Statistics unavailable.			
1995—Navarro College			Statistics unavailable.			
1996—New Mexico		11	6	78	13.0	1
1997—New Mexico		12	5	134	26.8	0
College totals (2 years)		23	11	212	19.3	1

McENDOO, JASON   G   SEAHAWKS

PERSONAL: Born February 25, 1975, in San Diego. ... 6-5/315. ... Full name: Jason Howard McEndoo. ... Nephew of Jim Winn, pitcher with Pittsburgh Pirates (1983-86), Chicago White Sox (1987) and Minnesota Twins (1988).
HIGH SCHOOL: Aberdeen (Cosmopolis, Wash.).
COLLEGE: Washington State.
TRANSACTIONS/CAREER NOTES: Selected by Seattle Seahawks in seventh round (197th pick overall) of 1998 NFL draft. ... Signed by Seahawks (June 5, 1998).
COLLEGE PLAYING EXPERIENCE: Washington State, 1993-1997. ... Games: 1993 (redshirted), 1994 (11), 1995 (11), 1996 (11), 1997 (11), Total: 44.

McGARRAHAN, SCOTT — S — PACKERS

PERSONAL: Born February 12, 1974, in Dallas. ... 6-1/200. ... Full name: John Scott McGarrahan.
HIGH SCHOOL: Lamar (Arlington, Texas).
COLLEGE: New Mexico.
TRANSACTIONS/CAREER NOTES: Selected by Green Bay Packers in sixth round (156th pick overall) of 1998 NFL draft.

		INTERCEPTIONS				SACKS
Year Team	G	No.	Yds.	Avg.	TD	No.
1993—New Mexico			Redshirted.			
1994—New Mexico	12	0	0	...	0	0.0
1995—New Mexico	11	1	2	2.0	0	0.0
1996—New Mexico	11	0	0	...	0	1.0
1997—New Mexico	12	2	96	48.0	0	4.0
College totals (4 years)	46	3	98	32.7	0	5.0

McKINNEY, STEVE — G — COLTS

PERSONAL: Born October 15, 1975, in Houston. ... 6-4/297. ... Full name: Stephen Michael McKinney.
HIGH SCHOOL: Clear Lake (Houston).
COLLEGE: Texas A&M.
TRANSACTIONS/CAREER NOTES: Selected by Indianapolis Colts in fourth round (93rd pick overall) of 1998 NFL draft.
COLLEGE NOTES: Played defensive end during 1994 season.
COLLEGE PLAYING EXPERIENCE: Texas A&M, 1994-1997. ... Games: 1994 (5), 1995 (11), 1996 (12), 1997 (12). Total. 40.

McLEOD, KEVIN — FB — JAGUARS

PERSONAL: Born October 17, 1974, in Kingston, Jamaica. ... 6-1/237. ... Full name: Kevin Aston McLeod.
HIGH SCHOOL: Clarkston (Ga.).
COLLEGE: Auburn.
TRANSACTIONS/CAREER NOTES: Selected by Jacksonville Jaguars in sixth round (182nd pick overall) of 1998 NFL draft. ... Signed by Jaguars (May 14, 1998).
COLLEGE NOTES: Played tight end during 1997 season.

		RUSHING				RECEIVING				TOTALS	
Year Team	G	Att.	Yds.	Avg.	TD	No.	Yds.	Avg.	TD	TD	Pts.
1994—Auburn	8	8	59	7.4	0	0	0	...	0	0	0
1995—Auburn	12	30	135	4.5	4	7	61	8.7	0	5	30
1996—Auburn	12	28	62	2.2	3	2	6	3.0	0	3	18
1997—Auburn	12	0	0	...	0	7	162	23.1	0	1	6
College totals (4 years)	44	66	256	3.9	7	16	229	14.3	0	9	54

McQUARTERS, R.W. — CB — 49ERS

PERSONAL: Born December 21, 1976, in Tulsa, Okla. ... 5-9/198.
HIGH SCHOOL: Washington (Tulsa, Okla.).
COLLEGE: Oklahoma State.
TRANSACTIONS/CAREER NOTES: Selected after junior season by San Francisco 49ers in first round (28th pick overall) of 1998 NFL draft.
COLLEGE NOTES: Rushed twice for four yards and credited with one sack (1995); and rushed twice for 69 yards and one touchdown (1997).

		INTERCEPTIONS				RECEIVING				PUNT RETURNS				KICKOFF RETURNS				TOTALS	
Year Team	G	No.	Yds.	Avg.	TD	No.	Yds.	Avg.	TD	No.	Yds.	Avg.	TD	No.	Yds.	Avg.	TD	TD	Pts.
1995—Oklahoma State	12	3	21	7.0	0	11	125	11.4	1	1	5	5.0	0	27	645	23.9	0	1	6
1996—Oklahoma State	7	2	0	0.0	0	0	0	...	0	10	134	13.4	0	15	331	22.1	0	0	0
1997—Oklahoma State	11	1	0	0.0	0	8	245	30.6	2	32	521	16.3	1	8	195	24.4	0	4	24
College totals (3 years)	30	6	21	3.5	0	19	370	19.5	3	43	660	15.3	1	50	1171	23.4	0	5	30

MERKERSON, RON — LB — PATRIOTS

PERSONAL: Born August 30, 1975, in Clarksville, Tenn. ... 6-2/247. ... Cousin of Harry Galbreath, offensive lineman with Miami Dolphins (1992), Green Bay Packers (1993-95) and New York Jets (1996).
HIGH SCHOOL: Clark (Las Vegas).
COLLEGE: Colorado.
TRANSACTIONS/CAREER NOTES: Selected by New England Patriots in fifth round (145th pick overall) of 1998 NFL draft.
COLLEGE NOTES: Credited with one sack (1995).
COLLEGE PLAYING EXPERIENCE: Colorado, 1993-1997. ... Games: 1993 (redshirted), 1994 (4), 1995 (10), 1996 (11), 1997 (5). Total: 30.

MIXON, KENNY — DE — DOLPHINS

PERSONAL: Born May 31, 1975, in Sun Valley, Calif. ... 6-4/270. ... Full name: Kenneth Jermaine Mixon.
HIGH SCHOOL: Pineville (La.).
COLLEGE: Louisiana State.
TRANSACTIONS/CAREER NOTES: Selected by Miami Dolphins in second round (49th pick overall) of 1998 NFL draft.
COLLEGE NOTES: Returned one blocked punt for 23 yards and a touchdown (1994).

Year—Team	G	SACKS
1993—Louisiana State		Redshirted.
1994—Louisiana State	9	0.0
1995—Louisiana State	7	2.0
1996—Louisiana State	3	1.0
1997—Louisiana State	11	7.0
College totals (4 years)	30	10.0

MONROE, RODRICK — TE — COWBOYS

PERSONAL: Born July 30, 1975, in Hearne, Texas. ... 6-4/244.
HIGH SCHOOL: Hearne (Texas).
JUNIOR COLLEGE: McLennan Community College (Texas); did not play.
COLLEGE: Cincinnati.
TRANSACTIONS/CAREER NOTES: Selected by Dallas Cowboys in seventh round (237th pick overall) of 1998 NFL draft.

			RECEIVING		
Year—Team	G	No.	Yds.	Avg.	TD
1993—McLennan			Did not play.		
1994—McLennan			Did not play.		
1995—Cincinnati			Did not play.		
1996—Cincinnati			Did not play.		
1997—Cincinnati	11	2	33	16.5	1
College totals (1 years)	11	2	33	16.5	1

MORENO, MOSES — QB — BEARS

PERSONAL: Born September 5, 1975, in Chula Vista, Calif. ... 6-1/195. ... Full name: Moses Nathaniel Moreno.
HIGH SCHOOL: Castle Park (Chula Vista, Calif.).
COLLEGE: Colorado State.
TRANSACTIONS/CAREER NOTES: Selected by Chicago Bears in seventh round (232nd pick overall) of 1998 NFL draft.

					PASSING						RUSHING				TOTALS	
Year—Team	G	Att.	Cmp.	Pct.	Yds.	TD	Int.	Avg.	Rat.	Att.	Yds.	Avg.	TD	TD	Pts.
1993—Colorado State						Redshirted.									
1994—Colorado State	3	20	8	40.0	72	0	1	3.60	60.2	8	8	1.0	0	0	0
1995—Colorado State	10	175	99	56.6	1439	11	6	8.22	139.5	35	-139	-4.0	1	1	6
1996—Colorado State	12	335	193	57.6	2921	18	12	8.72	141.4	70	-18	-0.3	2	2	12
1997—Colorado State	12	257	157	61.1	2257	20	9	8.78	153.5	56	-97	-1.7	1	1	6
College totals (4 years)	37	787	457	58.1	6689	49	28	8.50	142.9	169	-246	-1.5	4	4	24

MOSS, RANDY — WR — VIKINGS

PERSONAL: Born February 13, 1977, in Rand, W.Va. ... 6-4/194. ... Half brother of Eric Moss, guard, Minnesota Vikings. ... Nickname: The Freak.
HIGH SCHOOL: DuPont (Rand, W.Va.).
COLLEGE: Florida State (did not play), then Marshall (W.Va.).
TRANSACTIONS/CAREER NOTES: Selected after sophomore season by Minnesota Vikings in first round (21st pick overall) of 1998 NFL draft.
HONORS: Fred Biletnikoff Award winner (1997). ... Named wide receiver on THE SPORTING NEWS college All-America first team (1997).

		RUSHING				RECEIVING				PUNT RETURNS				KICKOFF RETURNS				TOTALS	
Year—Team	G	Att.	Yds.	Avg.	TD	No.	Yds.	Avg.	TD	No.	Yds.	Avg.	TD	No.	Yds.	Avg.	TD	TD	Pts.
1995—Florida State							Redshirted.												
1996—Marshall	15	2	29	14.5	1	78	1709	21.9	28	0	0	...	0	18	612	34.0	0	29	174
1997—Marshall	12	1	2	2.0	0	90	1647	18.3	25	24	266	11.1	0	14	263	18.8	0	25	150
College totals (2 years)	27	3	31	10.3	1	168	3356	20.0	53	24	266	11.1	0	32	875	27.3	0	54	324

MYERS, MICHAEL — DL — COWBOYS

PERSONAL: Born January 20, 1976, in Vicksburg, Miss. ... 6-2/286.
HIGH SCHOOL: Vicksburg (Miss.).
JUNIOR COLLEGE: Hinds Community College (Miss.).
COLLEGE: Alabama.
TRANSACTIONS/CAREER NOTES: Selected by Dallas Cowboys in fourth round (100th pick overall) of 1998 NFL draft.
HONORS: Named defensive tackle on THE SPORTING NEWS college All-America first team (1996).

Year—Team	G	SACKS
1994—Hinds	10	20.0
1995—Hinds	10	8.0
1996—Alabama	12	13.0
1997—Alabama	1	0.5
Junior college totals (2 years)	20	28.0
College totals (2 years)	13	13.5

MYLES, DESHONE — LB — SEAHAWKS

PERSONAL: Born October 31, 1974, in Las Vegas. ... 6-2/235.
HIGH SCHOOL: Cheyenne (Las Vegas).
COLLEGE: Nevada.
TRANSACTIONS/CAREER NOTES: Selected by Seattle Seahawks in fourth round (108th pick overall) of 1998 NFL draft.

Year Team	G	No.	Yds.	Avg.	TD	No.
			INTERCEPTIONS			SACKS
1993—Nevada			Redshirted.			
1994—Nevada	11	1	0	0.0	0	2.0
1995—Nevada	11	0	0	...	0	3.0
1996—Nevada	11	1	0	0.0	0	3.0
1997—Nevada	11	0	0	...	0	5.0
College totals (4 years)	44	2	0	0.0	0	13.0

MYLES, TOBY — OT — GIANTS

PERSONAL: Born July 23, 1975, in Jackson, Miss. ... 6-4/313. ... Full name: Tobiath Myles.
HIGH SCHOOL: Callaway (Jackson, Miss.).
COLLEGE: Mississippi State, then Jackson State.
TRANSACTIONS/CAREER NOTES: Selected by New York Giants in fifth round (147th pick overall) of 1998 NFL draft.
COLLEGE PLAYING EXPERIENCE: Mississippi State, 1993-1995; Jackson State, 1996 and 1997. ... Games: 1993 (redshirted); 1994 (2), 1995 (10), 1996 (12), 1997 (12). Total: 36.

NASH, MARCUS — WR — BRONCOS

PERSONAL: Born February 1, 1976, in Tulsa, Okla. ... 6-3/195. ... Full name: Marcus DeLando Nash.
HIGH SCHOOL: Edmond Memorial (Tulsa, Okla.).
COLLEGE: Tennessee.
TRANSACTIONS/CAREER NOTES: Selected by Denver Broncos in first round (30th pick overall) of 1998 NFL draft.
COLLEGE NOTES: Rushed once for six yards and attempted one pass with one completion for 28 yards (1995).

Year Team	G	No.	Yds.	Avg.	TD
			RECEIVING		
1994—Tennessee	10	5	77	15.4	0
1995—Tennessee	11	43	512	11.9	4
1996—Tennessee	11	53	688	13.0	3
1997—Tennessee	12	76	1170	15.4	13
College totals (4 years)	44	177	2447	13.8	20

NEWBERRY, JEREMY — C — 49ERS

PERSONAL: Born March 23, 1976, in Antioch, Calif. ... 6-5/315.
HIGH SCHOOL: Antioch (Calif.).
COLLEGE: California.
TRANSACTIONS/CAREER NOTES: Selected by after junior season San Francisco 49ers in second round (58th pick overall) of 1998 NFL draft.
COLLEGE NOTES: California, 1994-1997. ... Games: 1994 (redshirted), 1995 (8), 1996 (11), 1997 (11). Total: 30.

OGBOGU, ERIC — DE — JETS

PERSONAL: Born July 18, 1975, in Irvington, N.Y. ... 6-4/266.
HIGH SCHOOL: Archbishop Stepinac (Irvington, N.Y.).
COLLEGE: Maryland.
TRANSACTIONS/CAREER NOTES: Selected by New York Jets in sixth round (163rd pick overall) of 1998 NFL draft.
COLLEGE NOTES: Caught one pass for 11 yards (1995); and returned one kickoff for minus one yard (1997).

Year Team	G	SACKS
1994—Maryland	5	1.5
1995—Maryland	11	6.0
1996—Maryland	11	7.0
1997—Maryland	10	4.0
College totals (4 years)	37	18.5

OLSON, BENJI — G — OILERS

PERSONAL: Born June 5, 1975, in Bremerton, Wash. ... 6-4/313. ... Full name: Benjamin Dempsey Olson.
HIGH SCHOOL: South Kitsap (Port Orchard, Wash.).
COLLEGE: Washington.
TRANSACTIONS/CAREER NOTES: Selected after junior season by Tennessee Oilers in fifth round (139th pick overall) of 1998 NFL draft.
HONORS: Named guard on THE SPORTING NEWS college All-America first team (1996).
COLLEGE PLAYING EXPERIENCE: Washington, 1994-1997. ... Games: 1994 (redshirted), 1995 (11), 1996 (11), 1997 (11). Total: 33.

OLSON, RYAN — LB — STEELERS

PERSONAL: Born June 27, 1975, in Wheat Ridge, Colo. ... 6-2/275.
HIGH SCHOOL: Green Mountain (Lakewood, Colo.).
COLLEGE: Colorado.
TRANSACTIONS/CAREER NOTES: Selected by Pittsburgh Steelers in sixth round (186th pick overall) of 1998 NFL draft.

Year Team	G	SACKS
1993—Colorado		Redshirted.
1994—Colorado	7	1.0
1995—Colorado	11	4.0
1996—Colorado	11	8.5
1997—Colorado	11	3.0
College totals (4 years)	40	16.5

OSTROWSKI, PHIL   G   49ERS

PERSONAL: Born September 23, 1975, in Wilkes-Barre, Pa. ... 6-4/291. ... Full name: Phillip Lucas Ostrowski.
HIGH SCHOOL: E.L. Meyers (Wilkes-Barre, Pa.).
COLLEGE: Penn State.
TRANSACTIONS/CAREER NOTES: Selected by San Francisco 49ers in fifth round (151st pick overall) of 1998 NFL draft.
COLLEGE PLAYING EXPERIENCE: Penn State, 1993-1997. ... Games: 1993 (redshirted), 1994 (4), 1995 (5), 1996 (12), 1997 (11). Total: 32.

OVERHAUSER, CHAD   OT   BEARS

PERSONAL: Born June 17, 1975, in Sacramento. ... 6-4/296. ... Full name: Chad Michael Overhauser.
HIGH SCHOOL: Rio Americano (Sacramento).
COLLEGE: UCLA.
TRANSACTIONS/CAREER NOTES: Selected by Chicago Bears in seventh round (217th pick overall) of 1998 NFL draft.
HONORS: Named offensive tackle on THE SPORTING NEWS college All-America first team (1997).
COLLEGE PLAYING EXPERIENCE: UCLA,1993-1997. ... Games: 1993 (redshirted), 1994 (11), 1995 (11), 1996 (11), 1997 (11). Total: 44.

OXENDINE, KEN   RB   FALCONS

PERSONAL: Born October 4, 1975, in Richmond, Va. ... 6-1/228. ... Full name: Ken Qwarious Oxendine.
HIGH SCHOOL: Thomas Dale (Chester, Va.).
COLLEGE: Virginia Tech.
TRANSACTIONS/CAREER NOTES: Selected by Atlanta Falcons in seventh round (201st pick overall) of 1998 NFL draft. ... Signed by Falcons (May 29, 1998).

		RUSHING				RECEIVING				TOTALS	
Year Team	G	Att.	Yds.	Avg.	TD	No.	Yds.	Avg.	TD	TD	Pts.
1994—Virginia Tech	10	33	258	7.8	2	8	30	3.8	0	2	12
1995—Virginia Tech	9	106	593	5.6	4	13	89	6.8	0	4	24
1996—Virginia Tech	9	150	890	5.9	13	4	74	18.5	0	13	78
1997—Virginia Tech	11	237	904	3.8	8	13	96	7.4	0	8	48
College totals (4 years)	39	526	2645	5.0	27	38	289	7.6	0	27	162

PALMER, PAT   WR   REDSKINS

PERSONAL: Born July 13, 1975, in Port Arthur, Texas. ... 6-2/181. ... Full name: Patrick Palmer.
HIGH SCHOOL: Lincoln (Port Arthur, Texas).
COLLEGE: Northwestern State (La.).
TRANSACTIONS/CAREER NOTES: Selected by Washington Redskins in sixth round (170th pick overall) of 1998 NFL draft. ... Signed by Redskins (May 27, 1998).

		RUSHING				RECEIVING				PUNT RETURNS				KICKOFF RETURNS				TOTALS	
Year Team	G	Att.	Yds.	Avg.	TD	No.	Yds.	Avg.	TD	No.	Yds.	Avg.	TD	No.	Yds.	Avg.	TD	TD	Pts.
1994—Nortwestern State	11	0	0	...	0	9	153	17.0	1	0	0	...	0	0	0	...	0	1	6
1995—Nortwestern State	10	3	27	9.0	0	26	584	22.5	2	2	1	0.5	0	2	30	15.0	0	2	12
1996—Nortwestern State	11	2	19	9.5	0	32	829	25.9	8	15	111	7.4	0	0	0	...	0	8	48
1997—Nortwestern State	11	3	15	5.0	0	32	657	20.5	4	27	180	6.7	0	1	23	23.0	0	4	24
College totals (4 years)	43	8	61	7.6	0	99	2223	22.5	15	44	292	6.6	0	3	53	17.7	0	15	90

PARKER, MARCUS   FB   BENGALS

PERSONAL: Born November 12, 1976, in Roanoke, Va. ... 5-10/221. ... Full name: Marcus Jermaine Parker.
HIGH SCHOOL: Salem (Roanoke, Va.).
COLLEGE: Virginia Tech.
TRANSACTIONS/CAREER NOTES: Selected by Cincinnati Bengals in seventh round (202nd pick overall) of 1998 NFL draft. ... Signed by Bengals (May 18, 1998).

		RUSHING				RECEIVING				TOTALS	
Year Team	G	Att.	Yds.	Avg.	TD	No.	Yds.	Avg.	TD	TD	Pts.
1994—Virginia Tech	9	16	83	5.2	0	2	30	15.0	1	1	6
1995—Virginia Tech	11	46	267	5.8	5	3	50	16.7	0	5	30
1996—Virginia Tech	7	82	467	5.7	4	7	50	7.1	0	4	24
1997—Virginia Tech	10	67	363	5.4	4	20	212	10.6	0	4	24
College totals (4 years)	37	211	1180	5.6	13	32	342	10.7	1	14	84

PARRISH, TONY   S   BEARS

PERSONAL: Born November 23, 1975, in Huntington Beach, Calif. ... 5-11/205.
HIGH SCHOOL: Marina (Huntington Beach, Calif.).
COLLEGE: Washington.
TRANSACTIONS/CAREER NOTES: Selected by Chicago Bears in second round (35th pick overall) of 1990 NFL draft.

Year Team		G	No.	Yds.	Avg.	TD
	INTERCEPTIONS					
1993—Washington				Redshirted.		
1994—Washington		11	2	24	12.0	0
1995—Washington		10	1	0	0.0	0
1996—Washington		11	2	45	22.5	1
1997—Washington		11	4	82	20.5	1
College totals (4 years)		43	9	151	16.8	2

PATHON, JEROME — WR — COLTS

PERSONAL: Born December 16, 1975, in Capetown, South Africa. ... 6-0/187. ... Name pronounced PAY-thon.
HIGH SCHOOL: Carson Graham Secondary School (North Vancouver).
COLLEGE: Acadia (Nova Scotia), then Washington.
TRANSACTIONS/CAREER NOTES: Selected by Indianapolis Colts in second round (32nd pick overall) of 1998 NFL draft.
HONORS: Named wide receiver on The Sporting News college All-America second team (1997).

Year Team		G	**RECEIVING** No.	Yds.	Avg.	TD	**PUNT RETURNS** No.	Yds.	Avg.	TD	**KICKOFF RETURNS** No.	Yds.	Avg.	TD	**TOTALS** TD	Pts.
1993—Acadia		10	44	868	19.7	10	0	0	...	0	0	0	...	0	10	60
1994—Washington									Redshirted.							
1995—Washington		11	15	200	13.3	1	1	2	2.0	0	1	30	30.0	0	1	6
1996—Washington		11	41	618	15.1	7	18	217	12.1	0	7	204	29.1	0	7	42
1997—Washington		11	69	1245	18.0	8	19	209	11.0	0	16	386	24.1	0	8	48
College totals (4 years)		43	169	2931	17.3	26	38	428	11.3	0	24	620	25.8	0	26	156

PERRY, WILMONT — FB — SAINTS

PERSONAL: Born February 24, 1975, in Franklinton, N.C. ... 6-1/230. ... Full name: Wilmont Darnell Perry.
HIGH SCHOOL: Garner (Franklinton, N.C.).
COLLEGE: Barber-Scotia, N.C. (did not play), then Livingstone (N.C.).
TRANSACTIONS/CAREER NOTES: Selected by New Orleans Saints in fifth round (132nd pick overall) of 1998 NFL draft. ... Signed by Saints (June 11, 1998).

Year Team		G	**RUSHING** Att.	Yds.	Avg.	TD	**RECEIVING** No.	Yds.	Avg.	TD	**TOTALS** TD	Pts.
1994—Livingstone		10	109	799	7.3	11	0	0	...	0	11	66
1995—Livingstone							Did not play.					
1996—Livingstone		10	143	912	6.4	10	12	235	19.6	1	11	66
1997—Livingstone		10	195	1770	9.1	20	9	92	10.2	1	21	126
College totals (3 years)		30	447	3481	7.8	41	21	327	15.6	2	43	258

PETER, JASON — DT — PANTHERS

PERSONAL: Born September 13, 1974, in Locust, N.J. ... 6-5/288. ... Brother of Christian Peter, defensive tackle, New York Giants.
HIGH SCHOOL: Middletown South (Middleton, N.J.), then Milford (Conn.) Academy.
COLLEGE: Nebraska (degree in communication studies, 1997).
TRANSACTIONS/CAREER NOTES: Selected by Carolina Panthers in first round (14th pick overall) of 1998 NFL draft.
HONORS: Named defensive tackle on The Sporting News college All-America first team (1997).

Year Team		G	SACKS
1993—Nebraska			Redshirted.
1994—Nebraska		7	0.0
1995—Nebraska		11	0.0
1996—Nebraska		12	4.0
1997—Nebraska		12	7.0
College totals (4 years)		42	11.0

PITTMAN, JULIAN — DT — SAINTS

PERSONAL: Born April 22, 1975, in Niceville, Fla. ... 6-4/286.
HIGH SCHOOL: Niceville (Fla.).
COLLEGE: Florida State.
TRANSACTIONS/CAREER NOTES: Selected by New Orleans Saints in fourth round (99th pick overall) of 1998 NFL draft.
COLLEGE NOTES: Credited with one sack (1996).
COLLEGE PLAYING EXPERIENCE: Florida State, 1993-1997. ... Games: 1993 (redshirted), 1994 (10), 1995 (11), 1996 (11), 1997 (4). Total: 36.

PITTMAN, MICHAEL — RB — CARDINALS

PERSONAL: Born August 14, 1975, in New Orleans ... 6-0/214.
HIGH SCHOOL: Mira Mesa (San Diego).
COLLEGE: Fresno State.
TRANSACTIONS/CAREER NOTES: Selected by Arizona Cardinals in fourth round (95th pick overall) of 1998 NFL draft. ... Signed by Cardinals (May 20, 1998).
COLLEGE NOTES: Granted medical redshirt due to broken collarbone (1994).

Year	Team	G	RUSHING				RECEIVING				KICKOFF RETURNS				TOTALS	
			Att.	Yds.	Avg.	TD	No.	Yds.	Avg.	TD	No.	Yds.	Avg.	TD	TD	Pts.
1993—Fresno State		7	20	93	4.7	1	1	18	18.0	0	1	12	12.0	0	1	6
1994—Fresno State		3	48	174	3.6	0	7	48	6.9	1	0	0	...	0	1	6
1995—Fresno State		10	127	561	4.4	7	15	111	7.4	0	0	0	...	0	7	42
1996—Fresno State		11	214	1132	5.3	13	15	109	7.3	0	0	0	...	0	13	78
1997—Fresno State		10	238	1057	4.4	8	32	255	8.0	2	1	15	15.0	0	10	60
College totals (5 years)		41	647	3017	4.7	29	70	541	7.7	3	2	27	13.5	0	32	192

POLLACK, TODD — TE — GIANTS

PERSONAL: Born December 10, 1974, in Rye, N.Y. ... 6-4/241. ... Full name: Todd Luce Pollack.
HIGH SCHOOL: Brunswick (Conn.).
COLLEGE: Boston College.
TRANSACTIONS/CAREER NOTES: Selected by New York Giants in sixth round (177th pick overall) of 1998 NFL draft.
COLLEGE NOTES: Attempted one pass with one completion for 29 yards and a touchdown (1995); and attempted one pass without a completion (1996).

Year	Team	G	RECEIVING			
			No.	Yds.	Avg.	TD
1993—Boston College			Redshirted.			
1994—Boston College		5	2	16	8.0	0
1995—Boston College		12	25	182	7.3	5
1996—Boston College		8	22	249	11.3	2
1997—Boston College		11	28	296	10.6	1
College totals (4 years)		36	77	743	9.6	8

PONDS, ANTWUANE — LB — REDSKINS

PERSONAL: Born June 29, 1975, in Harrisburg, Pa. ... 6-2/252.
HIGH SCHOOL: Paxon (Jacksonville, Fla.).
COLLEGE: Syracuse.
TRANSACTIONS/CAREER NOTES: Selected by Washington Redskins in seventh round (206th pick overall) of 1998 NFL draft.
COLLEGE NOTES: Intercepted one pass for three yards (1995).

Year	Team	G	SACKS
1993—Syracuse			Redshirted.
1994—Syracuse		11	1.0
1995—Syracuse		9	1.0
1996—Syracuse		11	5.5
1997—Syracuse		12	2.0
College totals (4 years)		43	9.5

PRIESTER, RAYMOND — RB — RAMS

PERSONAL: Born February 3, 1975, in Allendale, S.C. ... 6-2/242.
HIGH SCHOOL: Allendale-Fairfax (Fairfax, S.C.).
COLLEGE: Clemson.
TRANSACTIONS/CAREER NOTES: Selected by St. Louis Rams in fifth round (129th pick overall) of 1998 NFL draft.

Year	Team	G	RUSHING				RECEIVING				TOTALS	
			Att.	Yds.	Avg.	TD	No.	Yds.	Avg.	TD	TD	Pts.
1994—Clemson		11	87	343	3.9	3	4	14	3.5	0	3	18
1995—Clemson		11	223	1286	5.8	6	10	58	5.8	0	6	36
1996—Clemson		11	232	1194	5.1	6	15	115	7.7	1	7	42
1997—Clemson		10	204	894	4.4	6	14	113	8.1	0	6	36
College totals (4 years)		43	746	3717	5.0	21	43	300	7.0	1	22	132

QUAYLE, CAM — TE — RAVENS

PERSONAL: Born September 24, 1972, in Ogden, Utah. ... 6-7/255. ... Full name: Cameron Paul Quayle.
HIGH SCHOOL: Ben Lomond (Ogden, Utah).
COLLEGE: Weber State (degree in intergraded studies).
TRANSACTIONS/CAREER NOTES: Selected by Baltimore Ravens in seventh round (241st pick overall) of 1998 NFL draft.
COLLEGE NOTES: On Mormon mission (1992 and 1993).

Year	Team	G	RECEIVING			
			No.	Yds.	Avg.	TD
1991—Weber State			Redshirted.			
1992—Weber State			Did not play.			
1993—Weber State			Did not play.			
1994—Weber State		11	5	44	8.8	0
1995—Weber State		10	29	233	8.0	0
1996—Weber State		11	62	658	10.6	7
1997—Weber State		11	53	479	9.0	3
College totals (4 years)		43	149	1414	9.5	10

QUINN, JONATHON — QB — JAGUARS

PERSONAL: Born February 27, 1975, in Turlock, Calif. ... 6-5/242. ... Full name: Jonathon Ryan Quinn.
HIGH SCHOOL: McGavock (Nashville).
COLLEGE: Tulane, then Middle Tennessee State.
TRANSACTIONS/CAREER NOTES: Selected by Jacksonville Jaguars in third round (86th pick overall) of 1998 NFL draft. ... Signed by Jaguars (May 14, 1998).

		PASSING								RUSHING				TOTALS	
Year Team	G	Att.	Cmp.	Pct.	Yds.	TD	Int.	Avg.	Rat.	Att.	Yds.	Avg.	TD	TD	Pts.
1993—Tulane							Redshirted.								
1994—Tulane	5	68	33	48.5	379	2	7	5.57	84.5	18	-37	-2.1	0	0	0
1995—Middle Tennessee State	11	223	108	48.4	1724	8	7	7.73	118.9	46	-16	-0.3	2	2	12
1996—Middle Tennessee State	11	159	71	44.7	931	4	9	5.86	90.8	39	8	0.2	1	1	6
1997—Middle Tennessee State	10	293	167	57.0	2209	16	10	7.54	131.5	66	170	2.6	4	4	24
College totals (4 years)	37	743	379	51.0	5243	30	33	7.06	114.7	169	125	0.7	7	7	42

RANSOM, DERRICK — DT — CHIEFS

PERSONAL: Born September 13, 1976, in Indianapolis. ... 6-3/286.
HIGH SCHOOL: Lawrence Central (Indianapolis).
COLLEGE: Cincinnati.
TRANSACTIONS/CAREER NOTES: Selected by Kansas City Chiefs in sixth round (181st pick overall) of 1998 NFL draft. ... Signed by Chiefs (June 3, 1998).

Year Team	G	SACKS
1994—Cincinnati NFL	11	1.0
1995—Cincinnati NFL	11	2.0
1996—Cincinnati NFL	11	6.0
1997—Cincinnati NFL	11	6.0
College totals (4 years)	44	15.0

REESE, IKE — LB — EAGLES

PERSONAL: Born October 16, 1973, in Jacksonville, N.C. ... 6-2/222. ... Full name: Isaiah Reese.
HIGH SCHOOL: Woodard (Cincinnati), then Aiken (Cincinnati).
COLLEGE: Michigan State.
TRANSACTIONS/CAREER NOTES: Selected by Philadelphia Eagles in fifth round (142nd pick overall) of 1998 NFL draft.

		INTERCEPTIONS				SACKS
Year Team	G	No.	Yds.	Avg.	TD	No.
1993—Michigan State			Redshirted.			
1994—Michigan State	11	0	0	...	0	3.0
1995—Michigan State	9	0	0	...	0	2.0
1996—Michigan State	11	1	21	21.0	0	2.0
1997—Michigan State	11	2	17	8.5	...	2.0
College totals (4 years)	42	3	38	12.7	0	9.0

REESE, IZELL — S — COWBOYS

PERSONAL: Born May 7, 1974, in Dothan, Ala. ... 6-2/193.
HIGH SCHOOL: Northview (Dothan, Ala.).
COLLEGE: Alabama-Birmingham.
TRANSACTIONS/CAREER NOTES: Selected by Dallas Cowboys in sixth round (188th pick overall) of 1998 NFL draft.
COLLEGE NOTES: Credited with three sacks (1996).

		INTERCEPTIONS			
Year Team	G	No.	Yds.	Avg.	TD
1994—Alabama-Birmingham	11	4	5	1.3	0
1995—Alabama-Birmingham	11	1	0	0.0	0
1996—Alabama-Birmingham	11	1	0	0.0	0
1997—Alabama-Birmingham	11	2	130	65.0	1
College totals (4 years)	44	8	135	16.9	1

RHEAMS, LEONTA — DT — PATRIOTS

PERSONAL: Born August 1, 1976, in Tyler, Texas. ... 6-2/280.
HIGH SCHOOL: Robert E. Lee (Tyler, Texas).
COLLEGE: Houston.
TRANSACTIONS/CAREER NOTES: Selected by New England Patriots in fourth round (115th pick overall) of 1998 NFL draft.

Year Team	G	SACKS
1994—Houston	10	1.0
1995—Houston	11	0.0
1996—Houston	11	1.0
1997—Houston	11	4.0
College totals (4 years)	43	6.0

RICHARDSON, DAMIEN　　　　S　　　　PANTHERS

PERSONAL: Born April 3, 1976, in Los Angeles. ... 6-1/210. ... Full name: Damien A. Richardson.
HIGH SCHOOL: Clovis West (Fresno, Calif.).
COLLEGE: Arizona State.
TRANSACTIONS/CAREER NOTES: Selected by Carolina Panthers in sixth round (165th pick overall) of 1998 NFL draft.
COLLEGE NOTES: Returned one blocked punt for eight yards and a touchdown (1994).

		INTERCEPTIONS			
Year　Team	G	No.	Yds.	Avg.	TD
1994—Arizona State	11	0	0	...	0
1995—Arizona State	11	0	0	...	0
1996—Arizona State	11	1	51	51.0	0
1997—Arizona State	11	1	1	1.0	0
College totals (4 years)	44	2	52	26.0	0

RICKS, MIKHAEL　　　　WR　　　　CHARGERS

PERSONAL: Born November 14, 1974, in Anahuac, Texas. ... 6-5/237. ... Name pronounced MICHAEL.
HIGH SCHOOL: Anahuac (Texas).
COLLEGE: Stephen F. Austin.
TRANSACTIONS/CAREER NOTES: Selected by San Diego Chargers in second round (59th pick overall) of 1998 NFL draft.
COLLEGE NOTES: Attempted one pass with one completion for 47 yards (1997).

		RUSHING				RECEIVING				TOTALS	
Year　Team	G	Att.	Yds.	Avg.	TD	No.	Yds.	Avg.	TD	TD	Pts.
1993—Stephen F. Austin State				Redshirted.							
1994—Stephen F. Austin State	11	0	0	...	0	9	202	22.4	0	0	0
1995—Stephen F. Austin State	12	1	-8	-8.0	0	14	259	18.5	5	5	30
1996—Stephen F. Austin State	10	3	23	7.7	1	16	218	13.6	4	5	30
1997—Stephen F. Austin State	11	1	7	7.0	0	47	1358	28.9	13	13	78
College totals (4 years)	44	5	22	4.4	1	86	2037	23.7	22	23	138

RILEY, VICTOR　　　　OT　　　　CHIEFS

PERSONAL: Born November 4, 1974, in Swansea, S.C. ... 6-5/321. ... Full name: Victor Allan Riley.
HIGH SCHOOL: Swansea (S.C.).
COLLEGE: Auburn.
TRANSACTIONS/CAREER NOTES: Selected by Kansas City Chiefs in first round (27th pick overall) of 1998 NFL draft.
COLLEGE PLAYING EXPERIENCE: Auburn, 1994-1997. ... Games: 1994 (11), 1995 (9), 1996 (10), 1997 (11). Total. 41.

RITCHIE, JON　　　　FB　　　　RAIDERS

PERSONAL: Born September 4, 1974, in Mechanicsburgh, Pa. ... 6-2/248.
HIGH SCHOOL: Cumberland Valley (Pa.).
COLLEGE: Michigan, then Stanford.
TRANSACTIONS/CAREER NOTES: Selected by Oakland Raiders in third round (63rd pick overall) of 1998 NFL draft.

		RUSHING				RECEIVING				TOTALS	
Year　Team	G	Att.	Yds.	Avg.	TD	No.	Yds.	Avg.	TD	TD	Pts.
1993—Michigan	11	31	95	3.1	2	2	13	6.5	0	2	12
1994—Michigan	11	2	25	12.5	0	0	0	...	0	0	0
1995—Stanford				Redshirted.							
1996—Stanford	8	9	27	3.0	1	4	26	6.5	1	2	12
1997—Stanford	11	17	95	5.6	0	8	61	7.6	2	2	12
College totals (4 years)	41	59	242	4.1	3	14	100	7.1	3	6	36

ROGERS, RON　　　　LB　　　　RAVENS

PERSONAL: Born April 20, 1975, in Dublin, Ga. ... 6-0/245. ... Full name: Ronald William Rogers Jr.
HIGH SCHOOL: Dodge City (Ga.).
COLLEGE: Georgia Tech.
TRANSACTIONS/CAREER NOTES: Selected by Baltimore Ravens in sixth round (154th pick overall) of 1998 NFL draft.

		INTERCEPTIONS				SACKS
Year　Team	G	No.	Yds.	Avg.	TD	No.
1993—Georgia Tech			Redshirted.			
1994—Georgia Tech	11	1	0	0.0	0	0.0
1995—Georgia Tech	11	1	8	8.0	0	1.0
1996—Georgia Tech	10	1	5	5.0	0	3.0
1997—Georgia Tech	11	1	4	4.0	0	0.0
College totals (4 years)	43	4	17	4.3	0	4.0

ROLLE, SAMARI　　　　CB　　　　OILERS

PERSONAL: Born August 10, 1976, in Miami. ... 5-11/173. ... Name pronounced suh-MAHR-ree ROLL.
HIGH SCHOOL: Miami Beach.

COLLEGE: Florida State.
TRANSACTIONS/CAREER NOTES: Selected by Tennessee Oilers in second round (46th pick overall) of 1998 NFL draft.

Year—Team	G	INTERCEPTIONS				PUNT RETURNS				TOTALS	
		No.	Yds.	Avg.	TD	No.	Yds.	Avg.	TD	TD	Pts.
1994—Florida State	5	0	0	...	0	5	29	5.8	0	0	0
1995—Florida State	11	3	111	37.0	0	4	30	7.5	0	0	0
1996—Florida State	11	2	1	0.5	0	0	0	...	0	0	0
1997—Florida State	11	7	32	4.6	0	0	0	...	0	0	0
College totals (4 years)	38	12	144	12.0	0	9	59	6.6	0	0	0

ROSS, OLIVER — OL — COWBOYS

PERSONAL: Born September 27, 1974, in Culver City, Calif. ... 6-4/300.
HIGH SCHOOL: Washington (Los Angeles).
JUNIOR COLLEGE: Southwestern College (Calif.).
COLLEGE: Iowa State.
TRANSACTIONS/CAREER NOTES: Selected by Dallas Cowboys in fifth round (138th pick overall) of 1998 NFL draft.
COLLEGE NOTES: Played defensive tackle during 1993, 1994 and 1995 seasons. ... Credited with nine sacks (1994).
COLLEGE PLAYING EXPERIENCE: Southwestern 1994; Iowa State, 1995-97. ... Games: 1993 (games played unavailable), 1994 (10), 1995 (2), 1996 (redshirted), 1997 (11). Total: 23.

ROSSUM, ALLEN — CB/KR — EAGLES

PERSONAL: Born October 22, 1975, in Dallas. ... 5-8/178.
HIGH SCHOOL: Skyline (Dallas).
COLLEGE: Notre Dame.
TRANSACTIONS/CAREER NOTES: Selected by Philadelphia Eagles in third round (85th pick overall) of 1998 NFL draft.

Year—Team	G	INTERCEPTIONS				PUNT RETURNS				KICKOFF RETURNS				TOTALS	
		No.	Yds.	Avg.	TD	No.	Yds.	Avg.	TD	No.	Yds.	Avg.	TD	TD	Pts.
1994—Notre Dame	8	0	0	...	0	0	0	...	0	0	0	...	0	0	0
1995—Notre Dame	11	3	105	35.0	2	0	0	...	0	3	94	31.3	0	2	12
1996—Notre Dame	11	2	8	4.0	0	15	344	22.9	3	6	227	37.8	1	4	24
1997—Notre Dame	12	2	38	19.0	1	12	83	6.9	0	20	570	28.5	2	3	18
College totals (4 years)	42	7	151	21.6	3	27	427	15.8	3	29	891	30.7	3	9	54

ROUNTREE, GLENN — G — RAMS

PERSONAL: Born November 24, 1973, in Suffolk, Va. ... 6-3/304.
HIGH SCHOOL: Suffolk (Va.) Academy.
COLLEGE: Clemson (degree in agricultural education, 1997).
TRANSACTIONS/CAREER NOTES: Selected by St. Louis Rams in sixth round (159th pick overall) of 1998 NFL draft.
COLLEGE PLAYING EXPERIENCE: Clemson, 1993-1997. ... Games: 1993 (redshirted), 1994 (11), 1995 (12), 1996 (12), 1997 (12). Total: 47.

RUBIO, ANGEL — DE — STEELERS

PERSONAL: Born April 12, 1975, in Modesto, Calif. ... 6-2/300.
HIGH SCHOOL: Ceres (Calif.).
COLLEGE: Southeast Missouri State.
TRANSACTIONS/CAREER NOTES: Selected by Pittsburgh Steelers in seventh round (221st pick overall) of 1998 NFL draft. ... Signed by Steelers (May 21, 1998).
COLLEGE NOTES: Granted medical redshirt due to knee injury (1995).

Year—Team	G	INTERCEPTIONS				SACKS
		No.	Yds.	Avg.	TD	No.
1993—Southeast Missouri State	11	0	0	...	0	3.0
1994—Southeast Missouri State	12	0	0	...	0	3.5
1995—Southeast Missouri State	1	0	0	...	0	0.0
1996—Southeast Missouri State	11	1	40	40.0	0	7.0
1997—Southeast Missouri State	11	0	0	...	0	7.0
College totals (5 years)	46	1	40	40.0	0	20.5

RUHMAN, CHRIS — OT — 49ERS

PERSONAL: Born December 19, 1974, in Houston. ... 6-5/321. ... Full name: Christopher Aamon Ruhman.
HIGH SCHOOL: Nimitz (Irving, Texas).
COLLEGE: Texas A&M.
TRANSACTIONS/CAREER NOTES: Selected by San Francisco 49ers in third round (89th pick overall) of 1998 NFL draft.
COLLEGE NOTES: Granted medical redshirt due to shoulder injury (1993).
COLLEGE PLAYING EXPERIENCE: Texas A&M, 1993-1997. ... Games: 1993 (2), 1994 (5), 1995 (11), 1996 (12), 1997 (9). Total: 37.

RUTLEDGE, ROD — TE — PATRIOTS

PERSONAL: Born August 12, 1975, in Birmingham, Ala. ... 6-5/262. ... Full name: Roderick Rutledge.
HIGH SCHOOL: Erwin (Birmingham, Ala.).

COLLEGE: Alabama.
TRANSACTIONS/CAREER NOTES: Selected by New England Patriots in second round (54th pick overall) of 1998 NFL draft. ... Signed by Patriots (June 15, 1998).

			RECEIVING		
Year Team	G	No.	Yds.	Avg.	TD
1994—Alabama	12	0	0	...	0
1995—Alabama	11	1	8	8.0	0
1996—Alabama	12	7	91	13.0	0
1997—Alabama	11	15	160	10.7	1
College totals (4 years)	46	23	259	11.3	1

SALAAM, EPHRAIM — OT — FALCONS

PERSONAL: Born June 19, 1976, in Chicago. ... 6-7/290. ... Full name: Ephraim Mateen Salaam. ... Name pronounced EE-frum sah-LAHM.
HIGH SCHOOL: Florin (Sacramento).
COLLEGE: San Diego State.
TRANSACTIONS/CAREER NOTES: Selected by Atlanta Falcons in seventh round (199th pick overall) of 1998 NFL draft. ... Signed by Falcons (June 3, 1998).
COLLEGE NOTES: Played defensive line during 1994 season.
COLLEGE PLAYING EXPERIENCE: San Diego State, 1993-1997. ... Games: 1993 (redshirted), 1994 (1), 1995 (12), 1996 (10), 1997 (9). Total: 32.

SALAVE'A, JOE — DT — OILERS

PERSONAL: Born March 23, 1975, in Leone, American Samoa. ... 6-4/285. ... Full name: Joe Fagaone Salave'a. ... Name pronounced sal-ah-VAY-ah.
HIGH SCHOOL: Oceanside (Calif.).
COLLEGE: Arizona (degree in sociology, 1997).
TRANSACTIONS/CAREER NOTES: Selected by Tennessee Oilers in fourth round (107th pick overall) of 1998 NFL draft.
HONORS: Named defensive tackle on THE SPORTING NEWS college All-America third team (1997).

Year Team	G	SACKS
1993—Arizona		Did not play.
1994—Arizona	...	3.0
1995—Arizona	...	1.0
1996—Arizona	...	6.0
1997—Arizona	...	11.5
College totals (4 years)	...	21.5

SANDERS, DAVID — DE — RAIDERS

PERSONAL: Born July 25, 1975, in Jackson, Miss. ... 6-4/284.
HIGH SCHOOL: Provine (Jackson, Miss.).
COLLEGE: Arkansas.
TRANSACTIONS/CAREER NOTES: Selected by Oakland Raiders in seventh round (235th pick overall) of 1998 NFL draft.

Year Team	G	SACKS
1993—Arkansas		Redshirted.
1994—Arkansas	5	1.0
1995—Arkansas	11	0.0
1996—Arkansas	11	4.0
1997—Arkansas	10	1.0
College totals (4 years)	37	6.0

SANFORD, KIO — WR — CHARGERS

PERSONAL: Born January 8, 1975, in Lexington, Ky. ... 5-10/180. ... Full name: Kiota Jermain Sanford.
HIGH SCHOOL: Bryan Station (Lexington, Ky.).
COLLEGE: Kentucky (degree in social work).
TRANSACTIONS/CAREER NOTES: Selected by San Diego Chargers in seventh round (234th pick overall) of 1998 NFL draft.
COLLEGE NOTES: Rushed three times for minus five yards (1994); and rushed once for 12 yards (1995).

		RECEIVING				PUNT RETURNS				KICKOFF RETURNS				TOTALS	
Year Team	G	No.	Yds.	Avg.	TD	No.	Yds.	Avg.	TD	No.	Yds.	Avg.	TD	TD	Pts.
1993—Kentucky									Redshirted.						
1994—Kentucky	11	12	145	12.1	0	24	202	8.4	0	33	820	24.8	1	1	6
1995—Kentucky	9	11	176	16.0	0	13	52	4.0	0	23	554	24.1	0	0	0
1996—Kentucky	10	5	51	10.2	0	16	126	7.9	0	15	240	16.0	0	0	0
1997—Kentucky	9	36	516	14.3	5	3	1	0.3	0	3	55	18.3	0	5	30
College totals (4 years)	39	64	888	13.9	5	56	381	6.8	0	74	1669	22.6	1	6	36

SAVOY, PHIL — WR — CARDINALS

PERSONAL: Born February 16, 1975, in Washington, D.C. ... 6-2/195.
HIGH SCHOOL: Achbishop Carroll (Washington, D.C.).
COLLEGE: Colorado.
TRANSACTIONS/CAREER NOTES: Selected by Arizona Cardinals in seventh round (193rd pick overall) of 1998 NFL draft.

Year Team	G	No.	RECEIVING Yds.	Avg.	TD
1993—Colorado			Redshirted.		
1994—Colorado	9	17	283	16.6	1
1995—Colorado	10	49	582	11.9	5
1996—Colorado	11	43	652	15.2	3
1997—Colorado	10	43	659	15.3	5
College totals (4 years)	40	152	2176	14.3	14

SCHULTERS, LANCE   S   49ERS

PERSONAL: Born May 27, 1975, in Brooklyn, N.Y. ... 6-2/188.
HIGH SCHOOL: Canarsie (Brooklyn, N.Y.).
JUNIOR COLLEGE: Nassau (N.Y.) Community College.
COLLEGE: Hofstra.
TRANSACTIONS/CAREER NOTES: Selected by San Francisco 49ers in fourth round (119th pick overall) of 1998 NFL draft.

Year Team	G	No.	INTERCEPTIONS Yds.	Avg.	TD	SACKS No.	No.	KICKOFF RETURNS Yds.	Avg. TD		TOTALS TD	Pts.
1994—Nassau						Statistics unavailable.						
1995—Nassau						Statistics unavailable.						
1996—Hofstra	10	5	48	9.6	1	1.0	0	0	...	0	1	6
1997—Hofstra	11	4	98	24.5	1	0.0	3	24	8.0	0	1	6
College totals (2 years)	21	9	146	16.2	2	1.0	3	24	8.0	0	2	12

SHANNON, LARRY   WR   DOLPHINS

PERSONAL: Born February 2, 1975, in Starke, Fla. ... 6-4/210.
HIGH SCHOOL: Bradford (Starke, Fla.).
COLLEGE: East Carolina.
TRANSACTIONS/CAREER NOTES: Selected by Miami Dolphins in third round (82nd pick overall) of 1998 NFL draft.

Year Team	G	No.	RECEIVING Yds.	Avg.	TD
1993—East Carolina			Redshirted.		
1994—East Carolina	11	17	226	13.3	6
1995—East Carolina	11	24	346	14.4	5
1996—East Carolina	11	39	834	21.4	9
1997—East Carolina	7	21	308	14.7	1
College totals (4 years)	40	101	1714	17.0	21

SHAW, BOBBY   WR   SEAHAWKS

PERSONAL: Born April 23, 1975, in San Francisco ... 6-0/186.
HIGH SCHOOL: Galileo (San Francisco).
COLLEGE: California.
TRANSACTIONS/CAREER NOTES: Selected by Seattle Seahawks in sixth round (169th pick overall) of 1998 NFL draft. ... Signed by Seahawks (June 5, 1998).
HONORS: Named wide receiver on The Sporting News college All-America first team (1997).
COLLEGE NOTES: Returned three kickoffs for 31 yards and returned one punt for 10 yards (1995); rushed once for 16 yards (1996); and attempted one pass with one completion for 19 yards, rushed twice for 16 yards and returned seven punts for 57 yards (1997).

Year Team	G	No.	RECEIVING Yds.	Avg.	TD
1993—California			Redshirted.		
1994—California	11	6	53	8.8	0
1995—California	11	38	658	17.3	6
1996—California	11	58	888	15.3	9
1997—California	11	75	1093	14.6	10
College totals (4 years)	44	177	2692	15.2	25

SHAW, HAROLD   RB   PATRIOTS

PERSONAL: Born September 3, 1974, in Magee, Miss. ... 6-0/228.
HIGH SCHOOL: Magee (Miss.).
COLLEGE: Southern Mississippi.
TRANSACTIONS/CAREER NOTES: Selected by New England Patriots in sixth round (176th pick overall) of 1998 NFL draft.

Year Team	G	RUSHING Att.	Yds.	Avg.	TD	RECEIVING No.	Yds.	Avg.	TD	KICKOFF RETURNS No.	Yds.	Avg.	TD	TOTALS TD	Pts.
1994—Southern Mississippi	11	82	393	4.8	7	3	20	6.7	0	4	82	20.5	0	7	42
1995—Southern Mississippi	11	87	295	3.4	1	16	101	6.3	1	4	56	14.0	0	2	12
1996—Southern Mississippi	11	178	486	2.7	8	17	162	9.5	1	2	50	25.0	0	9	54
1997—Southern Mississippi	11	245	1110	4.5	16	26	147	5.7	0	4	51	12.8	0	16	96
College totals (4 years)	44	592	2284	3.9	32	62	430	6.9	2	14	239	17.1	0	34	204

SHAW, SCOTT   G   DOLPHINS

PERSONAL: Born June 2, 1974, in Sterling Heights, Mich. ... 6-3/303.
HIGH SCHOOL: Henry Ford II (Sterling Heights, Mich.).

COLLEGE: Michigan State.
TRANSACTIONS/CAREER NOTES: Selected by Miami Dolphins in fifth round (143rd pick overall) of 1998 NFL draft.
COLLEGE PLAYING EXPERIENCE: Michigan State, 1993-1997. ... Games: 1993 (redshirted), 1994 (did not play), 1995 (8), 1996 (11), 1997 (11). Total: 30.

SHEHEE, RASHAAN — RB — CHIEFS

PERSONAL: Born June 20, 1975, in Bakersfield, Calif. ... 5-10/207. ... Name pronounced ruh-SHAHN.
HIGH SCHOOL: Foothill (Bakersfield, Calif.).
COLLEGE: Washington.
TRANSACTIONS/CAREER NOTES: Selected by Kansas City Chiefs in third round (88th pick overall) of 1998 NFL draft.

		RUSHING				RECEIVING				KICKOFF RETURNS				TOTALS	
Year Team	G	Att.	Yds.	Avg.	TD	No.	Yds.	Avg.	TD	No.	Yds.	Avg.	TD	TD	Pts.
1993—Washington						Redshirted.									
1994—Washington	10	14	89	6.4	0	0	0	...	0	9	159	17.7	0	0	0
1995—Washington	11	166	957	5.8	15	21	183	8.7	0	9	174	19.3	0	15	90
1996—Washington	4	65	242	3.7	4	8	47	5.9	0	0	0	...	0	4	24
1997—Washington	8	139	862	6.2	8	15	146	9.7	1	0	0	...	0	9	54
College totals (4 years)	33	384	2150	5.6	27	44	376	8.5	1	18	333	18.5	0	28	168

SIDNEY, DAINON — CB — OILERS

PERSONAL: Born May 30, 1975, in Atlanta. ... 6-0/186. ... Full name: Dainon Tarquinius Sidney.
HIGH SCHOOL: Riverdale (Ga.).
COLLEGE: East Tennessee State, then Alabama-Birmingham.
TRANSACTIONS/CAREER NOTES: Selected by Tennessee Oilers in third round (77th pick overall) of 1998 NFL draft.

		INTERCEPTIONS				KICKOFF RETURNS				TOTALS	
Year Team	G	No.	Yds.	Avg.	TD	No.	Yds.	Avg.	TD	TD	Pts.
1993—East Tennessee State	10	0	0	...	0	1	29	29.0	0	0	0
1994—East Tennessee State	5	0	0	...	0	7	242	34.6	1	1	6
1995—Alabama-Birmingham						Redshirted.					
1996—Alabama-Birmingham	11	5	60	12.0	1	0	0	...	0	1	6
1997—Alabama-Birmingham	11	4	28	7.0	1	2	29	14.5	0	1	6
College totals (4 years)	37	9	88	9.8	2	10	300	30.0	1	3	18

SIMMONS, ANTHONY — LB — SEAHAWKS

PERSONAL: Born June 20, 1976, in Spartanburg, S.C. ... 6-0/230.
HIGH SCHOOL: Spartanburg (S.C.).
COLLEGE: Clemson.
TRANSACTIONS/CAREER NOTES: Selected after junior season by Seattle Seahawks in first round (15th pick overall) of 1998 NFL draft.
HONORS: Named inside linebacker on THE SPORTING NEWS college All-America first team (1996 and 1997).

Year Team	G	SACKS
1995—Clemson	11	3.5
1996—Clemson	11	7.0
1997—Clemson	11	6.0
College totals (3 years)	33	16.5

SIMMONS, BRIAN — LB — BENGALS

PERSONAL: Born June 21, 1975, in New Bern, N.C. ... 6-3/233. ... Full name: Brian Eugene Simmons.
HIGH SCHOOL: New Bern (N.C.).
COLLEGE: North Carolina.
TRANSACTIONS/CAREER NOTES: Selected by Cincinnati Bengals in first round (17th pick overall) of 1998 NFL draft.
HONORS: Named outside linebacker on THE SPORTING NEWS college All-America second team (1996). ... Named outside linebacker on THE SPORTING NEWS college All-America third team (1997).

		INTERCEPTIONS				SACKS
Year Team	G	No.	Yds.	Avg.	TD	No.
1993—North Carolina			Redshirted.			
1994—North Carolina	11	0	0	...	0	1.0
1995—North Carolina	11	2	1	0.5	0	5.0
1996—North Carolina	10	4	160	40.0	1	2.0
1997—North Carolina	11	0	0	...	0	3.0
College totals (4 years)	43	6	161	26.8	1	11.0

SIMMONS, JASON — CB — STEELERS

PERSONAL: Born March 30, 1976, in Inglewood, Calif. ... 5-8/188. ... Full name: Jason Lawrence Simmons.
HIGH SCHOOL: Leuzinger (Lawndale, Calif.).
COLLEGE: Arizona State.
TRANSACTIONS/CAREER NOTES: Selected by Pittsburgh Steelers in fifth round (137th pick overall) of 1998 NFL draft.

Year Team	G	No.	Yds.	Avg.	TD
1994—Arizona State	11	0	0	...	0
1995—Arizona State	10	2	27	13.5	0
1996—Arizona State	11	1	0	0.0	0
1997—Arizona State	10	3	5	1.7	0
College totals (4 years)	42	6	32	5.3	0

SIMMONS, TONY — WR — PATRIOTS

PERSONAL: Born December 8, 1974, in Chicago. ... 6-0/206.
HIGH SCHOOL: St. Rita (Chicago).
COLLEGE: Wisconsin.
TRANSACTIONS/CAREER NOTES: Selected by New England Patriots in second round (52nd pick overall) of 1998 NFL draft.

			RECEIVING		
Year Team	G	No.	Yds.	Avg.	TD
1993—Wisconsin			Redshirted.		
1994—Wisconsin	11	21	536	25.5	8
1995—Wisconsin	11	29	504	17.4	7
1996—Wisconsin	8	20	346	17.3	3
1997—Wisconsin	12	27	537	19.9	5
College totals (4 years)	42	97	1923	19.8	23

SLAY, HENRY — DT — FALCONS

PERSONAL: Born April 28, 1975, in Elyria, Ohio. ... 6-2/290.
HIGH SCHOOL: Elyria (Ohio) West.
COLLEGE: West Virginia.
TRANSACTIONS/CAREER NOTES: Selected by Atlanta Falcons in seventh round (203rd pick overall) of 1998 NFL draft. ... Signed by Falcons (June 1, 1998).

Year Team	G	SACKS
1993—West Virginia		Redshirted.
1994—West Virginia	12	1.0
1995—West Virginia	11	4.0
1996—West Virginia	12	3.0
1997—West Virginia	12	8.0
College totals (4 years)	47	16.0

SMITH, SHEVIN — S — BUCCANEERS

PERSONAL: Born June 17, 1975, in Miami. ... 5-11/196.
HIGH SCHOOL: Southridge (Miami).
COLLEGE: Florida State.
TRANSACTIONS/CAREER NOTES: Selected by Tampa Bay Buccaneers in sixth round (184th pick overall) of 1998 NFL draft. ... Signed by Buccaneers (June 4, 1998).
COLLEGE NOTES: Credited with one sack (1995).

			INTERCEPTIONS		
Year Team	G	No.	Yds.	Avg.	TD
1993—Florida State			Redshirted.		
1994—Florida State	5	0	0	...	0
1995—Florida State	9	2	16	8.0	0
1996—Florida State	11	3	61	20.3	1
1997—Florida State	11	3	71	23.7	0
College totals (4 years)	36	8	148	18.5	1

SMITH, TARIK — RB — COWBOYS

PERSONAL: Born April 16, 1975, in Fort Worth, Texas. ... 5-10/200.
HIGH SCHOOL: Oak Park (Agoura, Calif.).
COLLEGE: California.
TRANSACTIONS/CAREER NOTES: Selected by Dallas Cowboys in seventh round (223rd pick overall) of 1998 NFL draft.
COLLEGE NOTES: Granted medical redshirt due to leg injury (1994).

		RUSHING				RECEIVING				TOTALS	
Year Team	G	Att.	Yds.	Avg.	TD	No.	Yds.	Avg.	TD	TD	Pts.
1993—California	5	32	112	3.5	1	1	9	9.0	0	1	6
1994—California	1	0	0	...	0	1	31	31.0	0	0	0
1995—California	10	74	391	5.3	2	6	27	4.5	0	2	12
1996—California	3	56	400	7.1	4	8	63	7.9	1	5	30
1997—California	10	162	636	3.9	7	8	54	6.8	0	7	42
College totals (5 years)	29	324	1539	4.8	14	24	184	7.7	1	15	90

SMITH, TRAVIAN — LB — RAIDERS

PERSONAL: Born August 26, 1975, in Good Shepard, Texas. ... 6-4/238.
HIGH SCHOOL: Tatum (Texas).
COLLEGE: Oklahoma.

TRANSACTIONS/CAREER NOTES: Selected by Oakland Raiders in fifth round (152nd pick overall) of 1998 NFL draft.
COLLEGE NOTES: Intercepted two passes for 93 yards and one touchdown and returned two punts for 39 yards (1997).

Year Team	G	SACKS
1994—Oklahoma	9	1.0
1995—Oklahoma	11	1.0
1996—Oklahoma	11	6.0
1997—Oklahoma	10	5.0
College totals (4 years)	41	13.0

SPENCE, BLAKE TE JETS

PERSONAL: Born June 20, 1975, in Garden Grove, Calif. ... 6-4/249. ... Full name: Blake Andrew Spence.
HIGH SCHOOL: Capistrano Valley (San Juan Capistrano, Calif.).
COLLEGE: Oregon.
TRANSACTIONS/CAREER NOTES: Selected by New York Jets in fifth round (146th pick overall) of 1998 NFL draft.

Year Team	G	RECEIVING No.	Yds.	Avg.	TD
1993—Oregon		Redshirted.			
1994—Oregon	11	8	109	13.6	1
1995—Oregon	12	24	247	10.3	1
1996—Oregon	11	21	380	18.1	2
1997—Oregon	12	38	632	16.6	6
College totals (4 years)	46	91	1368	15.0	10

SPIKES, TAKEO LB BENGALS

PERSONAL: Born December 17, 1976, in Sandersville, Ga. ... 6-2/221. ... Full name: Takeo Gerard Spikes. ... Name pronounced tuh-KEY-oh.
HIGH SCHOOL: Washington County (Sandersville, Ga.).
COLLEGE: Auburn.
TRANSACTIONS/CAREER NOTES: Selected after junior season by Cincinnati Bengals in first round (13th pick overall) of 1998 NFL draft.
HONORS: Named inside linebacker on THE SPORTING NEWS college All-America first team (1997).

Year Team	G	INTERCEPTIONS No.	Yds.	Avg.	TD	SACKS No.
1995—Auburn	11	0	0	...	0	3.0
1996—Auburn	11	1	0	0.0	0	1.0
1997—Auburn	12	2	80	40.0	1	2.0
College totals (3 years)	34	3	80	26.7	1	6.0

SPIRES, GREG DE PATRIOTS

PERSONAL: Born August 12, 1974, in Cape Coral, Fla. ... 6-1/260.
HIGH SCHOOL: Mariner (Cape Coral, Fla.).
COLLEGE: Florida State.
TRANSACTIONS/CAREER NOTES: Selected by New England Patriots in third round (83rd pick overall) of 1998 NFL draft.

Year Team	G	SACKS
1993—Florida State		Redshirted.
1994—Florida State	5	0.0
1995—Florida State	10	1.0
1996—Florida State	10	6.0
1997—Florida State	8	10.0
College totals (4 years)	33	17.0

SPROTTE, JIMMY LB OILERS

PERSONAL: Born October 2, 1974, in Olathe, Kan. ... 6-3/245. ... Full name: John Wild Sprotte. ... Name pronounced SPRAHT.
HIGH SCHOOL: Blue Ridge (Lakeside, Ariz.).
COLLEGE: Arizona.
TRANSACTIONS/CAREER NOTES: Selected by Tennessee Oilers in seventh round (205th pick overall) of 1998 NFL draft.

Year Team	G	SACKS
1993—Arizona		Redshirted.
1994—Arizona	11	0.0
1995—Arizona	11	0.0
1996—Arizona	10	3.0
1997—Arizona	10	3.0
College totals (4 years)	42	6.0

STAAT, JEREMY DT STEELERS

PERSONAL: Born October 10, 1976, in Bakersfield, Calif. ... 6-5/300. ... Full name: Jeremy Ray Staat. ... Name pronounced STOT.
HIGH SCHOOL: Bakersfield (Calif.).
JUNIOR COLLEGE: Bakersfield (Calif.) College.
COLLEGE: Arizona State.
TRANSACTIONS/CAREER NOTES: Selected by Pittsburgh Steelers in second round (41st pick overall) of 1998 NFL draft.
HONORS: Named defensive tackle on THE SPORTING NEWS college All-America second team (1997).

Year Team	G	SACKS
1994—Bakersfield	Statistics unavailable.	
1995—Bakersfield	Statistics unavailable.	
1996—Arizona State	11	0.0
1997—Arizona State	11	9.5
College totals (2 years)	22	9.5

STARKS, DUANE — CB — RAVENS

PERSONAL: Born May 23, 1974, in Miami. ... 5-10/170. ... Full name: Duane Lonell Starks.
HIGH SCHOOL: Miami Beach Senior.
JUNIOR COLLEGE: Holmes Junior College (Miss.).
COLLEGE: Miami.
TRANSACTIONS/CAREER NOTES: Selected by Baltimore Ravens in first round (10th pick overall) of 1998 NFL draft.
COLLEGE NOTES: Recovered one fumble for 27 yards and a touchdown (1994).

Year Team	G	INTERCEPTIONS				PUNT RETURNS				TOTALS	
		No.	Yds.	Avg.	TD	No.	Yds.	Avg.	TD	TD	Pts.
1994—Holmes	10	2	30	19.0	0	13	149	11.5	1	2	12
1995—Miami (Fla.)	1	0	0	...	0	0	0	...	0	0	0
1996—Miami (Fla.)	11	3	60	20.0	1	10	127	12.7	0	1	6
1997—Miami (Fla.)	11	3	79	26.3	1	26	298	11.5	1	2	12
Junior college totals (1 year)	10	2	38	19.0	0	13	149	11.5	1	2	12
College totals (3 years)	23	6	139	23.2	2	36	425	11.8	1	3	18

STEELE, GLEN — DL — BENGALS

PERSONAL: Born October 4, 1974, in Ligonier, Ind. ... 6-4/295. ... Full name: James Lendale Steele Jr.
HIGH SCHOOL: West Noble (Ligonier, Ind.).
COLLEGE: Michigan.
TRANSACTIONS/CAREER NOTES: Selected by Cincinnati Bengals in fourth round (105th pick overall) of 1998 NFL draft.
COLLEGE NOTES: Granted medical redshirt (1993).

Year Team	G	SACKS
1993—Michigan	1	0.0
1994—Michigan	11	3.0
1995—Michigan	12	8.0
1996—Michigan	11	4.0
1997—Michigan	11	7.0
College totals (5 years)	46	22.0

STRIKWERDA, NATHAN — C — DOLPHINS

PERSONAL: Born August 20, 1975, in Madison, Wis. ... 6-4/295. ... Full name: Nathan John Strikwerda.
HIGH SCHOOL: West (Madison, Wis.).
COLLEGE: Northwestern.
TRANSACTIONS/CAREER NOTES: Selected by Miami Dolphins in sixth round (171st pick overall) of 1998 NFL draft.
COLLEGE PLAYING EXPERIENCE: Northwestern, 1993-1997. ... Games: 1993 (redshirted), 1994 (3), 1995 (10), 1996 (11), 1997 (12). Totals: 36.

SURTAIN, PATRICK — CB — DOLPHINS

PERSONAL: Born May 19, 1976, in New Orleans. ... 5-11/197.
HIGH SCHOOL: Edna Karr (New Orleans).
COLLEGE: Southern Mississippi.
TRANSACTIONS/CAREER NOTES: Selected by Miami Dolphins in second round (44th pick overall) of 1998 NFL draft.
HONORS: Named cornerback on THE SPORTING NEWS college All-America second team (1997).

Year Team	G	INTERCEPTIONS				SACKS
		No.	Yds.	Avg.	TD	No.
1994—Southern Mississippi	7	1	8	8.0	0	1.0
1995—Southern Mississippi	11	0	0	...	0	0.0
1996—Southern Mississippi	11	6	77	12.8	0	0.0
1997—Southern Mississippi	11	6	127	21.2	0	0.0
College totals (4 years)	40	13	212	16.3	0	1.0

SUTTER, RYAN — S — RAVENS

PERSONAL: Born September 14, 1974, in Fort Collins, Colo. ... 6-1/203.
HIGH SCHOOL: Fort Collins (Colo.).
COLLEGE: Colorado.
TRANSACTIONS/CAREER NOTES: Selected by Baltimore Ravens in fifth round (133rd pick overall) of 1998 NFL draft.
COLLEGE NOTES: Intercepted three passes for 34 yards and one touchdown (1997).
COLLEGE PLAYING EXPERIENCE: Colorado, 1993-1997. ... Games: 1993 (redshirted), 1994 (11), 1995 (11), 1996 (11), 1997 (11). Total: 44.

TAYLOR, AARON   G   COLTS

PERSONAL: Born January 21, 1975, in Wichita Falls, Texas. ... 6-1/320.
HIGH SCHOOL: Rider (Wichita Falls, Texas).
COLLEGE: Nebraska.
TRANSACTIONS/CAREER NOTES: Selected by Indianapolis Colts in seventh round (190th pick overall) of 1998 NFL draft.
HONORS: Named center on THE SPORTING NEWS college All-America second team (1996). ... Lombardi Award winner (1997). ... Named guard on THE SPORTING NEWS college All-America first team (1997).
COLLEGE NOTES: Nebraska, 1993-1997. ... Games: 1993 (redshirted), 1994 (12), 1995 (11), 1996 (12), 1997 (12). Total: 47.

TAYLOR, CORDELL   CB   JAGUARS

PERSONAL: Born December 22, 1973, in Norfolk, Va. ... 6-0/192.
HIGH SCHOOL: Booker T. Washington (Norfolk, Va.).
COLLEGE: Hampton (Va.).
TRANSACTIONS/CAREER NOTES: Selected by Jacksonville Jaguars in second round (57th pick overall) of 1998 NFL draft. ... Signed by Jaguars (May 14, 1998).
COLLEGE NOTES: Returned one fumble for 57 yards and a touchdown (1997).

		INTERCEPTIONS				SACKS	PUNT RETURNS				TOTALS	
Year Team	G	No.	Yds.	Avg.	TD	No.	No.	Yds.	Avg.	TD	TD	Pts.
1993—Hampton						Redshirted.						
1994—Hampton	11	1	0	0.0	0	3.0	1	0	0.0	0	0	0
1995—Hampton	11	4	48	12.0	0	0.0	1	0	0.0	0	0	0
1996—Hampton	11	1	23	23.0	0	0.0	1	-1	-1.0	0	0	0
1997—Hampton	11	3	73	24.3	0	0.0	0	0	...	0	1	6
College totals (4 years)	44	9	144	16.0	0	3.0	3	-1	-0.3	0	1	6

TAYLOR, FRED   RB   JAGUARS

PERSONAL: Born June 27, 1976, in Belle Glade, Fla. ... 6-0/227. ... Full name: Frederick A. Taylor.
HIGH SCHOOL: Glades Central (Belle Glade, Fla.).
COLLEGE: Florida.
TRANSACTIONS/CAREER NOTES: Selected by Jacksonville Jaguars in first round (ninth pick overall) of 1998 NFL draft.
HONORS: Named running back on THE SPORTING NEWS college All-America third team (1997).

		RUSHING				RECEIVING				TOTALS	
Year Team	G	Att.	Yds.	Avg.	TD	No.	Yds.	Avg.	TD	TD	Pts.
1994—Florida	12	171	873	5.1	8	29	271	9.3	0	8	48
1995—Florida	6	48	281	5.9	5	6	88	14.7	0	5	30
1996—Florida	9	104	629	6.0	5	8	120	15.0	0	5	30
1997—Florida	11	214	1292	6.0	13	24	238	9.9	0	13	78
College totals (4 years)	38	537	3075	5.7	31	67	717	10.7	0	31	186

TEAGUE, TREY   OT   BRONCOS

PERSONAL: Born December 27, 1974, in Jackson, Tenn. ... 6-5/307. ... Full name: Fred Everette Teague III.
HIGH SCHOOL: University (Jackson, Tenn.).
COLLEGE: Tennessee.
TRANSACTIONS/CAREER NOTES: Selected by Denver Broncos in seventh round (200th pick overall) of 1998 NFL draft.
COLLEGE PLAYING EXPERIENCE: Tennessee, 1993-1997. ... Games: 1993 (redshirted), 1994 (10), 1995 (11), 1996 (12), 1997 (12). Total: 45.

TERRELL, DAVID   DB   REDSKINS

PERSONAL: Born July 8, 1975, in Floyada, Texas. ... 6-2/172.
HIGH SCHOOL: Sweetwater (Texas).
COLLEGE: Texas-El Paso.
TRANSACTIONS/CAREER NOTES: Selected by Washington Redskins in seventh round (191st pick overall) of 1998 NFL draft. ... Signed by Redskins (May 13, 1998).

		INTERCEPTIONS			
Year Team	G	No.	Yds.	Avg.	TD
1993—Texas-El Paso			Redshirted.		
1994—Texas-El Paso	11	1	2	2.0	0
1995—Texas-El Paso	12	3	11	3.7	0
1996—Texas-El Paso	11	1	0	0.0	0
1997—Texas-El Paso			Did not play.		
College totals (3 years)	34	5	13	2.6	0

THELWELL, RYAN   WR   49ERS

PERSONAL: Born April 6, 1973, in London, Ont. ... 6-2/188.
HIGH SCHOOL: Catholic Central (London, Ont.).
COLLEGE: Minnesota.
TRANSACTIONS/CAREER NOTES: Selected by San Francisco 49ers in seventh round (215th pick overall) of 1998 NFL draft.

1998 DRAFT PICKS

Year Team	G	RECEIVING			
		No.	Yds.	Avg.	TD
1994—Minnesota	7	24	406	16.9	3
1995—Minnesota	11	58	775	13.4	6
1996—Minnesota	11	54	1051	19.5	5
1997—Minnesota		Did not play.			
College totals (3 years)	29	136	2232	16.4	14

THOMAS, MELVIN　　　　　G　　　　　EAGLES

PERSONAL: Born June 11, 1975, in New Orleans. ... 6-3/322.
HIGH SCHOOL: Lawless (New Orleans).
COLLEGE: Colorado.
TRANSACTIONS/CAREER NOTES: Selected by Philadelphia Eagles in seventh round (240th pick overall) of 1998 NFL draft. ... Signed by Eagles (June 15, 1998).
COLLEGE PLAYING EXPERIENCE: Colorado, 1993-1997. ... Games: 1993 (redshirted), 1994 (5), 1995 (11), 1996 (11), 1997 (11). Total: 38.

THOMAS, TRA　　　　　OT　　　　　EAGLES

PERSONAL: Born November 20, 1974, in Deland, Fla. ... 6-7/349. ... Name pronounced TRAY.
HIGH SCHOOL: Deland (Fla.).
COLLEGE: Florida State.
TRANSACTIONS/CAREER NOTES: Selected by Philadelphia Eagles in first round (11th pick overall) of 1998 NFL draft.
COLLEGE PLAYING EXPERIENCE: Florida State, 1993-1997. ... Games: 1993 (redshirted), 1994 (games played unavailable), 1995 (11), 1996 (11), 1997 (11). Total: games played unavailable.

TILLMAN, PAT　　　　　DB　　　　　CARDINALS

PERSONAL: Born November 6, 1976, in Fremont, Calif. ... 5-11/204. ... Full name: Patrick Daniel Tillman.
HIGH SCHOOL: Leland (San Jose, Calif.).
COLLEGE: Arizona State.
TRANSACTIONS/CAREER NOTES: Selected by Arizona Cardinals in seventh round (226th pick overall) of 1998 NFL draft.
HONORS: Named outside linebacker on THE SPORTING NEWS college All-America first team (1997).

Year Team	G	INTERCEPTIONS				SACKS
		No.	Yds.	Avg.	TD	No.
1994—Arizona State	11	0	0	...	0	1.0
1995—Arizona State	11	0	0	...	0	1.0
1996—Arizona State	11	4	17	4.3	1	2.0
1997—Arizona State	11	3	2	0.7	0	4.0
College totals (4 years)	44	7	19	2.7	1	8.0

TOLBERT, BRANDON　　　　　LB　　　　　JAGUARS

PERSONAL: Born April 6, 1975, in Villa Rica, Ga. ... 6-2/225.
HIGH SCHOOL: Villa Rica (Ga.).
COLLEGE: Georgia.
TRANSACTIONS/CAREER NOTES: Selected by Jacksonville Jaguars in seventh round (214th pick overall) of 1998 NFL draft. ... Signed by Jaguars (May 14, 1998).

Year Team	G	INTERCEPTIONS				SACKS
		No.	Yds.	Avg.	TD	No.
1993—Georgia		Redshirted.				
1994—Georgia	9	0	0	...	0	0.0
1995—Georgia	9	1	0	0.0	0	1.0
1996—Georgia	11	0	0	...	0	3.5
1997—Georgia	11	1	4	4.0	0	2.0
College totals (4 years)	40	2	4	2.0	0	6.5

TOWNSEND, DESHEA　　　　　CB　　　　　STEELERS

PERSONAL: Born September 8, 1975, in Batesville, Miss. ... 5-10/180.
HIGH SCHOOL: South Panola (Batesville, Miss.).
COLLEGE: Alabama.
TRANSACTIONS/CAREER NOTES: Selected by Pittsburgh Steelers in fourth round (117th pick overall) of 1998 NFL draft.
COLLEGE NOTES: Returned blocked field-goal attempt for 90 yards and a touchdown (1995).

Year Team	G	INTERCEPTIONS				SACKS	PUNT RETURNS				TOTALS	
		No.	Yds.	Avg.	TD	No.	No.	Yds.	Avg.	TD	TD	Pts.
1994—Alabama	12	1	42	42.0	0	0.0	12	151	12.6	0	0	0
1995—Alabama	11	4	40	10.0	0	0.0	13	75	5.8	0	1	6
1996—Alabama	12	2	29	14.5	0	1.0	6	25	4.2	0	0	0
1997—Alabama	10	0	0	...	0	1.0	1	5	5.0	0	0	0
College totals (4 years)	45	7	111	15.9	0	2.0	32	256	8.0	0	1	6

TROTTER, JEREMIAH   LB   EAGLES

PERSONAL: Born January 20, 1977, in Hooks, Texas. ... 6-0/261.
HIGH SCHOOL: Hooks (Texas).
COLLEGE: Stephen F. Austin.
TRANSACTIONS/CAREER NOTES: Selected after junior season by Philadelphia Eagles in third round (72nd pick overall) of 1998 NFL draft.

		INTERCEPTIONS			SACKS
Year Team	G	No.	Yds.	Avg.	TD	No.
1995—Stephen F. Austin	13	2	13	6.5	1	0.5
1996—Stephen F. Austin	9	1	3	3.0	0	3.0
1997—Stephen F. Austin	10	0	0	...	0	4.0
College totals (3 years)	32	3	16	5.3	1	7.5

TUCKER, JASON   WR   BENGALS

PERSONAL: Born June 24, 1976, in Waco, Texas. ... 6-1/182.
HIGH SCHOOL: Robinson (Waco, Texas).
COLLEGE: Texas Christian.
TRANSACTIONS/CAREER NOTES: Selected after junior season by Cincinnati Bengals in sixth round (167th pick overall) of 1998 NFL draft.
COLLEGE NOTES: Returned one kickoff fo 26 yards (1994); returned two kickoffs for 53 yards (1995); and rushed four times for 20 yards and returned six punts for 26 yards (1996).

		RECEIVING			
Year Team	G	No.	Yds.	Avg.	TD
1994—Texas Christian	11	8	72	9.0	0
1995—Texas Christian	9	31	433	14.0	1
1996—Texas Christian	11	39	692	17.7	4
1997—Texas Christian		Did not play.			
College totals (3 years)	31	78	1197	15.3	5

TURLEY, KYLE   OT   SAINTS

PERSONAL: Born September 24, 1975, in Provo, Utah. ... 6-5/307. ... Full name: Kyle John Turley.
HIGH SCHOOL: Valley View (Moreno Valley, Calif.).
COLLEGE: San Diego State.
TRANSACTIONS/CAREER NOTES: Selected by New Orleans Saints in first round (seventh pick overall) of 1998 NFL draft.
HONORS: Named offensive tackle on THE SPORTING NEWS college All-America first team (1997).
COLLEGE PLAYING EXPERIENCE: San Diego State, 1994-1997. ... Games: 1994 (7), 1995 (12), 1996 (11), 1997 (12). Total: 42.

TURNER, JIM   WR   PANTHERS

PERSONAL: Born November 13, 1975, in Chicago. ... 6-4/212. ... Full name: Jim Allen Turner.
HIGH SCHOOL: Bishop Kenny (Jacksonville).
COLLEGE: Syracuse (degree in psychology).
TRANSACTIONS/CAREER NOTES: Selected by Carolina Panthers in seventh round (228th pick overall) of 1998 NFL draft.
COLLEGE NOTES: Rushed twice for 18 yards and returned one punt for 13 yards (1996); and rushed one for one yard (1997).

		RECEIVING				KICKOFF RETURNS				TOTALS	
Year Team	G	No.	Yds.	Avg.	TD	No.	Yds.	Avg.	TD	TD	Pts.
1993—Syracuse				Redshirted.							
1994—Syracuse	11	0	0	...	0	16	394	24.6	1	1	6
1995—Syracuse	12	7	110	15.7	0	17	411	24.2	0	0	0
1996—Syracuse	11	20	383	19.2	2	23	633	27.5	1	2	3
1997—Syracuse	12	23	488	21.2	4	12	250	20.8	0	4	24
College totals (4 years)	46	50	981	19.6	6	68	1688	24.8	2	7	33

VAUGHN, DAMIAN   TE   BENGALS

PERSONAL: Born June 14, 1975, in Orrville, Ohio. ... 6-4/247. ... Full name: Damian Joseph Vaughn.
HIGH SCHOOL: Orrville (Ohio).
COLLEGE: Miami of Ohio.
TRANSACTIONS/CAREER NOTES: Selected by Cincinnati Bengals in seventh round (222nd pick overall) of 1998 NFL draft. ... Signed by Bengals (May 28, 1998).

		RECEIVING			
Year Team	G	No.	Yds.	Avg.	TD
1993—Miami of Ohio		Redshirted.			
1994—Miami of Ohio	11	2	13	6.5	0
1995—Miami of Ohio	10	5	33	6.6	0
1996—Miami of Ohio	11	13	147	11.3	1
1997—Miami of Ohio	11	27	340	12.6	1
College totals (4 years)	43	47	533	11.3	2

WADE, JOHN   C   JAGUARS

PERSONAL: Born January 25, 1975, in Port Republic, Va. ... 6-6/302. ... Full name: Robert J. Wade.
HIGH SCHOOL: Harrisonburg (Va.).

COLLEGE: Marshall.
TRANSACTIONS/CAREER NOTES: Selected by Jacksonville Jaguars in fifth round (148th pick overall) of 1998 NFL draft. ... Signed by Jaguars (May 14, 1998).
COLLEGE PLAYING EXPERIENCE: Marshall, 1993-1997. ... Games: 1993 (redshirted), 1994 (games played unavailable), 1995 (games played unavailable), 1996 (15), 1997 (11). Total. 26.

WADSWORTH, ANDRE   DE   CARDINALS

PERSONAL: Born October 19, 1974, in Miami. ... 6-4/278.
HIGH SCHOOL: Florida Christian (Miami).
COLLEGE: Florida State.
TRANSACTIONS/CAREER NOTES: Selected by Arizona Cardinals in first round (third pick overall) of 1998 NFL draft.
HONORS: Named defensive end on THE SPORTING NEWS college All-America first team (1997).

Year Team	G	SACKS
1994—Florida State	11	2.5
1995—Florida State	11	2.5
1996—Florida State	9	2.0
1997—Florida State	11	16.0
College totals (4 years)	42	23.0

WALZ, ZACK   LB   CARDINALS

PERSONAL: Born February 13, 1976, in Los Altos, Calif. ... 6-4/228. ... Full name: Zachary Christian Walz.
HIGH SCHOOL: Saint Francis (Mountain View, Calif.).
COLLEGE: Dartmouth (degree in government and economics, 1998).
TRANSACTIONS/CAREER NOTES: Selected by Arizona Cardinals in sixth round (158th pick overall) of 1998 NFL draft. ... Signed by Cardinals (June 4, 1998).

Year Team	G	INTERCEPTIONS No.	Yds.	Avg.	TD	SACKS No.
1994—Dartmouth	10	0	0	...	0	0.0
1995—Dartmouth	10	1	0	0.0	0	5.0
1996—Dartmouth	10	0	0	...	0	5.0
1997—Dartmouth	10	1	17	17.0	0	0.0
College totals (4 years)	40	2	17	8.5	0	10.0

WARD, HINES   WR   STEELERS

PERSONAL: Born March 8, 1976, in Rex, Ga. ... 6-0/194.
HIGH SCHOOL: Forest Park (Ga.).
COLLEGE: Georgia.
TRANSACTIONS/CAREER NOTES: Selected by Pittsburgh Steelers in third round (92nd pick overall) of 1998 NFL draft.
COLLEGE NOTES: Played flanker, tailback and quarterback during career. ... Attempted one pass without a completion (1994); attempted 122 passes with 69 completions for 872 yards, two touchdowns and three interceptions (1995); attempted three passes with one completion for 18 yards and one touchdown (1996); and attempted five passes with two completions for 27 yards.

Year Team	G	RUSHING Att.	Yds.	Avg.	TD	RECEIVING No.	Yds.	Avg.	TD	PUNT RETURNS No.	Yds.	Avg.	TD	KICKOFF RETURNS No.	Yds.	Avg.	TD	TOTALS TD	Pts.
1994—Georgia	11	77	425	5.5	3	19	101	5.3	1	0	0	...	0	18	353	19.6	0	4	24
1995—Georgia	10	70	248	3.5	2	18	249	13.8	0	0	0	...	0	0	0	...	0	2	12
1996—Georgia	11	27	170	6.3	0	52	900	17.3	5	5	47	9.4	0	12	234	19.5	0	5	30
1997—Georgia	10	30	223	7.4	0	55	715	13.0	6	6	55	9.2	0	6	153	25.5	0	6	36
College totals (4 years)	42	204	1066	5.2	5	144	1965	13.6	12	11	102	9.3	0	36	740	20.6	0	17	102

WARFIELD, ERIC   S   CHIEFS

PERSONAL: Born March 3, 1976, in Texarkana, Ark. ... 6-0/192.
HIGH SCHOOL: Arkansas (Texarkana, Ark.).
COLLEGE: Nebraska.
TRANSACTIONS/CAREER NOTES: Selected by Kansas City Chiefs in seventh round (216th pick overall) of 1998 NFL draft. ... Signed by Chiefs (May 27, 1998).
COLLEGE NOTES: Returned one punt for two yards (1996).

Year Team	G	INTERCEPTIONS No.	Yds.	Avg.	TD
1994—Nebraska		Did not play.			
1995—Nebraska	11	0	0	...	0
1996—Nebraska	12	3	1	0.3	0
1997—Nebraska	12	2	26	13.0	0
College totals (3 years)	35	5	27	5.4	0

WARNER, RON   LB   SAINTS

PERSONAL: Born September 26, 1975, in Independence, Kan. ... 6-2/247.
HIGH SCHOOL: Independence (Kan.).
JUNIOR COLLEGE: Independence (Kan.) Community College.
COLLEGE: Kansas.

TRANSACTIONS/CAREER NOTES: Selected by New Orleans Saints in seventh round (239th pick overall) of 1998 NFL draft.
HONORS: Named outside linebacker on The Sporting News college All-America second team (1997).

Year Team	G	SACKS
1994—Independence	Statistics unavailable.	
1995—Independence	Statistics unavailable.	
1996—Kansas	11	6.0
1997—Kansas	10	14.5
College totals (2 years)	21	20.5

WASHINGTON, TODD   G   BUCCANEERS

PERSONAL: Born July 19, 1976, in Nassawadox, Va. ... 6-3/312. ... Full name: Todd Page Washington.
HIGH SCHOOL: Nandua (Melfa, Va.).
COLLEGE: Virginia Tech.
TRANSACTIONS/CAREER NOTES: Selected by Tampa Bay Buccaneers in fourth round (104th pick overall) of 1998 NFL draft. ... Signed by Buccaneers (June 11, 1998).
COLLEGE PLAYING EXPERIENCE: Virginia Tech, 1994-1997. ... Games: 1994 (6), 1995 (11), 1996 (11), 1997 (11). Total: 39.

WATSON, EDWIN   FB   PACKERS

PERSONAL: Born September 29, 1976, in Pontiac, Mich. ... 6-0/229. ... Full name: Edwin D. Watson.
HIGH SCHOOL: Northern (Pontiac, Mich.).
COLLEGE: Purdue.
TRANSACTIONS/CAREER NOTES: Selected by Green Bay Packers in seventh round (218th pick overall) of 1998 NFL draft. ... Signed by Packers (June 9, 1998).

		RUSHING				RECEIVING				TOTALS	
Year Team	G	Att.	Yds.	Avg.	TD	No.	Yds.	Avg.	TD	TD	Pts.
1994—Purdue	7	59	272	4.6	3	1	4	4.0	0	3	18
1995—Purdue	11	102	553	5.4	5	6	41	6.8	0	5	30
1996—Purdue	11	194	768	4.0	6	25	220	8.8	0	6	36
1997—Purdue	11	162	886	5.5	11	26	309	11.9	2	13	78
College totals (4 years)	40	517	2479	4.8	25	58	574	9.9	2	27	162

WAYNE, NATE   LB   BRONCOS

PERSONAL: Born January 12, 1975, in Macon, Miss. ... 6-0/229.
HIGH SCHOOL: Noxubee County (Macon, Miss.).
COLLEGE: Mississippi.
TRANSACTIONS/CAREER NOTES: Selected by Denver Broncos in seventh round (219th pick overall) of 1998 NFL draft.

		INTERCEPTIONS				SACKS
Year Team	G	No.	Yds.	Avg.	TD	No.
1993—Mississippi		Redshirted.				
1994—Mississippi	11	0	0	...	0	1.0
1995—Mississippi	11	1	0	0.0	0	3.5
1996—Mississippi	11	2	29	14.5	1	2.5
1997—Mississippi	11	0	0	...	0	1.5
College totals (4 years)	44	3	29	9.7	1	8.5

WEARY, FRED   CB   SAINTS

PERSONAL: Born April 12, 1974, in Jacksonville. ... 5-10/177. ... Full name: Joseph Fredrick Weary.
HIGH SCHOOL: Mandarin (Jacksonville).
COLLEGE: Florida.
TRANSACTIONS/CAREER NOTES: Selected by New Orleans Saints in fourth round (97th pick overall) of 1998 NFL draft.
HONORS: Named cornerback on The Sporting News college All-America first team (1997).
COLLEGE NOTES: Returned one fumble for 64 yards and a touchdown (1996).

		INTERCEPTIONS			
Year Team	G	No.	Yds.	Avg.	TD
1993—Florida		Redshirted.			
1994—Florida	12	2	0	0.0	0
1995—Florida	11	2	56	28.0	1
1996—Florida	12	5	117	23.4	1
1997—Florida	11	6	113	18.8	0
College totals (4 years)	46	15	286	19.1	2

WEINER, TODD   OT   SEAHAWKS

PERSONAL: Born September 16, 1975, in Bristol, Pa. ... 6-4/300.
HIGH SCHOOL: Taravella (Coral Springs, Fla.).
COLLEGE: Kansas State.
TRANSACTIONS/CAREER NOTES: Selected by Seattle Seahawks in second round (47th pick overall) of 1998 NFL draft.
HONORS: Named offensive tackle on The Sporting News college All-America second team (1997).
COLLEGE PLAYING EXPERIENCE: Kansas State, 1993-1997. ... Games: 1993 (redshirted), 1994 (games played unavailable), 1995 (games played unavailable), 1996 (11), 1997 (11). Total: games played unavailable.

WHITING, BRANDON   DT   EAGLES

PERSONAL: Born July 30, 1976, in Sante Rosa, Calif. ... 6-3/278.
HIGH SCHOOL: Long Beach (Calif.) Polytechnic.
COLLEGE: California.
TRANSACTIONS/CAREER NOTES: Selected by Philadelphia Eagles in fourth round (112th pick overall) of 1998 NFL draft.

Year Team	G	SACKS
1994—California	11	8.5
1995—California	7	2.5
1996—California	11	5.5
1997—California	11	8.0
College totals (4 years)	40	24.5

WHITTED, ALVIS   WR   JAGUARS

PERSONAL: Born September 4, 1974, in Hillsborough, N.C. ... 5-11/184.
HIGH SCHOOL: Orange (Hillsborough, N.C.).
COLLEGE: North Carolina State.
TRANSACTIONS/CAREER NOTES: Selected by Jacksonville Jaguars in seventh round (192nd pick overall) of 1998 NFL draft. ... Signed by Jaguars (May 14, 1998).

Year Team	G	RECEIVING				KICKOFF RETURNS				TOTALS	
		No.	Yds.	Avg.	TD	No.	Yds.	Avg.	TD	TD	Pts.
1994—North Carolina State	11	0	0	...	0	18	452	25.1	1	1	6
1995—North Carolina State	11	2	13	6.5	0	26	533	20.5	0	0	0
1996—North Carolina State	11	14	268	19.1	0	20	455	22.8	1	1	6
1997—North Carolina State	11	13	180	13.8	0	20	489	24.5	0	0	0
College totals (4 years)	44	29	461	15.9	0	84	1929	23.0	2	2	12

WIGGINS, LEE   CB   OILERS

PERSONAL: Born April 27, 1975, in Hartsville, S.C. ... 5-11/187.
HIGH SCHOOL: Hartsville (S.C.).
COLLEGE: South Carolina.
TRANSACTIONS/CAREER NOTES: Selected by Tennessee Oilers in sixth round (168th pick overall) of 1998 NFL draft.

Year Team	G	INTERCEPTIONS			
		No.	Yds.	Avg.	TD
1993—South Carolina		Redshirted.			
1994—South Carolina	11	1	16	16.0	0
1995—South Carolina	11	1	10	10.0	0
1996—South Carolina	11	0	0	...	0
1997—South Carolina	11	1	5	5.0	0
College totals (4 years)	44	3	31	10.3	0

WILEY, CHUCK   DE   PANTHERS

PERSONAL: Born July 16, 1975, in Baton Rouge, La. ... 6-4/275. ... Full name: Samuel Charles Wiley.
HIGH SCHOOL: Southern University Lab (Baton Rouge, La.).
COLLEGE: Louisiana State.
TRANSACTIONS/CAREER NOTES: Selected by Carolina Panthers in third round (62nd pick overall) of 1998 NFL draft. ... Signed by Panthers (June 10, 1998).

Year Team	G	SACKS
1993—Louisiana State		Redshirted.
1994—Louisiana State	11	1.0
1995—Louisiana State	11	7.0
1996—Louisiana State	11	6.0
1997—Louisiana State	11	5.0
College totals (4 years)	44	19.0

WILLIAMS, ELIJAH   CB   FALCONS

PERSONAL: Born August 20, 1975, in Milton, Fla. ... 5-10/181. ... Full name: Elijah Elgebra Williams.
HIGH SCHOOL: Milton (Fla.).
COLLEGE: Florida.
TRANSACTIONS/CAREER NOTES: Selected by Atlanta Falcons in sixth round (166th pick overall) of 1998 NFL draft.
COLLEGE NOTES: Played running back during 1994, 1995 and 1996 seasons. ... Rushed 123 times for 652 yards and four touchdowns and caught 27 passes for 312 yards and one touchdown (1994); rushed 114 times for 858 yards and seven touchdowns and caught 22 passes for 277 yards and two touchdowns (1995); and rushed 106 times for 671 yards and four touchdowns, caught 14 passes for 253 yards and one touchdown and returned two kickoffs for 19 yards (1996).

Year Team	G	INTERCEPTIONS			
		No.	Yds.	Avg.	TD
1993—Florida		Redshirted.			
1994—Florida	11	0	0	...	0
1995—Florida	11	0	0	...	0
1996—Florida	11	0	0	...	0
1997—Florida	10	1	11	11.0	0
College totals (4 years)	43	1	11	11.0	0

WILLIAMS, KEVIN   CB   JETS

PERSONAL: Born August 4, 1975, in Pine Bluff, Ark. ... 6-0/190.
HIGH SCHOOL: Watson Chapel (Pine Bluff, Ark.).
COLLEGE: Oklahoma State.
TRANSACTIONS/CAREER NOTES: Selected by New York Jets in third round (87th pick overall) of 1998 NFL draft.

		INTERCEPTIONS				KICKOFF RETURNS				TOTALS	
Year Team	G	No.	Yds.	Avg.	TD	No.	Yds.	Avg.	TD	TD	Pts.
1993—Oklahoma State	11	0	0	...	0	0	0	...	0	0	0
1994—Oklahoma State	11	1	4	4.0	0	0	0	...	0	0	0
1995—Oklahoma State	11	2	31	15.5	0	2	35	17.5	0	0	0
1996—Oklahoma State						Redshirted.					
1997—Oklahoma State	12	6	107	17.8	1	4	37	9.3	0	1	6
College totals (4 years)	45	9	142	15.8	1	6	72	12.0	0	1	6

WILLIAMS, LAMANZER   DE   JAGUARS

PERSONAL: Born November 17, 1974, in Ypsilanti, Mich. ... 6-4/262. ... Brother of Dan Williams, defensive end, Kansas City Chiefs.
HIGH SCHOOL: Willow Run (Ypsilanti, Mich.).
COLLEGE: Minnesota.
TRANSACTIONS/CAREER NOTES: Selected by Jacksonville Jaguars in sixth round (179th pick overall) of 1998 NFL draft. ... Signed by Jaguars (May 14, 1998).
HONORS: Named defensive end on THE SPORTING NEWS college All-America third team (1997).

Year Team	G	SACKS
1993—Minnesota		Redshirted.
1994—Minnesota	11	2.0
1995—Minnesota	10	3.0
1996—Minnesota	10	0.0
1997—Minnesota	12	18.5
College totals (4 years)	43	23.5

WILLIAMS, ROBERT   CB   CHIEFS

PERSONAL: Born May 29, 1977, in Shelby, N.C. ... 5-10/172. ... Full name: Robert M. Williams.
HIGH SCHOOL: Shelby (N.C.).
COLLEGE: North Carolina.
TRANSACTIONS/CAREER NOTES: Selected after junior season by Kansas City Chiefs in fifth round (128th pick overall) of 1998 NFL draft.

		INTERCEPTIONS			
Year Team	G	No.	Yds.	Avg.	TD
1995—North Carolina	5	0	0	...	0
1996—North Carolina	11	1	0	0.0	0
1997—North Carolina	11	2	22	11.0	0
College totals (3 years)	27	3	22	7.3	0

WILLIAMS, ROLAND   TE   RAMS

PERSONAL: Born April 27, 1975, in Rochester, N.Y. ... 6-5/269. ... Full name: Roland Lamar Williams.
HIGH SCHOOL: East (Rochester, N.Y.).
COLLEGE: Syracuse.
TRANSACTIONS/CAREER NOTES: Selected by St. Louis Rams in fourth round (98th pick overall) of 1998 NFL draft.

		RECEIVING			
Year Team	G	No.	Yds.	Avg.	TD
1993—Syracuse			Redshirted.		
1994—Syracuse	11	0	0	...	0
1995—Syracuse	11	6	64	10.7	2
1996—Syracuse	11	13	140	10.8	5
1997—Syracuse	12	8	132	16.5	1
College totals (4 years)	45	27	336	12.4	8

WILLIAMS, SAMMY   OT   RAVENS

PERSONAL: Born December 14, 1974, in Harvey, Ill. ... 6-5/318.
HIGH SCHOOL: Thornton (Harvey, Ill.).
JUNIOR COLLEGE: Coffeyville (Kan.) Community College.
COLLEGE: Oklahoma.
TRANSACTIONS/CAREER NOTES: Selected by Baltimore Ravens in sixth round (164th pick overall) of 1998 NFL draft.
COLLEGE NOTES: Coffeyville, 1994 and 1995; Oklahoma, 1996 and 1997. ... Games: 1994 (games played unavailable), 1995 (games played unavailable), 1996 (11), 1997 (12). Total: 23.

WILLIAMS, SHAUN   S   GIANTS

PERSONAL: Born October 10, 1976, in Los Angeles. ... 6-2/204. ... Full name: Shaun LeJon Williams.
HIGH SCHOOL: Crespi (Encino, Calif.).

COLLEGE: UCLA.

TRANSACTIONS/CAREER NOTES: Selected by New York Giants in first round (24th pick overall) of 1998 NFL draft.

HONORS: Named free safety on THE SPORTING NEWS college All-America second team (1997).

| Year Team | G | INTERCEPTIONS | | | | SACKS |
		No.	Yds.	Avg.	TD	No.
1994—UCLA	11	0	0	...	0	0.0
1995—UCLA	11	0	0	...	0	0.0
1996—UCLA	9	1	0	0.0	0	3.0
1997—UCLA	9	2	3	1.5	0	1.0
College totals (4 years)	40	3	3	1.0	0	4.0

WISTROM, GRANT　　　DE　　　RAMS

PERSONAL: Born July 3, 1976, in Webb City, Mo. ... 6-5/273.

HIGH SCHOOL: Webb City (Mo.).

COLLEGE: Nebraska.

TRANSACTIONS/CAREER NOTES: Selected by St. Louis Rams in first round (sixth pick overall) of 1998 NFL draft.

HONORS: Named defensive end on THE SPORTING NEWS college All-America first team (1996 and 1997).

Year Team	G	SACKS
1994—Nebraska	12	4.5
1995—Nebraska	11	4.0
1996—Nebraska	12	9.5
1997—Nebraska	12	8.5
College totals (4 years)	47	26.5

WONG, KAILEE　　　DE　　　VIKINGS

PERSONAL: Born May 23, 1976, in Eugene, Ore. ... 6-2/267.

HIGH SCHOOL: North Eugene (Ore.).

COLLEGE: Stanford.

TRANSACTIONS/CAREER NOTES: Selected by Minnesota Vikings in second round (51st pick overall) of 1998 NFL draft.

| Year Team | G | INTERCEPTIONS | | | | SACKS |
		No.	Yds.	Avg.	TD	No.
1994—Stanford	11	0	0	...	0	1.0
1995—Stanford	11	0	0	...	0	1.0
1996—Stanford	11	1	53	53.0	1	12.0
1997—Stanford	11	0	0	...	0	12.0
College totals (4 years)	44	1	53	53.0	1	26.0

WOODSON, CHARLES　　　CB　　　RAIDERS

PERSONAL: Born October 7, 1976, in Fremont, Ohio. ... 6-1/197.

HIGH SCHOOL: Ross (Fremont, Ohio).

COLLEGE: Michigan.

TRANSACTIONS/CAREER NOTES: Selected after junior season by Oakland Raiders in first round (fourth pick overall) of 1998 NFL draft.

HONORS: Named cornerback on THE SPORTING NEWS college All-America second team (1996). ... Heisman Trophy winner (1997). ... Jim Thorpe Award winner (1997). ... Maxwell Award winner (1997). ... Named College Football Player of the Year by THE SPORTING NEWS (1997). ... Named cornerback on THE SPORTING NEWS college All-America first team (1997).

COLLEGE NOTES: Rushed six times for 152 yards and one touchdown (1996); and rushed three times for 15 yards and one touchdown, attempted one pass with one completion for 28 yards, returned 33 punts for 283 yards and one touchdown and credited with one sack (1997).

| Year Team | G | INTERCEPTIONS | | | | RECEIVING | | | | TOTALS | |
		No.	Yds.	Avg.	TD	No.	Yds.	Avg.	TD	TD	Pts.
1995—Michigan	12	5	46	9.2	0	0	0	...	0	0	0
1996—Michigan	11	4	28	7.0	0	10	139	13.9	1	2	12
1997—Michigan	11	7	7	1.0	0	11	231	21.0	2	4	24
College totals (3 years)	34	16	81	5.1	0	21	370	17.6	3	6	36

HEAD COACHES

CAPERS, DOM — PANTHERS

PERSONAL: Born August 7, 1950, in Cambridge, Ohio. ... Full name: Dominic Capers.
HIGH SCHOOL: Meadowbrook (Byesville, Ohio).
COLLEGE: Mount Union, Ohio (bachelor's degree in psychology and physical education), then Kent (master's degree in administration).

HEAD COACHING RECORD
BACKGROUND: Graduate assistant, Kent State (1972-1974). ... Graduate assistant, Washington (1975). ... Defensive backs coach, Hawaii (1975). ... Defensive coordinator, Hawaii (1976). ... Defensive assistant coach, San Jose State (1977). ... Defensive assistant coach, California (1978 and 1979). ... Defensive backs coach, Tennessee (1980 and 1981). ... Defensive backs coach, Ohio State (1982 and 1983). ... Defensive backs coach, Philadelphia Stars USFL (1984). ... Defensive backs coach, Baltimore Stars USFL (1985). ... Defensive backs coach, New Orleans Saints NFL (1986-1991). ... Defensive coordinator, Pittsburgh Steelers NFL (1992-1994).
HONORS: Named NFL Coach of the Year by THE SPORTING NEWS (1996).

		REGULAR SEASON				POST-SEASON	
	W	L	T	Pct.	Finish	W	L
1995—Carolina NFL	7	9	0	.438	T3rd/NFC Western Division	—	—
1996—Carolina NFL	12	4	0	.750	T1st/NFC Western Division	1	1
1997—Carolina NFL	7	9	0	.438	T2nd/NFC Western Division	—	—
Pro totals (3 years)	26	22	0	.542	**Pro totals (1 year)**	1	1

NOTES:
1996—Defeated Dallas, 26-17, in conference playoff game; lost to Green Bay, 30-13, in NFC championship game.

CARROLL, PETE — PATRIOTS

PERSONAL: Born September 15, 1951, in San Francisco. ... Full name: Peter C. Carroll.
HIGH SCHOOL: Larkspur (Calif.)-Redwood.
COLLEGE: Pacific (bachelor's degree in business administration, 1974; master's degree in physical education, 1978).

HEAD COACHING RECORD
BACKGROUND: Assistant coach, Arkansas (1977). ... Assistant coach, Iowa State (1978). ... Assistant coach, Ohio State (1979). ... Assistant coach, North Carolina State (1980-82). ... Assistant coach, Pacific (1983). ... Defensive backs coach, Buffalo Bills NFL (1984). ... Defensive backs coach, Minnesota Vikings NFL (1985-89). ... Defensive coordinator, New York Jets NFL (1990-93). ... Defensive coordinator, San Francisco 49ers (1995 and 1996).

		REGULAR SEASON				POST-SEASON	
	W	L	T	Pct.	Finish	W	L
1994—New York Jets NFL	6	10	0	.375	5th/AFC Eastern Division	—	—
1997—New England NFL	10	6	0	.625	1st/AFC Eastern Division	1	1
Pro totals (2 years)	16	16	0	.500	**Pro totals (1 year)**	1	1

NOTES:
1997—Defeated Miami, 17-3, in first-round playoff game; lost to Pittsburgh, 7-6, in conference playoff game.

COSLET, BRUCE — BENGALS

PERSONAL: Born August 5, 1946, in Oakdale, Calif. ... Full name: Bruce Noel Coslet. ... Played tight end.
HIGH SCHOOL: Joint Union (Oakdale, Calif.).
COLLEGE: Pacific (bachelor of arts degree in history and psychology).
TRANSACTIONS/CAREER NOTES: Signed as non-drafted free agent by Cincinnati Bengals (1969).
PRO STATISTICS: 1973—Returned one kickoff for no yards and recovered one fumble. 1975—Rushed once for one yard and recovered two fumbles for two yards. 1976—Recovered two fumbles.

		RECEIVING			TOTALS			
Year Team	G	No.	Yds.	Avg.	TD	TD	Pts.	Fum.
1969—Cincinnati AFL	8	1	39	39.0	1	1	6	0
1970—Cincinnati NFL	14	8	97	12.1	1	1	6	0
1971—Cincinnati NFL	14	21	356	17.0	4	4	24	3
1972—Cincinnati NFL	10	5	48	9.6	1	1	6	0
1973—Cincinnati NFL	13	9	123	13.7	0	0	0	0
1974—Cincinnati NFL	14	2	24	12.0	0	0	0	0
1975—Cincinnati NFL	14	10	117	11.7	0	0	0	0
1976—Cincinnati NFL	14	5	73	14.6	2	2	12	0
AFL totals (1 year)	8	1	39	39.0	1	1	6	0
NFL totals (7 years)	93	60	838	14.0	8	8	48	3
Pro totals (8 years)	101	61	877	14.4	9	9	54	3

HEAD COACHING RECORD
BACKGROUND: Special teams/tight ends coach, San Francisco 49ers NFL (1980). ... Special teams/tight ends coach, Cincinnati Bengals NFL (1981-83). ... Wide receivers coach, Bengals (1984 and 1985). ... Offensive coordinator, Bengals (1986-1989). ... Offensive coordinator, Bengals (1994-October 21, 1996).

	REGULAR SEASON					POST-SEASON	
	W	L	T	Pct.	Finish	W	L
1990—New York Jets NFL	6	10	0	.375	4th/AFC Eastern Division	—	—
1991—New York Jets NFL	8	8	0	.500	T2nd/AFC Eastern Division	0	1
1992—New York Jets NFL	4	12	0	.250	4th/AFC Eastern Division	—	—
1993—New York Jets NFL	8	8	0	.500	3rd/AFC Eastern Division	—	—
1996—Cincinnati NFL	7	2	0	.778	T3rd/AFC Central Division	—	—
1997—Cincinnati NFL	7	9	0	.438	4th/AFC Central Division	—	—
Pro totals (6 years)	40	49	0	.449	**Pro totals (1 year)**	0	1

NOTES:

1991—Lost to Houston, 17-10, in first-round playoff game.
1996—Replaced Dave Shula as coach of Cincinnati (October 21), with 1-6 record and in fifth place.

COUGHLIN, TOM   JAGUARS

PERSONAL: Born August 31, 1946, in Waterloo, N.Y.
HIGH SCHOOL: Waterloo (N.Y.).
COLLEGE: Syracuse (bachelor's degree in education, 1968; master's degree in education, 1969).

HEAD COACHING RECORD

BACKGROUND: Graduate assistant/freshman coach, Syracuse (1969). ... Assistant coach, Rochester Institute of Technology (1969). ... Offensive coordinator, Syracuse (1974-79). ... Quarterbacks coach, Boston College (1980-83). ... Receivers coach, Philadelphia Eagles NFL (1984 and 1985). ... Receivers coach, Green Bay Packers NFL (1986 and 1987). ... Receivers coach, New York Giants NFL (1988-90).

	REGULAR SEASON					POST-SEASON	
	W	L	T	Pct.	Finish	W	L
1970—Rochester Tech	4	3	0	.571	Eastern College Athletic Conference	—	—
1971—Rochester Tech	5	2	1	.688	Eastern College Athletic Conference	—	—
1972—Rochester Tech	4	5	0	.444	Eastern College Athletic Conference	—	—
1973—Rochester Tech	3	5	1	.389	Eastern College Athletic Conference	—	—
1991—Boston College	4	7	0	.364	7th/Big East Conference	—	—
1992—Boston College	8	2	1	.773	3rd/Big East Conference	0	1
1993—Boston College	8	3	0	.727	3rd/Big East Conference	1	0
1995—Jacksonville NFL	4	12	0	.250	5th/AFC Central Division	—	—
1996—Jacksonville NFL	9	7	0	.563	2nd/AFC Central Division	2	1
1997—Jacksonville NFL	11	5	0	.688	T1st/AFC Central Division	0	1
College totals (7 years)	36	27	3	.568	**College totals (2 years)**	1	1
Pro totals (3 years)	24	24	0	.500	**Pro totals (2 years)**	2	2

NOTES:

1992—Lost to Tennessee, 38-23, in Hall of Fame Bowl.
1993—Defeated Virginia, 31-13, in CarQuest Bowl.
1996—Defeated Buffalo, 30-27, in first-round playoff game; defeated Denver, 30-27, in conference playoff game; lost to New England, 20-6, in AFC championship game.
1997—Lost to Denver, 42-17, in first-round playoff game.

COWHER, BILL   STEELERS

PERSONAL: Born May 8, 1957, in Pittsburgh. ... Full name: William Laird Cowher. ... Played linebacker.
HIGH SCHOOL: Carlynton (Crafton, Pa.).
COLLEGE: North Carolina State (degree in education, 1979).
TRANSACTIONS/CAREER NOTES: Signed as non-drafted free agent by Philadelphia Eagles (May 8, 1979). ... Released by Eagles (August 14, 1979). ... Signed by Cleveland Browns (February 27, 1980). ... On injured reserve with knee injury (August 20, 1981-entire season). ... Traded by Browns to Eagles for ninth-round pick (WR Don Jones) in 1984 draft (August 21, 1983). ... On injured reserve with knee injury (September 25, 1984-remainder of season).
PLAYING EXPERIENCE: Cleveland NFL, 1980 and 1982; Philadelphia NFL, 1983 and 1984. ... Games: 1980 (16), 1982 (9), 1983 (16), 1984 (4). Total: 45.
PRO STATISTICS: 1983—Recovered one fumble.

HEAD COACHING RECORD

BACKGROUND: Special teams coach, Cleveland Browns NFL (1985 and 1986). ... Defensive backs coach, Browns (1987 and 1988). ... Defensive coordinator, Kansas City Chiefs NFL (1989-91).
HONORS: Named NFL Coach of the Year by THE SPORTING NEWS (1992).

	REGULAR SEASON					POST-SEASON	
	W	L	T	Pct.	Finish	W	L
1992—Pittsburgh NFL	11	5	0	.688	1st/AFC Central Division	0	1
1993—Pittsburgh NFL	9	7	0	.563	2nd/AFC Central Division	0	1
1994—Pittsburgh NFL	12	4	0	.750	1st/AFC Central Division	1	1
1995—Pittsburgh NFL	11	5	0	.688	1st/AFC Central Division	2	1
1996—Pittsburgh NFL	10	6	0	.625	1st/AFC Central Division	1	1
1997—Pittsburgh NFL	11	5	0	.688	T1st/AFC Central Division	1	1
Pro totals (6 years)	64	32	0	.667	**Pro totals (6 years)**	5	6

NOTES:
1992—Lost to Buffalo, 24-3, in conference playoff game.
1993—Lost to Kansas City, 27-24 (OT), in first-round playoff game.
1994—Defeated Cleveland, 29-9, in conference playoff game; lost to San Diego, 17-13, in AFC championship game.
1995—Defeated Buffalo, 40-21, in conference playoff game; defeated Indianapolis, 20-16, in AFC championship game; lost to Dallas, 27-17, in Super Bowl XXX.
1996—Defeated Indianapolis, 42-14, in first-round playoff game; lost to New England, 28-3, in conference playoff game.
1997—Defeated New England, 7-6, in conference playoff game; lost to Denver, 24-21, in AFC championship game.

DITKA, MIKE   SAINTS

PERSONAL: Born October 18, 1939, in Carnegie, Pa. ... Full name: Michael Keller Ditka. ... Played tight end.
HIGH SCHOOL: Aliquippa (Pa.).
COLLEGE: Pittsburgh.
TRANSACTIONS/CAREER NOTES: Selected by Chicago Bears in first round of 1961 NFL draft. ... Traded by Bears to Philadelphia Eagles for quarterback Jack Concannon and a pick in 1968 draft (April 26, 1967). ... Traded by Eagles to Dallas Cowboys for WR Dave McDaniels (January 18, 1969).
CHAMPIONSHIP GAME EXPERIENCE: Played in NFL championship game (1963 season). ... Played in NFC championship game (1970-1972 seasons). ... Played in Super Bowl V (1970 season). ... Member of Super Bowl championship team (1971 season).
HONORS: Named end on THE SPORTING NEWS college All-America first team (1960). ... Named NFL Rookie of the Year by THE SPORTING NEWS (1961). ... Named tight end on THE SPORTING NEWS NFL Western Conference All-Star team (1961-1965). ... Played in Pro Bowl (1961-1965 seasons). ... Inducted into Pro Football Hall of Fame (1988).
RECORDS: Shares NFL career record for most touchdowns by recovery of own fumbles—2.
PRO STATISTICS: 1962—Recovered one fumble for a touchdown. 1964—Recovered one fumble for a touchdown. 1969—Fumbled once. 1971—Rushed twice for two yards, returned three kickoffs for 30 yards and recovered one fumble.

		RECEIVING				TOTALS		
Year Team	G	No.	Yds.	Avg.	TD	TD	Pts.	Fum.
1961—Chicago NFL	14	56	1076	19.2	12	12	72	0
1962—Chicago NFL	14	58	904	15.6	5	6	36	0
1963—Chicago NFL	14	59	794	13.5	8	3	48	0
1964—Chicago NFL	14	75	897	12.0	5	6	36	0
1965—Chicago NFL	14	36	454	12.6	2	2	12	0
1966—Chicago NFL	14	32	378	11.8	2	2	12	0
1967—Philadelphia NFL	9	26	274	10.5	2	2	12	0
1968—Philadelphia NFL	11	13	111	8.5	2	3	12	0
1969—Dallas NFL	12	17	268	15.8	3	3	18	1
1970—Dallas NFL	14	8	98	12.3	0	0	0	0
1971—Dallas NFL	14	30	360	12.0	1	1	6	0
1972—Dallas NFL	14	17	198	11.6	1	1	6	0
Pro totals (12 years)	158	427	5812	13.6	43	43	258	1

HEAD COACHING RECORD

BACKGROUND: Receivers coach, Dallas Cowboys NFL (1973 and 1974). ... Special teams/tight ends coach, Cowboys (1975, 1976 and 1980). ... Special teams/receivers coach, Cowboys (1977-1979 and 1981).
HONORS: Named NFL Coach of the Year by THE SPORTING NEWS (1985).

		REGULAR SEASON					POST-SEASON	
	W	L	T	Pct.	Finish		W	L
1982—Chicago NFL	3	6	0	.333	T11th/NFC		—	—
1983—Chicago NFL	8	8	0	.500	T2nd/NFC Central Division		—	—
1984—Chicago NFL	10	6	0	.625	1st/NFC Central Division		1	1
1985—Chicago NFL	15	1	0	.938	1st/NFC Central Division		3	0
1986—Chicago NFL	14	2	0	.875	1st/NFC Central Division		0	1
1987—Chicago NFL	11	4	0	.733	1st/NFC Central Division		0	1
1988—Chicago NFL	12	4	0	.750	1st/NFC Central Division		1	1
1989—Chicago NFL	6	10	0	.375	4th/NFC Central Division		—	—
1990—Chicago NFL	11	5	0	.688	1st/NFC Central Division		1	1
1991—Chicago NFL	11	5	0	.688	2nd/NFC Central Division		0	1
1992—Chicago NFL	5	11	0	.313	T3rd/NFC Central Division		—	—
1997—New Orleans NFL	6	10	0	.375	4th/NFC Western Division		—	—
Pro totals (12 years)	112	72	0	.609	Pro totals (7 years)		6	6

NOTES:
1984—Defeated Washington, 23-19, in conference playoff game; lost to San Francisco, 23-0, in NFC championship game.
1985—Defeated New York Giants, 21-0, in conference playoff game; defeated Los Angeles Rams, 24-0, in NFC championship game; defeated New England, 46-10, in Super Bowl XX.
1986—Lost to Washington, 27-13, in conference playoff game.
1987—Lost to Washington, 21-17, in conference playoff game.
1988—Record includes two games missed due to heart attack suffered on November 1; assistant coach Vince Tobin was 2-0 during that time. Defeated Philadelphia, 20-12, in conference playoff game; lost to San Francisco, 28-3, in NFC championship game.
1990—Defeated New Orleans, 16-6, in first-round playoff game; lost to New York Giants, 31-3, in conference playoff game.
1991—Lost to Dallas, 17-13, in first-round playoff game.

DUNGY, TONY   BUCCANEERS

PERSONAL: Born October 6, 1955, in Jackson, Mich. ... Full name: Anthony Kevin Dungy. ... Name pronounced DUN-gee. ... Played defensive back and quarterback.
HIGH SCHOOL: Parkside (Jackson, Mich.).

COLLEGE: Minnesota (degree in business administration, 1978).

TRANSACTIONS/CAREER NOTES: Signed as non-drafted free agent by Pittsburgh Steelers (May 1977). ... Traded by Steelers to San Francisco 49ers for 10th-round pick in 1980 draft (August 21, 1979). ... Traded by 49ers with RB Mike Hogan to New York Giants for WR Jimmy Robinson and CB Ray Rhodes (March 27, 1980).

CHAMPIONSHIP GAME EXPERIENCE: Played in AFC championship game (1978 season). ... Played in Super Bowl XIII (1978 season).

PRO STATISTICS: 1977—Attempted eight passes with three completions for 43 yards and two interceptions, rushed three times for eight yards and fumbled once. 1978—Recovered two fumbles for eight yards. 1979—Recovered two fumbles.

		INTERCEPTIONS			
Year Team	G	No.	Yds.	Avg.	TD
1977—Pittsburgh NFL	14	3	37	12.3	0
1978—Pittsburgh NFL	16	6	95	15.8	0
1979—San Francisco NFL	15	0	0	...	0
Pro totals (3 years)	45	9	132	14.7	0

HEAD COACHING RECORD

BACKGROUND: Defensive backs coach, Minnesota (1980). ... Defensive assistant, Pittsburgh Steelers NFL (1981). ... Defensive backs coach, Steelers (1982 and 1983). ... Defensive coordinator, Steelers (1984-1988). ... Defensive backs coach, Kansas City Chiefs NFL (1989-1991). ... Defensive coordinator, Minnesota Vikings NFL (1992-1995).

		REGULAR SEASON				POST-SEASON	
	W	L	T	Pct.	Finish	W	L
1996—Tampa Bay NFL	6	10	0	.375	4th/NFC Central Division	—	—
1997—Tampa Bay NFL	10	6	0	.625	2nd/NFC Central Division	1	1
Pro totals (2 years)	16	16	0	.500	Pro totals (1 year)	1	1

NOTES:

1997—Defeated Detroit, 20-10, in first-round playoff game; lost to Green Bay, 21-7, in conference playoff game.

ERICKSON, DENNIS — SEAHAWKS

PERSONAL: Born March 24, 1947, in Everett, Wash.
HIGH SCHOOL: Everett (Wash.).
COLLEGE: Montana State (degree in physical education, 1970).

HEAD COACHING RECORD

BACKGROUND: Graduate assistant, Montana State (1969). ... Graduate assistant, Washington State (spring 1970). ... Head coach, Billings (Mont.) Central High (1970; record: 7-2). ... Offensive backs coach, Montana State (1971-73). ... Offensive coordinator, Idaho (1974 and 1975). ... Offensive coordinator, Fresno State (1976-78). ... Offensive coordinator, San Jose State (1979-81).

HONORS: Named College Football Coach of the Year by THE SPORTING NEWS (1992).

		REGULAR SEASON				POST-SEASON	
	W	L	T	Pct.	Finish	W	L
1982—Idaho	8	3	0	.727	T2nd/Big Sky Conference	1	1
1983—Idaho	8	3	0	.727	T3rd/Big Sky Conference	—	—
1984—Idaho	6	5	0	.545	T3rd/Big Sky Conference	—	—
1985—Idaho	9	2	0	.818	1st/Big Sky Conference	0	1
1986—Wyoming	6	6	0	.500	T4th/Western Athletic Conference	—	—
1987—Washington State	3	7	1	.318	9th/Pacific-10 Conference	—	—
1988—Washington State	8	3	0	.727	T3rd/Pacific-10 Conference	1	0
1989—Miami (Fla.)	10	1	0	.909	Independent	1	0
1990—Miami (Fla.)	9	2	0	.818	Independent	1	0
1991—Miami (Fla.)	11	0	0	1.000	Independent	1	0
1992—Miami (Fla.)	11	0	0	1.000	1st/Big East Conference	0	1
1993—Miami (Fla.)	9	2	0	.818	2nd/Big East Conference	0	1
1994—Miami (Fla.)	10	1	0	.909	1st/Big East Conference	0	1
1995—Seattle NFL	8	8	0	.500	T3rd/AFC Western Division	—	—
1996—Seattle NFL	7	9	0	.438	T4th/AFC Western Division	—	—
1997—Seattle NFL	8	8	0	.500	3rd/AFC Western Division	—	—
College totals (13 years)	108	35	1	.753	College totals (9 years)	5	5
Pro totals (3 years)	23	25	0	.479			

NOTES:

1982—Defeated Montana, 21-7, in first round of NCAA Division I-AA playoffs; lost to Eastern Kentucky, 38-30, in second round of NCAA Division I-AA playoffs.
1985—Lost to Eastern Washington, 42-38, in first round of NCAA Division I-AA playoffs.
1988—Defeated Houston, 24-22, in Aloha Bowl.
1989—Defeated Alabama, 33-25, in Sugar Bowl.
1990—Defeated Texas, 46-3, in Cotton Bowl.
1991—Defeated Nebraska, 22-0, in Orange Bowl.
1992—Lost to Alabama, 34-13, in Sugar Bowl.
1993—Lost to Arizona, 29-0, in Fiesta Bowl.
1994—Lost to Nebraska, 24-17, in Orange Bowl.

FASSEL, JIM — GIANTS

PERSONAL: Born August 31, 1949, in Anaheim, Calif. ... Full name: James Fassel.
HIGH SCHOOL: Anaheim (Calif.).
JUNIOR COLLEGE: Fullerton College (Calif.).

COLLEGE: Southern California, then Long Beach State (degree in physical education, 1972).
TRANSACTIONS/CAREER NOTES: Selected by Chicago Bears in seventh round of 1972 NFL draft.

HEAD COACHING RECORD
BACKGROUND: Coach, Fullerton College (1973). ... Player/coach, Hawaii Hawaiians WFL (1974). ... Quarterbacks/receivers coach, Utah (1976). ... Offensive coordinator, Weber State (1977 and 1978). ... Offensive coordinator, Stanford (1979-1983). ... Offensive coordinator, New Orleans Breakers USFL (1984) ... Quarterbacks coach, New York Giants NFL (1991). ... Offensive coordinator, Giants (1992) ... Assistant head coach/offensive coordinator, Denver Broncos NFL (1993 and 1994). ... Quarterbacks coach, Oakland Raiders NFL (1995). ... Offensive coordinator/quarterbacks coach, Arizona Cardinals NFL (1996).
HONORS: Named NFL Coach of the Year by THE SPORTING NEWS (1997).

		REGULAR SEASON				POST-SEASON	
	W	L	T	Pct.	Finish	W	L
1985—Utah	8	4	0	.667	2nd/Western Athletic Conference	—	—
1986—Utah	2	9	0	.182	9th/Western Athletic Conference	—	—
1987—Utah	5	7	0	.417	7th/Western Athletic Conference	—	—
1988—Utah	6	5	0	.545	4th/Western Athletic Conference	—	—
1989—Utah	4	8	0	.333	7th/Western Athletic Conference	—	—
1997—New York Giants NFL	10	5	1	.656	1st/NFC Eastern Division	0	1
College totals (5 years)	25	33	0	.431	**College totals**	—	—
Pro totals (1 year)	10	5	1	.656	**Pro totals (1 year)**	0	1

NOTES:
1997—Lost to Minnesota, 23-22, in first-round playoff game.

FISHER, JEFF — OILERS

PERSONAL: Born February 25, 1958, in Culver City, Calif. ... Full name: Jeffrey Michael Fisher. ... Played safety.
HIGH SCHOOL: Woodland Hills (Calif.)-Taft.
COLLEGE: Southern California (degree in public administration, 1981).
TRANSACTIONS/CAREER NOTES: Selected by Chicago Bears in seventh round (177th pick overall) of 1981 NFL draft. ... On injured reserve with broken leg (October 24, 1983-remainder of season). ... On injured reserve with ankle injury (entire 1985 season).
CHAMPIONSHIP GAME EXPERIENCE: Played in NFC championship game (1984 season).
PRO STATISTICS: 1981—Recovered one fumble. 1984—Recovered one fumble.

		INTERCEPTIONS				PUNT RETURNS				KICKOFF RETURNS				TOTALS		
Year Team	G	No.	Yds.	Avg.	TD	No.	Yds.	Avg.	TD	No.	Yds.	Avg.	TD	TD	Pts.	Fum.
1981—Chicago NFL	16	2	3	1.5	0	43	509	11.8	1	7	102	14.6	0	1	6	3
1982—Chicago NFL	9	3	19	6.3	0	7	53	7.6	0	7	102	14.6	0	0	0	2
1983—Chicago NFL	8	0	0	...	0	13	71	5.5	0	0	0	...	0	0	0	0
1984—Chicago NFL	16	0	0	...	0	57	492	8.6	0	0	0	...	0	0	0	4
1985—Chicago NFL								Did not play.								
Pro totals (4 years)	49	5	22	4.4	0	120	1125	9.4	1	14	204	14.6	0	1	6	9

HEAD COACHING RECORD
BACKGROUND: Defensive backs coach, Philadelphia Eagles NFL (1986-88). ... Defensive coordinator, Eagles (1989 and 1990). ... Defensive coordinator, Los Angeles Rams NFL (1991). ... Defensive backs coach, San Francisco 49ers NFL (1992 and 1993). ... Defensive coordinator, Houston Oilers NFL (February 9-November 14, 1994). ... Oilers franchise moved to Tennessee for 1997 season.

		REGULAR SEASON				POST-SEASON	
	W	L	T	Pct.	Finish	W	L
1994—Houston NFL	1	5	0	.167	4th/AFC Central Division	—	—
1995—Houston NFL	7	9	0	.438	T2nd/AFC Central Division	—	—
1996—Houston NFL	8	8	0	.500	T3rd/AFC Central Division	—	—
1997—Tennessee NFL	8	8	0	.500	3rd/AFC Central Division	—	—
Pro totals (4 years)	24	30	0	.444			

NOTES:
1994—Replaced Jack Pardee as coach of Houston (November 14), with 1-9 record and in fourth place.

GAILEY, CHAN — COWBOYS

PERSONAL: Born January 5, 1952, in Gainesville, Ga. ... Full name: Thomas Chandler Gailey.
COLLEGE: Florida (degree in physical education, 1974).

HEAD COACHING RECORD
BACKGROUND: Graduate assistant, Florida (1974-75). ... Defensive backfield coach, Troy State (1976-79). ... Defensive backfield coach, Air Force (1979-82). ... Head coach, Troy State (1983 and 1984). ... Assistant coach, Denver Broncos NFL (1985-88). ... Offensive coordinator/wide receivers coach, Broncos (1989 and 1990). ... Head coach, Birmingham Fire W.L. (1991 and 1992). ... Head coach, Samford (1993). ... Wide receivers coach, Pittsburgh Steelers NFL (1994 and 1995). ... Offensive coordinator, Steelers NFL (1996 and 1997).

		REGULAR SEASON				POST-SEASON	
	W	L	T	Pct.	Finish	W	L
1983—Troy State	7	4	0	.636	T2nd/Gulf Coast Conference		
1984—Troy State	9	1	0	.900	1st/Gulf Coast Conference	3	0
1991—Birmingham CFL	5	5	0	.500	1st/North American West Division	0	1
1992—Birmingham CFL	7	2	1	.750	2nd/North American West Division	0	1
1993—Samford	5	6	0	.455	Independent	—	—
College totals (3 years)	21	11	0	.656	**College totals (1 year)**	3	0
Pro totals (2 years)	12	7	1	.625	**Pro totals (2 years)**	0	2

NOTES:

1984—Defeated Central State, 31-21, in first-round playoff game; defeated Towson State, 45-3, in semifinal playoff game; defeated North Dakota, 18-17, in championship game.
1991—Lost to Barcelona, 10-3, in first-round playoff game.
1992—Lost to Orlando, 45-7, in first-round playoff game.

GILBRIDE, KEVIN — CHARGERS

PERSONAL: Born August 27, 1951, in New Haven, Conn.
HIGH SCHOOL: North Haven (Conn.).
COLLEGE: Southern Connecticut State (bachelor's degree in physical education), then Idaho State (master's degree in sports administration).

HEAD COACHING RECORD

BACKGROUND: Defensive coordinator, Tufts University (1976 and 1977). ... Defensive coordinator, American International (1978 and 1979). ... Quarterbacks/receivers coach, Ottawa Rough Riders of Canadian Football League (1985). ... Offensive coordinator, Rough Riders (1986). ... Passing game coordinator, East Carolina (1987). ... Offensive coordinator, East Carolina (1988). ... Assistant head coach/offensive coordinator, Houston Oilers (1993 and 1994). ... Offensive coordinator, Jacksonville Jaguars NFL (1995 and 1996).

	W	L	T	Pct.	Finish (REGULAR SEASON)	POST-SEASON W	L
1980—Southern Connecticut State.	5	4	1	.550	Independent	—	—
1981—Southern Connecticut State.	6	3	1	.650	Independent	—	—
1982—Southern Connecticut State.	9	1	0	.900	Independent	—	—
1983—Southern Connecticut State.	8	3	0	.727	Independent	—	—
1984—Southern Connecticut State.	7	3	0	.700	Independent	—	—
1997—San Diego NFL	4	12	0	.250	T4th/AFC Western Division	—	—
College totals (5 years)	35	14	2	.706			
Pro totals (1 year)	4	12	0	.250			

GREEN, DENNIS — VIKINGS

PERSONAL: Born February 17, 1949, in Harrisburg, Pa.
HIGH SCHOOL: John Harris (Harrisburg, Pa.).
COLLEGE: Iowa (degree in recreation education, 1971).

HEAD COACHING RECORD

BACKGROUND: Graduate assistant, Iowa (1972). ... Running backs/receivers coach, Dayton (1973). ... Running backs/receivers coach, Iowa (1974-1976). ... Running backs coach, Stanford (1977 and 1978). ... Special teams coach, San Francisco 49ers NFL (1979). ... Offensive coordinator, Stanford (1980). ... Receivers coach, 49ers (1986-1988).

	W	L	T	Pct.	Finish (REGULAR SEASON)	POST-SEASON W	L
1981—Northwestern	0	11	0	.000	10th/Big Ten Conference	—	—
1982—Northwestern	3	8	0	.273	T8th/Big Ten Conference	—	—
1983—Northwestern	2	9	0	.182	T8th/Big Ten Conference	—	—
1984—Northwestern	2	9	0	.182	9th/Big Ten Conference	—	—
1985—Northwestern	3	8	0	.273	T9th/Big Ten Conference	—	—
1989—Stanford	3	8	0	.273	T7th/Pacific-10 Conference	—	—
1990—Stanford	5	6	0	.455	T6th/Pacific-10 Conference	—	—
1991—Stanford	8	3	0	.727	T2nd/Pacific-10 Conference	0	1
1992—Minnesota NFL	11	5	0	.688	1st/NFC Central Division	0	1
1993—Minnesota NFL	9	7	0	.563	2nd/NFC Central Division	0	1
1994—Minnesota NFL	10	6	0	.625	1st/NFC Central Division	0	1
1995—Minnesota NFL	8	8	0	.500	4th/NFC Central Division	—	—
1996—Minnesota NFL	9	7	0	.563	2nd/NFC Central Division	0	1
1997—Minnesota NFL	9	7	0	.563	T3rd/NFC Central Division	1	1
College totals (8 years)	26	62	0	.295	College totals (1 year)	0	1
Pro totals (6 years)	56	40	0	.583	Pro totals (5 years)	1	5

NOTES:

1991—Lost to Georgia Tech, 18-17, in Aloha Bowl.
1992—Lost to Washington, 24-7, in first-round playoff game.
1993—Lost to New York Giants, 17-10, in first-round playoff game.
1994—Lost to Chicago, 35-18, in first-round playoff game.
1996—Lost to Dallas, 40-15, in first-round playoff game.
1997—Defeated New York Giants, 23-22, in first-round playoff game; lost to San Francisco, 38-22, in conference playoff game.

GRUDEN, JON — RAIDERS

PERSONAL: Born August 17, 1963, in Sandusky, Ohio. ... Son of Jim Gruden, scout with San Francisco 49ers; and brother of Jay Gruden, quarterback with Tampa Bay Storm of Arena League (1991-1996).
HIGH SCHOOL: Clay (South Bend, Ind.).
COLLEGE: Dayton (degree in communications, 1985), then Tennessee.

HEAD COACHING RECORD

BACKGROUND: Graduate assistant, Tennessee (1986-87). ... Passing game coordinator, Southeast Missouri State (1988). ... Wide receivers coach, Pacific (1989). ... Assistant coach, San Francisco 49ers NFL (1990) ... Wide receivers coach, Pittsburgh (1991). ... Offensive/quality control coach, Green Bay Packers NFL (1992). ... Wide receivers coach, Packers (1993 and 1994). ... Offensive coordinator, Philadelphia Eagles NFL (1995-97).

PERSONAL: Born June 15, 1948, in San Francisco. ... Full name: Michael George Holmgren.
HIGH SCHOOL: Lincoln (San Francisco).
COLLEGE: Southern California (degree in business finance, 1970).
TRANSACTIONS/CAREER NOTES: Selected by St. Louis Cardinals in eighth round of 1970 NFL draft. ... Released by Cardinals (1970).

HEAD COACHING RECORD
BACKGROUND: Assistant coach, Sacred Heart Cathedral Prep School, San Francisco (1972 and 1973). ... Assistant coach, Oak Grove High School, San Jose, Calif. (1975-1980). ... Offensive coordinator/quarterbacks coach, San Francisco State (1981). ... Quarterbacks coach, Brigham Young (1982-1985). ... Quarterbacks coach, San Francisco 49ers NFL (1986-1988). ... Offensive coordinator, 49ers (1989-1991).

		REGULAR SEASON				POST-SEASON	
	W	L	T	Pct.	Finish	W	L
1992—Green Bay NFL	9	7	0	.563	2nd/NFC Central Division	—	—
1993—Green Bay NFL	9	7	0	.563	T2nd/NFC Central Division	1	1
1994—Green Bay NFL	9	7	0	.563	T2nd/NFC Central Division	1	1
1995—Green Bay NFL	11	5	0	.688	1st/NFC Central Division	2	1
1996—Green Bay NFL	13	3	0	.813	1st/NFC Central Division	3	0
1997—Green Bay NFL	13	3	0	.813	1st/NFC Central Division	2	1
Pro totals (6 years)	**64**	**32**	**0**	**.667**	**Pro totals (5 years)**	**9**	**4**

NOTES:
1993—Defeated Detroit, 28-24, in first-round playoff game; lost to Dallas 27-17, in conference playoff game.
1994—Defeated Detroit, 16-12, in first-round playoff game; lost to Dallas, 35-9, in conference playoff game.
1995—Defeated Atlanta, 37-20, in first-round playoff game; defeated San Francisco, 27-17, in conference playoff game; lost to Dallas, 38-27, in NFC championship game.
1996—Defeated San Francisco, 35-14, in conference playoff game; defeated Carolina, 30-13, in NFC championship game; defeated New England, 35-21, in Super Bowl XXXI.
1997—Defeated Tampa Bay, 21-7, in conference playoff game; defeated San Francisco, 23-10, in NFC championship game; lost to Denver, 31-24, in Super Bowl XXXII.

PERSONAL: Born July 16, 1943, in Port Arthur, Texas. ... Full name: James William Johnson.
HIGH SCHOOL: Thomas Jefferson (Port Arthur, Texas).
COLLEGE: Arkansas (degree in psychology, 1965).

HEAD COACHING RECORD
BACKGROUND: Assistant coach, Louisiana Tech (1965). ... Assistant coach, Wichita State (1967). ... Assistant coach, Iowa State (1968 and 1969). ... Assistant coach, Oklahoma (1970-72). ... Assistant coach, Arkansas (1973-76). ... Assistant coach, Pittsburgh (1977 and 1978).

		REGULAR SEASON				POST-SEASON	
	W	L	T	Pct.	Finish	W	L
1979—Oklahoma State	7	4	0	.636	3rd/Big Eight Conference	—	—
1980—Oklahoma State	3	7	1	.318	5th/Big Eight Conference	—	—
1981—Oklahoma State	7	4	0	.636	T3rd/Big Eight Conference	—	—
1982—Oklahoma State	4	5	2	.455	3rd/Big Eight Conference	—	—
1983—Oklahoma State	7	4	0	.636	T4th/Big Eight Conference	—	—
1984—Miami (Fla.)	8	4	0	.667	Independent	—	—
1985—Miami (Fla.)	10	1	0	.909	Independent	—	—
1986—Miami (Fla.)	11	0	0	1.000	Independent	—	—
1987—Miami (Fla.)	11	0	0	1.000	Independent	—	—
1988—Miami (Fla.)	10	1	0	.909	Independent	—	—
1989—Dallas NFL	1	15	0	.063	5th/NFC Eastern Division	—	—
1990—Dallas NFL	7	9	0	.438	4th/NFC Eastern Division	—	—
1991—Dallas NFL	11	5	0	.688	2nd/NFC Eastern Division	1	1
1992—Dallas NFL	13	3	0	.813	1st/NFC Eastern Division	3	0
1993—Dallas NFL	12	4	0	.750	1st/NFC Eastern Division	3	0
1996—Miami NFL	8	8	0	.500	4th/AFC Eastern Division	—	—
1997—Miami NFL	9	7	0	.563	T2nd/AFC Eastern Division	0	1
College totals (10 years)	**78**	**30**	**3**	**.716**			
Pro totals (7 years)	**61**	**51**	**0**	**.545**	**Pro totals (4 years)**	**7**	**2**

NOTES:
1980—Oklahoma State played to a 14-14 forfeit tie against Kansas (October 25).
1981—Lost to Texas A&M, 33-16, in Independence Bowl.
1983—Defeated Baylor, 24-14, in Bluebonnet Bowl.
1984—Lost to UCLA, 39-37, in Fiesta Bowl.
1985—Lost to Tennessee, 35-7, in Sugar Bowl.
1986—Lost to Penn State, 14-10, in Fiesta Bowl.
1987—Defeated Oklahoma, 20-14, in Orange Bowl.
1988—Defeated Nebraska, 23-3, in Orange Bowl.
1991—Defeated Chicago, 17-13, in first-round playoff game; lost to Detroit, 38-6, in conference playoff game.
1992—Defeated Philadelphia, 34-10, in conference playoff game; defeated San Francisco, 30-20, in NFC championship game; defeated Buffalo, 52-17, in Super Bowl XXVII.
1993—Defeated Green Bay, 27-17, in conference playoff game; defeated San Francisco, 38-21, in NFC championship game; defeated Buffalo, 30-13, in Super Bowl XXVIII.
1997—Lost to New England, 17-3, in first-round playoff game.

MARCHIBRODA, TED — RAVENS

PERSONAL: Born March 15, 1931, in Franklin, Pa. ... Full name: Theodore Joseph Marchibroda. ... Played quarterback.
HIGH SCHOOL: Franklin (Pa.).
COLLEGE: St. Bonaventure, then Detroit (degree in physical education, 1953).
TRANSACTIONS/CAREER NOTES: Selected by Pittsburgh Steelers in first round of 1953 NFL draft. ... On military list (1954). ... Released by Steelers (1957). ... Signed by Chicago Cardinals (1957).
PRO STATISTICS: 1953—Returned one kickoff for 25 yards. 1957—Recovered one fumble.

Year Team	G	Att.	Cmp.	Pct.	Yds.	TD	Int.	Avg.	Rat.	Att.	Yds.	Avg.	TD	TD	Pts.
				PASSING							RUSHING			TOTALS	
1953—Pittsburgh NFL	4	22	9	40.9	66	1	2	3.00	25.9	1	15	15.0	0	0	0
1954—Pittsburgh NFL					Did not play.										
1955—Pittsburgh NFL	10	43	24	55.8	280	2	3	6.51	62.2	6	-1	-0.2	1	1	6
1956—Pittsburgh NFL	12	275	124	45.1	1585	12	19	5.76	49.4	39	152	3.9	2	2	12
1957—Chicago NFL	7	45	15	33.3	238	1	5	5.29	19.7	4	10	2.5	0	0	0
Pro totals (4 years)	33	385	172	44.7	2169	16	29	5.63	45.3	50	176	3.5	3	3	18

HEAD COACHING RECORD

BACKGROUND: Offensive backfield coach, Washington Redskins NFL (1961-65). ... Offensive assistant coach, Los Angeles Rams NFL (1966-70). ... Offensive coordinator, Redskins (1971-74). ... Consultant, Philadelphia Eagles NFL (1980). ... Quarterbacks coach, Chicago Bears (1981). ... Offensive coordinator, Detroit Lions NFL (1982 and 1983). ... Offensive coordinator, Eagles (1984 and 1985). ... Quarterbacks coach, Buffalo Bills NFL (1987 and 1988). ... Offensive coordinator, Bills (1989-91).
HONORS: Named NFL Coach of the Year by THE SPORTING NEWS (1975).

	W	L	T	Pct.	Finish	W	L
		REGULAR SEASON				POST-SEASON	
1975—Baltimore NFL	10	4	0	.714	T1st/AFC Eastern Division	0	1
1976—Baltimore NFL	11	3	0	.786	T1st/AFC Eastern Division	0	1
1977—Baltimore NFL	10	4	0	.714	T1st/AFC Eastern Division	0	1
1978—Baltimore NFL	5	11	0	.313	T4th/AFC Eastern Division	—	—
1979—Baltimore NFL	5	11	0	.313	5th/AFC Eastern Division	—	—
1992—Indianapolis NFL	9	7	0	.563	3rd/AFC Eastern Division	—	—
1993—Indianapolis NFL	4	12	0	.250	5th/AFC Eastern Division	—	—
1994—Indianapolis NFL	8	8	0	.500	3rd/AFC Eastern Division	—	—
1995—Indianapolis NFL	9	7	0	.563	T2nd/AFC Eastern Division	2	1
1996—Baltimore NFL	4	12	0	.250	5th/AFC Central Division	—	—
1997—Baltimore NFL	6	9	1	.406	5th/AFC Central Division	—	—
Pro totals (11 years)	81	88	1	.479	Pro totals (4 years)	2	4

NOTES:
1975—Lost to Pittsburgh, 28-10, in conference playoff game.
1976—Lost to Pittsburgh, 40-14, in conference playoff game.
1977—Lost to Oakland, 37-31 (OT), in conference playoff game.
1995—Defeated San Diego, 35-20, in first-round playoff game; defeated Kansas City, 10-7, in conference playoff game; lost to Pittsburgh, 20-16, in AFC championship game.

MARIUCCI, STEVE — 49ERS

PERSONAL: Born November 4, 1955, in Iron Mountain, Mich. ... Full name: Steven Mariucci.
HIGH SCHOOL: Iron Mountain (Mich.).
COLLEGE: Northern Michigan.
TRANSACTIONS/CAREER NOTES: Signed with Hamilton of the CFL for 1978 season.

HEAD COACHING RECORD

BACKGROUND: Quarterbacks/running backs coach, Northern Michigan (1978 and 1979). ... Quarterbacks/special teams coordinator, Cal State Fullerton (1980-1982). ... Assistant head coach, Louisville (1983 and 1984). ... Receivers coach, Orlando Renegades USFL (1985). ... Quality control coach, Los Angeles Rams NFL (fall, 1985). ... Wide receivers/special teams coach, California (1987-1989). ... Offensive coordinator/quarterbacks coach, Cal (1990 and 1991). ... Quarterbacks coach, Green Bay Packers NFL (1992-1995).

	W	L	T	Pct.	Finish	W	L
		REGULAR SEASON				POST-SEASON	
1996—California	6	6	0	.500	T5th/Pacific-10 Conference	0	1
1997—San Francisco NFL	13	3	0	.813	1st/NFC Western Division	1	1
College totals (1 year)	6	6	0	.500	College totals (1 year)	0	1
Pro totals (1 year)	13	3	0	.813	Pro totals (1 year)	1	1

NOTES:
1996—Lost to Navy, 42-38, in Aloha Bowl.
1997—Defeated Minnesota, 38-22, in conference playoff game; lost to Green Bay, 23-10, in NFC championship game.

MORA, JIM — COLTS

PERSONAL: Born May 24, 1935, in Los Angeles. ... Full name: James Ernest Mora.
HIGH SCHOOL: University (Los Angeles).
COLLEGE: Occidental College (degree in physical education, 1957), then Southern California (master's degree in education, 1967).
MISCELLANEOUS: Played for U.S. Marines at Quantico (1957) and Camp Lejeune (1958 and 1959).

HEAD COACHING RECORD
BACKGROUND: Assistant coach, Occidental College (1960-1963). ... Linebackers coach, Stanford (1967).
HONORS: Named USFL Coach of the Year by THE SPORTING NEWS (1984). ... Name NFL Coach of the Year by THE SPORTING NEWS (1987).

			REGULAR SEASON				POST-SEASON	
	W	L	T	Pct.	Finish		W	L
1964—Occidental	5	4	0	.556	3rd/Southern Calif. Intercollegiate Conference		—	—
1965—Occidental	8	1	0	.889	1st/Southern Calif. Intercollegiate Conference		—	—
1966—Occidental	5	4	0	.556	4th/Southern Calif. Intercollegiate Conference		—	—
1983—Philadelphia USFL	15	3	0	.833	1st/Atlantic Division		1	1
1984—Philadelphia USFL	16	2	0	.889	1st/Eastern Conference Atlantic Division		3	0
1985—Baltimore USFL	10	7	1	.583	4th/Eastern Conference		3	0
1986—New Orleans NFL	7	9	0	.438	4th/Western Division		—	—
1987—New Orleans NFL	12	3	0	.800	2nd/Western Division		0	1
1988—New Orleans NFL	10	6	0	.625	T1st/Western Division		—	—
1989—New Orleans NFL	9	7	0	.563	3rd/Western Division		—	—
1990—New Orleans NFL	8	8	0	.500	2nd/Western Division		0	1
1991—New Orleans NFL	11	5	0	.688	1st/Western Division		0	1
1992—New Orleans NFL	12	4	0	.750	2nd/Western Division		0	1
1993—New Orleans NFL	8	8	0	.500	2nd/Western Division		—	—
1994—New Orleans NFL	7	9	0	.438	T2nd/Western Division		—	—
1995—New Orleans NFL	7	9	0	.438	T3rd/Western Division		—	—
College totals (3 years)	18	9	0	.667				
USFL totals (3 years)	41	12	1	.769	USFL totals (3 years)		7	1
NFL totals (10 years)	91	68	0	.572	NFL totals (4 years)		0	4
Pro totals (13 years)	132	80	1	.622	Pro totals (7 years)		7	5

PARCELLS, BILL — JETS

PERSONAL: Born August 22, 1941, in Englewood, N.J. ... Full name: Duane Charles Parcells.
HIGH SCHOOL: River Dell (Oradell, N.J.).
COLLEGE: Colgate, then Wichita State (degree in education, 1964).

HEAD COACHING RECORD
BACKGROUND: Defensive assistant coach, Hasting (Neb.) College (1964). ... Defensive line coach, Wichita State (1965). ... Linebackers coach, Army (1966-69). ... Linebackers coach, Florida State (1970-72). ... Defensive coordinator, Vanderbilt (1973 an 1974). ... Defensive coordinator, Texas Tech (1975-77). ... Lineackers coach, New England NFL (1980). ... Defensive coordinator and linebackers coach, New York Giants NFL (1981 and 1982).
HONORS: Named NFL Coach of the Year (1986).

			REGULAR SEASON				POST-SEASON	
	W	L	T	Pct.	Finish		W	L
1978—Air Force	3	8	0	.273	Independent		—	—
1983—New York Giants NFL	3	12	1	.219	5th/NFC Eastern Division		—	—
1984—New York Giants NFL	9	7	0	.563	T2nd/NFC Eastern Division		1	1
1985—New York Giants NFL	10	6	0	.625	T1st/NFC Eastern Division		1	1
1986—New York Giants NFL	14	2	0	.875	1st/NFC Eastern Division		3	0
1987—New York Giants NFL	6	9	0	.400	5th/NFC Eastern Division		—	—
1988—New York Giants NFL	10	6	0	.625	T1st/NFC Eastern Division		—	—
1989—New York Giants NFL	12	4	0	.750	1st/NFC Eastern Division		0	1
1990—New York Giants NFL	13	3	0	.813	1st/NFC Eastern Division		3	0
1993—New England NFL	5	11	0	.313	4th/AFC Eastern Division		—	—
1994—New England NFL	10	6	0	.625	T1st/AFC Eastern Division		0	1
1995—New England NFL	6	10	0	.375	4lh/AFC Eastern Division		—	—
1996—New England NFL	11	5	0	.688	1st/AFC Eastern Division		2	1
1997—New York Jets NFL	9	7	0	.563	T2nd/AFC Eastern Division		—	—
College totals (1 year)	3	8	0	.273				
Pro totals (13 years)	118	88	1	.572	Pro totals (7 years)		10	5

NOTES:
1984—Defeated Los Angeles Rams, 16-10, in wild-card playoff game; lost to San Francisco, 21-10, in conference playoff game.
1985—Defeated San Francisco, 17-3, in wild-card playoff game; lost to Chicago, 21-0, in conference playoff game.
1986—Defeated San Francisco, 49-3, in conference playoff game; defeated Washington, 17-0, in NFC championship game; defeated Denver, 39-20, in Super Bowl XXI.
1989—Lost to Los Angeles Rams, 19-13 (OT), in conference playoff game.
1990—Defeated Chicago, 31-3, in conference playoff game; defeated San Francisco, 15-13, in NFC championship game; defeated Buffalo, 20-19, in Super Bowl XXV.
1994—Lost to Cleveland, 20-13, in first-round playoff game.
1996—Defeated Pittsburgh, 28-3, in conference playoff game; defeated Jacksonville, 20-6, in AFC championship game; lost to Green Bay, 35-21, in Super Bowl XXXI.

PHILLIPS, WADE — BILLS

PERSONAL: Born June 21, 1947, in Orange, Texas. ... Son of O.A. (Bum) Phillips, head coach with Houston Oilers (1975-80) and New Orleans Saints (1981-85).
HIGH SCHOOL: Port Neches-Groves (Neches, Texas).
COLLEGE: Houston (bachelor of science degree in physical education and speech).

HEAD COACHING RECORD

BACKGROUND: Assistant coach, Houston (1969). ... Assistant coach, Orange (Texas) High School (1970-72). ... Assistant coach, Oklahoma State (1973 and 1974). ... Assistant coach, Kansas (1975). ... Assistant coach, Houston Oilers NFL (1976-80). ... Assistant coach, New Orleans Saints NFL (1981-November 25, 1985). ... Assistant coach, Philadelphia Eagles NFL (1986-88). ... Assistant coach, Denver Broncos NFL (1989-January 25, 1993). ... Defensive coordinator, Buffalo Bills (1995-97).

		REGULAR SEASON				POST-SEASON	
	W	L	T	Pct.	Finish	W	L
1985—New Orleans NFL...............	1	3	0	.250	3rd/NFC Western Division	—	—
1993—Denver NFL	9	7	0	.563	3rd/AFC Western Division	0	1
1994—Denver NFL	7	9	0	.438	4th/AFC Western Division	—	—
Pro totals (3 years)	**17**	**19**	**0**	**.472**	**Pro totals (1 year)**	**0**	**1**

NOTES:
1993—Lost to Los Angeles Raiders, 42-24, in first-round playoff game.

REEVES, DAN — FALCONS

PERSONAL: Born January 19, 1944, in Rome, Ga. ... Full name: Daniel Edward Reeves. ... Played running back.
HIGH SCHOOL: Americus (Ga.).
COLLEGE: South Carolina.
TRANSACTIONS/CAREER NOTES: Signed as non-drafted free agent by Dallas Cowboys for 1965 season.
CHAMPIONSHIP GAME EXPERIENCE: Played in NFL championship game (1966 and 1967 seasons). ... Played in NFC championship game (1970 and 1971 seasons). ... Played in Super Bowl V (1970 season). ... Member of Super Bowl championship team (1971 season).
HONORS: Named halfback on THE SPORTING NEWS NFL Eastern Conference All-Star team (1966).
PRO STATISTICS: 1965—Returned two kickoffs for 45 yards. 1966—Returned two punts for minus one yard, returned three kickoffs for 56 yards and fumbled six times. 1967—Fumbled seven times. 1969—Fumbled twice. 1970—Fumbled four times. 1971—Fumbled once.

		PASSING						RUSHING				RECEIVING				TOTALS	
Year Team	G	Att.	Cmp.	Pct.	Yds.	TD	Int.	Avg.	Att.	Yds.	Avg.	TD	No.	Yds.	Avg.	TD	TD	Pts.
1965—Dallas NFL..........	13	2	1	50.0	11	0	0	5.50	33	102	3.1	2	9	210	23.3	1	3	18
1966—Dallas NFL..........	14	6	3	50.0	48	0	0	8.00	175	757	4.3	8	41	557	13.6	8	16	96
1967—Dallas NFL..........	14	7	4	57.1	195	2	1	27.86	173	603	3.5	5	39	490	12.6	6	11	66
1968—Dallas NFL..........	4	4	2	50.0	43	0	0	10.75	40	178	4.5	4	7	84	12.0	1	5	30
1969—Dallas NFL..........	13	3	1	33.3	35	0	1	11.67	59	173	2.9	4	18	187	10.4	1	5	30
1970—Dallas NFL..........	14	3	1	33.3	14	0	1	4.67	35	84	2.4	2	12	140	11.7	0	2	12
1971—Dallas NFL..........	14	5	2	40.0	24	0	1	4.80	17	79	4.6	0	3	25	8.3	0	0	0
1972—Dallas NFL..........	14	2	0	0.0	0	0	0	...	3	14	4.7	0	0	0	...	0	0	0
Pro totals (8 years)	**100**	**32**	**14**	**43.8**	**370**	**2**	**4**	**11.56**	**535**	**1990**	**3.7**	**25**	**129**	**1693**	**13.1**	**17**	**42**	**252**

HEAD COACHING RECORD

BACKGROUND: Player/coach, Dallas Cowboys NFL (1970 and 1971). ... Offensive backs coach, Cowboys (1972 and 1974-1976). ... Offensive coordinator, Cowboys (1977-1980).
HONORS: Named NFL Coach of the Year by THE SPORTING NEWS (1993).

		REGULAR SEASON				POST-SEASON	
	W	L	T	Pct.	Finish	W	L
1981—Denver NFL	10	6	0	.625	T1st/AFC Western Division	—	—
1982—Denver NFL	2	7	0	.222	12th/AFC	—	—
1983—Denver NFL	9	7	0	.563	T2nd/AFC Western Division	0	1
1984—Denver NFL	13	3	0	.813	1st/AFC Western Division	0	1
1985—Denver NFL	11	5	0	.688	2nd/AFC Western Division	—	—
1986—Denver NFL	11	5	0	.688	1st/AFC Western Division	2	1
1987—Denver NFL	10	4	1	.700	1st/AFC Western Division	2	1
1988—Denver NFL	8	8	0	.500	2nd/AFC Western Division	—	—
1989—Denver NFL	11	5	0	.688	1st/AFC Western Division	2	1
1990—Denver NFL	5	11	0	.313	5th/AFC Western Division	—	—
1991—Denver NFL	12	4	0	.750	1st/AFC Western Division	1	1
1992—Denver NFL	8	8	0	.500	3rd/AFC Western Division	—	—
1993—New York Giants NFL	11	5	0	.688	2nd/NFC Eastern Division	1	1
1994—New York Giants NFL	9	7	0	.563	2nd/NFC Eastern Division	—	—
1995—New York Giants NFL	5	11	0	.313	4th/NFC Eastern Division	—	—
1996—New York Giants NFL	6	10	0	.375	5th/NFC Eastern Division	—	—
1997—Atlanta NFL	7	9	0	.438	T2nd/NFC Western Division	—	—
Pro totals (17 years)	**148**	**115**	**1**	**.563**	**Pro totals (7 years)**	**8**	**7**

NOTES:
1983—Lost to Seattle, 31-7, in wild-card playoff game.
1984—Lost to Pittsburgh, 24-17, in conference playoff game.
1986—Defeated New England, 22-17, in conference playoff game; defeated Cleveland, 23-20 (OT), in AFC championship game; lost to New York Giants, 39-20, in Super Bowl XXI.
1987—Defeated Houston, 34-10, in conference playoff game; defeated Cleveland, 38-33, in AFC championship game; lost to Washington, 42-10, in Super Bowl XXII.
1989—Defeated Pittsburgh, 24-23, in conference playoff game; defeated Cleveland, 37-21, in AFC championship game; lost to San Francisco, 55-10, in Super Bowl XXIV.
1991—Defeated Houston, 26-24, in conference playoff game; lost to Buffalo, 10-7, in AFC championship game.
1993—Defeated Minnesota, 17-10, in first-round playoff game; lost to San Francisco, 44-3, in conference playoff game.

PERSONAL: Born October 20, 1950, in Mexia, Texas. ... Full name: Raymond Earl Rhodes. ... Played wide receiver and defensive back.
HIGH SCHOOL: Mexia (Texas).
COLLEGE: Texas Christian, then Tulsa.
TRANSACTIONS/CAREER NOTES: Selected by New York Giants in 10th round of 1974 NFL draft. ... Traded by Giants with WR Jimmy Robinson to San Francisco 49ers for RB Mike Hogan and S Tony Dungy (March 27, 1980).
PRO STATISTICS: 1974—Rushed once for minus six yards, returned 10 punts for 124 yards and returned one kickoff for 27 yards. 1975—Rushed three times for minus four yards and recovered two fumbles. 1976—Rushed twice for 10 yards. 1977—Recovered two fumbles for 77 yards. 1979—Recovered two fumbles for seven yards. 1980—Recovered one fumble.

		INTERCEPTIONS				RECEIVING				TOTALS		
Year Team	G	No.	Yds.	Avg.	TD	No.	Yds.	Avg.	TD	TD	Pts.	Fum.
1974—New York Giants NFL	14	0	0	...	0	9	138	15.3	0	0	0	1
1975—New York Giants NFL	14	0	0	...	0	26	537	20.7	6	6	36	3
1976—New York Giants NFL	13	0	0	...	0	16	305	19.1	1	1	6	1
1977—New York Giants NFL	14	2	59	29.5	0	0	0	...	0	0	0	0
1978—New York Giants NFL	13	3	74	24.7	0	0	0	...	0	0	0	0
1979—New York Giants NFL	14	2	0	0.0	0	0	0	...	0	0	0	0
1980—San Francisco NFL	14	1	25	25.0	0	0	0	...	0	0	0	0
Pro totals (7 years)	96	8	158	19.8	0	51	980	19.2	7	7	42	5

HEAD COACHING RECORD

BACKGROUND: Assistant defensive backs coach, San Francisco 49ers NFL (1981). ... Defensive backs coach, 49ers (1982-1991). ... Defensive coordinator, Green Bay Packers NFL (1992 and 1993). ... Defensive coordinator, 49ers (1994).
HONORS: Named NFL Coach of the Year by THE SPORTING NEWS (1995).

		REGULAR SEASON				POST-SEASON	
	W	L	T	Pct.	Finish	W	L
1995—Philadelphia NFL	10	6	0	.625	2nd/NFC Eastern Division	1	1
1996—Philadelphia NFL	10	6	0	.625	T1st/NFC Eastern Division	0	1
1997—Philadelphia NFL	6	9	1	.406	3rd/NFC Western Division	—	—
Pro totals (3 years)	26	21	1	.552	**Pro totals (2 years)**	1	2

NOTES:

1995—Defeated Detroit, 58-37, in first-round playoff game; lost to Dallas, 30-11, in conference playoff game.
1996—Lost to San Francisco, 14-0, in first-round playoff game.

PERSONAL: Born December 23, 1936, in Richmond, Va. ... Full name: Robert Joseph Ross.
HIGH SCHOOL: Benedictine (Richmond, Va.).
COLLEGE: Virginia Military Institute (degrees in English and history).

HEAD COACHING RECORD

BACKGROUND: Head coach, Benedictine High School, Richmond, Va. (1959; record: 1-8-1). ... Served in military (1960-1962). ... Assistant coach, Colonial Heights (Va.) High School (1962). ... Head coach, Colonial Heights (Va.) High School (1963 and 1964). ... Freshman coach, Virginia Military Institute (1965). ... Defensive backs coach, VMI (1966). ... Offensive backs coach, William & Mary (1967 and 1968). ... Defensive backs coach, William & Mary (1969). ... Defensive coordinator, William & Mary (1970). ... Linebackers coach, Rice (1971). ... Linebackers coach, Maryland (1972). ... Special teams coach, Kansas City Chiefs NFL (1978 and 1979). ... Offensive backs coach, Chiefs (1980 and 1981).
HONORS: Named College Football Coach of the Year by THE SPORTING NEWS (1990).

		REGULAR SEASON				POST-SEASON	
	W	L	T	Pct.	Finish	W	L
1973—The Citadel	3	8	0	.273	T7th/Southern Conference	—	—
1974—The Citadel	4	7	0	.364	5th/Southern Conference	—	—
1975—The Citadel	6	5	0	.545	4th/Southern Conference	—	—
1976—The Citadel	6	5	0	.545	6th/Southern Conference	—	—
1977—The Citadel	5	6	0	.455	T3rd/Southern Conference	—	—
1982—Maryland	8	3	0	.727	2nd/Atlantic Coast Conference	0	1
1983—Maryland	8	3	0	.727	1st/Atlantic Coast Conference	0	1
1984—Maryland	8	3	0	.727	1st/Atlantic Coast Conference	1	0
1985—Maryland	8	3	0	.727	1st/Atlantic Coast Conference	1	0
1986—Maryland	5	5	1	.500	5th/Atlantic Coast Conference	—	—
1987—Georgia Tech	2	9	0	.182	8th/Atlantic Coast Conference	—	—
1988—Georgia Tech	3	8	0	.273	8th/Atlantic Coast Conference	—	—
1989—Georgia Tech	7	4	0	.636	T4th/Atlantic Coast Conference	—	—
1990—Georgia Tech	10	0	1	.955	1st/Atlantic Coast Conference	1	0
1991—Georgia Tech	7	5	0	.583	T2nd/Atlantic Coast Conference	1	0
1992—San Diego NFL	11	5	0	.688	1st/AFC Western Division	1	1
1993—San Diego NFL	8	8	0	.500	4th/AFC Western Division	—	—
1994—San Diego NFL	11	5	0	.688	1st/AFC Western Division	2	1
1995—San Diego NFL	9	7	0	.563	2nd/AFC Western Division	0	1
1996—San Diego NFL	8	8	0	.500	3rd/AFC Western Division	—	—
1997—Detroit NFL	9	7	0	.563	T3rd/NFC Central Division	0	1
College totals (15 years)	90	74	2	.548	**College totals (6 years)**	4	2
Pro totals (6 years)	56	40	0	.583	**Pro totals (4 years)**	3	4

HEAD COACHES

NOTES:
1982—Lost to Washington, 21-10, in Aloha Bowl.
1983—Lost to Tennessee, 30-23, in Florida Citrus Bowl.
1984—Defeated Tennessee, 28-27, in Sun Bowl.
1985—Defeated Syracuse, 35-18, in Cherry Bowl.
1990—Defeated Nebraska, 45-21, in Florida Citrus Bowl.
1991—Defeated Stanford, 18-17, in Aloha Bowl.
1992—Defeated Kansas City, 17-0, in first-round playoff game; lost to Miami, 31-0, in conference playoff game.
1994—Defeated Miami, 22-21, in conference playoff game; defeated Pittsburgh, 17-13, in AFC championship game; lost to San Francisco, 49-26, in Super Bowl XXIX.
1995—Lost to Indianapolis, 35-20, in first-round playoff game.
1997—Lost to Tampa Bay, 20-10, in first-round playoff game.

SCHOTTENHEIMER, MARTY — CHIEFS

PERSONAL: Born September 23, 1943, in Canonsburg, Pa. ... Full name: Martin Edward Schottenheimer. ... Played linebacker. ... Brother of Kurt Schottenheimer, defensive backs coach, Kansas City Chiefs.
HIGH SCHOOL: McDonald (Pa.).
COLLEGE: Pittsburgh (degree in English, 1964).
TRANSACTIONS/CAREER NOTES: Selected by Buffalo Bills in seventh round of 1965 AFL draft. ... Released by Bills (1969). ... Signed by Boston Patriots (1969). ... Patriots franchise renamed New England Patriots for 1971 season. ... Traded by New England Patriots to Pittsburgh Steelers for OT Mike Haggerty and a draft choice (July 10, 1971). ... Released by Steelers (1971).
CHAMPIONSHIP GAME EXPERIENCE: Member of AFL championship team (1965 season). ... Played in AFL championship game (1966 season).
HONORS: Played in AFL All-Star Game (1965 season).
PRO STATISTICS: 1969—Returned one kickoff for 13 yards. 1970—Returned one kickoff for eight yards.

			INTERCEPTIONS		
Year Team	G	No.	Yds.	Avg.	TD
1965—Buffalo AFL	14	0	0	...	0
1966—Buffalo AFL	14	1	20	20.0	0
1967—Buffalo AFL	14	3	88	29.3	1
1968—Buffalo AFL	14	1	22	22.0	0
1969—Boston AFL	11	1	3	3.0	0
1970—Boston NFL	12	0	0	...	0
AFL totals (5 years)	67	6	133	22.2	1
NFL totals (1 year)	12	0	0		0
Pro totals (6 years)	79	6	133	22.2	1

HEAD COACHING RECORD
BACKGROUND: Linebackers coach, Portland Storm WFL (1974). ... Linebackers coach, New York Giants NFL (1975 and 1976). ... Defensive coordinator, Giants (1977). ... Linebackers coach, Detroit Lions NFL (1978 and 1979). ... Defensive coordinator, Cleveland Browns NFL (1989-October 22, 1984).

		REGULAR SEASON				POST-SEASON	
	W	L	T	Pct.	Finish	W	L
1984—Cleveland NFL	4	4	—	.500	3rd/AFC Central Division	—	—
1985—Cleveland NFL	8	8	—	.500	3rd/AFC Central Division	0	1
1986—Cleveland NFL	12	4	0	.750	1st/AFC Central Division	1	1
1987—Cleveland NFL	10	5	0	.667	1st/AFC Central Division	1	1
1988—Cleveland NFL	10	6	0	.625	T2nd/AFC Central Division	0	1
1989—Kansas City NFL	8	7	1	.531	2nd/AFC Western Division	—	—
1990—Kansas City NFL	11	5	0	.688	2nd/AFC Western Division	0	1
1991—Kansas City NFL	10	6	0	.625	2nd/AFC Western Division	1	1
1992—Kansas City NFL	10	6	0	.625	2nd/AFC Western Division	0	1
1993—Kansas City NFL	11	5	0	.688	1st/AFC Western Division	2	1
1994—Kansas City NFL	9	7	0	.563	T2nd/AFC Western Division	0	1
1995—Kansas City NFL	13	3	0	.813	1st/AFC Western Division	0	1
1996—Kansas City NFL	9	7	0	.563	2nd/AFC Western Division	—	—
1997—Kansas City NFL	13	3	0	.813	1st/AFC Western Division	0	1
Pro totals (14 years)	138	76	1	.644	Pro totals (11 years)	5	11

NOTES:
1984—Replaced Sam Rutigliano as coach of Cleveland (October 22), with 1-7 record and in third place.
1985—Lost to Miami, 24-21, in conference playoff game.
1986—Defeated Ney York Jets, 23-20 (2 OT), in conference playoff game; lost to Denver, 23-20 (OT), in AFC championship game.
1987—Defeated Indianapolis, 38-21, in conference playoff game; lost to Denver, 38-33, in AFC championship game.
1988—Lost to Houston, 24-23, in wild-card playoff game.
1990—Lost to Miami, 17-16, in conference playoff game.
1991—Defeated Los Angeles Raiders, 10-6, in first-round playoff game; lost to Buffalo, 37-14, in conference playoff game.
1992—Lost to San Diego, 17-0, in first-round playoff game.
1993—Defeated Pittsburgh, 27-24 (OT), in first-round playoff game; defeated Houston, 28-20, in conference playoff game; lost to Buffalo, 30-13, in AFC championship game.
1994—Lost to Miami, 27-17, in first-round playoff game.
1995—Lost to Indianapolis, 10-7, in conference playoff game.
1997—Lost to Denver, 14-10, in conference playoff game.

SHANAHAN, MIKE — BRONCOS

PERSONAL: Born August 24, 1952, in Oak Park, Ill. ... Full name: Michael Edward Shanahan.
HIGH SCHOOL: Franklin Park (East Leyden, Ill.).
COLLEGE: Eastern Illinois (bachelor's degree in physical education, 1974; master's degree in education, 1975).

HEAD COACHING RECORD

BACKGROUND: Graduate assistant, Eastern Illinois (1973 and 1974). ... Running backs/wide receivers coach, Oklahoma (1975 and 1976). ... Assistant coach, Northern Arizona (1977). ... Offensive coordinator, Eastern Illinois (1978). ... Offensive coordinator, Minnesota (1979). ... Offensive coordinator, Florida (1980-83). ... Quarterbacks coach, Denver Broncos NFL (1984, 1989 and 1990). ... Offensive coordinator, Broncos (1985-87 and 1991). ... Offensive coordinator, San Francisco NFL (1992-94).

	W	L	T	Pct.	Finish		W	L
			REGULAR SEASON				POST-SEASON	
1988—Los Angeles Raiders NFL	7	9	0	.438	3rd/AFC Western Division		—	—
1989—Los Angeles Raiders NFL	1	3	0	.250	—		—	—
1995—Denver NFL	8	8	0	.500	T3rd/AFC Western Division		—	—
1996—Denver NFL	13	3	0	.813	1st/AFC Western Division		0	1
1997—Denver NFL	12	4	0	.750	2nd/AFC Western Conference		4	0
Pro totals (5 years)	**41**	**27**	**0**	**.603**	**Pro totals (2 years)**		**4**	**1**

NOTES:

1989—Replaced as Raiders coach by Art Shell (October 3) with club tied for fourth place.

1996—Lost to Jacksonville, 30-27, in conference playoff game.

1997—Defeated Jacksonville, 42-17, in first-round playoff game; defeated Kansas City, 14-10, in conference playoff game; defeated Pittsburgh, 24-21, in AFC championship game; defeated Green Bay, 31-24, in Super Bowl XXXII.

TOBIN, VINCE — CARDINALS

PERSONAL: Born September 29, 1943, in Burlington Junction, Mo.
HIGH SCHOOL: Maryville (Mo.).
COLLEGE: Missouri (degree in physical education, 1965; master's degree in guidance and counseling, 1966).

HEAD COACHING RECORD

BACKGROUND: Defensive ends coach, Missouri (1967-1970). ... Defensive coordinator, Missouri (1971-1976). ... Defensive coordinator, British Columbia Lions CFL (1977-1982). ... Defensive coordinator, Philadelphia/Baltimore Stars USFL (1983-1985). ... Defensive coordinator, Chicago Bears NFL (1986-1992). ... Defensive coordinator, Indianapolis Colts NFL (1994 ad 1995).

	W	L	T	Pct.	Finish		W	L
			REGULAR SEASON				POST-SEASON	
1996—Arizona NFL........................	7	9	0	.438	4th/NFC Eastern Division		—	—
1997—Arizona NFL........................	4	12	0	.250	5th/NFC Eastern Division		—	—
Pro totals (2 years)	**11**	**21**	**0**	**.344**				

TURNER, NORV — REDSKINS

PERSONAL: Born May 17, 1952, in LeJeune, N.C. ... Full name: Norval Eugene Turner. ... Brother of Ron Turner, offensive coordinator, Chicago Bears.
HIGH SCHOOL: Alhambra (Calif.).
COLLEGE: Oregon (degree in history, 1975).

HEAD COACHING RECORD

BACKGROUND: Graduate assistant, Oregon (1975). ... Receivers coach, Southern California (1976-1979). ... Defensive backs coach, USC (1980). ... Quarterbacks coach, USC (1981-1983). ... Offensive coordinator, USC (1984). ... Receivers coach, Los Angeles Rams NFL (1985-1990). ... Offensive coordinator, Dallas Cowboys NFL (1991-1993).

	W	L	T	Pct.	Finish		W	L
			REGULAR SEASON				POST-SEASON	
1994—Washington NFL..................	3	13	0	.188	5th/NFC Eastern Division		—	—
1995—Washington NFL..................	6	10	0	.375	3rd/NFC Eastern Division		—	—
1996—Washington NFL..................	9	7	0	.563	3rd/NFC Eastern Division		—	—
1997—Washington NFL..................	8	7	1	.531	2nd/NFC Eastern Division		—	—
Pro totals (4 years)	**26**	**37**	**1**	**.414**				

VERMEIL, DICK — RAMS

PERSONAL: Born October 30, 1936, in Calistoga, Calif. ... Full name: Richard Albert Vermeil. ... Brother of Al Vermeil, conditioning coach with San Francisco 49ers (1979-1982) and brother-in-law of Louie Giammona, running back with Philadelphia Eagles (1978-1982).
HIGH SCHOOL: Calistoga (Calif.).
JUNIOR COLLEGE: Napa College (degree in physical education, 1958).
COLLEGE: San Jose State (master's degree in physical education, 1959).

HEAD COACHING RECORD

BACKGROUND: Assistant coach, Del Mar High School, San Jose, Calif. (1959). ... Head coach, Hillsdale High School, San Mateo, Calif. (1960-1962; record: 17-9-1). ... Assistant coach, College of San Mateo (1963). ... Assistant coach, Stanford (1965-1968). ... Assistant coach, Los Angeles Rams NFL (1969 and 1971-1973). ... Assistant coach, UCLA (1970).
HONORS: Named NFL Coach of the Year by THE SPORTING NEWS (1979).

				REGULAR SEASON		POST-SEASON	
	W	L	T	Pct.	Finish	W	L
1964—Napa College	8	1	0	.889	2nd/Golden Valley Conference	—	—
1974—UCLA	6	3	2	.636	T3rd/Pacific-8 Conference	—	—
1975—UCLA	8	2	1	.773	T1st/Pacific-8 Conference	1	0
1976—Philadelphia NFL	4	10	0	.286	4th/NFC Eastern Division	—	—
1977—Philadelphia NFL	5	9	0	.357	T4th/NFC Eastern Division	—	—
1978—Philadelphia NFL	9	7	0	.563	2nd/NFC Eastern Division	0	1
1979—Philadelphia NFL	11	5	0	.688	T1st/NFC Eastern Division	1	1
1980—Philadelphia NFL	12	4	0	.750	T1st/NFC Eastern Division	2	1
1981—Philadelphia NFL	10	6	0	.625	2nd/NFC Eastern Division	0	1
1982—Philadelphia NFL	3	6	0	.333	5th/NFC Eastern Division	—	—
1997—St. Louis NFL	5	11	0	.313	5th/NFC Western Division	—	—
College totals (3 years)	**22**	**6**	**3**	**.758**	**College totals (1 year)**	**1**	**0**
Pro totals (8 years)	**59**	**58**	**0**	**.504**	**Pro totals (4 years)**	**3**	**4**

NOTES:
1975—Defeated Ohio State, 23-10, in Rose Bowl.
1978—Lost to Atlanta, 14-13, in conference playoff game.
1979—Defeated Chicago, 27-17, in first-round playoff game; lost to Tampa Bay, 24-17, in conference playoff game.
1980—Defeated Minnesota, 31-16, in conference playoff game; defeated Dallas, 20-7, in NFC championship game; lost to Oakland, 27-10, in Super Bowl XV.
1981—Lost to New York Giants, 27-21, in conference playoff game.
1982—Only nine of 16 games were played due to the cancellation of games because of a players strike.

WANNSTEDT, DAVE — BEARS

PERSONAL: Born May 21, 1952, in Pittsburgh. ... Full name: David Raymond Wannstedt.
HIGH SCHOOL: Baldwin (Pittsburgh).
COLLEGE: Pittsburgh (bachelor of science degree in physical education, 1974; master's degree in education, 1975).
TRANSACTIONS/CAREER NOTES: Selected by Green Bay Packers in 15th round (376th pick overall) of 1974 NFL draft. ... On injured reserve with neck injury (entire 1974 season).

HEAD COACHING RECORD

BACKGROUND: Graduate assistant, Pittsburgh (1975). ... Defensive line coach, Pittsburgh (1976-1978). ... Defensive line coach, Oklahoma State (1979 and 1980). ... Defensive coordinator, Oklahoma State (1981 and 1982). ... Defensive line coach, Southern California (1983-1985). ... Defensive coordinator, Miami, Fla. (1986-1988). ... Defensive coordinator, Dallas Cowboys NFL (1989-1992).

				REGULAR SEASON		POST-SEASON	
	W	L	T	Pct.	Finish	W	L
1993—Chicago NFL	7	9	0	.438	4th/NFC Central Division	—	—
1994—Chicago NFL	9	7	0	.563	T2nd/NFC Central Division	1	1
1995—Chicago NFL	9	7	0	.563	3rd/NFC Central Division	—	—
1996—Chicago NFL	7	9	0	.438	3rd/NFC Central Division	—	—
1997—Chicago NFL	4	12	0	.250	5th/NFC Central Division	—	—
Pro totals (5 years)	**36**	**44**	**0**	**.450**	**Pro totals (1 year)**	**1**	**1**

NOTES:
1994—Defeated Minnesota, 35-18, in first-round playoff game; lost to San Francisco, 44-15, in conference playoff game.